MARVEL FIRSTS THE 1980s

VOL. 3

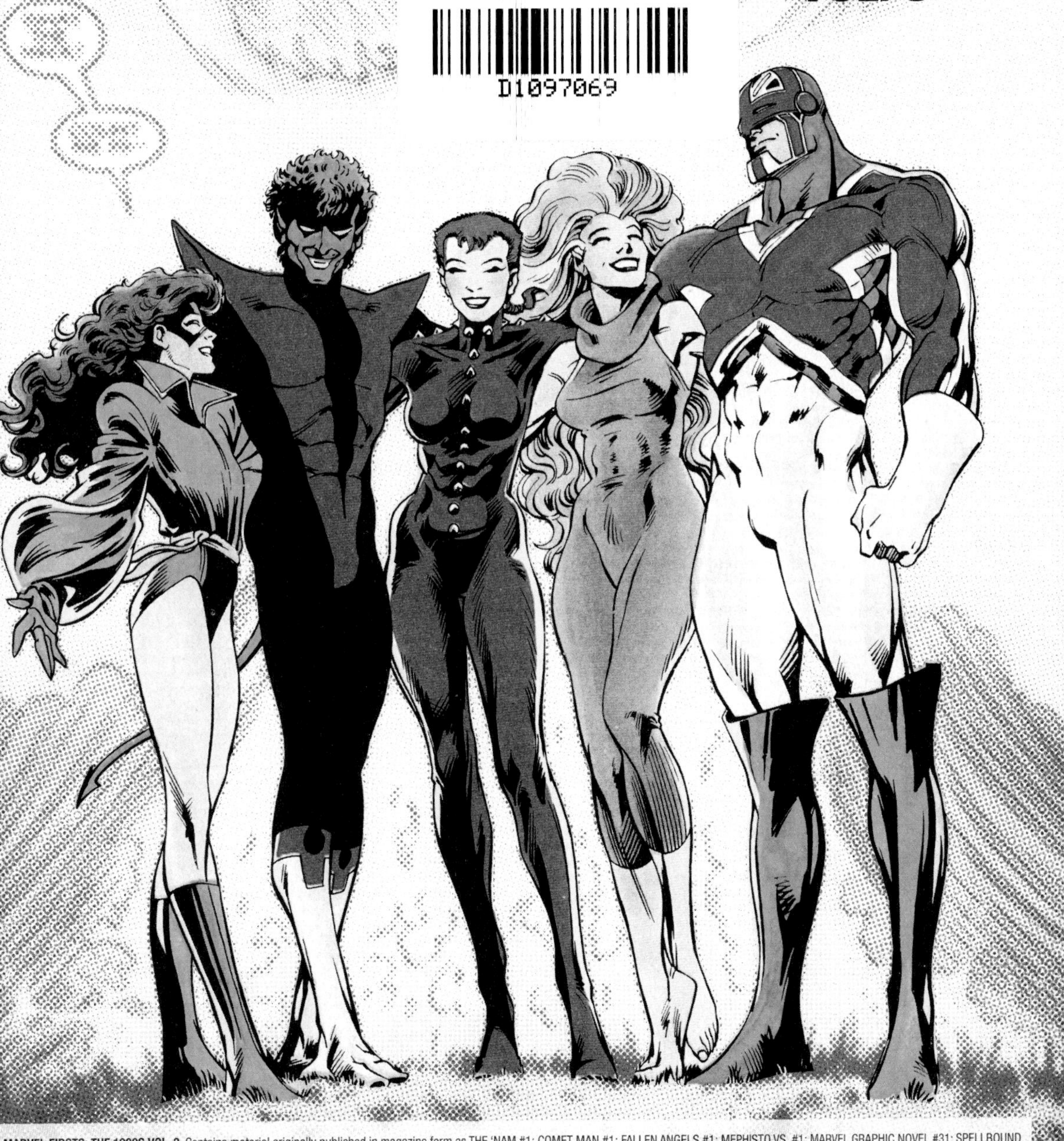

MARVEL FIRSTS: THE 1980S VOL. 3. Contains material originally published in magazine form as THE 'NAM #1; COMET MAN #1; FALLEN ANGELS #1; MEPHISTO VS. #1; MARVEL GRAPHIC NOVEL #31; SPELLBOUND #1; EXCALIBUR SPECIAL EDITION; X-TERMINATORS #1; HAVOK & WOLVERINE: MELTDOWN #1; SHADOWMASTERS #1; AMAZING SPIDER-MAN ANNUAL #22; MARVEL AGE ANNUAL #4; and MARVEL COMICS PRESENTS #10, #17, #25, #26, #29 and #38. First printing 2014. ISBN# 978-0-7851-9004-2. Published by MARVEL WORLDWIDE, INC., a subsidiary of MARVEL ENTERTAINMENT, LLC. OFFICE OF PUBLICATION: 135 West 50th Street, New York, NY 10020. **Printed in the U.S.A.** ALAN FINE, EVP - Office of the President, Marvel Worldwide, Inc. and EVP & CMO Marvel Characters B.V.; DAN BUCKLEY, Publisher & President - Print, Animation & Digital Divisions; JOE QUESADA, Chief Creative Officer; TOM BREVOORT, SVP of Publishing; DAVID BOGART, SVP of Operations & Procurement, Publishing; C.B. CEBULSKI, SVP of Creator & Content Development; DAVID GABRIEL, SVP Print, Sales & Marketing; JIM O'KEEFE, VP of Operations & Logistics; DAN CARR, Executive Director of Publishing Technology; SUSAN CRESPI, Editorial Operations Manager; ALEX MORALES, Publishing Operations Manager; STAN LEE, Chairman Emeritus. For information regarding advertising in Marvel Comics or on Marvel.com, please contact Niza Disla, Director of Marvel Partnerships, at ndisla@marvel.com. For Marvel subscription inquiries, please call 800-217-9158. **Manufactured between 10/24/2014 and 12/1/2014 by R.R. DONNELLEY, INC., SALEM, VA, USA.**

10 9 8 7 6 5 4 3 2 1

THE 'NAM #1
"'Nam: First Patrol"
WRITER: Doug Murray
PENCILER & COLORIST: Michael Golden
INKER: Armando Gil
LETTERER: Phil Felix
ASSISTANT EDITOR: Pat Redding
EDITOR: Larry Hama

COMET MAN #1
"The Coming of the Comet Man"
WRITERS: Bill Mumy & Miguel Ferrer
PENCILER: Kelly Jones
INKER: Gerry Talaoc
COLORIST: Daina Graziunas
LETTERER: Bill Oakley
EDITOR: Ann Nocenti

FALLEN ANGELS #1
"Runaway"
WRITER: Jo Duffy
PENCILER: Kerry Gammill
INKER: Tom Palmer
COLORIST: Petra Scotese
LETTERER: Jim Novak
EDITOR: Ann Nocenti

MEPHISTO VS. ... #1
"Give the Devil His Due!"
WRITER: Al Milgrom
PENCILER: John Buscema
INKER: Bob Wiacek
COLORIST: George Roussos
LETTERER: Rick Parker
EDITOR: Ralph Macchio

SPELLBOUND #1
"Power!"
CO-PLOTTER & SCRIPTER: Louise Simonson
CO-PLOTTER & INKER: Carl Potts
PENCILER: Terry Shoemaker
COLORIST: Christie Scheele
LETTERER: Joe Rosen
MANAGING EDITOR: Bobbie Chase
EDITOR: Bob Harras

MARVEL GRAPHIC NOVEL #31
"Chapter 1: Rafael / Chapter 2: The Crucible / Chapter 3: Transfiguration"
starring THE WOLFPACK
WRITER: Larry Hama
PENCILER: Ron Wilson
INKERS: Whilce Portacio & Kyle Baker
COLORISTS: Petra Scotese, Christie Scheele & Glynis Oliver
LETTERER: Joe Rosen
ASSISTANT EDITOR: Terry Kavanagh
EDITOR: Ann Nocenti

EXCALIBUR SPECIAL EDITION
"The Sword Is Drawn"
WRITER: Chris Claremont
PENCILER: Alan Davis
INKERS: Paul Neary with Mark Farmer
COLORIST: Glynis Oliver
LETTERER: Tom Orzechowski
EDITOR: Ann Nocenti

AMAZING SPIDER-MAN ANNUAL #22
"He Who Laughs..."
starring SPEEDBALL
PLOTTER & PENCILER: Steve Ditko
SCRIPTER: Roger Stern
INKER: Jackson Guice
COLORIST: Tom Vincent
LETTERER: Rick Parker
EDITOR: Jim Salicrup

MARVEL AGE ANNUAL #4
"The Sales Pitch"
starring DAMAGE CONTROL
WRITER: Dwayne McDuffie
PENCILER: Ernie Colón
INKER: Jon D'Agostino
COLORIST: Gregory Wright
LETTERER: Rick Parker
MANAGING EDITOR: Dwight Zimmerman
EDITOR: Jim Salicrup

X-TERMINATORS #1
"Invasion of the Baby-Snatchers"
WRITER: Louise Simonson
PENCILER: Jon Bogdanove
INKERS: Al Williamson & Al Milgrom
COLORIST: John Wellington
LETTERER: Joe Rosen
EDITOR: Bob Harras

MARVEL COMICS PRESENTS #10
"God's Country, Part I: Eating American Pie"
starring COLOSSUS
WRITER: Ann Nocenti
PENCILER: Rick Leonardi
INKER: P. Craig Russell
COLORIST: Glynis Oliver
LETTERER: Ken Lopez
ASSISTANT EDITOR: Mike Rockwitz
EDITOR: Ann Nocenti

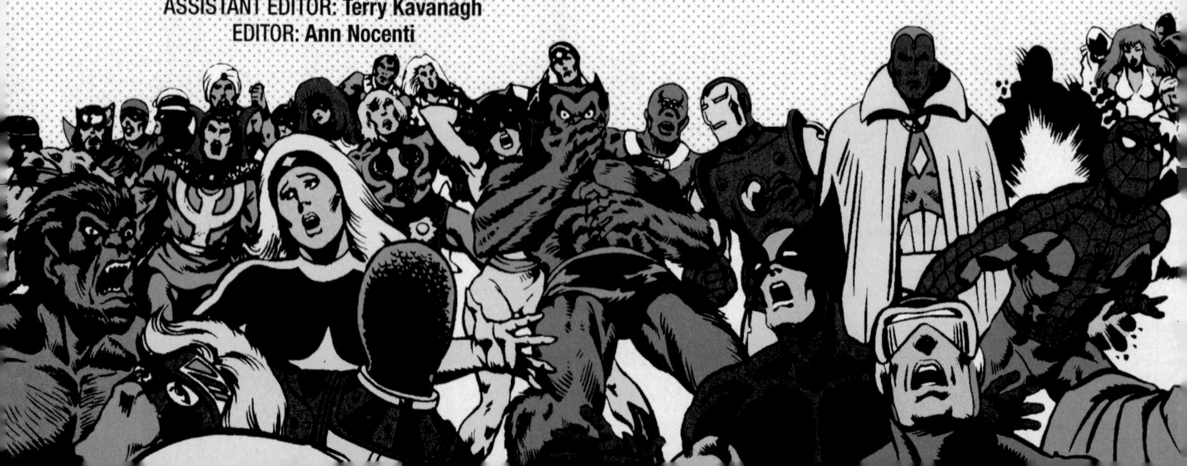

HAVOK & WOLVERINE: MELTDOWN #1
"Mexican Standoff"
WRITERS: Walter Simonson & Louise Simonson
ARTISTS & COLORISTS: Jon J Muth & Kent Williams
with Sherilyn van Valkenburgh
LETTERER: Bill Oakley
DESIGNER: Robbin Brosterman
EDITORS: Margaret Clark & Steve Buccellato

MARVEL COMICS PRESENTS #17
"The Retribution Affair! Part 1: Blinded by the Light"
starring CYCLOPS
WRITER: Bob Harras
PENCILER: Ron Lim
INKER: Bruce Patterson
COLORIST: Andy Yanchus
LETTERER: Agustin Mas
ASSISTANT EDITOR: Mike Rockwitz
EDITOR: Terry Kavanagh

MARVEL COMICS PRESENTS #25
"…From Little Acorns Grow"
starring NTH MAN
WRITER: Larry Hama
PENCILER: Ron Wagner
INKER: Fred Fredericks
COLORIST: Mark Chiarello
LETTERER: Janice Chiang
ASSISTANT EDITOR: Mike Rockwitz
EDITOR: Terry Kavanagh

MARVEL COMICS PRESENTS #26
"Rise, and Shine Chapter I: New York"
starring COLDBLOOD
WRITER: Doug Moench
ARTIST: Paul Gulacy
COLORIST: Glynis Oliver
LETTERER: Tim Harkins
ASSISTANT EDITOR: Mike Rockwitz
EDITOR: Terry Kavanagh

MARVEL COMICS PRESENTS #29
"It Came From Within"
starring QUASAR
WRITER: Mark Gruenwald
PENCILER: Paul Ryan
INKER: Danny Bulanadi
COLORIST: Paul Becton
LETTERER: Janice Chiang
ASSISTANT EDITOR: Mike Rockwitz
EDITOR: Terry Kavanagh

SHADOWMASTERS #1
"Shadows of the Past"
WRITER: Carl Potts
PENCILER: Dan Lawlis
INKER: Russ Heath
COLORIST: Steve Oliff
LETTERER: Jim Novak
ASSISTANT EDITOR: Marc McLaurin
EDITOR: Al Milgrom

MARVEL COMICS PRESENTS #38
"Stardust Miseries, Part 1: Something in the Air"
starring WONDER MAN
WRITER: Michael Higgins
PENCILER: Javier Saltares
INKER: Jose Marzan
COLORIST: Tom Vincent
LETTERER: Ken Lopez
ASSISTANT EDITOR: Kelly Corvese
EDITOR: Terry Kavanagh

COLLECTION EDITOR: Mark D. Beazley
DIGITAL TRAFFIC COORDINATOR: Joe Hochstein
ASSOCIATE MANAGING EDITOR: Alex Starbuck
EDITOR, SPECIAL PROJECTS: Jennifer Grünwald
SENIOR EDITOR, SPECIAL PROJECTS: Jeff Youngquist
RESEARCH & LAYOUT: Jeph York
PRODUCTION & COLOR RECONSTRUCTION: ColorTek,
Jerron Quality Color & Joe Frontirre
BOOK DESIGN: Jeff Powell
SVP PRINT, SALES & MARKETING: David Gabriel

EDITOR IN CHIEF: Axel Alonso
CHIEF CREATIVE OFFICER: Joe Quesada
PUBLISHER: Dan Buckley
EXECUTIVE PRODUCER: Alan Fine

Special Thanks to Jeremy Hall, Mike Hansen, Jess Harrold,
Gregory Hecht, Gary Henderson, David Kolf, Stuart Mann,
Marc Riemer, Jacob Rougemont, Jeff Stoltman, Steve Topper,
Mario Trabucco, Antoine Verville, Chuck Rozanski & Chris
Boyd of Mile High Comics, and Buddy Saunders & Doug Shark
of mycomicshop.com.

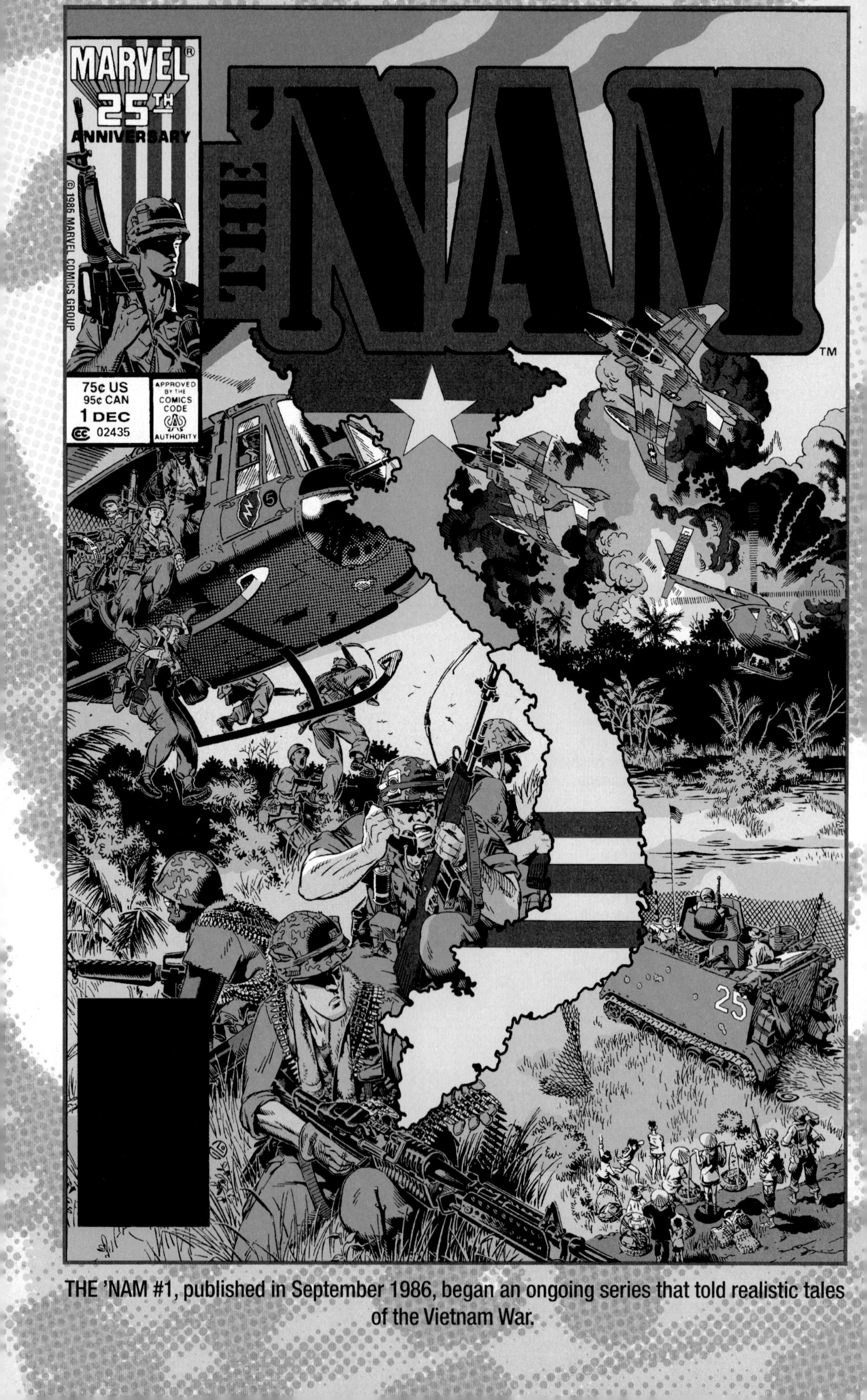
MARVEL®
25TH ANNIVERSARY
© 1986 MARVEL COMICS GROUP
THE 'NAM
TM
75¢ US
95¢ CAN
1 DEC
02435
APPROVED BY THE COMICS CODE AUTHORITY
5
25
THE 'NAM #1, published in September 1986, began an ongoing series that told realistic tales of the Vietnam War.

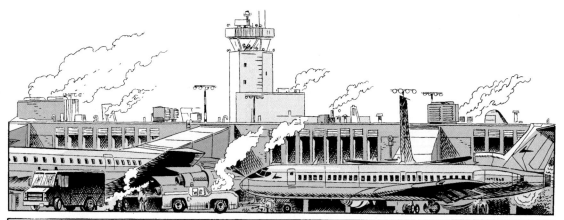

EARLY IN 1966, A YOUNG SOLDIER LEAVES HOME FOR HIS FIRST TASTE OF INDEPENDENCE, AND **WAR**.

'NAM: FIRST PATROL

STORY: DOUG MURRAY. PENCILS, COLORING: MICHAEL GOLDEN. INKS: ARMANDO GIL. LETTERS: PHIL FELIX. EDITOR: LARRY HAMA. EDITOR IN CHIEF: JIM SHOOTER.

GOODBYE, SON! DON'T FORGET TO WRITE! PLEASE... BE CAREFUL!

THAT'S RIGHT, SON! BE CAREFUL!

DON'T FORGET YOUR DRAMAMINE!

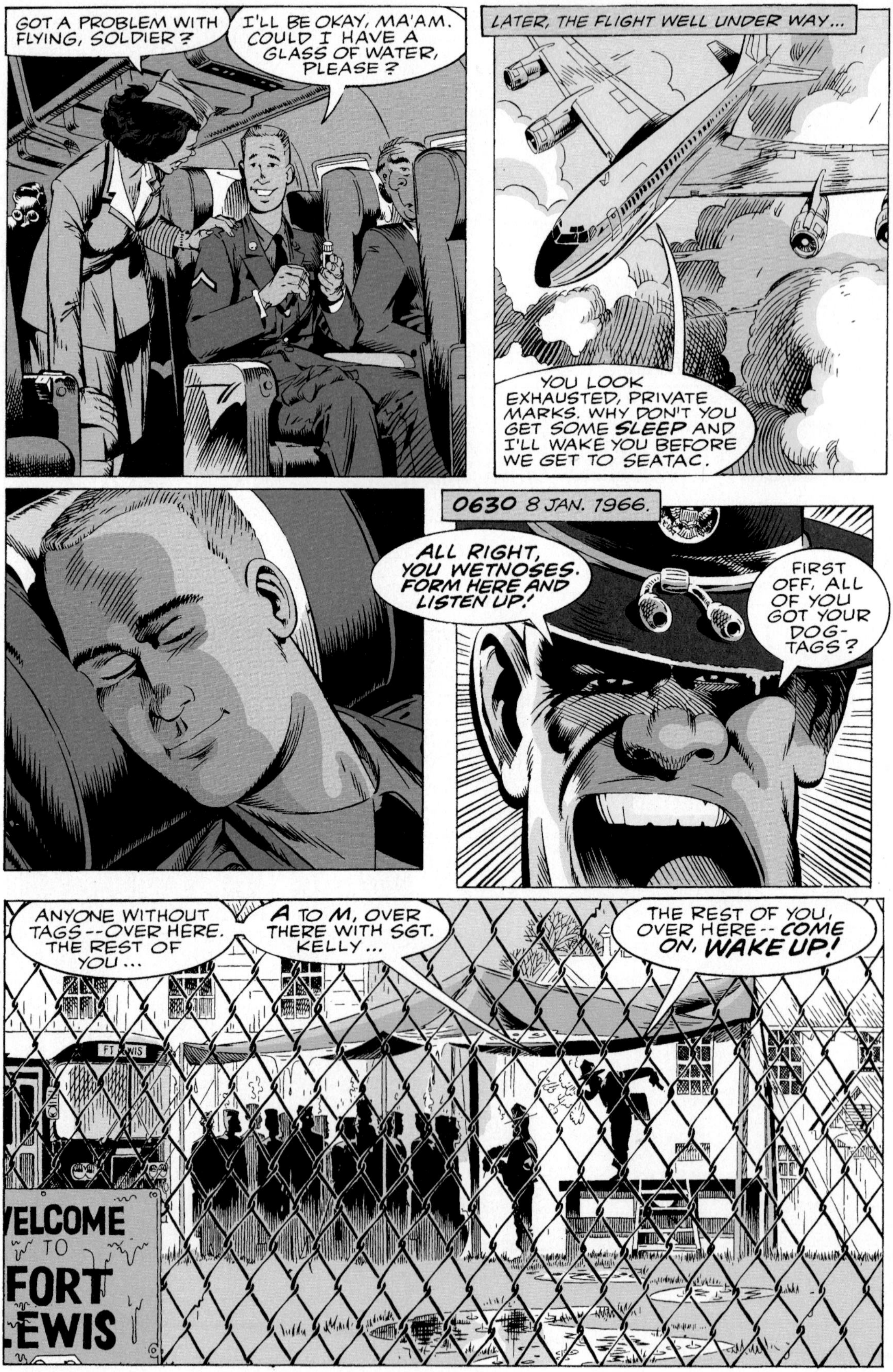
GOT A PROBLEM WITH FLYING, SOLDIER?
I'LL BE OKAY, MA'AM. COULD I HAVE A GLASS OF WATER, PLEASE?
LATER, THE FLIGHT WELL UNDER WAY...
YOU LOOK EXHAUSTED, PRIVATE MARKS. WHY DON'T YOU GET SOME SLEEP AND I'LL WAKE YOU BEFORE WE GET TO SEATAC.
0630 8 JAN. 1966.
ALL RIGHT, YOU WETNOSES. FORM HERE AND LISTEN UP!
FIRST OFF, ALL OF YOU GOT YOUR DOG-TAGS?
ANYONE WITHOUT TAGS--OVER HERE. THE REST OF YOU...
A TO M, OVER THERE WITH SGT. KELLY...
THE REST OF YOU, OVER HERE--COME ON, WAKE UP!
FT LEWIS
WELCOME TO FORT LEWIS

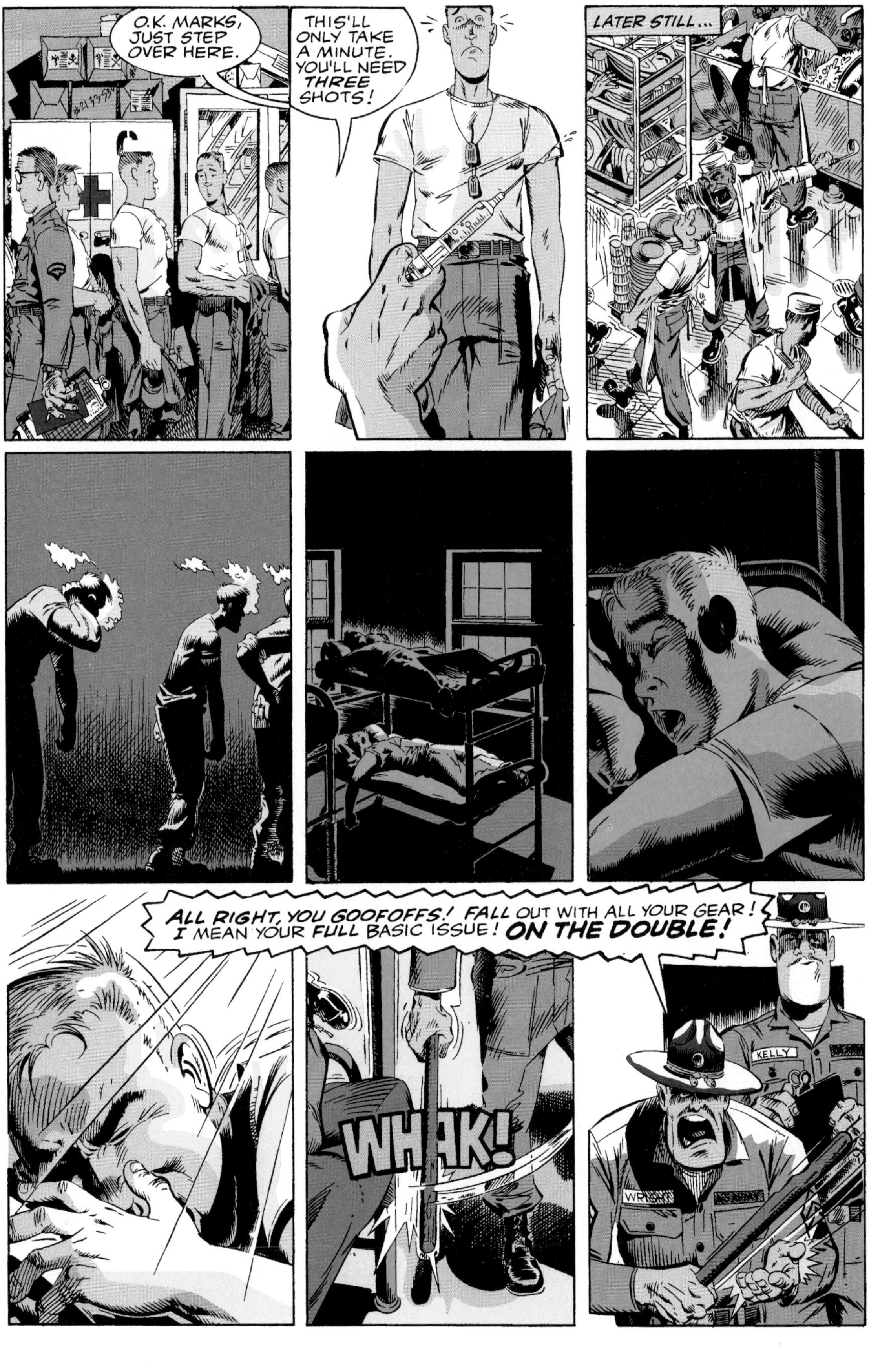
O.K. MARKS, JUST STEP OVER HERE.
THIS'LL ONLY TAKE A MINUTE. YOU'LL NEED THREE SHOTS!
LATER STILL...
ALL RIGHT, YOU GOOFOFFS! FALL OUT WITH ALL YOUR GEAR! I MEAN YOUR FULL BASIC ISSUE! ON THE DOUBLE!
WHAK!
KELLY

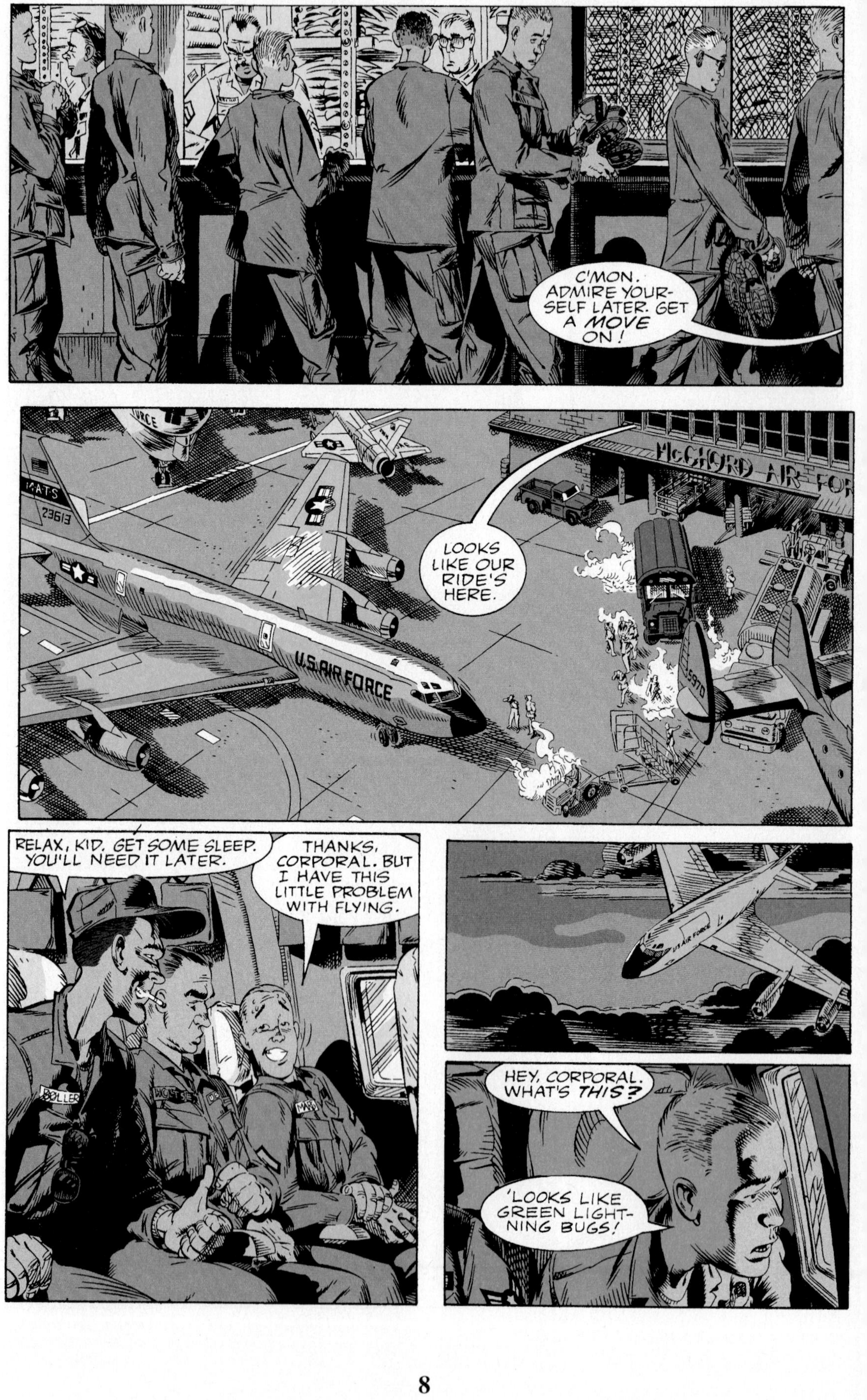
C'MON. ADMIRE YOURSELF LATER. GET A *MOVE* ON!
M.A.T.S
23613
U.S. AIR FORCE
McCHORD AIR FOR
LOOKS LIKE OUR RIDE'S HERE.
RELAX, KID. GET SOME SLEEP. YOU'LL NEED IT LATER.
THANKS, CORPORAL. BUT I HAVE THIS LITTLE PROBLEM WITH FLYING.
HEY, CORPORAL. WHAT'S *THIS?*
'LOOKS LIKE GREEN LIGHTNING BUGS!

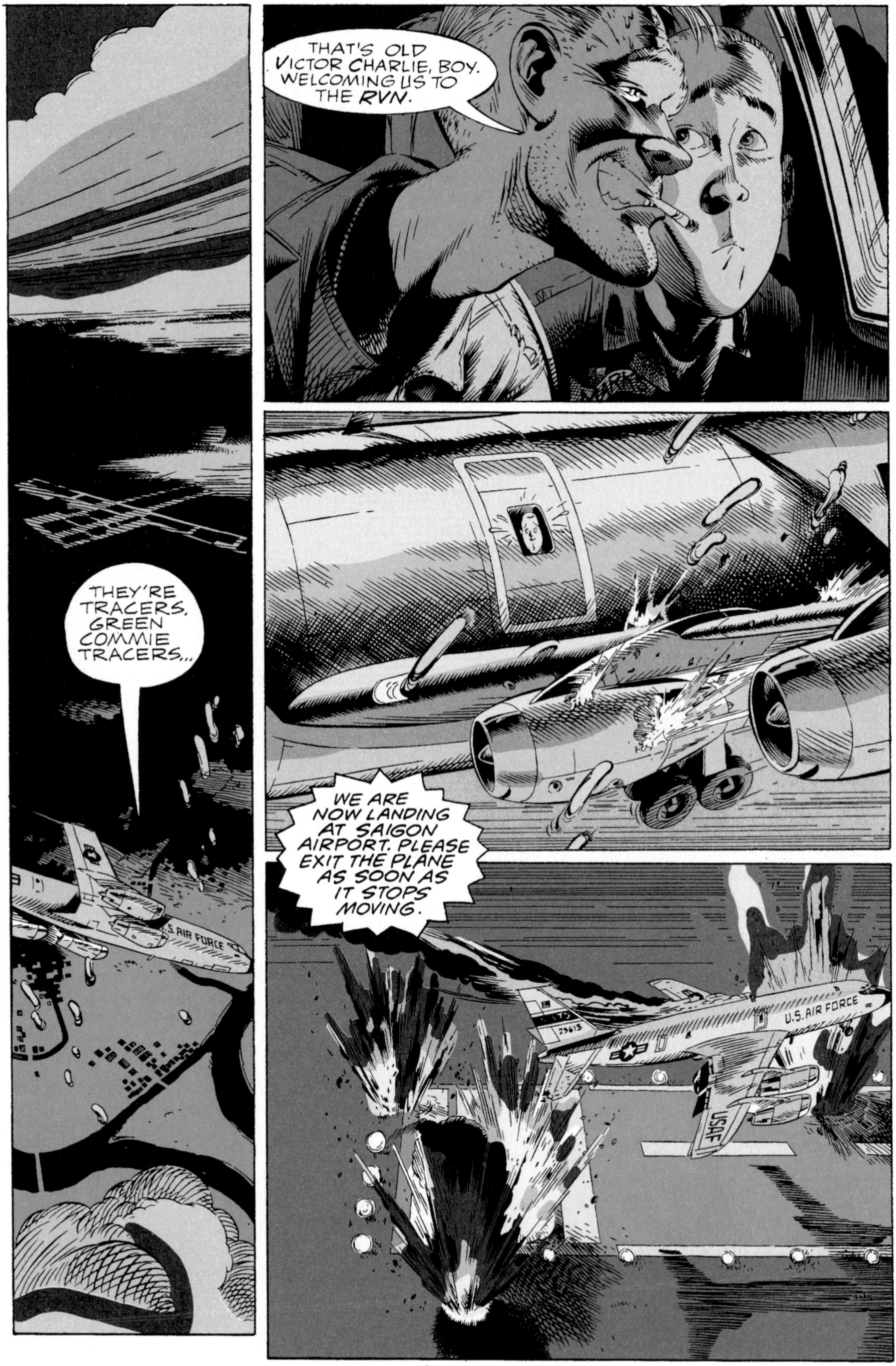
THEY'RE TRACERS, GREEN COMMIE TRACERS...
THAT'S OLD VICTOR CHARLIE, BOY. WELCOMING US TO THE RVN.
WE ARE NOW LANDING AT SAIGON AIRPORT. PLEASE EXIT THE PLANE AS SOON AS IT STOPS MOVING.
U.S. AIR FORCE
USAF

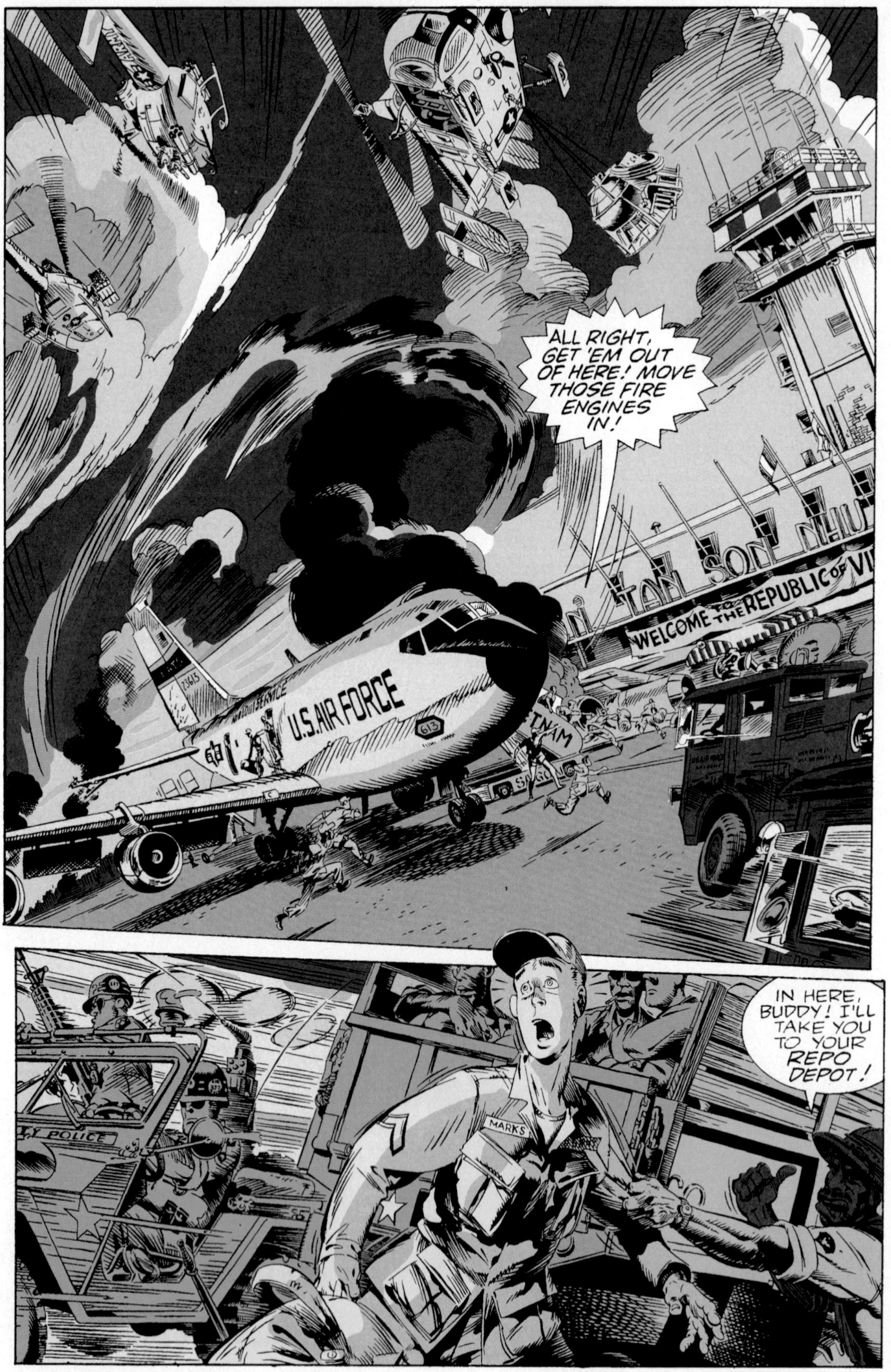
ALL RIGHT, GET 'EM OUT OF HERE! MOVE THOSE FIRE ENGINES IN!
U.S. AIR FORCE
MARKS
IN HERE, BUDDY! I'LL TAKE YOU TO YOUR REPO DEPOT!

A FEW MINUTES LATER, SAFELY AWAY FROM THE BELEAGUERED AIRSTRIP...

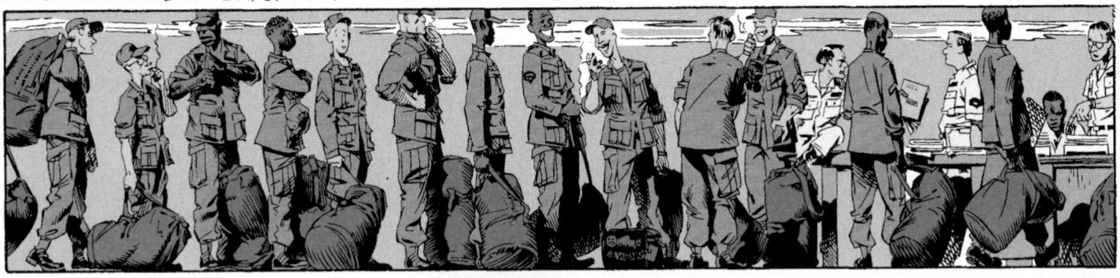

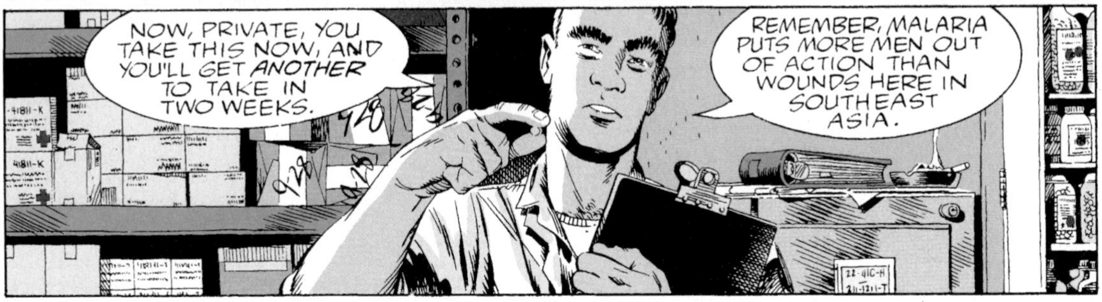
NOW, PRIVATE, YOU TAKE THIS NOW, AND YOU'LL GET *ANOTHER* TO TAKE IN TWO WEEKS.
REMEMBER, MALARIA PUTS MORE MEN OUT OF ACTION THAN WOUNDS HERE IN SOUTHEAST ASIA.

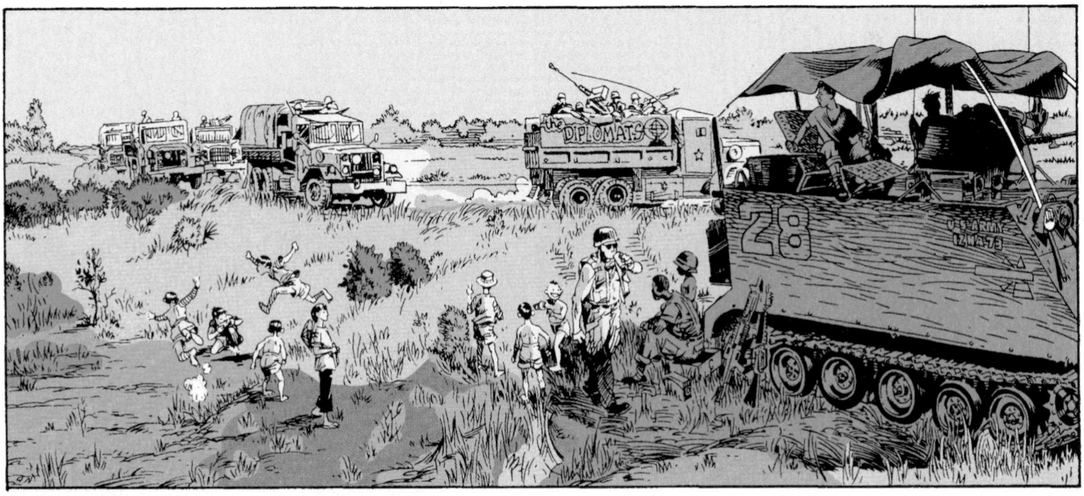
DIPLOMATS
28

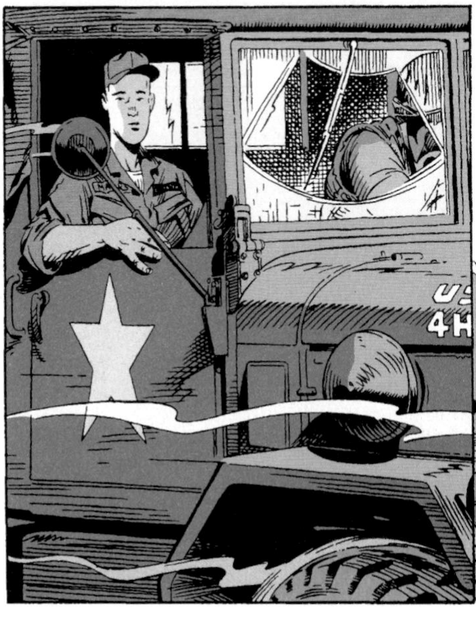

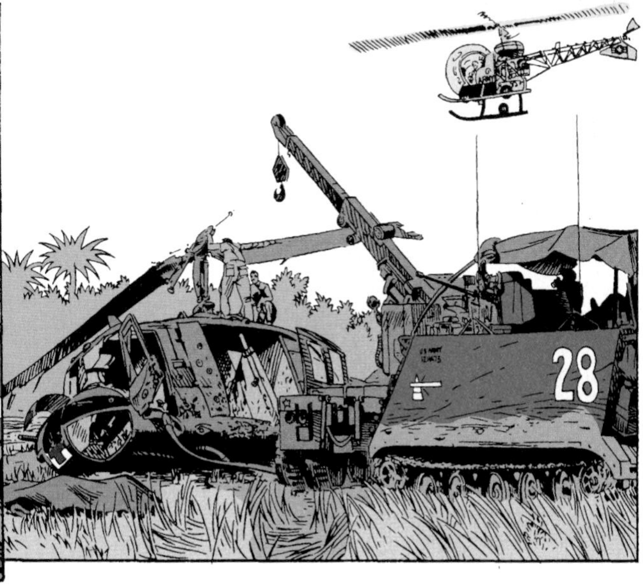
28

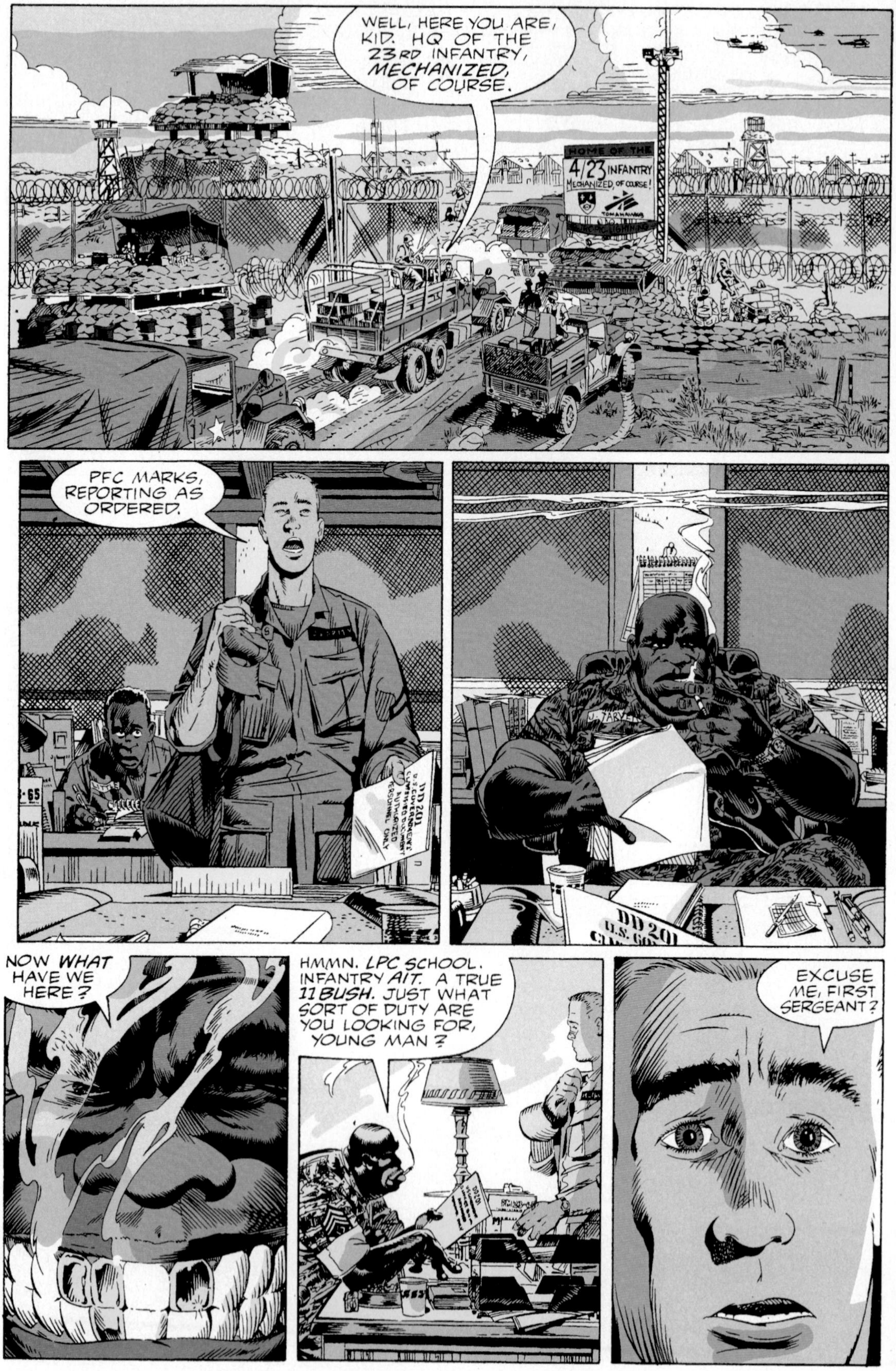
WELL, HERE YOU ARE, KID. HQ OF THE 23rd INFANTRY, MECHANIZED, OF COURSE.
HOME OF THE 4/23 INFANTRY MECHANIZED, OF COURSE!
PFC MARKS, REPORTING AS ORDERED.
DD 201
NOW WHAT HAVE WE HERE?
HMMN. LPC SCHOOL. INFANTRY AIT. A TRUE 11 BUSH. JUST WHAT SORT OF DUTY ARE YOU LOOKING FOR, YOUNG MAN?
EXCUSE ME, FIRST SERGEANT?

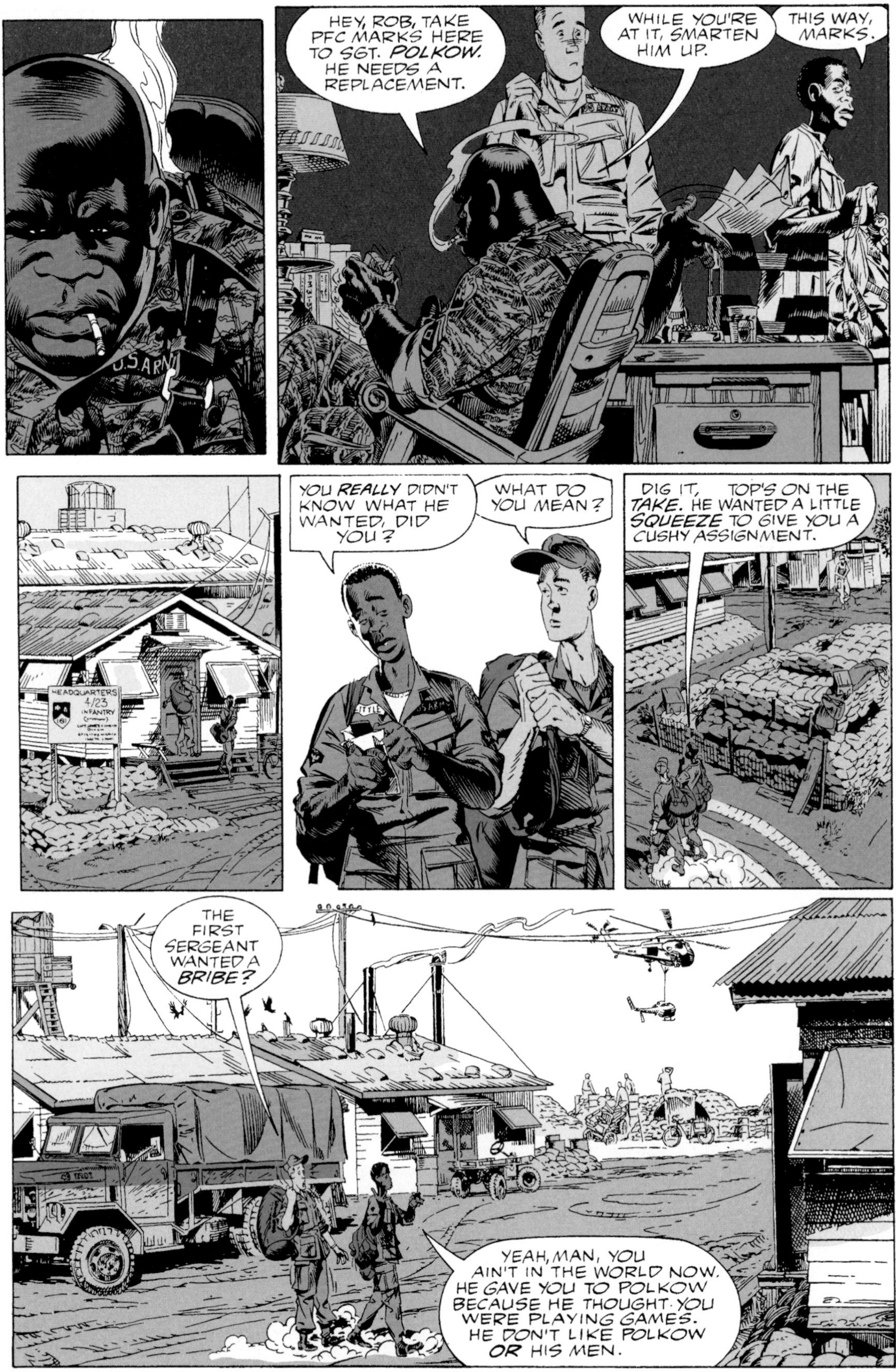
HEY, ROB, TAKE PFC MARKS HERE TO SGT. POLKOW. HE NEEDS A REPLACEMENT.
WHILE YOU'RE AT IT, SMARTEN HIM UP.
THIS WAY, MARKS.
HEADQUARTERS 4/23 INFANTRY
YOU REALLY DIDN'T KNOW WHAT HE WANTED, DID YOU?
WHAT DO YOU MEAN?
DIG IT, TOP'S ON THE TAKE. HE WANTED A LITTLE SQUEEZE TO GIVE YOU A CUSHY ASSIGNMENT.
THE FIRST SERGEANT WANTED A BRIBE?
YEAH, MAN, YOU AIN'T IN THE WORLD NOW. HE GAVE YOU TO POLKOW BECAUSE HE THOUGHT YOU WERE PLAYING GAMES. HE DON'T LIKE POLKOW OR HIS MEN.

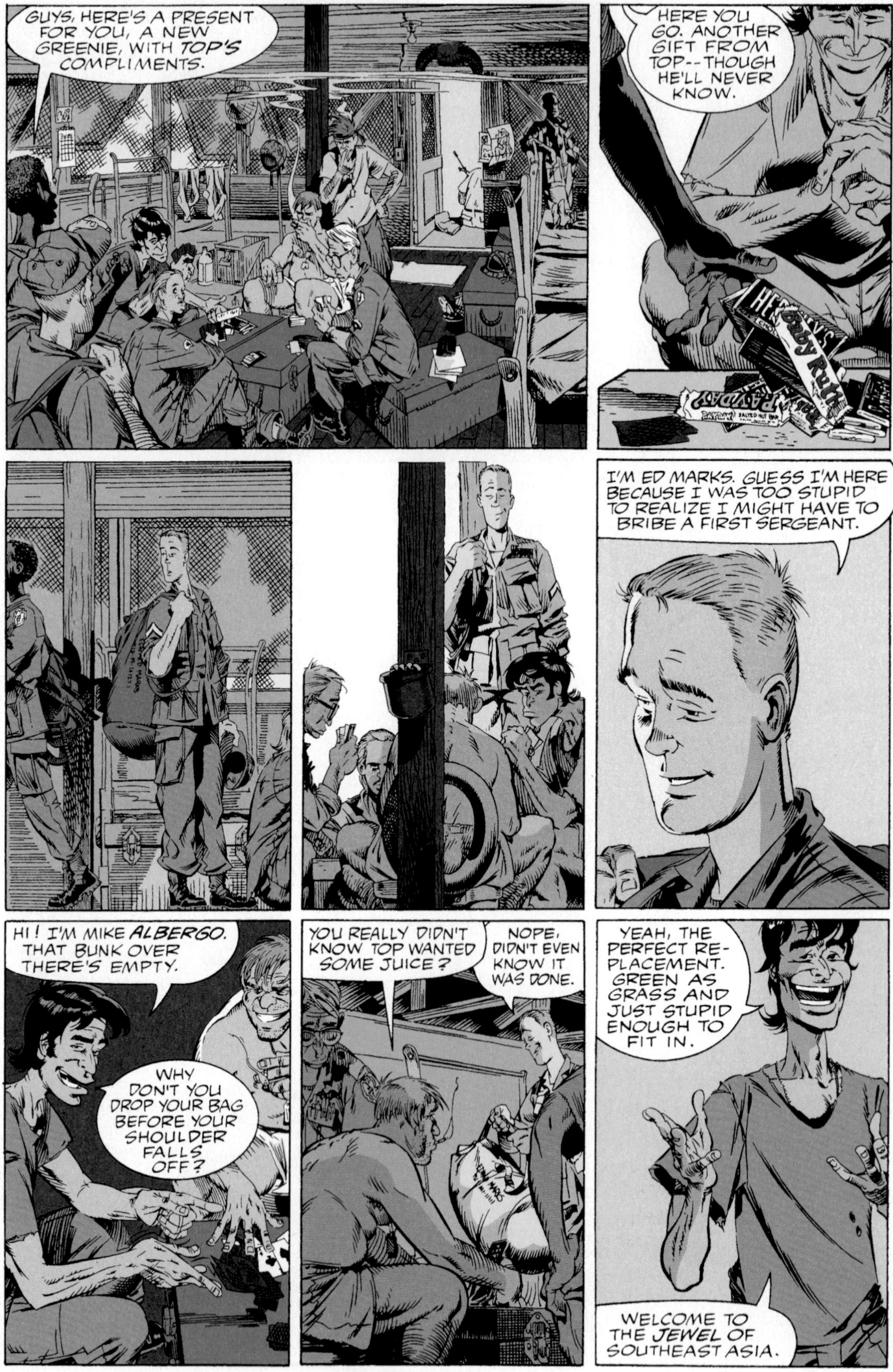
GUYS, HERE'S A PRESENT FOR YOU, A NEW GREENIE, WITH *TOP'S* COMPLIMENTS.
HERE YOU GO. ANOTHER GIFT FROM TOP--THOUGH HE'LL NEVER KNOW.
I'M ED MARKS. GUESS I'M HERE BECAUSE I WAS TOO STUPID TO REALIZE I MIGHT HAVE TO BRIBE A FIRST SERGEANT.
HI! I'M MIKE *ALBERGO*. THAT BUNK OVER THERE'S EMPTY.
WHY DON'T YOU DROP YOUR BAG BEFORE YOUR SHOULDER FALLS OFF?
YOU REALLY DIDN'T KNOW TOP WANTED SOME JUICE?
NOPE. DIDN'T EVEN KNOW IT WAS DONE.
YEAH, THE PERFECT RE-PLACEMENT. GREEN AS GRASS AND JUST STUPID ENOUGH TO FIT IN.
WELCOME TO THE *JEWEL* OF SOUTHEAST ASIA.

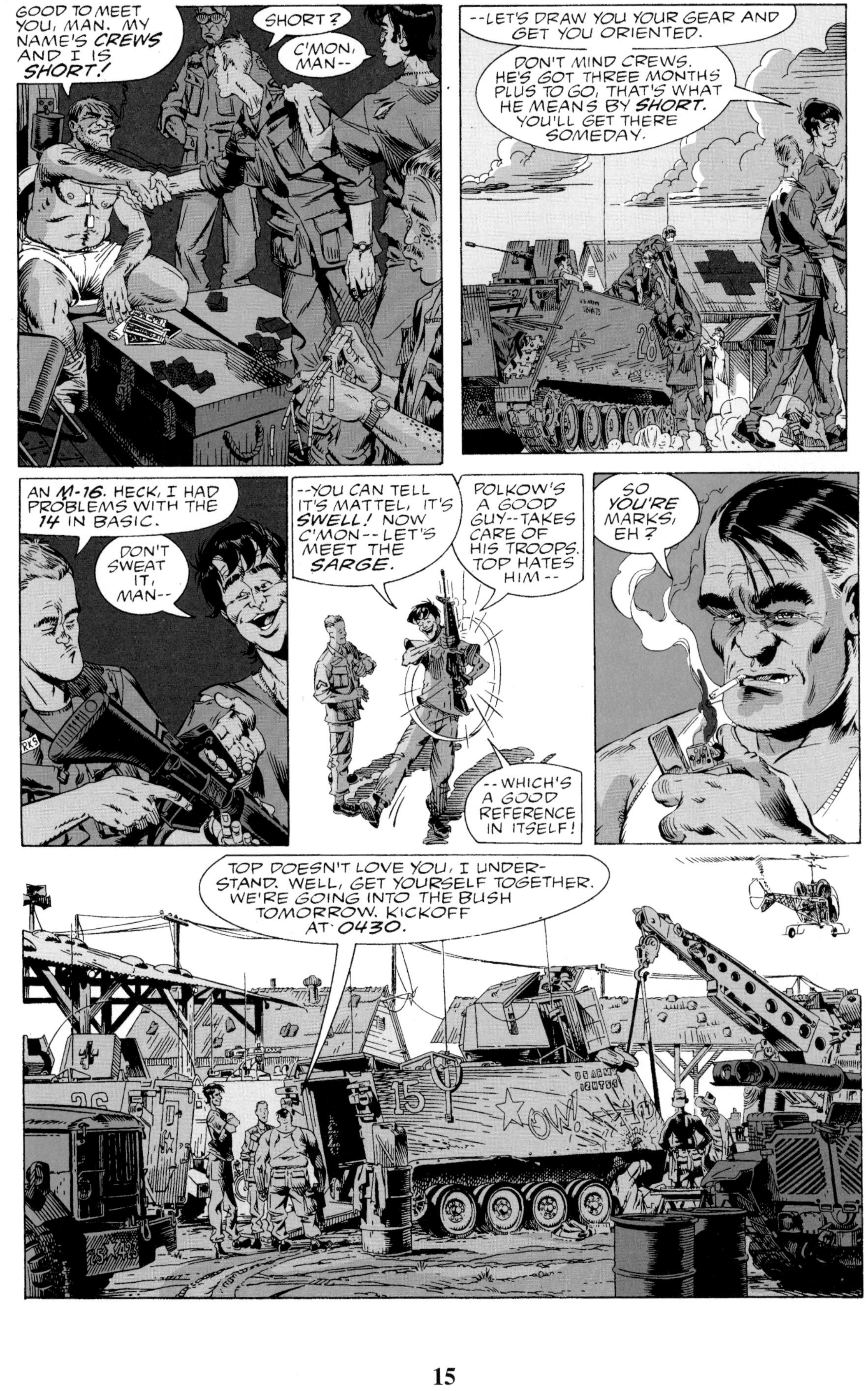
GOOD TO MEET YOU, MAN. MY NAME'S CREWS AND I IS SHORT!
SHORT?
C'MON, MAN--
--LET'S DRAW YOU YOUR GEAR AND GET YOU ORIENTED.
DON'T MIND CREWS. HE'S GOT THREE MONTHS PLUS TO GO, THAT'S WHAT HE MEANS BY SHORT. YOU'LL GET THERE SOMEDAY.
AN M-16. HECK, I HAD PROBLEMS WITH THE 14 IN BASIC.
DON'T SWEAT IT, MAN--
--YOU CAN TELL IT'S MATTEL, IT'S SWELL! NOW C'MON--LET'S MEET THE SARGE.
POLKOW'S A GOOD GUY--TAKES CARE OF HIS TROOPS. TOP HATES HIM--
--WHICH'S A GOOD REFERENCE IN ITSELF!
SO YOU'RE MARKS, EH?
TOP DOESN'T LOVE YOU, I UNDERSTAND. WELL, GET YOURSELF TOGETHER. WE'RE GOING INTO THE BUSH TOMORROW. KICKOFF AT 0430.

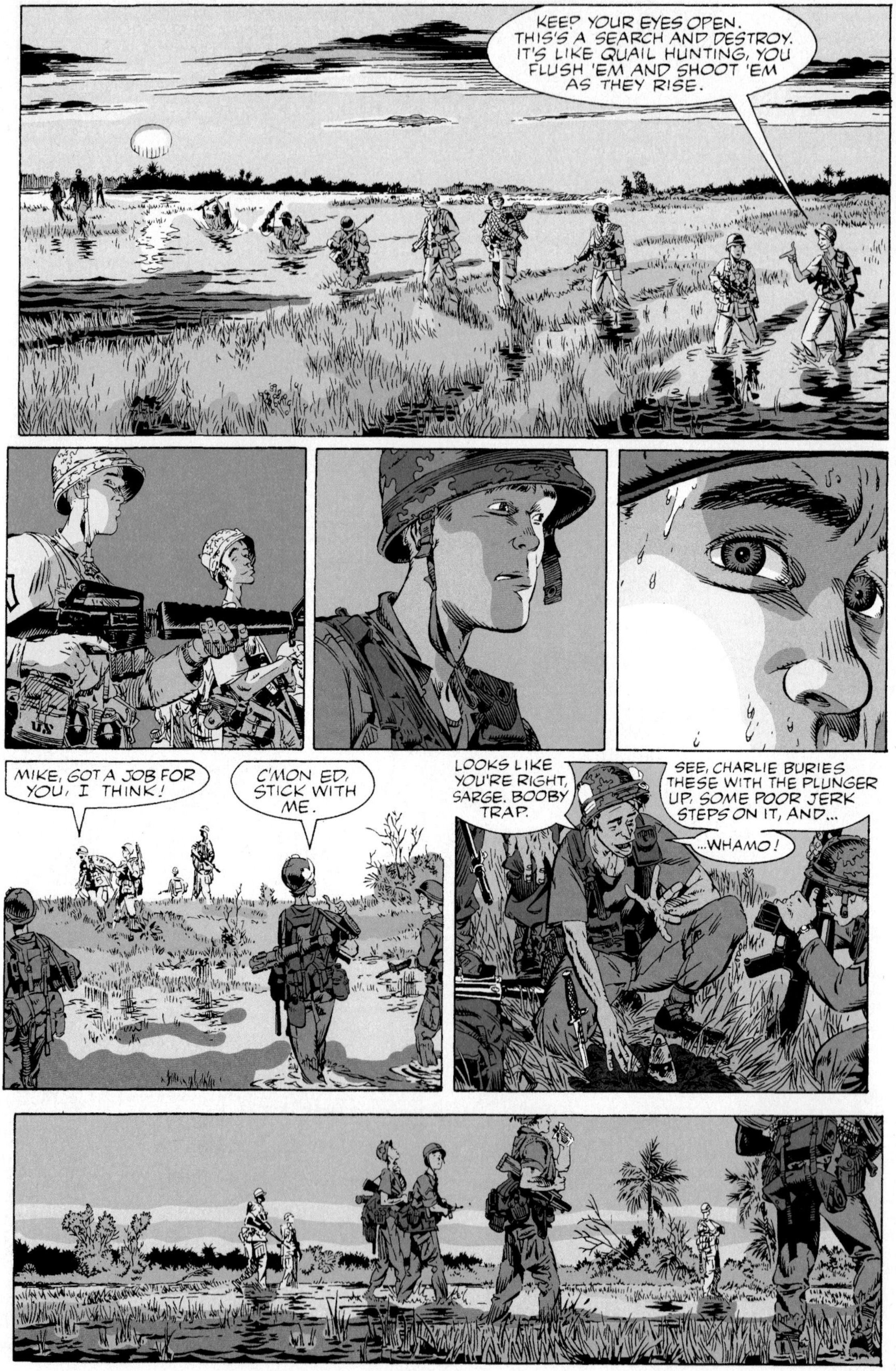
KEEP YOUR EYES OPEN. THIS'S A SEARCH AND DESTROY. IT'S LIKE QUAIL HUNTING, YOU FLUSH 'EM AND SHOOT 'EM AS THEY RISE.
MIKE, GOT A JOB FOR YOU, I THINK!
C'MON ED, STICK WITH ME.
LOOKS LIKE YOU'RE RIGHT, SARGE. BOOBY TRAP.
SEE, CHARLIE BURIES THESE WITH THE PLUNGER UP, SOME POOR JERK STEPS ON IT, AND...
...WHAMO!

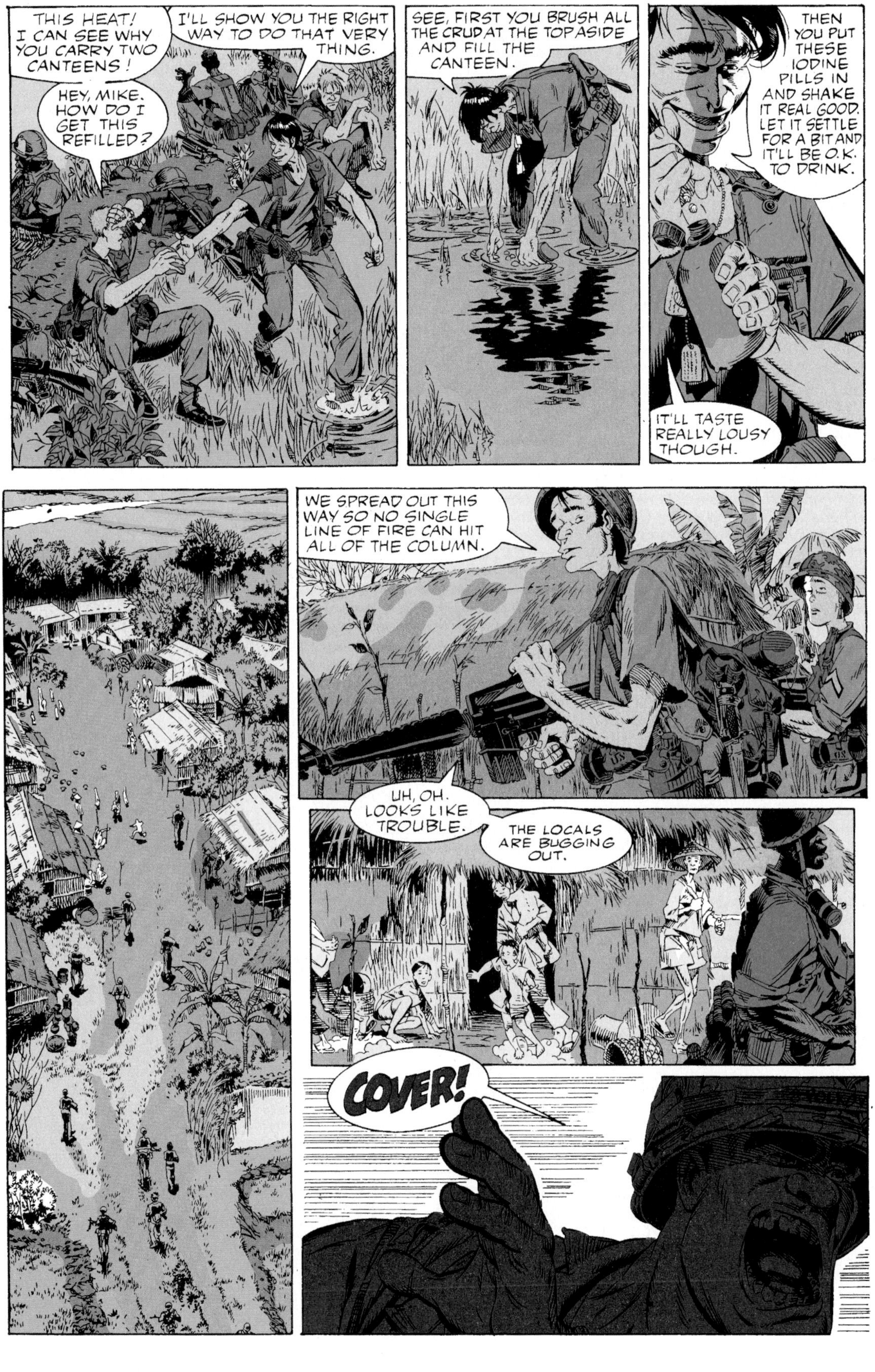
THIS HEAT! I CAN SEE WHY YOU CARRY TWO CANTEENS!
HEY, MIKE. HOW DO I GET THIS REFILLED?
I'LL SHOW YOU THE RIGHT WAY TO DO THAT VERY THING.
SEE, FIRST YOU BRUSH ALL THE CRUD AT THE TOP ASIDE AND FILL THE CANTEEN.
THEN YOU PUT THESE IODINE PILLS IN AND SHAKE IT REAL GOOD. LET IT SETTLE FOR A BIT AND IT'LL BE O.K. TO DRINK.
IT'LL TASTE REALLY LOUSY THOUGH.
WE SPREAD OUT THIS WAY SO NO SINGLE LINE OF FIRE CAN HIT ALL OF THE COLUMN.
UH, OH. LOOKS LIKE TROUBLE.
THE LOCALS ARE BUGGING OUT.
COVER!

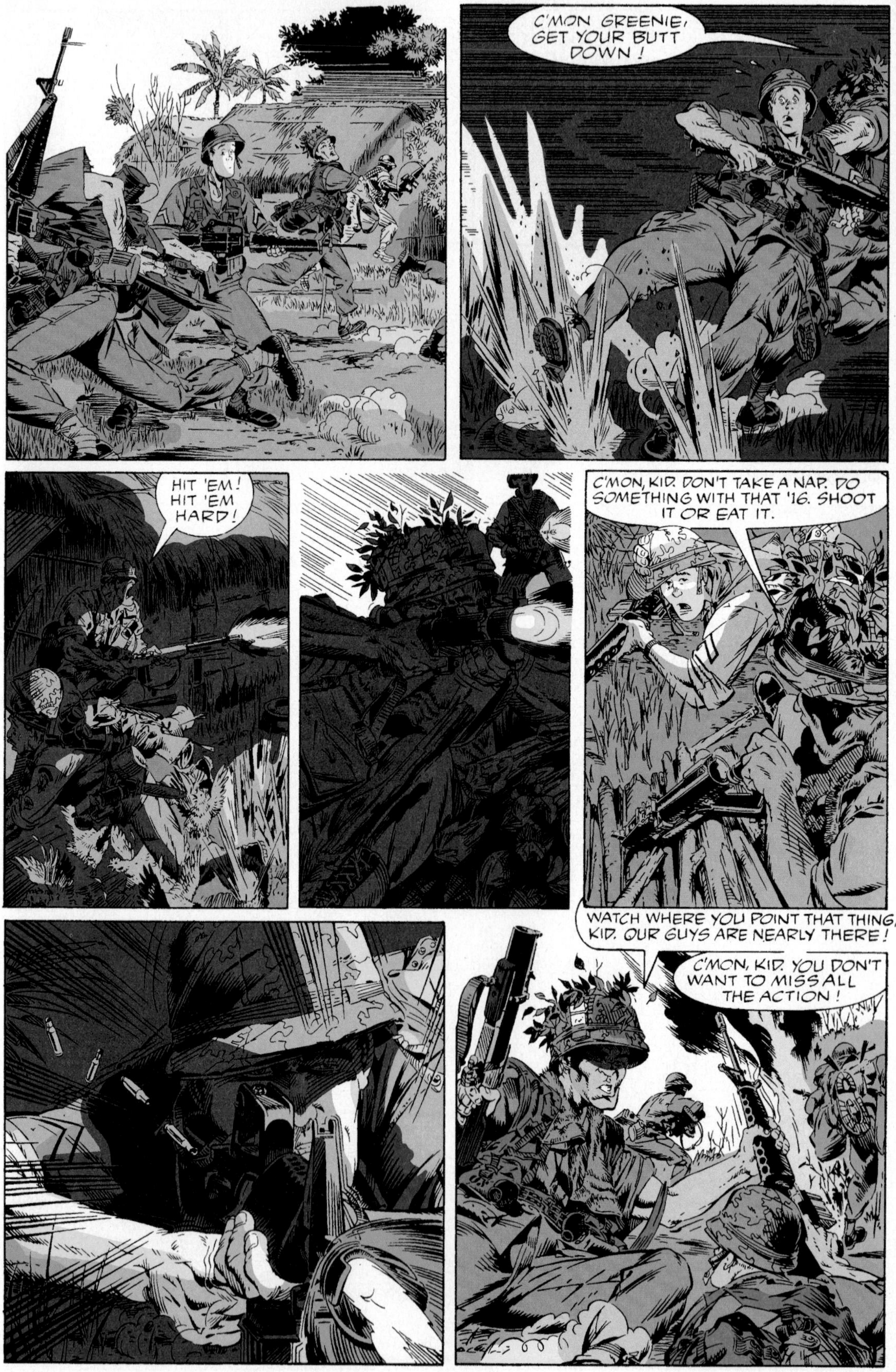
C'MON GREENIE, GET YOUR BUTT DOWN!
HIT 'EM! HIT 'EM HARD!
C'MON, KID. DON'T TAKE A NAP. DO SOMETHING WITH THAT '16. SHOOT IT OR EAT IT.
WATCH WHERE YOU POINT THAT THING, KID. OUR GUYS ARE NEARLY THERE!
C'MON, KID. YOU DON'T WANT TO MISS ALL THE ACTION!

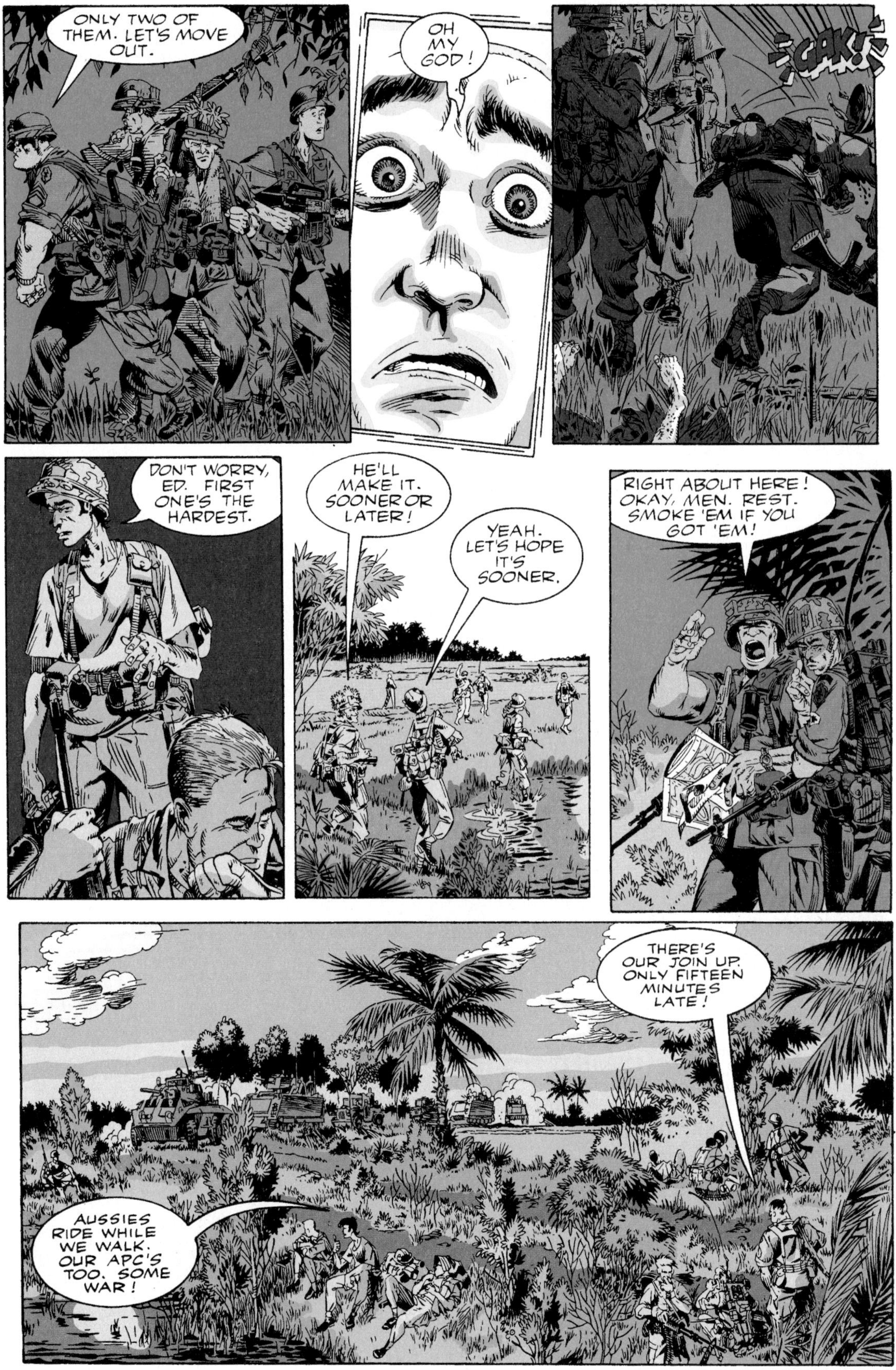
ONLY TWO OF THEM. LET'S MOVE OUT.
OH MY GOD!
GAK!
DON'T WORRY, ED. FIRST ONE'S THE HARDEST.
HE'LL MAKE IT. SOONER OR LATER!
YEAH. LET'S HOPE IT'S SOONER.
RIGHT ABOUT HERE! OKAY, MEN. REST. SMOKE 'EM IF YOU GOT 'EM!
THERE'S OUR JOIN UP. ONLY FIFTEEN MINUTES LATE!
AUSSIES RIDE WHILE WE WALK. OUR APC'S TOO. SOME WAR!

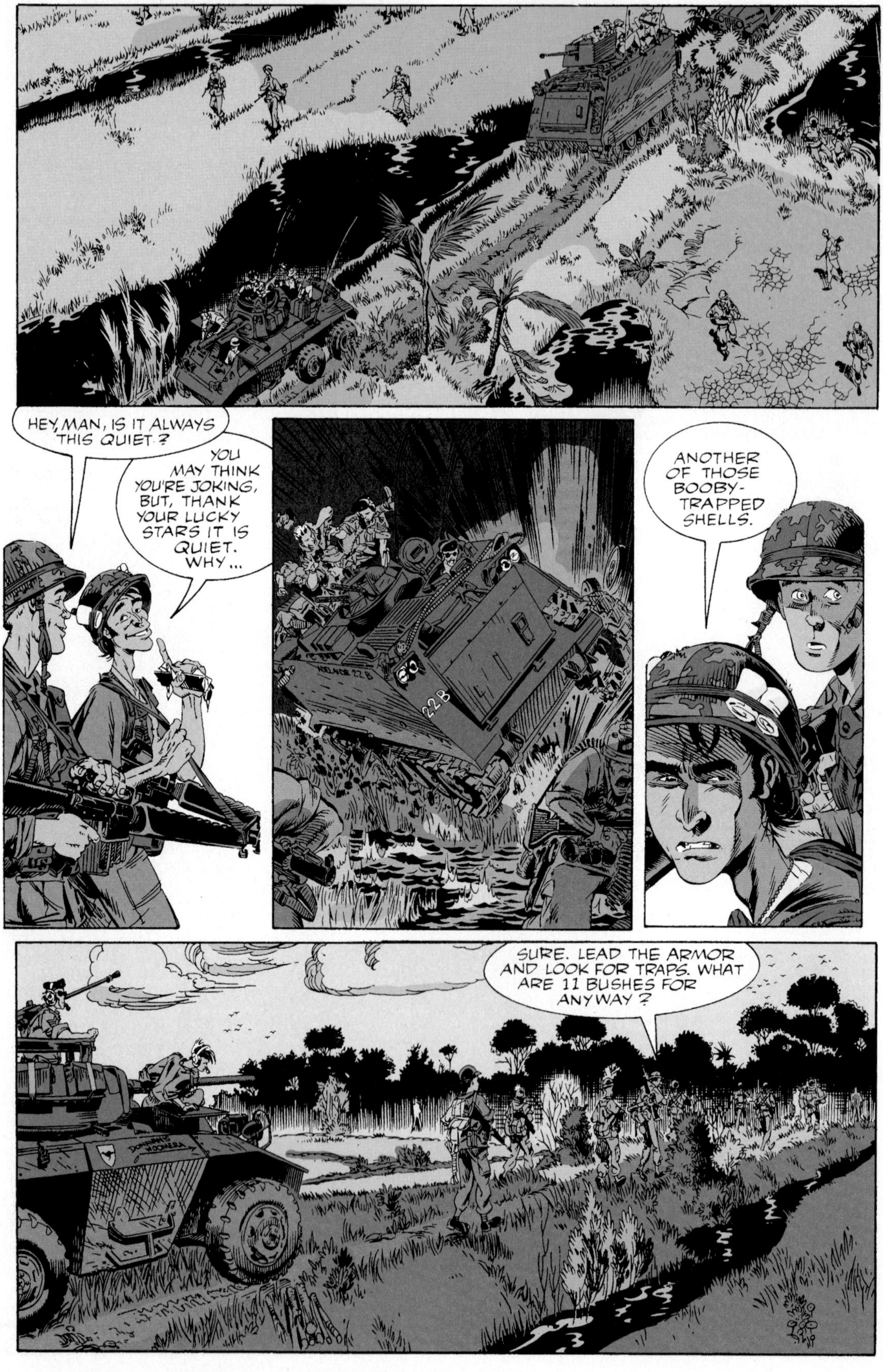
HEY, MAN, IS IT ALWAYS THIS QUIET ?
YOU MAY THINK YOU'RE JOKING, BUT, THANK YOUR LUCKY STARS IT IS QUIET. WHY...
ANOTHER OF THOSE BOOBY-TRAPPED SHELLS.
SURE. LEAD THE ARMOR AND LOOK FOR TRAPS. WHAT ARE 11 BUSHES FOR ANYWAY ?

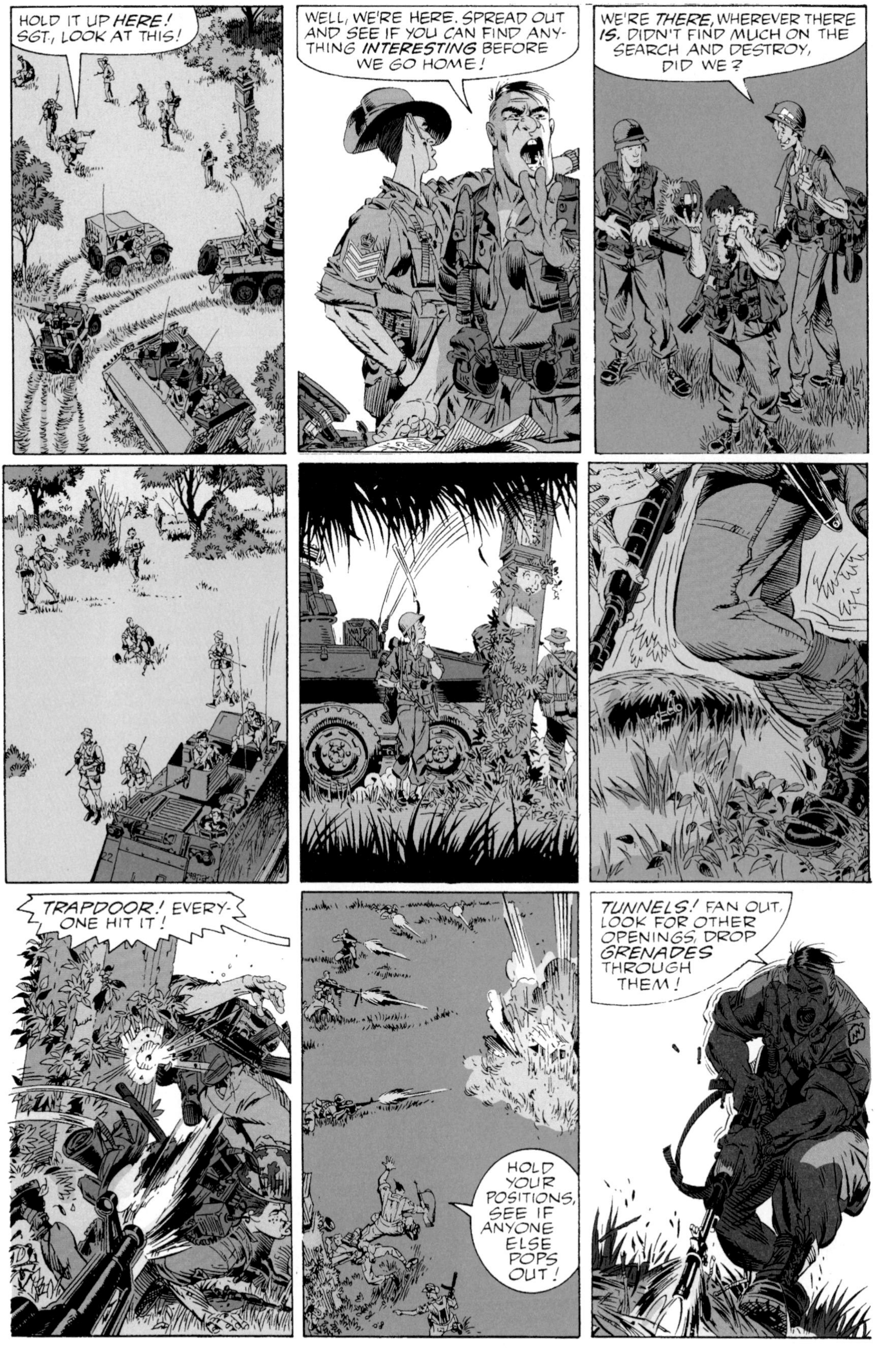
HOLD IT UP HERE! SGT., LOOK AT THIS!
WELL, WE'RE HERE. SPREAD OUT AND SEE IF YOU CAN FIND ANYTHING INTERESTING BEFORE WE GO HOME!
WE'RE THERE, WHEREVER THERE IS. DIDN'T FIND MUCH ON THE SEARCH AND DESTROY, DID WE?
WATER
TRAPDOOR! EVERYONE HIT IT!
HOLD YOUR POSITIONS, SEE IF ANYONE ELSE POPS OUT!
TUNNELS! FAN OUT, LOOK FOR OTHER OPENINGS, DROP GRENADES THROUGH THEM!

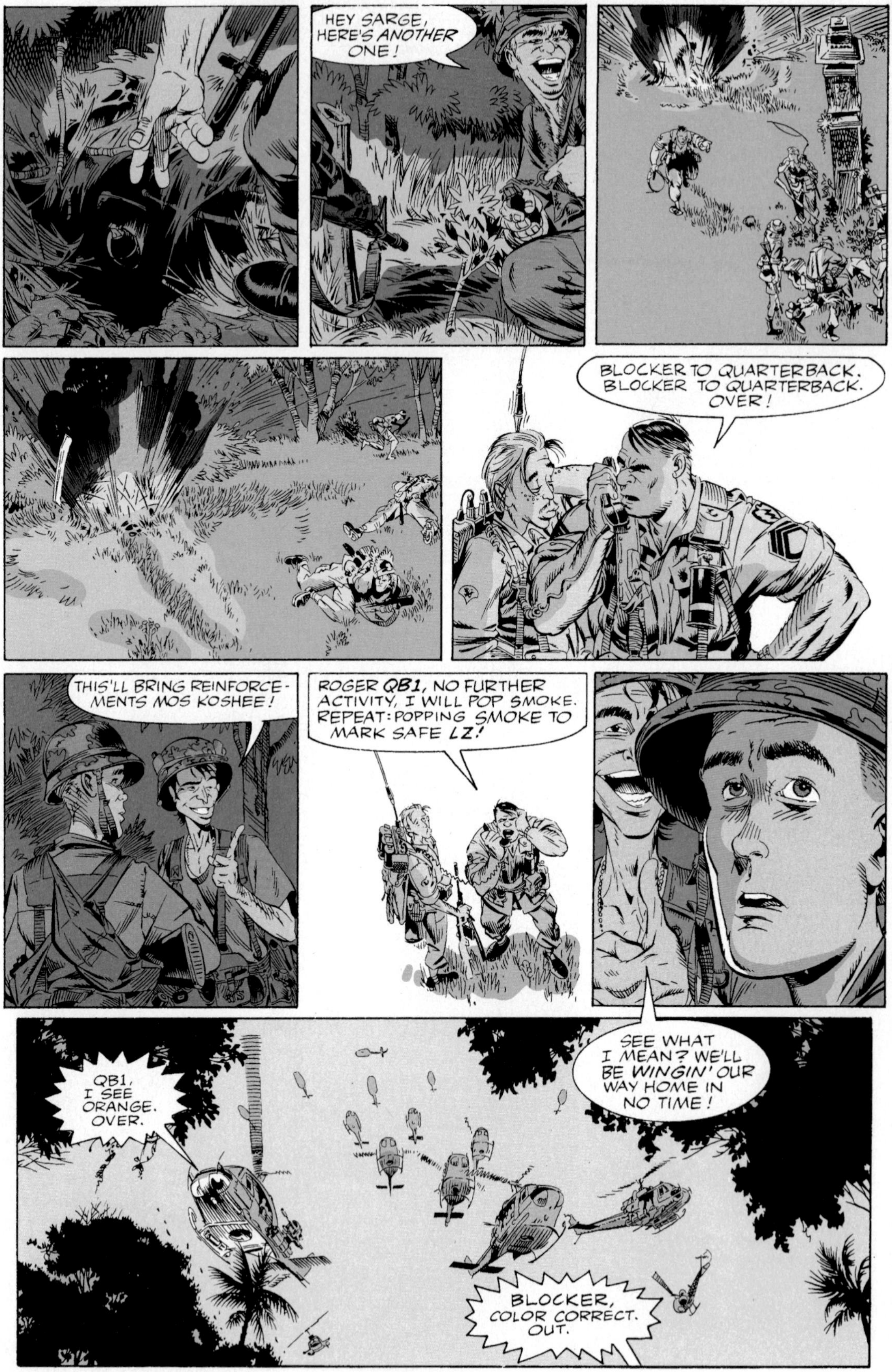
HEY SARGE, HERE'S ANOTHER ONE!
BLOCKER TO QUARTERBACK. BLOCKER TO QUARTERBACK. OVER!
THIS'LL BRING REINFORCE-MENTS MOS KOSHEE!
ROGER QB1, NO FURTHER ACTIVITY, I WILL POP SMOKE. REPEAT: POPPING SMOKE TO MARK SAFE LZ!
QB1, I SEE ORANGE. OVER.
SEE WHAT I MEAN? WE'LL BE WINGIN' OUR WAY HOME IN NO TIME!
BLOCKER, COLOR CORRECT. OUT.

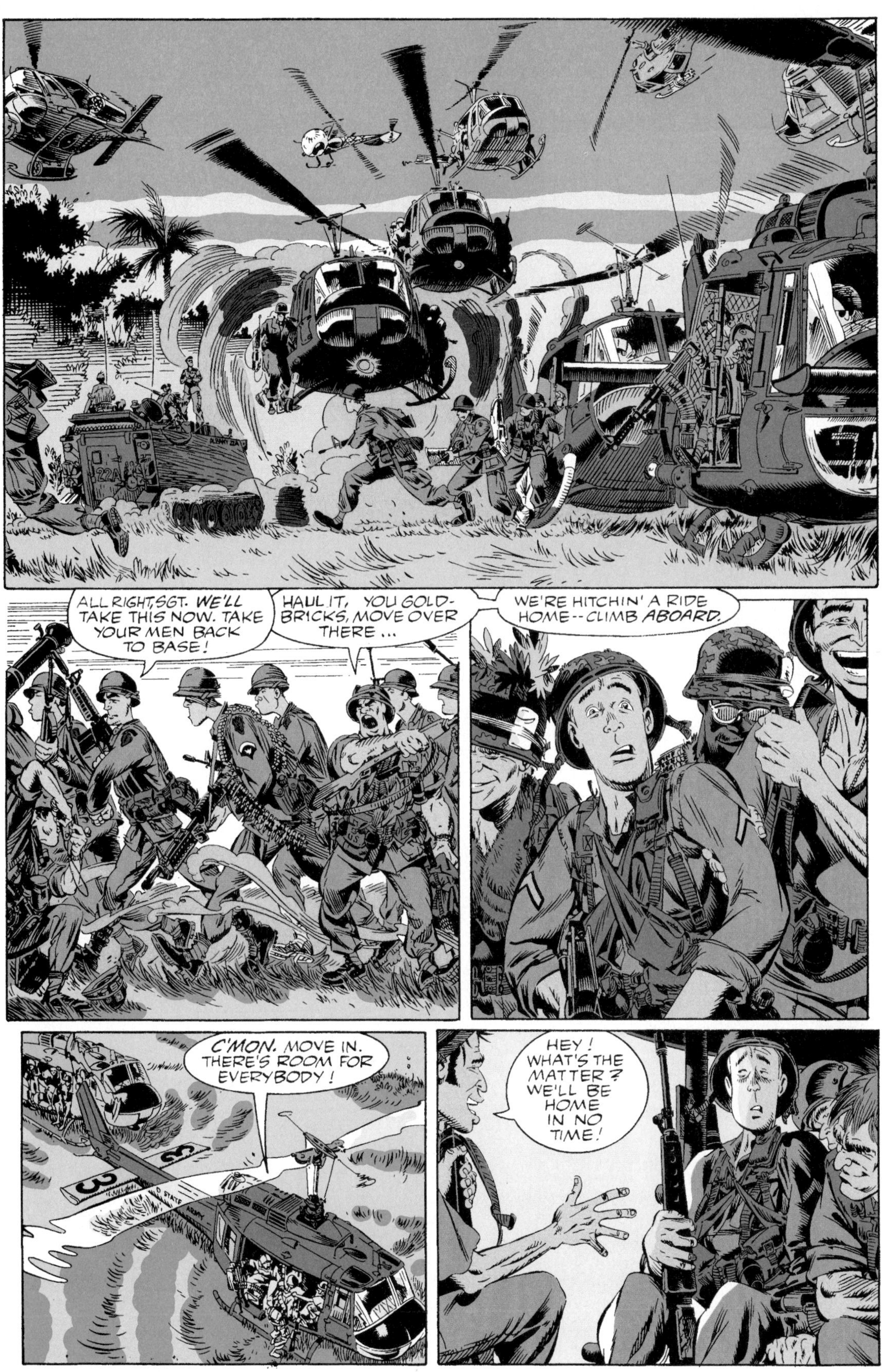
ALL RIGHT, SGT. WE'LL TAKE THIS NOW. TAKE YOUR MEN BACK TO BASE!
HAUL IT, YOU GOLD-BRICKS, MOVE OVER THERE...
WE'RE HITCHIN' A RIDE HOME--CLIMB ABOARD.
C'MON. MOVE IN. THERE'S ROOM FOR EVERYBODY!
HEY! WHAT'S THE MATTER? WE'LL BE HOME IN NO TIME!

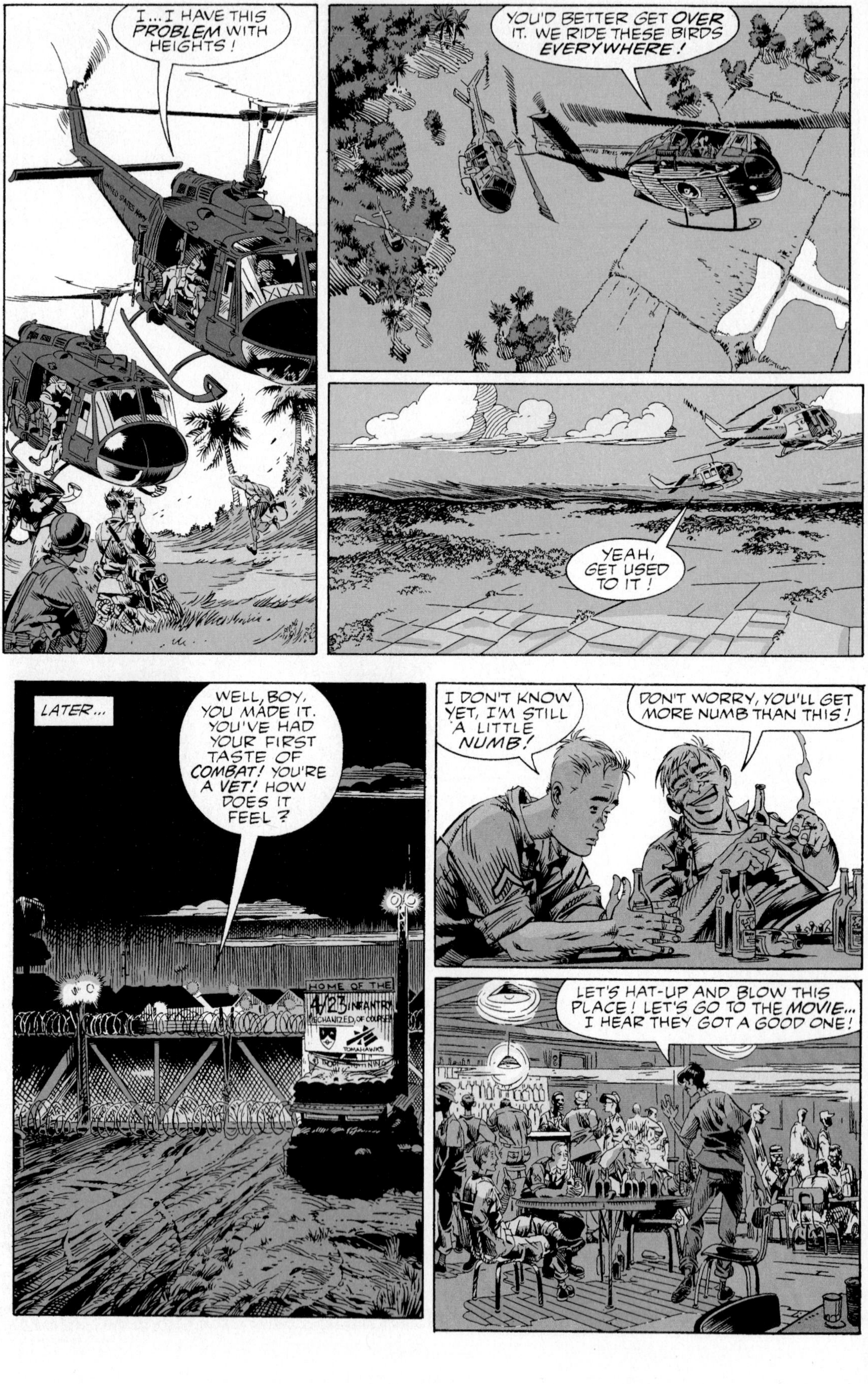
I... I HAVE THIS PROBLEM WITH HEIGHTS!
YOU'D BETTER GET OVER IT. WE RIDE THESE BIRDS EVERYWHERE!
YEAH, GET USED TO IT!
LATER...
WELL, BOY, YOU MADE IT. YOU'VE HAD YOUR FIRST TASTE OF COMBAT! YOU'RE A VET! HOW DOES IT FEEL?
HOME OF THE
4/23 INFANTRY
MECHANIZED, OF COURSE
TOMAHAWKS
I DON'T KNOW YET, I'M STILL A LITTLE NUMB!
DON'T WORRY, YOU'LL GET MORE NUMB THAN THIS!
LET'S HAT-UP AND BLOW THIS PLACE! LET'S GO TO THE MOVIE... I HEAR THEY GOT A GOOD ONE!

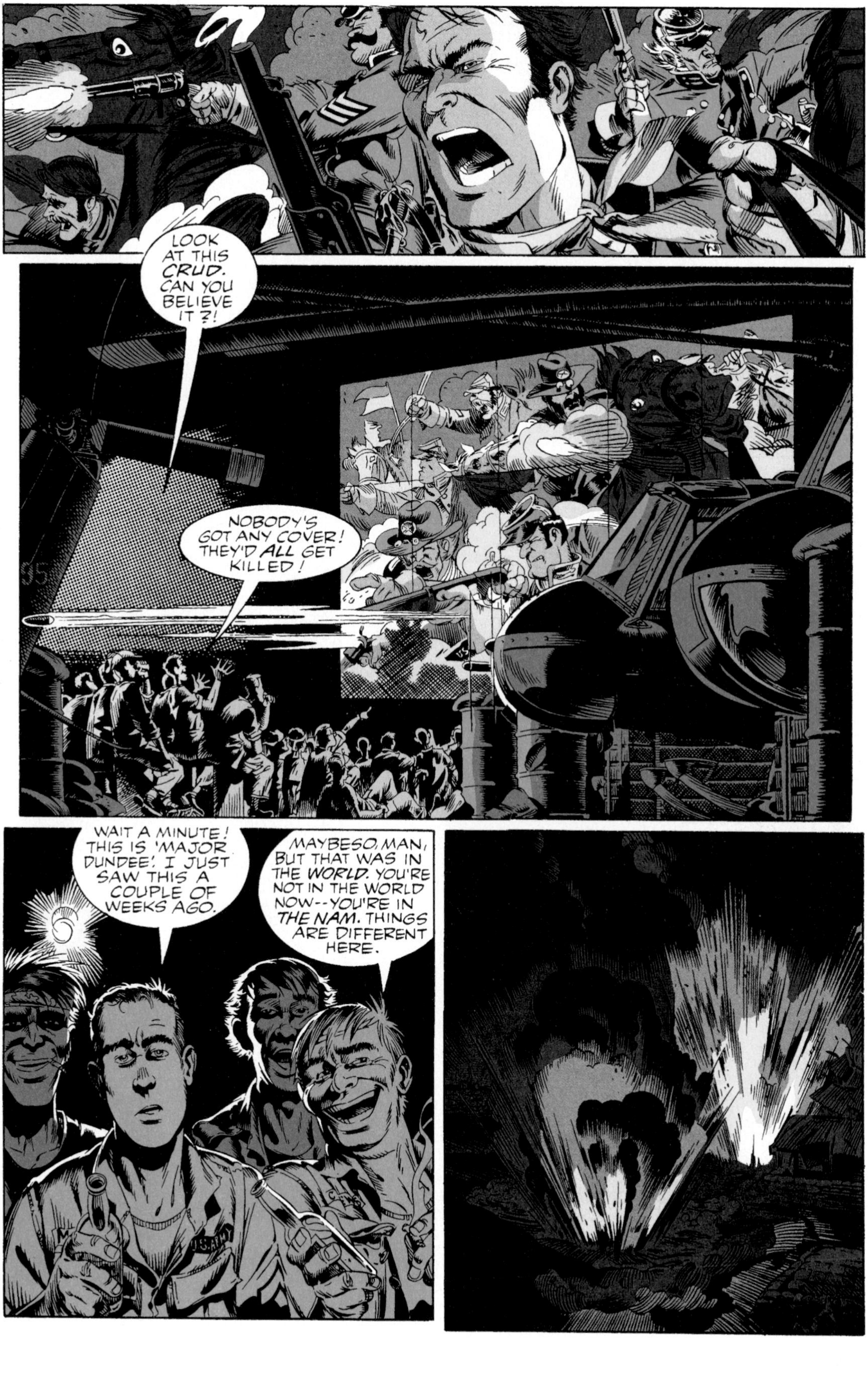
LOOK AT THIS CRUD. CAN YOU BELIEVE IT ?!
NOBODY'S GOT ANY COVER! THEY'D ALL GET KILLED!
WAIT A MINUTE! THIS IS 'MAJOR DUNDEE.' I JUST SAW THIS A COUPLE OF WEEKS AGO.
MAYBESO, MAN, BUT THAT WAS IN THE WORLD. YOU'RE NOT IN THE WORLD NOW--YOU'RE IN THE NAM. THINGS ARE DIFFERENT HERE.

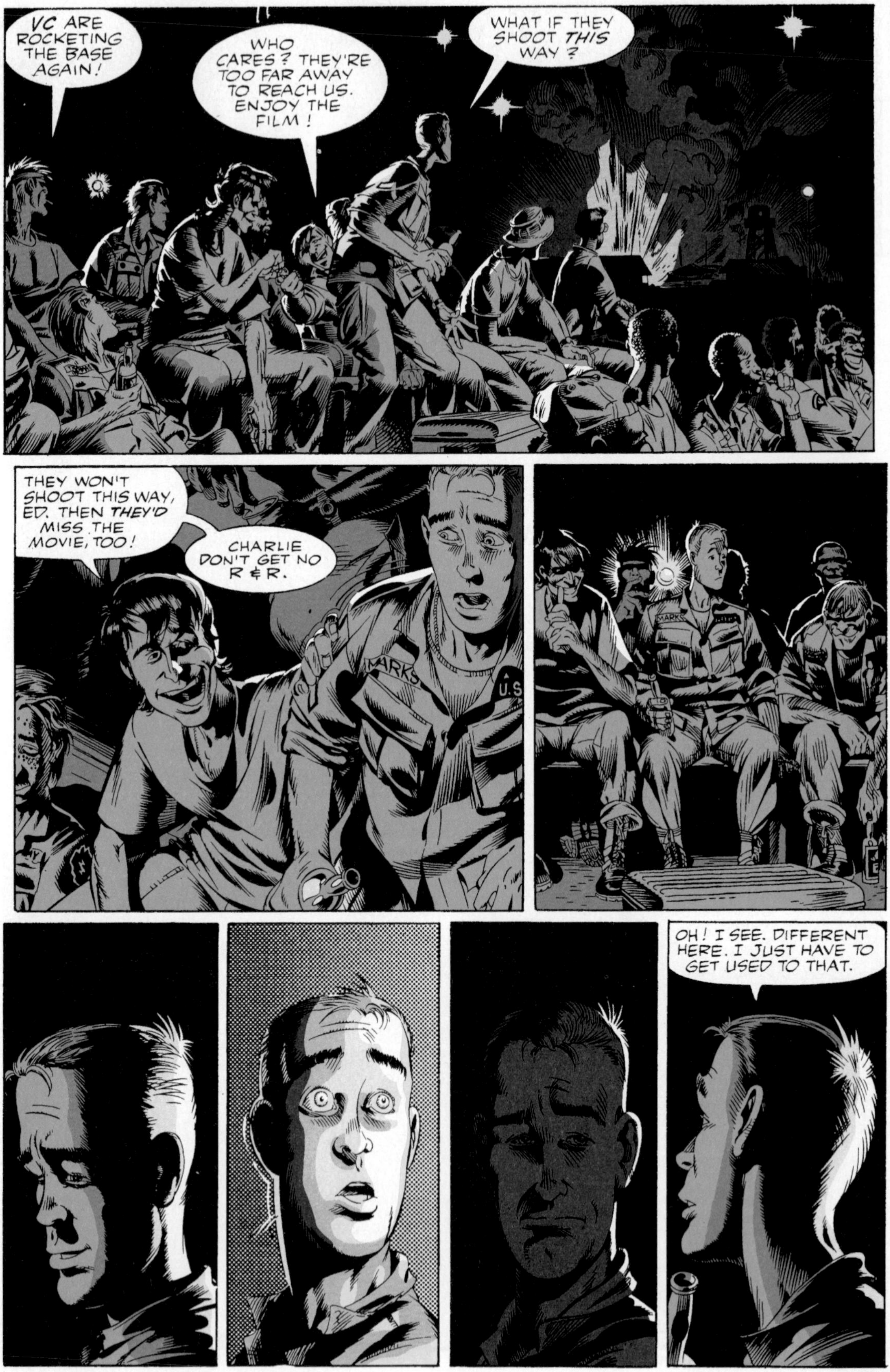
VC ARE ROCKETING THE BASE AGAIN!
WHO CARES? THEY'RE TOO FAR AWAY TO REACH US. ENJOY THE FILM!
WHAT IF THEY SHOOT THIS WAY?
THEY WON'T SHOOT THIS WAY, ED. THEN THEY'D MISS THE MOVIE, TOO!
CHARLIE DON'T GET NO R & R.
MARKS
U.S.
MARKS
OH! I SEE. DIFFERENT HERE. I JUST HAVE TO GET USED TO THAT.

LARRY HAMA: editor — PAT REDDING: assistant editor
℅ MARVEL COMICS GROUP-387 Park Avenue South-New York, New York-10016
Attention correspondents: if you don't want your full address printed, please be sure to tell us so!

INCOMING

The 'NAM is the real thing—or at least as close to the real thing as we can get—in a newsstand comic bearing the Comics Code seal. Every action, every fire fight is based on fact. That doesn't mean that the 23rd Infantry was in every action we show—it does mean that, in February of 1966, a contingent of U.S. Infantry met with a mechanized group of Aussie Infantry and together they discovered a Viet Cong tunnel system, just as shown in issue #1.

Furthermore, the events in the 'Nam happen in real time. When thirty days pass for the reader, thirty days also pass for the characters in the story. When a full year—12 issues—have gone by of the 'Nam, characters introduced in issue #1 will all have rotated back to the states, just like in the real world.

Yes, we had to make some compromises. The real language used by soldiers in the field can be quite raw. The most common appellation for a new troop was not "greenie." The word itself was printable, but the explanation gets a bit touchy. We all know that General McAuliffe didn't really say "nuts" to the German commander at Bastogne . . .

Now, I can't promise that we will show everything, every action that everyone's father or brother ever took part in during the Viet Nam War. But I will promise that we will show, in basic terms, what the War was really like for those who fought in it.

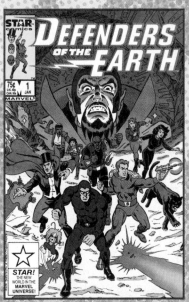

STAR comics
DEFENDERS OF THE EARTH
75¢ U.K. 40p CAN. 95¢ M 1 JAN
MARVEL
STAR! THE NEW WORLD IN THE MARVEL UNIVERSE!
DEFENDERS OF THE EARTH #1, published in September 1986, began a short Star series based on the Marvel Productions/King Features animated TV series.

STAR comics
CHUCK NORRIS
KARATE KOMMANDOS
75¢ U.K. 40p CAN. 95¢ M 1 JAN
MARVEL
STAR! THE NEW WORLD IN THE MARVEL UNIVERSE!
CHUCK NORRIS KARATE KOMMANDOS #1, published in September 1986, began a short Star series based on the Ruby-Spears animated TV series.

MARVEL 25th ANNIVERSARY
#1 IN A FOUR-ISSUE LIMITED SERIES
G.I. JOE AND THE TRANSFORMERS
75¢ U.K. 40p CAN. 95¢ M 1 JAN
UNITED STATES
G.I. JOE AND THE TRANSFORMERS #1, published in September 1986, began a miniseries featuring a crossover between the two Hasbro toy lines.

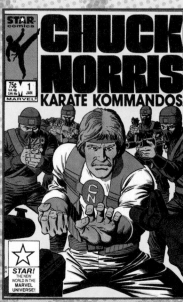

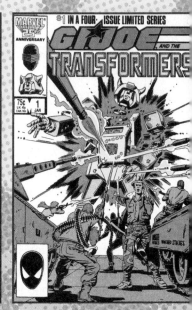

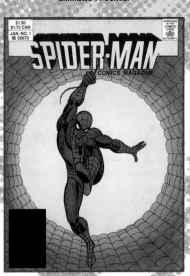

$1.50 $1.75 CAN
JAN. NO. 1
02670
APPROVED BY THE COMICS CODE AUTHORITY
SPIDER-MAN
COMICS MAGAZINE
SPIDER-MAN COMICS MAGAZINE #1, published in September 1986, began a digest-sized reprint series.

$1.50 $1.75 CAN
JAN. NO. 1
02672
APPROVED BY THE COMICS CODE AUTHORITY
THE TRANSFORMERS
COMICS MAGAZINE
TRANSFORMERS COMICS MAGAZINE #1, published in October 1986, began a digest-sized reprint series.

STAR comics
THE FEROCIOUS FIRST ISSUE OF
THE INHUMANOIDS
75¢ U.K. 40p CAN. 95¢ M 1 JAN
MARVEL
FEATURING: THE BEAST-BUSTING EARTH CORPS!
STAR! THE NEW WORLD IN THE MARVEL UNIVERSE!
INHUMANOIDS #1, published in October 1986, began a short Star series based on the Marvel Productions/Sunbow animated TV series.

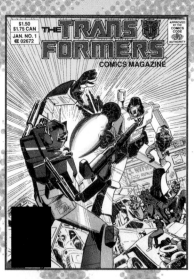

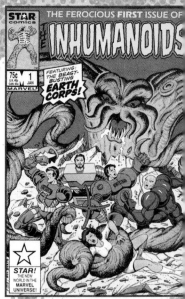

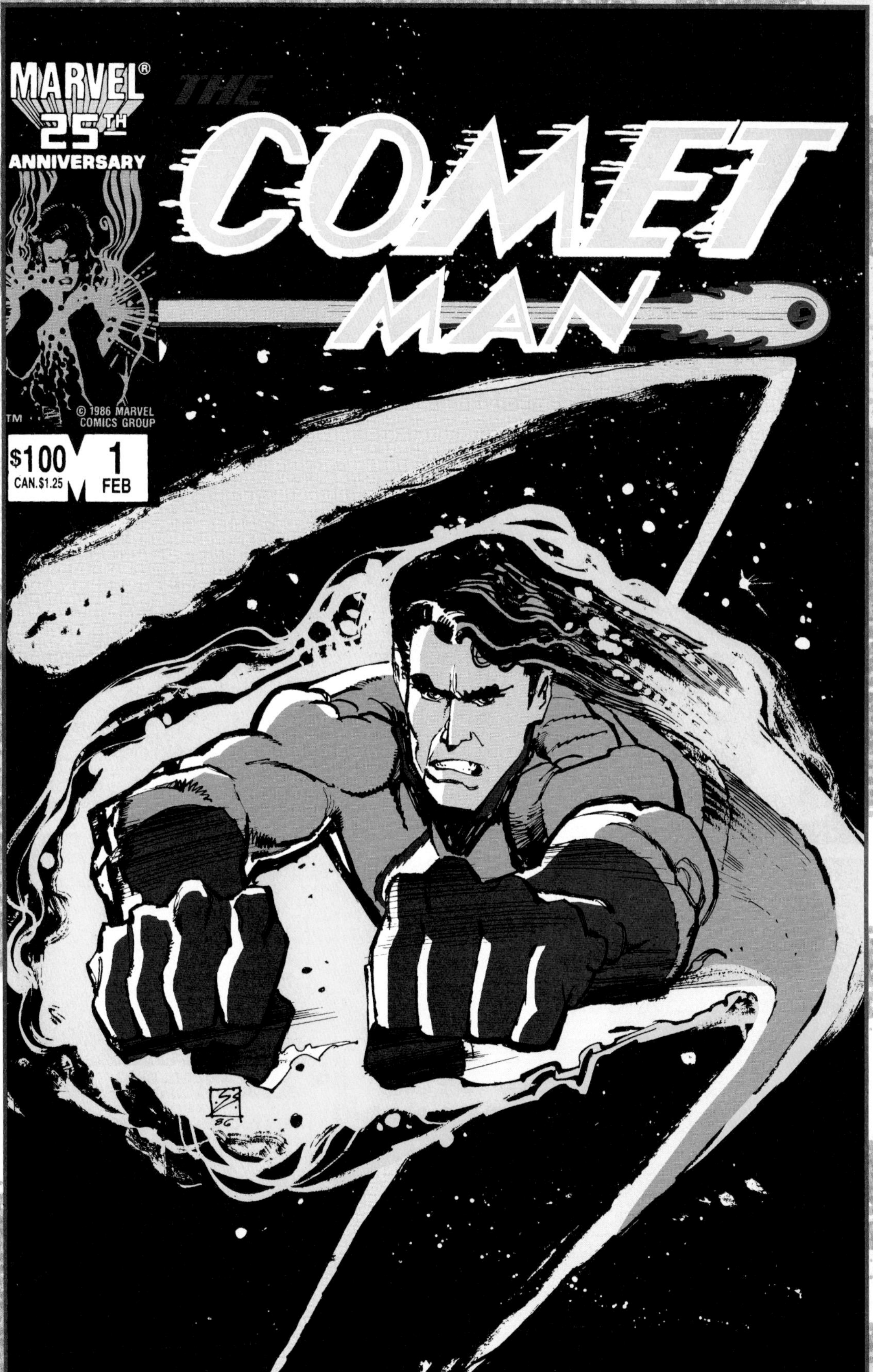
MARVEL®
25TH
ANNIVERSARY
THE
COMET
MAN
TM
TM
© 1986 MARVEL
COMICS GROUP
$100
CAN.$1.25
1
FEB

COMET MAN #1, published in October 1986, introduced the scientist-turned-super hero in a limited series.

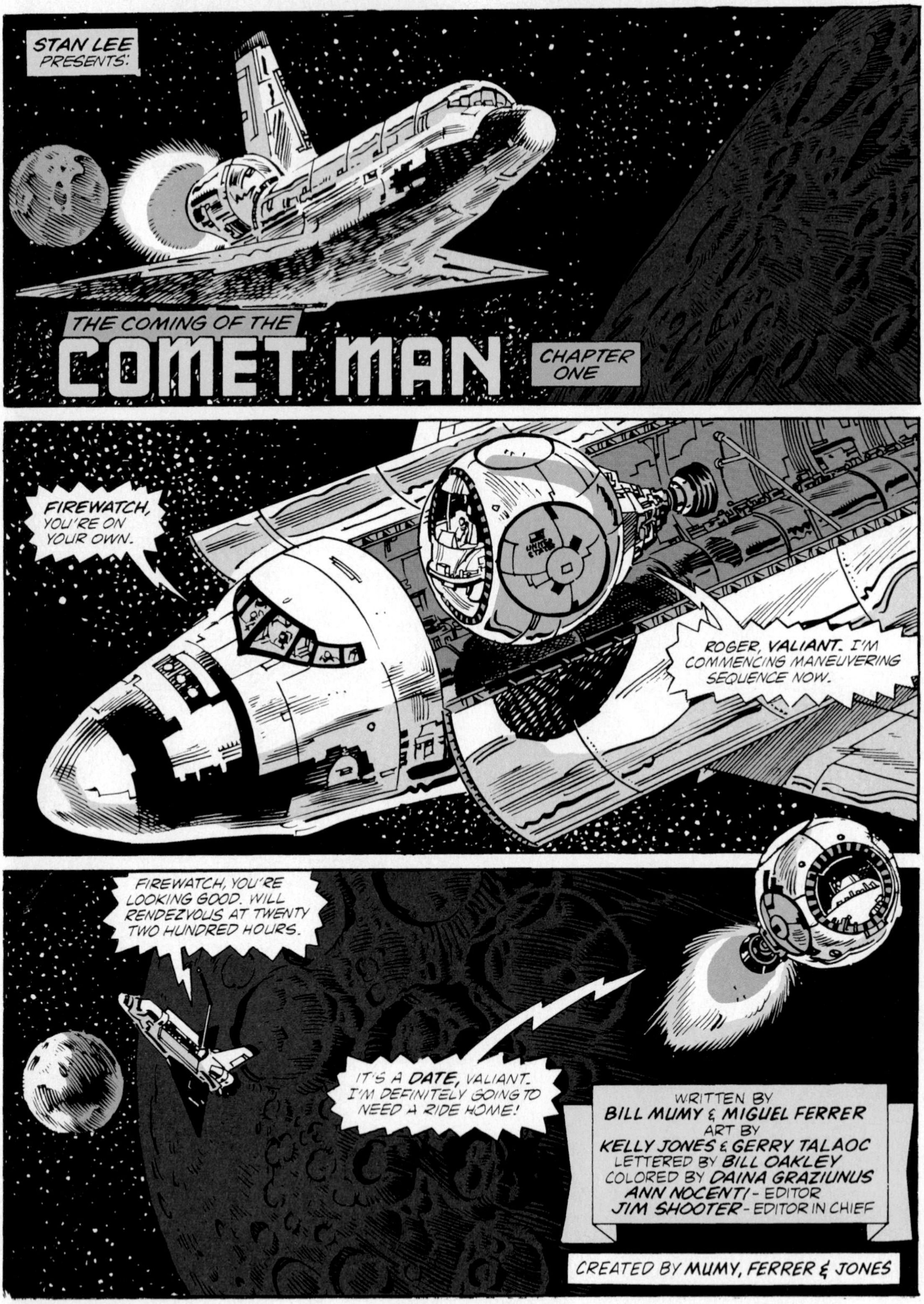
STAN LEE PRESENTS:
THE COMING OF THE COMET MAN
CHAPTER ONE
FIREWATCH, YOU'RE ON YOUR OWN.
ROGER, VALIANT. I'M COMMENCING MANEUVERING SEQUENCE NOW.
FIREWATCH, YOU'RE LOOKING GOOD. WILL RENDEZVOUS AT TWENTY TWO HUNDRED HOURS.
IT'S A DATE, VALIANT. I'M DEFINITELY GOING TO NEED A RIDE HOME!
WRITTEN BY BILL MUMY & MIGUEL FERRER ART BY KELLY JONES & GERRY TALAOC LETTERED BY BILL OAKLEY COLORED BY DAINA GRAZIUNUS ANN NOCENTI - EDITOR JIM SHOOTER - EDITOR IN CHIEF
CREATED BY MUMY, FERRER & JONES

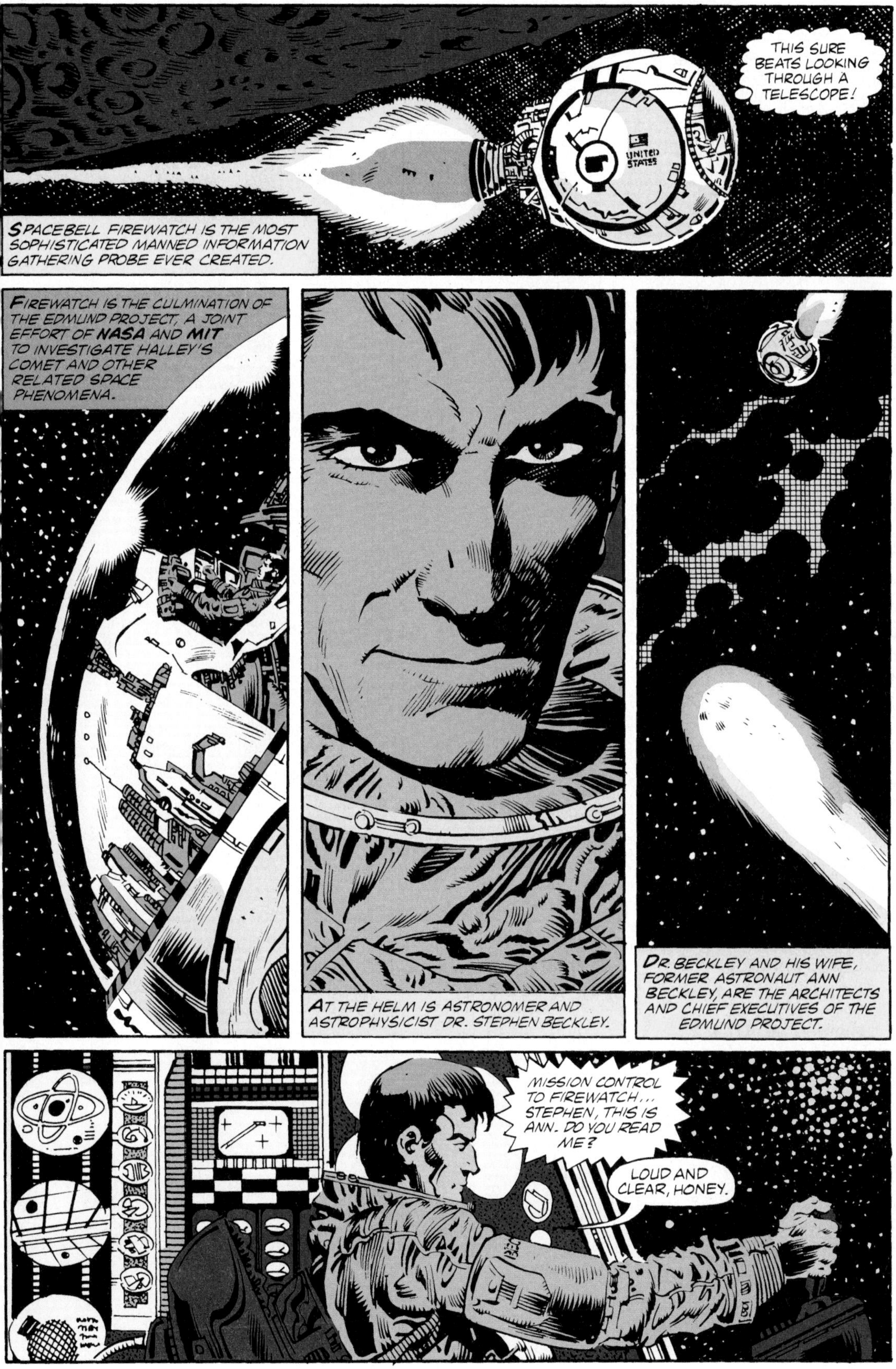
THIS SURE BEATS LOOKING THROUGH A TELESCOPE!
UNITED STATES
SPACEBELL FIREWATCH IS THE MOST SOPHISTICATED MANNED INFORMATION GATHERING PROBE EVER CREATED.
FIREWATCH IS THE CULMINATION OF THE EDMUND PROJECT, A JOINT EFFORT OF NASA AND MIT TO INVESTIGATE HALLEY'S COMET AND OTHER RELATED SPACE PHENOMENA.
AT THE HELM IS ASTRONOMER AND ASTROPHYSICIST DR. STEPHEN BECKLEY.
DR. BECKLEY AND HIS WIFE, FORMER ASTRONAUT ANN BECKLEY, ARE THE ARCHITECTS AND CHIEF EXECUTIVES OF THE EDMUND PROJECT.
MISSION CONTROL TO FIREWATCH... STEPHEN, THIS IS ANN. DO YOU READ ME?
LOUD AND CLEAR, HONEY.

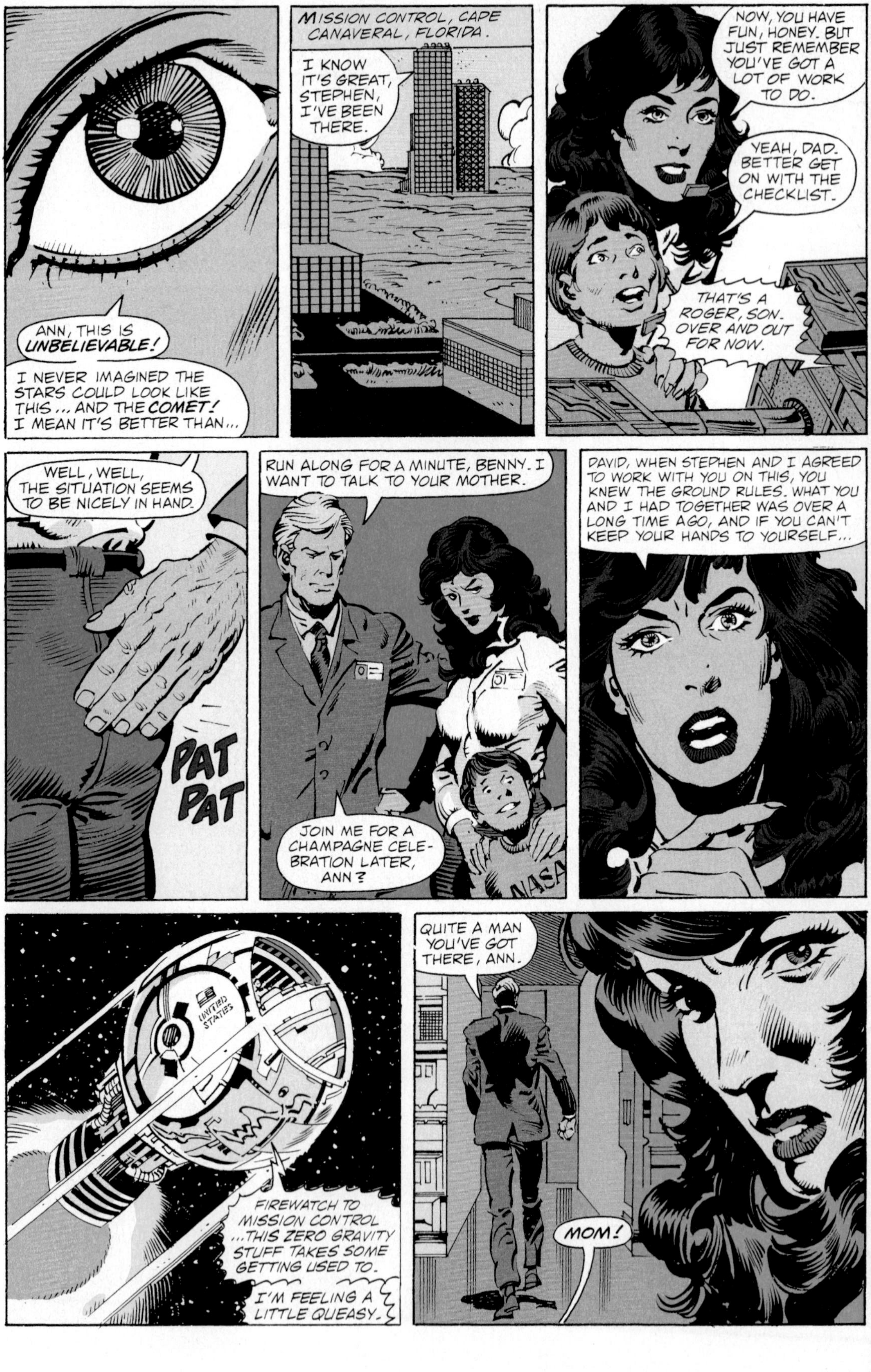
ANN, THIS IS UNBELIEVABLE!
I NEVER IMAGINED THE STARS COULD LOOK LIKE THIS... AND THE COMET! I MEAN IT'S BETTER THAN...
MISSION CONTROL, CAPE CANAVERAL, FLORIDA.
I KNOW IT'S GREAT, STEPHEN, I'VE BEEN THERE.
NOW, YOU HAVE FUN, HONEY. BUT JUST REMEMBER YOU'VE GOT A LOT OF WORK TO DO.
YEAH, DAD. BETTER GET ON WITH THE CHECKLIST.
THAT'S A ROGER, SON. OVER AND OUT FOR NOW.
WELL, WELL, THE SITUATION SEEMS TO BE NICELY IN HAND.
PAT PAT
RUN ALONG FOR A MINUTE, BENNY. I WANT TO TALK TO YOUR MOTHER.
JOIN ME FOR A CHAMPAGNE CELEBRATION LATER, ANN?
NASA
DAVID, WHEN STEPHEN AND I AGREED TO WORK WITH YOU ON THIS, YOU KNEW THE GROUND RULES. WHAT YOU AND I HAD TOGETHER WAS OVER A LONG TIME AGO, AND IF YOU CAN'T KEEP YOUR HANDS TO YOURSELF...
UNITED STATES
FIREWATCH TO MISSION CONTROL ...THIS ZERO GRAVITY STUFF TAKES SOME GETTING USED TO.
I'M FEELING A LITTLE QUEASY.
QUITE A MAN YOU'VE GOT THERE, ANN.
MOM!

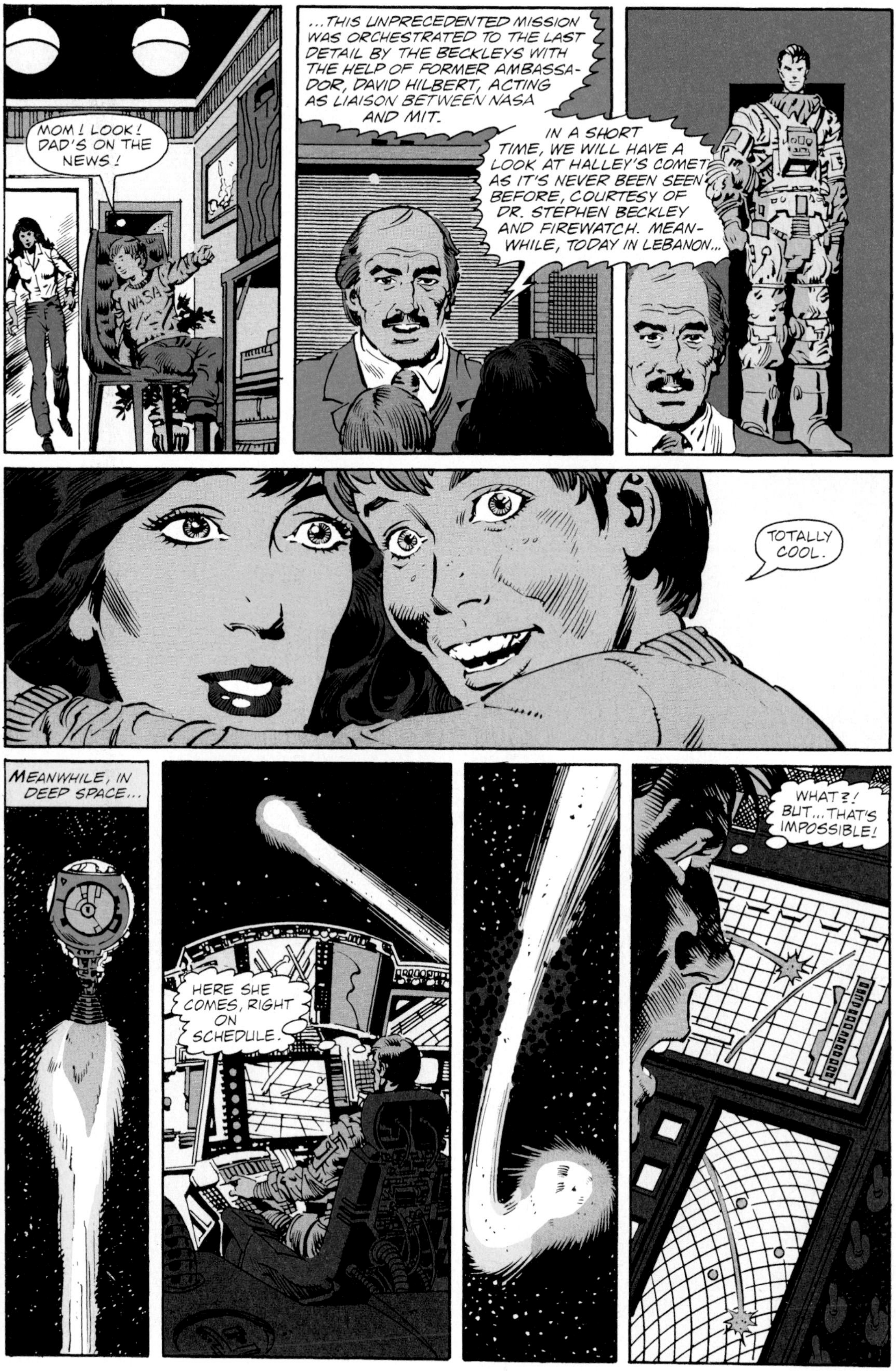
MOM! LOOK! DAD'S ON THE NEWS!
NASA
...THIS UNPRECEDENTED MISSION WAS ORCHESTRATED TO THE LAST DETAIL BY THE BECKLEYS WITH THE HELP OF FORMER AMBASSADOR, DAVID HILBERT, ACTING AS LIAISON BETWEEN NASA AND MIT.
IN A SHORT TIME, WE WILL HAVE A LOOK AT HALLEY'S COMET AS IT'S NEVER BEEN SEEN BEFORE, COURTESY OF DR. STEPHEN BECKLEY AND FIREWATCH. MEANWHILE, TODAY IN LEBANON...
TOTALLY COOL.
MEANWHILE, IN DEEP SPACE...
HERE SHE COMES, RIGHT ON SCHEDULE.
WHAT?! BUT... THAT'S IMPOSSIBLE!

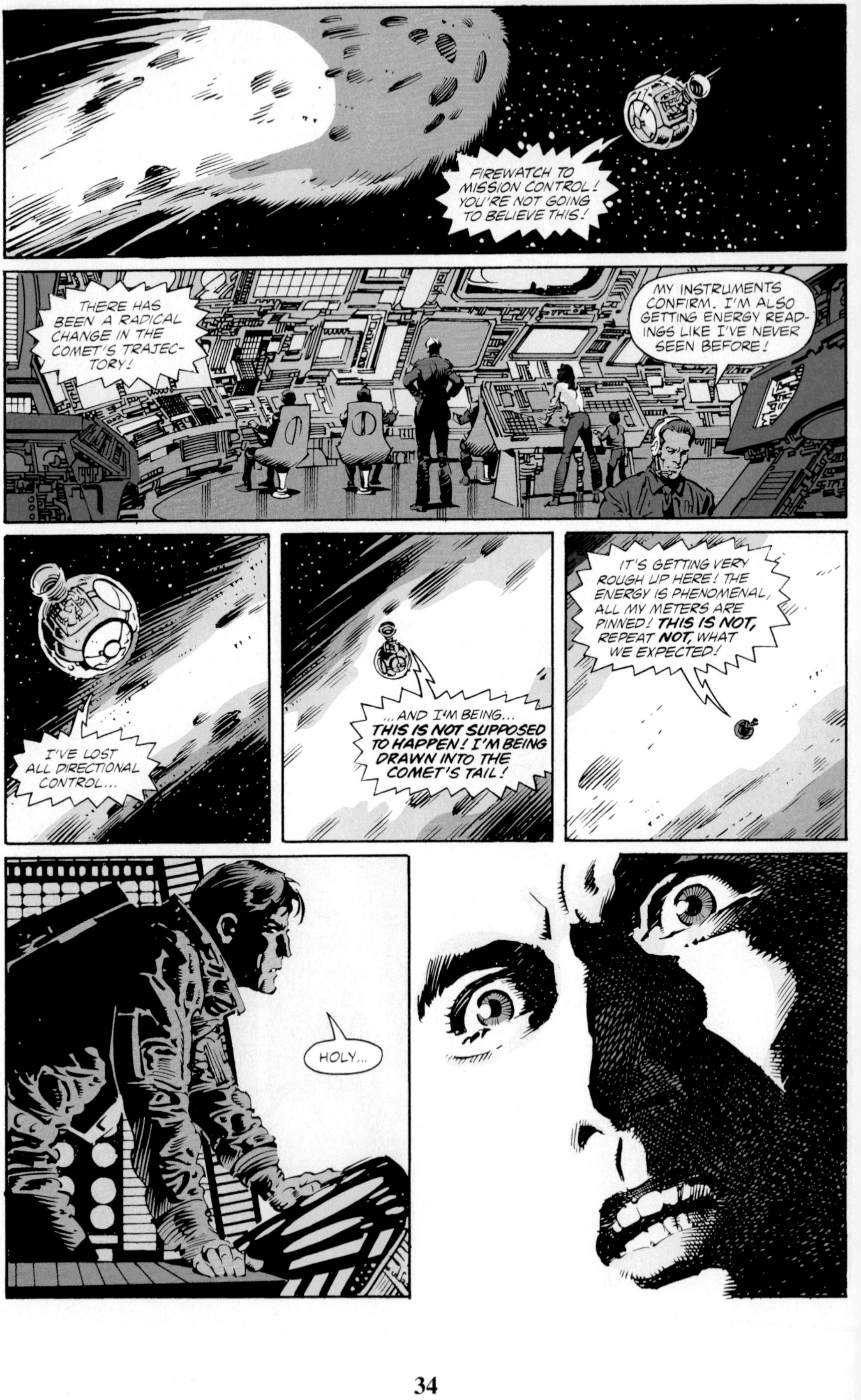

FIREWATCH TO MISSION CONTROL! YOU'RE NOT GOING TO BELIEVE THIS!
THERE HAS BEEN A RADICAL CHANGE IN THE COMET'S TRAJECTORY!
MY INSTRUMENTS CONFIRM. I'M ALSO GETTING ENERGY READINGS LIKE I'VE NEVER SEEN BEFORE!
I'VE LOST ALL DIRECTIONAL CONTROL...
...AND I'M BEING... **THIS IS NOT SUPPOSED TO HAPPEN! I'M BEING DRAWN INTO THE COMET'S TAIL!**
IT'S GETTING VERY ROUGH UP HERE! THE ENERGY IS PHENOMENAL, ALL MY METERS ARE PINNED! **THIS IS NOT,** REPEAT **NOT,** WHAT WE EXPECTED!
HOLY...

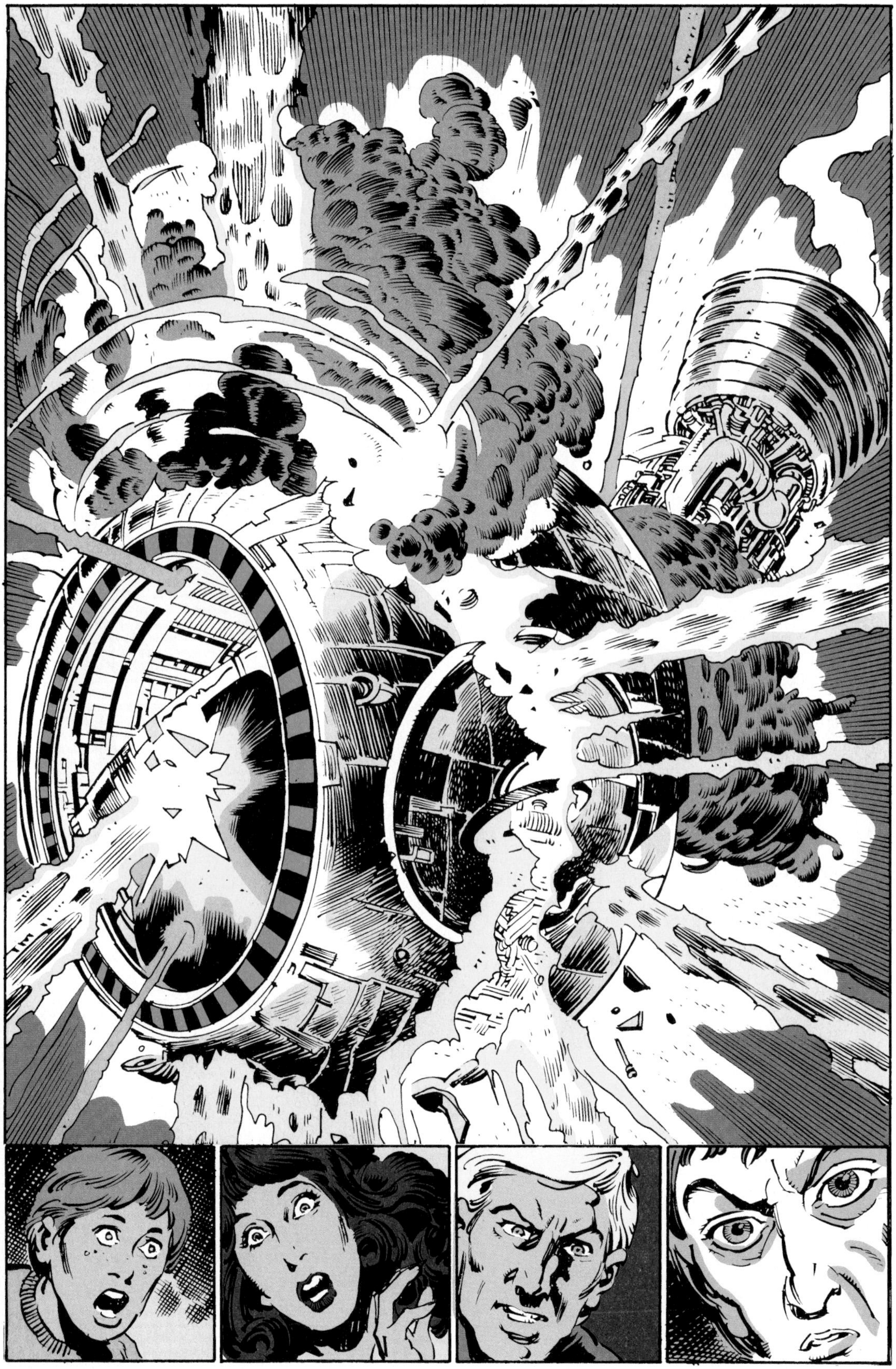

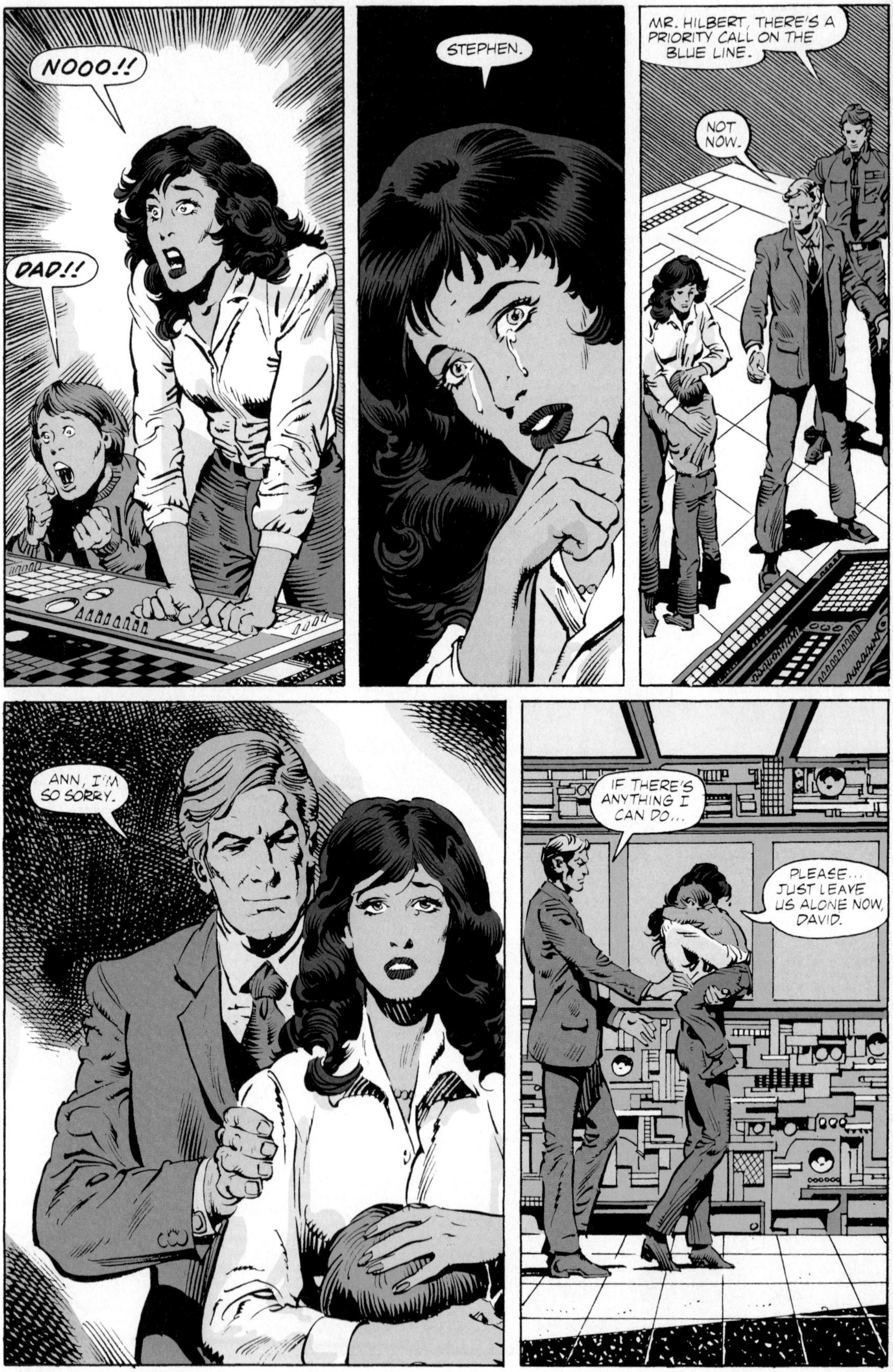
NOOO!!
DAD!!
STEPHEN.
MR. HILBERT, THERE'S A PRIORITY CALL ON THE BLUE LINE.
NOT NOW.
ANN, I'M SO SORRY.
IF THERE'S ANYTHING I CAN DO...
PLEASE... JUST LEAVE US ALONE NOW, DAVID.

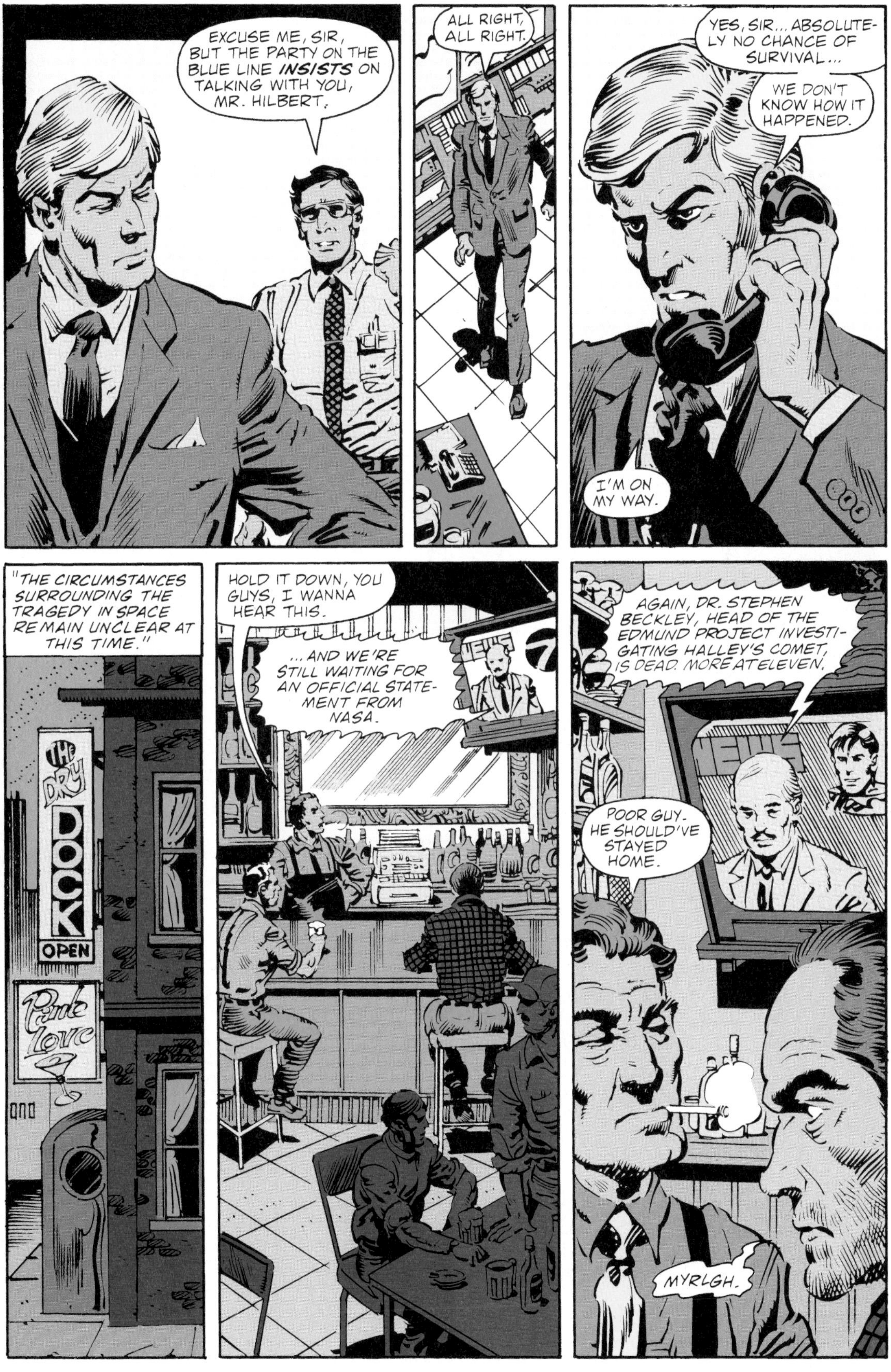
EXCUSE ME, SIR, BUT THE PARTY ON THE BLUE LINE **INSISTS** ON TALKING WITH YOU, MR. HILBERT.
ALL RIGHT, ALL RIGHT.
YES, SIR... ABSOLUTE-LY NO CHANCE OF SURVIVAL...
WE DON'T KNOW HOW IT HAPPENED.
I'M ON MY WAY.
"THE CIRCUMSTANCES SURROUNDING THE TRAGEDY IN SPACE REMAIN UNCLEAR AT THIS TIME."
THE DRY DOCK
OPEN
Pink Love
HOLD IT DOWN, YOU GUYS, I WANNA HEAR THIS.
...AND WE'RE STILL WAITING FOR AN OFFICIAL STATE-MENT FROM NASA.
AGAIN, DR. STEPHEN BECKLEY, HEAD OF THE EDMUND PROJECT INVESTI-GATING HALLEY'S COMET, IS DEAD. MORE AT ELEVEN.
POOR GUY. HE SHOULD'VE STAYED HOME.
MYRLGH.

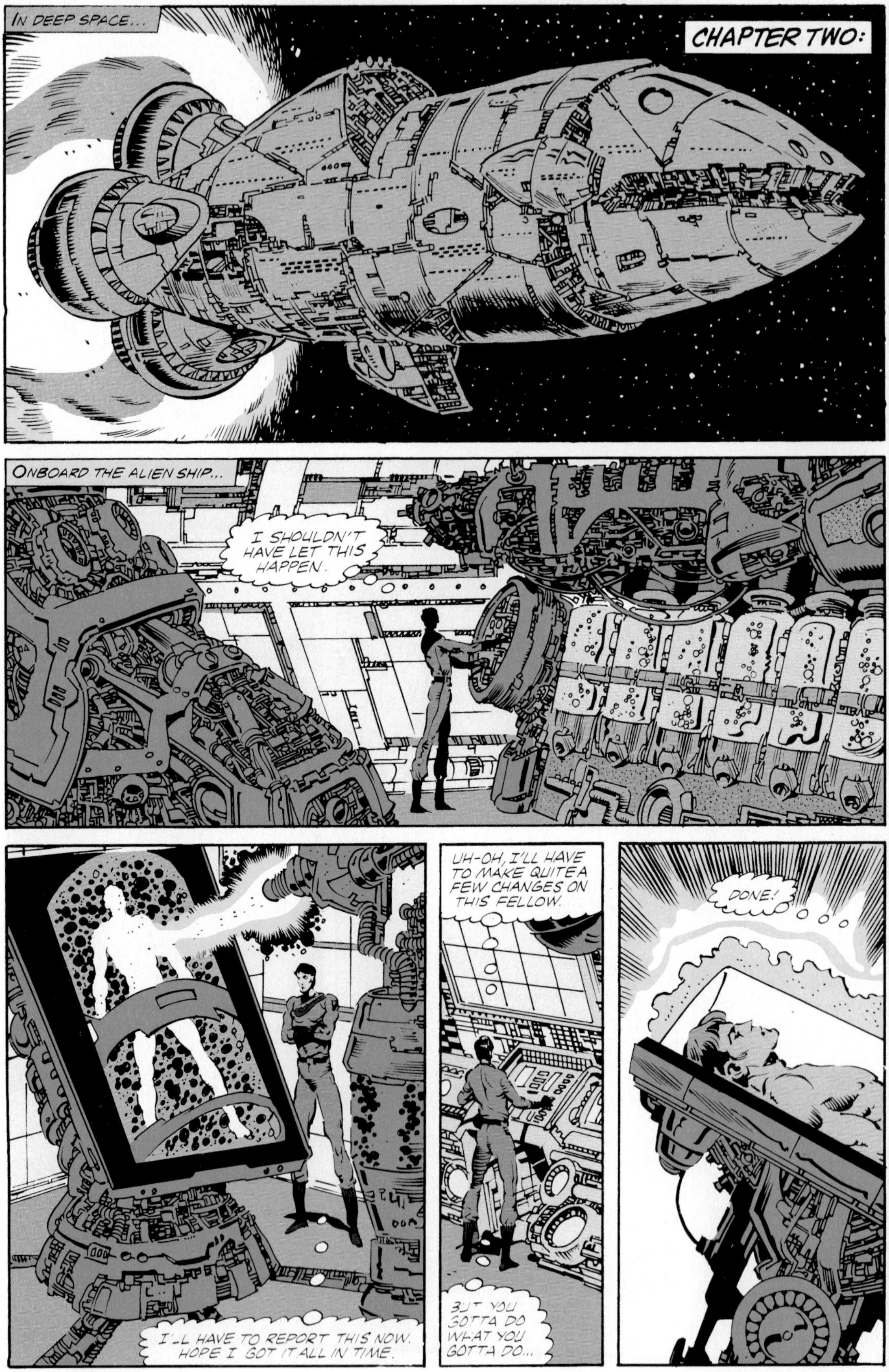
IN DEEP SPACE...
CHAPTER TWO:
ONBOARD THE ALIEN SHIP...
I SHOULDN'T HAVE LET THIS HAPPEN.
I'LL HAVE TO REPORT THIS NOW. HOPE I GOT IT ALL IN TIME.
UH-OH, I'LL HAVE TO MAKE QUITE A FEW CHANGES ON THIS FELLOW.
BUT YOU GOTTA DO WHAT YOU GOTTA DO...
DONE!

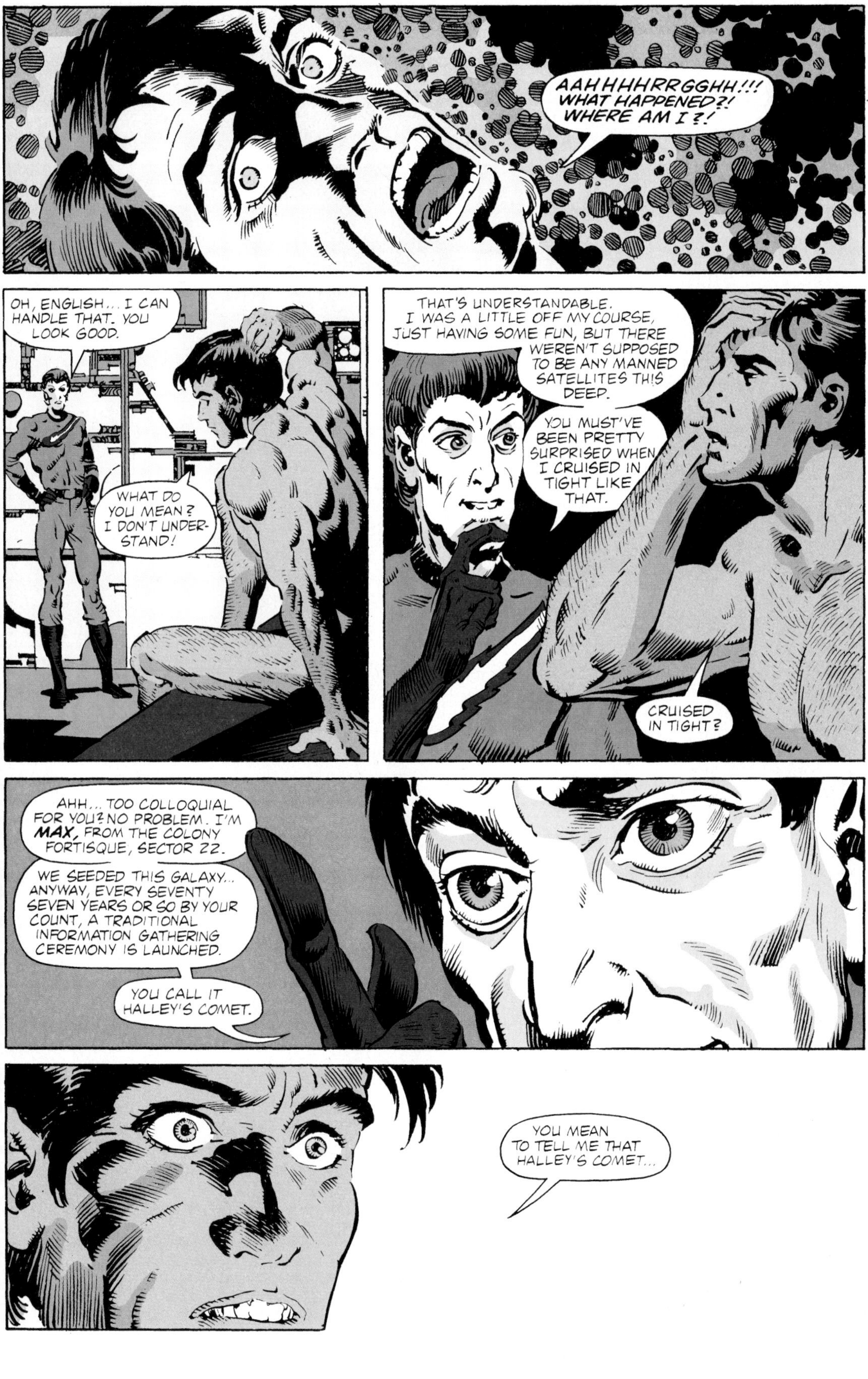
AAHHHHRRGGHH!!! WHAT HAPPENED?! WHERE AM I?!
OH, ENGLISH... I CAN HANDLE THAT. YOU LOOK GOOD.
WHAT DO YOU MEAN? I DON'T UNDERSTAND!
THAT'S UNDERSTANDABLE. I WAS A LITTLE OFF MY COURSE, JUST HAVING SOME FUN, BUT THERE WEREN'T SUPPOSED TO BE ANY MANNED SATELLITES THIS DEEP.
YOU MUST'VE BEEN PRETTY SURPRISED WHEN I CRUISED IN TIGHT LIKE THAT.
CRUISED IN TIGHT?
AHH... TOO COLLOQUIAL FOR YOU? NO PROBLEM. I'M **MAX,** FROM THE COLONY FORTISQUE, SECTOR 22.
WE SEEDED THIS GALAXY... ANYWAY, EVERY SEVENTY SEVEN YEARS OR SO BY YOUR COUNT, A TRADITIONAL INFORMATION GATHERING CEREMONY IS LAUNCHED.
YOU CALL IT HALLEY'S COMET.
YOU MEAN TO TELL ME THAT HALLEY'S COMET...

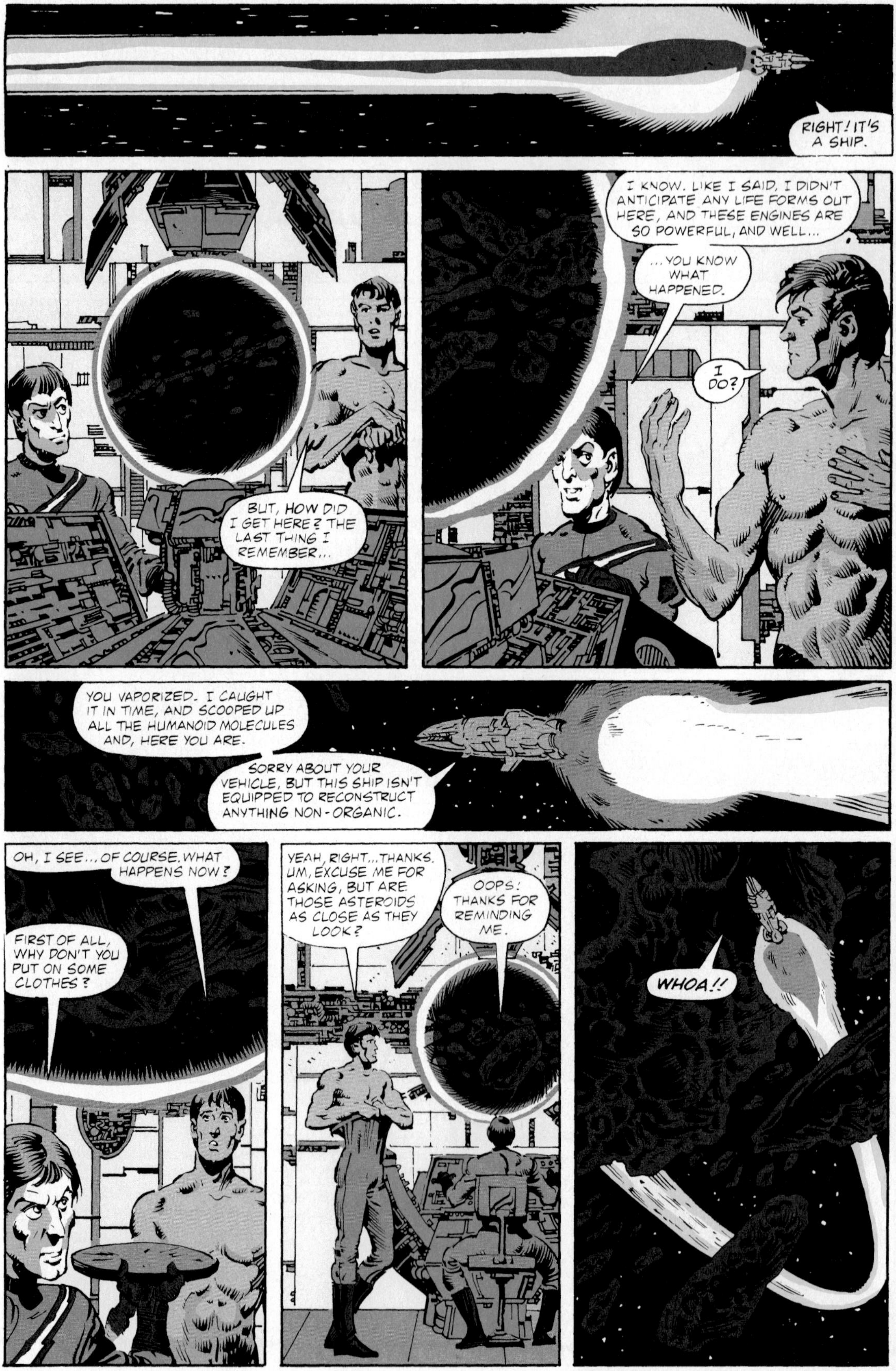
RIGHT! IT'S A SHIP.
BUT, HOW DID I GET HERE? THE LAST THING I REMEMBER...
I KNOW. LIKE I SAID, I DIDN'T ANTICIPATE ANY LIFE FORMS OUT HERE, AND THESE ENGINES ARE SO POWERFUL, AND WELL...
...YOU KNOW WHAT HAPPENED.
I DO?
YOU VAPORIZED. I CAUGHT IT IN TIME, AND SCOOPED UP ALL THE HUMANOID MOLECULES AND, HERE YOU ARE.
SORRY ABOUT YOUR VEHICLE, BUT THIS SHIP ISN'T EQUIPPED TO RECONSTRUCT ANYTHING NON-ORGANIC.
OH, I SEE... OF COURSE. WHAT HAPPENS NOW?
FIRST OF ALL, WHY DON'T YOU PUT ON SOME CLOTHES?
YEAH, RIGHT... THANKS. UM, EXCUSE ME FOR ASKING, BUT ARE THOSE ASTEROIDS AS CLOSE AS THEY LOOK?
OOPS! THANKS FOR REMINDING ME.
WHOA!!

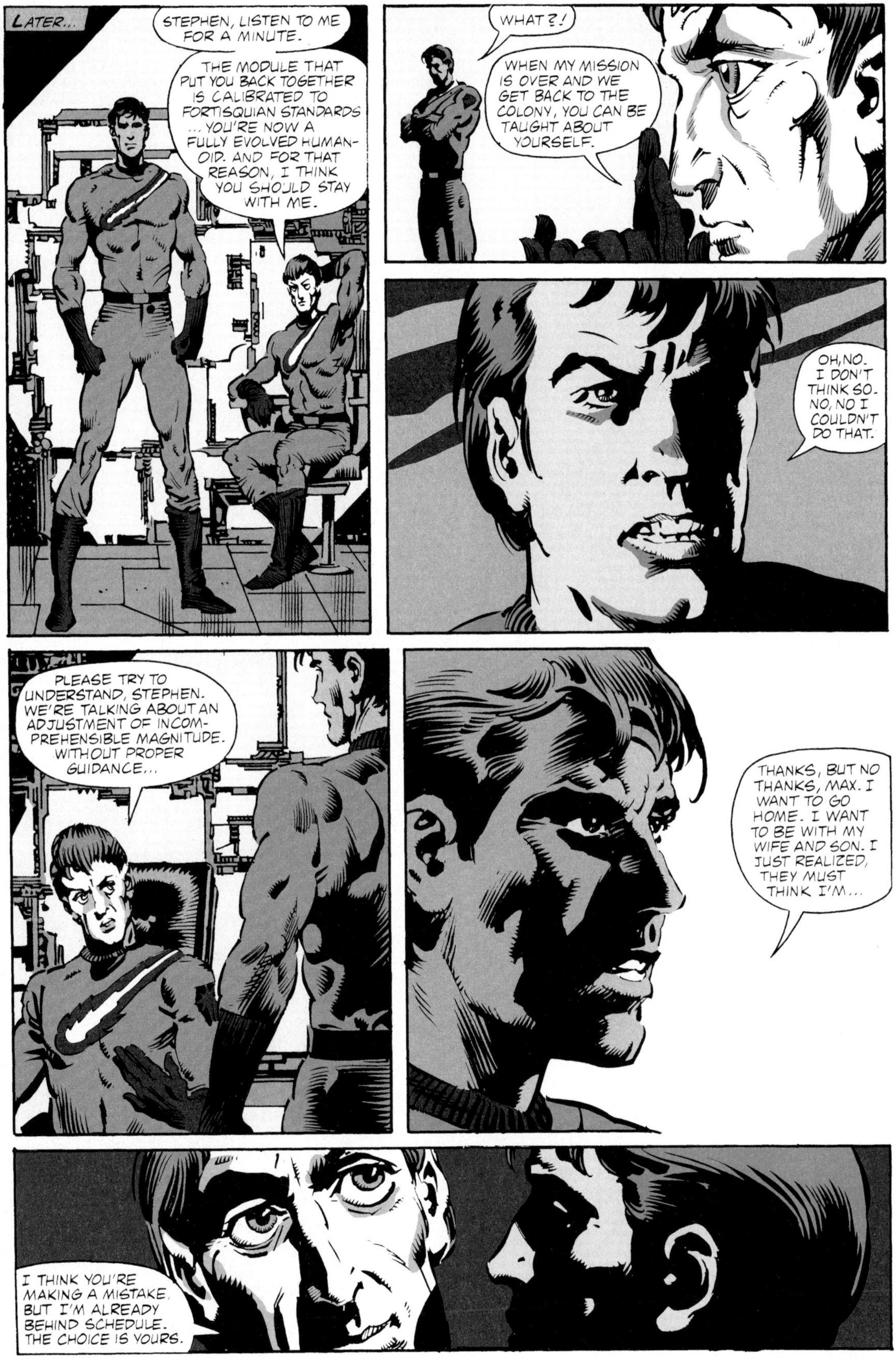
LATER...
STEPHEN, LISTEN TO ME FOR A MINUTE.
THE MODULE THAT PUT YOU BACK TOGETHER IS CALIBRATED TO FORTISQUIAN STANDARDS ...YOU'RE NOW A FULLY EVOLVED HUMAN-OID. AND FOR THAT REASON, I THINK YOU SHOULD STAY WITH ME.
WHAT?!
WHEN MY MISSION IS OVER AND WE GET BACK TO THE COLONY, YOU CAN BE TAUGHT ABOUT YOURSELF.
OH, NO. I DON'T THINK SO. NO, NO I COULDN'T DO THAT.
PLEASE TRY TO UNDERSTAND, STEPHEN. WE'RE TALKING ABOUT AN ADJUSTMENT OF INCOM-PREHENSIBLE MAGNITUDE. WITHOUT PROPER GUIDANCE...
THANKS, BUT NO THANKS, MAX. I WANT TO GO HOME. I WANT TO BE WITH MY WIFE AND SON. I JUST REALIZED, THEY MUST THINK I'M...
I THINK YOU'RE MAKING A MISTAKE. BUT I'M ALREADY BEHIND SCHEDULE. THE CHOICE IS YOURS.

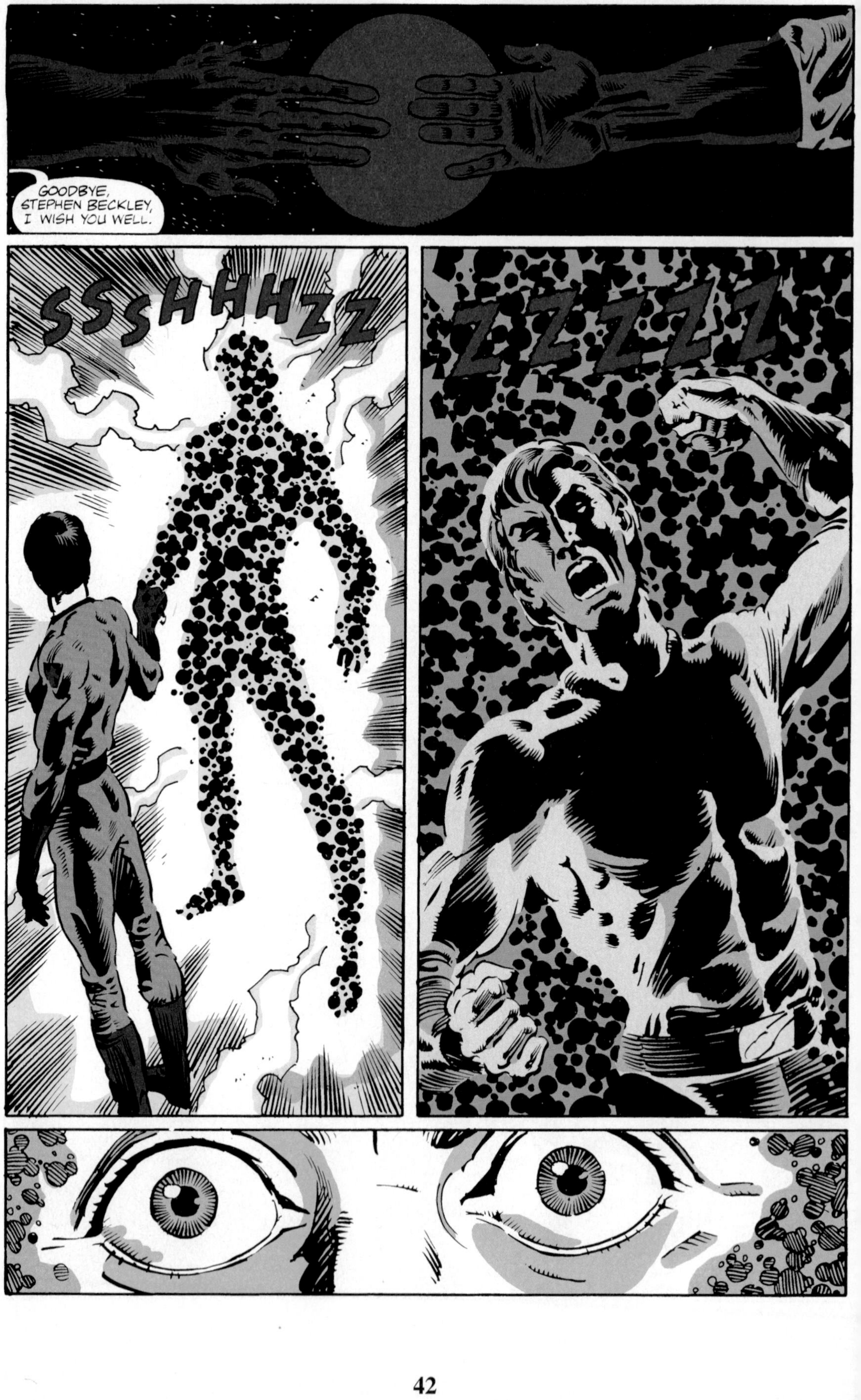
GOODBYE, STEPHEN BECKLEY, I WISH YOU WELL.
SSSHHHZZ
ZZZZZ

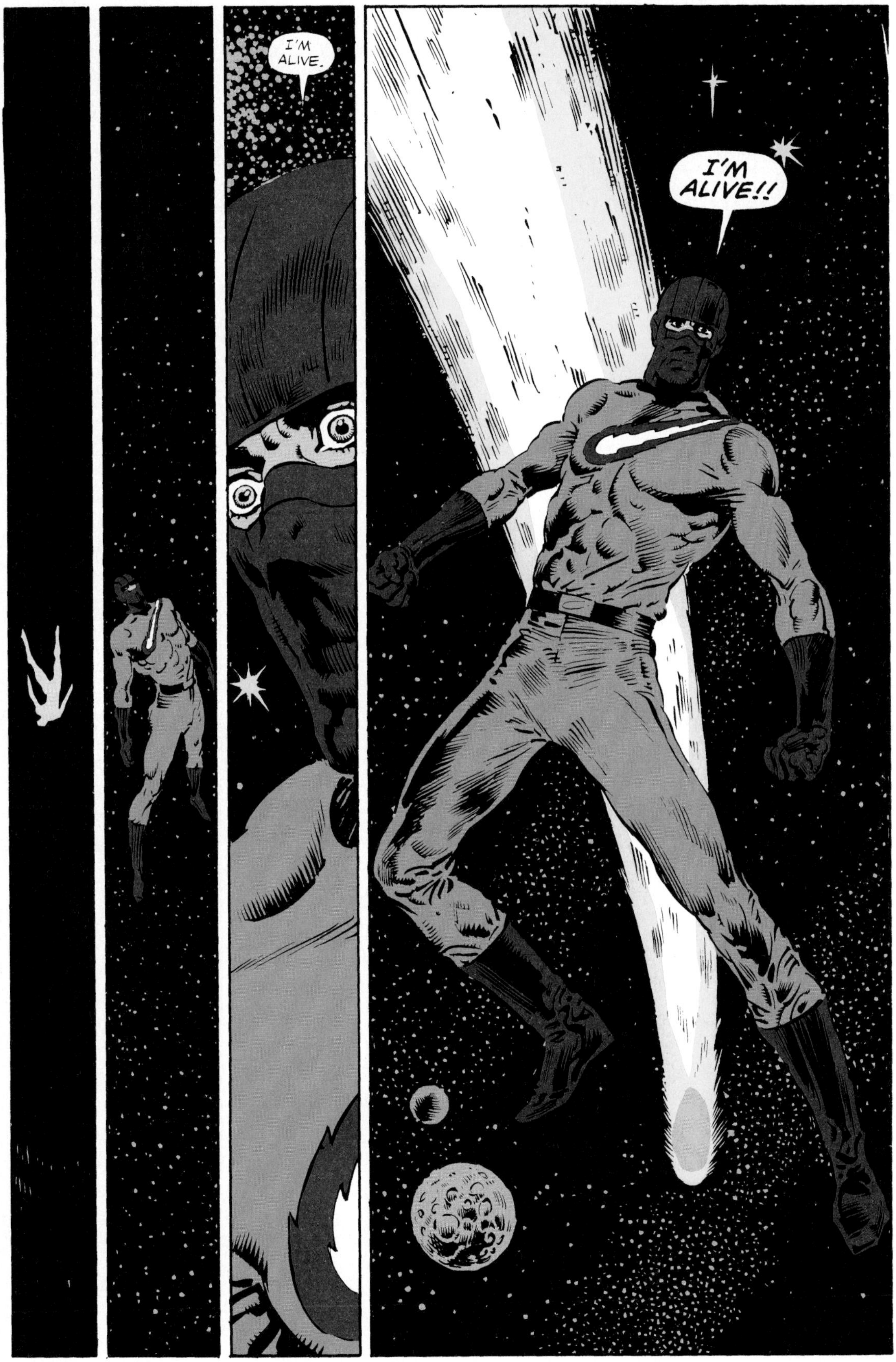
I'M ALIVE.
I'M ALIVE!!

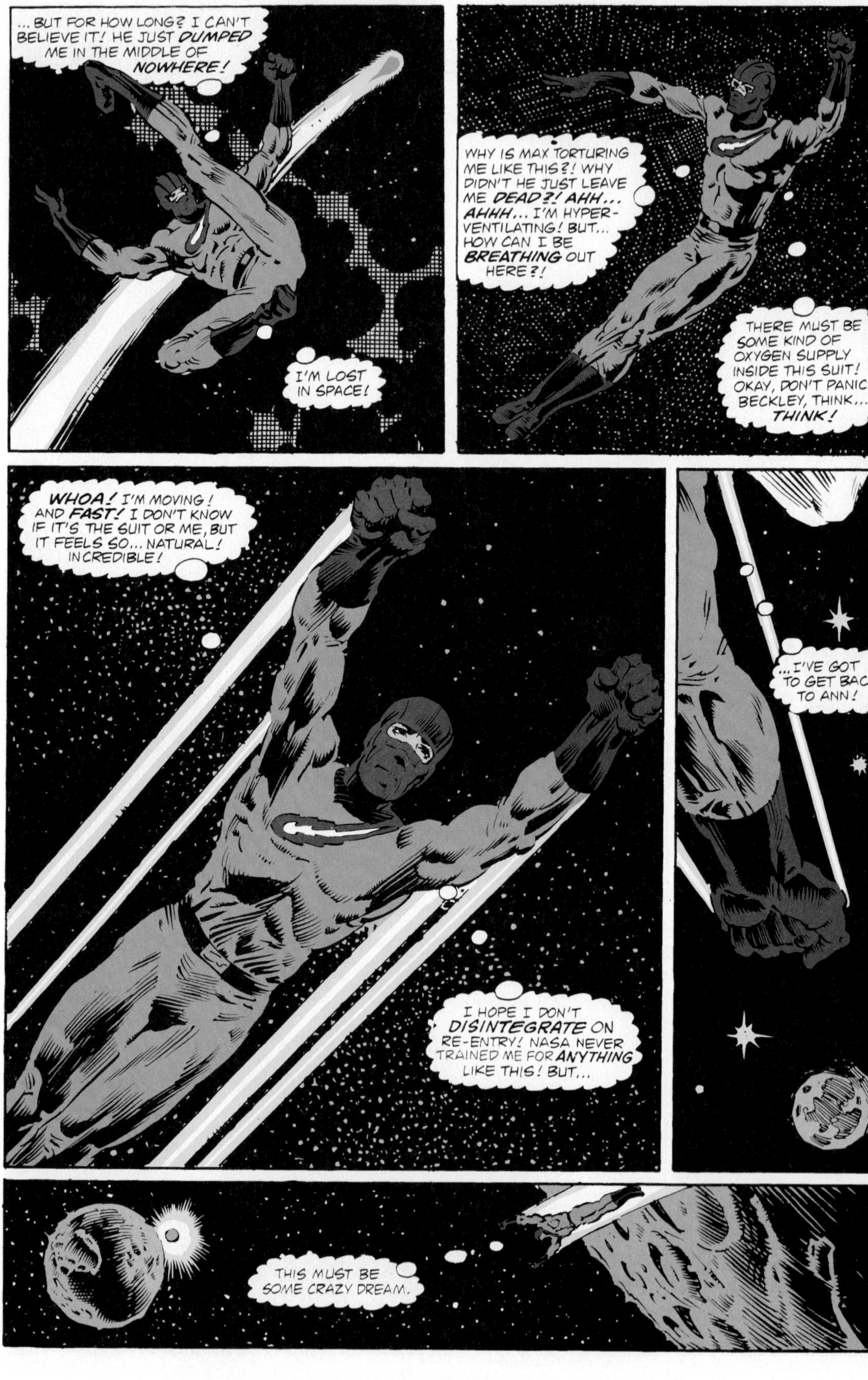
... BUT FOR HOW LONG? I CAN'T BELIEVE IT! HE JUST DUMPED ME IN THE MIDDLE OF NOWHERE!
I'M LOST IN SPACE!
WHY IS MAX TORTURING ME LIKE THIS?! WHY DIDN'T HE JUST LEAVE ME DEAD?! AHH... AHHH... I'M HYPER-VENTILATING! BUT... HOW CAN I BE BREATHING OUT HERE?!
THERE MUST BE SOME KIND OF OXYGEN SUPPLY INSIDE THIS SUIT! OKAY, DON'T PANIC BECKLEY, THINK... THINK!
WHOA! I'M MOVING! AND FAST! I DON'T KNOW IF IT'S THE SUIT OR ME, BUT IT FEELS SO... NATURAL! INCREDIBLE!
I HOPE I DON'T DISINTEGRATE ON RE-ENTRY! NASA NEVER TRAINED ME FOR ANYTHING LIKE THIS! BUT...
...I'VE GOT TO GET BACK TO ANN!
THIS MUST BE SOME CRAZY DREAM.

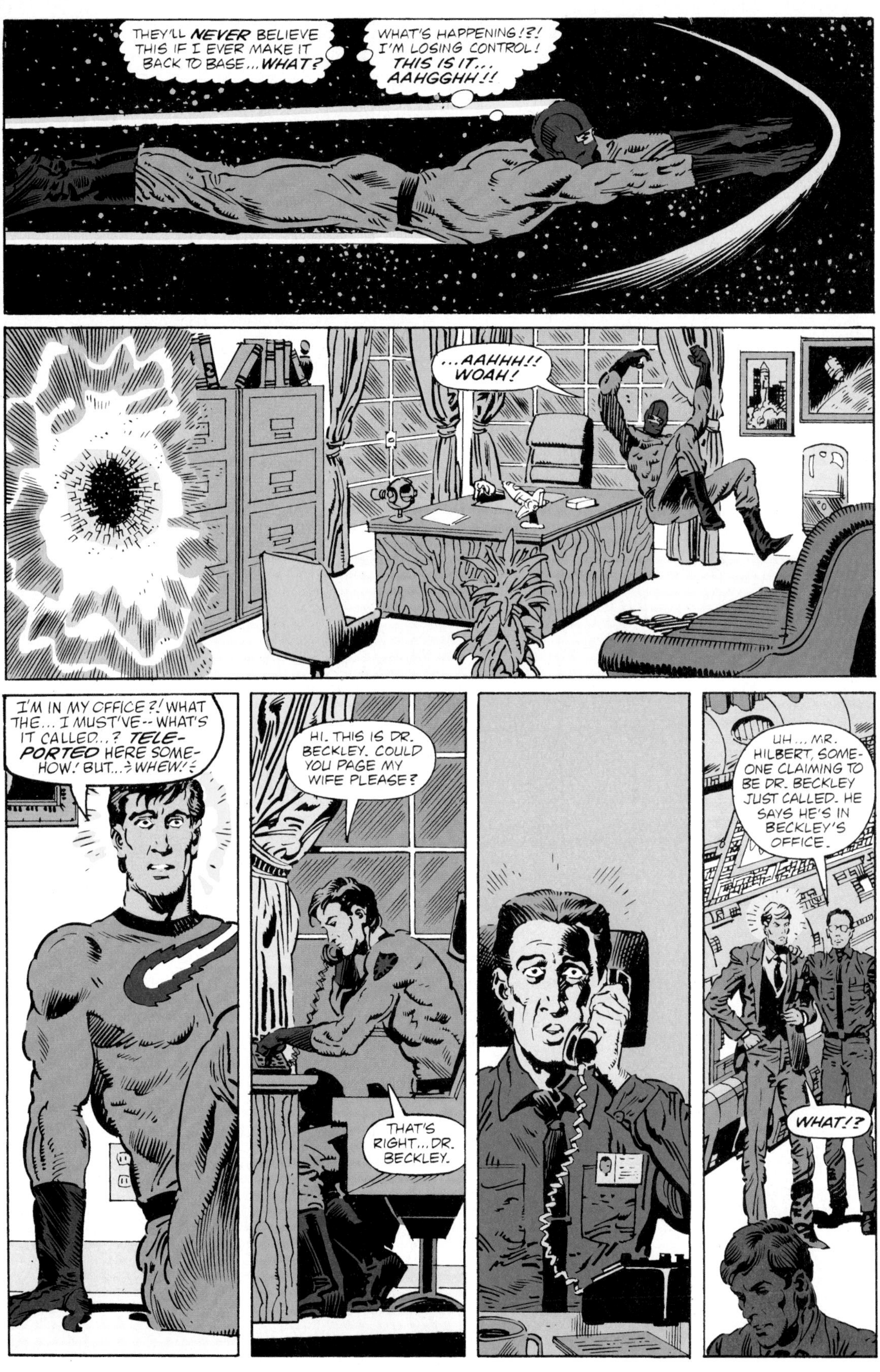
THEY'LL NEVER BELIEVE THIS IF I EVER MAKE IT BACK TO BASE... WHAT?
WHAT'S HAPPENING!?! I'M LOSING CONTROL! THIS IS IT... AAHGGHH!!
...AAHHH!! WOAH!
I'M IN MY OFFICE?! WHAT THE... I MUST'VE-- WHAT'S IT CALLED...? TELE-PORTED HERE SOME-HOW! BUT... WHEW!
HI. THIS IS DR. BECKLEY. COULD YOU PAGE MY WIFE PLEASE?
THAT'S RIGHT... DR. BECKLEY.
UH... MR. HILBERT, SOME-ONE CLAIMING TO BE DR. BECKLEY JUST CALLED. HE SAYS HE'S IN BECKLEY'S OFFICE.
WHAT!?

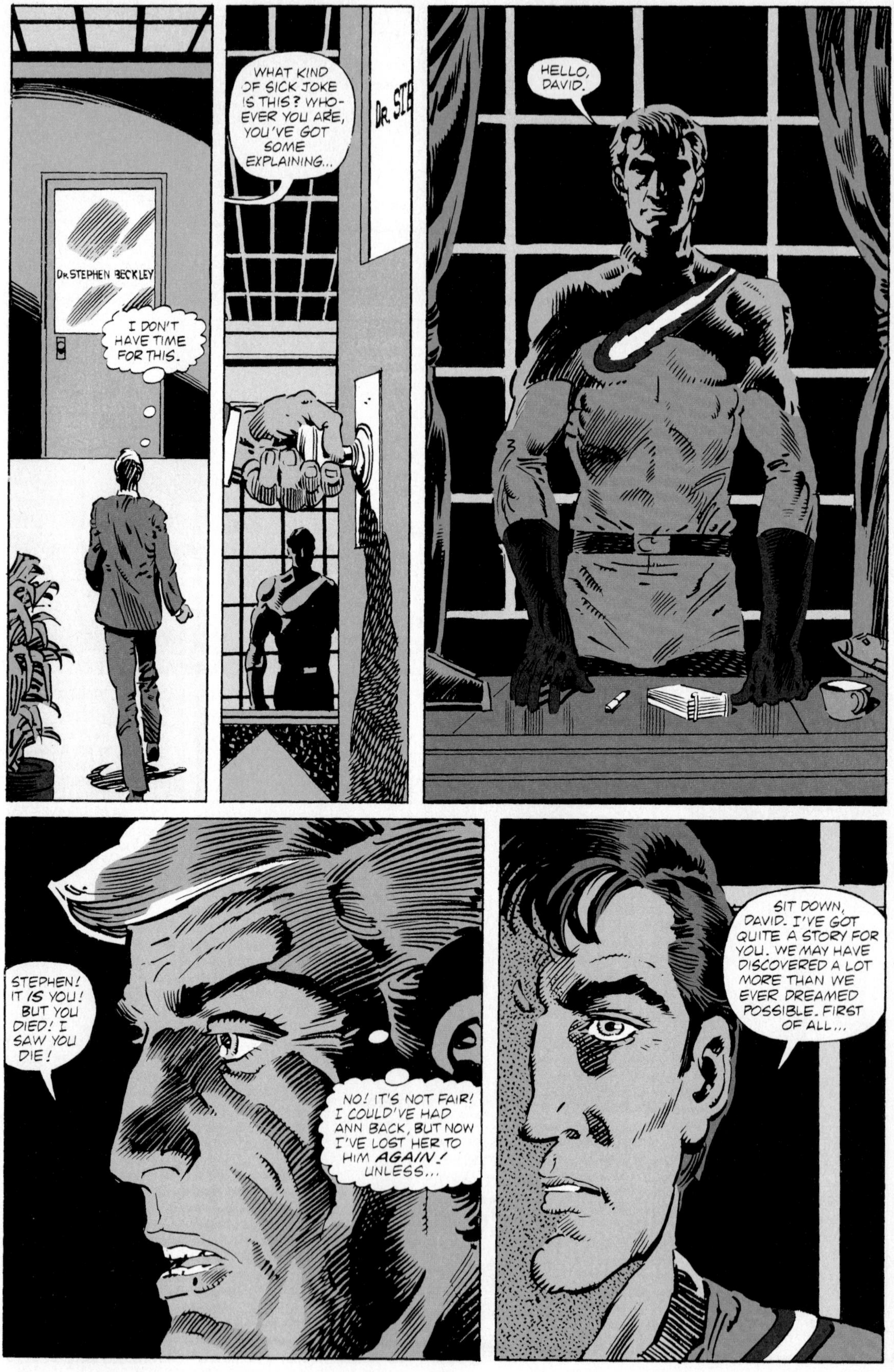
DR. STEPHEN BECKLEY
I DON'T HAVE TIME FOR THIS.
WHAT KIND OF SICK JOKE IS THIS? WHO-EVER YOU ARE, YOU'VE GOT SOME EXPLAINING...
HELLO, DAVID.
STEPHEN! IT IS YOU! BUT YOU DIED! I SAW YOU DIE!
NO! IT'S NOT FAIR! I COULD'VE HAD ANN BACK, BUT NOW I'VE LOST HER TO HIM AGAIN! UNLESS...
SIT DOWN, DAVID. I'VE GOT QUITE A STORY FOR YOU. WE MAY HAVE DISCOVERED A LOT MORE THAN WE EVER DREAMED POSSIBLE. FIRST OF ALL...

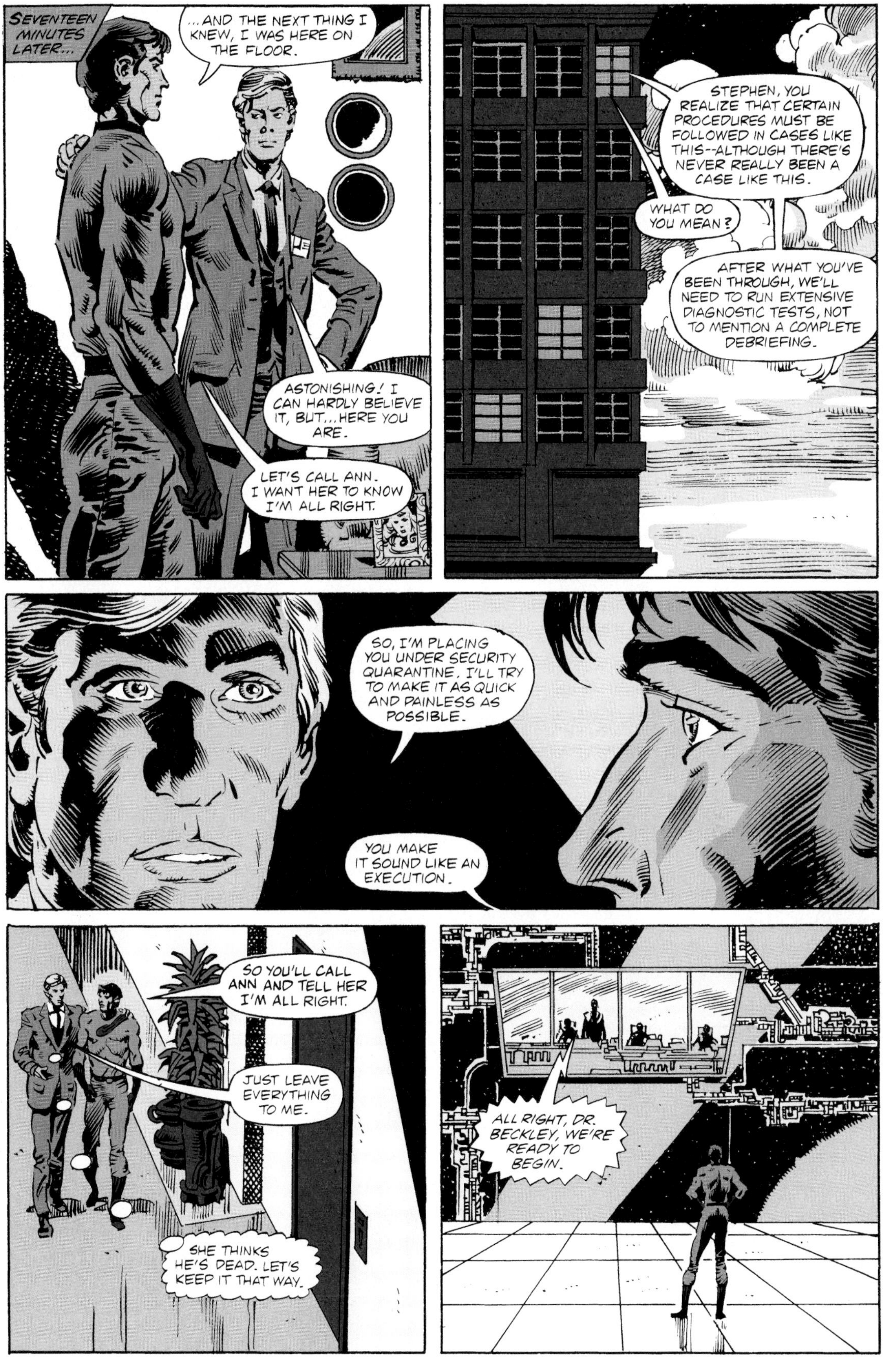
SEVENTEEN MINUTES LATER...
...AND THE NEXT THING I KNEW, I WAS HERE ON THE FLOOR.
ASTONISHING! I CAN HARDLY BELIEVE IT, BUT... HERE YOU ARE.
LET'S CALL ANN. I WANT HER TO KNOW I'M ALL RIGHT.
STEPHEN, YOU REALIZE THAT CERTAIN PROCEDURES MUST BE FOLLOWED IN CASES LIKE THIS--ALTHOUGH THERE'S NEVER REALLY BEEN A CASE LIKE THIS.
WHAT DO YOU MEAN?
AFTER WHAT YOU'VE BEEN THROUGH, WE'LL NEED TO RUN EXTENSIVE DIAGNOSTIC TESTS, NOT TO MENTION A COMPLETE DEBRIEFING.
SO, I'M PLACING YOU UNDER SECURITY QUARANTINE. I'LL TRY TO MAKE IT AS QUICK AND PAINLESS AS POSSIBLE.
YOU MAKE IT SOUND LIKE AN EXECUTION.
SO YOU'LL CALL ANN AND TELL HER I'M ALL RIGHT.
JUST LEAVE EVERYTHING TO ME.
SHE THINKS HE'S DEAD. LET'S KEEP IT THAT WAY.
ALL RIGHT, DR. BECKLEY, WE'RE READY TO BEGIN.

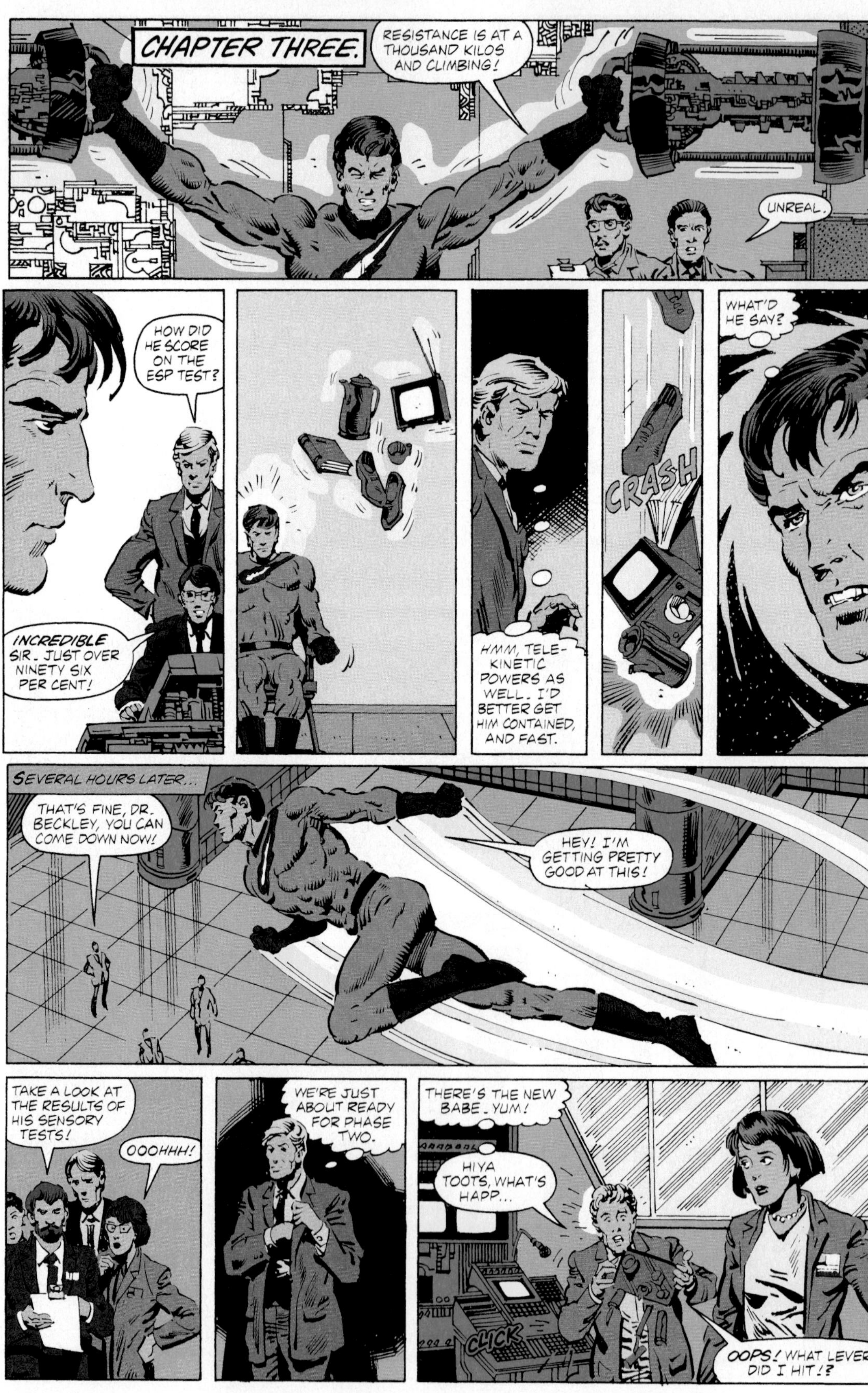

CHAPTER THREE.
RESISTANCE IS AT A THOUSAND KILOS AND CLIMBING!
UNREAL.
HOW DID HE SCORE ON THE ESP TEST?
INCREDIBLE SIR. JUST OVER NINETY SIX PER CENT!
HMM, TELE-KINETIC POWERS AS WELL. I'D BETTER GET HIM CONTAINED, AND FAST.
CRASH
WHAT'D HE SAY?
SEVERAL HOURS LATER...
THAT'S FINE, DR. BECKLEY, YOU CAN COME DOWN NOW!
HEY! I'M GETTING PRETTY GOOD AT THIS!
TAKE A LOOK AT THE RESULTS OF HIS SENSORY TESTS!
OOOHHH!
WE'RE JUST ABOUT READY FOR PHASE TWO.
THERE'S THE NEW BABE. YUM!
HIYA TOOTS, WHAT'S HAPP...
CLICK
OOPS! WHAT LEVER DID I HIT!?

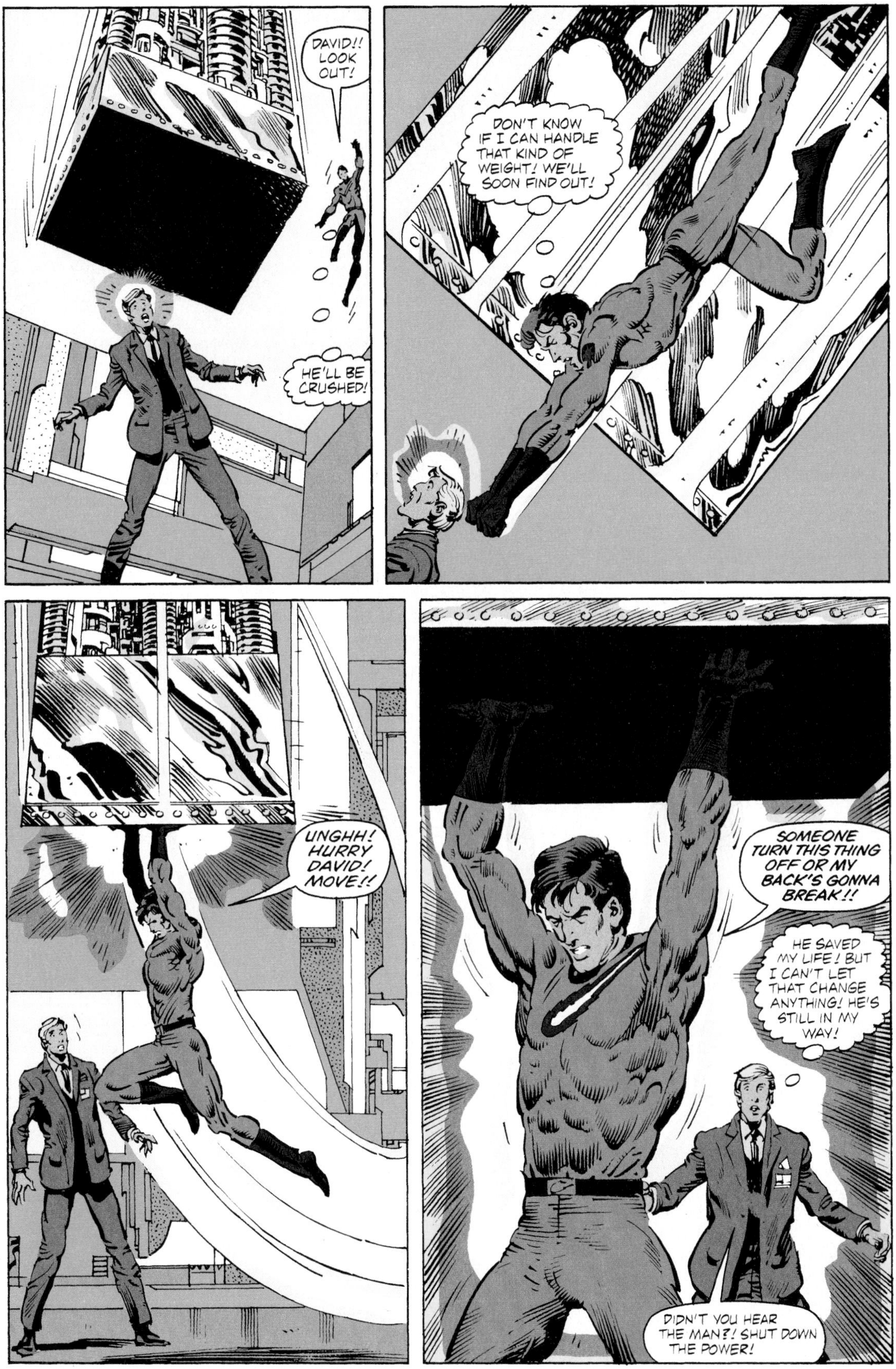
DAVID!! LOOK OUT!
HE'LL BE CRUSHED!
DON'T KNOW IF I CAN HANDLE THAT KIND OF WEIGHT! WE'LL SOON FIND OUT!
UNGHH! HURRY DAVID! MOVE!!
SOMEONE TURN THIS THING OFF OR MY BACK'S GONNA BREAK!!
HE SAVED MY LIFE! BUT I CAN'T LET THAT CHANGE ANYTHING! HE'S STILL IN MY WAY!
DIDN'T YOU HEAR THE MAN?! SHUT DOWN THE POWER!

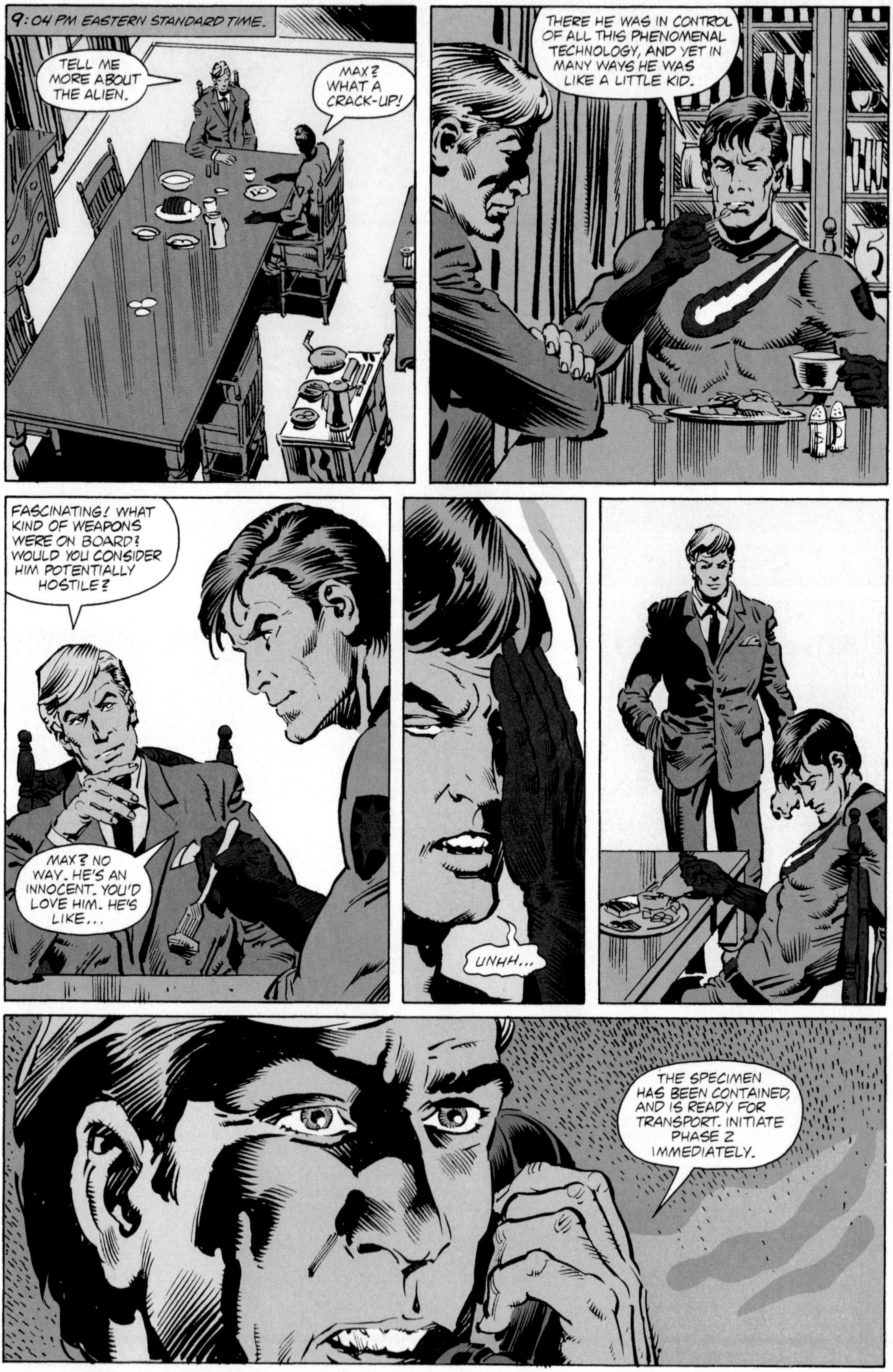
9:04 PM EASTERN STANDARD TIME.
TELL ME MORE ABOUT THE ALIEN.
MAX? WHAT A CRACK-UP!
THERE HE WAS IN CONTROL OF ALL THIS PHENOMENAL TECHNOLOGY, AND YET IN MANY WAYS HE WAS LIKE A LITTLE KID.
FASCINATING! WHAT KIND OF WEAPONS WERE ON BOARD? WOULD YOU CONSIDER HIM POTENTIALLY HOSTILE?
MAX? NO WAY. HE'S AN INNOCENT. YOU'D LOVE HIM. HE'S LIKE...
UNHH...
THE SPECIMEN HAS BEEN CONTAINED, AND IS READY FOR TRANSPORT. INITIATE PHASE 2 IMMEDIATELY.

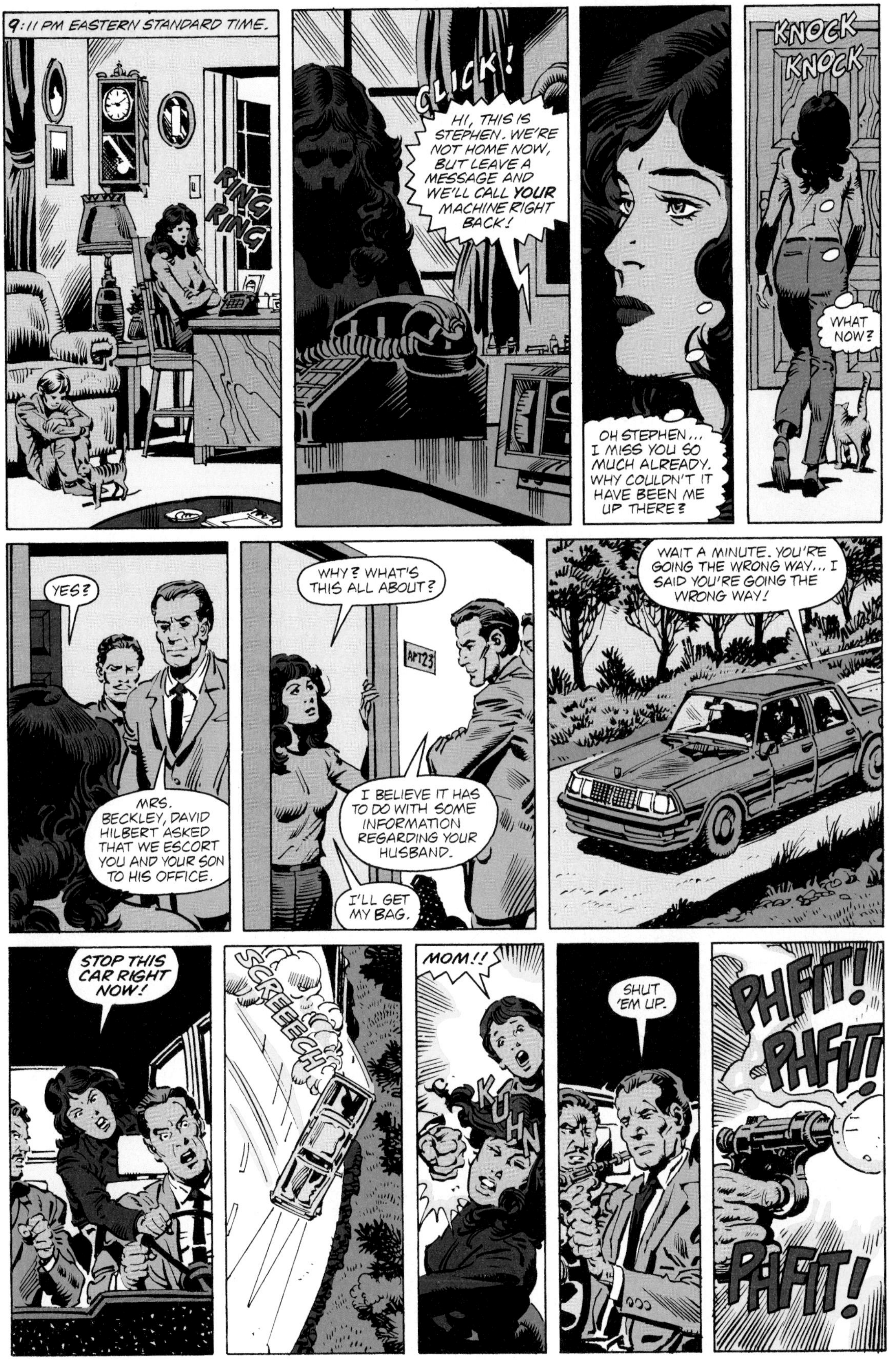
9:11 PM EASTERN STANDARD TIME.
RING RING
CLICK!
HI, THIS IS STEPHEN. WE'RE NOT HOME NOW, BUT LEAVE A MESSAGE AND WE'LL CALL YOUR MACHINE RIGHT BACK!
OH STEPHEN... I MISS YOU SO MUCH ALREADY. WHY COULDN'T IT HAVE BEEN ME UP THERE?
KNOCK KNOCK
WHAT NOW?
YES?
MRS. BECKLEY, DAVID HILBERT ASKED THAT WE ESCORT YOU AND YOUR SON TO HIS OFFICE.
WHY? WHAT'S THIS ALL ABOUT?
APT 23
I BELIEVE IT HAS TO DO WITH SOME INFORMATION REGARDING YOUR HUSBAND.
I'LL GET MY BAG.
WAIT A MINUTE. YOU'RE GOING THE WRONG WAY... I SAID YOU'RE GOING THE WRONG WAY!
STOP THIS CAR RIGHT NOW!
SCREEECH
MOM!!
KUHN
SHUT 'EM UP.
PHFIT! PHFIT! PHFIT!

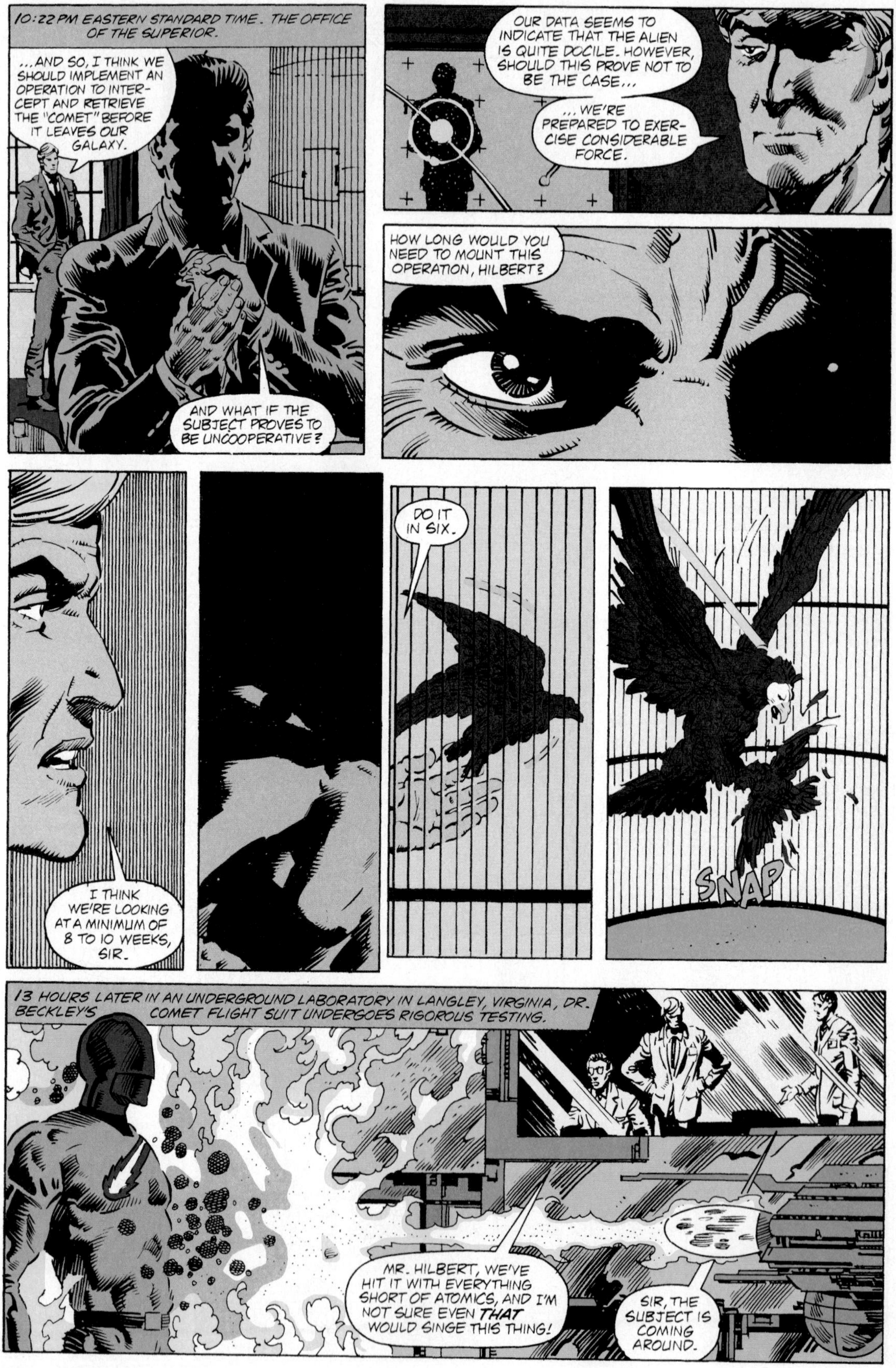
10:22 PM EASTERN STANDARD TIME. THE OFFICE OF THE SUPERIOR.
...AND SO, I THINK WE SHOULD IMPLEMENT AN OPERATION TO INTERCEPT AND RETRIEVE THE "COMET" BEFORE IT LEAVES OUR GALAXY.
AND WHAT IF THE SUBJECT PROVES TO BE UNCOOPERATIVE?
OUR DATA SEEMS TO INDICATE THAT THE ALIEN IS QUITE DOCILE. HOWEVER, SHOULD THIS PROVE NOT TO BE THE CASE...
...WE'RE PREPARED TO EXERCISE CONSIDERABLE FORCE.
HOW LONG WOULD YOU NEED TO MOUNT THIS OPERATION, HILBERT?
I THINK WE'RE LOOKING AT A MINIMUM OF 8 TO 10 WEEKS, SIR.
DO IT IN SIX.
SNAP
13 HOURS LATER IN AN UNDERGROUND LABORATORY IN LANGLEY, VIRGINIA, DR. BECKLEY'S COMET FLIGHT SUIT UNDERGOES RIGOROUS TESTING.
MR. HILBERT, WE'VE HIT IT WITH EVERYTHING SHORT OF ATOMICS, AND I'M NOT SURE EVEN *THAT* WOULD SINGE THIS THING!
SIR, THE SUBJECT IS COMING AROUND.

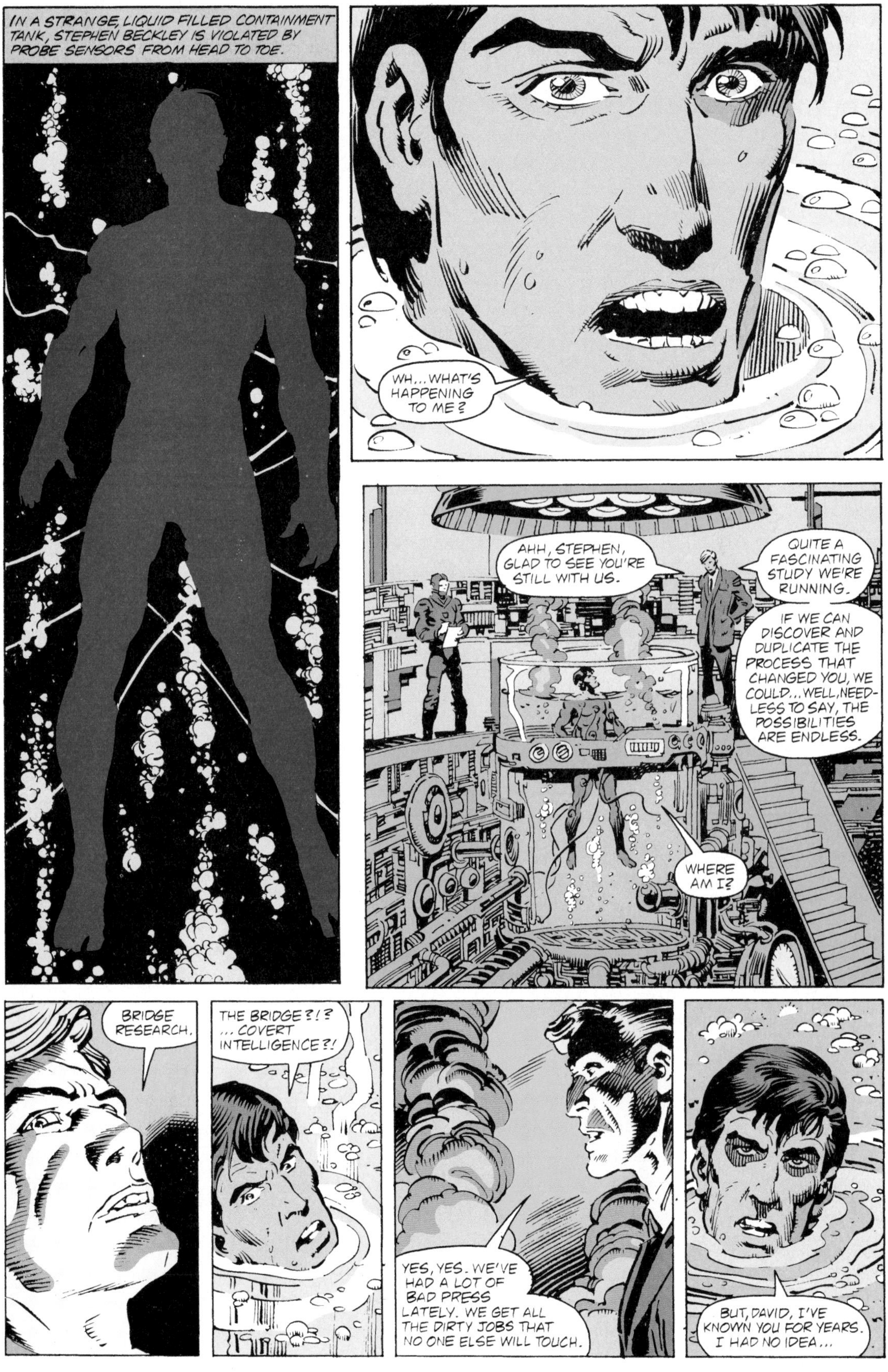
IN A STRANGE, LIQUID FILLED CONTAINMENT TANK, STEPHEN BECKLEY IS VIOLATED BY PROBE SENSORS FROM HEAD TO TOE.
WH... WHAT'S HAPPENING TO ME?
AHH, STEPHEN, GLAD TO SEE YOU'RE STILL WITH US.
QUITE A FASCINATING STUDY WE'RE RUNNING.
IF WE CAN DISCOVER AND DUPLICATE THE PROCESS THAT CHANGED YOU, WE COULD... WELL, NEEDLESS TO SAY, THE POSSIBILITIES ARE ENDLESS.
WHERE AM I?
BRIDGE RESEARCH.
THE BRIDGE?!? ... COVERT INTELLIGENCE?!
YES, YES. WE'VE HAD A LOT OF BAD PRESS LATELY. WE GET ALL THE DIRTY JOBS THAT NO ONE ELSE WILL TOUCH.
BUT, DAVID, I'VE KNOWN YOU FOR YEARS. I HAD NO IDEA...

THAT I WAS CHIEF OF BRIDGE OPERATIONS? LIFE IS FULL OF LITTLE SURPRISES.

DOES ANN KNOW ABOUT THIS?

YOU'RE MY TICKET INTO THE HISTORY BOOKS, STEPHEN.

IN "FIREWATCH'S" LAST MOMENTS, THE ENERGY READINGS YOU TRANSMITTED WERE PHENOMENAL. NO ONE EXPECTED NUMBERS LIKE THAT.

WHERE'S MY WIFE? I WANT TO SEE ANN *RIGHT NOW!*

DO YOU THINK I'M STUPID? YOU COOPERATE WITH US STEPHEN, AND I'LL SEE THAT ANN AND BENNY ARE TAKEN CARE OF. YOU'LL BE TOGETHER AGAIN--

--AFTER THE RESEARCH ON YOU IS COMPLETED!

IN THE MEANTIME, I'LL *PERSONALLY* SEE TO IT ANN HAS *EVERYTHING* SHE NEEDS!

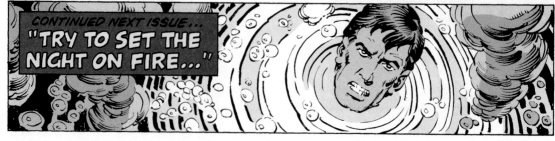

CONTINUED NEXT ISSUE...

"TRY TO SET THE NIGHT ON FIRE..."

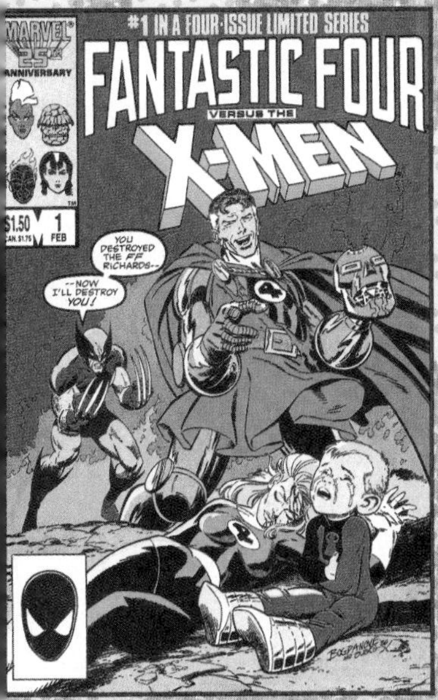
MARVEL 25th ANNIVERSARY
#1 IN A FOUR-ISSUE LIMITED SERIES
FANTASTIC FOUR
VERSUS THE
X-MEN
$1.50 CAN. $1.75 1 FEB
YOU DESTROYED THE FF RICHARDS--
--NOW I'LL DESTROY YOU!

FANTASTIC FOUR VERSUS THE X-MEN #1, published in November 1986, began a miniseries featuring a clash between the two teams.

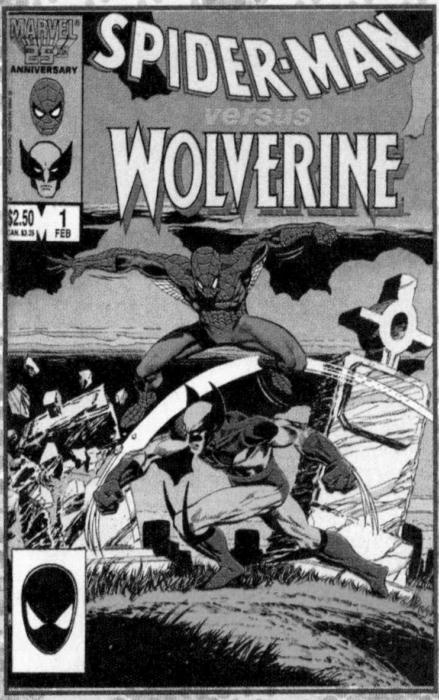
MARVEL 25th ANNIVERSARY
SPIDER-MAN
versus
WOLVERINE
$2.50 CAN. $3.25 1 FEB

SPIDER-MAN VERSUS WOLVERINE, published in November 1986, was a one-shot starring the two popular heroes.

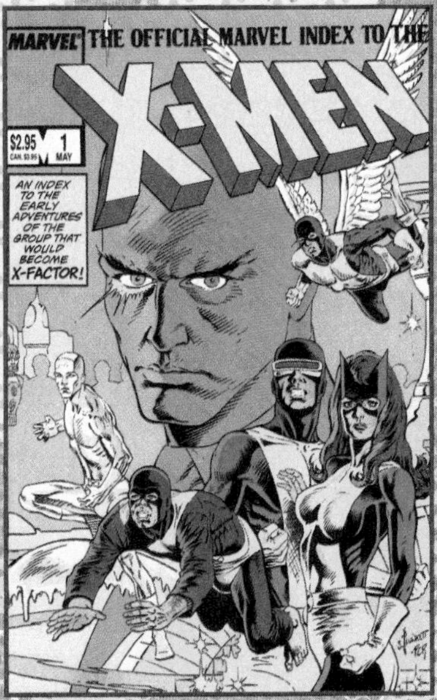
MARVEL
THE OFFICIAL MARVEL INDEX TO THE
X-MEN
$2.95 CAN. $3.95 1 MAY
AN INDEX TO THE EARLY ADVENTURES OF THE GROUP THAT WOULD BECOME X-FACTOR!

OFFICIAL MARVEL INDEX TO THE X-MEN #1, published in December 1986, began a short series providing information about every issue of *Uncanny X-Men*.

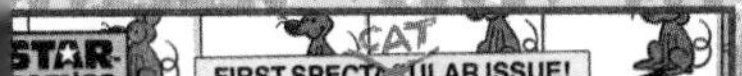
STAR comics
FIRST SPECTACULAR ISSUE!
HEATHCLIFF'S
FUNHOUSE
75¢ US 1 MAY
MARVEL
STAR! THE NEW WORLD IN THE MARVEL UNIVERSE!

HEATHCLIFF'S FUNHOUSE #1, published in December 1986, began the cartoon cat's second ongoing Star series, running concurrently with *Heathcliff*.

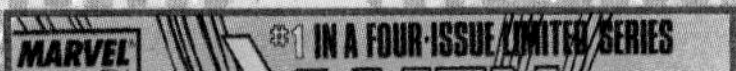
MARVEL
#1 IN A FOUR-ISSUE LIMITED SERIES
THE X-MEN VS. THE
AVENGERS
$1.50 US 1 APR

X-MEN VS. THE AVENGERS #1, published in December 1986, began a miniseries featuring a clash between the two teams.

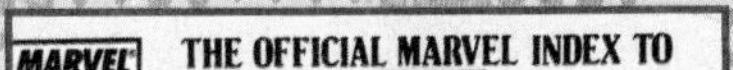
MARVEL
THE OFFICIAL MARVEL INDEX TO
THE
AVENGERS
$2.95 US 1 JUNE
MILGROM

OFFICIAL MARVEL INDEX TO THE AVENGERS #1, published in December 1986, began a short series providing information about every issue of *Avengers*.

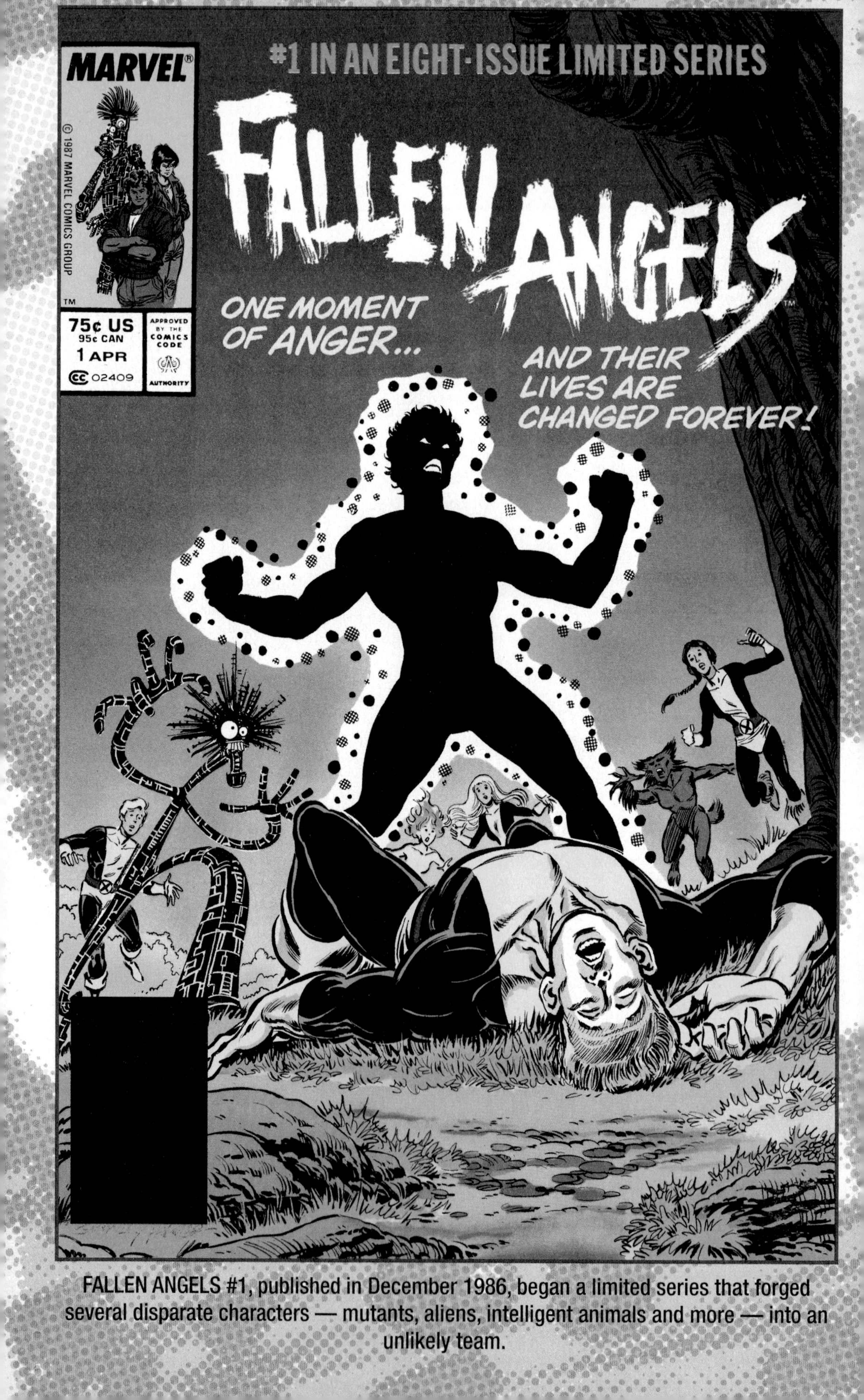
MARVEL®
© 1987 MARVEL COMICS GROUP
75¢ US
95¢ CAN
1 APR
02409
APPROVED BY THE COMICS CODE AUTHORITY
#1 IN AN EIGHT-ISSUE LIMITED SERIES
FALLEN ANGELS
ONE MOMENT OF ANGER...
AND THEIR LIVES ARE CHANGED FOREVER!

FALLEN ANGELS #1, published in December 1986, began a limited series that forged several disparate characters — mutants, aliens, intelligent animals and more — into an unlikely team.

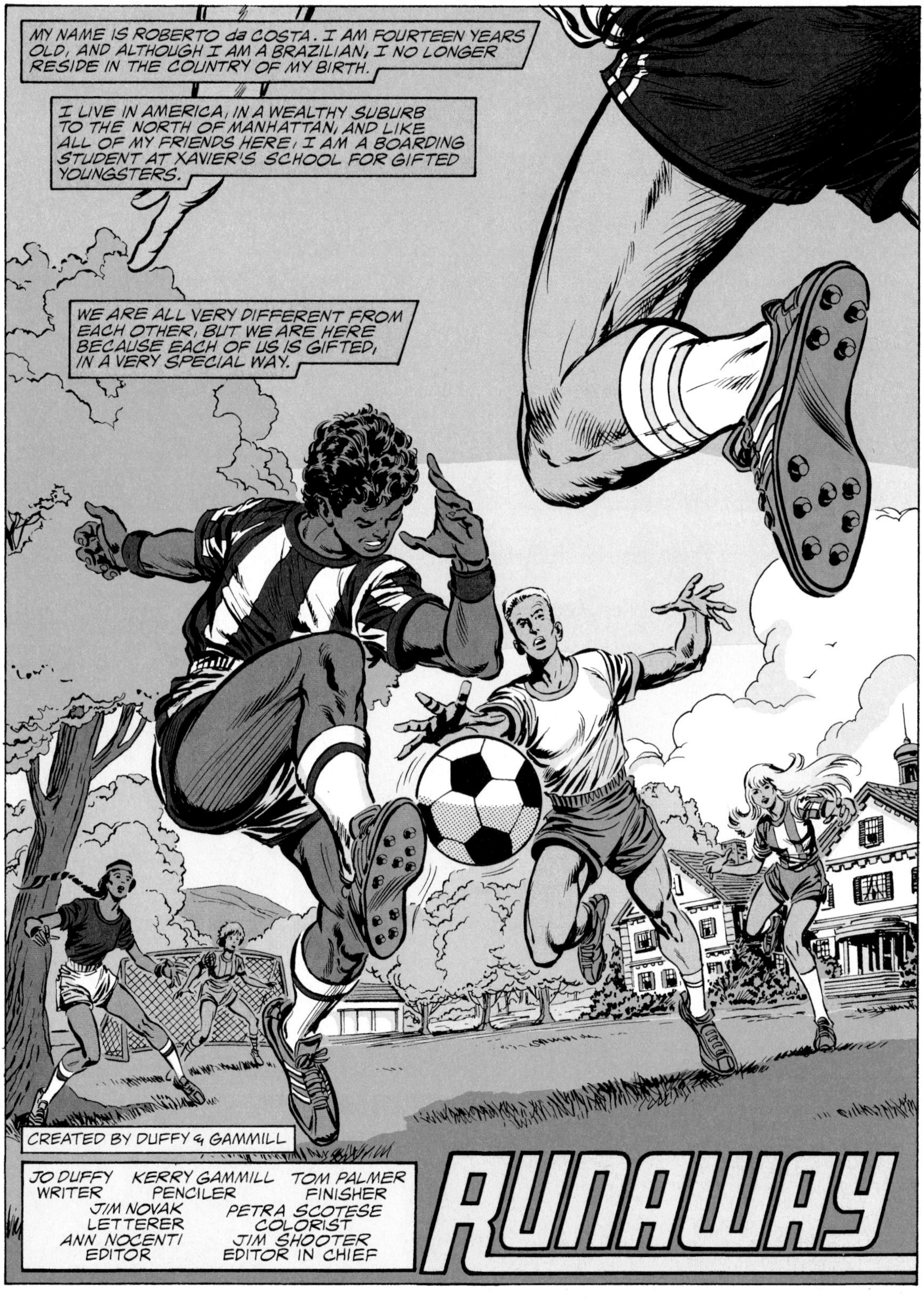
MY NAME IS ROBERTO da COSTA. I AM FOURTEEN YEARS OLD, AND ALTHOUGH I AM A BRAZILIAN, I NO LONGER RESIDE IN THE COUNTRY OF MY BIRTH.
I LIVE IN AMERICA, IN A WEALTHY SUBURB TO THE NORTH OF MANHATTAN, AND LIKE ALL OF MY FRIENDS HERE, I AM A BOARDING STUDENT AT XAVIER'S SCHOOL FOR GIFTED YOUNGSTERS.
WE ARE ALL VERY DIFFERENT FROM EACH OTHER, BUT WE ARE HERE BECAUSE EACH OF US IS GIFTED, IN A VERY SPECIAL WAY.
CREATED BY DUFFY & GAMMILL
JO DUFFY WRITER
KERRY GAMMILL PENCILER
TOM PALMER FINISHER
JIM NOVAK LETTERER
PETRA SCOTESE COLORIST
ANN NOCENTI EDITOR
JIM SHOOTER EDITOR IN CHIEF
RUNAWAY

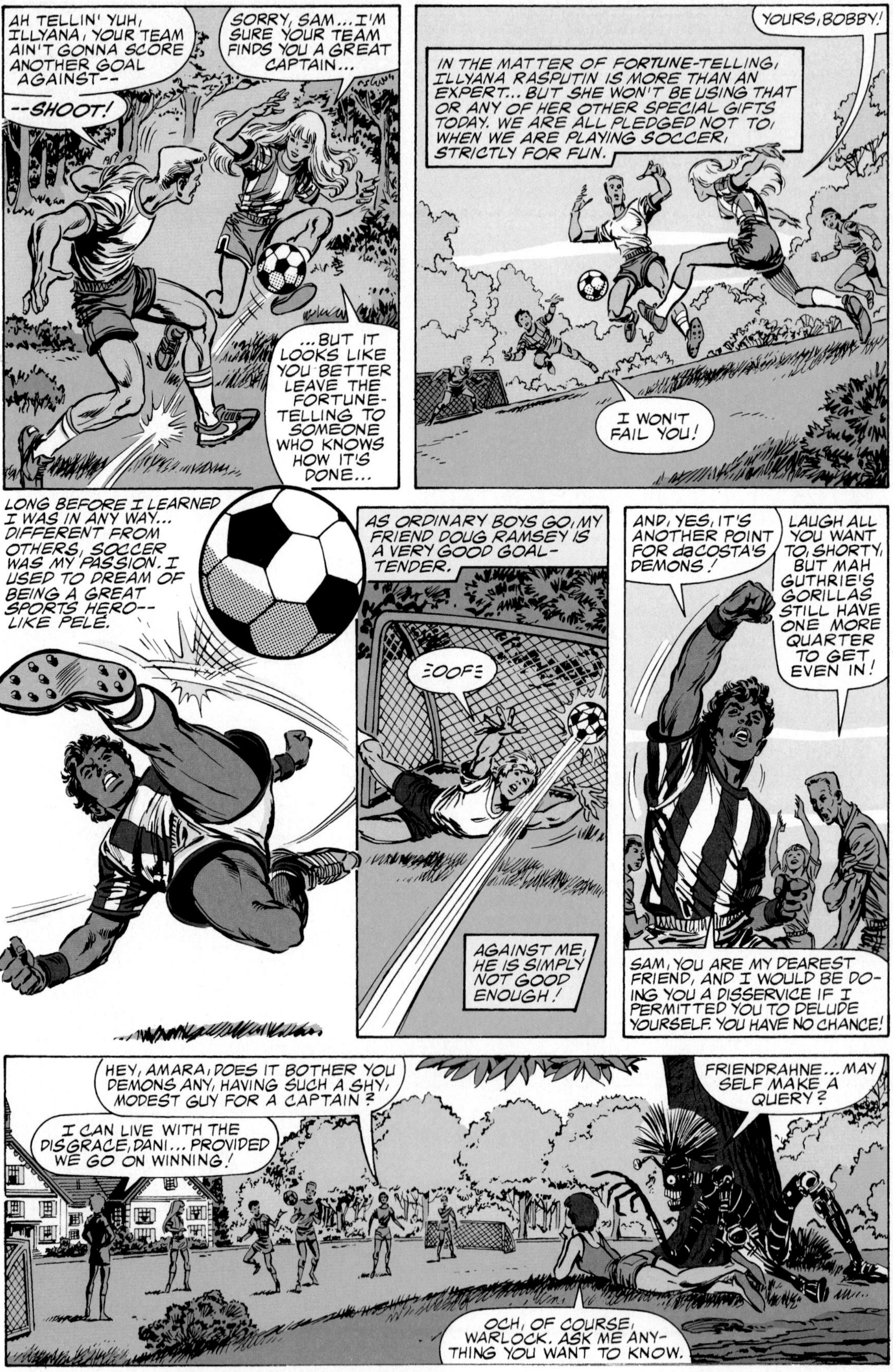
AH TELLIN' YUH, ILLYANA, YOUR TEAM AIN'T GONNA SCORE ANOTHER GOAL AGAINST--
--SHOOT!
SORRY, SAM...I'M SURE YOUR TEAM FINDS YOU A GREAT CAPTAIN...
...BUT IT LOOKS LIKE YOU BETTER LEAVE THE FORTUNE-TELLING TO SOMEONE WHO KNOWS HOW IT'S DONE...
YOURS, BOBBY!
IN THE MATTER OF FORTUNE-TELLING, ILLYANA RASPUTIN IS MORE THAN AN EXPERT... BUT SHE WON'T BE USING THAT OR ANY OF HER OTHER SPECIAL GIFTS TODAY. WE ARE ALL PLEDGED NOT TO, WHEN WE ARE PLAYING SOCCER, STRICTLY FOR FUN.
I WON'T FAIL YOU!
LONG BEFORE I LEARNED I WAS IN ANY WAY... DIFFERENT FROM OTHERS, SOCCER WAS MY PASSION. I USED TO DREAM OF BEING A GREAT SPORTS HERO-- LIKE PELÉ.
AS ORDINARY BOYS GO, MY FRIEND DOUG RAMSEY IS A VERY GOOD GOAL-TENDER.
OOF
AGAINST ME, HE IS SIMPLY NOT GOOD ENOUGH!
AND, YES, IT'S ANOTHER POINT FOR daCOSTA'S DEMONS!
LAUGH ALL YOU WANT TO, SHORTY, BUT MAH GUTHRIE'S GORILLAS STILL HAVE ONE MORE QUARTER TO GET EVEN IN!
SAM, YOU ARE MY DEAREST FRIEND, AND I WOULD BE DOING YOU A DISSERVICE IF I PERMITTED YOU TO DELUDE YOURSELF. YOU HAVE NO CHANCE!
HEY, AMARA, DOES IT BOTHER YOU DEMONS ANY, HAVING SUCH A SHY, MODEST GUY FOR A CAPTAIN?
I CAN LIVE WITH THE DISGRACE, DANI... PROVIDED WE GO ON WINNING!
FRIENDRAHNE... MAY SELF MAKE A QUERY?
OCH, OF COURSE, WARLOCK. ASK ME ANYTHING YOU WANT TO KNOW.

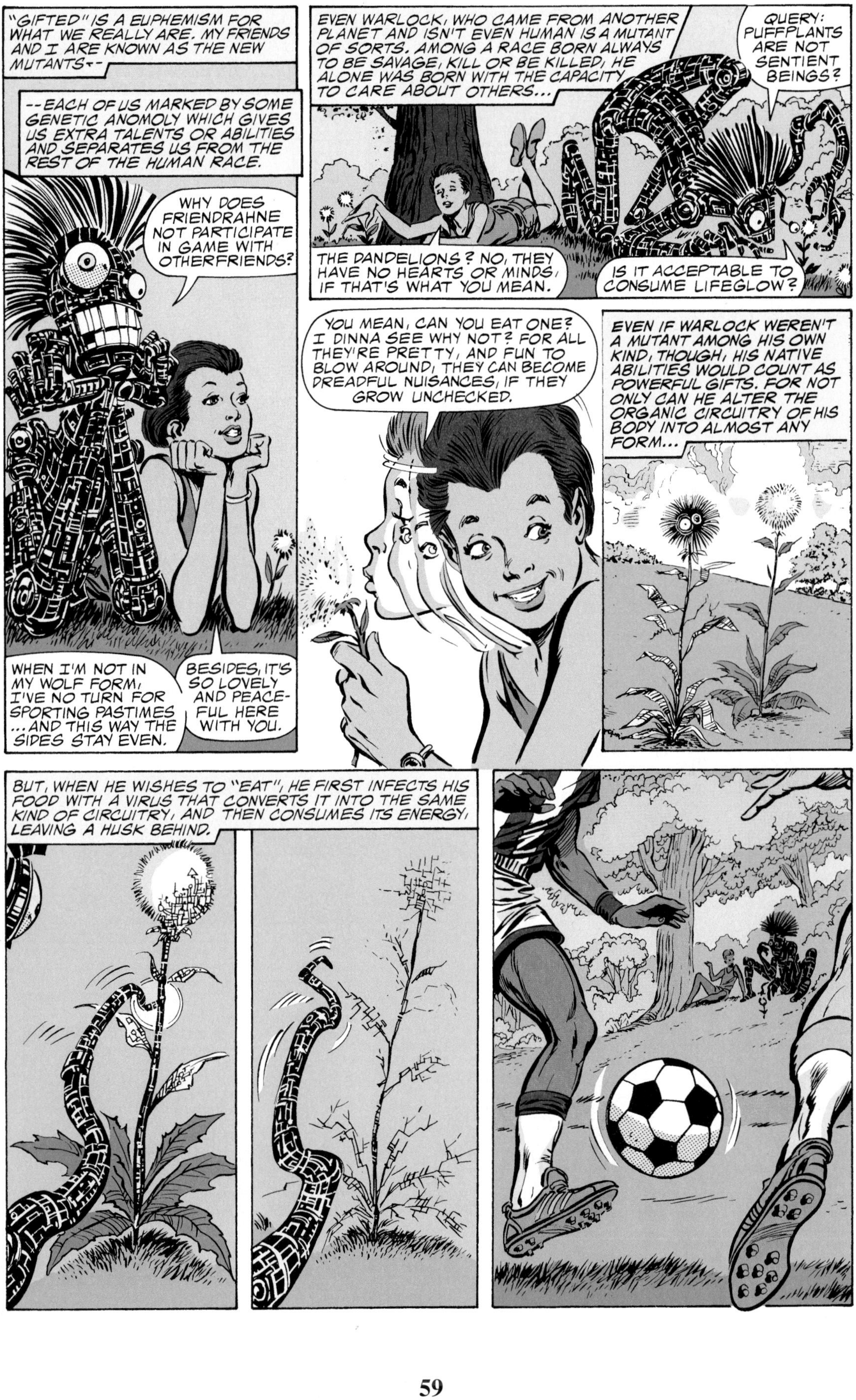
"GIFTED" IS A EUPHEMISM FOR WHAT WE REALLY ARE. MY FRIENDS AND I ARE KNOWN AS THE NEW MUTANTS--
--EACH OF US MARKED BY SOME GENETIC ANOMOLY WHICH GIVES US EXTRA TALENTS OR ABILITIES AND SEPARATES US FROM THE REST OF THE HUMAN RACE.
WHY DOES FRIENDRAHNE NOT PARTICIPATE IN GAME WITH OTHERFRIENDS?
WHEN I'M NOT IN MY WOLF FORM, I'VE NO TURN FOR SPORTING PASTIMES ...AND THIS WAY THE SIDES STAY EVEN.
BESIDES, IT'S SO LOVELY AND PEACEFUL HERE WITH YOU.
EVEN WARLOCK, WHO CAME FROM ANOTHER PLANET AND ISN'T EVEN HUMAN IS A MUTANT OF SORTS. AMONG A RACE BORN ALWAYS TO BE SAVAGE, KILL OR BE KILLED, HE ALONE WAS BORN WITH THE CAPACITY TO CARE ABOUT OTHERS...
QUERY: PUFFPLANTS ARE NOT SENTIENT BEINGS?
THE DANDELIONS? NO, THEY HAVE NO HEARTS OR MINDS, IF THAT'S WHAT YOU MEAN.
IS IT ACCEPTABLE TO CONSUME LIFEGLOW?
YOU MEAN, CAN YOU EAT ONE? I DINNA SEE WHY NOT? FOR ALL THEY'RE PRETTY, AND FUN TO BLOW AROUND, THEY CAN BECOME DREADFUL NUISANCES, IF THEY GROW UNCHECKED.
EVEN IF WARLOCK WEREN'T A MUTANT AMONG HIS OWN KIND, THOUGH, HIS NATIVE ABILITIES WOULD COUNT AS POWERFUL GIFTS. FOR NOT ONLY CAN HE ALTER THE ORGANIC CIRCUITRY OF HIS BODY INTO ALMOST ANY FORM...
BUT, WHEN HE WISHES TO "EAT", HE FIRST INFECTS HIS FOOD WITH A VIRUS THAT CONVERTS IT INTO THE SAME KIND OF CIRCUITRY, AND THEN CONSUMES ITS ENERGY, LEAVING A HUSK BEHIND.

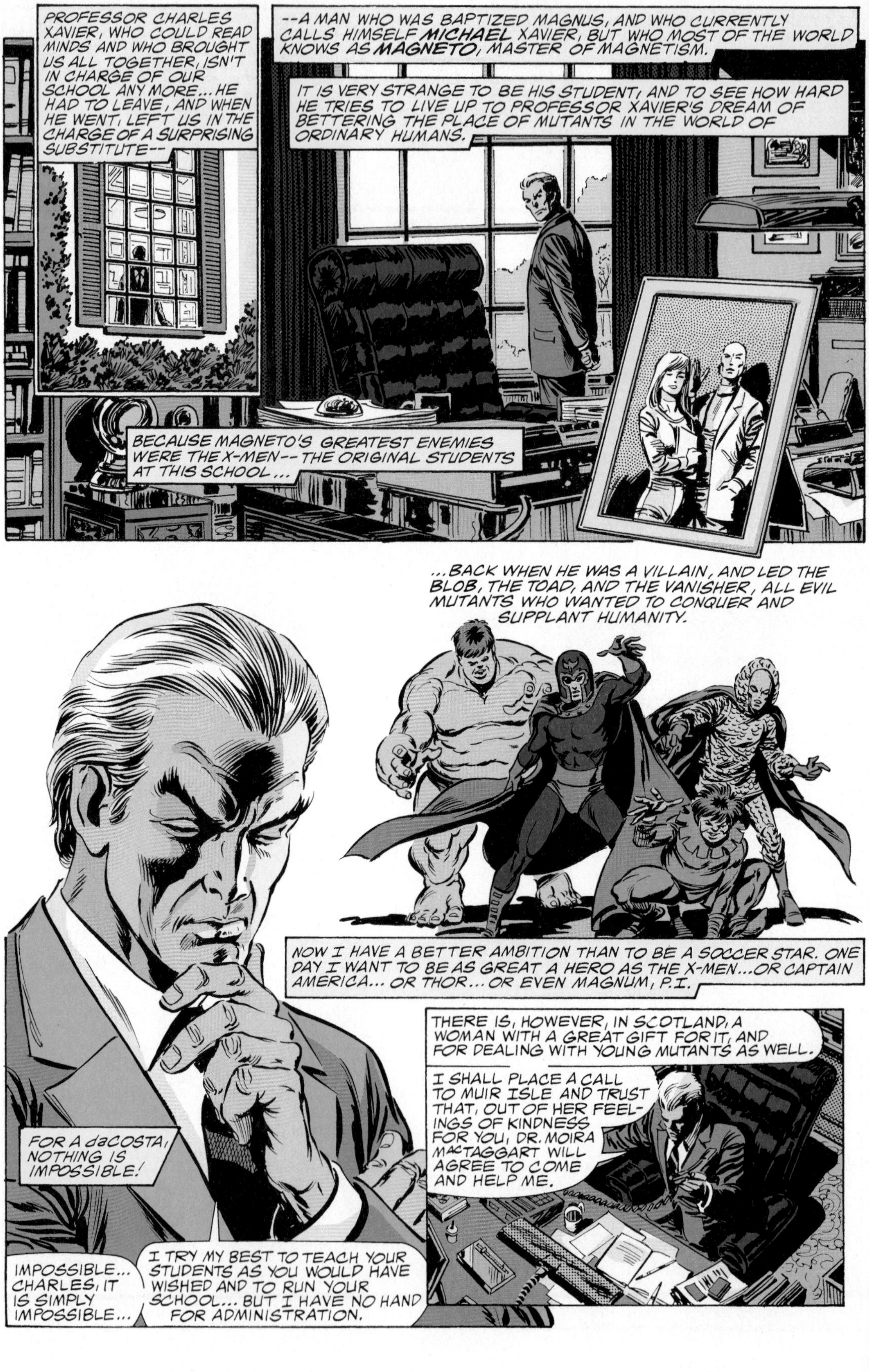
PROFESSOR CHARLES XAVIER, WHO COULD READ MINDS AND WHO BROUGHT US ALL TOGETHER, ISN'T IN CHARGE OF OUR SCHOOL ANY MORE... HE HAD TO LEAVE, AND WHEN HE WENT, LEFT US IN THE CHARGE OF A SURPRISING SUBSTITUTE--
--A MAN WHO WAS BAPTIZED MAGNUS, AND WHO CURRENTLY CALLS HIMSELF MICHAEL XAVIER, BUT WHO MOST OF THE WORLD KNOWS AS MAGNETO, MASTER OF MAGNETISM.
IT IS VERY STRANGE TO BE HIS STUDENT, AND TO SEE HOW HARD HE TRIES TO LIVE UP TO PROFESSOR XAVIER'S DREAM OF BETTERING THE PLACE OF MUTANTS IN THE WORLD OF ORDINARY HUMANS.
BECAUSE MAGNETO'S GREATEST ENEMIES WERE THE X-MEN--THE ORIGINAL STUDENTS AT THIS SCHOOL...
...BACK WHEN HE WAS A VILLAIN, AND LED THE BLOB, THE TOAD, AND THE VANISHER, ALL EVIL MUTANTS WHO WANTED TO CONQUER AND SUPPLANT HUMANITY.
NOW I HAVE A BETTER AMBITION THAN TO BE A SOCCER STAR. ONE DAY I WANT TO BE AS GREAT A HERO AS THE X-MEN...OR CAPTAIN AMERICA... OR THOR... OR EVEN MAGNUM, P.I.
FOR A daCOSTA, NOTHING IS IMPOSSIBLE!
IMPOSSIBLE... CHARLES, IT IS SIMPLY IMPOSSIBLE...
I TRY MY BEST TO TEACH YOUR STUDENTS AS YOU WOULD HAVE WISHED AND TO RUN YOUR SCHOOL... BUT I HAVE NO HAND FOR ADMINISTRATION.
THERE IS, HOWEVER, IN SCOTLAND, A WOMAN WITH A GREAT GIFT FOR IT, AND FOR DEALING WITH YOUNG MUTANTS AS WELL.
I SHALL PLACE A CALL TO MUIR ISLE AND TRUST THAT, OUT OF HER FEELINGS OF KINDNESS FOR YOU, DR. MOIRA MacTAGGART WILL AGREE TO COME AND HELP ME.

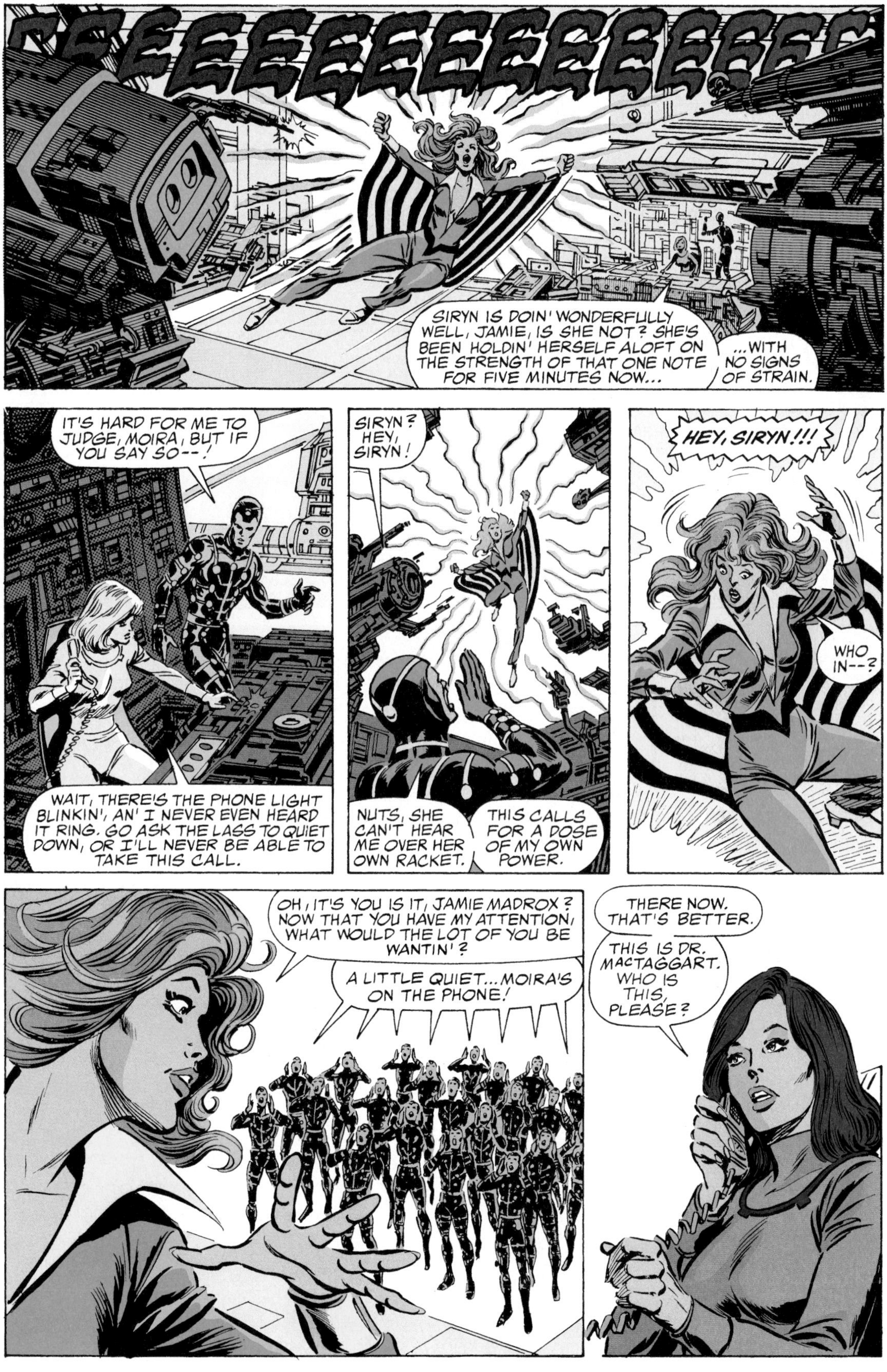

EEEEEEEEEEEEEEEEE
SIRYN IS DOIN' WONDERFULLY WELL, JAMIE, IS SHE NOT? SHE'S BEEN HOLDIN' HERSELF ALOFT ON THE STRENGTH OF THAT ONE NOTE FOR FIVE MINUTES NOW...
...WITH NO SIGNS OF STRAIN.
IT'S HARD FOR ME TO JUDGE, MOIRA, BUT IF YOU SAY SO--!
WAIT, THERE'S THE PHONE LIGHT BLINKIN', AN' I NEVER EVEN HEARD IT RING. GO ASK THE LASS TO QUIET DOWN, OR I'LL NEVER BE ABLE TO TAKE THIS CALL.
SIRYN? HEY, SIRYN!
NUTS, SHE CAN'T HEAR ME OVER HER OWN RACKET.
THIS CALLS FOR A DOSE OF MY OWN POWER.
HEY, SIRYN!!!
WHO IN--?
OH, IT'S YOU IS IT, JAMIE MADROX? NOW THAT YOU HAVE MY ATTENTION, WHAT WOULD THE LOT OF YOU BE WANTIN'?
A LITTLE QUIET... MOIRA'S ON THE PHONE!
THERE NOW. THAT'S BETTER.
THIS IS DR. MACTAGGART. WHO IS THIS, PLEASE?

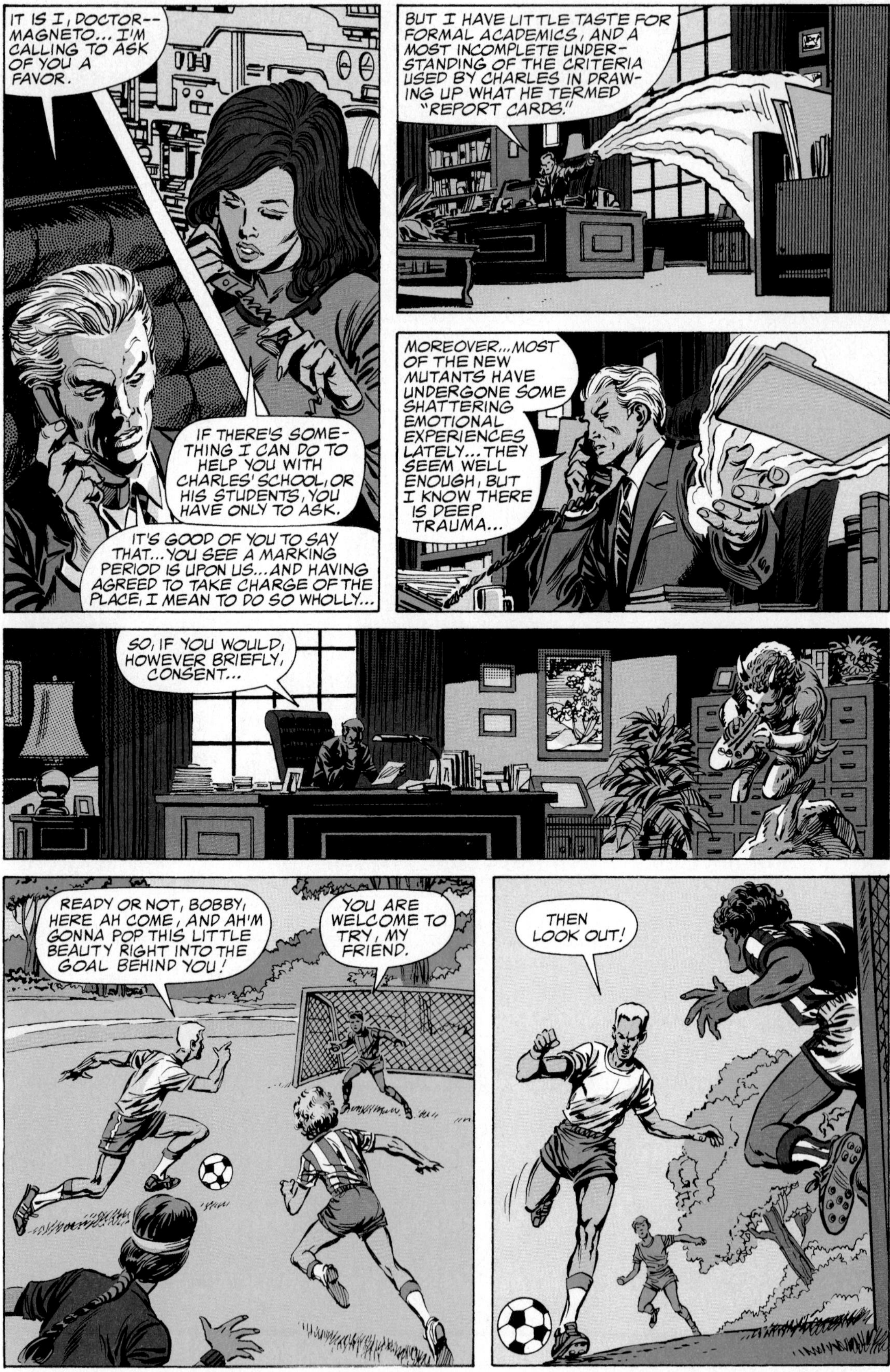
IT IS I, DOCTOR-- MAGNETO... I'M CALLING TO ASK OF YOU A FAVOR.
IF THERE'S SOMETHING I CAN DO TO HELP YOU WITH CHARLES' SCHOOL, OR HIS STUDENTS, YOU HAVE ONLY TO ASK.
IT'S GOOD OF YOU TO SAY THAT... YOU SEE A MARKING PERIOD IS UPON US... AND HAVING AGREED TO TAKE CHARGE OF THE PLACE, I MEAN TO DO SO WHOLLY...
BUT I HAVE LITTLE TASTE FOR FORMAL ACADEMICS, AND A MOST INCOMPLETE UNDERSTANDING OF THE CRITERIA USED BY CHARLES IN DRAWING UP WHAT HE TERMED "REPORT CARDS."
MOREOVER... MOST OF THE NEW MUTANTS HAVE UNDERGONE SOME SHATTERING EMOTIONAL EXPERIENCES LATELY... THEY SEEM WELL ENOUGH, BUT I KNOW THERE IS DEEP TRAUMA...
SO, IF YOU WOULD, HOWEVER BRIEFLY, CONSENT...
READY OR NOT, BOBBY, HERE AH COME, AND AH'M GONNA POP THIS LITTLE BEAUTY RIGHT INTO THE GOAL BEHIND YOU!
YOU ARE WELCOME TO TRY, MY FRIEND.
THEN LOOK OUT!

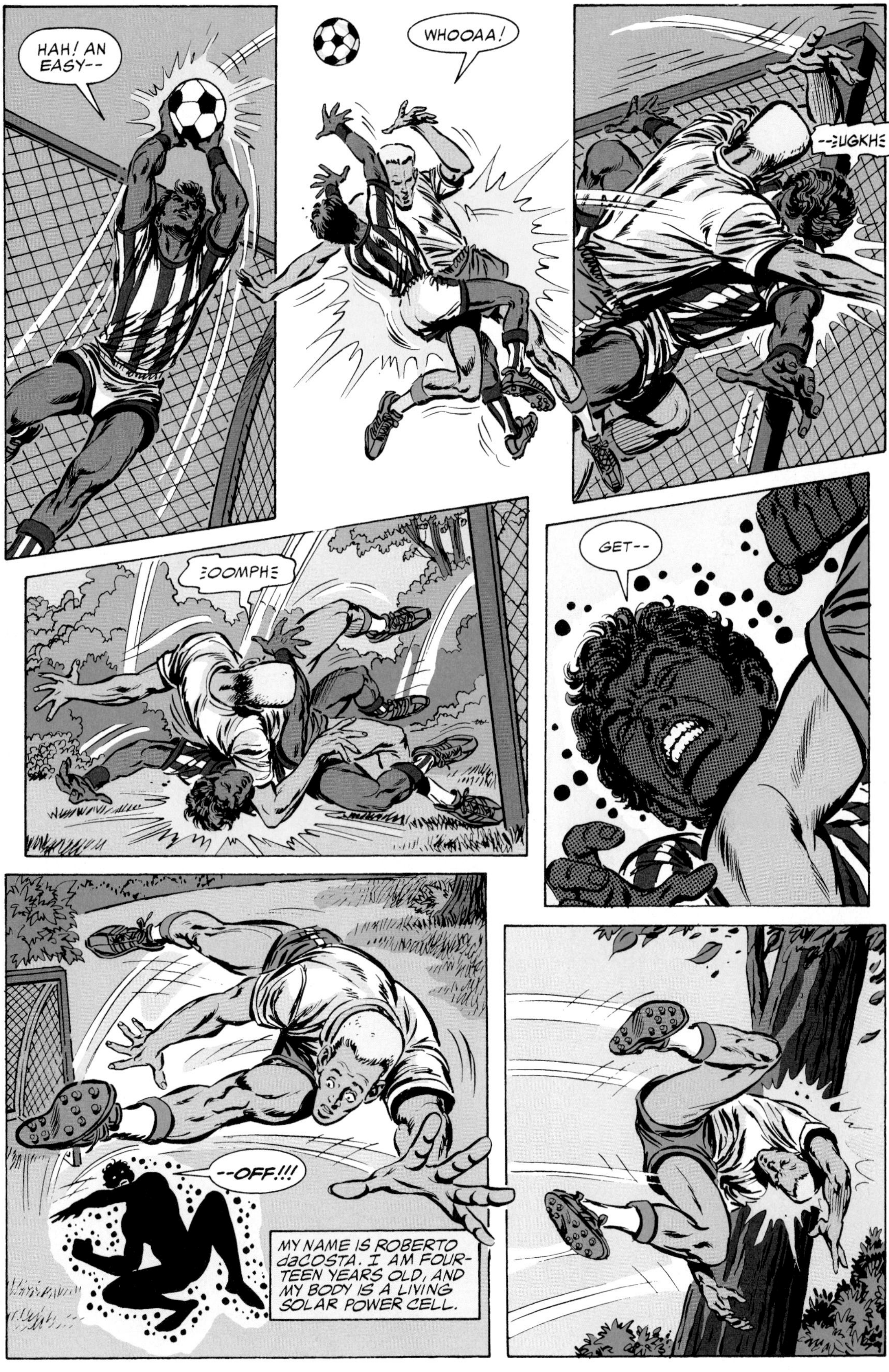
HAH! AN EASY--
WHOOAA!
--UGKH
OOMPH
GET--
--OFF!!!
MY NAME IS ROBERTO daCOSTA. I AM FOURTEEN YEARS OLD, AND MY BODY IS A LIVING SOLAR POWER CELL.

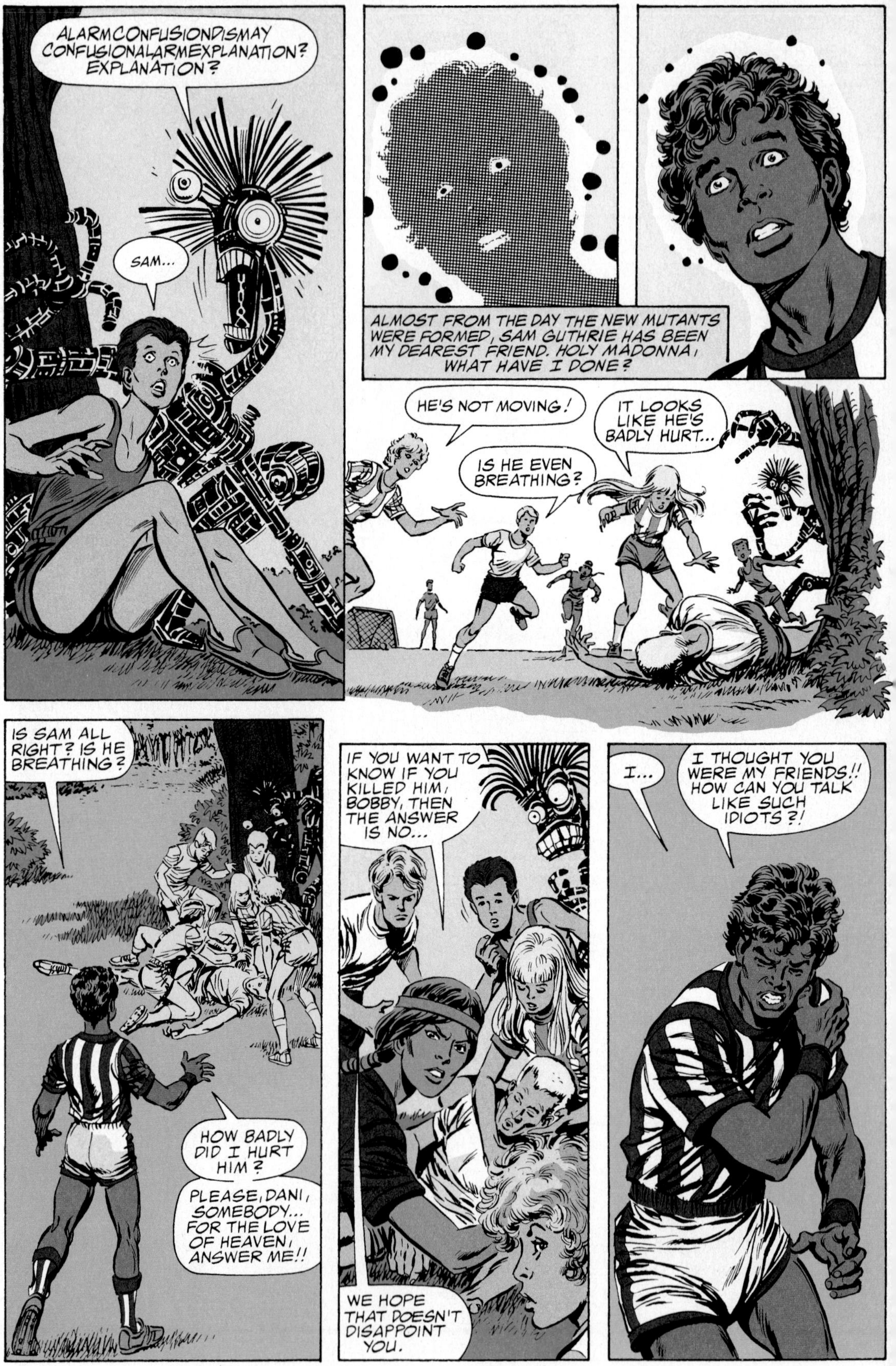

ALARMCONFUSIONDISMAY CONFUSIONALARMEXPLANATION? EXPLANATION?
SAM...
ALMOST FROM THE DAY THE NEW MUTANTS WERE FORMED, SAM GUTHRIE HAS BEEN MY DEAREST FRIEND. HOLY MADONNA, WHAT HAVE I DONE?
HE'S NOT MOVING!
IS HE EVEN BREATHING?
IT LOOKS LIKE HE'S BADLY HURT...
IS SAM ALL RIGHT? IS HE BREATHING?
HOW BADLY DID I HURT HIM?
PLEASE, DANI, SOMEBODY... FOR THE LOVE OF HEAVEN, ANSWER ME!!
IF YOU WANT TO KNOW IF YOU KILLED HIM, BOBBY, THEN THE ANSWER IS NO...
WE HOPE THAT DOESN'T DISAPPOINT YOU.
I...
I THOUGHT YOU WERE MY FRIENDS!! HOW CAN YOU TALK LIKE SUCH IDIOTS?!

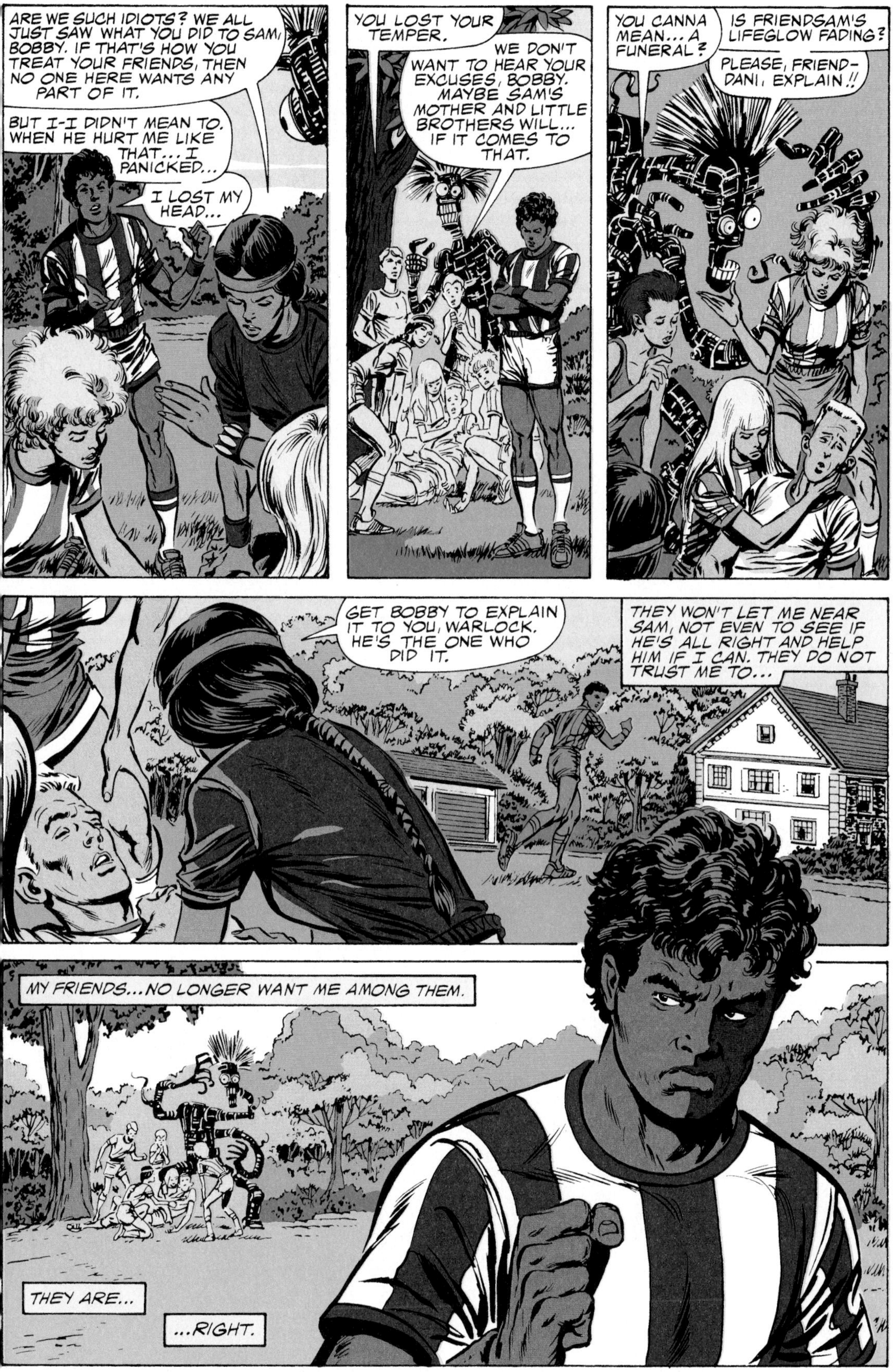
ARE WE SUCH IDIOTS? WE ALL JUST SAW WHAT YOU DID TO SAM, BOBBY. IF THAT'S HOW YOU TREAT YOUR FRIENDS, THEN NO ONE HERE WANTS ANY PART OF IT.
BUT I-I DIDN'T MEAN TO. WHEN HE HURT ME LIKE THAT... I PANICKED...
I LOST MY HEAD...
YOU LOST YOUR TEMPER.
WE DON'T WANT TO HEAR YOUR EXCUSES, BOBBY. MAYBE SAM'S MOTHER AND LITTLE BROTHERS WILL... IF IT COMES TO THAT.
YOU CANNA MEAN... A FUNERAL?
IS FRIENDSAM'S LIFEGLOW FADING?
PLEASE, FRIEND-DANI, EXPLAIN!!
GET BOBBY TO EXPLAIN IT TO YOU, WARLOCK. HE'S THE ONE WHO DID IT.
THEY WON'T LET ME NEAR SAM, NOT EVEN TO SEE IF HE'S ALL RIGHT AND HELP HIM IF I CAN. THEY DO NOT TRUST ME TO...
MY FRIENDS... NO LONGER WANT ME AMONG THEM.
THEY ARE...
...RIGHT.

ATTENTION! ALERT! FRIENDSHAN AND MAGNETO ENTITY ARE APPROACHING!

SURELY MAGNETO'LL KNOW WHAT'S TO BE DONE!

WHAT HAPPENED HERE?

IT WAS BOBBY, SIR. HE USED HIS SUN-SPOT POWER TO HURL SAM HEAD-LONG INTO A TREE!

WHAT IS CURRENT STATUS OF FRIENDSAM'S LIFEGLOW?!

HE'S MOVING, WARLOCK! THAT'S A GOOD SIGN!

BOBBY, ARE YOU OKAY? DID WE GET THE GOAL?

WHAT A RELIEF!

JUBILATION! JUBILATION!

TAKE IT EASY, SAM. YOU'VE HAD A NASTY SHOCK.

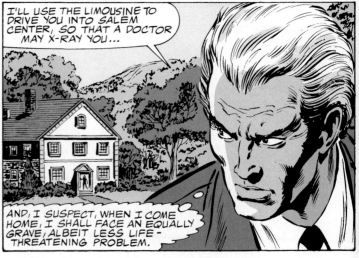

I'LL USE THE LIMOUSINE TO DRIVE YOU INTO SALEM CENTER, SO THAT A DOCTOR MAY X-RAY YOU...

AND, I SUSPECT, WHEN I COME HOME, I SHALL FACE AN EQUALLY GRAVE, ALBEIT LESS LIFE-THREATENING PROBLEM.

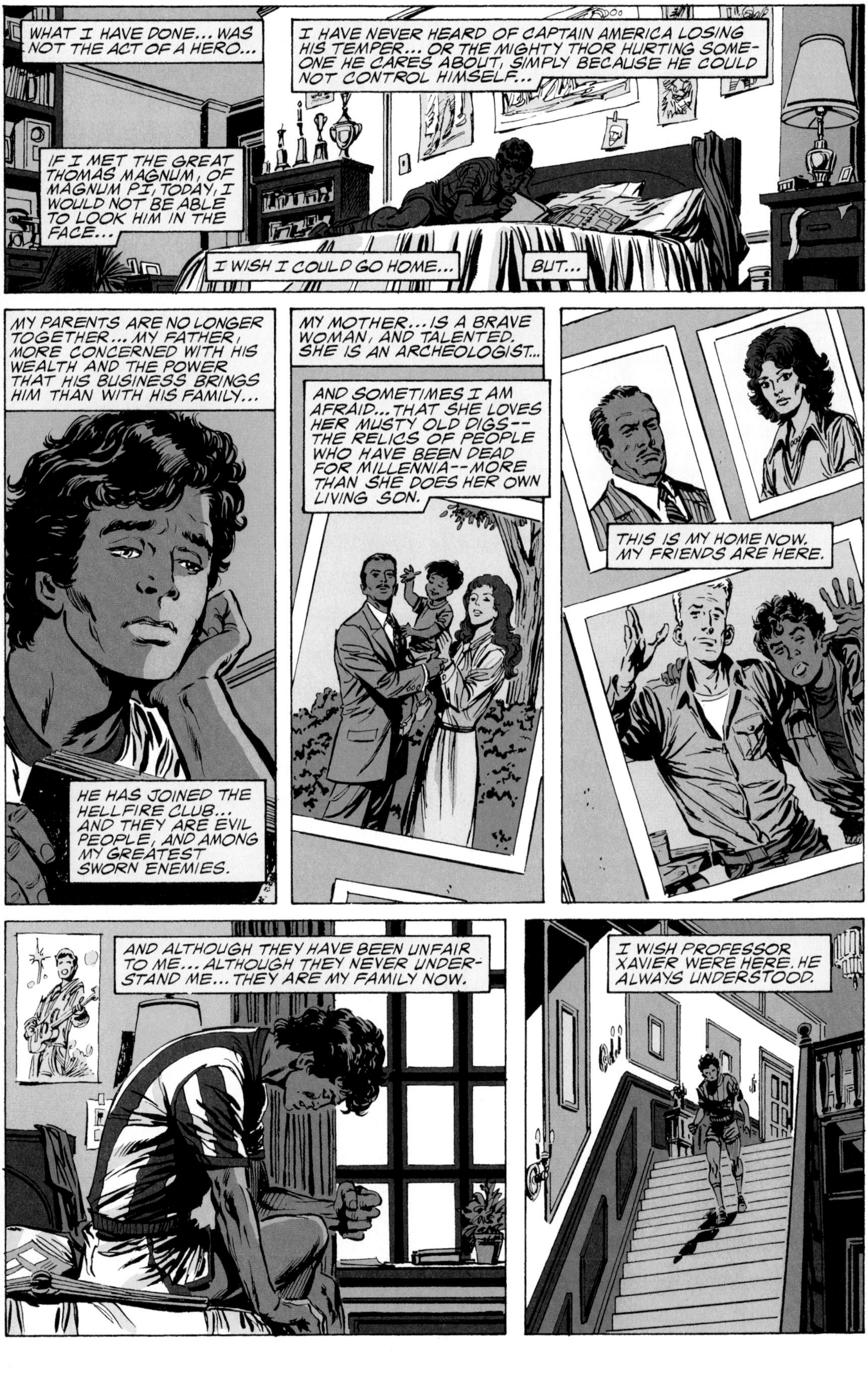
WHAT I HAVE DONE... WAS NOT THE ACT OF A HERO...
I HAVE NEVER HEARD OF CAPTAIN AMERICA LOSING HIS TEMPER... OR THE MIGHTY THOR HURTING SOMEONE HE CARES ABOUT, SIMPLY BECAUSE HE COULD NOT CONTROL HIMSELF...
IF I MET THE GREAT THOMAS MAGNUM, OF MAGNUM PI, TODAY, I WOULD NOT BE ABLE TO LOOK HIM IN THE FACE...
I WISH I COULD GO HOME...
BUT...
MY PARENTS ARE NO LONGER TOGETHER... MY FATHER, MORE CONCERNED WITH HIS WEALTH AND THE POWER THAT HIS BUSINESS BRINGS HIM THAN WITH HIS FAMILY...
HE HAS JOINED THE HELLFIRE CLUB... AND THEY ARE EVIL PEOPLE, AND AMONG MY GREATEST SWORN ENEMIES.
MY MOTHER... IS A BRAVE WOMAN, AND TALENTED. SHE IS AN ARCHEOLOGIST...
AND SOMETIMES I AM AFRAID... THAT SHE LOVES HER MUSTY OLD DIGS-- THE RELICS OF PEOPLE WHO HAVE BEEN DEAD FOR MILLENNIA--MORE THAN SHE DOES HER OWN LIVING SON.
THIS IS MY HOME NOW. MY FRIENDS ARE HERE.
AND ALTHOUGH THEY HAVE BEEN UNFAIR TO ME... ALTHOUGH THEY NEVER UNDERSTAND ME... THEY ARE MY FAMILY NOW.
I WISH PROFESSOR XAVIER WERE HERE. HE ALWAYS UNDERSTOOD.

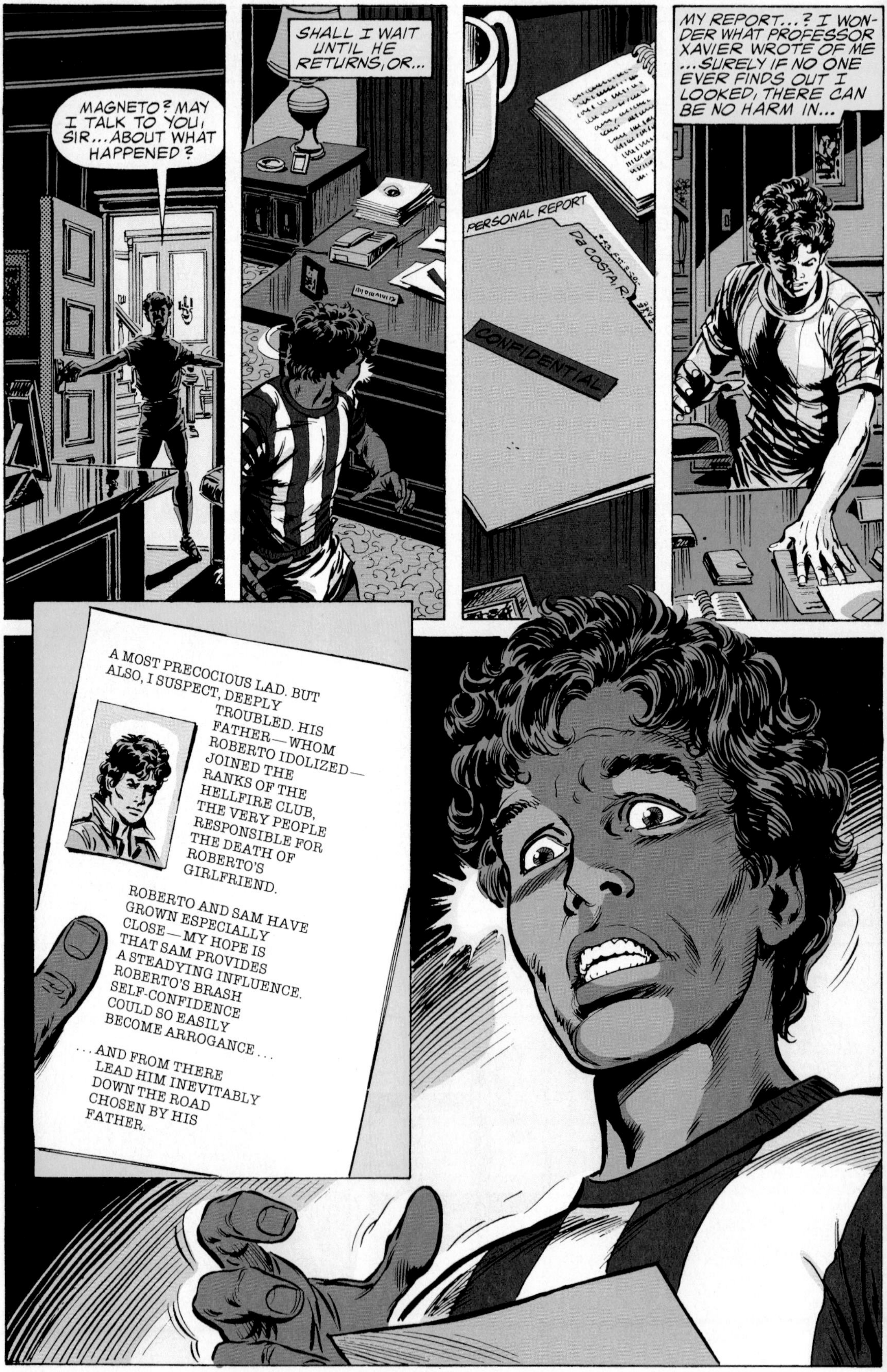
MAGNETO? MAY I TALK TO YOU, SIR... ABOUT WHAT HAPPENED?
SHALL I WAIT UNTIL HE RETURNS, OR...
PERSONAL REPORT
DaCOSTA, R.
CONFIDENTIAL
MY REPORT...? I WONDER WHAT PROFESSOR XAVIER WROTE OF ME ...SURELY IF NO ONE EVER FINDS OUT I LOOKED, THERE CAN BE NO HARM IN...
A MOST PRECOCIOUS LAD. BUT ALSO, I SUSPECT, DEEPLY TROUBLED. HIS FATHER—WHOM ROBERTO IDOLIZED—JOINED THE RANKS OF THE HELLFIRE CLUB, THE VERY PEOPLE RESPONSIBLE FOR THE DEATH OF ROBERTO'S GIRLFRIEND.
ROBERTO AND SAM HAVE GROWN ESPECIALLY CLOSE—MY HOPE IS THAT SAM PROVIDES A STEADYING INFLUENCE. ROBERTO'S BRASH SELF-CONFIDENCE COULD SO EASILY BECOME ARROGANCE...
...AND FROM THERE LEAD HIM INEVITABLY DOWN THE ROAD CHOSEN BY HIS FATHER.

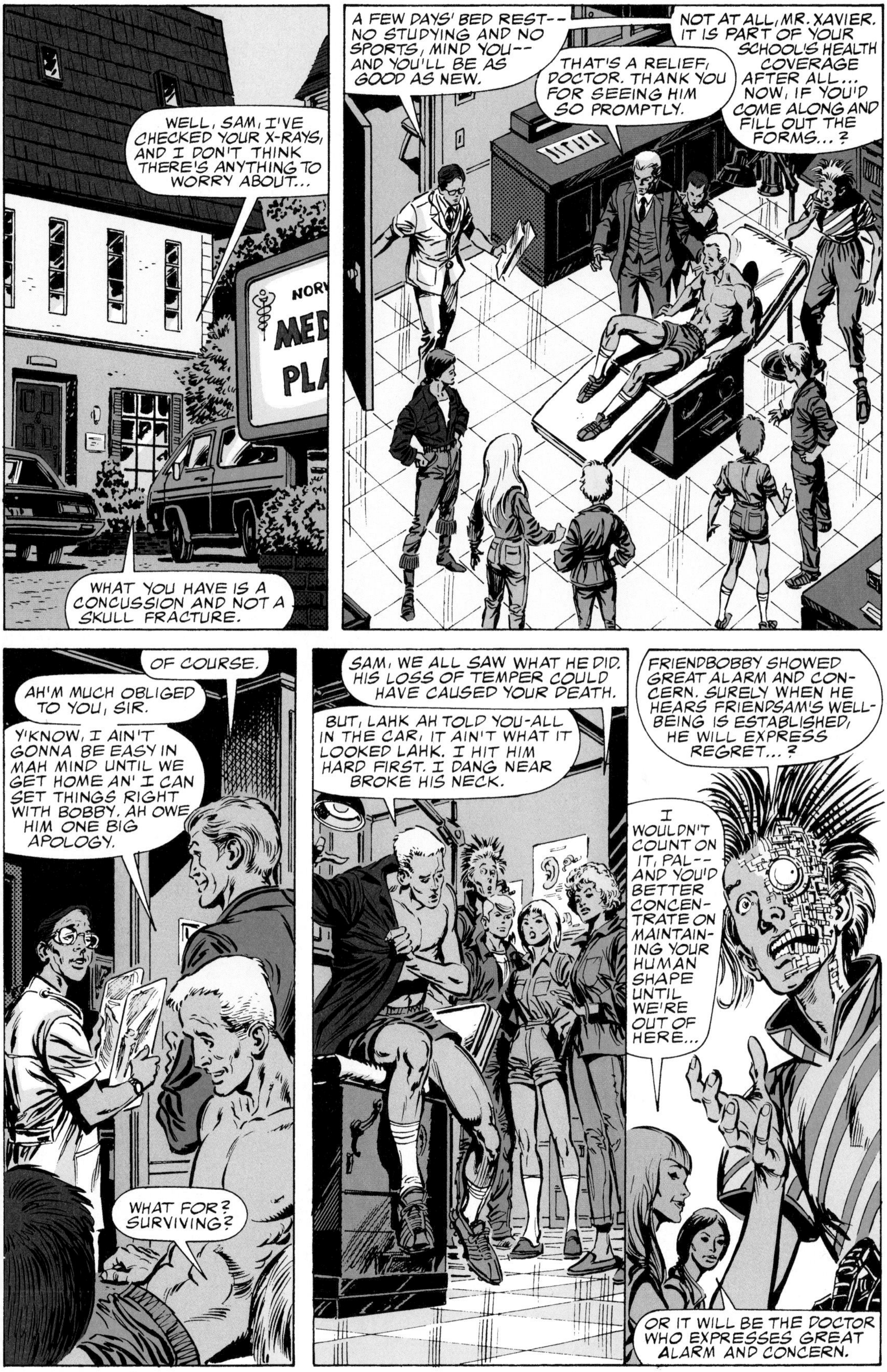
WELL, SAM, I'VE CHECKED YOUR X-RAYS, AND I DON'T THINK THERE'S ANYTHING TO WORRY ABOUT...
NORV
MED
PLA
WHAT YOU HAVE IS A CONCUSSION AND NOT A SKULL FRACTURE.
A FEW DAYS' BED REST-- NO STUDYING AND NO SPORTS, MIND YOU-- AND YOU'LL BE AS GOOD AS NEW.
THAT'S A RELIEF, DOCTOR. THANK YOU FOR SEEING HIM SO PROMPTLY.
NOT AT ALL, MR. XAVIER. IT IS PART OF YOUR SCHOOL'S HEALTH COVERAGE AFTER ALL... NOW, IF YOU'D COME ALONG AND FILL OUT THE FORMS...?
OF COURSE.
AH'M MUCH OBLIGED TO YOU, SIR.
Y'KNOW, I AIN'T GONNA BE EASY IN MAH MIND UNTIL WE GET HOME AN' I CAN SET THINGS RIGHT WITH BOBBY. AH OWE HIM ONE BIG APOLOGY.
WHAT FOR? SURVIVING?
SAM, WE ALL SAW WHAT HE DID. HIS LOSS OF TEMPER COULD HAVE CAUSED YOUR DEATH.
BUT, LAHK AH TOLD YOU-ALL IN THE CAR, IT AIN'T WHAT IT LOOKED LAHK. I HIT HIM HARD FIRST. I DANG NEAR BROKE HIS NECK.
FRIENDBOBBY SHOWED GREAT ALARM AND CONCERN. SURELY WHEN HE HEARS FRIENDSAM'S WELL-BEING IS ESTABLISHED, HE WILL EXPRESS REGRET...?
I WOULDN'T COUNT ON IT, PAL-- AND YOU'D BETTER CONCENTRATE ON MAINTAINING YOUR HUMAN SHAPE UNTIL WE'RE OUT OF HERE...
OR IT WILL BE THE DOCTOR WHO EXPRESSES GREAT ALARM AND CONCERN.

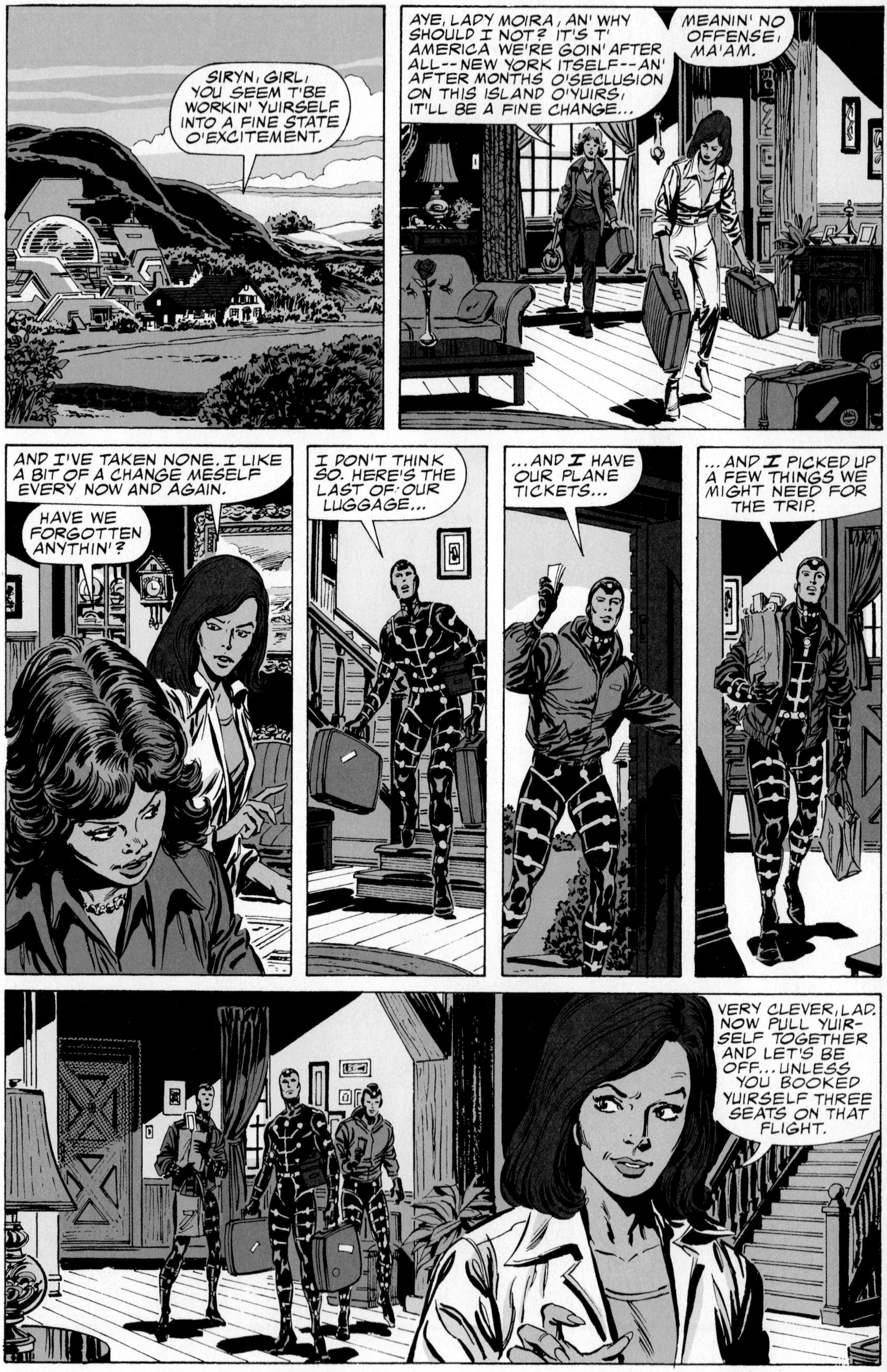
SIRYN, GIRL, YOU SEEM T'BE WORKIN' YUIRSELF INTO A FINE STATE O'EXCITEMENT.
AYE, LADY MOIRA, AN' WHY SHOULD I NOT? IT'S T' AMERICA WE'RE GOIN' AFTER ALL-- NEW YORK ITSELF-- AN' AFTER MONTHS O'SECLUSION ON THIS ISLAND O'YUIRS, IT'LL BE A FINE CHANGE...
MEANIN' NO OFFENSE, MA'AM.
AND I'VE TAKEN NONE. I LIKE A BIT OF A CHANGE MESELF EVERY NOW AND AGAIN.
HAVE WE FORGOTTEN ANYTHIN'?
I DON'T THINK SO. HERE'S THE LAST OF OUR LUGGAGE...
...AND I HAVE OUR PLANE TICKETS...
...AND I PICKED UP A FEW THINGS WE MIGHT NEED FOR THE TRIP.
VERY CLEVER, LAD. NOW PULL YUIRSELF TOGETHER AND LET'S BE OFF... UNLESS YOU BOOKED YUIRSELF THREE SEATS ON THAT FLIGHT.

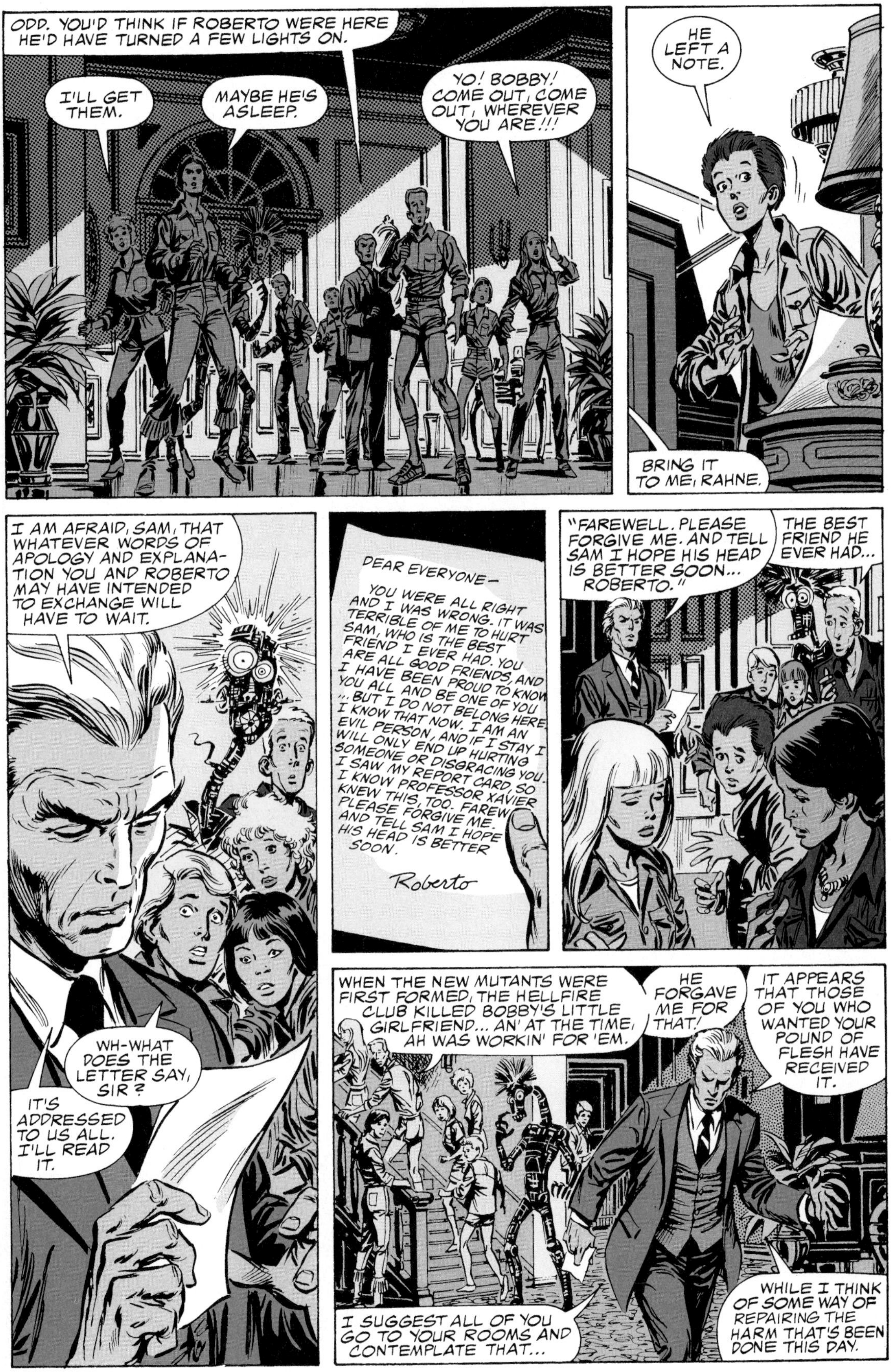
ODD. YOU'D THINK IF ROBERTO WERE HERE HE'D HAVE TURNED A FEW LIGHTS ON.
I'LL GET THEM.
MAYBE HE'S ASLEEP.
YO! BOBBY! COME OUT, COME OUT, WHEREVER YOU ARE!!!
HE LEFT A NOTE.
BRING IT TO ME, RAHNE.
I AM AFRAID, SAM, THAT WHATEVER WORDS OF APOLOGY AND EXPLANATION YOU AND ROBERTO MAY HAVE INTENDED TO EXCHANGE WILL HAVE TO WAIT.
WH-WHAT DOES THE LETTER SAY, SIR?
IT'S ADDRESSED TO US ALL. I'LL READ IT.
DEAR EVERYONE—
YOU WERE ALL RIGHT AND I WAS WRONG. IT WAS TERRIBLE OF ME TO HURT SAM, WHO IS THE BEST FRIEND I EVER HAD. YOU ARE ALL GOOD FRIENDS, AND I HAVE BEEN PROUD TO KNOW YOU ALL AND BE ONE OF YOU ...BUT I DO NOT BELONG HERE. I KNOW THAT NOW. I AM AN EVIL PERSON, AND IF I STAY I WILL ONLY END UP HURTING SOMEONE OR DISGRACING YOU. I SAW MY REPORT CARD, SO I KNOW PROFESSOR XAVIER KNEW THIS, TOO. FAREW PLEASE FORGIVE ME. AND TELL SAM I HOPE HIS HEAD IS BETTER SOON.
Roberto
"FAREWELL. PLEASE FORGIVE ME. AND TELL SAM I HOPE HIS HEAD IS BETTER SOON... ROBERTO."
THE BEST FRIEND HE EVER HAD...
WHEN THE NEW MUTANTS WERE FIRST FORMED, THE HELLFIRE CLUB KILLED BOBBY'S LITTLE GIRLFRIEND... AN' AT THE TIME, AH WAS WORKIN' FOR 'EM.
HE FORGAVE ME FOR THAT!
IT APPEARS THAT THOSE OF YOU WHO WANTED YOUR POUND OF FLESH HAVE RECEIVED IT.
I SUGGEST ALL OF YOU GO TO YOUR ROOMS AND CONTEMPLATE THAT...
WHILE I THINK OF SOME WAY OF REPAIRING THE HARM THAT'S BEEN DONE THIS DAY.

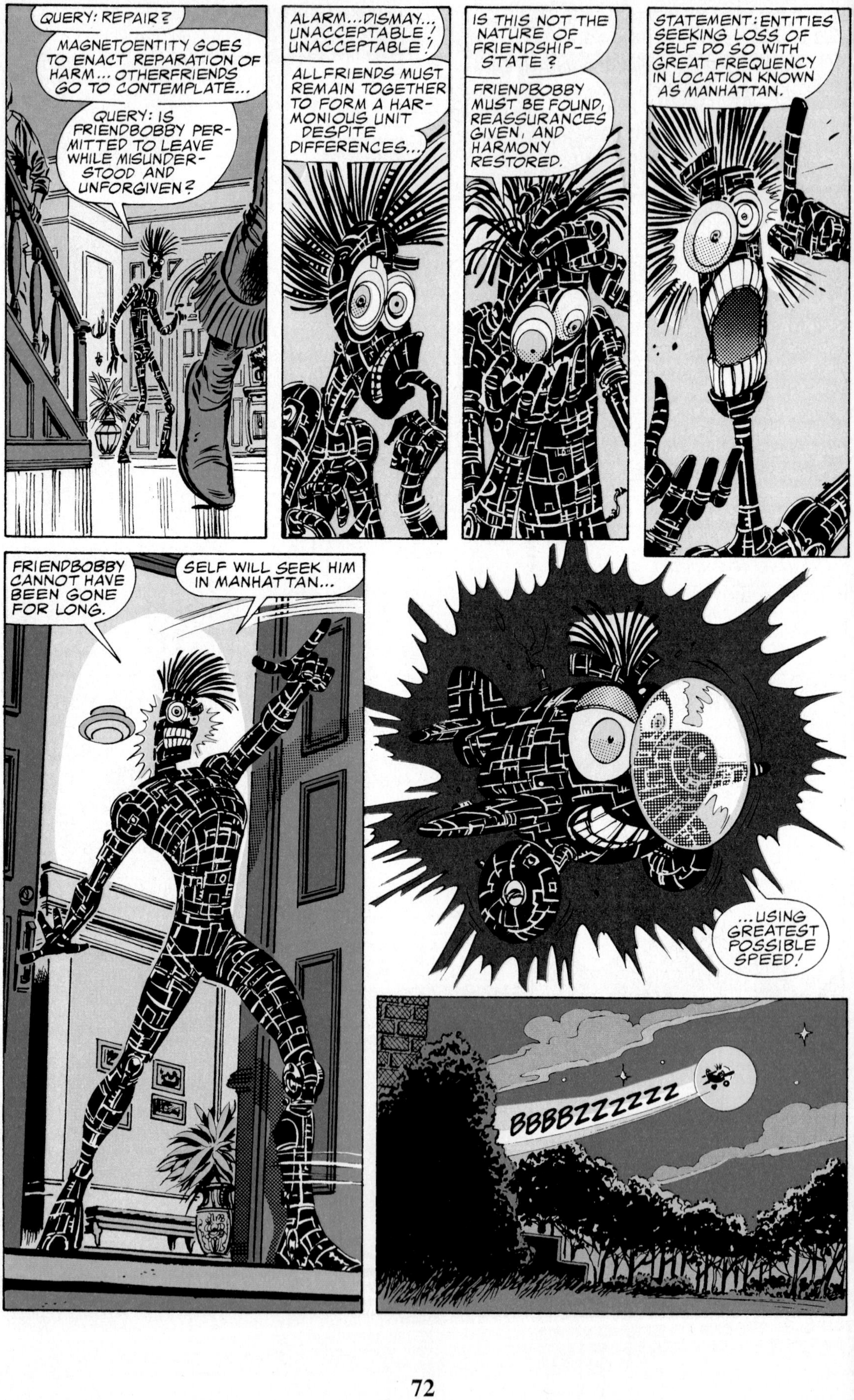
QUERY: REPAIR?
MAGNETOENTITY GOES TO ENACT REPARATION OF HARM... OTHERFRIENDS GO TO CONTEMPLATE...
QUERY: IS FRIENDBOBBY PERMITTED TO LEAVE WHILE MISUNDERSTOOD AND UNFORGIVEN?
ALARM...DISMAY... UNACCEPTABLE! UNACCEPTABLE!
ALLFRIENDS MUST REMAIN TOGETHER TO FORM A HARMONIOUS UNIT DESPITE DIFFERENCES...
IS THIS NOT THE NATURE OF FRIENDSHIP-STATE?
FRIENDBOBBY MUST BE FOUND, REASSURANCES GIVEN, AND HARMONY RESTORED.
STATEMENT: ENTITIES SEEKING LOSS OF SELF DO SO WITH GREAT FREQUENCY IN LOCATION KNOWN AS MANHATTAN.
FRIENDBOBBY CANNOT HAVE BEEN GONE FOR LONG.
SELF WILL SEEK HIM IN MANHATTAN...
...USING GREATEST POSSIBLE SPEED!
BBBBZZZZZZ

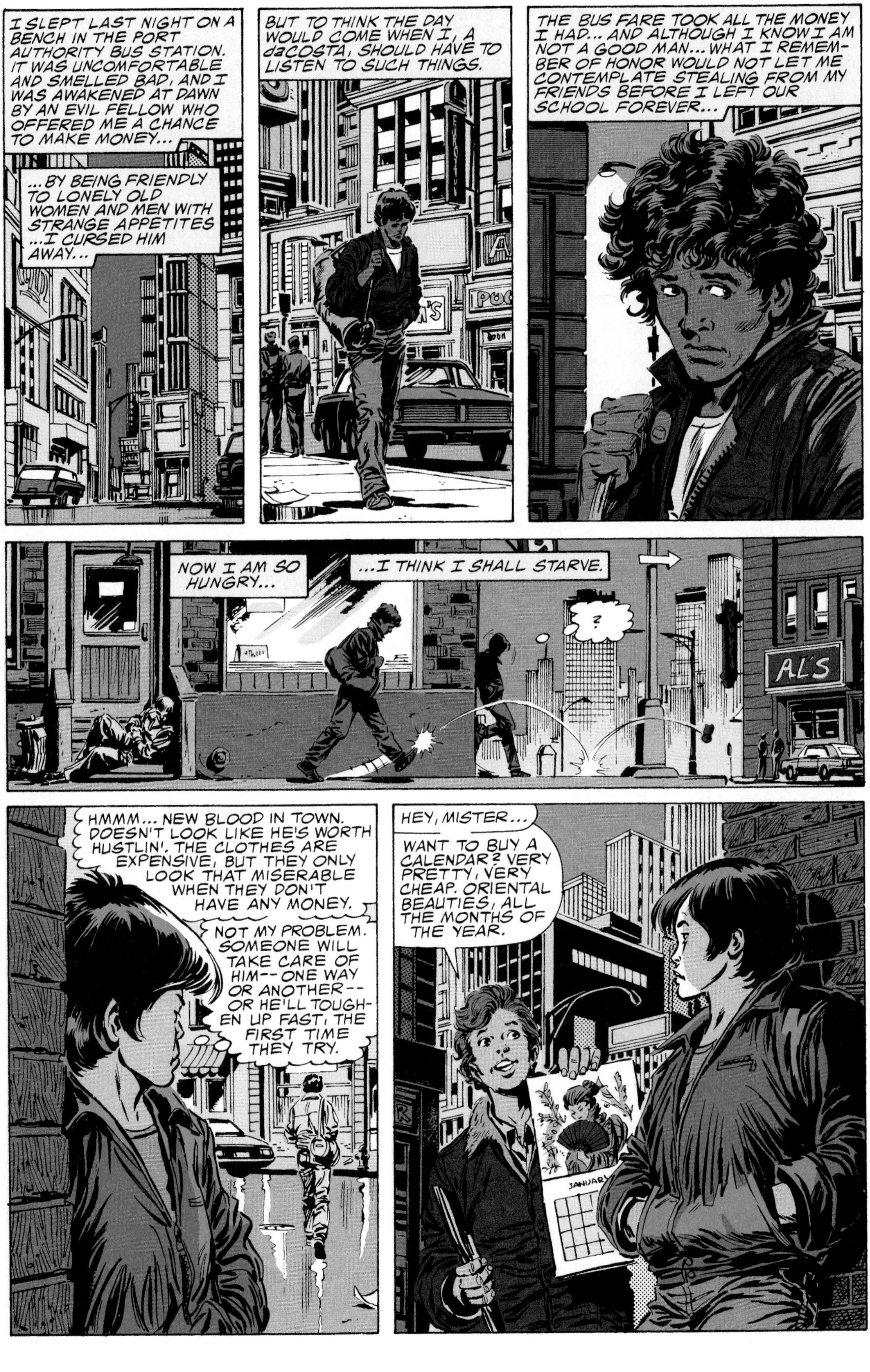
I SLEPT LAST NIGHT ON A BENCH IN THE PORT AUTHORITY BUS STATION. IT WAS UNCOMFORTABLE AND SMELLED BAD, AND I WAS AWAKENED AT DAWN BY AN EVIL FELLOW WHO OFFERED ME A CHANCE TO MAKE MONEY...
...BY BEING FRIENDLY TO LONELY OLD WOMEN AND MEN WITH STRANGE APPETITES ...I CURSED HIM AWAY...
BUT TO THINK THE DAY WOULD COME WHEN I, A daCOSTA, SHOULD HAVE TO LISTEN TO SUCH THINGS.
THE BUS FARE TOOK ALL THE MONEY I HAD... AND ALTHOUGH I KNOW I AM NOT A GOOD MAN... WHAT I REMEMBER OF HONOR WOULD NOT LET ME CONTEMPLATE STEALING FROM MY FRIENDS BEFORE I LEFT OUR SCHOOL FOREVER...
NOW I AM SO HUNGRY...
...I THINK I SHALL STARVE.
AL'S
?
HMMM... NEW BLOOD IN TOWN. DOESN'T LOOK LIKE HE'S WORTH HUSTLIN'. THE CLOTHES ARE EXPENSIVE, BUT THEY ONLY LOOK THAT MISERABLE WHEN THEY DON'T HAVE ANY MONEY.
NOT MY PROBLEM. SOMEONE WILL TAKE CARE OF HIM-- ONE WAY OR ANOTHER-- OR HE'LL TOUGHEN UP FAST, THE FIRST TIME THEY TRY.
HEY, MISTER...
WANT TO BUY A CALENDAR? VERY PRETTY, VERY CHEAP. ORIENTAL BEAUTIES, ALL THE MONTHS OF THE YEAR.
JANUARY

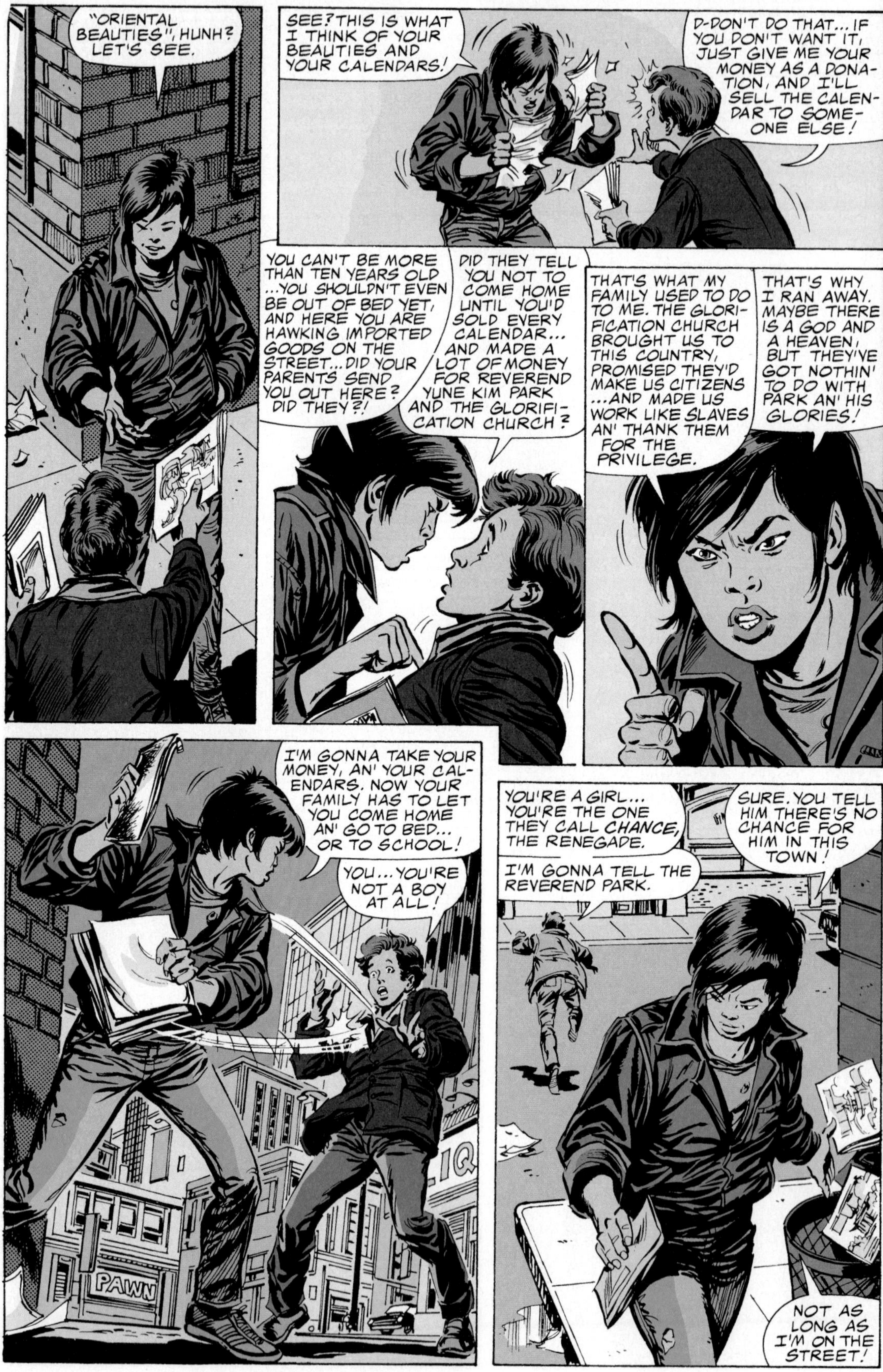
"ORIENTAL BEAUTIES", HUNH? LET'S SEE.
SEE? THIS IS WHAT I THINK OF YOUR BEAUTIES AND YOUR CALENDARS!
D-DON'T DO THAT... IF YOU DON'T WANT IT, JUST GIVE ME YOUR MONEY AS A DONATION, AND I'LL SELL THE CALENDAR TO SOMEONE ELSE!
YOU CAN'T BE MORE THAN TEN YEARS OLD ...YOU SHOULDN'T EVEN BE OUT OF BED YET, AND HERE YOU ARE HAWKING IMPORTED GOODS ON THE STREET... DID YOUR PARENTS SEND YOU OUT HERE? DID THEY?!
DID THEY TELL YOU NOT TO COME HOME UNTIL YOU'D SOLD EVERY CALENDAR... AND MADE A LOT OF MONEY FOR REVEREND YUNE KIM PARK AND THE GLORIFICATION CHURCH?
THAT'S WHAT MY FAMILY USED TO DO TO ME. THE GLORIFICATION CHURCH BROUGHT US TO THIS COUNTRY, PROMISED THEY'D MAKE US CITIZENS ...AND MADE US WORK LIKE SLAVES AN' THANK THEM FOR THE PRIVILEGE.
THAT'S WHY I RAN AWAY. MAYBE THERE IS A GOD AND A HEAVEN, BUT THEY'VE GOT NOTHIN' TO DO WITH PARK AN' HIS GLORIES!
I'M GONNA TAKE YOUR MONEY, AN' YOUR CALENDARS. NOW YOUR FAMILY HAS TO LET YOU COME HOME AN' GO TO BED... OR TO SCHOOL!
YOU... YOU'RE NOT A BOY AT ALL!
PAWN
YOU'RE A GIRL... YOU'RE THE ONE THEY CALL *CHANCE*, THE RENEGADE.
I'M GONNA TELL THE REVEREND PARK.
SURE. YOU TELL HIM THERE'S NO CHANCE FOR HIM IN THIS TOWN!
NOT AS LONG AS I'M ON THE STREET!

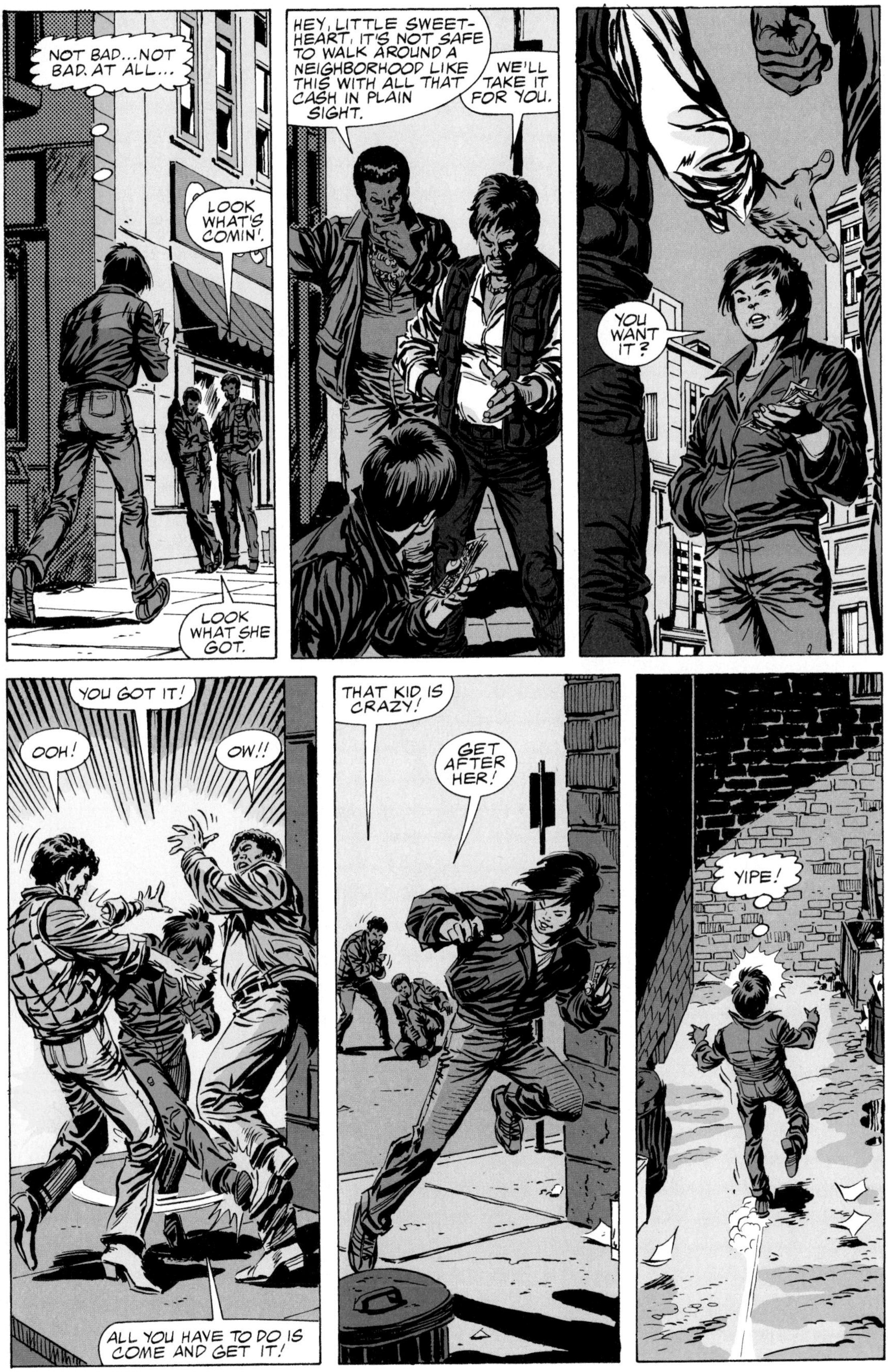
NOT BAD...NOT BAD. AT ALL...
LOOK WHAT'S COMIN'.
LOOK WHAT SHE GOT.
HEY, LITTLE SWEET-HEART. IT'S NOT SAFE TO WALK AROUND A NEIGHBORHOOD LIKE THIS WITH ALL THAT CASH IN PLAIN SIGHT.
WE'LL TAKE IT FOR YOU.
YOU WANT IT?
YOU GOT IT!
OOH!
OW!!
ALL YOU HAVE TO DO IS COME AND GET IT!
THAT KID IS CRAZY!
GET AFTER HER!
YIPE!

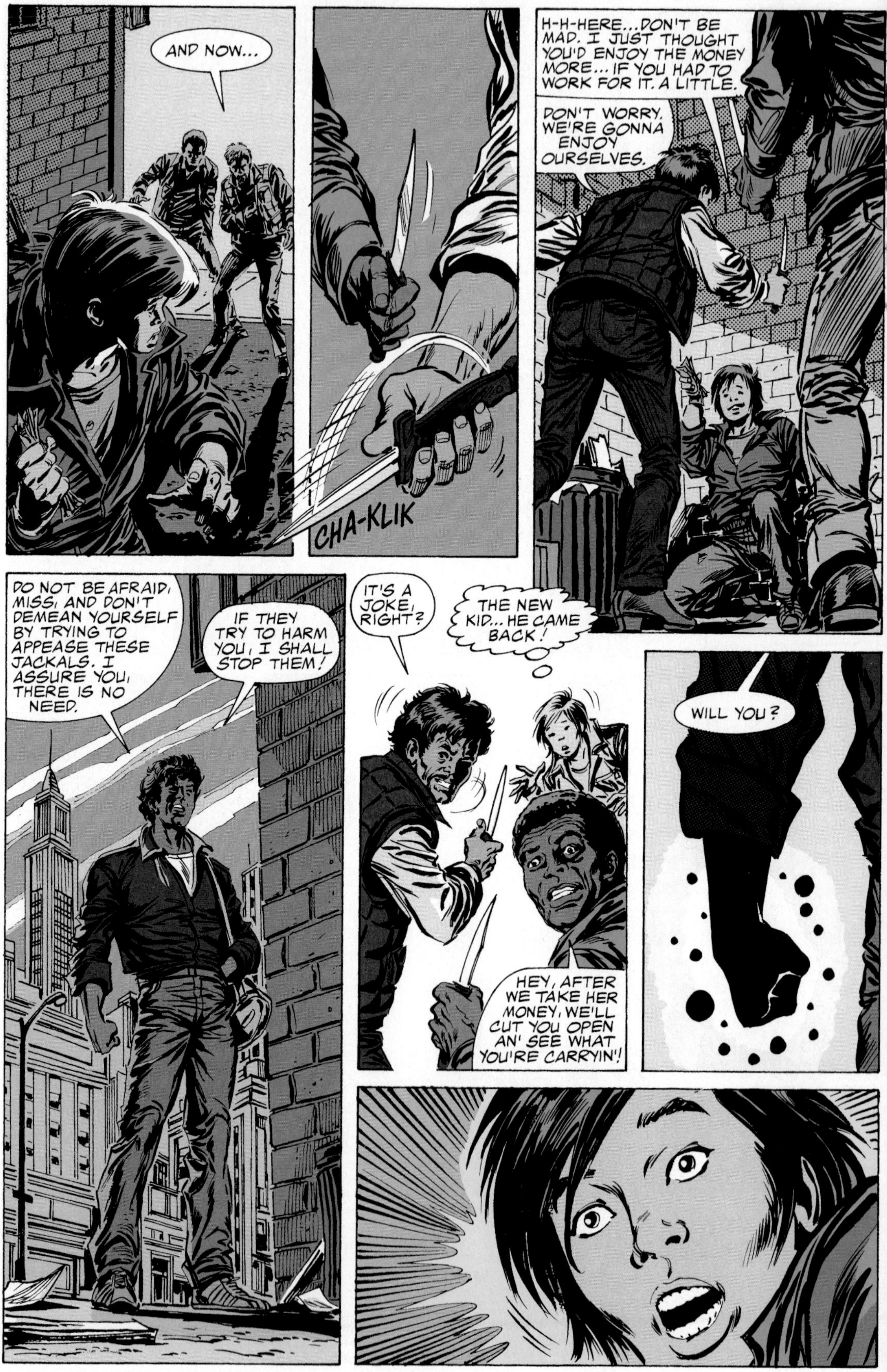
AND NOW...
CHA-KLIK
H-H-HERE...DON'T BE MAD. I JUST THOUGHT YOU'D ENJOY THE MONEY MORE... IF YOU HAD TO WORK FOR IT. A LITTLE.
DON'T WORRY. WE'RE GONNA ENJOY OURSELVES.
DO NOT BE AFRAID, MISS, AND DON'T DEMEAN YOURSELF BY TRYING TO APPEASE THESE JACKALS. I ASSURE YOU, THERE IS NO NEED.
IF THEY TRY TO HARM YOU, I SHALL STOP THEM!
IT'S A JOKE, RIGHT?
THE NEW KID... HE CAME BACK!
HEY, AFTER WE TAKE HER MONEY, WE'LL CUT YOU OPEN AN' SEE WHAT YOU'RE CARRYIN'!
WILL YOU?

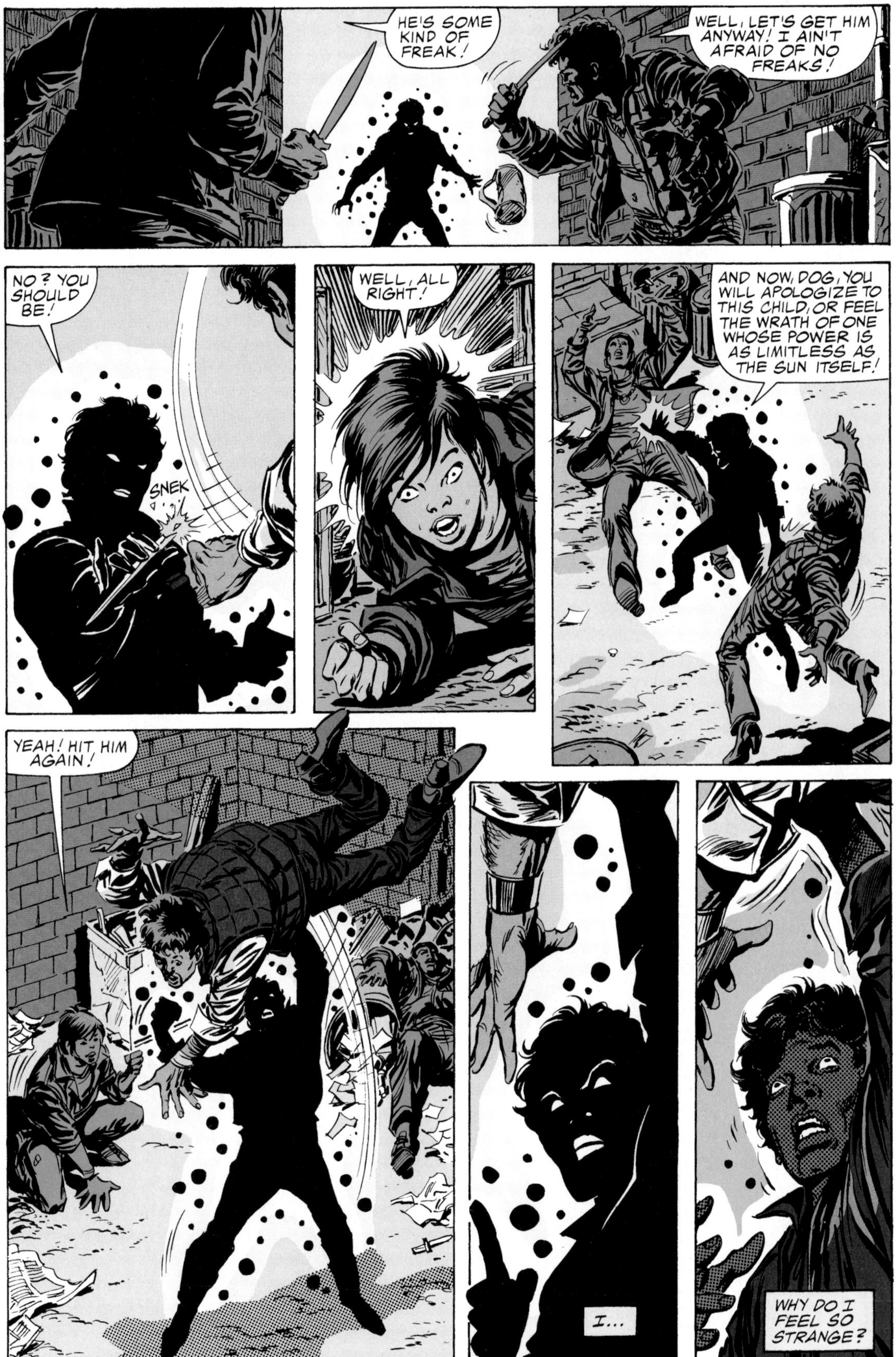
HE'S SOME KIND OF FREAK!
WELL, LET'S GET HIM ANYWAY! I AIN'T AFRAID OF NO FREAKS!
NO? YOU SHOULD BE!
SNEK
WELL, ALL RIGHT!
AND NOW, DOG, YOU WILL APOLOGIZE TO THIS CHILD, OR FEEL THE WRATH OF ONE WHOSE POWER IS AS LIMITLESS AS THE SUN ITSELF!
YEAH! HIT HIM AGAIN!
I...
WHY DO I FEEL SO STRANGE?

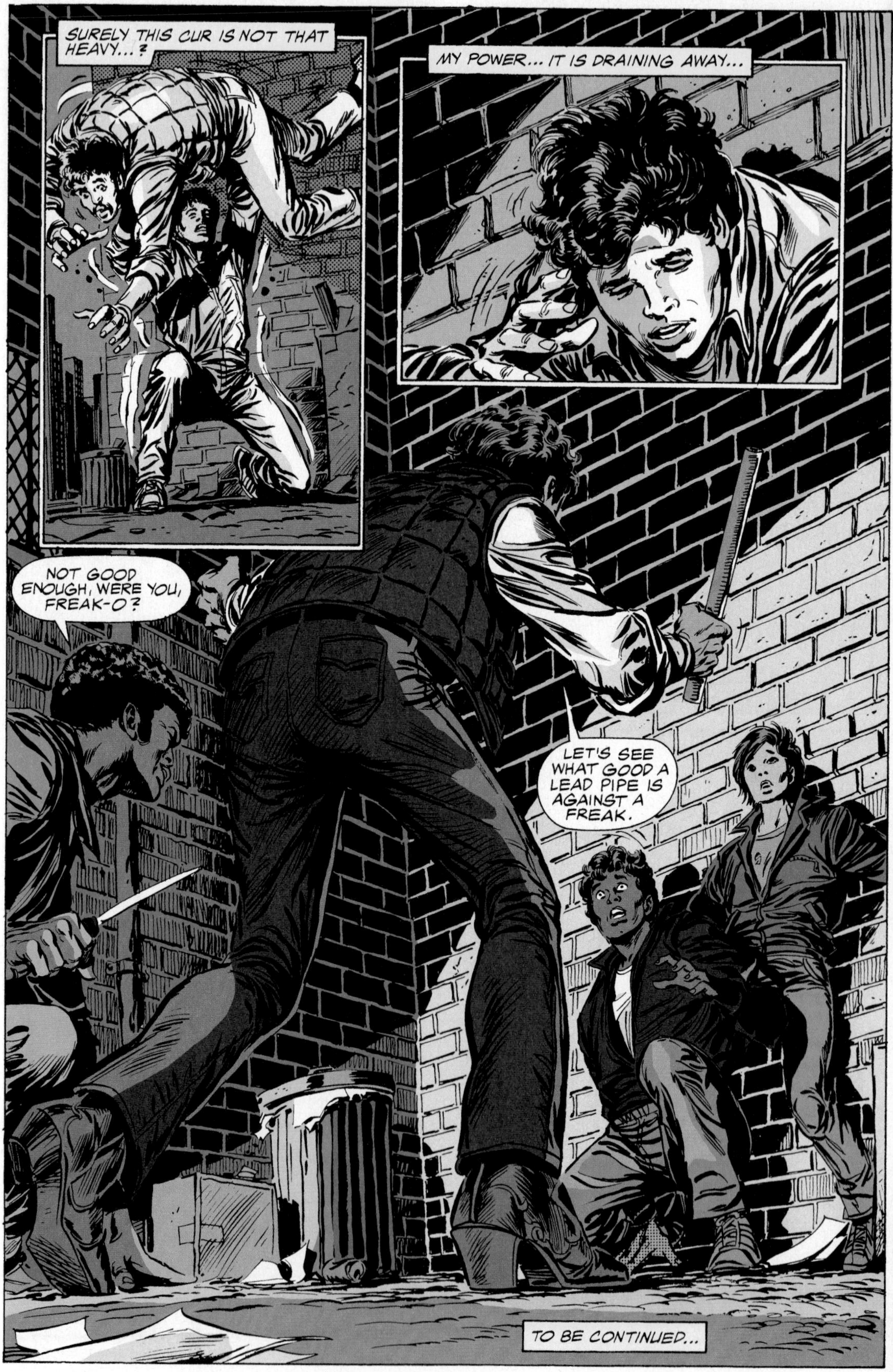

SURELY THIS CUR IS NOT THAT HEAVY...?
MY POWER... IT IS DRAINING AWAY...
NOT GOOD ENOUGH, WERE YOU, FREAK-O?
LET'S SEE WHAT GOOD A LEAD PIPE IS AGAINST A FREAK.
TO BE CONTINUED...

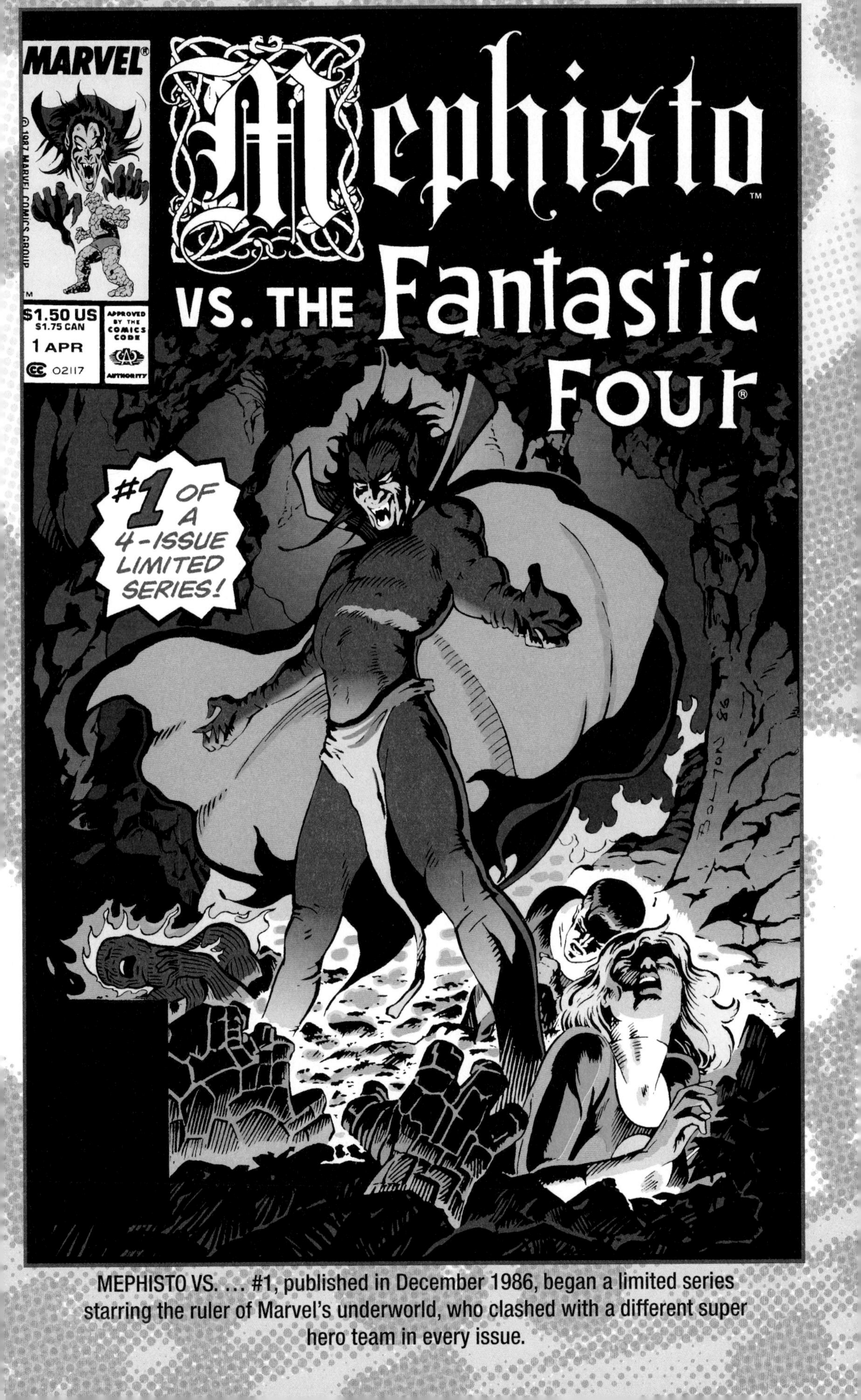
MARVEL
© 1987 MARVEL COMICS GROUP
Mephisto™
VS. THE Fantastic Four®
$1.50 US
$1.75 CAN
1 APR
02117
APPROVED BY THE COMICS CODE AUTHORITY
#1 OF A 4-ISSUE LIMITED SERIES!

MEPHISTO VS. … #1, published in December 1986, began a limited series starring the ruler of Marvel's underworld, who clashed with a different super hero team in every issue.

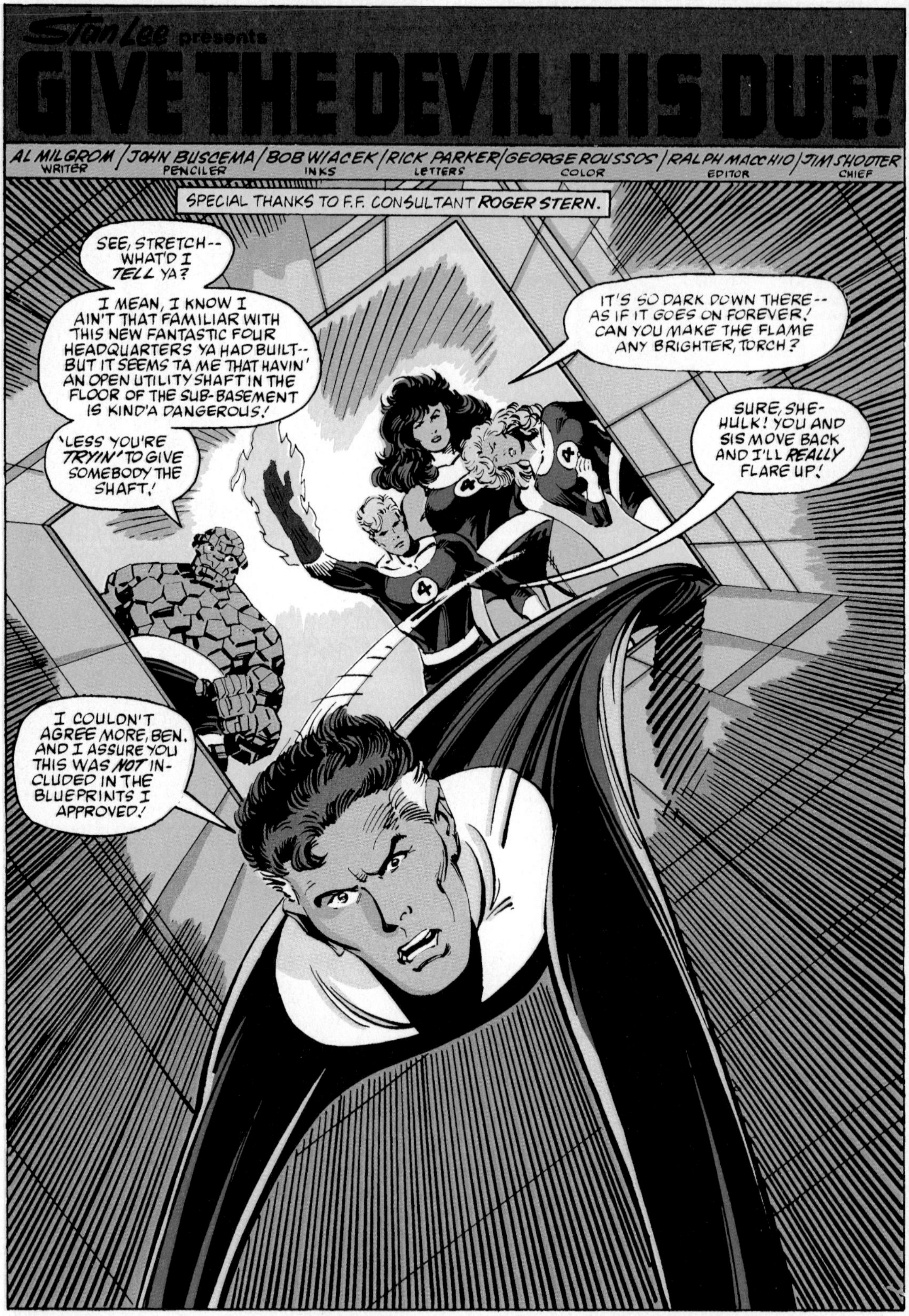

Stan Lee presents
GIVE THE DEVIL HIS DUE!
AL MILGROM WRITER / JOHN BUSCEMA PENCILER / BOB WIACEK INKS / RICK PARKER LETTERS / GEORGE ROUSSOS COLOR / RALPH MACCHIO EDITOR / JIM SHOOTER CHIEF
SPECIAL THANKS TO F.F. CONSULTANT ROGER STERN.
SEE, STRETCH-- WHAT'D I TELL YA?
I MEAN, I KNOW I AIN'T THAT FAMILIAR WITH THIS NEW FANTASTIC FOUR HEADQUARTERS YA HAD BUILT-- BUT IT SEEMS TA ME THAT HAVIN' AN OPEN UTILITY SHAFT IN THE FLOOR OF THE SUB-BASEMENT IS KIND'A DANGEROUS!
'LESS YOU'RE TRYIN' TO GIVE SOMEBODY THE SHAFT!
IT'S SO DARK DOWN THERE-- AS IF IT GOES ON FOREVER! CAN YOU MAKE THE FLAME ANY BRIGHTER, TORCH?
SURE, SHE-HULK! YOU AND SIS MOVE BACK AND I'LL REALLY FLARE UP!
I COULDN'T AGREE MORE, BEN. AND I ASSURE YOU THIS WAS NOT IN-CLUDED IN THE BLUEPRINTS I APPROVED!

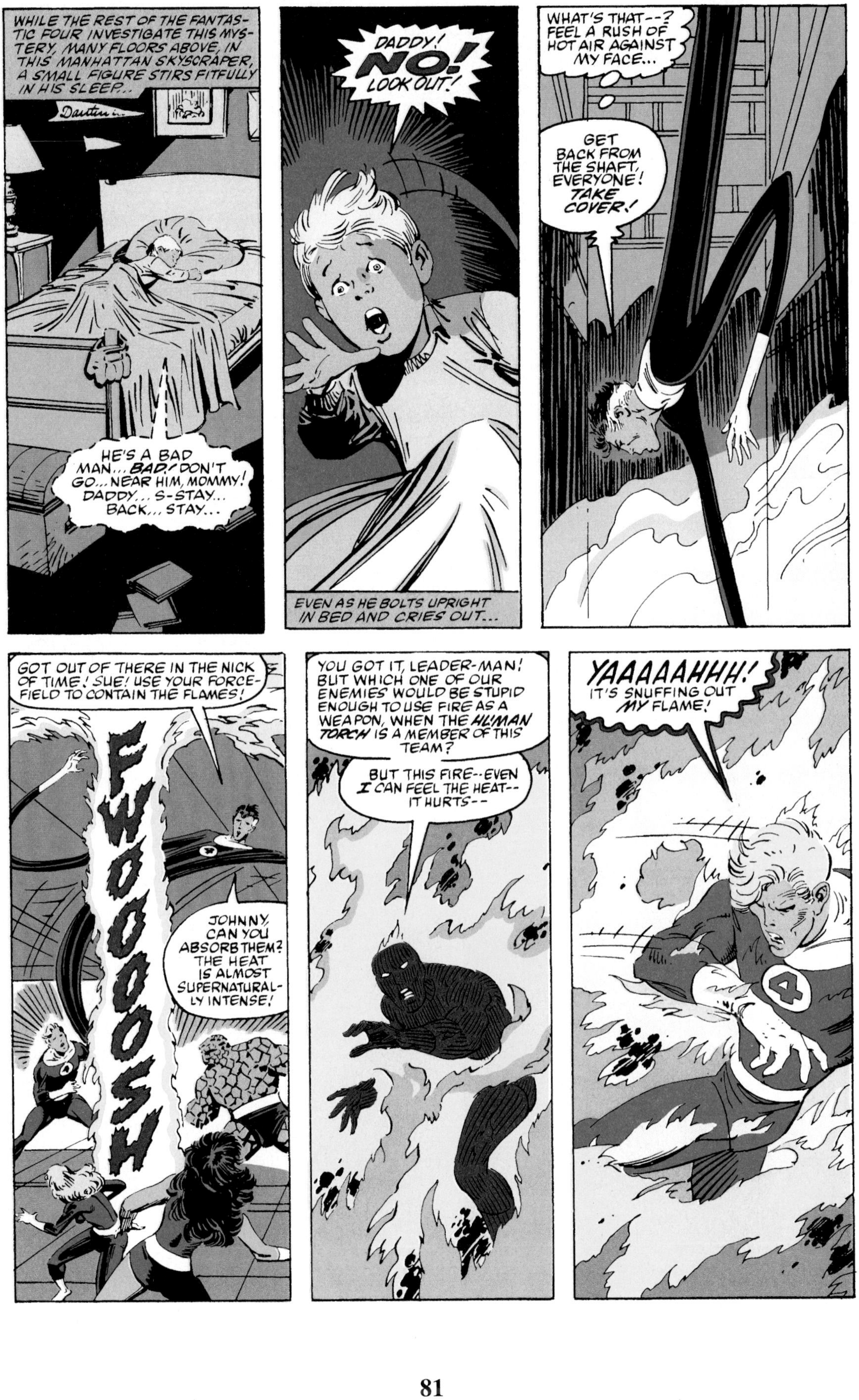
WHILE THE REST OF THE FANTASTIC FOUR INVESTIGATE THIS MYSTERY, MANY FLOORS ABOVE, IN THIS MANHATTAN SKYSCRAPER, A SMALL FIGURE STIRS FITFULLY IN HIS SLEEP...
HE'S A BAD MAN... BAD! DON'T GO... NEAR HIM, MOMMY! DADDY... S-STAY... BACK... STAY...
DADDY! NO! LOOK OUT!
EVEN AS HE BOLTS UPRIGHT IN BED AND CRIES OUT...
WHAT'S THAT--? FEEL A RUSH OF HOT AIR AGAINST MY FACE...
GET BACK FROM THE SHAFT, EVERYONE! TAKE COVER!
GOT OUT OF THERE IN THE NICK OF TIME! SUE! USE YOUR FORCE-FIELD TO CONTAIN THE FLAMES!
FWOOOOOSH
JOHNNY, CAN YOU ABSORB THEM? THE HEAT IS ALMOST SUPERNATURALLY INTENSE!
YOU GOT IT, LEADER-MAN! BUT WHICH ONE OF OUR ENEMIES WOULD BE STUPID ENOUGH TO USE FIRE AS A WEAPON, WHEN THE HUMAN TORCH IS A MEMBER OF THIS TEAM?
BUT THIS FIRE--EVEN I CAN FEEL THE HEAT--IT HURTS--
YAAAAAHHH! IT'S SNUFFING OUT MY FLAME!

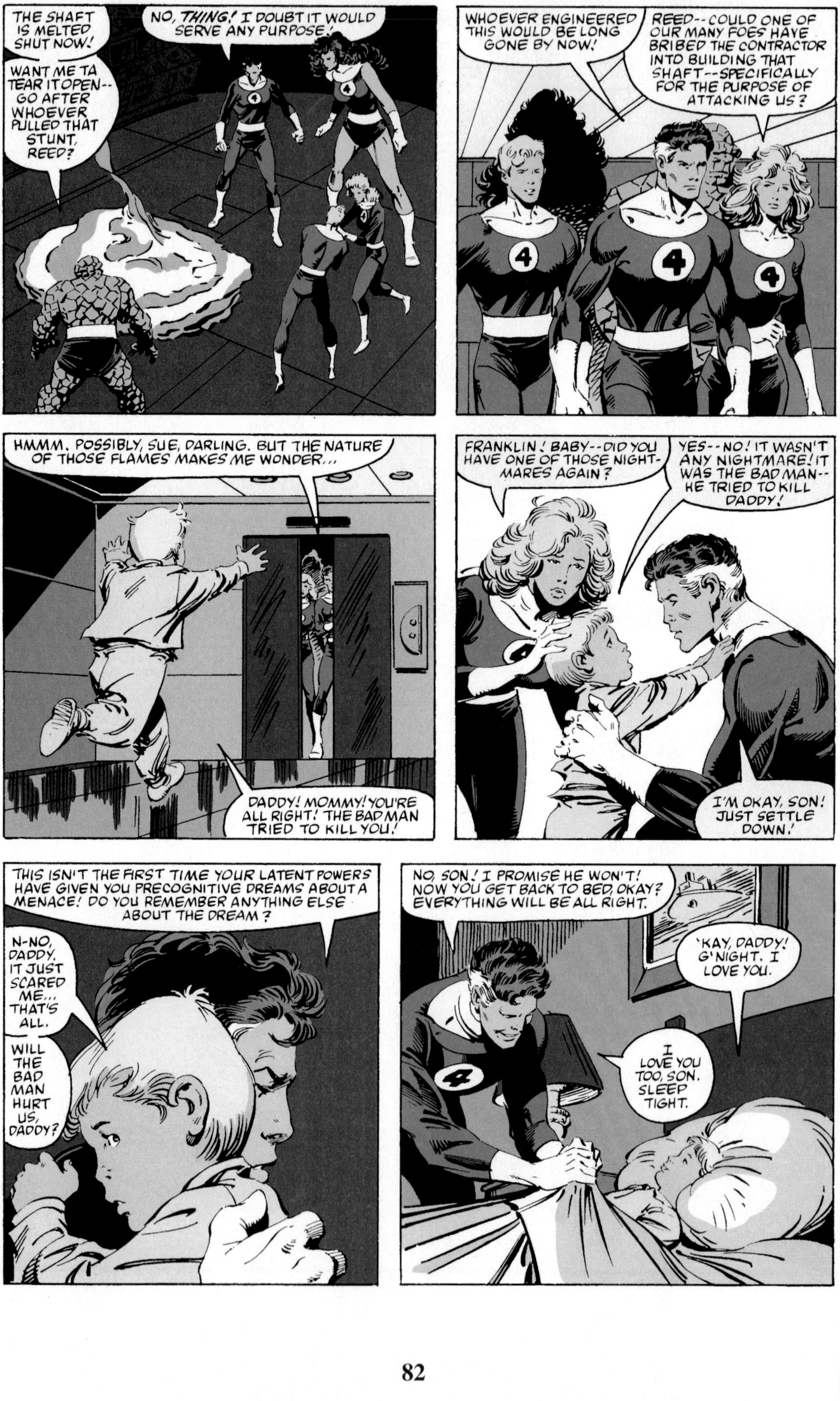
THE SHAFT IS MELTED SHUT NOW!
WANT ME TA TEAR IT OPEN-- GO AFTER WHOEVER PULLED THAT STUNT, REED?
NO, THING! I DOUBT IT WOULD SERVE ANY PURPOSE!
WHOEVER ENGINEERED THIS WOULD BE LONG GONE BY NOW!
REED--COULD ONE OF OUR MANY FOES HAVE BRIBED THE CONTRACTOR INTO BUILDING THAT SHAFT--SPECIFICALLY FOR THE PURPOSE OF ATTACKING US?
HMMM. POSSIBLY, SUE, DARLING. BUT THE NATURE OF THOSE FLAMES MAKES ME WONDER...
DADDY! MOMMY! YOU'RE ALL RIGHT! THE BAD MAN TRIED TO KILL YOU!
FRANKLIN! BABY--DID YOU HAVE ONE OF THOSE NIGHT-MARES AGAIN?
YES--NO! IT WASN'T ANY NIGHTMARE! IT WAS THE BAD MAN--HE TRIED TO KILL DADDY!
I'M OKAY, SON! JUST SETTLE DOWN!
THIS ISN'T THE FIRST TIME YOUR LATENT POWERS HAVE GIVEN YOU PRECOGNITIVE DREAMS ABOUT A MENACE! DO YOU REMEMBER ANYTHING ELSE ABOUT THE DREAM?
N-NO, DADDY, IT JUST SCARED ME... THAT'S ALL.
WILL THE BAD MAN HURT US, DADDY?
NO, SON! I PROMISE HE WON'T! NOW YOU GET BACK TO BED, OKAY? EVERYTHING WILL BE ALL RIGHT.
'KAY, DADDY! G'NIGHT. I LOVE YOU.
I LOVE YOU TOO, SON. SLEEP TIGHT.

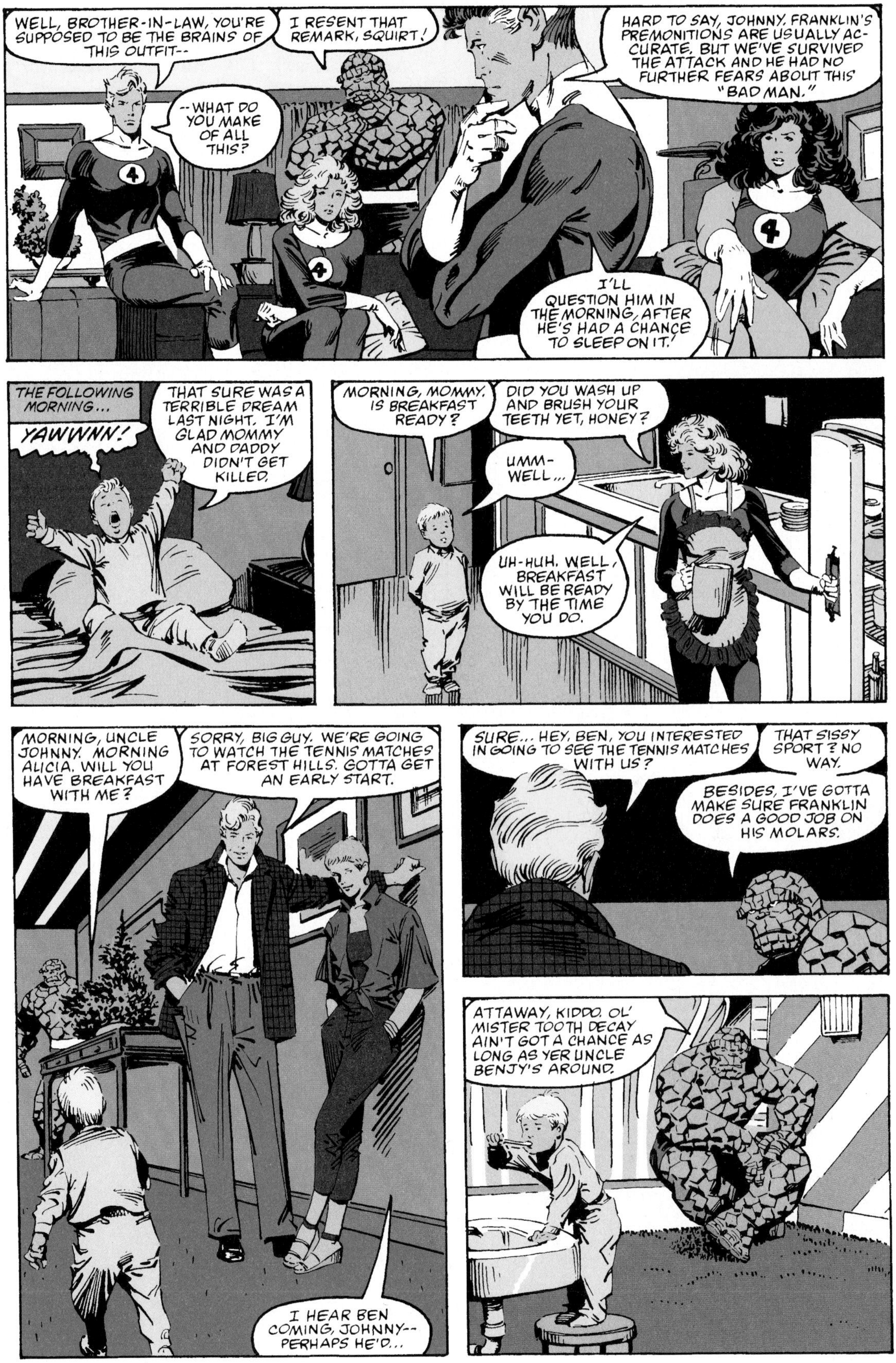
WELL, BROTHER-IN-LAW, YOU'RE SUPPOSED TO BE THE BRAINS OF THIS OUTFIT--
--WHAT DO YOU MAKE OF ALL THIS?
I RESENT THAT REMARK, SQUIRT!
HARD TO SAY, JOHNNY. FRANKLIN'S PREMONITIONS ARE USUALLY ACCURATE. BUT WE'VE SURVIVED THE ATTACK AND HE HAD NO FURTHER FEARS ABOUT THIS "BAD MAN."
I'LL QUESTION HIM IN THE MORNING, AFTER HE'S HAD A CHANCE TO SLEEP ON IT.
THE FOLLOWING MORNING...
YAWWNN!
THAT SURE WAS A TERRIBLE DREAM LAST NIGHT. I'M GLAD MOMMY AND DADDY DIDN'T GET KILLED.
MORNING, MOMMY. IS BREAKFAST READY?
DID YOU WASH UP AND BRUSH YOUR TEETH YET, HONEY?
UMM-WELL...
UH-HUH. WELL, BREAKFAST WILL BE READY BY THE TIME YOU DO.
MORNING, UNCLE JOHNNY. MORNING ALICIA. WILL YOU HAVE BREAKFAST WITH ME?
SORRY, BIG GUY. WE'RE GOING TO WATCH THE TENNIS MATCHES AT FOREST HILLS. GOTTA GET AN EARLY START.
I HEAR BEN COMING, JOHNNY-- PERHAPS HE'D...
SURE... HEY, BEN, YOU INTERESTED IN GOING TO SEE THE TENNIS MATCHES WITH US?
THAT SISSY SPORT? NO WAY.
BESIDES, I'VE GOTTA MAKE SURE FRANKLIN DOES A GOOD JOB ON HIS MOLARS.
ATTAWAY, KIDDO. OL' MISTER TOOTH DECAY AIN'T GOT A CHANCE AS LONG AS YER UNCLE BENJY'S AROUND.

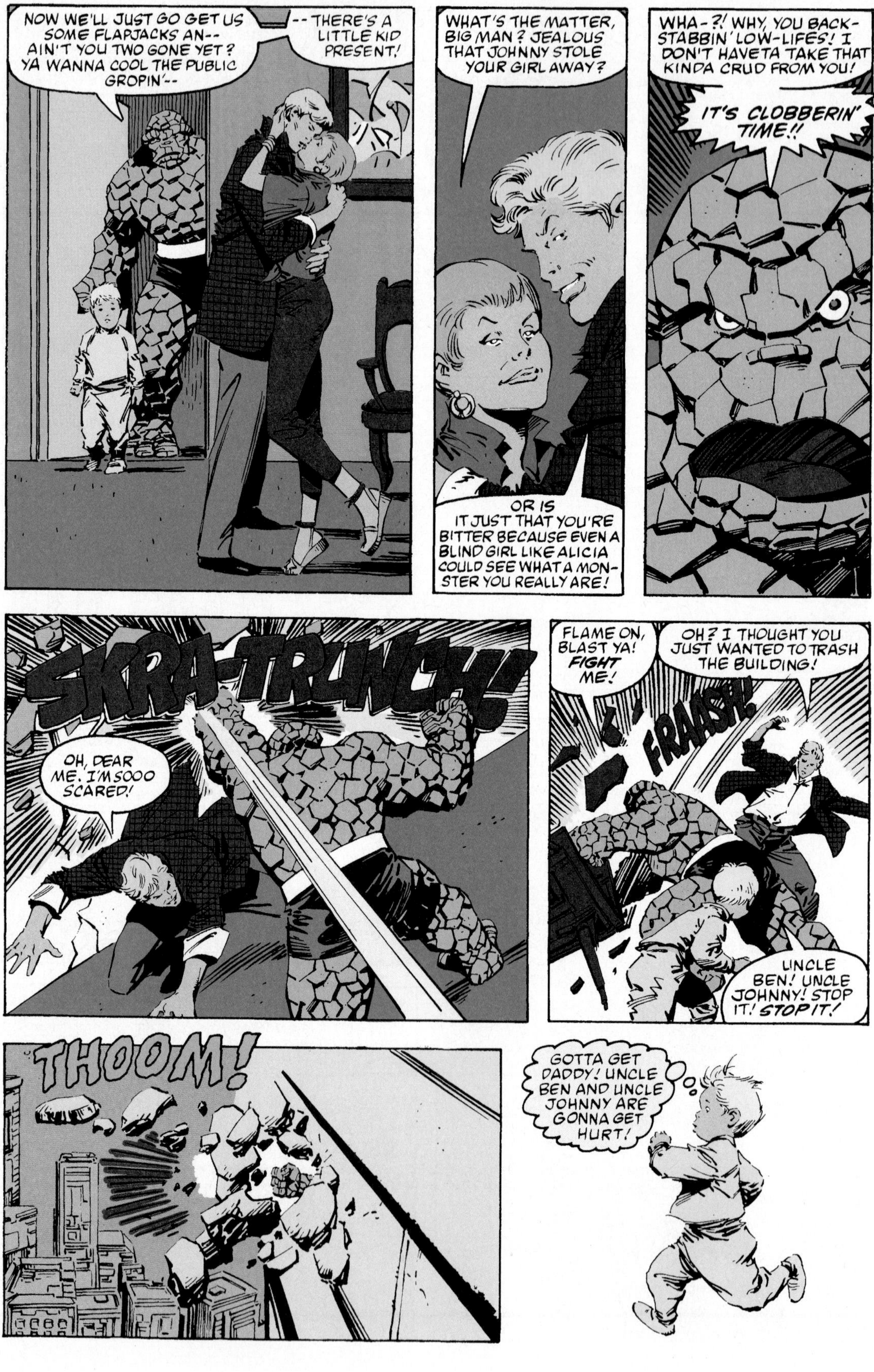
NOW WE'LL JUST GO GET US SOME FLAPJACKS AN-- AIN'T YOU TWO GONE YET? YA WANNA COOL THE PUBLIC GROPIN'--
--THERE'S A LITTLE KID PRESENT!
WHAT'S THE MATTER, BIG MAN? JEALOUS THAT JOHNNY STOLE YOUR GIRL AWAY?
OR IS IT JUST THAT YOU'RE BITTER BECAUSE EVEN A BLIND GIRL LIKE ALICIA COULD SEE WHAT A MONSTER YOU REALLY ARE!
WHA-?! WHY, YOU BACK-STABBIN' LOW-LIFES! I DON'T HAVETA TAKE THAT KINDA CRUD FROM YOU!
IT'S CLOBBERIN' TIME!!
SKRA-TRUNCH!
OH, DEAR ME. I'M SOOO SCARED!
FLAME ON, BLAST YA! FIGHT ME!
OH? I THOUGHT YOU JUST WANTED TO TRASH THE BUILDING!
FRAASH!
UNCLE BEN! UNCLE JOHNNY! STOP IT! STOP IT!
THOOM!
GOTTA GET DADDY! UNCLE BEN AND UNCLE JOHNNY ARE GONNA GET HURT!

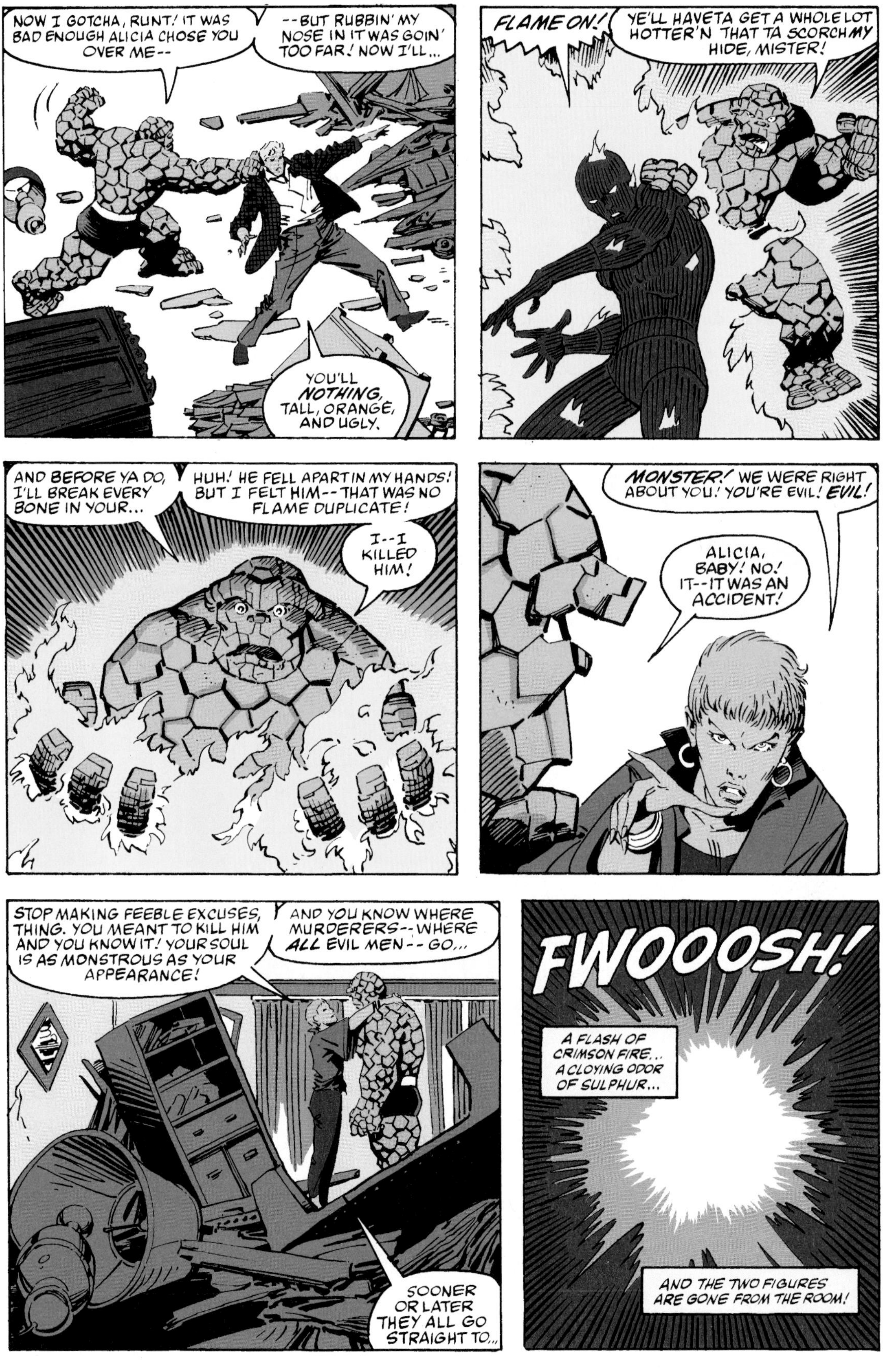
NOW I GOTCHA, RUNT! IT WAS BAD ENOUGH ALICIA CHOSE YOU OVER ME--
--BUT RUBBIN' MY NOSE IN IT WAS GOIN' TOO FAR! NOW I'LL...
YOU'LL NOTHING, TALL, ORANGE, AND UGLY.
FLAME ON!
YE'LL HAVETA GET A WHOLE LOT HOTTER'N THAT TA SCORCH MY HIDE, MISTER!
AND BEFORE YA DO, I'LL BREAK EVERY BONE IN YOUR...
HUH! HE FELL APART IN MY HANDS! BUT I FELT HIM--THAT WAS NO FLAME DUPLICATE!
I--I KILLED HIM!
MONSTER! WE WERE RIGHT ABOUT YOU! YOU'RE EVIL! EVIL!
ALICIA, BABY! NO! IT--IT WAS AN ACCIDENT!
STOP MAKING FEEBLE EXCUSES, THING. YOU MEANT TO KILL HIM AND YOU KNOW IT! YOUR SOUL IS AS MONSTROUS AS YOUR APPEARANCE!
AND YOU KNOW WHERE MURDERERS--WHERE ALL EVIL MEN--GO,..
SOONER OR LATER THEY ALL GO STRAIGHT TO,..
FWOOOSH!
A FLASH OF CRIMSON FIRE... A CLOYING ODOR OF SULPHUR...
AND THE TWO FIGURES ARE GONE FROM THE ROOM!

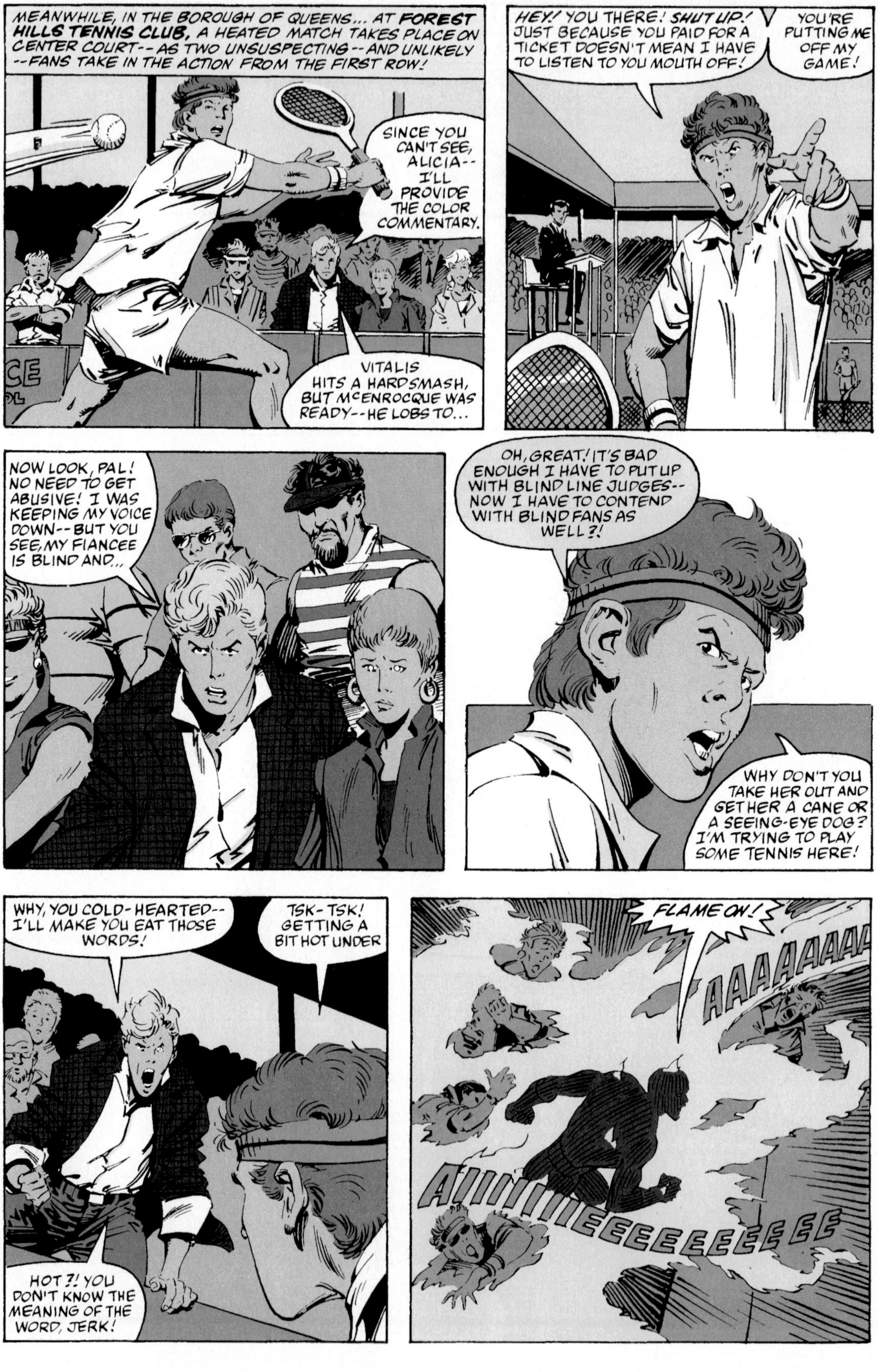
MEANWHILE, IN THE BOROUGH OF QUEENS... AT FOREST HILLS TENNIS CLUB, A HEATED MATCH TAKES PLACE ON CENTER COURT-- AS TWO UNSUSPECTING -- AND UNLIKELY --FANS TAKE IN THE ACTION FROM THE FIRST ROW!
SINCE YOU CAN'T SEE, ALICIA-- I'LL PROVIDE THE COLOR COMMENTARY.
VITALIS HITS A HARDSMASH, BUT McENROCQUE WAS READY--HE LOBS TO...
HEY! YOU THERE! SHUT UP! JUST BECAUSE YOU PAID FOR A TICKET DOESN'T MEAN I HAVE TO LISTEN TO YOU MOUTH OFF!
YOU'RE PUTTING ME OFF MY GAME!
NOW LOOK, PAL! NO NEED TO GET ABUSIVE! I WAS KEEPING MY VOICE DOWN-- BUT YOU SEE, MY FIANCEE IS BLIND AND...
OH, GREAT! IT'S BAD ENOUGH I HAVE TO PUT UP WITH BLIND LINE JUDGES-- NOW I HAVE TO CONTEND WITH BLIND FANS AS WELL?!
WHY DON'T YOU TAKE HER OUT AND GET HER A CANE OR A SEEING-EYE DOG? I'M TRYING TO PLAY SOME TENNIS HERE!
WHY, YOU COLD-HEARTED-- I'LL MAKE YOU EAT THOSE WORDS!
TSK-TSK! GETTING A BIT HOT UNDER
HOT?! YOU DON'T KNOW THE MEANING OF THE WORD, JERK!
FLAME ON!
AAAAAAAA
AIIIIIIIEEEEEEEEEEEE

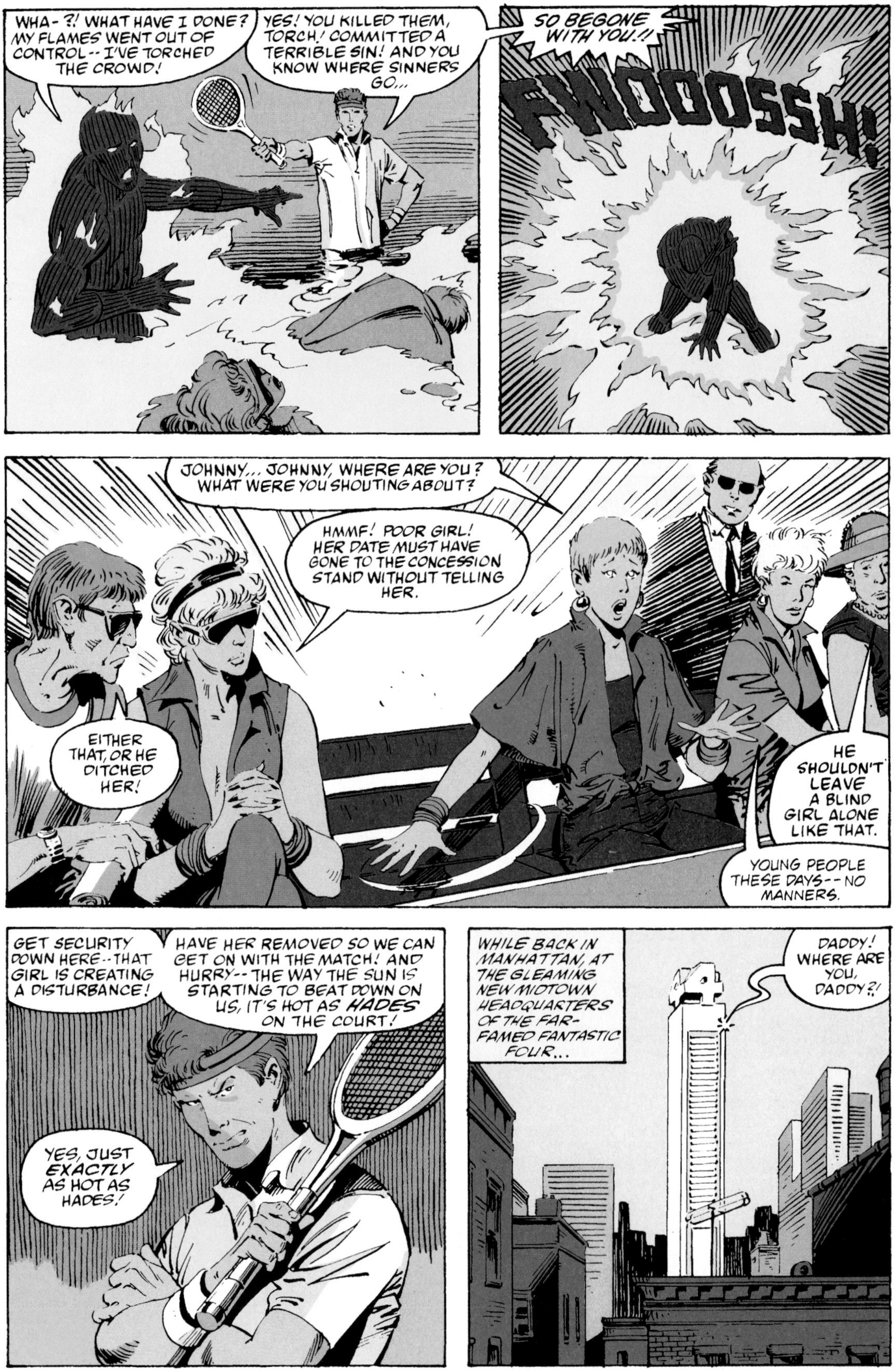
WHA-?! WHAT HAVE I DONE? MY FLAMES WENT OUT OF CONTROL-- I'VE TORCHED THE CROWD!
YES! YOU KILLED THEM, TORCH! COMMITTED A TERRIBLE SIN! AND YOU KNOW WHERE SINNERS GO...
SO BEGONE WITH YOU!!
FWOOOSSH!
JOHNNY... JOHNNY, WHERE ARE YOU? WHAT WERE YOU SHOUTING ABOUT?
HMMF! POOR GIRL! HER DATE MUST HAVE GONE TO THE CONCESSION STAND WITHOUT TELLING HER.
EITHER THAT, OR HE DITCHED HER!
HE SHOULDN'T LEAVE A BLIND GIRL ALONE LIKE THAT.
YOUNG PEOPLE THESE DAYS-- NO MANNERS.
GET SECURITY DOWN HERE-- THAT GIRL IS CREATING A DISTURBANCE!
HAVE HER REMOVED SO WE CAN GET ON WITH THE MATCH! AND HURRY-- THE WAY THE SUN IS STARTING TO BEAT DOWN ON US, IT'S HOT AS HADES ON THE COURT!
YES, JUST EXACTLY AS HOT AS HADES!
WHILE BACK IN MANHATTAN, AT THE GLEAMING NEW MIDTOWN HEADQUARTERS OF THE FAR-FAMED FANTASTIC FOUR...
DADDY! WHERE ARE YOU, DADDY?!

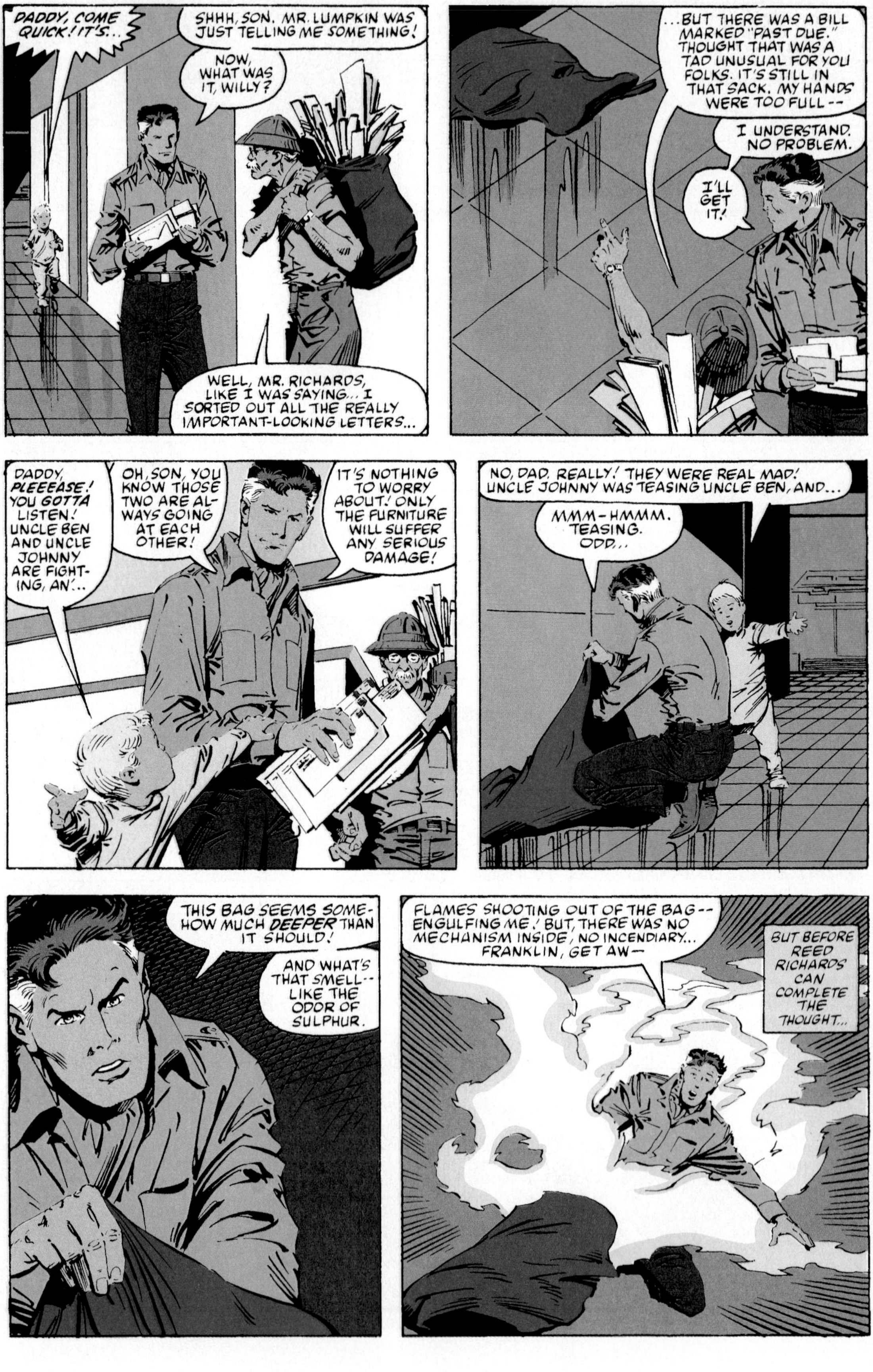
DADDY, COME QUICK! IT'S...
SHHH, SON. MR. LUMPKIN WAS JUST TELLING ME SOMETHING!
NOW, WHAT WAS IT, WILLY?
WELL, MR. RICHARDS, LIKE I WAS SAYING... I SORTED OUT ALL THE REALLY IMPORTANT-LOOKING LETTERS...
...BUT THERE WAS A BILL MARKED "PAST DUE." THOUGHT THAT WAS A TAD UNUSUAL FOR YOU FOLKS. IT'S STILL IN THAT SACK. MY HANDS WERE TOO FULL--
I UNDERSTAND. NO PROBLEM.
I'LL GET IT!
DADDY, PLEEEASE! YOU GOTTA LISTEN! UNCLE BEN AND UNCLE JOHNNY ARE FIGHTING, AN'...
OH, SON, YOU KNOW THOSE TWO ARE ALWAYS GOING AT EACH OTHER!
IT'S NOTHING TO WORRY ABOUT! ONLY THE FURNITURE WILL SUFFER ANY SERIOUS DAMAGE!
NO, DAD. REALLY! THEY WERE REAL MAD! UNCLE JOHNNY WAS TEASING UNCLE BEN, AND...
MMM-HMMM. TEASING. ODD...
THIS BAG SEEMS SOMEHOW MUCH DEEPER THAN IT SHOULD!
AND WHAT'S THAT SMELL-- LIKE THE ODOR OF SULPHUR.
FLAMES SHOOTING OUT OF THE BAG-- ENGULFING ME! BUT, THERE WAS NO MECHANISM INSIDE, NO INCENDIARY... FRANKLIN, GET AW—
BUT BEFORE REED RICHARDS CAN COMPLETE THE THOUGHT...

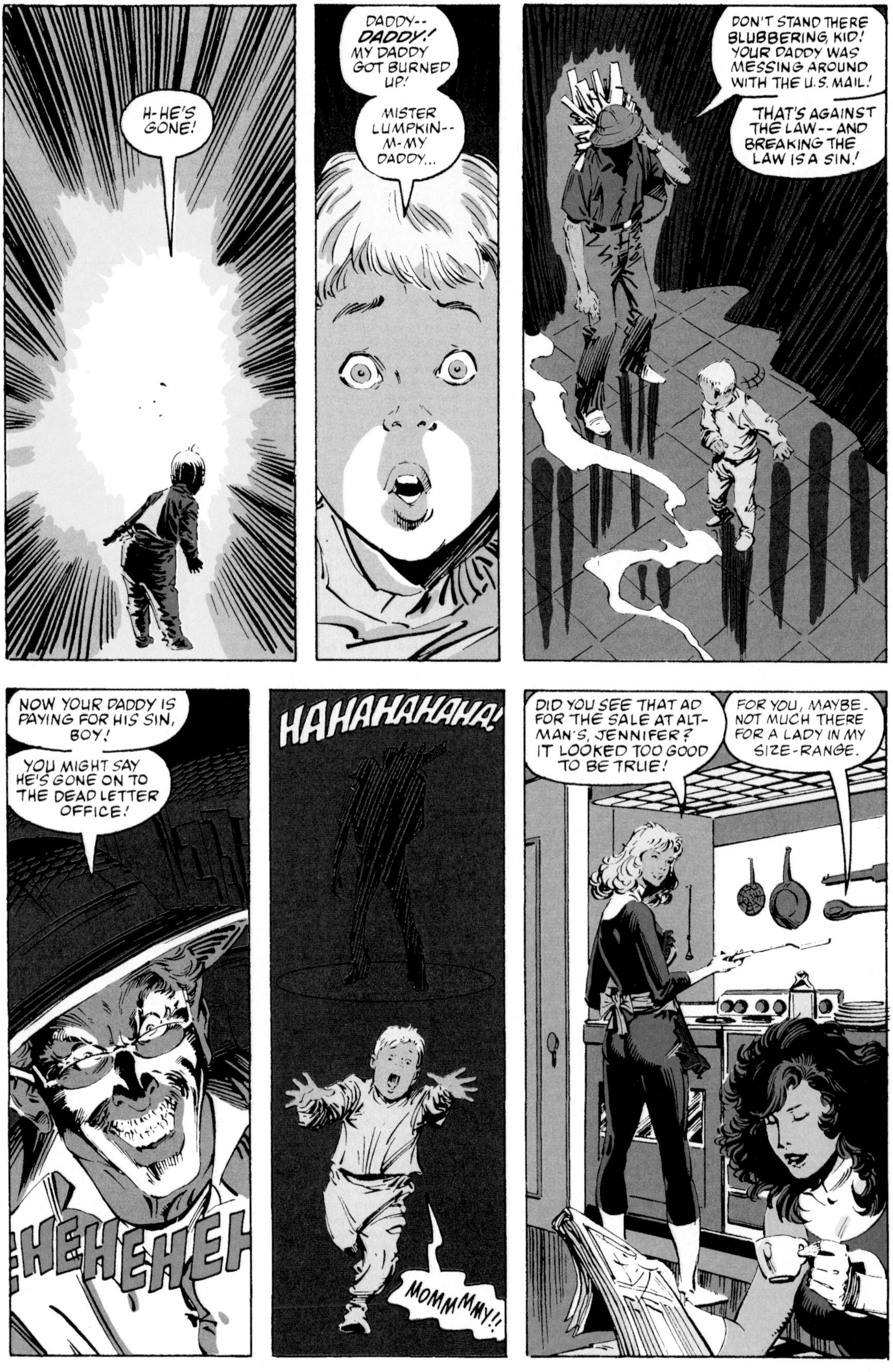
H-HE'S GONE!
DADDY-- DADDY! MY DADDY GOT BURNED UP!
MISTER LUMPKIN-- M-MY DADDY...
DON'T STAND THERE BLUBBERING, KID! YOUR DADDY WAS MESSING AROUND WITH THE U.S. MAIL!
THAT'S AGAINST THE LAW-- AND BREAKING THE LAW IS A SIN!
NOW YOUR DADDY IS PAYING FOR HIS SIN, BOY!
YOU MIGHT SAY HE'S GONE ON TO THE DEAD LETTER OFFICE!
EHEHEHEH
HAHAHAHAHA!
MOMMMMY!!
DID YOU SEE THAT AD FOR THE SALE AT ALT-MAN'S, JENNIFER? IT LOOKED TOO GOOD TO BE TRUE!
FOR YOU, MAYBE. NOT MUCH THERE FOR A LADY IN MY SIZE-RANGE.

MOMMY, MOMMY-- DADDY GOT KILLED! HE GOT BURNED UP!

WHAT?! FRANKLIN ARE YOU--

HE GOT KILLED! WILLY LUMPKIN KILLED HIM!

WILLY LUMPKIN--OH, HONEY DID YOU DOZE OFF AND HAVE ANOTHER BAD DREAM?

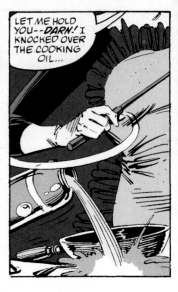

MR. LUMPKIN WOULD NEVER HURT ANYONE! HERE, COME TO MOMMY.

LET ME HOLD YOU--*DARN!* I KNOCKED OVER THE COOKING OIL....

GAS STOVE--IGNITING THE OIL! THE FLAMES...*AAAAAAHHHHHHH....*

FWOOSH!

OH ≩SOB≩ NO! N-NOT MOMMY TOO...

FRANKLIN, HONEY... DON'T CRY! YOUR MOTHER WAS CARELESS... AND IT'S VERY DANGEROUS TO BE CARE- LESS WITH FIRE.

IT'S HARDLY A *SIN*-- CARELESSNESS-- BUT IN THIS CASE WE WERE WILLING TO MAKE AN EXCEPTION!

BUT IF YOU REALLY *WANT* YOUR MOMMY--

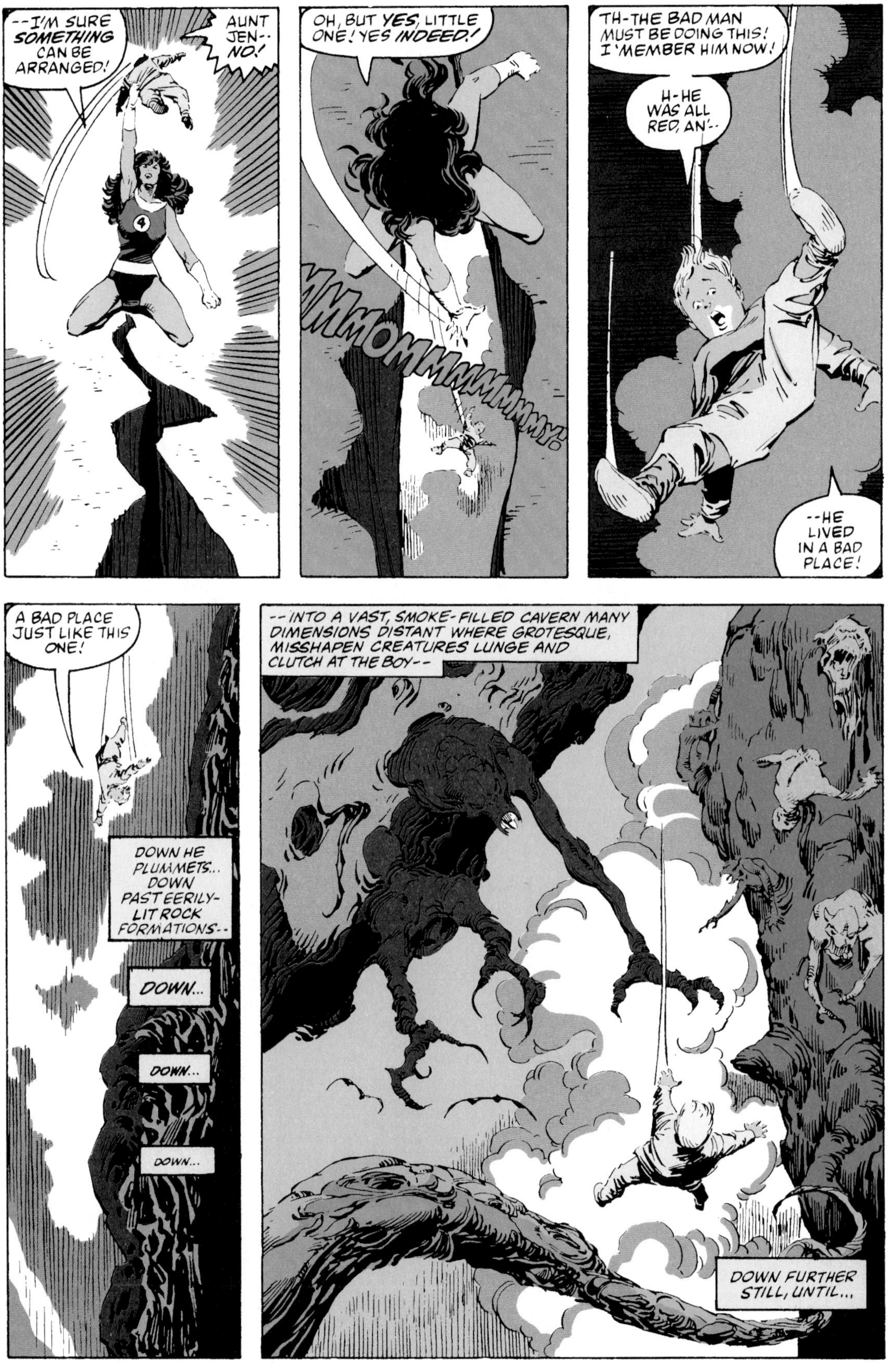
--I'M SURE SOMETHING CAN BE ARRANGED!
AUNT JEN--NO!
OH, BUT YES, LITTLE ONE! YES INDEED!
MMMOMMMMMMMMY!
TH-THE BAD MAN MUST BE DOING THIS! I 'MEMBER HIM NOW!
H-HE WAS ALL RED, AN'--
--HE LIVED IN A BAD PLACE!
A BAD PLACE JUST LIKE THIS ONE!
DOWN HE PLUMMETS... DOWN PAST EERILY-LIT ROCK FORMATIONS--
DOWN...
DOWN...
DOWN...
--INTO A VAST, SMOKE-FILLED CAVERN MANY DIMENSIONS DISTANT WHERE GROTESQUE, MISSHAPEN CREATURES LUNGE AND CLUTCH AT THE BOY--
DOWN FURTHER STILL, UNTIL...

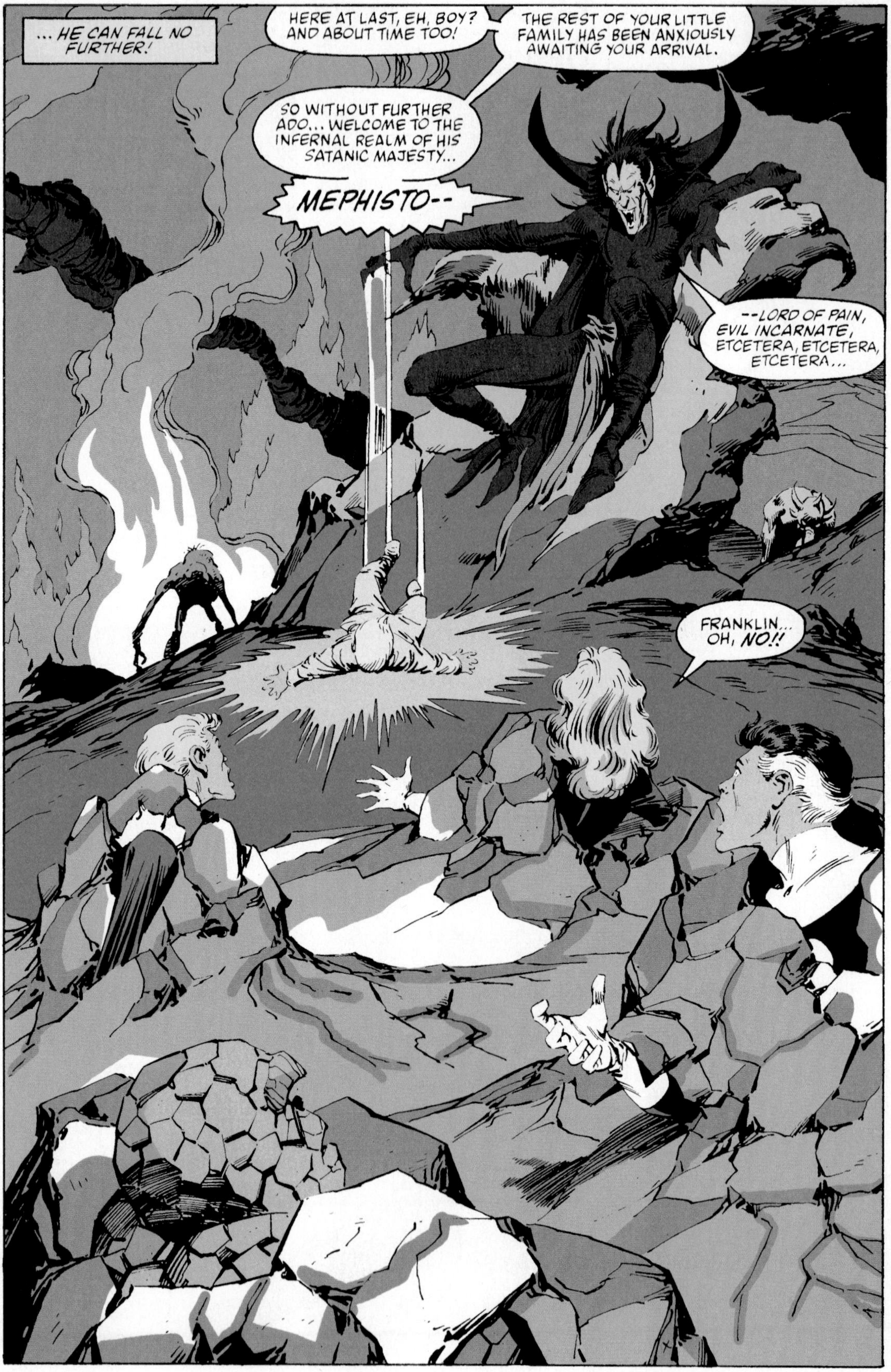

...HE CAN FALL NO FURTHER!
HERE AT LAST, EH, BOY? AND ABOUT TIME TOO!
THE REST OF YOUR LITTLE FAMILY HAS BEEN ANXIOUSLY AWAITING YOUR ARRIVAL.
SO WITHOUT FURTHER ADO... WELCOME TO THE INFERNAL REALM OF HIS SATANIC MAJESTY...
MEPHISTO--
--LORD OF PAIN, EVIL INCARNATE, ETCETERA, ETCETERA, ETCETERA...
FRANKLIN... OH, NO!!

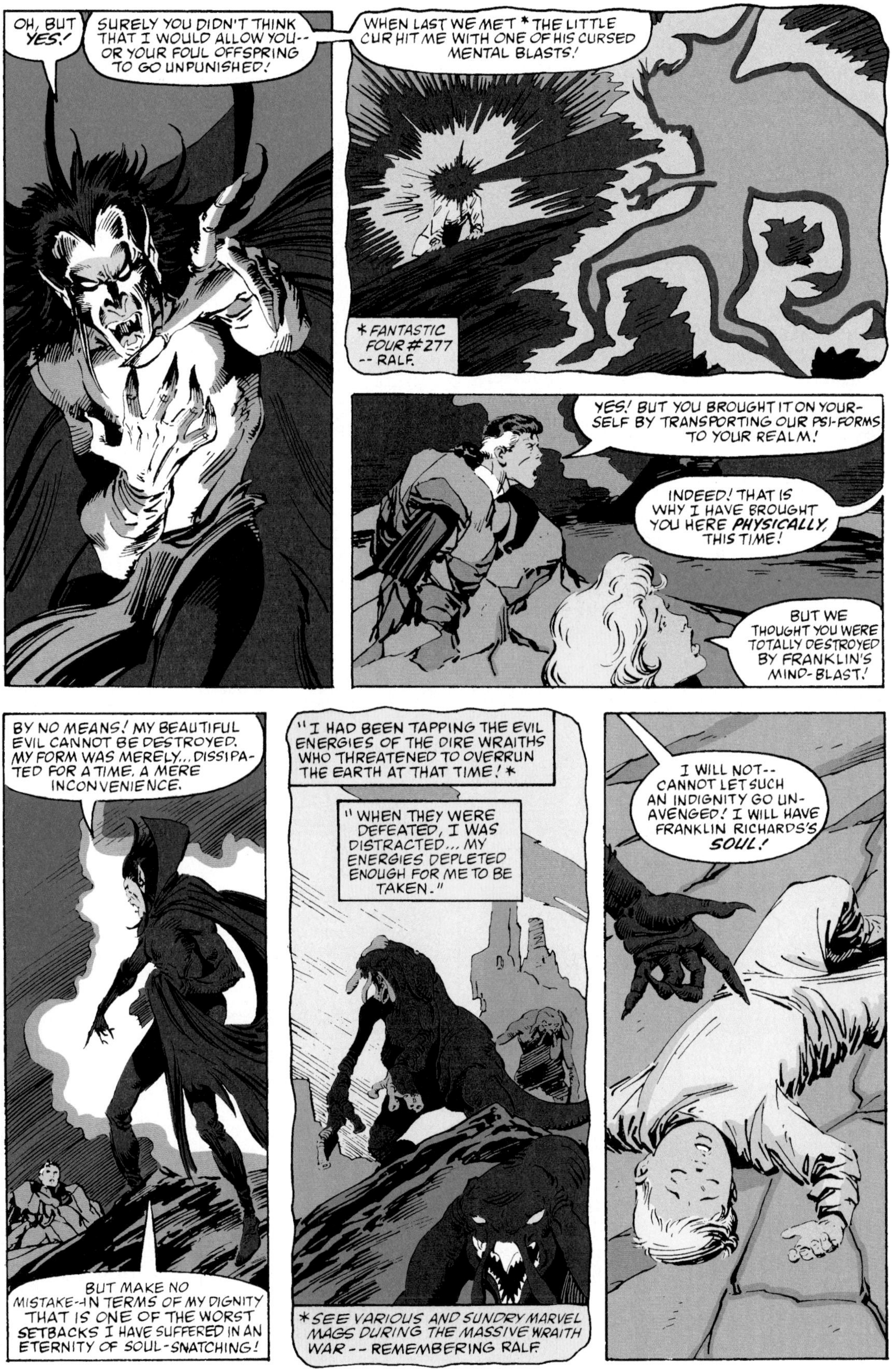

OH, BUT YES!
SURELY YOU DIDN'T THINK THAT I WOULD ALLOW YOU-- OR YOUR FOUL OFFSPRING TO GO UNPUNISHED!
WHEN LAST WE MET * THE LITTLE CUR HIT ME WITH ONE OF HIS CURSED MENTAL BLASTS!
* FANTASTIC FOUR #277 -- RALF.
YES! BUT YOU BROUGHT IT ON YOURSELF BY TRANSPORTING OUR PSI-FORMS TO YOUR REALM!
INDEED! THAT IS WHY I HAVE BROUGHT YOU HERE PHYSICALLY, THIS TIME!
BUT WE THOUGHT YOU WERE TOTALLY DESTROYED BY FRANKLIN'S MIND-BLAST!
BY NO MEANS! MY BEAUTIFUL EVIL CANNOT BE DESTROYED. MY FORM WAS MERELY... DISSIPATED FOR A TIME. A MERE INCONVENIENCE.
BUT MAKE NO MISTAKE--IN TERMS OF MY DIGNITY THAT IS ONE OF THE WORST SETBACKS I HAVE SUFFERED IN AN ETERNITY OF SOUL-SNATCHING!
"I HAD BEEN TAPPING THE EVIL ENERGIES OF THE DIRE WRAITHS WHO THREATENED TO OVERRUN THE EARTH AT THAT TIME! *
"WHEN THEY WERE DEFEATED, I WAS DISTRACTED... MY ENERGIES DEPLETED ENOUGH FOR ME TO BE TAKEN."
* SEE VARIOUS AND SUNDRY MARVEL MAGS DURING THE MASSIVE WRAITH WAR -- REMEMBERING RALF.
I WILL NOT-- CANNOT LET SUCH AN INDIGNITY GO UNAVENGED! I WILL HAVE FRANKLIN RICHARDS'S SOUL!

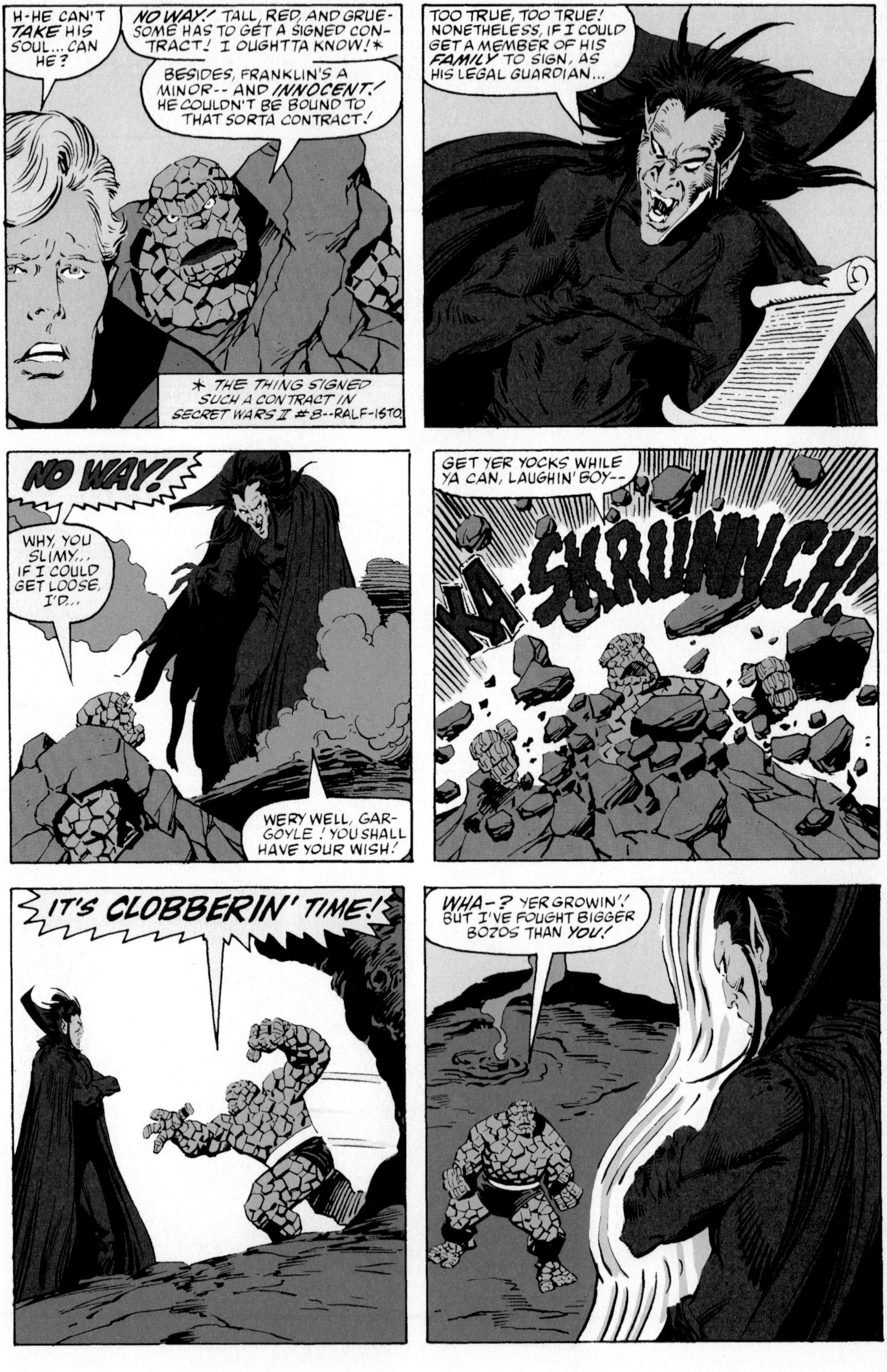
H-HE CAN'T TAKE HIS SOUL... CAN HE?
NO WAY! TALL, RED, AND GRUESOME HAS TO GET A SIGNED CONTRACT! I OUGHTTA KNOW!*
BESIDES, FRANKLIN'S A MINOR-- AND INNOCENT! HE COULDN'T BE BOUND TO THAT SORTA CONTRACT!
* THE THING SIGNED SUCH A CONTRACT IN SECRET WARS II #8--RALF-I$TO.
TOO TRUE, TOO TRUE! NONETHELESS, IF I COULD GET A MEMBER OF HIS FAMILY TO SIGN, AS HIS LEGAL GUARDIAN...
NO WAY!
WHY, YOU SLIMY... IF I COULD GET LOOSE, I'D...
WERY WELL, GARGOYLE! YOU SHALL HAVE YOUR WISH!
GET YER YOCKS WHILE YA CAN, LAUGHIN' BOY--
KA-SKRUNNCH!
IT'S CLOBBERIN' TIME!
WHA-? YER GROWIN'! BUT I'VE FOUGHT BIGGER BOZOS THAN YOU!

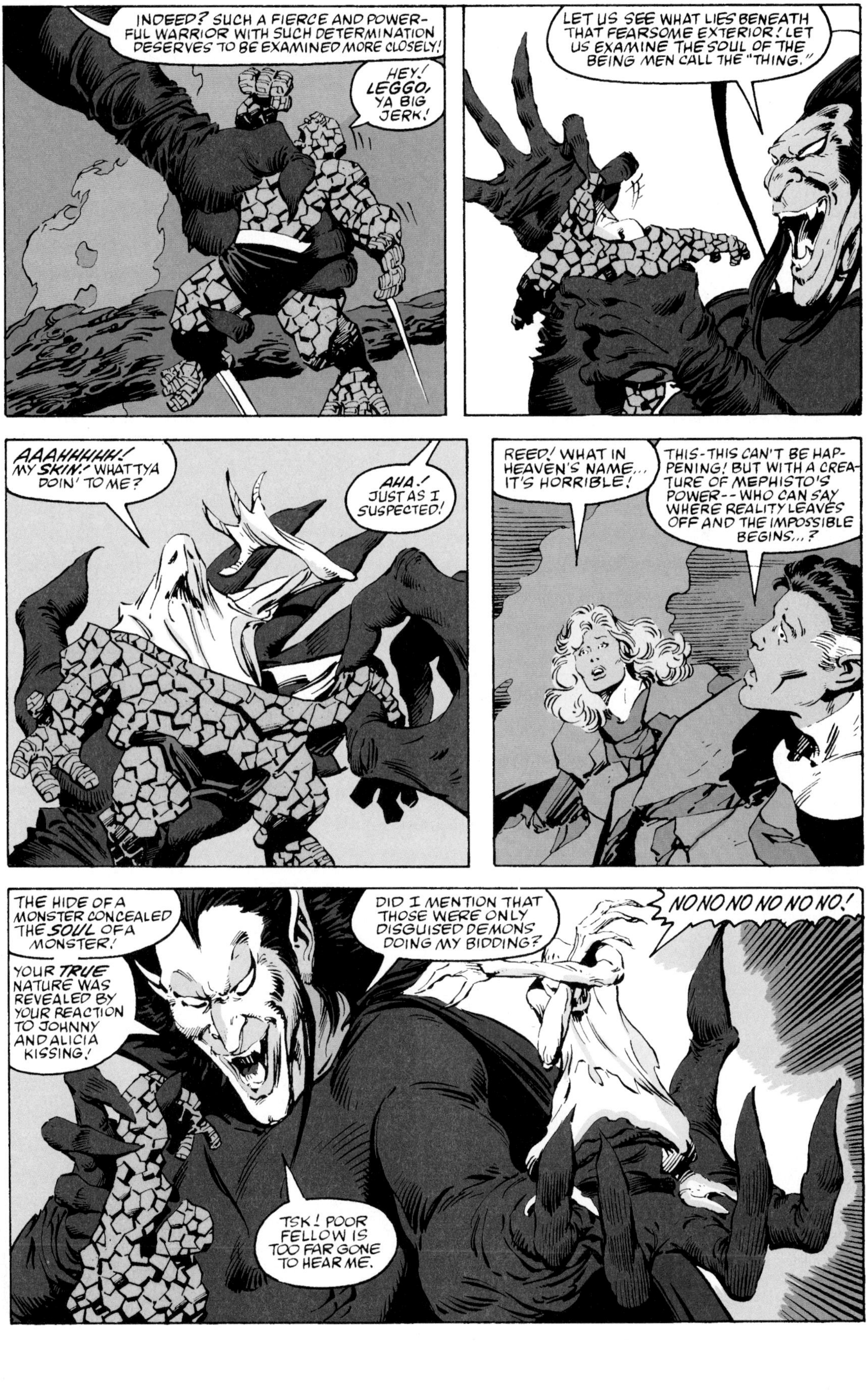
INDEED? SUCH A FIERCE AND POWERFUL WARRIOR WITH SUCH DETERMINATION DESERVES TO BE EXAMINED MORE CLOSELY!
HEY! LEGGO, YA BIG JERK!
LET US SEE WHAT LIES BENEATH THAT FEARSOME EXTERIOR! LET US EXAMINE THE SOUL OF THE BEING MEN CALL THE "THING."
AAAHHHHH! MY SKIN! WHATTYA DOIN' TO ME?
AHA! JUST AS I SUSPECTED!
REED! WHAT IN HEAVEN'S NAME... IT'S HORRIBLE!
THIS-THIS CAN'T BE HAPPENING! BUT WITH A CREATURE OF MEPHISTO'S POWER--WHO CAN SAY WHERE REALITY LEAVES OFF AND THE IMPOSSIBLE BEGINS...?
THE HIDE OF A MONSTER CONCEALED THE SOUL OF A MONSTER!
YOUR TRUE NATURE WAS REVEALED BY YOUR REACTION TO JOHNNY AND ALICIA KISSING!
DID I MENTION THAT THOSE WERE ONLY DISGUISED DEMONS DOING MY BIDDING?
NO NO NO NO NO NO!
TSK! POOR FELLOW IS TOO FAR GONE TO HEAR ME.

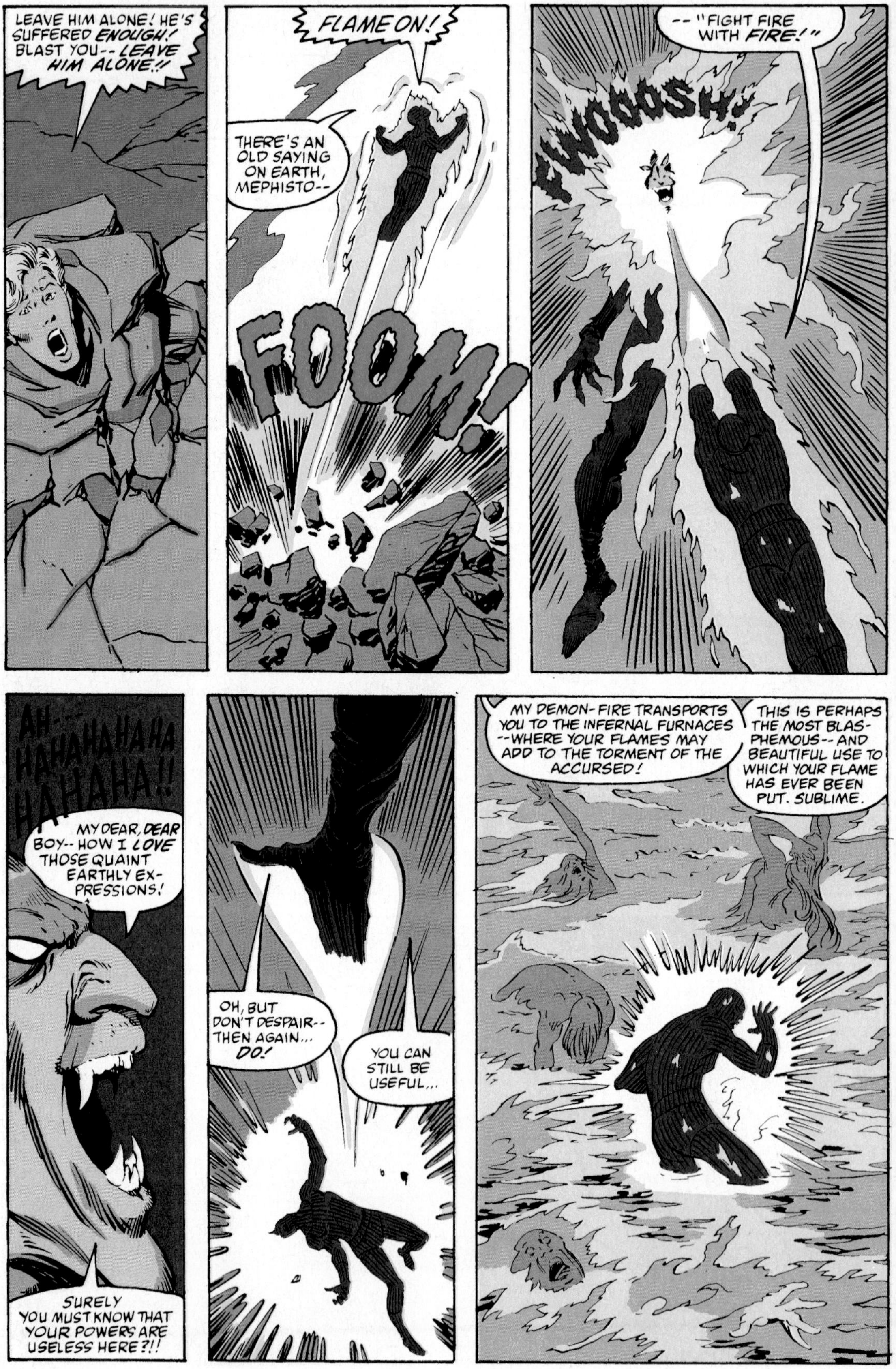
LEAVE HIM ALONE! HE'S SUFFERED ENOUGH! BLAST YOU-- LEAVE HIM ALONE!!
FLAME ON!
THERE'S AN OLD SAYING ON EARTH, MEPHISTO--
FOOM!
-- "FIGHT FIRE WITH FIRE!"
FWOOOSH!
AH--HAHAHAHAHAHA HAHAHAHA!!
MY DEAR, DEAR BOY-- HOW I LOVE THOSE QUAINT EARTHLY EXPRESSIONS!
SURELY YOU MUST KNOW THAT YOUR POWERS ARE USELESS HERE?!!
OH, BUT DON'T DESPAIR-- THEN AGAIN... DO!
YOU CAN STILL BE USEFUL...
MY DEMON-FIRE TRANSPORTS YOU TO THE INFERNAL FURNACES --WHERE YOUR FLAMES MAY ADD TO THE TORMENT OF THE ACCURSED!
THIS IS PERHAPS THE MOST BLASPHEMOUS-- AND BEAUTIFUL USE TO WHICH YOUR FLAME HAS EVER BEEN PUT. SUBLIME.

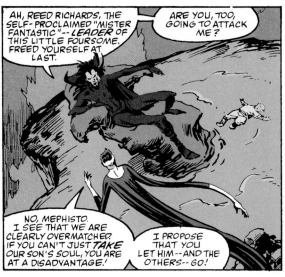

AH, REED RICHARDS, THE SELF-PROCLAIMED "MISTER FANTASTIC"-- *LEADER* OF THIS LITTLE FOURSOME, FREED YOURSELF AT LAST.

ARE YOU, TOO, GOING TO ATTACK ME?

NO, MEPHISTO. I SEE THAT WE ARE CLEARLY OVERMATCHED! IF YOU CAN'T JUST *TAKE* OUR SON'S SOUL, YOU ARE AT A DISADVANTAGE!

I PROPOSE THAT YOU LET HIM--AND THE OTHERS-- GO!

I'LL REMAIN BEHIND TO BATTLE YOU ON WHATEVER TERMS YOU SAY!

HMMM. A TEMPTING OFFER-- AND ONE WORTHY OF YOUR VAST INTELLECT, EXCEPT FOR ONE SMALL DETAIL...

I HAVE NO NEED OF BARGAINS WITH YOU, REED RICHARDS, FOR I ALREADY OWN YOUR SOUL!

WHAT?! IMPOSSIBLE! YOU'RE BLUFFING!

OH, NO! NOT AT ALL! HAVE YOU SO SOON FORGOTTEN OUR AGREEMENT? 'TWAS IN THE EARLY DAYS OF YOUR COLLEGE CAREER...

YOU HAD JUST MET THE YOUTHFUL, BUT ALREADY ARROGANT VICTOR VON DOOM-- WHO WOULD GO ON TO BECOME *DOCTOR DOOM*, THE FANTASTIC FOUR'S GREATEST FOE.

DOOM-- I THINK YOU HAD BETTER CHECK YOUR CALCU-LATIONS. IT SEEMS TO ME YOU'RE OFF A FEW DECIMAL POINTS IN SOME OF TH'...

GET OUT, RICHARDS! YOUR PUNY MIND CANNOT BEGIN TO COMPRE-HEND THE BRILLIANCE OF MY EXPERIMENTS!

BUT, DOOM, IT COULD BE DAN-GEROUS!

BAH! THE IGNORANT PEASANT! HOW COULD HE *HOPE* TO UNDERSTAND THAT I AM DELVING INTO THE REALM OF *SORCERY*-- NOT MERE SCIENCE!

WHO KNOWS WHAT UNNAMED POWERS I MAY TAP IF THIS PROVES SUCCESSFUL.

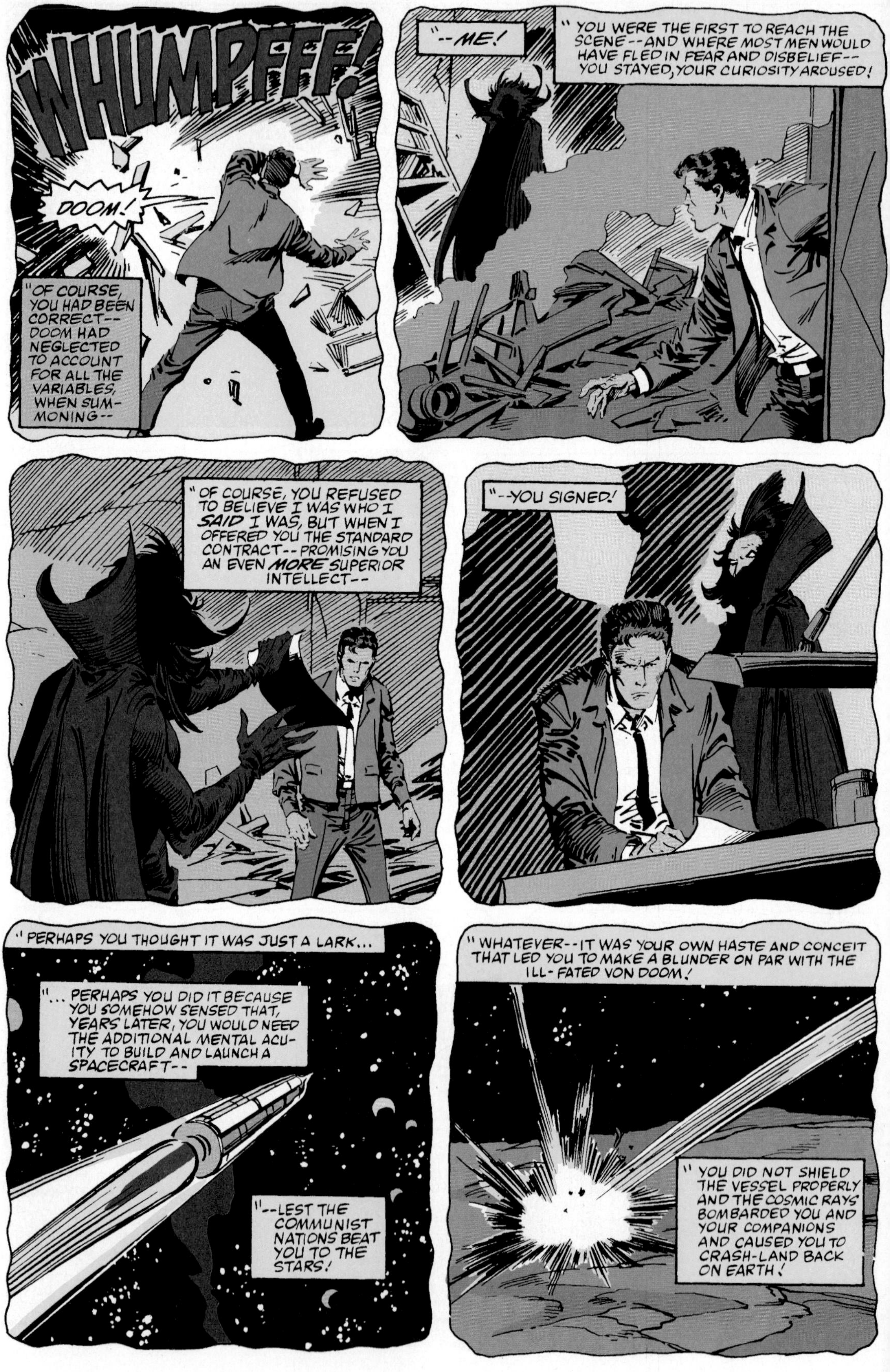
WHUMPFFF!
DOOM!
"OF COURSE, YOU HAD BEEN CORRECT-- DOOM HAD NEGLECTED TO ACCOUNT FOR ALL THE VARIABLES, WHEN SUMMONING--
"--ME!
"YOU WERE THE FIRST TO REACH THE SCENE--AND WHERE MOST MEN WOULD HAVE FLED IN FEAR AND DISBELIEF-- YOU STAYED, YOUR CURIOSITY AROUSED!
"OF COURSE, YOU REFUSED TO BELIEVE I WAS WHO I SAID I WAS, BUT WHEN I OFFERED YOU THE STANDARD CONTRACT--PROMISING YOU AN EVEN MORE SUPERIOR INTELLECT--
"--YOU SIGNED!
"PERHAPS YOU THOUGHT IT WAS JUST A LARK...
"...PERHAPS YOU DID IT BECAUSE YOU SOMEHOW SENSED THAT, YEARS LATER, YOU WOULD NEED THE ADDITIONAL MENTAL ACUITY TO BUILD AND LAUNCH A SPACECRAFT--
"--LEST THE COMMUNIST NATIONS BEAT YOU TO THE STARS!
"WHATEVER--IT WAS YOUR OWN HASTE AND CONCEIT THAT LED YOU TO MAKE A BLUNDER ON PAR WITH THE ILL-FATED VON DOOM!
"YOU DID NOT SHIELD THE VESSEL PROPERLY AND THE COSMIC RAYS BOMBARDED YOU AND YOUR COMPANIONS AND CAUSED YOU TO CRASH-LAND BACK ON EARTH!

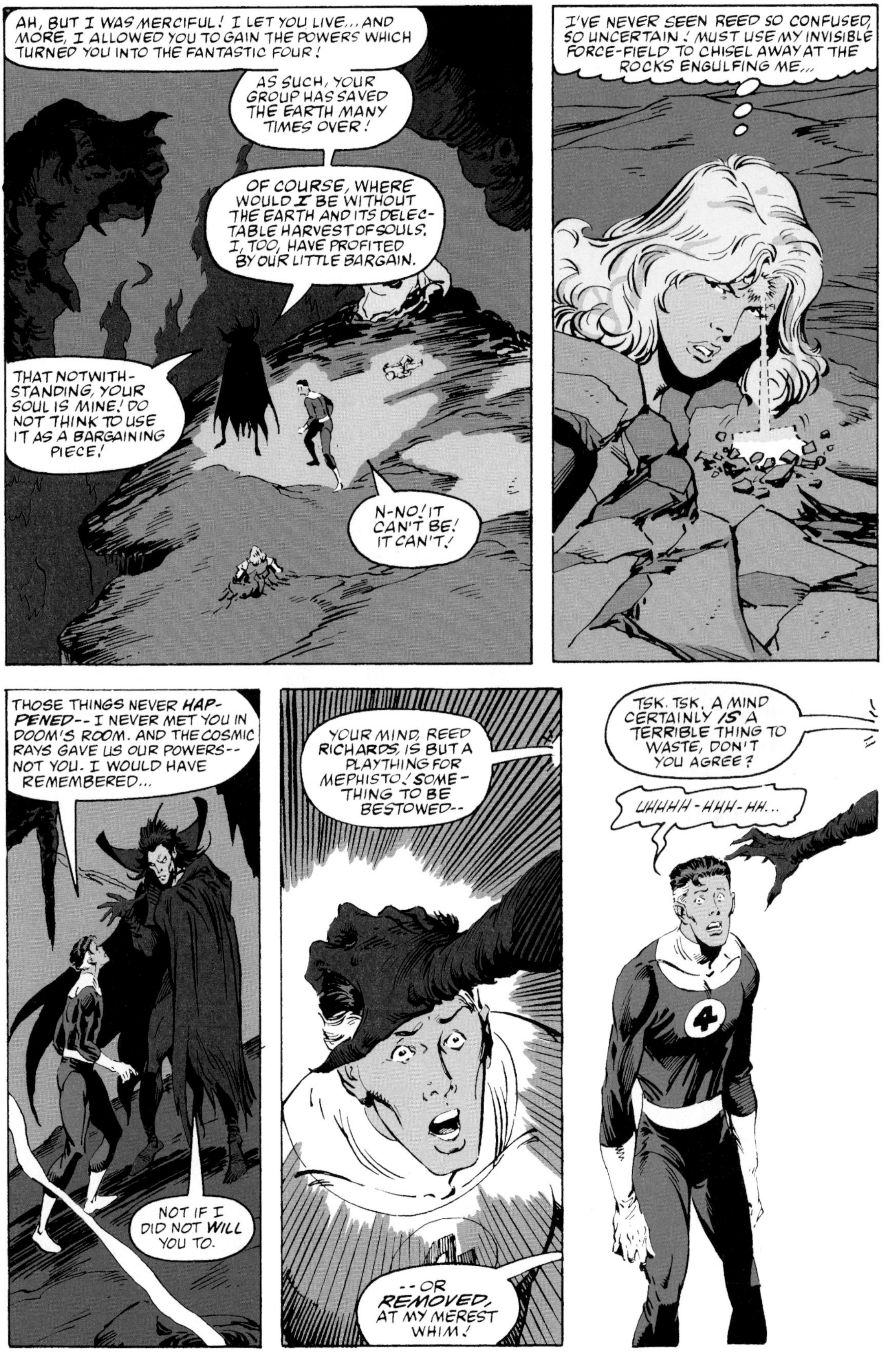
AH, BUT I WAS MERCIFUL! I LET YOU LIVE... AND MORE, I ALLOWED YOU TO GAIN THE POWERS WHICH TURNED YOU INTO THE FANTASTIC FOUR!
AS SUCH, YOUR GROUP HAS SAVED THE EARTH MANY TIMES OVER!
OF COURSE, WHERE WOULD I BE WITHOUT THE EARTH AND ITS DELECTABLE HARVEST OF SOULS. I, TOO, HAVE PROFITED BY OUR LITTLE BARGAIN.
THAT NOTWITHSTANDING, YOUR SOUL IS MINE! DO NOT THINK TO USE IT AS A BARGAINING PIECE!
N-NO! IT CAN'T BE! IT CAN'T!
I'VE NEVER SEEN REED SO CONFUSED, SO UNCERTAIN! MUST USE MY INVISIBLE FORCE-FIELD TO CHISEL AWAY AT THE ROCKS ENGULFING ME...
THOSE THINGS NEVER HAPPENED-- I NEVER MET YOU IN DOOM'S ROOM. AND THE COSMIC RAYS GAVE US OUR POWERS-- NOT YOU. I WOULD HAVE REMEMBERED...
NOT IF I DID NOT WILL YOU TO.
YOUR MIND, REED RICHARDS, IS BUT A PLAYTHING FOR MEPHISTO! SOMETHING TO BE BESTOWED--
--OR REMOVED, AT MY MEREST WHIM!
TSK. TSK, A MIND CERTAINLY IS A TERRIBLE THING TO WASTE, DON'T YOU AGREE?
UHHHH-HHH-HH...

REED.!!

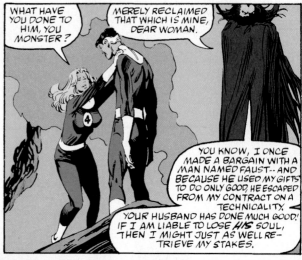

WHAT HAVE YOU DONE TO HIM, YOU MONSTER?

MERELY RECLAIMED THAT WHICH IS MINE, DEAR WOMAN.

YOU KNOW, I ONCE MADE A BARGAIN WITH A MAN NAMED FAUST-- AND BECAUSE HE USED MY GIFTS TO DO ONLY GOOD, HE ESCAPED FROM MY CONTRACT ON A TECHNICALITY. YOUR HUSBAND HAS DONE MUCH GOOD! IF I AM LIABLE TO LOSE HIS SOUL, THEN I MIGHT JUST AS WELL RETRIEVE MY STAKES.

FIEND!

FLATTERER!

YOU THINK THIS IS FUNNY, MEPHISTO?!

YOU TAKE MY CHILD-- CRIPPLE MY HUSBAND--AND YOU LAUGH AT ME?!

HOW...

...DARE...

YOU!

ENOUGH, WOMAN! ENOUGH, I SAY!

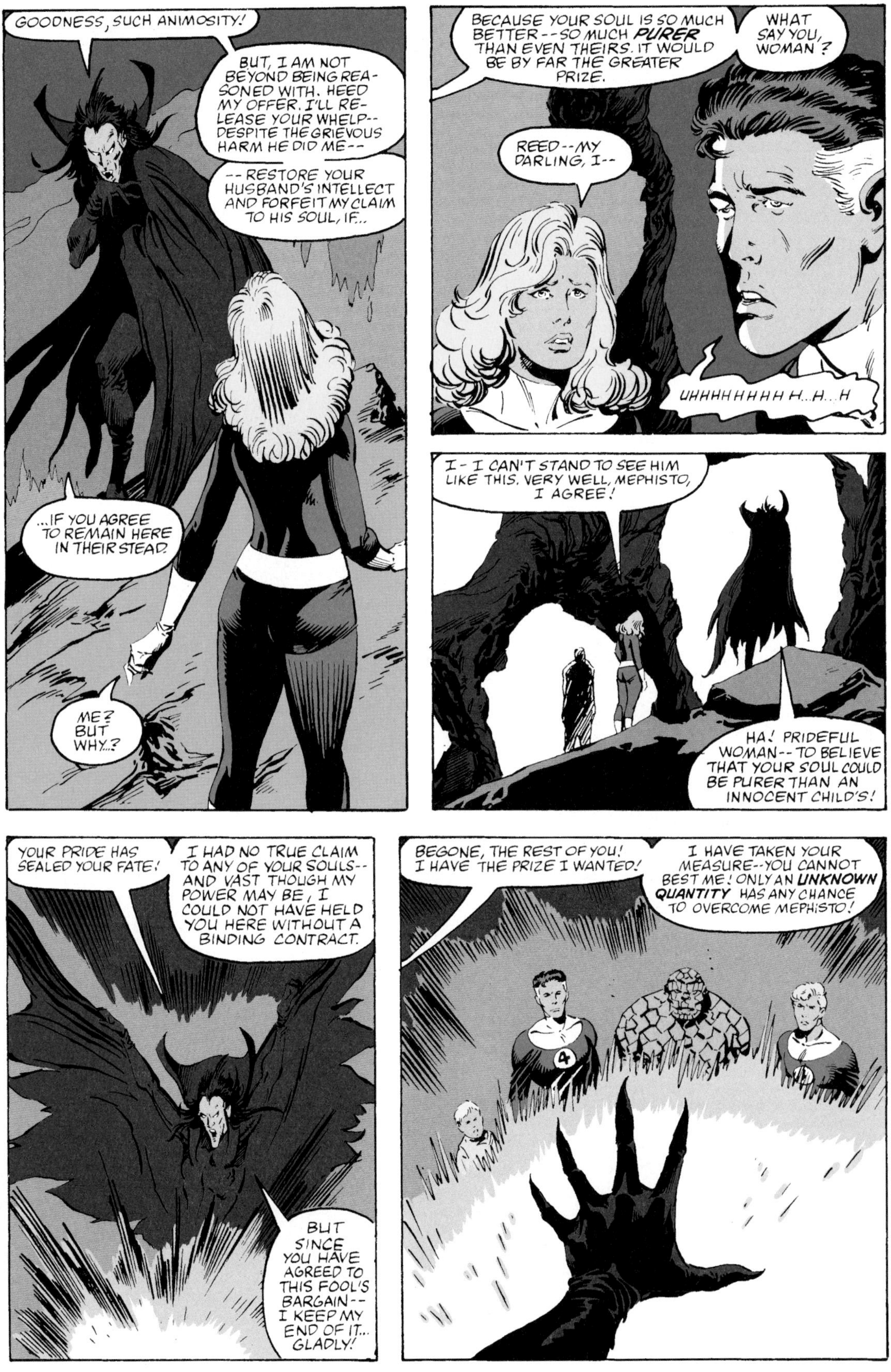
GOODNESS, SUCH ANIMOSITY!
BUT, I AM NOT BEYOND BEING REASONED WITH. HEED MY OFFER. I'LL RELEASE YOUR WHELP-- DESPITE THE GRIEVOUS HARM HE DID ME--
--RESTORE YOUR HUSBAND'S INTELLECT AND FORFEIT MY CLAIM TO HIS SOUL, IF...
...IF YOU AGREE TO REMAIN HERE IN THEIR STEAD.
ME? BUT WHY...?
BECAUSE YOUR SOUL IS SO MUCH BETTER--SO MUCH PURER THAN EVEN THEIRS. IT WOULD BE BY FAR THE GREATER PRIZE.
WHAT SAY YOU, WOMAN?
REED--MY DARLING, I--
UHHHHHHHHH H...H...H
I-I CAN'T STAND TO SEE HIM LIKE THIS. VERY WELL, MEPHISTO, I AGREE!
HA! PRIDEFUL WOMAN--TO BELIEVE THAT YOUR SOUL COULD BE PURER THAN AN INNOCENT CHILD'S!
YOUR PRIDE HAS SEALED YOUR FATE!
I HAD NO TRUE CLAIM TO ANY OF YOUR SOULS-- AND VAST THOUGH MY POWER MAY BE, I COULD NOT HAVE HELD YOU HERE WITHOUT A BINDING CONTRACT.
BUT SINCE YOU HAVE AGREED TO THIS FOOL'S BARGAIN-- I KEEP MY END OF IT... GLADLY!
BEGONE, THE REST OF YOU! I HAVE THE PRIZE I WANTED!
I HAVE TAKEN YOUR MEASURE--YOU CANNOT BEST ME! ONLY AN UNKNOWN QUANTITY HAS ANY CHANCE TO OVERCOME MEPHISTO!

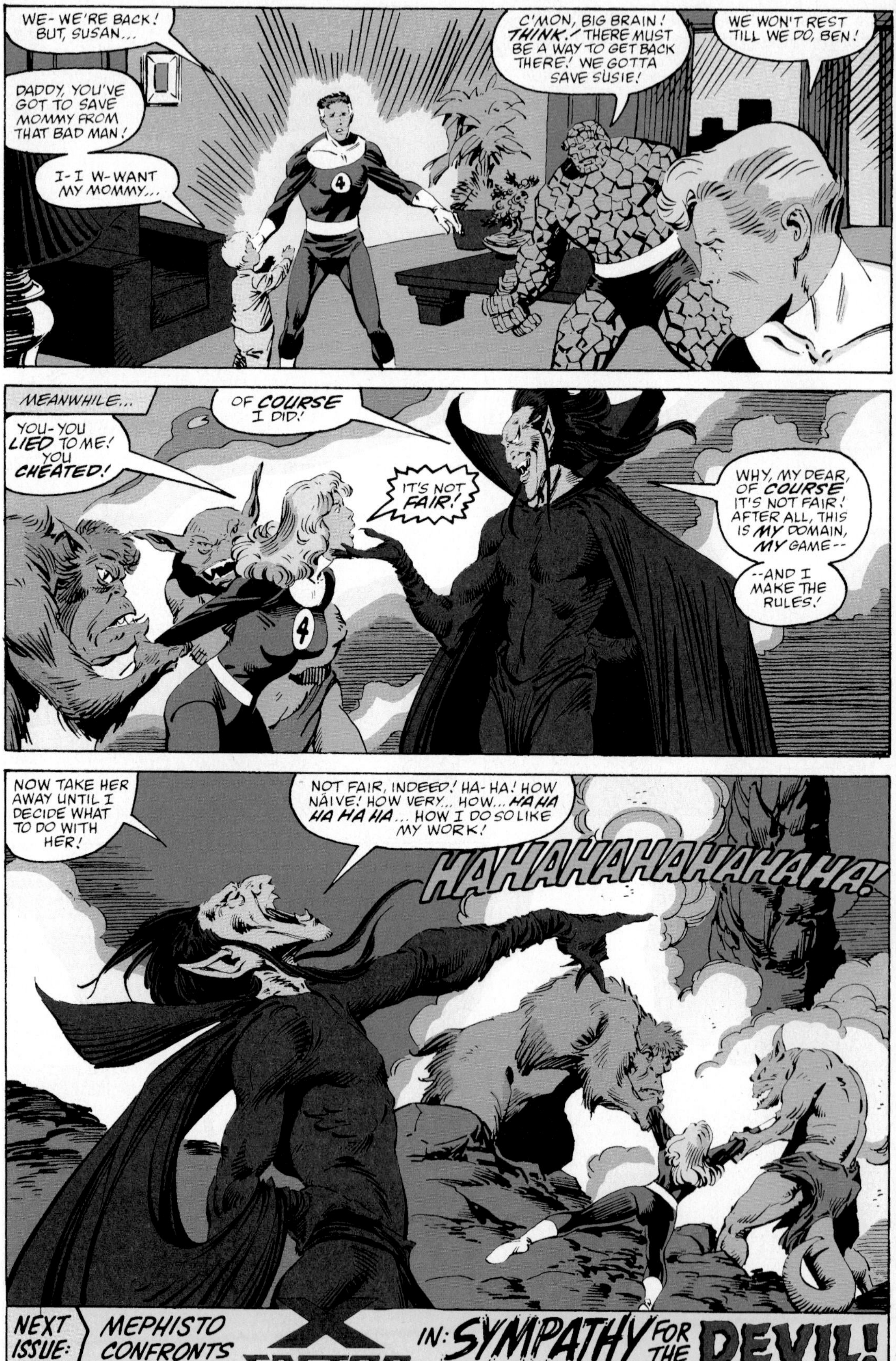
WE- WE'RE BACK! BUT, SUSAN...
DADDY, YOU'VE GOT TO SAVE MOMMY FROM THAT BAD MAN!
I- I W-WANT MY MOMMY...
C'MON, BIG BRAIN! THINK! THERE MUST BE A WAY TO GET BACK THERE! WE GOTTA SAVE SUSIE!
WE WON'T REST TILL WE DO, BEN!
MEANWHILE...
YOU- YOU LIED TO ME! YOU CHEATED!
OF COURSE I DID!
IT'S NOT FAIR!
WHY, MY DEAR, OF COURSE IT'S NOT FAIR! AFTER ALL, THIS IS MY DOMAIN, MY GAME--
--AND I MAKE THE RULES!
NOW TAKE HER AWAY UNTIL I DECIDE WHAT TO DO WITH HER!
NOT FAIR, INDEED! HA-HA! HOW NÄIVE! HOW VERY... HOW... HA HA HA HA HA... HOW I DO SO LIKE MY WORK!
HAHAHAHAHAHAHAHA!
NEXT ISSUE: MEPHISTO CONFRONTS X-FACTOR IN: SYMPATHY FOR THE DEVIL!

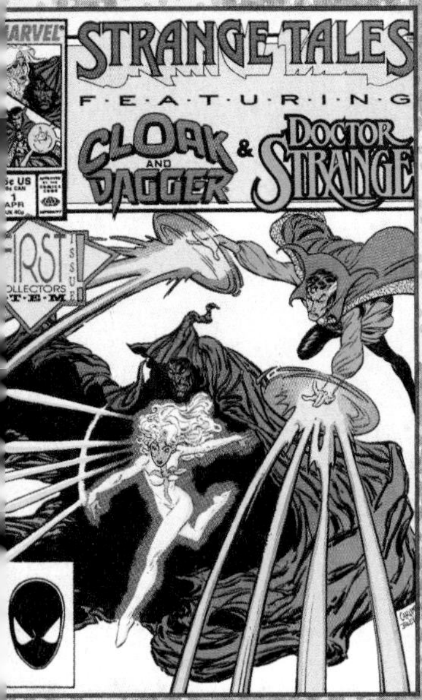
MARVEL
STRANGE TALES
FEATURING
CLOAK AND DAGGER & DOCTOR STRANGE
FIRST ISSUE
COLLECTORS ITEM

TRANGE TALES #1, published in December 1986, egan a split-format series with ongoing serials starring Cloak & Dagger and Dr. Strange.

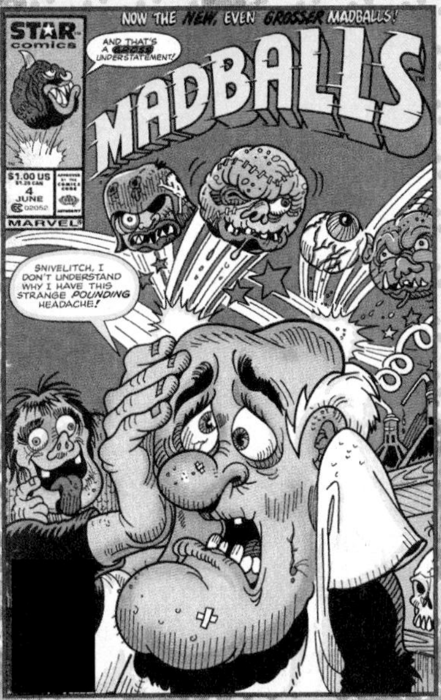
NOW THE NEW, EVEN GROSSER MADBALLS!
STAR comics
AND THAT'S A GROSS UNDERSTATEMENT!
MADBALLS
$1.00 US
4
JUNE
SNIVELITCH, I DON'T UNDERSTAND WHY I HAVE THIS STRANGE POUNDING HEADACHE!

MADBALLS #4, published in February 1987, revived the completed Star miniseries, extending it into an ongoing.

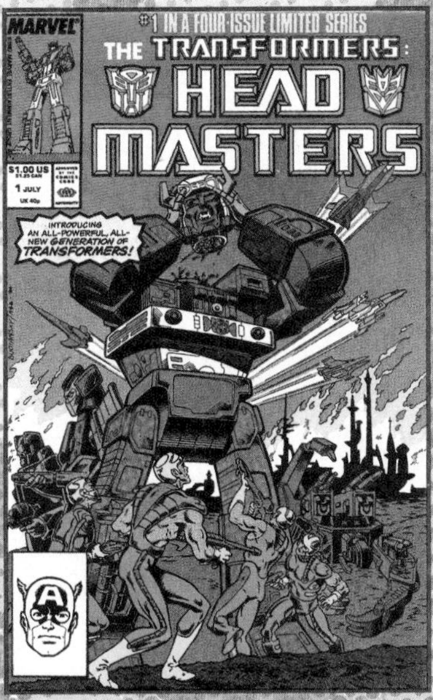
#1 IN A FOUR-ISSUE LIMITED SERIES
MARVEL
THE TRANSFORMERS:
HEAD MASTERS
$1.00 US
1 JULY
INTRODUCING AN ALL-POWERFUL, ALL-NEW GENERATION OF TRANSFORMERS!

HEADMASTERS #1, published in March 1987, began a miniseries based on Hasbro's *Transformers* toy line.

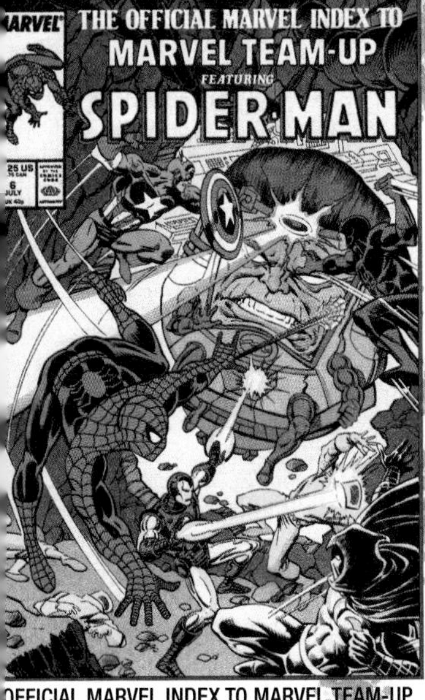
MARVEL
THE OFFICIAL MARVEL INDEX TO
MARVEL TEAM-UP
FEATURING
SPIDER-MAN
6
JULY

OFFICIAL MARVEL INDEX TO MARVEL TEAM-UP #6, published in March 1987, revived the title after a 7-month hiatus; however, it was the series' final issue.

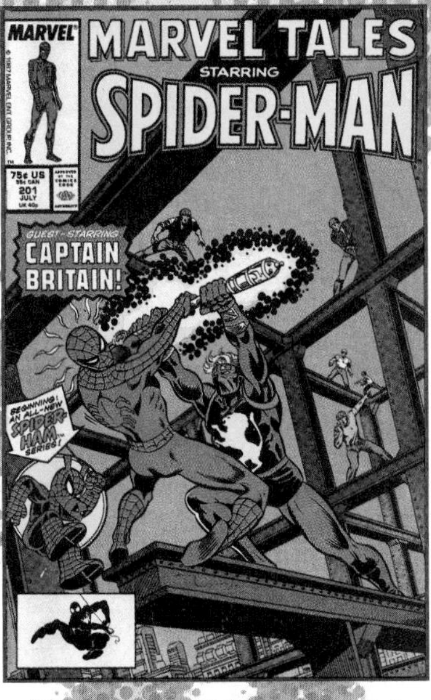
MARVEL
MARVEL TALES
STARRING
SPIDER-MAN
75¢ US
201
JULY
GUEST-STARRING
CAPTAIN BRITAIN!
BEGINNING! AN ALL-NEW SPIDER-HAM SERIES!

MARVEL TALES #201, published in March 1987, began a humor backup serial starring Spider-Ham.

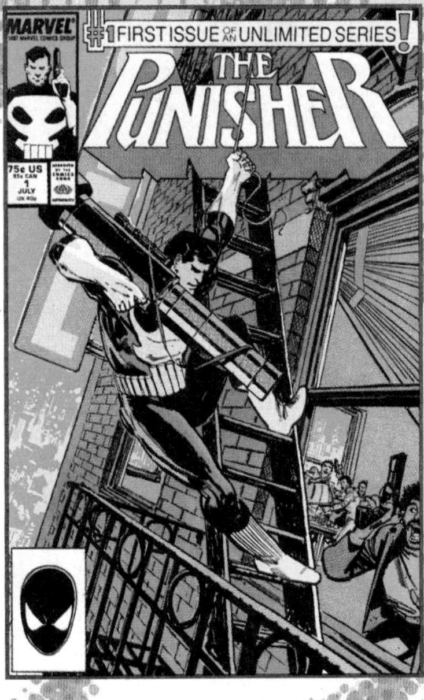
MARVEL
#1 FIRST ISSUE OF AN UNLIMITED SERIES!
THE PUNISHER
75¢ US
1
JULY

PUNISHER #1, published in March 1987, began the lethal crimefighter's new ongoing series.

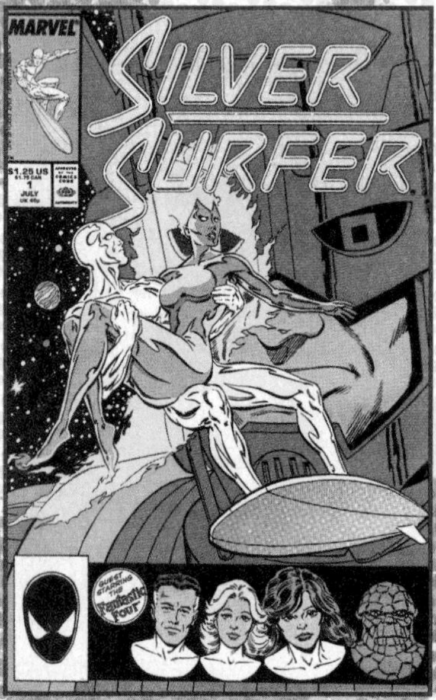
MARVEL
SILVER SURFER
$1.25 US
1
JULY

SILVER SURFER #1, published in March 1987, began the sentinel of the spaceways' new ongoing series.

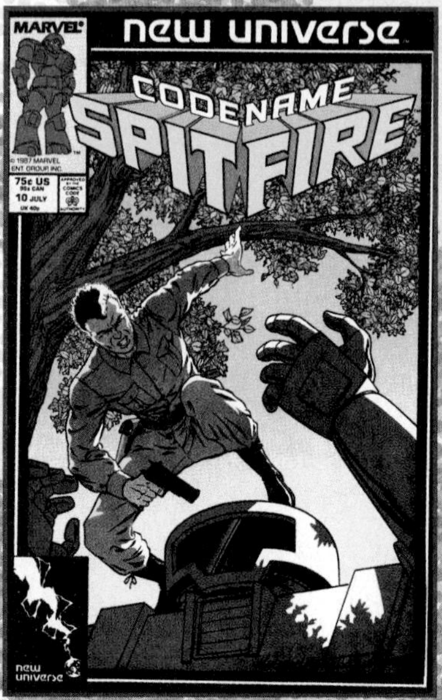
MARVEL
new universe
CODENAME
SPITFIRE
75¢ US
10 JULY
new universe

Spitfire and the Troubleshooters changed its title to CODENAME: SPITFIRE with #10, published in March 1987.

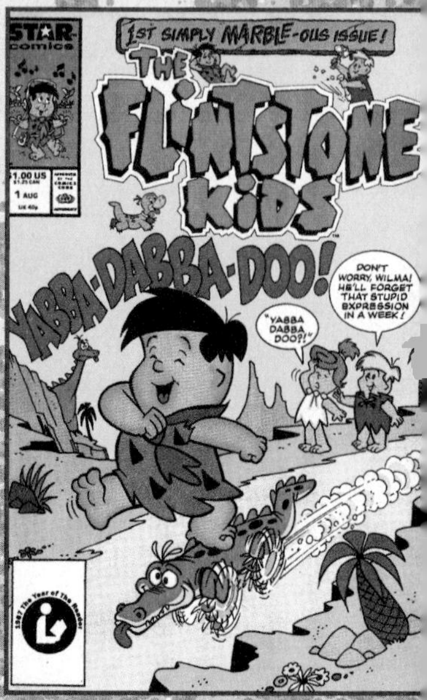
STAR comics
1ST SIMPLY MARBLE-OUS ISSUE!
THE FLINTSTONE KIDS
$1.00 US
1 AUG
YABBA-DABBA-DOO!
DON'T WORRY, WILMA! HE'LL FORGET THAT STUPID EXPRESSION IN A WEEK!
"YABBA DABBA DOO?!"

FLINTSTONE KIDS #1, published in April 1987, began an ongoing Star series based on the Hanna-Barbera animated TV series.

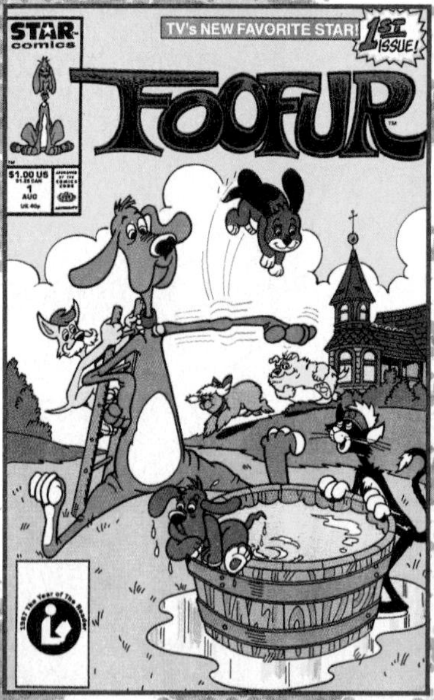
STAR comics
TV's NEW FAVORITE STAR!
1ST ISSUE!
FOOFUR
$1.00 US
1
AUG

FOOFUR #1, published in April 1987, began a short Star series based on the Hanna-Barbera animated TV series.

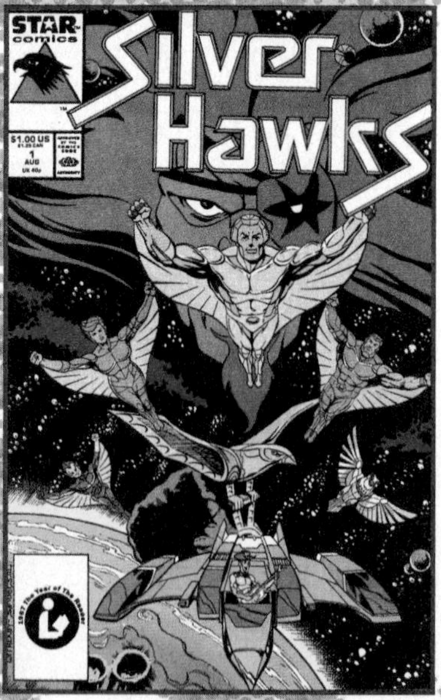
STAR comics
Silver Hawks
$1.00 US
1
AUG

SILVERHAWKS #1, published in April 1987, began an ongoing Star series based on the Rankin/Bass Productions animated TV series.

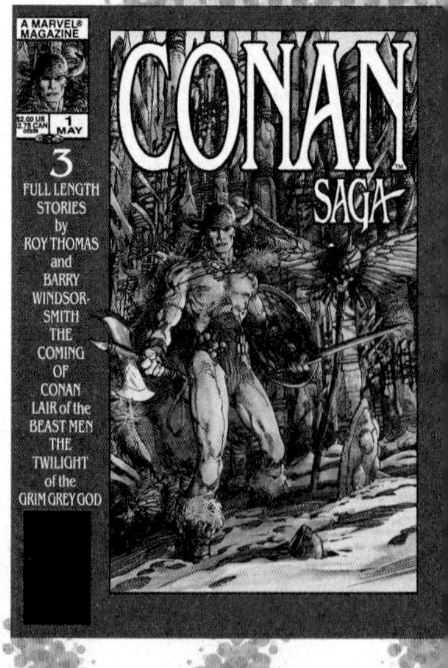
A MARVEL MAGAZINE
1
MAY
CONAN
SAGA
3
FULL LENGTH STORIES
by
ROY THOMAS
and
BARRY WINDSOR-SMITH
THE COMING OF CONAN
LAIR of the BEAST MEN
THE TWILIGHT of the GRIM GREY GOD

CONAN SAGA #1, published in April 1987, began an ongoing magazine-sized reprint series.

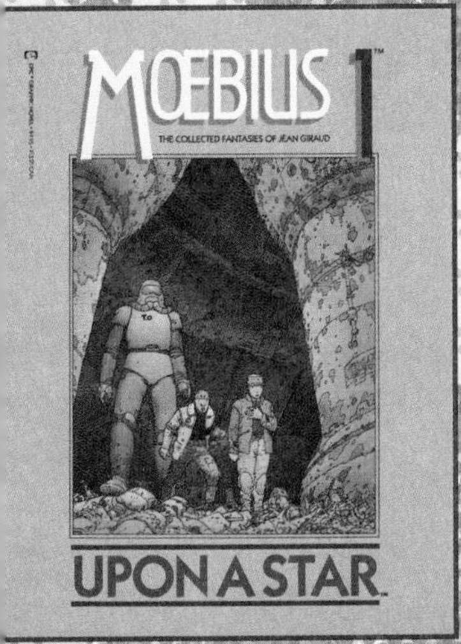
MOEBIUS 1
THE COLLECTED FANTASIES OF JEAN GIRAUD
UPON A STAR

MOEBIUS #1, published in May 1987, began a series of magazine-sized Epic Graphic Novels reprinting and translating the French work of Jean "Moebius" Giraud.

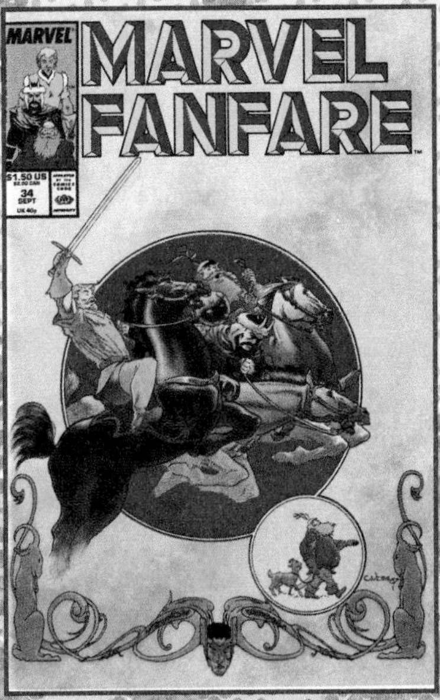
MARVEL
MARVEL FANFARE
$1.50 US
34
SEPT

MARVEL FANFARE #34, published in May 1987, began a short serial starring the Asgardian Warriors Three.

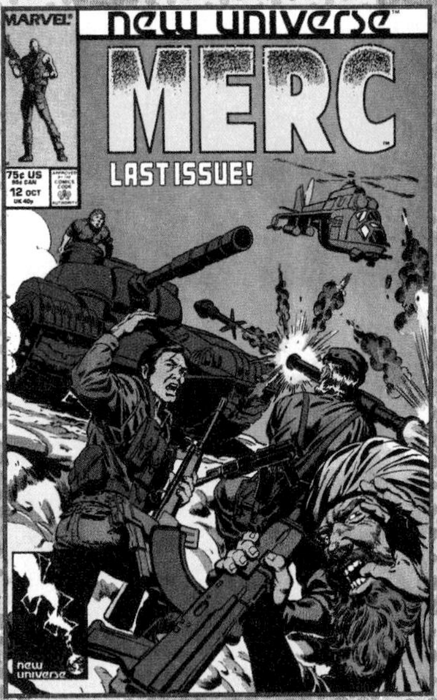
MARVEL
new universe
MERC
75¢ US
12 OCT
LAST ISSUE!
new universe

After the death of its main character, *Mark Hazzard: Merc* changed its title to MERC with #12, the series' final issue, published in June 1987.

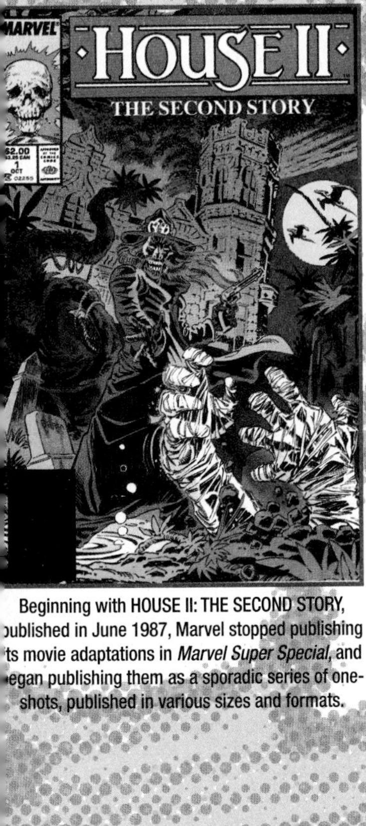
MARVEL
HOUSE II
THE SECOND STORY
$2.00
1
OCT

Beginning with HOUSE II: THE SECOND STORY, ublished in June 1987, Marvel stopped publishing ts movie adaptations in *Marvel Super Special,* and egan publishing them as a sporadic series of one-shots, published in various sizes and formats.

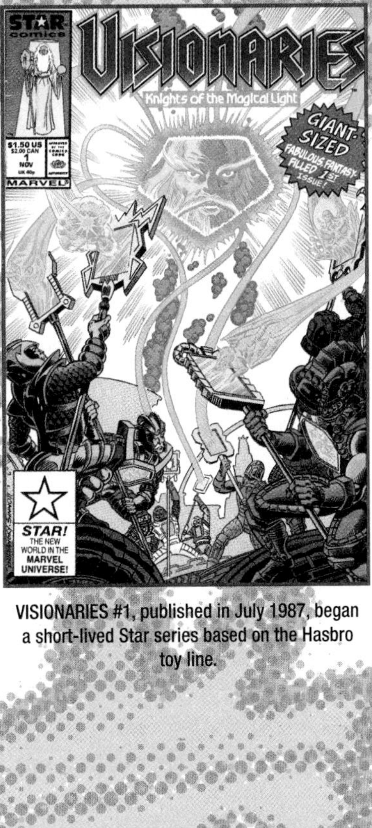
STAR comics
VISIONARIES
Knights of the Magical Light
$1.50 US
1
NOV
MARVEL
GIANT-SIZED
FABULOUS FANTASY-FILLED 1ST ISSUE!
STAR!
THE NEW WORLD IN THE MARVEL UNIVERSE!

VISIONARIES #1, published in July 1987, began a short-lived Star series based on the Hasbro toy line.

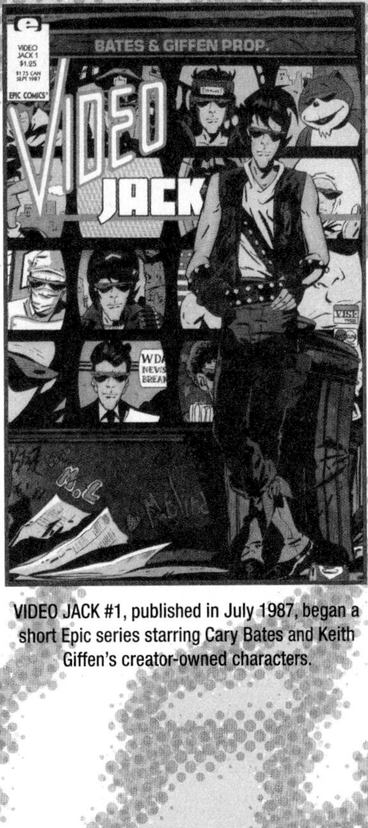
VIDEO JACK 1
$1.25
EPIC COMICS
BATES & GIFFEN PROP.
VIDEO
JACK

VIDEO JACK #1, published in July 1987, began a short Epic series starring Cary Bates and Keith Giffen's creator-owned characters.

STAR comics
FABULOUS FIRST ISSUE!
AIR Raiders
THE POWER IS IN THE AIR
SWASHBUCKLING SUPER-ACTION ON A FAR-OUT FANTASY-FILLED WORLD!
$1.00 US
1 NOV
MARVEL

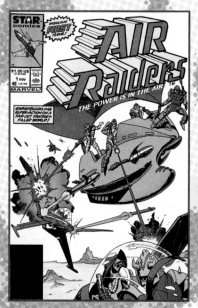

AIR RAIDERS #1, published in July 1987, began a short Star series based on the Hasbro toy line.

STAR comics
THE FUNTASTIC RETURN OF...
No 1!
BULLWINKLE
AND ROCKY
FROSTBITE FALLS
WITH ALL THEIR FRIENDS!
AND THEIR NOT SO FRIENDS! HEH, HEH!
$1.00 US
1 NOV
MARVEL
STAR! THE NEW WORLD IN THE MARVEL UNIVERSE!
THIS ISSUE: "THE INVISIBLE RAY"
OR... "________________!"

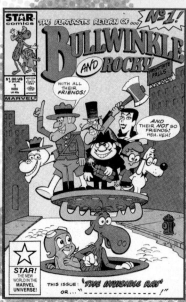

BULLWINKLE AND ROCKY #1, published in July 1987, began an ongoing Star series based on the Jay Ward Productions animated TV series.

MARVEL
SOLO AVENGERS STARRING
HAWKEYE
AND MOCKINGBIRD
75¢ US
1 DEC
BECAUSE YOU DEMANDED IT— THE AVENGING ARCHER IN HIS OWN SERIES OF SOLO ADVENTURES!
THE FALL OF THE MUTANTS IS COMING!
PLUS! HAWKEYE'S BATTLING BRIDE IN HER FIRST SOLO EXPLOIT EVER!

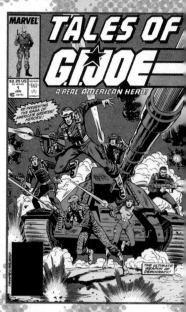

SOLO AVENGERS #1, published in August 1987, began an ongoing series with a main serial starring Hawkeye, and backup stories starring different Avengers.

MILLS O'NEILL
MARSHAL LAW
EPIC COMICS
FEAR AND LOATHING

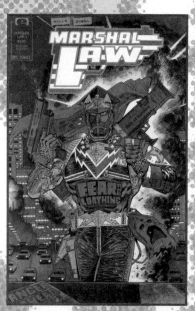

MARSHAL LAW #1, published in August 1987, began Pat Mills and Kevin O'Neill's short Epic series.

FIRST ISSUE! NEW FORMAT!
ALIEN LEGION
EPIC COMICS

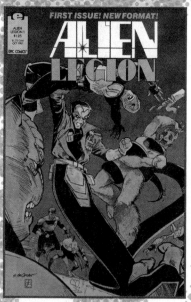

ALIEN LEGION #1, published in August 1987, began the Legion's new ongoing Epic series.

MARVEL
TALES OF G.I. JOE
A REAL AMERICAN HERO!
$2.25 US
1 JAN
RE-PRESENTING THE SAGA OF AMERICA'S GREATEST HEROES!
THE ULTIMATE WEAPON OF DEMOCRACY!

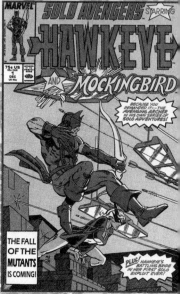

TALES OF G.I. JOE #1, published in September 1987, began an ongoing reprint series.

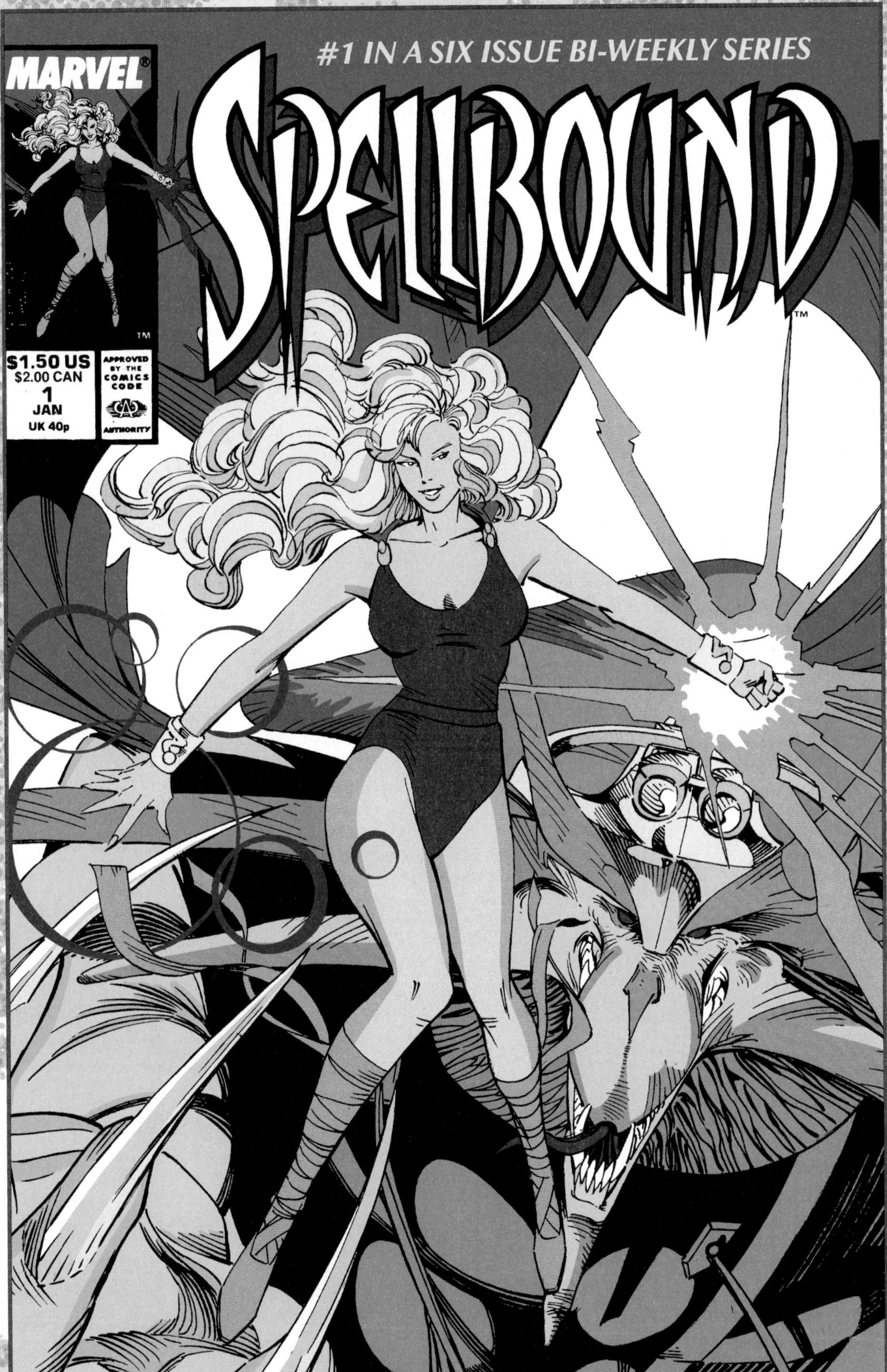
MARVEL
#1 IN A SIX ISSUE BI-WEEKLY SERIES
SPELLBOUND
$1.50 US
$2.00 CAN
1
JAN
UK 40p
APPROVED BY THE COMICS CODE AUTHORITY

SPELLBOUND #1, published in September 1987, introduced the telekinetic heroine in a limited series.

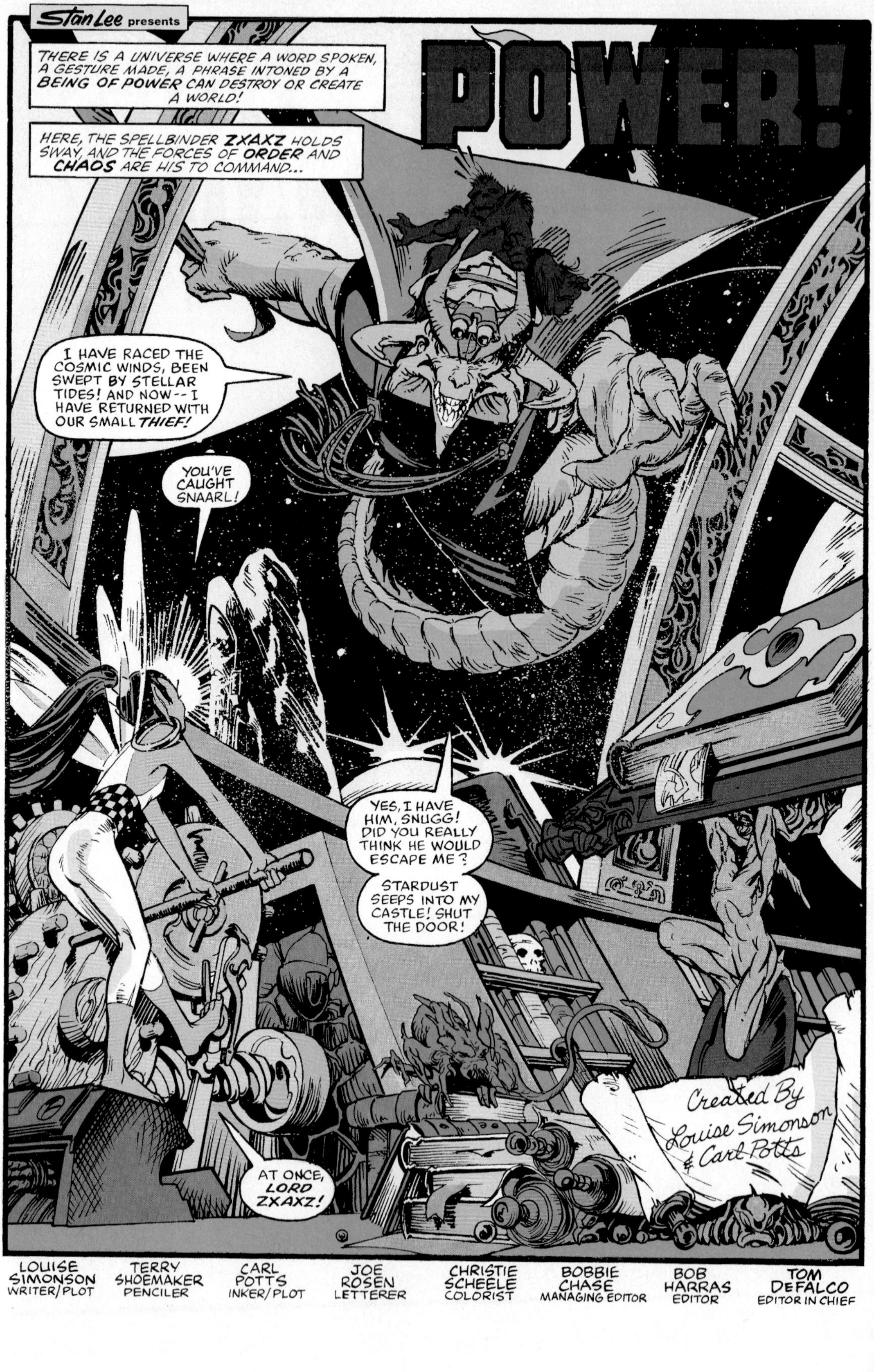
Stan Lee presents
POWER!
THERE IS A UNIVERSE WHERE A WORD SPOKEN, A GESTURE MADE, A PHRASE INTONED BY A BEING OF POWER CAN DESTROY OR CREATE A WORLD!
HERE, THE SPELLBINDER ZXAXZ HOLDS SWAY, AND THE FORCES OF ORDER AND CHAOS ARE HIS TO COMMAND...
I HAVE RACED THE COSMIC WINDS, BEEN SWEPT BY STELLAR TIDES! AND NOW-- I HAVE RETURNED WITH OUR SMALL THIEF!
YOU'VE CAUGHT SNAARL!
YES, I HAVE HIM, SNUGG! DID YOU REALLY THINK HE WOULD ESCAPE ME?
STARDUST SEEPS INTO MY CASTLE! SHUT THE DOOR!
AT ONCE, LORD ZXAXZ!
Created By Louise Simonson & Carl Potts

LOUISE SIMONSON WRITER/PLOT · TERRY SHOEMAKER PENCILER · CARL POTTS INKER/PLOT · JOE ROSEN LETTERER · CHRISTIE SCHEELE COLORIST · BOBBIE CHASE MANAGING EDITOR · BOB HARRAS EDITOR · TOM DEFALCO EDITOR IN CHIEF

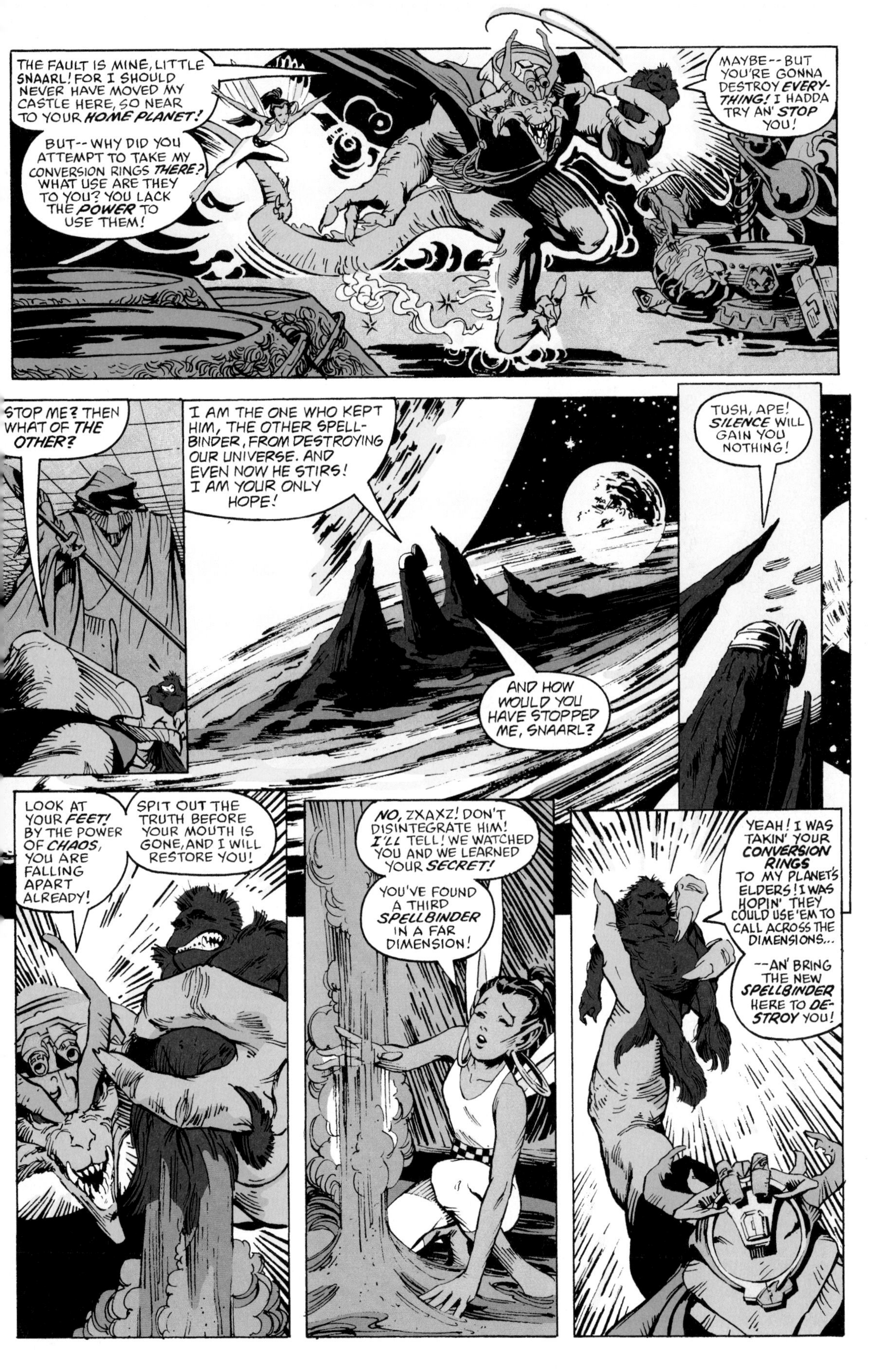
THE FAULT IS MINE, LITTLE SNAARL! FOR I SHOULD NEVER HAVE MOVED MY CASTLE HERE, SO NEAR TO YOUR HOME PLANET!
BUT-- WHY DID YOU ATTEMPT TO TAKE MY CONVERSION RINGS THERE? WHAT USE ARE THEY TO YOU? YOU LACK THE POWER TO USE THEM!
MAYBE-- BUT YOU'RE GONNA DESTROY EVERY-THING! I HADDA TRY AN' STOP YOU!
STOP ME? THEN WHAT OF THE OTHER?
I AM THE ONE WHO KEPT HIM, THE OTHER SPELL-BINDER, FROM DESTROYING OUR UNIVERSE. AND EVEN NOW HE STIRS! I AM YOUR ONLY HOPE!
AND HOW WOULD YOU HAVE STOPPED ME, SNAARL?
TUSH, APE! SILENCE WILL GAIN YOU NOTHING!
LOOK AT YOUR FEET! BY THE POWER OF CHAOS, YOU ARE FALLING APART ALREADY!
SPIT OUT THE TRUTH BEFORE YOUR MOUTH IS GONE, AND I WILL RESTORE YOU!
NO, ZXAXZ! DON'T DISINTEGRATE HIM! I'LL TELL! WE WATCHED YOU AND WE LEARNED YOUR SECRET!
YOU'VE FOUND A THIRD SPELLBINDER IN A FAR DIMENSION!
YEAH! I WAS TAKIN' YOUR CONVERSION RINGS TO MY PLANET'S ELDERS! I WAS HOPIN' THEY COULD USE 'EM TO CALL ACROSS THE DIMENSIONS...
--AN' BRING THE NEW SPELLBINDER HERE TO DE-STROY YOU!

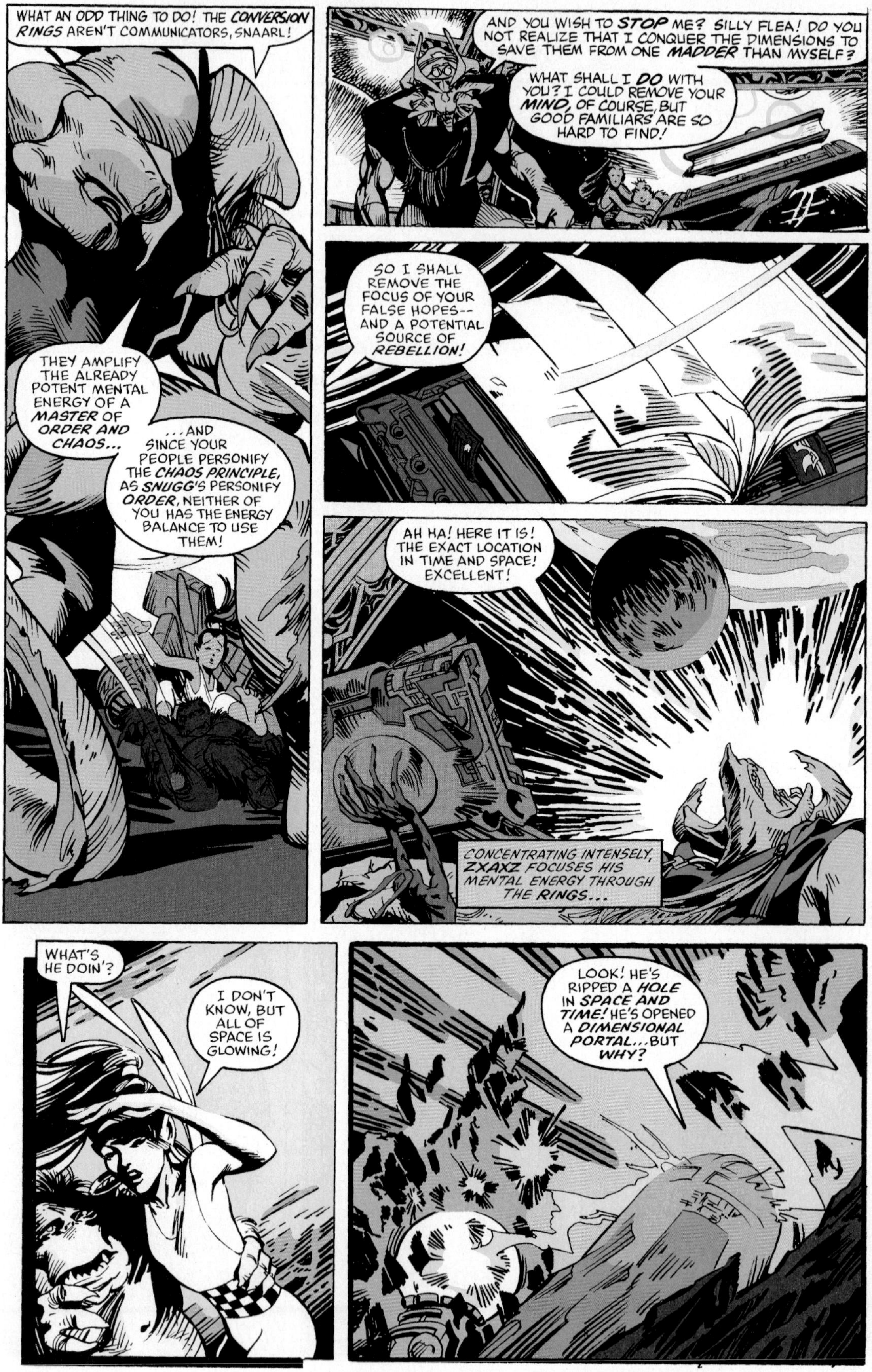
WHAT AN ODD THING TO DO! THE CONVERSION RINGS AREN'T COMMUNICATORS, SNAARL!
THEY AMPLIFY THE ALREADY POTENT MENTAL ENERGY OF A MASTER OF ORDER AND CHAOS...
...AND SINCE YOUR PEOPLE PERSONIFY THE CHAOS PRINCIPLE, AS SNUGG'S PERSONIFY ORDER, NEITHER OF YOU HAS THE ENERGY BALANCE TO USE THEM!
AND YOU WISH TO STOP ME? SILLY FLEA! DO YOU NOT REALIZE THAT I CONQUER THE DIMENSIONS TO SAVE THEM FROM ONE MADDER THAN MYSELF?
WHAT SHALL I DO WITH YOU? I COULD REMOVE YOUR MIND, OF COURSE, BUT GOOD FAMILIARS ARE SO HARD TO FIND!
SO I SHALL REMOVE THE FOCUS OF YOUR FALSE HOPES-- AND A POTENTIAL SOURCE OF REBELLION!
AH HA! HERE IT IS! THE EXACT LOCATION IN TIME AND SPACE! EXCELLENT!
CONCENTRATING INTENSELY, ZXAXZ FOCUSES HIS MENTAL ENERGY THROUGH THE RINGS...
WHAT'S HE DOIN'?
I DON'T KNOW, BUT ALL OF SPACE IS GLOWING!
LOOK! HE'S RIPPED A HOLE IN SPACE AND TIME! HE'S OPENED A DIMENSIONAL PORTAL... BUT WHY?

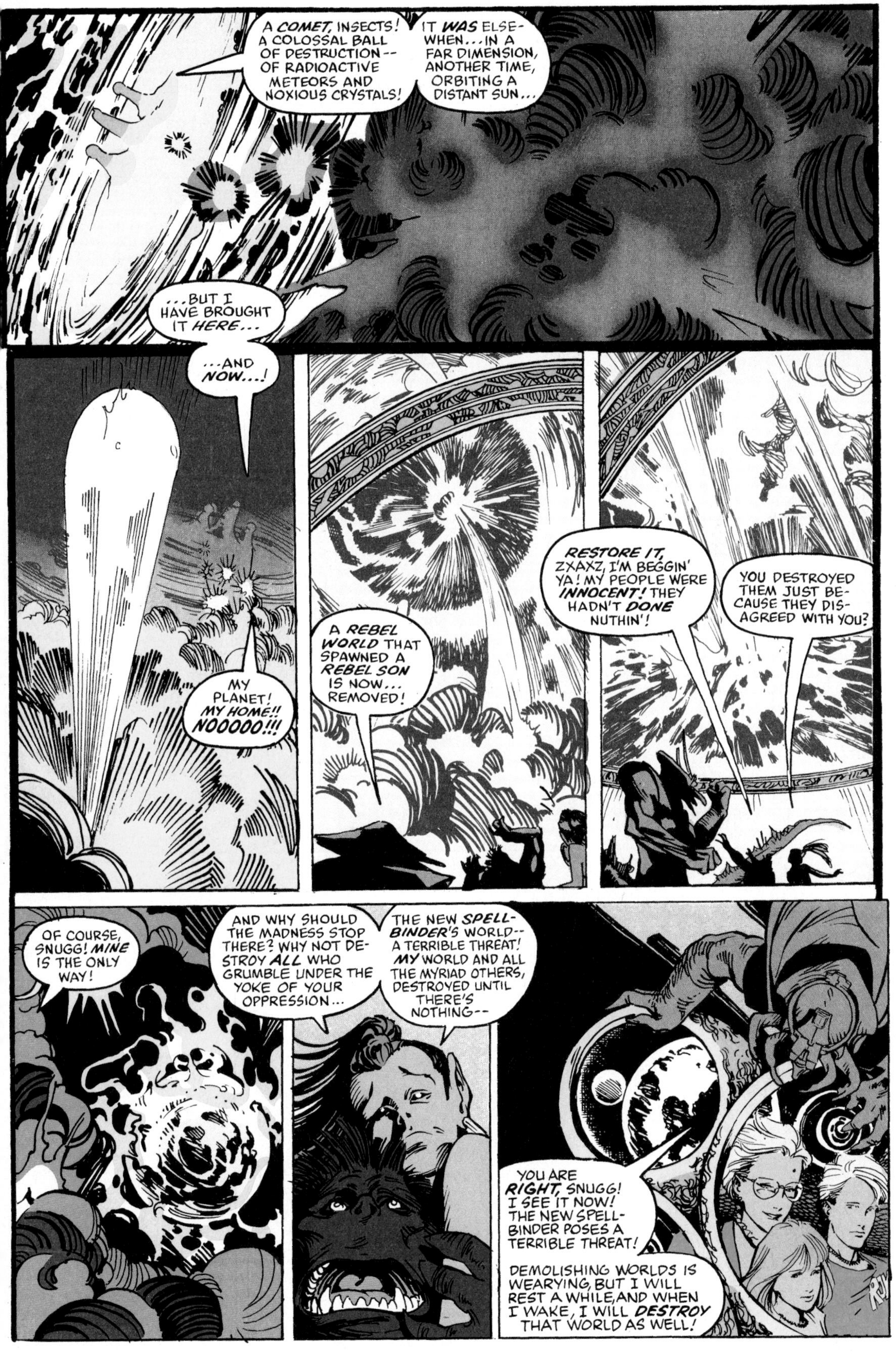
A COMET, INSECTS! A COLOSSAL BALL OF DESTRUCTION -- OF RADIOACTIVE METEORS AND NOXIOUS CRYSTALS!
IT WAS ELSEWHEN... IN A FAR DIMENSION, ANOTHER TIME, ORBITING A DISTANT SUN...
...BUT I HAVE BROUGHT IT HERE...
...AND NOW...!
MY PLANET! MY HOME!! NOOOOO!!!
A REBEL WORLD THAT SPAWNED A REBEL SON IS NOW... REMOVED!
RESTORE IT, ZXAXZ, I'M BEGGIN' YA! MY PEOPLE WERE INNOCENT! THEY HADN'T DONE NUTHIN'!
YOU DESTROYED THEM JUST BECAUSE THEY DISAGREED WITH YOU?
OF COURSE, SNUGG! MINE IS THE ONLY WAY!
AND WHY SHOULD THE MADNESS STOP THERE? WHY NOT DESTROY ALL WHO GRUMBLE UNDER THE YOKE OF YOUR OPPRESSION...
THE NEW SPELLBINDER'S WORLD-- A TERRIBLE THREAT! MY WORLD AND ALL THE MYRIAD OTHERS, DESTROYED UNTIL THERE'S NOTHING--
YOU ARE RIGHT, SNUGG! I SEE IT NOW! THE NEW SPELLBINDER POSES A TERRIBLE THREAT!
DEMOLISHING WORLDS IS WEARYING, BUT I WILL REST A WHILE, AND WHEN I WAKE, I WILL DESTROY THAT WORLD AS WELL!

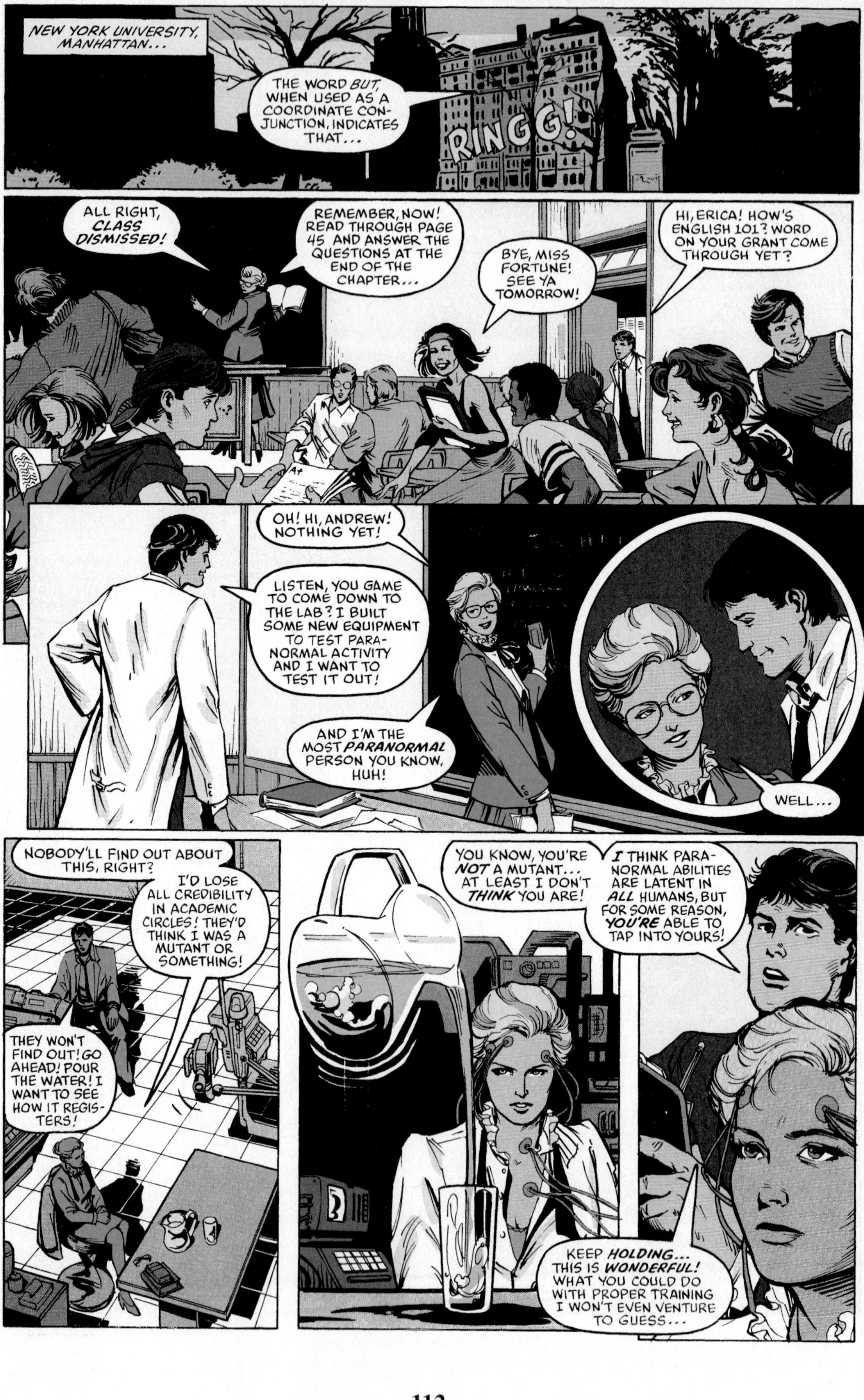
NEW YORK UNIVERSITY, MANHATTAN...
THE WORD *BUT*, WHEN USED AS A COORDINATE CONJUNCTION, INDICATES THAT...
RINGG!
ALL RIGHT, *CLASS DISMISSED!*
REMEMBER, NOW! READ THROUGH PAGE 45 AND ANSWER THE QUESTIONS AT THE END OF THE CHAPTER...
BYE, MISS FORTUNE! SEE YA TOMORROW!
HI, ERICA! HOW'S ENGLISH 101? WORD ON YOUR GRANT COME THROUGH YET?
OH! HI, ANDREW! NOTHING YET!
LISTEN, YOU GAME TO COME DOWN TO THE LAB? I BUILT SOME NEW EQUIPMENT TO TEST PARANORMAL ACTIVITY AND I WANT TO TEST IT OUT!
AND I'M THE MOST *PARANORMAL* PERSON YOU KNOW, HUH!
WELL...
NOBODY'LL FIND OUT ABOUT THIS, RIGHT?
I'D LOSE ALL CREDIBILITY IN ACADEMIC CIRCLES! THEY'D THINK I WAS A MUTANT OR SOMETHING!
THEY WON'T FIND OUT! GO AHEAD! POUR THE WATER! I WANT TO SEE HOW IT REGISTERS!
YOU KNOW, YOU'RE *NOT* A MUTANT... AT LEAST I DON'T *THINK* YOU ARE!
I THINK PARANORMAL ABILITIES ARE LATENT IN *ALL* HUMANS, BUT FOR SOME REASON, *YOU'RE* ABLE TO TAP INTO YOURS!
KEEP *HOLDING*... THIS IS *WONDERFUL!* WHAT YOU COULD DO WITH PROPER TRAINING I WON'T EVEN VENTURE TO GUESS...

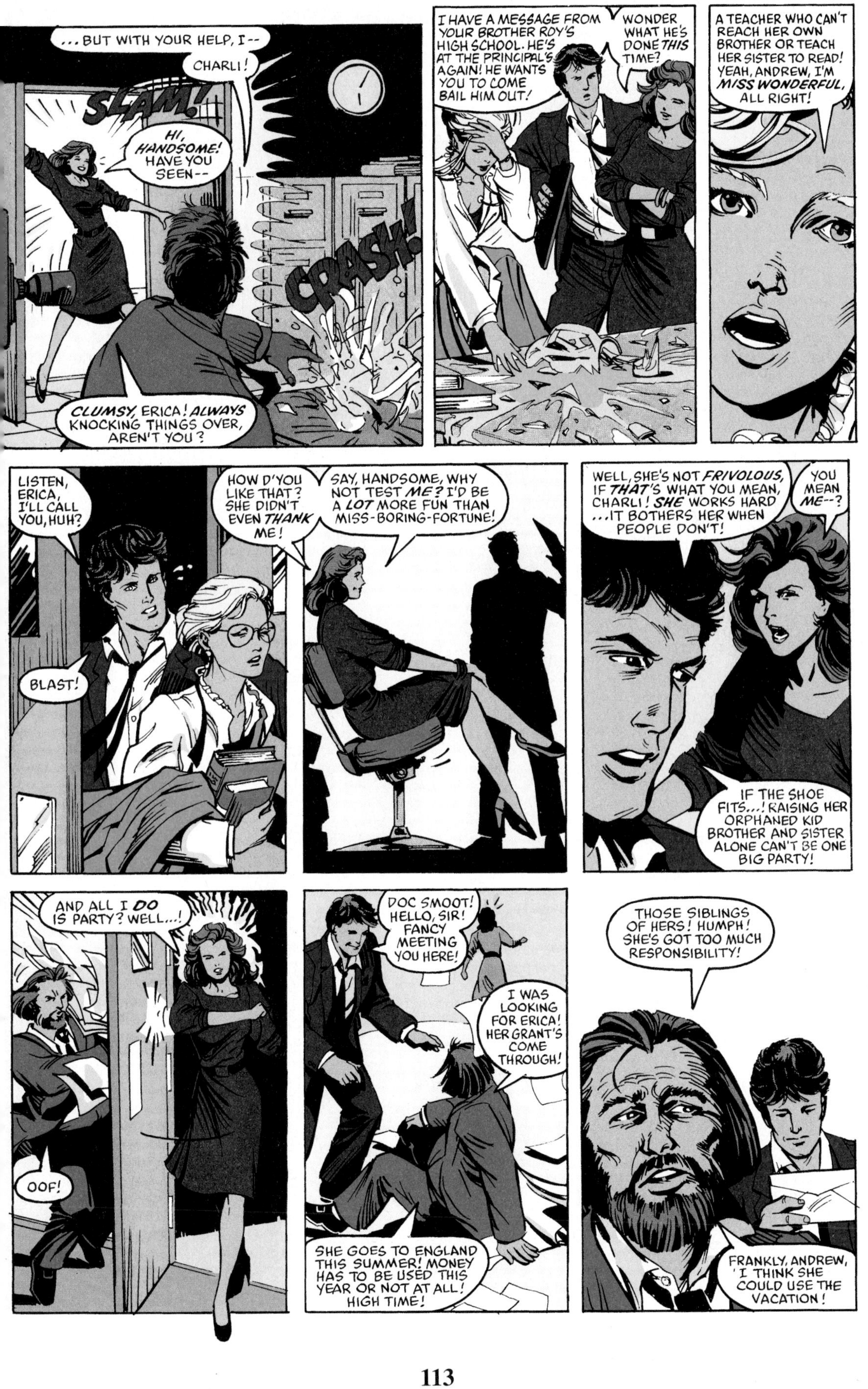
...BUT WITH YOUR HELP, I--
CHARLI!
SLAM!
HI, HANDSOME! HAVE YOU SEEN--
CRASH!
CLUMSY, ERICA! ALWAYS KNOCKING THINGS OVER, AREN'T YOU?
I HAVE A MESSAGE FROM YOUR BROTHER ROY'S HIGH SCHOOL. HE'S AT THE PRINCIPAL'S AGAIN! HE WANTS YOU TO COME BAIL HIM OUT!
WONDER WHAT HE'S DONE THIS TIME?
A TEACHER WHO CAN'T REACH HER OWN BROTHER OR TEACH HER SISTER TO READ! YEAH, ANDREW, I'M MISS WONDERFUL, ALL RIGHT!
LISTEN, ERICA, I'LL CALL YOU, HUH?
BLAST!
HOW D'YOU LIKE THAT? SHE DIDN'T EVEN THANK ME!
SAY, HANDSOME, WHY NOT TEST ME? I'D BE A LOT MORE FUN THAN MISS-BORING-FORTUNE!
WELL, SHE'S NOT FRIVOLOUS, IF THAT'S WHAT YOU MEAN, CHARLI! SHE WORKS HARD ...IT BOTHERS HER WHEN PEOPLE DON'T!
YOU MEAN ME--?
IF THE SHOE FITS...! RAISING HER ORPHANED KID BROTHER AND SISTER ALONE CAN'T BE ONE BIG PARTY!
AND ALL I DO IS PARTY? WELL...!
OOF!
DOC SMOOT! HELLO, SIR! FANCY MEETING YOU HERE!
I WAS LOOKING FOR ERICA! HER GRANT'S COME THROUGH!
SHE GOES TO ENGLAND THIS SUMMER! MONEY HAS TO BE USED THIS YEAR OR NOT AT ALL! HIGH TIME!
THOSE SIBLINGS OF HERS! HUMPH! SHE'S GOT TOO MUCH RESPONSIBILITY!
FRANKLY, ANDREW, I THINK SHE COULD USE THE VACATION!

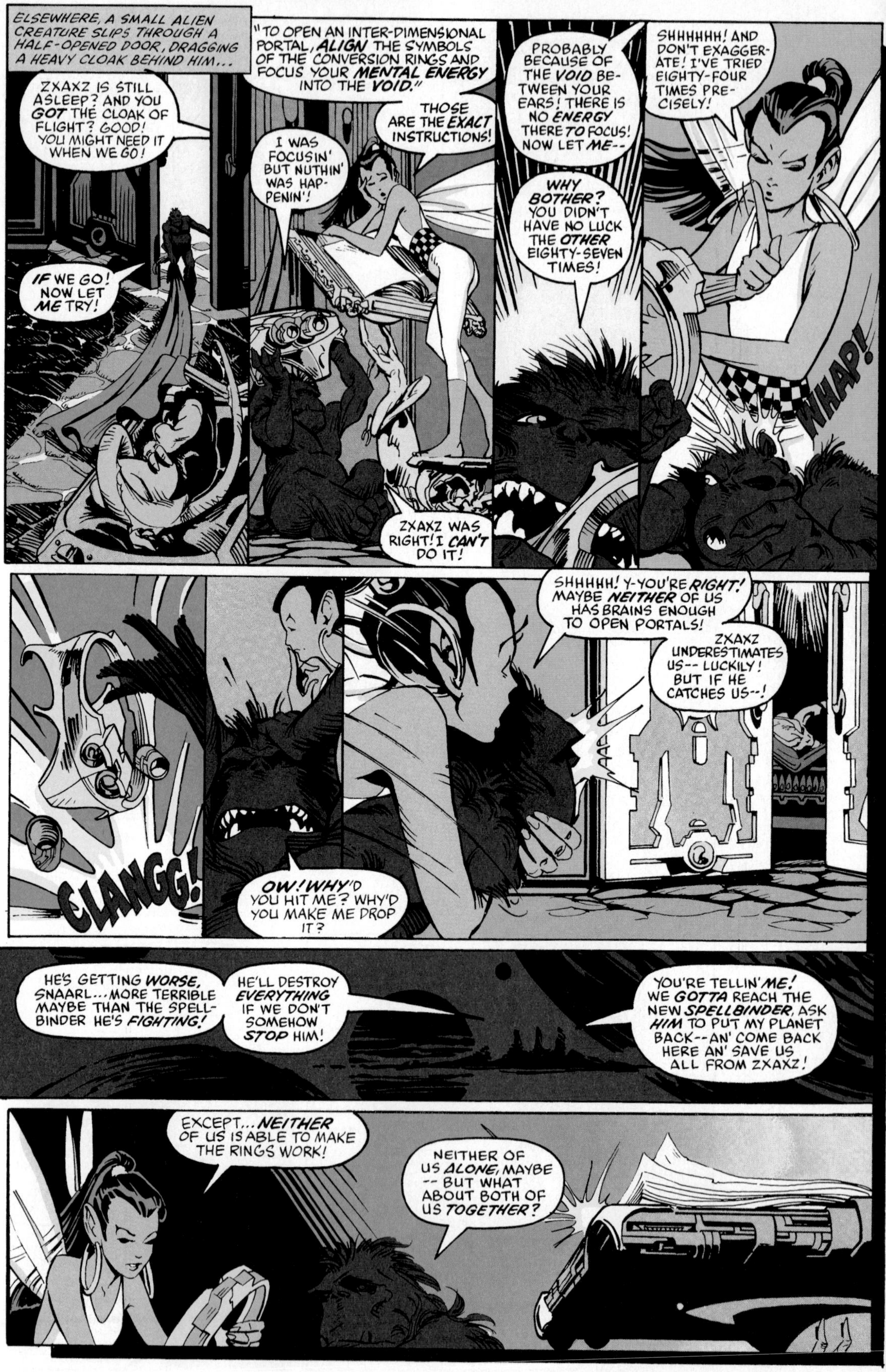
ELSEWHERE, A SMALL ALIEN CREATURE SLIPS THROUGH A HALF-OPENED DOOR, DRAGGING A HEAVY CLOAK BEHIND HIM...
ZXAXZ IS STILL ASLEEP? AND YOU GOT THE CLOAK OF FLIGHT? GOOD! YOU MIGHT NEED IT WHEN WE GO!
IF WE GO! NOW LET ME TRY!
"TO OPEN AN INTER-DIMENSIONAL PORTAL, ALIGN THE SYMBOLS OF THE CONVERSION RINGS AND FOCUS YOUR MENTAL ENERGY INTO THE VOID."
THOSE ARE THE EXACT INSTRUCTIONS!
I WAS FOCUSIN' BUT NUTHIN' WAS HAP-PENIN'!
ZXAXZ WAS RIGHT! I CAN'T DO IT!
PROBABLY BECAUSE OF THE VOID BE-TWEEN YOUR EARS! THERE IS NO ENERGY THERE TO FOCUS! NOW LET ME--
WHY BOTHER? YOU DIDN'T HAVE NO LUCK THE OTHER EIGHTY-SEVEN TIMES!
SHHHHHH! AND DON'T EXAGGER-ATE! I'VE TRIED EIGHTY-FOUR TIMES PRE-CISELY!
WHAP!
CLANGG!
OW! WHY'D YOU HIT ME? WHY'D YOU MAKE ME DROP IT?
SHHHHH! Y-YOU'RE RIGHT! MAYBE NEITHER OF US HAS BRAINS ENOUGH TO OPEN PORTALS!
ZXAXZ UNDERESTIMATES US-- LUCKILY! BUT IF HE CATCHES US--!
HE'S GETTING WORSE, SNAARL... MORE TERRIBLE MAYBE THAN THE SPELL-BINDER HE'S FIGHTING!
HE'LL DESTROY EVERYTHING IF WE DON'T SOMEHOW STOP HIM!
YOU'RE TELLIN' ME! WE GOTTA REACH THE NEW SPELLBINDER, ASK HIM TO PUT MY PLANET BACK--AN' COME BACK HERE AN' SAVE US ALL FROM ZXAXZ!
EXCEPT... NEITHER OF US IS ABLE TO MAKE THE RINGS WORK!
NEITHER OF US ALONE, MAYBE -- BUT WHAT ABOUT BOTH OF US TOGETHER?

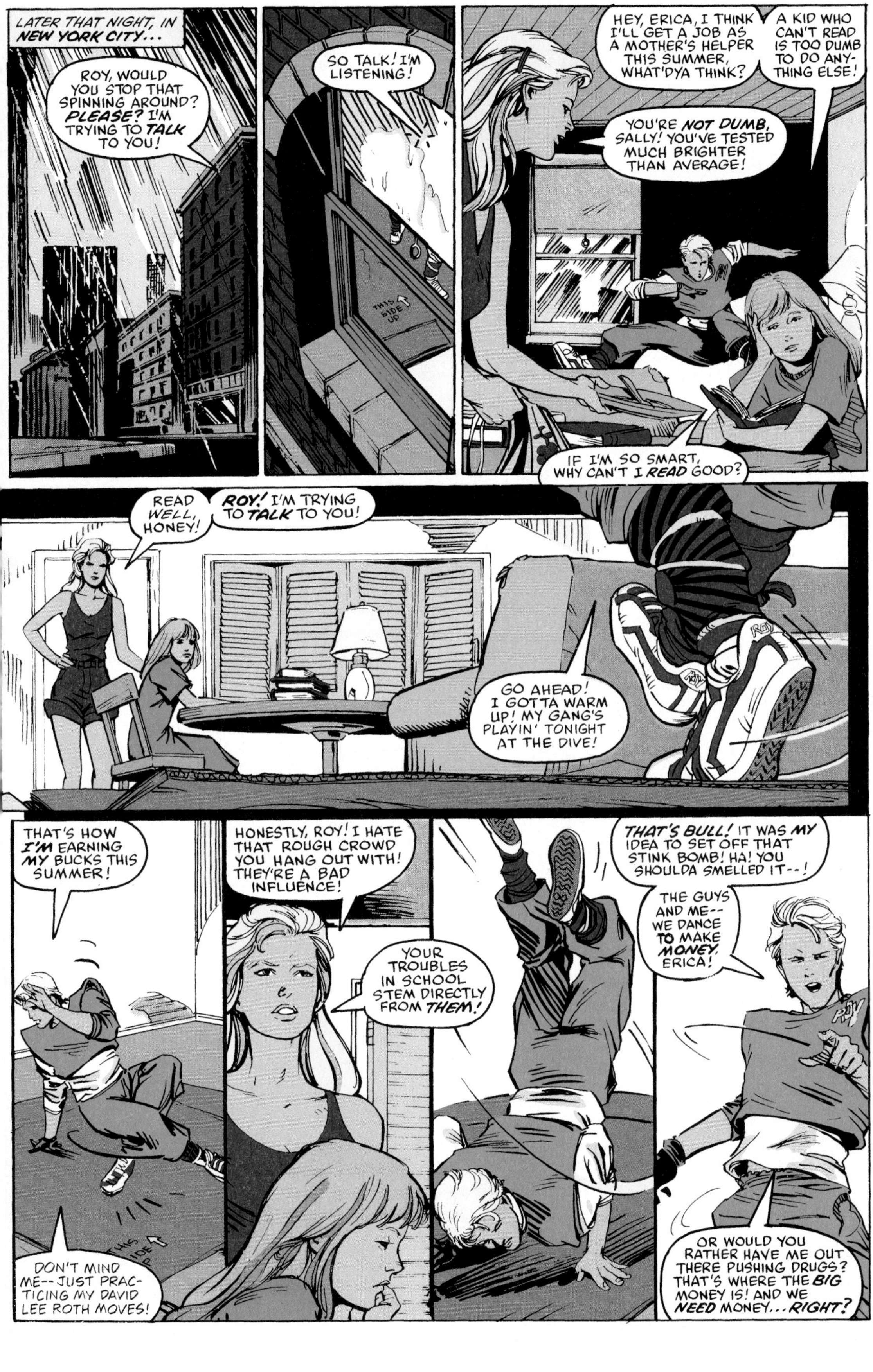
LATER THAT NIGHT, IN NEW YORK CITY...
ROY, WOULD YOU STOP THAT SPINNING AROUND? PLEASE? I'M TRYING TO TALK TO YOU!
SO TALK! I'M LISTENING!
THIS SIDE UP
HEY, ERICA, I THINK I'LL GET A JOB AS A MOTHER'S HELPER THIS SUMMER, WHAT'DYA THINK?
A KID WHO CAN'T READ IS TOO DUMB TO DO ANYTHING ELSE!
YOU'RE NOT DUMB, SALLY! YOU'VE TESTED MUCH BRIGHTER THAN AVERAGE!
IF I'M SO SMART, WHY CAN'T I READ GOOD?
READ WELL, HONEY!
ROY! I'M TRYING TO TALK TO YOU!
GO AHEAD! I GOTTA WARM UP! MY GANG'S PLAYIN' TONIGHT AT THE DIVE!
THAT'S HOW I'M EARNING MY BUCKS THIS SUMMER!
DON'T MIND ME--JUST PRACTICING MY DAVID LEE ROTH MOVES!
HONESTLY, ROY! I HATE THAT ROUGH CROWD YOU HANG OUT WITH! THEY'RE A BAD INFLUENCE!
YOUR TROUBLES IN SCHOOL STEM DIRECTLY FROM THEM!
THAT'S BULL! IT WAS MY IDEA TO SET OFF THAT STINK BOMB! HA! YOU SHOULDA SMELLED IT--!
THE GUYS AND ME--WE DANCE TO MAKE MONEY, ERICA!
OR WOULD YOU RATHER HAVE ME OUT THERE PUSHING DRUGS? THAT'S WHERE THE BIG MONEY IS! AND WE NEED MONEY...RIGHT?

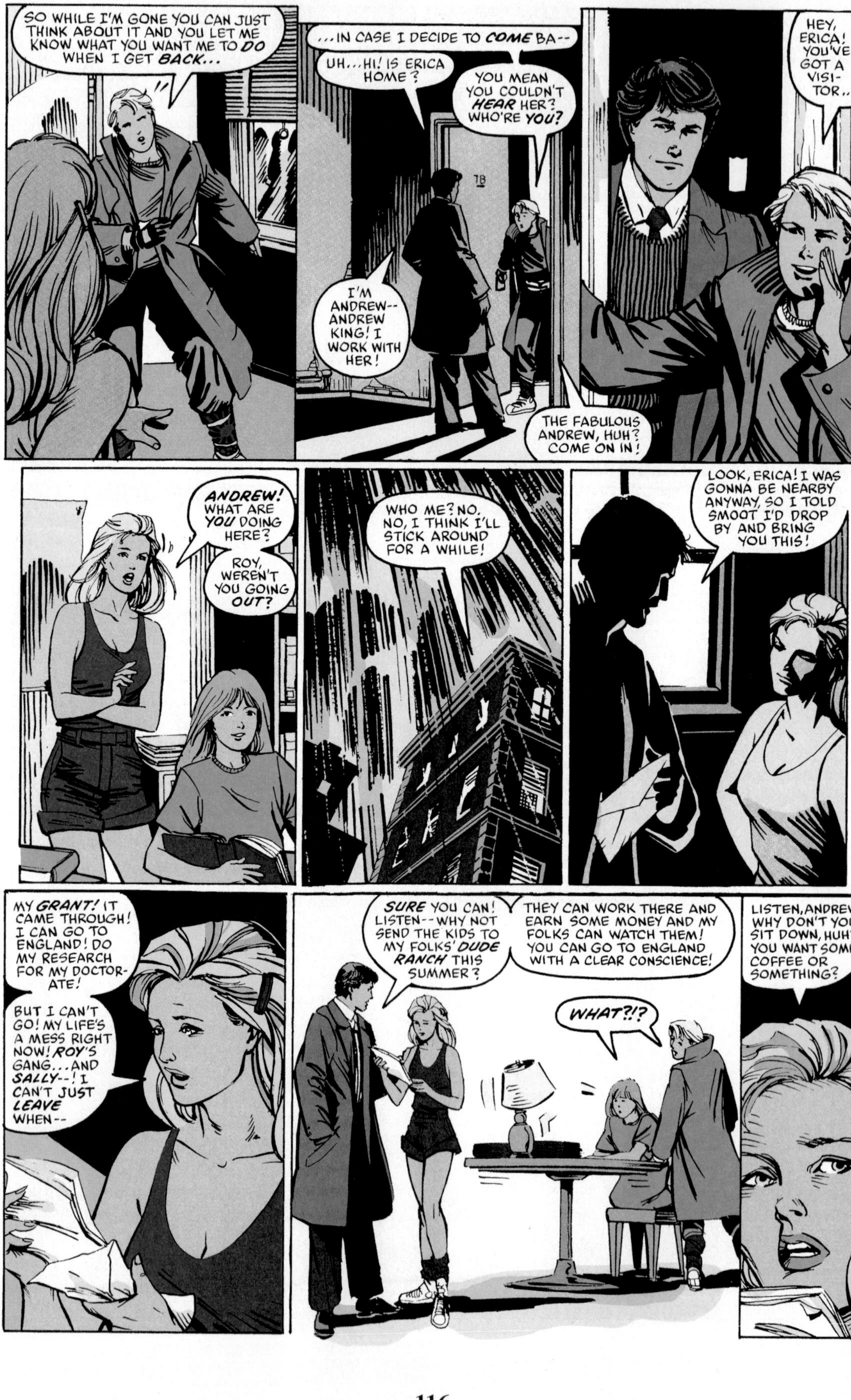
SO WHILE I'M GONE YOU CAN JUST THINK ABOUT IT AND YOU LET ME KNOW WHAT YOU WANT ME TO DO WHEN I GET BACK...
...IN CASE I DECIDE TO COME BA--
UH...HI! IS ERICA HOME?
YOU MEAN YOU COULDN'T HEAR HER? WHO'RE YOU?
I'M ANDREW-- ANDREW KING! I WORK WITH HER!
HEY, ERICA! YOU'VE GOT A VISI- TOR...!
THE FABULOUS ANDREW, HUH? COME ON IN!
ANDREW! WHAT ARE YOU DOING HERE?
ROY, WEREN'T YOU GOING OUT?
WHO ME? NO. NO, I THINK I'LL STICK AROUND FOR A WHILE!
LOOK, ERICA! I WAS GONNA BE NEARBY ANYWAY, SO I TOLD SMOOT I'D DROP BY AND BRING YOU THIS!
MY GRANT! IT CAME THROUGH! I CAN GO TO ENGLAND! DO MY RESEARCH FOR MY DOCTOR- ATE!
BUT I CAN'T GO! MY LIFE'S A MESS RIGHT NOW! ROY'S GANG...AND SALLY--! I CAN'T JUST LEAVE WHEN--
SURE YOU CAN! LISTEN--WHY NOT SEND THE KIDS TO MY FOLKS' DUDE RANCH THIS SUMMER?
THEY CAN WORK THERE AND EARN SOME MONEY AND MY FOLKS CAN WATCH THEM! YOU CAN GO TO ENGLAND WITH A CLEAR CONSCIENCE!
WHAT?!?
LISTEN, ANDREW, WHY DON'T YOU SIT DOWN, HUH? YOU WANT SOME COFFEE OR SOMETHING?

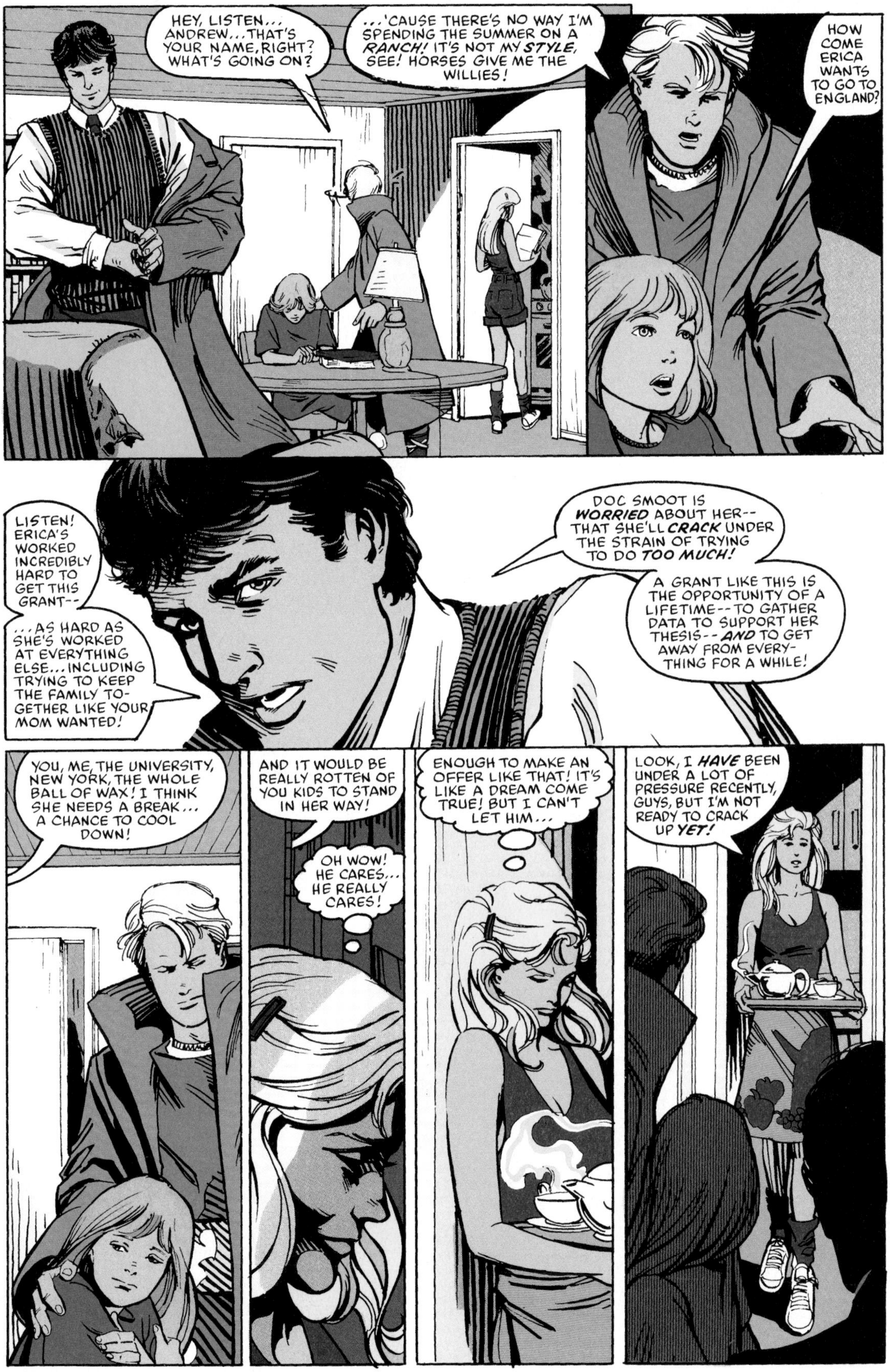
HEY, LISTEN... ANDREW...THAT'S YOUR NAME, RIGHT? WHAT'S GOING ON?
...'CAUSE THERE'S NO WAY I'M SPENDING THE SUMMER ON A RANCH! IT'S NOT MY STYLE, SEE! HORSES GIVE ME THE WILLIES!
HOW COME ERICA WANTS TO GO TO ENGLAND?
LISTEN! ERICA'S WORKED INCREDIBLY HARD TO GET THIS GRANT--
...AS HARD AS SHE'S WORKED AT EVERYTHING ELSE...INCLUDING TRYING TO KEEP THE FAMILY TOGETHER LIKE YOUR MOM WANTED!
DOC SMOOT IS WORRIED ABOUT HER--THAT SHE'LL CRACK UNDER THE STRAIN OF TRYING TO DO TOO MUCH!
A GRANT LIKE THIS IS THE OPPORTUNITY OF A LIFETIME--TO GATHER DATA TO SUPPORT HER THESIS--AND TO GET AWAY FROM EVERYTHING FOR A WHILE!
YOU, ME, THE UNIVERSITY, NEW YORK, THE WHOLE BALL OF WAX! I THINK SHE NEEDS A BREAK... A CHANCE TO COOL DOWN!
AND IT WOULD BE REALLY ROTTEN OF YOU KIDS TO STAND IN HER WAY!
OH WOW! HE CARES... HE REALLY CARES!
ENOUGH TO MAKE AN OFFER LIKE THAT! IT'S LIKE A DREAM COME TRUE! BUT I CAN'T LET HIM...
LOOK, I HAVE BEEN UNDER A LOT OF PRESSURE RECENTLY, GUYS, BUT I'M NOT READY TO CRACK UP YET!

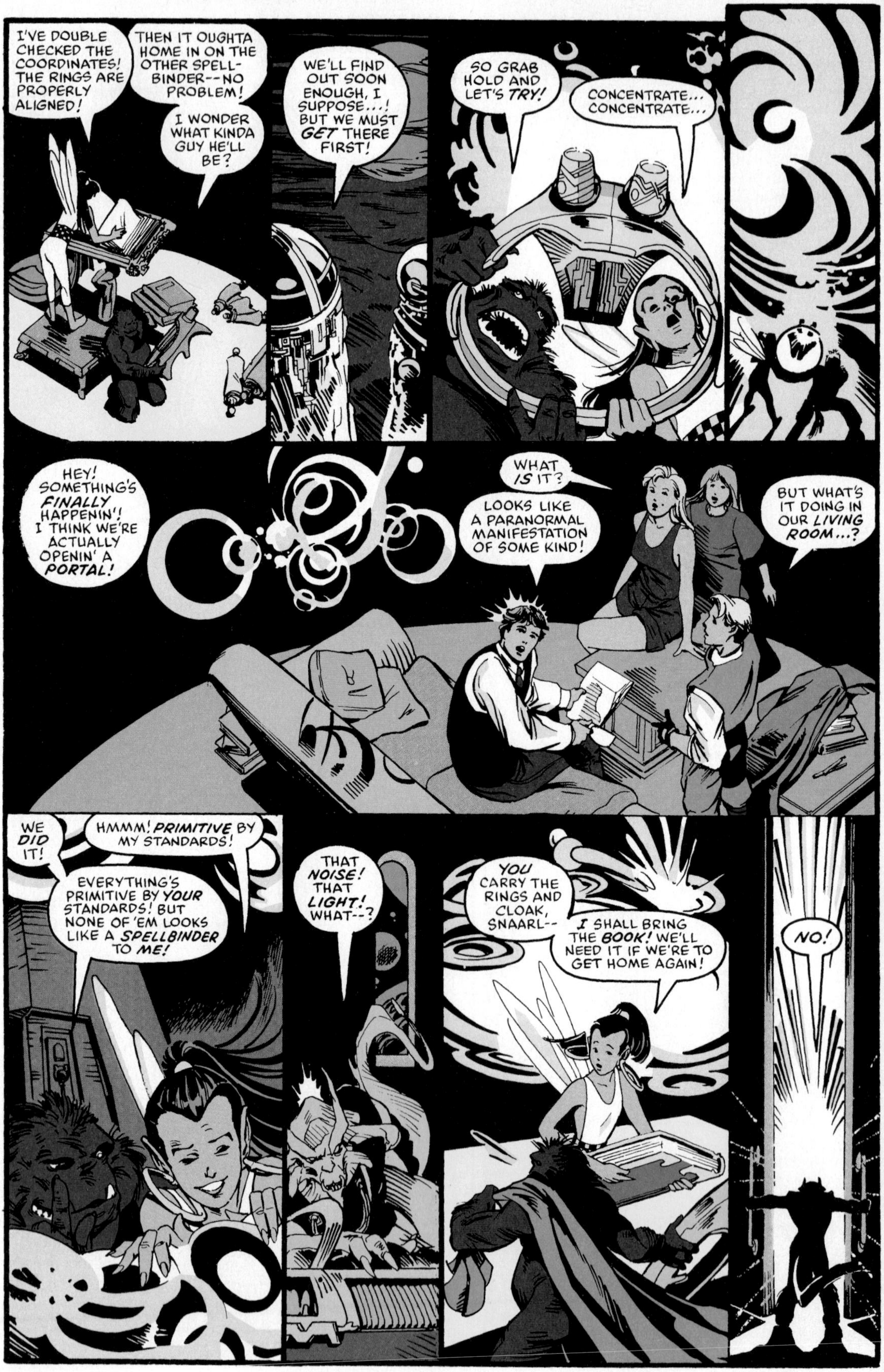
I'VE DOUBLE CHECKED THE COORDINATES! THE RINGS ARE PROPERLY ALIGNED!
THEN IT OUGHTA HOME IN ON THE OTHER SPELL-BINDER--NO PROBLEM!
I WONDER WHAT KINDA GUY HE'LL BE?
WE'LL FIND OUT SOON ENOUGH, I SUPPOSE...! BUT WE MUST GET THERE FIRST!
SO GRAB HOLD AND LET'S TRY!
CONCENTRATE... CONCENTRATE...
HEY! SOMETHING'S FINALLY HAPPENIN'! I THINK WE'RE ACTUALLY OPENIN' A PORTAL!
WHAT IS IT?
LOOKS LIKE A PARANORMAL MANIFESTATION OF SOME KIND!
BUT WHAT'S IT DOING IN OUR LIVING ROOM...?
WE DID IT!
HMMM! PRIMITIVE BY MY STANDARDS!
EVERYTHING'S PRIMITIVE BY YOUR STANDARDS! BUT NONE OF 'EM LOOKS LIKE A SPELLBINDER TO ME!
THAT NOISE! THAT LIGHT! WHAT--?
YOU CARRY THE RINGS AND CLOAK, SNAARL--
I SHALL BRING THE BOOK! WE'LL NEED IT IF WE'RE TO GET HOME AGAIN!
NO!

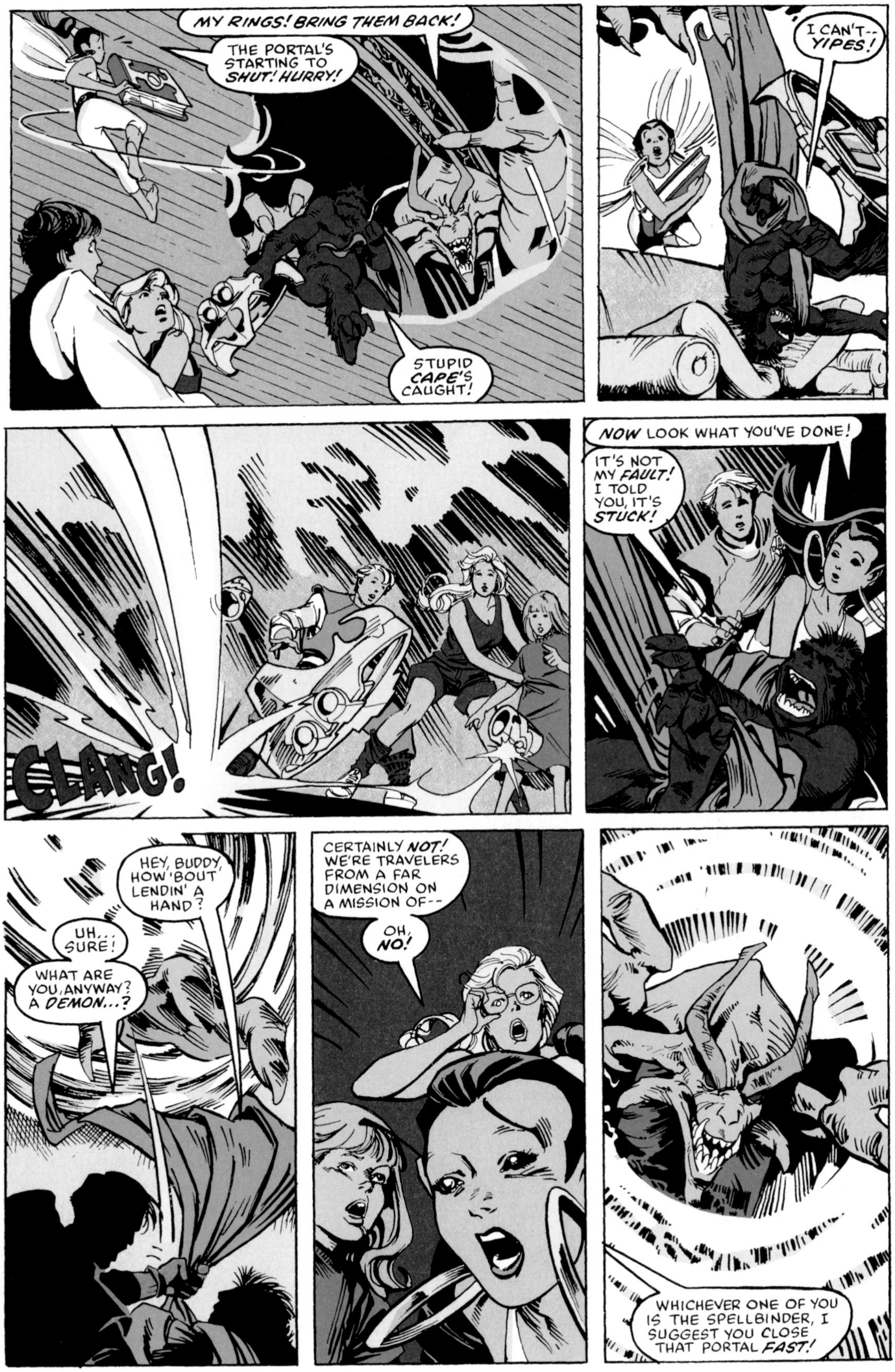
MY RINGS! BRING THEM BACK!
THE PORTAL'S STARTING TO SHUT! HURRY!
STUPID CAPE'S CAUGHT!
I CAN'T-- YIPES!
CLANG!
NOW LOOK WHAT YOU'VE DONE!
IT'S NOT MY FAULT! I TOLD YOU, IT'S STUCK!
HEY, BUDDY, HOW 'BOUT LENDIN' A HAND?
UH... SURE!
WHAT ARE YOU, ANYWAY? A DEMON...?
CERTAINLY NOT! WE'RE TRAVELERS FROM A FAR DIMENSION ON A MISSION OF--
OH, NO!
WHICHEVER ONE OF YOU IS THE SPELLBINDER, I SUGGEST YOU CLOSE THAT PORTAL FAST!

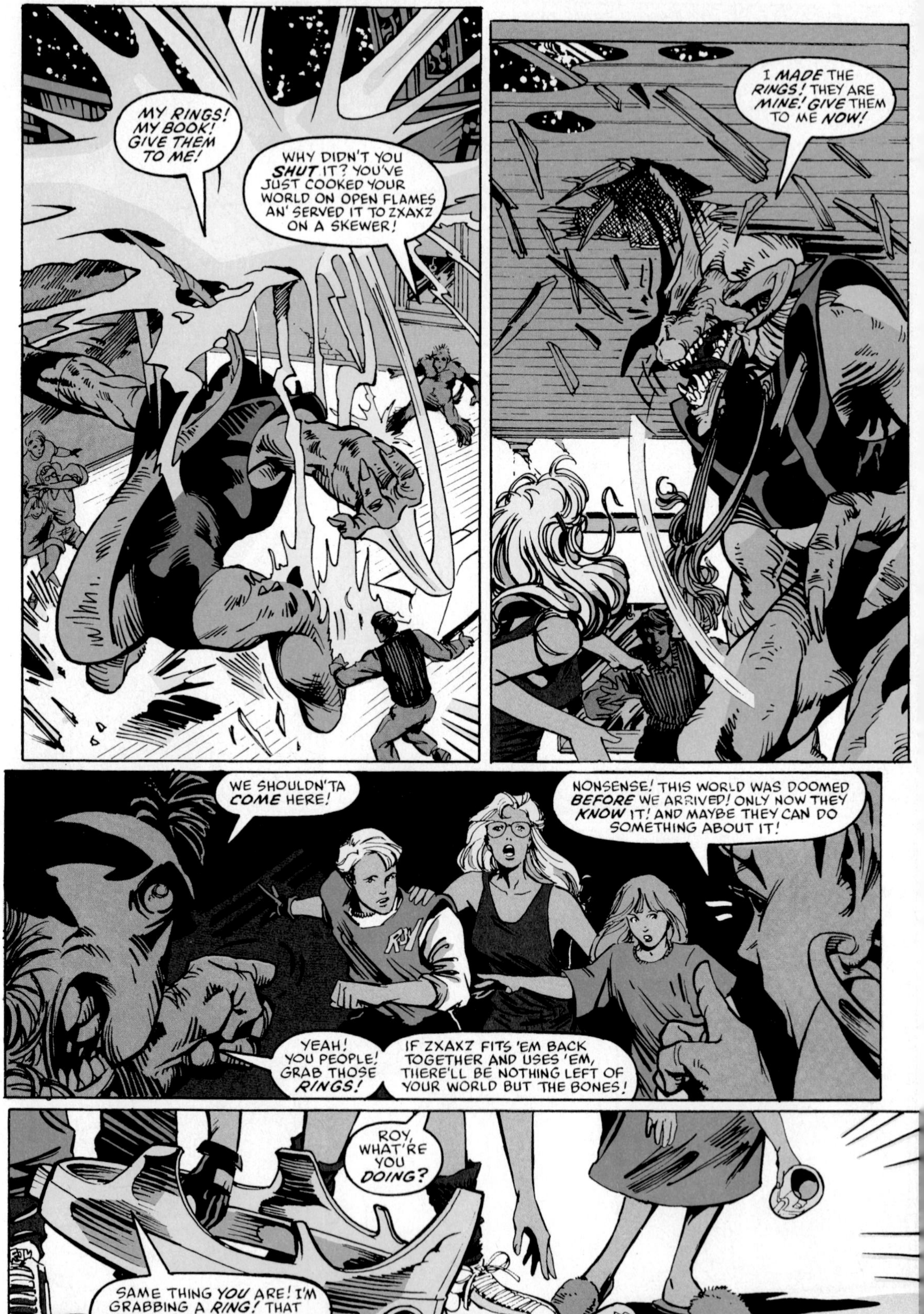
MY RINGS! MY BOOK! GIVE THEM TO ME!
WHY DIDN'T YOU SHUT IT? YOU'VE JUST COOKED YOUR WORLD ON OPEN FLAMES AN' SERVED IT TO ZXAXZ ON A SKEWER!
I MADE THE RINGS! THEY ARE MINE! GIVE THEM TO ME NOW!
WE SHOULDN'TA COME HERE!
NONSENSE! THIS WORLD WAS DOOMED BEFORE WE ARRIVED! ONLY NOW THEY KNOW IT! AND MAYBE THEY CAN DO SOMETHING ABOUT IT!
YEAH! YOU PEOPLE! GRAB THOSE RINGS!
IF ZXAXZ FITS 'EM BACK TOGETHER AND USES 'EM, THERE'LL BE NOTHING LEFT OF YOUR WORLD BUT THE BONES!
ROY, WHAT'RE YOU DOING?
SAME THING YOU ARE! I'M GRABBING A RING! THAT BIG GUY ZXAXZ LOOKS CRAZED ENOUGH TO DO ANYTHING!

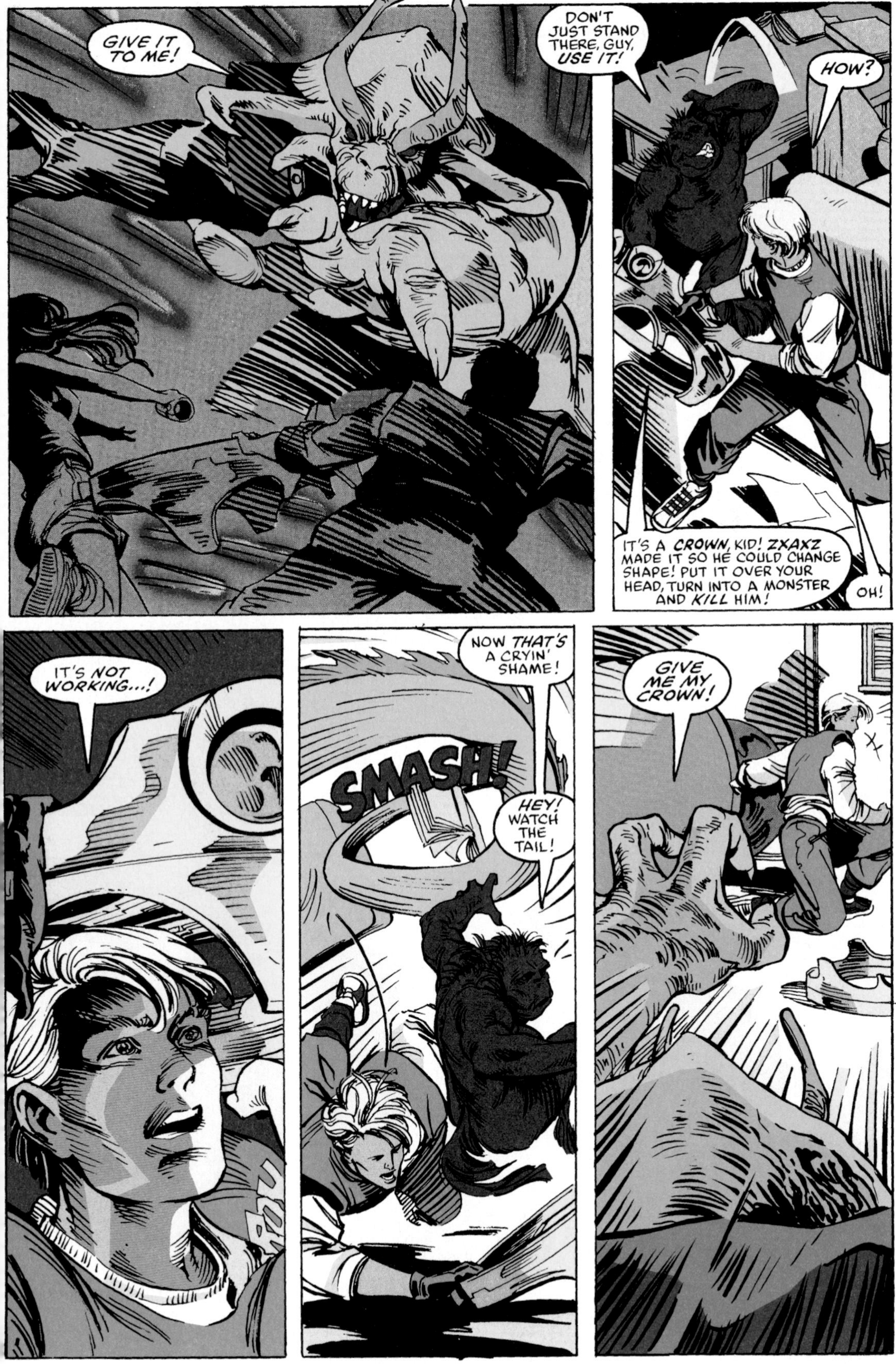
GIVE IT TO ME!
DON'T JUST STAND THERE, GUY, USE IT!
HOW?
IT'S A CROWN, KID! ZXAXZ MADE IT SO HE COULD CHANGE SHAPE! PUT IT OVER YOUR HEAD, TURN INTO A MONSTER AND KILL HIM!
OH!
IT'S NOT WORKING...!
NOW THAT'S A CRYIN' SHAME!
SMASH!
HEY! WATCH THE TAIL!
GIVE ME MY CROWN!

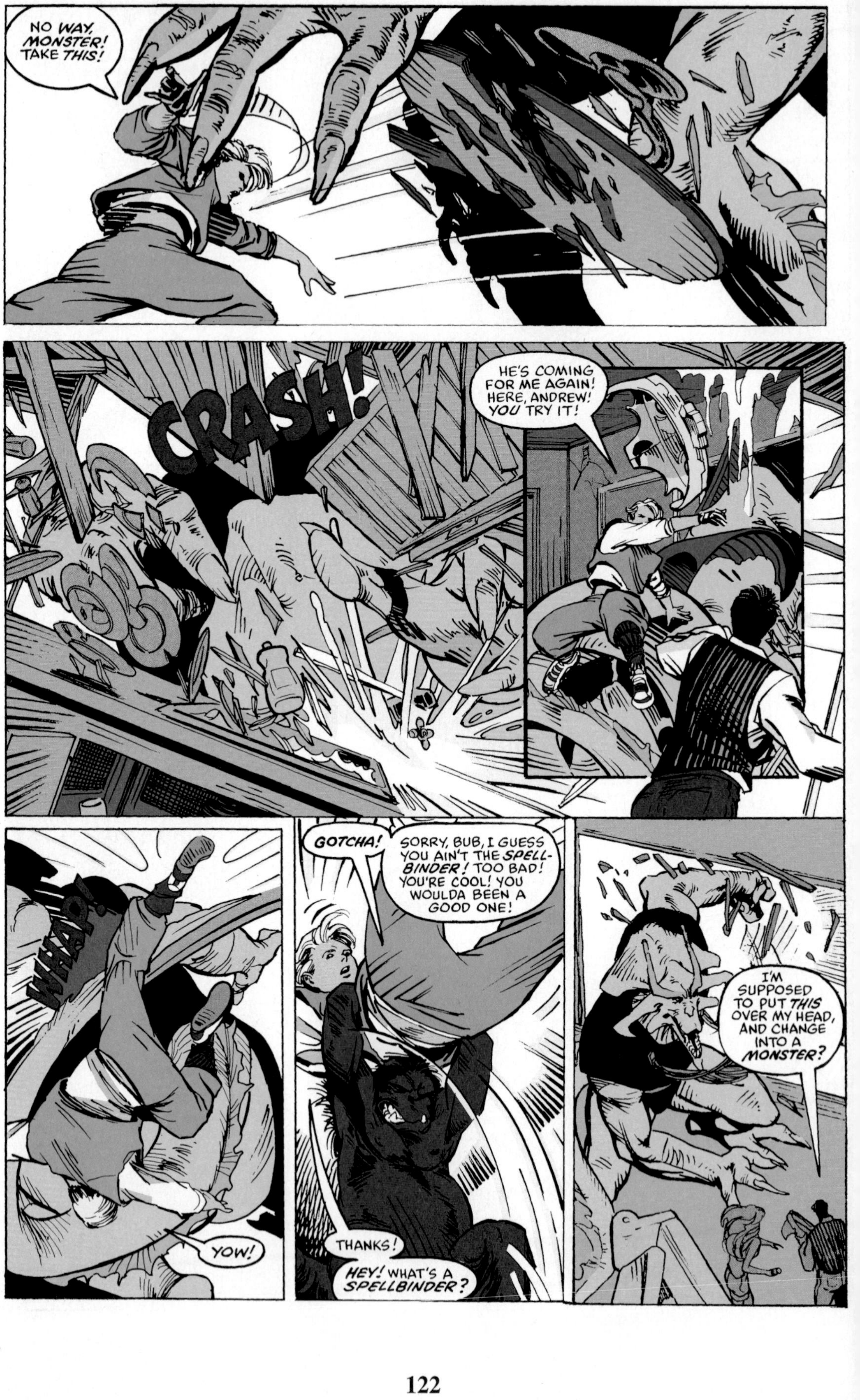
NO WAY, MONSTER! TAKE THIS!
CRASH!
HE'S COMING FOR ME AGAIN! HERE, ANDREW! YOU TRY IT!
WHAP!
YOW!
GOTCHA!
SORRY, BUB, I GUESS YOU AIN'T THE SPELL-BINDER! TOO BAD! YOU'RE COOL! YOU WOULDA BEEN A GOOD ONE!
THANKS!
HEY! WHAT'S A SPELLBINDER?
I'M SUPPOSED TO PUT THIS OVER MY HEAD, AND CHANGE INTO A MONSTER?

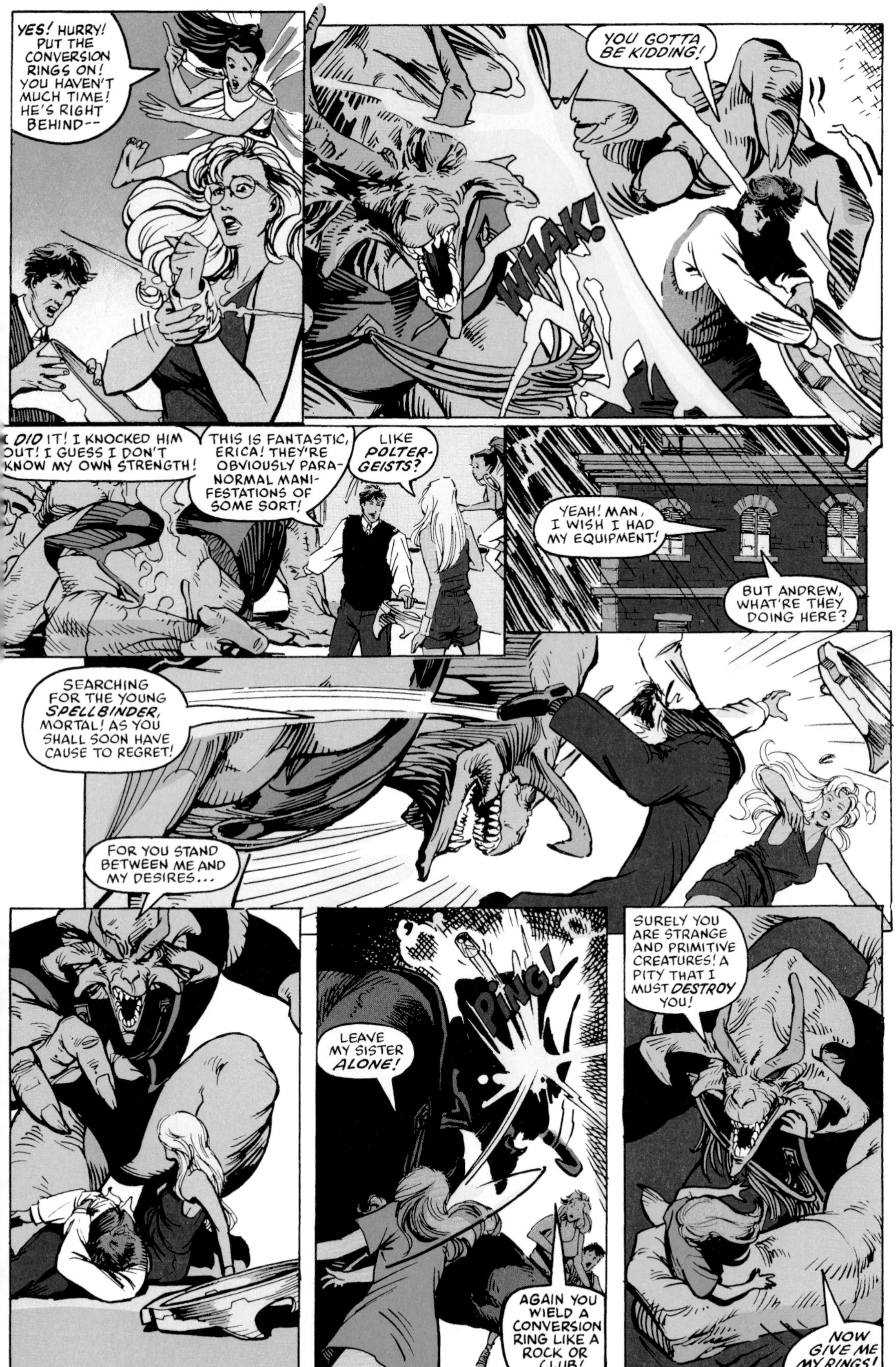

YES! HURRY! PUT THE CONVERSION RINGS ON! YOU HAVEN'T MUCH TIME! HE'S RIGHT BEHIND--
YOU GOTTA BE KIDDING!
WHAK!
I DID IT! I KNOCKED HIM OUT! I GUESS I DON'T KNOW MY OWN STRENGTH!
THIS IS FANTASTIC, ERICA! THEY'RE OBVIOUSLY PARA-NORMAL MANI-FESTATIONS OF SOME SORT!
LIKE POLTER-GEISTS?
YEAH! MAN, I WISH I HAD MY EQUIPMENT!
BUT ANDREW, WHAT'RE THEY DOING HERE?
SEARCHING FOR THE YOUNG SPELLBINDER, MORTAL! AS YOU SHALL SOON HAVE CAUSE TO REGRET!
FOR YOU STAND BETWEEN ME AND MY DESIRES...
LEAVE MY SISTER ALONE!
PING!
AGAIN YOU WIELD A CONVERSION RING LIKE A ROCK OR CLUB!
SURELY YOU ARE STRANGE AND PRIMITIVE CREATURES! A PITY THAT I MUST DESTROY YOU!
NOW GIVE ME MY RINGS!

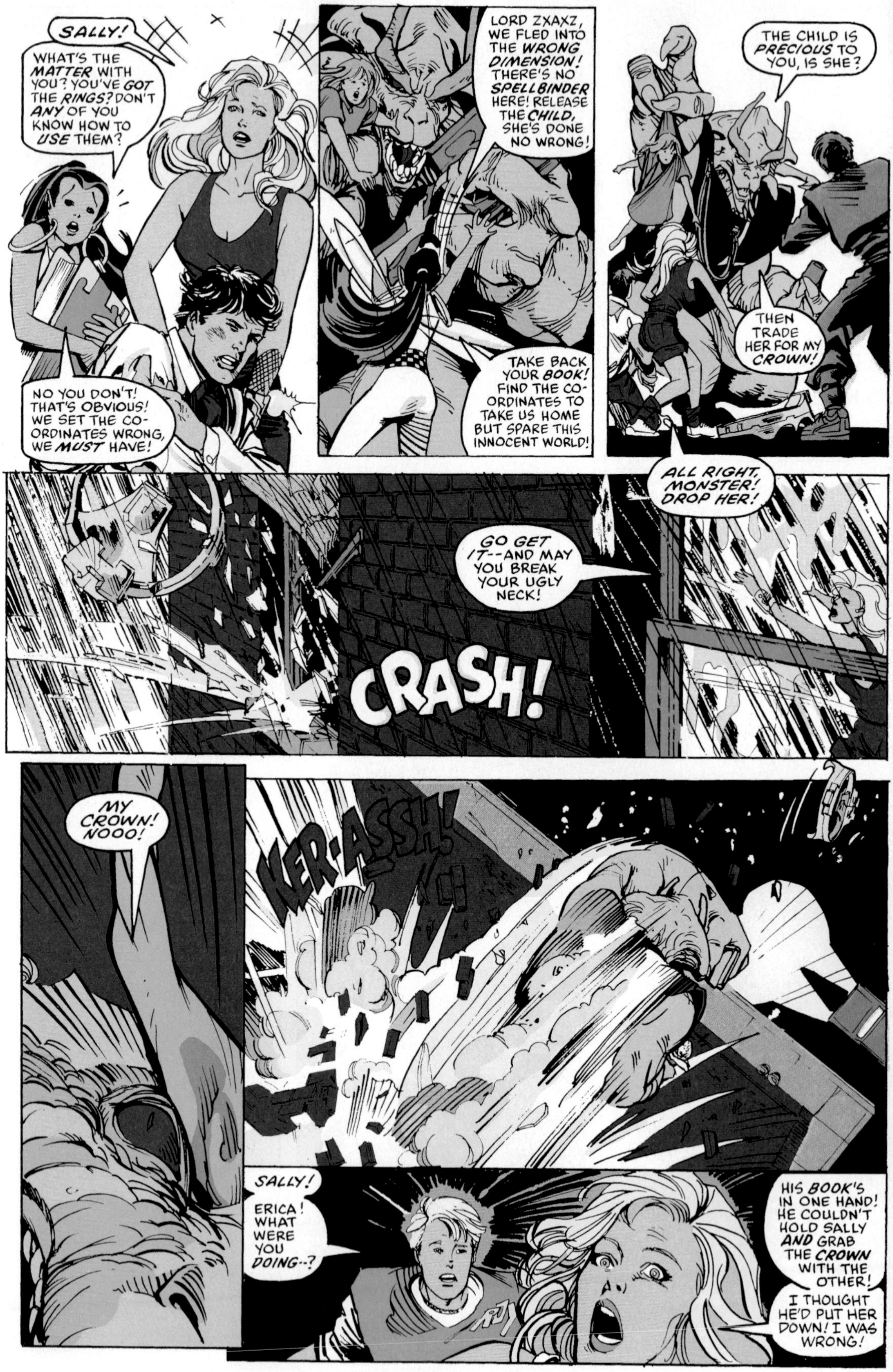
SALLY!
WHAT'S THE MATTER WITH YOU? YOU'VE GOT THE RINGS? DON'T ANY OF YOU KNOW HOW TO USE THEM?
NO YOU DON'T! THAT'S OBVIOUS! WE SET THE CO-ORDINATES WRONG, WE MUST HAVE!
LORD ZXAXZ, WE FLED INTO THE WRONG DIMENSION! THERE'S NO SPELLBINDER HERE! RELEASE THE CHILD, SHE'S DONE NO WRONG!
TAKE BACK YOUR BOOK! FIND THE CO-ORDINATES TO TAKE US HOME BUT SPARE THIS INNOCENT WORLD!
THE CHILD IS PRECIOUS TO YOU, IS SHE?
THEN TRADE HER FOR MY CROWN!
ALL RIGHT, MONSTER! DROP HER!
GO GET IT--AND MAY YOU BREAK YOUR UGLY NECK!
CRASH!
MY CROWN! NOOO!
KER-ASSH!
SALLY!
ERICA! WHAT WERE YOU DOING--?
HIS BOOK'S IN ONE HAND! HE COULDN'T HOLD SALLY AND GRAB THE CROWN WITH THE OTHER!
I THOUGHT HE'D PUT HER DOWN! I WAS WRONG!

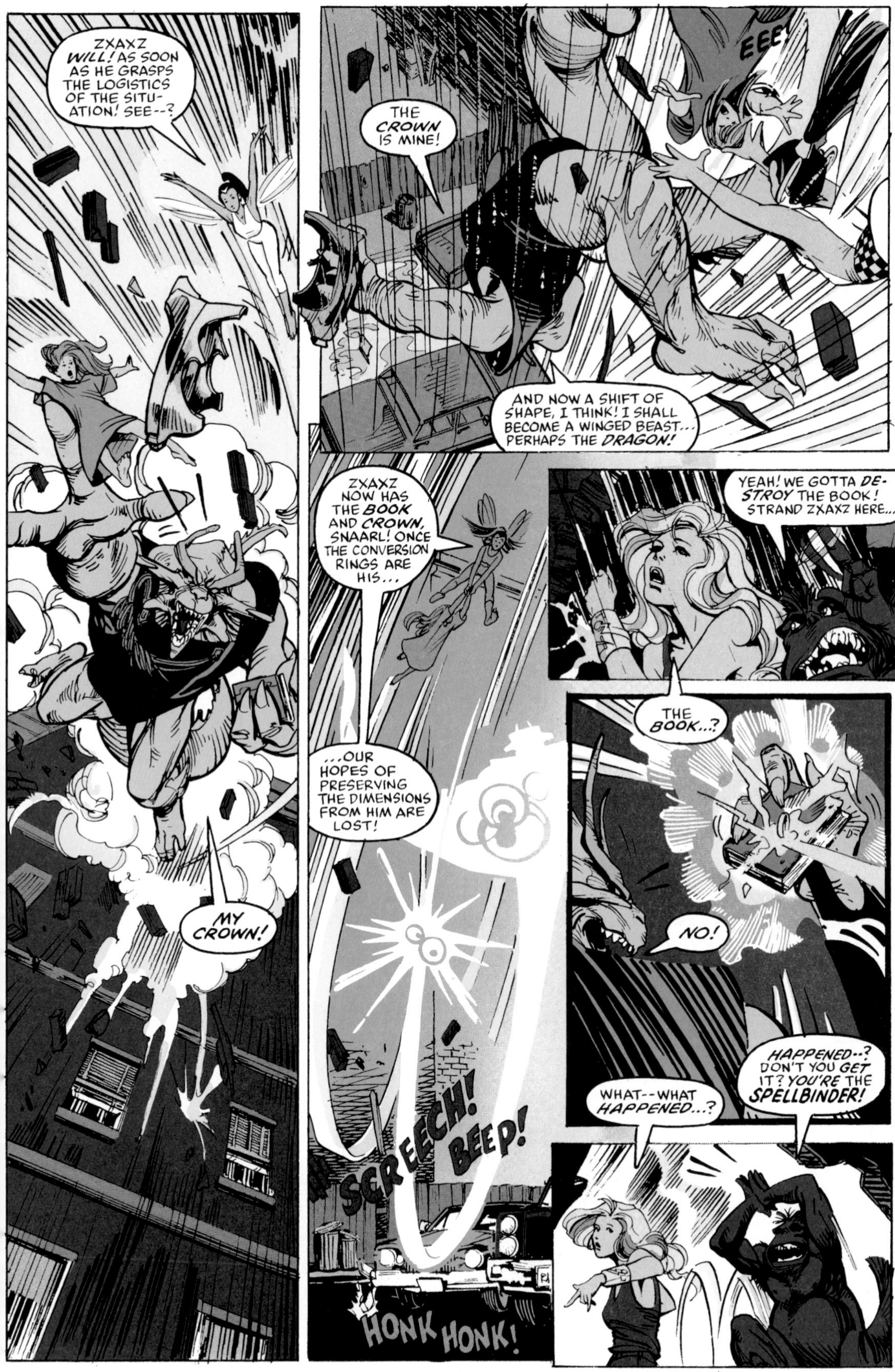
ZXAXZ *WILL!* AS SOON AS HE GRASPS THE LOGISTICS OF THE SITUATION! SEE--?
MY CROWN!
EEE
THE *CROWN* IS MINE!
AND NOW A SHIFT OF SHAPE, I THINK! I SHALL BECOME A WINGED BEAST... PERHAPS THE *DRAGON!*
ZXAXZ NOW HAS THE *BOOK* AND *CROWN,* SNAARL! ONCE THE CONVERSION RINGS ARE HIS...
...OUR HOPES OF PRESERVING THE DIMENSIONS FROM HIM ARE LOST!
SCREECH! BEEP!
HONK HONK!
YEAH! WE GOTTA *DESTROY* THE BOOK! STRAND ZXAXZ HERE...!
THE *BOOK*...?
NO!
WHAT--WHAT *HAPPENED*...?
HAPPENED..? DON'T YOU *GET* IT? YOU'RE THE *SPELLBINDER!*

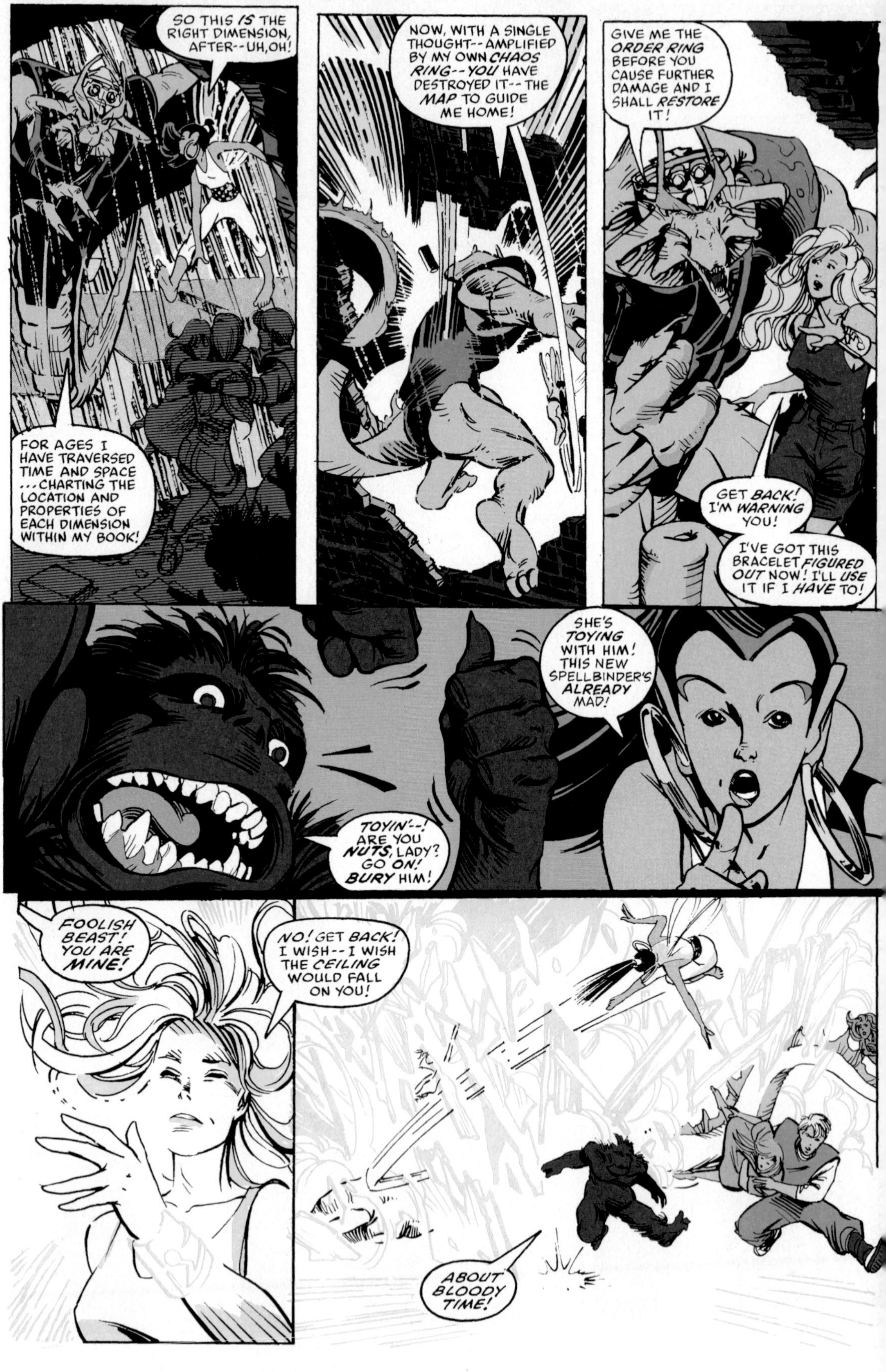
SO THIS *IS* THE RIGHT DIMENSION, AFTER--UH,OH!
FOR AGES I HAVE TRAVERSED TIME AND SPACE ...CHARTING THE LOCATION AND PROPERTIES OF EACH DIMENSION WITHIN MY BOOK!
NOW, WITH A SINGLE THOUGHT--AMPLIFIED BY MY OWN *CHAOS RING--YOU* HAVE DESTROYED IT--THE *MAP* TO GUIDE ME HOME!
GIVE ME THE *ORDER RING* BEFORE YOU CAUSE FURTHER DAMAGE AND I SHALL *RESTORE* IT!
GET *BACK!* I'M *WARNING* YOU!
I'VE GOT THIS BRACELET *FIGURED OUT* NOW! I'LL *USE* IT IF I *HAVE* TO!
SHE'S *TOYING* WITH HIM! THIS NEW SPELLBINDER'S *ALREADY* MAD!
TOYIN'--! ARE YOU **NUTS**, LADY? GO *ON!* **BURY** HIM!
FOOLISH BEAST! YOU ARE MINE!
NO! GET *BACK!* I WISH--I WISH THE *CEILING* WOULD FALL ON YOU!
ABOUT BLOODY TIME!

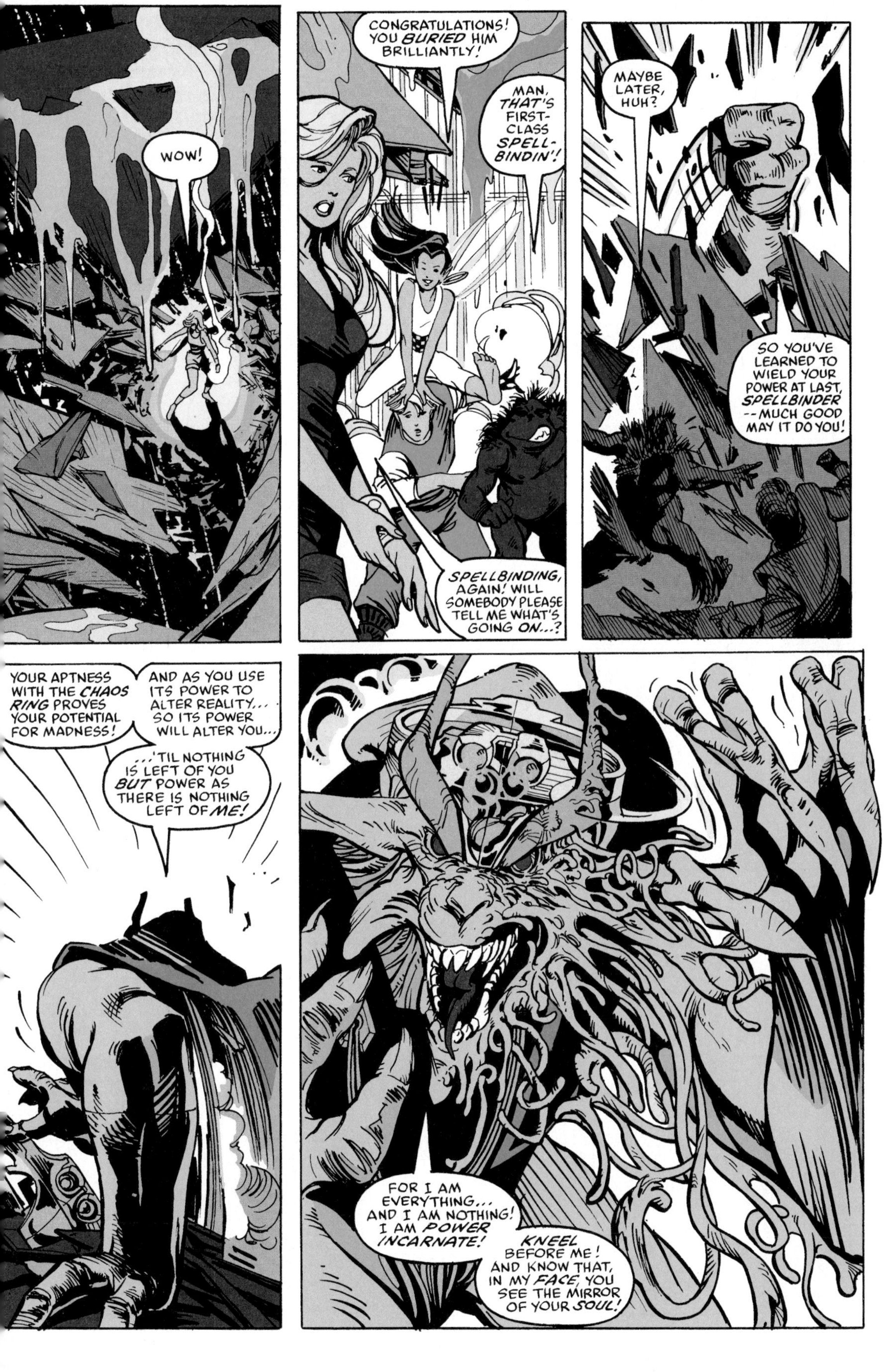
WOW!
CONGRATULATIONS! YOU *BURIED* HIM BRILLIANTLY!
MAN, *THAT'S* FIRST-CLASS *SPELL-BINDIN'!*
SPELLBINDING, AGAIN! WILL SOMEBODY PLEASE TELL ME WHAT'S GOING *ON*...?
MAYBE LATER, HUH?
SO YOU'VE LEARNED TO WIELD YOUR POWER AT LAST, *SPELLBINDER* --MUCH GOOD MAY IT DO YOU!
YOUR APTNESS WITH THE *CHAOS RING* PROVES YOUR POTENTIAL FOR MADNESS!
AND AS YOU USE ITS POWER TO ALTER REALITY... SO ITS POWER WILL ALTER YOU...
...'TIL NOTHING IS LEFT OF YOU *BUT* POWER AS THERE IS NOTHING LEFT OF *ME!*
FOR I AM EVERYTHING... AND I AM NOTHING! I AM *POWER INCARNATE!*
KNEEL BEFORE ME! AND KNOW THAT, IN MY *FACE,* YOU SEE THE MIRROR OF YOUR *SOUL!*

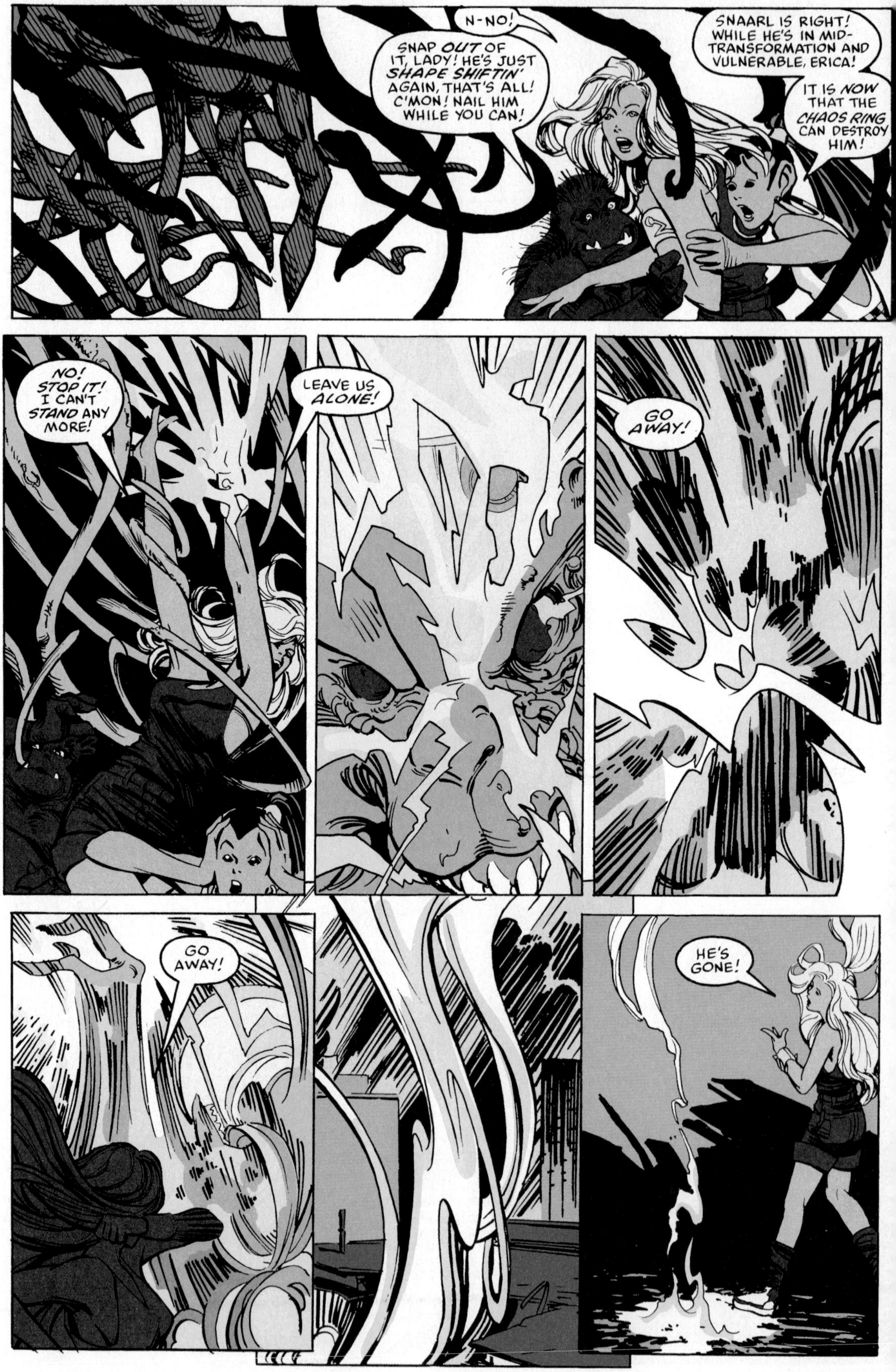
N-NO!
SNAP OUT OF IT, LADY! HE'S JUST SHAPE SHIFTIN' AGAIN, THAT'S ALL! C'MON! NAIL HIM WHILE YOU CAN!
SNAARL IS RIGHT! WHILE HE'S IN MID-TRANSFORMATION AND VULNERABLE, ERICA!
IT IS NOW THAT THE CHAOS RING CAN DESTROY HIM!
NO! STOP IT! I CAN'T STAND ANY MORE!
LEAVE US ALONE!
GO AWAY!
GO AWAY!
HE'S GONE!

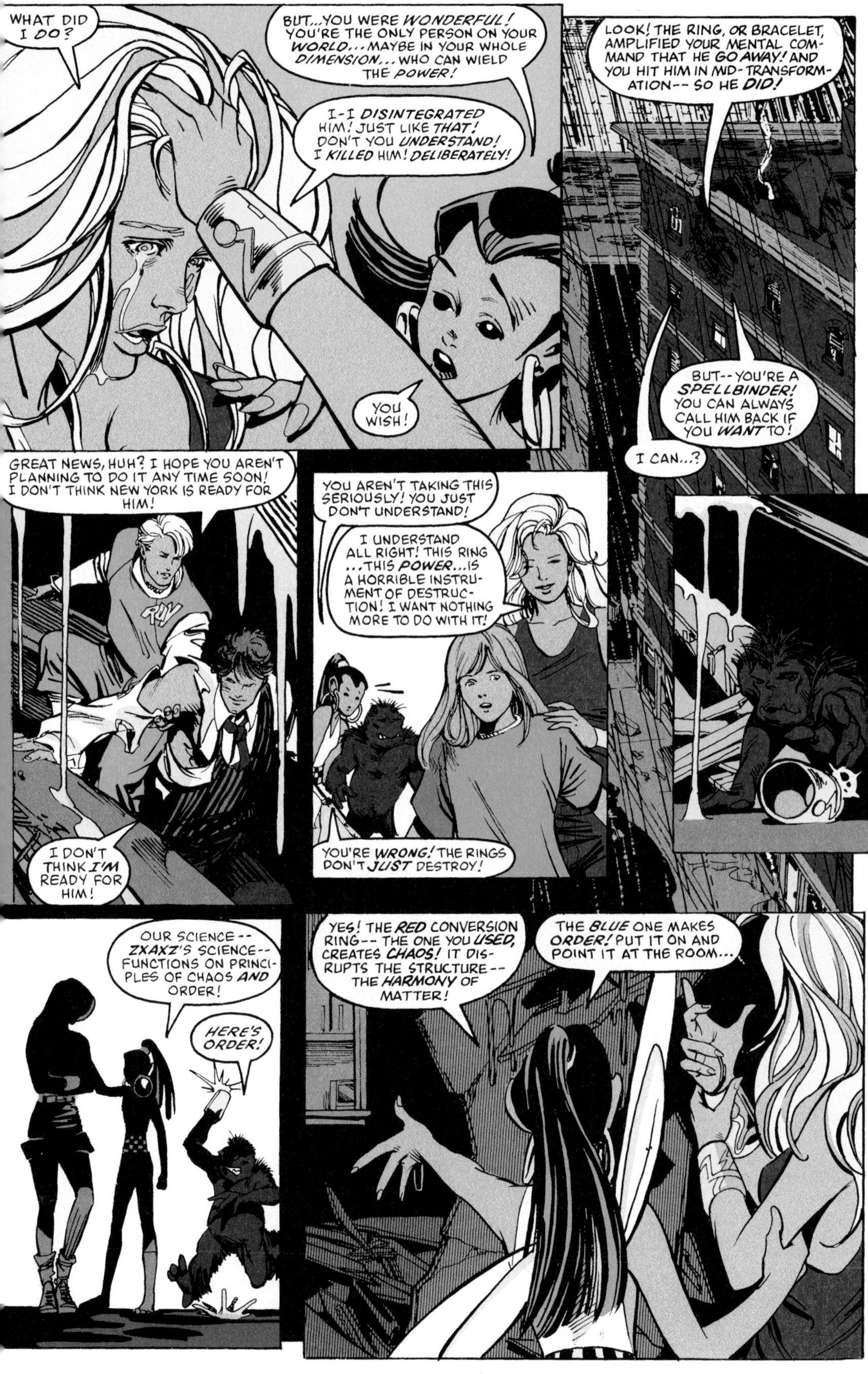
WHAT DID I DO?
BUT...YOU WERE WONDERFUL! YOU'RE THE ONLY PERSON ON YOUR WORLD...MAYBE IN YOUR WHOLE DIMENSION...WHO CAN WIELD THE POWER!
I-I DISINTEGRATED HIM! JUST LIKE THAT! DON'T YOU UNDERSTAND! I KILLED HIM! DELIBERATELY!
YOU WISH!
LOOK! THE RING, OR BRACELET, AMPLIFIED YOUR MENTAL COMMAND THAT HE GO AWAY! AND YOU HIT HIM IN MID-TRANSFORMATION-- SO HE DID!
BUT--YOU'RE A SPELLBINDER! YOU CAN ALWAYS CALL HIM BACK IF YOU WANT TO!
I CAN...?
GREAT NEWS, HUH? I HOPE YOU AREN'T PLANNING TO DO IT ANY TIME SOON! I DON'T THINK NEW YORK IS READY FOR HIM!
I DON'T THINK I'M READY FOR HIM!
YOU AREN'T TAKING THIS SERIOUSLY! YOU JUST DON'T UNDERSTAND!
I UNDERSTAND ALL RIGHT! THIS RING ...THIS POWER...IS A HORRIBLE INSTRUMENT OF DESTRUCTION! I WANT NOTHING MORE TO DO WITH IT!
YOU'RE WRONG! THE RINGS DON'T JUST DESTROY!
OUR SCIENCE--ZXAXZ'S SCIENCE--FUNCTIONS ON PRINCIPLES OF CHAOS AND ORDER!
HERE'S ORDER!
YES! THE RED CONVERSION RING--THE ONE YOU USED, CREATES CHAOS! IT DISRUPTS THE STRUCTURE--THE HARMONY OF MATTER!
THE BLUE ONE MAKES ORDER! PUT IT ON AND POINT IT AT THE ROOM...

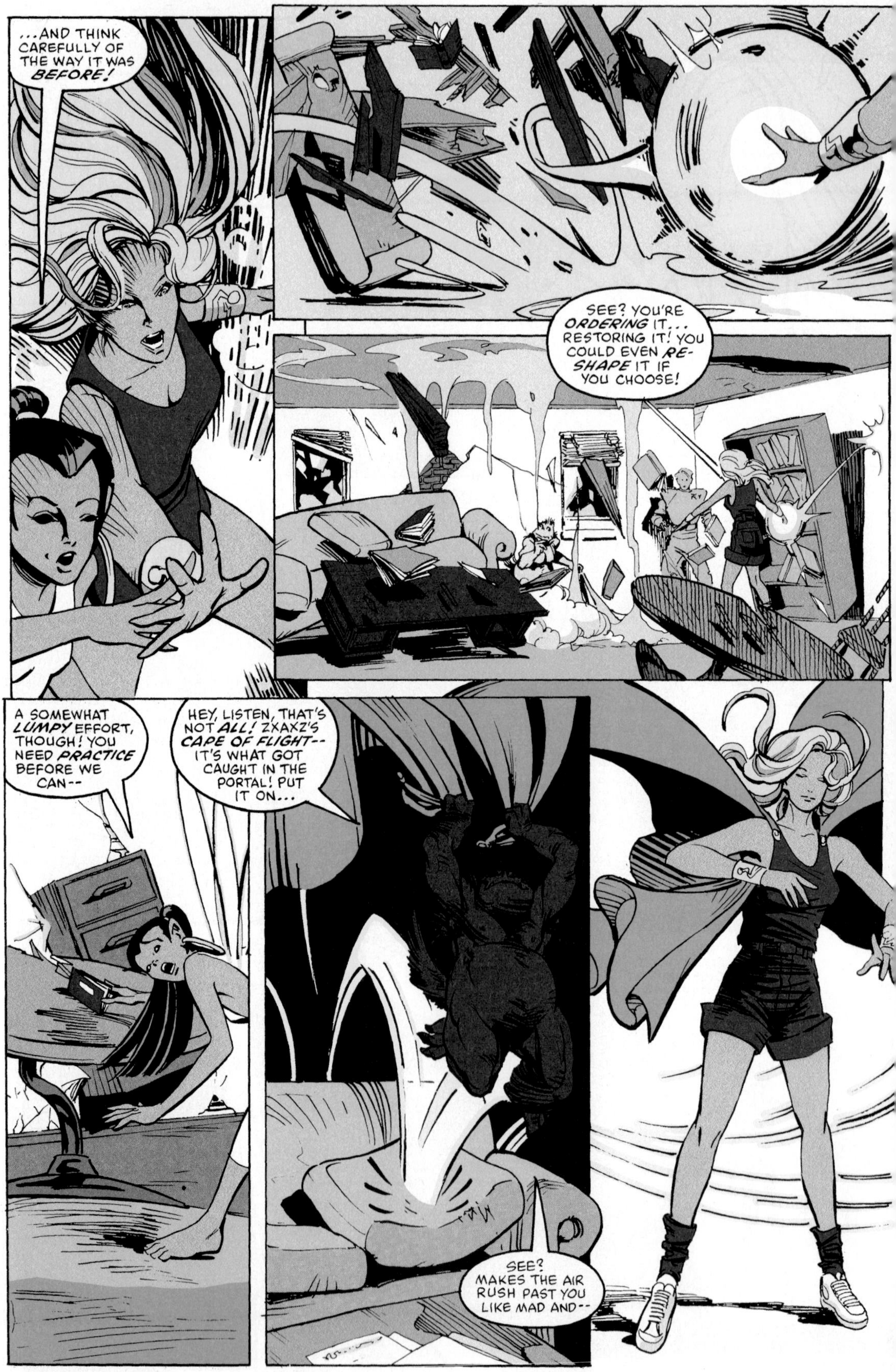
...AND THINK CAREFULLY OF THE WAY IT WAS BEFORE!
SEE? YOU'RE ORDERING IT... RESTORING IT! YOU COULD EVEN RE-SHAPE IT IF YOU CHOOSE!
A SOMEWHAT LUMPY EFFORT, THOUGH! YOU NEED PRACTICE BEFORE WE CAN--
HEY, LISTEN, THAT'S NOT ALL! ZXAXZ'S CAPE OF FLIGHT-- IT'S WHAT GOT CAUGHT IN THE PORTAL! PUT IT ON...
SEE? MAKES THE AIR RUSH PAST YOU LIKE MAD AND--

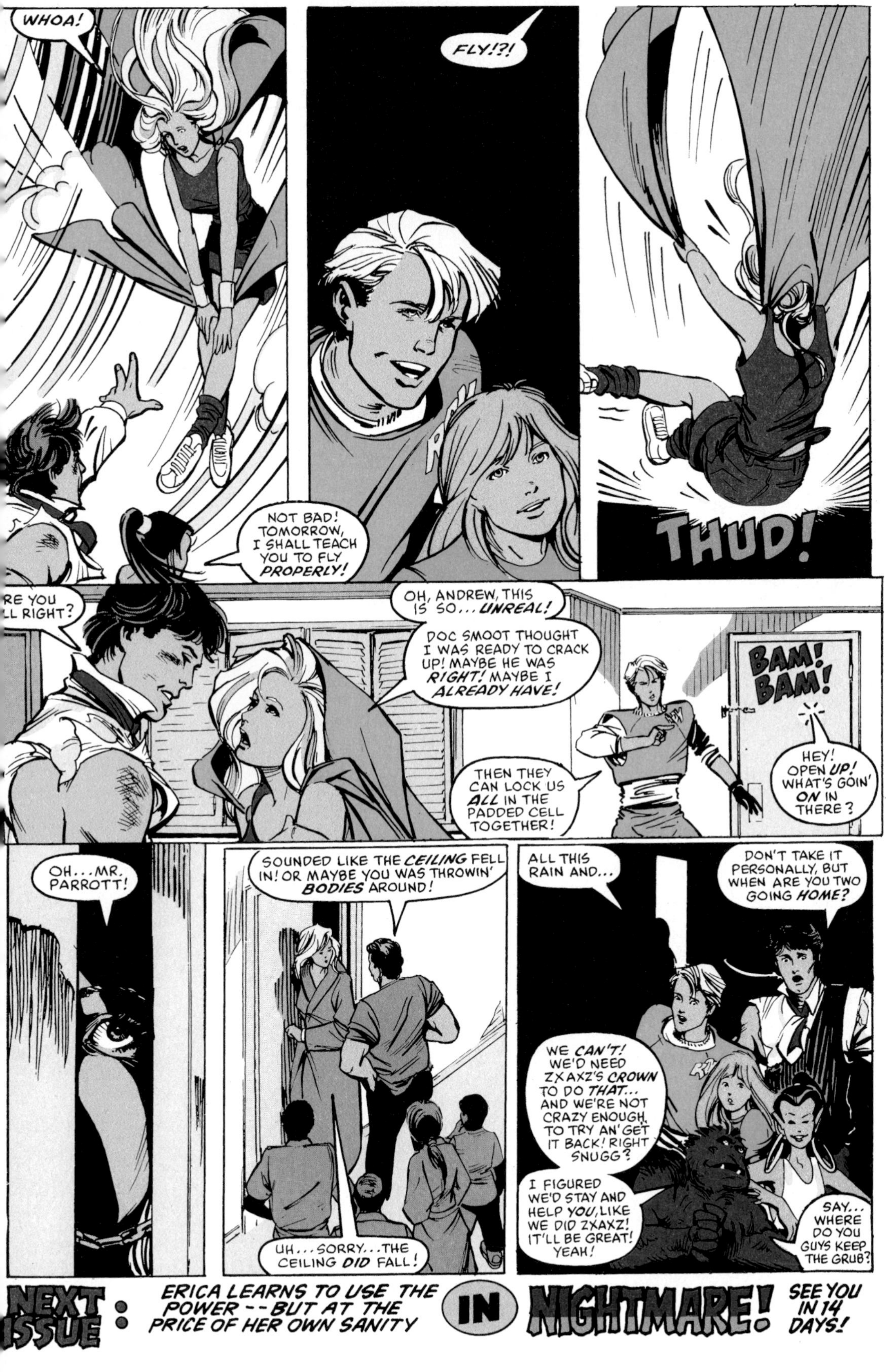
WHOA!
FLY!?!
NOT BAD! TOMORROW, I SHALL TEACH YOU TO FLY PROPERLY!
THUD!
...RE YOU ...LL RIGHT?
OH, ANDREW, THIS IS SO... UNREAL!
DOC SMOOT THOUGHT I WAS READY TO CRACK UP! MAYBE HE WAS RIGHT! MAYBE I ALREADY HAVE!
THEN THEY CAN LOCK US ALL IN THE PADDED CELL TOGETHER!
BAM! BAM!
HEY! OPEN UP! WHAT'S GOIN' ON IN THERE?
OH... MR. PARROTT!
SOUNDED LIKE THE CEILING FELL IN! OR MAYBE YOU WAS THROWIN' BODIES AROUND!
UH... SORRY... THE CEILING DID FALL!
ALL THIS RAIN AND...
DON'T TAKE IT PERSONALLY, BUT WHEN ARE YOU TWO GOING HOME?
WE CAN'T! WE'D NEED ZXAXZ'S CROWN TO DO THAT... AND WE'RE NOT CRAZY ENOUGH TO TRY AN' GET IT BACK! RIGHT SNUGG?
I FIGURED WE'D STAY AND HELP YOU, LIKE WE DID ZXAXZ! IT'LL BE GREAT! YEAH!
SAY... WHERE DO YOU GUYS KEEP THE GRUB?
NEXT ISSUE: ERICA LEARNS TO USE THE POWER -- BUT AT THE PRICE OF HER OWN SANITY IN NIGHTMARE! SEE YOU IN 14 DAYS!

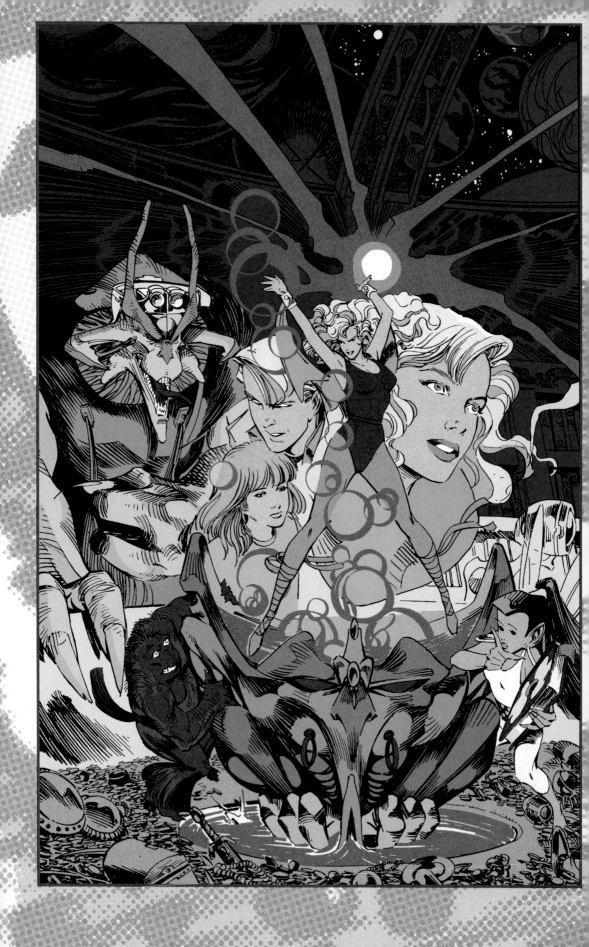

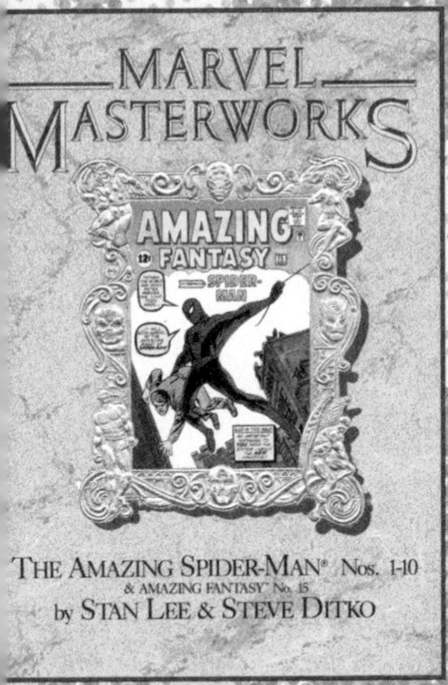
MARVEL
MASTERWORKS
AMAZING FANTASY
SPIDER-MAN
THE AMAZING SPIDER-MAN® Nos. 1-10
& AMAZING FANTASY™ No. 15
by STAN LEE & STEVE DITKO

ARVEL MASTERWORKS VOL. 1 HC, published in
ptember 1987, began a line of hardcovers that
eprinted several of Marvel's earliest and most
popular titles.

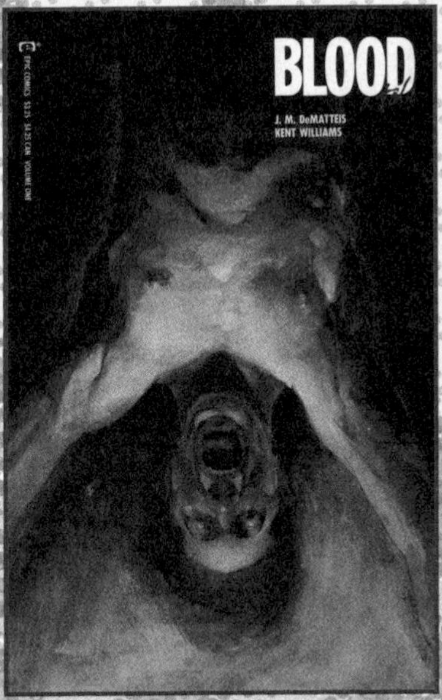
BLOOD
J. M. DeMATTEIS
KENT WILLIAMS

BLOOD: A TALE #1, published in September 1987, began J.M. DeMatteis and Kent Williams' Epic miniseries.

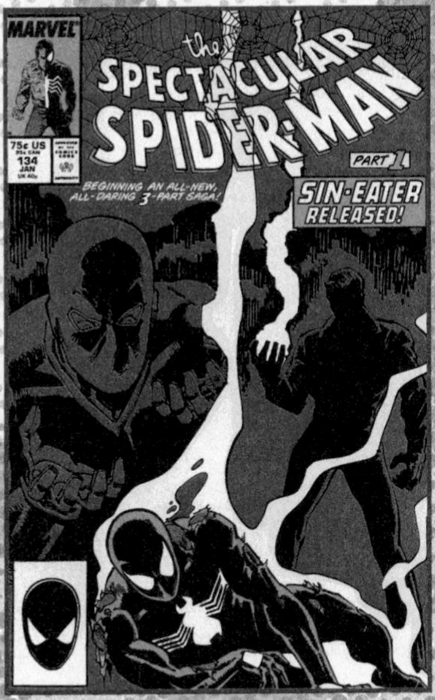
MARVEL
the SPECTACULAR SPIDER-MAN
75¢ US
134
JAN
BEGINNING AN ALL-NEW, ALL-DARING 3rd-PART SAGA!
PART 1
SIN-EATER RELEASED!

Peter Parker, the Spectacular Spider-Man changed its title to SPECTACULAR SPIDER-MAN with #134, published in September 1987.

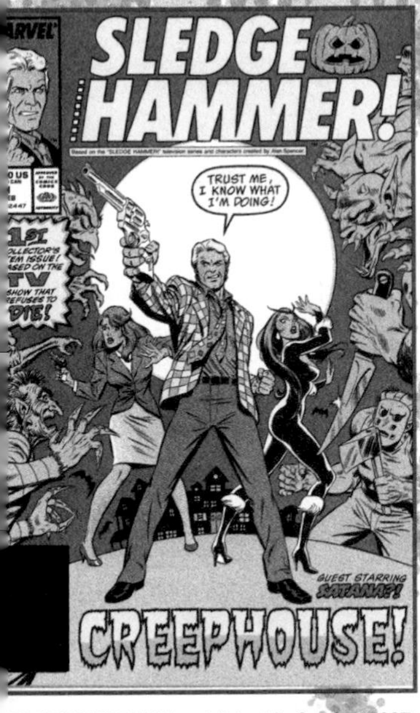
MARVEL
SLEDGE HAMMER!
TRUST ME, I KNOW WHAT I'M DOING!
GUEST STARRING SATANIKA!
CREEPHOUSE!

EDGE HAMMER! #1, published in October 1987, began a miniseries based on the New World Television TV series.

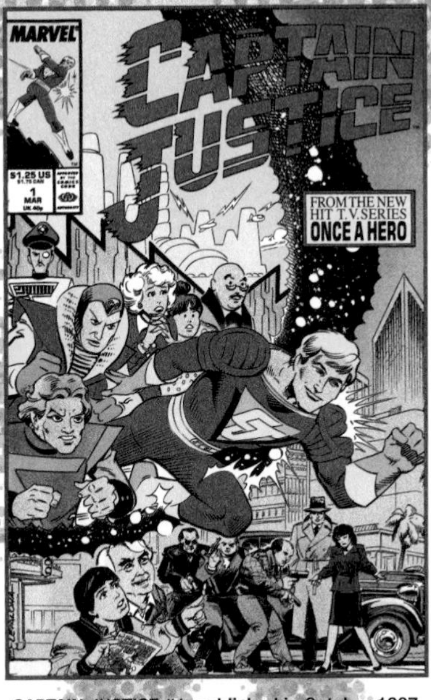
MARVEL
CAPTAIN JUSTICE
$1.25 US
1
MAR
FROM THE NEW HIT T.V. SERIES
ONCE A HERO

CAPTAIN JUSTICE #1, published in October 1987, began a miniseries based on the ABC TV series *Once a Hero.*

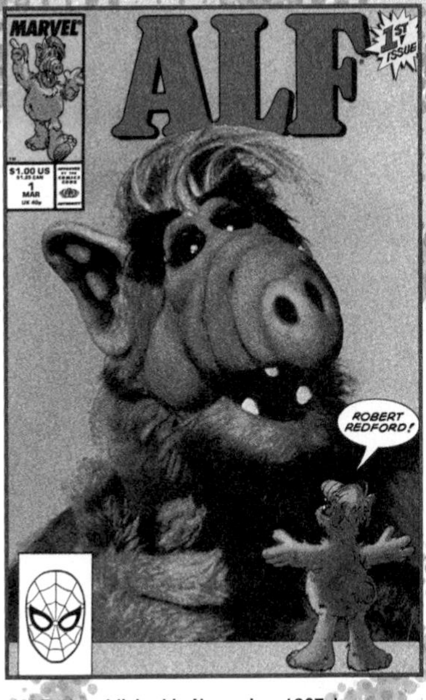
MARVEL
ALF
1ST ISSUE
$1.00 US
1
MAR
ROBERT REDFORD!

ALF #1, published in November 1987, began an ongoing Star series based on the Warner Brothers TV series.

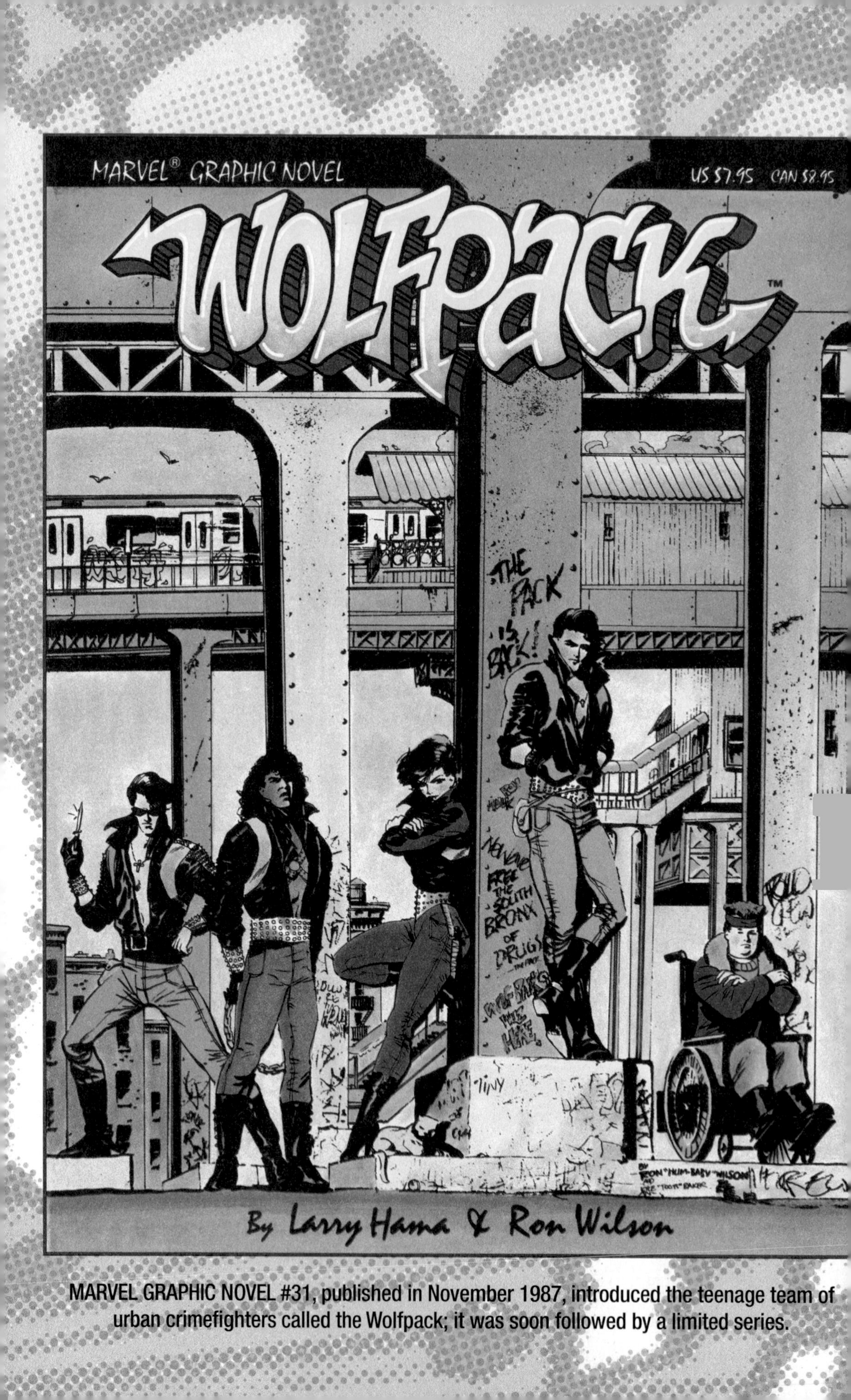
MARVEL® GRAPHIC NOVEL
US $7.95 CAN $8.95
WOLFPACK™
THE PACK IS BACK!
FREE THE SOUTH BRONX OF DRUGS
By Larry Hama & Ron Wilson

MARVEL GRAPHIC NOVEL #31, published in November 1987, introduced the teenage team of urban crimefighters called the Wolfpack; it was soon followed by a limited series.

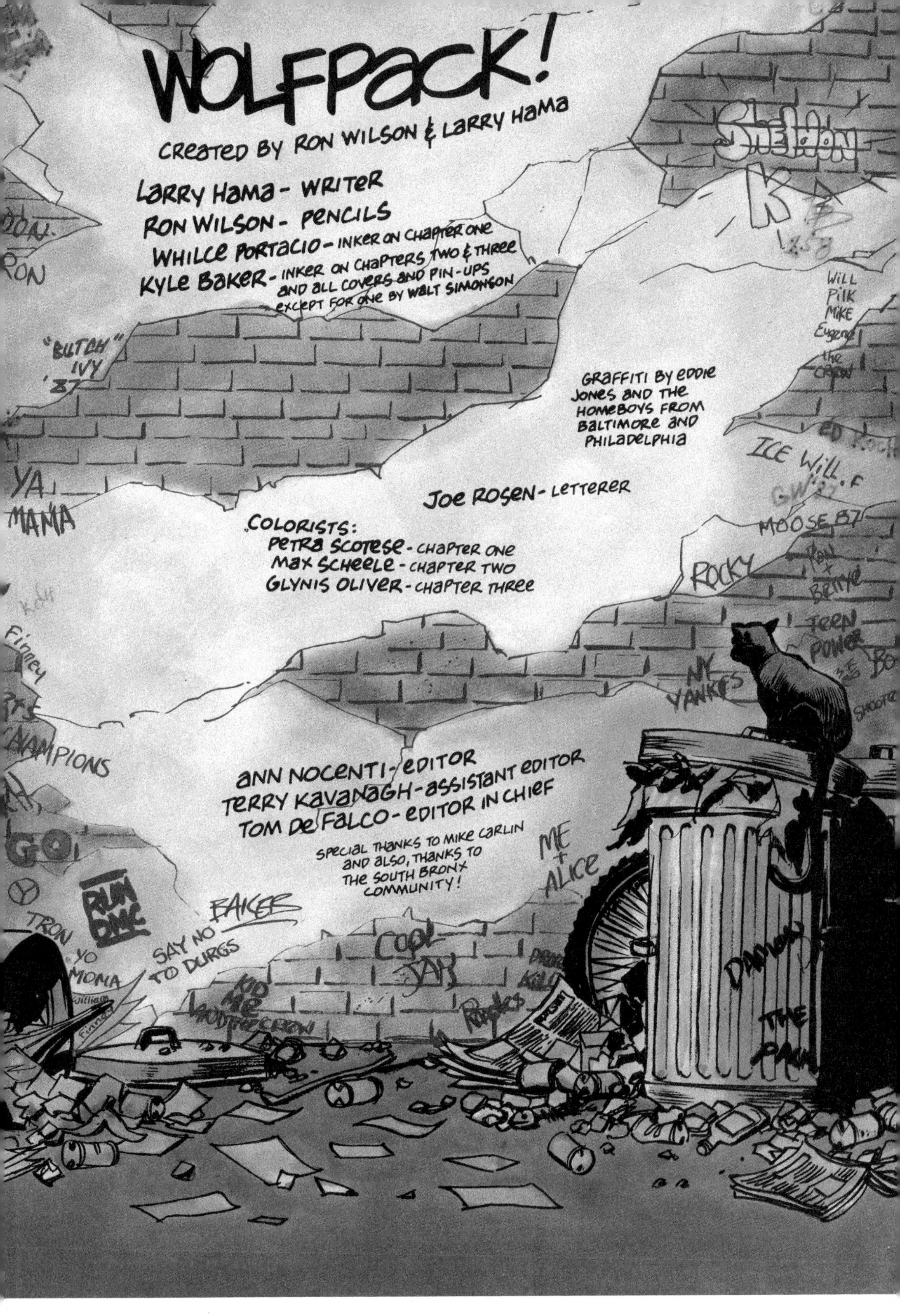
WOLFPACK!
CREATED BY RON WILSON & LARRY HAMA
LARRY HAMA - WRITER
RON WILSON - PENCILS
WHILCE PORTACIO - INKER ON CHAPTER ONE
KYLE BAKER - INKER ON CHAPTERS TWO & THREE AND ALL COVERS AND PIN-UPS EXCEPT FOR ONE BY WALT SIMONSON
GRAFFITI BY EDDIE JONES AND THE HOMEBOYS FROM BALTIMORE AND PHILADELPHIA
JOE ROSEN - LETTERER
COLORISTS:
PETRA SCOTESE - CHAPTER ONE
MAX SCHEELE - CHAPTER TWO
GLYNIS OLIVER - CHAPTER THREE
ANN NOCENTI - EDITOR
TERRY KAVANAGH - ASSISTANT EDITOR
TOM DE FALCO - EDITOR IN CHIEF
SPECIAL THANKS TO MIKE CARLIN AND ALSO, THANKS TO THE SOUTH BRONX COMMUNITY!

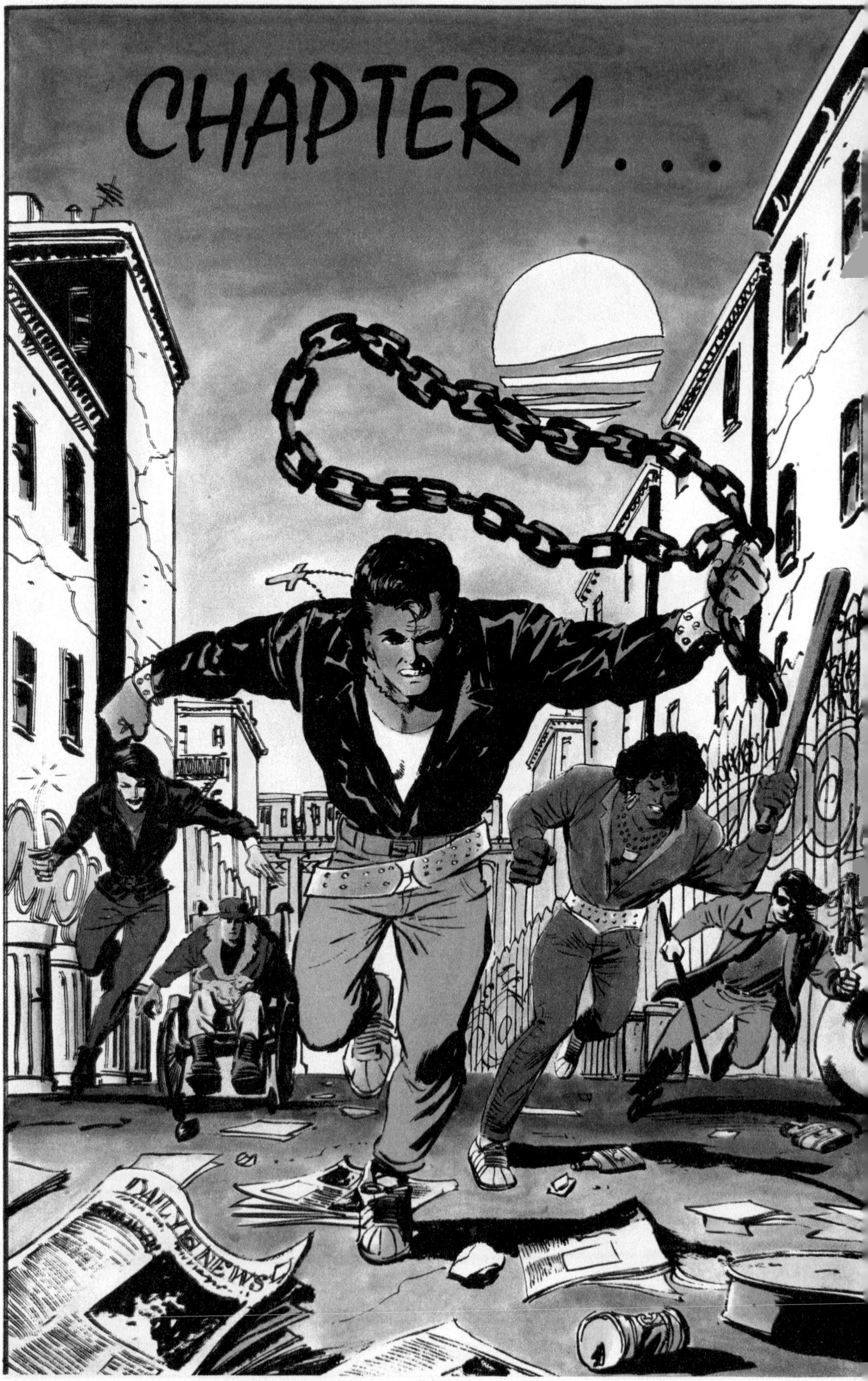
CHAPTER 1 . . .
DAILY NEWS

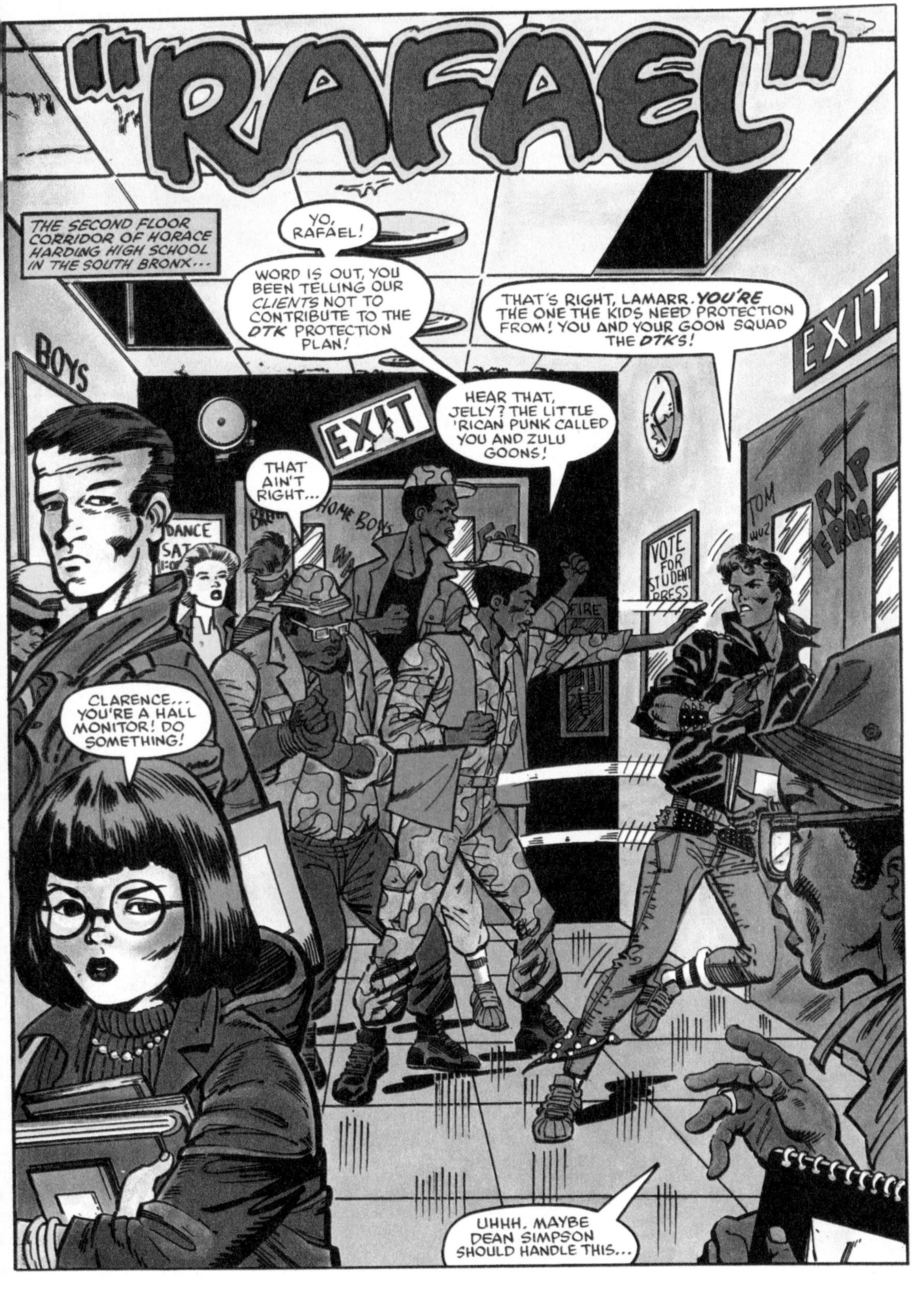
"RAFAEL"
THE SECOND FLOOR CORRIDOR OF HORACE HARDING HIGH SCHOOL IN THE SOUTH BRONX...
YO, RAFAEL!
WORD IS OUT, YOU BEEN TELLING OUR CLIENTS NOT TO CONTRIBUTE TO THE DTK PROTECTION PLAN!
THAT'S RIGHT, LAMARR. YOU'RE THE ONE THE KIDS NEED PROTECTION FROM! YOU AND YOUR GOON SQUAD THE DTKS!
EXIT
BOYS
EXIT
HEAR THAT, JELLY? THE LITTLE 'RICAN PUNK CALLED YOU AND ZULU GOONS!
THAT AIN'T RIGHT...
HOME BOYS
DANCE SAT
VOTE FOR STUDENT PRESS
FIRE
TOM WUZ
RAP FROG
CLARENCE... YOU'RE A HALL MONITOR! DO SOMETHING!
UHHH, MAYBE DEAN SIMPSON SHOULD HANDLE THIS...

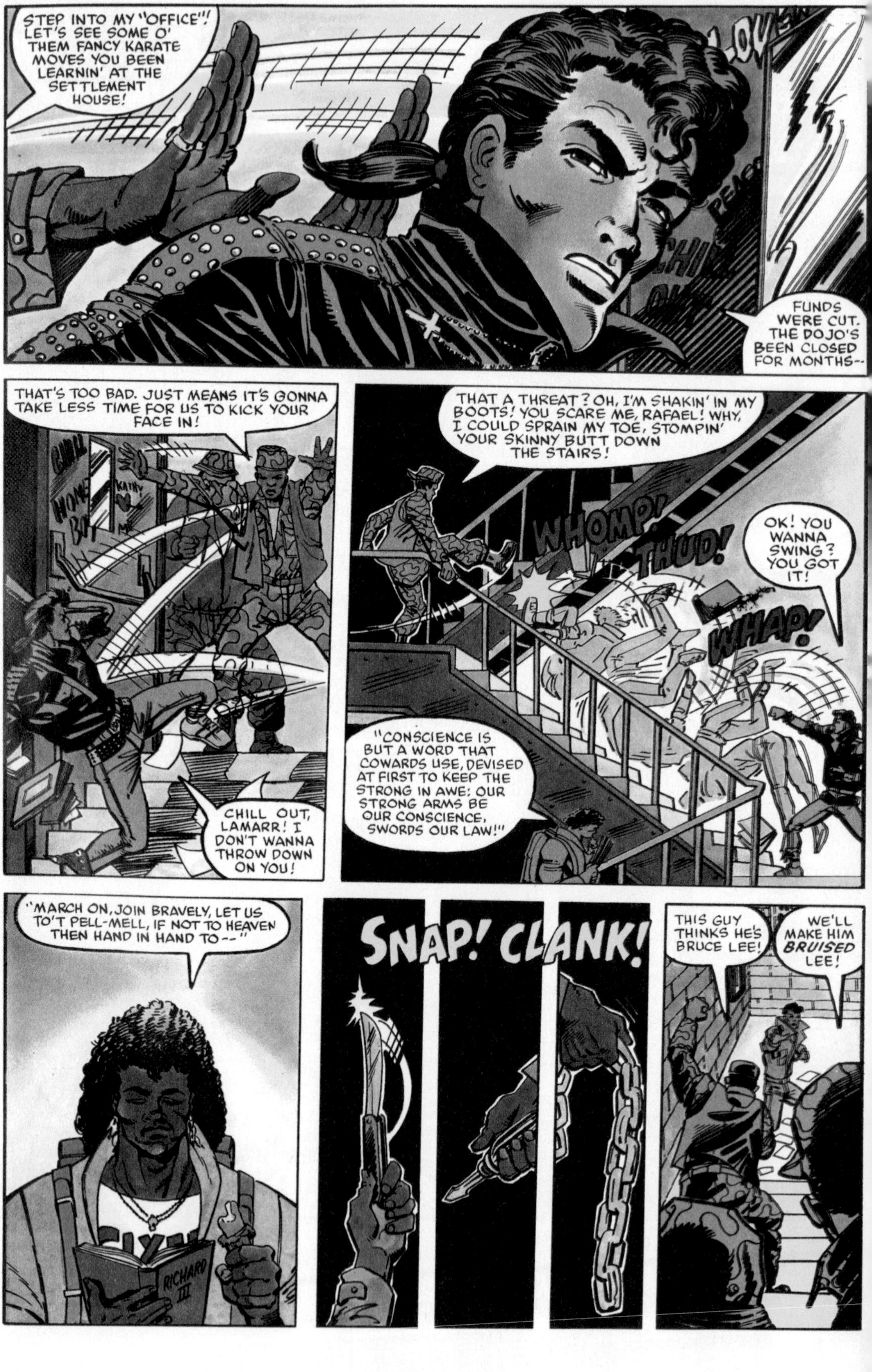
STEP INTO MY "OFFICE"! LET'S SEE SOME O' THEM FANCY KARATE MOVES YOU BEEN LEARNIN' AT THE SETTLEMENT HOUSE!
FUNDS WERE CUT. THE DOJO'S BEEN CLOSED FOR MONTHS--
THAT'S TOO BAD. JUST MEANS IT'S GONNA TAKE LESS TIME FOR US TO KICK YOUR FACE IN!
CHILL OUT, LAMARR! I DON'T WANNA THROW DOWN ON YOU!
THAT A THREAT? OH, I'M SHAKIN' IN MY BOOTS! YOU SCARE ME, RAFAEL! WHY, I COULD SPRAIN MY TOE, STOMPIN' YOUR SKINNY BUTT DOWN THE STAIRS!
WHOMP!
THUD!
OK! YOU WANNA SWING? YOU GOT IT!
WHAP!
"CONSCIENCE IS BUT A WORD THAT COWARDS USE, DEVISED AT FIRST TO KEEP THE STRONG IN AWE: OUR STRONG ARMS BE OUR CONSCIENCE, SWORDS OUR LAW!"
"MARCH ON, JOIN BRAVELY, LET US TO'T PELL-MELL, IF NOT TO HEAVEN THEN HAND IN HAND TO--"
RICHARD III
SNAP! CLANK!
THIS GUY THINKS HE'S BRUCE LEE!
WE'LL MAKE HIM *BRUISED* LEE!

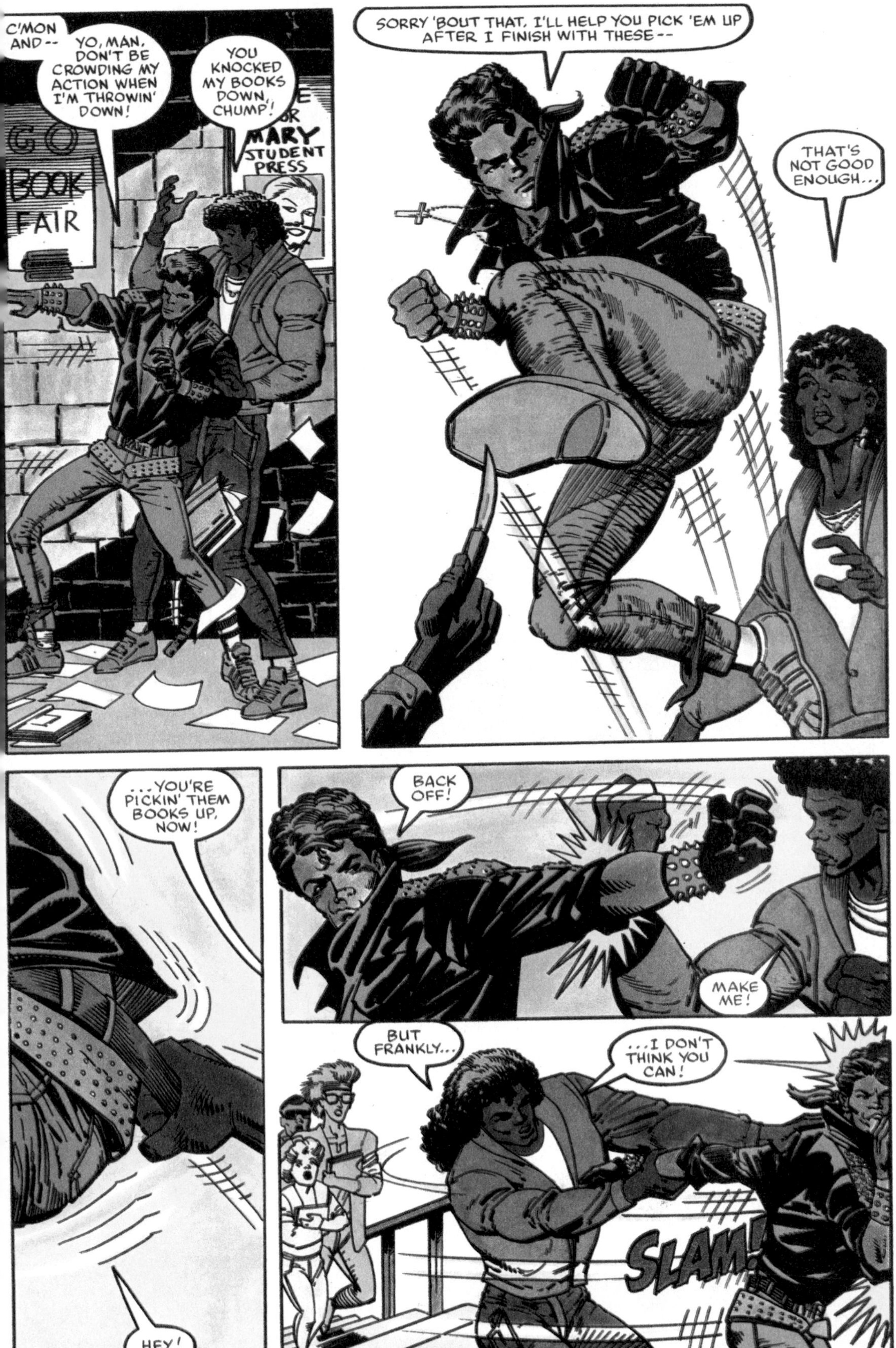
C'MON AND--
YO, MAN, DON'T BE CROWDING MY ACTION WHEN I'M THROWIN' DOWN!
YOU KNOCKED MY BOOKS DOWN, CHUMP!
GO BOOK FAIR
MARY STUDENT PRESS
SORRY 'BOUT THAT, I'LL HELP YOU PICK 'EM UP AFTER I FINISH WITH THESE--
THAT'S NOT GOOD ENOUGH...
...YOU'RE PICKIN' THEM BOOKS UP, NOW!
HEY!
BACK OFF!
MAKE ME!
BUT FRANKLY...
...I DON'T THINK YOU CAN!
SLAM!

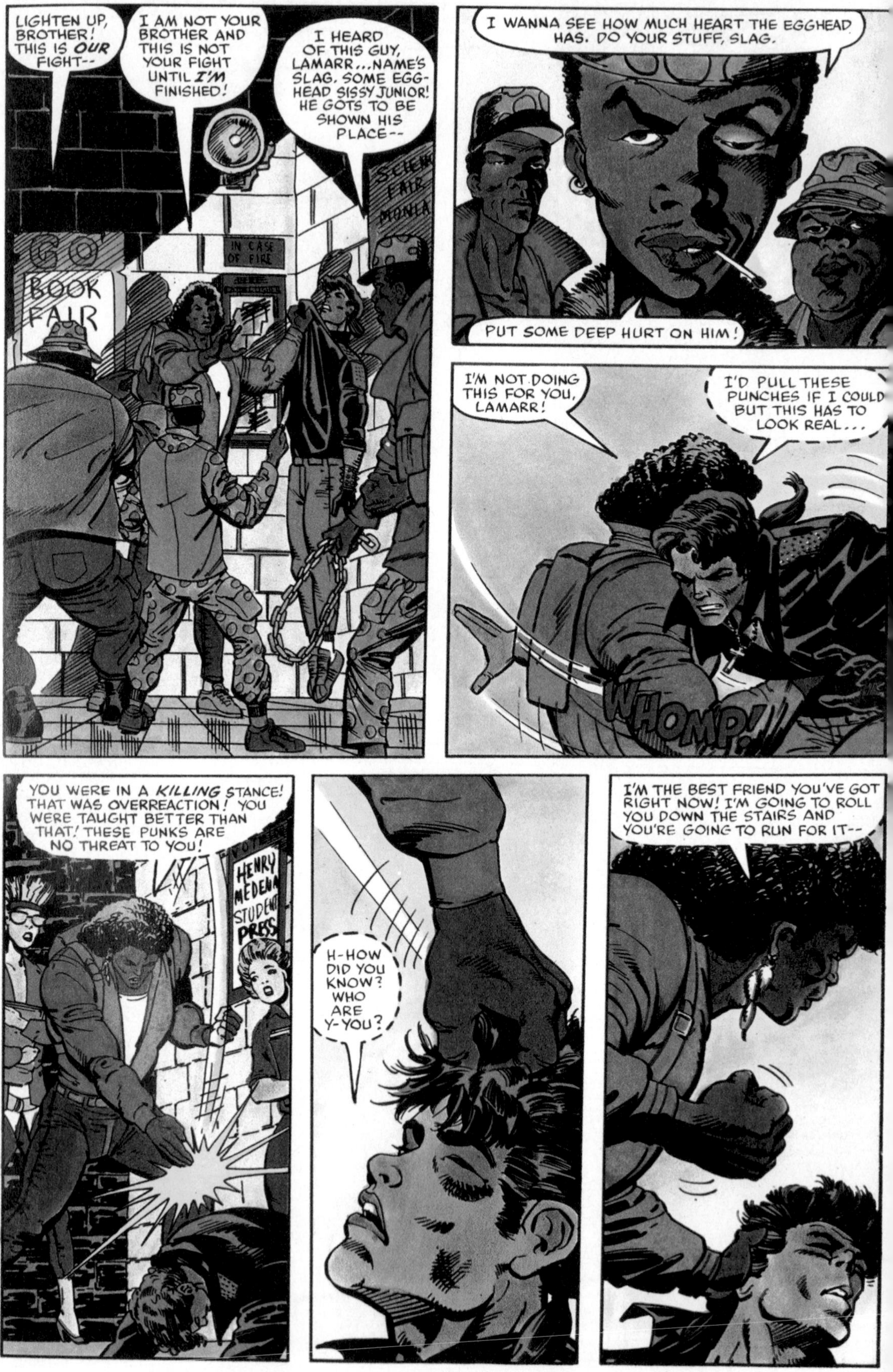
LIGHTEN UP, BROTHER! THIS IS OUR FIGHT--
I AM NOT YOUR BROTHER AND THIS IS NOT YOUR FIGHT UNTIL I'M FINISHED!
I HEARD OF THIS GUY, LAMARR...NAME'S SLAG. SOME EGG-HEAD SISSY JUNIOR! HE GOTS TO BE SHOWN HIS PLACE--
IN CASE OF FIRE
BOOK FAIR
I WANNA SEE HOW MUCH HEART THE EGGHEAD HAS. DO YOUR STUFF, SLAG.
PUT SOME DEEP HURT ON HIM!
I'M NOT DOING THIS FOR YOU, LAMARR!
I'D PULL THESE PUNCHES IF I COULD BUT THIS HAS TO LOOK REAL...
WHOMP!
YOU WERE IN A KILLING STANCE! THAT WAS OVERREACTION! YOU WERE TAUGHT BETTER THAN THAT! THESE PUNKS ARE NO THREAT TO YOU!
H-HOW DID YOU KNOW? WHO ARE Y-YOU?
I'M THE BEST FRIEND YOU'VE GOT RIGHT NOW! I'M GOING TO ROLL YOU DOWN THE STAIRS AND YOU'RE GOING TO RUN FOR IT--

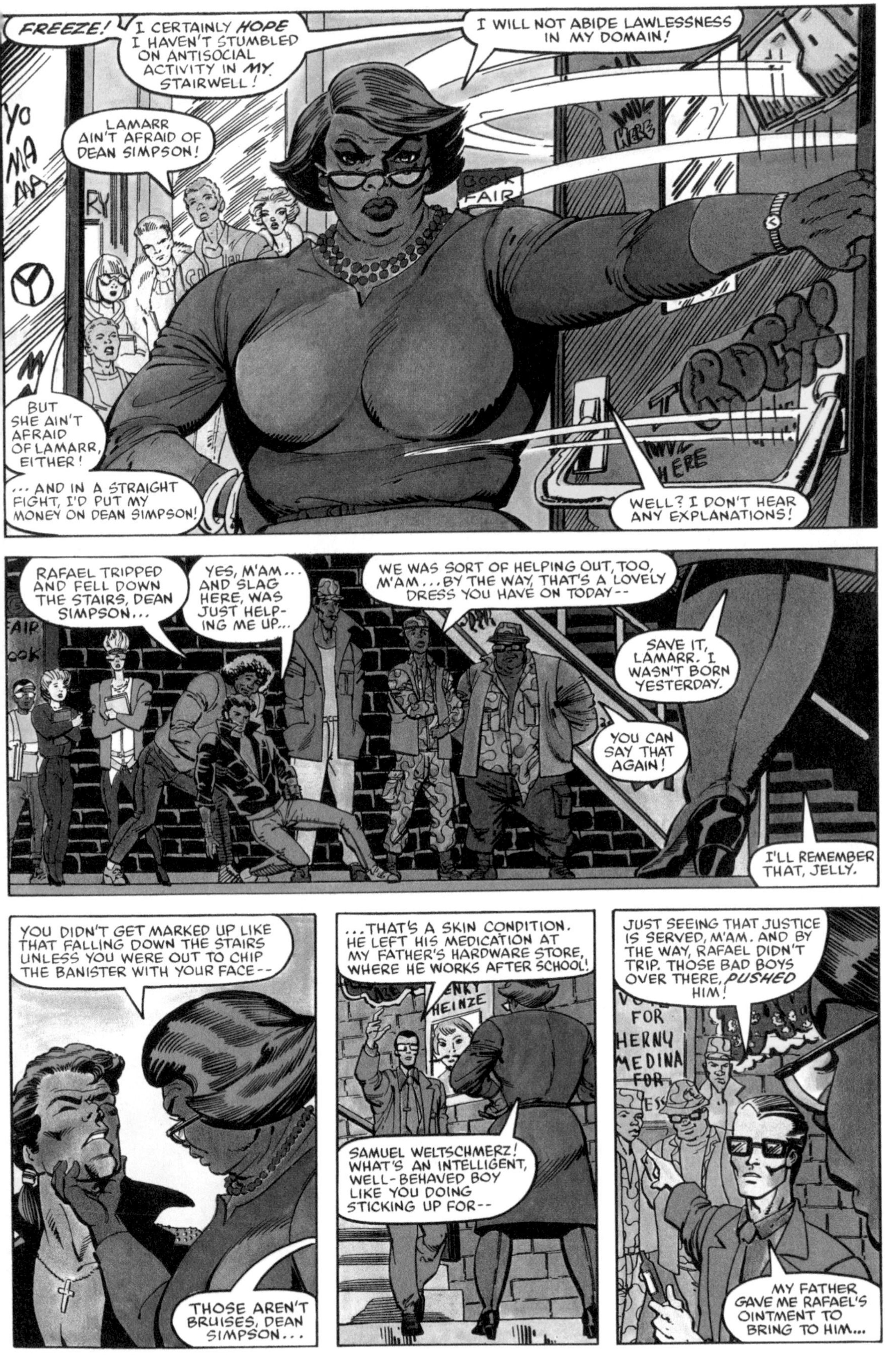
FREEZE!
I CERTAINLY HOPE I HAVEN'T STUMBLED ON ANTISOCIAL ACTIVITY IN MY STAIRWELL!
I WILL NOT ABIDE LAWLESSNESS IN MY DOMAIN!
LAMARR AIN'T AFRAID OF DEAN SIMPSON!
BUT SHE AIN'T AFRAID OF LAMARR, EITHER!
...AND IN A STRAIGHT FIGHT, I'D PUT MY MONEY ON DEAN SIMPSON!
WELL? I DON'T HEAR ANY EXPLANATIONS!
RAFAEL TRIPPED AND FELL DOWN THE STAIRS, DEAN SIMPSON...
YES, M'AM... AND SLAG HERE, WAS JUST HELPING ME UP...
WE WAS SORT OF HELPING OUT, TOO, M'AM... BY THE WAY, THAT'S A LOVELY DRESS YOU HAVE ON TODAY--
SAVE IT, LAMARR. I WASN'T BORN YESTERDAY.
YOU CAN SAY THAT AGAIN!
I'LL REMEMBER THAT, JELLY.
YOU DIDN'T GET MARKED UP LIKE THAT FALLING DOWN THE STAIRS UNLESS YOU WERE OUT TO CHIP THE BANISTER WITH YOUR FACE--
THOSE AREN'T BRUISES, DEAN SIMPSON...
...THAT'S A SKIN CONDITION. HE LEFT HIS MEDICATION AT MY FATHER'S HARDWARE STORE, WHERE HE WORKS AFTER SCHOOL!
SAMUEL WELTSCHMERZ! WHAT'S AN INTELLIGENT, WELL-BEHAVED BOY LIKE YOU DOING STICKING UP FOR--
JUST SEEING THAT JUSTICE IS SERVED, M'AM. AND BY THE WAY, RAFAEL DIDN'T TRIP. THOSE BAD BOYS OVER THERE, PUSHED HIM!
MY FATHER GAVE ME RAFAEL'S OINTMENT TO BRING TO HIM...

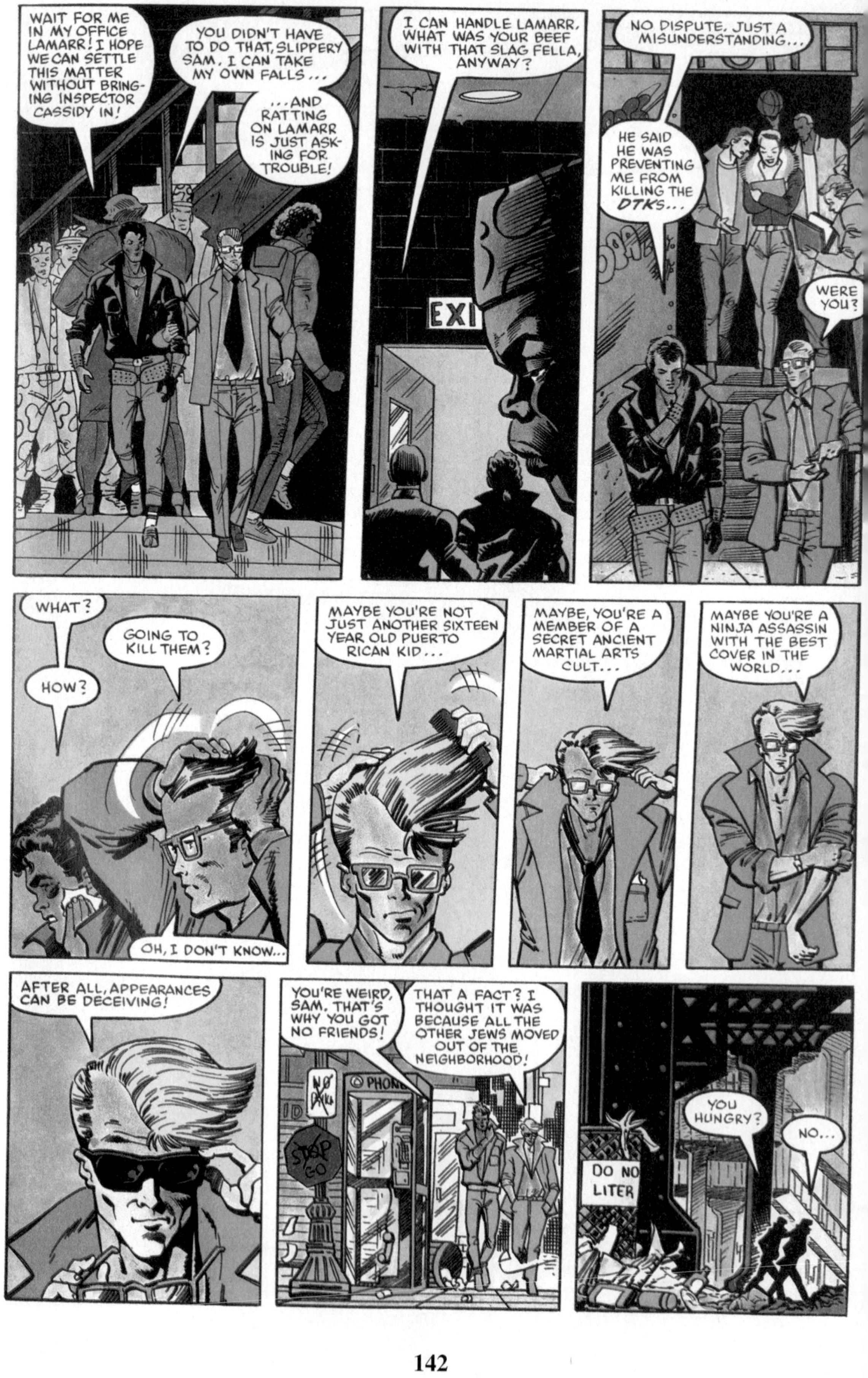
WAIT FOR ME IN MY OFFICE LAMARR! I HOPE WE CAN SETTLE THIS MATTER WITHOUT BRINGING INSPECTOR CASSIDY IN!
YOU DIDN'T HAVE TO DO THAT, SLIPPERY SAM. I CAN TAKE MY OWN FALLS...
...AND RATTING ON LAMARR IS JUST ASKING FOR TROUBLE!
I CAN HANDLE LAMARR. WHAT WAS YOUR BEEF WITH THAT SLAG FELLA, ANYWAY?
EXI
NO DISPUTE. JUST A MISUNDERSTANDING...
HE SAID HE WAS PREVENTING ME FROM KILLING THE *DTKS*...
WERE YOU?
WHAT?
HOW?
GOING TO KILL THEM?
OH, I DON'T KNOW...
MAYBE YOU'RE NOT JUST ANOTHER SIXTEEN YEAR OLD PUERTO RICAN KID...
MAYBE, YOU'RE A MEMBER OF A SECRET ANCIENT MARTIAL ARTS CULT...
MAYBE YOU'RE A NINJA ASSASSIN WITH THE BEST COVER IN THE WORLD...
AFTER ALL, APPEARANCES CAN BE DECEIVING!
YOU'RE WEIRD, SAM. THAT'S WHY YOU GOT NO FRIENDS!
THAT A FACT? I THOUGHT IT WAS BECAUSE ALL THE OTHER JEWS MOVED OUT OF THE NEIGHBORHOOD!
PHONE
STOP GO
YOU HUNGRY?
NO...
DO NO
LITER

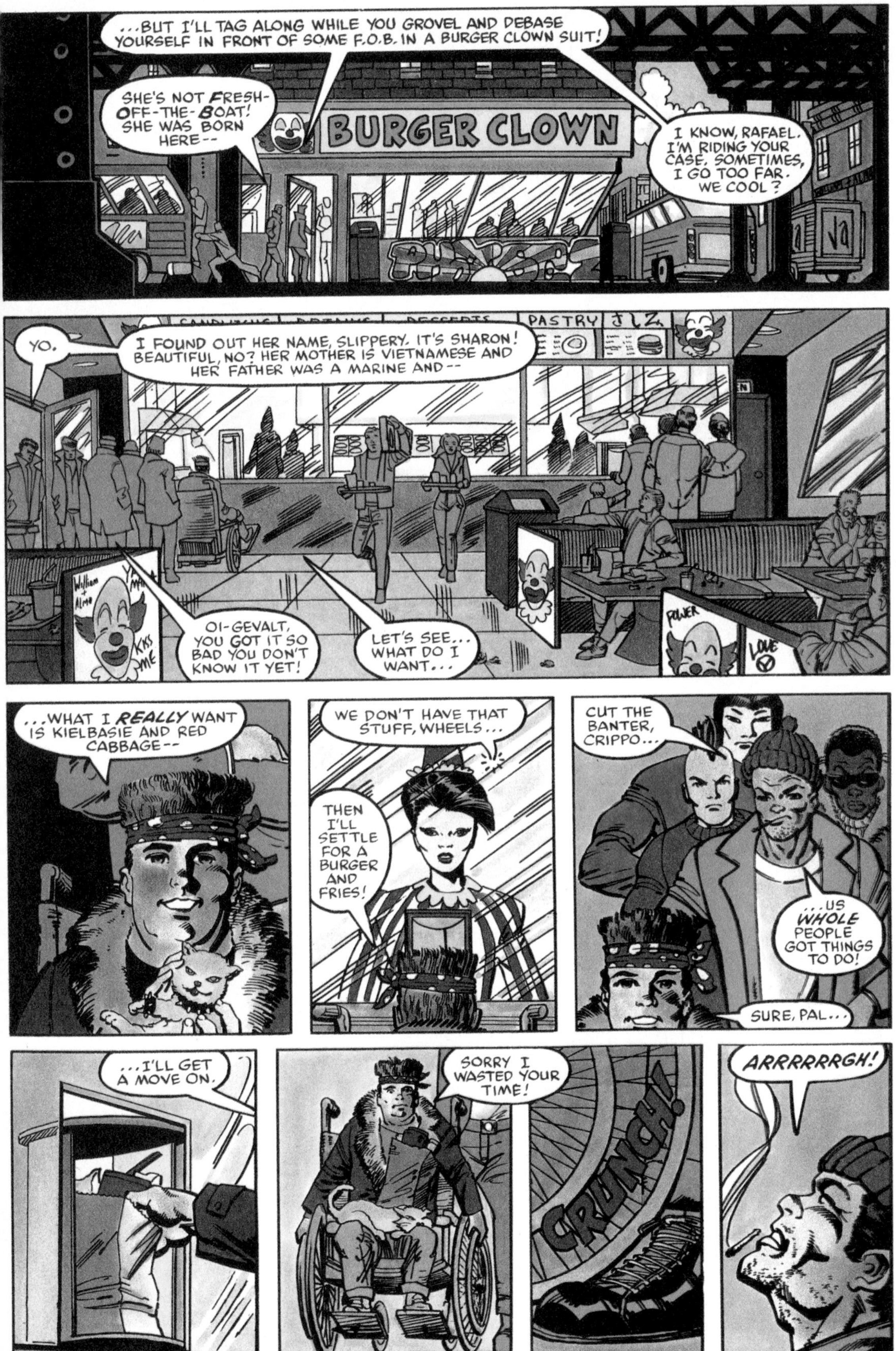
...BUT I'LL TAG ALONG WHILE YOU GROVEL AND DEBASE YOURSELF IN FRONT OF SOME F.O.B. IN A BURGER CLOWN SUIT!
SHE'S NOT FRESH-OFF-THE-BOAT! SHE WAS BORN HERE--
BURGER CLOWN
I KNOW, RAFAEL. I'M RIDING YOUR CASE. SOMETIMES, I GO TOO FAR. WE COOL?
PASTRY
YO.
I FOUND OUT HER NAME, SLIPPERY. IT'S SHARON! BEAUTIFUL, NO? HER MOTHER IS VIETNAMESE AND HER FATHER WAS A MARINE AND--
OI-GEVALT, YOU GOT IT SO BAD YOU DON'T KNOW IT YET!
LET'S SEE... WHAT DO I WANT...
...WHAT I REALLY WANT IS KIELBASIE AND RED CABBAGE--
WE DON'T HAVE THAT STUFF, WHEELS...
THEN I'LL SETTLE FOR A BURGER AND FRIES!
CUT THE BANTER, CRIPPO...
...US WHOLE PEOPLE GOT THINGS TO DO!
SURE, PAL...
...I'LL GET A MOVE ON.
SORRY I WASTED YOUR TIME!
CRUNCH!
ARRRRRRGH!

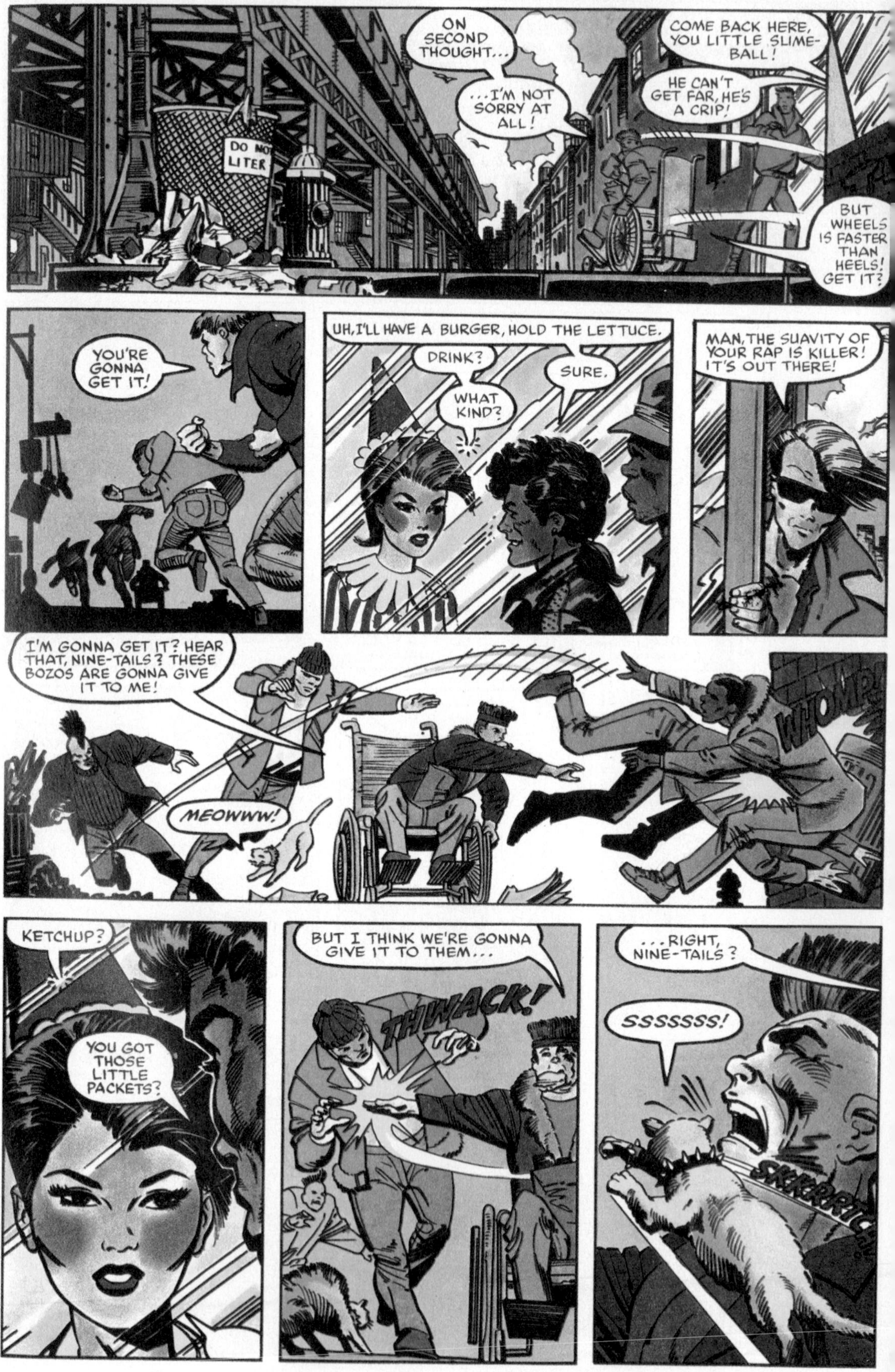
DO NOT LITER
ON SECOND THOUGHT...
...I'M NOT SORRY AT ALL!
COME BACK HERE, YOU LITTLE SLIME-BALL!
HE CAN'T GET FAR, HE'S A CRIP!
BUT WHEELS IS FASTER THAN HEELS! GET IT?
YOU'RE GONNA GET IT!
UH, I'LL HAVE A BURGER, HOLD THE LETTUCE.
DRINK?
SURE.
WHAT KIND?
MAN, THE SUAVITY OF YOUR RAP IS KILLER! IT'S OUT THERE!
I'M GONNA GET IT? HEAR THAT, NINE-TAILS? THESE BOZOS ARE GONNA GIVE IT TO ME!
WHOMP!
MEOWWW!
KETCHUP?
YOU GOT THOSE LITTLE PACKETS?
BUT I THINK WE'RE GONNA GIVE IT TO THEM...
THWACK!
...RIGHT, NINE-TAILS?
SSSSSSS!

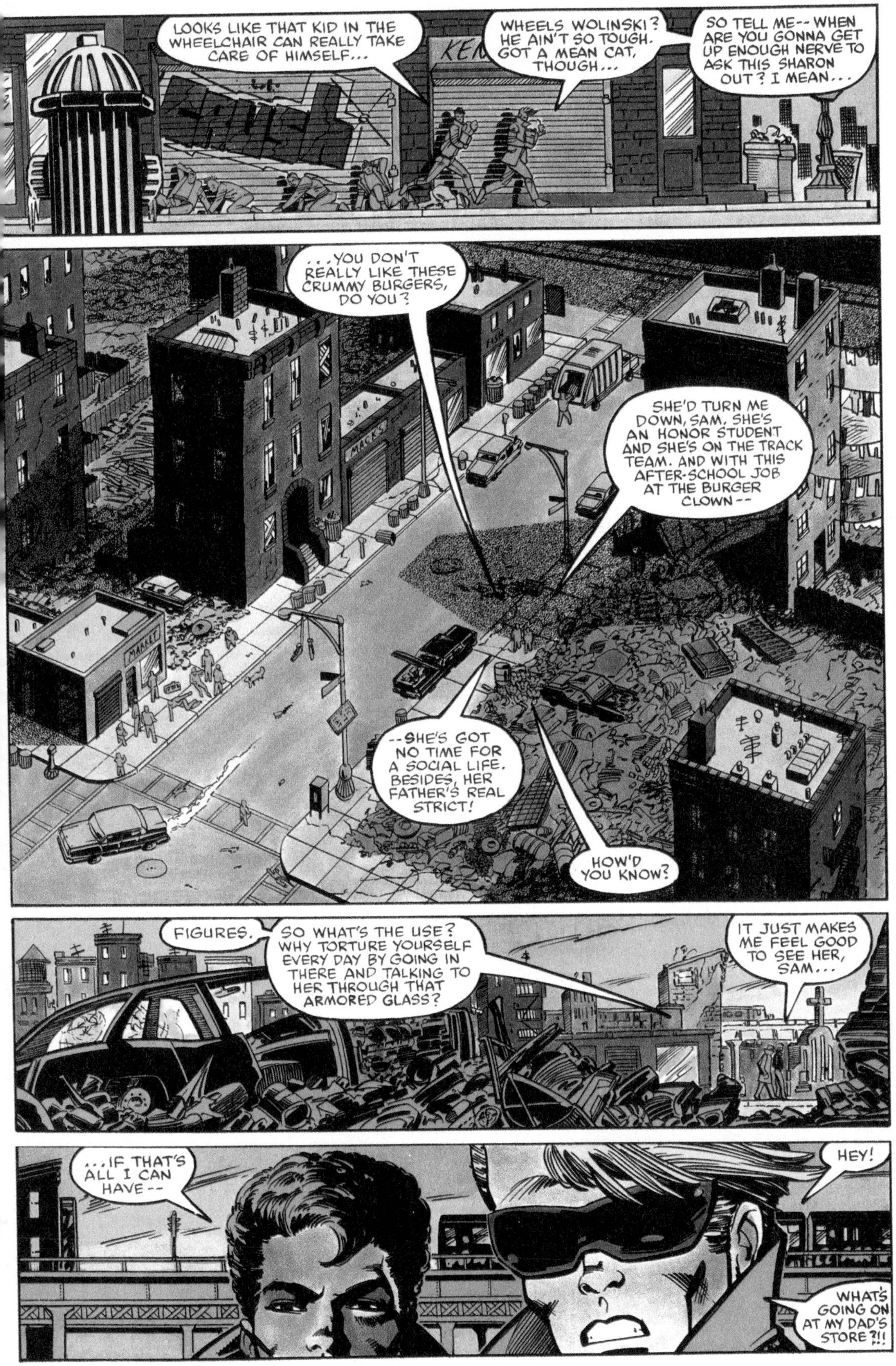
LOOKS LIKE THAT KID IN THE WHEELCHAIR CAN REALLY TAKE CARE OF HIMSELF...
WHEELS WOLINSKI? HE AIN'T SO TOUGH. GOT A MEAN CAT, THOUGH...
SO TELL ME-- WHEN ARE YOU GONNA GET UP ENOUGH NERVE TO ASK THIS SHARON OUT? I MEAN...
...YOU DON'T REALLY LIKE THESE CRUMMY BURGERS, DO YOU?
SHE'D TURN ME DOWN, SAM. SHE'S AN HONOR STUDENT AND SHE'S ON THE TRACK TEAM. AND WITH THIS AFTER-SCHOOL JOB AT THE BURGER CLOWN--
--SHE'S GOT NO TIME FOR A SOCIAL LIFE. BESIDES, HER FATHER'S REAL STRICT!
HOW'D YOU KNOW?
FIGURES.
SO WHAT'S THE USE? WHY TORTURE YOURSELF EVERY DAY BY GOING IN THERE AND TALKING TO HER THROUGH THAT ARMORED GLASS?
IT JUST MAKES ME FEEL GOOD TO SEE HER, SAM...
...IF THAT'S ALL I CAN HAVE--
HEY!
WHAT'S GOING ON AT MY DAD'S STORE?!!

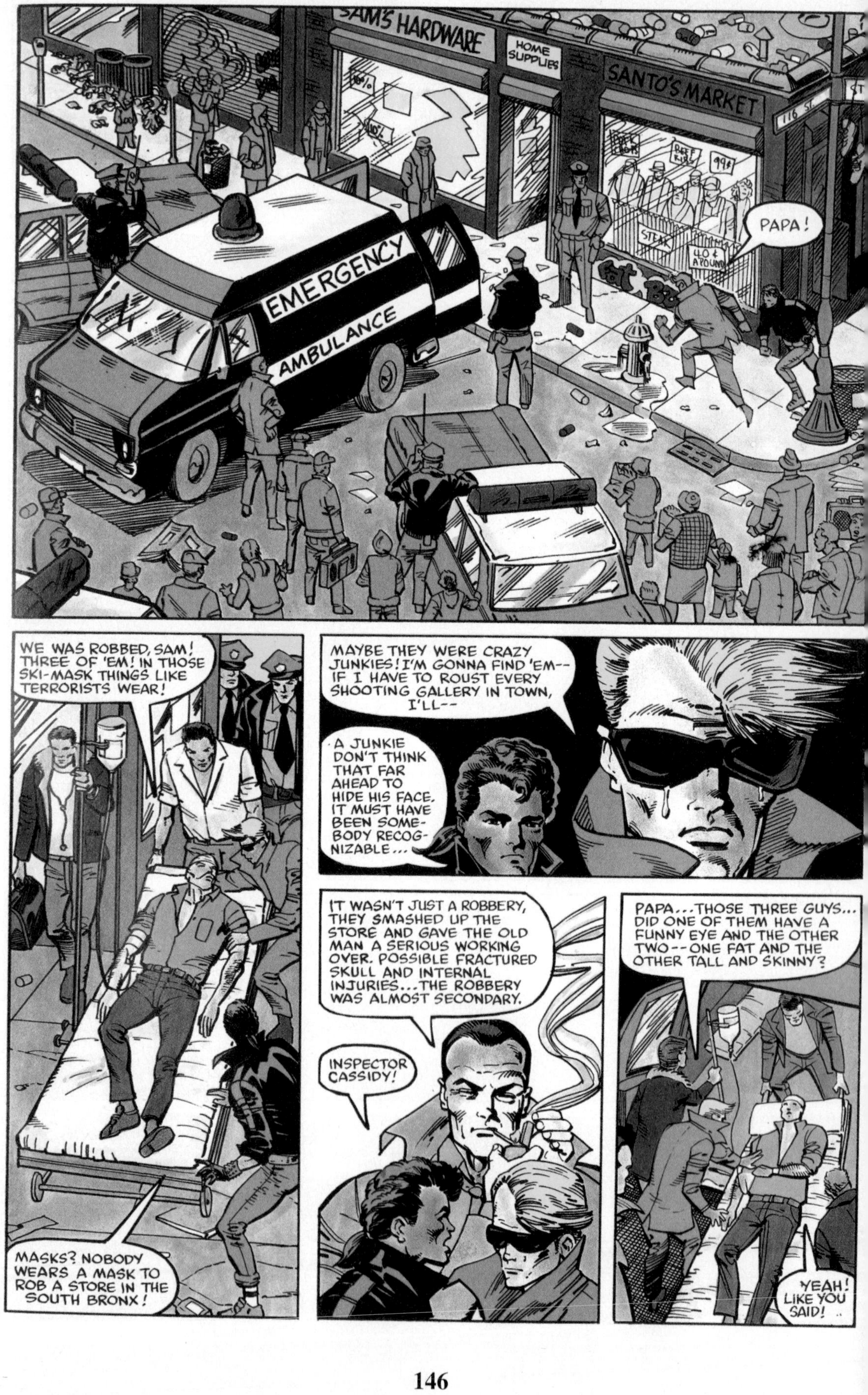
SAM'S HARDWARE
HOME SUPPLIES
SANTO'S MARKET
116 ST
EMERGENCY
AMBULANCE
99¢
STEAK
PAPA!
WE WAS ROBBED, SAM! THREE OF 'EM! IN THOSE SKI-MASK THINGS LIKE TERRORISTS WEAR!
MASKS? NOBODY WEARS A MASK TO ROB A STORE IN THE SOUTH BRONX!
MAYBE THEY WERE CRAZY JUNKIES! I'M GONNA FIND 'EM-- IF I HAVE TO ROUST EVERY SHOOTING GALLERY IN TOWN, I'LL--
A JUNKIE DON'T THINK THAT FAR AHEAD TO HIDE HIS FACE. IT MUST HAVE BEEN SOMEBODY RECOGNIZABLE...
IT WASN'T JUST A ROBBERY, THEY SMASHED UP THE STORE AND GAVE THE OLD MAN A SERIOUS WORKING OVER. POSSIBLE FRACTURED SKULL AND INTERNAL INJURIES... THE ROBBERY WAS ALMOST SECONDARY.
INSPECTOR CASSIDY!
PAPA... THOSE THREE GUYS... DID ONE OF THEM HAVE A FUNNY EYE AND THE OTHER TWO-- ONE FAT AND THE OTHER TALL AND SKINNY?
YEAH! LIKE YOU SAID!

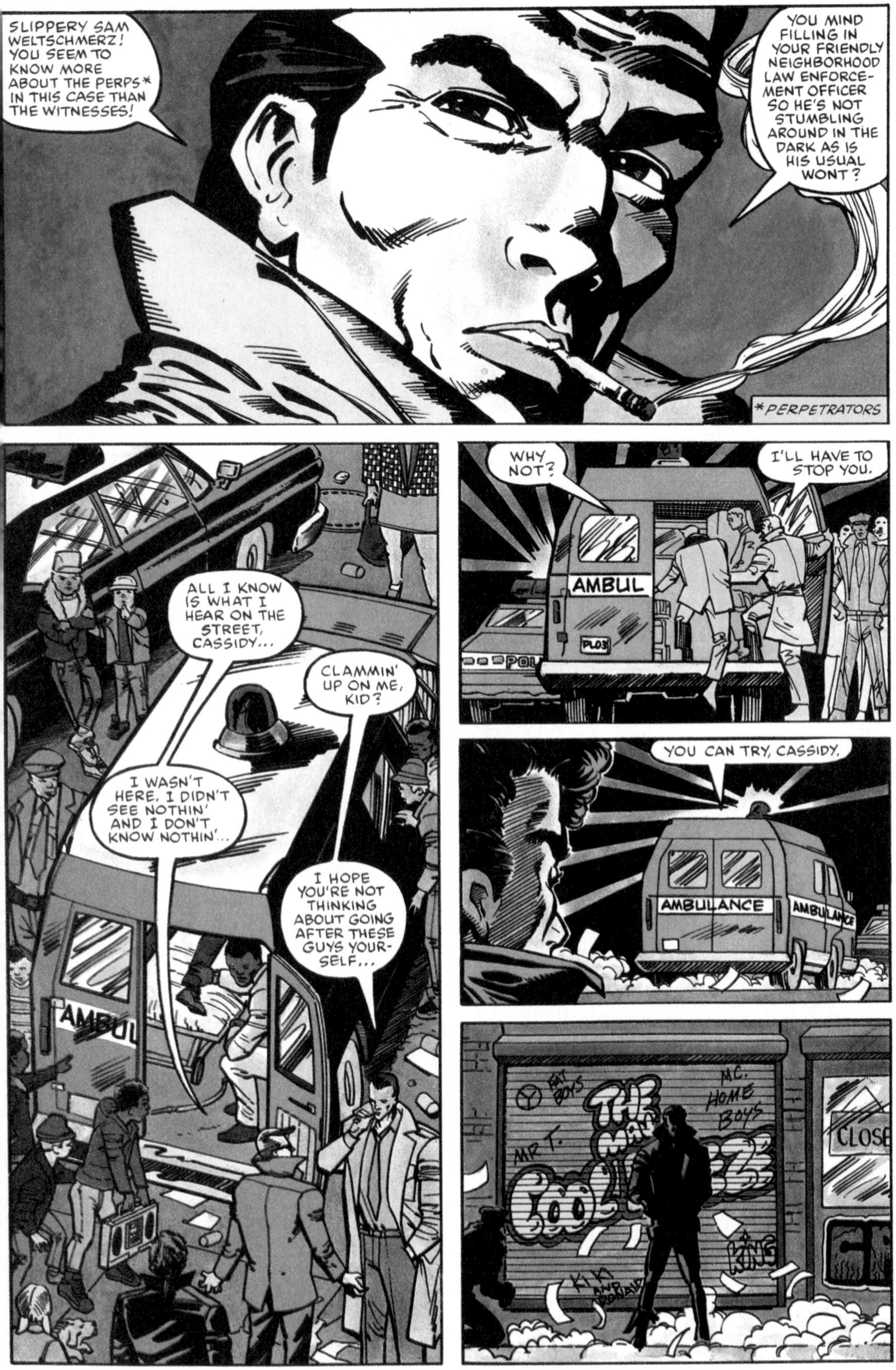
SLIPPERY SAM WELTSCHMERZ! YOU SEEM TO KNOW MORE ABOUT THE PERPS* IN THIS CASE THAN THE WITNESSES!
YOU MIND FILLING IN YOUR FRIENDLY NEIGHBORHOOD LAW ENFORCEMENT OFFICER SO HE'S NOT STUMBLING AROUND IN THE DARK AS IS HIS USUAL WONT?
*PERPETRATORS
ALL I KNOW IS WHAT I HEAR ON THE STREET, CASSIDY...
CLAMMIN' UP ON ME, KID?
I WASN'T HERE. I DIDN'T SEE NOTHIN' AND I DON'T KNOW NOTHIN'...
I HOPE YOU'RE NOT THINKING ABOUT GOING AFTER THESE GUYS YOURSELF...
AMBUL
WHY NOT?
I'LL HAVE TO STOP YOU.
AMBUL
YOU CAN TRY, CASSIDY.
AMBULANCE
MC. HOME BOYS
MR T.
CLOSE

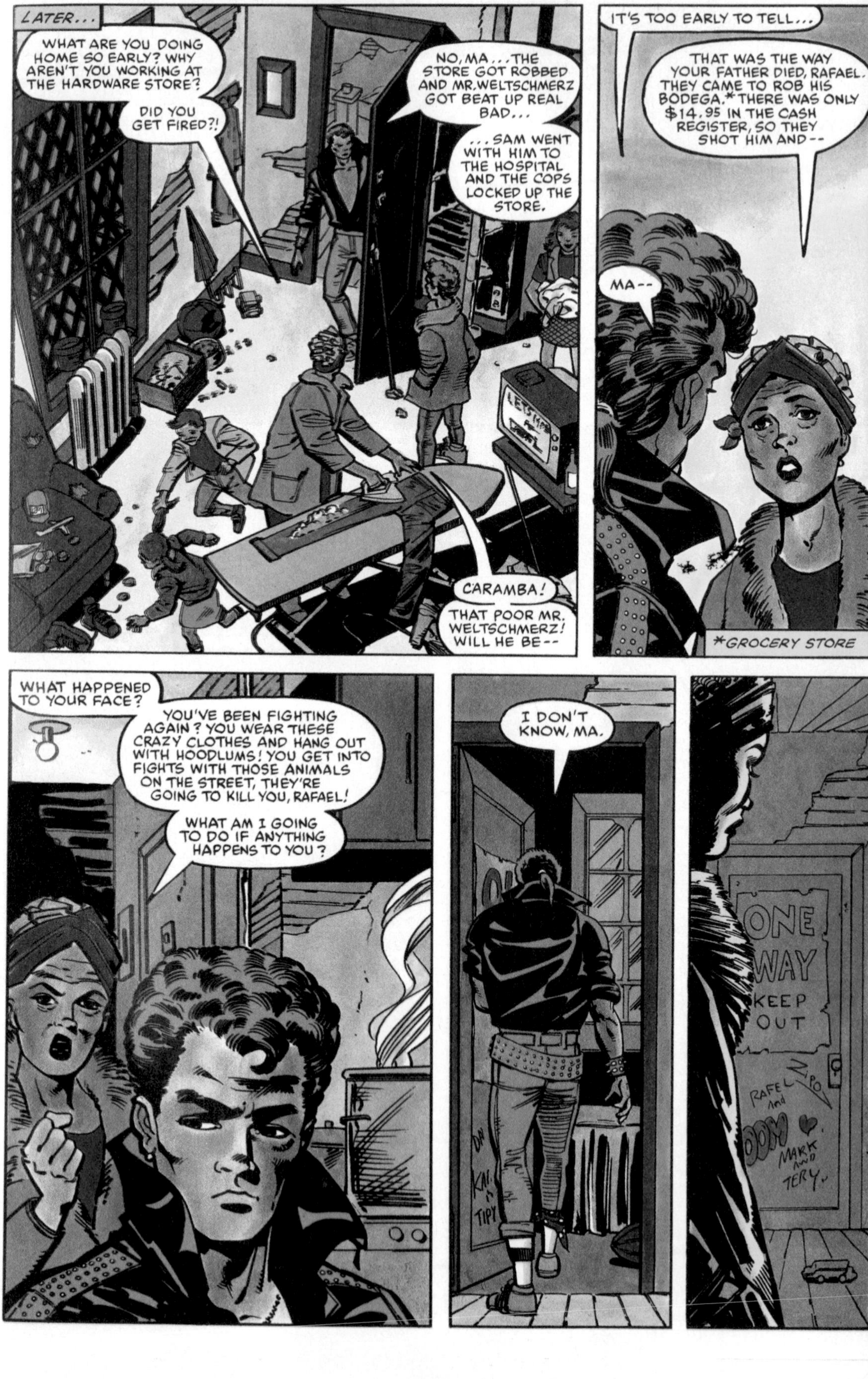
LATER...
WHAT ARE YOU DOING HOME SO EARLY? WHY AREN'T YOU WORKING AT THE HARDWARE STORE?
DID YOU GET FIRED?!
NO, MA... THE STORE GOT ROBBED AND MR. WELTSCHMERZ GOT BEAT UP REAL BAD...
...SAM WENT WITH HIM TO THE HOSPITAL AND THE COPS LOCKED UP THE STORE.
CARAMBA!
THAT POOR MR. WELTSCHMERZ! WILL HE BE--
IT'S TOO EARLY TO TELL...
THAT WAS THE WAY YOUR FATHER DIED, RAFAEL. THEY CAME TO ROB HIS BODEGA.* THERE WAS ONLY $14.95 IN THE CASH REGISTER, SO THEY SHOT HIM AND--
MA--
*GROCERY STORE
WHAT HAPPENED TO YOUR FACE?
YOU'VE BEEN FIGHTING AGAIN? YOU WEAR THESE CRAZY CLOTHES AND HANG OUT WITH HOODLUMS! YOU GET INTO FIGHTS WITH THOSE ANIMALS ON THE STREET, THEY'RE GOING TO KILL YOU, RAFAEL!
WHAT AM I GOING TO DO IF ANYTHING HAPPENS TO YOU?
I DON'T KNOW, MA.
ONE WAY
KEEP OUT
RAFEL And ZIPO
MARK AND TERY

THAT NIGHT...

AIR JORDON

"IT'S TIME."

"HECTOR AND LUIS ARE ASLEEP, GOOD."

"TIME TO FALL INTO THE NIGHT...!"

"TIME TO BREATHE THE DARKNESS..."

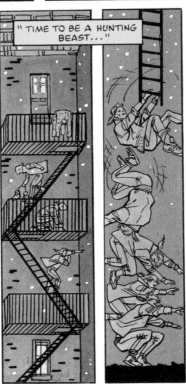

"TIME TO BE A HUNTING BEAST..."

"...A WOLF!"

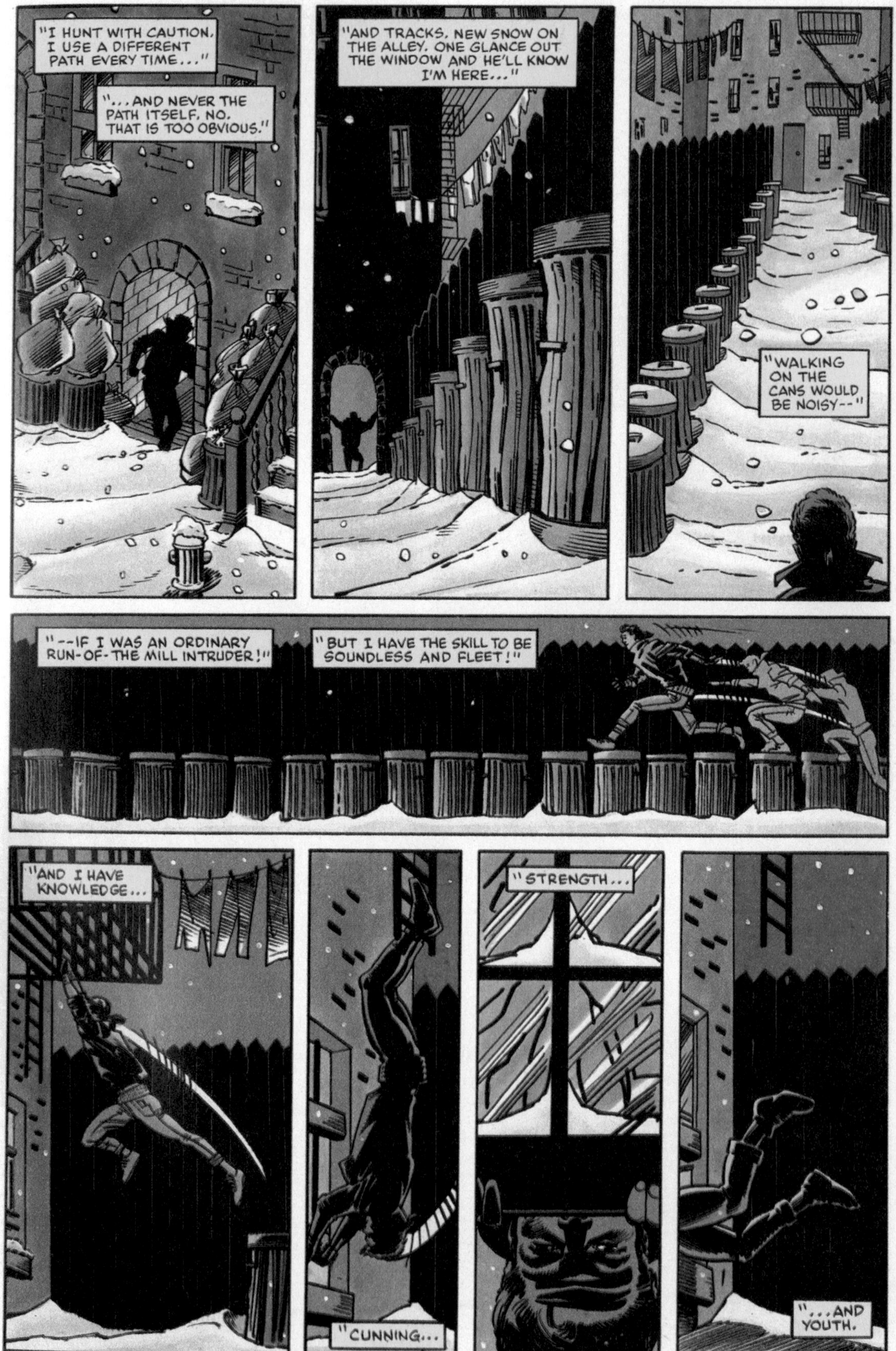
"I HUNT WITH CAUTION. I USE A DIFFERENT PATH EVERY TIME..."
"...AND NEVER THE PATH ITSELF, NO. THAT IS TOO OBVIOUS."
"AND TRACKS, NEW SNOW ON THE ALLEY. ONE GLANCE OUT THE WINDOW AND HE'LL KNOW I'M HERE..."
"WALKING ON THE CANS WOULD BE NOISY--"
"--IF I WAS AN ORDINARY RUN-OF-THE MILL INTRUDER!"
"BUT I HAVE THE SKILL TO BE SOUNDLESS AND FLEET!"
"AND I HAVE KNOWLEDGE...
"CUNNING...
"STRENGTH...
"...AND YOUTH.

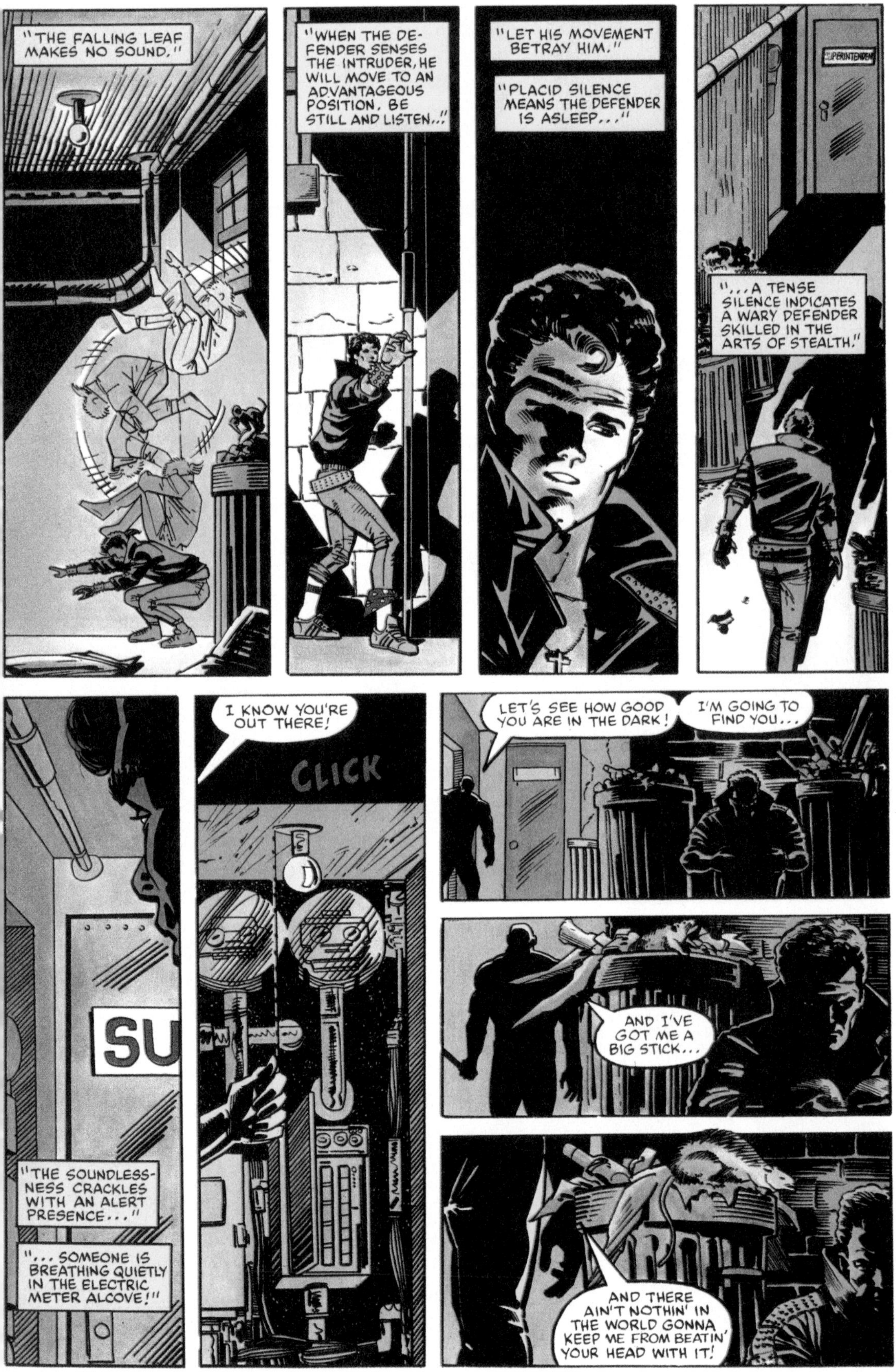
"THE FALLING LEAF MAKES NO SOUND."
"WHEN THE DEFENDER SENSES THE INTRUDER, HE WILL MOVE TO AN ADVANTAGEOUS POSITION. BE STILL AND LISTEN..."
"LET HIS MOVEMENT BETRAY HIM."
"PLACID SILENCE MEANS THE DEFENDER IS ASLEEP..."
SUPERINTENDENT
"...A TENSE SILENCE INDICATES A WARY DEFENDER SKILLED IN THE ARTS OF STEALTH."
SU
"THE SOUNDLESSNESS CRACKLES WITH AN ALERT PRESENCE..."
"...SOMEONE IS BREATHING QUIETLY IN THE ELECTRIC METER ALCOVE!"
I KNOW YOU'RE OUT THERE!
CLICK
LET'S SEE HOW GOOD YOU ARE IN THE DARK!
I'M GOING TO FIND YOU...
AND I'VE GOT ME A BIG STICK...
AND THERE AIN'T NOTHIN' IN THE WORLD GONNA KEEP ME FROM BEATIN' YOUR HEAD WITH IT!

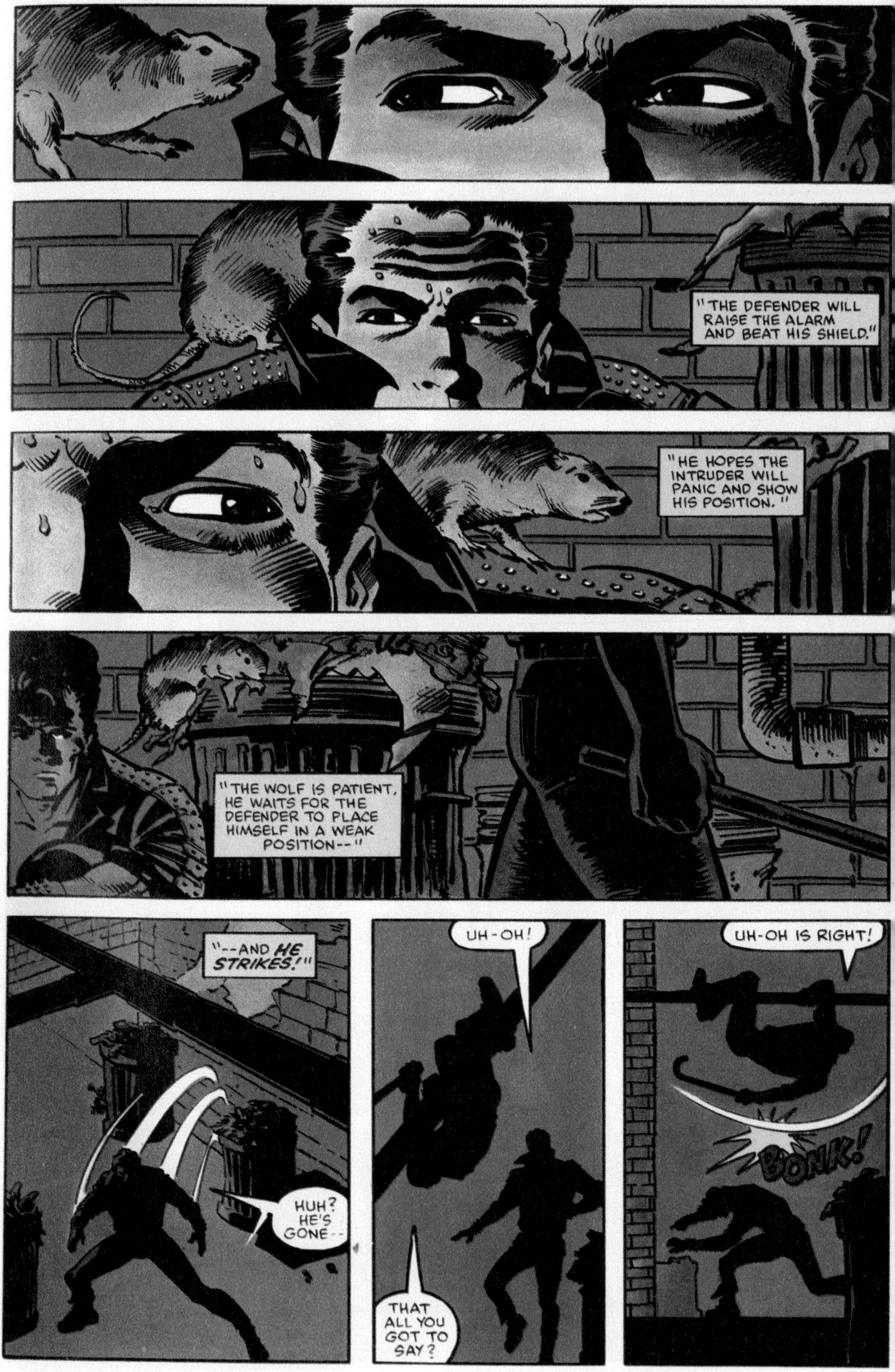
"THE DEFENDER WILL RAISE THE ALARM AND BEAT HIS SHIELD."
"HE HOPES THE INTRUDER WILL PANIC AND SHOW HIS POSITION."
"THE WOLF IS PATIENT. HE WAITS FOR THE DEFENDER TO PLACE HIMSELF IN A WEAK POSITION--"
"--AND HE STRIKES!"
HUH? HE'S GONE--
UH-OH!
THAT ALL YOU GOT TO SAY?
UH-OH IS RIGHT!
BONK!

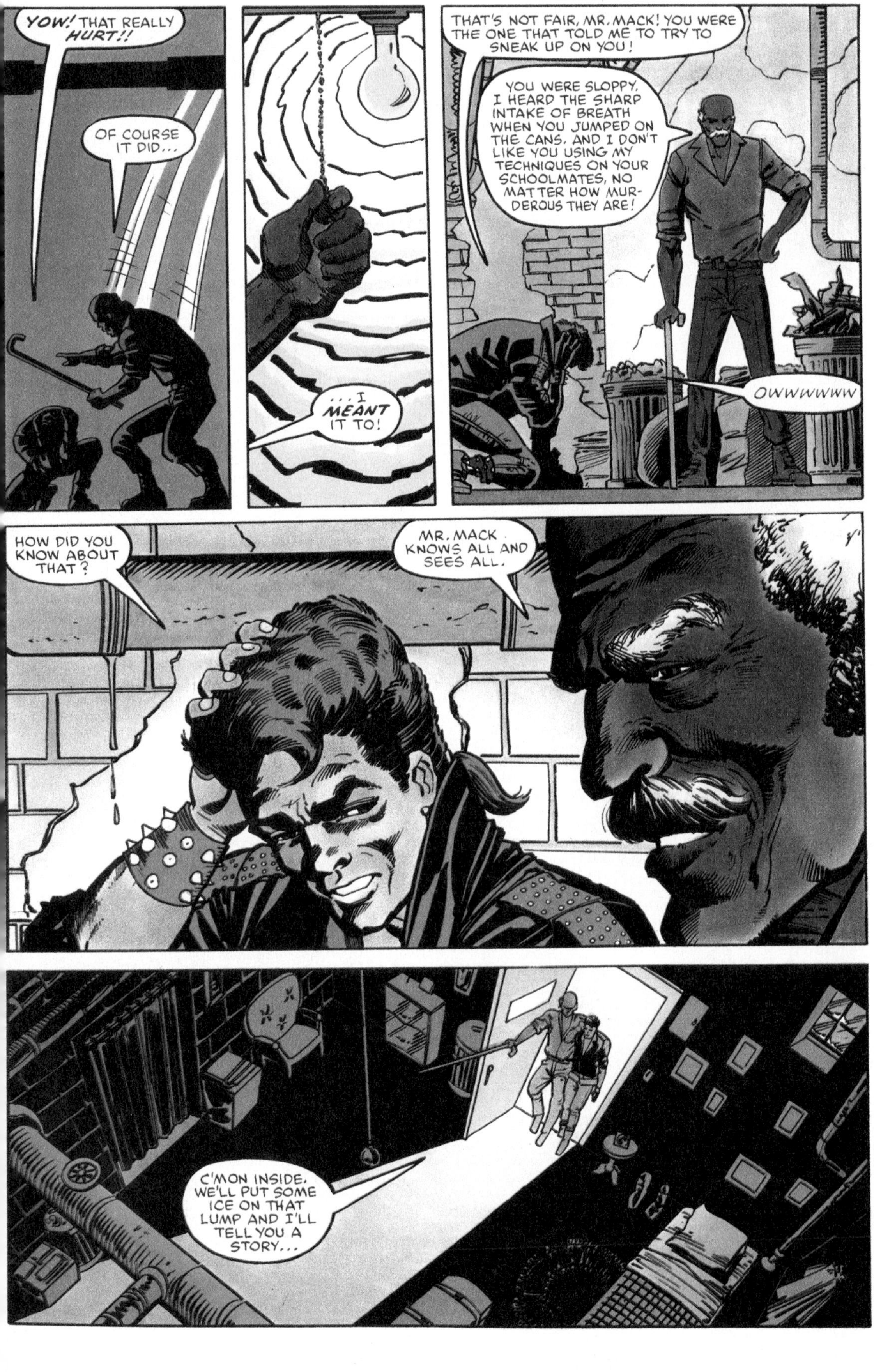
YOW! THAT REALLY HURT!!
OF COURSE IT DID...
...I MEANT IT TO!
THAT'S NOT FAIR, MR. MACK! YOU WERE THE ONE THAT TOLD ME TO TRY TO SNEAK UP ON YOU!
YOU WERE SLOPPY. I HEARD THE SHARP INTAKE OF BREATH WHEN YOU JUMPED ON THE CANS. AND I DON'T LIKE YOU USING MY TECHNIQUES ON YOUR SCHOOLMATES, NO MATTER HOW MURDEROUS THEY ARE!
OWWWWWW
HOW DID YOU KNOW ABOUT THAT?
MR. MACK KNOWS ALL AND SEES ALL.
C'MON INSIDE. WE'LL PUT SOME ICE ON THAT LUMP AND I'LL TELL YOU A STORY...

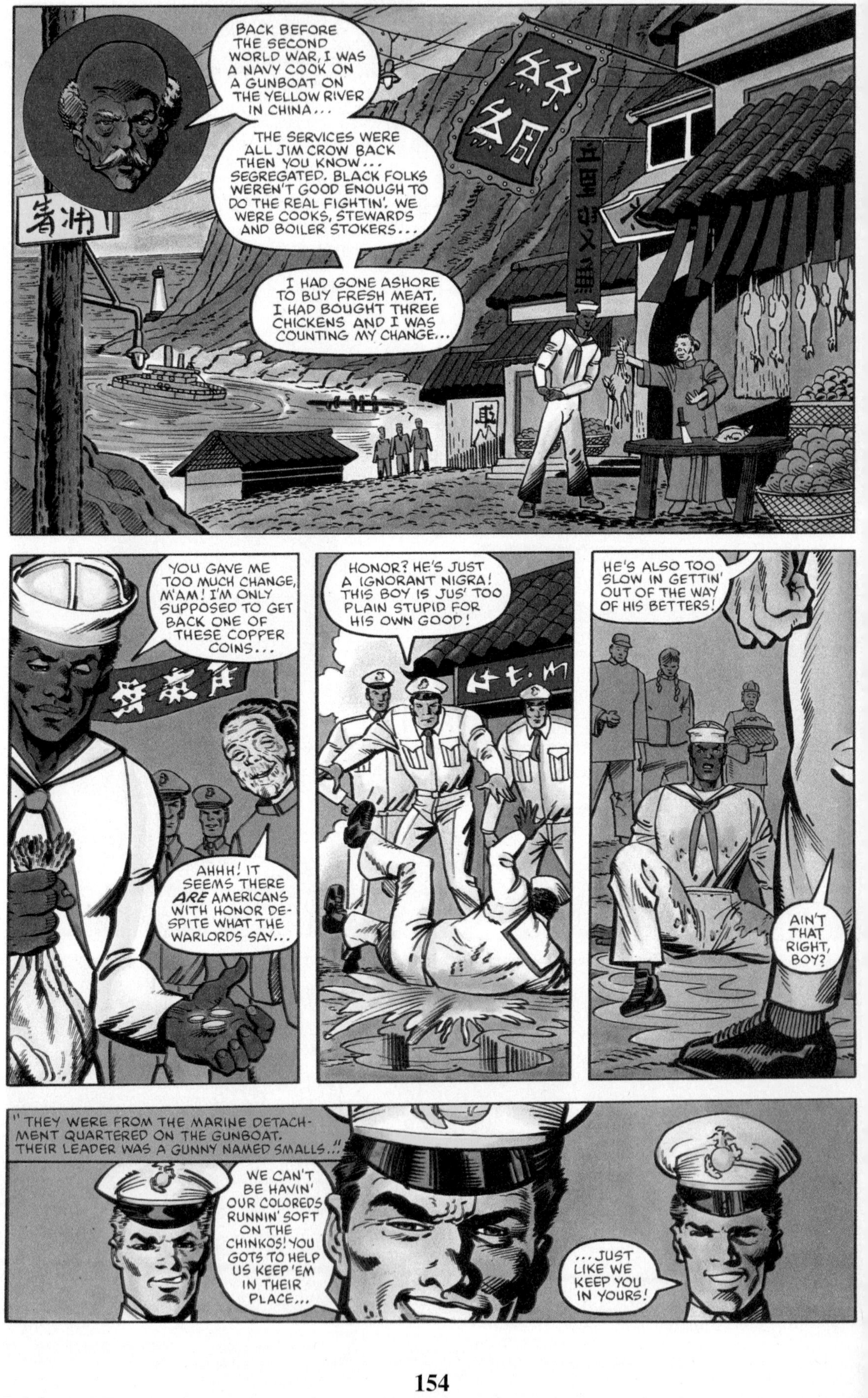
BACK BEFORE THE SECOND WORLD WAR, I WAS A NAVY COOK ON A GUNBOAT ON THE YELLOW RIVER IN CHINA...
THE SERVICES WERE ALL JIM CROW BACK THEN YOU KNOW... SEGREGATED. BLACK FOLKS WEREN'T GOOD ENOUGH TO DO THE REAL FIGHTIN'. WE WERE COOKS, STEWARDS AND BOILER STOKERS...
I HAD GONE ASHORE TO BUY FRESH MEAT. I HAD BOUGHT THREE CHICKENS AND I WAS COUNTING MY CHANGE...
YOU GAVE ME TOO MUCH CHANGE, M'AM! I'M ONLY SUPPOSED TO GET BACK ONE OF THESE COPPER COINS...
AHHH! IT SEEMS THERE *ARE* AMERICANS WITH HONOR DE-SPITE WHAT THE WARLORDS SAY...
HONOR? HE'S JUST A IGNORANT NIGRA! THIS BOY IS JUS' TOO PLAIN STUPID FOR HIS OWN GOOD!
HE'S ALSO TOO SLOW IN GETTIN' OUT OF THE WAY OF HIS BETTERS!
AIN'T THAT RIGHT, BOY?
"THEY WERE FROM THE MARINE DETACH-MENT QUARTERED ON THE GUNBOAT. THEIR LEADER WAS A GUNNY NAMED SMALLS..."
WE CAN'T BE HAVIN' OUR COLOREDS RUNNIN' SOFT ON THE CHINKOS! YOU GOTS TO HELP US KEEP 'EM IN THEIR PLACE...
...JUST LIKE WE KEEP YOU IN YOURS!

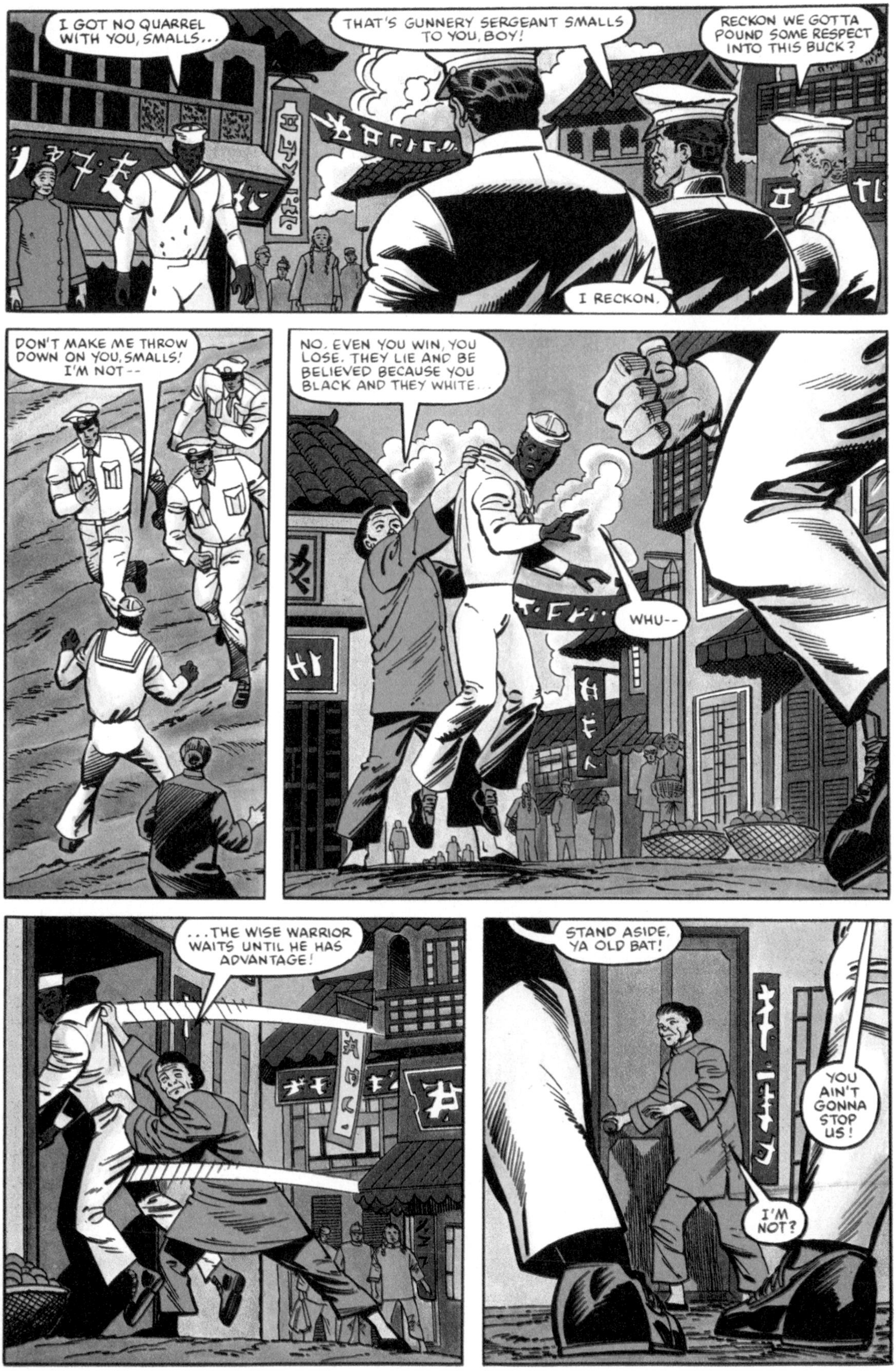
I GOT NO QUARREL WITH YOU, SMALLS...
THAT'S GUNNERY SERGEANT SMALLS TO YOU, BOY!
RECKON WE GOTTA POUND SOME RESPECT INTO THIS BUCK?
I RECKON.
DON'T MAKE ME THROW DOWN ON YOU, SMALLS! I'M NOT--
NO. EVEN YOU WIN, YOU LOSE. THEY LIE AND BE BELIEVED BECAUSE YOU BLACK AND THEY WHITE...
WHU--
...THE WISE WARRIOR WAITS UNTIL HE HAS ADVANTAGE!
STAND ASIDE, YA OLD BAT!
YOU AIN'T GONNA STOP US!
I'M NOT?

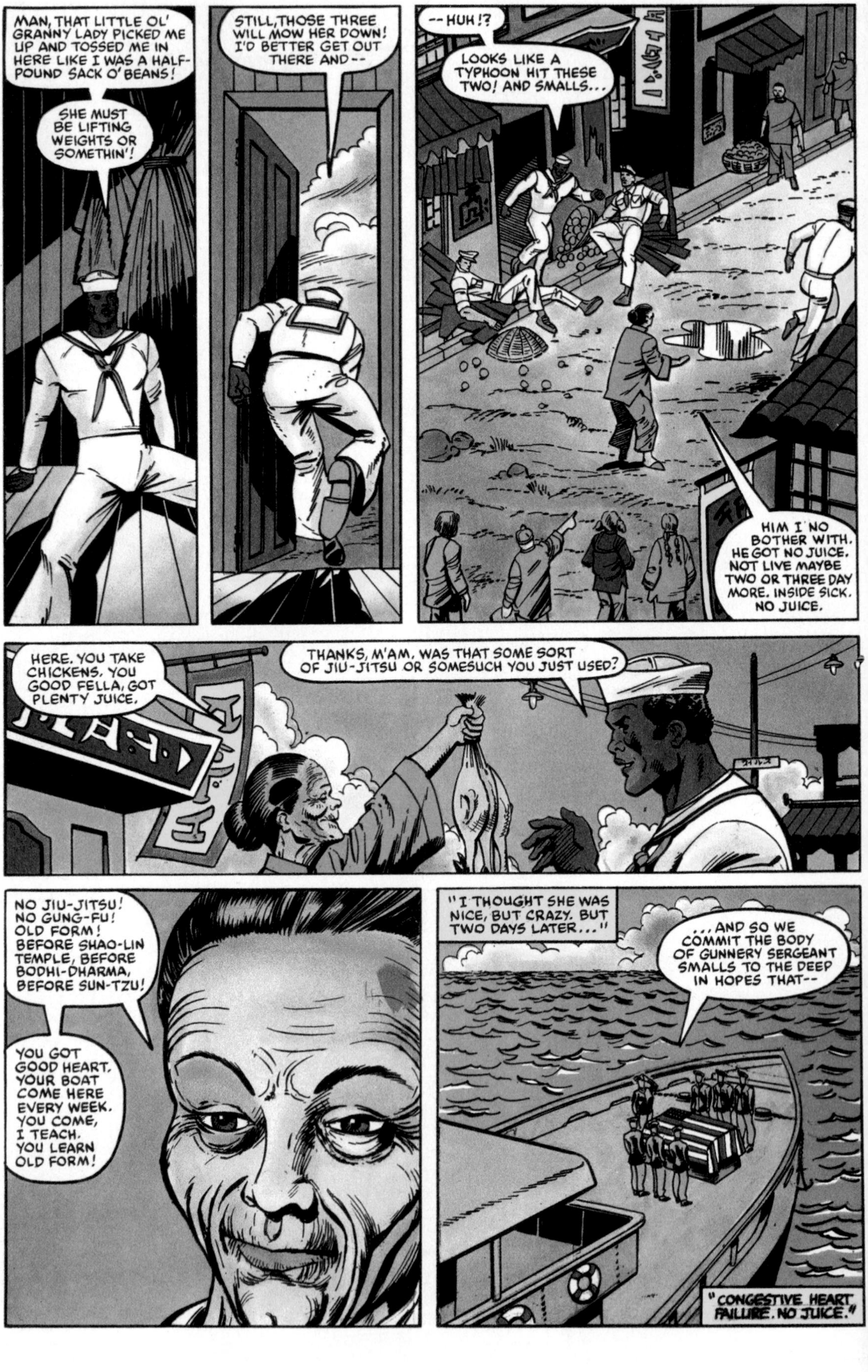
MAN, THAT LITTLE OL' GRANNY LADY PICKED ME UP AND TOSSED ME IN HERE LIKE I WAS A HALF-POUND SACK O' BEANS!
SHE MUST BE LIFTING WEIGHTS OR SOMETHIN'!
STILL, THOSE THREE WILL MOW HER DOWN! I'D BETTER GET OUT THERE AND--
--HUH!?
LOOKS LIKE A TYPHOON HIT THESE TWO! AND SMALLS...
HIM I NO BOTHER WITH. HE GOT NO JUICE. NOT LIVE MAYBE TWO OR THREE DAY MORE. INSIDE SICK. NO JUICE.
HERE. YOU TAKE CHICKENS. YOU GOOD FELLA, GOT PLENTY JUICE.
THANKS, M'AM. WAS THAT SOME SORT OF JIU-JITSU OR SOMESUCH YOU JUST USED?
NO JIU-JITSU! NO GUNG-FU! OLD FORM! BEFORE SHAO-LIN TEMPLE, BEFORE BODHI-DHARMA, BEFORE SUN-TZU!
YOU GOT GOOD HEART. YOUR BOAT COME HERE EVERY WEEK. YOU COME, I TEACH. YOU LEARN OLD FORM!
"I THOUGHT SHE WAS NICE, BUT CRAZY. BUT TWO DAYS LATER..."
...AND SO WE COMMIT THE BODY OF GUNNERY SERGEANT SMALLS TO THE DEEP IN HOPES THAT--
"CONGESTIVE HEART FAILURE. NO JUICE."

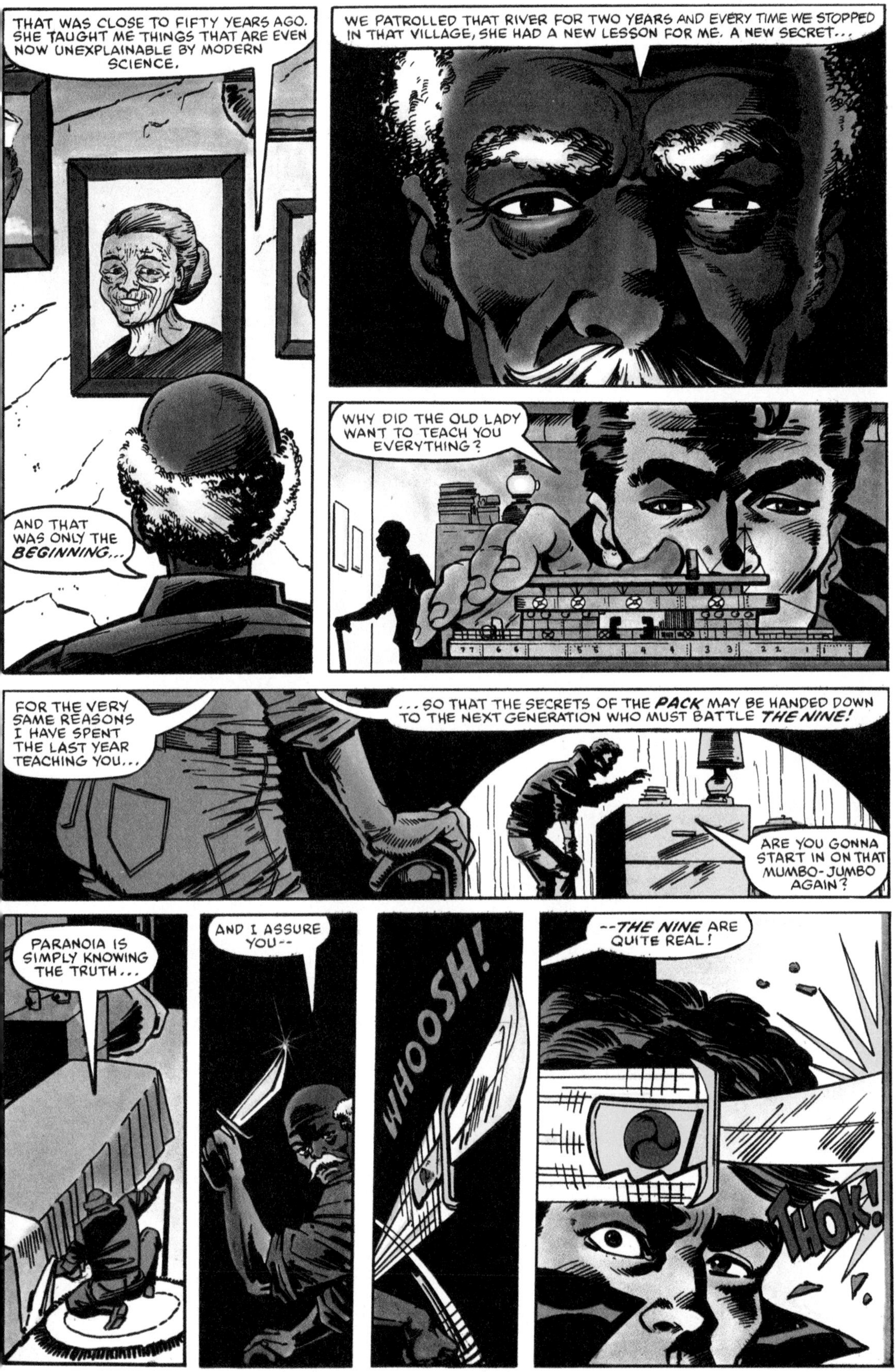

THAT WAS CLOSE TO FIFTY YEARS AGO. SHE TAUGHT ME THINGS THAT ARE EVEN NOW UNEXPLAINABLE BY MODERN SCIENCE.
AND THAT WAS ONLY THE BEGINNING...
WE PATROLLED THAT RIVER FOR TWO YEARS AND EVERY TIME WE STOPPED IN THAT VILLAGE, SHE HAD A NEW LESSON FOR ME. A NEW SECRET...
WHY DID THE OLD LADY WANT TO TEACH YOU EVERYTHING?
FOR THE VERY SAME REASONS I HAVE SPENT THE LAST YEAR TEACHING YOU...
...SO THAT THE SECRETS OF THE PACK MAY BE HANDED DOWN TO THE NEXT GENERATION WHO MUST BATTLE THE NINE!
ARE YOU GONNA START IN ON THAT MUMBO-JUMBO AGAIN?
PARANOIA IS SIMPLY KNOWING THE TRUTH...
AND I ASSURE YOU--
WHOOSH!
--THE NINE ARE QUITE REAL!
THOK!

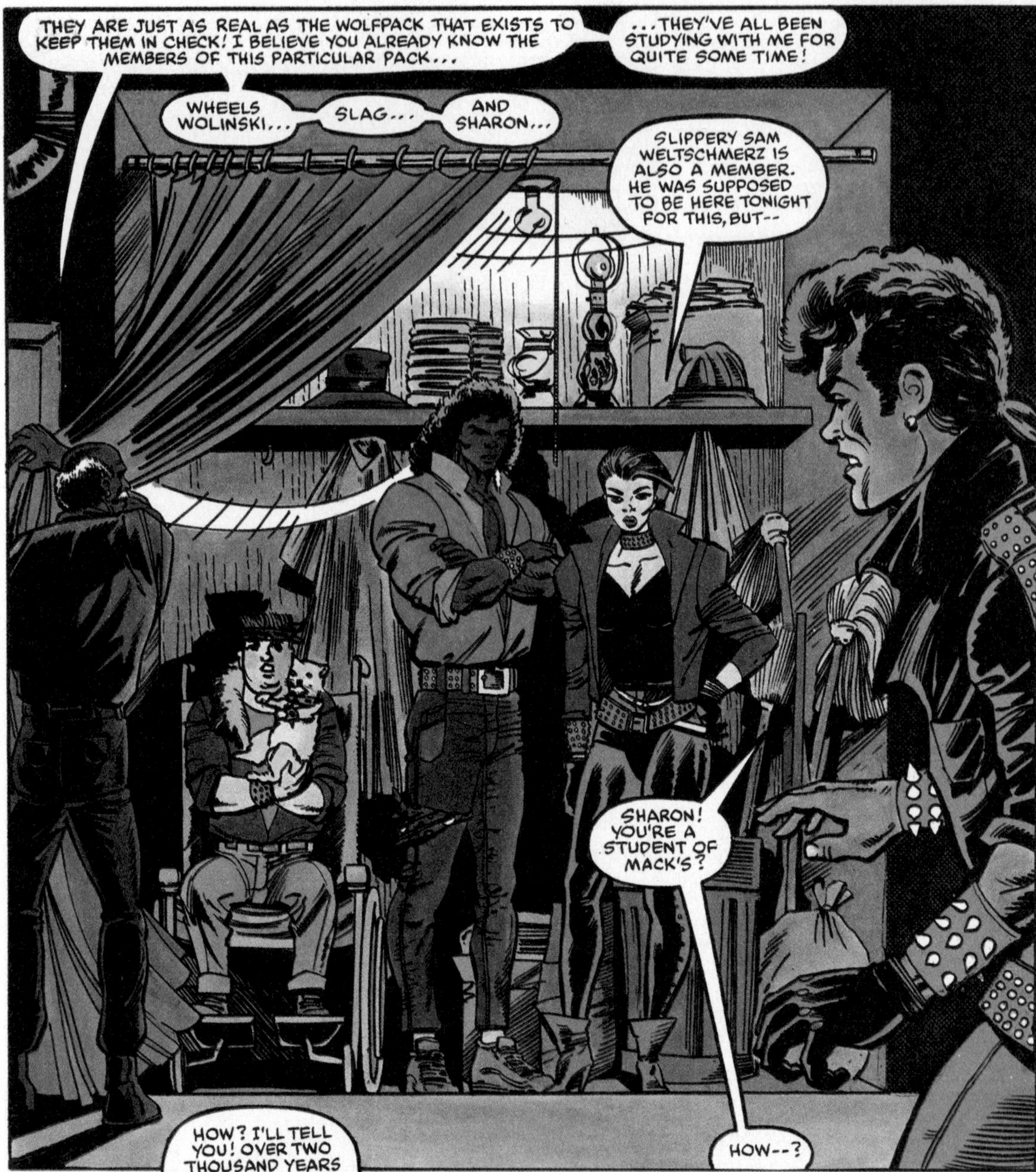
THEY ARE JUST AS REAL AS THE WOLFPACK THAT EXISTS TO KEEP THEM IN CHECK! I BELIEVE YOU ALREADY KNOW THE MEMBERS OF THIS PARTICULAR PACK...
WHEELS WOLINSKI...
SLAG...
AND SHARON...
...THEY'VE ALL BEEN STUDYING WITH ME FOR QUITE SOME TIME!
SLIPPERY SAM WELTSCHMERZ IS ALSO A MEMBER. HE WAS SUPPOSED TO BE HERE TONIGHT FOR THIS, BUT--
SHARON! YOU'RE A STUDENT OF MACK'S?
HOW--?
HOW? I'LL TELL YOU! OVER TWO THOUSAND YEARS AGO, A LOST TRIBE OF ISRAEL WANDERED INTO CHINA...

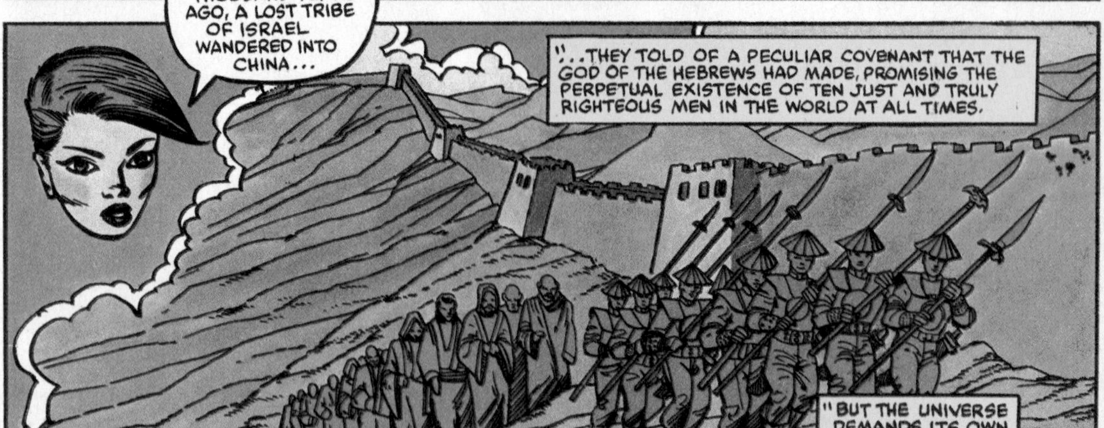
"...THEY TOLD OF A PECULIAR COVENANT THAT THE GOD OF THE HEBREWS HAD MADE, PROMISING THE PERPETUAL EXISTENCE OF TEN JUST AND TRULY RIGHTEOUS MEN IN THE WORLD AT ALL TIMES.
"BUT THE UNIVERSE DEMANDS ITS OWN BALANCE..."

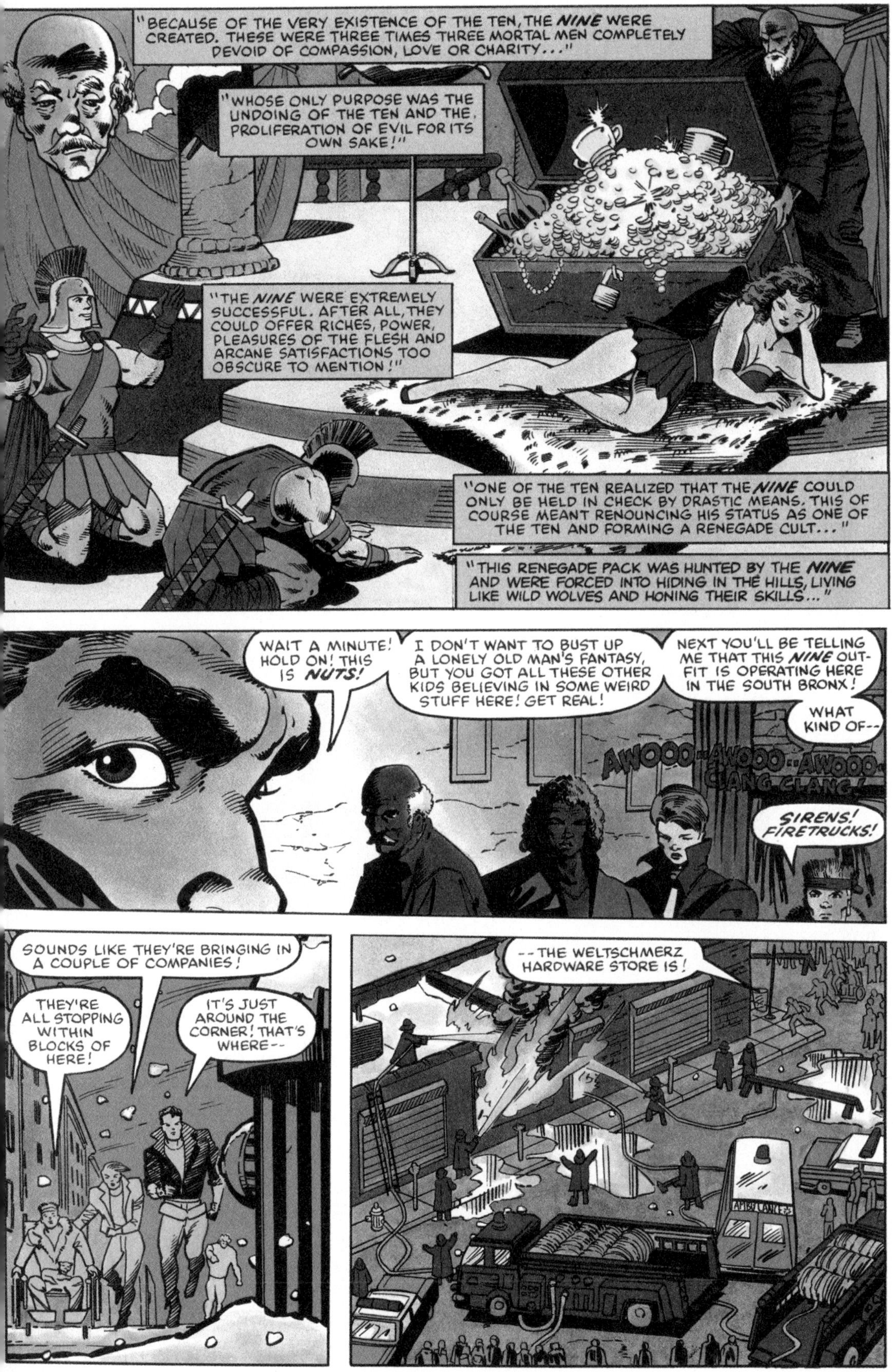
"BECAUSE OF THE VERY EXISTENCE OF THE TEN, THE NINE WERE CREATED. THESE WERE THREE TIMES THREE MORTAL MEN COMPLETELY DEVOID OF COMPASSION, LOVE OR CHARITY..."
"WHOSE ONLY PURPOSE WAS THE UNDOING OF THE TEN AND THE PROLIFERATION OF EVIL FOR ITS OWN SAKE!"
"THE NINE WERE EXTREMELY SUCCESSFUL. AFTER ALL, THEY COULD OFFER RICHES, POWER, PLEASURES OF THE FLESH AND ARCANE SATISFACTIONS TOO OBSCURE TO MENTION!"
"ONE OF THE TEN REALIZED THAT THE NINE COULD ONLY BE HELD IN CHECK BY DRASTIC MEANS. THIS OF COURSE MEANT RENOUNCING HIS STATUS AS ONE OF THE TEN AND FORMING A RENEGADE CULT..."
"THIS RENEGADE PACK WAS HUNTED BY THE NINE AND WERE FORCED INTO HIDING IN THE HILLS, LIVING LIKE WILD WOLVES AND HONING THEIR SKILLS..."
WAIT A MINUTE! HOLD ON! THIS IS NUTS!
I DON'T WANT TO BUST UP A LONELY OLD MAN'S FANTASY, BUT YOU GOT ALL THESE OTHER KIDS BELIEVING IN SOME WEIRD STUFF HERE! GET REAL!
NEXT YOU'LL BE TELLING ME THAT THIS NINE OUTFIT IS OPERATING HERE IN THE SOUTH BRONX!
WHAT KIND OF--
AWOOO--AWOOO--AWOOO
CLANG CLANG!
SIRENS! FIRETRUCKS!
SOUNDS LIKE THEY'RE BRINGING IN A COUPLE OF COMPANIES!
THEY'RE ALL STOPPING WITHIN BLOCKS OF HERE!
IT'S JUST AROUND THE CORNER! THAT'S WHERE--
--THE WELTSCHMERZ HARDWARE STORE IS!

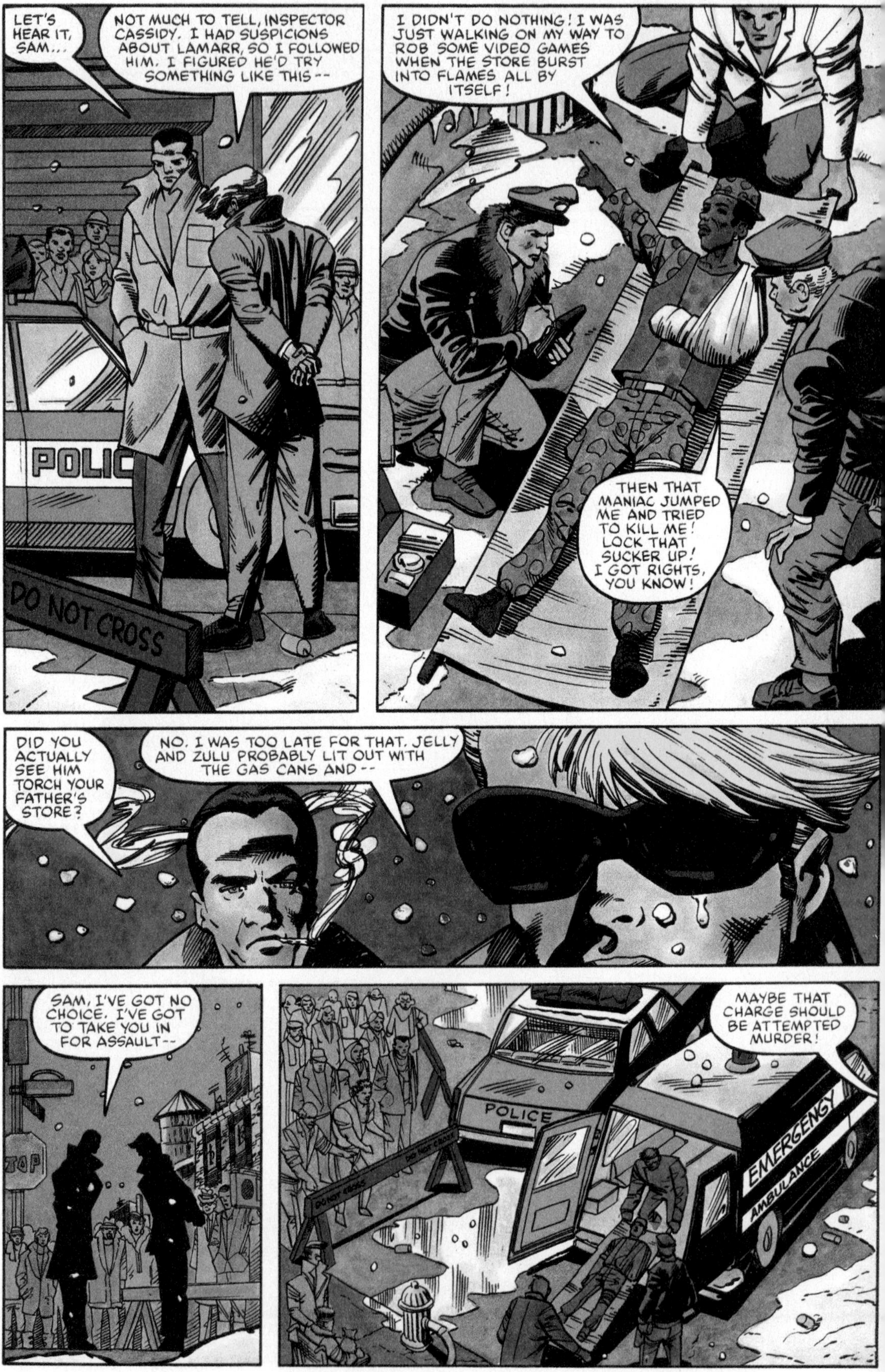
LET'S HEAR IT, SAM...
NOT MUCH TO TELL, INSPECTOR CASSIDY. I HAD SUSPICIONS ABOUT LAMARR, SO I FOLLOWED HIM. I FIGURED HE'D TRY SOMETHING LIKE THIS--
POLIC
DO NOT CROSS
I DIDN'T DO NOTHING! I WAS JUST WALKING ON MY WAY TO ROB SOME VIDEO GAMES WHEN THE STORE BURST INTO FLAMES ALL BY ITSELF!
THEN THAT MANIAC JUMPED ME AND TRIED TO KILL ME! LOCK THAT SUCKER UP! I GOT RIGHTS, YOU KNOW!
DID YOU ACTUALLY SEE HIM TORCH YOUR FATHER'S STORE?
NO. I WAS TOO LATE FOR THAT. JELLY AND ZULU PROBABLY LIT OUT WITH THE GAS CANS AND--
SAM, I'VE GOT NO CHOICE. I'VE GOT TO TAKE YOU IN FOR ASSAULT--
STOP
POLICE
EMERGENCY
AMBULANCE
MAYBE THAT CHARGE SHOULD BE ATTEMPTED MURDER!

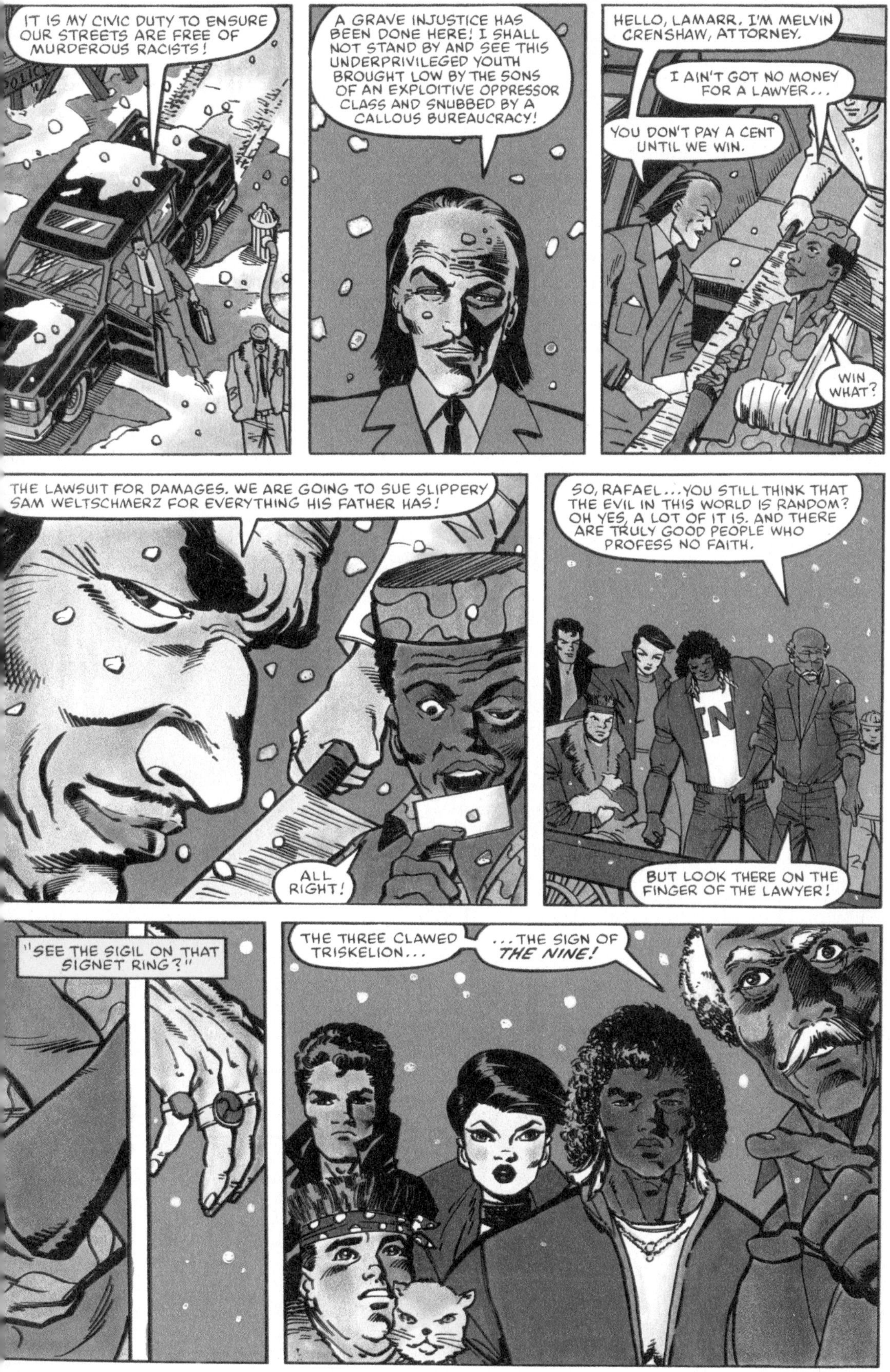
IT IS MY CIVIC DUTY TO ENSURE OUR STREETS ARE FREE OF MURDEROUS RACISTS!
POLICE
A GRAVE INJUSTICE HAS BEEN DONE HERE! I SHALL NOT STAND BY AND SEE THIS UNDERPRIVILEGED YOUTH BROUGHT LOW BY THE SONS OF AN EXPLOITIVE OPPRESSOR CLASS AND SNUBBED BY A CALLOUS BUREAUCRACY!
HELLO, LAMARR. I'M MELVIN CRENSHAW, ATTORNEY.
I AIN'T GOT NO MONEY FOR A LAWYER...
YOU DON'T PAY A CENT UNTIL WE WIN.
WIN WHAT?
THE LAWSUIT FOR DAMAGES. WE ARE GOING TO SUE SLIPPERY SAM WELTSCHMERZ FOR EVERYTHING HIS FATHER HAS!
ALL RIGHT!
SO, RAFAEL...YOU STILL THINK THAT THE EVIL IN THIS WORLD IS RANDOM? OH YES, A LOT OF IT IS. AND THERE ARE TRULY GOOD PEOPLE WHO PROFESS NO FAITH.
BUT LOOK THERE ON THE FINGER OF THE LAWYER!
"SEE THE SIGIL ON THAT SIGNET RING?"
THE THREE CLAWED TRISKELION...
...THE SIGN OF THE NINE!

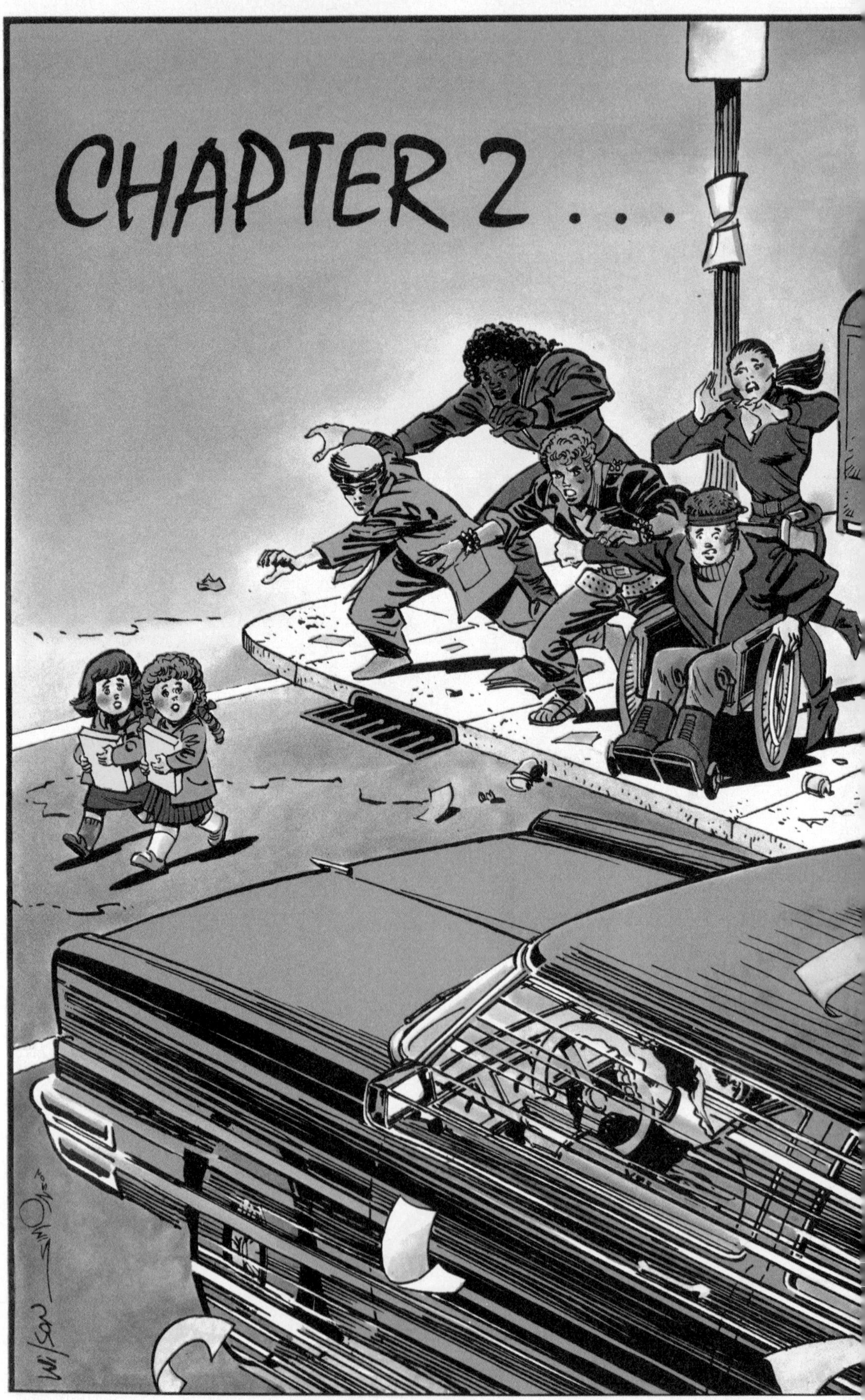
CHAPTER 2 . . .

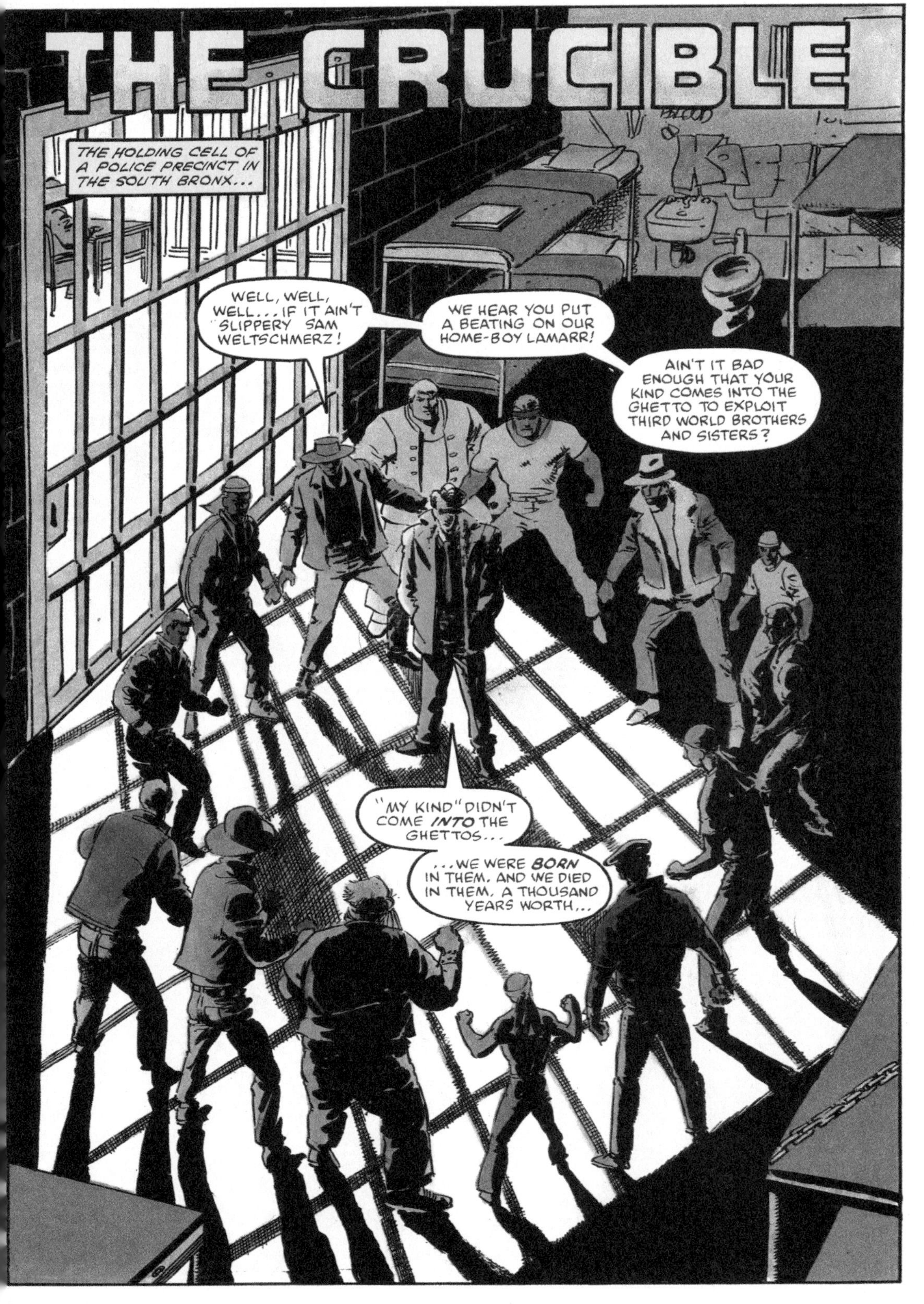
THE CRUCIBLE
THE HOLDING CELL OF A POLICE PRECINCT IN THE SOUTH BRONX...
WELL, WELL, WELL... IF IT AIN'T SLIPPERY SAM WELTSCHMERZ!
WE HEAR YOU PUT A BEATING ON OUR HOME-BOY LAMARR!
AIN'T IT BAD ENOUGH THAT YOUR KIND COMES INTO THE GHETTO TO EXPLOIT THIRD WORLD BROTHERS AND SISTERS?
"MY KIND" DIDN'T COME INTO THE GHETTOS...
...WE WERE BORN IN THEM. AND WE DIED IN THEM. A THOUSAND YEARS WORTH...

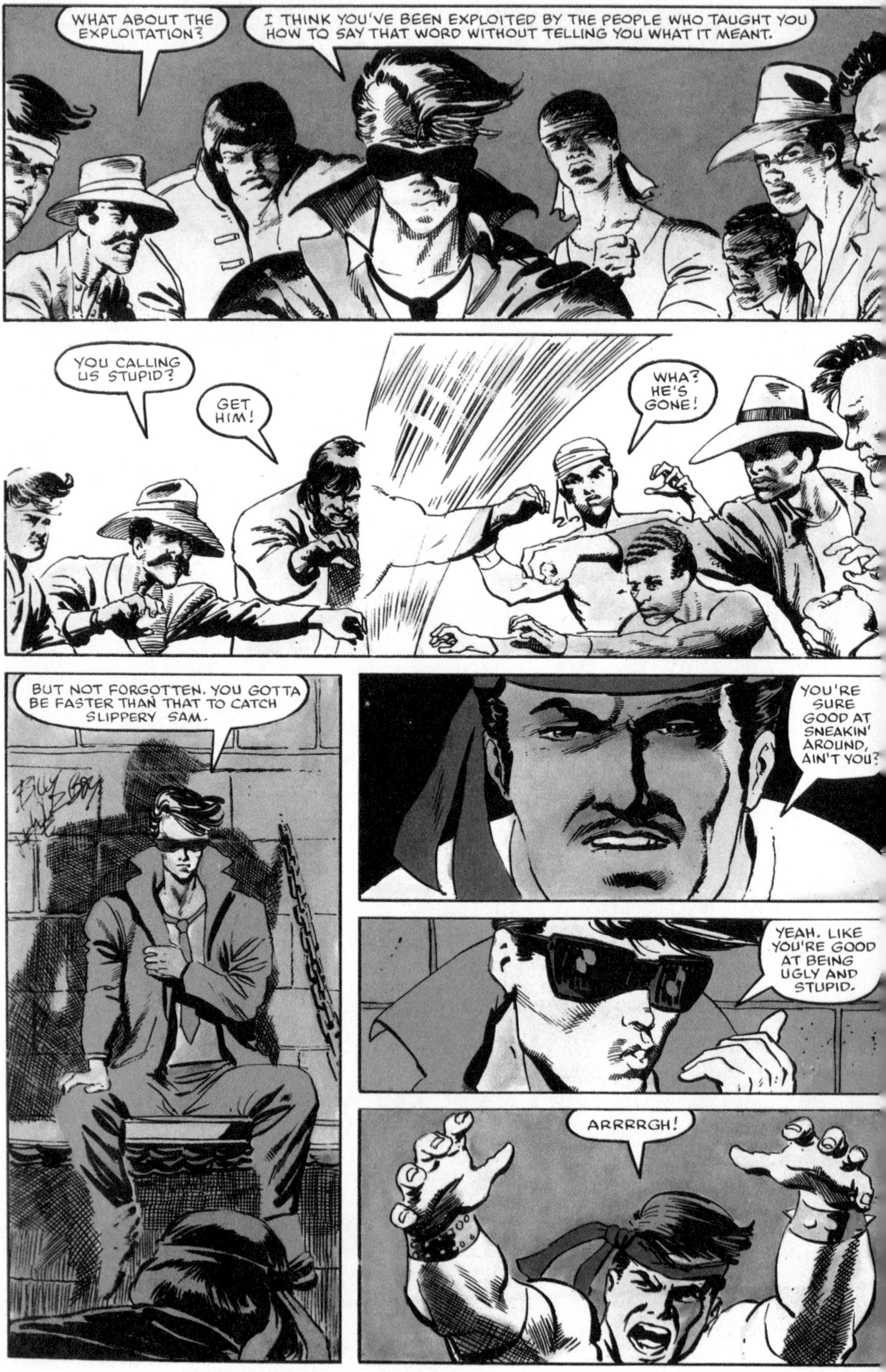
WHAT ABOUT THE EXPLOITATION?
I THINK YOU'VE BEEN EXPLOITED BY THE PEOPLE WHO TAUGHT YOU HOW TO SAY THAT WORD WITHOUT TELLING YOU WHAT IT MEANT.
YOU CALLING US STUPID?
GET HIM!
WHA? HE'S GONE!
BUT NOT FORGOTTEN. YOU GOTTA BE FASTER THAN THAT TO CATCH SLIPPERY SAM.
YOU'RE SURE GOOD AT SNEAKIN' AROUND, AIN'T YOU?
YEAH. LIKE YOU'RE GOOD AT BEING UGLY AND STUPID.
ARRRRGH!

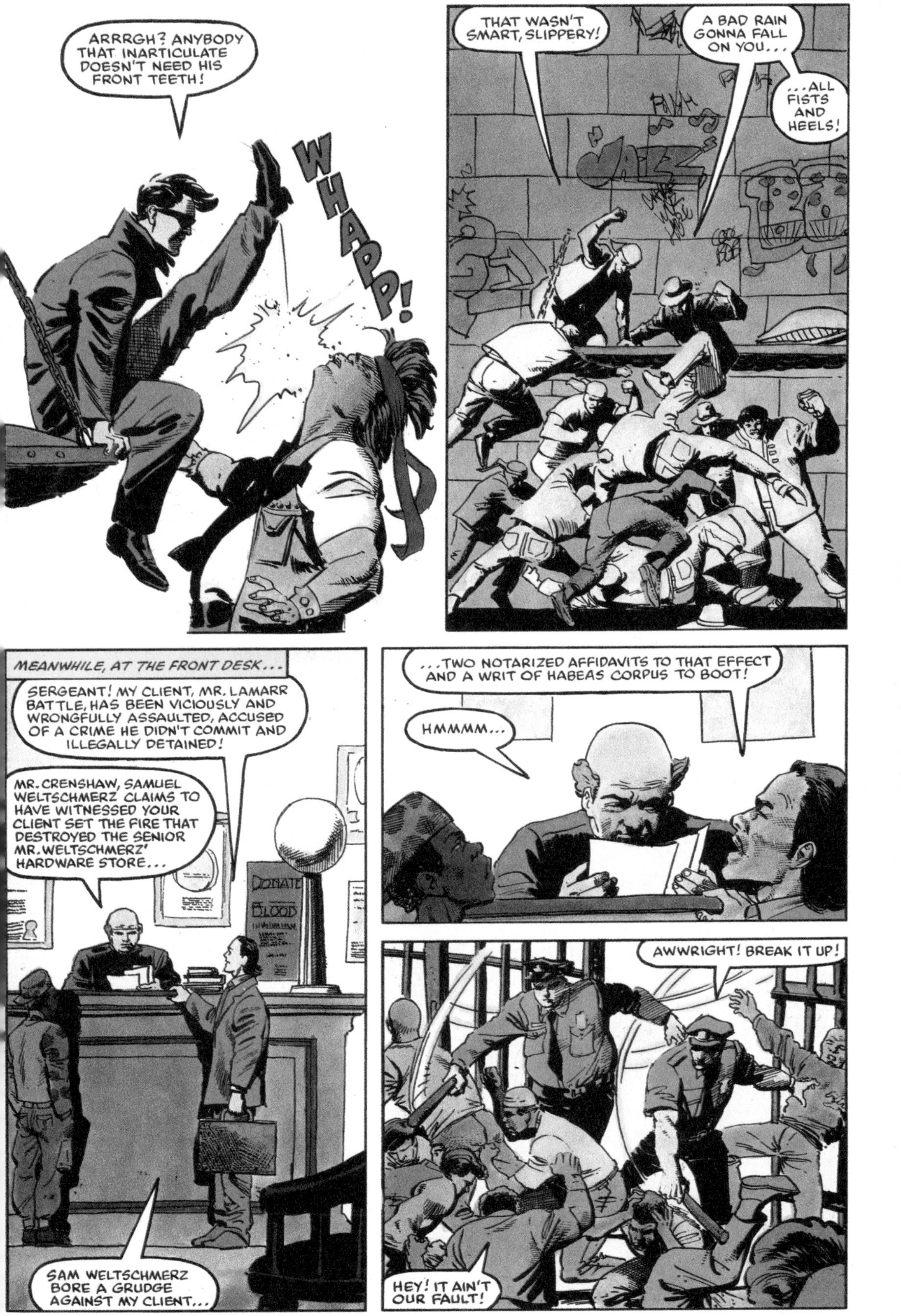
ARRRGH? ANYBODY THAT INARTICULATE DOESN'T NEED HIS FRONT TEETH!
WHAPP!
THAT WASN'T SMART, SLIPPERY!
A BAD RAIN GONNA FALL ON YOU...
...ALL FISTS AND HEELS!
MEANWHILE, AT THE FRONT DESK...
SERGEANT! MY CLIENT, MR. LAMARR BATTLE, HAS BEEN VICIOUSLY AND WRONGFULLY ASSAULTED, ACCUSED OF A CRIME HE DIDN'T COMMIT AND ILLEGALLY DETAINED!
MR. CRENSHAW, SAMUEL WELTSCHMERZ CLAIMS TO HAVE WITNESSED YOUR CLIENT SET THE FIRE THAT DESTROYED THE SENIOR MR. WELTSCHMERZ' HARDWARE STORE...
DONATE
BLOOD
SAM WELTSCHMERZ BORE A GRUDGE AGAINST MY CLIENT...
...TWO NOTARIZED AFFIDAVITS TO THAT EFFECT AND A WRIT OF HABEAS CORPUS TO BOOT!
HMMMM...
AWWRIGHT! BREAK IT UP!
HEY! IT AIN'T OUR FAULT!

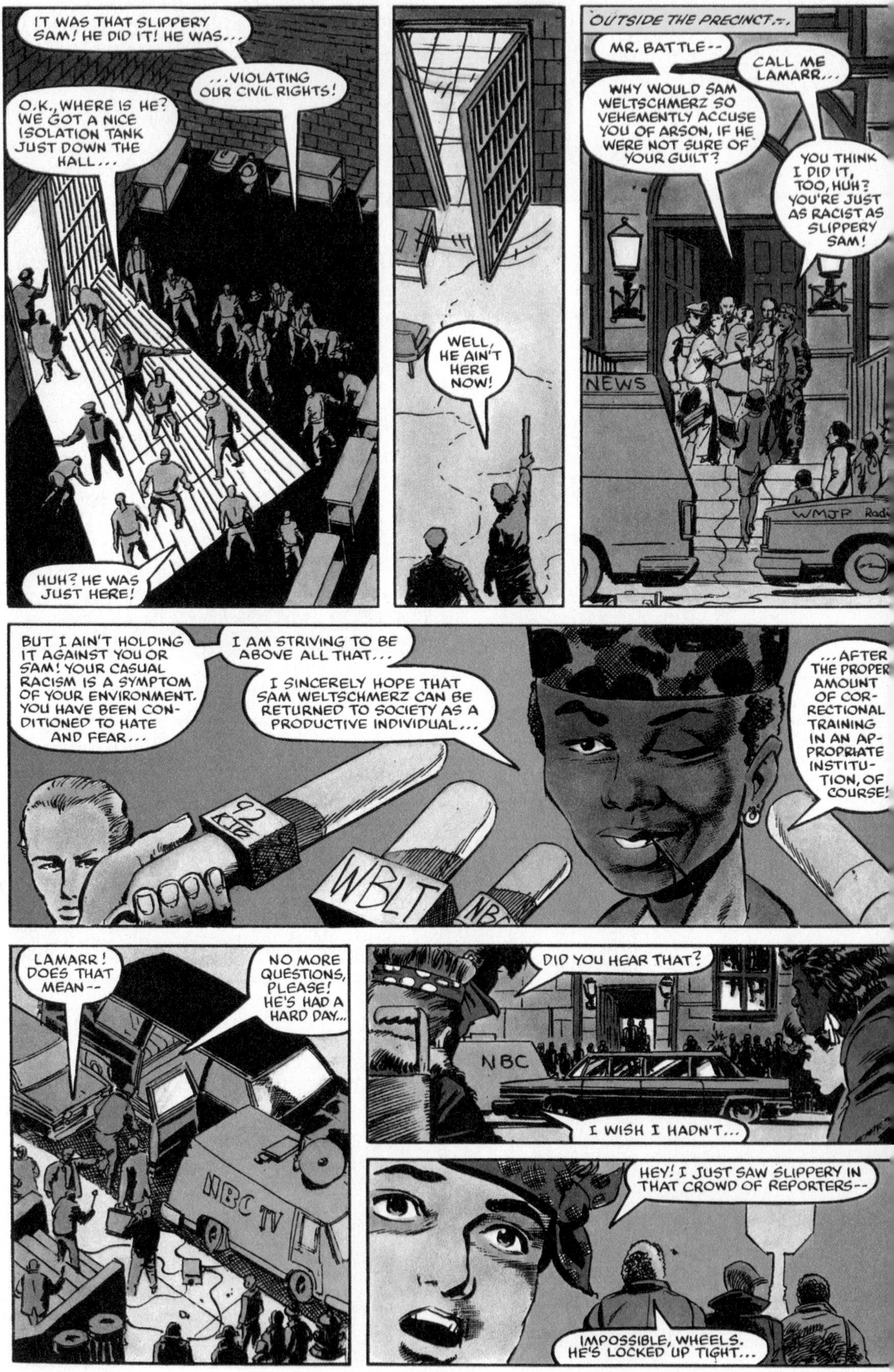
IT WAS THAT SLIPPERY SAM! HE DID IT! HE WAS...
...VIOLATING OUR CIVIL RIGHTS!
O.K., WHERE IS HE? WE GOT A NICE ISOLATION TANK JUST DOWN THE HALL...
HUH? HE WAS JUST HERE!
WELL, HE AIN'T HERE NOW!
OUTSIDE THE PRECINCT...
MR. BATTLE--
WHY WOULD SAM WELTSCHMERZ SO VEHEMENTLY ACCUSE YOU OF ARSON, IF HE WERE NOT SURE OF YOUR GUILT?
CALL ME LAMARR...
YOU THINK I DID IT, TOO, HUH? YOU'RE JUST AS RACIST AS SLIPPERY SAM!
NEWS
WMJP
BUT I AIN'T HOLDING IT AGAINST YOU OR SAM! YOUR CASUAL RACISM IS A SYMPTOM OF YOUR ENVIRONMENT. YOU HAVE BEEN CONDITIONED TO HATE AND FEAR...
I AM STRIVING TO BE ABOVE ALL THAT...
I SINCERELY HOPE THAT SAM WELTSCHMERZ CAN BE RETURNED TO SOCIETY AS A PRODUCTIVE INDIVIDUAL...
...AFTER THE PROPER AMOUNT OF CORRECTIONAL TRAINING IN AN APPROPRIATE INSTITUTION, OF COURSE!
92 KJB
WBLT
NBC
LAMARR! DOES THAT MEAN--
NO MORE QUESTIONS, PLEASE! HE'S HAD A HARD DAY...
NBC TV
DID YOU HEAR THAT?
NBC
I WISH I HADN'T...
HEY! I JUST SAW SLIPPERY IN THAT CROWD OF REPORTERS--
IMPOSSIBLE, WHEELS. HE'S LOCKED UP TIGHT...

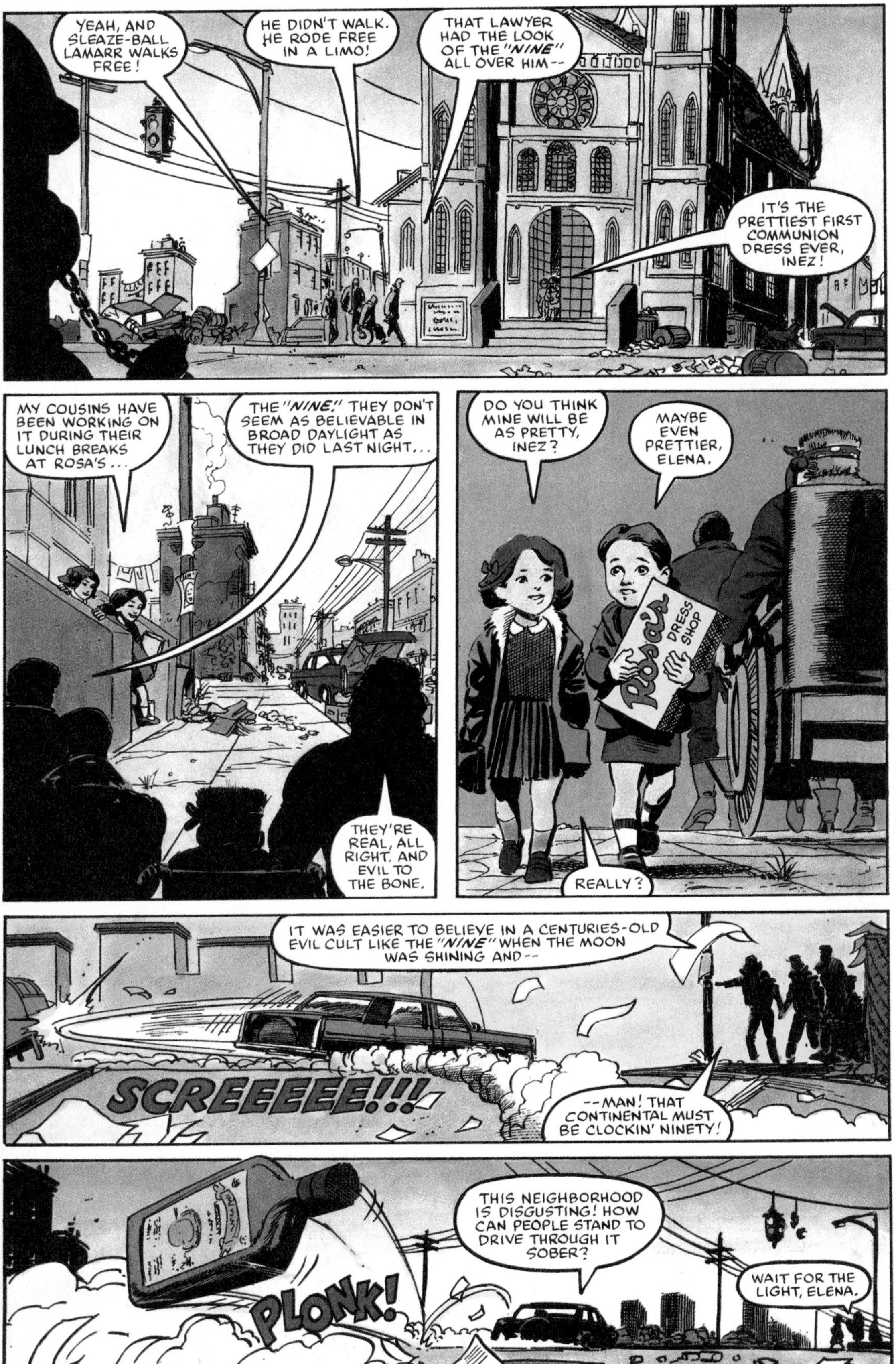
YEAH, AND SLEAZE-BALL LAMARR WALKS FREE!
HE DIDN'T WALK. HE RODE FREE IN A LIMO!
THAT LAWYER HAD THE LOOK OF THE "NINE" ALL OVER HIM--
IT'S THE PRETTIEST FIRST COMMUNION DRESS EVER, INEZ!
MY COUSINS HAVE BEEN WORKING ON IT DURING THEIR LUNCH BREAKS AT ROSA'S...
THE "NINE." THEY DON'T SEEM AS BELIEVABLE IN BROAD DAYLIGHT AS THEY DID LAST NIGHT...
THEY'RE REAL, ALL RIGHT. AND EVIL TO THE BONE.
DO YOU THINK MINE WILL BE AS PRETTY, INEZ?
MAYBE EVEN PRETTIER, ELENA.
ROSA'S DRESS SHOP
REALLY?
IT WAS EASIER TO BELIEVE IN A CENTURIES-OLD EVIL CULT LIKE THE "NINE" WHEN THE MOON WAS SHINING AND--
SCREEEEEE!!!
--MAN! THAT CONTINENTAL MUST BE CLOCKIN' NINETY!
THIS NEIGHBORHOOD IS DISGUSTING! HOW CAN PEOPLE STAND TO DRIVE THROUGH IT SOBER?
PLONK!
WAIT FOR THE LIGHT, ELENA.

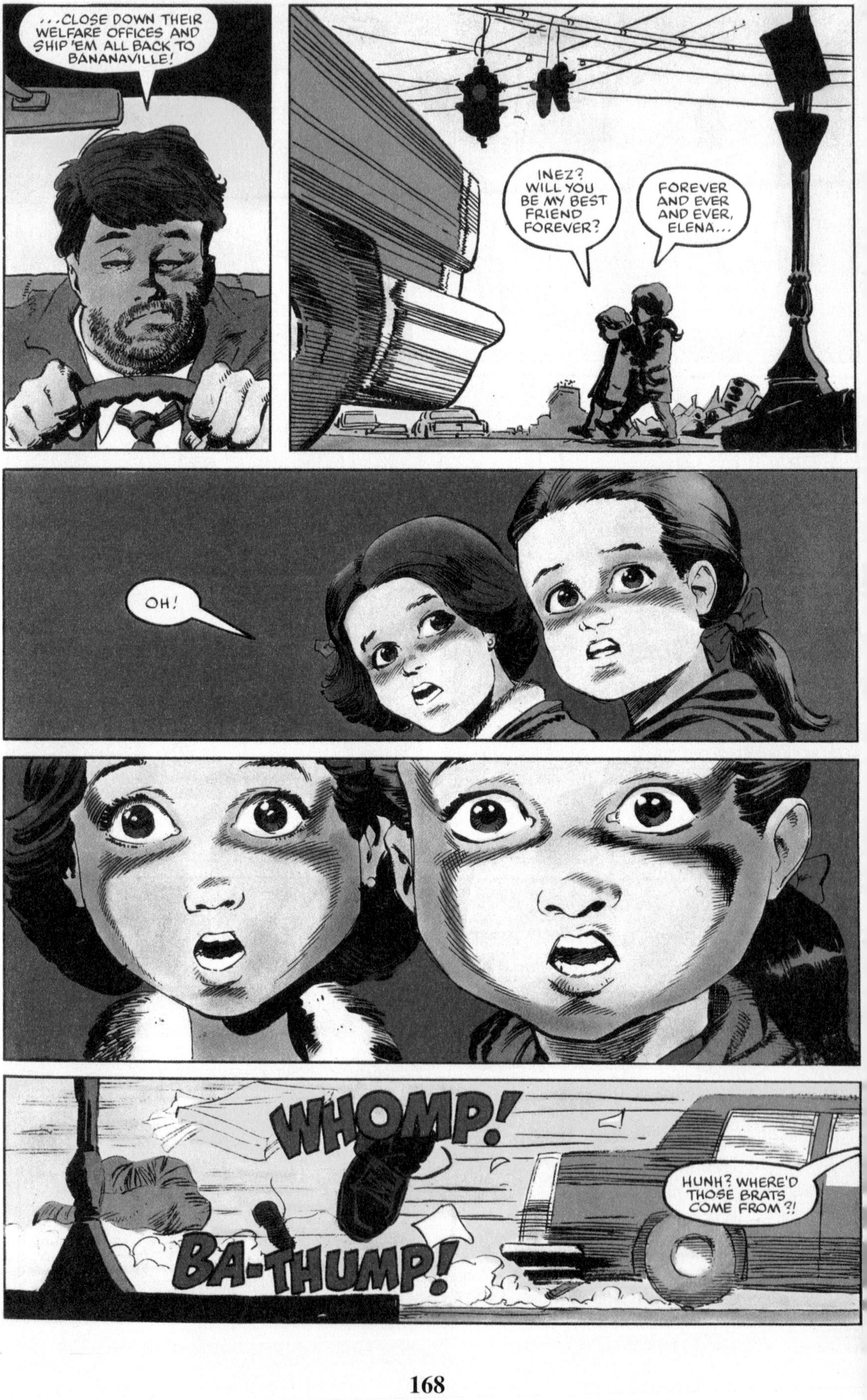
...CLOSE DOWN THEIR WELFARE OFFICES AND SHIP 'EM ALL BACK TO BANANAVILLE!
INEZ? WILL YOU BE MY BEST FRIEND FOREVER?
FOREVER AND EVER AND EVER, ELENA...
OH!
WHOMP!
BA-THUMP!
HUNH? WHERE'D THOSE BRATS COME FROM?!

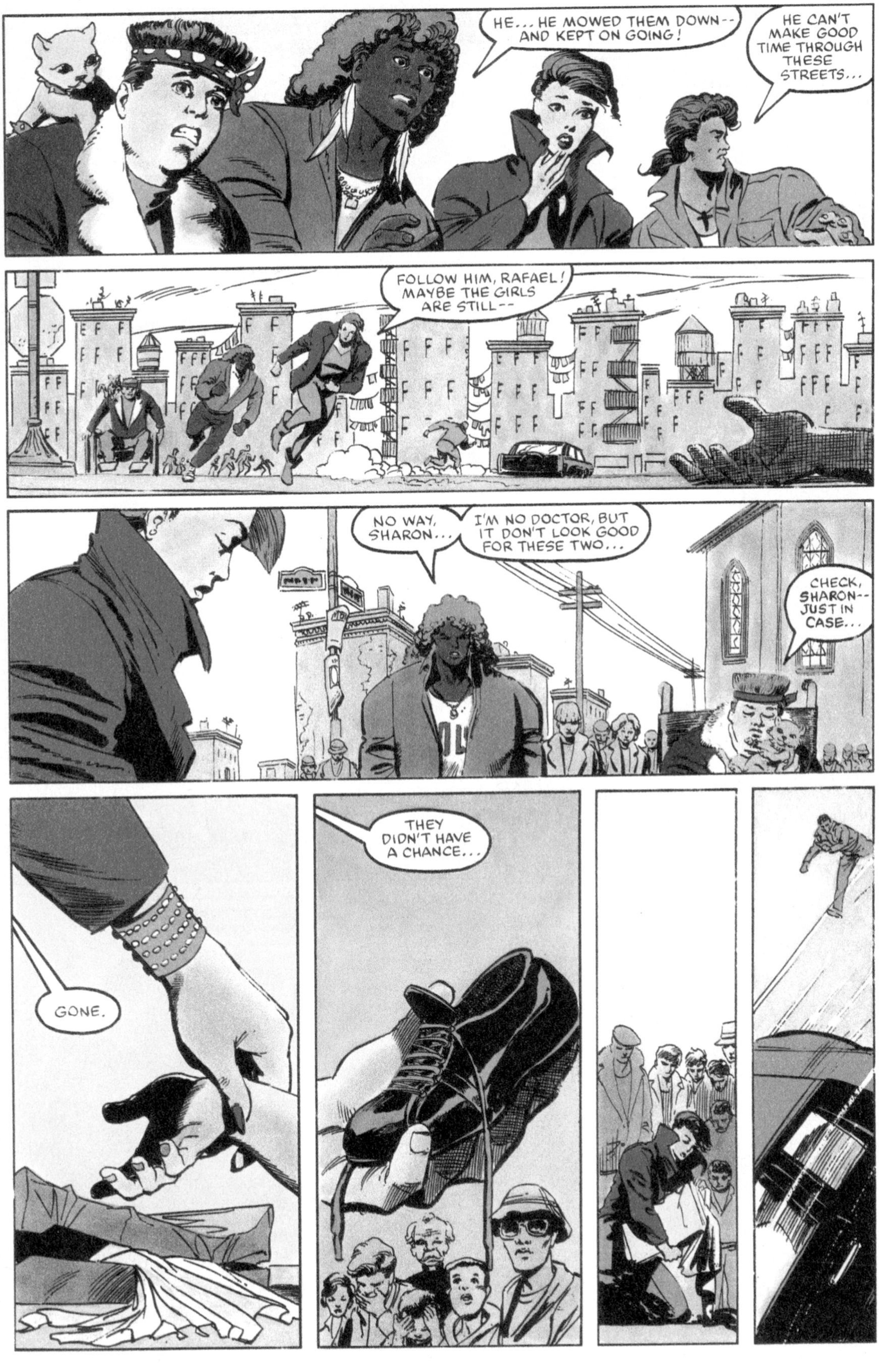

HE... HE MOWED THEM DOWN-- AND KEPT ON GOING!
HE CAN'T MAKE GOOD TIME THROUGH THESE STREETS...
FOLLOW HIM, RAFAEL! MAYBE THE GIRLS ARE STILL--
NO WAY, SHARON...
I'M NO DOCTOR, BUT IT DON'T LOOK GOOD FOR THESE TWO...
CHECK, SHARON-- JUST IN CASE...
GONE.
THEY DIDN'T HAVE A CHANCE...

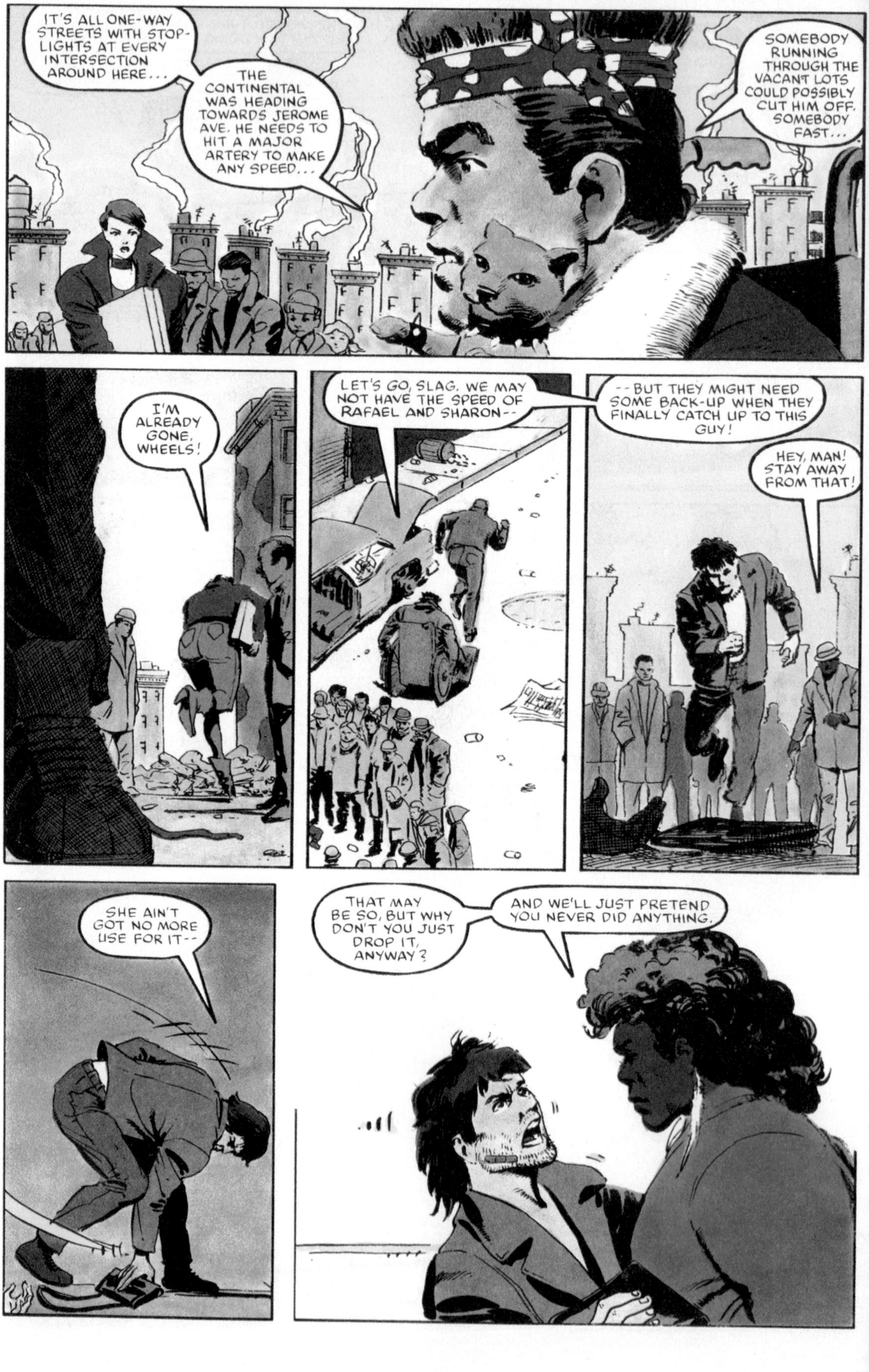
IT'S ALL ONE-WAY STREETS WITH STOP-LIGHTS AT EVERY INTERSECTION AROUND HERE...
THE CONTINENTAL WAS HEADING TOWARDS JEROME AVE. HE NEEDS TO HIT A MAJOR ARTERY TO MAKE ANY SPEED...
SOMEBODY RUNNING THROUGH THE VACANT LOTS COULD POSSIBLY CUT HIM OFF. SOMEBODY FAST...
I'M ALREADY GONE, WHEELS!
LET'S GO, SLAG. WE MAY NOT HAVE THE SPEED OF RAFAEL AND SHARON--
--BUT THEY MIGHT NEED SOME BACK-UP WHEN THEY FINALLY CATCH UP TO THIS GUY!
HEY, MAN! STAY AWAY FROM THAT!
SHE AIN'T GOT NO MORE USE FOR IT--
THAT MAY BE SO, BUT WHY DON'T YOU JUST DROP IT, ANYWAY?
AND WE'LL JUST PRETEND YOU NEVER DID ANYTHING.

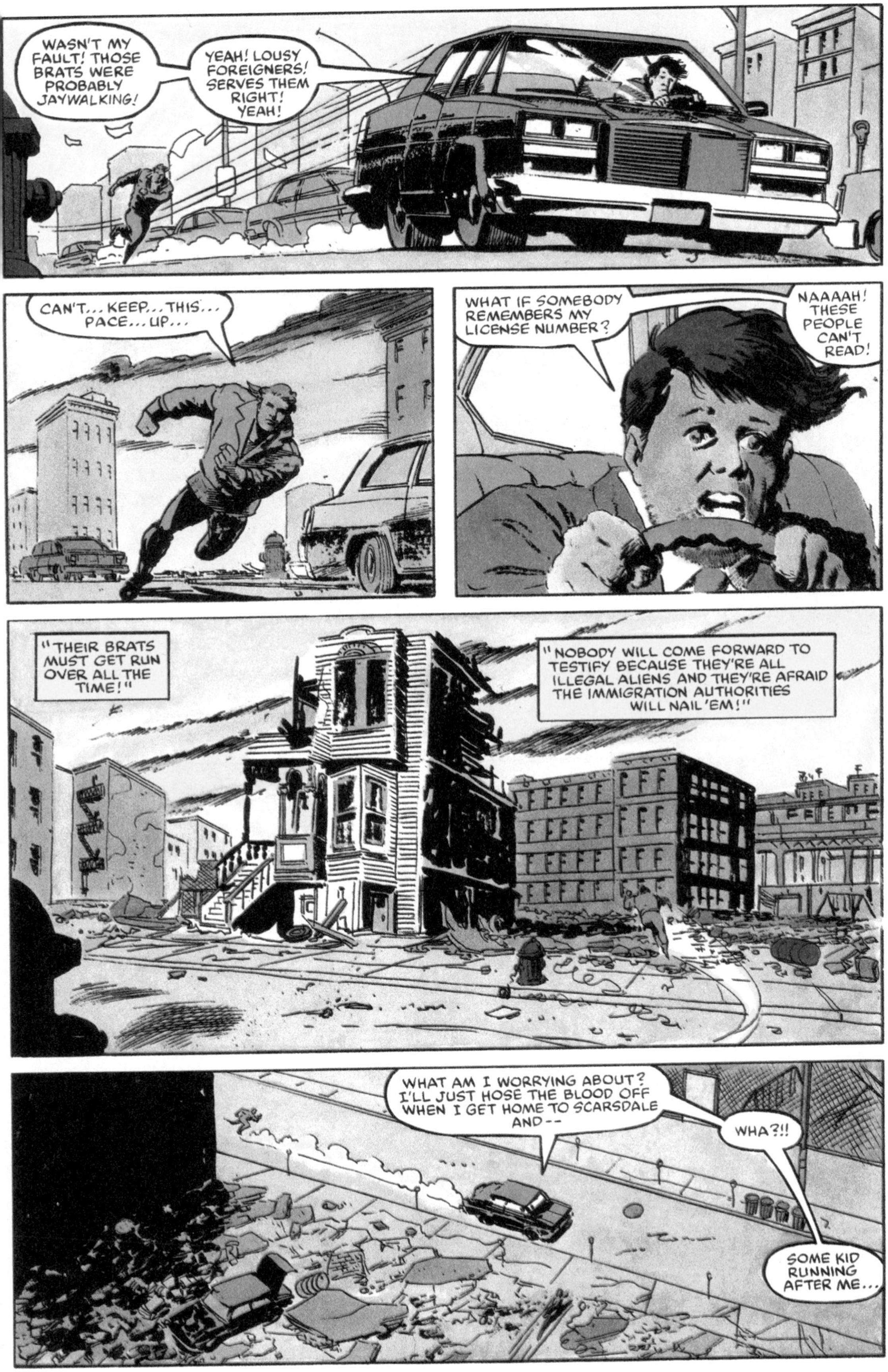
WASN'T MY FAULT! THOSE BRATS WERE PROBABLY JAYWALKING!
YEAH! LOUSY FOREIGNERS! SERVES THEM RIGHT! YEAH!
CAN'T... KEEP... THIS... PACE... UP...
WHAT IF SOMEBODY REMEMBERS MY LICENSE NUMBER?
NAAAAH! THESE PEOPLE CAN'T READ!
"THEIR BRATS MUST GET RUN OVER ALL THE TIME!"
"NOBODY WILL COME FORWARD TO TESTIFY BECAUSE THEY'RE ALL ILLEGAL ALIENS AND THEY'RE AFRAID THE IMMIGRATION AUTHORITIES WILL NAIL 'EM!"
WHAT AM I WORRYING ABOUT? I'LL JUST HOSE THE BLOOD OFF WHEN I GET HOME TO SCARSDALE AND--
WHA?!!
SOME KID RUNNING AFTER ME...

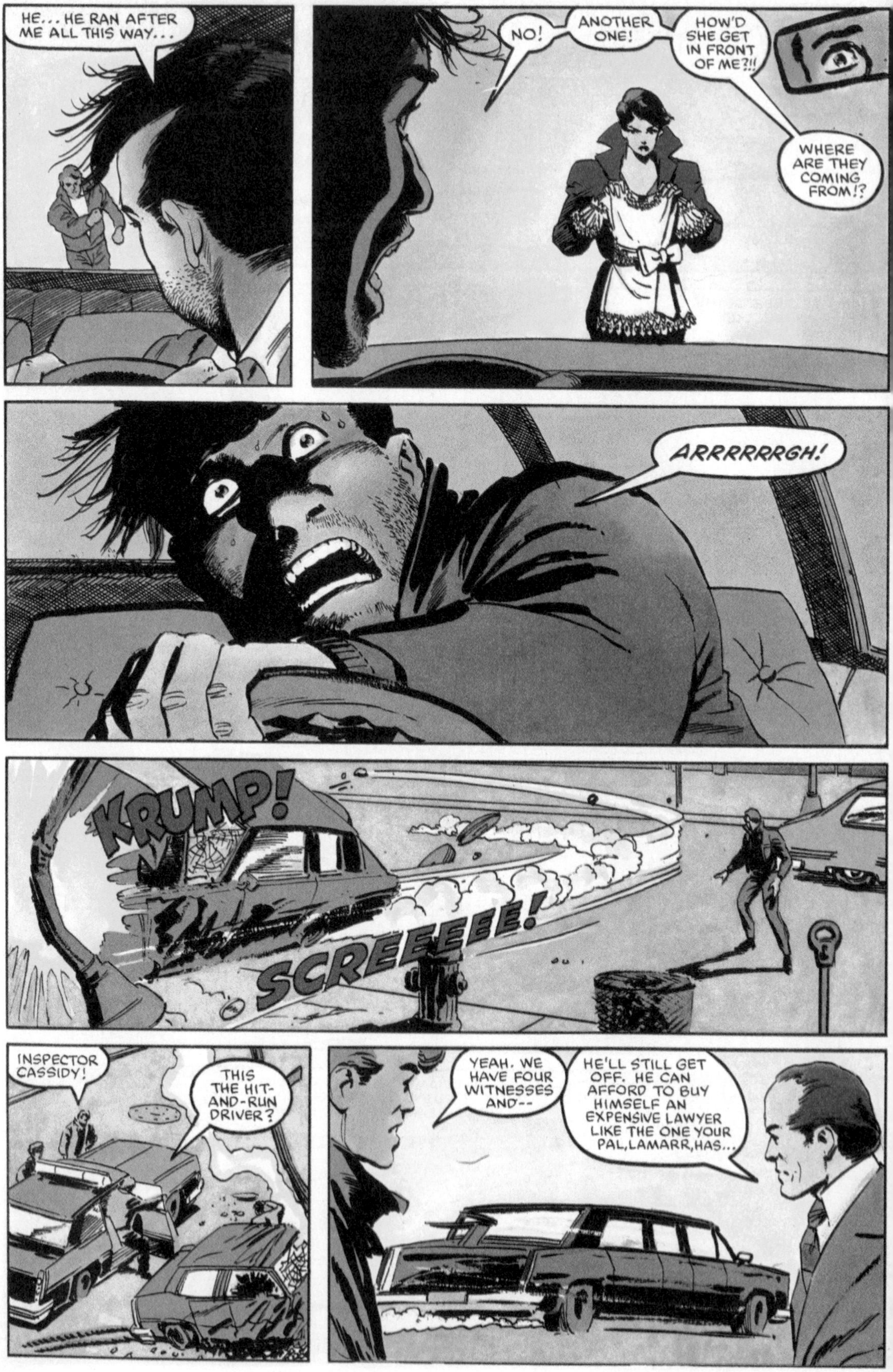

HE... HE RAN AFTER ME ALL THIS WAY...
NO!
ANOTHER ONE!
HOW'D SHE GET IN FRONT OF ME?!!
WHERE ARE THEY COMING FROM!?
ARRRRRRGH!
KRUMP!
SCREEEEEE!
INSPECTOR CASSIDY!
THIS THE HIT-AND-RUN DRIVER?
YEAH. WE HAVE FOUR WITNESSES AND--
HE'LL STILL GET OFF. HE CAN AFFORD TO BUY HIMSELF AN EXPENSIVE LAWYER LIKE THE ONE YOUR PAL, LAMARR, HAS...

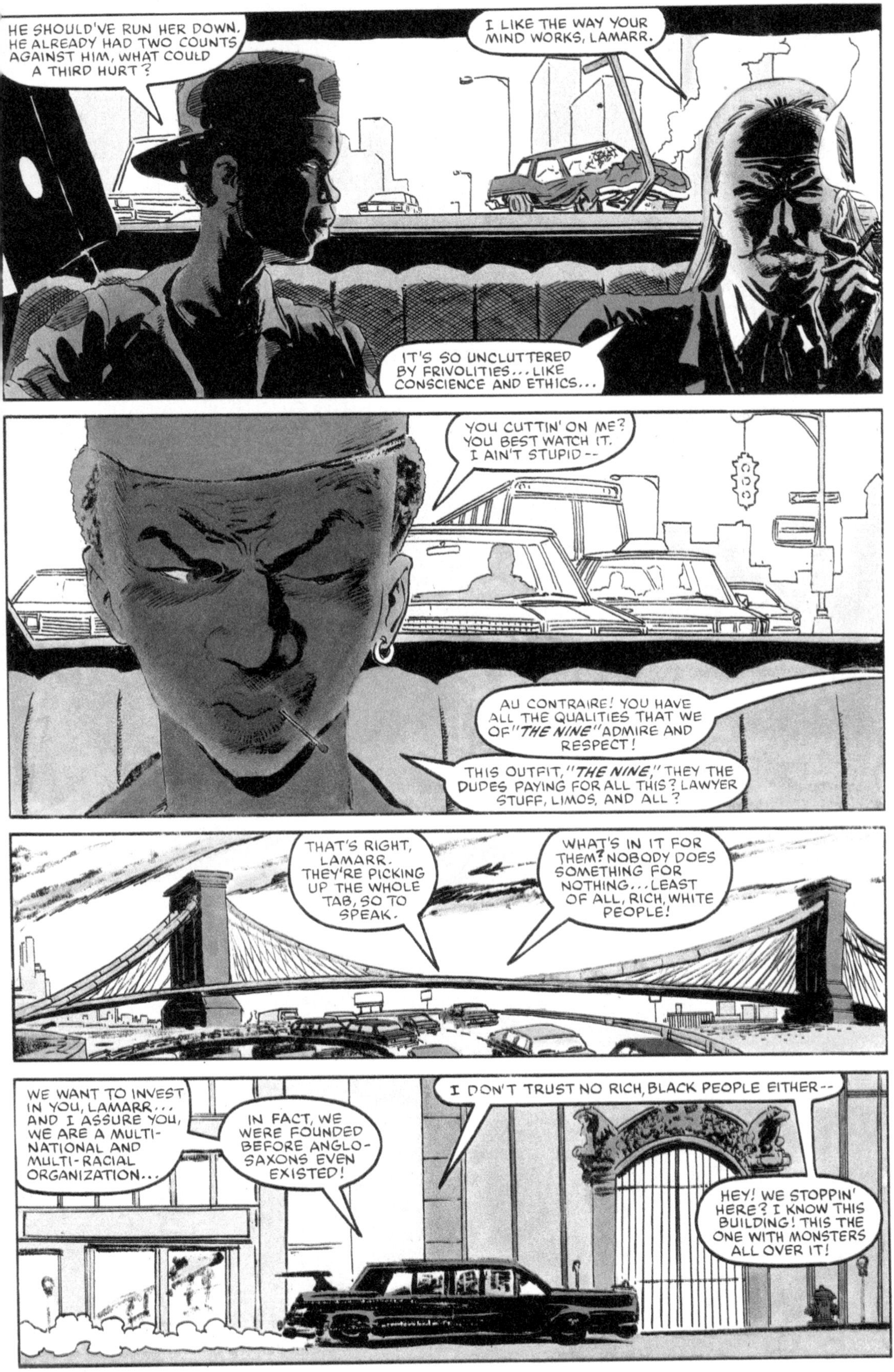
HE SHOULD'VE RUN HER DOWN. HE ALREADY HAD TWO COUNTS AGAINST HIM, WHAT COULD A THIRD HURT?
I LIKE THE WAY YOUR MIND WORKS, LAMARR.
IT'S SO UNCLUTTERED BY FRIVOLITIES... LIKE CONSCIENCE AND ETHICS...
YOU CUTTIN' ON ME? YOU BEST WATCH IT. I AIN'T STUPID--
AU CONTRAIRE! YOU HAVE ALL THE QUALITIES THAT WE OF "THE NINE" ADMIRE AND RESPECT!
THIS OUTFIT, "THE NINE," THEY THE DUDES PAYING FOR ALL THIS? LAWYER STUFF, LIMOS, AND ALL?
THAT'S RIGHT, LAMARR. THEY'RE PICKING UP THE WHOLE TAB, SO TO SPEAK.
WHAT'S IN IT FOR THEM? NOBODY DOES SOMETHING FOR NOTHING... LEAST OF ALL, RICH, WHITE PEOPLE!
WE WANT TO INVEST IN YOU, LAMARR... AND I ASSURE YOU, WE ARE A MULTI-NATIONAL AND MULTI-RACIAL ORGANIZATION...
IN FACT, WE WERE FOUNDED BEFORE ANGLO-SAXONS EVEN EXISTED!
I DON'T TRUST NO RICH, BLACK PEOPLE EITHER--
HEY! WE STOPPIN' HERE? I KNOW THIS BUILDING! THIS THE ONE WITH MONSTERS ALL OVER IT!

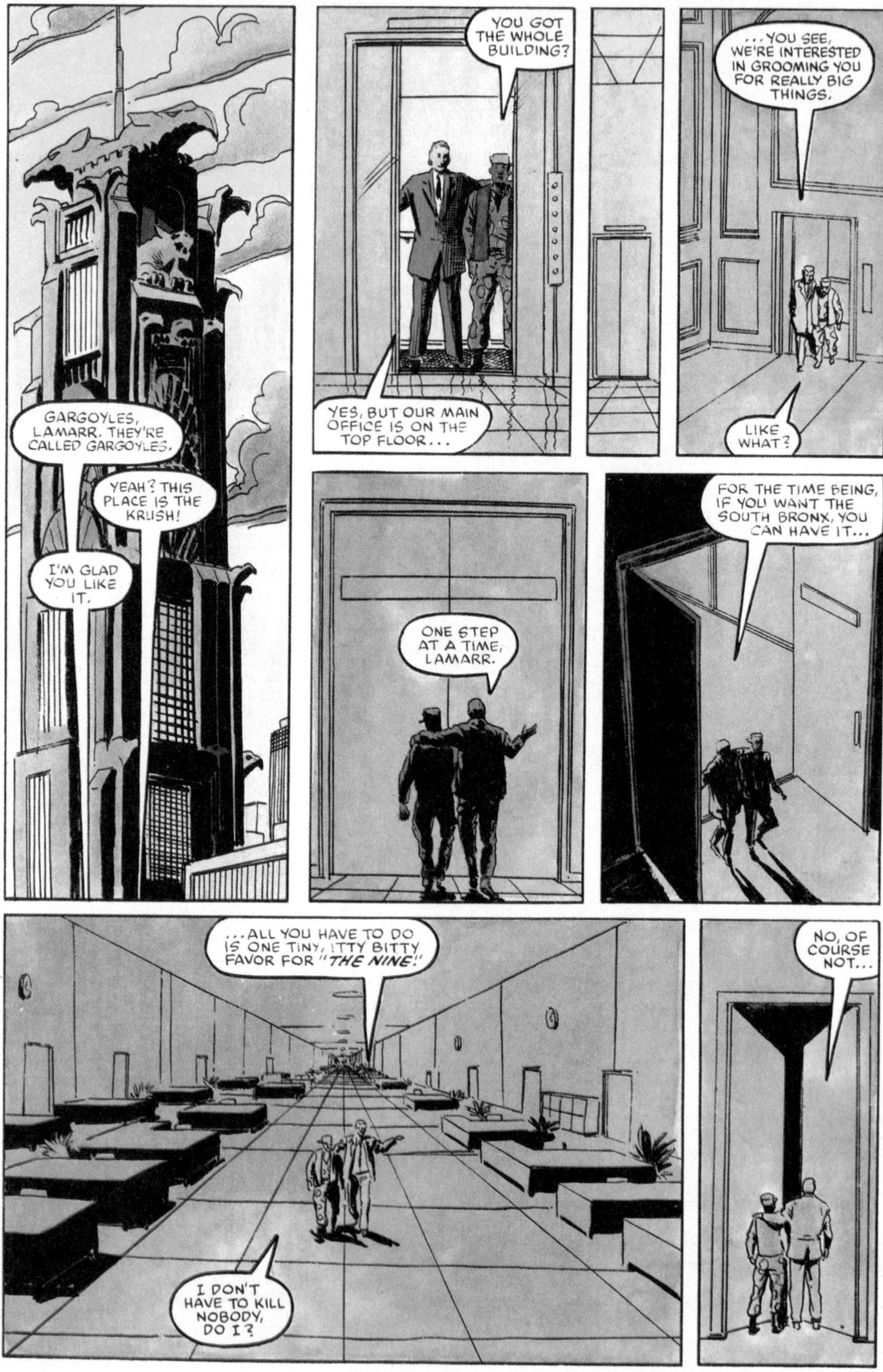
GARGOYLES, LAMARR. THEY'RE CALLED GARGOYLES.
YEAH? THIS PLACE IS THE KRUSH!
I'M GLAD YOU LIKE IT.
YOU GOT THE WHOLE BUILDING?
YES, BUT OUR MAIN OFFICE IS ON THE TOP FLOOR...
...YOU SEE, WE'RE INTERESTED IN GROOMING YOU FOR REALLY BIG THINGS.
LIKE WHAT?
ONE STEP AT A TIME, LAMARR.
FOR THE TIME BEING, IF YOU WANT THE SOUTH BRONX, YOU CAN HAVE IT...
...ALL YOU HAVE TO DO IS ONE TINY, ITTY BITTY FAVOR FOR "THE NINE."
I DON'T HAVE TO KILL NOBODY, DO I?
NO, OF COURSE NOT...

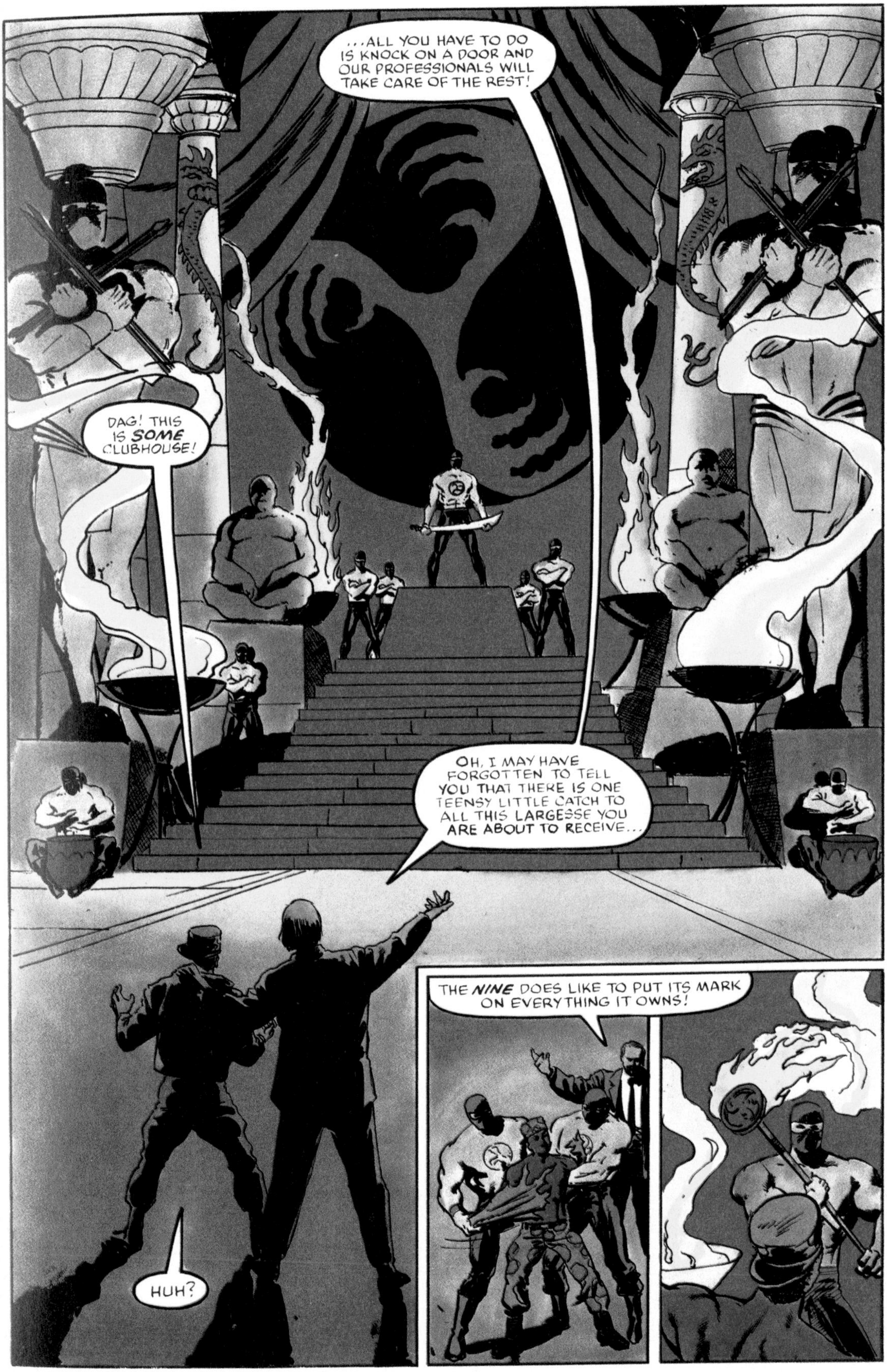
...ALL YOU HAVE TO DO IS KNOCK ON A DOOR AND OUR PROFESSIONALS WILL TAKE CARE OF THE REST!
DAG! THIS IS **SOME** CLUBHOUSE!
OH, I MAY HAVE FORGOTTEN TO TELL YOU THAT THERE IS ONE TEENSY LITTLE CATCH TO ALL THIS LARGESSE YOU ARE ABOUT TO RECEIVE...
HUH?
THE ***NINE*** DOES LIKE TO PUT ITS MARK ON EVERYTHING IT OWNS!

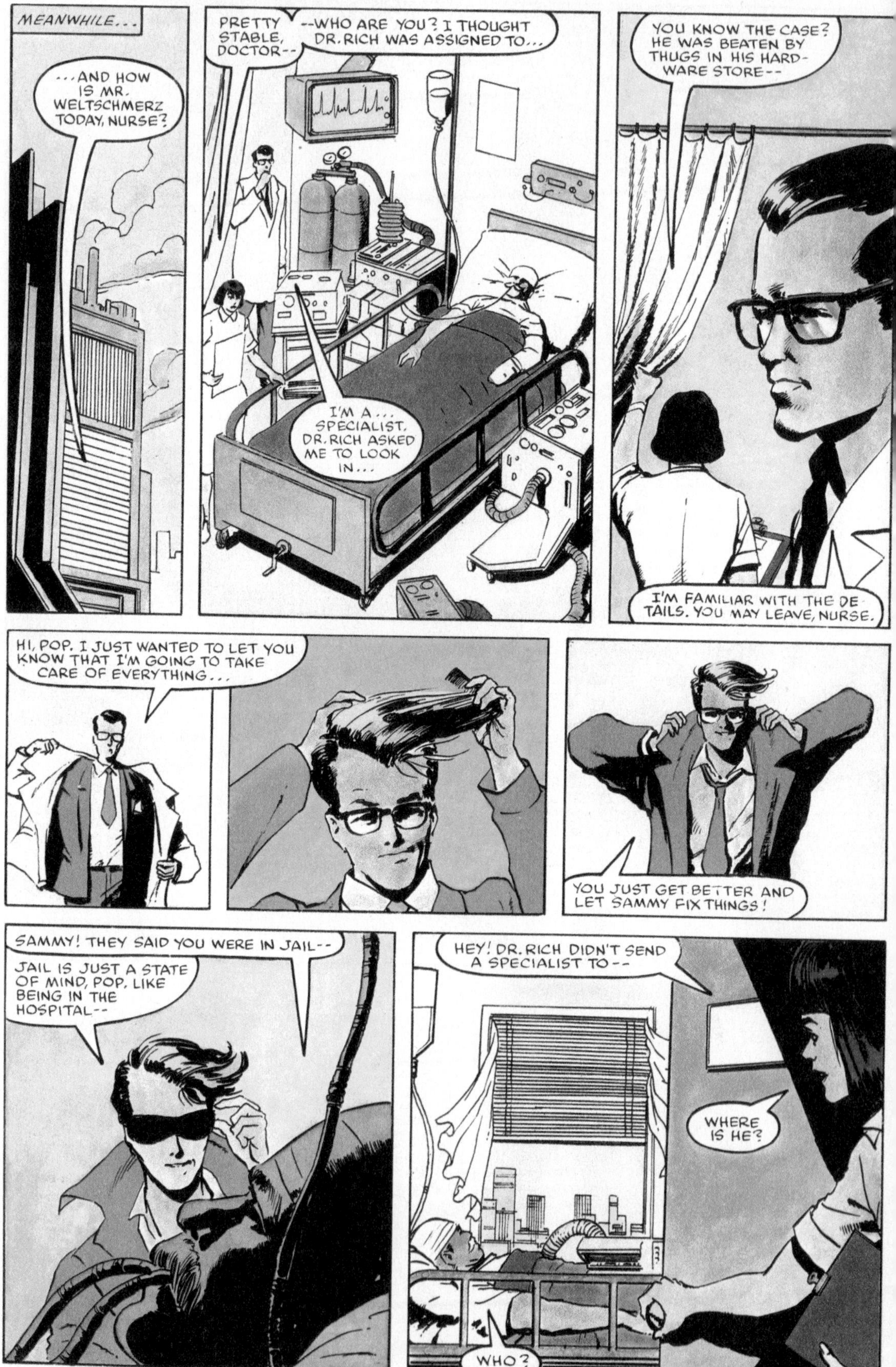
MEANWHILE...
...AND HOW IS MR. WELTSCHMERZ TODAY, NURSE?
PRETTY STABLE, DOCTOR--
--WHO ARE YOU? I THOUGHT DR. RICH WAS ASSIGNED TO...
I'M A... SPECIALIST. DR. RICH ASKED ME TO LOOK IN...
YOU KNOW THE CASE? HE WAS BEATEN BY THUGS IN HIS HARDWARE STORE--
I'M FAMILIAR WITH THE DETAILS. YOU MAY LEAVE, NURSE.
HI, POP. I JUST WANTED TO LET YOU KNOW THAT I'M GOING TO TAKE CARE OF EVERYTHING...
YOU JUST GET BETTER AND LET SAMMY FIX THINGS!
SAMMY! THEY SAID YOU WERE IN JAIL--
JAIL IS JUST A STATE OF MIND, POP, LIKE BEING IN THE HOSPITAL--
HEY! DR. RICH DIDN'T SEND A SPECIALIST TO--
WHERE IS HE?
WHO?

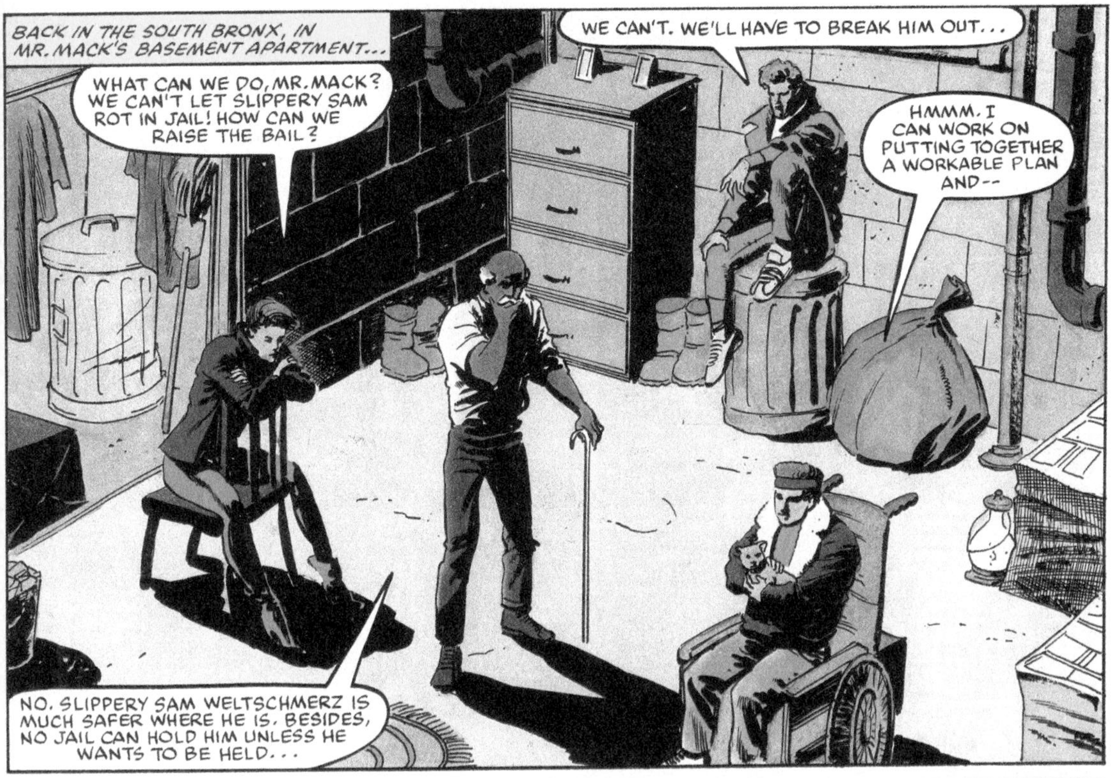
BACK IN THE SOUTH BRONX, IN MR. MACK'S BASEMENT APARTMENT...
WHAT CAN WE DO, MR. MACK? WE CAN'T LET SLIPPERY SAM ROT IN JAIL! HOW CAN WE RAISE THE BAIL?
WE CAN'T. WE'LL HAVE TO BREAK HIM OUT...
HMMM. I CAN WORK ON PUTTING TOGETHER A WORKABLE PLAN AND--
NO. SLIPPERY SAM WELTSCHMERZ IS MUCH SAFER WHERE HE IS. BESIDES, NO JAIL CAN HOLD HIM UNLESS HE WANTS TO BE HELD...

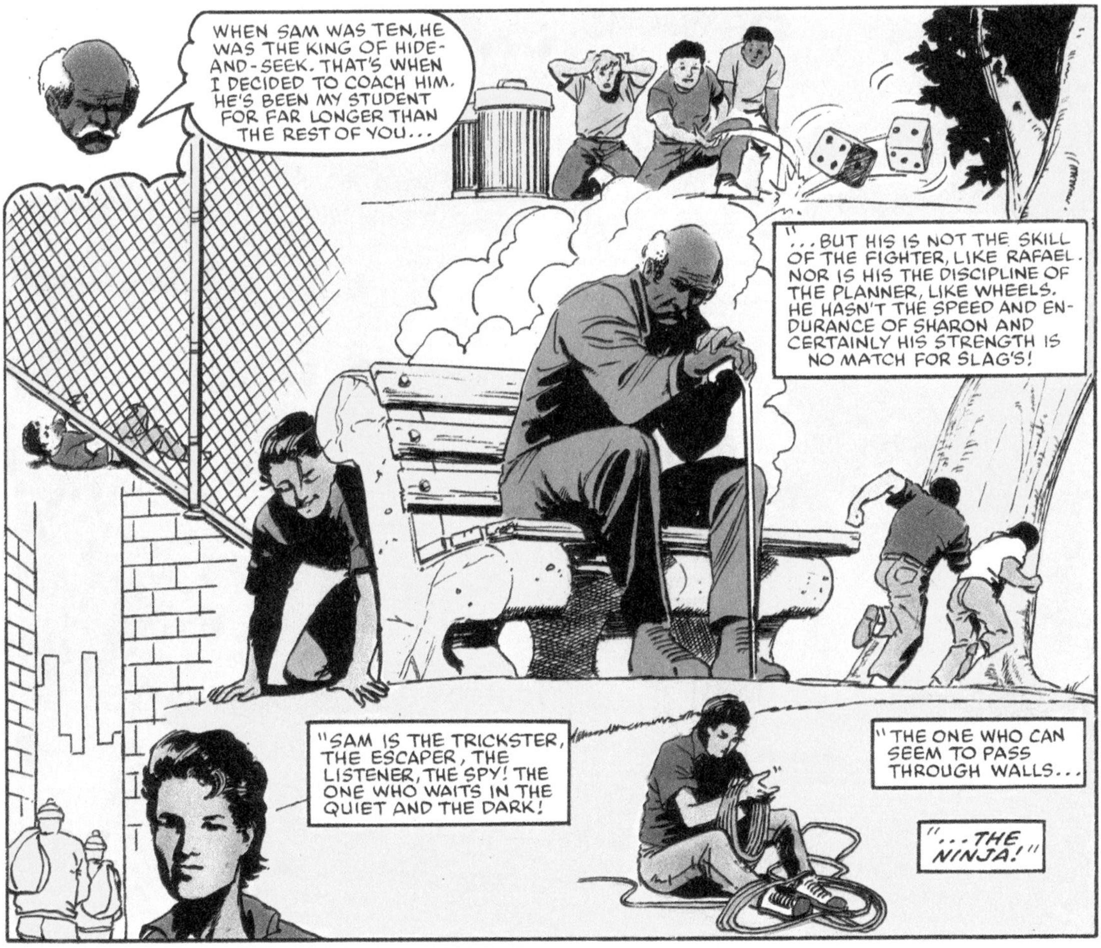
WHEN SAM WAS TEN, HE WAS THE KING OF HIDE-AND-SEEK. THAT'S WHEN I DECIDED TO COACH HIM. HE'S BEEN MY STUDENT FOR FAR LONGER THAN THE REST OF YOU...
"...BUT HIS IS NOT THE SKILL OF THE FIGHTER, LIKE RAFAEL. NOR IS HIS THE DISCIPLINE OF THE PLANNER, LIKE WHEELS. HE HASN'T THE SPEED AND ENDURANCE OF SHARON AND CERTAINLY HIS STRENGTH IS NO MATCH FOR SLAG'S!
"SAM IS THE TRICKSTER, THE ESCAPER, THE LISTENER, THE SPY! THE ONE WHO WAITS IN THE QUIET AND THE DARK!
"THE ONE WHO CAN SEEM TO PASS THROUGH WALLS...
"...THE NINJA!"

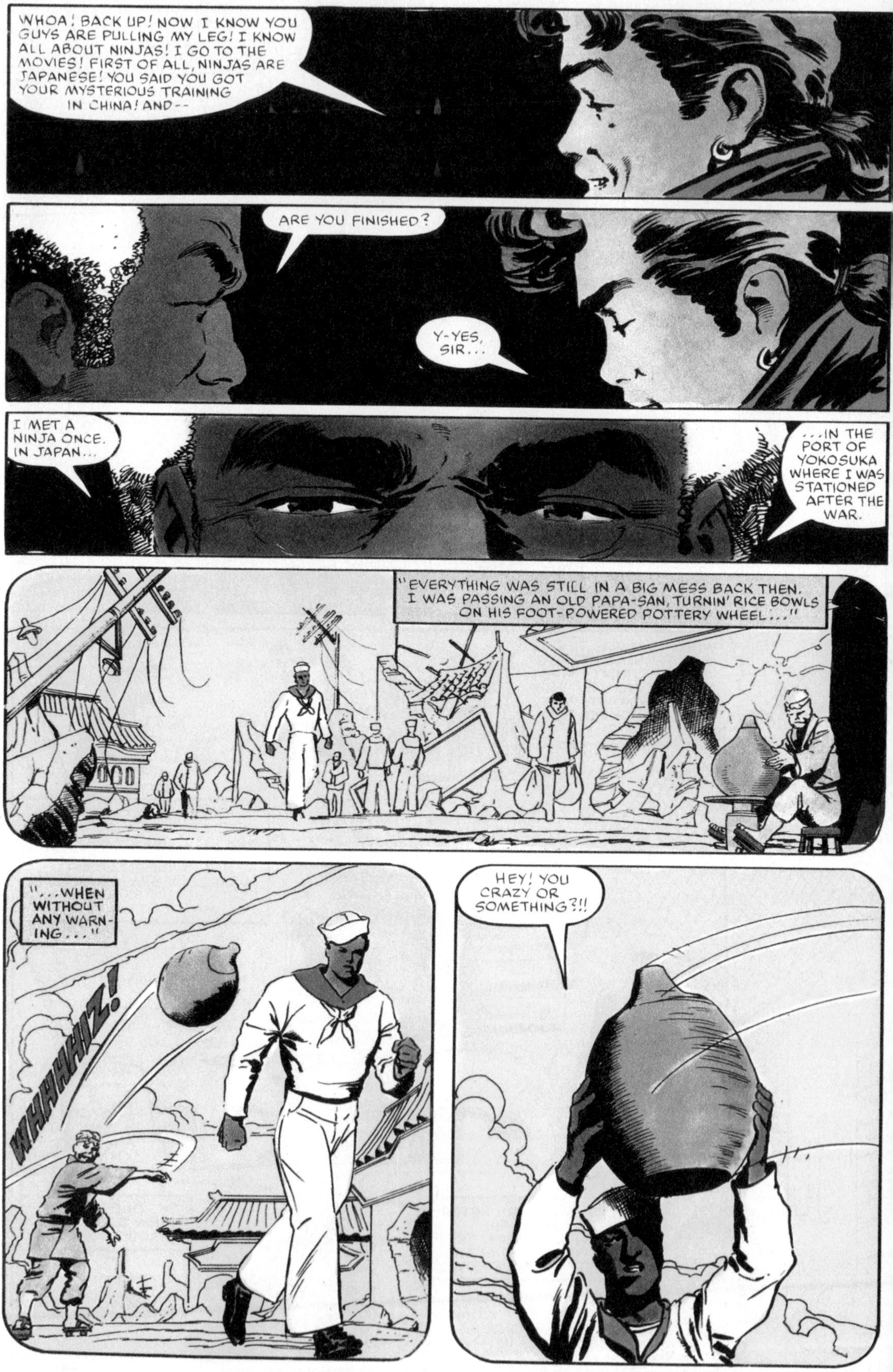
WHOA! BACK UP! NOW I KNOW YOU GUYS ARE PULLING MY LEG! I KNOW ALL ABOUT NINJAS! I GO TO THE MOVIES! FIRST OF ALL, NINJAS ARE JAPANESE! YOU SAID YOU GOT YOUR MYSTERIOUS TRAINING IN CHINA! AND--
ARE YOU FINISHED?
Y-YES, SIR...
I MET A NINJA ONCE. IN JAPAN...
...IN THE PORT OF YOKOSUKA WHERE I WAS STATIONED AFTER THE WAR.
"EVERYTHING WAS STILL IN A BIG MESS BACK THEN. I WAS PASSING AN OLD PAPA-SAN, TURNIN' RICE BOWLS ON HIS FOOT-POWERED POTTERY WHEEL..."
"...WHEN WITHOUT ANY WARNING..."
WHHHHIZ!
HEY! YOU CRAZY OR SOMETHING?!!

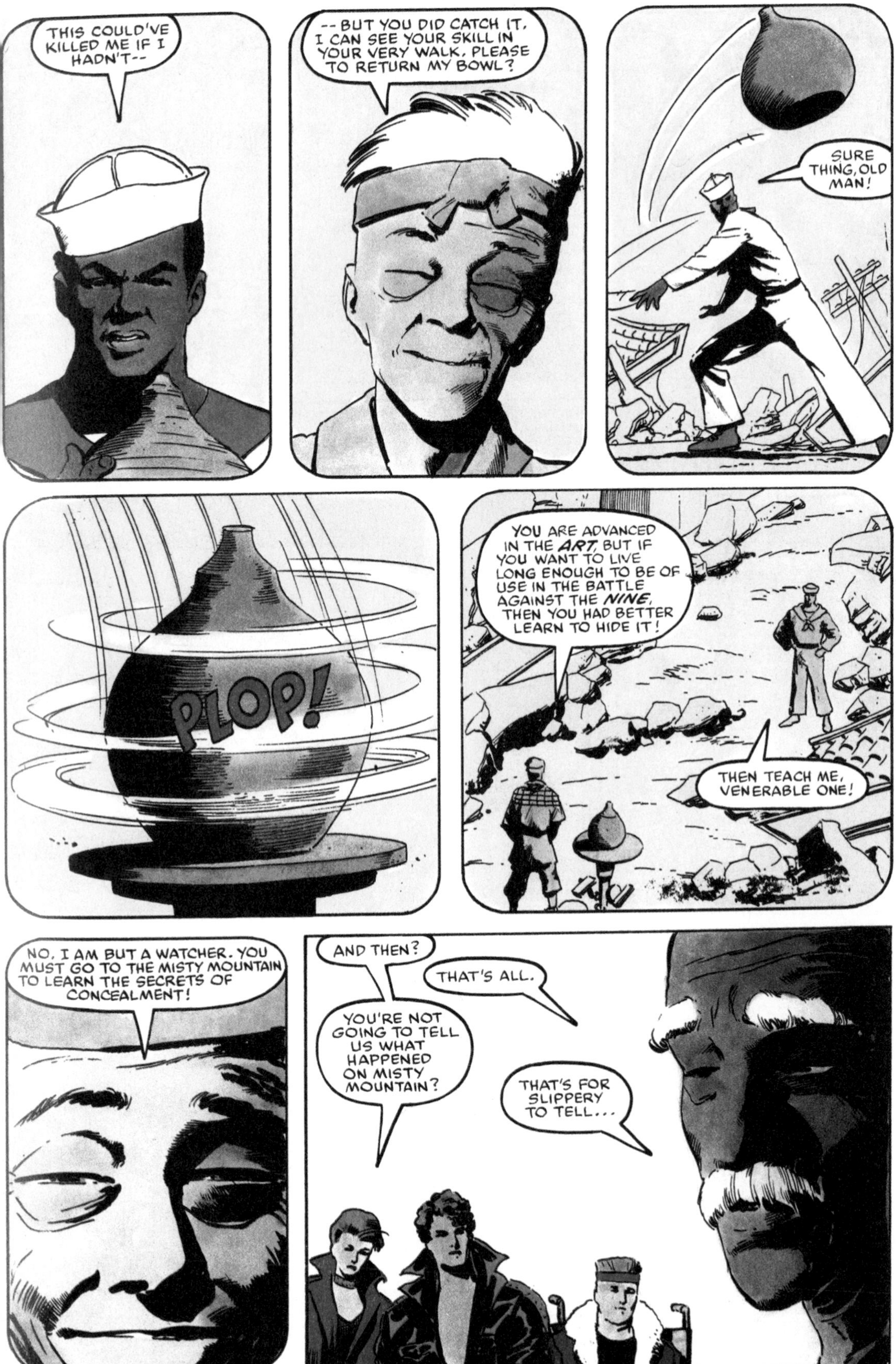
THIS COULD'VE KILLED ME IF I HADN'T--
-- BUT YOU DID CATCH IT. I CAN SEE YOUR SKILL IN YOUR VERY WALK. PLEASE TO RETURN MY BOWL?
SURE THING, OLD MAN!
PLOP!
YOU ARE ADVANCED IN THE ART, BUT IF YOU WANT TO LIVE LONG ENOUGH TO BE OF USE IN THE BATTLE AGAINST THE NINE, THEN YOU HAD BETTER LEARN TO HIDE IT!
THEN TEACH ME, VENERABLE ONE!
NO, I AM BUT A WATCHER. YOU MUST GO TO THE MISTY MOUNTAIN TO LEARN THE SECRETS OF CONCEALMENT!
AND THEN?
THAT'S ALL.
YOU'RE NOT GOING TO TELL US WHAT HAPPENED ON MISTY MOUNTAIN?
THAT'S FOR SLIPPERY TO TELL...

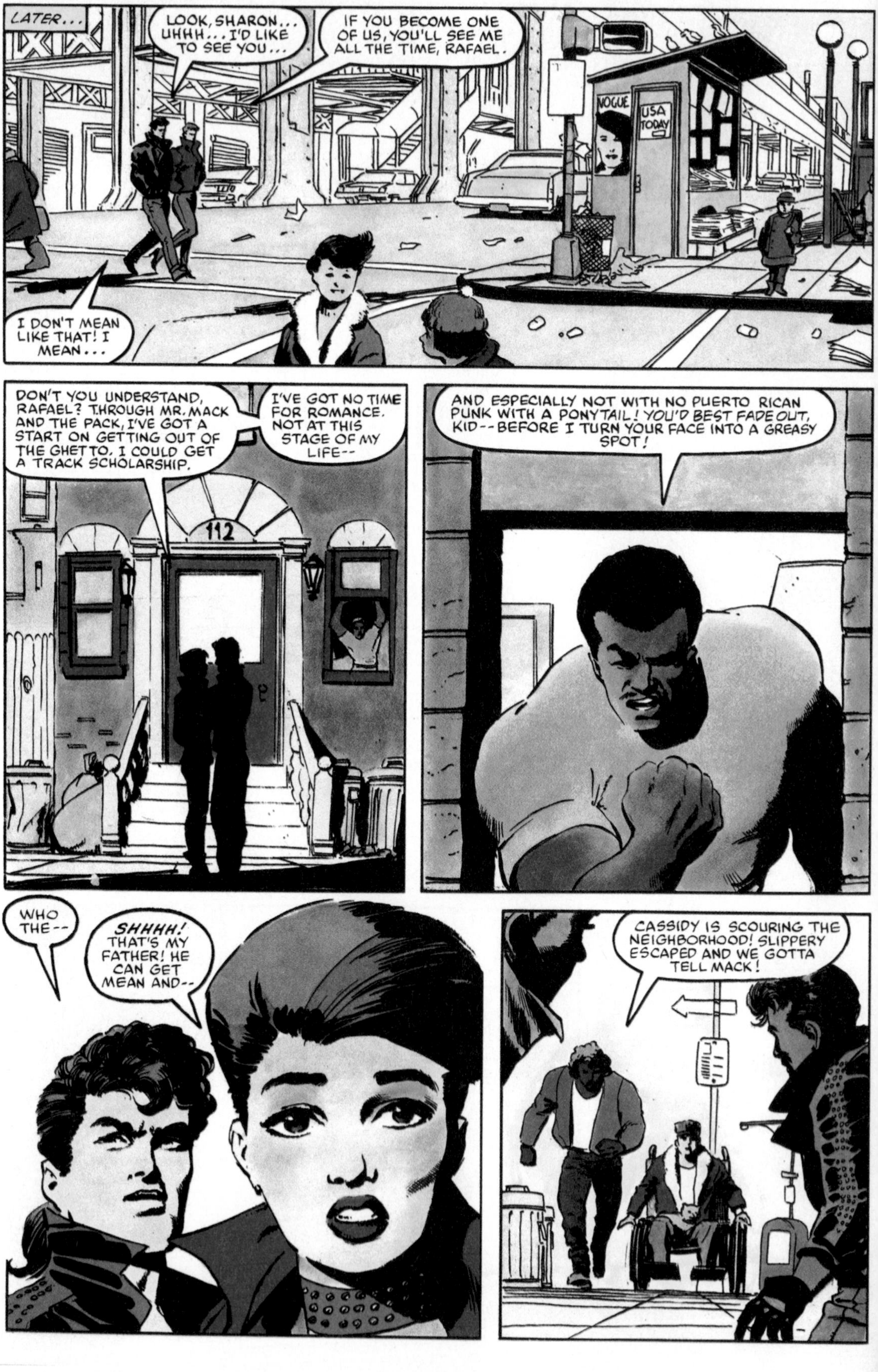
LATER...
LOOK, SHARON... UHHH... I'D LIKE TO SEE YOU...
IF YOU BECOME ONE OF US, YOU'LL SEE ME ALL THE TIME, RAFAEL.
I DON'T MEAN LIKE THAT! I MEAN...
VOGUE
USA TODAY
DON'T YOU UNDERSTAND, RAFAEL? THROUGH MR. MACK AND THE PACK, I'VE GOT A START ON GETTING OUT OF THE GHETTO. I COULD GET A TRACK SCHOLARSHIP.
I'VE GOT NO TIME FOR ROMANCE. NOT AT THIS STAGE OF MY LIFE--
112
AND ESPECIALLY NOT WITH NO PUERTO RICAN PUNK WITH A PONYTAIL! YOU'D BEST FADE OUT, KID--BEFORE I TURN YOUR FACE INTO A GREASY SPOT!
WHO THE--
SHHHH! THAT'S MY FATHER! HE CAN GET MEAN AND--
CASSIDY IS SCOURING THE NEIGHBORHOOD! SLIPPERY ESCAPED AND WE GOTTA TELL MACK!

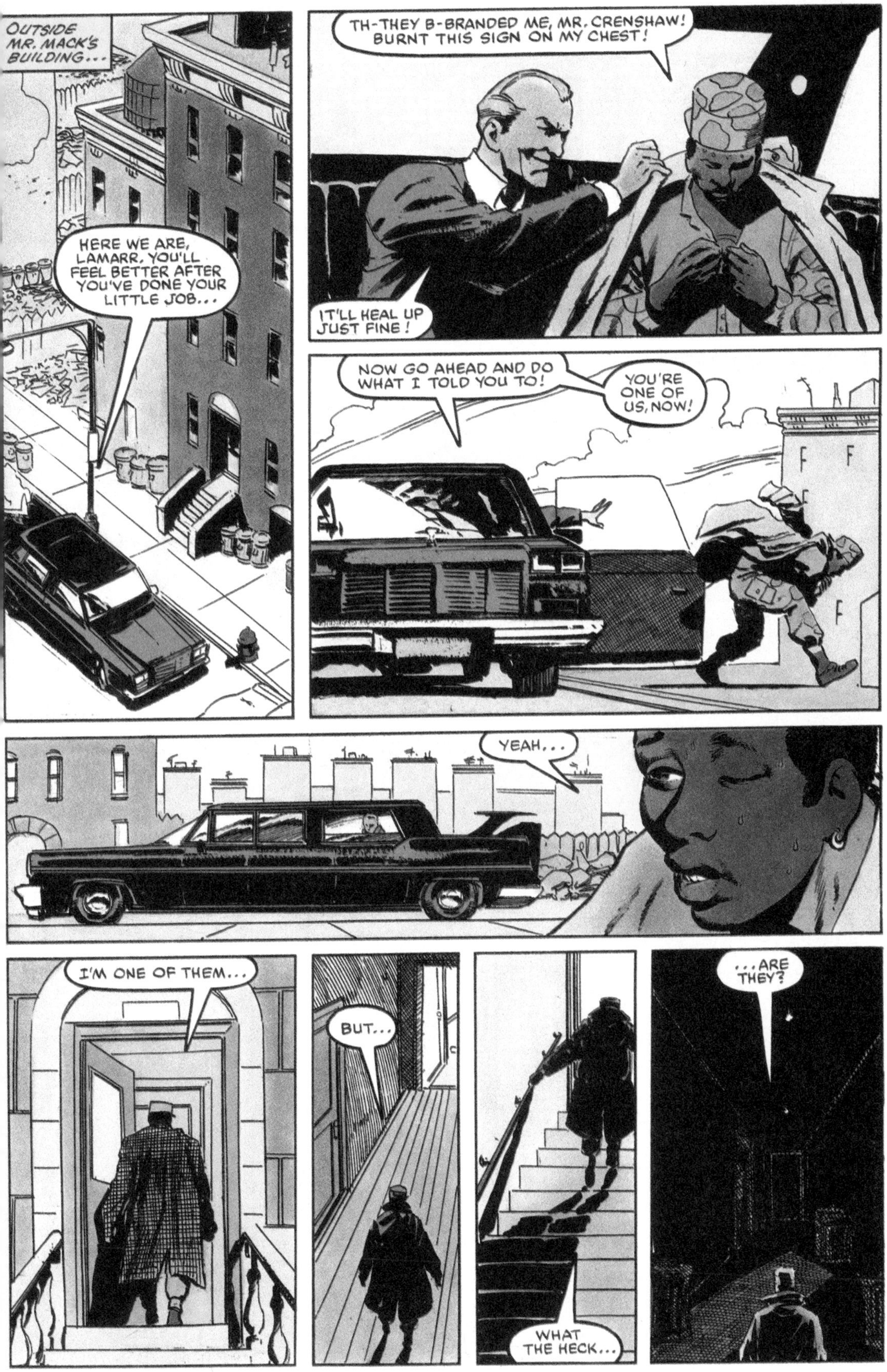
OUTSIDE MR. MACK'S BUILDING...
HERE WE ARE, LAMARR. YOU'LL FEEL BETTER AFTER YOU'VE DONE YOUR LITTLE JOB...
TH-THEY B-BRANDED ME, MR. CRENSHAW! BURNT THIS SIGN ON MY CHEST!
IT'LL HEAL UP JUST FINE!
NOW GO AHEAD AND DO WHAT I TOLD YOU TO!
YOU'RE ONE OF US, NOW!
YEAH...
I'M ONE OF THEM...
BUT...
WHAT THE HECK...
...ARE THEY?

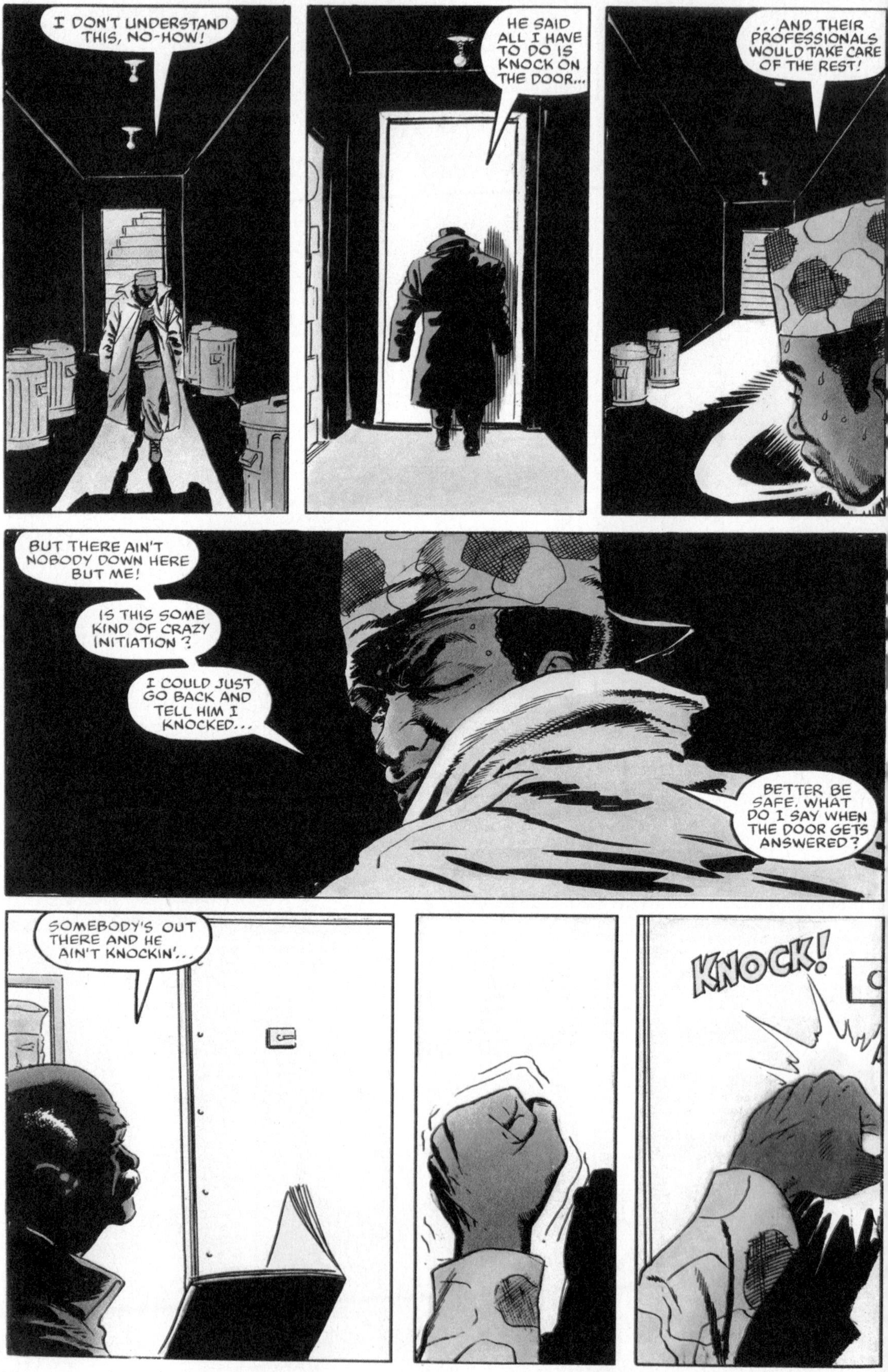
I DON'T UNDERSTAND THIS, NO-HOW!
HE SAID ALL I HAVE TO DO IS KNOCK ON THE DOOR...
...AND THEIR PROFESSIONALS WOULD TAKE CARE OF THE REST!
BUT THERE AIN'T NOBODY DOWN HERE BUT ME!
IS THIS SOME KIND OF CRAZY INITIATION?
I COULD JUST GO BACK AND TELL HIM I KNOCKED...
BETTER BE SAFE. WHAT DO I SAY WHEN THE DOOR GETS ANSWERED?
SOMEBODY'S OUT THERE AND HE AIN'T KNOCKIN'...
KNOCK!

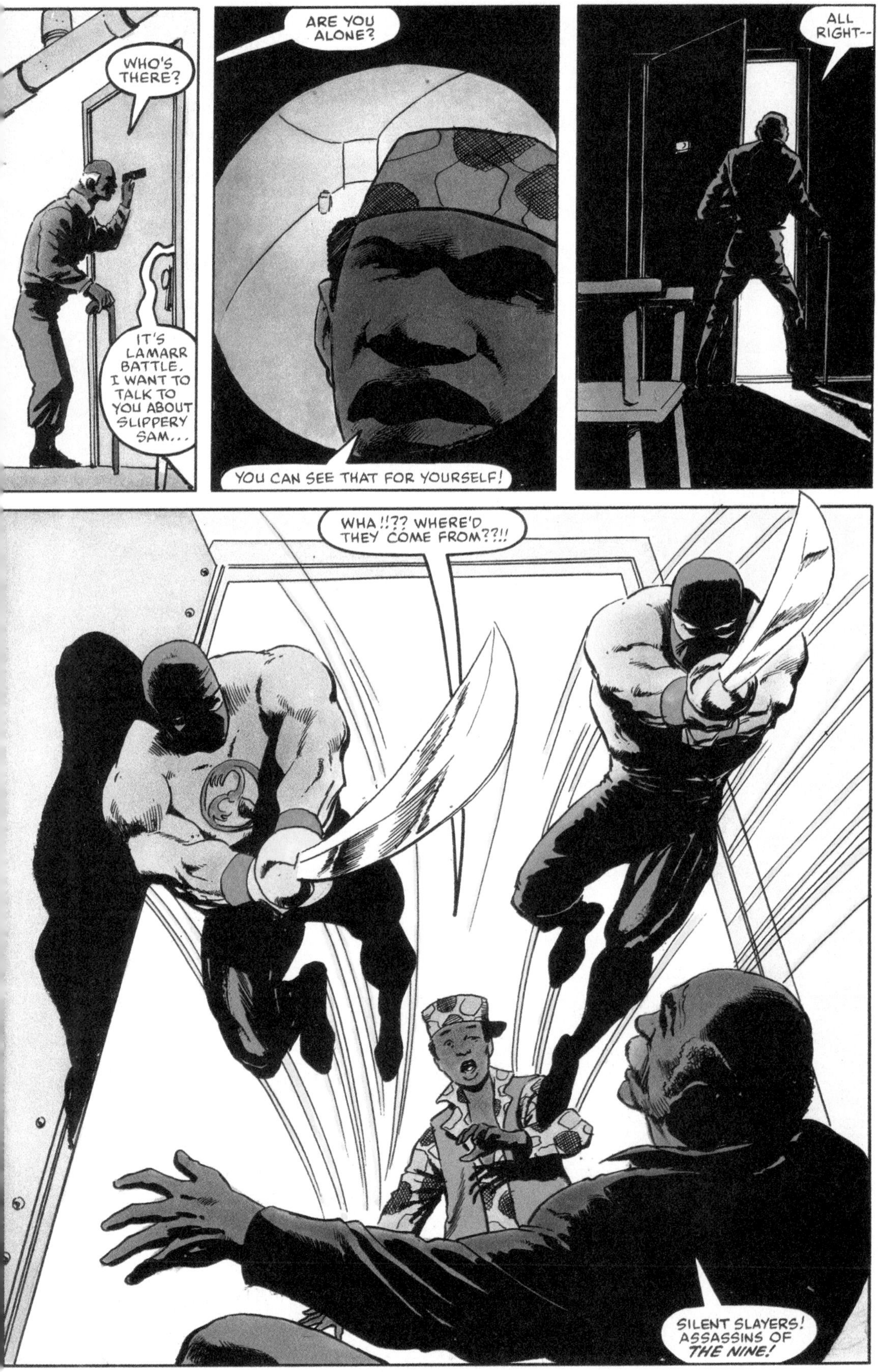
WHO'S THERE?
IT'S LAMARR BATTLE. I WANT TO TALK TO YOU ABOUT SLIPPERY SAM...
ARE YOU ALONE?
YOU CAN SEE THAT FOR YOURSELF!
ALL RIGHT--
WHA!!?? WHERE'D THEY COME FROM??!!
SILENT SLAYERS! ASSASSINS OF *THE NINE!*

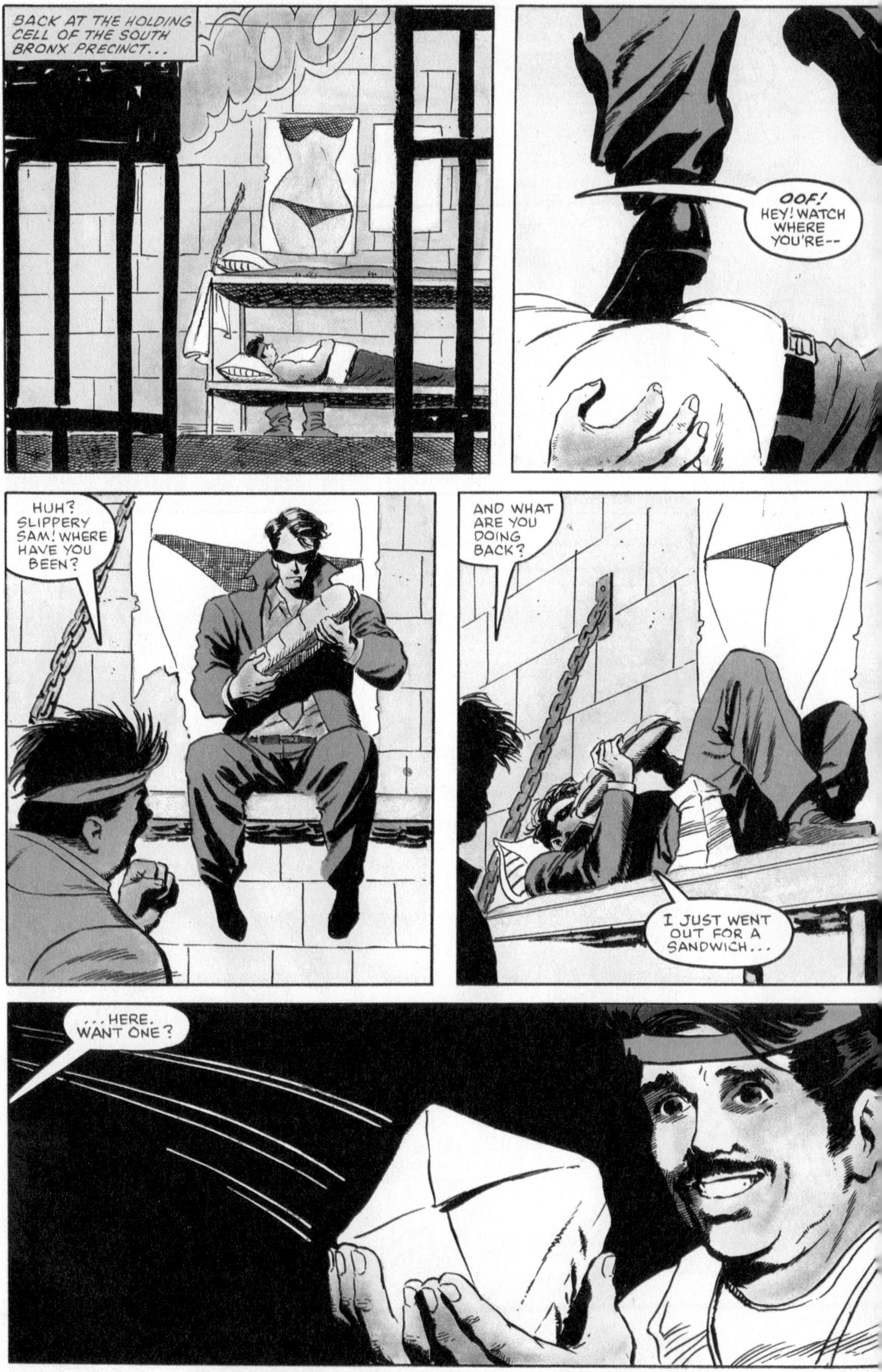
BACK AT THE HOLDING CELL OF THE SOUTH BRONX PRECINCT...
OOF! HEY! WATCH WHERE YOU'RE--
HUH? SLIPPERY SAM! WHERE HAVE YOU BEEN?
AND WHAT ARE YOU DOING BACK?
I JUST WENT OUT FOR A SANDWICH...
...HERE. WANT ONE?

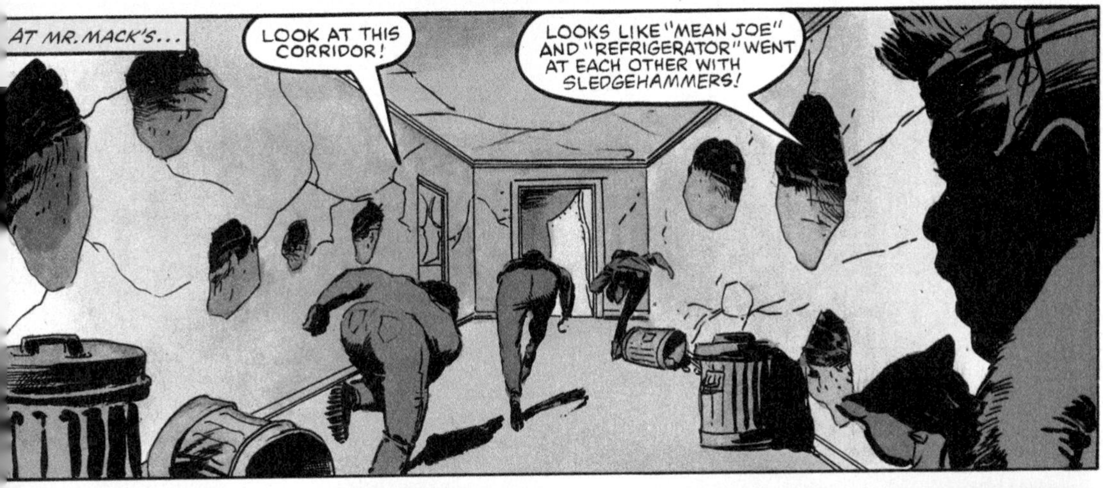
AT MR. MACK'S...
LOOK AT THIS CORRIDOR!
LOOKS LIKE "MEAN JOE" AND "REFRIGERATOR" WENT AT EACH OTHER WITH SLEDGEHAMMERS!

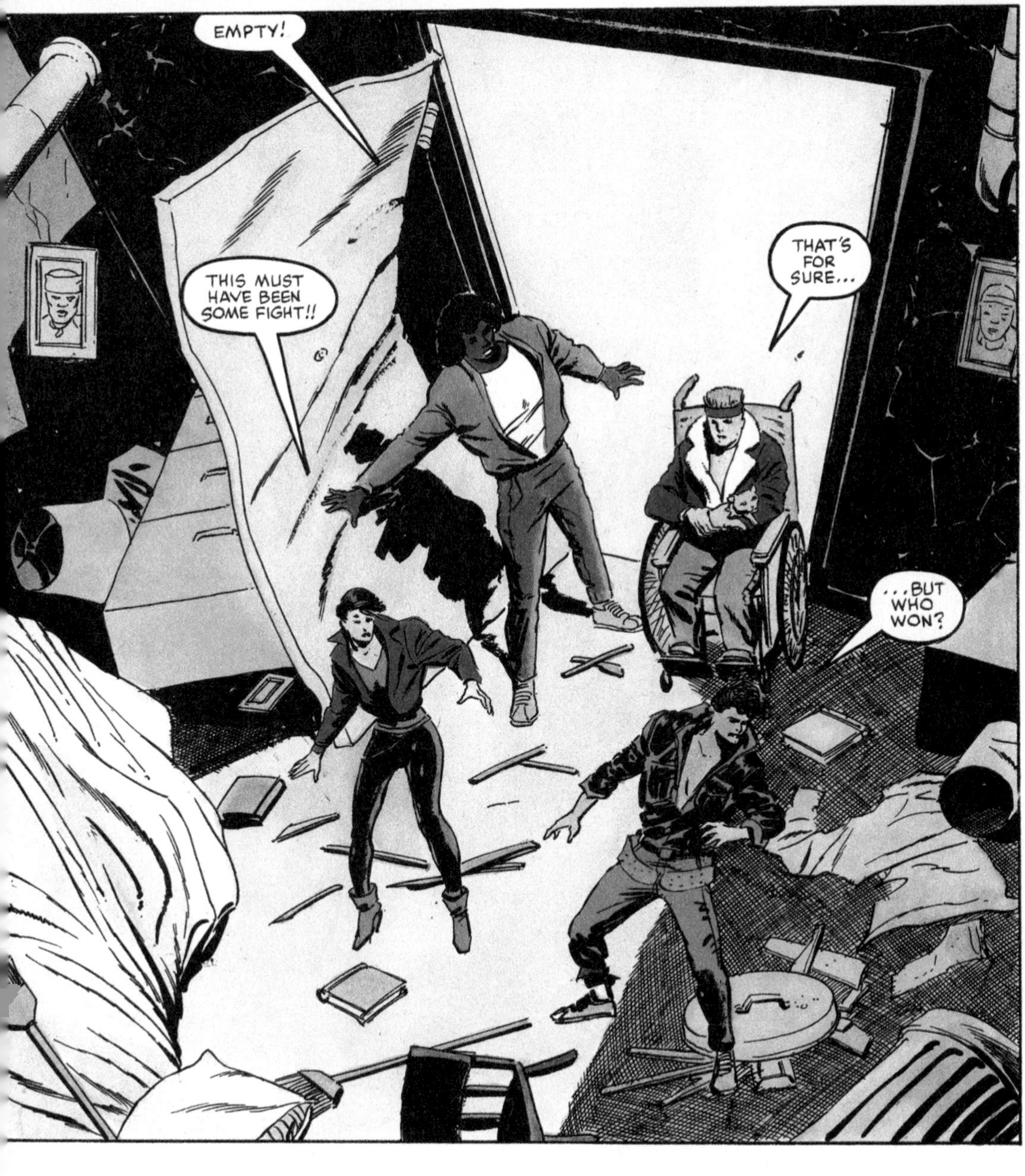
EMPTY!
THIS MUST HAVE BEEN SOME FIGHT!!
THAT'S FOR SURE...
...BUT WHO WON?

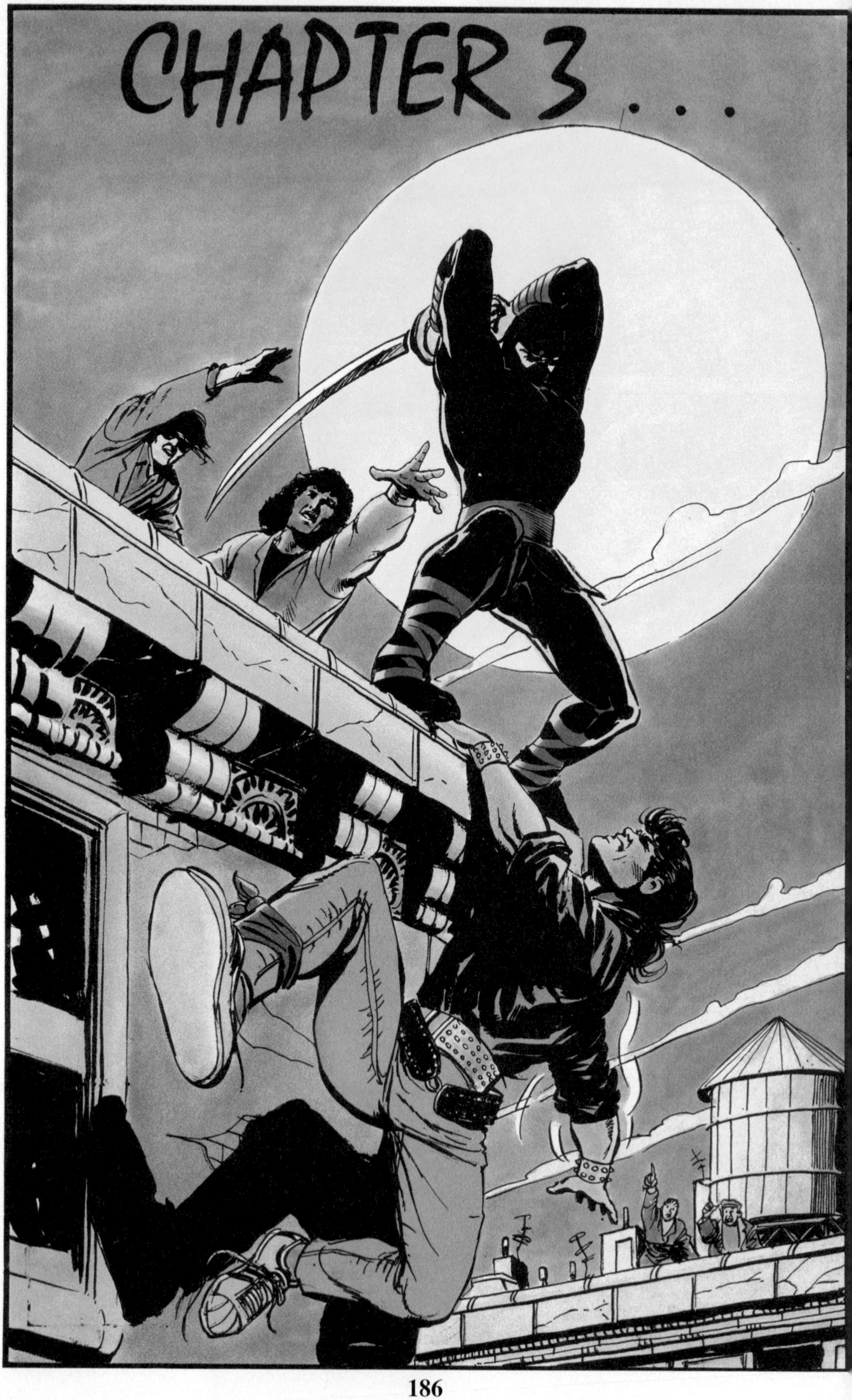
CHAPTER 3 . . .

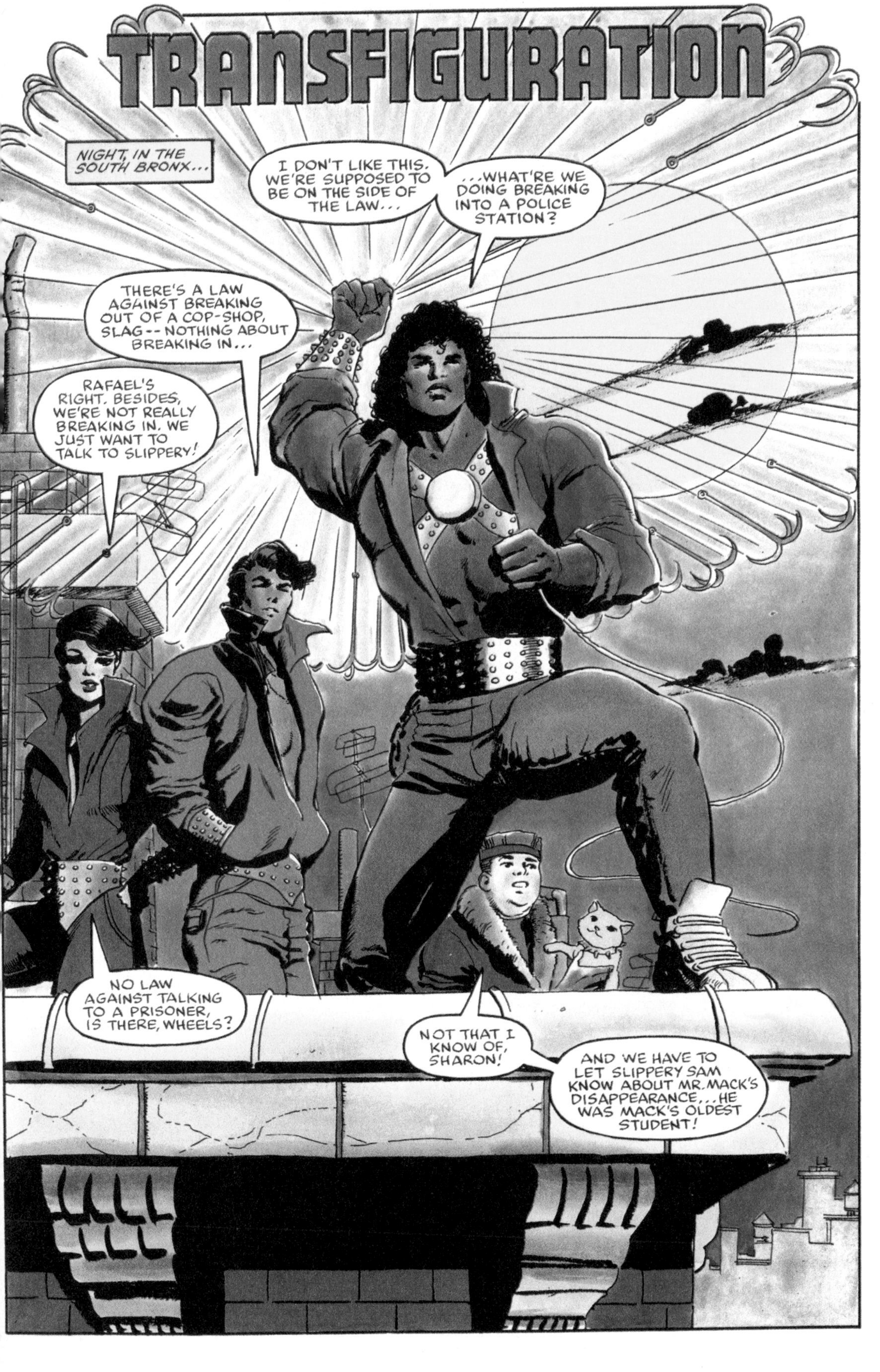
TRANSFIGURATION
NIGHT, IN THE SOUTH BRONX...
I DON'T LIKE THIS. WE'RE SUPPOSED TO BE ON THE SIDE OF THE LAW...
...WHAT'RE WE DOING BREAKING INTO A POLICE STATION?
THERE'S A LAW AGAINST BREAKING OUT OF A COP-SHOP, SLAG--NOTHING ABOUT BREAKING IN...
RAFAEL'S RIGHT. BESIDES, WE'RE NOT REALLY BREAKING IN. WE JUST WANT TO TALK TO SLIPPERY!
NO LAW AGAINST TALKING TO A PRISONER, IS THERE, WHEELS?
NOT THAT I KNOW OF, SHARON!
AND WE HAVE TO LET SLIPPERY SAM KNOW ABOUT MR. MACK'S DISAPPEARANCE... HE WAS MACK'S OLDEST STUDENT!

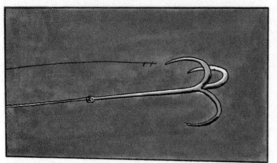

CLUNK!

THE WINDOWS TO THE CELLS ARE ON THE TOP FLOOR, FACING THE ALLEY!

BE CAREFUL, RAFAEL!

PSSSSST! SLIPPERY!

DID YOU REALLY JUST SAY "PSSST"!? RAFAEL, YOU'RE HOPELESS!

THEY DON'T EVEN SAY "PSSST" ON BAD SATURDAY MORNING CARTOONS ANYMORE! YOU DIDN'T BRING A CAKE WITH A FILE IN IT, DID YOU?

SLIPPERY! THIS IS REALLY IMPORTANT! SOMETHING'S HAPPENED TO MR. MACK! YOU KNEW HIM LONGER THAN ANYBODY ELSE... MAYBE YOU CAN FIGURE OUT WHAT TO DO!

KEEP YOUR VOICE DOWN. THE SQUAD ROOM IS RIGHT BELOW US...

ON THE STREETS BELOW...

...YOU LIED TO ME, MR. CRENSHAW! YOU SAID THAT ALL I HAD TO DO WAS RING THAT MR. MACK'S DOOR BELL!

YOU DIDN'T SAY NOTHING ABOUT THOSE TWO GUYS WITH THE SWORDS THAT WERE WAITING TO JUMP INSIDE AND KILL HIM!

AND THEN I HAD TO BURY THAT OLD MAN IN THE VACANT LOT AND ME WITH MY CHEST STILL HURTIN' FROM THAT HOT BRANDING IRON--

GET TO THE POINT, LAMARR.

I FIGURE WE'RE EVEN NOW FOR ALL THAT FANCY LAWYER WORK YOU DONE FOR ME. IN FACT, I THINK YOU OWE ME A LITTLE SOMETHING...

NOW WHAT COULD THAT SOMETHING BE, LAMARR?

CLYDE? PULL UP HERE ON THE LEFT...

THIS IS THE PRECINCT HOUSE WHERE "SLIPPERY" SAM WELTSCHMERZ IS BEING HELD. YOU STILL HOLD A GRUDGE AGAINST HIM, DON'T YOU, LAMARR?

IS THAT THE LITTLE SOMETHING WE OWE YOU?

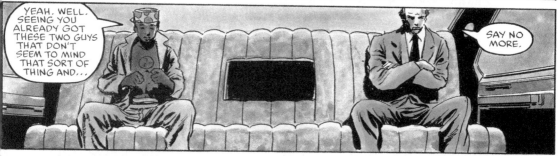

YEAH. WELL, SEEING YOU ALREADY GOT THESE TWO GUYS THAT DON'T SEEM TO MIND THAT SORT OF THING AND...

SAY NO MORE.

YOW!

MR. CRENSHAW! THEY'RE GOING TO DO IT RIGHT HERE AND NOW? WITH US SITTING OUTSIDE? WHAT IF--

WHAT'S THE MATTER WITH YOU, LAMARR? FIRST YOU WANT SOMETHING AND THEN YOU DON'T...

189

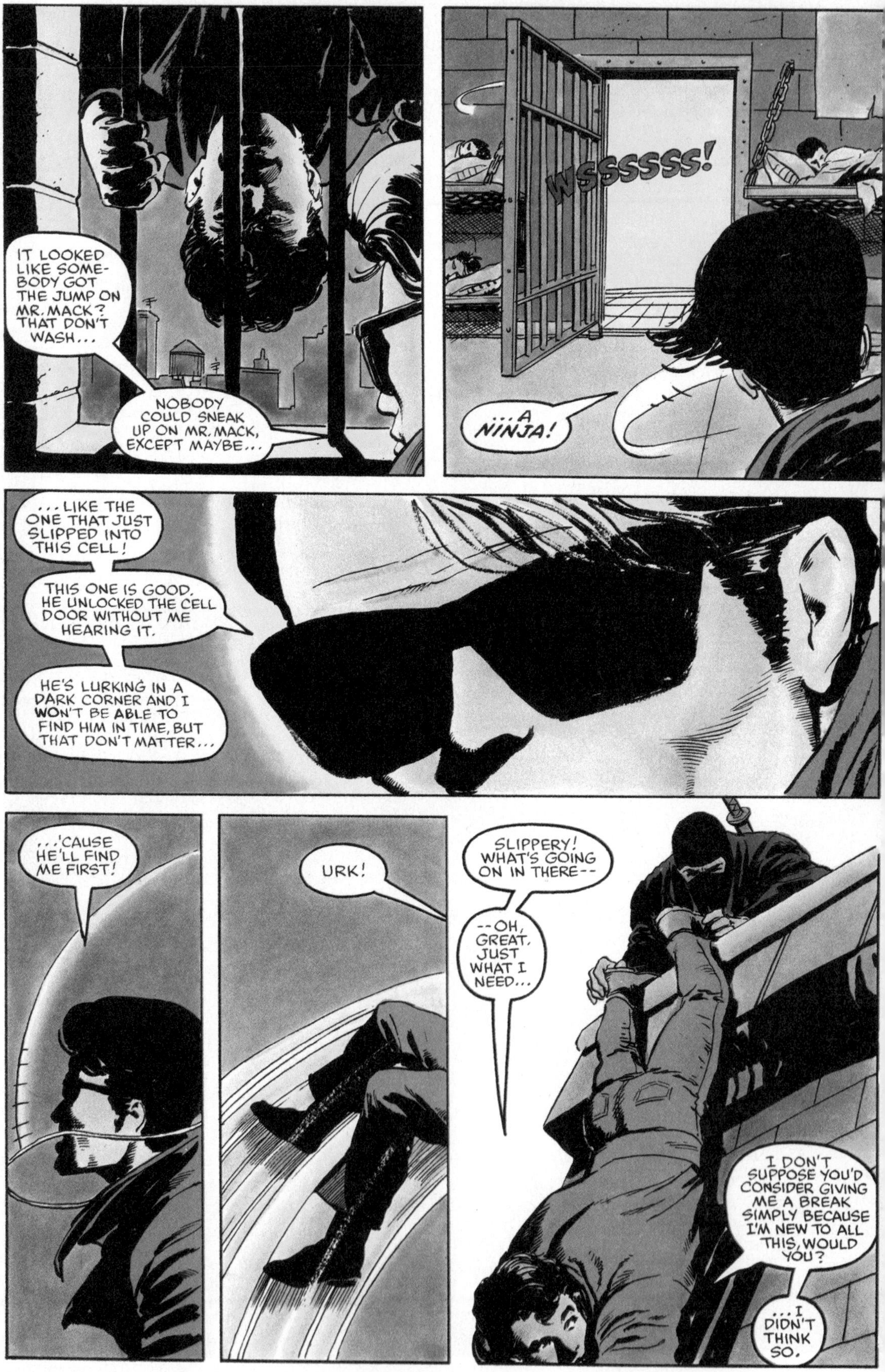
IT LOOKED LIKE SOMEBODY GOT THE JUMP ON MR. MACK? THAT DON'T WASH...
NOBODY COULD SNEAK UP ON MR. MACK, EXCEPT MAYBE...
WSSSSSS!
...A NINJA!
...LIKE THE ONE THAT JUST SLIPPED INTO THIS CELL!
THIS ONE IS GOOD. HE UNLOCKED THE CELL DOOR WITHOUT ME HEARING IT.
HE'S LURKING IN A DARK CORNER AND I WON'T BE ABLE TO FIND HIM IN TIME, BUT THAT DON'T MATTER...
...'CAUSE HE'LL FIND ME FIRST!
URK!
SLIPPERY! WHAT'S GOING ON IN THERE--
--OH, GREAT. JUST WHAT I NEED...
I DON'T SUPPOSE YOU'D CONSIDER GIVING ME A BREAK SIMPLY BECAUSE I'M NEW TO ALL THIS, WOULD YOU?
...I DIDN'T THINK SO.

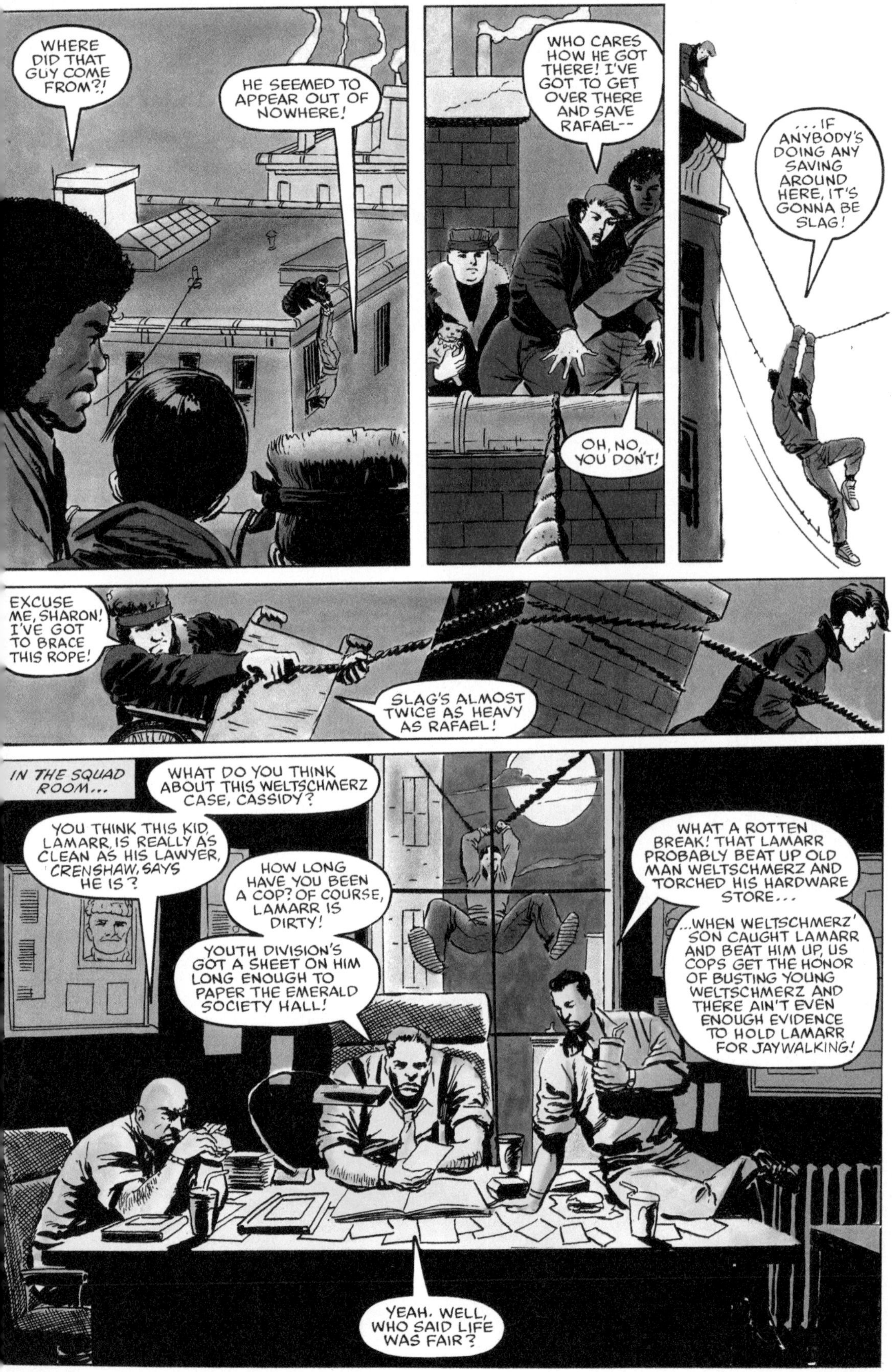
WHERE DID THAT GUY COME FROM?!
HE SEEMED TO APPEAR OUT OF NOWHERE!
WHO CARES HOW HE GOT THERE! I'VE GOT TO GET OVER THERE AND SAVE RAFAEL--
OH, NO, YOU DON'T!
...IF ANYBODY'S DOING ANY SAVING AROUND HERE, IT'S GONNA BE SLAG!
EXCUSE ME, SHARON! I'VE GOT TO BRACE THIS ROPE!
SLAG'S ALMOST TWICE AS HEAVY AS RAFAEL!
IN THE SQUAD ROOM...
WHAT DO YOU THINK ABOUT THIS WELTSCHMERZ CASE, CASSIDY?
YOU THINK THIS KID, LAMARR, IS REALLY AS CLEAN AS HIS LAWYER, CRENSHAW, SAYS HE IS?
HOW LONG HAVE YOU BEEN A COP? OF COURSE, LAMARR IS DIRTY!
YOUTH DIVISION'S GOT A SHEET ON HIM LONG ENOUGH TO PAPER THE EMERALD SOCIETY HALL!
WHAT A ROTTEN BREAK! THAT LAMARR PROBABLY BEAT UP OLD MAN WELTSCHMERZ AND TORCHED HIS HARDWARE STORE...
...WHEN WELTSCHMERZ' SON CAUGHT LAMARR AND BEAT HIM UP, US COPS GET THE HONOR OF BUSTING YOUNG WELTSCHMERZ AND THERE AIN'T EVEN ENOUGH EVIDENCE TO HOLD LAMARR FOR JAYWALKING!
YEAH. WELL, WHO SAID LIFE WAS FAIR?

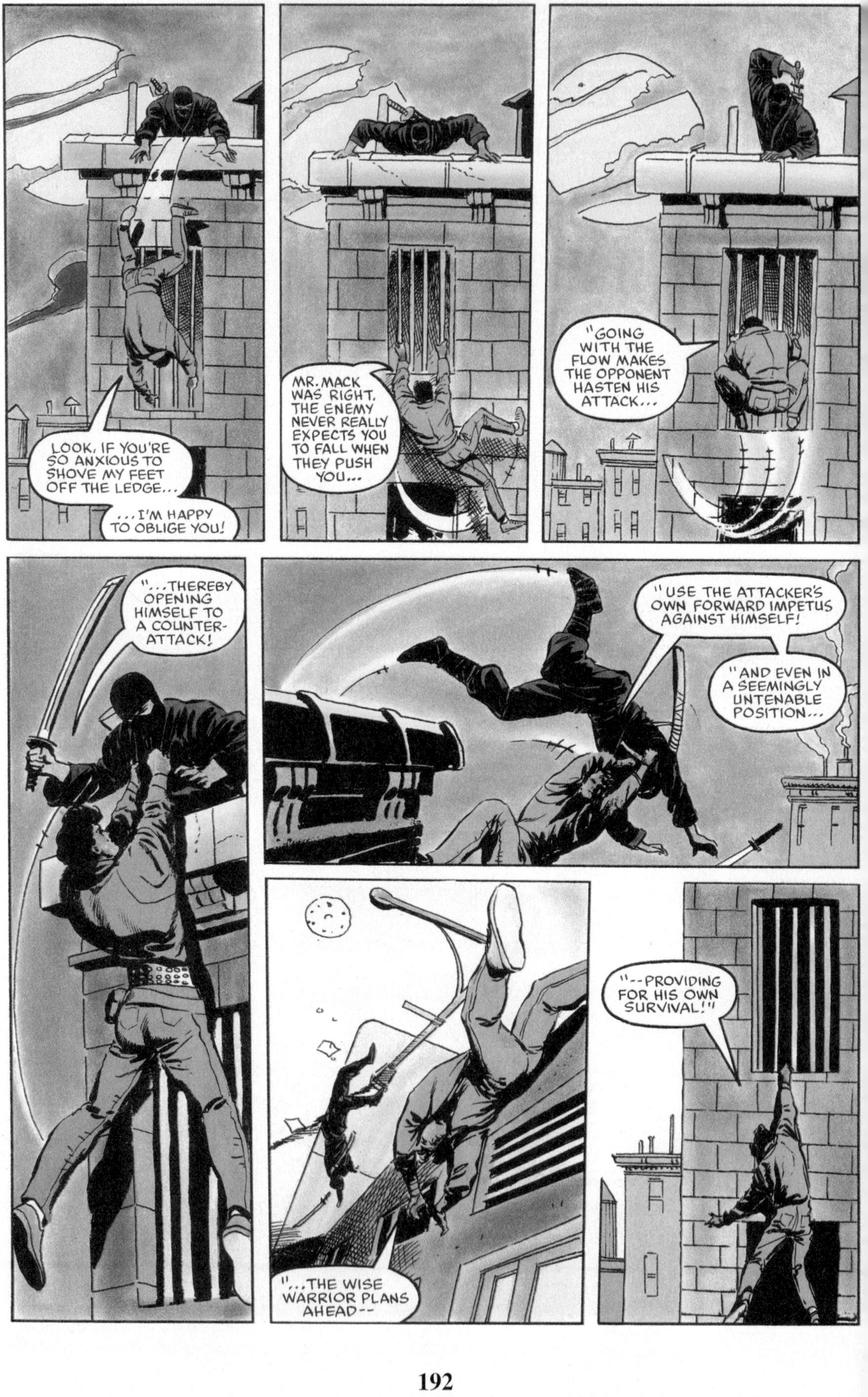
LOOK, IF YOU'RE SO ANXIOUS TO SHOVE MY FEET OFF THE LEDGE...
...I'M HAPPY TO OBLIGE YOU!
MR. MACK WAS RIGHT. THE ENEMY NEVER REALLY EXPECTS YOU TO FALL WHEN THEY PUSH YOU...
"GOING WITH THE FLOW MAKES THE OPPONENT HASTEN HIS ATTACK...
"...THEREBY OPENING HIMSELF TO A COUNTER-ATTACK!
"USE THE ATTACKER'S OWN FORWARD IMPETUS AGAINST HIMSELF!
"AND EVEN IN A SEEMINGLY UNTENABLE POSITION...
"...THE WISE WARRIOR PLANS AHEAD--
"--PROVIDING FOR HIS OWN SURVIVAL!"

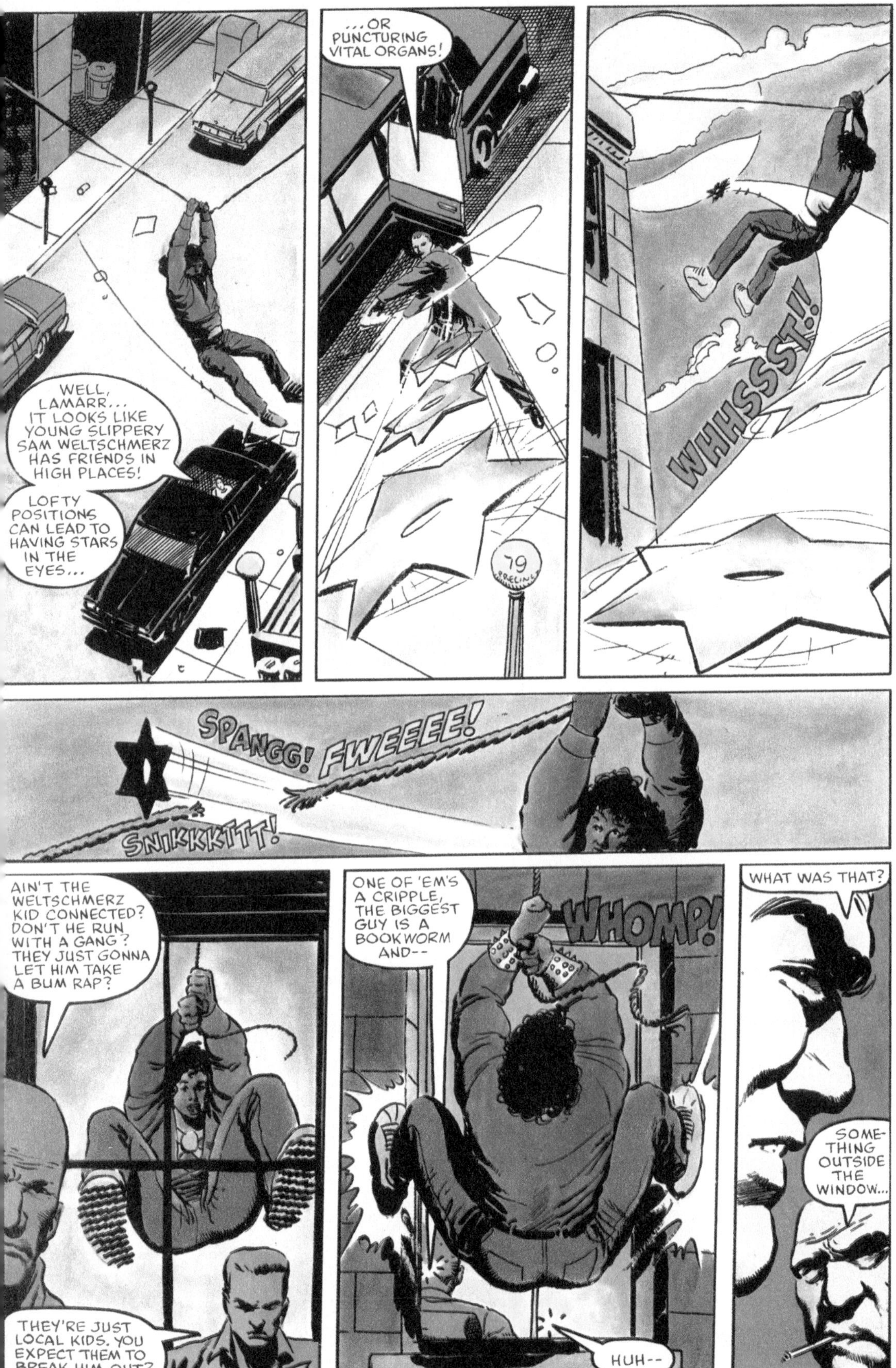
WELL, LAMARR... IT LOOKS LIKE YOUNG SLIPPERY SAM WELTSCHMERZ HAS FRIENDS IN HIGH PLACES!
LOFTY POSITIONS CAN LEAD TO HAVING STARS IN THE EYES...
...OR PUNCTURING VITAL ORGANS!
79
WHHSSSST!!
SPANGG!
FWEEEEE!
SNIKKKTTT!
AIN'T THE WELTSCHMERZ KID CONNECTED? DON'T HE RUN WITH A GANG? THEY JUST GONNA LET HIM TAKE A BUM RAP?
THEY'RE JUST LOCAL KIDS. YOU EXPECT THEM TO BREAK HIM OUT?
ONE OF 'EM'S A CRIPPLE, THE BIGGEST GUY IS A BOOKWORM AND--
WHOMP!
HUH--
WHAT WAS THAT?
SOME-THING OUTSIDE THE WINDOW...

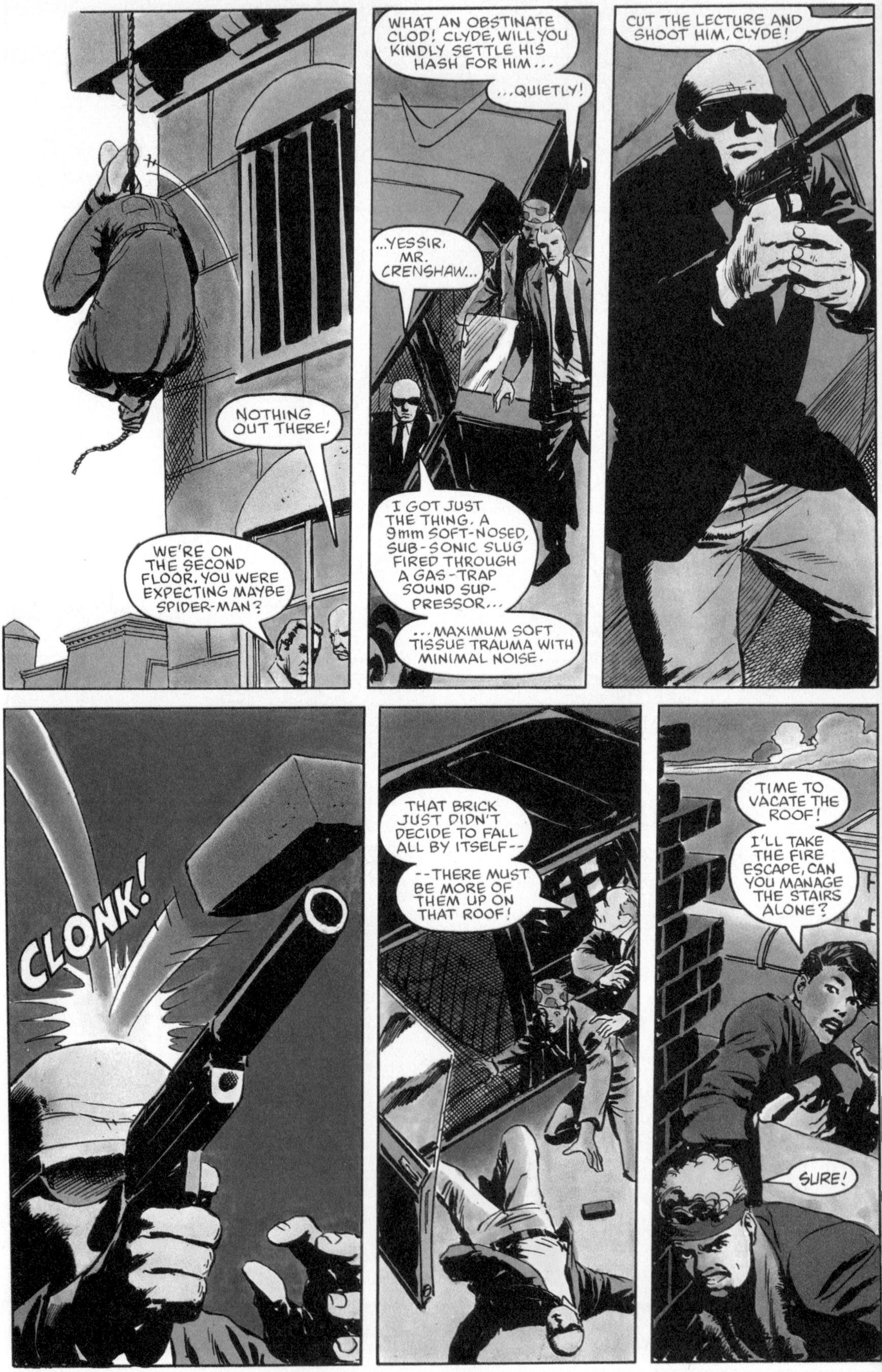
NOTHING OUT THERE!
WE'RE ON THE SECOND FLOOR. YOU WERE EXPECTING MAYBE SPIDER-MAN?
WHAT AN OBSTINATE CLOD! CLYDE, WILL YOU KINDLY SETTLE HIS HASH FOR HIM...
...QUIETLY!
...YESSIR, MR. CRENSHAW...
I GOT JUST THE THING. A 9mm SOFT-NOSED, SUB-SONIC SLUG FIRED THROUGH A GAS-TRAP SOUND SUPPRESSOR...
...MAXIMUM SOFT TISSUE TRAUMA WITH MINIMAL NOISE.
CUT THE LECTURE AND SHOOT HIM, CLYDE!
CLONK!
THAT BRICK JUST DIDN'T DECIDE TO FALL ALL BY ITSELF--
--THERE MUST BE MORE OF THEM UP ON THAT ROOF!
TIME TO VACATE THE ROOF!
I'LL TAKE THE FIRE ESCAPE, CAN YOU MANAGE THE STAIRS ALONE?
SURE!

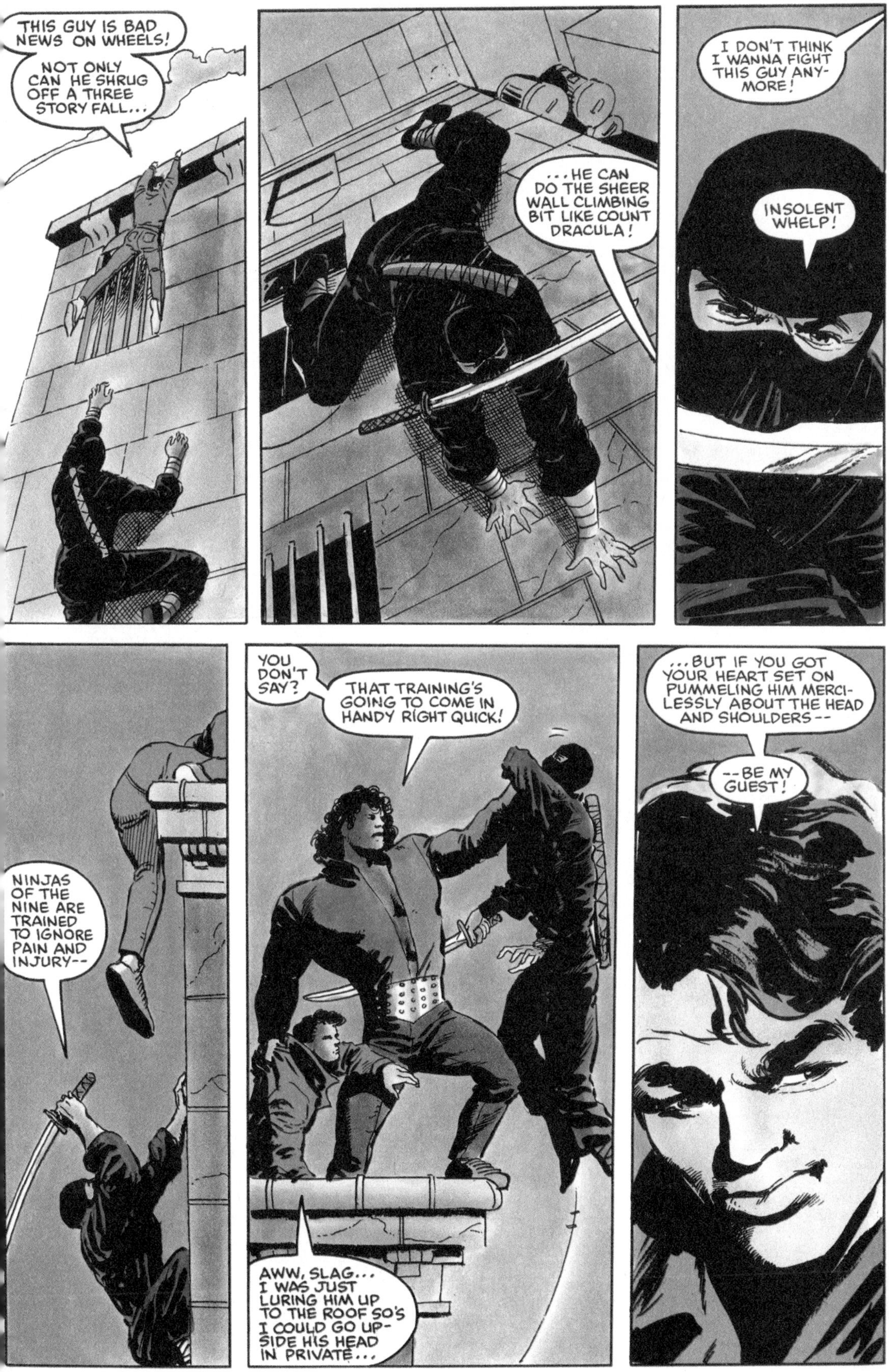
THIS GUY IS BAD NEWS ON WHEELS!
NOT ONLY CAN HE SHRUG OFF A THREE STORY FALL...
...HE CAN DO THE SHEER WALL CLIMBING BIT LIKE COUNT DRACULA!
I DON'T THINK I WANNA FIGHT THIS GUY ANY-MORE!
INSOLENT WHELP!
NINJAS OF THE NINE ARE TRAINED TO IGNORE PAIN AND INJURY--
YOU DON'T SAY?
THAT TRAINING'S GOING TO COME IN HANDY RIGHT QUICK!
AWW, SLAG... I WAS JUST LURING HIM UP TO THE ROOF SO'S I COULD GO UP-SIDE HIS HEAD IN PRIVATE...
...BUT IF YOU GOT YOUR HEART SET ON PUMMELING HIM MERCI-LESSLY ABOUT THE HEAD AND SHOULDERS--
--BE MY GUEST!

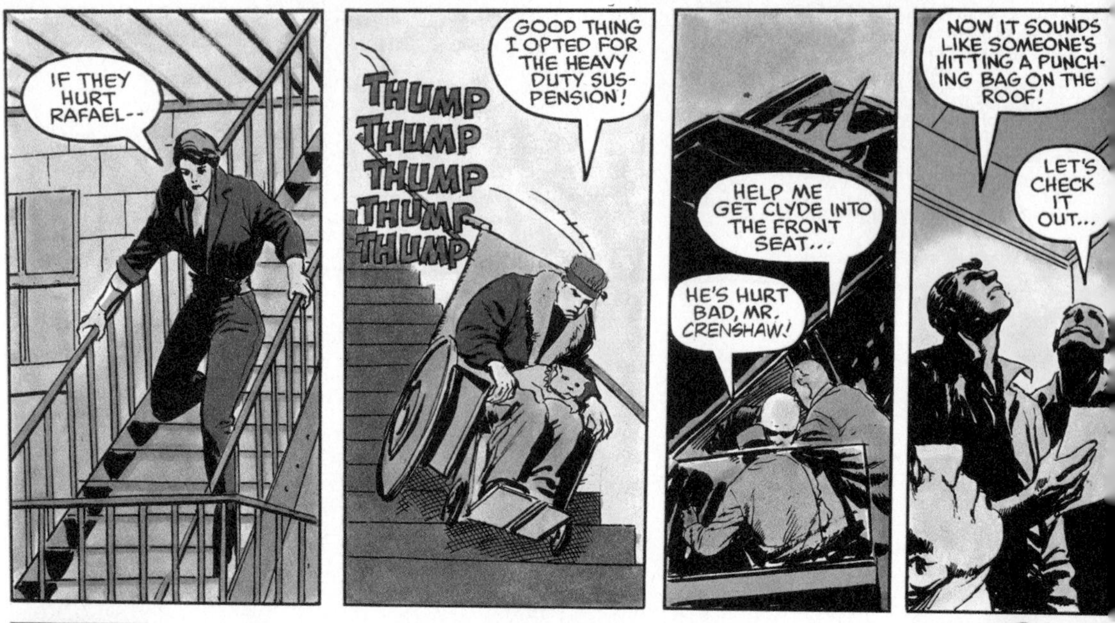
IF THEY HURT RAFAEL--
THUMP THUMP THUMP THUMP THUMP
GOOD THING I OPTED FOR THE HEAVY DUTY SUSPENSION!
HELP ME GET CLYDE INTO THE FRONT SEAT...
HE'S HURT BAD, MR. CRENSHAW!
NOW IT SOUNDS LIKE SOMEONE'S HITTING A PUNCHING BAG ON THE ROOF!
LET'S CHECK IT OUT...

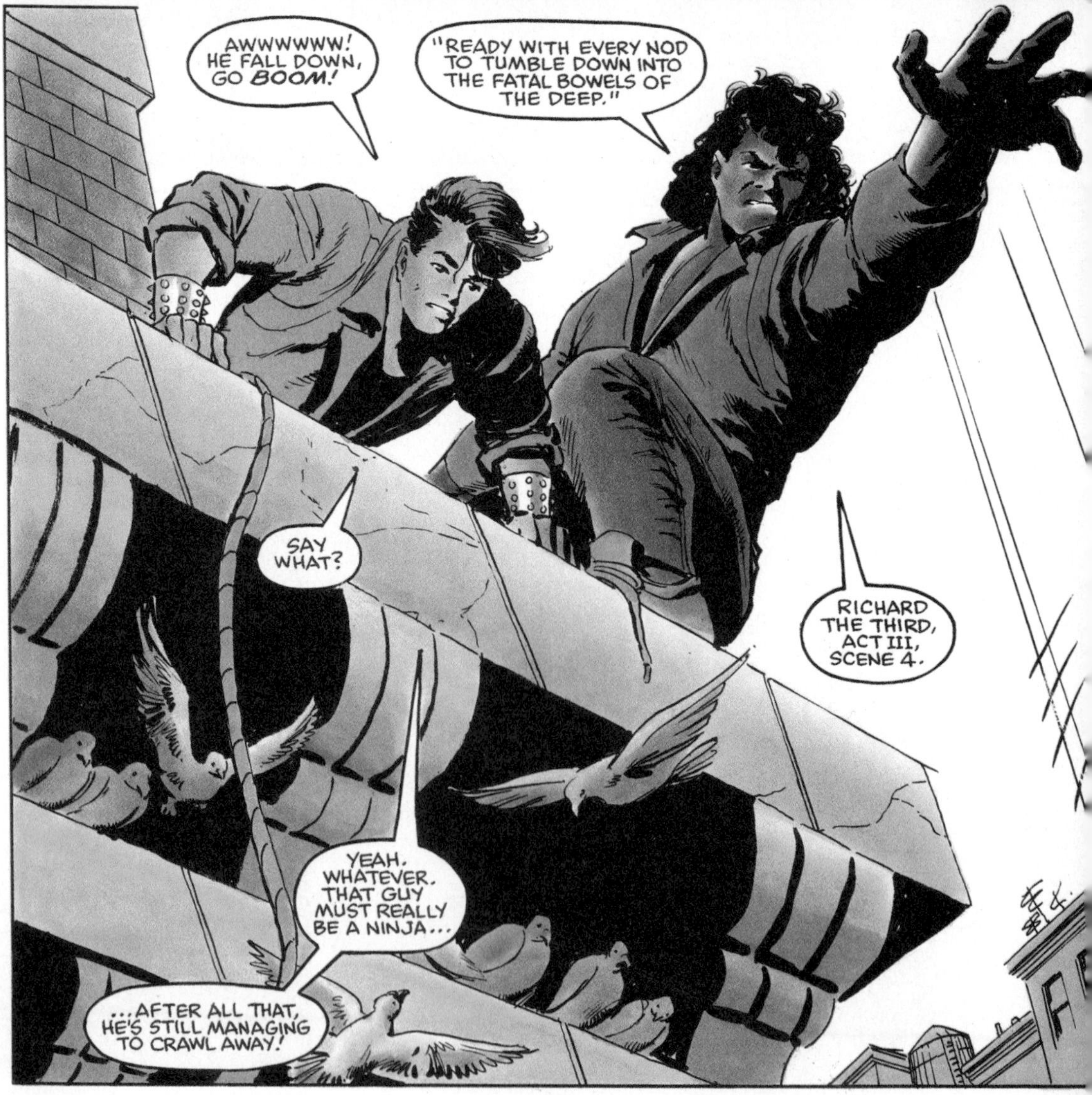
AWWWWWW! HE FALL DOWN, GO *BOOM*!
"READY WITH EVERY NOD TO TUMBLE DOWN INTO THE FATAL BOWELS OF THE DEEP."
SAY WHAT?
RICHARD THE THIRD, ACT III, SCENE 4.
YEAH. WHATEVER. THAT GUY MUST REALLY BE A NINJA...
...AFTER ALL THAT, HE'S STILL MANAGING TO CRAWL AWAY!

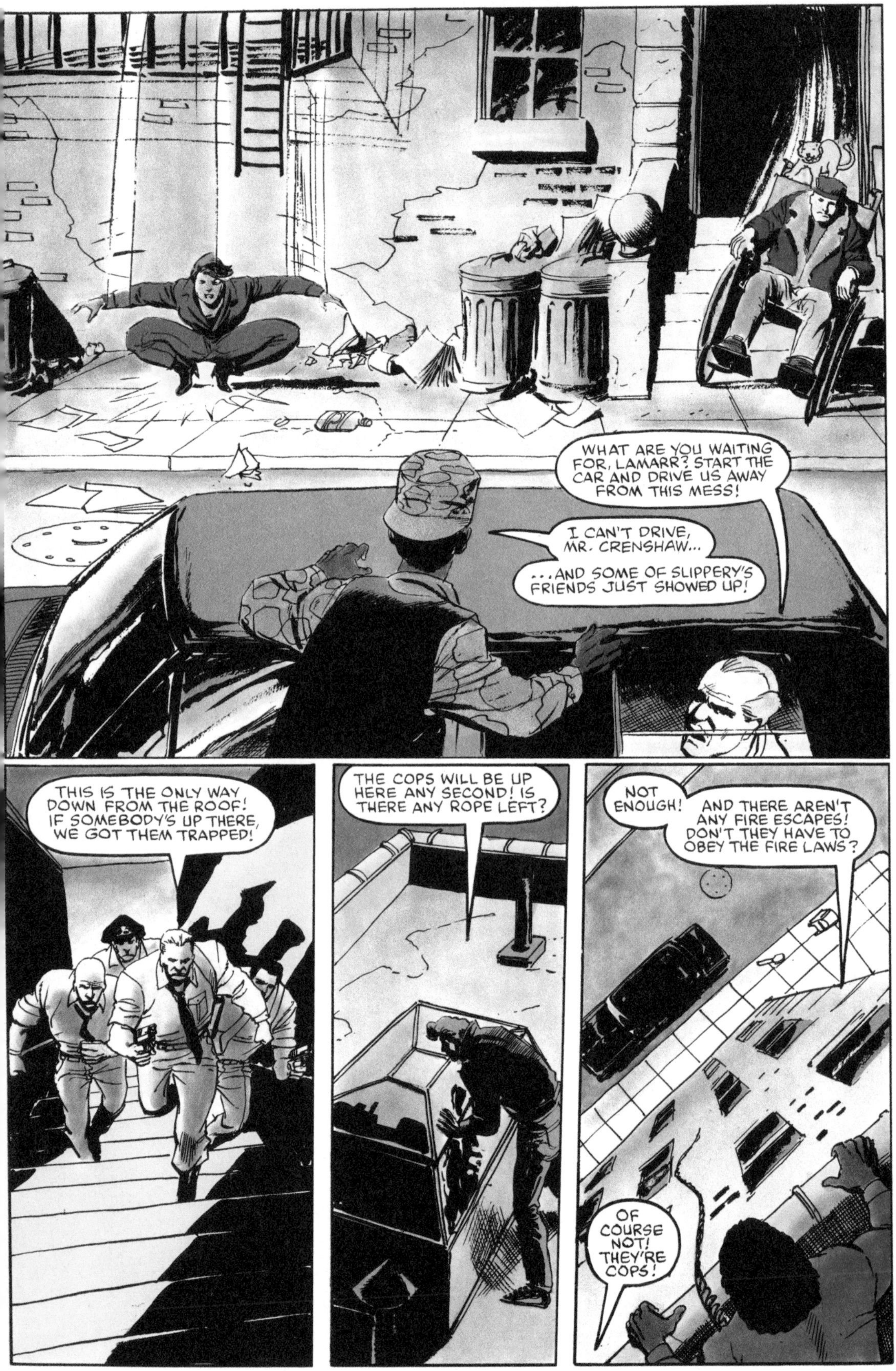
WHAT ARE YOU WAITING FOR, LAMARR? START THE CAR AND DRIVE US AWAY FROM THIS MESS!
I CAN'T DRIVE, MR. CRENSHAW...
...AND SOME OF SLIPPERY'S FRIENDS JUST SHOWED UP!
THIS IS THE ONLY WAY DOWN FROM THE ROOF! IF SOMEBODY'S UP THERE, WE GOT THEM TRAPPED!
THE COPS WILL BE UP HERE ANY SECOND! IS THERE ANY ROPE LEFT?
NOT ENOUGH!
AND THERE AREN'T ANY FIRE ESCAPES! DON'T THEY HAVE TO OBEY THE FIRE LAWS?
OF COURSE NOT! THEY'RE COPS!

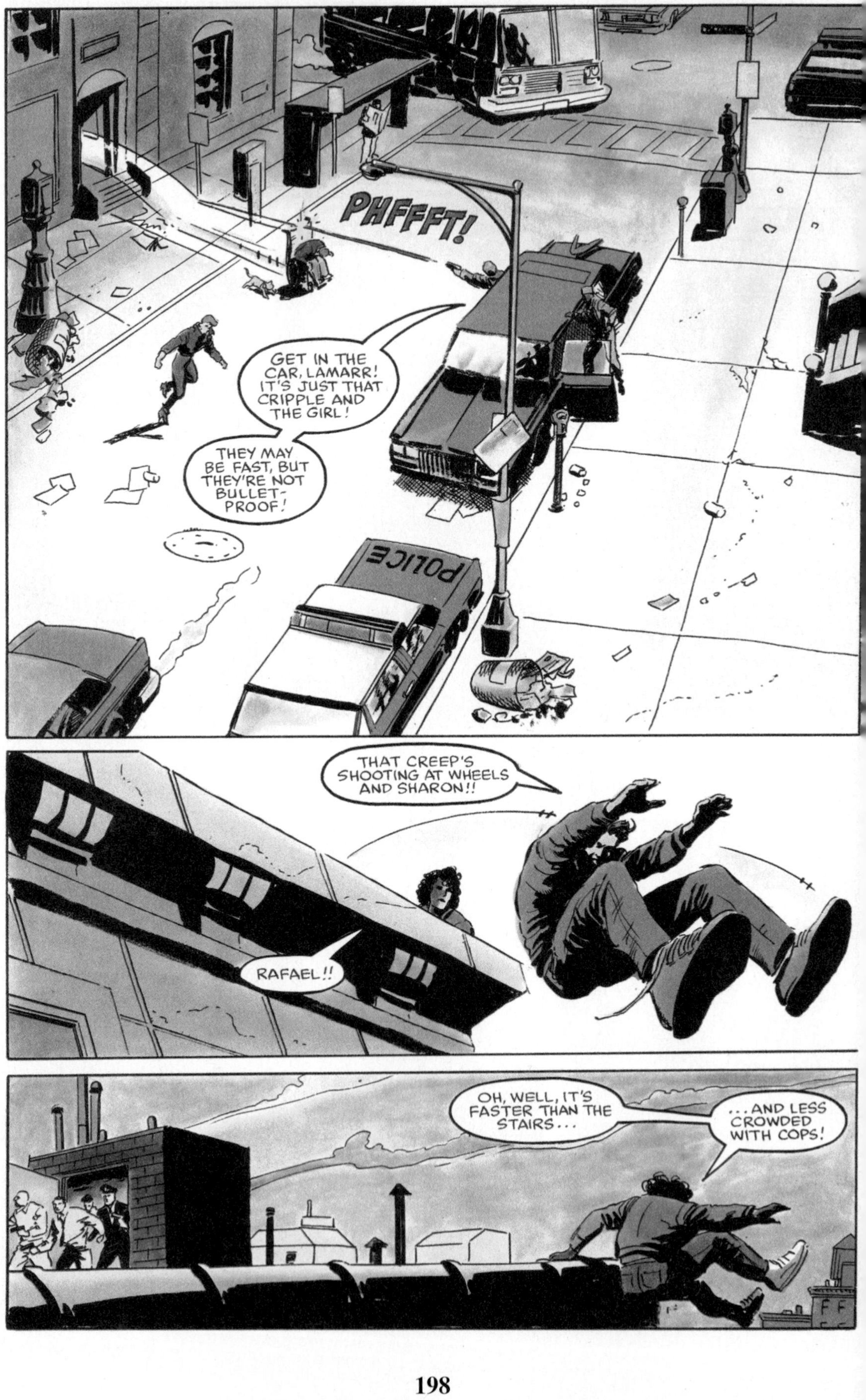
PHFFFT!
GET IN THE CAR, LAMARR! IT'S JUST THAT CRIPPLE AND THE GIRL!
THEY MAY BE FAST, BUT THEY'RE NOT BULLET-PROOF!
POLICE
THAT CREEP'S SHOOTING AT WHEELS AND SHARON!!
RAFAEL!!
OH, WELL, IT'S FASTER THAN THE STAIRS...
...AND LESS CROWDED WITH COPS!

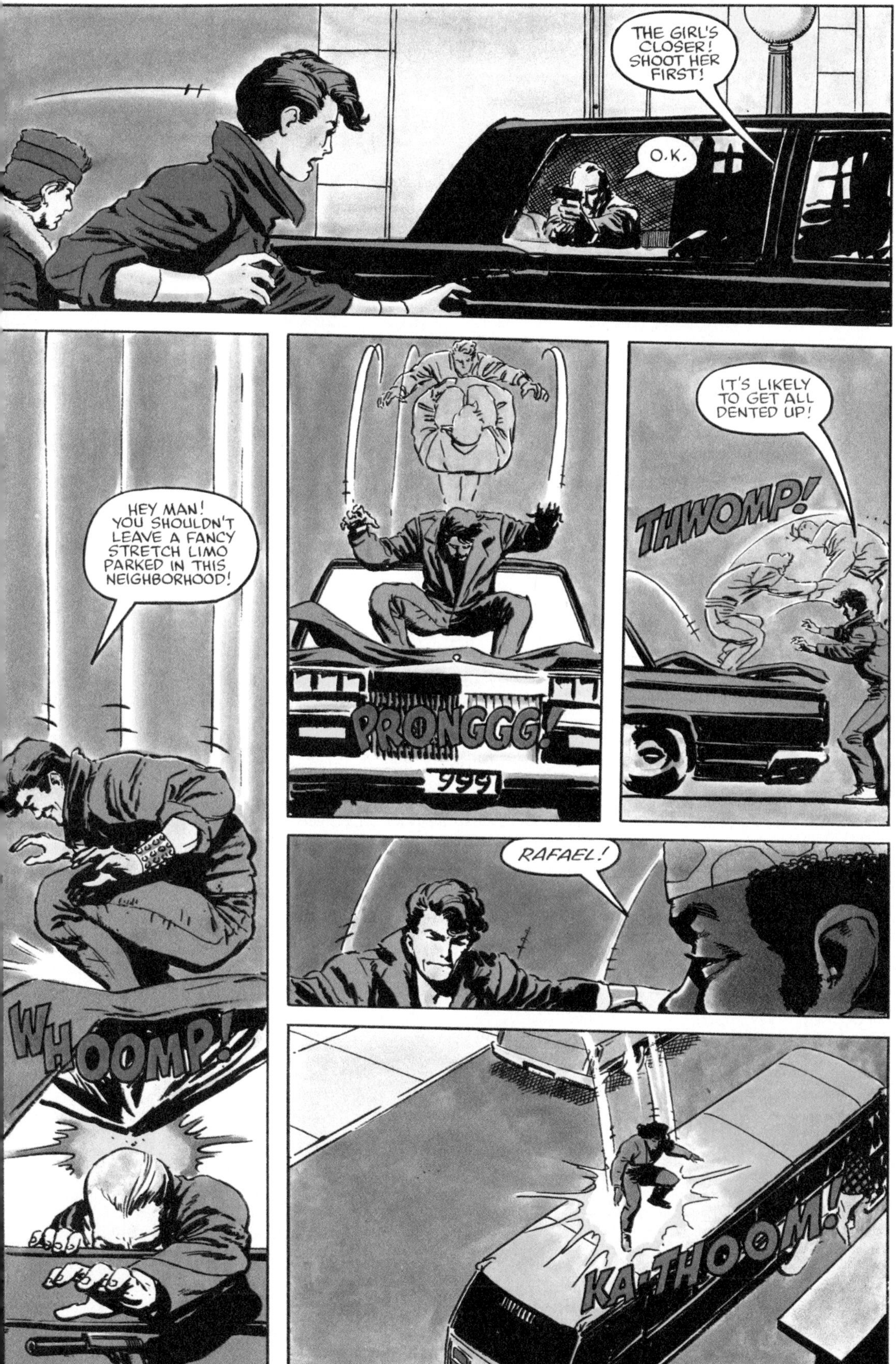
THE GIRL'S CLOSER! SHOOT HER FIRST!
O.K.
HEY MAN! YOU SHOULDN'T LEAVE A FANCY STRETCH LIMO PARKED IN THIS NEIGHBORHOOD!
WHOOMP!
PRONGGG!
999
IT'S LIKELY TO GET ALL DENTED UP!
THWOMP!
RAFAEL!
KA-THOOOM!

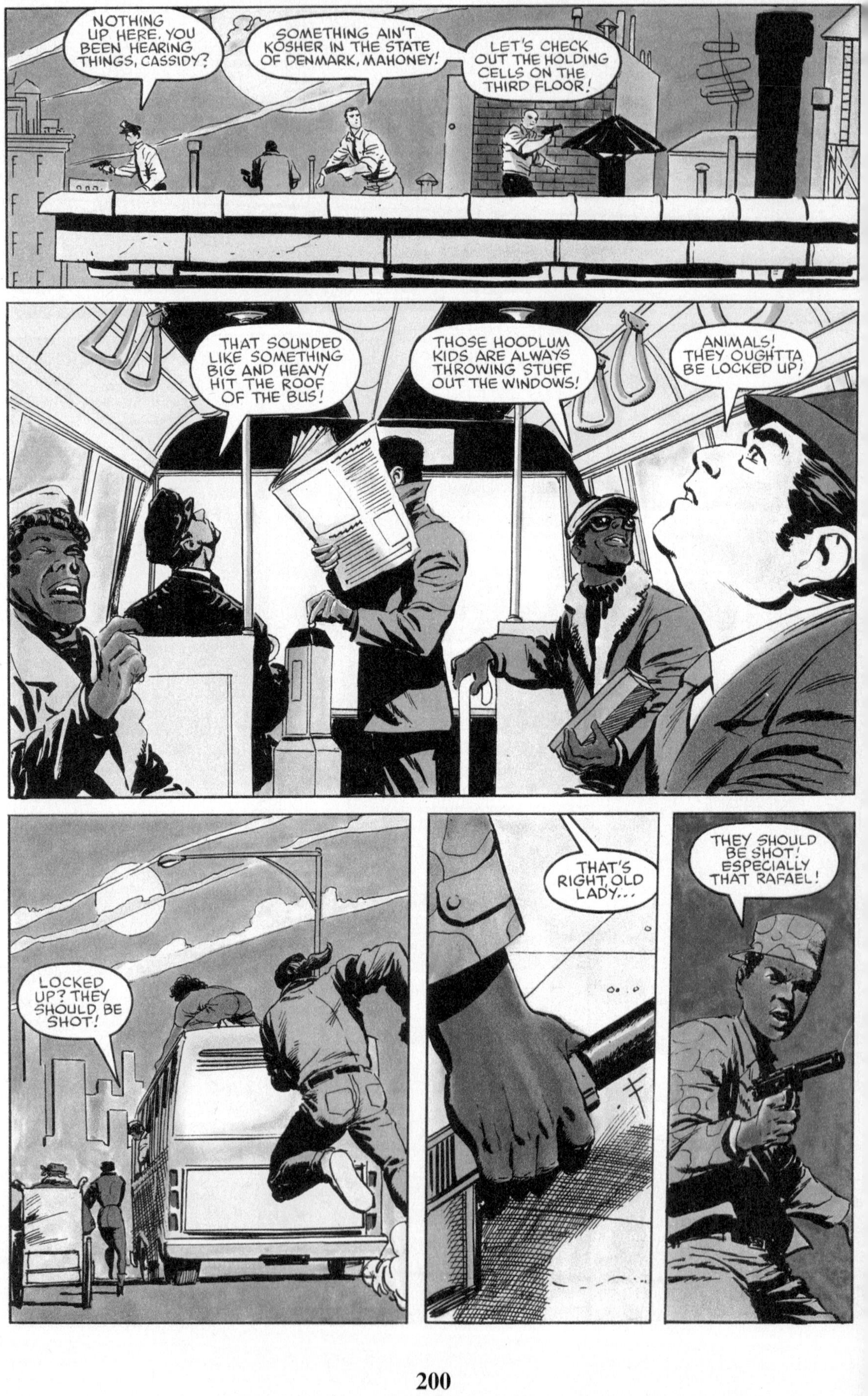
NOTHING UP HERE. YOU BEEN HEARING THINGS, CASSIDY?
SOMETHING AIN'T KOSHER IN THE STATE OF DENMARK, MAHONEY!
LET'S CHECK OUT THE HOLDING CELLS ON THE THIRD FLOOR!
THAT SOUNDED LIKE SOMETHING BIG AND HEAVY HIT THE ROOF OF THE BUS!
THOSE HOODLUM KIDS ARE ALWAYS THROWING STUFF OUT THE WINDOWS!
ANIMALS! THEY OUGHTTA BE LOCKED UP!
LOCKED UP? THEY SHOULD BE SHOT!
THAT'S RIGHT, OLD LADY...
THEY SHOULD BE SHOT! ESPECIALLY THAT RAFAEL!

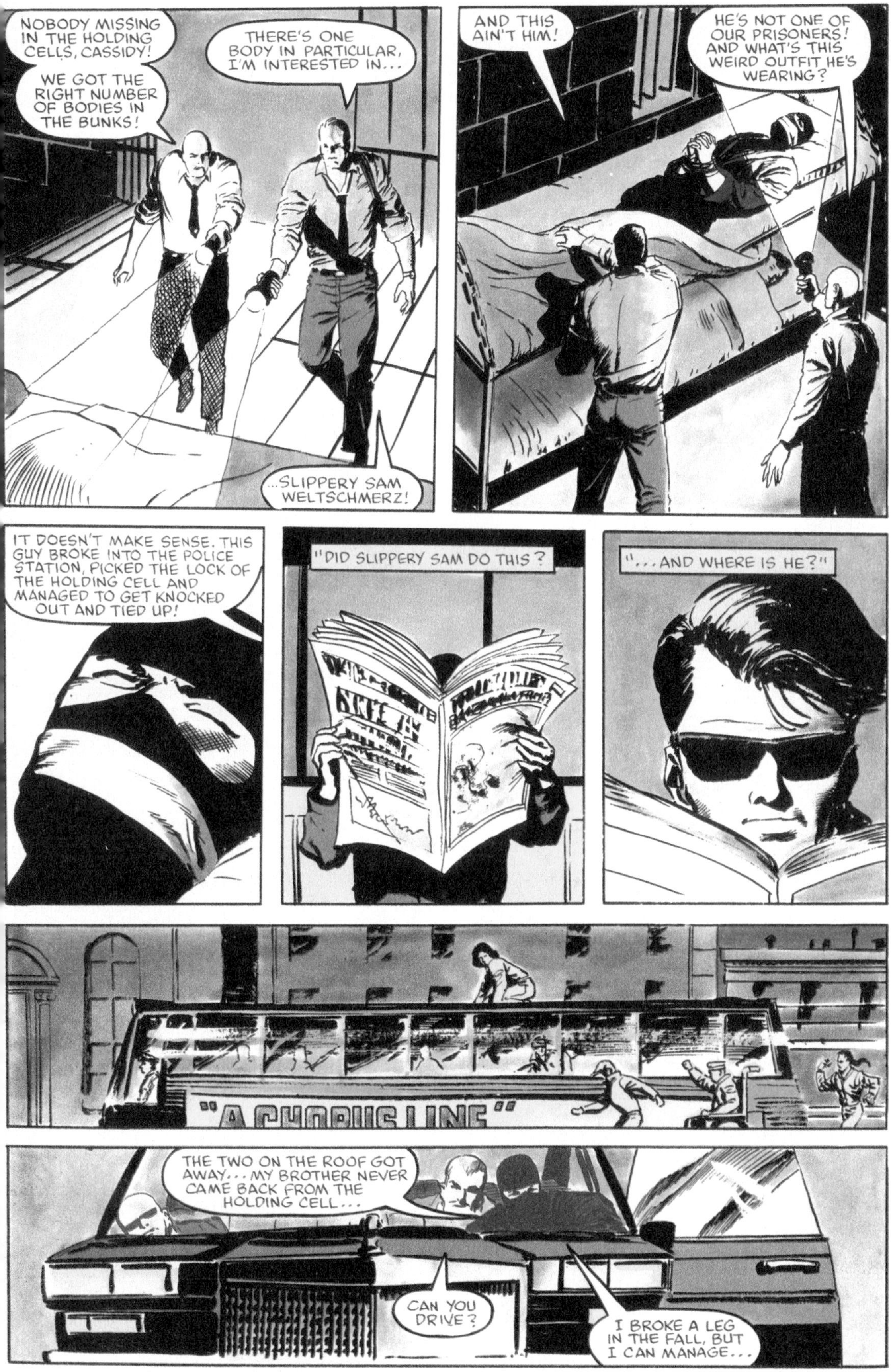
NOBODY MISSING IN THE HOLDING CELLS, CASSIDY!
WE GOT THE RIGHT NUMBER OF BODIES IN THE BUNKS!
THERE'S ONE BODY IN PARTICULAR, I'M INTERESTED IN...
...SLIPPERY SAM WELTSCHMERZ!
AND THIS AIN'T HIM!
HE'S NOT ONE OF OUR PRISONERS! AND WHAT'S THIS WEIRD OUTFIT HE'S WEARING?
IT DOESN'T MAKE SENSE. THIS GUY BROKE INTO THE POLICE STATION, PICKED THE LOCK OF THE HOLDING CELL AND MANAGED TO GET KNOCKED OUT AND TIED UP!
"DID SLIPPERY SAM DO THIS?
"...AND WHERE IS HE?"
"A CHORUS LINE"
THE TWO ON THE ROOF GOT AWAY... MY BROTHER NEVER CAME BACK FROM THE HOLDING CELL...
CAN YOU DRIVE?
I BROKE A LEG IN THE FALL, BUT I CAN MANAGE...

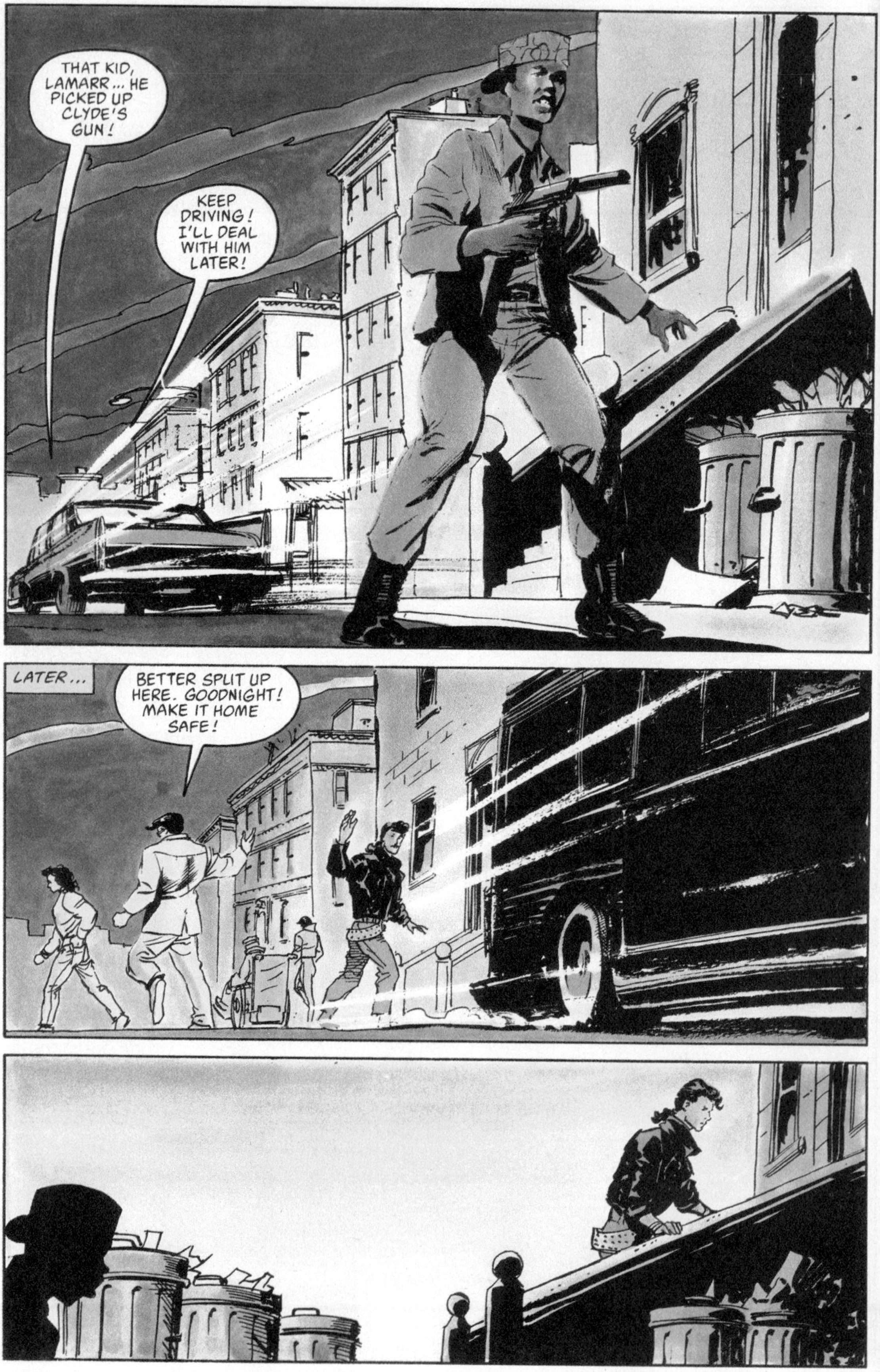
THAT KID, LAMARR... HE PICKED UP CLYDE'S GUN!
KEEP DRIVING! I'LL DEAL WITH HIM LATER!
LATER...
BETTER SPLIT UP HERE. GOODNIGHT! MAKE IT HOME SAFE!

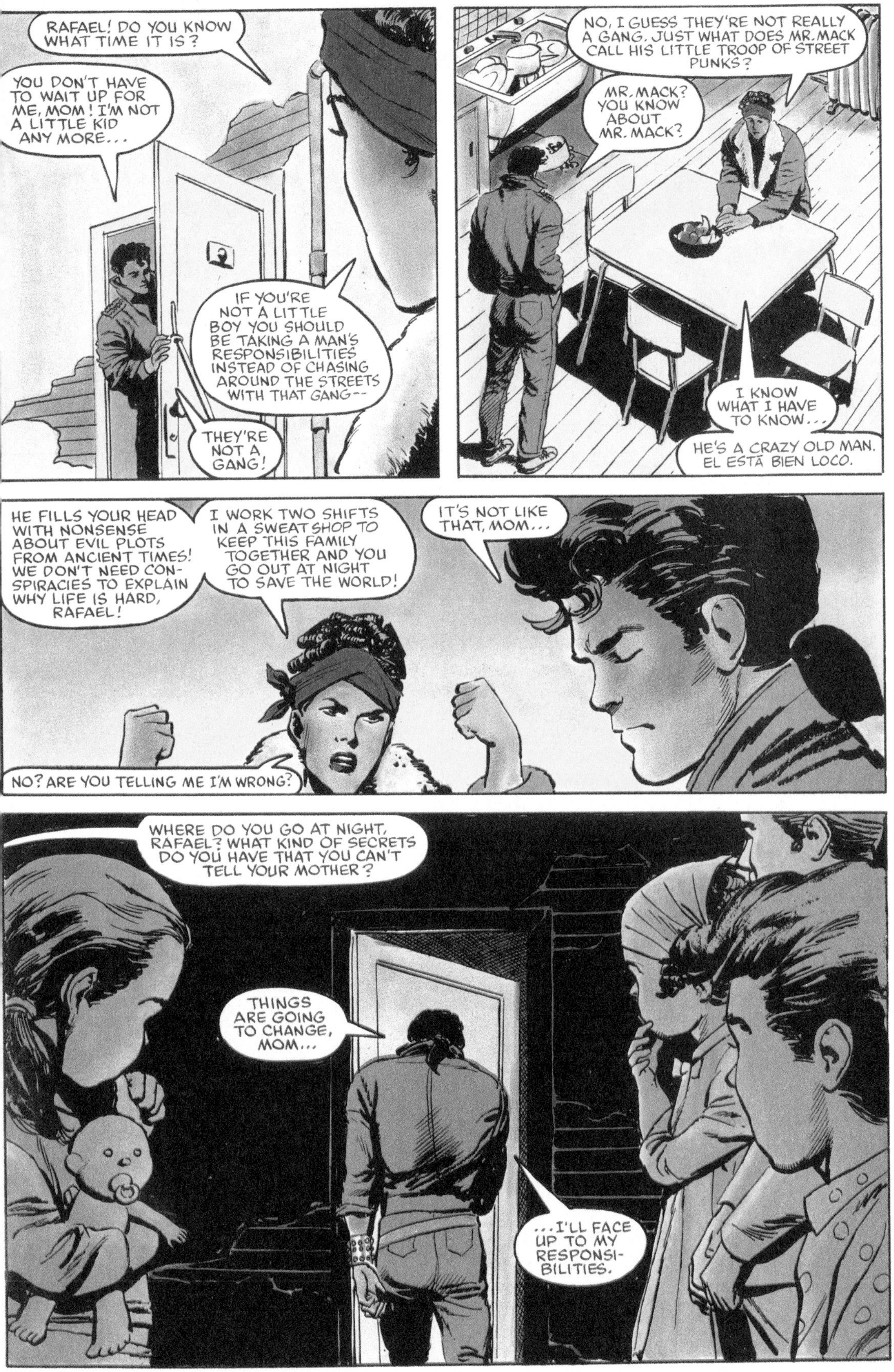
RAFAEL! DO YOU KNOW WHAT TIME IT IS?
YOU DON'T HAVE TO WAIT UP FOR ME, MOM! I'M NOT A LITTLE KID ANY MORE...
IF YOU'RE NOT A LITTLE BOY YOU SHOULD BE TAKING A MAN'S RESPONSIBILITIES INSTEAD OF CHASING AROUND THE STREETS WITH THAT GANG--
THEY'RE NOT A GANG!
NO, I GUESS THEY'RE NOT REALLY A GANG. JUST WHAT DOES MR. MACK CALL HIS LITTLE TROOP OF STREET PUNKS?
MR. MACK? YOU KNOW ABOUT MR. MACK?
I KNOW WHAT I HAVE TO KNOW...
HE'S A CRAZY OLD MAN. EL ESTÁ BIEN LOCO.
HE FILLS YOUR HEAD WITH NONSENSE ABOUT EVIL PLOTS FROM ANCIENT TIMES! WE DON'T NEED CON-SPIRACIES TO EXPLAIN WHY LIFE IS HARD, RAFAEL!
I WORK TWO SHIFTS IN A SWEATSHOP TO KEEP THIS FAMILY TOGETHER AND YOU GO OUT AT NIGHT TO SAVE THE WORLD!
IT'S NOT LIKE THAT, MOM...
NO? ARE YOU TELLING ME I'M WRONG?
WHERE DO YOU GO AT NIGHT, RAFAEL? WHAT KIND OF SECRETS DO YOU HAVE THAT YOU CAN'T TELL YOUR MOTHER?
THINGS ARE GOING TO CHANGE, MOM...
...I'LL FACE UP TO MY RESPONSI-BILITIES.

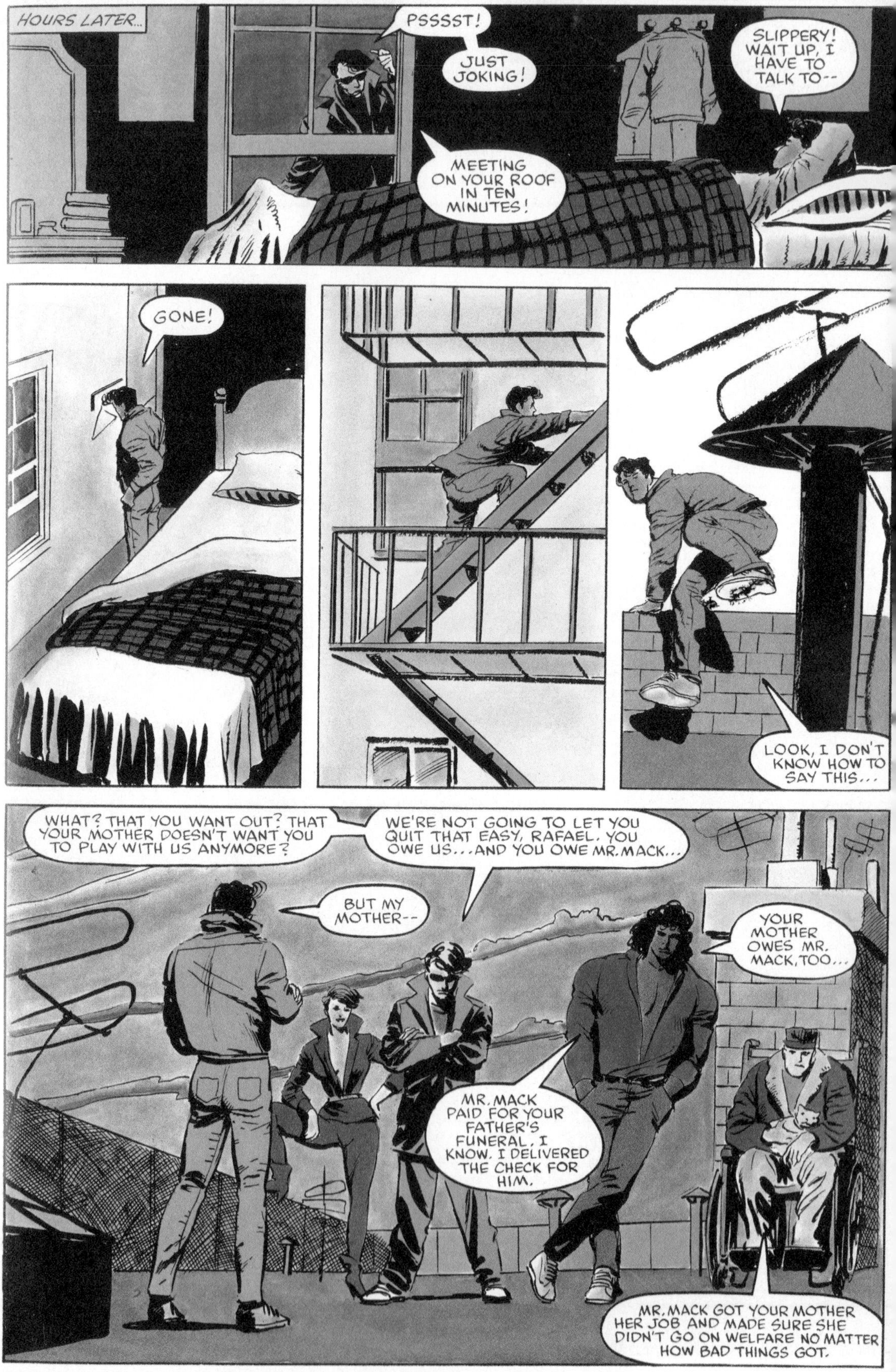
HOURS LATER...
PSSSST!
JUST JOKING!
MEETING ON YOUR ROOF IN TEN MINUTES!
SLIPPERY! WAIT UP, I HAVE TO TALK TO--
GONE!
LOOK, I DON'T KNOW HOW TO SAY THIS...
WHAT? THAT YOU WANT OUT? THAT YOUR MOTHER DOESN'T WANT YOU TO PLAY WITH US ANYMORE?
WE'RE NOT GOING TO LET YOU QUIT THAT EASY, RAFAEL. YOU OWE US...AND YOU OWE MR. MACK...
BUT MY MOTHER--
YOUR MOTHER OWES MR. MACK, TOO...
MR. MACK PAID FOR YOUR FATHER'S FUNERAL, I KNOW. I DELIVERED THE CHECK FOR HIM.
MR. MACK GOT YOUR MOTHER HER JOB AND MADE SURE SHE DIDN'T GO ON WELFARE NO MATTER HOW BAD THINGS GOT.

MR. MACK TRACKED DOWN THE TWO PUNKS THAT KILLED YOUR FATHER. HE SETTLED YOUR MOTHER'S DEBTS, ALL OF THEM.

MR. MACK NEVER WENT BEHIND YOUR MOTHER'S BACK. HE ASKED HER IF HE COULD TRAIN YOU AND SHE AGREED.

A MOTHER'S LOVE GOES BEYOND HONOR, RAFAEL. SHE WANTED OUT ON HER BARGAIN AND YOU CAN'T BLAME HER FOR THAT. SHE WOULD DO ANYTHING TO PROTECT YOU...

WE'RE NOT ASKING YOU TO BETRAY HER TRUST. WE'RE JUST ASKING YOU TO CONFIRM YOUR TRUST...

...IN US.

THE CEREMONY FOR THE FORMATION OF A NEW PACK IS OVER TWO THOUSAND YEARS OLD. MR. MACK TOLD ME ABOUT IT SO MANY TIMES, I KNOW IT BY HEART.

THERE ARE NO WORDS OR PLEDGES. WORDS CAN BE TWISTED AND PLEDGES SPOKEN WITH A FALSE HEART.

THIS DAGGER WAS FORGED FROM THE BROKEN SWORD OF ONE OF THE TEN JUST MEN...

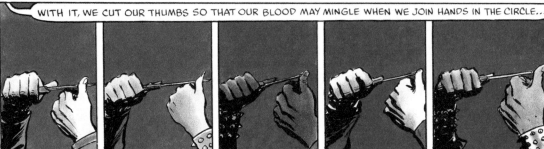

WITH IT, WE CUT OUR THUMBS SO THAT OUR BLOOD MAY MINGLE WHEN WE JOIN HANDS IN THE CIRCLE...

...A CIRCLE OF BLOOD AND STEEL.

MR. MACK MENTIONED THAT THE CEREMONY WASN'T COMPLETE WITHOUT FIRE. DID SOMEBODY BRING FIRE?

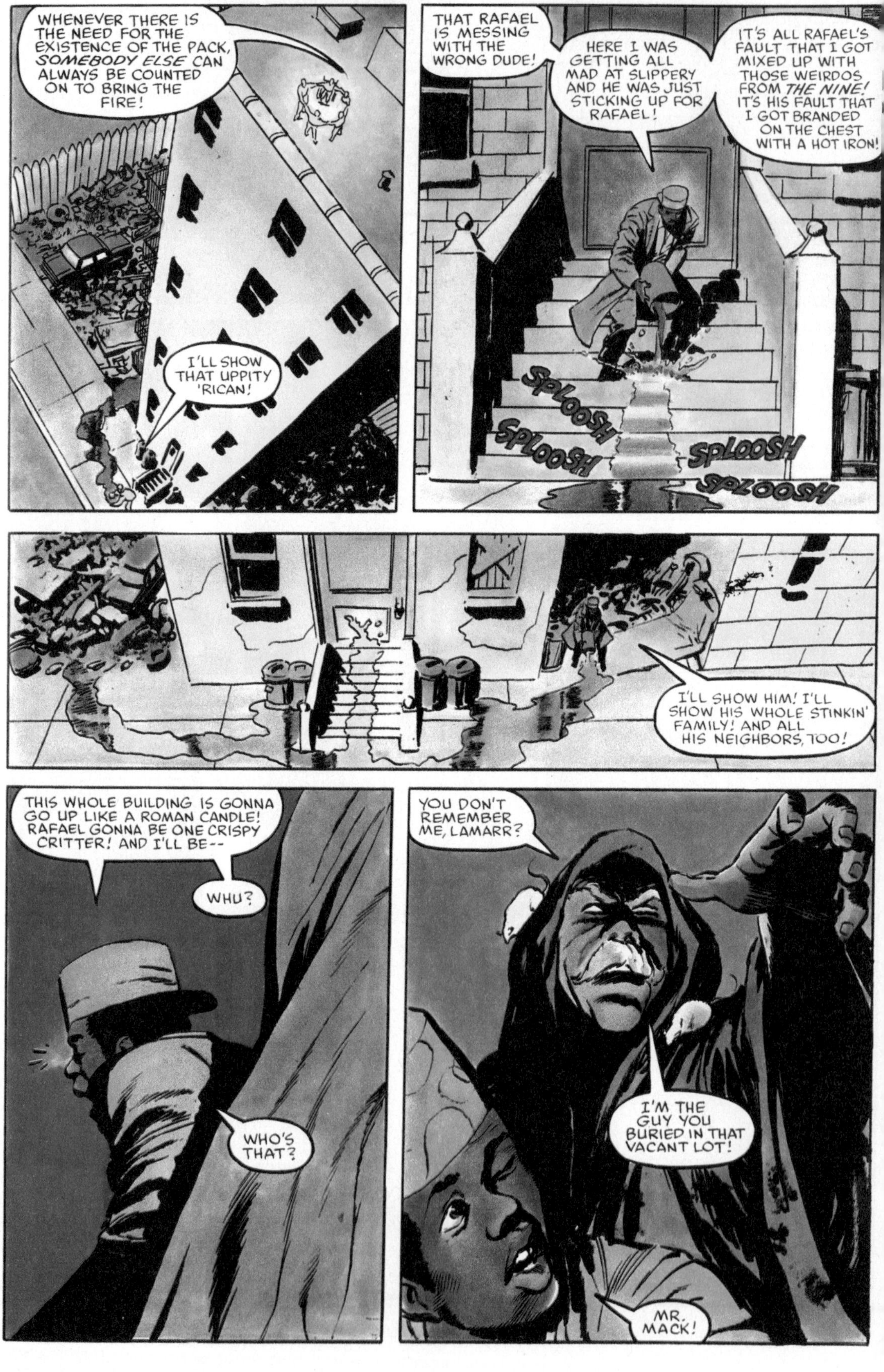

WHENEVER THERE IS THE NEED FOR THE EXISTENCE OF THE PACK, SOMEBODY ELSE CAN ALWAYS BE COUNTED ON TO BRING THE FIRE!
I'LL SHOW THAT UPPITY 'RICAN!
THAT RAFAEL IS MESSING WITH THE WRONG DUDE!
HERE I WAS GETTING ALL MAD AT SLIPPERY AND HE WAS JUST STICKING UP FOR RAFAEL!
IT'S ALL RAFAEL'S FAULT THAT I GOT MIXED UP WITH THOSE WEIRDOS FROM THE NINE! IT'S HIS FAULT THAT I GOT BRANDED ON THE CHEST WITH A HOT IRON!
SPLOOSH
SPLOOSH
SPLOOSH
SPLOOSH
SPLOOSH
I'LL SHOW HIM! I'LL SHOW HIS WHOLE STINKIN' FAMILY! AND ALL HIS NEIGHBORS, TOO!
THIS WHOLE BUILDING IS GONNA GO UP LIKE A ROMAN CANDLE! RAFAEL GONNA BE ONE CRISPY CRITTER! AND I'LL BE--
WHU?
WHO'S THAT?
YOU DON'T REMEMBER ME, LAMARR?
I'M THE GUY YOU BURIED IN THAT VACANT LOT!
MR. MACK!

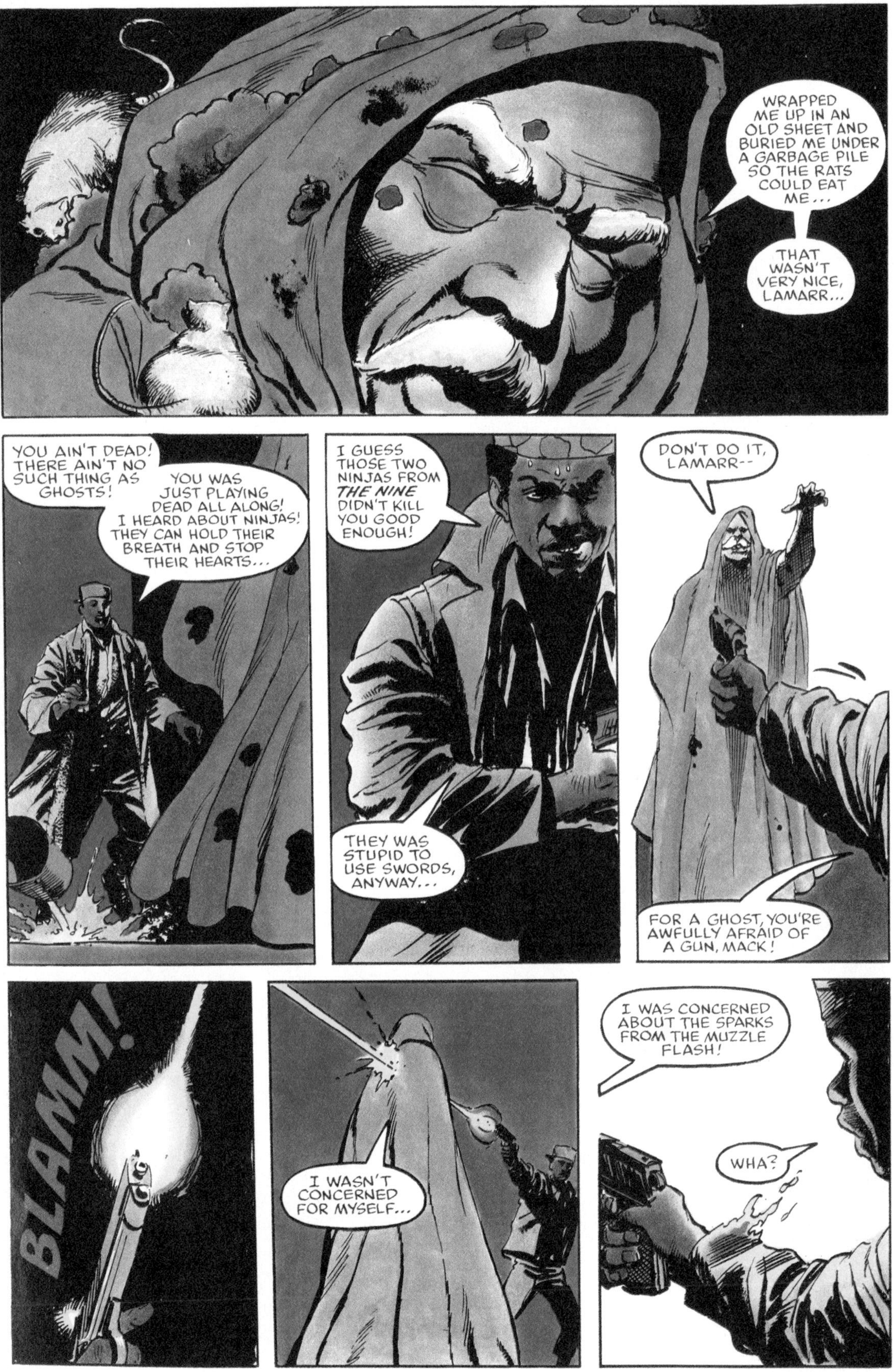
WRAPPED ME UP IN AN OLD SHEET AND BURIED ME UNDER A GARBAGE PILE SO THE RATS COULD EAT ME...
THAT WASN'T VERY NICE, LAMARR...
YOU AIN'T DEAD! THERE AIN'T NO SUCH THING AS GHOSTS!
YOU WAS JUST PLAYING DEAD ALL ALONG! I HEARD ABOUT NINJAS! THEY CAN HOLD THEIR BREATH AND STOP THEIR HEARTS...
I GUESS THOSE TWO NINJAS FROM ***THE NINE*** DIDN'T KILL YOU GOOD ENOUGH!
THEY WAS STUPID TO USE SWORDS, ANYWAY...
DON'T DO IT, LAMARR--
FOR A GHOST, YOU'RE AWFULLY AFRAID OF A GUN, MACK!
BLAMM!
I WASN'T CONCERNED FOR MYSELF...
I WAS CONCERNED ABOUT THE SPARKS FROM THE MUZZLE FLASH!
WHA?

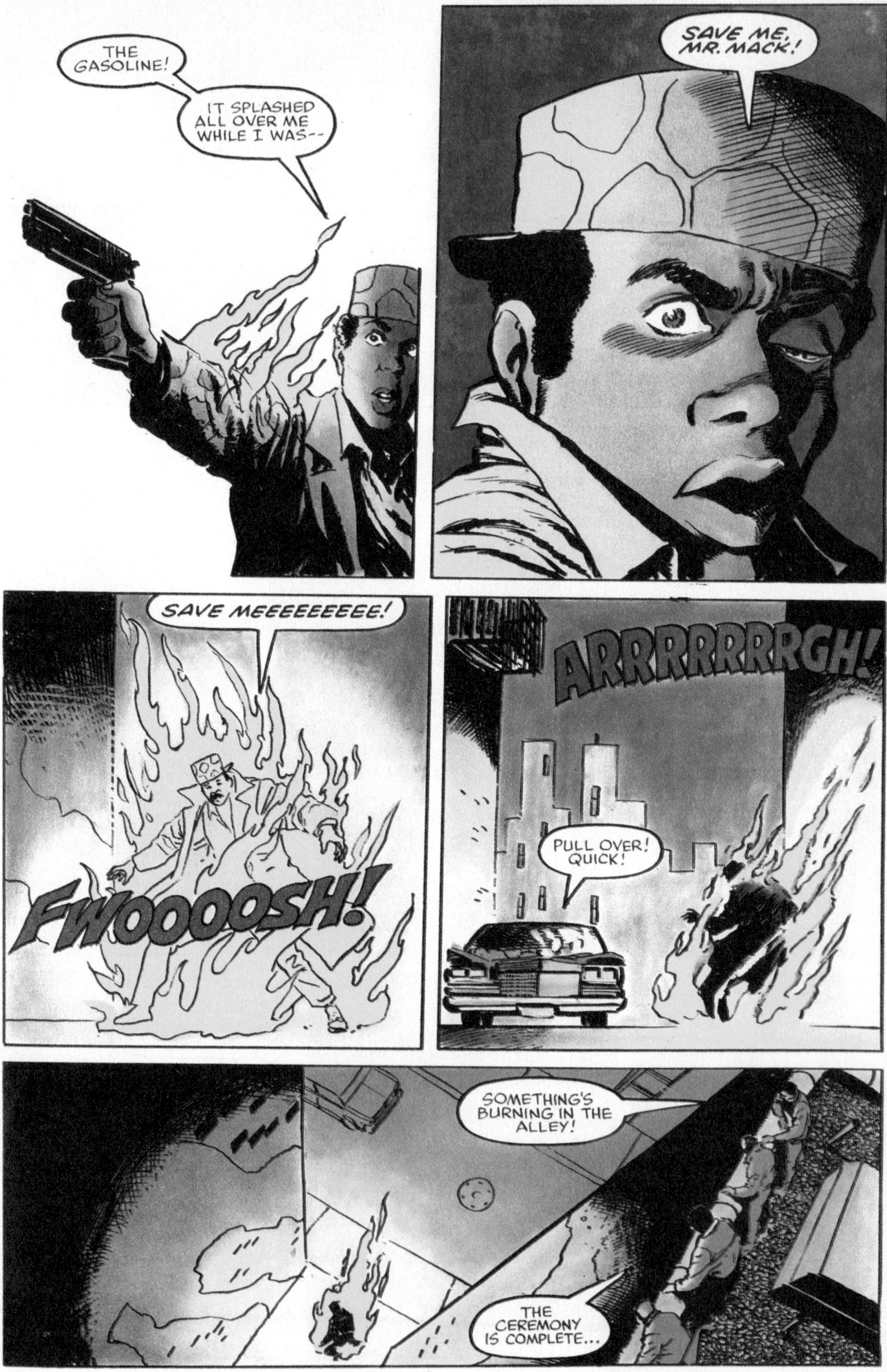
THE GASOLINE!
IT SPLASHED ALL OVER ME WHILE I WAS--
SAVE ME, MR. MACK!
SAVE MEEEEEEEEE!
FWOOOOSH!
ARRRRRRRGH!
PULL OVER! QUICK!
SOMETHING'S BURNING IN THE ALLEY!
THE CEREMONY IS COMPLETE...

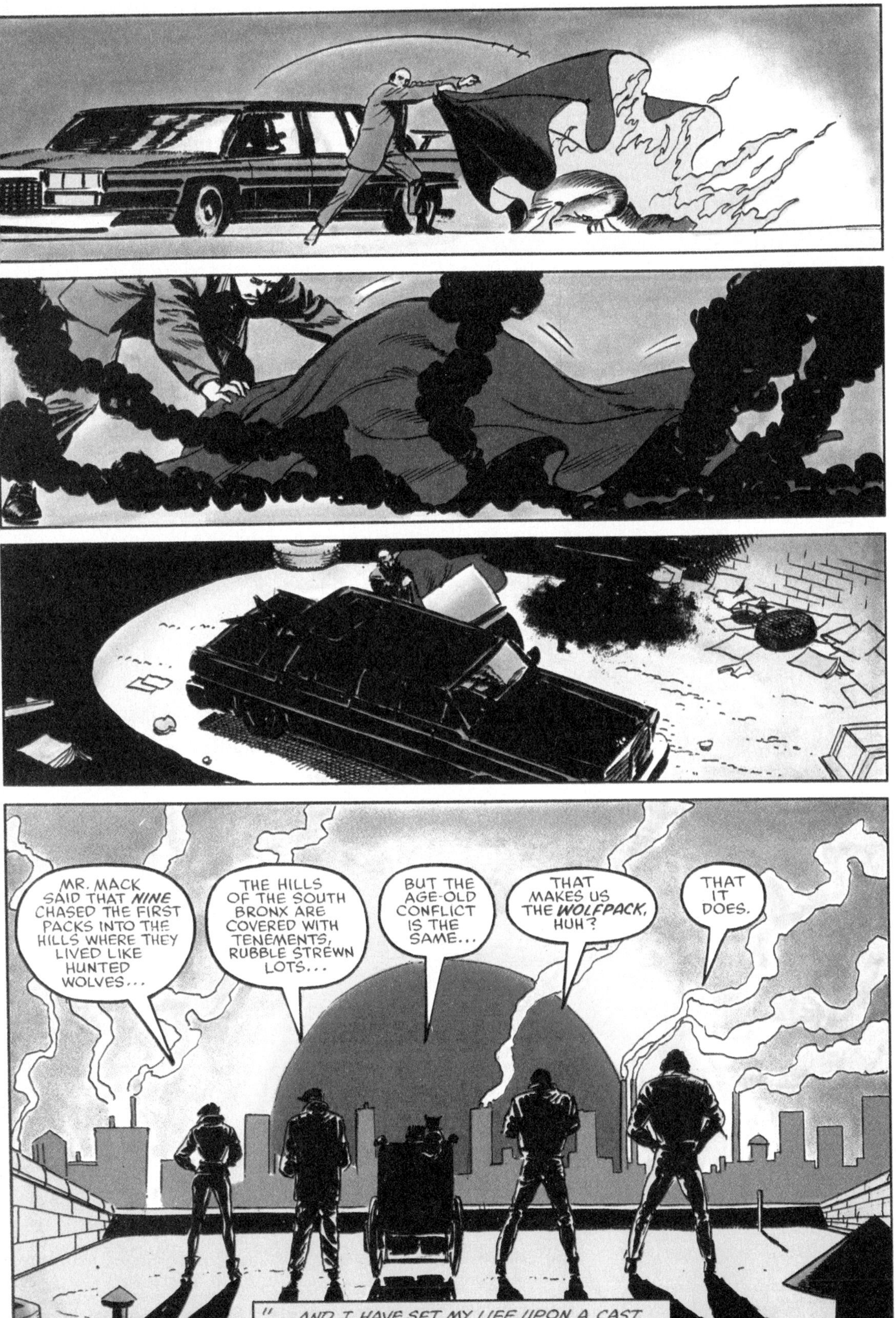
MR. MACK SAID THAT NINE CHASED THE FIRST PACKS INTO THE HILLS WHERE THEY LIVED LIKE HUNTED WOLVES...
THE HILLS OF THE SOUTH BRONX ARE COVERED WITH TENEMENTS, RUBBLE STREWN LOTS...
BUT THE AGE-OLD CONFLICT IS THE SAME...
THAT MAKES US THE WOLFPACK, HUH?
THAT IT DOES.
"...AND I HAVE SET MY LIFE UPON A CAST, AND I WILL STAND THE HAZARD OF THE DIE."
RICHARD III ACT V, SCENE IV

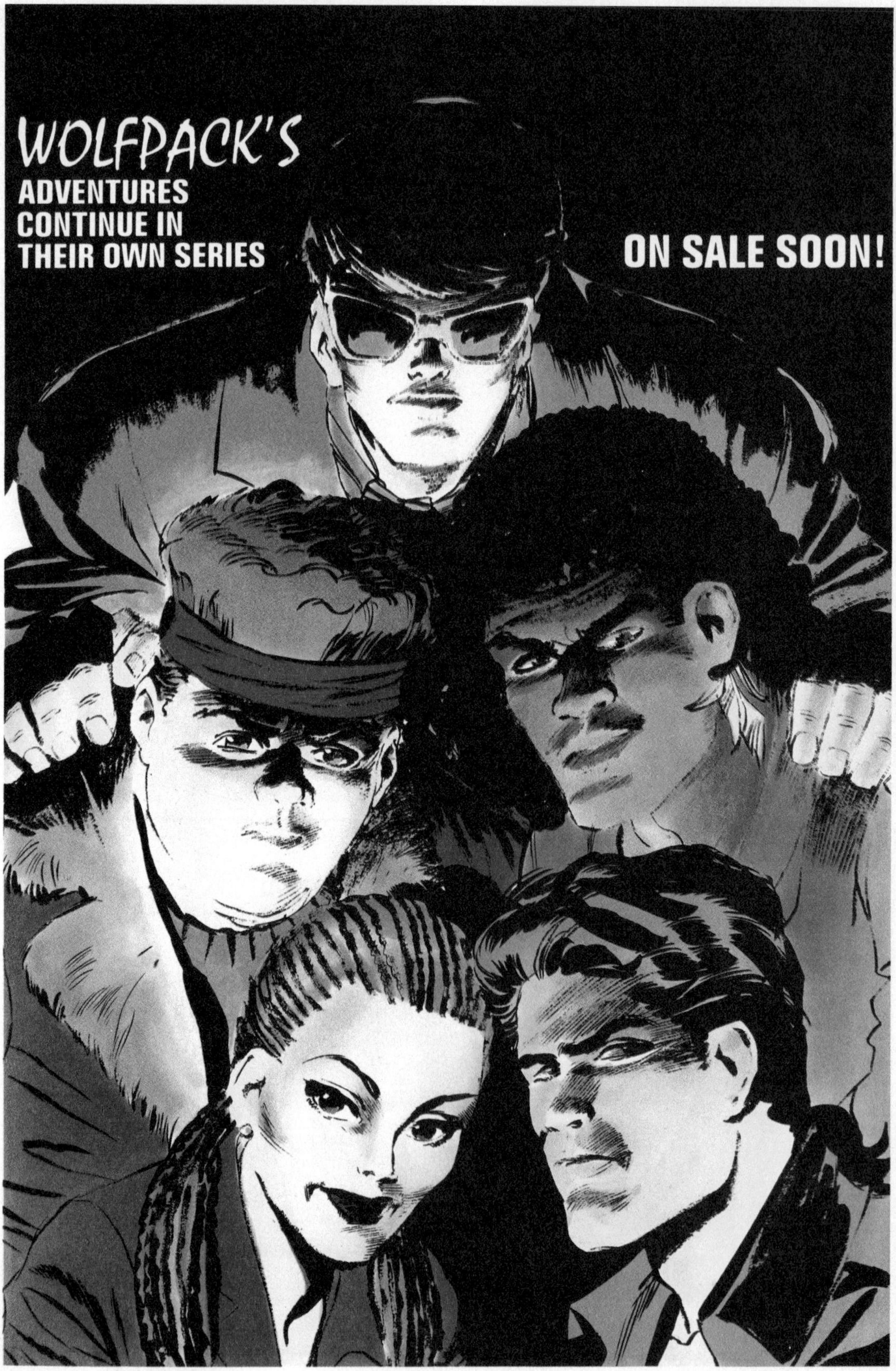
WOLFPACK'S
ADVENTURES
CONTINUE IN
THEIR OWN SERIES
ON SALE SOON!

US $7.95
CAN $8.95

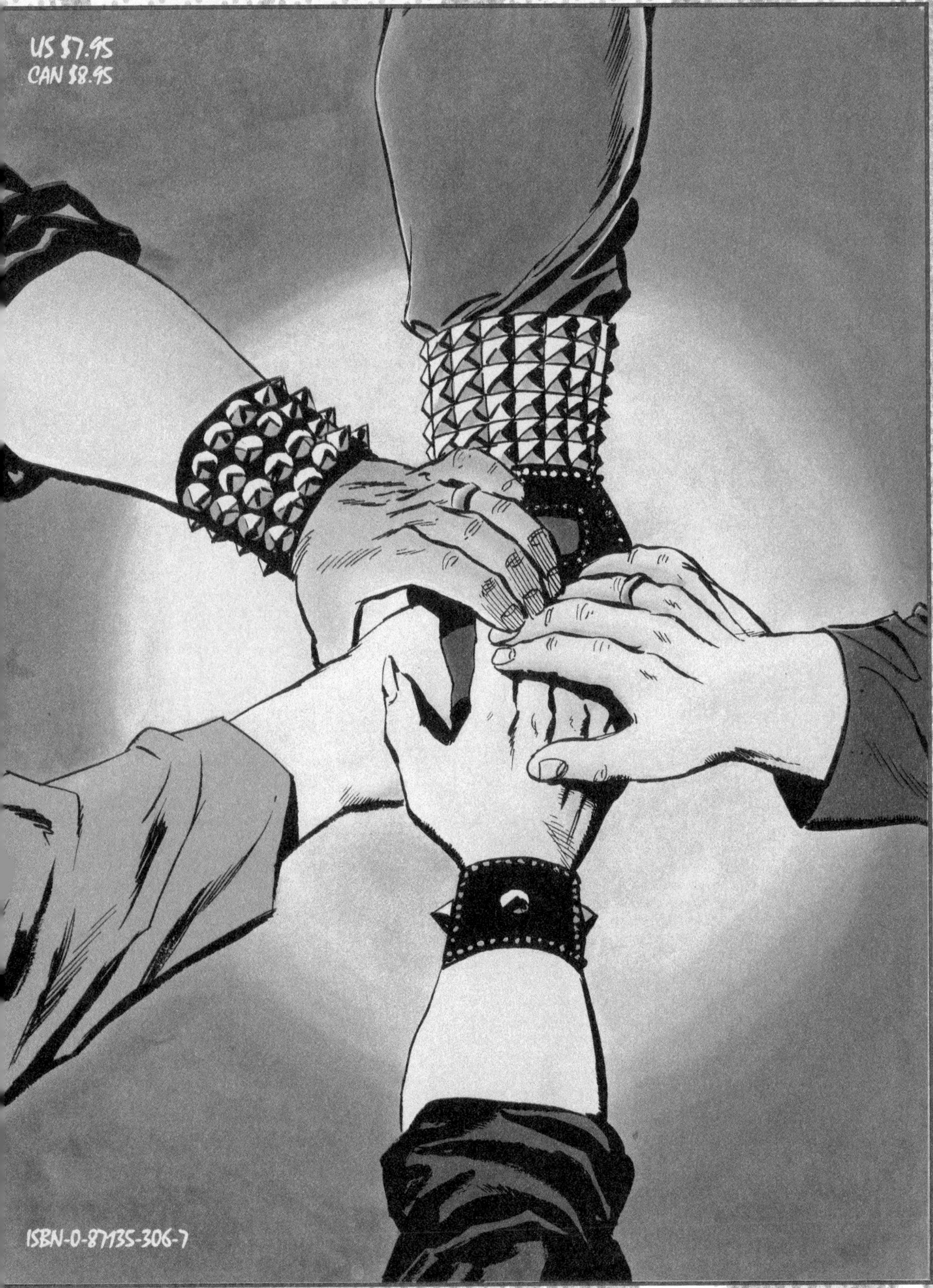

ISBN-0-87135-306-7

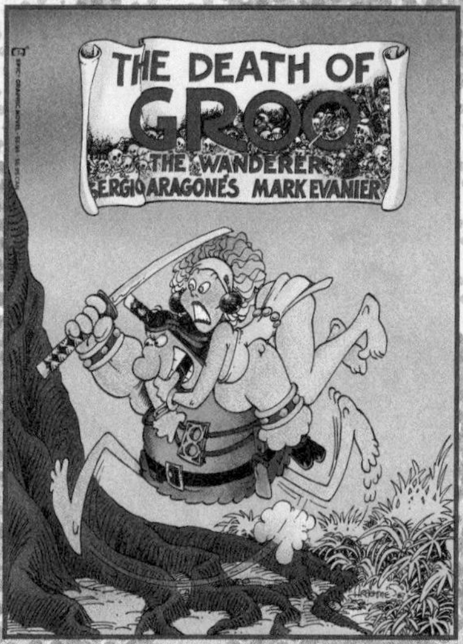
THE DEATH OF
GROO
THE WANDERER
SERGIO ARAGONÉS MARK EVANIER

Although DEATH OF GROO THE WANDERER, published in November 1987, is commonly considered part of the *Marvel Graphic Novel* line, it is actually the first non-reprint Epic Graphic Novel.

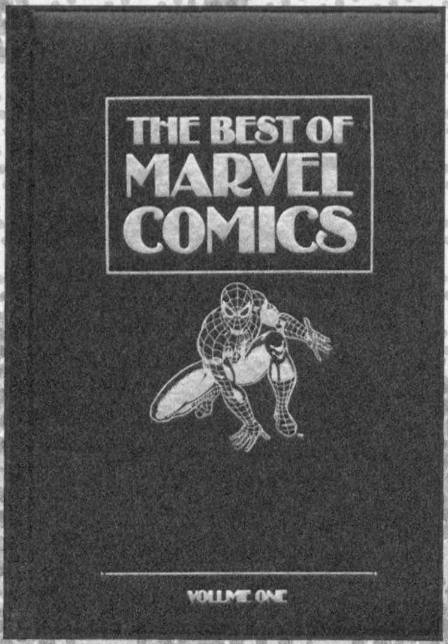
THE BEST OF
MARVEL
COMICS
VOLUME ONE

BEST OF MARVEL COMICS HC, published in December 1987, was a hardcover reprint volume that also contained a new short story starring Wolverine.

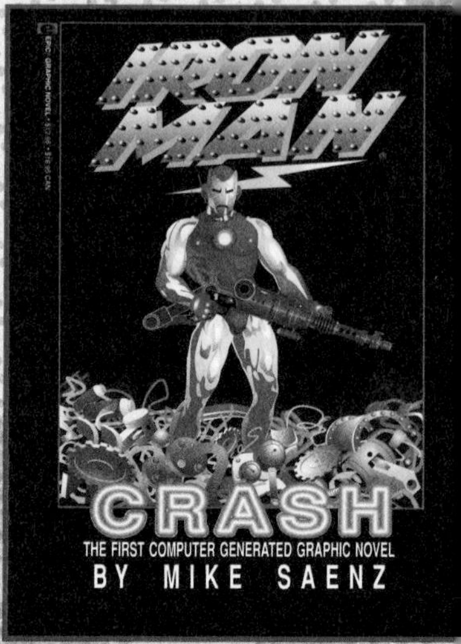
IRON MAN
CRASH
THE FIRST COMPUTER GENERATED GRAPHIC NOVEL
BY MIKE SAENZ

IRON MAN: CRASH, published in December 1987 was an Epic Graphic Novel starring the armored Avenger; its artwork was entirely computer-generated.

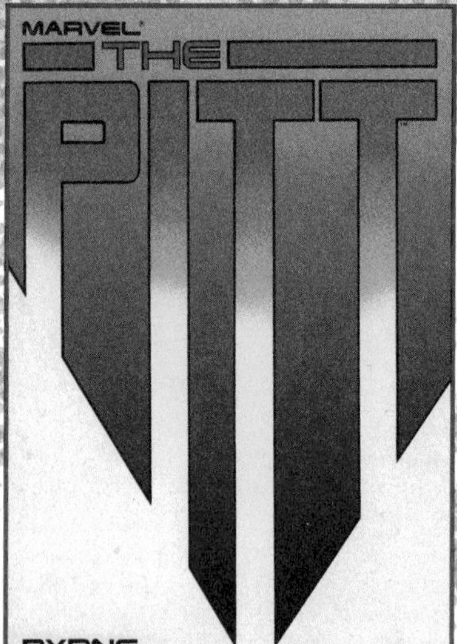
MARVEL
THE
PITT
BYRNE
GRUENWALD
BUSCEMA
DRAKE

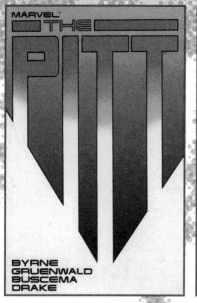

THE PITT, published in December 1987, was a one-shot set in the New Universe.

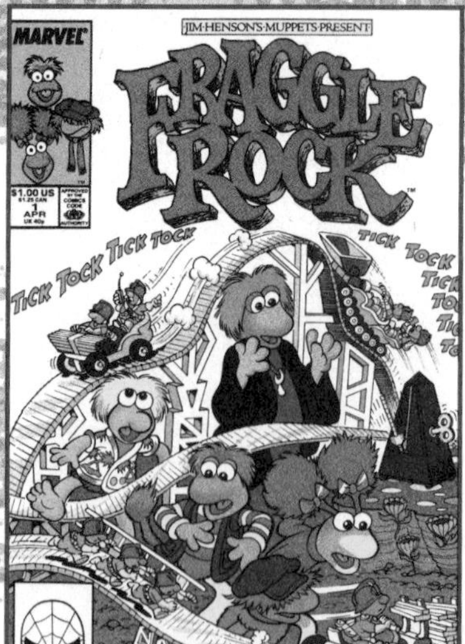
JIM HENSON'S MUPPETS PRESENT
MARVEL
FRAGGLE ROCK
TICK TOCK TICK TOCK
TICK TOCK TICK TOCK TICK TOCK
"THE MAGIC TIME MACHINE" TAKES OVER FRAGGLE ROCK!

FRAGGLE ROCK #1, published in January 1988, began a short reprint series.

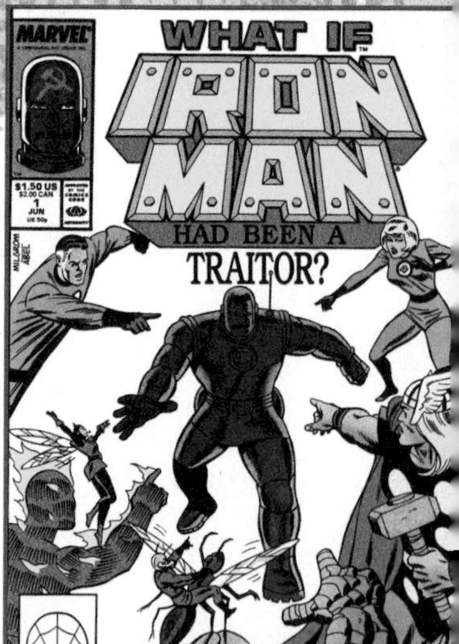
MARVEL
WHAT IF
IRON MAN
HAD BEEN A
TRAITOR?

WHAT IF? SPECIAL, published in February 1988, was a one-shot reviving the alternate-universe showcase title.

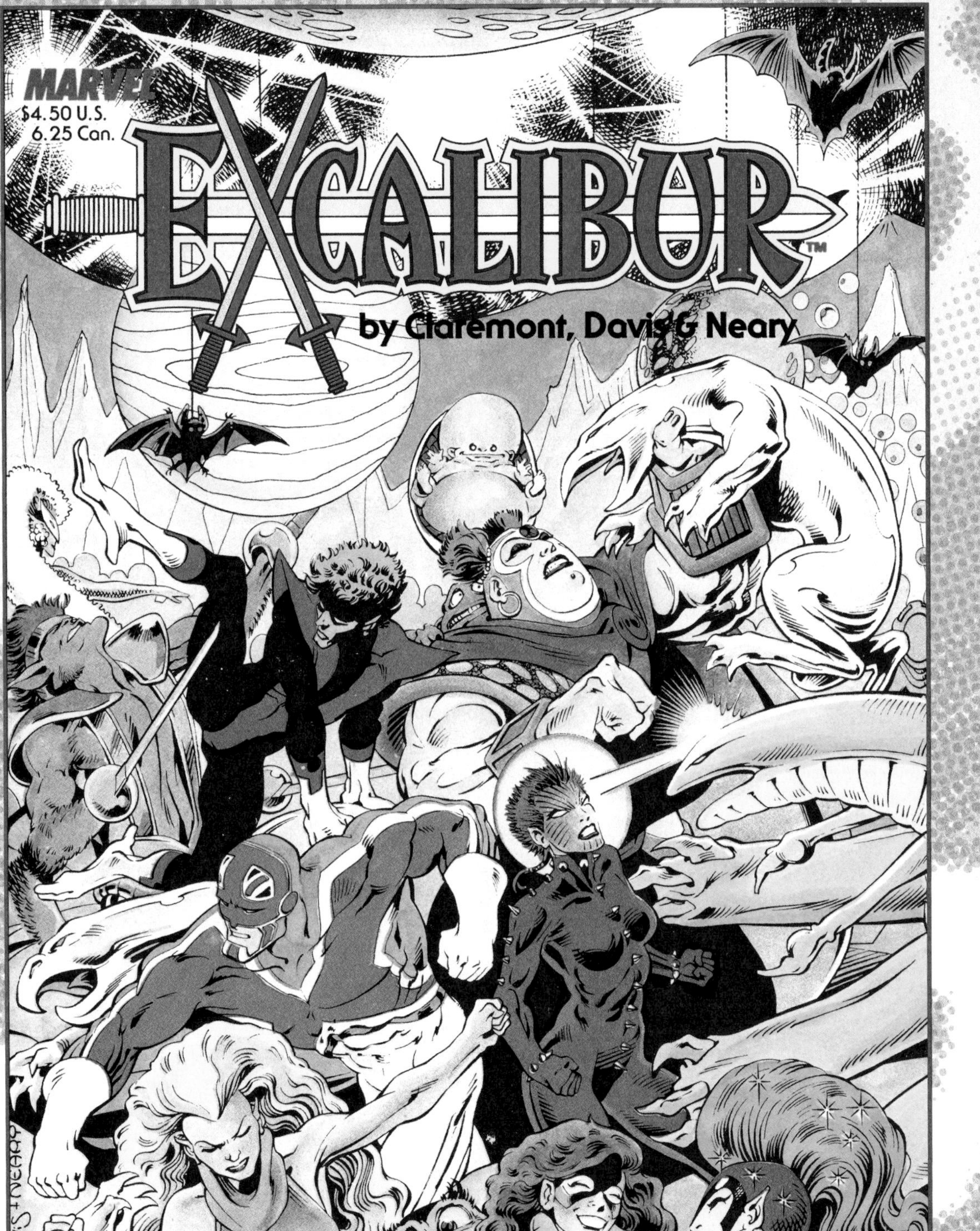
MARVEL
$4.50 U.S.
6.25 Can.
EXCALIBUR™
by Claremont, Davis & Neary
THE SWORD IS DRAWN

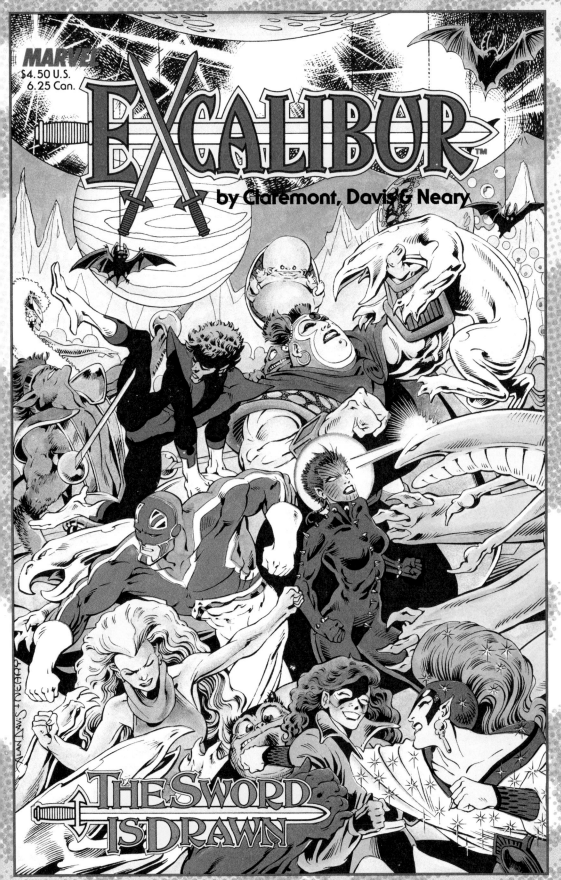

EXCALIBUR SPECIAL EDITION, published in December 1987, founded the Britain-based X-Men spinoff team; it was soon followed by an ongoing series.

"THE SWORD IS DRAWN"

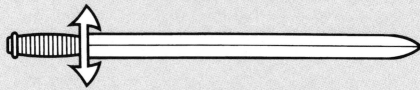

writer — **CHRIS CLAREMONT**

penciler — **ALAN DAVIS**

inker — **PAUL NEARY** (WITH SPECIAL THANKS TO MARK FARMER FOR ASSISTANCE)

letterer — **TOM ORZECHOWSKI**

colorist — **GLYNIS OLIVER**

editor — **ANN NOCENTI**

assistant editor — **TERRY KAVANAGH**

editor in chief — **TOM DeFALCO**

CREATED BY CHRIS CLAREMONT & ALAN DAVIS

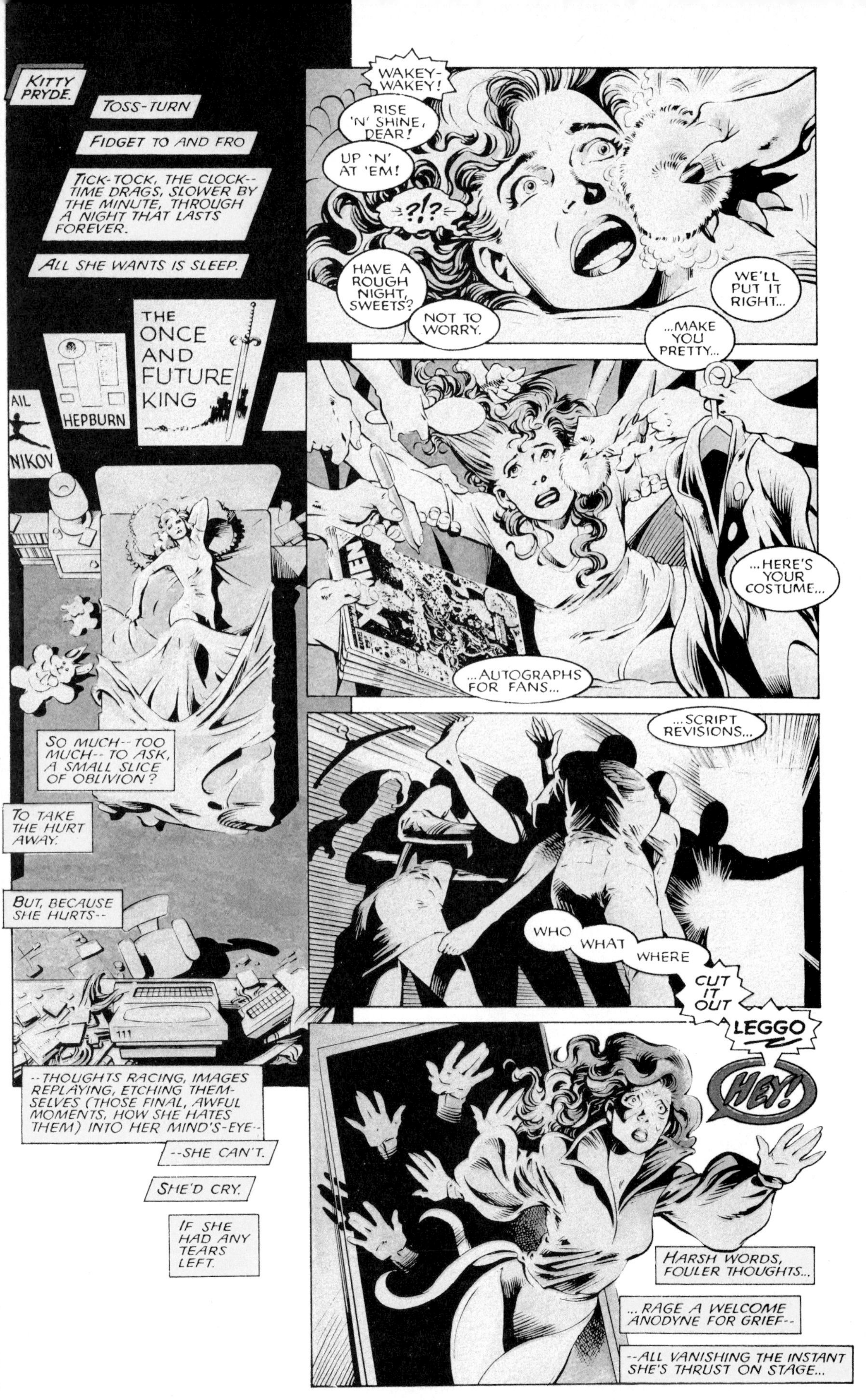

KITTY PRYDE.
TOSS-TURN
FIDGET TO AND FRO
TICK-TOCK, THE CLOCK-- TIME DRAGS, SLOWER BY THE MINUTE, THROUGH A NIGHT THAT LASTS FOREVER.
ALL SHE WANTS IS SLEEP.
THE ONCE AND FUTURE KING
HEPBURN
SO MUCH-- TOO MUCH-- TO ASK, A SMALL SLICE OF OBLIVION?
TO TAKE THE HURT AWAY.
BUT, BECAUSE SHE HURTS--
--THOUGHTS RACING, IMAGES REPLAYING, ETCHING THEMSELVES (THOSE FINAL, AWFUL MOMENTS, HOW SHE HATES THEM) INTO HER MIND'S-EYE--
--SHE CAN'T.
SHE'D CRY.
IF SHE HAD ANY TEARS LEFT.
WAKEY-WAKEY!
RISE 'N' SHINE, DEAR!
UP 'N' AT 'EM!
?!?
HAVE A ROUGH NIGHT, SWEETS?
NOT TO WORRY.
WE'LL PUT IT RIGHT...
...MAKE YOU PRETTY...
...HERE'S YOUR COSTUME...
...AUTOGRAPHS FOR FANS...
...SCRIPT REVISIONS...
WHO
WHAT
WHERE
CUT IT OUT
LEGGO
HEY!
HARSH WORDS, FOULER THOUGHTS...
...RAGE A WELCOME ANODYNE FOR GRIEF--
--ALL VANISHING THE INSTANT SHE'S THRUST ON STAGE...

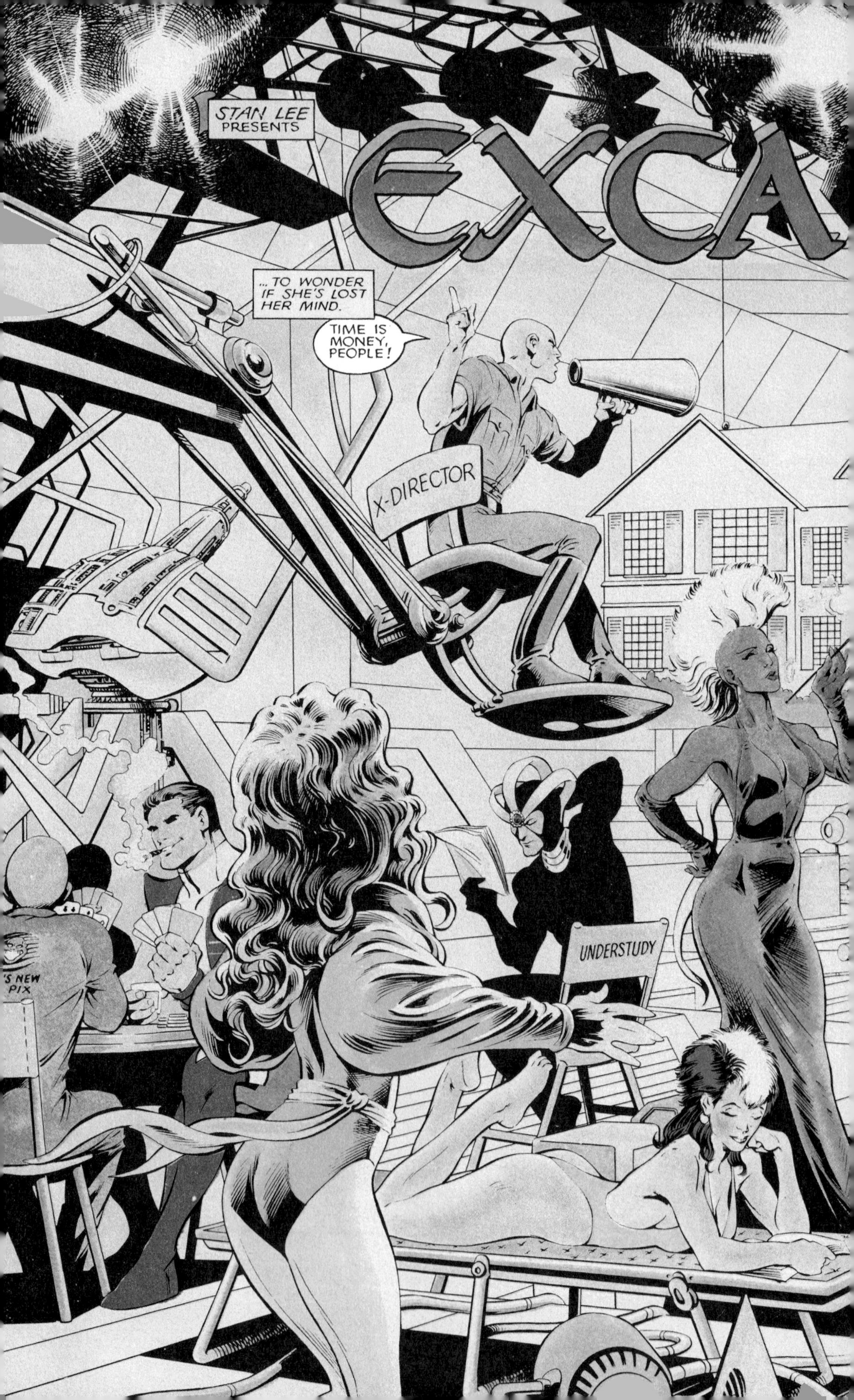
STAN LEE PRESENTS
EXCA
...TO WONDER IF SHE'S LOST HER MIND.
TIME IS MONEY, PEOPLE!
X-DIRECTOR
UNDERSTUDY
'S NEW PIX

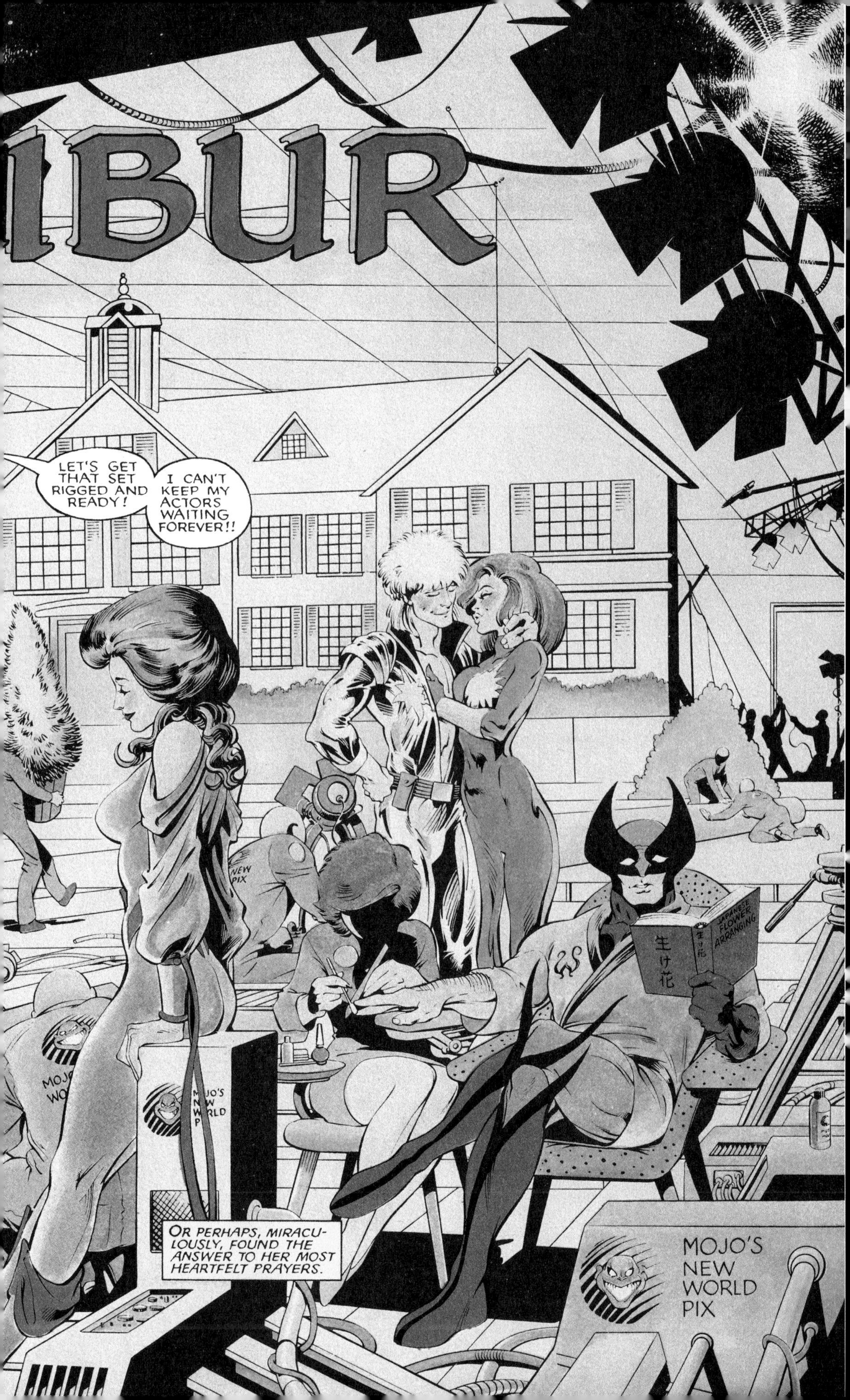
IBUR
LET'S GET THAT SET RIGGED AND READY!
I CAN'T KEEP MY ACTORS WAITING FOREVER!!
NEW PIX
JAPANESE FLOWER ARRANGING
生け花
MOJO'S NEW WORLD P
OR PERHAPS, MIRACULOUSLY, FOUND THE ANSWER TO HER MOST HEARTFELT PRAYERS.
MOJO'S NEW WORLD PIX

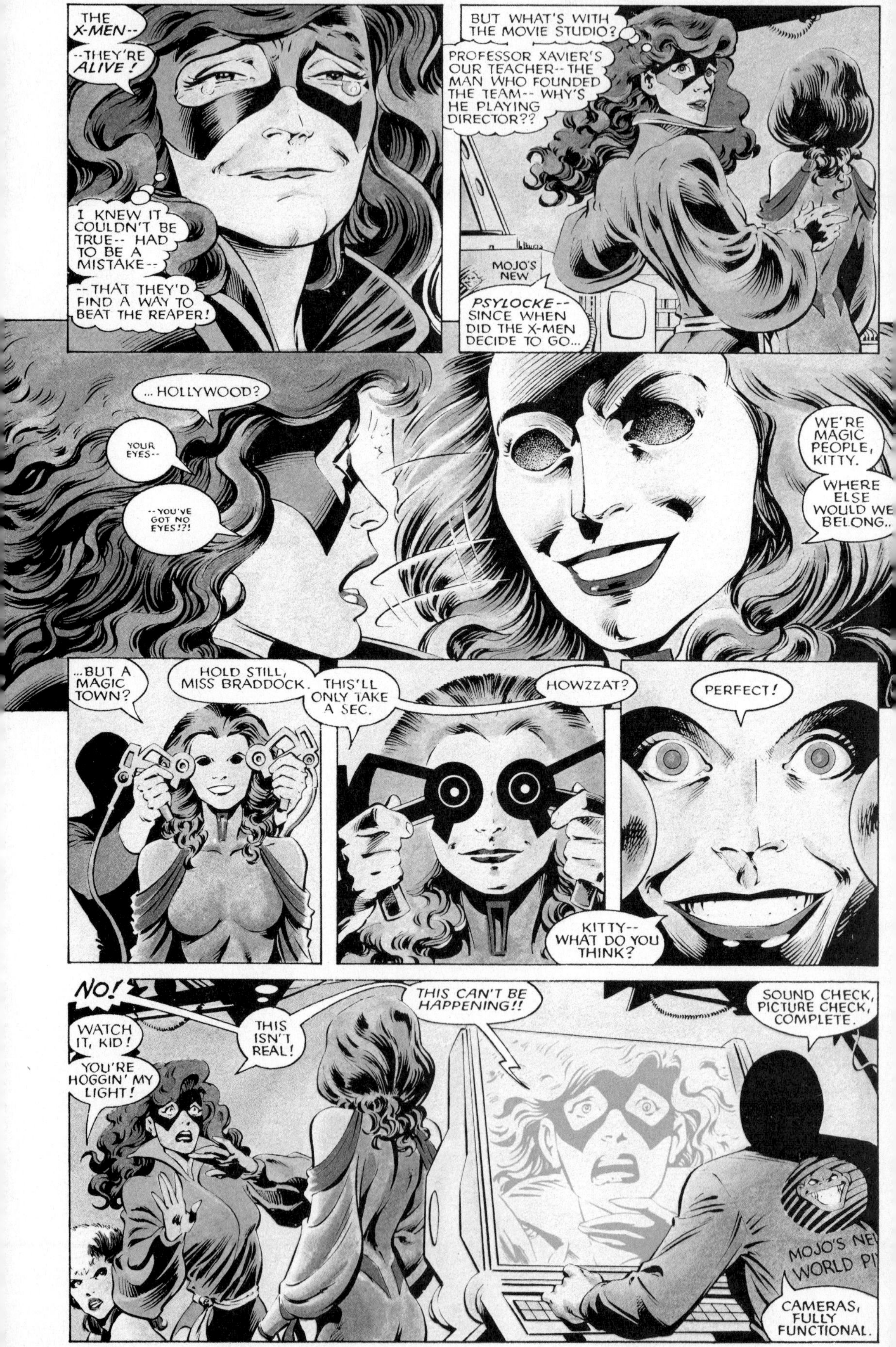

THE X-MEN--
--THEY'RE ALIVE!
I KNEW IT COULDN'T BE TRUE-- HAD TO BE A MISTAKE--
--THAT THEY'D FIND A WAY TO BEAT THE REAPER!
BUT WHAT'S WITH THE MOVIE STUDIO?
PROFESSOR XAVIER'S OUR TEACHER-- THE MAN WHO FOUNDED THE TEAM-- WHY'S HE PLAYING DIRECTOR??
MOJO'S NEW
PSYLOCKE-- SINCE WHEN DID THE X-MEN DECIDE TO GO...
...HOLLYWOOD?
YOUR EYES--
--YOU'VE GOT NO EYES!?!
WE'RE MAGIC PEOPLE, KITTY.
WHERE ELSE WOULD WE BELONG..
...BUT A MAGIC TOWN?
HOLD STILL, MISS BRADDOCK.
THIS'LL ONLY TAKE A SEC.
HOWZZAT?
PERFECT!
KITTY-- WHAT DO YOU THINK?
NO!
WATCH IT, KID!
YOU'RE HOGGIN' MY LIGHT!
THIS ISN'T REAL!
THIS CAN'T BE HAPPENING!!
SOUND CHECK, PICTURE CHECK, COMPLETE.
MOJO'S NE
WORLD PI
CAMERAS, FULLY FUNCTIONAL.

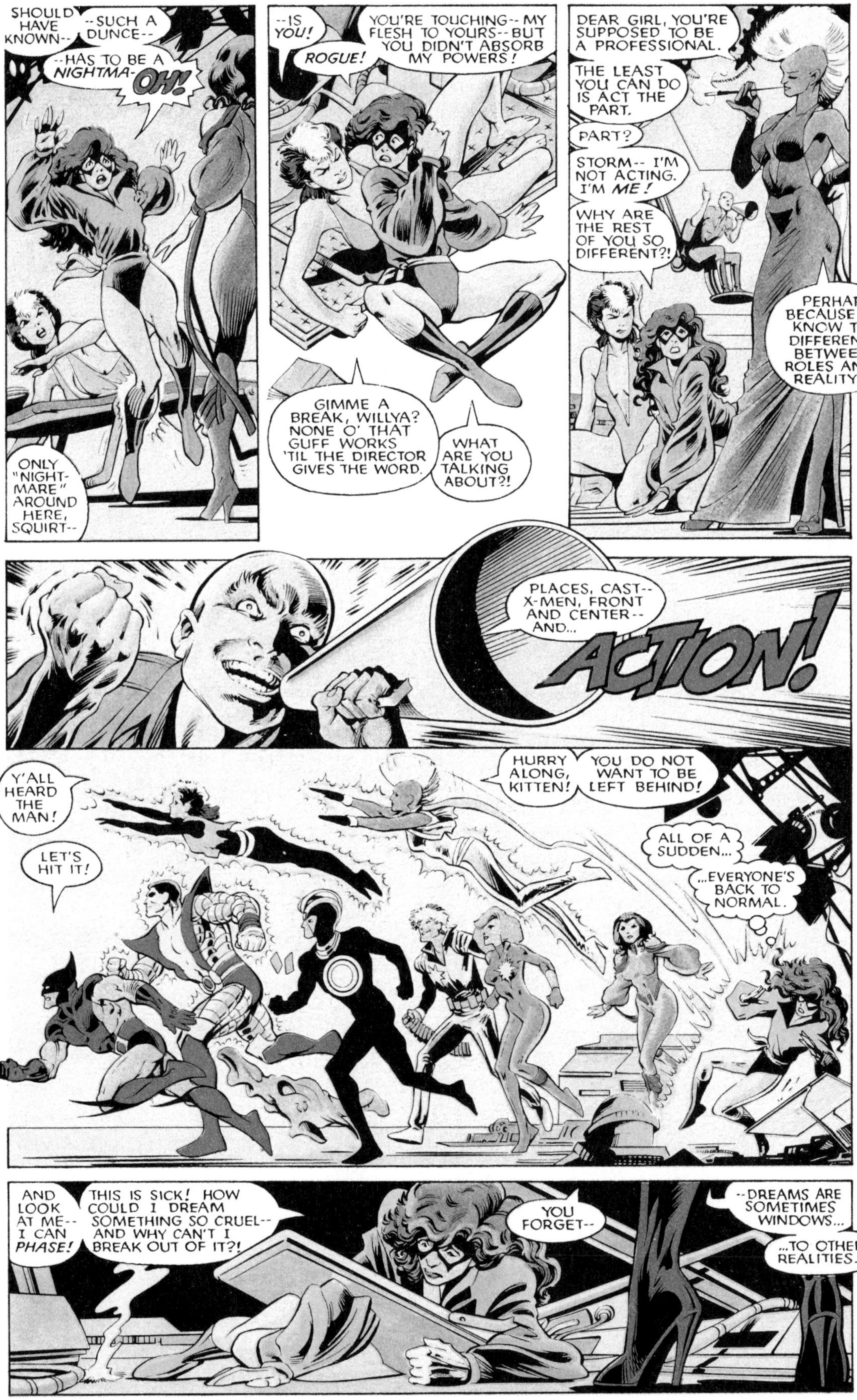
SHOULD HAVE KNOWN--
--SUCH A DUNCE--
--HAS TO BE A *NIGHTMA-* *OH!*
ONLY "NIGHT-MARE" AROUND HERE, SQUIRT--
--IS *YOU!*
ROGUE!
YOU'RE TOUCHING-- MY FLESH TO YOURS-- BUT YOU DIDN'T ABSORB MY POWERS!
GIMME A BREAK, WILLYA? NONE O' THAT GUFF WORKS 'TIL THE DIRECTOR GIVES THE WORD.
WHAT ARE YOU TALKING ABOUT?!
DEAR GIRL, YOU'RE SUPPOSED TO BE A PROFESSIONAL.
THE LEAST YOU CAN DO IS ACT THE PART.
PART?
STORM-- I'M NOT ACTING. I'M *ME!*
WHY ARE THE REST OF YOU SO DIFFERENT?!
PERHAPS, BECAUSE WE KNOW THE DIFFERENCE BETWEEN ROLES AND REALITY.
PLACES, CAST-- X-MEN, FRONT AND CENTER-- AND...
ACTION!
Y'ALL HEARD THE MAN!
LET'S HIT IT!
HURRY ALONG, KITTEN!
YOU DO NOT WANT TO BE LEFT BEHIND!
ALL OF A SUDDEN...
...EVERYONE'S BACK TO NORMAL.
AND LOOK AT ME-- I CAN *PHASE!*
THIS IS SICK! HOW COULD I DREAM SOMETHING SO CRUEL-- AND WHY CAN'T I BREAK OUT OF IT?!
YOU FORGET--
--DREAMS ARE SOMETIMES WINDOWS...
...TO OTHER REALITIES.

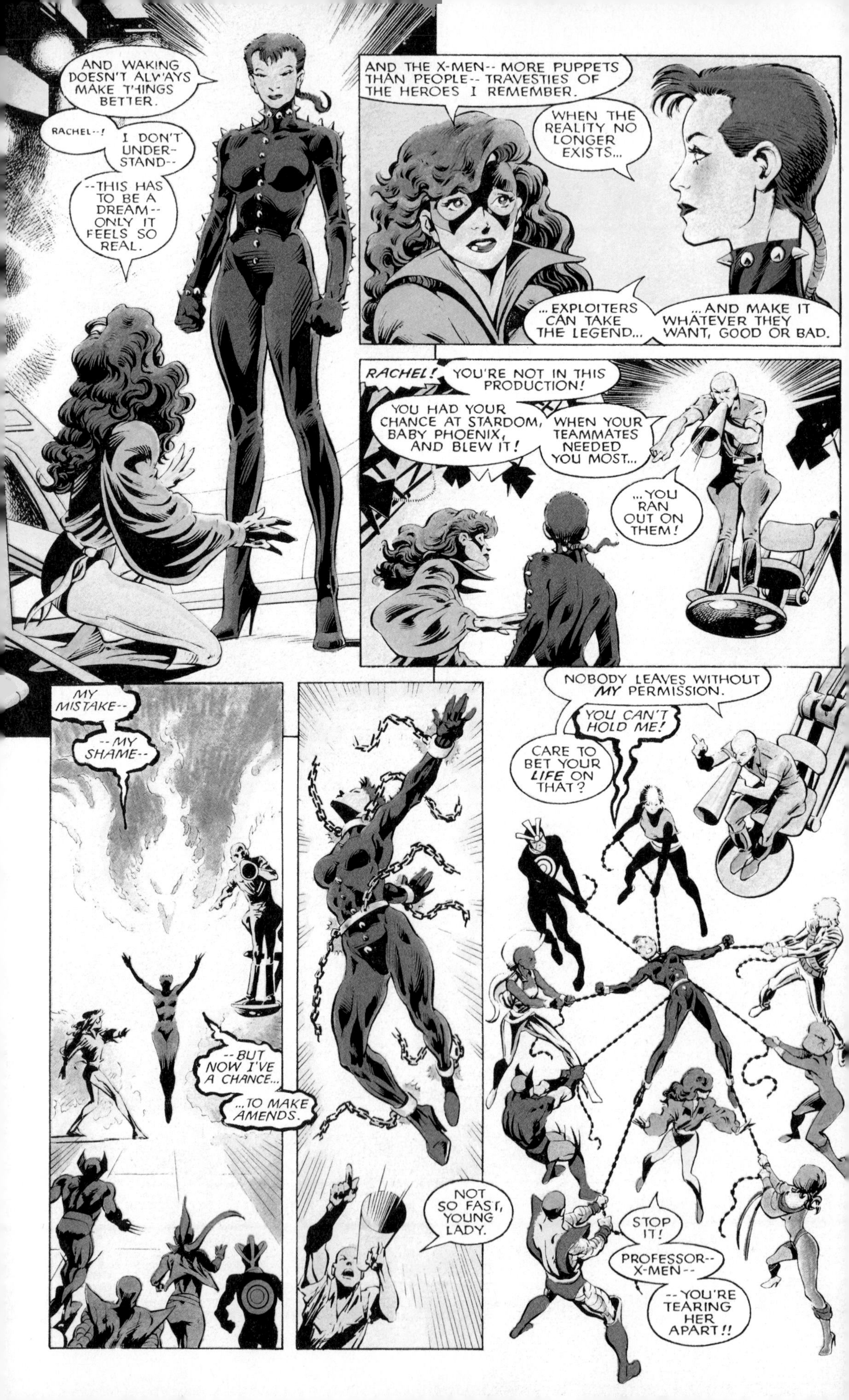
AND WAKING DOESN'T ALWAYS MAKE THINGS BETTER.
RACHEL--!
I DON'T UNDER-STAND--
--THIS HAS TO BE A DREAM-- ONLY IT FEELS SO REAL.
AND THE X-MEN-- MORE PUPPETS THAN PEOPLE-- TRAVESTIES OF THE HEROES I REMEMBER.
WHEN THE REALITY NO LONGER EXISTS...
...EXPLOITERS CAN TAKE THE LEGEND...
...AND MAKE IT WHATEVER THEY WANT, GOOD OR BAD.
RACHEL!
YOU'RE NOT IN THIS PRODUCTION!
YOU HAD YOUR CHANCE AT STARDOM, BABY PHOENIX, AND BLEW IT!
WHEN YOUR TEAMMATES NEEDED YOU MOST...
...YOU RAN OUT ON THEM!
MY MISTAKE--
--MY SHAME--
--BUT NOW I'VE A CHANCE...
...TO MAKE AMENDS.
NOT SO FAST, YOUNG LADY.
NOBODY LEAVES WITHOUT MY PERMISSION.
YOU CAN'T HOLD ME!
CARE TO BET YOUR LIFE ON THAT?
STOP IT!
PROFESSOR-- X-MEN--
--YOU'RE TEARING HER APART!!

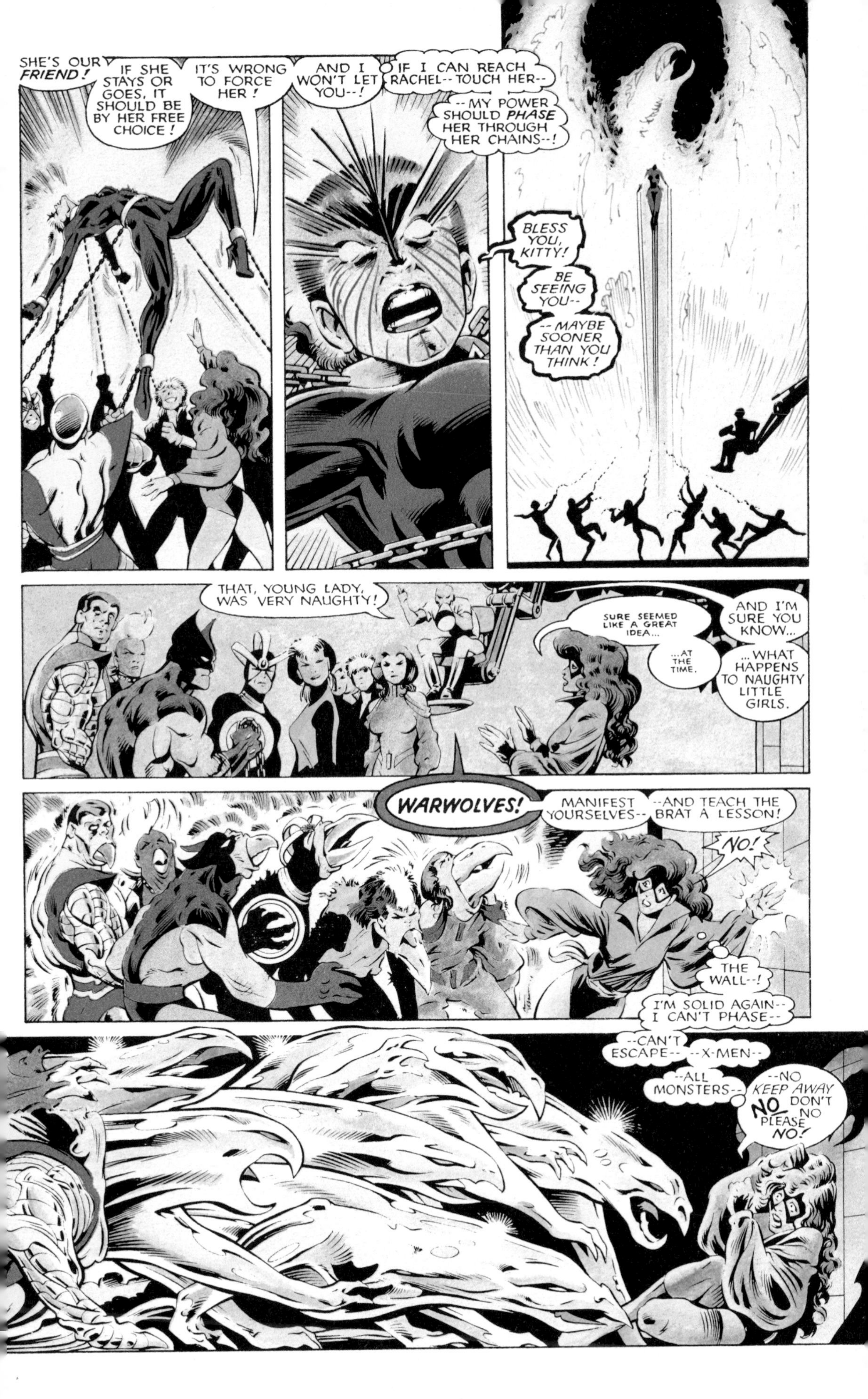
SHE'S OUR *FRIEND*!
IF SHE STAYS OR GOES, IT SHOULD BE BY HER FREE CHOICE!
IT'S WRONG TO FORCE HER!
AND I WON'T LET YOU--!
IF I CAN REACH RACHEL--TOUCH HER--
--MY POWER SHOULD *PHASE* HER THROUGH HER CHAINS--!
BLESS YOU, KITTY!
BE SEEING YOU--
--MAYBE SOONER THAN YOU THINK!
THAT, YOUNG LADY, WAS VERY NAUGHTY!
SURE SEEMED LIKE A GREAT IDEA...
...AT THE TIME.
AND I'M SURE YOU KNOW...
...WHAT HAPPENS TO NAUGHTY LITTLE GIRLS.
WARWOLVES!
MANIFEST YOURSELVES--
--AND TEACH THE BRAT A LESSON!
NO!
THE WALL--!
I'M SOLID AGAIN--I CAN'T PHASE--
--CAN'T ESCAPE--
--X-MEN--
--ALL MONSTERS--
--NO *KEEP AWAY* DON'T NO NO PLEASE *NO!*

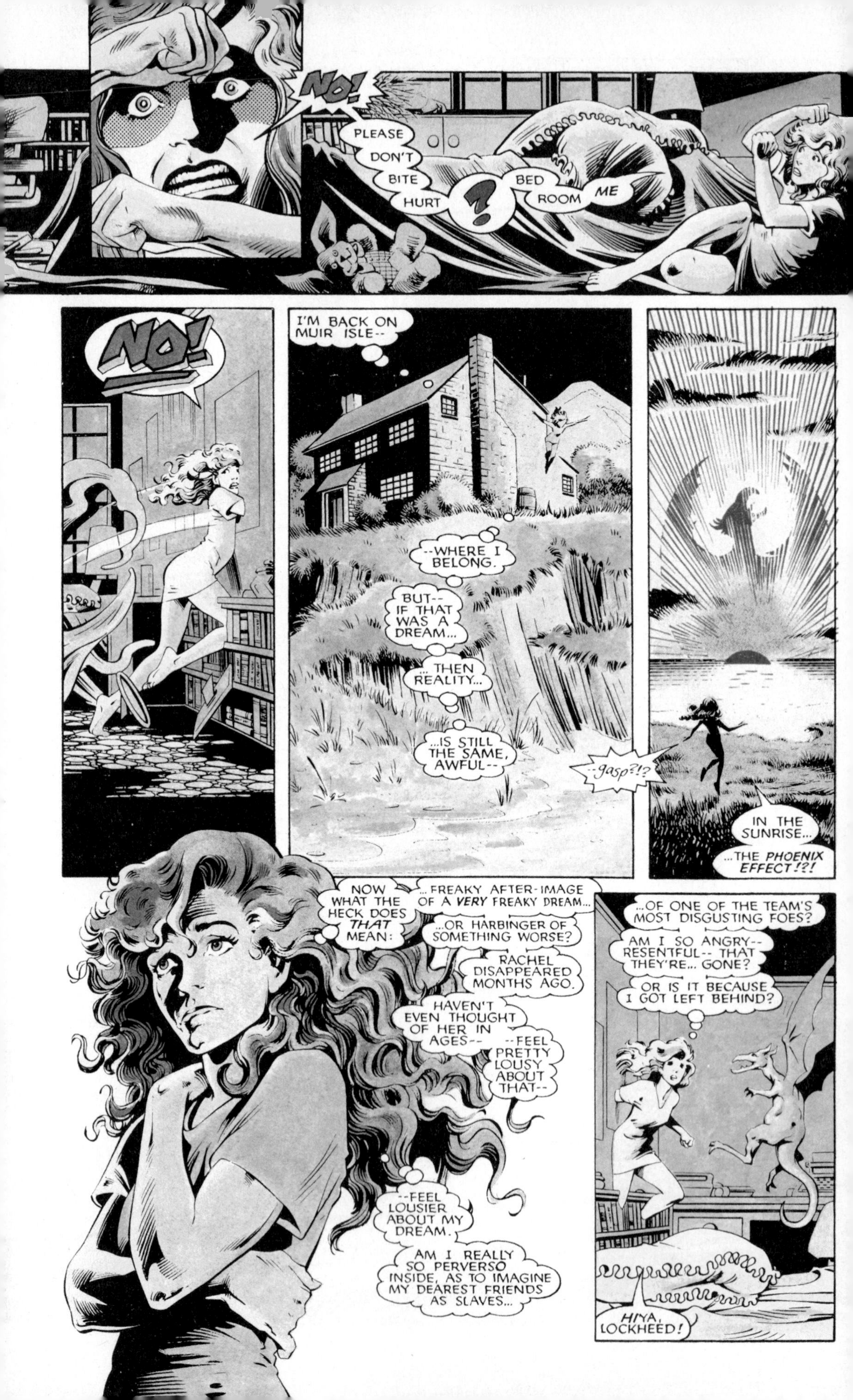
NO!
PLEASE
DON'T
BITE
HURT
?
BED
ROOM
ME
NO!
I'M BACK ON MUIR ISLE--
--WHERE I BELONG.
BUT-- IF THAT WAS A DREAM...
...THEN REALITY...
...IS STILL THE SAME, AWFUL--
--gasp?!?
IN THE SUNRISE...
...THE PHOENIX EFFECT!?!
NOW WHAT THE HECK DOES THAT MEAN:
...FREAKY AFTER-IMAGE OF A VERY FREAKY DREAM...
...OR HARBINGER OF SOMETHING WORSE?
RACHEL DISAPPEARED MONTHS AGO.
HAVEN'T EVEN THOUGHT OF HER IN AGES--
--FEEL PRETTY LOUSY ABOUT THAT--
--FEEL LOUSIER ABOUT MY DREAM.
AM I REALLY SO PERVERSO INSIDE, AS TO IMAGINE MY DEAREST FRIENDS AS SLAVES...
...OF ONE OF THE TEAM'S MOST DISGUSTING FOES?
AM I SO ANGRY-- RESENTFUL-- THAT THEY'RE... GONE?
OR IS IT BECAUSE I GOT LEFT BEHIND?
HIYA, LOCKHEED!

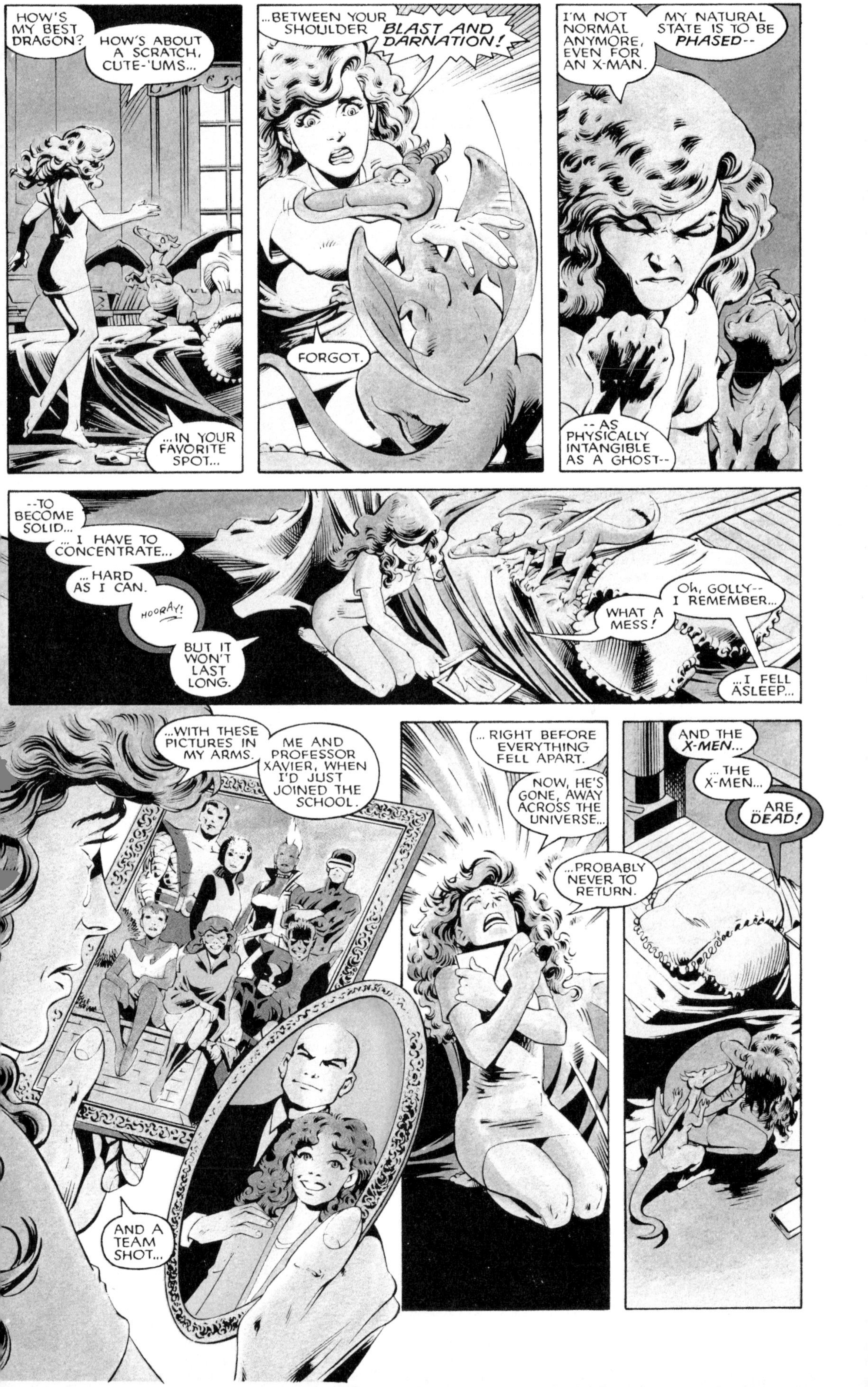
HOW'S MY BEST DRAGON?
HOW'S ABOUT A SCRATCH, CUTE-'UMS...
...IN YOUR FAVORITE SPOT...
...BETWEEN YOUR SHOULDER
BLAST AND DARNATION!
FORGOT.
I'M NOT NORMAL ANYMORE, EVEN FOR AN X-MAN.
MY NATURAL STATE IS TO BE PHASED--
--AS PHYSICALLY INTANGIBLE AS A GHOST--
--TO BECOME SOLID...
...I HAVE TO CONCENTRATE...
...HARD AS I CAN.
HOORAY!
BUT IT WON'T LAST LONG.
WHAT A MESS!
Oh, GOLLY-- I REMEMBER...
...I FELL ASLEEP...
...WITH THESE PICTURES IN MY ARMS.
ME AND PROFESSOR XAVIER, WHEN I'D JUST JOINED THE SCHOOL.
AND A TEAM SHOT...
...RIGHT BEFORE EVERYTHING FELL APART.
NOW, HE'S GONE, AWAY ACROSS THE UNIVERSE...
...PROBABLY NEVER TO RETURN.
AND THE X-MEN...
...THE X-MEN...
...ARE DEAD!

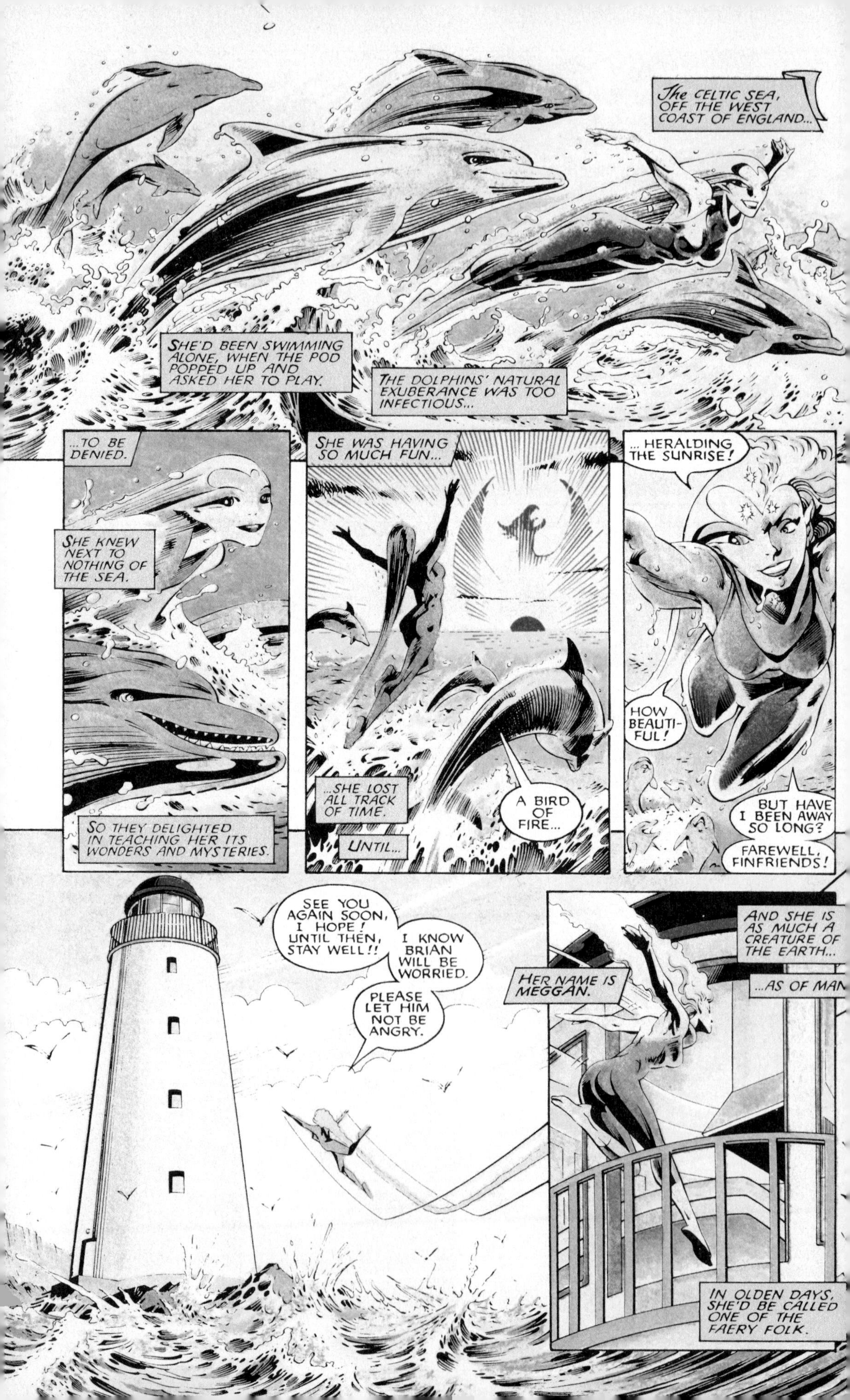
The CELTIC SEA, OFF THE WEST COAST OF ENGLAND...
SHE'D BEEN SWIMMING ALONE, WHEN THE POD POPPED UP AND ASKED HER TO PLAY.
THE DOLPHINS' NATURAL EXUBERANCE WAS TOO INFECTIOUS...
...TO BE DENIED.
SHE KNEW NEXT TO NOTHING OF THE SEA.
SO THEY DELIGHTED IN TEACHING HER ITS WONDERS AND MYSTERIES.
SHE WAS HAVING SO MUCH FUN...
...SHE LOST ALL TRACK OF TIME.
UNTIL...
A BIRD OF FIRE...
... HERALDING THE SUNRISE!
HOW BEAUTIFUL!
BUT HAVE I BEEN AWAY SO LONG?
FAREWELL, FINFRIENDS!
SEE YOU AGAIN SOON, I HOPE! UNTIL THEN, STAY WELL!!
I KNOW BRIAN WILL BE WORRIED.
PLEASE LET HIM NOT BE ANGRY.
HER NAME IS MEGGAN.
AND SHE IS AS MUCH A CREATURE OF THE EARTH...
...AS OF MAN
IN OLDEN DAYS, SHE'D BE CALLED ONE OF THE FAERY FOLK.

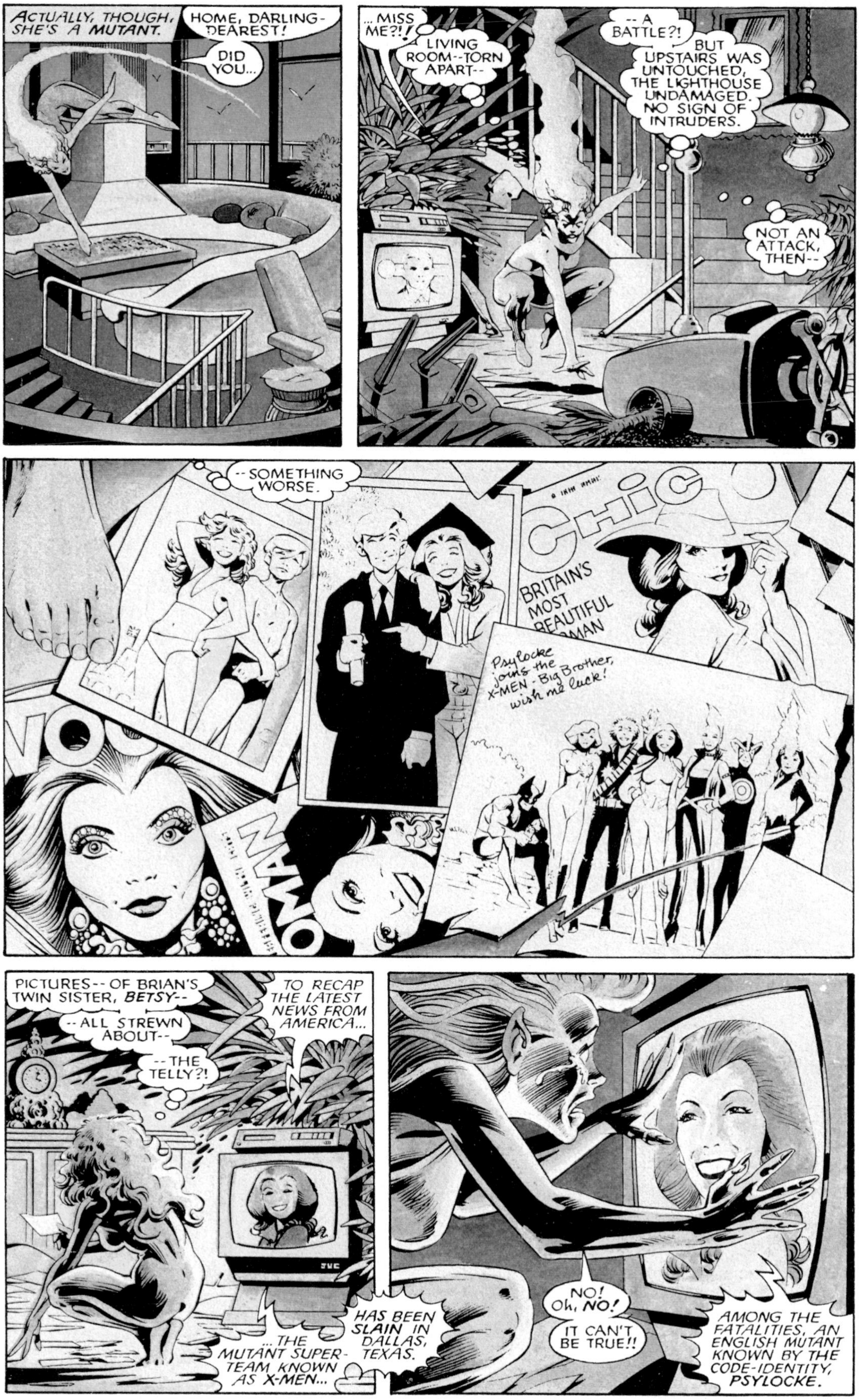

ACTUALLY, THOUGH, SHE'S A MUTANT.
HOME, DARLING-DEAREST!
DID YOU...
...MISS ME?!
LIVING ROOM--TORN APART--
--A BATTLE?!
BUT UPSTAIRS WAS UNTOUCHED, THE LIGHTHOUSE UNDAMAGED. NO SIGN OF INTRUDERS.
NOT AN ATTACK, THEN--
--SOMETHING WORSE.
CHIC
BRITAIN'S MOST BEAUTIFUL
Psylocke joins the X-MEN - Big Brother, wish me luck!
PICTURES--OF BRIAN'S TWIN SISTER, BETSY--
--ALL STREWN ABOUT--
--THE TELLY?!
TO RECAP THE LATEST NEWS FROM AMERICA...
JVC
...THE MUTANT SUPER-TEAM KNOWN AS X-MEN...
HAS BEEN SLAIN IN DALLAS, TEXAS.
NO! Oh, NO!
IT CAN'T BE TRUE!!
AMONG THE FATALITIES, AN ENGLISH MUTANT KNOWN BY THE CODE-IDENTITY, PSYLOCKE.

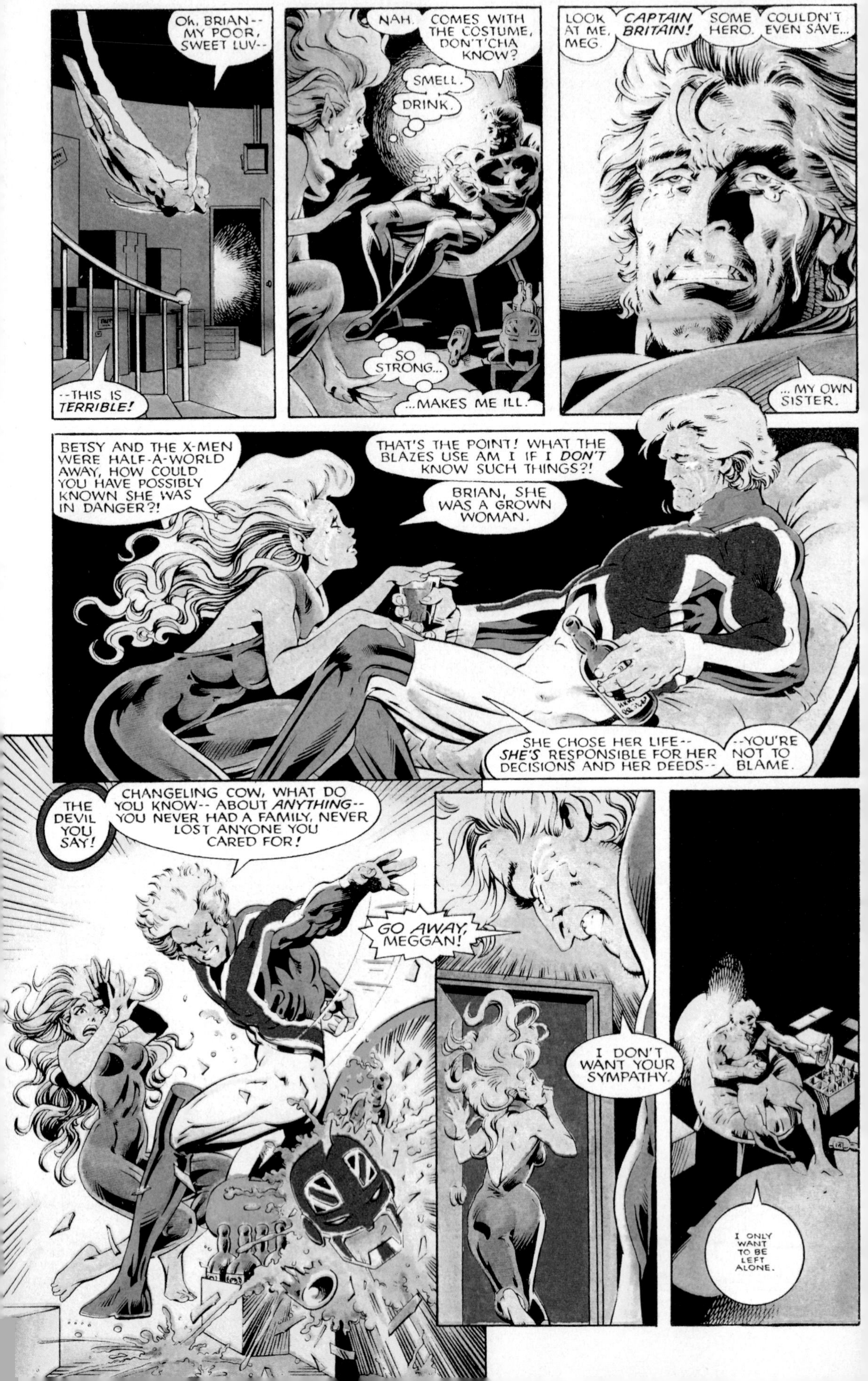
Oh, BRIAN-- MY POOR, SWEET LUV--
--THIS IS *TERRIBLE!*
NAH.
COMES WITH THE COSTUME, DON'T'CHA KNOW?
SMELL.
DRINK.
SO STRONG...
...MAKES ME ILL.
LOOK AT ME, MEG.
CAPTAIN BRITAIN!
SOME HERO.
COULDN'T EVEN SAVE...
... MY OWN SISTER.
BETSY AND THE X-MEN WERE HALF-A-WORLD AWAY, HOW COULD YOU HAVE POSSIBLY KNOWN SHE WAS IN DANGER?!
THAT'S THE POINT! WHAT THE BLAZES USE AM I IF I *DON'T* KNOW SUCH THINGS?!
BRIAN, SHE WAS A GROWN WOMAN.
SHE CHOSE HER LIFE-- *SHE'S* RESPONSIBLE FOR HER DECISIONS AND HER DEEDS--
--YOU'RE NOT TO BLAME.
THE DEVIL YOU SAY!
CHANGELING COW, WHAT DO YOU KNOW-- ABOUT *ANYTHING*-- YOU NEVER HAD A FAMILY, NEVER LOST ANYONE YOU CARED FOR!
GO AWAY, MEGGAN!
I DON'T WANT YOUR SYMPATHY.
I ONLY WANT TO BE LEFT ALONE.

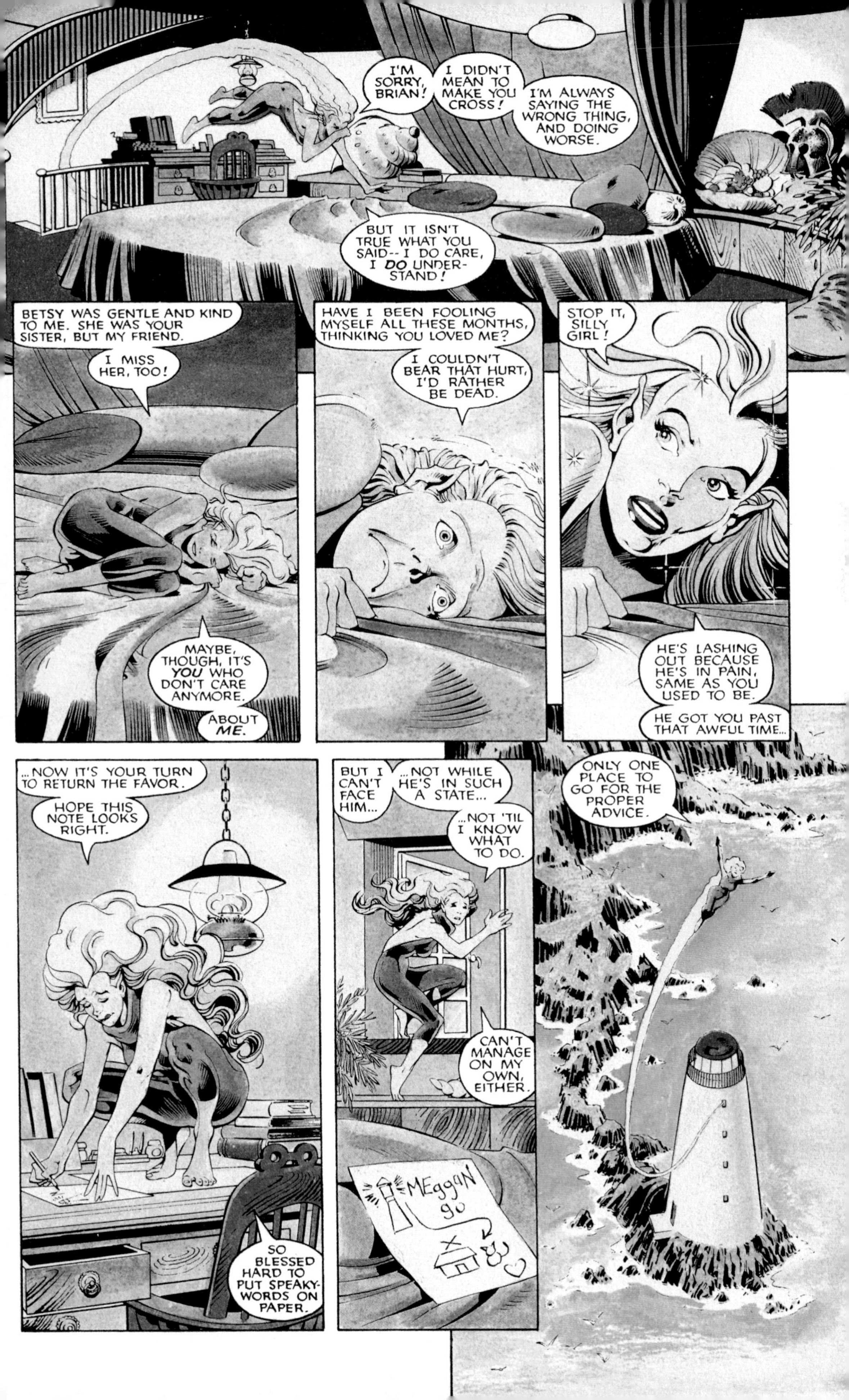
I'M SORRY, BRIAN!
I DIDN'T MEAN TO MAKE YOU CROSS!
I'M ALWAYS SAYING THE WRONG THING, AND DOING WORSE.
BUT IT ISN'T TRUE WHAT YOU SAID-- I DO CARE, I DO UNDERSTAND!
BETSY WAS GENTLE AND KIND TO ME. SHE WAS YOUR SISTER, BUT MY FRIEND.
I MISS HER, TOO!
MAYBE, THOUGH, IT'S YOU WHO DON'T CARE ANYMORE.
ABOUT ME.
HAVE I BEEN FOOLING MYSELF ALL THESE MONTHS, THINKING YOU LOVED ME?
I COULDN'T BEAR THAT HURT, I'D RATHER BE DEAD.
STOP IT, SILLY GIRL!
HE'S LASHING OUT BECAUSE HE'S IN PAIN, SAME AS YOU USED TO BE.
HE GOT YOU PAST THAT AWFUL TIME...
...NOW IT'S YOUR TURN TO RETURN THE FAVOR.
HOPE THIS NOTE LOOKS RIGHT.
SO BLESSED HARD TO PUT SPEAKY-WORDS ON PAPER.
BUT I CAN'T FACE HIM...
...NOT WHILE HE'S IN SUCH A STATE...
...NOT 'TIL I KNOW WHAT TO DO.
CAN'T MANAGE ON MY OWN, EITHER.
MEggaN
go
ONLY ONE PLACE TO GO FOR THE PROPER ADVICE.

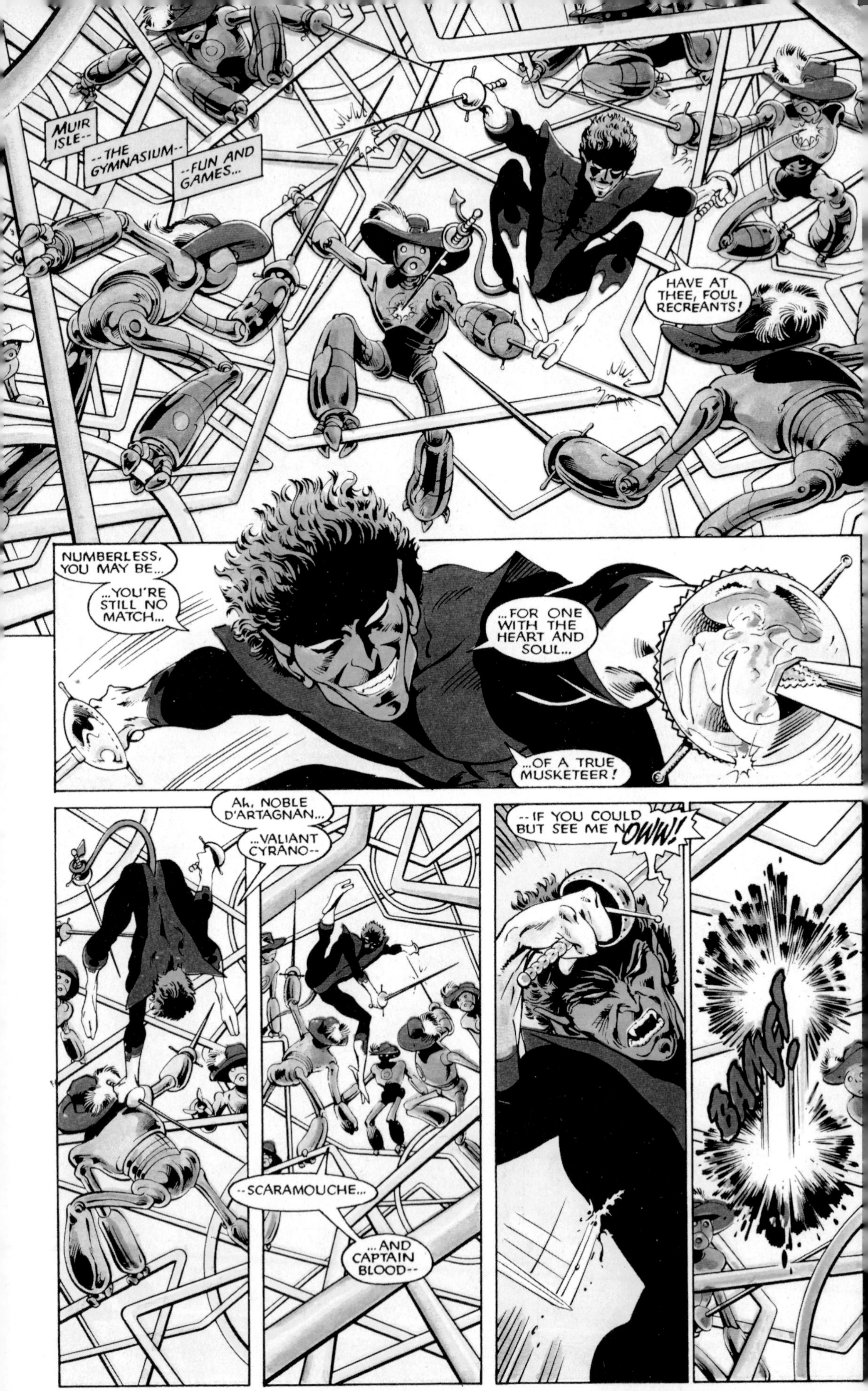
MUIR ISLE--
--THE GYMNASIUM--
--FUN AND GAMES...
HAVE AT THEE, FOUL RECREANTS!
NUMBERLESS, YOU MAY BE...
...YOU'RE STILL NO MATCH...
...FOR ONE WITH THE HEART AND SOUL...
...OF A TRUE MUSKETEER!
Ah, NOBLE D'ARTAGNAN...
...VALIANT CYRANO--
--SCARAMOUCHE...
...AND CAPTAIN BLOOD--
--IF YOU COULD BUT SEE ME N
OWW!
BAMF!

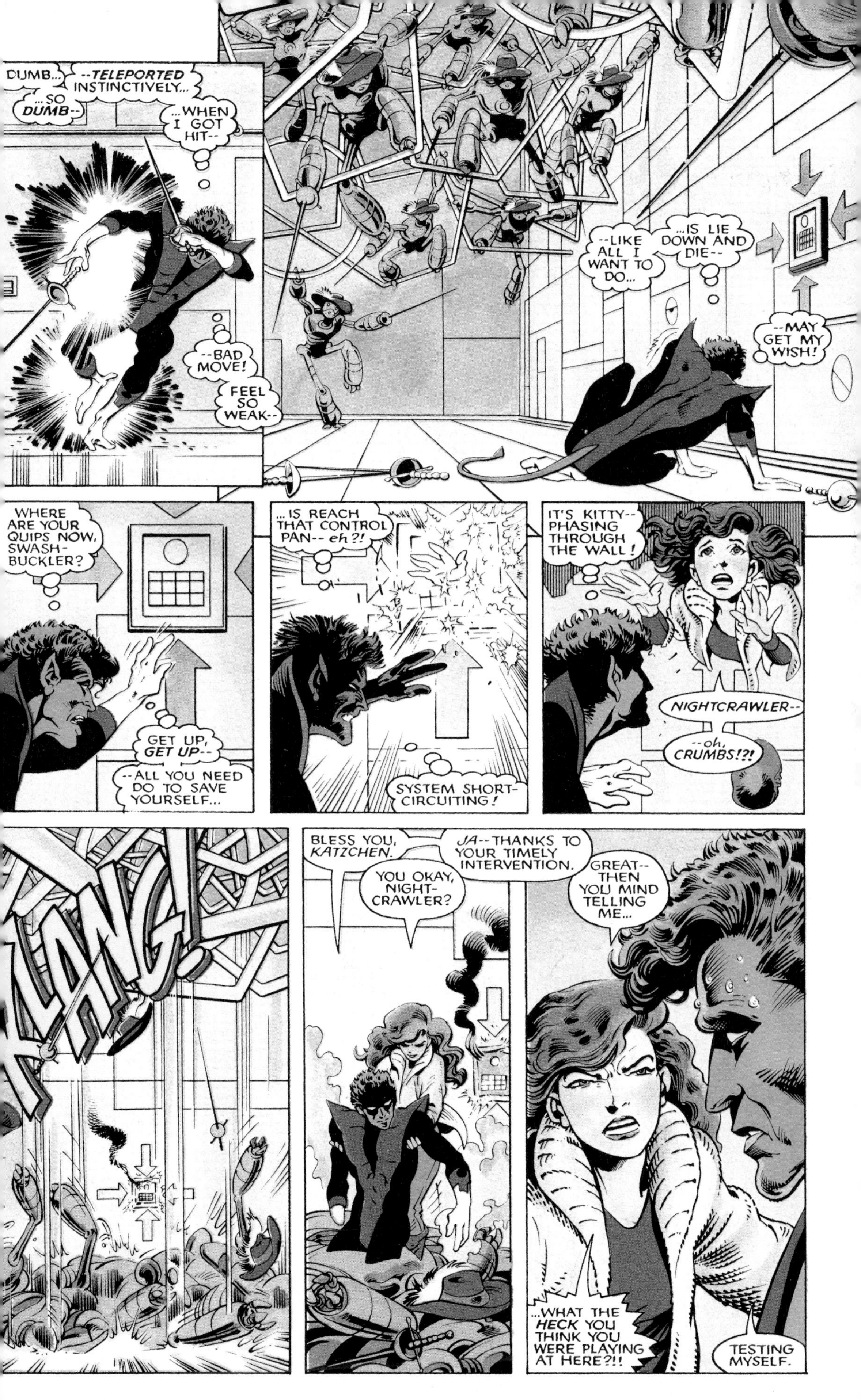
DUMB...
...SO DUMB--
--TELEPORTED INSTINCTIVELY...
...WHEN I GOT HIT--
--BAD MOVE!
FEEL SO WEAK--
--LIKE ALL I WANT TO DO...
...IS LIE DOWN AND DIE--
--MAY GET MY WISH!
WHERE ARE YOUR QUIPS NOW, SWASH-BUCKLER?
GET UP, GET UP--
--ALL YOU NEED DO TO SAVE YOURSELF...
...IS REACH THAT CONTROL PAN-- eh?!
SYSTEM SHORT-CIRCUITING!
IT'S KITTY--PHASING THROUGH THE WALL!
NIGHTCRAWLER--
--oh, CRUMBS!?!
KLANG!
BLESS YOU, KATZCHEN.
YOU OKAY, NIGHT-CRAWLER?
JA--THANKS TO YOUR TIMELY INTERVENTION.
GREAT--THEN YOU MIND TELLING ME...
...WHAT THE HECK YOU THINK YOU WERE PLAYING AT HERE?!!
TESTING MYSELF.

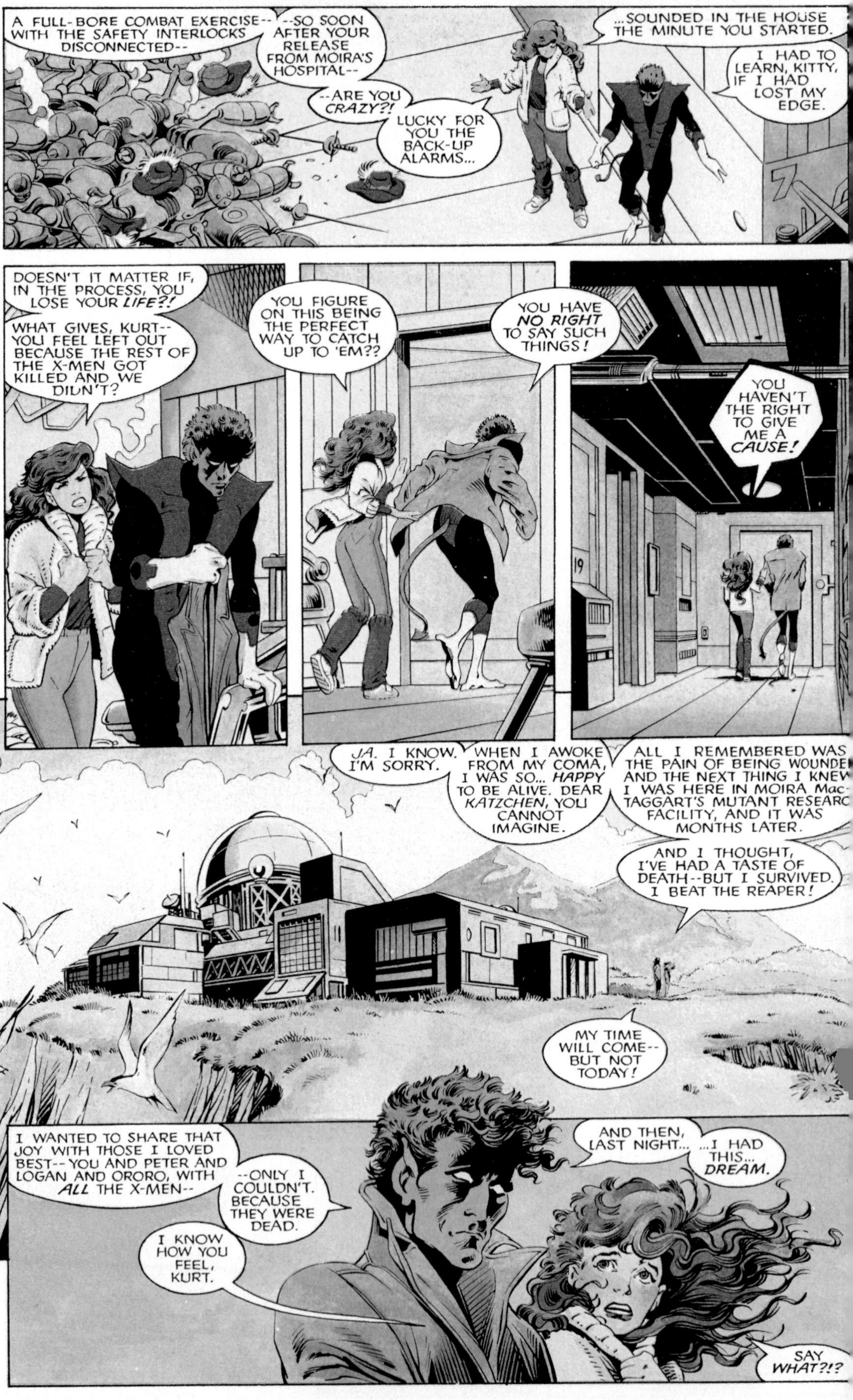
A FULL-BORE COMBAT EXERCISE--WITH THE SAFETY INTERLOCKS DISCONNECTED--
--SO SOON AFTER YOUR RELEASE FROM MOIRA'S HOSPITAL--
--ARE YOU *CRAZY?!*
LUCKY FOR YOU THE BACK-UP ALARMS...
...SOUNDED IN THE HOUSE THE MINUTE YOU STARTED.
I HAD TO LEARN, KITTY, IF I HAD LOST MY EDGE.
DOESN'T IT MATTER IF, IN THE PROCESS, YOU LOSE YOUR *LIFE?!*
WHAT GIVES, KURT--YOU FEEL LEFT OUT BECAUSE THE REST OF THE X-MEN GOT KILLED AND WE DIDN'T?
YOU FIGURE ON THIS BEING THE PERFECT WAY TO CATCH UP TO 'EM??
YOU HAVE **NO RIGHT** TO SAY SUCH THINGS!
YOU HAVEN'T THE RIGHT TO GIVE ME A *CAUSE!*
JA. I KNOW. I'M SORRY.
WHEN I AWOKE FROM MY COMA, I WAS SO... *HAPPY* TO BE ALIVE. DEAR *KATZCHEN*, YOU CANNOT IMAGINE.
ALL I REMEMBERED WAS THE PAIN OF BEING WOUNDE AND THE NEXT THING I KNEW I WAS HERE IN MOIRA Mac-TAGGART'S MUTANT RESEARC FACILITY, AND IT WAS MONTHS LATER.
AND I THOUGHT, I'VE HAD A TASTE OF DEATH--BUT I SURVIVED. I BEAT THE REAPER!
MY TIME WILL COME--BUT NOT TODAY!
I WANTED TO SHARE THAT JOY WITH THOSE I LOVED BEST--YOU AND PETER AND LOGAN AND ORORO, WITH *ALL* THE X-MEN--
--ONLY I COULDN'T. BECAUSE THEY WERE DEAD.
I KNOW HOW YOU FEEL, KURT.
AND THEN, LAST NIGHT...
...I HAD THIS... *DREAM.*
SAY *WHAT?!?*

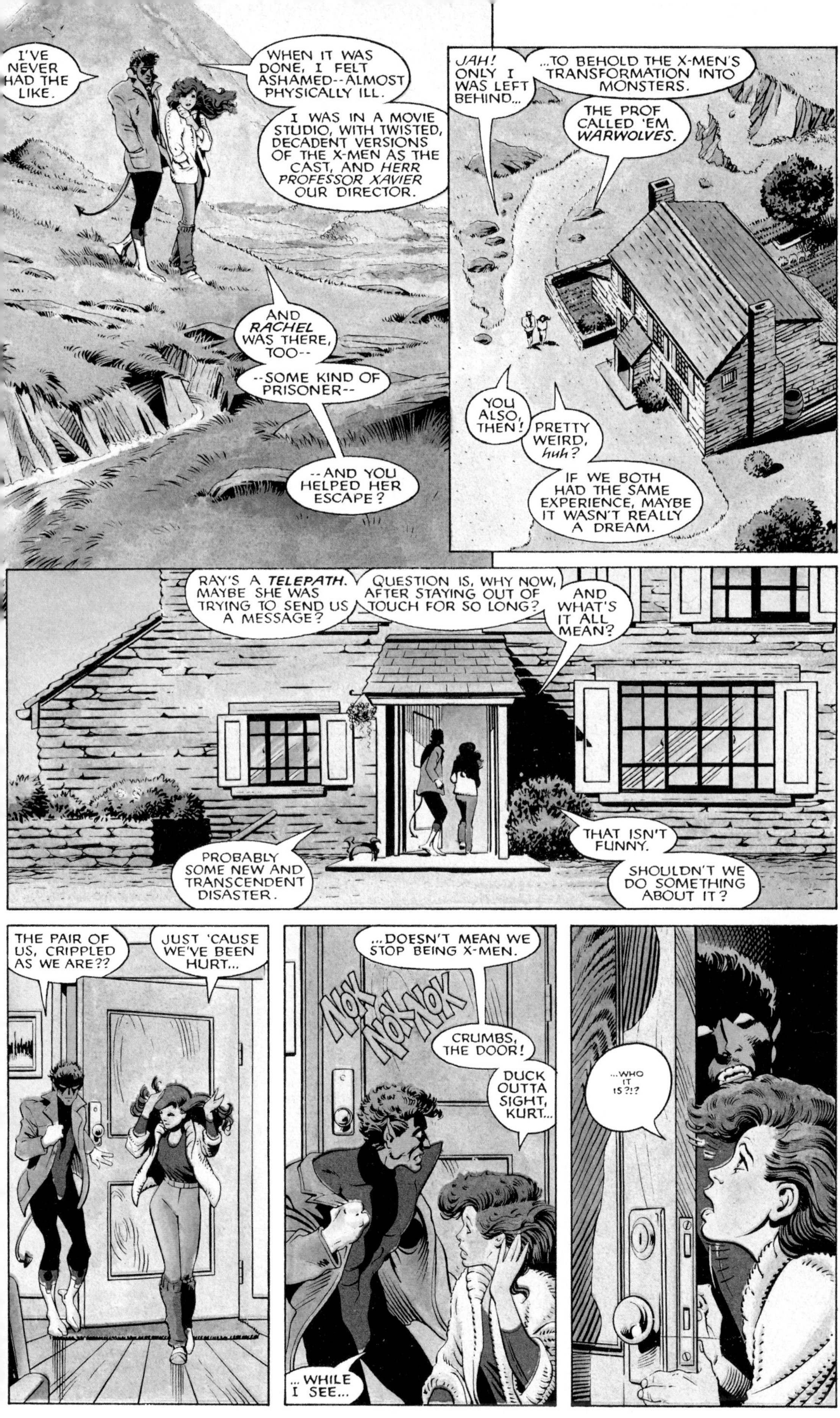
I'VE NEVER HAD THE LIKE.
WHEN IT WAS DONE, I FELT ASHAMED--ALMOST PHYSICALLY ILL.
I WAS IN A MOVIE STUDIO, WITH TWISTED, DECADENT VERSIONS OF THE X-MEN AS THE CAST, AND *HERR PROFESSOR XAVIER* OUR DIRECTOR.
AND *RACHEL* WAS THERE, TOO--
--SOME KIND OF PRISONER--
--AND YOU HELPED HER ESCAPE?
JAH! ONLY I WAS LEFT BEHIND...
...TO BEHOLD THE X-MEN'S TRANSFORMATION INTO MONSTERS.
THE PROF CALLED 'EM *WARWOLVES.*
YOU ALSO, THEN!
PRETTY WEIRD, *huh?*
IF WE BOTH HAD THE SAME EXPERIENCE, MAYBE IT WASN'T REALLY A DREAM.
RAY'S A *TELEPATH.* MAYBE SHE WAS TRYING TO SEND US A MESSAGE?
QUESTION IS, WHY NOW, AFTER STAYING OUT OF TOUCH FOR SO LONG?
AND WHAT'S IT ALL MEAN?
PROBABLY SOME NEW AND TRANSCENDENT DISASTER.
THAT ISN'T FUNNY.
SHOULDN'T WE DO SOMETHING ABOUT IT?
THE PAIR OF US, CRIPPLED AS WE ARE??
JUST 'CAUSE WE'VE BEEN HURT...
...DOESN'T MEAN WE STOP BEING X-MEN.
NOK NOK NOK
CRUMBS, THE DOOR!
DUCK OUTTA SIGHT, KURT...
... WHILE I SEE...
...WHO IT IS?!?

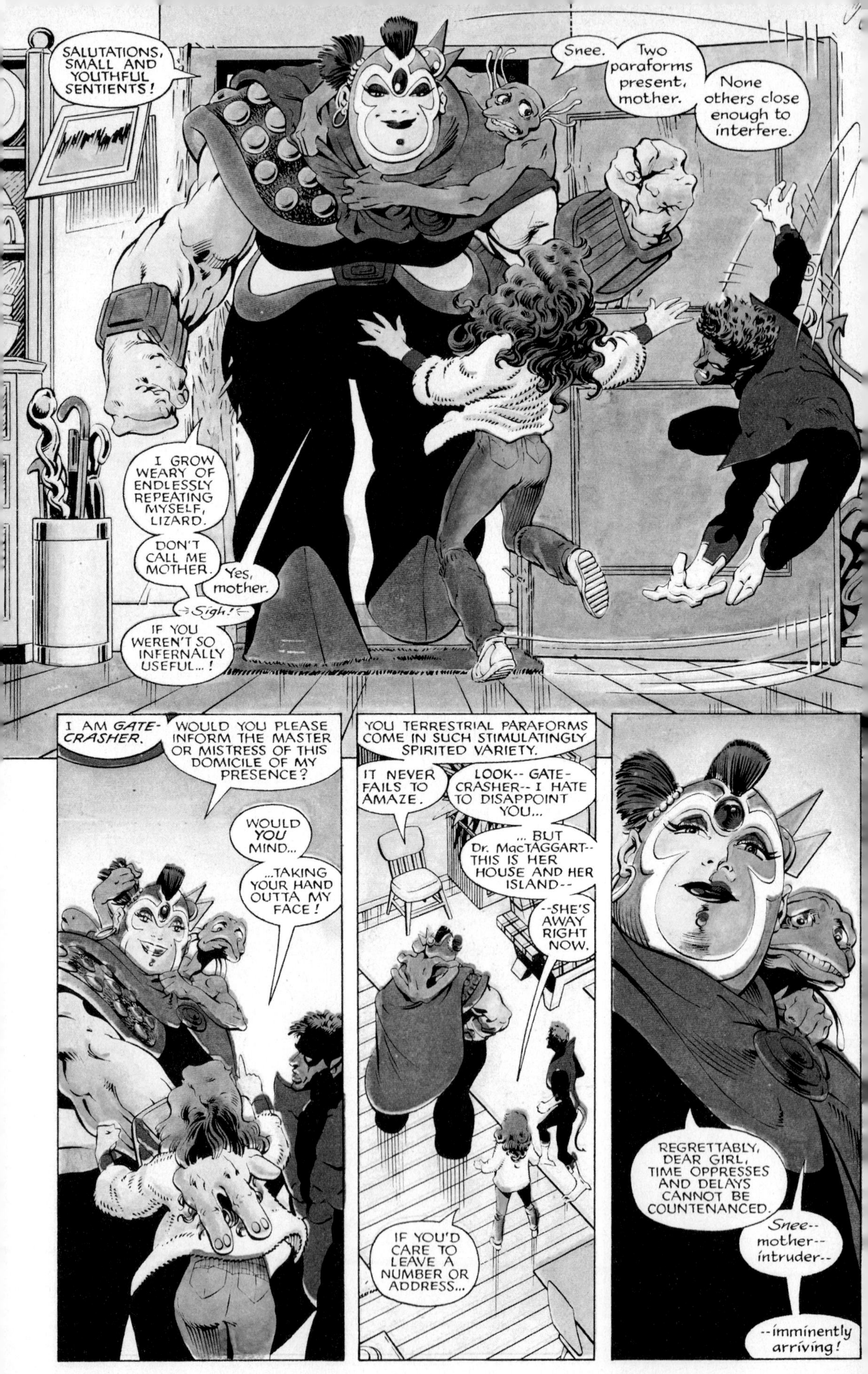
SALUTATIONS, SMALL AND YOUTHFUL SENTIENTS!
Snee.
Two paraforms present, mother.
None others close enough to interfere.
I GROW WEARY OF ENDLESSLY REPEATING MYSELF, LIZARD.
DON'T CALL ME MOTHER.
Yes, mother.
Sigh!
IF YOU WEREN'T SO INFERNALLY USEFUL...!
I AM GATE-CRASHER.
WOULD YOU PLEASE INFORM THE MASTER OR MISTRESS OF THIS DOMICILE OF MY PRESENCE?
WOULD YOU MIND...
...TAKING YOUR HAND OUTTA MY FACE!
YOU TERRESTRIAL PARAFORMS COME IN SUCH STIMULATINGLY SPIRITED VARIETY.
IT NEVER FAILS TO AMAZE.
LOOK-- GATE-CRASHER-- I HATE TO DISAPPOINT YOU...
... BUT Dr. MacTAGGART-- THIS IS HER HOUSE AND HER ISLAND--
--SHE'S AWAY RIGHT NOW.
IF YOU'D CARE TO LEAVE A NUMBER OR ADDRESS...
REGRETTABLY, DEAR GIRL, TIME OPPRESSES AND DELAYS CANNOT BE COUNTENANCED.
Snee-- mother-- intruder--
--imminently arriving!

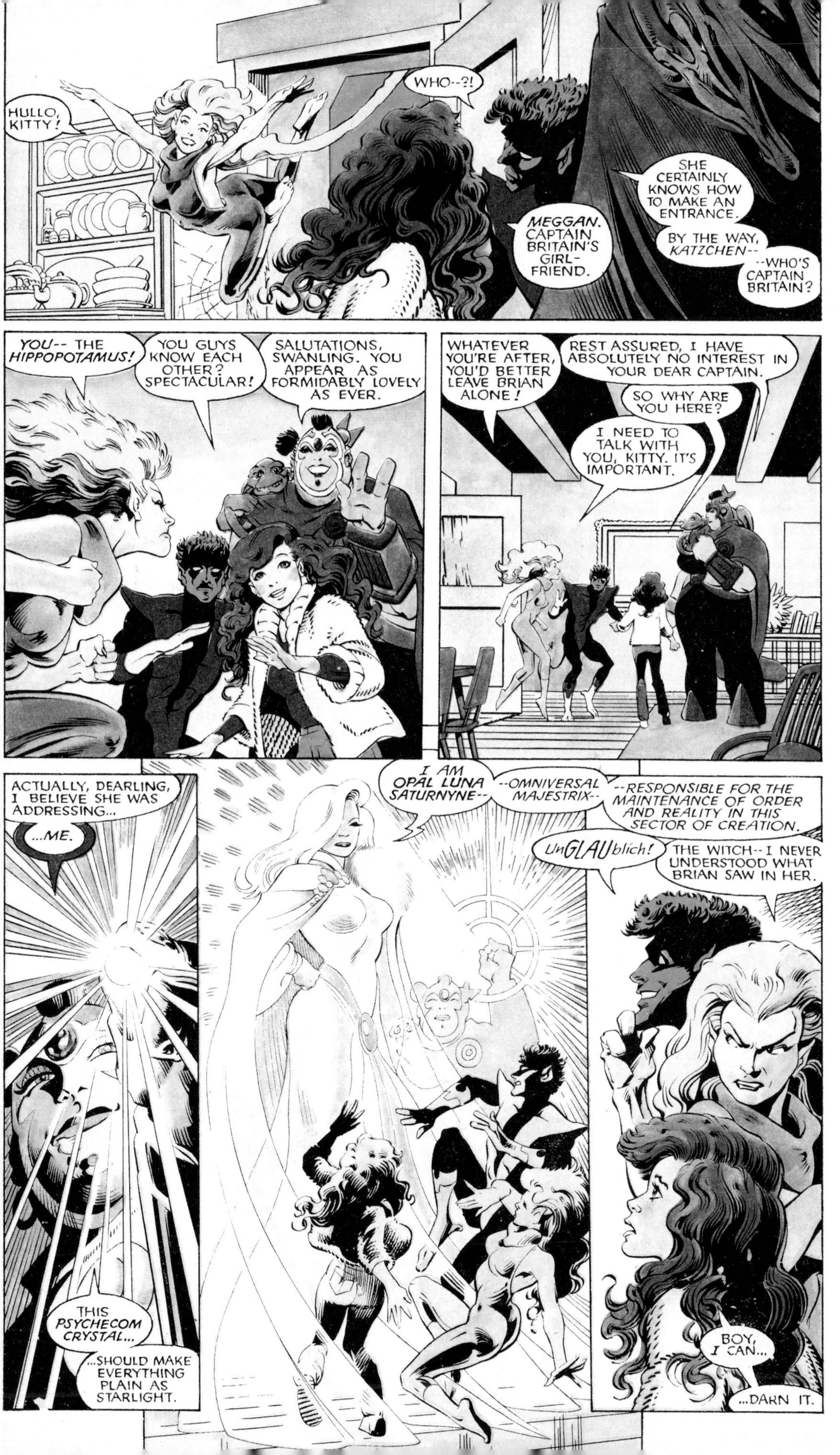
HULLO, KITTY!
WHO--?!
MEGGAN. CAPTAIN BRITAIN'S GIRL-FRIEND.
SHE CERTAINLY KNOWS HOW TO MAKE AN ENTRANCE.
BY THE WAY, KATZCHEN--
--WHO'S CAPTAIN BRITAIN?
YOU-- THE HIPPOPOTAMUS!
YOU GUYS KNOW EACH OTHER? SPECTACULAR!
SALUTATIONS, SWANLING. YOU APPEAR AS FORMIDABLY LOVELY AS EVER.
WHATEVER YOU'RE AFTER, YOU'D BETTER LEAVE BRIAN ALONE!
REST ASSURED, I HAVE ABSOLUTELY NO INTEREST IN YOUR DEAR CAPTAIN.
SO WHY ARE YOU HERE?
I NEED TO TALK WITH YOU, KITTY. IT'S IMPORTANT.
ACTUALLY, DEARLING, I BELIEVE SHE WAS ADDRESSING...
...ME.
THIS PSYCHECOM CRYSTAL...
...SHOULD MAKE EVERYTHING PLAIN AS STARLIGHT.
I AM OPAL LUNA SATURNYNE--
--OMNIVERSAL MAJESTRIX--
--RESPONSIBLE FOR THE MAINTENANCE OF ORDER AND REALITY IN THIS SECTOR OF CREATION.
UnGLAUblich!
THE WITCH-- I NEVER UNDERSTOOD WHAT BRIAN SAW IN HER.
BOY, I CAN...
...DARN IT.

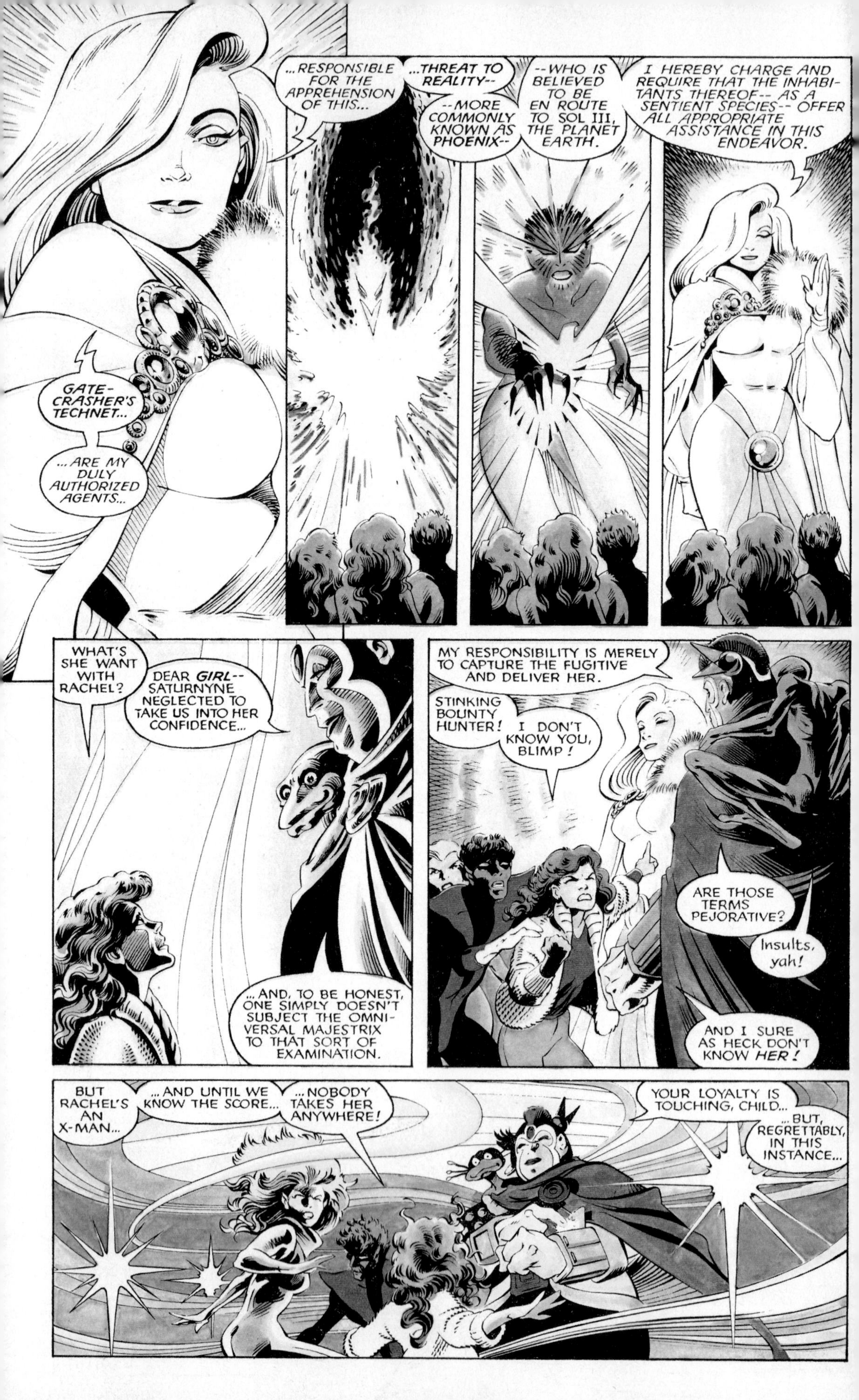
GATE-CRASHER'S TECHNET...
...ARE MY DULY AUTHORIZED AGENTS...
...RESPONSIBLE FOR THE APPREHENSION OF THIS...
...THREAT TO REALITY--
--MORE COMMONLY KNOWN AS PHOENIX--
--WHO IS BELIEVED TO BE EN ROUTE TO SOL III, THE PLANET EARTH.
I HEREBY CHARGE AND REQUIRE THAT THE INHABITANTS THEREOF-- AS A SENTIENT SPECIES-- OFFER ALL APPROPRIATE ASSISTANCE IN THIS ENDEAVOR.
WHAT'S SHE WANT WITH RACHEL?
DEAR GIRL-- SATURNYNE NEGLECTED TO TAKE US INTO HER CONFIDENCE...
...AND, TO BE HONEST, ONE SIMPLY DOESN'T SUBJECT THE OMNIVERSAL MAJESTRIX TO THAT SORT OF EXAMINATION.
MY RESPONSIBILITY IS MERELY TO CAPTURE THE FUGITIVE AND DELIVER HER.
STINKING BOUNTY HUNTER!
I DON'T KNOW YOU, BLIMP!
ARE THOSE TERMS PEJORATIVE?
Insults, yah!
AND I SURE AS HECK DON'T KNOW HER!
BUT RACHEL'S AN X-MAN...
...AND UNTIL WE KNOW THE SCORE...
...NOBODY TAKES HER ANYWHERE!
YOUR LOYALTY IS TOUCHING, CHILD...
...BUT, REGRETTABLY, IN THIS INSTANCE...

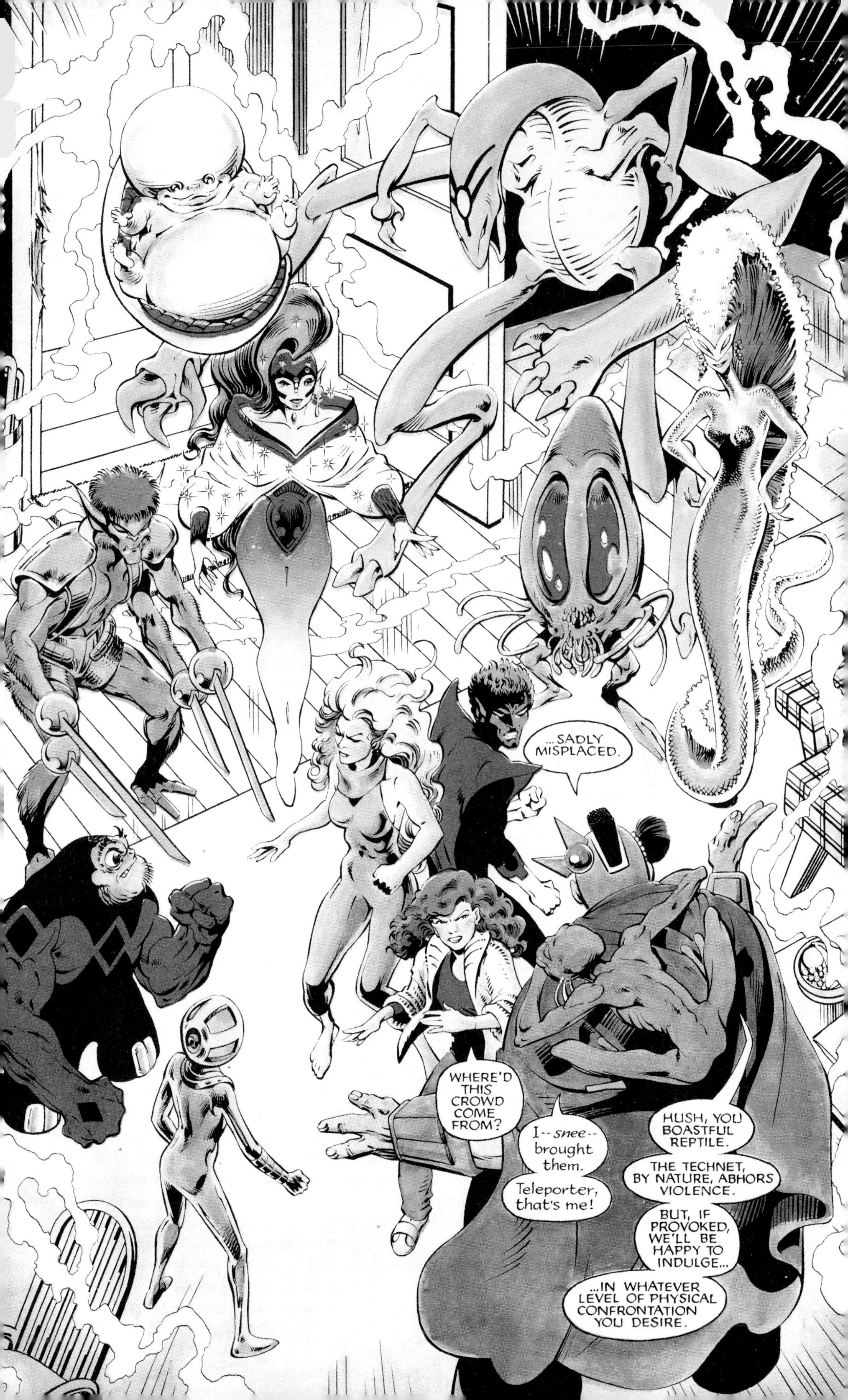
...SADLY MISPLACED.
WHERE'D THIS CROWD COME FROM?
I--snee--brought them.
Teleporter, that's me!
HUSH, YOU BOASTFUL REPTILE.
THE TECHNET, BY NATURE, ABHORS VIOLENCE.
BUT, IF PROVOKED, WE'LL BE HAPPY TO INDULGE...
...IN WHATEVER LEVEL OF PHYSICAL CONFRONTATION YOU DESIRE.

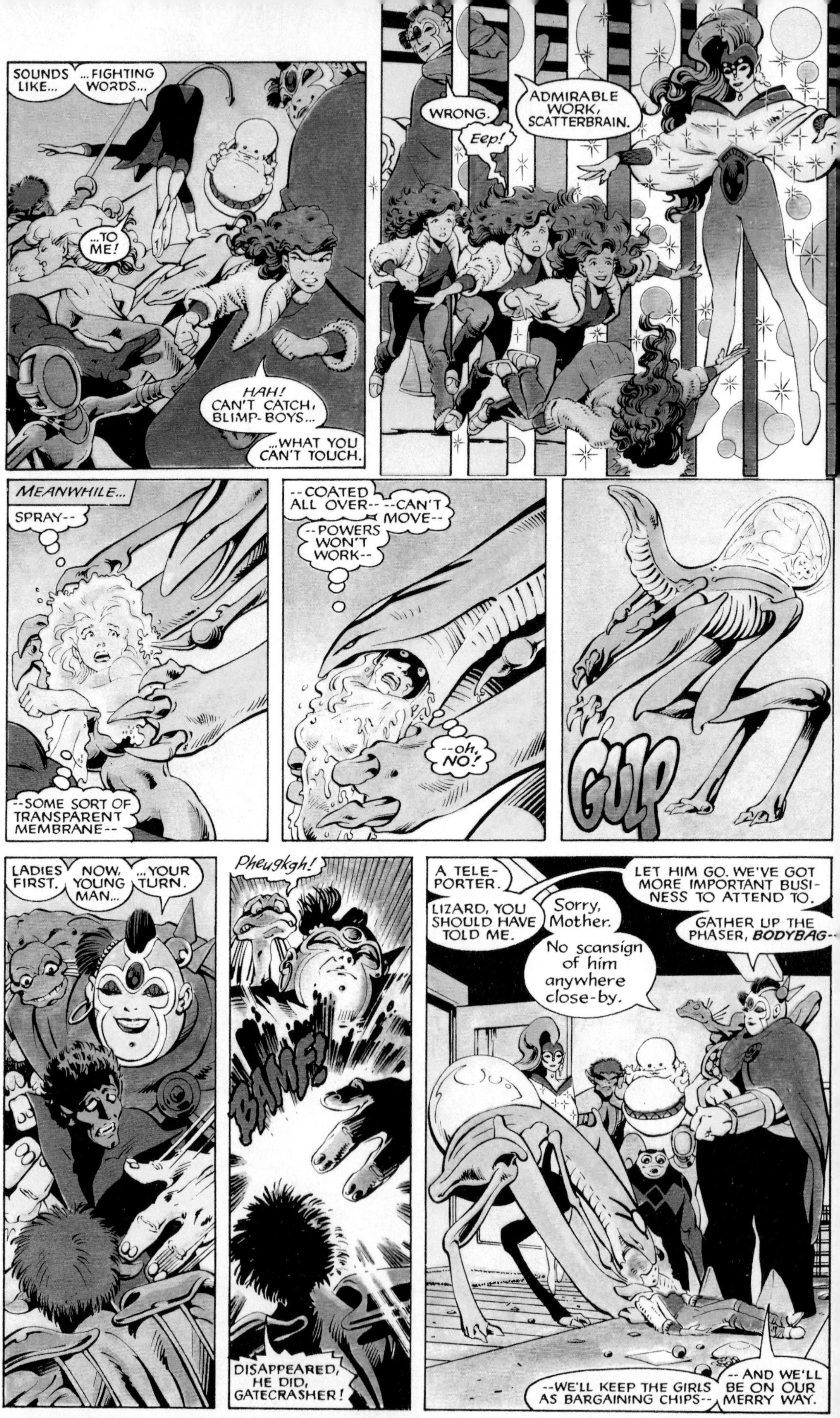
SOUNDS LIKE...
...FIGHTING WORDS...
...TO ME!
HAH! CAN'T CATCH, BLIMP-BOYS...
...WHAT YOU CAN'T TOUCH.
WRONG.
Eep!
ADMIRABLE WORK, SCATTERBRAIN.
MEANWHILE...
SPRAY--
--SOME SORT OF TRANSPARENT MEMBRANE--
--COATED ALL OVER--
--CAN'T MOVE--
--POWERS WON'T WORK--
--oh, NO!
GULP
LADIES FIRST.
NOW, YOUNG MAN...
...YOUR TURN.
Pheugkgh!
BAMF!
DISAPPEARED, HE DID, GATECRASHER!
A TELE-PORTER.
LIZARD, YOU SHOULD HAVE TOLD ME.
Sorry, Mother.
No scansign of him anywhere close-by.
LET HIM GO. WE'VE GOT MORE IMPORTANT BUSINESS TO ATTEND TO.
GATHER UP THE PHASER, BODYBAG--
--WE'LL KEEP THE GIRLS AS BARGAINING CHIPS--
--AND WE'LL BE ON OUR MERRY WAY.

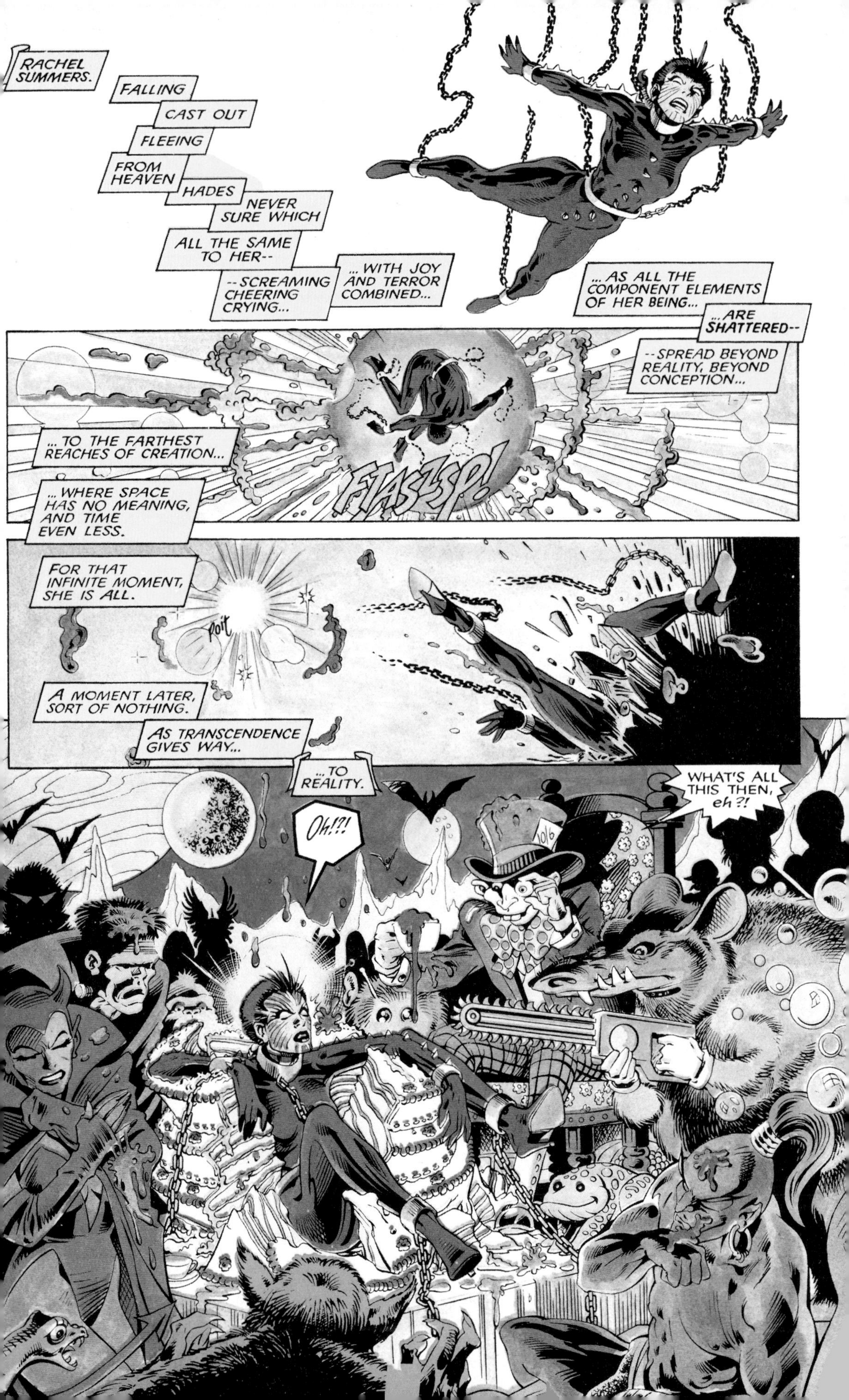
RACHEL SUMMERS.
FALLING
CAST OUT
FLEEING
FROM HEAVEN
HADES
NEVER SURE WHICH
ALL THE SAME TO HER--
--SCREAMING CHEERING CRYING...
...WITH JOY AND TERROR COMBINED...
...AS ALL THE COMPONENT ELEMENTS OF HER BEING...
...ARE SHATTERED--
--SPREAD BEYOND REALITY, BEYOND CONCEPTION...
...TO THE FARTHEST REACHES OF CREATION...
...WHERE SPACE HAS NO MEANING, AND TIME EVEN LESS.
FTASZSP!
FOR THAT INFINITE MOMENT, SHE IS ALL.
poit
A MOMENT LATER, SORT OF NOTHING.
AS TRANSCENDENCE GIVES WAY...
...TO REALITY.
Oh!?!
WHAT'S ALL THIS THEN, eh?!
10/6

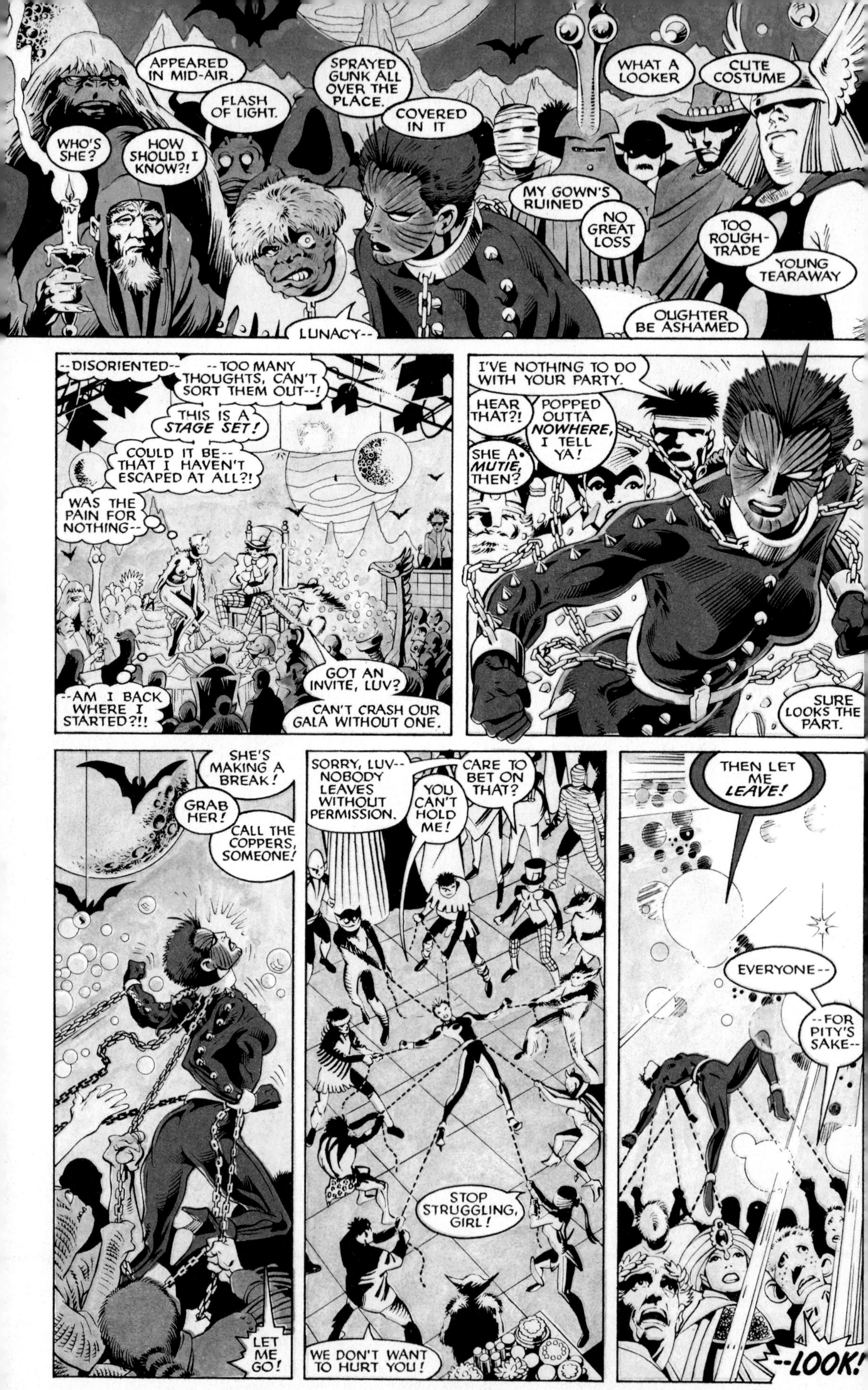
APPEARED IN MID-AIR.
FLASH OF LIGHT.
WHO'S SHE?
HOW SHOULD I KNOW?!
SPRAYED GUNK ALL OVER THE PLACE.
COVERED IN IT
WHAT A LOOKER
CUTE COSTUME
MY GOWN'S RUINED
NO GREAT LOSS
TOO ROUGH-TRADE
YOUNG TEARAWAY
LUNACY--
OUGHTER BE ASHAMED
--DISORIENTED--
--TOO MANY THOUGHTS, CAN'T SORT THEM OUT--!
THIS IS A STAGE SET!
COULD IT BE-- THAT I HAVEN'T ESCAPED AT ALL?!
WAS THE PAIN FOR NOTHING--
--AM I BACK WHERE I STARTED?!!
GOT AN INVITE, LUV?
CAN'T CRASH OUR GALA WITHOUT ONE.
I'VE NOTHING TO DO WITH YOUR PARTY.
HEAR THAT?!
POPPED OUTTA NOWHERE, I TELL YA!
SHE A MUTIE, THEN?
SURE LOOKS THE PART.
SHE'S MAKING A BREAK!
GRAB HER!
CALL THE COPPERS, SOMEONE!
LET ME GO!
SORRY, LUV-- NOBODY LEAVES WITHOUT PERMISSION.
YOU CAN'T HOLD ME!
CARE TO BET ON THAT?
STOP STRUGGLING, GIRL!
WE DON'T WANT TO HURT YOU!
THEN LET ME LEAVE!
EVERYONE--
--FOR PITY'S SAKE--
--LOOK!

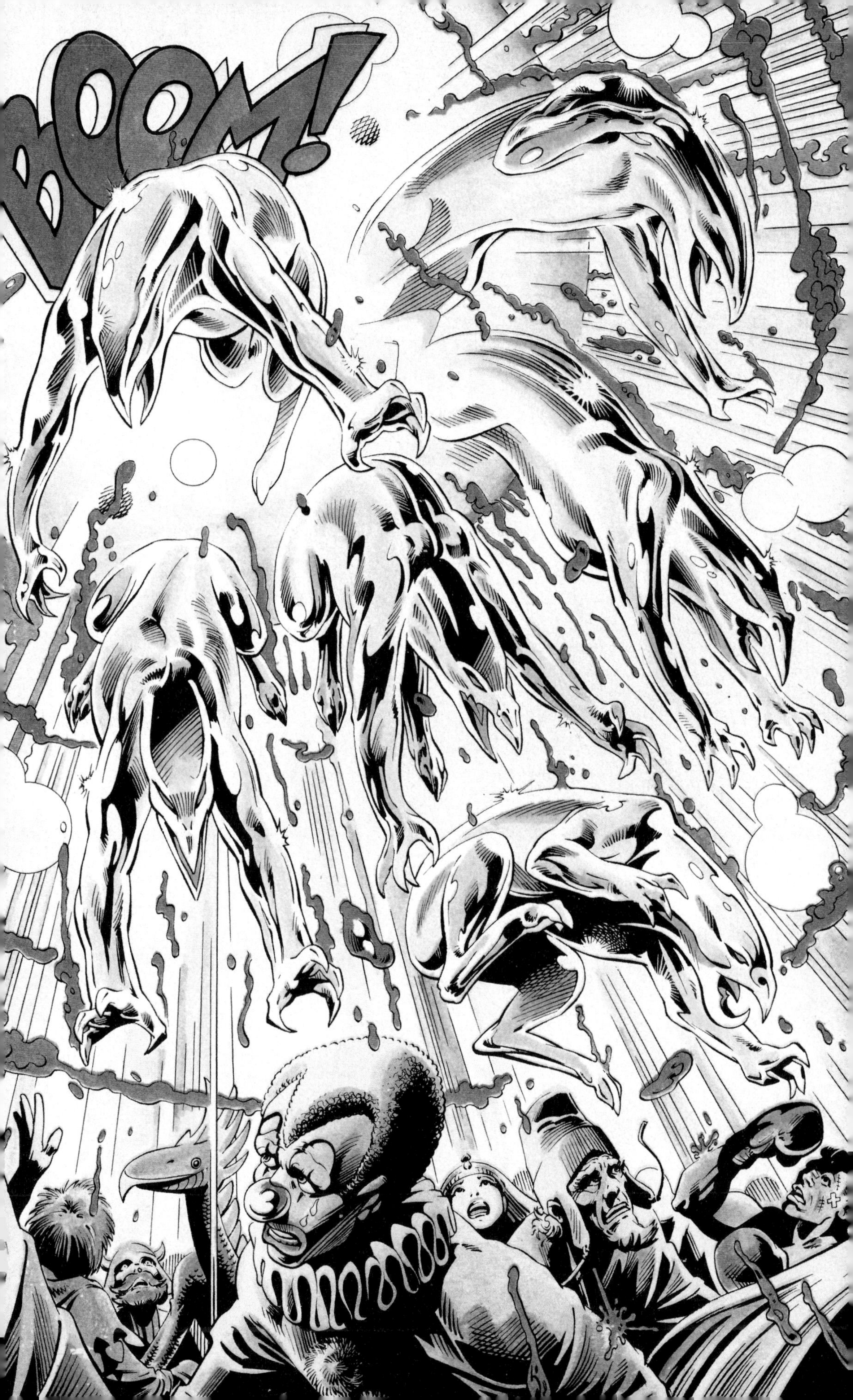
BOOM!

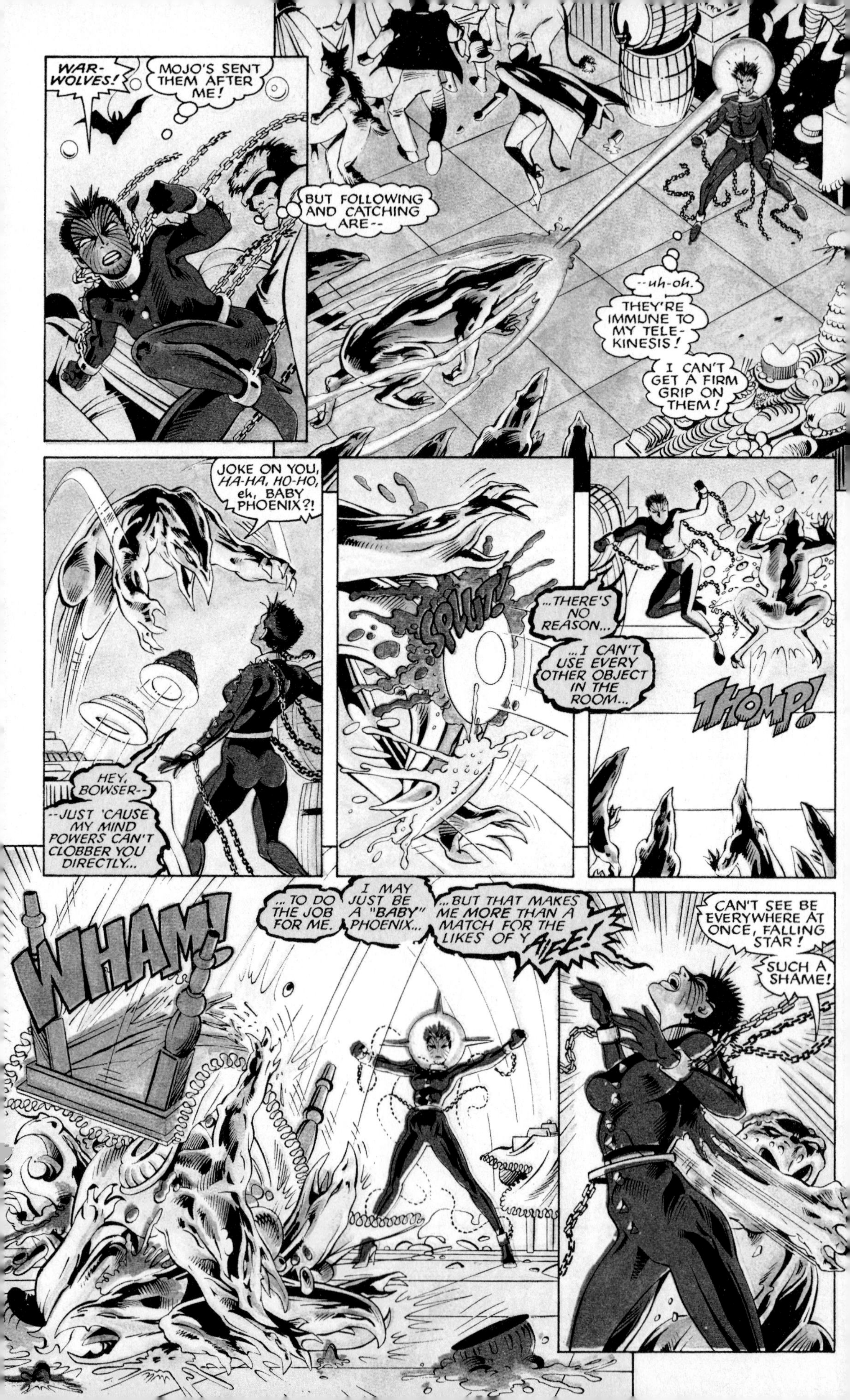
WAR-WOLVES!
MOJO'S SENT THEM AFTER ME!
BUT FOLLOWING AND CATCHING ARE--
--uh-oh.
THEY'RE IMMUNE TO MY TELE-KINESIS!
I CAN'T GET A FIRM GRIP ON THEM!
JOKE ON YOU, HA-HA, HO-HO, eh, BABY PHOENIX?!
HEY, BOWSER--
--JUST 'CAUSE MY MIND POWERS CAN'T CLOBBER YOU DIRECTLY...
SPLUT!
...THERE'S NO REASON...
...I CAN'T USE EVERY OTHER OBJECT IN THE ROOM...
THOMP!
WHAM!
...TO DO THE JOB FOR ME.
I MAY JUST BE A "BABY" PHOENIX...
...BUT THAT MAKES ME MORE THAN A MATCH FOR THE LIKES OF Y
AIEE!
CAN'T SEE BE EVERYWHERE AT ONCE, FALLING STAR!
SUCH A SHAME!

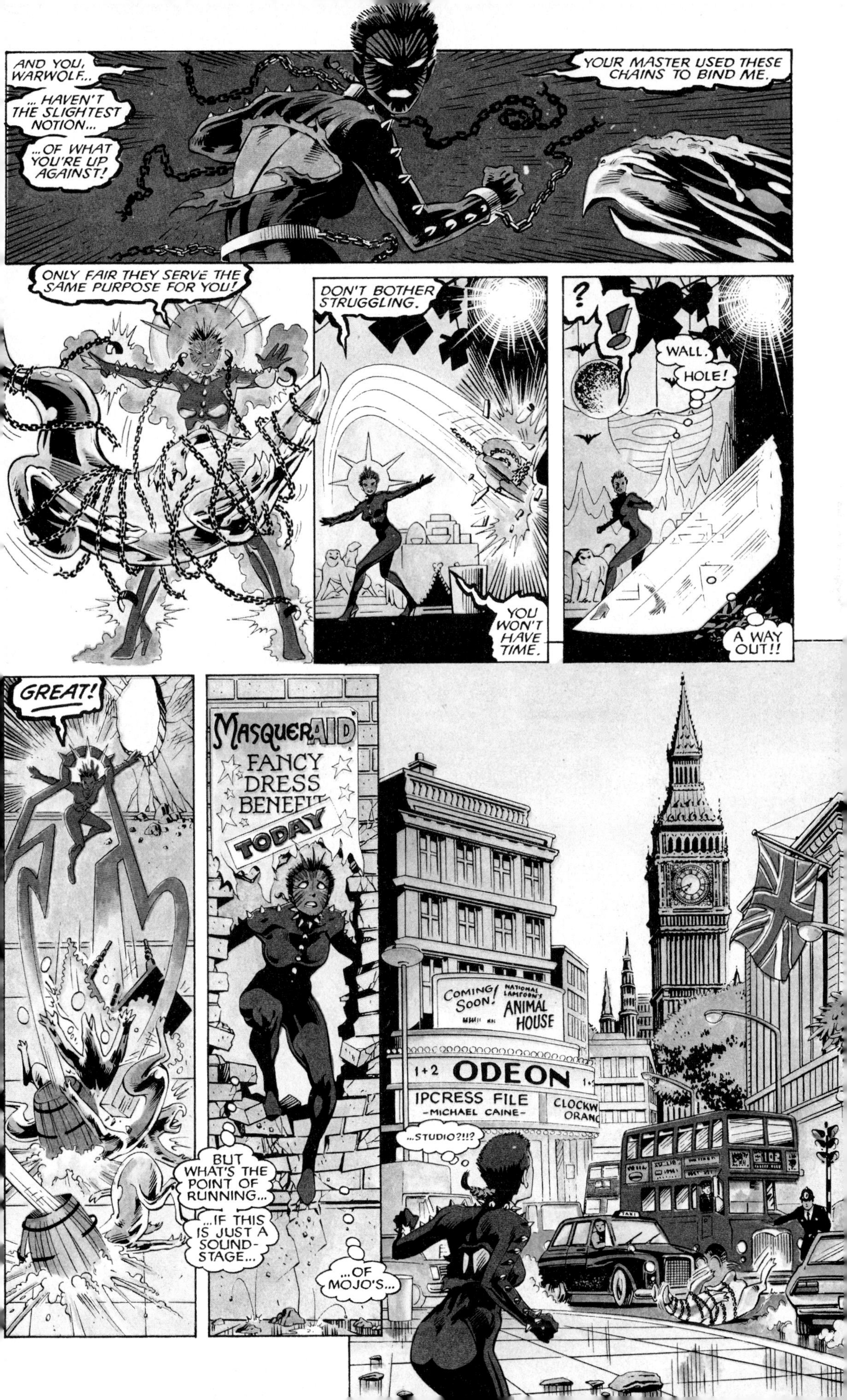
AND YOU, WARWOLF...
... HAVEN'T THE SLIGHTEST NOTION...
...OF WHAT YOU'RE UP AGAINST!
YOUR MASTER USED THESE CHAINS TO BIND ME.
ONLY FAIR THEY SERVE THE SAME PURPOSE FOR YOU!
DON'T BOTHER STRUGGLING.
YOU WON'T HAVE TIME.
?
WALL.
HOLE!
A WAY OUT!!
GREAT!
MASQUERAID
FANCY DRESS BENEFIT
TODAY
BUT WHAT'S THE POINT OF RUNNING...
...IF THIS IS JUST A SOUND-STAGE...
...OF MOJO'S...
COMING SOON! NATIONAL LAMPOON'S ANIMAL HOUSE
1+2 ODEON
IPCRESS FILE
-MICHAEL CAINE-
...STUDIO?!!?

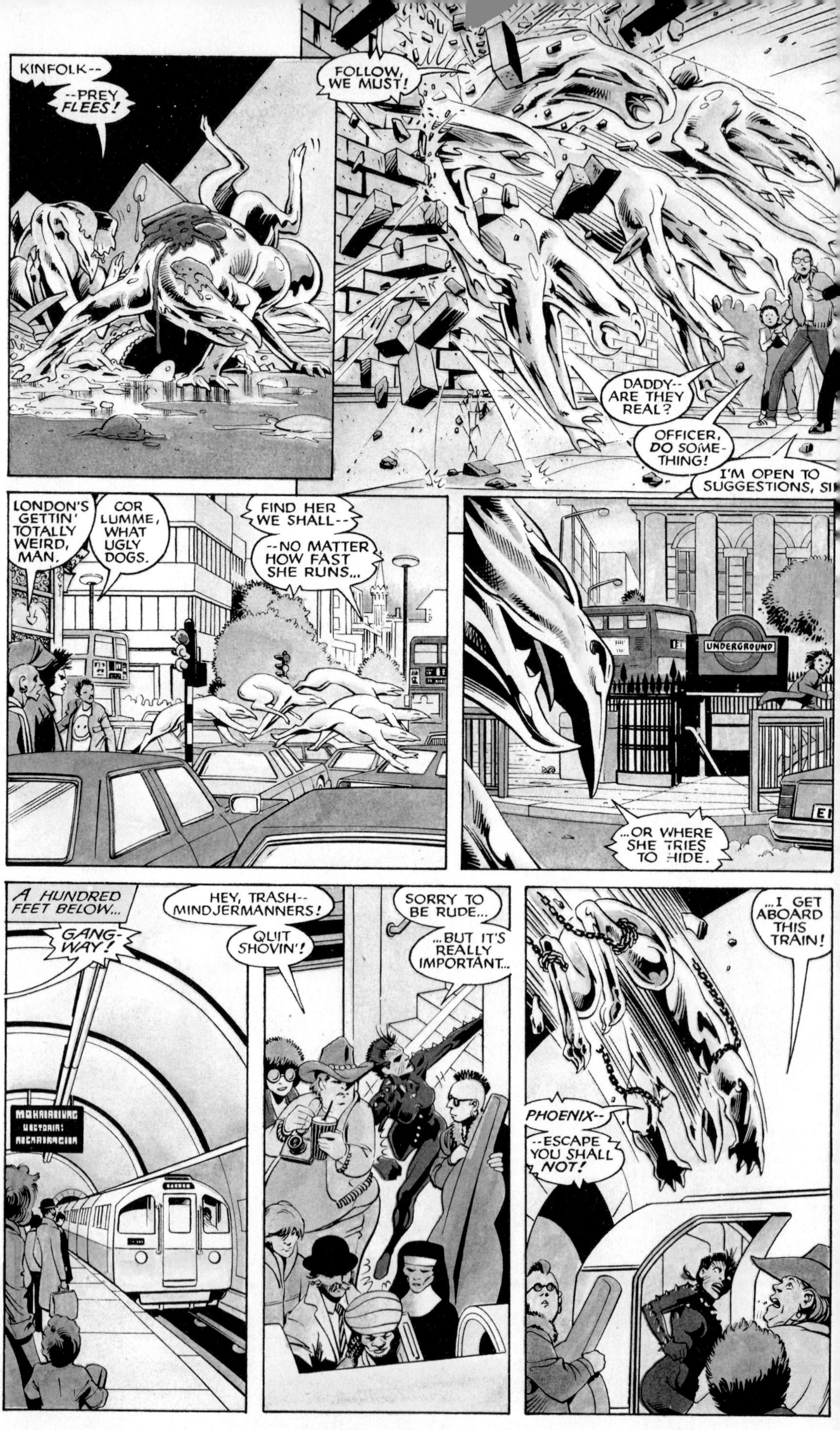

KINFOLK--
--PREY FLEES!
FOLLOW, WE MUST!
DADDY-- ARE THEY REAL?
OFFICER, DO SOME-THING!
I'M OPEN TO SUGGESTIONS, SI
LONDON'S GETTIN' TOTALLY WEIRD, MAN.
COR LUMME, WHAT UGLY DOGS.
FIND HER WE SHALL--
--NO MATTER HOW FAST SHE RUNS...
UNDERGROUND
...OR WHERE SHE TRIES TO HIDE.
A HUNDRED FEET BELOW...
GANG-WAY!
HEY, TRASH-- MINDJERMANNERS!
QUIT SHOVIN'!
SORRY TO BE RUDE...
...BUT IT'S REALLY IMPORTANT...
...I GET ABOARD THIS TRAIN!
PHOENIX--
--ESCAPE YOU SHALL NOT!

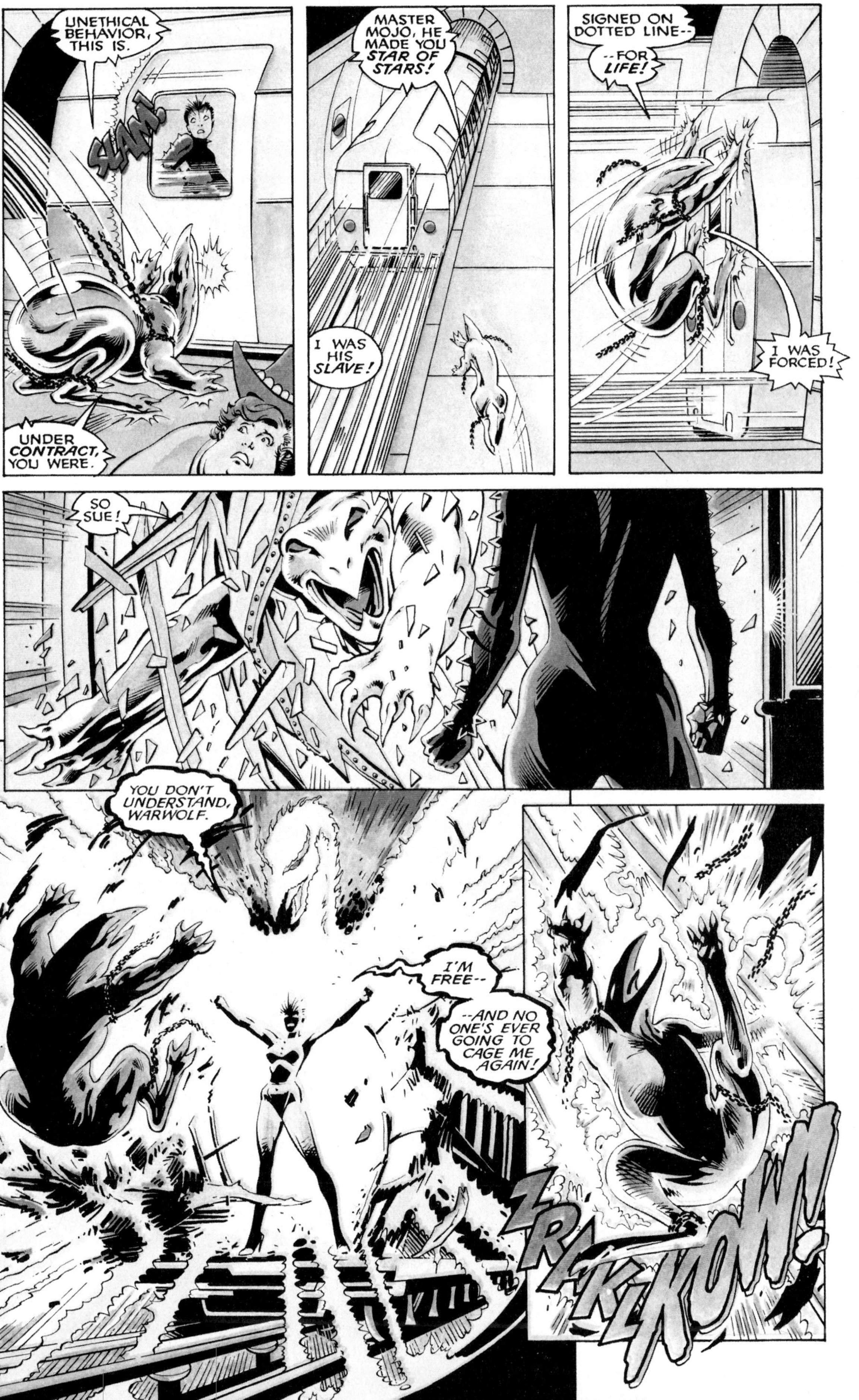
UNETHICAL BEHAVIOR, THIS IS.
SLAM!
UNDER CONTRACT, YOU WERE.
MASTER MOJO, HE MADE YOU STAR OF STARS!
I WAS HIS SLAVE!
SIGNED ON DOTTED LINE--
--FOR LIFE!
I WAS FORCED!
SO SUE!
YOU DON'T UNDERSTAND, WARWOLF.
I'M FREE--
--AND NO ONE'S EVER GOING TO CAGE ME AGAIN!
ZRAKKKOWW!

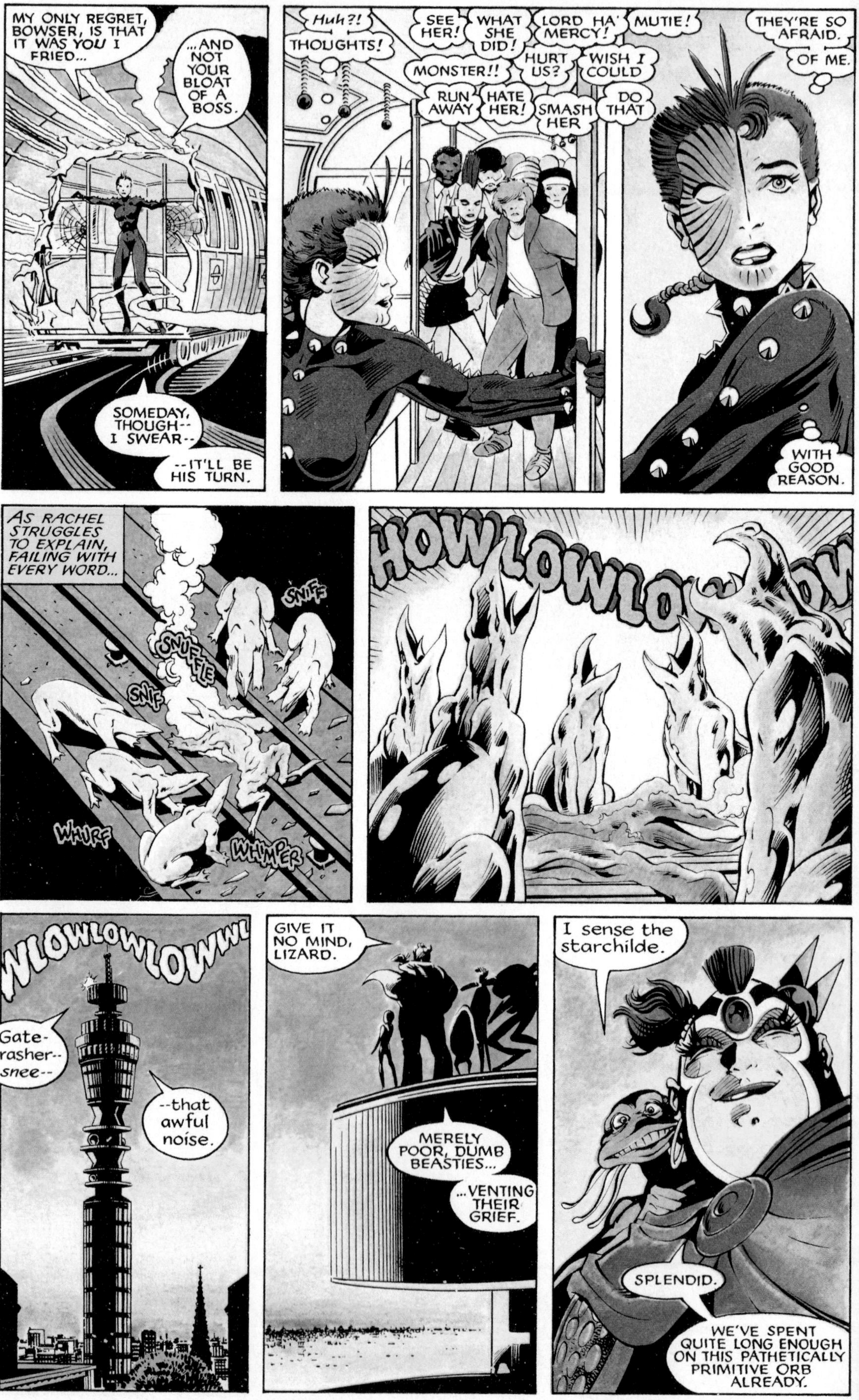

MY ONLY REGRET, BOWSER, IS THAT IT WAS YOU I FRIED...
...AND NOT YOUR BLOAT OF A BOSS.
SOMEDAY, THOUGH-- I SWEAR--
--IT'LL BE HIS TURN.
Huh?! THOUGHTS!
SEE HER!
WHAT SHE DID!
LORD HA' MERCY!
MUTIE!
MONSTER!!
HURT US?
WISH I COULD
RUN AWAY
HATE HER!
SMASH HER
DO THAT
THEY'RE SO AFRAID.
OF ME.
WITH GOOD REASON.
AS RACHEL STRUGGLES TO EXPLAIN, FAILING WITH EVERY WORD...
SNIF
SNUFFLE
SNIF
WHURF
WHIMPER
HOWLOWLOWLOWLOWLOW
WLOWLOWLOWLOWWL
Gate-crasher-- snee--
--that awful noise.
GIVE IT NO MIND, LIZARD.
MERELY POOR, DUMB BEASTIES...
...VENTING THEIR GRIEF.
I sense the starchilde.
SPLENDID.
WE'VE SPENT QUITE LONG ENOUGH ON THIS PATHETICALLY PRIMITIVE ORB ALREADY.

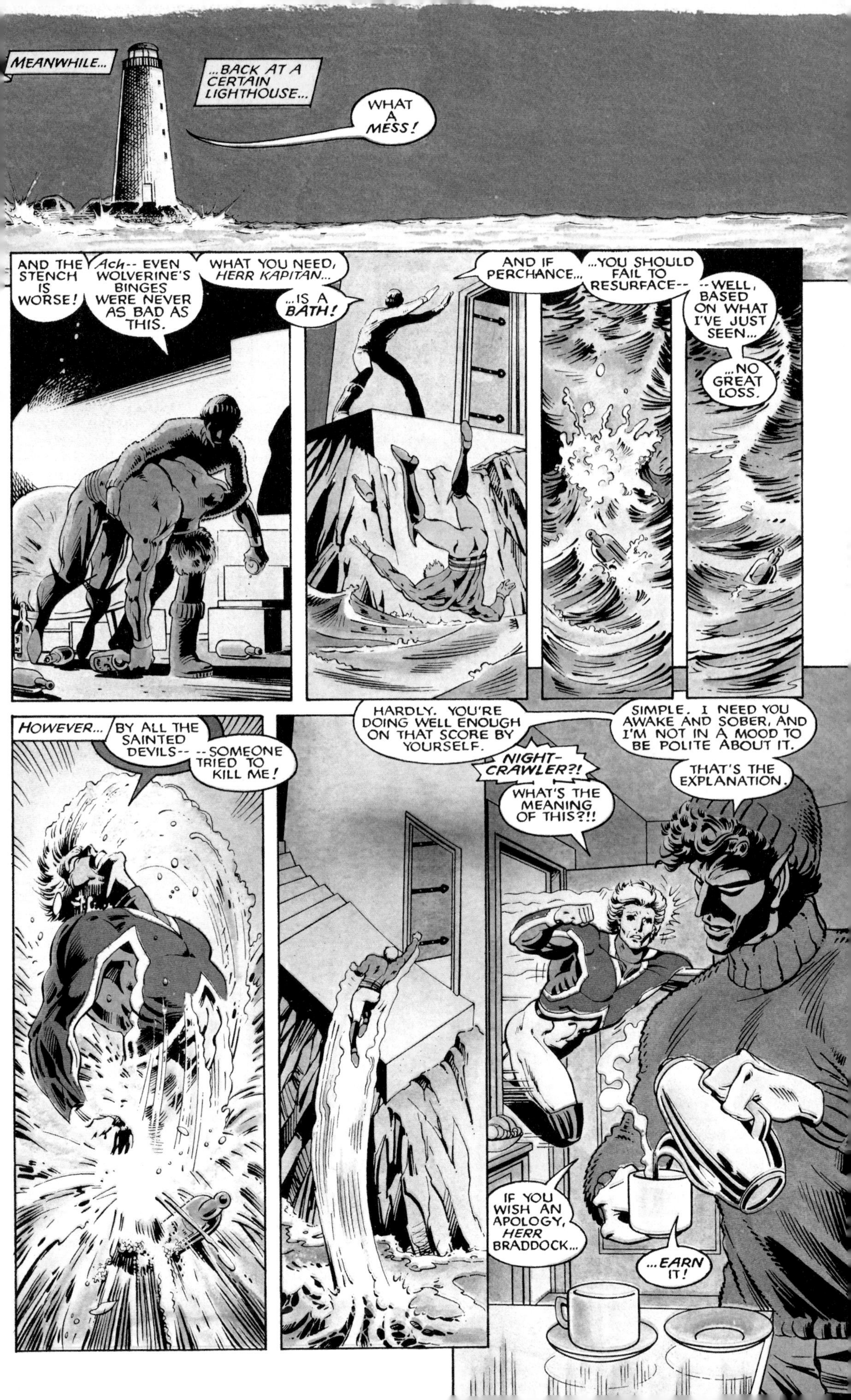
MEANWHILE...
...BACK AT A CERTAIN LIGHTHOUSE...
WHAT A MESS!
AND THE STENCH IS WORSE!
Ach-- EVEN WOLVERINE'S BINGES WERE NEVER AS BAD AS THIS.
WHAT YOU NEED, HERR KAPITAN...
...IS A BATH!
AND IF PERCHANCE...
...YOU SHOULD FAIL TO RESURFACE--
--WELL, BASED ON WHAT I'VE JUST SEEN...
...NO GREAT LOSS.
HOWEVER...
BY ALL THE SAINTED DEVILS--
--SOMEONE TRIED TO KILL ME!
HARDLY. YOU'RE DOING WELL ENOUGH ON THAT SCORE BY YOURSELF.
SIMPLE. I NEED YOU AWAKE AND SOBER, AND I'M NOT IN A MOOD TO BE POLITE ABOUT IT.
NIGHT-CRAWLER?!
WHAT'S THE MEANING OF THIS?!!
THAT'S THE EXPLANATION.
IF YOU WISH AN APOLOGY, HERR BRADDOCK...
...EARN IT!

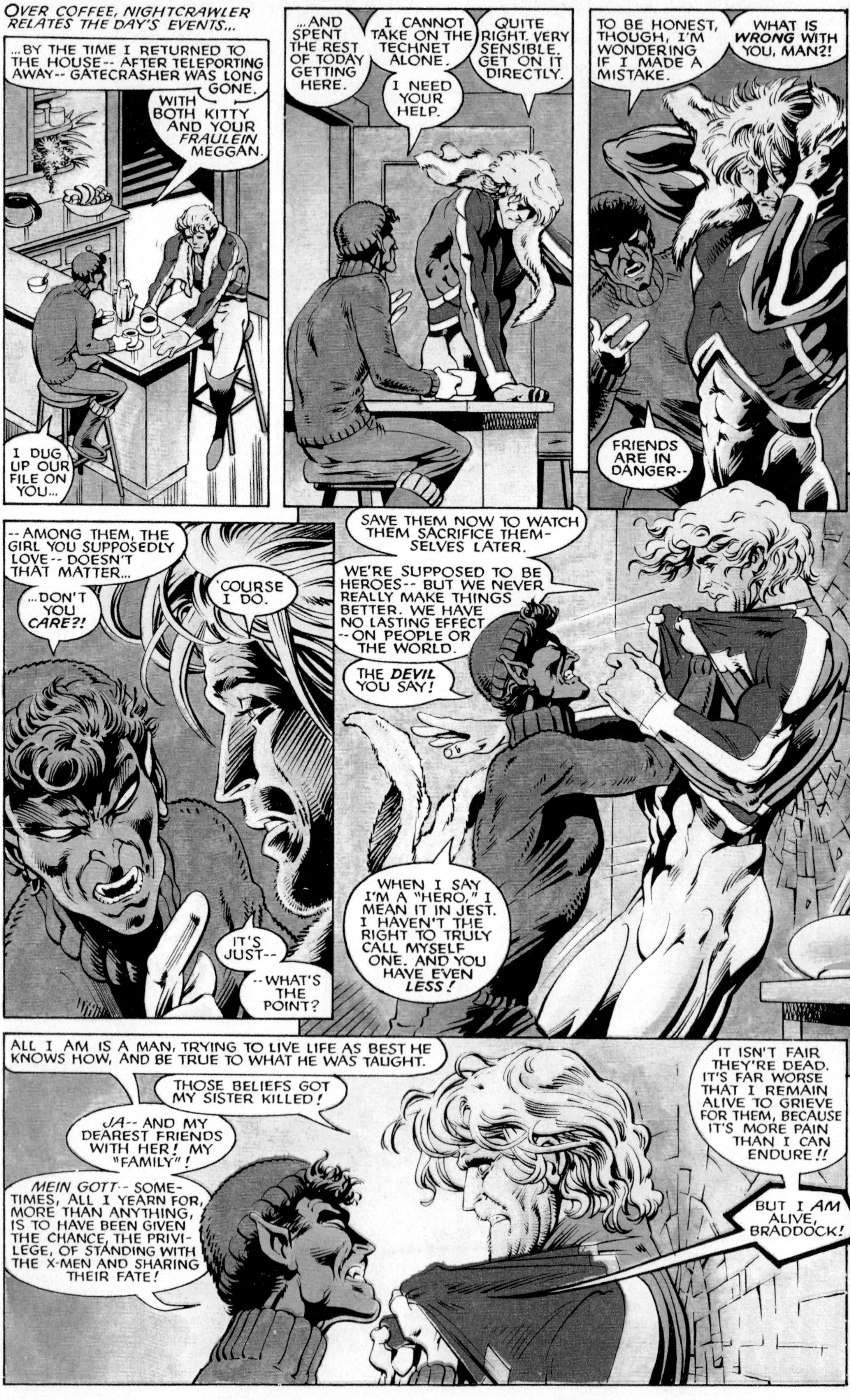
OVER COFFEE, NIGHTCRAWLER RELATES THE DAY'S EVENTS...
...BY THE TIME I RETURNED TO THE HOUSE-- AFTER TELEPORTING AWAY-- GATECRASHER WAS LONG GONE.
WITH BOTH KITTY AND YOUR FRAULEIN MEGGAN.
I DUG UP OUR FILE ON YOU...
...AND SPENT THE REST OF TODAY GETTING HERE.
I CANNOT TAKE ON THE TECHNET ALONE.
I NEED YOUR HELP.
QUITE RIGHT. VERY SENSIBLE. GET ON IT DIRECTLY.
TO BE HONEST, THOUGH, I'M WONDERING IF I MADE A MISTAKE.
WHAT IS WRONG WITH YOU, MAN?!
FRIENDS ARE IN DANGER--
--AMONG THEM, THE GIRL YOU SUPPOSEDLY LOVE-- DOESN'T THAT MATTER...
...DON'T YOU CARE?!
'COURSE I DO.
IT'S JUST--
--WHAT'S THE POINT?
SAVE THEM NOW TO WATCH THEM SACRIFICE THEMSELVES LATER.
WE'RE SUPPOSED TO BE HEROES-- BUT WE NEVER REALLY MAKE THINGS BETTER. WE HAVE NO LASTING EFFECT --ON PEOPLE OR THE WORLD.
THE DEVIL YOU SAY!
WHEN I SAY I'M A "HERO," I MEAN IT IN JEST. I HAVEN'T THE RIGHT TO TRULY CALL MYSELF ONE. AND YOU HAVE EVEN LESS!
ALL I AM IS A MAN, TRYING TO LIVE LIFE AS BEST HE KNOWS HOW, AND BE TRUE TO WHAT HE WAS TAUGHT.
THOSE BELIEFS GOT MY SISTER KILLED!
JA-- AND MY DEAREST FRIENDS WITH HER! MY "FAMILY"!
MEIN GOTT-- SOMETIMES, ALL I YEARN FOR, MORE THAN ANYTHING, IS TO HAVE BEEN GIVEN THE CHANCE, THE PRIVILEGE, OF STANDING WITH THE X-MEN AND SHARING THEIR FATE!
IT ISN'T FAIR THEY'RE DEAD. IT'S FAR WORSE THAT I REMAIN ALIVE TO GRIEVE FOR THEM, BECAUSE IT'S MORE PAIN THAN I CAN ENDURE!!
BUT I AM ALIVE, BRADDOCK!

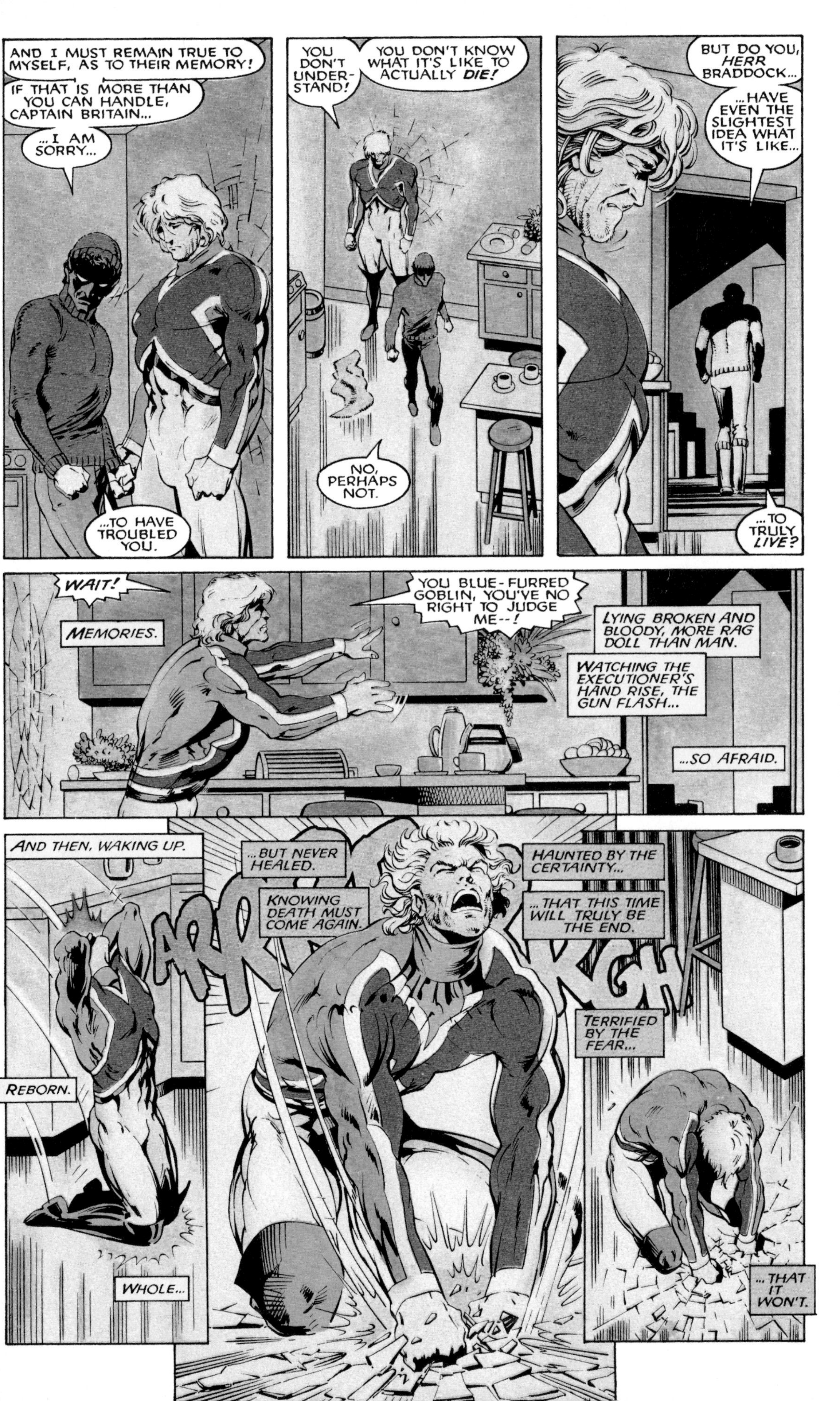
AND I MUST REMAIN TRUE TO MYSELF, AS TO THEIR MEMORY!
IF THAT IS MORE THAN YOU CAN HANDLE, CAPTAIN BRITAIN...
...I AM SORRY...
...TO HAVE TROUBLED YOU.
YOU DON'T UNDERSTAND!
YOU DON'T KNOW WHAT IT'S LIKE TO ACTUALLY DIE!
NO, PERHAPS NOT.
BUT DO YOU, HERR BRADDOCK...
...HAVE EVEN THE SLIGHTEST IDEA WHAT IT'S LIKE...
...TO TRULY LIVE?
WAIT!
MEMORIES.
YOU BLUE-FURRED GOBLIN, YOU'VE NO RIGHT TO JUDGE ME--!
LYING BROKEN AND BLOODY, MORE RAG DOLL THAN MAN.
WATCHING THE EXECUTIONER'S HAND RISE, THE GUN FLASH...
...SO AFRAID.
AND THEN, WAKING UP.
REBORN.
WHOLE...
...BUT NEVER HEALED.
KNOWING DEATH MUST COME AGAIN.
AARRGH
HAUNTED BY THE CERTAINTY...
...THAT THIS TIME WILL TRULY BE THE END.
TERRIFIED BY THE FEAR...
...THAT IT WON'T.

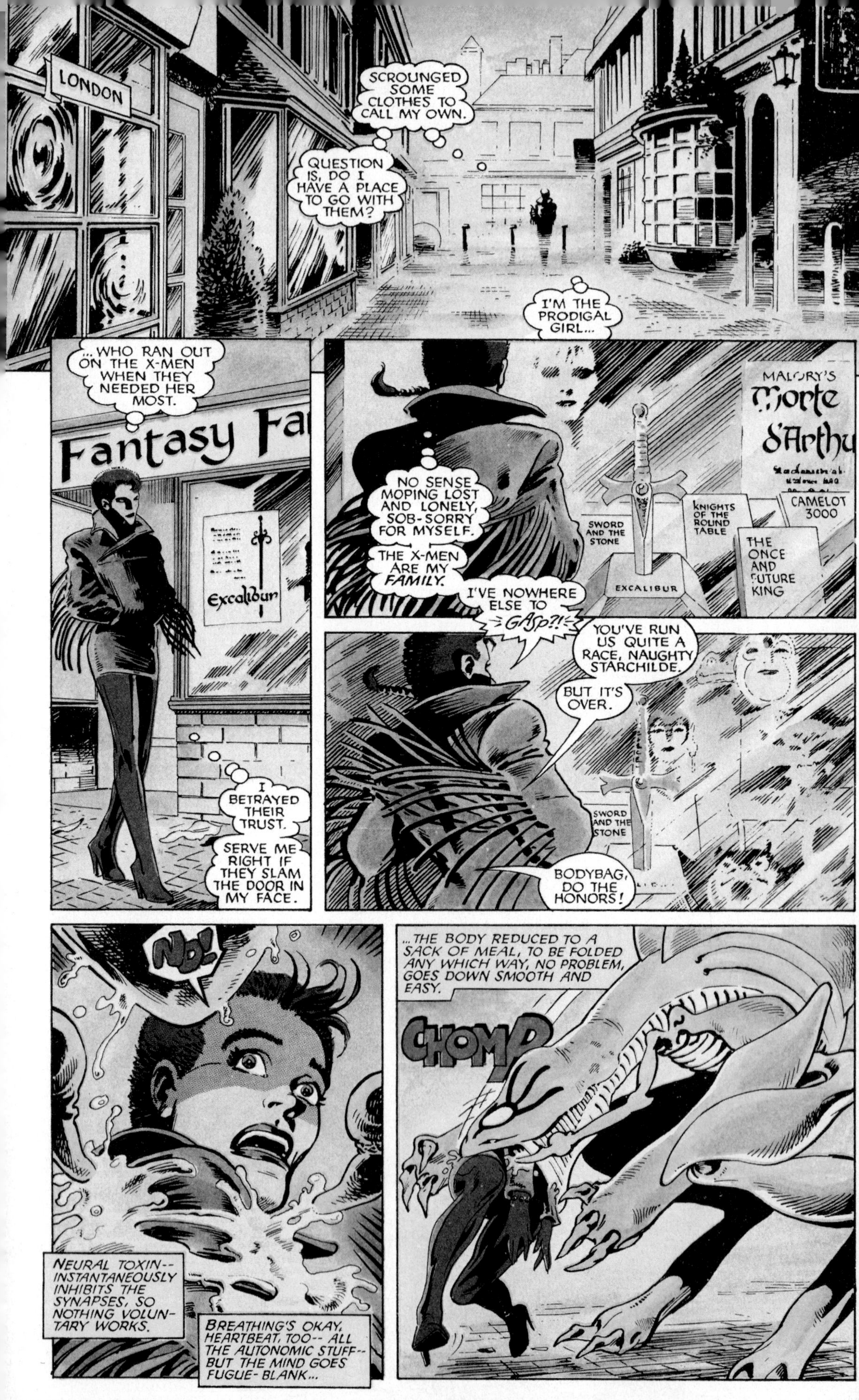
LONDON
SCROUNGED SOME CLOTHES TO CALL MY OWN.
QUESTION IS, DO I HAVE A PLACE TO GO WITH THEM?
I'M THE PRODIGAL GIRL...
...WHO RAN OUT ON THE X-MEN WHEN THEY NEEDED HER MOST.
Fantasy Fa
Excalibur
I BETRAYED THEIR TRUST.
SERVE ME RIGHT IF THEY SLAM THE DOOR IN MY FACE.
MALORY'S Morte d'Arthu
NO SENSE MOPING LOST AND LONELY, SOB-SORRY FOR MYSELF.
THE X-MEN ARE MY FAMILY.
I'VE NOWHERE ELSE TO
GASP?!
SWORD AND THE STONE
KNIGHTS OF THE ROUND TABLE
CAMELOT 3000
THE ONCE AND FUTURE KING
EXCALIBUR
YOU'VE RUN US QUITE A RACE, NAUGHTY STARCHILDE.
BUT IT'S OVER.
SWORD AND THE STONE
BODYBAG, DO THE HONORS!
NO!
NEURAL TOXIN-- INSTANTANEOUSLY INHIBITS THE SYNAPSES, SO NOTHING VOLUNTARY WORKS.
BREATHING'S OKAY, HEARTBEAT, TOO-- ALL THE AUTONOMIC STUFF-- BUT THE MIND GOES FUGUE-BLANK...
...THE BODY REDUCED TO A SACK OF MEAL, TO BE FOLDED ANY WHICH WAY, NO PROBLEM, GOES DOWN SMOOTH AND EASY.
CHOMP

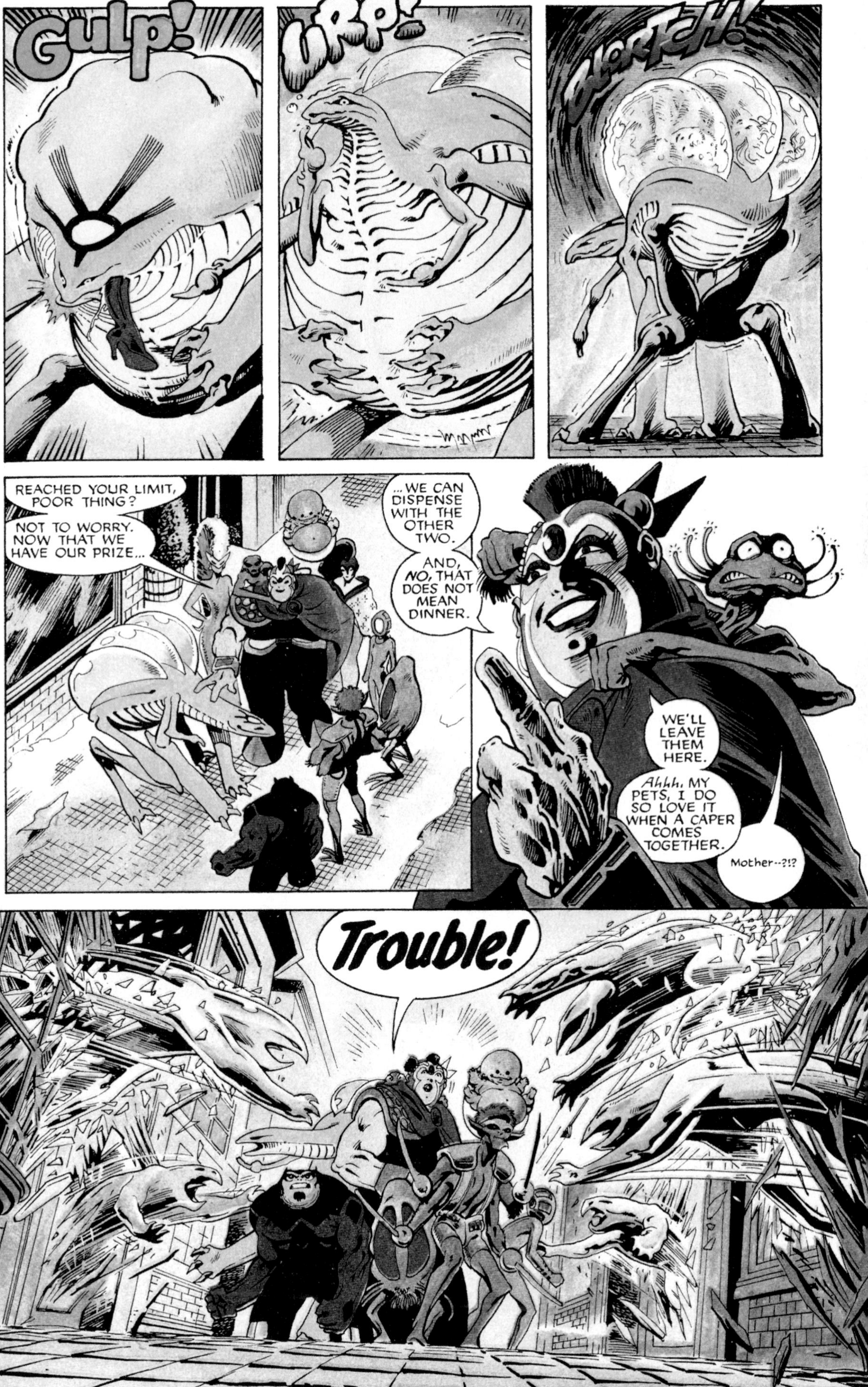

Gulp!
URP!
SKORTCH!
REACHED YOUR LIMIT, POOR THING?
NOT TO WORRY. NOW THAT WE HAVE OUR PRIZE...
...WE CAN DISPENSE WITH THE OTHER TWO.
AND, NO, THAT DOES NOT MEAN DINNER.
WE'LL LEAVE THEM HERE.
Ahhh, MY PETS, I DO SO LOVE IT WHEN A CAPER COMES TOGETHER.
Mother--?!?
Trouble!

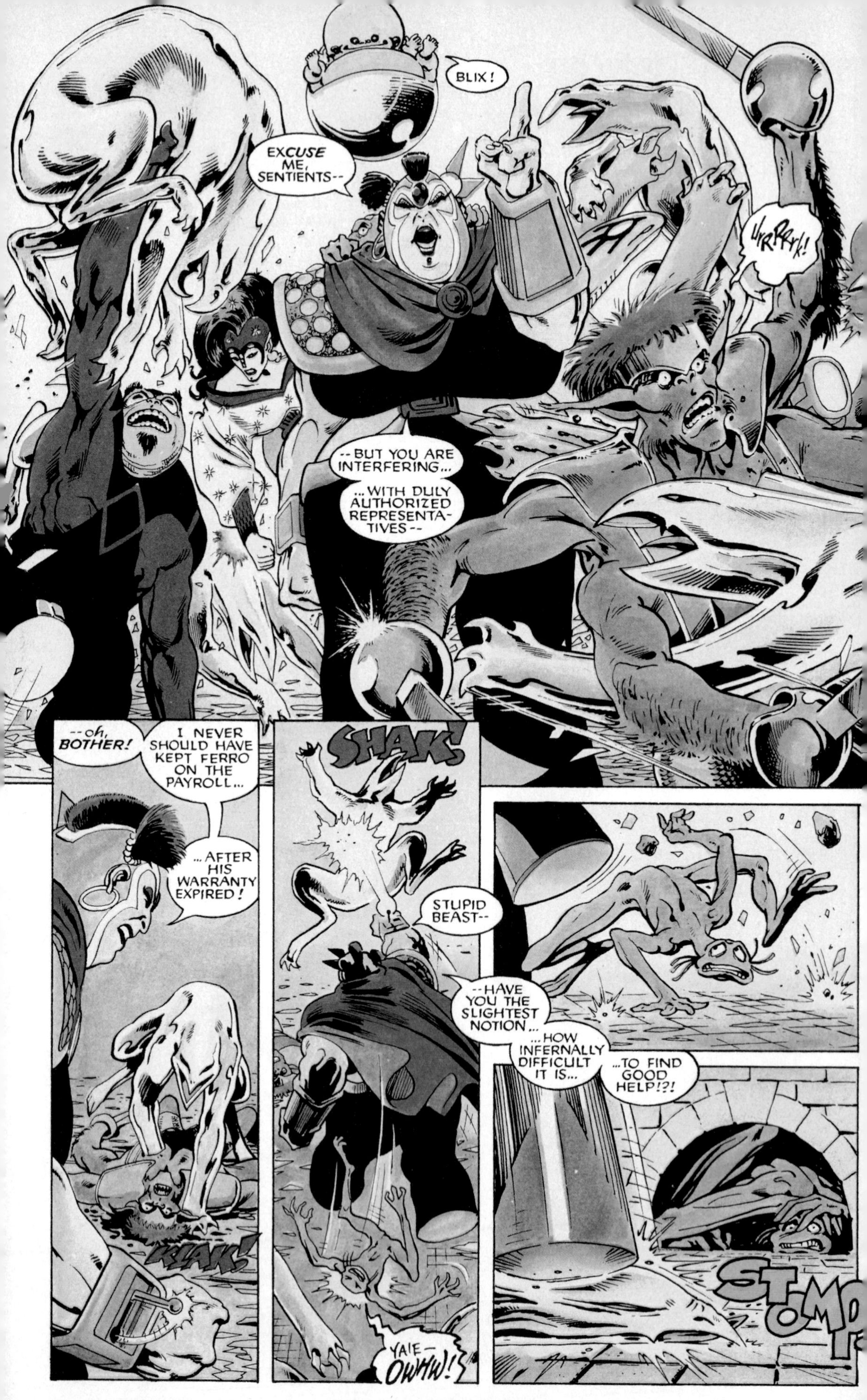
BLIX!
EXCUSE ME, SENTIENTS--
URRRRK!
--BUT YOU ARE INTERFERING...
...WITH DULY AUTHORIZED REPRESENTATIVES--
--oh, BOTHER!
I NEVER SHOULD HAVE KEPT FERRO ON THE PAYROLL...
...AFTER HIS WARRANTY EXPIRED!
KLAK!
SHAK!
STUPID BEAST--
--HAVE YOU THE SLIGHTEST NOTION...
...HOW INFERNALLY DIFFICULT IT IS...
...TO FIND GOOD HELP!?!
YAIE-OWHW!
STOMP

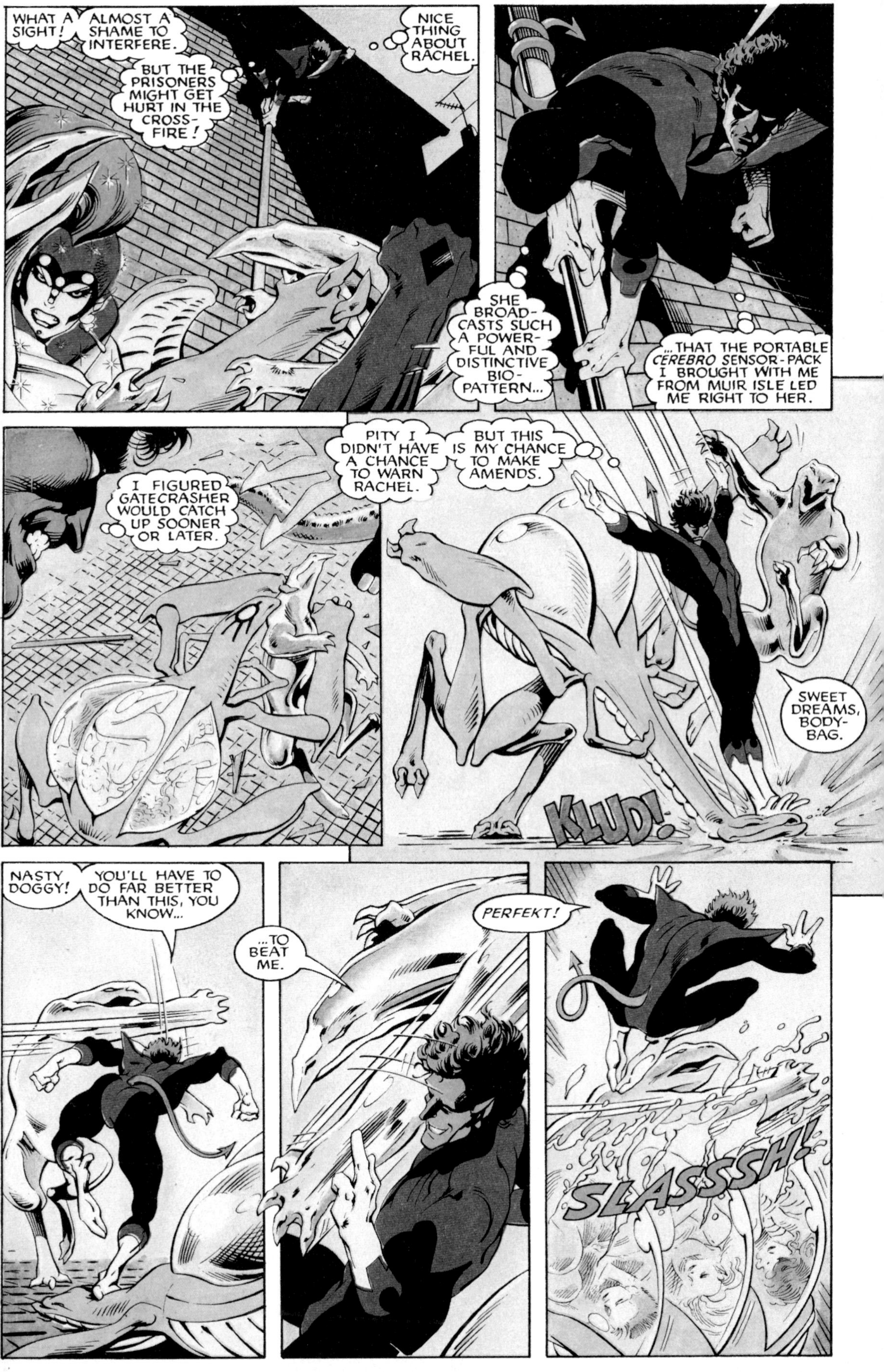
WHAT A SIGHT!
ALMOST A SHAME TO INTERFERE.
BUT THE PRISONERS MIGHT GET HURT IN THE CROSS-FIRE!
NICE THING ABOUT RACHEL.
SHE BROAD-CASTS SUCH A POWER-FUL AND DISTINCTIVE BIO-PATTERN...
...THAT THE PORTABLE CEREBRO SENSOR-PACK I BROUGHT WITH ME FROM MUIR ISLE LED ME RIGHT TO HER.
I FIGURED GATECRASHER WOULD CATCH UP SOONER OR LATER.
PITY I DIDN'T HAVE A CHANCE TO WARN RACHEL.
BUT THIS IS MY CHANCE TO MAKE AMENDS.
SWEET DREAMS, BODY-BAG.
KLUD!
NASTY DOGGY!
YOU'LL HAVE TO DO FAR BETTER THAN THIS, YOU KNOW...
...TO BEAT ME.
PERFEKT!
SLASSSH!

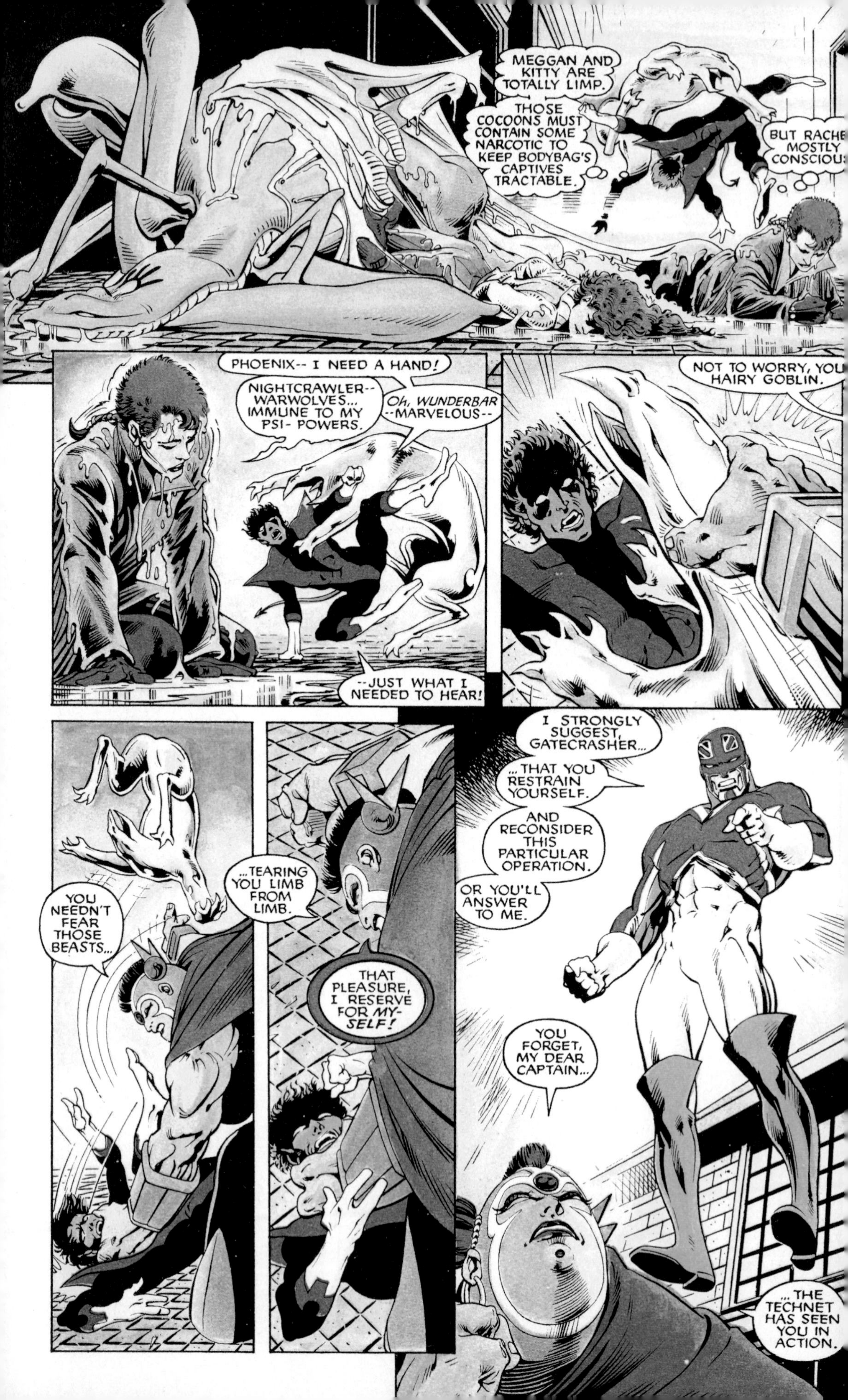
MEGGAN AND KITTY ARE TOTALLY LIMP.
THOSE COCOONS MUST CONTAIN SOME NARCOTIC TO KEEP BODYBAG'S CAPTIVES TRACTABLE.
BUT RACHE MOSTLY CONSCIOU
PHOENIX-- I NEED A HAND!
NIGHTCRAWLER-- WARWOLVES... IMMUNE TO MY PSI- POWERS.
Oh, WUNDERBAR --MARVELOUS--
--JUST WHAT I NEEDED TO HEAR!
NOT TO WORRY, YOU HAIRY GOBLIN.
YOU NEEDN'T FEAR THOSE BEASTS...
...TEARING YOU LIMB FROM LIMB.
THAT PLEASURE, I RESERVE FOR MY-SELF!
I STRONGLY SUGGEST, GATECRASHER...
...THAT YOU RESTRAIN YOURSELF.
AND RECONSIDER THIS PARTICULAR OPERATION.
OR YOU'LL ANSWER TO ME.
YOU FORGET, MY DEAR CAPTAIN...
...THE TECHNET HAS SEEN YOU IN ACTION.

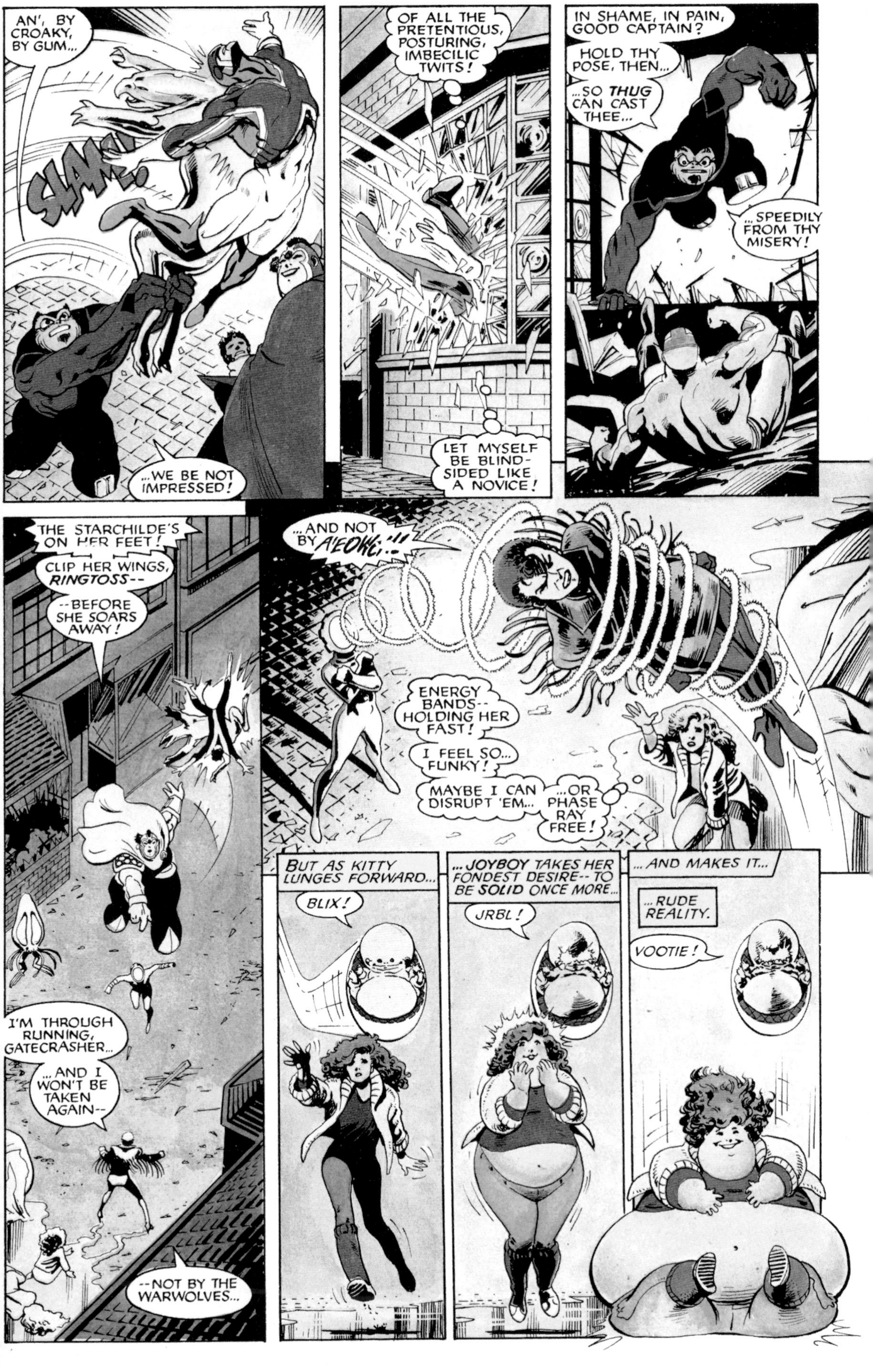
AN', BY CROAKY, BY GUM...
SLAM!
...WE BE NOT IMPRESSED!
OF ALL THE PRETENTIOUS, POSTURING, IMBECILIC TWITS!
LET MYSELF BE BLIND-SIDED LIKE A NOVICE!
IN SHAME, IN PAIN, GOOD CAPTAIN?
HOLD THY POSE, THEN...
...SO THUG CAN CAST THEE...
...SPEEDILY FROM THY MISERY!
THE STARCHILDE'S ON HER FEET!
CLIP HER WINGS, RINGTOSS--
--BEFORE SHE SOARS AWAY!
I'M THROUGH RUNNING, GATECRASHER...
...AND I WON'T BE TAKEN AGAIN--
--NOT BY THE WARWOLVES...
...AND NOT BY A'LEOKK!!
ENERGY BANDS-- HOLDING HER FAST!
I FEEL SO... FUNKY!
MAYBE I CAN DISRUPT 'EM...
...OR PHASE RAY FREE!
BUT AS KITTY LUNGES FORWARD...
BLIX!
...JOYBOY TAKES HER FONDEST DESIRE-- TO BE SOLID ONCE MORE...
JRBL!
...AND MAKES IT...
...RUDE REALITY.
VOOTIE!

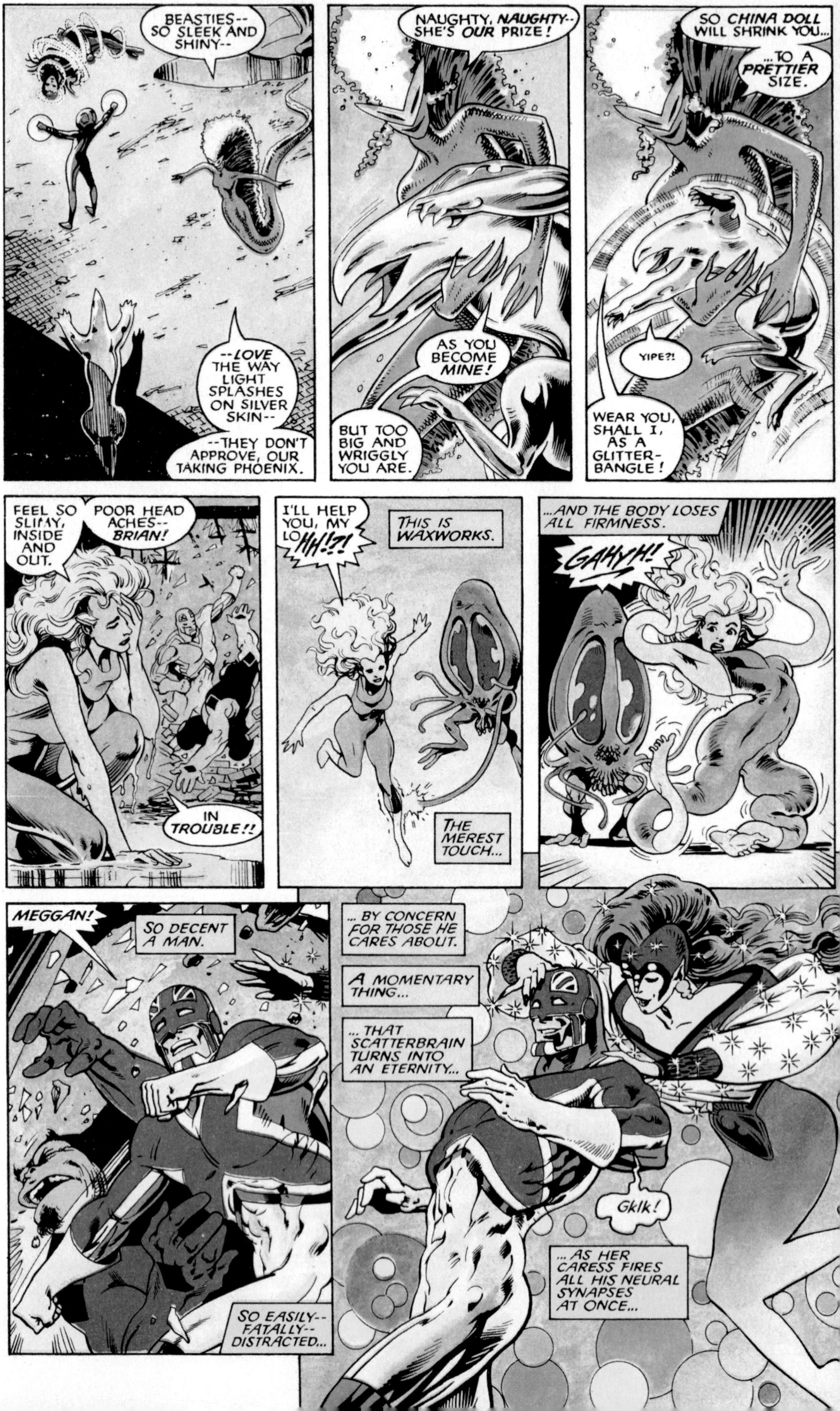
BEASTIES-- SO SLEEK AND SHINY--
--LOVE THE WAY LIGHT SPLASHES ON SILVER SKIN--
--THEY DON'T APPROVE, OUR TAKING PHOENIX.
NAUGHTY, NAUGHTY-- SHE'S OUR PRIZE!
AS YOU BECOME MINE!
BUT TOO BIG AND WRIGGLY YOU ARE.
SO CHINA DOLL WILL SHRINK YOU...
...TO A PRETTIER SIZE.
YIPE?!
WEAR YOU, SHALL I, AS A GLITTER-BANGLE!
FEEL SO SLIMY, INSIDE AND OUT.
POOR HEAD ACHES-- BRIAN!
IN TROUBLE!!
I'LL HELP YOU, MY LOHH!?!
THIS IS WAXWORKS.
THE MEREST TOUCH...
...AND THE BODY LOSES ALL FIRMNESS.
GAHYH!
MEGGAN!
SO DECENT A MAN.
SO EASILY-- FATALLY-- DISTRACTED...
...BY CONCERN FOR THOSE HE CARES ABOUT.
A MOMENTARY THING...
...THAT SCATTERBRAIN TURNS INTO AN ETERNITY...
Gklk!
...AS HER CARESS FIRES ALL HIS NEURAL SYNAPSES AT ONCE...

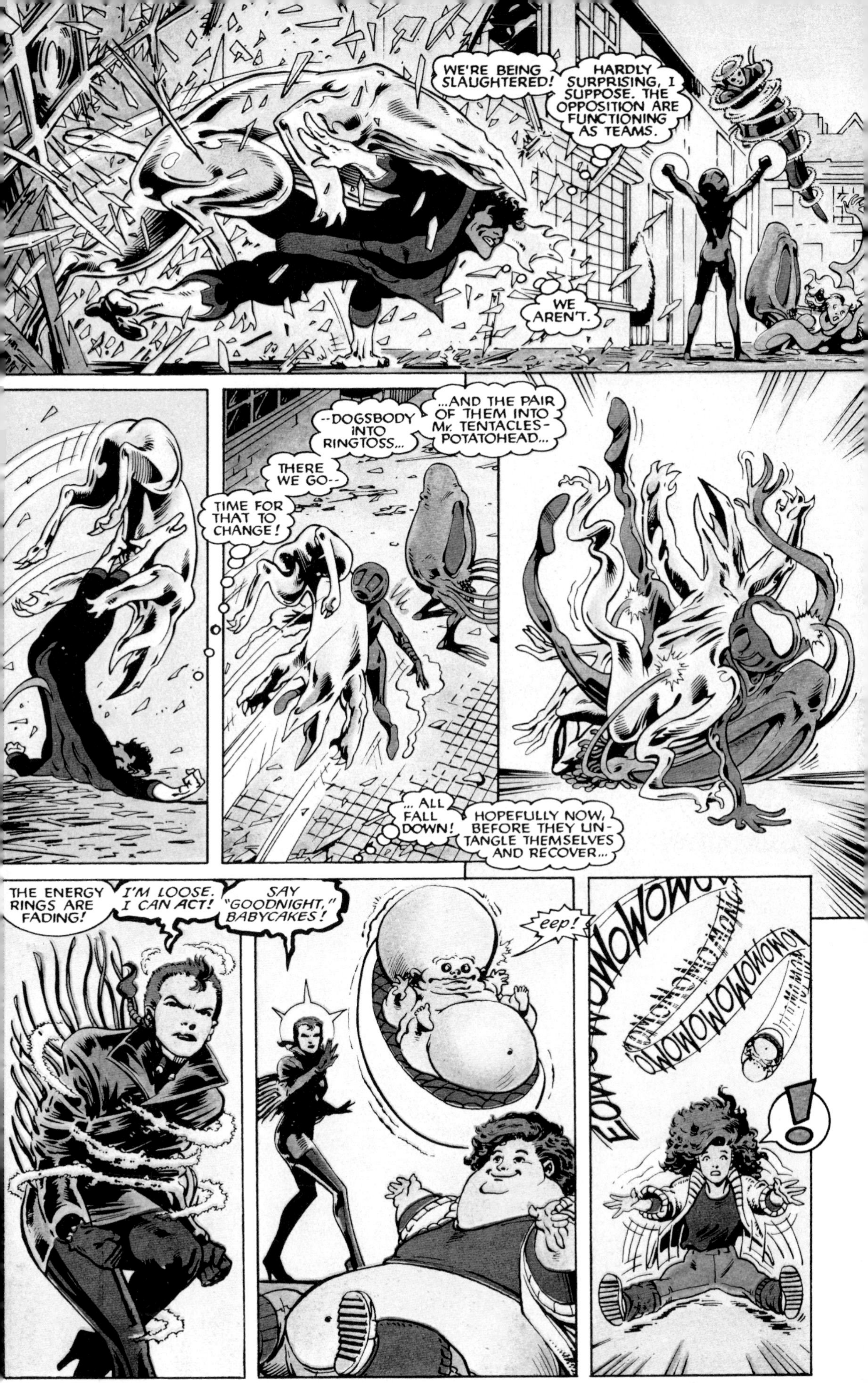
WE'RE BEING SLAUGHTERED!
HARDLY SURPRISING, I SUPPOSE. THE OPPOSITION ARE FUNCTIONING AS TEAMS.
WE AREN'T.
TIME FOR THAT TO CHANGE!
THERE WE GO--
--DOGSBODY INTO RINGTOSS...
...AND THE PAIR OF THEM INTO Mr. TENTACLES-POTATOHEAD...
...ALL FALL DOWN!
HOPEFULLY NOW, BEFORE THEY UNTANGLE THEMSELVES AND RECOVER...
THE ENERGY RINGS ARE FADING!
I'M LOOSE. I CAN ACT!
SAY "GOODNIGHT," BABYCAKES!
eep!
!

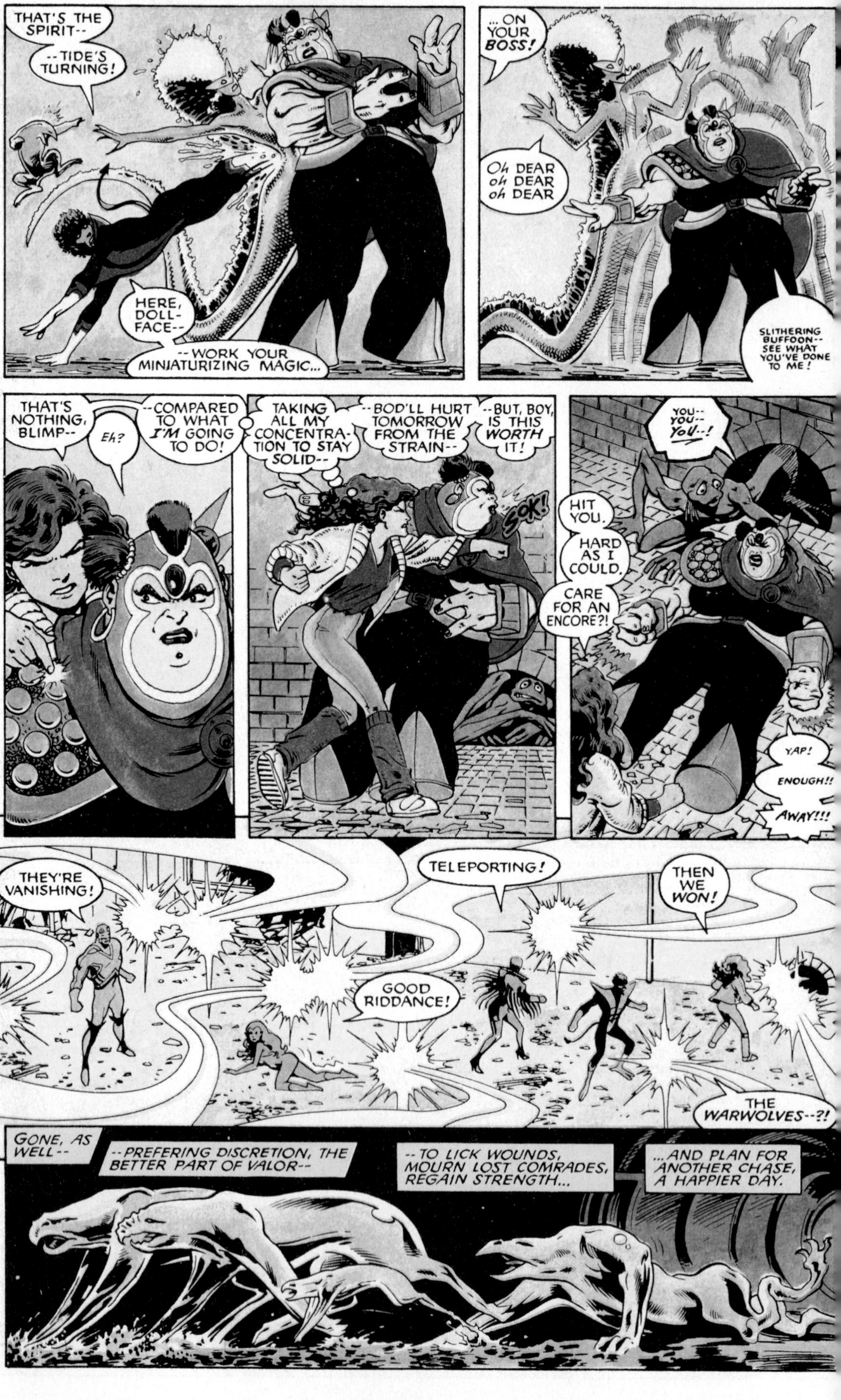
THAT'S THE SPIRIT--
--TIDE'S TURNING!
HERE, DOLL-FACE--
--WORK YOUR MINIATURIZING MAGIC...
...ON YOUR BOSS!
Oh DEAR oh DEAR oh DEAR
SLITHERING BUFFOON--SEE WHAT YOU'VE DONE TO ME!
THAT'S NOTHING, BLIMP--
Eh?
--COMPARED TO WHAT I'M GOING TO DO!
TAKING ALL MY CONCENTRATION TO STAY SOLID--
--BOD'LL HURT TOMORROW FROM THE STRAIN--
--BUT, BOY, IS THIS WORTH IT!
SOK!
YOU--YOU--YOU--!
HIT YOU.
HARD AS I COULD.
CARE FOR AN ENCORE?!
YAP!
ENOUGH!!
AWAY!!!
THEY'RE VANISHING!
TELEPORTING!
THEN WE WON!
GOOD RIDDANCE!
THE WARWOLVES--?!
GONE, AS WELL--
--PREFERING DISCRETION, THE BETTER PART OF VALOR--
--TO LICK WOUNDS, MOURN LOST COMRADES, REGAIN STRENGTH...
...AND PLAN FOR ANOTHER CHASE, A HAPPIER DAY.

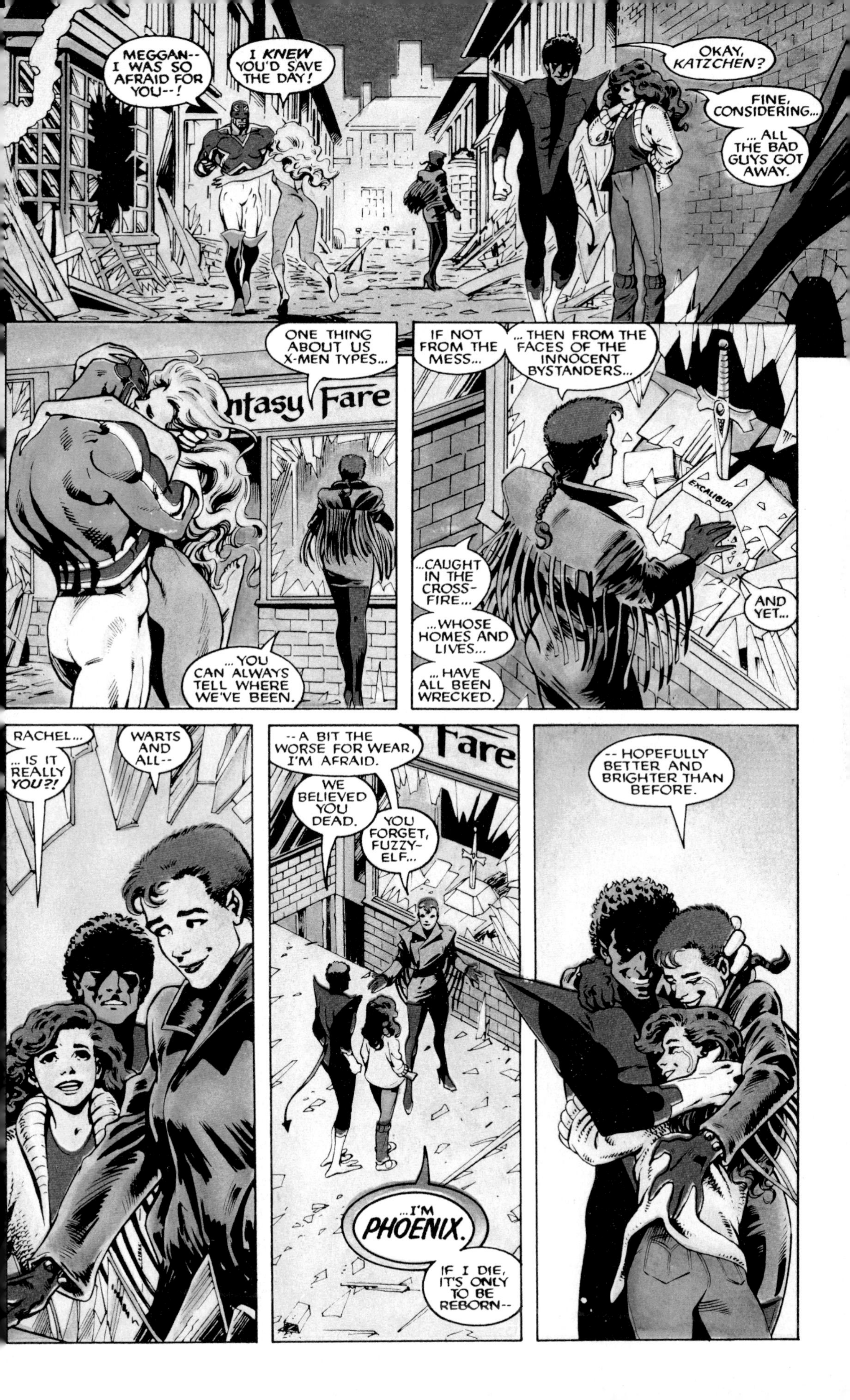
MEGGAN-- I WAS SO AFRAID FOR YOU--!
I KNEW YOU'D SAVE THE DAY!
OKAY, KATZCHEN?
FINE, CONSIDERING...
...ALL THE BAD GUYS GOT AWAY.
ONE THING ABOUT US X-MEN TYPES...
ntasy Fare
...YOU CAN ALWAYS TELL WHERE WE'VE BEEN.
IF NOT FROM THE MESS...
...THEN FROM THE FACES OF THE INNOCENT BYSTANDERS...
EXCALIBUR
...CAUGHT IN THE CROSS-FIRE...
...WHOSE HOMES AND LIVES...
...HAVE ALL BEEN WRECKED.
AND YET...
RACHEL...
...IS IT REALLY YOU?!
WARTS AND ALL--
--A BIT THE WORSE FOR WEAR, I'M AFRAID.
Fare
WE BELIEVED YOU DEAD.
YOU FORGET, FUZZY-ELF...
...I'M PHOENIX.
IF I DIE, IT'S ONLY TO BE REBORN--
--HOPEFULLY BETTER AND BRIGHTER THAN BEFORE.

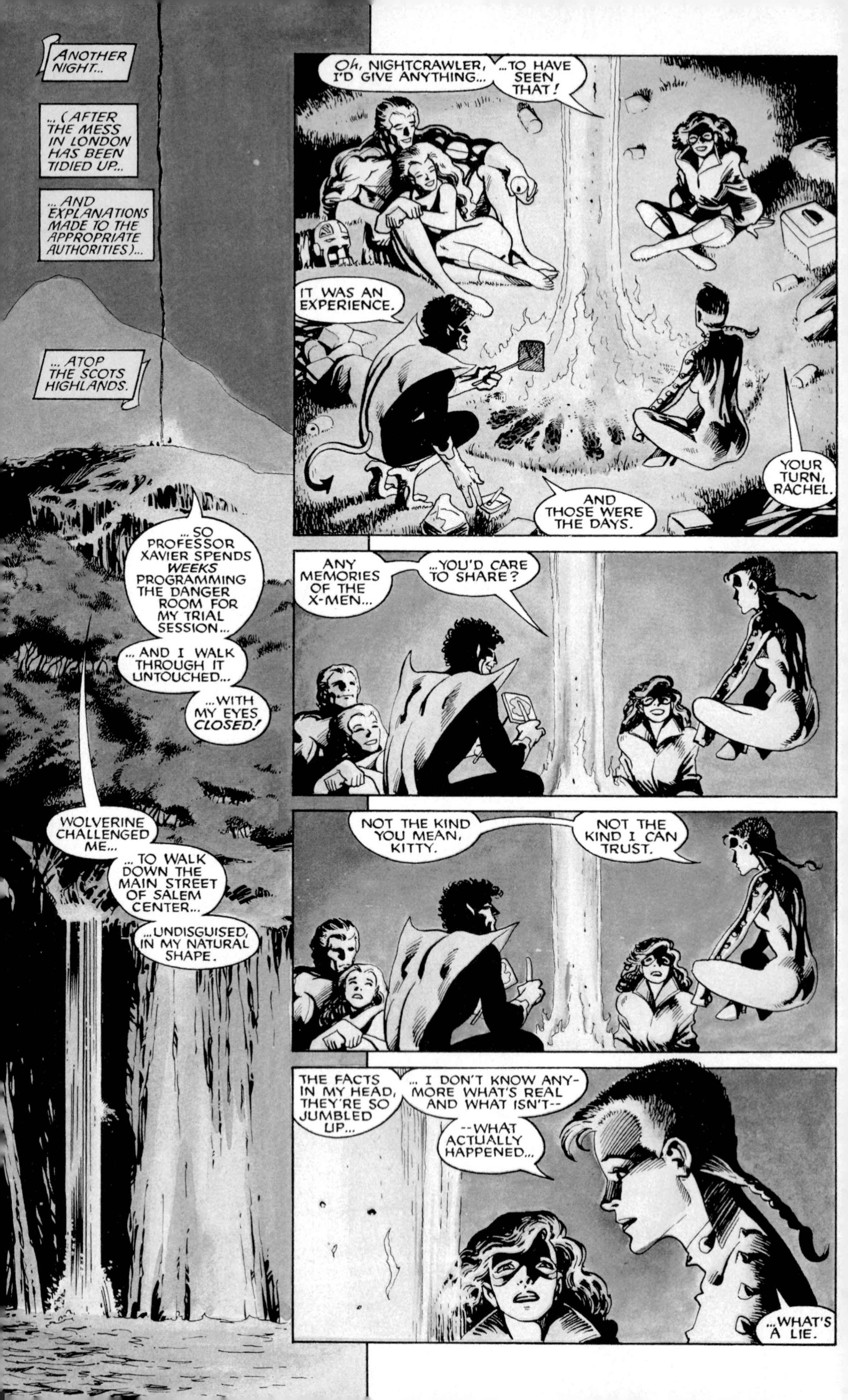
ANOTHER NIGHT...
...(AFTER THE MESS IN LONDON HAS BEEN TIDIED UP...
...AND EXPLANATIONS MADE TO THE APPROPRIATE AUTHORITIES)...
...ATOP THE SCOTS HIGHLANDS.
...SO PROFESSOR XAVIER SPENDS WEEKS PROGRAMMING THE DANGER ROOM FOR MY TRIAL SESSION...
...AND I WALK THROUGH IT UNTOUCHED...
...WITH MY EYES CLOSED!
WOLVERINE CHALLENGED ME...
...TO WALK DOWN THE MAIN STREET OF SALEM CENTER...
...UNDISGUISED, IN MY NATURAL SHAPE.
Oh, NIGHTCRAWLER, I'D GIVE ANYTHING...
...TO HAVE SEEN THAT!
IT WAS AN EXPERIENCE.
AND THOSE WERE THE DAYS.
YOUR TURN, RACHEL.
ANY MEMORIES OF THE X-MEN...
...YOU'D CARE TO SHARE?
NOT THE KIND YOU MEAN, KITTY.
NOT THE KIND I CAN TRUST.
THE FACTS IN MY HEAD, THEY'RE SO JUMBLED UP...
...I DON'T KNOW ANY-MORE WHAT'S REAL AND WHAT ISN'T--
--WHAT ACTUALLY HAPPENED...
...WHAT'S A LIE.

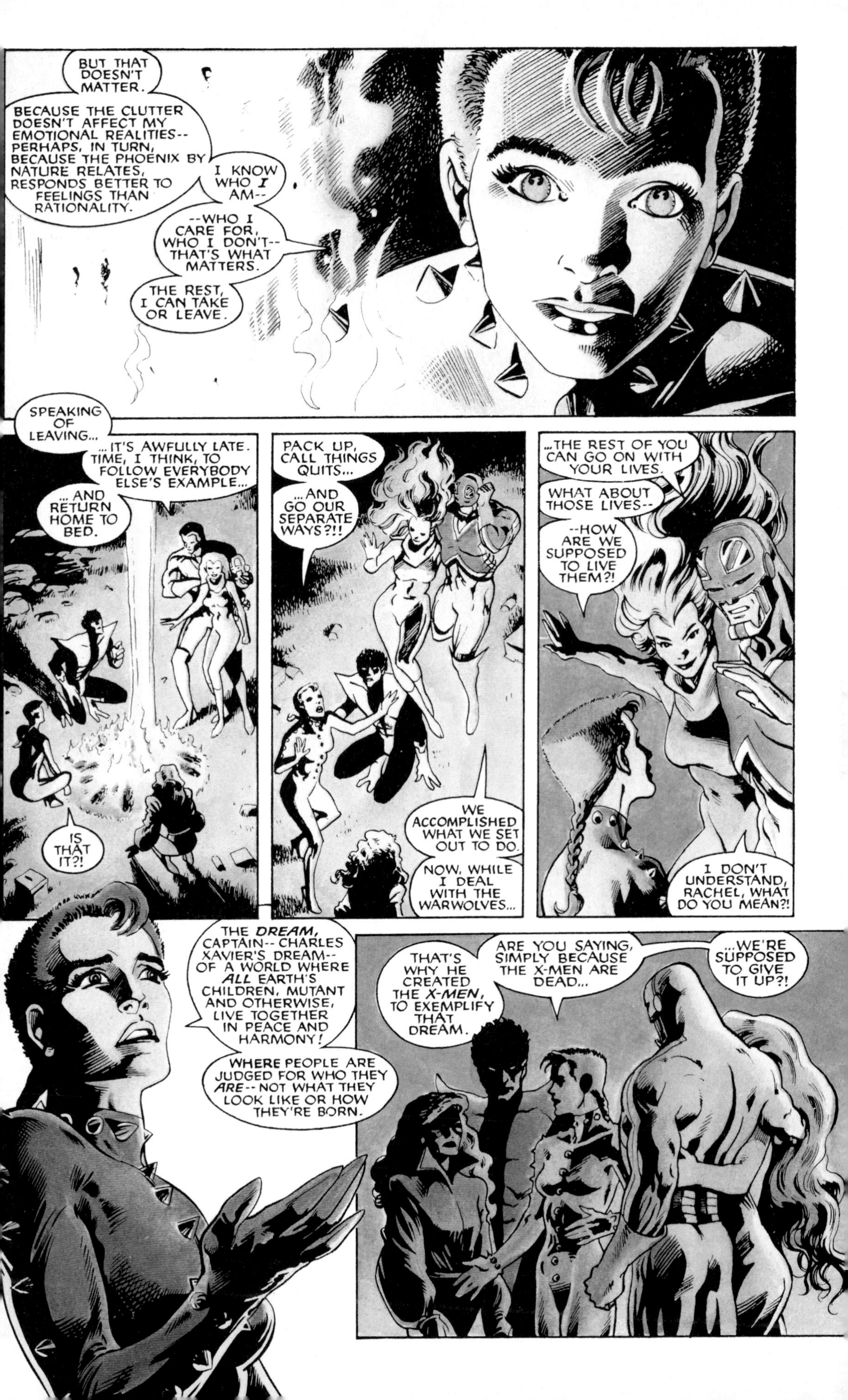
BUT THAT DOESN'T MATTER.
BECAUSE THE CLUTTER DOESN'T AFFECT MY EMOTIONAL REALITIES-- PERHAPS, IN TURN, BECAUSE THE PHOENIX BY NATURE RELATES, RESPONDS BETTER TO FEELINGS THAN RATIONALITY.
I KNOW WHO *I* AM--
--WHO I CARE FOR, WHO I DON'T-- THAT'S WHAT MATTERS.
THE REST, I CAN TAKE OR LEAVE.
SPEAKING OF LEAVING...
...IT'S AWFULLY LATE. TIME, I THINK, TO FOLLOW EVERYBODY ELSE'S EXAMPLE...
...AND RETURN HOME TO BED.
IS THAT IT?!
PACK UP, CALL THINGS QUITS...
...AND GO OUR SEPARATE WAYS?!!
WE ACCOMPLISHED WHAT WE SET OUT TO DO.
NOW, WHILE I DEAL WITH THE WARWOLVES...
...THE REST OF YOU CAN GO ON WITH YOUR LIVES.
WHAT ABOUT THOSE LIVES--
--HOW ARE WE SUPPOSED TO LIVE THEM?!
I DON'T UNDERSTAND, RACHEL, WHAT DO YOU MEAN?!
THE *DREAM*, CAPTAIN-- CHARLES XAVIER'S DREAM-- OF A WORLD WHERE *ALL* EARTH'S CHILDREN, MUTANT AND OTHERWISE, LIVE TOGETHER IN PEACE AND HARMONY!
WHERE PEOPLE ARE JUDGED FOR WHO THEY *ARE*-- NOT WHAT THEY LOOK LIKE OR HOW THEY'RE BORN.
THAT'S WHY HE CREATED THE *X-MEN*, TO EXEMPLIFY THAT DREAM.
ARE YOU SAYING, SIMPLY BECAUSE THE X-MEN ARE DEAD...
...WE'RE SUPPOSED TO GIVE IT UP?!

THE DREAM *WE* HAD, NIGHT-CRAWLER-- REMEMBER, BACK BEFORE THIS CRAZY CAPER BEGAN-- IN IT, RACHEL SAID TO ME:

"...WHEN THE REALITY NO LONGER EXISTS, EXPLOITERS CAN TAKE THE LEGEND...

"...AND MAKE IT WHATEVER THEY WANT...

"...GOOD OR BAD."

ARE YOU SUGGESTING WE TAKE THE X-MEN'S PLACE?

NOBODY CAN DO THAT. BUT *KING ARTHUR* HAD A DREAM, TOO.

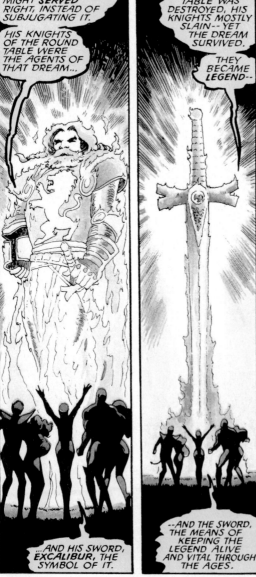

OF A WORLD WHERE MIGHT *SERVED* RIGHT, INSTEAD OF SUBJUGATING IT.

HIS KNIGHTS OF THE ROUND TABLE WERE THE AGENTS OF THAT DREAM...

...AND HIS SWORD, EXCALIBUR, THE SYMBOL OF IT.

HE DIED, THE TABLE WAS DESTROYED, HIS KNIGHTS MOSTLY SLAIN-- YET THE DREAM SURVIVED.

THEY BECAME *LEGEND*--

--AND THE SWORD, THE MEANS OF KEEPING THE LEGEND ALIVE AND VITAL THROUGH THE AGES.

THE X-MEN THOUGHT ENOUGH OF PROFESSOR XAVIER'S DREAM TO OFFER UP THEIR LIVES. IS IT SO MUCH TO ASK THAT WE FIGHT TO PRESERVE IT?

THE SWORD, EXCALIBUR, REPRESENTED *HOPE*.

IT WAS LIGHT IN THE DARKNESS OF FEAR AND IGNORANCE AND HATE.

DO WE WANT-- --HAVE WE THE RIGHT-- --TO SNUFF IT OUT?

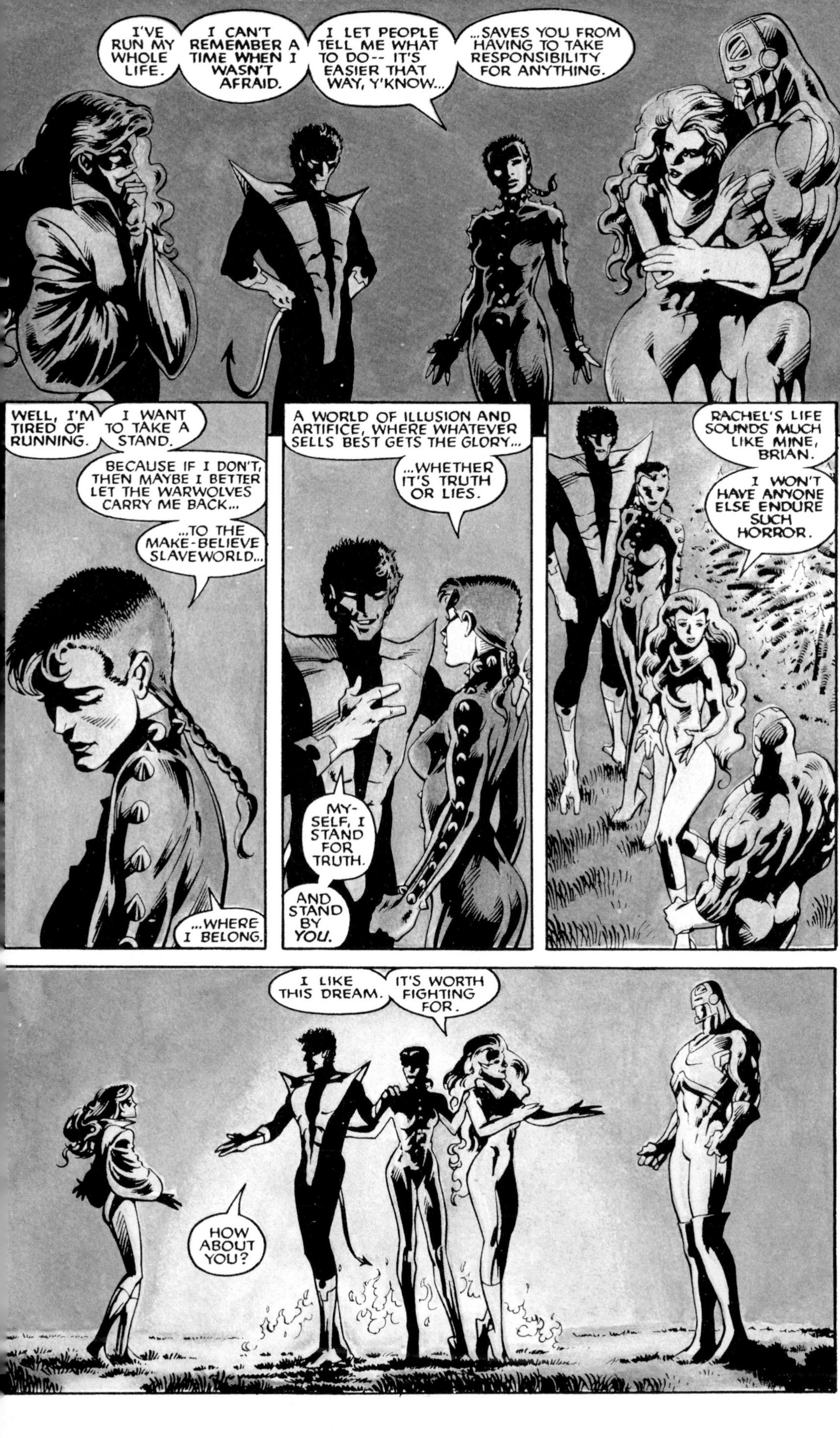
I'VE RUN MY WHOLE LIFE.
I CAN'T REMEMBER A TIME WHEN I WASN'T AFRAID.
I LET PEOPLE TELL ME WHAT TO DO-- IT'S EASIER THAT WAY, Y'KNOW...
...SAVES YOU FROM HAVING TO TAKE RESPONSIBILITY FOR ANYTHING.
WELL, I'M TIRED OF RUNNING.
I WANT TO TAKE A STAND.
BECAUSE IF I DON'T, THEN MAYBE I BETTER LET THE WARWOLVES CARRY ME BACK...
...TO THE MAKE-BELIEVE SLAVEWORLD...
...WHERE I BELONG.
A WORLD OF ILLUSION AND ARTIFICE, WHERE WHATEVER SELLS BEST GETS THE GLORY...
...WHETHER IT'S TRUTH OR LIES.
MY-SELF, I STAND FOR TRUTH.
AND STAND BY *YOU*.
RACHEL'S LIFE SOUNDS MUCH LIKE MINE, BRIAN.
I WON'T HAVE ANYONE ELSE ENDURE SUCH HORROR.
I LIKE THIS DREAM.
IT'S WORTH FIGHTING FOR.
HOW ABOUT YOU?

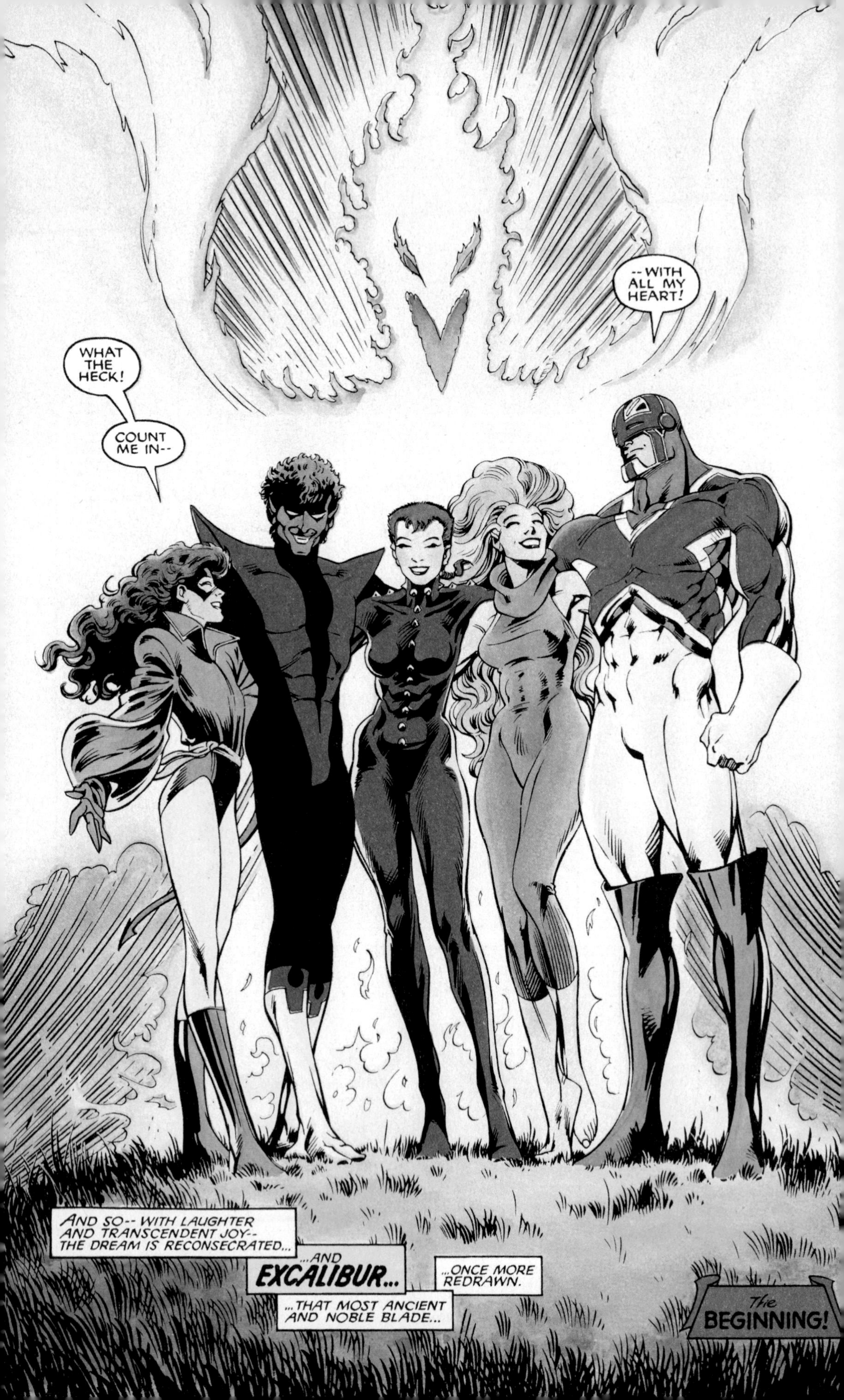
WHAT THE HECK!
COUNT ME IN--
--WITH ALL MY HEART!
AND SO-- WITH LAUGHTER AND TRANSCENDENT JOY-- THE DREAM IS RECONSECRATED...
...AND EXCALIBUR...
...THAT MOST ANCIENT AND NOBLE BLADE...
...ONCE MORE REDRAWN.
The BEGINNING!

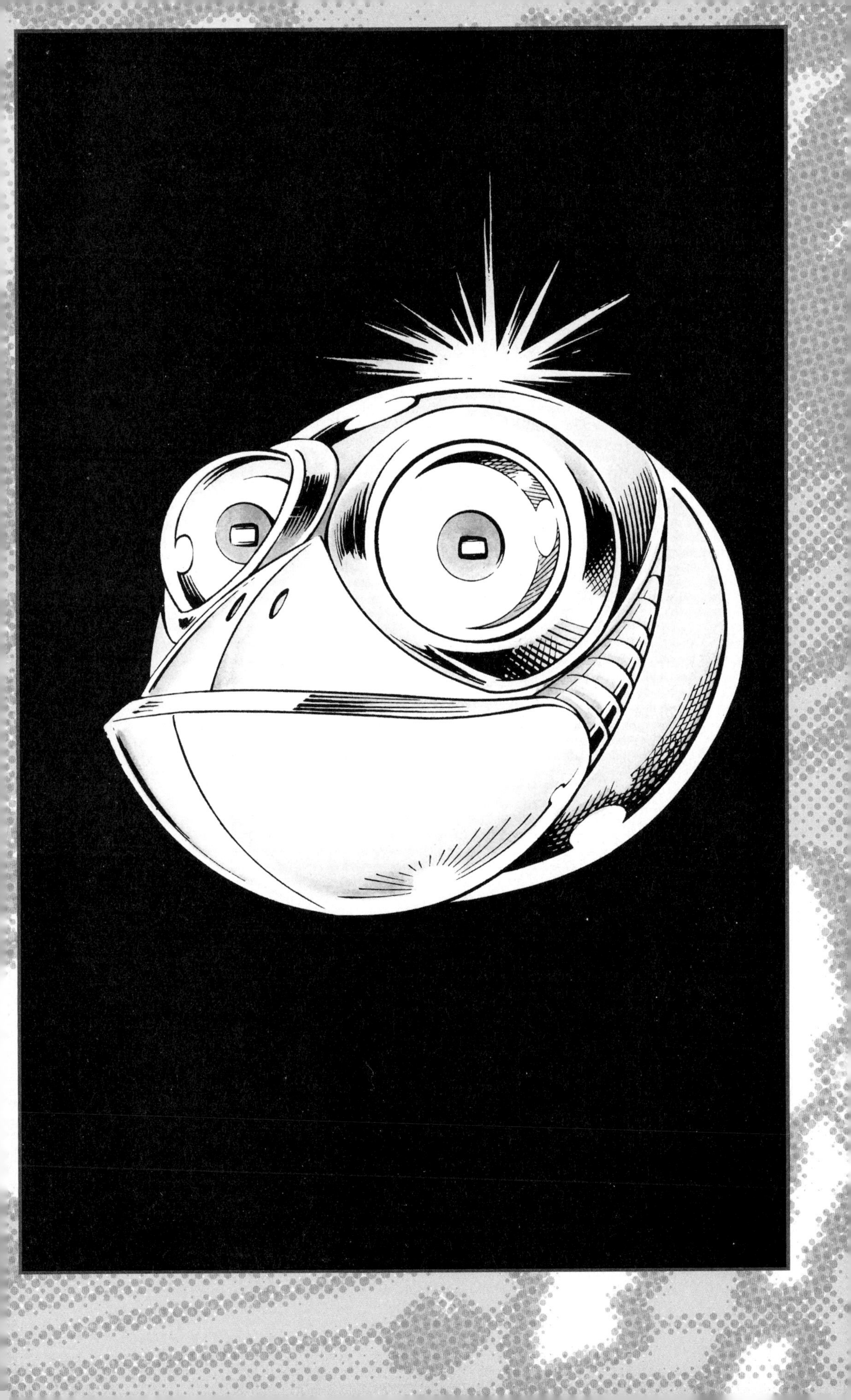

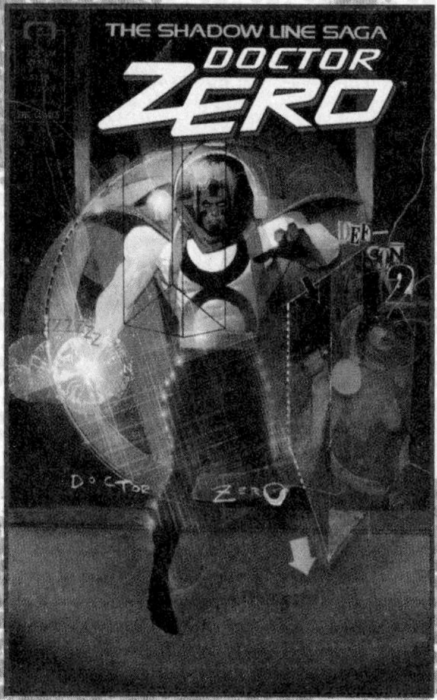
THE SHADOW LINE SAGA
DOCTOR
ZERO

DOCTOR ZERO #1, published in February 1988, introduced the manipulative Shadow Dweller in an ongoing Epic series; it also debuted the new Shadowline imprint, a shared super hero universe aimed at mature readers.

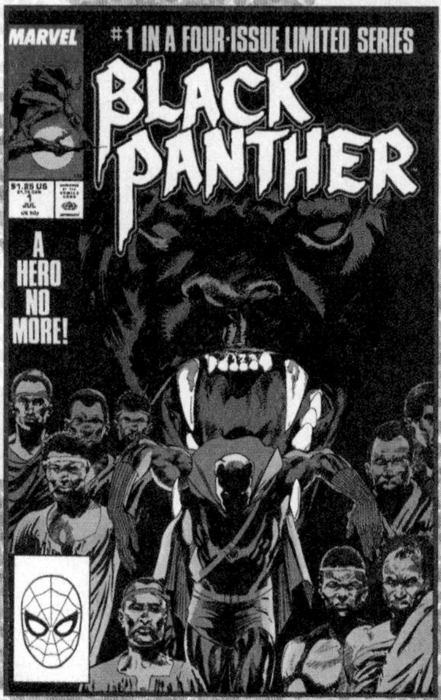
MARVEL
#1 IN A FOUR-ISSUE LIMITED SERIES
BLACK PANTHER
$1.25 US
A HERO NO MORE!

BLACK PANTHER #1, published in March 1988, began the Wakandan hero's new miniseries.

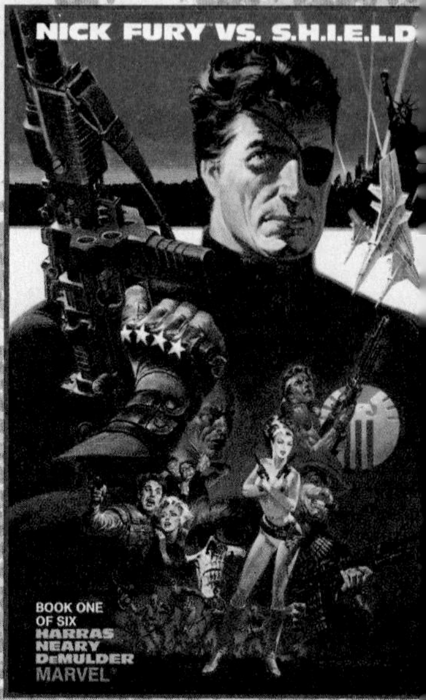
NICK FURY VS. S.H.I.E.L.D
BOOK ONE OF SIX
HARRAS
NEARY
DeMULDER
MARVEL

NICK FURY VS. S.H.I.E.L.D. #1, published in Marc 1988, began the spymaster's new miniseries.

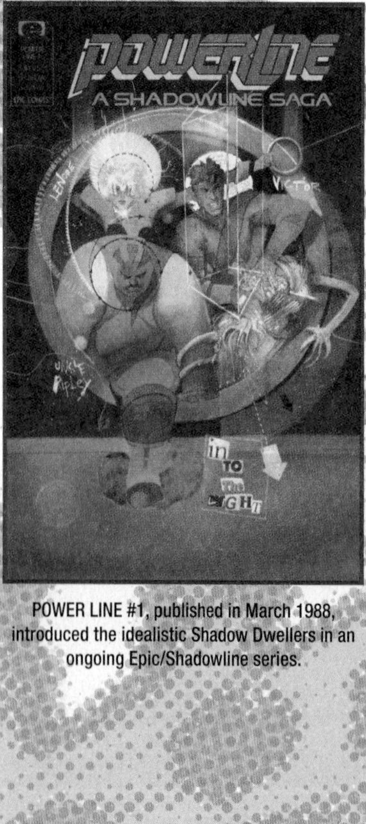
POWERLINE
A SHADOWLINE SAGA

POWER LINE #1, published in March 1988, introduced the idealistic Shadow Dwellers in an ongoing Epic/Shadowline series.

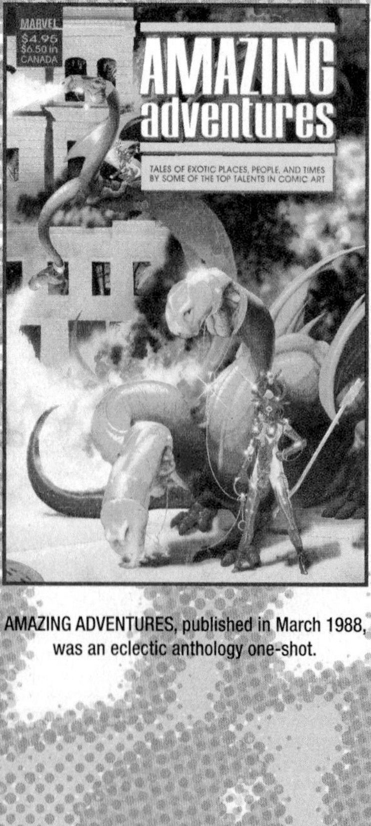
MARVEL
$4.95
$6.50 in CANADA
AMAZING
adventures
TALES OF EXOTIC PLACES, PEOPLE, AND TIMES BY SOME OF THE TOP TALENTS IN COMIC ART

AMAZING ADVENTURES, published in March 1988, was an eclectic anthology one-shot.

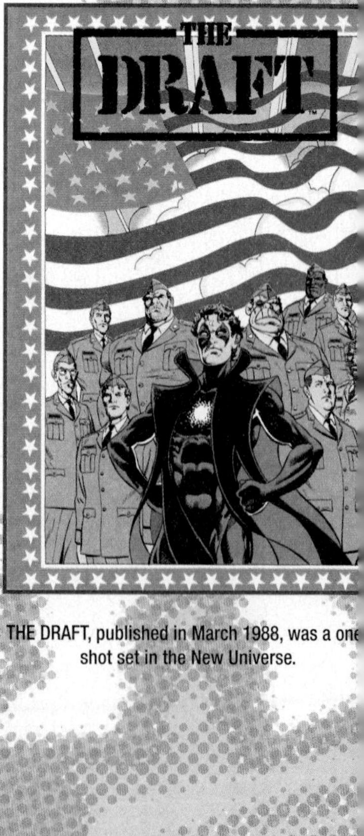
THE
DRAFT

THE DRAFT, published in March 1988, was a one shot set in the New Universe.

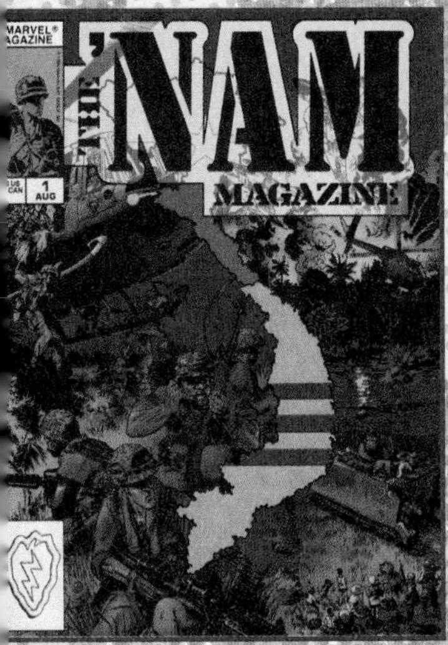
MARVEL
AGAZINE
THE
'NAM
MAGAZINE
1
AUG

'NAM MAGAZINE #1, published in April 1988, egan an ongoing magazine-sized reprint series.

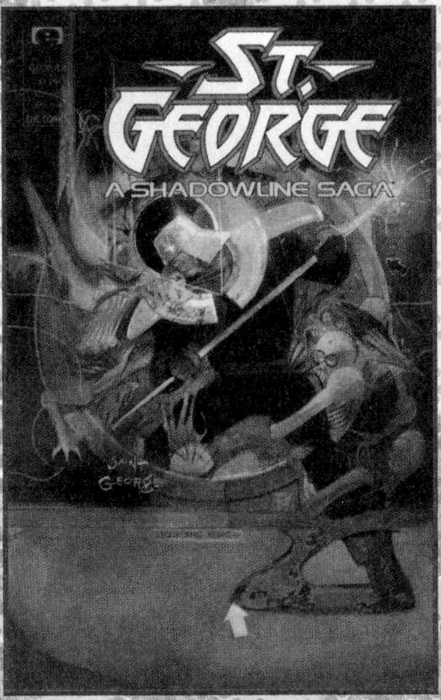
ST. GEORGE
A SHADOWLINE SAGA

ST. GEORGE #1, published in April 1988, introduced the armored knight in an ongoing Epic/Shadowline series.

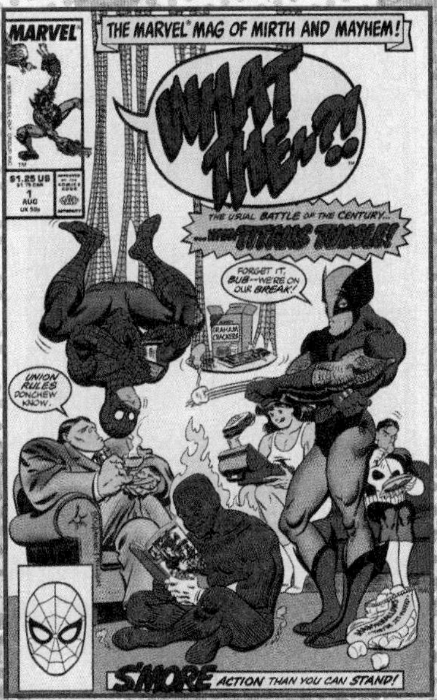
MARVEL
THE MARVEL MAG OF MIRTH AND MAYHEM!
WHAT THE--?!
$1.25 US
1
AUG
THE USUAL BATTLE OF THE CENTURY...
FORGET IT, BUB--WE'RE ON OUR BREAK!
GRAHAM CRACKERS
UNION RULES DONCHEW KNOW.
S'MORE ACTION THAN YOU CAN STAND!

WHAT THE--?! #1, published in April 1988, began a humor miniseries that parodied the Marvel Universe.

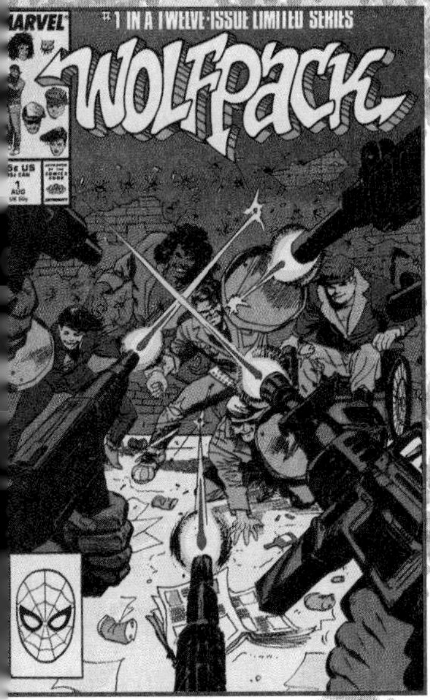
MARVEL
#1 IN A TWELVE-ISSUE LIMITED SERIES
WOLFPACK
1
AUG

VOLFPACK #1, published in April 1988, began the inner-city teens' miniseries.

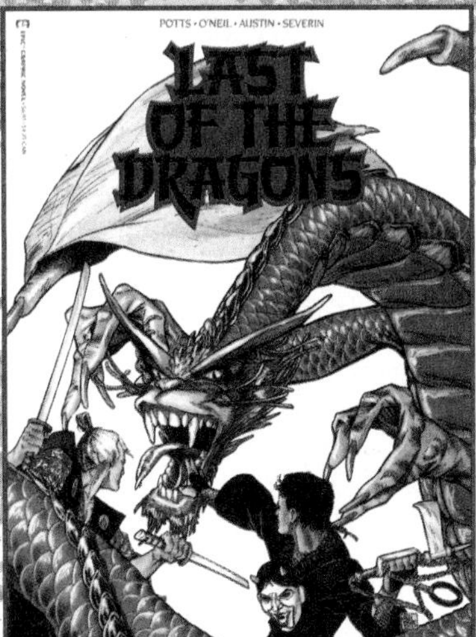
POTTS • O'NEIL • AUSTIN • SEVERIN
LAST OF THE DRAGONS

LAST OF THE DRAGONS, published in April 1988, was an Epic Graphic Novel reprint one-shot.

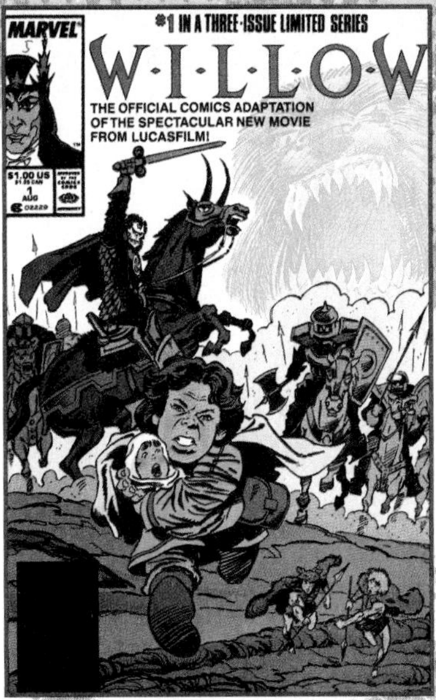
#1 IN A THREE-ISSUE LIMITED SERIES
MARVEL
W·I·L·L·O·W
THE OFFICIAL COMICS ADAPTATION OF THE SPECTACULAR NEW MOVIE FROM LUCASFILM!
$1.00 US
1
AUG

WILLOW #1, published in April 1988, began a miniseries reprinting Marvel's film adaptation.

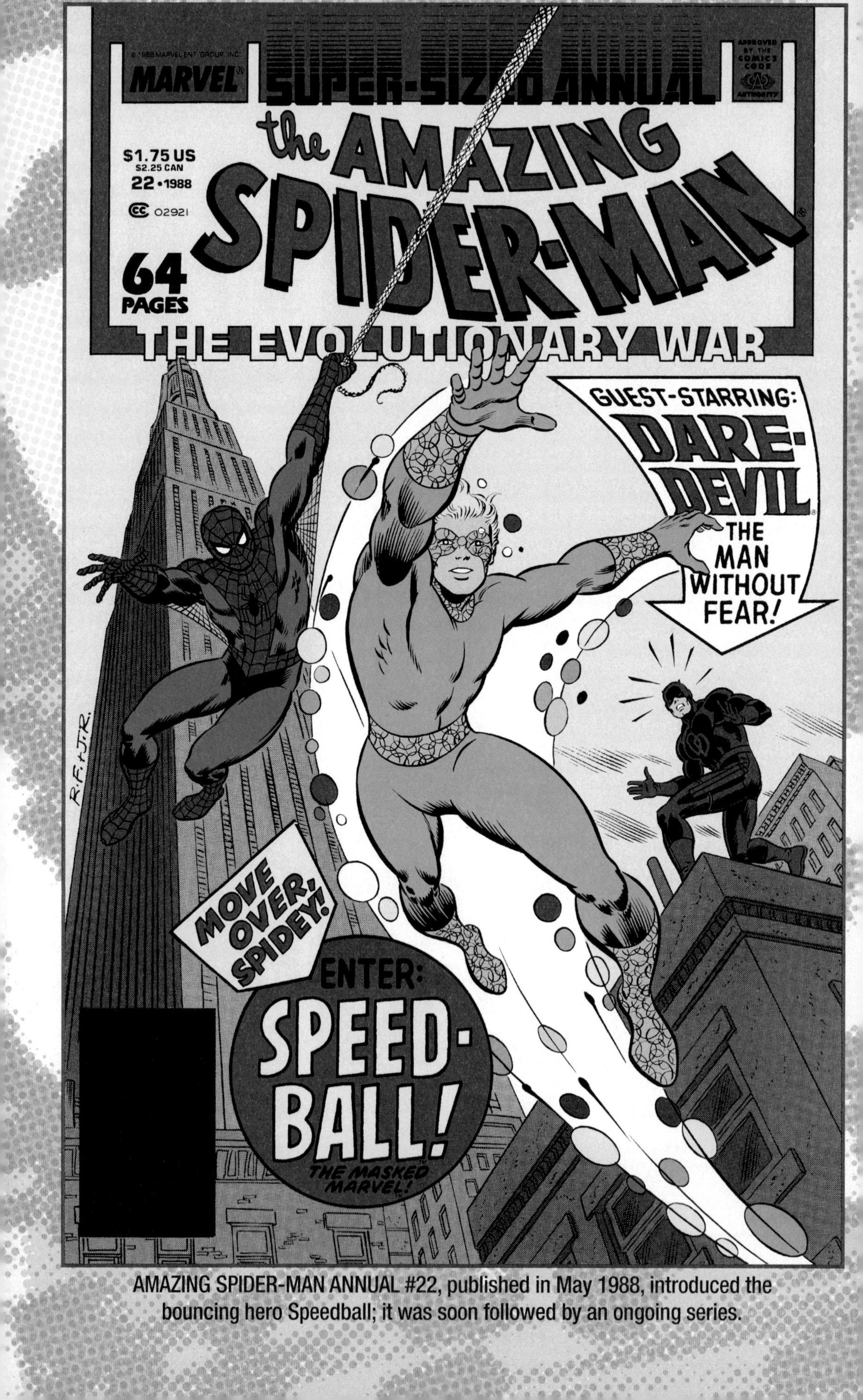
© 1988 MARVEL ENT. GROUP, INC.
MARVEL
SUPER-SIZED ANNUAL
APPROVED BY THE COMICS CODE AUTHORITY
the AMAZING SPIDER-MAN
$1.75 US
$2.25 CAN
22 • 1988
CC 02921
64 PAGES
THE EVOLUTIONARY WAR
GUEST-STARRING: DARE-DEVIL THE MAN WITHOUT FEAR!
R.F. + J.R.
MOVE OVER, SPIDEY!
ENTER: SPEED-BALL!
THE MASKED MARVEL!

AMAZING SPIDER-MAN ANNUAL #22, published in May 1988, introduced the bouncing hero Speedball; it was soon followed by an ongoing series.

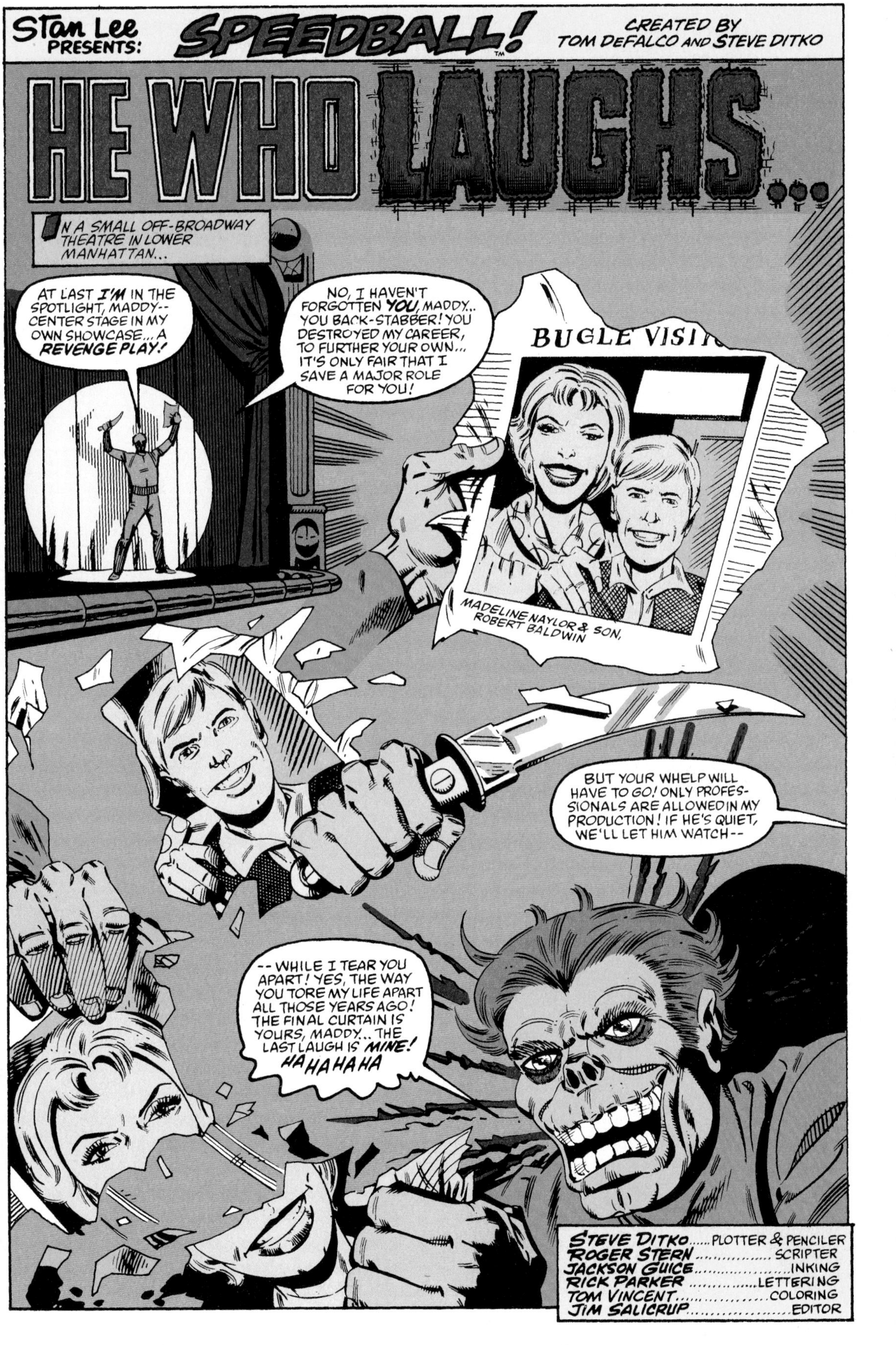
Stan Lee PRESENTS:
SPEEDBALL!
CREATED BY TOM DEFALCO AND STEVE DITKO
HE WHO LAUGHS...
IN A SMALL OFF-BROADWAY THEATRE IN LOWER MANHATTAN...
AT LAST I'M IN THE SPOTLIGHT, MADDY-- CENTER STAGE IN MY OWN SHOWCASE... A REVENGE PLAY!
NO, I HAVEN'T FORGOTTEN YOU, MADDY.. YOU BACK-STABBER! YOU DESTROYED MY CAREER, TO FURTHER YOUR OWN... IT'S ONLY FAIR THAT I SAVE A MAJOR ROLE FOR YOU!
BUGLE VISIT
MADELINE NAYLOR & SON, ROBERT BALDWIN
BUT YOUR WHELP WILL HAVE TO GO! ONLY PROFES-SIONALS ARE ALLOWED IN MY PRODUCTION! IF HE'S QUIET, WE'LL LET HIM WATCH--
--WHILE I TEAR YOU APART! YES, THE WAY YOU TORE MY LIFE APART ALL THOSE YEARS AGO! THE FINAL CURTAIN IS YOURS, MADDY... THE LAST LAUGH IS MINE! HA HA HA HA HA
STEVE DITKO......PLOTTER & PENCILER
ROGER STERN................SCRIPTER
JACKSON GUICE....................INKING
RICK PARKER...............LETTERING
TOM VINCENT..................COLORING
JIM SALICRUP........................EDITOR

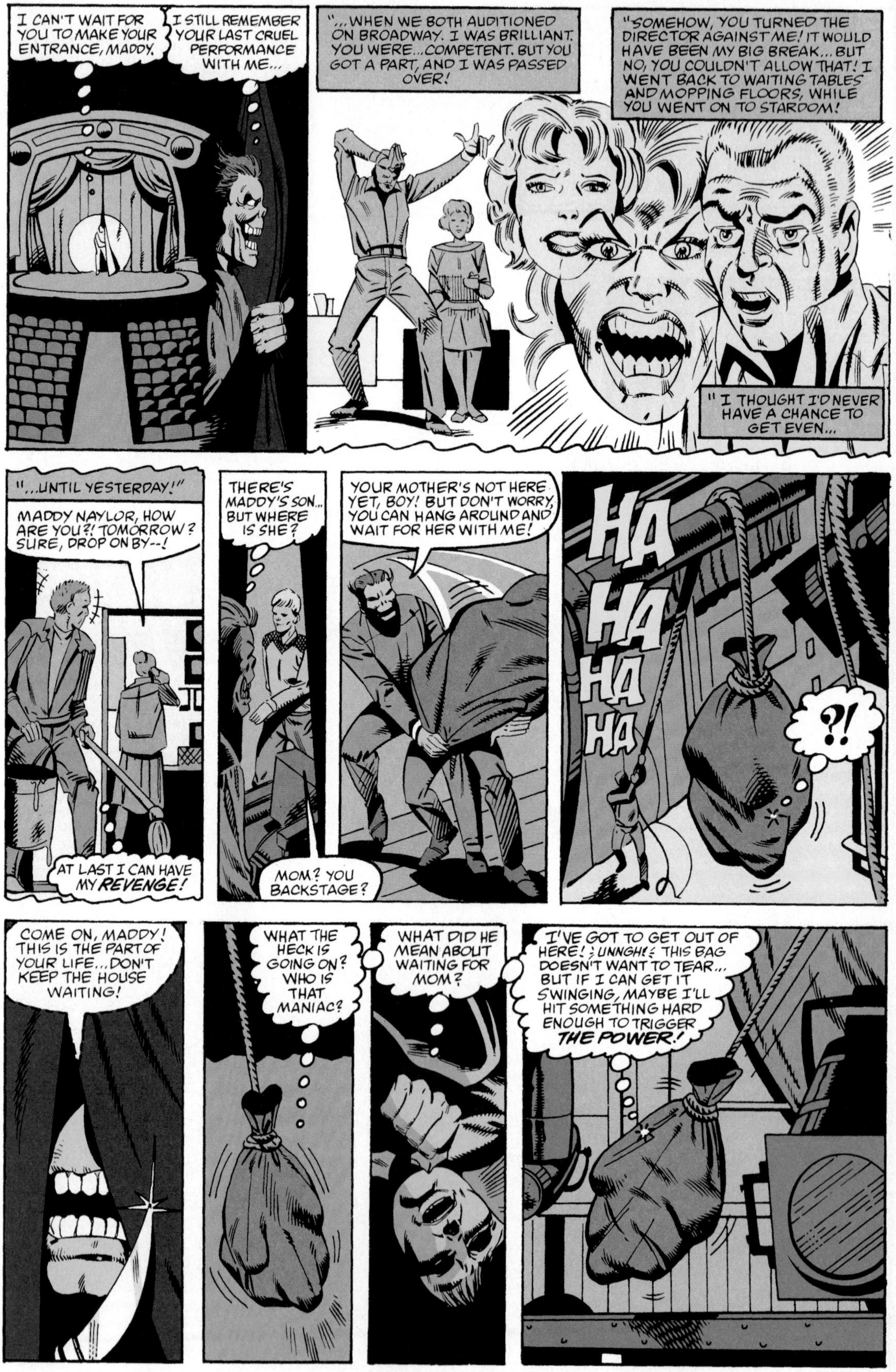

I CAN'T WAIT FOR YOU TO MAKE YOUR ENTRANCE, MADDY.
I STILL REMEMBER YOUR LAST CRUEL PERFORMANCE WITH ME...
"...WHEN WE BOTH AUDITIONED ON BROADWAY. I WAS BRILLIANT. YOU WERE...COMPETENT. BUT YOU GOT A PART, AND I WAS PASSED OVER!
"SOMEHOW, YOU TURNED THE DIRECTOR AGAINST ME! IT WOULD HAVE BEEN MY BIG BREAK... BUT NO, YOU COULDN'T ALLOW THAT! I WENT BACK TO WAITING TABLES AND MOPPING FLOORS, WHILE YOU WENT ON TO STARDOM!
"I THOUGHT I'D NEVER HAVE A CHANCE TO GET EVEN...
"...UNTIL YESTERDAY!"
MADDY NAYLOR, HOW ARE YOU?! TOMORROW? SURE, DROP ON BY--!
AT LAST I CAN HAVE MY REVENGE!
THERE'S MADDY'S SON... BUT WHERE IS SHE?
MOM? YOU BACKSTAGE?
YOUR MOTHER'S NOT HERE YET, BOY! BUT DON'T WORRY, YOU CAN HANG AROUND AND WAIT FOR HER WITH ME!
HA HA HA HA
?!
COME ON, MADDY! THIS IS THE PART OF YOUR LIFE... DON'T KEEP THE HOUSE WAITING!
WHAT THE HECK IS GOING ON? WHO IS THAT MANIAC?
WHAT DID HE MEAN ABOUT WAITING FOR MOM?
I'VE GOT TO GET OUT OF HERE! ¡UNNGH!¡ THIS BAG DOESN'T WANT TO TEAR... BUT IF I CAN GET IT SWINGING, MAYBE I'LL HIT SOMETHING HARD ENOUGH TO TRIGGER THE POWER!

HEL-LO? AMY... ROB? ANYBODY HERE?

YES, MADDY! KEEP COMING!

MAYBE THEY'RE BACKSTAGE.

IT'S WORKING... THE POWER IS BUILDING!

B-BUT THERE'S NOWHERE FOR IT TO GO! NOW WHAT--?

COME ON, MADDY! JUST CROSS THE FOOTLIGHTS!

...AND YOU'LL BE--

--HUH? WHO'S THERE?!?

HRIP

WHEW! THE POWER SHREDDED THE BAG JUST IN TIME!

ROB? AMY? IS THAT YOU?

BACK HERE, MADDY!

I HAD TO STEP OUT FOR A SEC! HOPE YOU WEREN'T WAITING LONG!

NOT AT ALL, AMY! I DID WONDER WHY THE PLACE WAS EMPTY!

OH, FINE! THE HANDYMAN MUST'VE SNUCK OUT FOR A DRINK AGAIN-- AND LEFT THE THEATRE UNLOCKED!

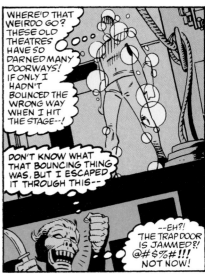

WHERE'D THAT WEIRDO GO? THESE OLD THEATRES HAVE SO DARNED MANY DOORWAYS! IF ONLY I HADN'T BOUNCED THE WRONG WAY WHEN I HIT THE STAGE--!

DON'T KNOW WHAT THAT BOUNCING THING WAS, BUT I ESCAPED IT THROUGH THIS--

--EH?! THE TRAP DOOR IS JAMMED?! @#$%#!!! NOT NOW!

MINUTES LATER...

HI, MOM! YOU READY TO GO? OUR TRAIN LEAVES IN...

RELAX, ROB! WE CAN ALWAYS TAKE A LATER TRAIN.

I HAVEN'T SEEN AMY IN YEARS! AND WE STILL HAVE TO ORDER COSTUMES AND PROPS FOR THE SPRINGDALE CIVIC THEATRE.

NO PROBLEM, DEAR! BROADWAY SUPPLY IS OPEN LATE!

THAT MANIAC COULD STILL BE AROUND SOMEWHERE. HOW CAN I GET MOM OUT OF HERE? IF I TELL HER WHAT HAPPENED--

--I'LL HAVE TO EXPLAIN MY POWER-- AND I'M NOT SURE I CAN!

I CAN JUST BARELY HEAR THROUGH THIS WALL. HOW DID MADDY'S KID GET LOOSE-- AND WHY ISN'T HE SQUAWKING? MAYBE HE HATES HER, TOO?

THAT'S A BREAK! I CAN CORNER HER AT BROADWAY SUPPLY...IF I CAN GET OUT OF HERE!

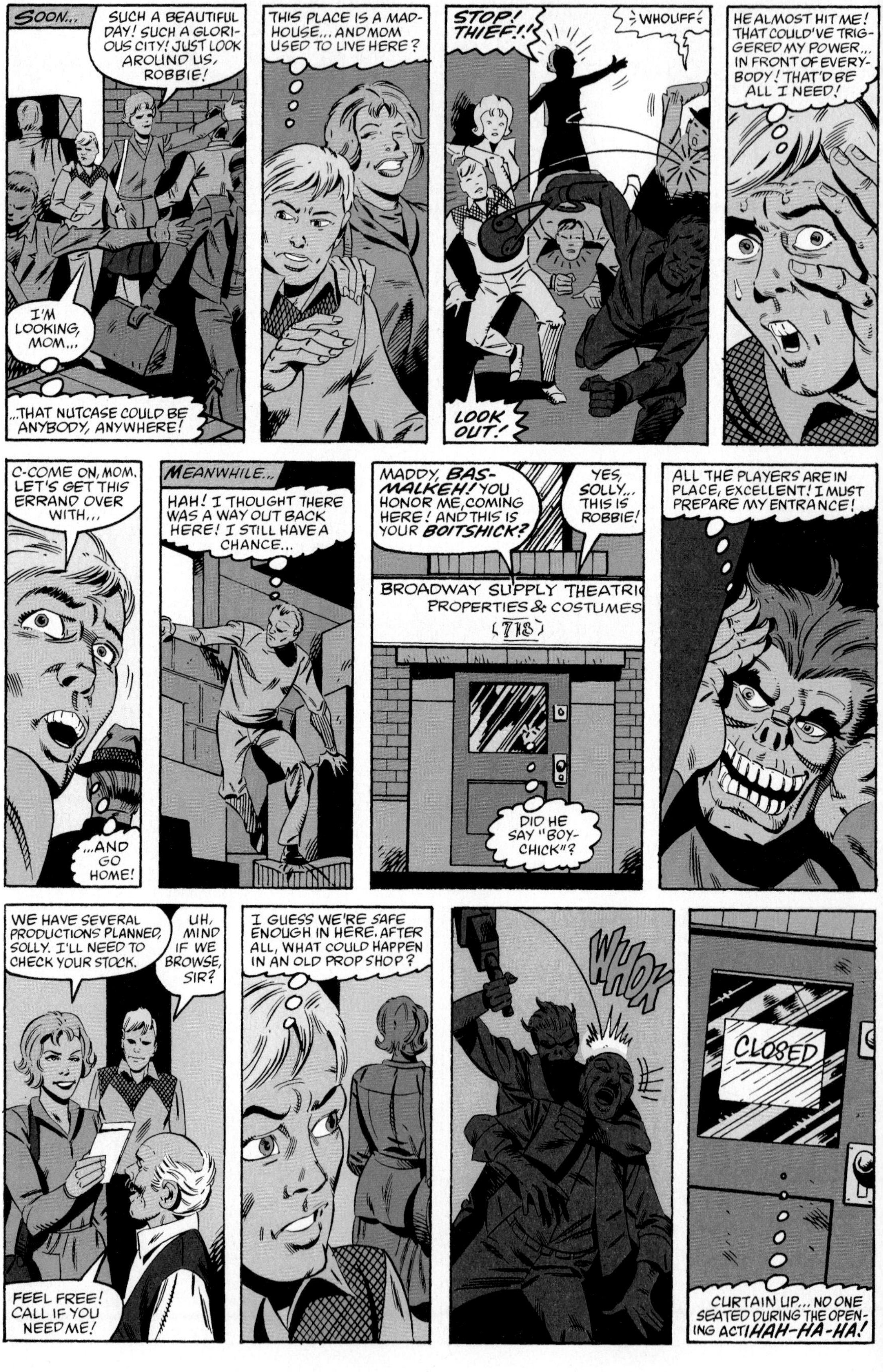
SOON...
SUCH A BEAUTIFUL DAY! SUCH A GLORIOUS CITY! JUST LOOK AROUND US, ROBBIE!
I'M LOOKING, MOM...
...THAT NUTCASE COULD BE ANYBODY, ANYWHERE!
THIS PLACE IS A MADHOUSE... AND MOM USED TO LIVE HERE?
STOP! THIEF!!
WHOUFF
LOOK OUT!
HE ALMOST HIT ME! THAT COULD'VE TRIGGERED MY POWER... IN FRONT OF EVERYBODY! THAT'D BE ALL I NEED!
C-COME ON, MOM. LET'S GET THIS ERRAND OVER WITH...
...AND GO HOME!
MEANWHILE...
HAH! I THOUGHT THERE WAS A WAY OUT BACK HERE! I STILL HAVE A CHANCE...
MADDY, BAS-MALKEH! YOU HONOR ME, COMING HERE! AND THIS IS YOUR BOITSHICK?
YES, SOLLY... THIS IS ROBBIE!
BROADWAY SUPPLY THEATRIC
PROPERTIES & COSTUMES
718
DID HE SAY "BOY-CHICK"?
ALL THE PLAYERS ARE IN PLACE, EXCELLENT! I MUST PREPARE MY ENTRANCE!
WE HAVE SEVERAL PRODUCTIONS PLANNED, SOLLY. I'LL NEED TO CHECK YOUR STOCK.
UH, MIND IF WE BROWSE, SIR?
FEEL FREE! CALL IF YOU NEED ME!
I GUESS WE'RE SAFE ENOUGH IN HERE. AFTER ALL, WHAT COULD HAPPEN IN AN OLD PROP SHOP?
WHOK
CLOSED
CURTAIN UP... NO ONE SEATED DURING THE OPENING ACT! HAH-HA-HA!

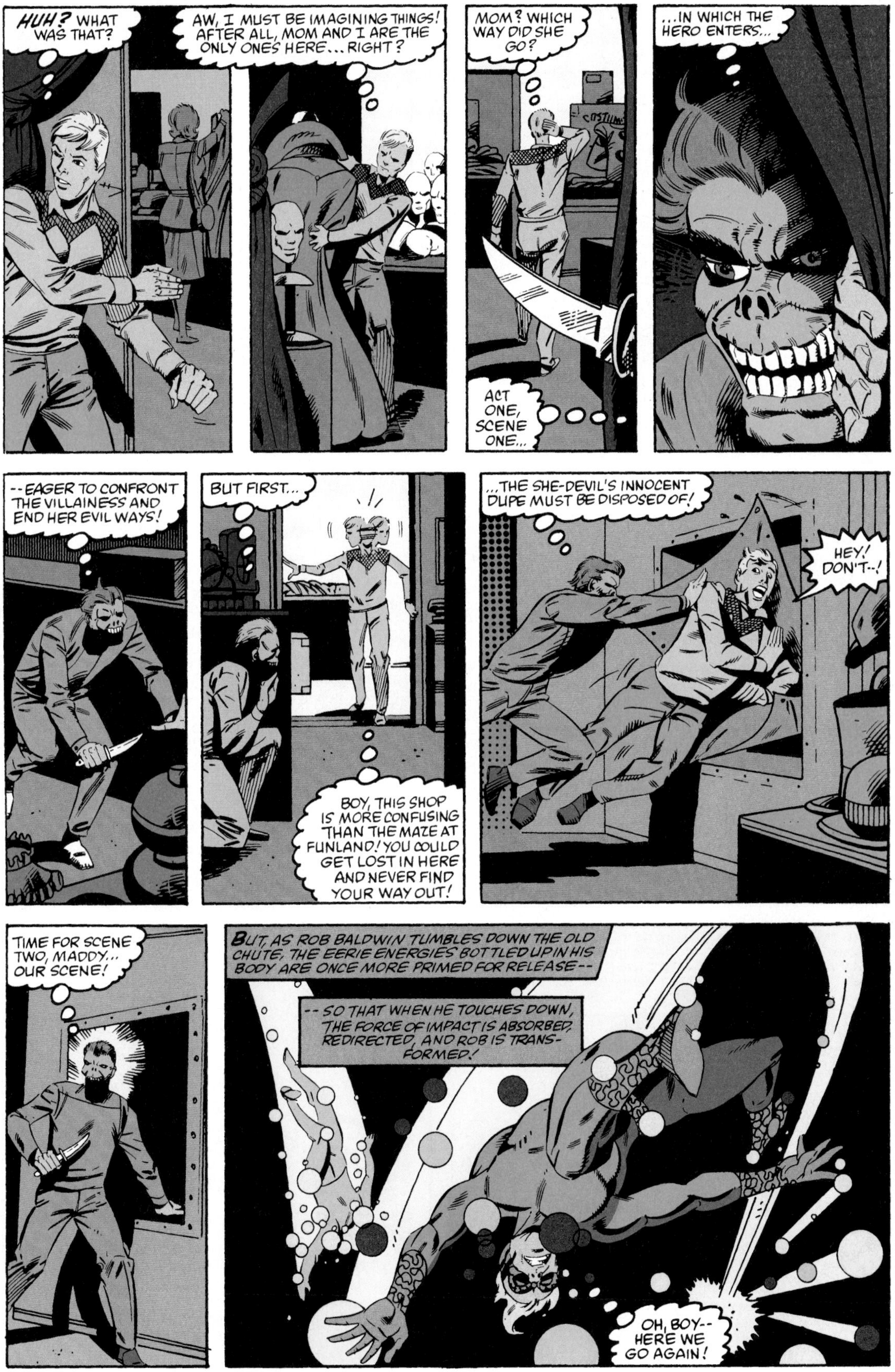
HUH? WHAT WAS THAT?
AW, I MUST BE IMAGINING THINGS! AFTER ALL, MOM AND I ARE THE ONLY ONES HERE... RIGHT?
MOM? WHICH WAY DID SHE GO?
ACT ONE, SCENE ONE...
...IN WHICH THE HERO ENTERS...
--EAGER TO CONFRONT THE VILLAINESS AND END HER EVIL WAYS!
BUT FIRST...
BOY, THIS SHOP IS MORE CONFUSING THAN THE MAZE AT FUNLAND! YOU COULD GET LOST IN HERE AND NEVER FIND YOUR WAY OUT!
...THE SHE-DEVIL'S INNOCENT DUPE MUST BE DISPOSED OF!
HEY! DON'T--!
TIME FOR SCENE TWO, MADDY... OUR SCENE!
BUT, AS ROB BALDWIN TUMBLES DOWN THE OLD CHUTE, THE EERIE ENERGIES BOTTLED UP IN HIS BODY ARE ONCE MORE PRIMED FOR RELEASE--
--SO THAT WHEN HE TOUCHES DOWN, THE FORCE OF IMPACT IS ABSORBED, REDIRECTED, AND ROB IS TRANSFORMED!
OH, BOY-- HERE WE GO AGAIN!

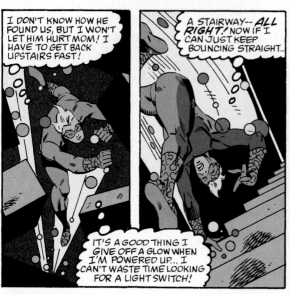

I DON'T KNOW HOW HE FOUND US, BUT I WON'T LET HIM HURT MOM! I HAVE TO GET BACK UPSTAIRS FAST!

A STAIRWAY-- *ALL RIGHT!* NOW IF I CAN JUST KEEP BOUNCING STRAIGHT...

IT'S A GOOD THING I GIVE OFF A GLOW WHEN I'M POWERED UP... I CAN'T WASTE TIME LOOKING FOR A LIGHT SWITCH!

MMM, BEAUTIFUL FABRIC... BUT MAYBE A BIT DARING FOR SPINGDALE!

FIRST, A TOUCH OF PAIN, AND THEN--!

I DID IT!

GYAHH!

WHAT A FACE! I HOPE THAT'S A MASK!

ROBBIE? IS THAT YOU?

UH-OH! BETTER NOT LET *MOM* SEE ME LIKE THIS!

WHO IS THIS ACROBATIC FOOL? WHY IS HE BUTTING IN?

IF MOM SEES THE *MASKED MARVEL* HERE, SHE'S BOUND TO GUESS WHO I AM! BUT I HAVE TO STICK CLOSE TO HER... I DON'T THINK THAT NUTCASE IS GOING TO GIVE UP!

LOST MY KNIFE... I'LL JUST HAVE TO *IMPROVISE!*

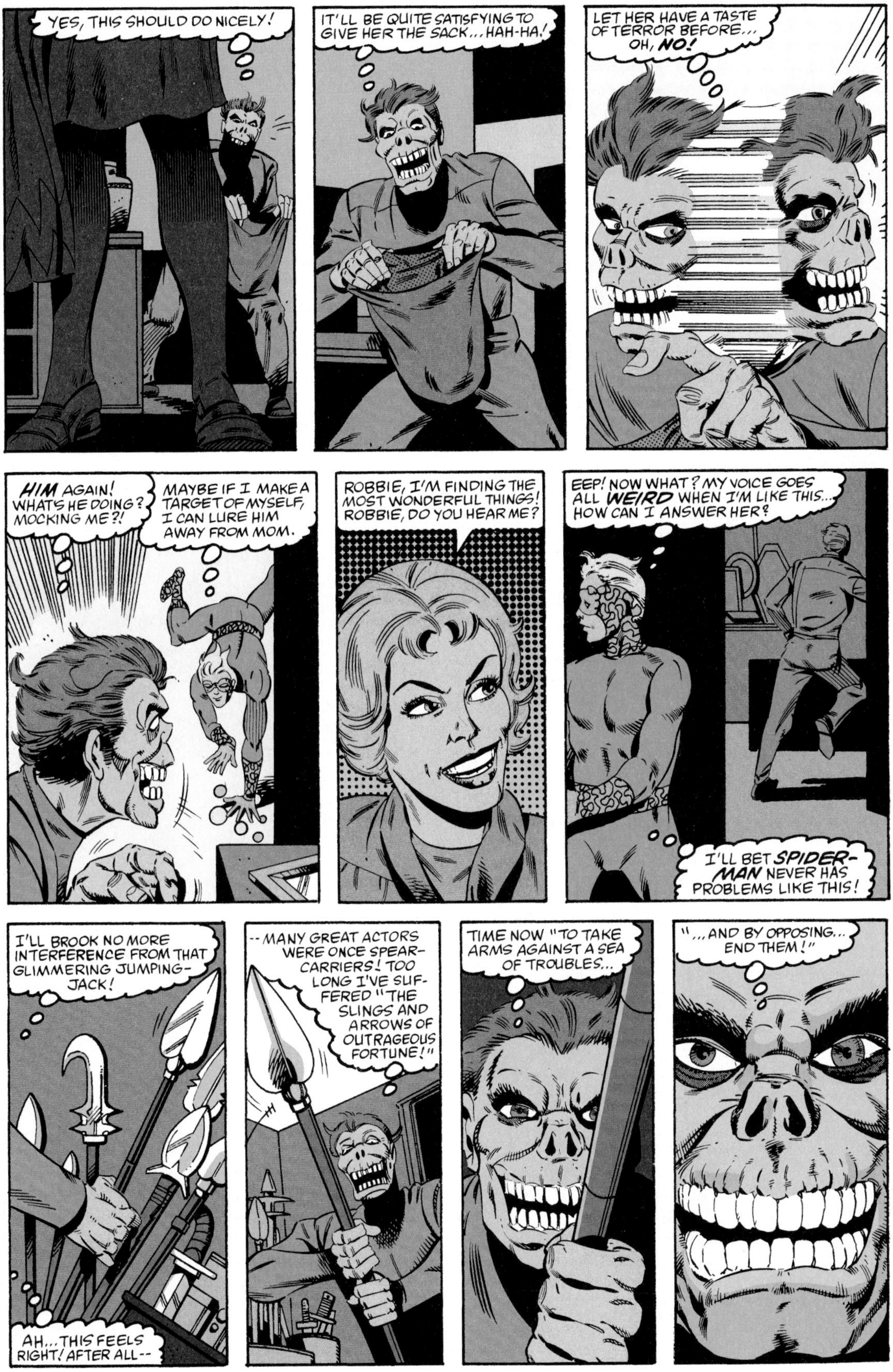
YES, THIS SHOULD DO NICELY!
IT'LL BE QUITE SATISFYING TO GIVE HER THE SACK... HAH-HA!
LET HER HAVE A TASTE OF TERROR BEFORE... OH, NO!
HIM AGAIN! WHAT'S HE DOING? MOCKING ME?!
MAYBE IF I MAKE A TARGET OF MYSELF, I CAN LURE HIM AWAY FROM MOM.
ROBBIE, I'M FINDING THE MOST WONDERFUL THINGS! ROBBIE, DO YOU HEAR ME?
EEP! NOW WHAT? MY VOICE GOES ALL WEIRD WHEN I'M LIKE THIS... HOW CAN I ANSWER HER?
I'LL BET SPIDER-MAN NEVER HAS PROBLEMS LIKE THIS!
I'LL BROOK NO MORE INTERFERENCE FROM THAT GLIMMERING JUMPING-JACK!
AH... THIS FEELS RIGHT! AFTER ALL--
--MANY GREAT ACTORS WERE ONCE SPEAR-CARRIERS! TOO LONG I'VE SUFFERED "THE SLINGS AND ARROWS OF OUTRAGEOUS FORTUNE!"
TIME NOW "TO TAKE ARMS AGAINST A SEA OF TROUBLES...
"...AND BY OPPOSING... END THEM!"

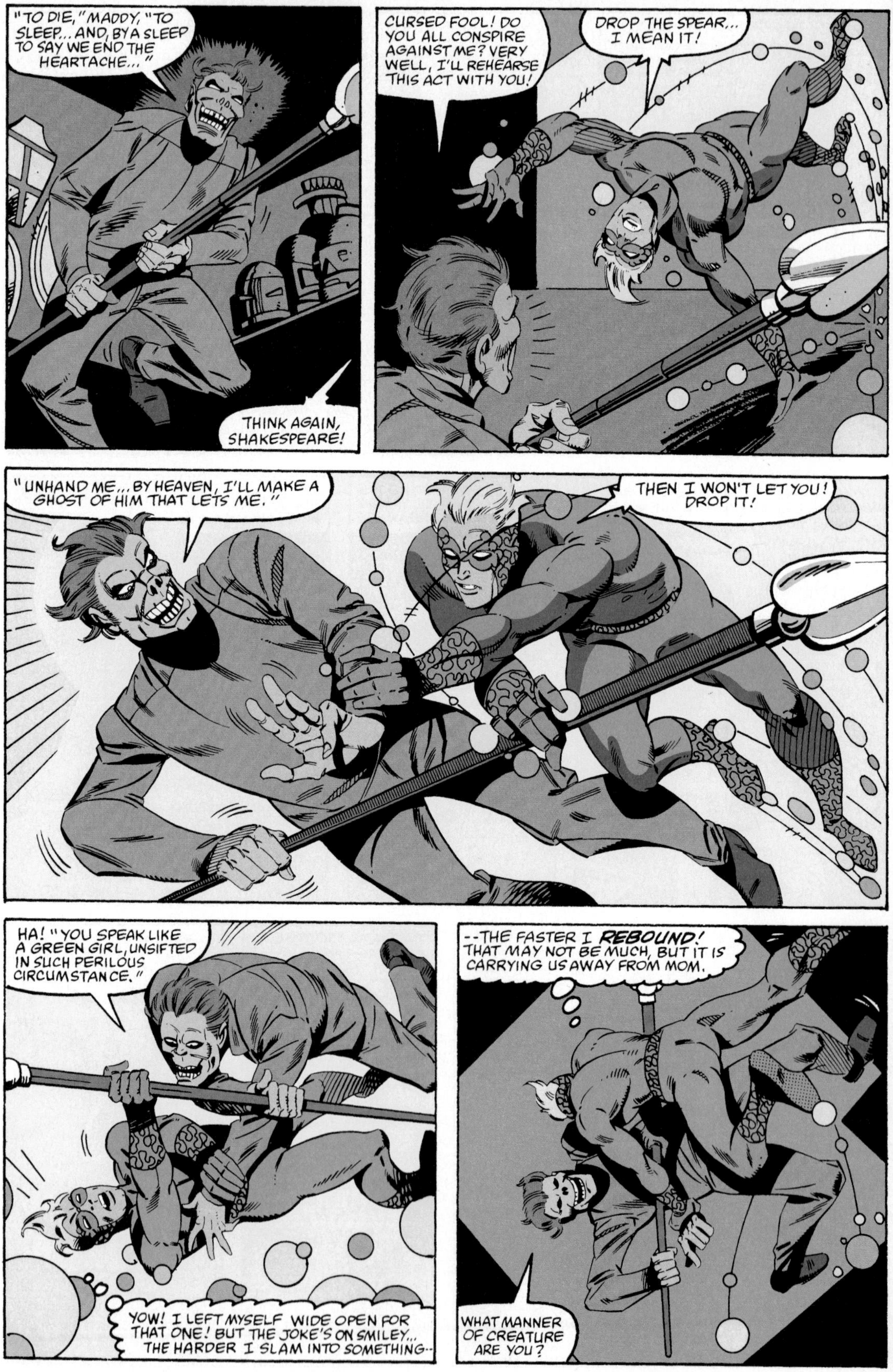
"TO DIE," MADDY, "TO SLEEP... AND, BY A SLEEP TO SAY WE END THE HEARTACHE..."
THINK AGAIN, SHAKESPEARE!
CURSED FOOL! DO YOU ALL CONSPIRE AGAINST ME? VERY WELL, I'LL REHEARSE THIS ACT WITH YOU!
DROP THE SPEAR... I MEAN IT!
"UNHAND ME... BY HEAVEN, I'LL MAKE A GHOST OF HIM THAT LETS ME."
THEN I WON'T LET YOU! DROP IT!
HA! "YOU SPEAK LIKE A GREEN GIRL, UNSIFTED IN SUCH PERILOUS CIRCUMSTANCE."
YOW! I LEFT MYSELF WIDE OPEN FOR THAT ONE! BUT THE JOKE'S ON SMILEY... THE HARDER I SLAM INTO SOMETHING--
--THE FASTER I REBOUND! THAT MAY NOT BE MUCH, BUT IT IS CARRYING US AWAY FROM MOM.
WHAT MANNER OF CREATURE ARE YOU?

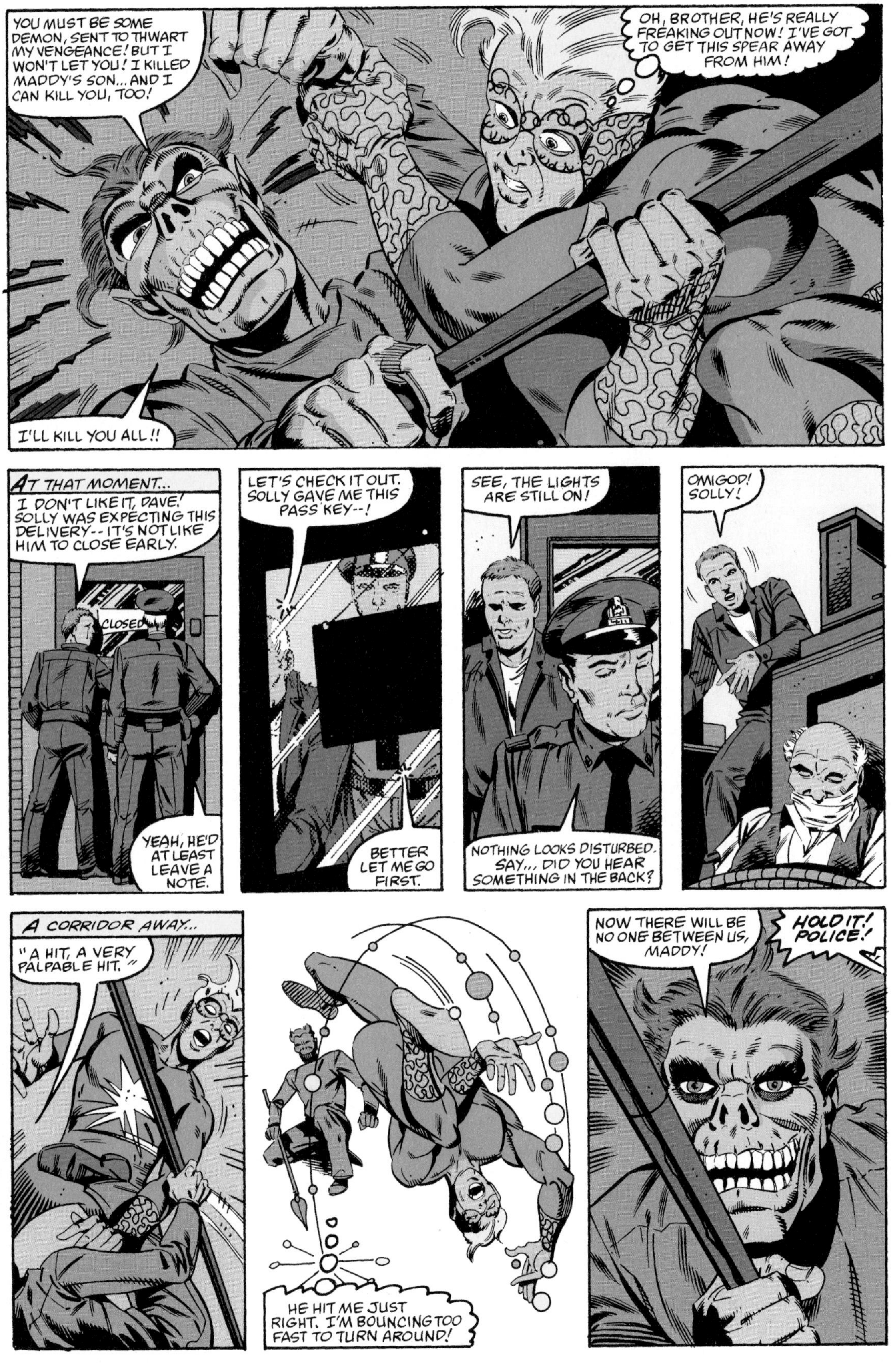
YOU MUST BE SOME DEMON, SENT TO THWART MY VENGEANCE! BUT I WON'T LET YOU! I KILLED MADDY'S SON... AND I CAN KILL YOU, TOO!
OH, BROTHER, HE'S REALLY FREAKING OUT NOW! I'VE GOT TO GET THIS SPEAR AWAY FROM HIM!
I'LL KILL YOU ALL!!
AT THAT MOMENT...
I DON'T LIKE IT, DAVE! SOLLY WAS EXPECTING THIS DELIVERY-- IT'S NOT LIKE HIM TO CLOSE EARLY.
CLOSED
YEAH, HE'D AT LEAST LEAVE A NOTE.
LET'S CHECK IT OUT. SOLLY GAVE ME THIS PASS KEY--!
BETTER LET ME GO FIRST.
SEE, THE LIGHTS ARE STILL ON!
NOTHING LOOKS DISTURBED. SAY... DID YOU HEAR SOMETHING IN THE BACK?
OMIGOD! SOLLY!
A CORRIDOR AWAY...
"A HIT, A VERY PALPABLE HIT."
HE HIT ME JUST RIGHT. I'M BOUNCING TOO FAST TO TURN AROUND!
NOW THERE WILL BE NO ONE BETWEEN US, MADDY!
HOLD IT! POLICE!

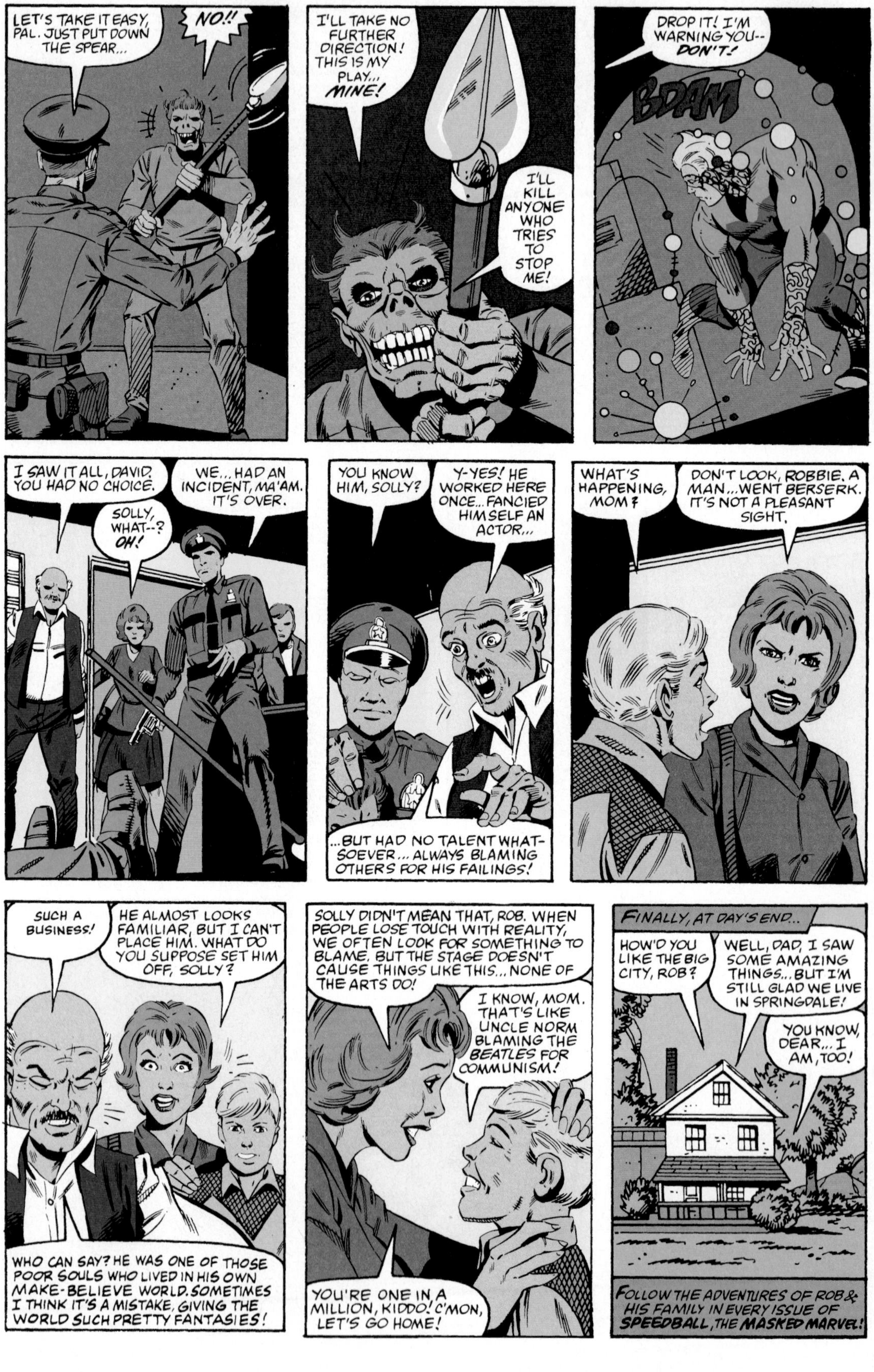
LET'S TAKE IT EASY, PAL. JUST PUT DOWN THE SPEAR...
NO!!
I'LL TAKE NO FURTHER DIRECTION! THIS IS MY PLAY... MINE!
I'LL KILL ANYONE WHO TRIES TO STOP ME!
DROP IT! I'M WARNING YOU-- DON'T!
BDAM
I SAW IT ALL, DAVID. YOU HAD NO CHOICE.
WE... HAD AN INCIDENT, MA'AM. IT'S OVER.
SOLLY, WHAT--? OH!
YOU KNOW HIM, SOLLY?
Y-YES! HE WORKED HERE ONCE... FANCIED HIMSELF AN ACTOR...
...BUT HAD NO TALENT WHATSOEVER... ALWAYS BLAMING OTHERS FOR HIS FAILINGS!
WHAT'S HAPPENING, MOM?
DON'T LOOK, ROBBIE. A MAN... WENT BERSERK. IT'S NOT A PLEASANT SIGHT.
SUCH A BUSINESS!
HE ALMOST LOOKS FAMILIAR, BUT I CAN'T PLACE HIM. WHAT DO YOU SUPPOSE SET HIM OFF, SOLLY?
WHO CAN SAY? HE WAS ONE OF THOSE POOR SOULS WHO LIVED IN HIS OWN MAKE-BELIEVE WORLD. SOMETIMES I THINK IT'S A MISTAKE, GIVING THE WORLD SUCH PRETTY FANTASIES!
SOLLY DIDN'T MEAN THAT, ROB. WHEN PEOPLE LOSE TOUCH WITH REALITY, WE OFTEN LOOK FOR SOMETHING TO BLAME. BUT THE STAGE DOESN'T CAUSE THINGS LIKE THIS... NONE OF THE ARTS DO!
I KNOW, MOM. THAT'S LIKE UNCLE NORM BLAMING THE BEATLES FOR COMMUNISM!
YOU'RE ONE IN A MILLION, KIDDO! C'MON, LET'S GO HOME!
FINALLY, AT DAY'S END...
HOW'D YOU LIKE THE BIG CITY, ROB?
WELL, DAD, I SAW SOME AMAZING THINGS... BUT I'M STILL GLAD WE LIVE IN SPRINGDALE!
YOU KNOW, DEAR... I AM, TOO!
FOLLOW THE ADVENTURES OF ROB & HIS FAMILY IN EVERY ISSUE OF SPEEDBALL, THE MASKED MARVEL!

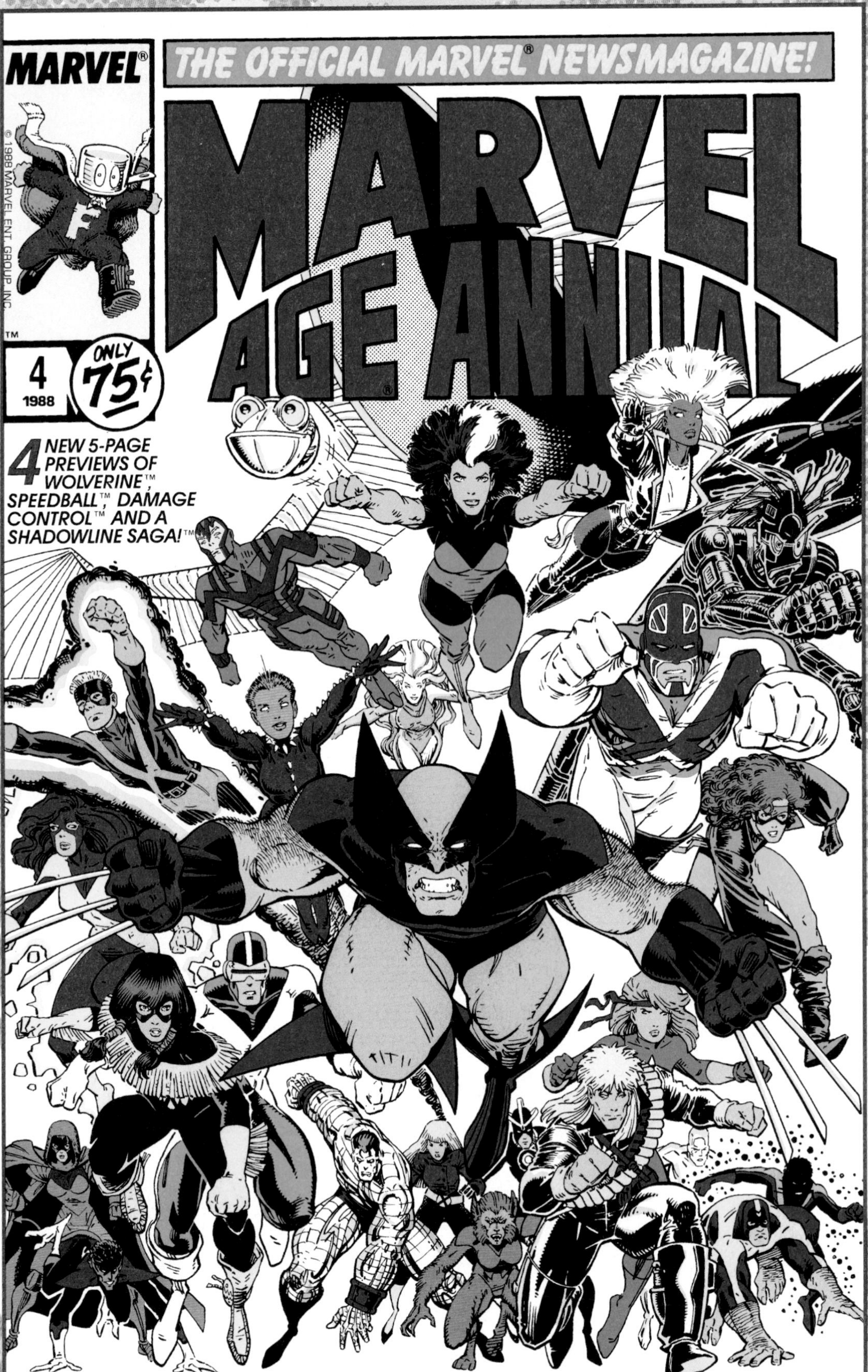
MARVEL®
THE OFFICIAL MARVEL® NEWSMAGAZINE!
MARVEL AGE ANNUAL®
© 1988 MARVEL ENT. GROUP, INC.
TM
4
1988
ONLY 75¢
4 NEW 5-PAGE PREVIEWS OF WOLVERINE™, SPEEDBALL™, DAMAGE CONTROL™ AND A SHADOWLINE SAGA!™

MARVEL AGE ANNUAL #4, published in June 1988, introduced Damage Control, a company that repaired destruction caused by superhuman battles; it was soon followed by another short story and a limited series.

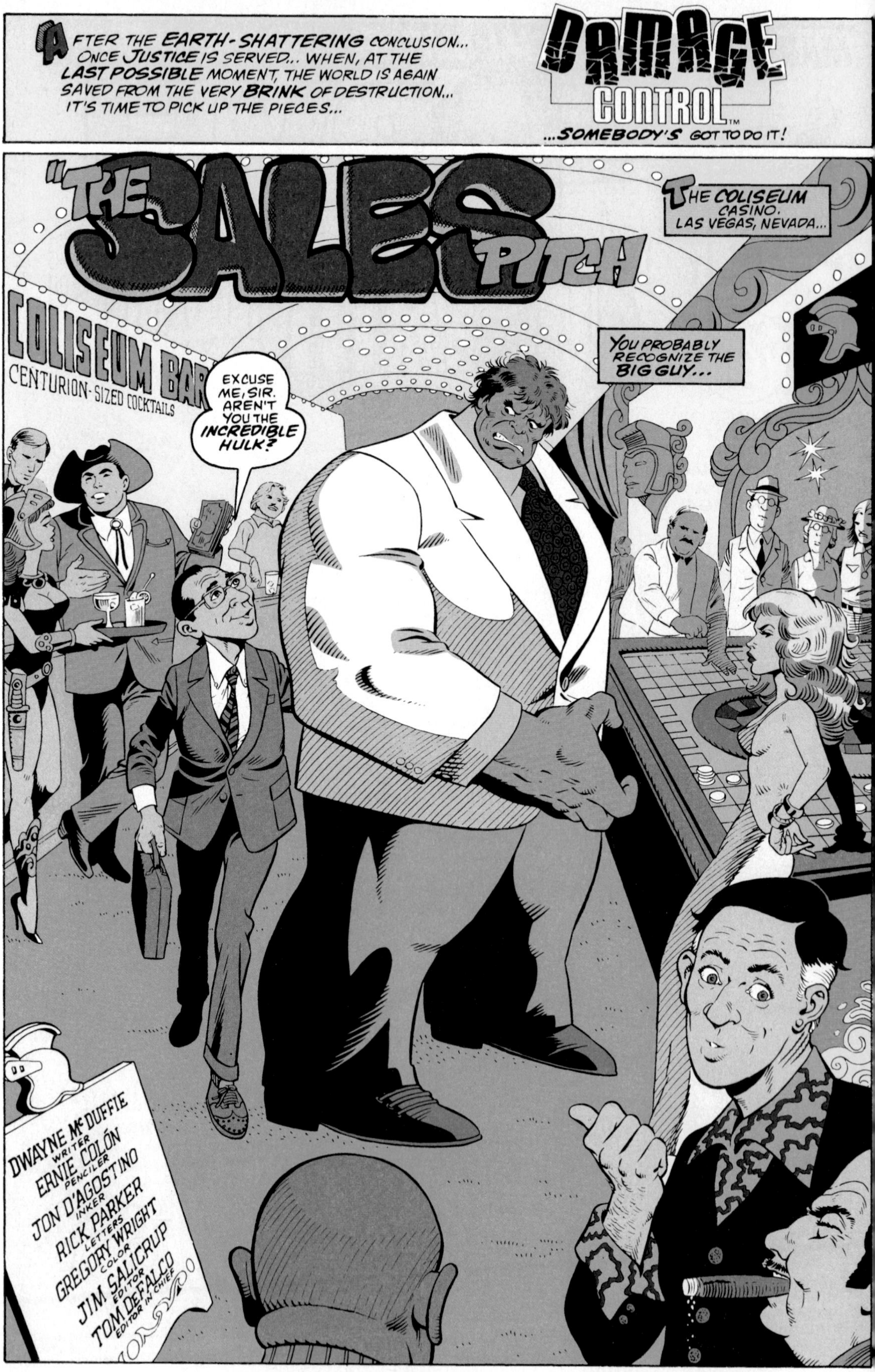
AFTER THE EARTH-SHATTERING CONCLUSION... ONCE JUSTICE IS SERVED... WHEN, AT THE LAST POSSIBLE MOMENT, THE WORLD IS AGAIN SAVED FROM THE VERY BRINK OF DESTRUCTION... IT'S TIME TO PICK UP THE PIECES...
DAMAGE CONTROL™
...SOMEBODY'S GOT TO DO IT!
"THE SALES PITCH"
THE COLISEUM CASINO. LAS VEGAS, NEVADA...
COLISEUM BAR
CENTURION-SIZED COCKTAILS
EXCUSE ME, SIR. AREN'T YOU THE INCREDIBLE HULK?
YOU PROBABLY RECOGNIZE THE BIG GUY...
DWAYNE McDUFFIE WRITER
ERNIE COLÓN PENCILER
JON D'AGOSTINO INKER
RICK PARKER LETTERS
GREGORY WRIGHT COLOR
JIM SALICRUP EDITOR
TOM DEFALCO EDITOR IN CHIEF

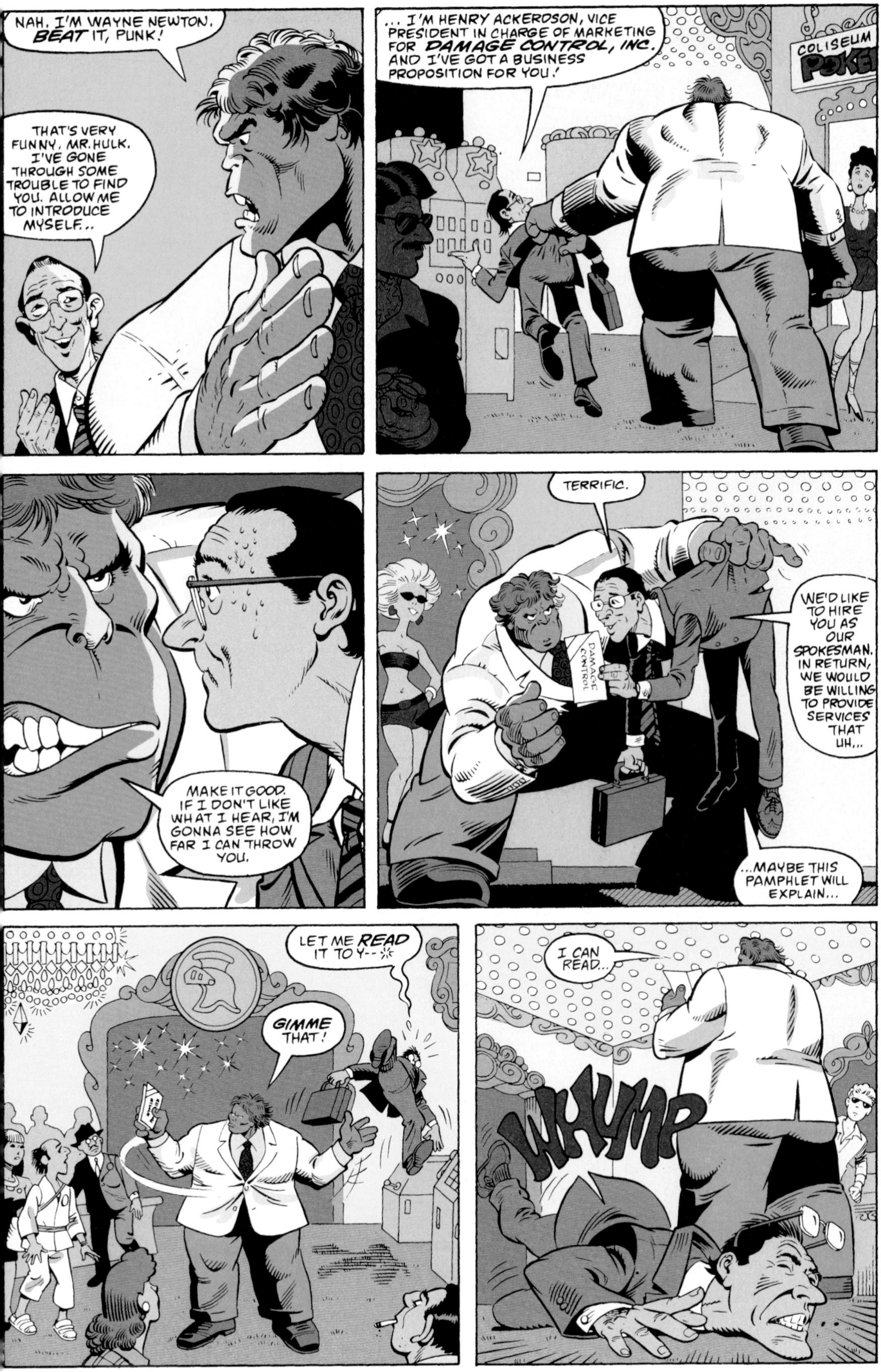
NAH. I'M WAYNE NEWTON. BEAT IT, PUNK!
THAT'S VERY FUNNY, MR. HULK. I'VE GONE THROUGH SOME TROUBLE TO FIND YOU. ALLOW ME TO INTRODUCE MYSELF...
... I'M HENRY ACKERDSON, VICE PRESIDENT IN CHARGE OF MARKETING FOR DAMAGE CONTROL, INC. AND I'VE GOT A BUSINESS PROPOSITION FOR YOU!
COLISEUM
POKER
MAKE IT GOOD. IF I DON'T LIKE WHAT I HEAR, I'M GONNA SEE HOW FAR I CAN THROW YOU.
TERRIFIC.
DAMAGE CONTROL
WE'D LIKE TO HIRE YOU AS OUR SPOKESMAN. IN RETURN, WE WOULD BE WILLING TO PROVIDE SERVICES THAT UH...
...MAYBE THIS PAMPHLET WILL EXPLAIN...
LET ME READ IT TO Y--
GIMME THAT!
I CAN READ...
WHUMP

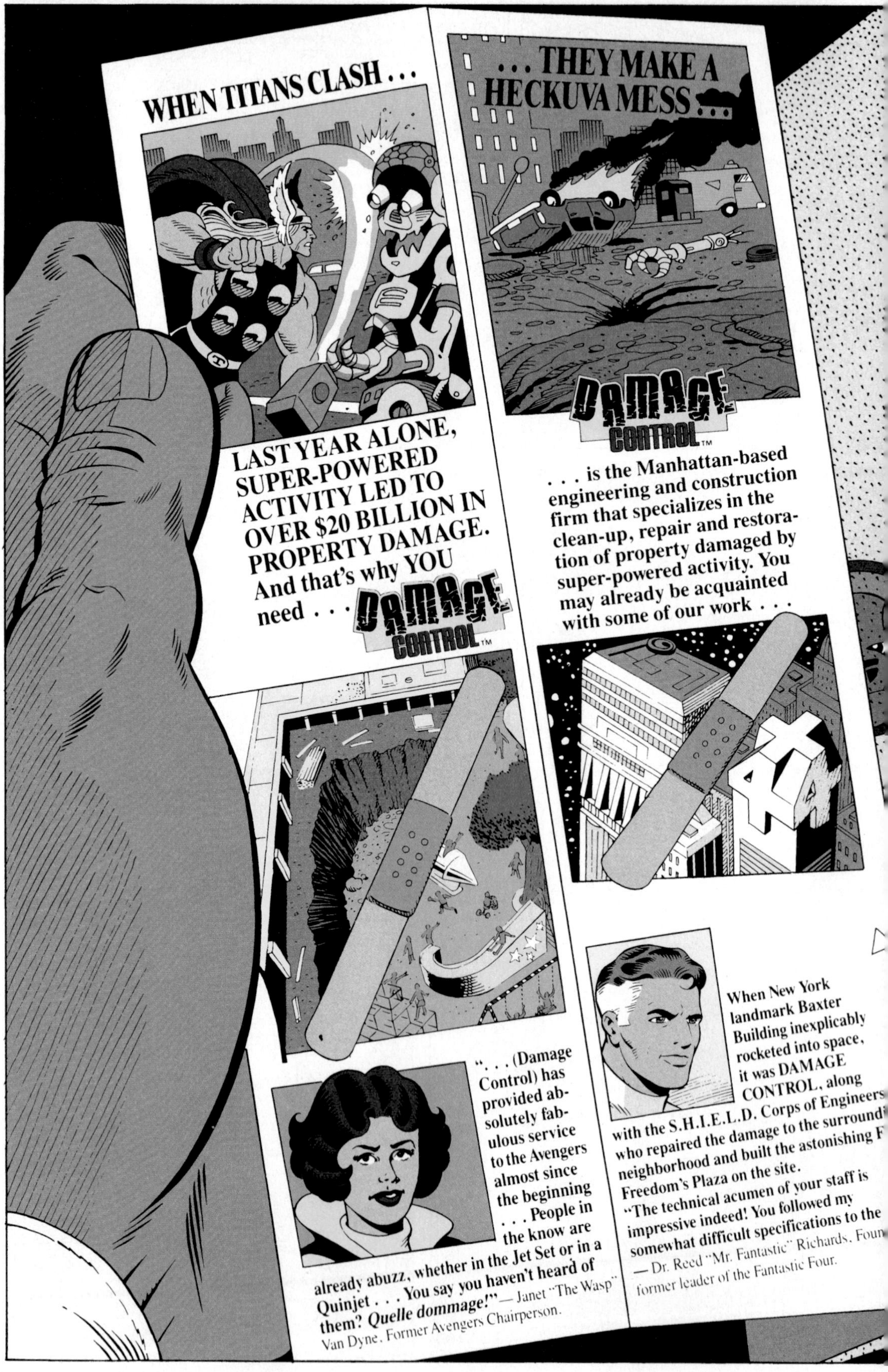

WHEN TITANS CLASH . . .
. . . THEY MAKE A HECKUVA MESS . . .
LAST YEAR ALONE, SUPER-POWERED ACTIVITY LED TO OVER $20 BILLION IN PROPERTY DAMAGE. And that's why YOU need . . . DAMAGE CONTROL™
DAMAGE CONTROL™
. . . is the Manhattan-based engineering and construction firm that specializes in the clean-up, repair and restoration of property damaged by super-powered activity. You may already be acquainted with some of our work . . .
"... (Damage Control) has provided absolutely fabulous service to the Avengers almost since the beginning . . . People in the know are already abuzz, whether in the Jet Set or in a Quinjet . . . You say you haven't heard of them? Quelle dommage!" — Janet "The Wasp" Van Dyne, Former Avengers Chairperson.
When New York landmark Baxter Building inexplicably rocketed into space, it was DAMAGE CONTROL, along with the S.H.I.E.L.D. Corps of Engineers who repaired the damage to the surroundi neighborhood and built the astonishing F Freedom's Plaza on the site.
"The technical acumen of your staff is impressive indeed! You followed my somewhat difficult specifications to the — Dr. Reed "Mr. Fantastic" Richards, Foun former leader of the Fantastic Four.

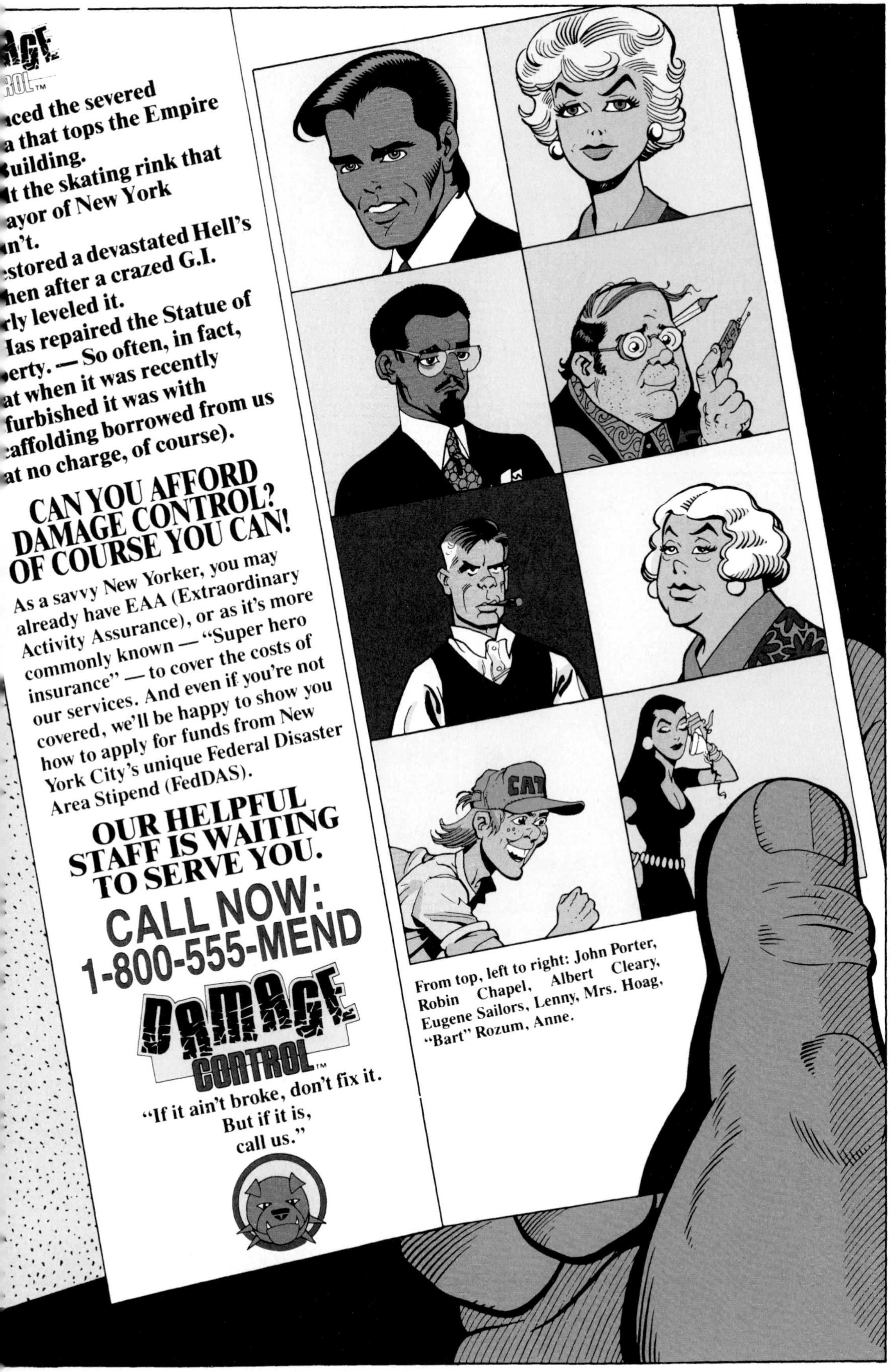

AGE
ROL™
aced the severed
a that tops the Empire
Building.
It the skating rink that
ayor of New York
n't.
estored a devastated Hell's
hen after a crazed G.I.
rly leveled it.
Has repaired the Statue of
berty. — So often, in fact,
at when it was recently
furbished it was with
scaffolding borrowed from us
at no charge, of course).
CAN YOU AFFORD DAMAGE CONTROL? OF COURSE YOU CAN!
As a savvy New Yorker, you may already have EAA (Extraordinary Activity Assurance), or as it's more commonly known — "Super hero insurance" — to cover the costs of our services. And even if you're not covered, we'll be happy to show you how to apply for funds from New York City's unique Federal Disaster Area Stipend (FedDAS).
OUR HELPFUL STAFF IS WAITING TO SERVE YOU.
CALL NOW: 1-800-555-MEND
DAMAGE CONTROL™
"If it ain't broke, don't fix it. But if it is, call us."
CAT
From top, left to right: John Porter, Robin Chapel, Albert Cleary, Eugene Sailors, Lenny, Mrs. Hoag, "Bart" Rozum, Anne.

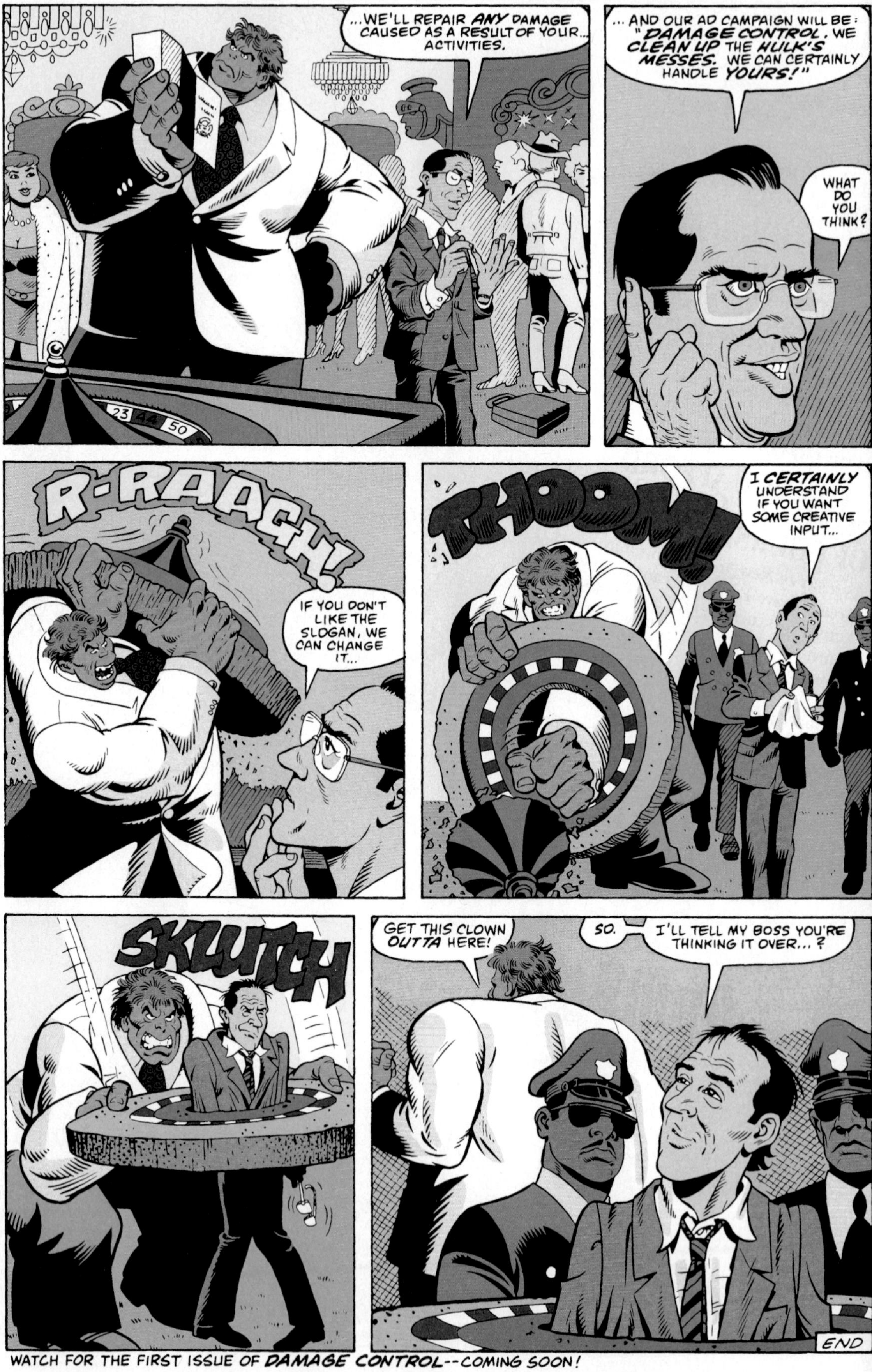
...WE'LL REPAIR ANY DAMAGE CAUSED AS A RESULT OF YOUR... ACTIVITIES.
... AND OUR AD CAMPAIGN WILL BE: "DAMAGE CONTROL. WE CLEAN UP THE HULK'S MESSES. WE CAN CERTAINLY HANDLE YOURS!"
WHAT DO YOU THINK?
R-RAAGH!
IF YOU DON'T LIKE THE SLOGAN, WE CAN CHANGE IT...
THOOM!
I CERTAINLY UNDERSTAND IF YOU WANT SOME CREATIVE INPUT...
SKLUTCH
GET THIS CLOWN OUTTA HERE!
SO.
I'LL TELL MY BOSS YOU'RE THINKING IT OVER... ?
END

WATCH FOR THE FIRST ISSUE OF ***DAMAGE CONTROL***--COMING SOON!

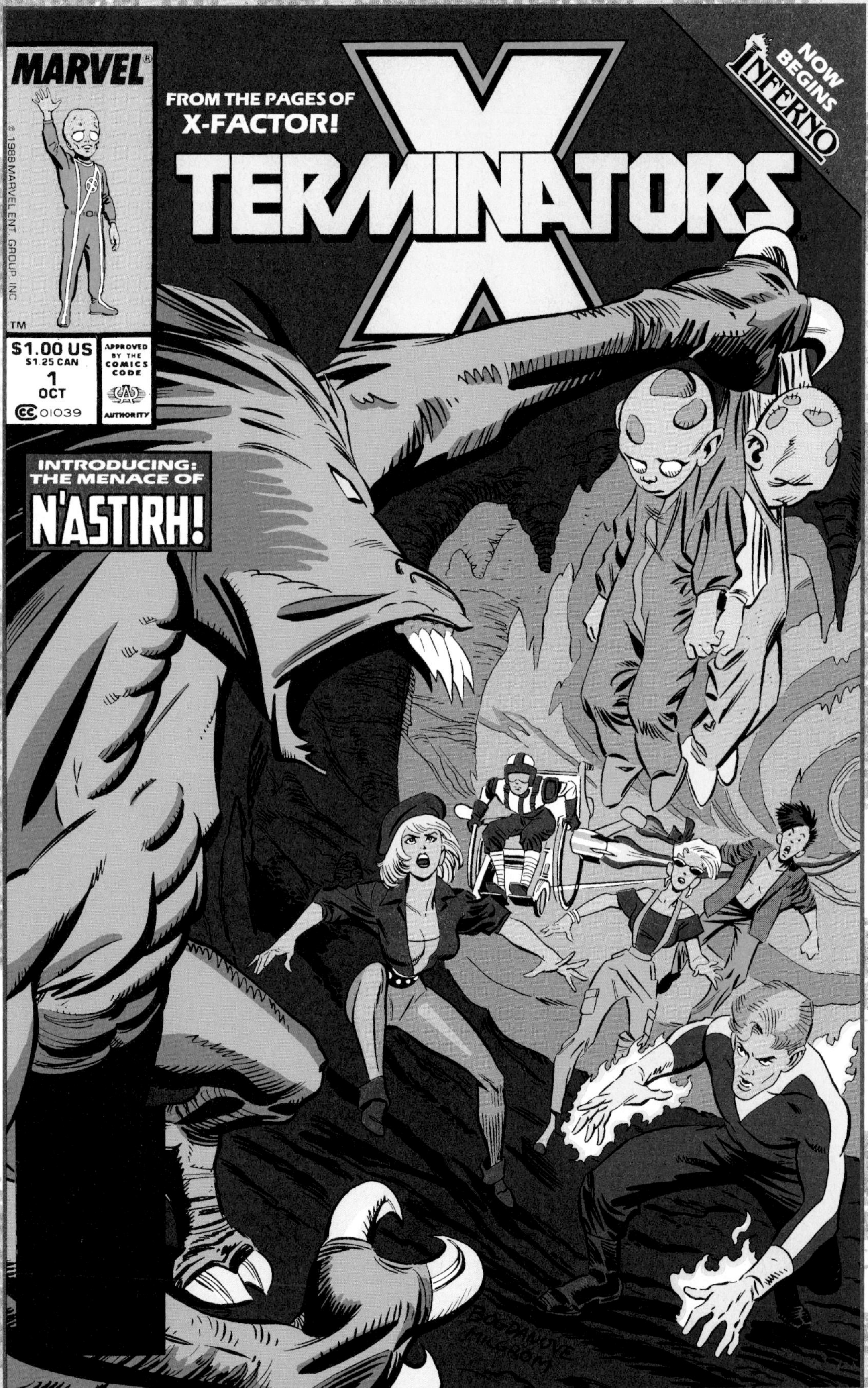
MARVEL®
© 1988 MARVEL ENT. GROUP, INC.
TM
$1.00 US
$1.25 CAN
1
OCT
01039
APPROVED BY THE COMICS CODE AUTHORITY
FROM THE PAGES OF
X-FACTOR!
X-TERMINATORS
NOW BEGINS
INFERNO
INTRODUCING:
THE MENACE OF
N'ASTIRH!

X-TERMINATORS #1, published in June 1988, began a limited series starring X-Factor's teenage wards; it tied heavily into the "Inferno" crossover event.

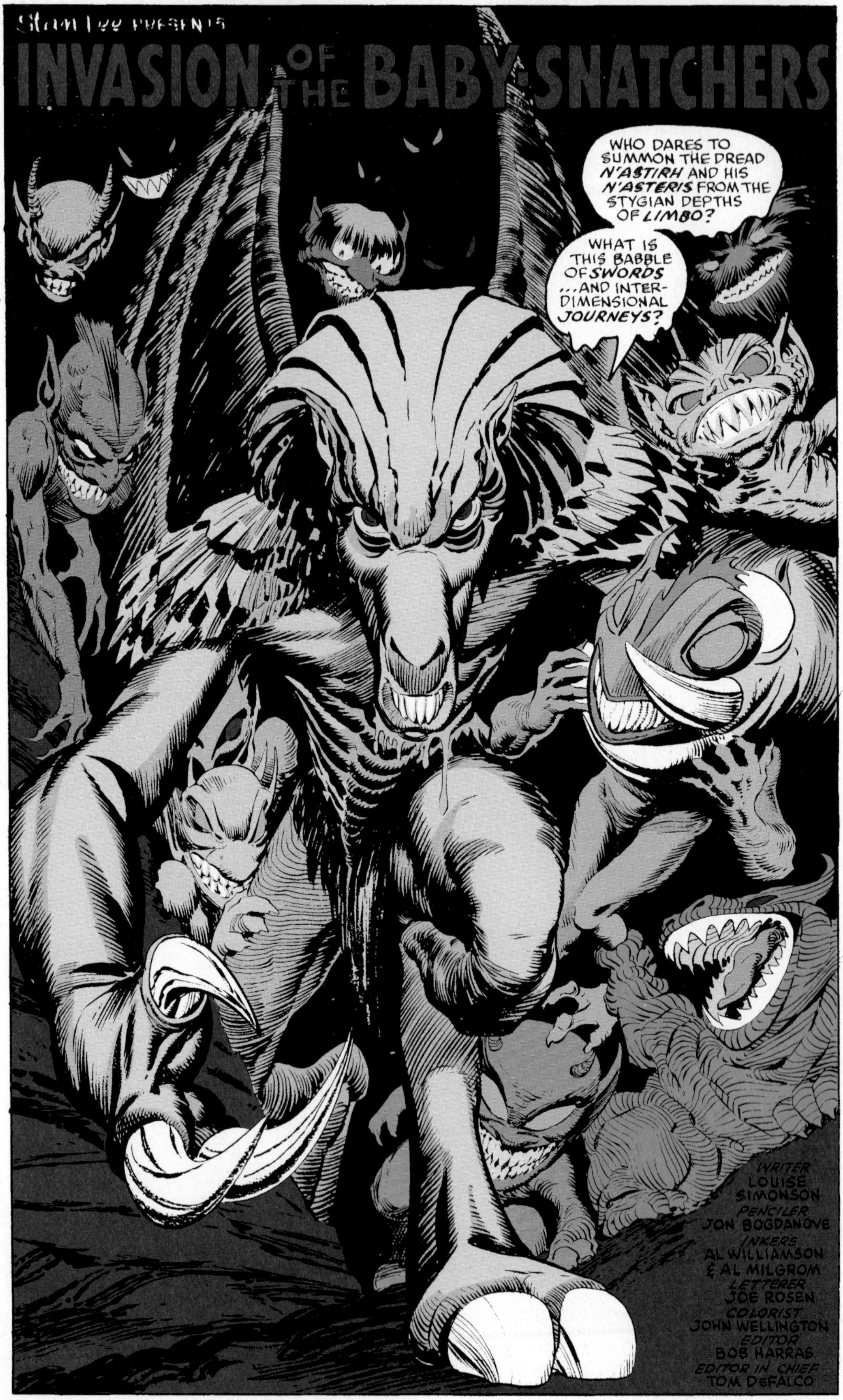
Stan Lee PRESENTS
INVASION OF THE BABY-SNATCHERS
WHO DARES TO SUMMON THE DREAD N'ASTIRH AND HIS N'ASTERIS FROM THE STYGIAN DEPTHS OF LIMBO?
WHAT IS THIS BABBLE OF SWORDS ...AND INTER-DIMENSIONAL JOURNEYS?
WRITER LOUISE SIMONSON
PENCILER JON BOGDANOVE
INKERS AL WILLIAMSON & AL MILGROM
LETTERER JOE ROSEN
COLORIST JOHN WELLINGTON
EDITOR BOB HARRAS
EDITOR IN CHIEF TOM DEFALCO

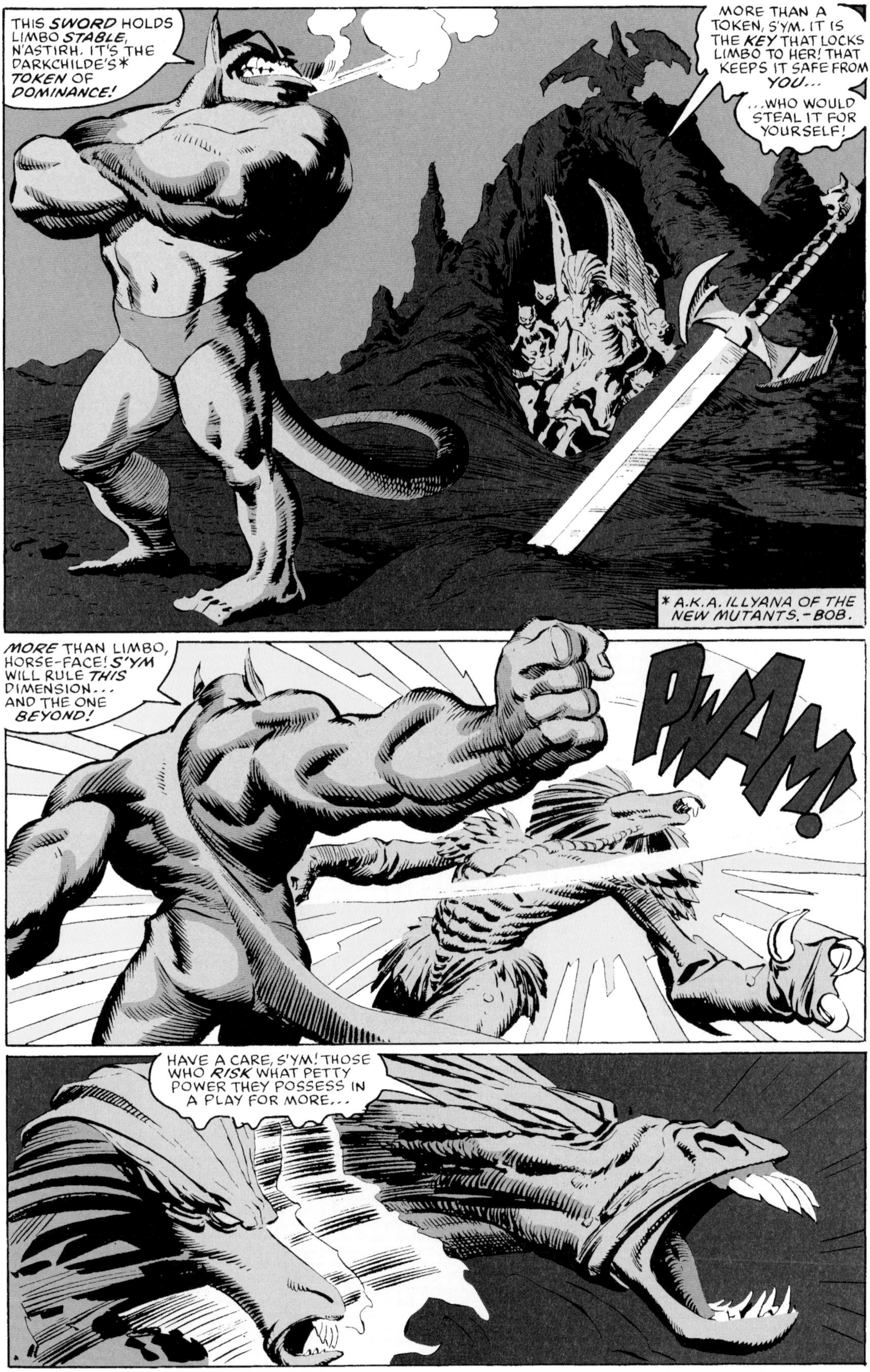
THIS SWORD HOLDS LIMBO STABLE, N'ASTIRH. IT'S THE DARKCHILDE'S* TOKEN OF DOMINANCE!
MORE THAN A TOKEN, S'YM. IT IS THE KEY THAT LOCKS LIMBO TO HER! THAT KEEPS IT SAFE FROM YOU...
...WHO WOULD STEAL IT FOR YOURSELF!
* A.K.A. ILLYANA OF THE NEW MUTANTS.-BOB.
MORE THAN LIMBO, HORSE-FACE! S'YM WILL RULE THIS DIMENSION... AND THE ONE BEYOND!
PWAM!
HAVE A CARE, S'YM! THOSE WHO RISK WHAT PETTY POWER THEY POSSESS IN A PLAY FOR MORE...

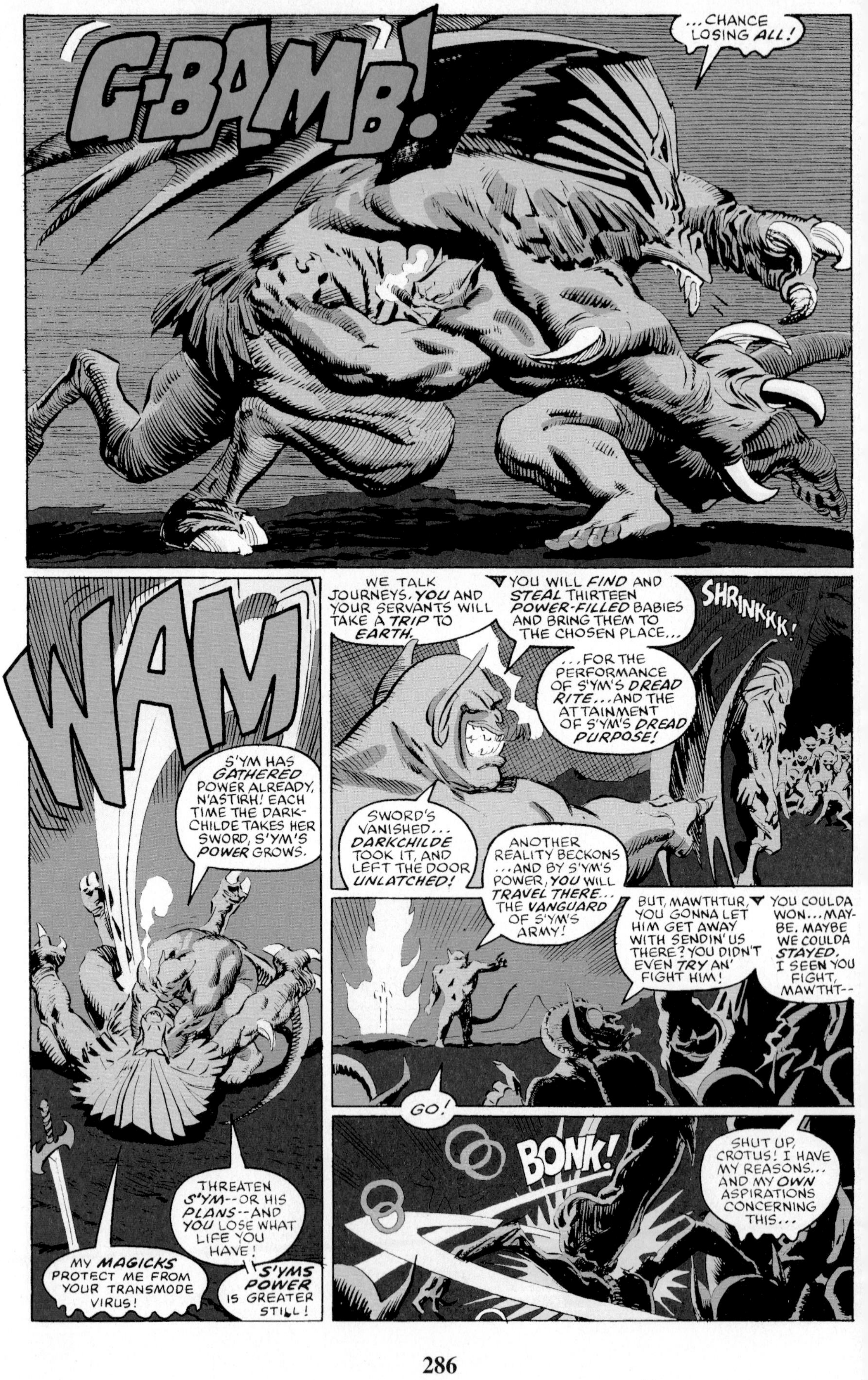

G-BAMB!
...CHANCE LOSING ALL!
WAM
S'YM HAS GATHERED POWER ALREADY, N'ASTIRH! EACH TIME THE DARKCHILDE TAKES HER SWORD, S'YM'S POWER GROWS.
THREATEN S'YM--OR HIS PLANS--AND YOU LOSE WHAT LIFE YOU HAVE!
MY MAGICKS PROTECT ME FROM YOUR TRANSMODE VIRUS!
S'YMS POWER IS GREATER STILL!
WE TALK JOURNEYS. YOU AND YOUR SERVANTS WILL TAKE A TRIP TO EARTH.
YOU WILL FIND AND STEAL THIRTEEN POWER-FILLED BABIES AND BRING THEM TO THE CHOSEN PLACE...
...FOR THE PERFORMANCE OF S'YM'S DREAD RITE...AND THE ATTAINMENT OF S'YM'S DREAD PURPOSE!
SHRINKKK!
SWORD'S VANISHED... DARKCHILDE TOOK IT, AND LEFT THE DOOR UNLATCHED!
ANOTHER REALITY BECKONS ...AND BY S'YM'S POWER, YOU WILL TRAVEL THERE... THE VANGUARD OF S'YM'S ARMY!
BUT, MAWTHTUR, YOU GONNA LET HIM GET AWAY WITH SENDIN' US THERE? YOU DIDN'T EVEN TRY AN' FIGHT HIM!
YOU COULDA WON...MAYBE. MAYBE WE COULDA STAYED. I SEEN YOU FIGHT, MAWTHT--
GO!
BONK!
SHUT UP, CROTUS! I HAVE MY REASONS... AND MY OWN ASPIRATIONS CONCERNING THIS...

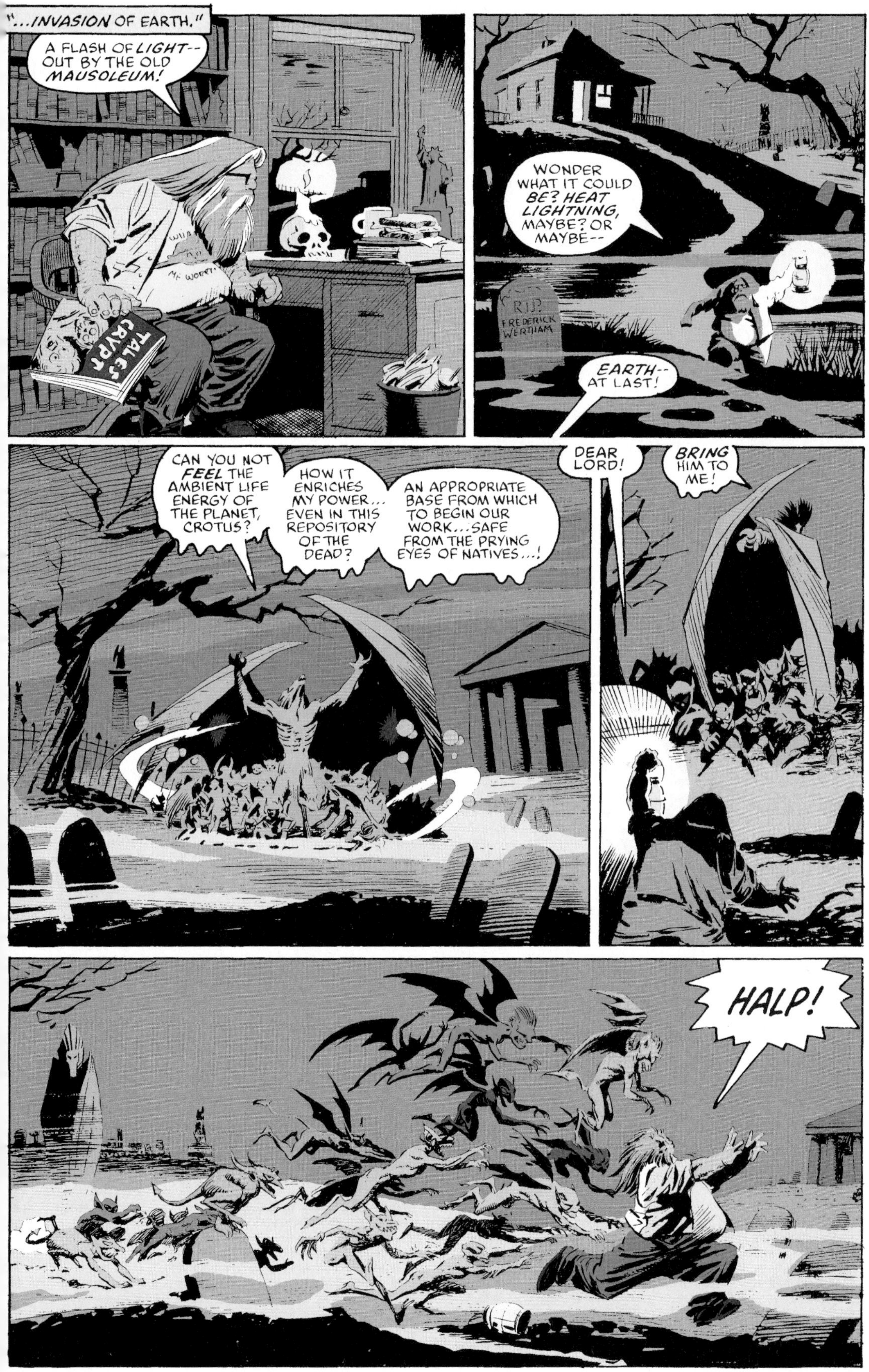
"...INVASION OF EARTH."
A FLASH OF LIGHT-- OUT BY THE OLD MAUSOLEUM!
TALES CRYPT
WONDER WHAT IT COULD BE? HEAT LIGHTNING, MAYBE? OR MAYBE--
R.I.P. FREDERICK WERTHAM
EARTH-- AT LAST!
CAN YOU NOT FEEL THE AMBIENT LIFE ENERGY OF THE PLANET, CROTUS?
HOW IT ENRICHES MY POWER... EVEN IN THIS REPOSITORY OF THE DEAD?
AN APPROPRIATE BASE FROM WHICH TO BEGIN OUR WORK... SAFE FROM THE PRYING EYES OF NATIVES...!
DEAR LORD!
BRING HIM TO ME!
HALP!

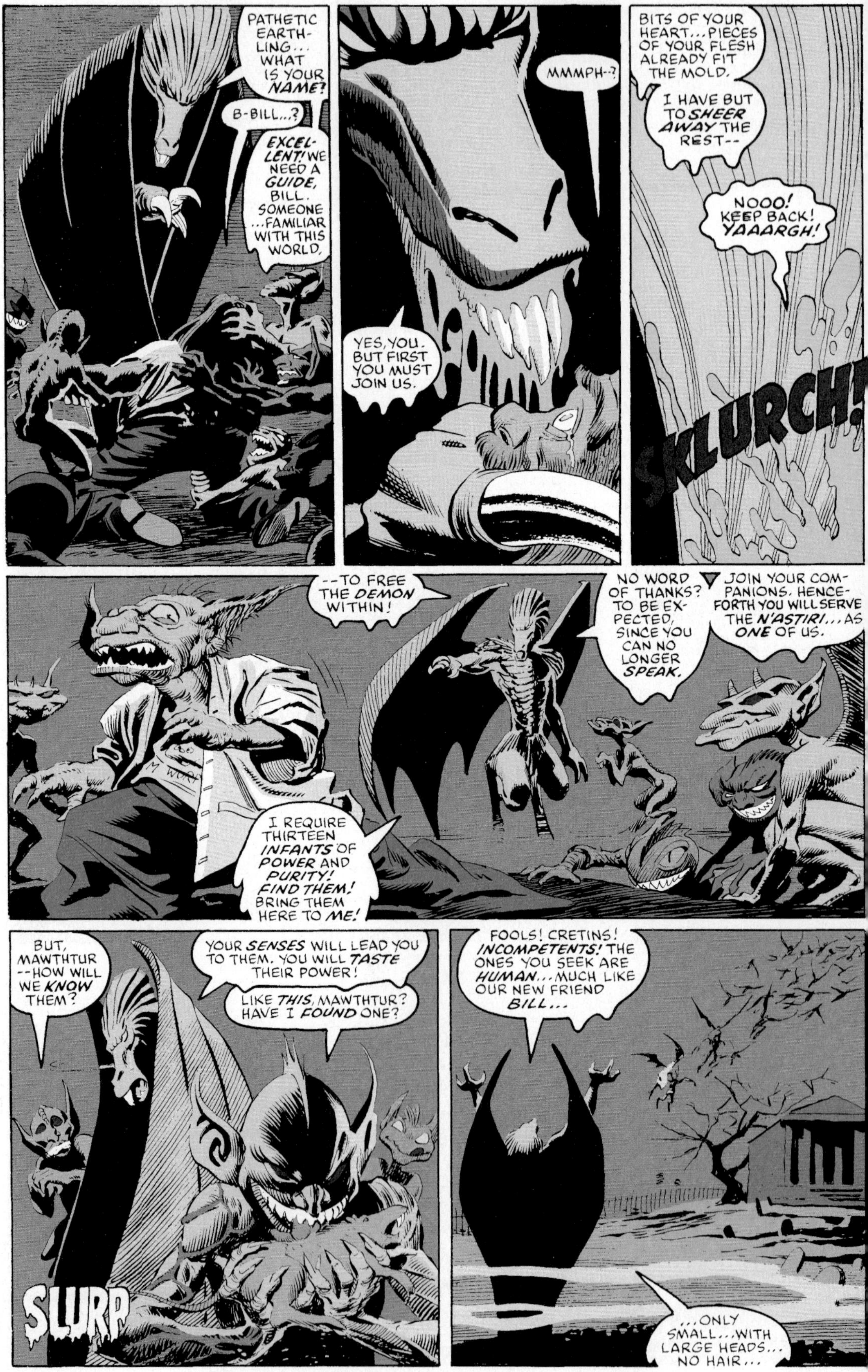
PATHETIC EARTHLING... WHAT IS YOUR NAME?
B-BILL...?
EXCELLENT! WE NEED A GUIDE, BILL. SOMEONE ...FAMILIAR WITH THIS WORLD.
MMMPH--?
YES, YOU. BUT FIRST YOU MUST JOIN US.
BITS OF YOUR HEART... PIECES OF YOUR FLESH ALREADY FIT THE MOLD.
I HAVE BUT TO SHEER AWAY THE REST--
NOOO! KEEP BACK! YAAARGH!
SKLURCH!
--TO FREE THE DEMON WITHIN!
I REQUIRE THIRTEEN INFANTS OF POWER AND PURITY! FIND THEM! BRING THEM HERE TO ME!
NO WORD OF THANKS? TO BE EXPECTED, SINCE YOU CAN NO LONGER SPEAK.
JOIN YOUR COMPANIONS. HENCEFORTH YOU WILL SERVE THE N'ASTIRI... AS ONE OF US.
BUT, MAWTHTUR --HOW WILL WE KNOW THEM?
YOUR SENSES WILL LEAD YOU TO THEM. YOU WILL TASTE THEIR POWER!
LIKE THIS, MAWTHTUR? HAVE I FOUND ONE?
SLURP
FOOLS! CRETINS! INCOMPETENTS! THE ONES YOU SEEK ARE HUMAN... MUCH LIKE OUR NEW FRIEND BILL...
...ONLY SMALL... WITH LARGE HEADS... NO HAIR...

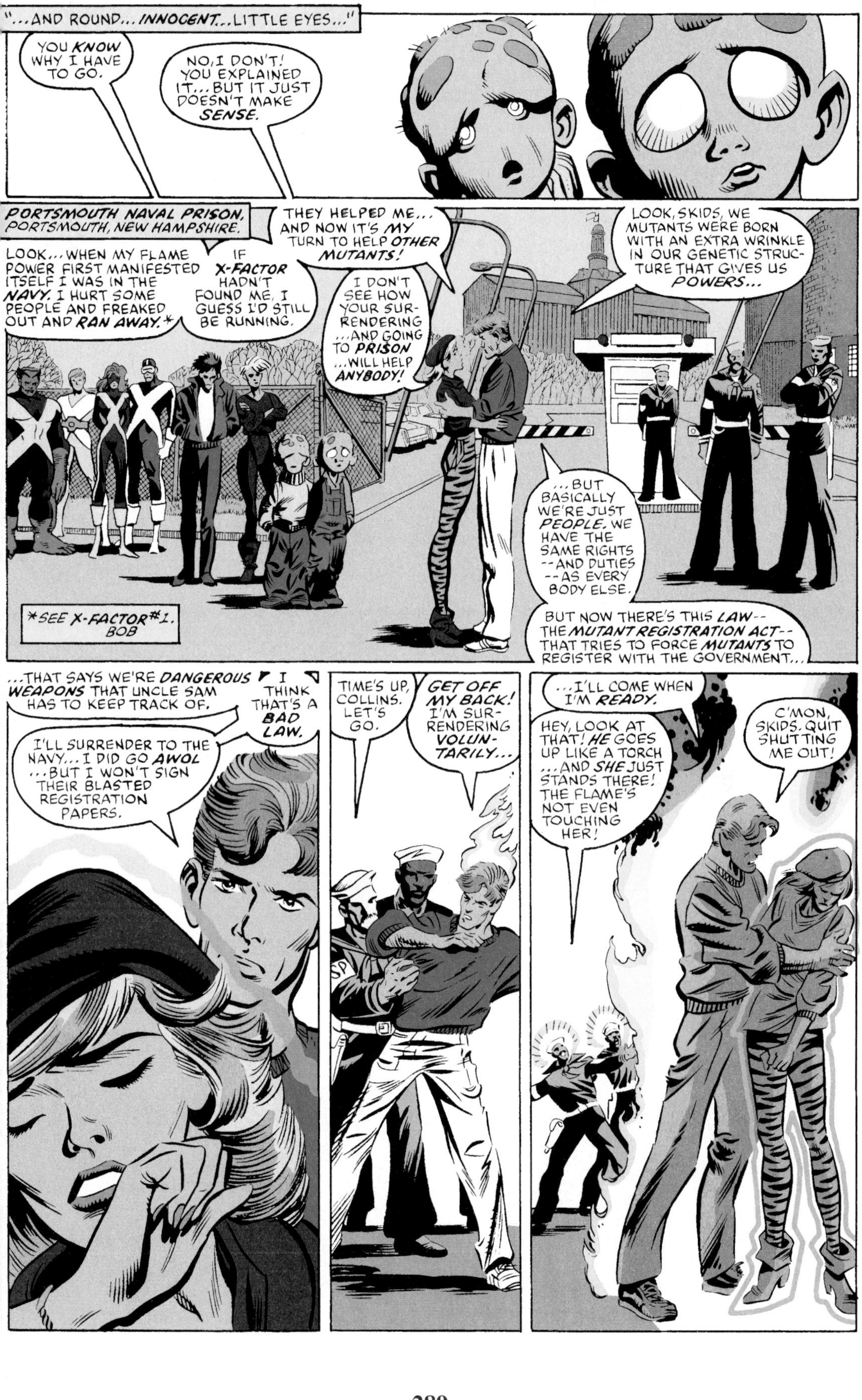
"...AND ROUND... INNOCENT... LITTLE EYES..."
YOU KNOW WHY I HAVE TO GO.
NO, I DON'T! YOU EXPLAINED IT... BUT IT JUST DOESN'T MAKE SENSE.
PORTSMOUTH NAVAL PRISON, PORTSMOUTH, NEW HAMPSHIRE.
LOOK... WHEN MY FLAME POWER FIRST MANIFESTED ITSELF I WAS IN THE NAVY. I HURT SOME PEOPLE AND FREAKED OUT AND RAN AWAY.*
IF X-FACTOR HADN'T FOUND ME, I GUESS I'D STILL BE RUNNING.
THEY HELPED ME... AND NOW IT'S MY TURN TO HELP OTHER MUTANTS!
I DON'T SEE HOW YOUR SURRENDERING ...AND GOING TO PRISON ...WILL HELP ANYBODY!
LOOK, SKIDS, WE MUTANTS WERE BORN WITH AN EXTRA WRINKLE IN OUR GENETIC STRUCTURE THAT GIVES US POWERS...
...BUT BASICALLY WE'RE JUST PEOPLE. WE HAVE THE SAME RIGHTS --AND DUTIES-- AS EVERY BODY ELSE.
*SEE X-FACTOR #1. BOB
BUT NOW THERE'S THIS LAW-- THE MUTANT REGISTRATION ACT-- THAT TRIES TO FORCE MUTANTS TO REGISTER WITH THE GOVERNMENT...
...THAT SAYS WE'RE DANGEROUS WEAPONS THAT UNCLE SAM HAS TO KEEP TRACK OF.
I THINK THAT'S A BAD LAW.
I'LL SURRENDER TO THE NAVY... I DID GO AWOL ...BUT I WON'T SIGN THEIR BLASTED REGISTRATION PAPERS.
TIME'S UP, COLLINS. LET'S GO.
GET OFF MY BACK! I'M SURRENDERING VOLUNTARILY...
SP
...I'LL COME WHEN I'M READY.
HEY, LOOK AT THAT! HE GOES UP LIKE A TORCH ...AND SHE JUST STANDS THERE! THE FLAME'S NOT EVEN TOUCHING HER!
C'MON, SKIDS. QUIT SHUTTING ME OUT!

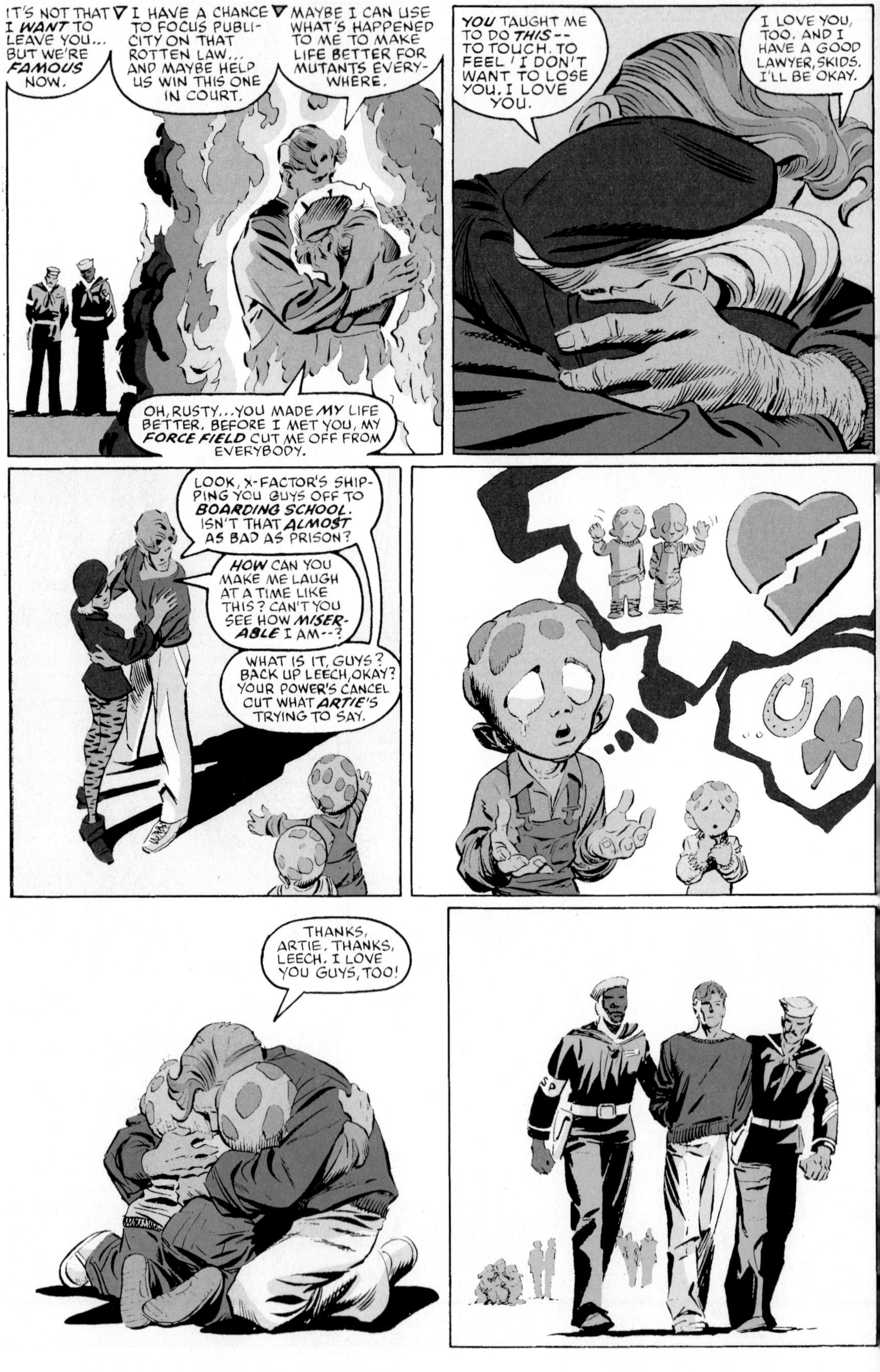
IT'S NOT THAT I WANT TO LEAVE YOU... BUT WE'RE FAMOUS NOW.
I HAVE A CHANCE TO FOCUS PUBLICITY ON THAT ROTTEN LAW... AND MAYBE HELP US WIN THIS ONE IN COURT.
MAYBE I CAN USE WHAT'S HAPPENED TO ME TO MAKE LIFE BETTER FOR MUTANTS EVERYWHERE.
OH, RUSTY...YOU MADE MY LIFE BETTER. BEFORE I MET YOU, MY FORCE FIELD CUT ME OFF FROM EVERYBODY.
YOU TAUGHT ME TO DO THIS-- TO TOUCH. TO FEEL! I DON'T WANT TO LOSE YOU. I LOVE YOU.
I LOVE YOU, TOO. AND I HAVE A GOOD LAWYER, SKIDS. I'LL BE OKAY.
LOOK, X-FACTOR'S SHIPPING YOU GUYS OFF TO BOARDING SCHOOL. ISN'T THAT ALMOST AS BAD AS PRISON?
HOW CAN YOU MAKE ME LAUGH AT A TIME LIKE THIS? CAN'T YOU SEE HOW MISERABLE I AM--?
WHAT IS IT, GUYS? BACK UP LEECH, OKAY? YOUR POWER'S CANCEL OUT WHAT ARTIE'S TRYING TO SAY.
THANKS, ARTIE. THANKS, LEECH. I LOVE YOU GUYS, TOO!

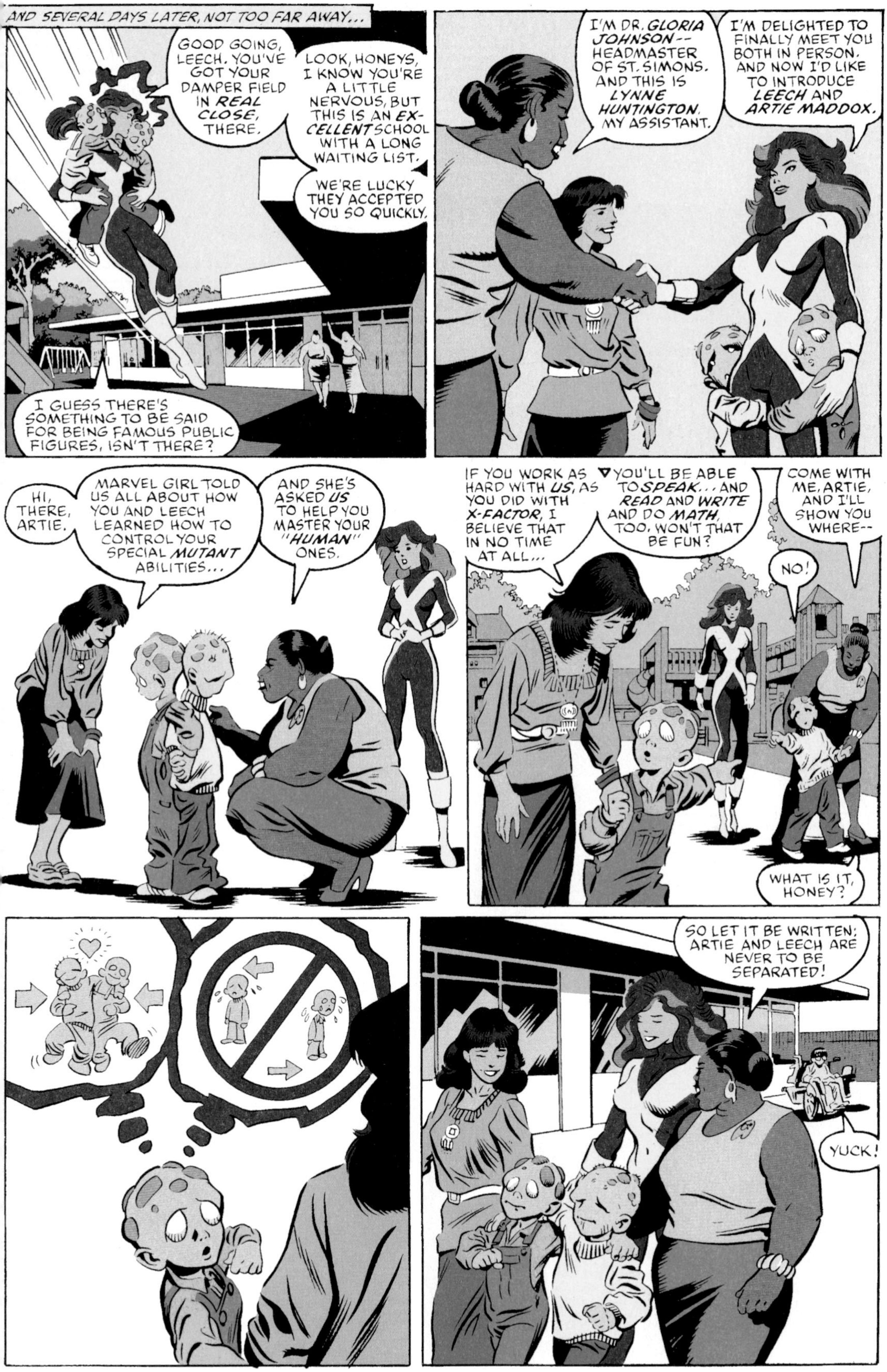
AND SEVERAL DAYS LATER, NOT TOO FAR AWAY...
GOOD GOING, LEECH. YOU'VE GOT YOUR DAMPER FIELD IN REAL CLOSE, THERE.
LOOK, HONEYS, I KNOW YOU'RE A LITTLE NERVOUS, BUT THIS IS AN EXCELLENT SCHOOL WITH A LONG WAITING LIST.
WE'RE LUCKY THEY ACCEPTED YOU SO QUICKLY.
I GUESS THERE'S SOMETHING TO BE SAID FOR BEING FAMOUS PUBLIC FIGURES, ISN'T THERE?
I'M DR. GLORIA JOHNSON-- HEADMASTER OF ST. SIMONS. AND THIS IS LYNNE HUNTINGTON, MY ASSISTANT.
I'M DELIGHTED TO FINALLY MEET YOU BOTH IN PERSON. AND NOW I'D LIKE TO INTRODUCE LEECH AND ARTIE MADDOX.
HI, THERE, ARTIE.
MARVEL GIRL TOLD US ALL ABOUT HOW YOU AND LEECH LEARNED HOW TO CONTROL YOUR SPECIAL MUTANT ABILITIES...
AND SHE'S ASKED US TO HELP YOU MASTER YOUR "HUMAN" ONES.
IF YOU WORK AS HARD WITH US, AS YOU DID WITH X-FACTOR, I BELIEVE THAT IN NO TIME AT ALL...
YOU'LL BE ABLE TO SPEAK... AND READ AND WRITE AND DO MATH, TOO. WON'T THAT BE FUN?
COME WITH ME, ARTIE, AND I'LL SHOW YOU WHERE--
NO!
WHAT IS IT, HONEY?
SO LET IT BE WRITTEN; ARTIE AND LEECH ARE NEVER TO BE SEPARATED!
YUCK!

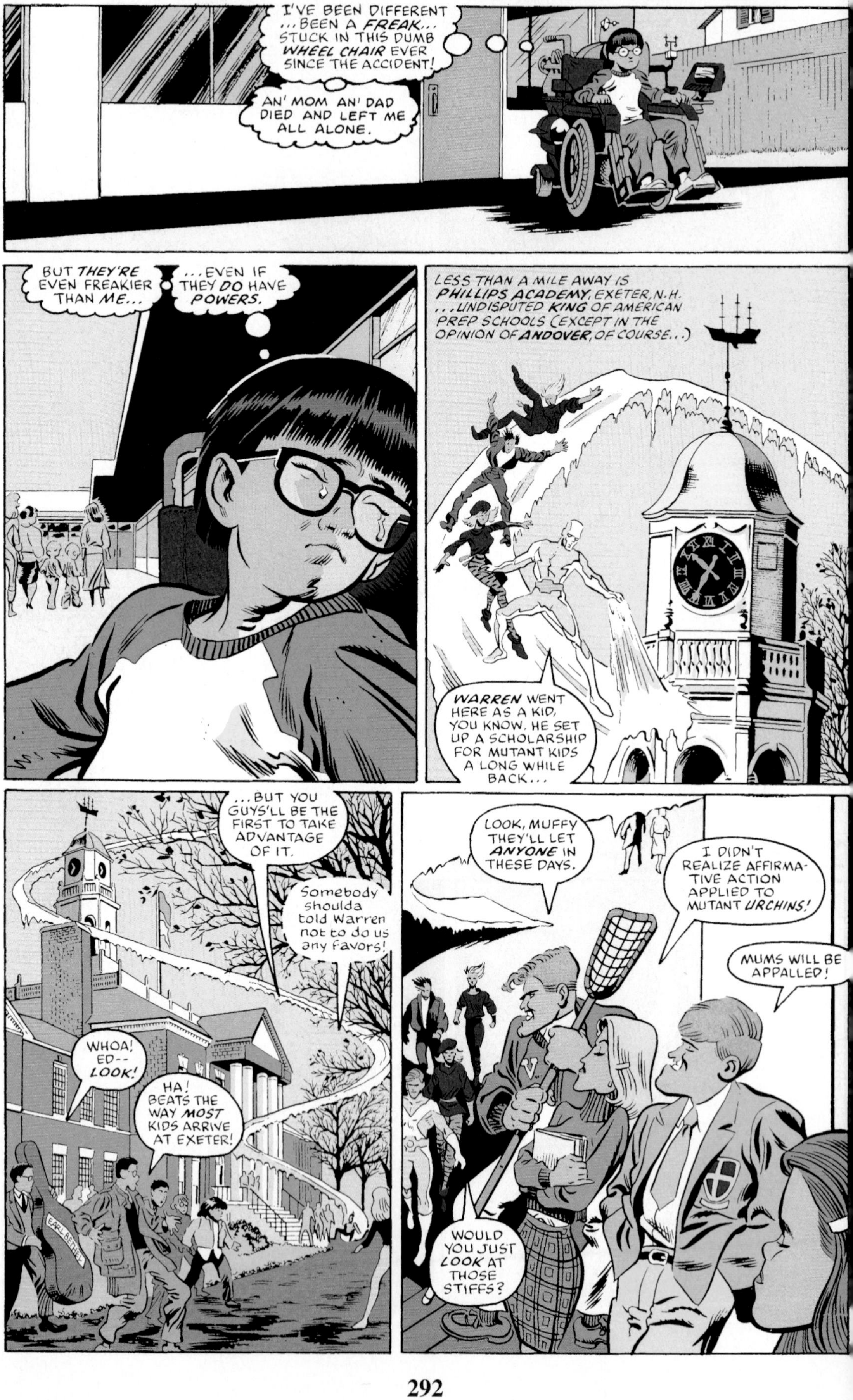
I'VE BEEN DIFFERENT ...BEEN A FREAK... STUCK IN THIS DUMB WHEEL CHAIR EVER SINCE THE ACCIDENT!
AN' MOM AN' DAD DIED AND LEFT ME ALL ALONE.
BUT THEY'RE EVEN FREAKIER THAN ME...
...EVEN IF THEY DO HAVE POWERS.
LESS THAN A MILE AWAY IS PHILLIPS ACADEMY, EXETER, N.H. ...UNDISPUTED KING OF AMERICAN PREP SCHOOLS (EXCEPT IN THE OPINION OF ANDOVER, OF COURSE...)
WARREN WENT HERE AS A KID, YOU KNOW. HE SET UP A SCHOLARSHIP FOR MUTANT KIDS A LONG WHILE BACK...
...BUT YOU GUYS'LL BE THE FIRST TO TAKE ADVANTAGE OF IT.
Somebody shoulda told Warren not to do us any favors!
WHOA! ED-- LOOK!
HA! BEATS THE WAY MOST KIDS ARRIVE AT EXETER!
LOOK, MUFFY THEY'LL LET ANYONE IN THESE DAYS.
I DIDN'T REALIZE AFFIRMATIVE ACTION APPLIED TO MUTANT URCHINS!
MUMS WILL BE APPALLED!
WOULD YOU JUST LOOK AT THOSE STIFFS?

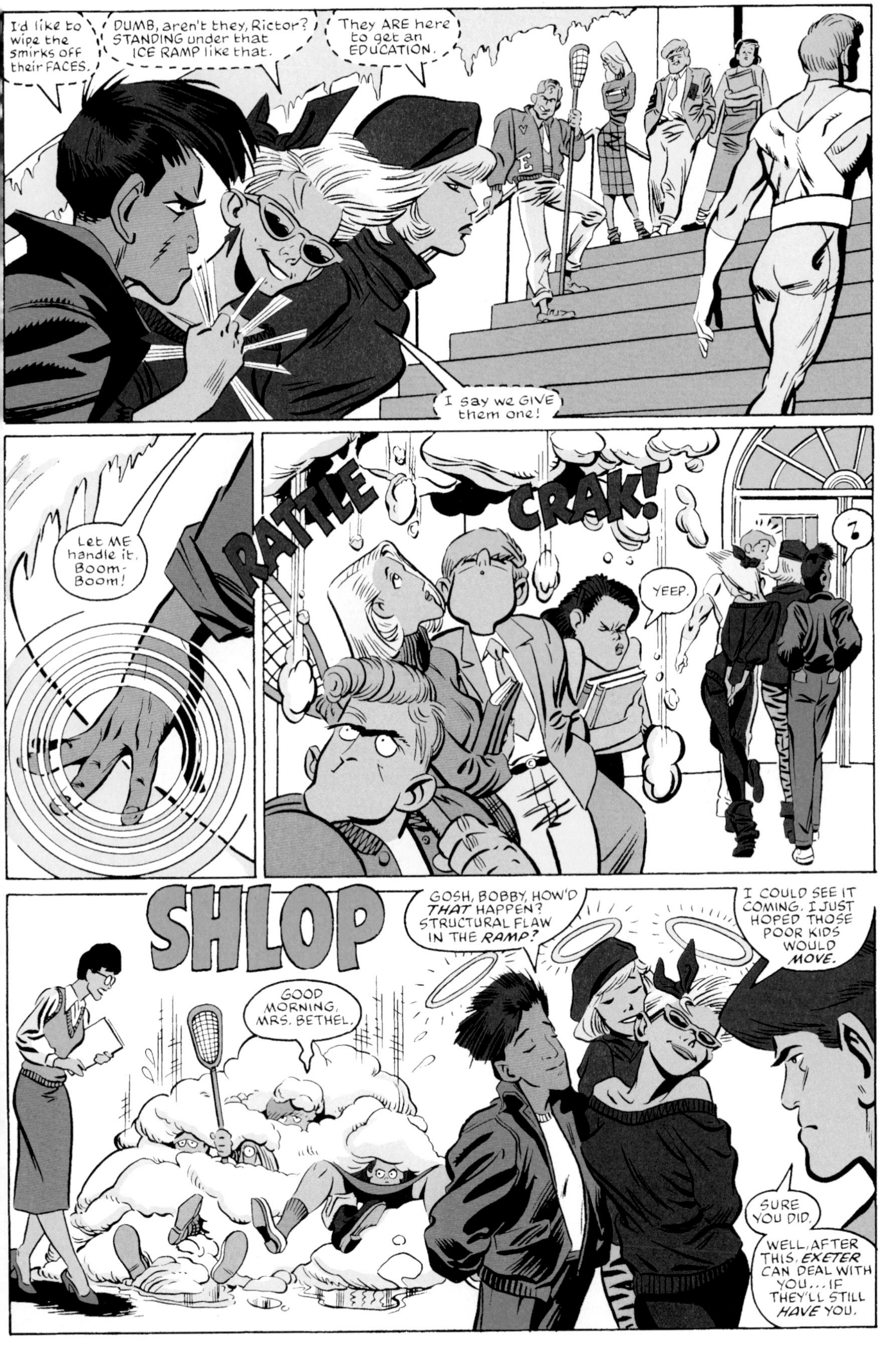
I'd like to wipe the smirks off their FACES.
DUMB, aren't they, Rictor? STANDING under that ICE RAMP like that.
They ARE here to get an EDUCATION.
I say we GIVE them one!
Let ME handle it, Boom-Boom!
RATTLE
CRAK!
YEEP.
?
SHLOP
GOSH, BOBBY, HOW'D THAT HAPPEN? STRUCTURAL FLAW IN THE RAMP?
I COULD SEE IT COMING. I JUST HOPED THOSE POOR KIDS WOULD MOVE.
GOOD MORNING, MRS. BETHEL.
SURE YOU DID.
WELL, AFTER THIS, EXETER CAN DEAL WITH YOU... IF THEY'LL STILL HAVE YOU.

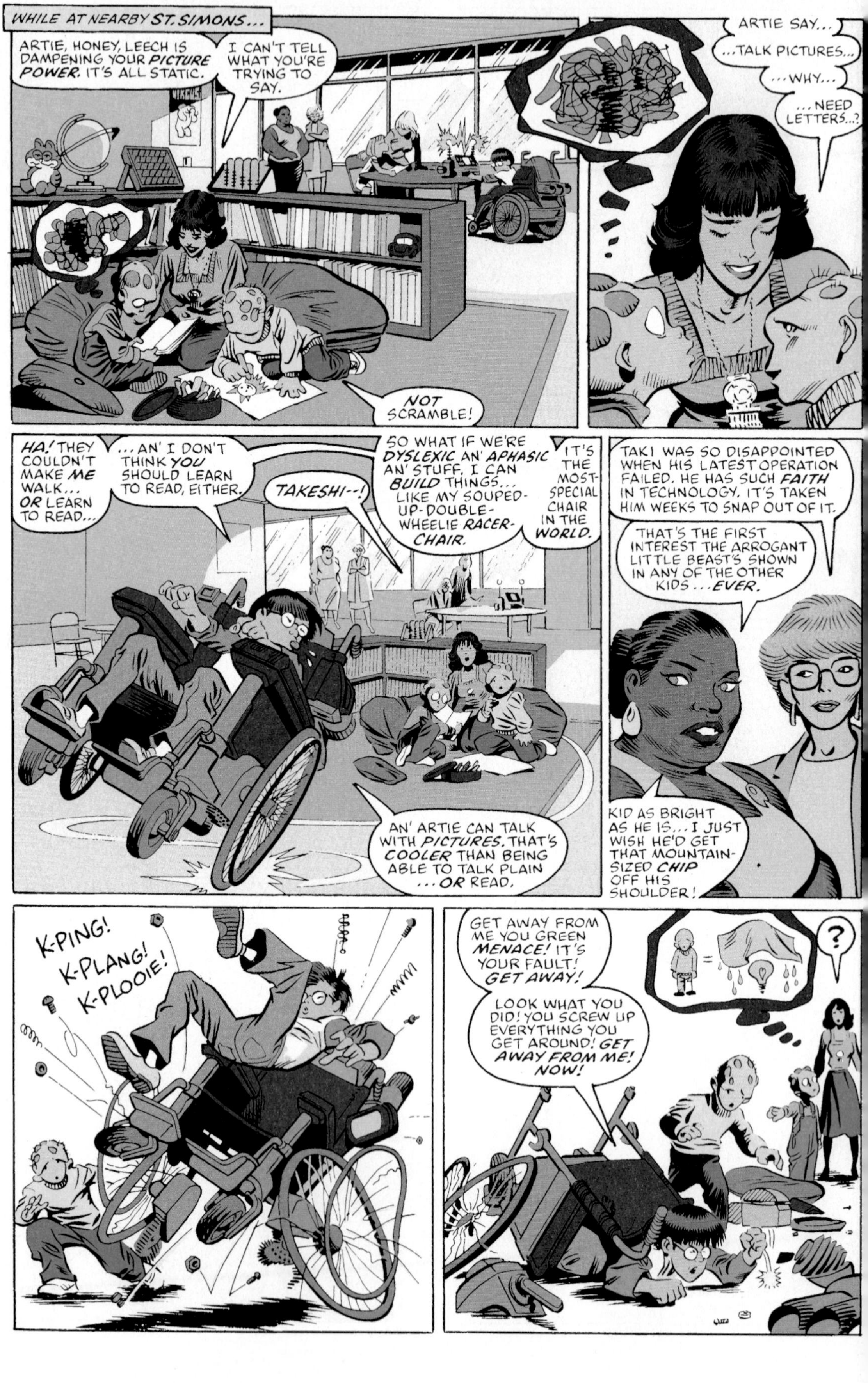
WHILE AT NEARBY ST. SIMONS...
ARTIE, HONEY, LEECH IS DAMPENING YOUR PICTURE POWER. IT'S ALL STATIC.
I CAN'T TELL WHAT YOU'RE TRYING TO SAY.
NOT SCRAMBLE!
ARTIE SAY...
...TALK PICTURES...
...WHY...
...NEED LETTERS...?
HA! THEY COULDN'T MAKE ME WALK... OR LEARN TO READ...
...AN' I DON'T THINK YOU SHOULD LEARN TO READ, EITHER.
TAKESHI--!
SO WHAT IF WE'RE DYSLEXIC AN' APHASIC AN' STUFF. I CAN BUILD THINGS... LIKE MY SOUPED-UP-DOUBLE-WHEELIE RACER-CHAIR.
IT'S THE MOST-SPECIAL CHAIR IN THE WORLD.
AN' ARTIE CAN TALK WITH PICTURES. THAT'S COOLER THAN BEING ABLE TO TALK PLAIN ...OR READ.
TAKI WAS SO DISAPPOINTED WHEN HIS LATEST OPERATION FAILED. HE HAS SUCH FAITH IN TECHNOLOGY. IT'S TAKEN HIM WEEKS TO SNAP OUT OF IT.
THAT'S THE FIRST INTEREST THE ARROGANT LITTLE BEAST'S SHOWN IN ANY OF THE OTHER KIDS ...EVER.
KID AS BRIGHT AS HE IS... I JUST WISH HE'D GET THAT MOUNTAIN-SIZED CHIP OFF HIS SHOULDER!
K-PING!
K-PLANG!
K-PLOOIE!
GET AWAY FROM ME YOU GREEN MENACE! IT'S YOUR FAULT! GET AWAY!
LOOK WHAT YOU DID! YOU SCREW UP EVERYTHING YOU GET AROUND! GET AWAY FROM ME! NOW!
?

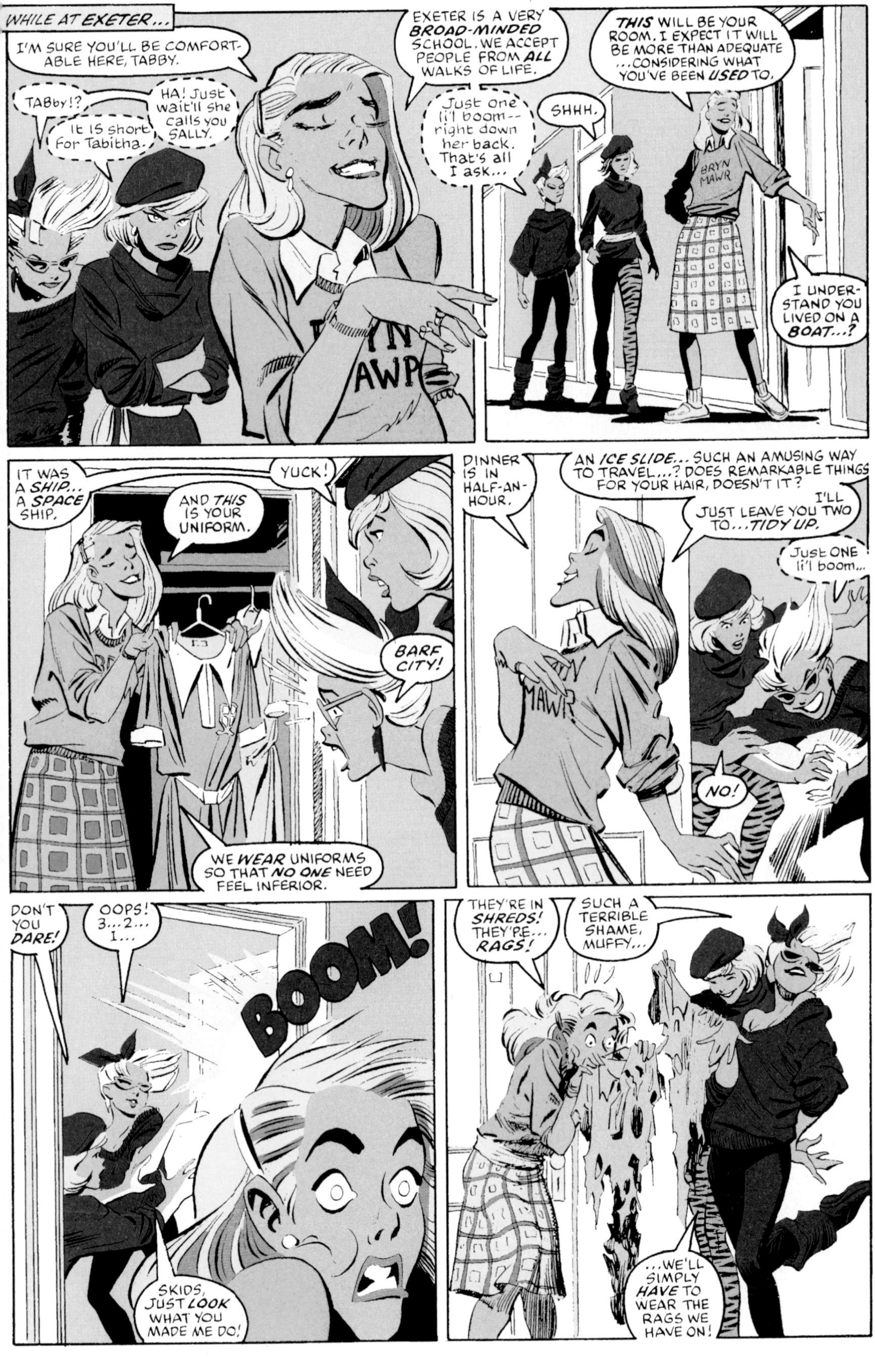

WHILE AT EXETER...
I'M SURE YOU'LL BE COMFORTABLE HERE, TABBY.
TABby!?
It IS short for Tabitha.
HA! Just wait'll she calls you SALLY.
EXETER IS A VERY BROAD-MINDED SCHOOL. WE ACCEPT PEOPLE FROM ALL WALKS OF LIFE.
Just one li'l boom-- right down her back. That's all I ask...
SHHH.
THIS WILL BE YOUR ROOM. I EXPECT IT WILL BE MORE THAN ADEQUATE ...CONSIDERING WHAT YOU'VE BEEN USED TO.
BRYN MAWR
I UNDERSTAND YOU LIVED ON A BOAT...?
IT WAS A SHIP... A SPACE SHIP.
AND THIS IS YOUR UNIFORM.
YUCK!
BARF CITY!
WE WEAR UNIFORMS SO THAT NO ONE NEED FEEL INFERIOR.
DINNER IS IN HALF-AN-HOUR.
AN ICE SLIDE... SUCH AN AMUSING WAY TO TRAVEL...? DOES REMARKABLE THINGS FOR YOUR HAIR, DOESN'T IT?
I'LL JUST LEAVE YOU TWO TO... TIDY UP.
Just ONE li'l boom...
NO!
DON'T YOU DARE!
OOPS! 3...2... 1...
BOOM!
SKIDS, JUST LOOK WHAT YOU MADE ME DO!
THEY'RE IN SHREDS! THEY'RE... RAGS!
SUCH A TERRIBLE SHAME, MUFFY...
...WE'LL SIMPLY HAVE TO WEAR THE RAGS WE HAVE ON!

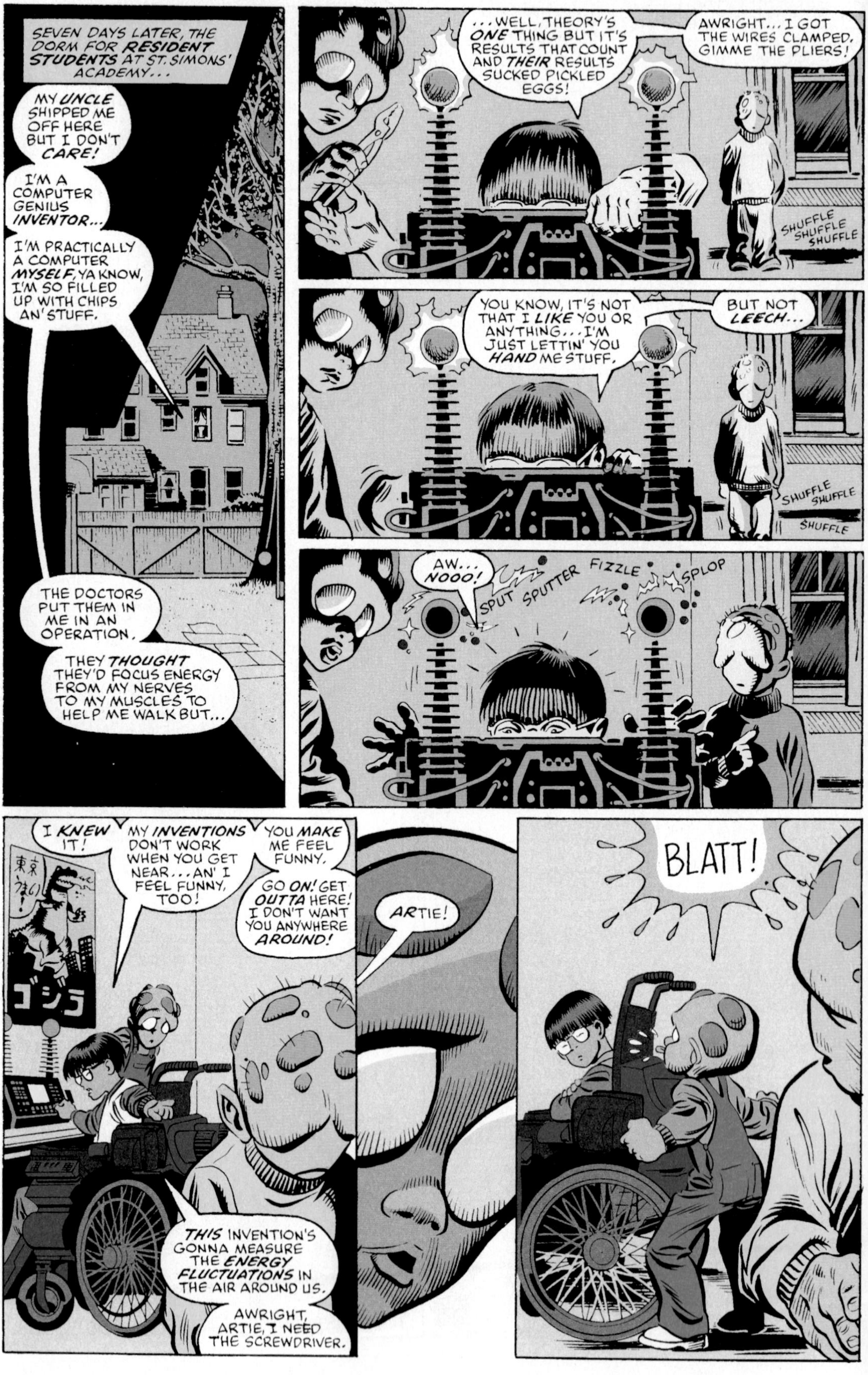
SEVEN DAYS LATER, THE DORM FOR RESIDENT STUDENTS AT ST. SIMONS' ACADEMY...
MY UNCLE SHIPPED ME OFF HERE BUT I DON'T CARE!
I'M A COMPUTER GENIUS INVENTOR...
I'M PRACTICALLY A COMPUTER MYSELF, YA KNOW, I'M SO FILLED UP WITH CHIPS AN' STUFF.
THE DOCTORS PUT THEM IN ME IN AN OPERATION.
THEY THOUGHT THEY'D FOCUS ENERGY FROM MY NERVES TO MY MUSCLES TO HELP ME WALK BUT...
...WELL, THEORY'S ONE THING BUT IT'S RESULTS THAT COUNT AND THEIR RESULTS SUCKED PICKLED EGGS!
AWRIGHT... I GOT THE WIRES CLAMPED. GIMME THE PLIERS!
SHUFFLE SHUFFLE SHUFFLE
YOU KNOW, IT'S NOT THAT I LIKE YOU OR ANYTHING... I'M JUST LETTIN' YOU HAND ME STUFF.
BUT NOT LEECH...
SHUFFLE SHUFFLE
SHUFFLE
AW... NOOO!
SPUT SPUTTER FIZZLE SPLOP
I KNEW IT!
東京
ゴジラ
MY INVENTIONS DON'T WORK WHEN YOU GET NEAR... AN' I FEEL FUNNY, TOO!
YOU MAKE ME FEEL FUNNY.
GO ON! GET OUTTA HERE! I DON'T WANT YOU ANYWHERE AROUND!
THIS INVENTION'S GONNA MEASURE THE ENERGY FLUCTUATIONS IN THE AIR AROUND US.
AWRIGHT, ARTIE, I NEED THE SCREWDRIVER.
ARTIE!
BLATT!

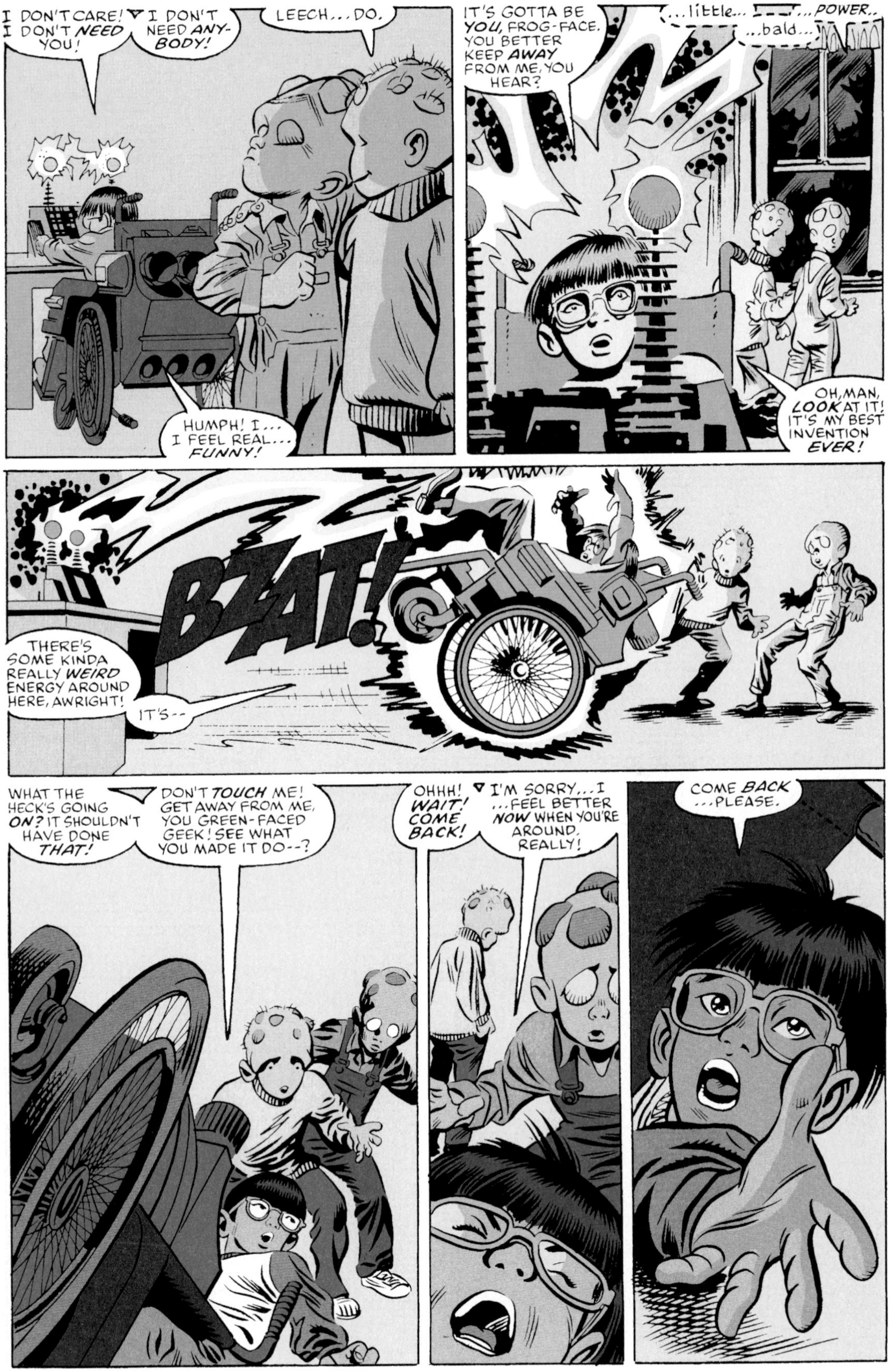
I DON'T CARE! I DON'T NEED YOU!
I DON'T NEED ANY-BODY!
LEECH... DO.
HUMPH! I... I FEEL REAL... FUNNY!
IT'S GOTTA BE YOU, FROG-FACE. YOU BETTER KEEP AWAY FROM ME, YOU HEAR?
...little...
...POWER...
...bald...
OH, MAN, LOOK AT IT! IT'S MY BEST INVENTION EVER!
BZAT!
THERE'S SOME KINDA REALLY WEIRD ENERGY AROUND HERE, AWRIGHT!
IT'S--
WHAT THE HECK'S GOING ON? IT SHOULDN'T HAVE DONE THAT!
DON'T TOUCH ME! GET AWAY FROM ME, YOU GREEN-FACED GEEK! SEE WHAT YOU MADE IT DO--?
OHHH! WAIT! COME BACK!
I'M SORRY... I ...FEEL BETTER NOW WHEN YOU'RE AROUND. REALLY!
COME BACK ...PLEASE.

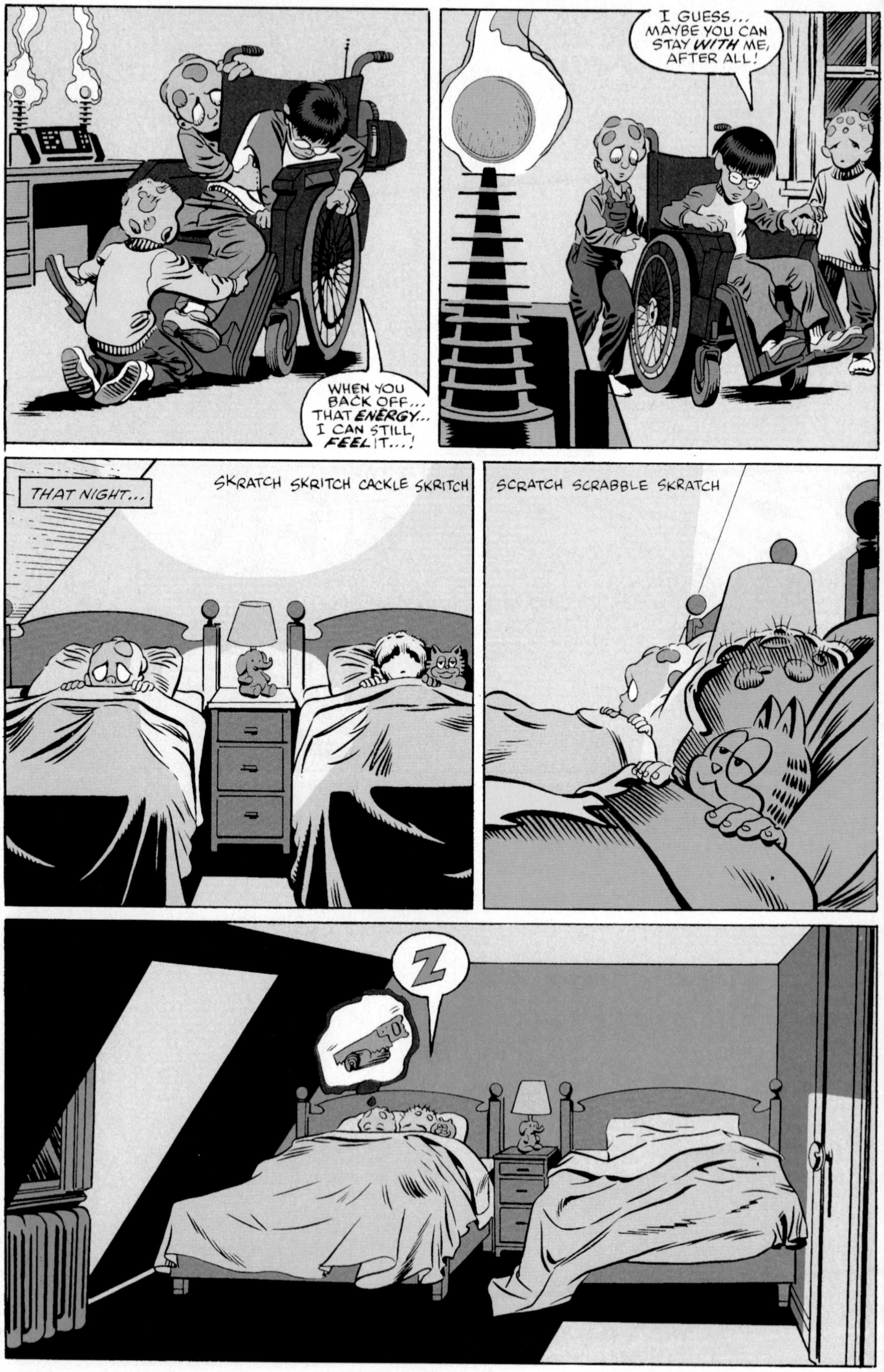
WHEN YOU BACK OFF... THAT ENERGY... I CAN STILL FEEL IT...!
I GUESS... MAYBE YOU CAN STAY WITH ME, AFTER ALL!
THAT NIGHT...
SKRATCH SKRITCH CACKLE SKRITCH
SCRATCH SCRABBLE SKRATCH
Z

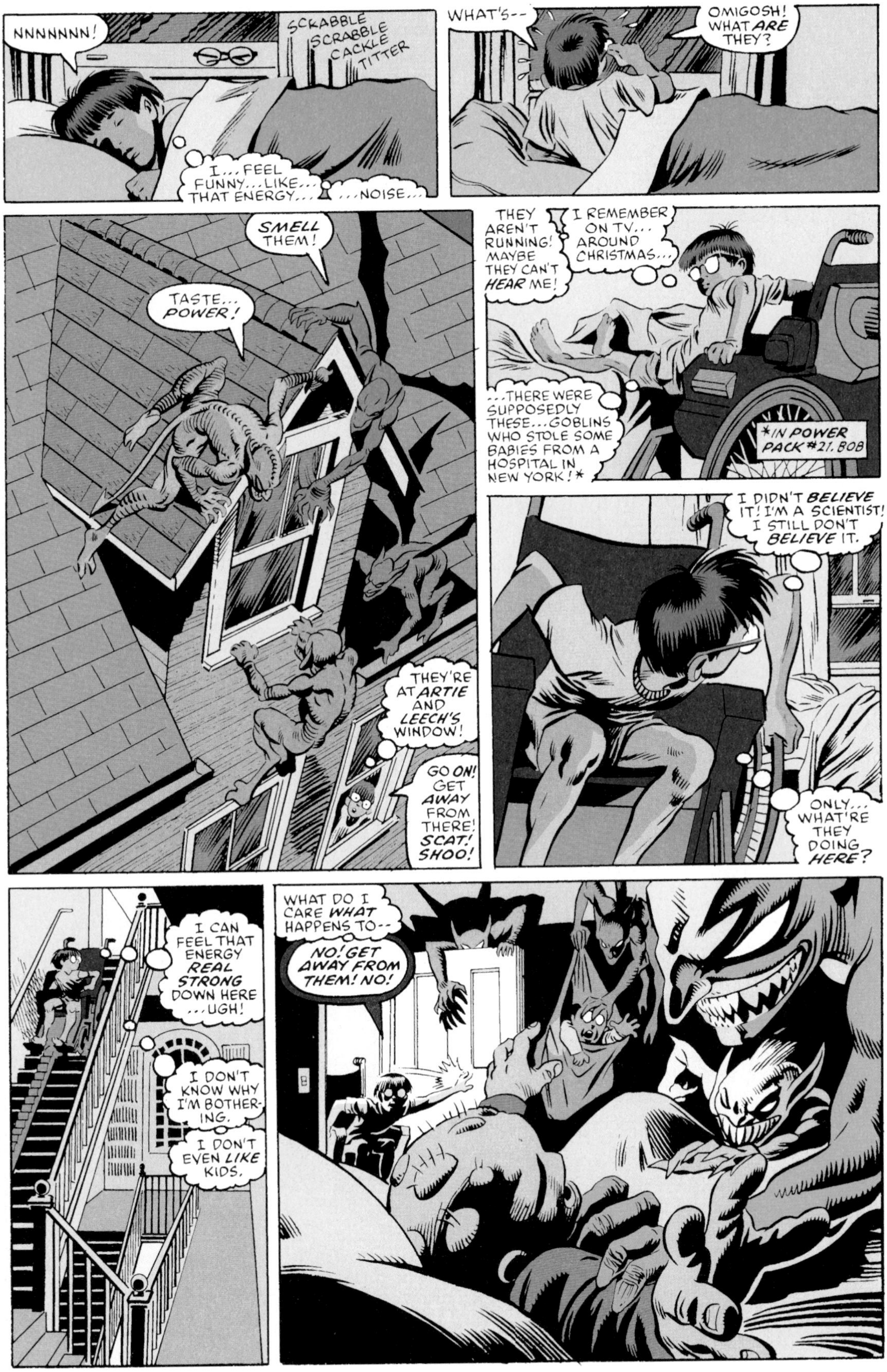
NNNNNNN!
SCKABBLE SCRABBLE CACKLE TITTER
I... FEEL FUNNY... LIKE... THAT ENERGY...
...NOISE...
WHAT'S--
OMIGOSH! WHAT ARE THEY?
SMELL THEM!
TASTE... POWER!
THEY'RE AT ARTIE AND LEECH'S WINDOW!
GO ON! GET AWAY FROM THERE! SCAT! SHOO!
THEY AREN'T RUNNING! MAYBE THEY CAN'T HEAR ME!
I REMEMBER ON TV... AROUND CHRISTMAS...
...THERE WERE SUPPOSEDLY THESE...GOBLINS WHO STOLE SOME BABIES FROM A HOSPITAL IN NEW YORK!*
*IN POWER PACK #21. BOB
I DIDN'T BELIEVE IT! I'M A SCIENTIST! I STILL DON'T BELIEVE IT.
ONLY... WHAT'RE THEY DOING HERE?
I CAN FEEL THAT ENERGY REAL STRONG DOWN HERE ...UGH!
I DON'T KNOW WHY I'M BOTHERING.
I DON'T EVEN LIKE KIDS.
WHAT DO I CARE WHAT HAPPENS TO--
NO! GET AWAY FROM THEM! NO!

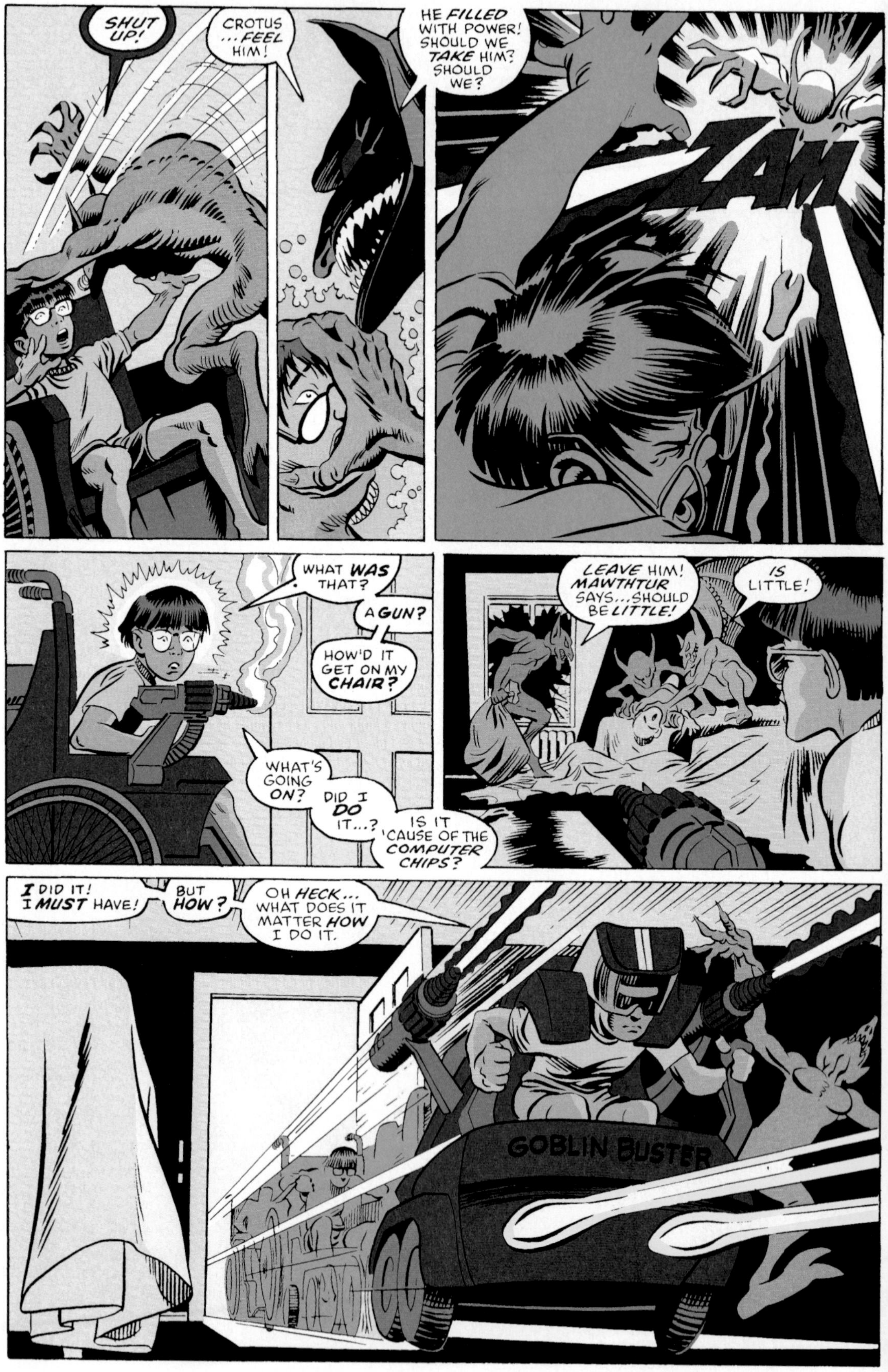
SHUT UP!
CROTUS ...FEEL HIM!
HE FILLED WITH POWER! SHOULD WE TAKE HIM? SHOULD WE?
ZAM
WHAT WAS THAT?
A GUN?
HOW'D IT GET ON MY CHAIR?
WHAT'S GOING ON?
DID I DO IT...?
IS IT 'CAUSE OF THE COMPUTER CHIPS?
LEAVE HIM! MAWTHTUR SAYS...SHOULD BE LITTLE!
IS LITTLE!
I DID IT! I MUST HAVE!
BUT HOW?
OH HECK... WHAT DOES IT MATTER HOW I DO IT.
GOBLIN BUSTER

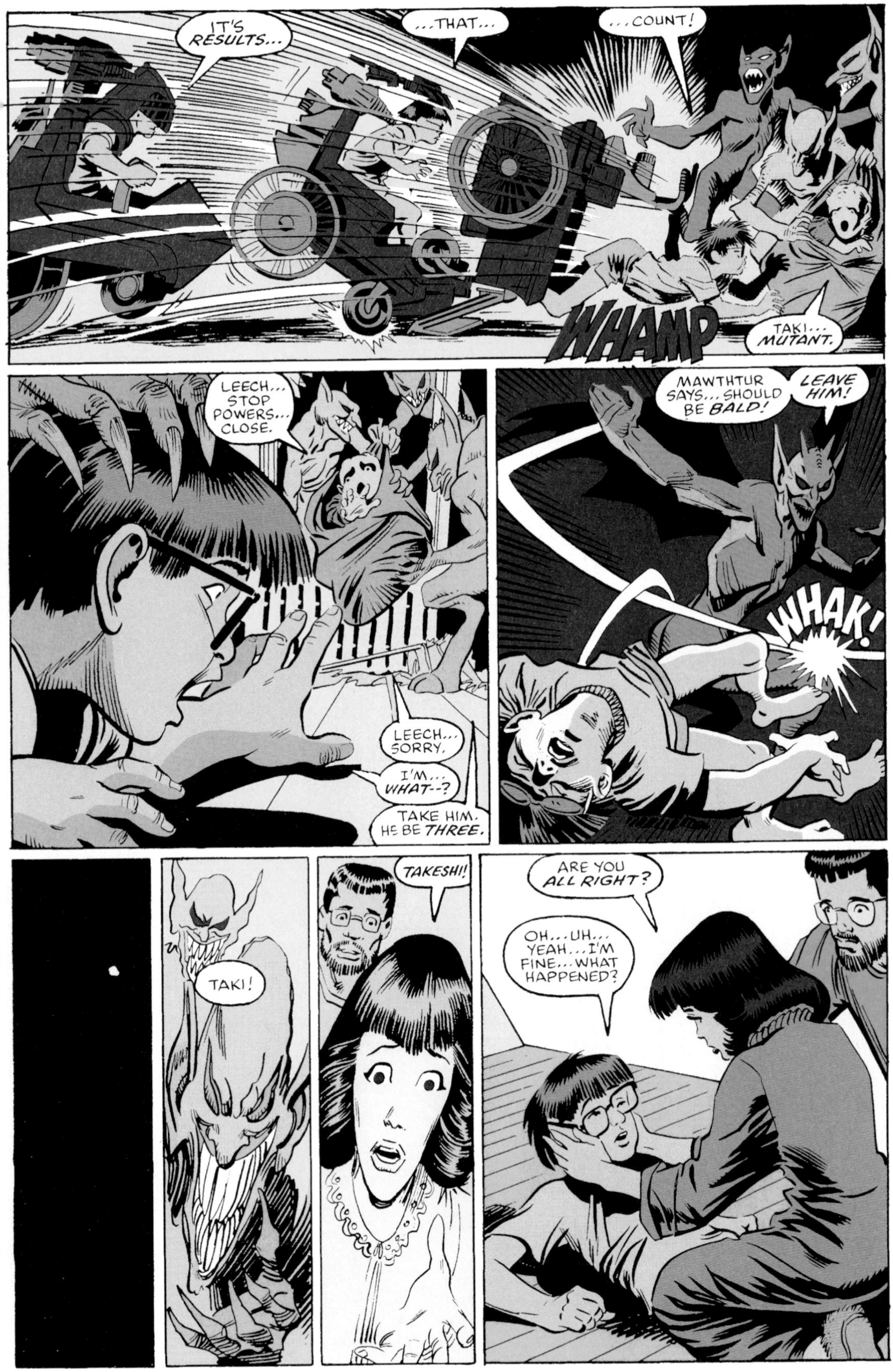
IT'S RESULTS...
...THAT...
...COUNT!
WHAMP
TAKI... MUTANT.
LEECH... STOP POWERS... CLOSE.
LEECH... SORRY.
I'M... WHAT--?
TAKE HIM. HE BE THREE.
MAWTHTUR SAYS... SHOULD BE BALD!
LEAVE HIM!
WHAK!
TAKI!
TAKESHI!
ARE YOU ALL RIGHT?
OH... UH... YEAH... I'M FINE... WHAT HAPPENED?

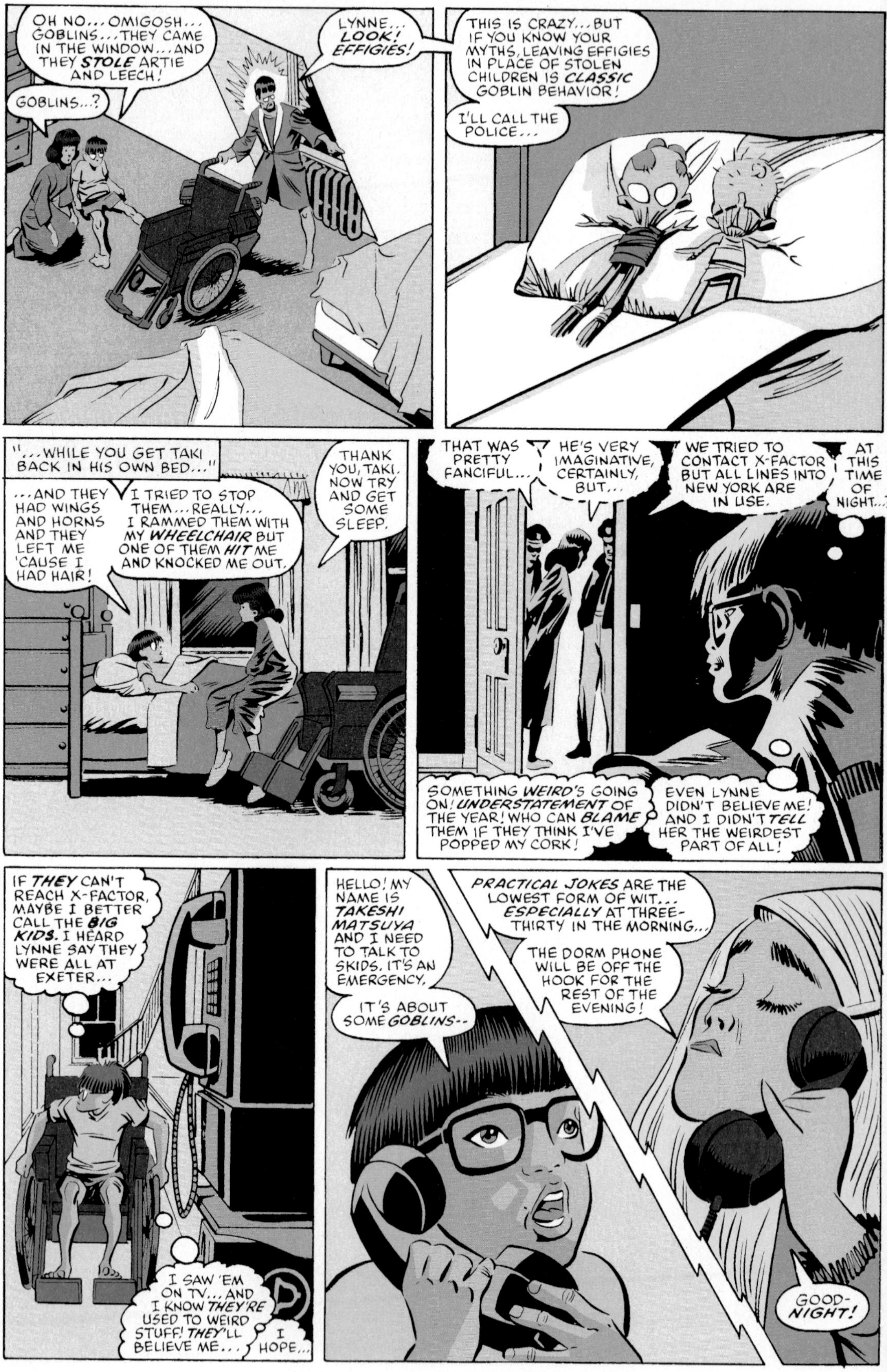
OH NO... OMIGOSH... GOBLINS... THEY CAME IN THE WINDOW... AND THEY STOLE ARTIE AND LEECH!
GOBLINS...?
LYNNE... LOOK! EFFIGIES!
THIS IS CRAZY... BUT IF YOU KNOW YOUR MYTHS, LEAVING EFFIGIES IN PLACE OF STOLEN CHILDREN IS CLASSIC GOBLIN BEHAVIOR!
I'LL CALL THE POLICE...
"...WHILE YOU GET TAKI BACK IN HIS OWN BED..."
...AND THEY HAD WINGS AND HORNS AND THEY LEFT ME 'CAUSE I HAD HAIR!
I TRIED TO STOP THEM... REALLY... I RAMMED THEM WITH MY WHEELCHAIR BUT ONE OF THEM HIT ME AND KNOCKED ME OUT.
THANK YOU, TAKI. NOW TRY AND GET SOME SLEEP.
THAT WAS PRETTY FANCIFUL...
HE'S VERY IMAGINATIVE, CERTAINLY, BUT...
WE TRIED TO CONTACT X-FACTOR BUT ALL LINES INTO NEW YORK ARE IN USE.
AT THIS TIME OF NIGHT...
SOMETHING WEIRD'S GOING ON! UNDERSTATEMENT OF THE YEAR! WHO CAN BLAME THEM IF THEY THINK I'VE POPPED MY CORK!
EVEN LYNNE DIDN'T BELIEVE ME! AND I DIDN'T TELL HER THE WEIRDEST PART OF ALL!
IF THEY CAN'T REACH X-FACTOR, MAYBE I BETTER CALL THE BIG KIDS. I HEARD LYNNE SAY THEY WERE ALL AT EXETER...
I SAW 'EM ON TV... AND I KNOW THEY'RE USED TO WEIRD STUFF! THEY'LL BELIEVE ME...
I HOPE...
HELLO! MY NAME IS TAKESHI MATSUYA AND I NEED TO TALK TO SKIDS. IT'S AN EMERGENCY.
IT'S ABOUT SOME GOBLINS--
PRACTICAL JOKES ARE THE LOWEST FORM OF WIT... ESPECIALLY AT THREE-THIRTY IN THE MORNING...
THE DORM PHONE WILL BE OFF THE HOOK FOR THE REST OF THE EVENING!
GOOD-NIGHT!

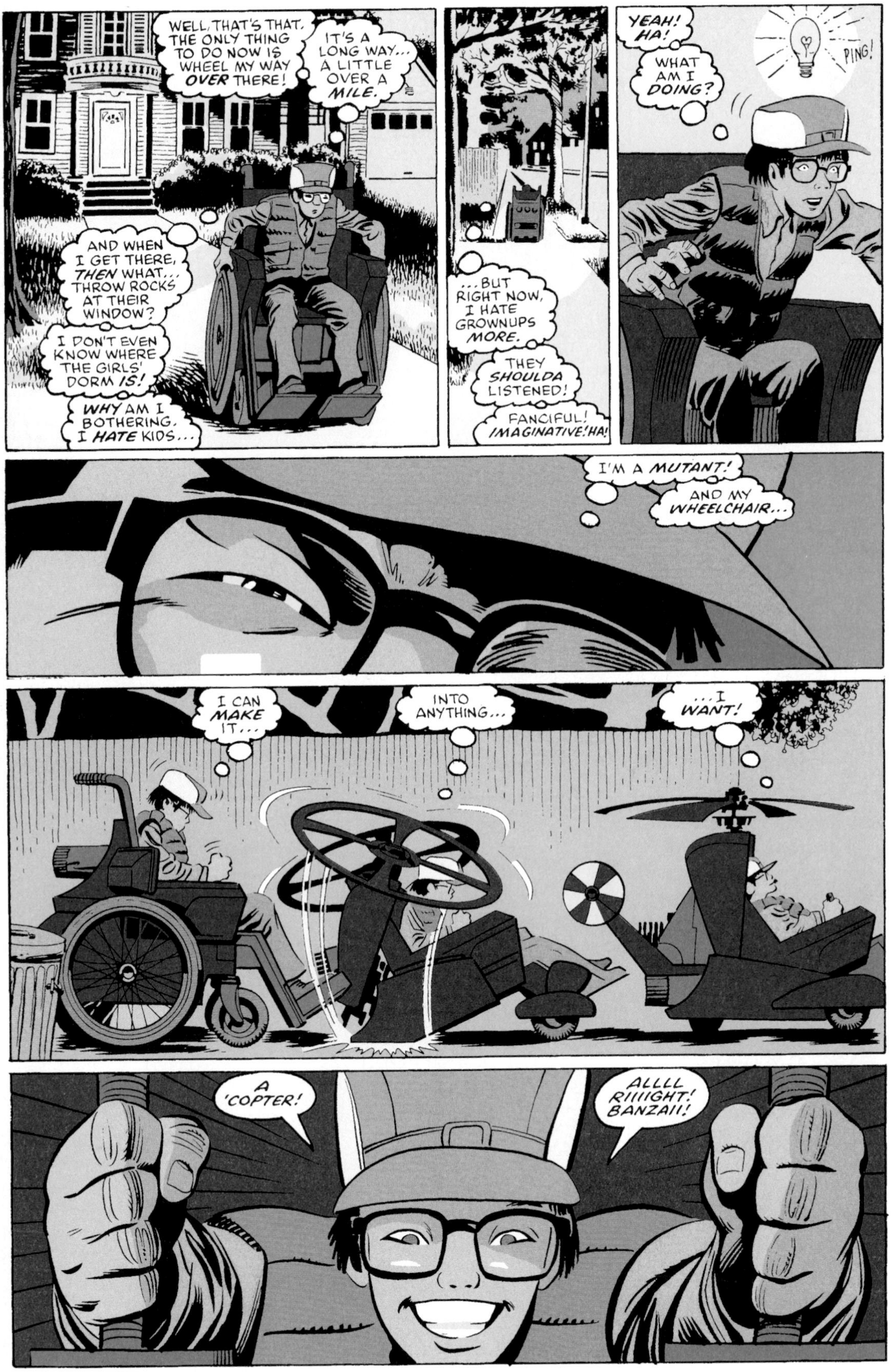
WELL, THAT'S THAT. THE ONLY THING TO DO NOW IS WHEEL MY WAY OVER THERE!
IT'S A LONG WAY... A LITTLE OVER A MILE.
AND WHEN I GET THERE, THEN WHAT... THROW ROCKS AT THEIR WINDOW?
I DON'T EVEN KNOW WHERE THE GIRLS' DORM IS!
WHY AM I BOTHERING. I HATE KIDS...
...BUT RIGHT NOW, I HATE GROWNUPS MORE.
THEY SHOULDA LISTENED!
FANCIFUL! IMAGINATIVE! HA!
YEAH! HA!
WHAT AM I DOING?
PING!
I'M A MUTANT!
AND MY WHEELCHAIR...
I CAN MAKE IT...
INTO ANYTHING...
...I WANT!
A 'COPTER!
ALLLL RIIIIGHT! BANZAII!

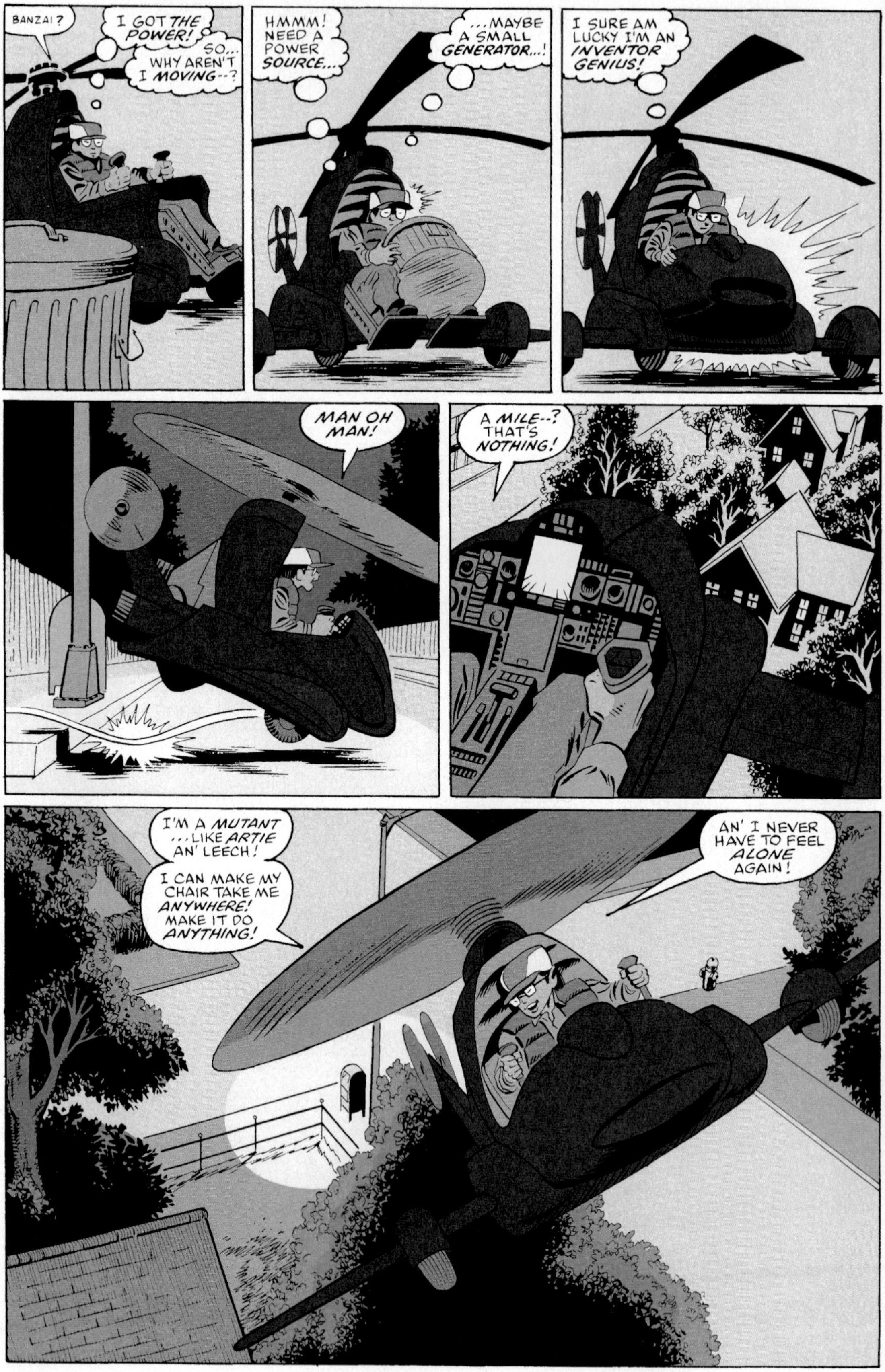
BANZAI?
I GOT THE POWER!
SO... WHY AREN'T I MOVING--?
HMMM! NEED A POWER SOURCE...
...MAYBE A SMALL GENERATOR...!
I SURE AM LUCKY I'M AN INVENTOR GENIUS!
MAN OH MAN!
A MILE--? THAT'S NOTHING!
I'M A MUTANT ...LIKE ARTIE AN' LEECH!
I CAN MAKE MY CHAIR TAKE ME ANYWHERE! MAKE IT DO ANYTHING!
AN' I NEVER HAVE TO FEEL ALONE AGAIN!

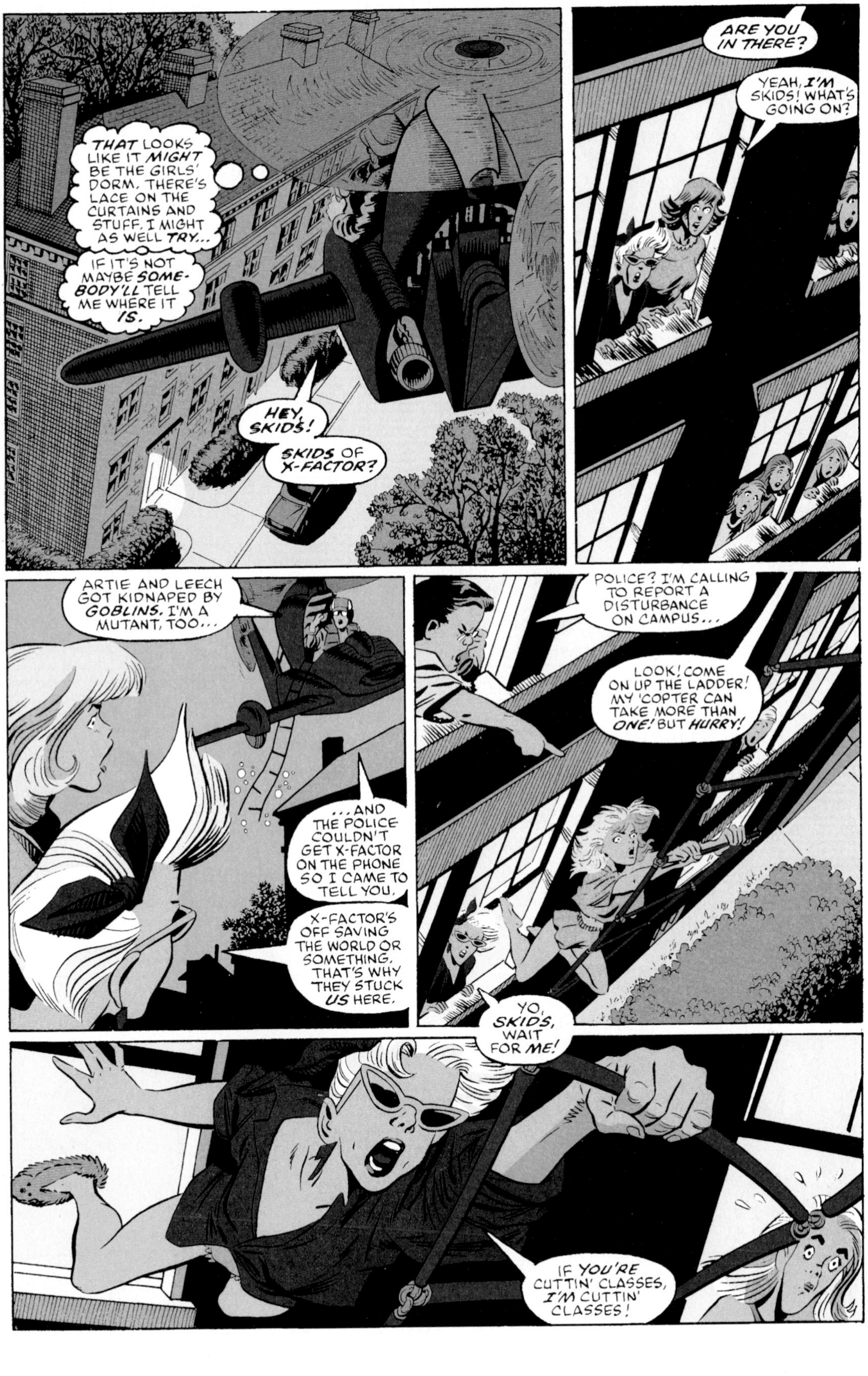
THAT LOOKS LIKE IT MIGHT BE THE GIRLS' DORM. THERE'S LACE ON THE CURTAINS AND STUFF. I MIGHT AS WELL TRY...
IF IT'S NOT MAYBE SOMEBODY'LL TELL ME WHERE IT IS.
HEY, SKIDS!
SKIDS OF X-FACTOR?
ARE YOU IN THERE?
YEAH, I'M SKIDS! WHAT'S GOING ON?
ARTIE AND LEECH GOT KIDNAPED BY GOBLINS. I'M A MUTANT, TOO...
...AND THE POLICE COULDN'T GET X-FACTOR ON THE PHONE SO I CAME TO TELL YOU.
X-FACTOR'S OFF SAVING THE WORLD OR SOMETHING. THAT'S WHY THEY STUCK US HERE.
POLICE? I'M CALLING TO REPORT A DISTURBANCE ON CAMPUS...
LOOK! COME ON UP THE LADDER! MY 'COPTER CAN TAKE MORE THAN ONE! BUT HURRY!
YO, SKIDS, WAIT FOR ME!
IF YOU'RE CUTTIN' CLASSES, I'M CUTTIN' CLASSES!

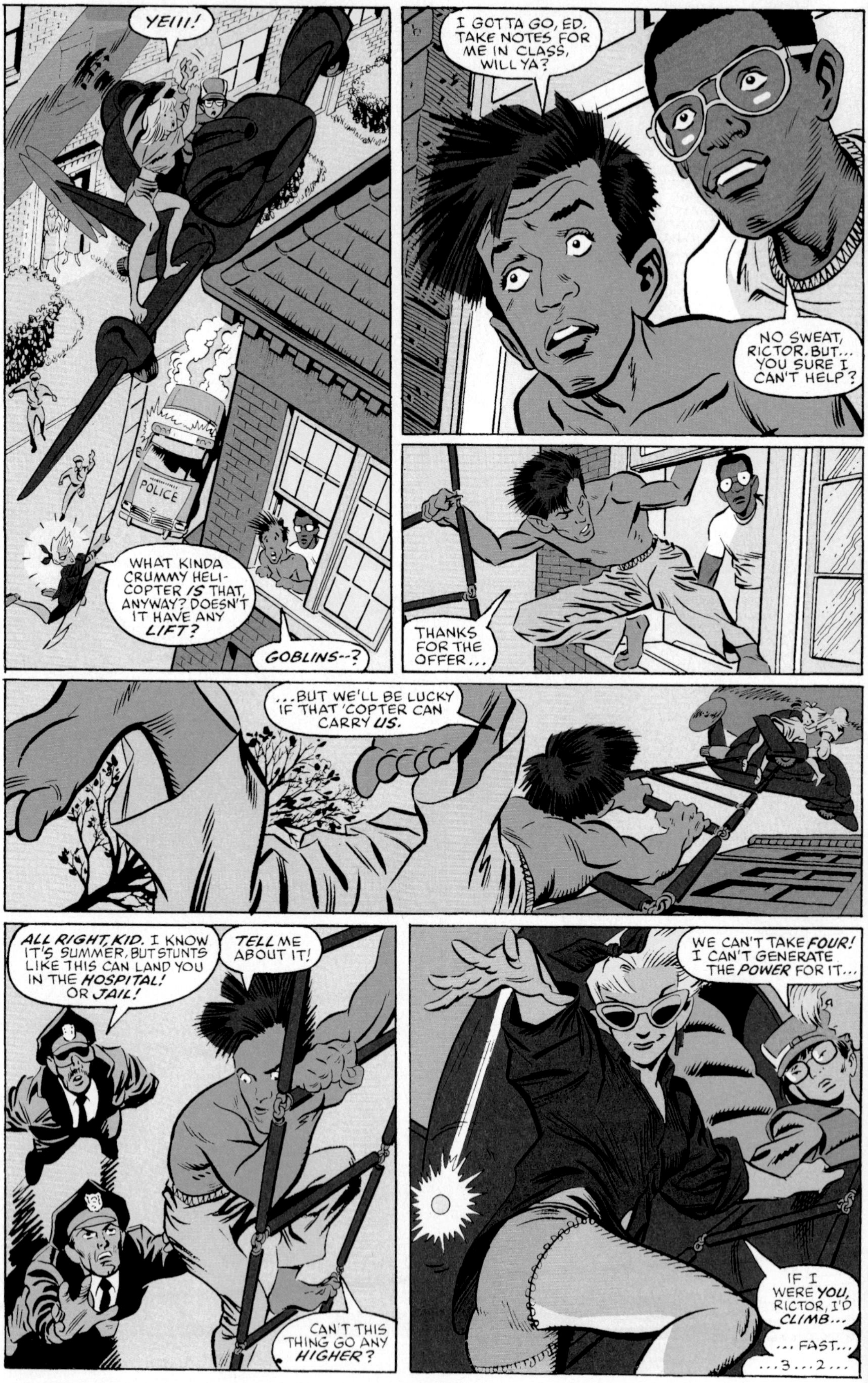
YEIII!
I GOTTA GO, ED. TAKE NOTES FOR ME IN CLASS, WILL YA?
NO SWEAT, RICTOR. BUT... YOU SURE I CAN'T HELP?
WHAT KINDA CRUMMY HELI-COPTER IS THAT, ANYWAY? DOESN'T IT HAVE ANY LIFT?
GOBLINS--?
POLICE
THANKS FOR THE OFFER...
...BUT WE'LL BE LUCKY IF THAT 'COPTER CAN CARRY US.
ALL RIGHT, KID. I KNOW IT'S SUMMER, BUT STUNTS LIKE THIS CAN LAND YOU IN THE HOSPITAL! OR JAIL!
TELL ME ABOUT IT!
CAN'T THIS THING GO ANY HIGHER?
WE CAN'T TAKE FOUR! I CAN'T GENERATE THE POWER FOR IT...
IF I WERE YOU, RICTOR, I'D CLIMB...
...FAST...
...3...2...

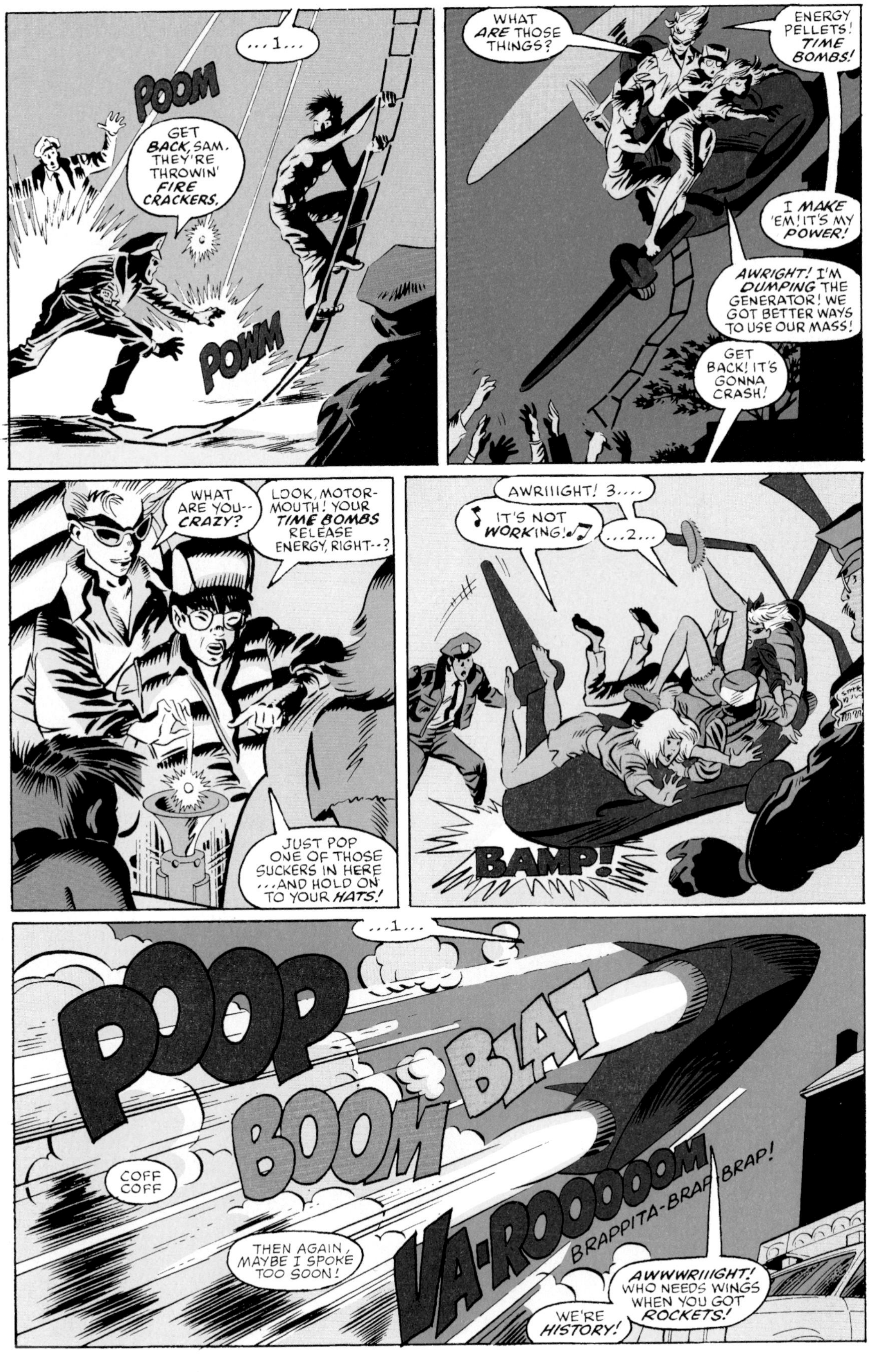
...1...
POOM
GET BACK, SAM. THEY'RE THROWIN' FIRE CRACKERS.
POWM
WHAT ARE THOSE THINGS?
ENERGY PELLETS! TIME BOMBS!
I MAKE 'EM! IT'S MY POWER!
AWRIGHT! I'M DUMPING THE GENERATOR! WE GOT BETTER WAYS TO USE OUR MASS!
GET BACK! IT'S GONNA CRASH!
WHAT ARE YOU-- CRAZY?
LOOK, MOTOR-MOUTH! YOUR TIME BOMBS RELEASE ENERGY, RIGHT--?
JUST POP ONE OF THOSE SUCKERS IN HERE ...AND HOLD ON TO YOUR HATS!
AWRIIIGHT! 3....
♪ IT'S NOT WORKING! ♫
...2...
BAMP!
...1...
POOP
BOOM
BLAT
COFF COFF
VA-ROOOOOOM
BRAPPITA-BRAP-BRAP!
THEN AGAIN, MAYBE I SPOKE TOO SOON!
AWWWRIIIGHT! WHO NEEDS WINGS WHEN YOU GOT ROCKETS!
WE'RE HISTORY!

WE'VE GOT *ALMOST* EVERYBODY NOW.

ALMOST--?

WE'VE GOT TO GO GET RUSTY...

WHAT DO WE NEED HIM FOR?

HE'S OUR *LEADER*! HE'LL KNOW WHAT TO DO! HE'S EVEN HAD *MILITARY EXPERIENCE*.

GREAT WHERE IS HE?

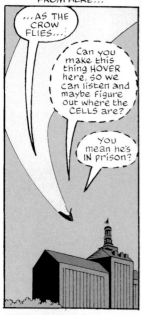

"AT *PORTSMOUTH NAVAL PRISON*. IT'S NOT TOO FAR FROM HERE..."

...*AS THE CROW FLIES*...!

Can you make this thing *HOVER* here, so we can listen and maybe figure out where the *CELLS* are?

You mean he's *IN* prison?

Sure. Don't you read the papers? SHHHH!

THE MUTANT KID'S QUIET AND WELL BEHAVED. SEEMS TO HAVE ADJUSTED TO *PRISON LIFE* JUST FINE!

JUST AS WELL. I HEAR THE ADMINISTRATION'S GONNA MAKE AN *EXAMPLE* OF HIM.

YEAH, I HEARD THAT, TOO. THEY'RE GONNA THROW AWAY THE KEY!

Oh NO! They *CAN'T*! We gotta get him OUT of here!

Uh... that's against the law ...isn't it?

Yeah! But we're *MINORS*...and we gotta think of what's best for *ARTIE* and *LEECH*...

...3...2 ...1...

BOOM!

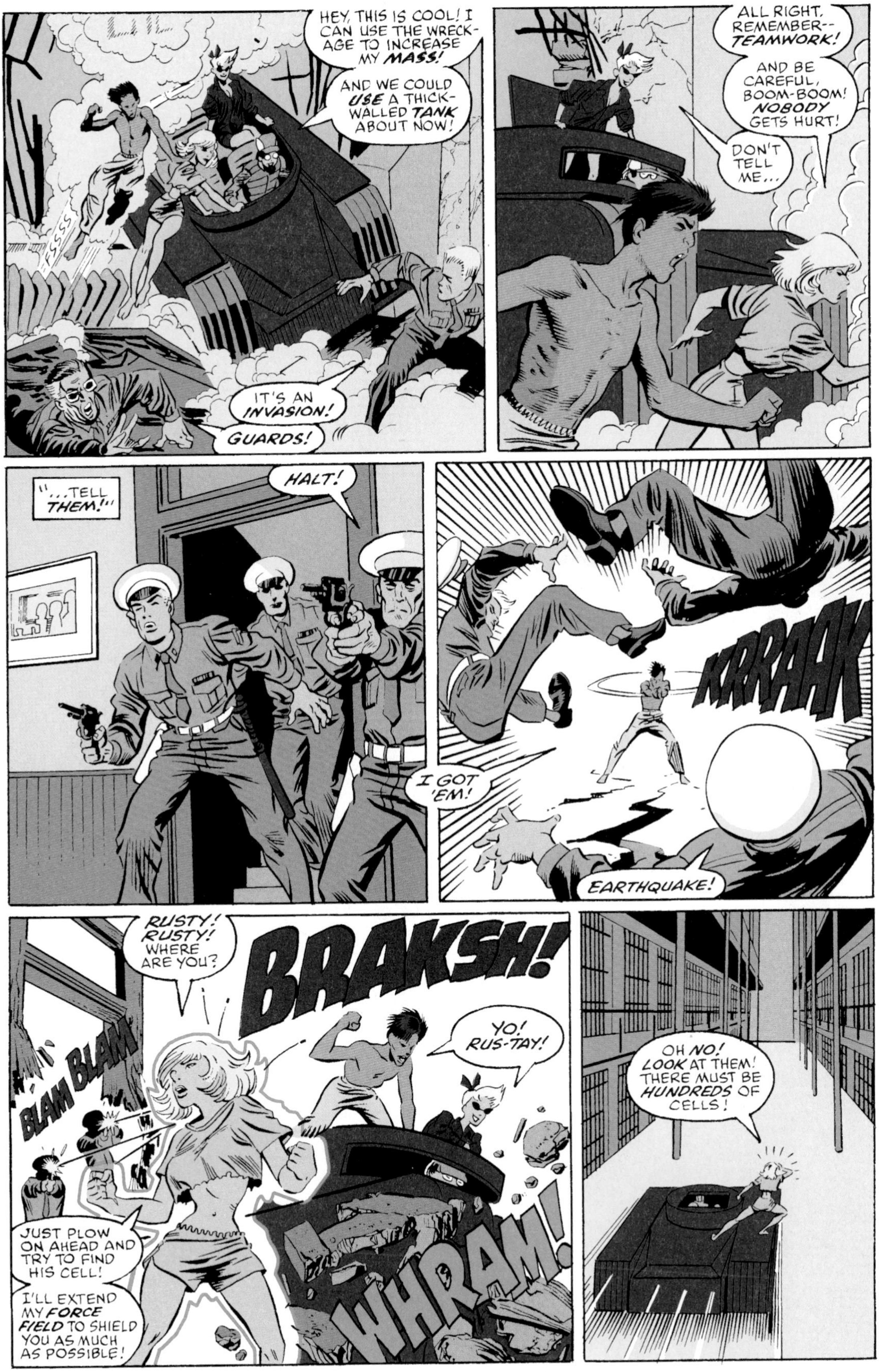
HEY, THIS IS COOL! I CAN USE THE WRECKAGE TO INCREASE MY MASS!
AND WE COULD USE A THICK-WALLED TANK ABOUT NOW!
FSSSS
IT'S AN INVASION!
GUARDS!
ALL RIGHT. REMEMBER--TEAMWORK!
AND BE CAREFUL, BOOM-BOOM! NOBODY GETS HURT!
DON'T TELL ME...
"...TELL THEM!"
HALT!
I GOT 'EM!
KRRAAK
EARTHQUAKE!
RUSTY! RUSTY! WHERE ARE YOU?
BRAKSH!
YO! RUS-TAY!
BLAM BLAM
JUST PLOW ON AHEAD AND TRY TO FIND HIS CELL!
I'LL EXTEND MY FORCE FIELD TO SHIELD YOU AS MUCH AS POSSIBLE!
WHRAM!
OH NO! LOOK AT THEM! THERE MUST BE HUNDREDS OF CELLS!

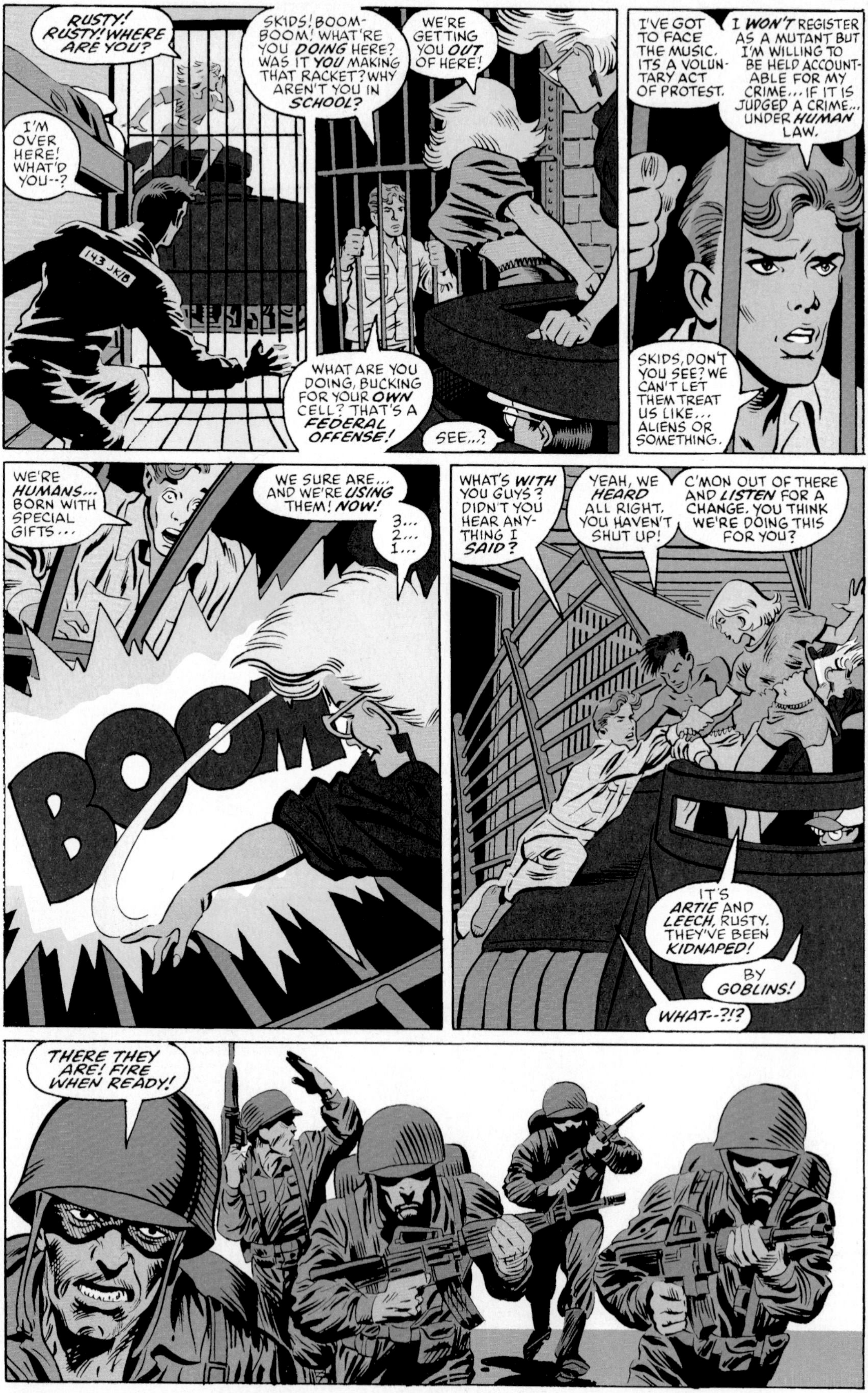
RUSTY! RUSTY! WHERE ARE YOU?
I'M OVER HERE! WHAT'D YOU--?
SKIDS! BOOM-BOOM! WHAT'RE YOU DOING HERE? WAS IT YOU MAKING THAT RACKET? WHY AREN'T YOU IN SCHOOL?
WE'RE GETTING YOU OUT OF HERE!
WHAT ARE YOU DOING, BUCKING FOR YOUR OWN CELL? THAT'S A FEDERAL OFFENSE!
SEE...?
I'VE GOT TO FACE THE MUSIC. ITS A VOLUNTARY ACT OF PROTEST.
I WON'T REGISTER AS A MUTANT BUT I'M WILLING TO BE HELD ACCOUNTABLE FOR MY CRIME... IF IT IS JUDGED A CRIME... UNDER HUMAN LAW.
SKIDS, DON'T YOU SEE? WE CAN'T LET THEM TREAT US LIKE... ALIENS OR SOMETHING.
WE'RE HUMANS... BORN WITH SPECIAL GIFTS...
WE SURE ARE... AND WE'RE USING THEM! NOW!
3... 2... 1...
BOOM
WHAT'S WITH YOU GUYS? DIDN'T YOU HEAR ANYTHING I SAID?
YEAH, WE HEARD ALL RIGHT. YOU HAVEN'T SHUT UP!
C'MON OUT OF THERE AND LISTEN FOR A CHANGE. YOU THINK WE'RE DOING THIS FOR YOU?
IT'S ARTIE AND LEECH, RUSTY. THEY'VE BEEN KIDNAPED!
BY GOBLINS!
WHAT--?!?
THERE THEY ARE! FIRE WHEN READY!

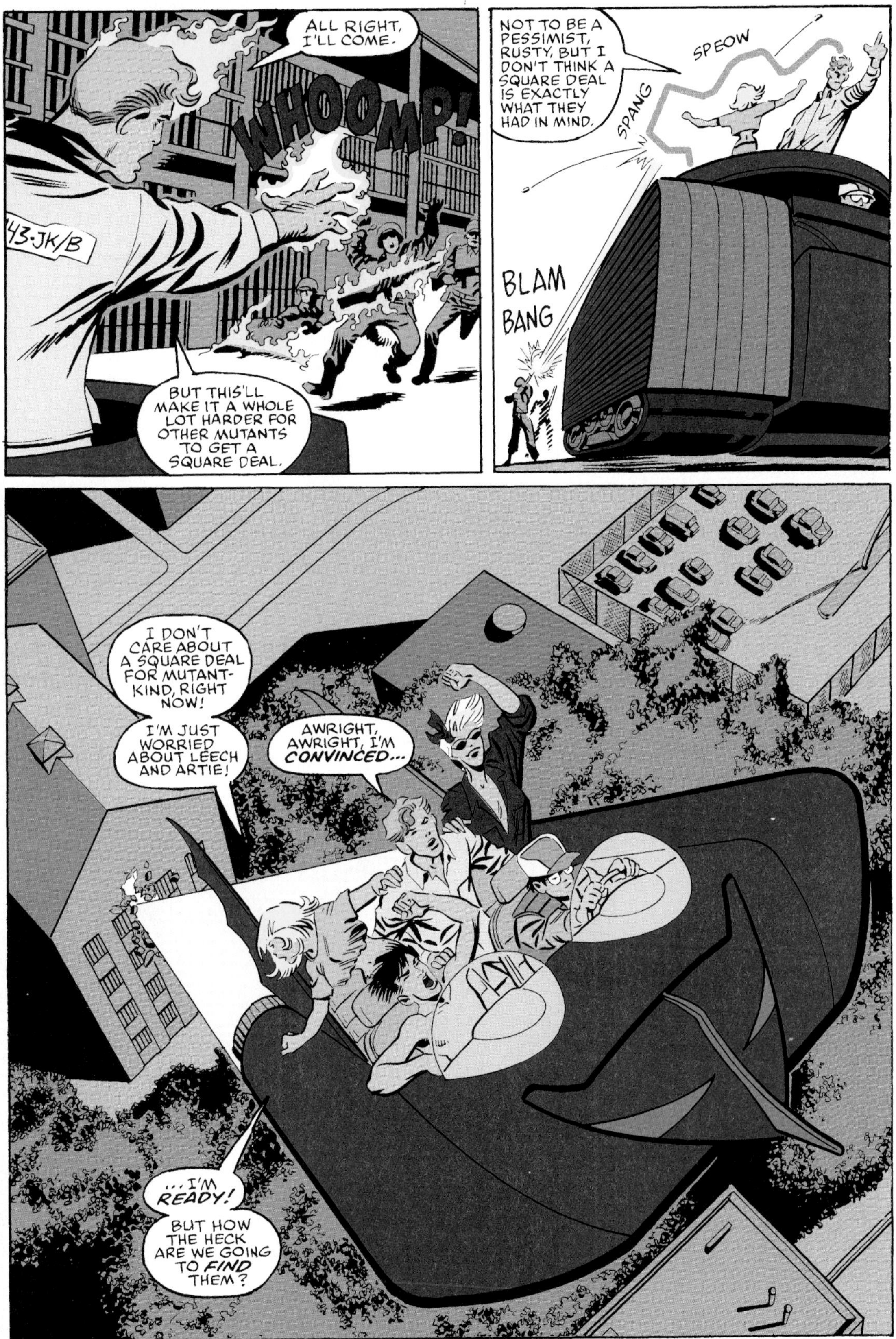
ALL RIGHT, I'LL COME.
WHOOMP!
43-JK/B
BUT THIS'LL MAKE IT A WHOLE LOT HARDER FOR OTHER MUTANTS TO GET A SQUARE DEAL.
NOT TO BE A PESSIMIST, RUSTY, BUT I DON'T THINK A SQUARE DEAL IS EXACTLY WHAT THEY HAD IN MIND.
SPEOW
SPANG
BLAM
BANG
I DON'T CARE ABOUT A SQUARE DEAL FOR MUTANT-KIND, RIGHT NOW!
I'M JUST WORRIED ABOUT LEECH AND ARTIE!
AWRIGHT, AWRIGHT, I'M ***CONVINCED...***
...I'M ***READY!***
BUT HOW THE HECK ARE WE GOING TO ***FIND*** THEM?

NEXT ISSUE: *THE* ***X-FACTOR KIDS*** *GET* ***NEW COSTUMES ...AND A NEW NAME!*** *AS* ***NEW YORK*** *GOES CRAZY AND* ***N'ASTIRH*** *GAINS A...* ***TECHNOLOGICAL ADVANTAGE*** *IN...* **-SPEED-DEMON!** ***INFERNO*** *IS JUST AROUND THE CORNER!*

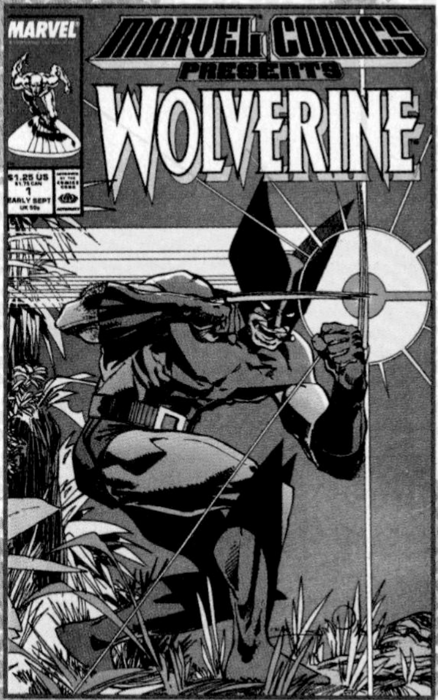
MARVEL
MARVEL COMICS
PRESENTS
WOLVERINE

MARVEL COMICS PRESENTS #1, published in May 1988, began an ongoing bi-weekly anthology series; the first issue began limited serials starring Wolverine, Man-Thing and Shang-Chi.

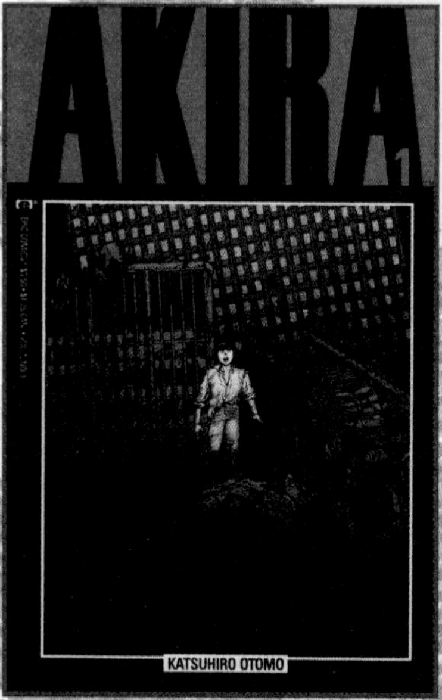
AKIRA 1
KATSUHIRO OTOMO

AKIRA #1, published in May 1988, began an ongoing Epic series reprinting and translating the Japanese manga.

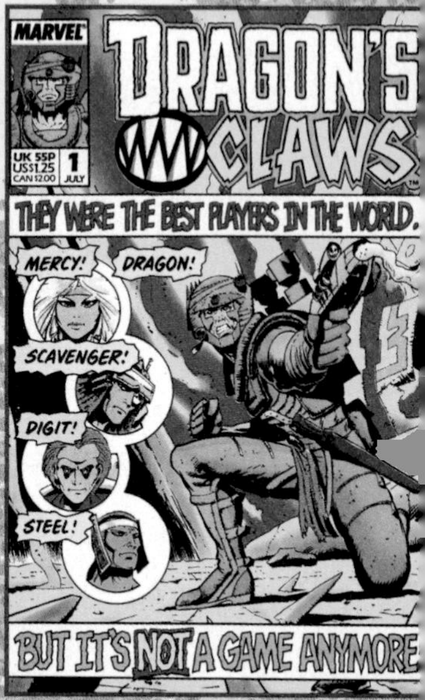
MARVEL
DRAGON'S CLAWS
UK 55P
US$1.25
CAN $2.00
1
JULY
THEY WERE THE BEST PLAYERS IN THE WORLD.
MERCY!
DRAGON!
SCAVENGER!
DIGIT!
STEEL!
BUT IT'S NOT A GAME ANYMORE

DRAGON'S CLAWS #1, published in May 1988, began an ongoing UK series starring the futurist law-enforcement group.

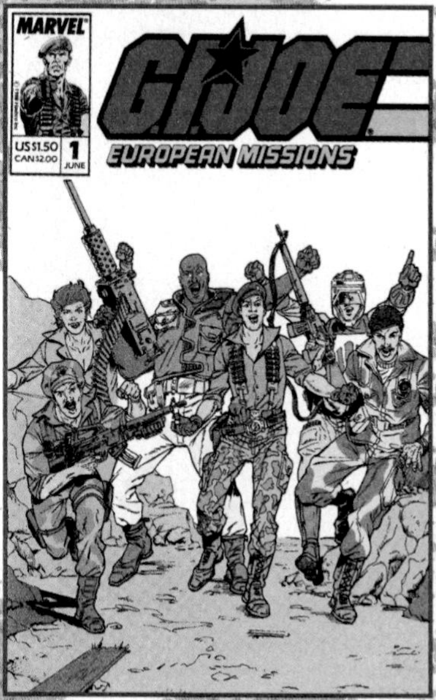
MARVEL
G.I. JOE
EUROPEAN MISSIONS
US$1.50
CAN$2.00
1
JUNE

G.I. JOE EUROPEAN MISSIONS #1, published in May 1988, began an ongoing series reprinting UK stories.

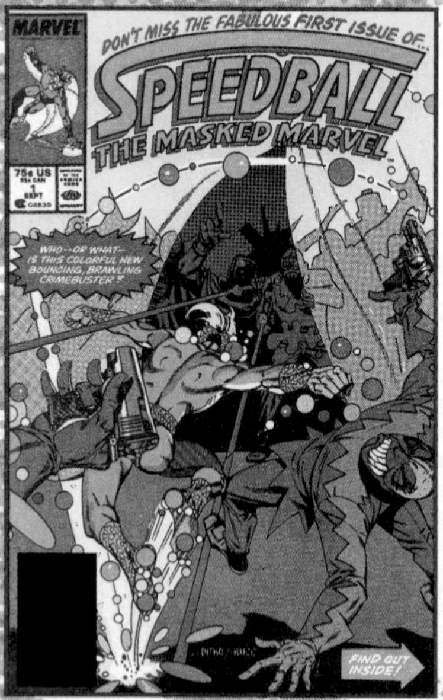
MARVEL
DON'T MISS THE FABULOUS FIRST ISSUE OF...
SPEEDBALL
THE MASKED MARVEL
WHO--OR WHAT--IS THIS COLORFUL NEW BOUNCING, BRAWLING CRIMEBUSTER?
FIND OUT INSIDE!

SPEEDBALL #1, published in June 1988, began the bouncing hero's ongoing series.

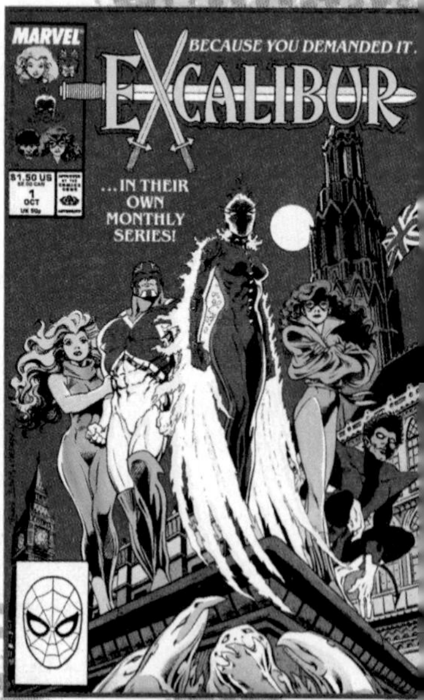
MARVEL
BECAUSE YOU DEMANDED IT...
EXCALIBUR
...IN THEIR OWN MONTHLY SERIES!

EXCALIBUR #1, published in June 1988, began the British X-team's ongong series.

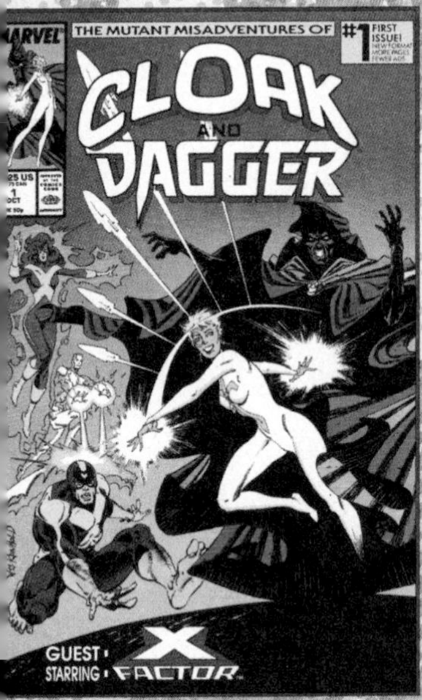
MARVEL
THE MUTANT MISADVENTURES OF
#1 FIRST ISSUE!
CLOAK AND DAGGER
GUEST-STARRING X-FACTOR

MUTANT MISADVENTURES OF CLOAK AND
AGGER #1, published in June 1988, began the crimefighting duo's new ongoing series.

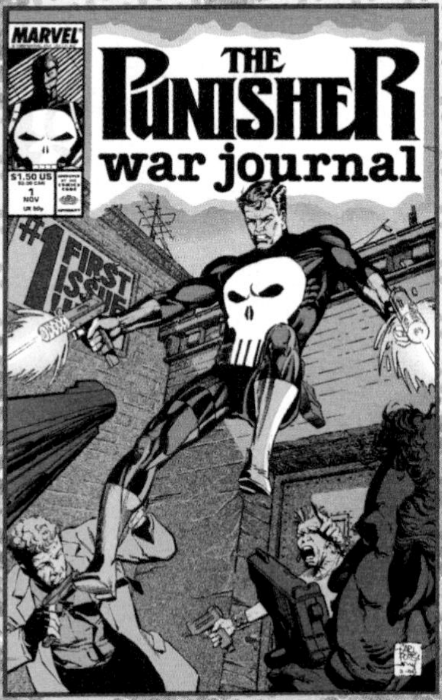
MARVEL
THE PUNISHER
war journal
#1 FIRST ISSUE

PUNISHER WAR JOURNAL #1, published in July 1988, began the lethal crimefighter's second ongoing solo series, running concurrently with Punisher.

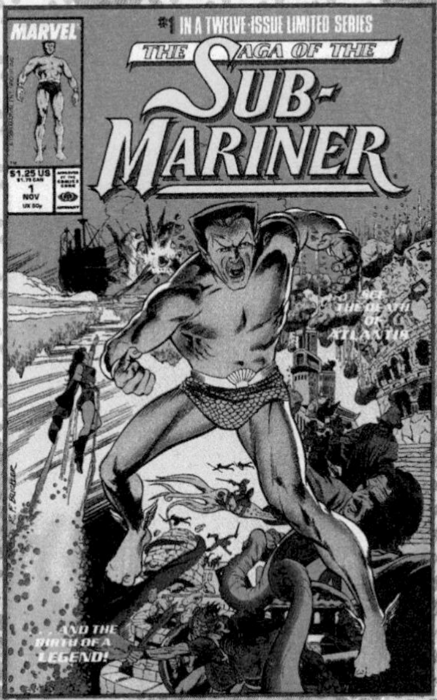
MARVEL
#1 IN A TWELVE-ISSUE LIMITED SERIES
THE SAGA OF THE SUB-MARINER
SEE THE DEATH OF ATLANTIS
...AND THE BIRTH OF A LEGEND!

SAGA OF THE SUB-MARINER #1, published in July 1988, began a miniseries providing an overview of the Sub-Mariner's lengthy history.

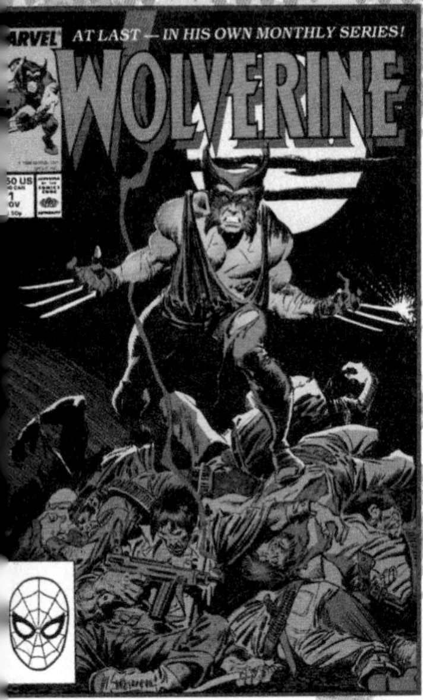
MARVEL
AT LAST — IN HIS OWN MONTHLY SERIES!
WOLVERINE

OLVERINE #1, published in July 1988, began the
lamantium-clawed X-Man's first ongoing series.

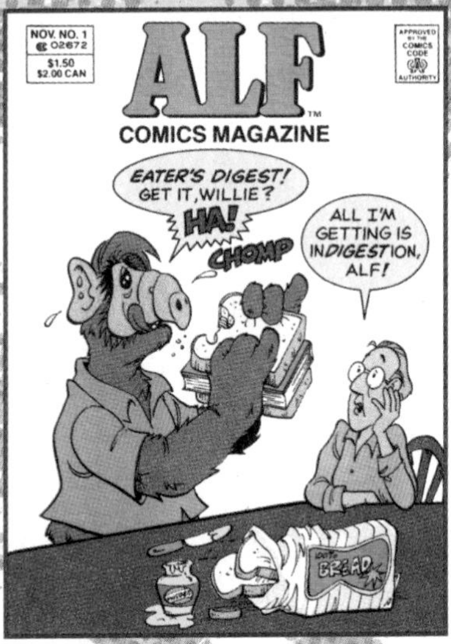
NOV. NO. 1
$1.50
$2.00 CAN
ALF
COMICS MAGAZINE
EATER'S DIGEST! GET IT, WILLIE?
HA!
CHOMP
ALL I'M GETTING IS INDIGESTION, ALF!
BREAD

ALF COMICS MAGAZINE #1, published in July 1988, began a short digest-sized reprint series.

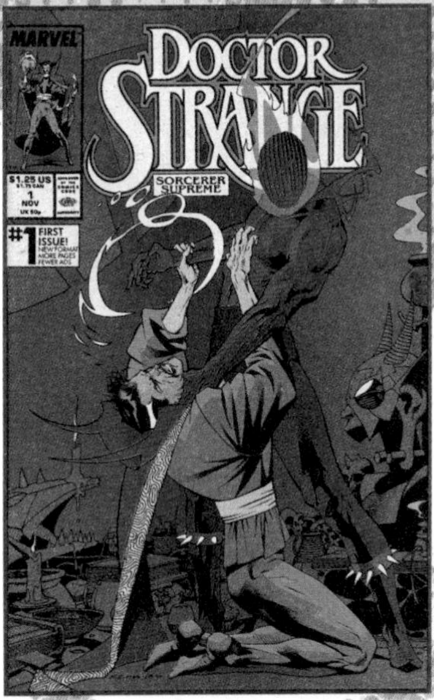
MARVEL
DOCTOR STRANGE
SORCERER SUPREME
#1 FIRST ISSUE!

DOCTOR STRANGE, SORCERER SUPREME #1, published in July 1988, began Dr. Strange's new ongoing series.

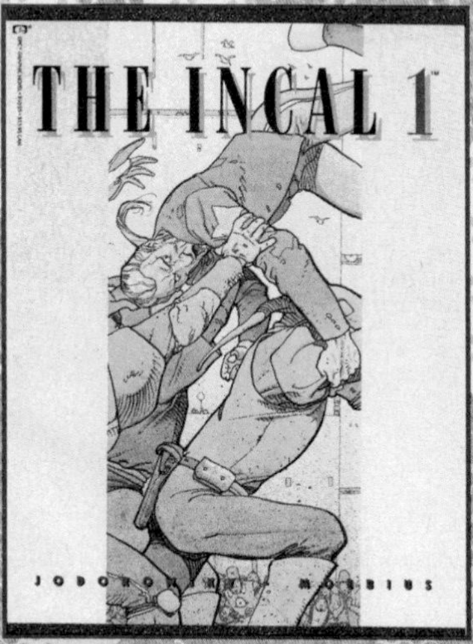
THE INCAL 1

THE INCAL #1, published in July 1988, began a series of Epic Graphic Novels reprinting and translating the French sci-fi series.

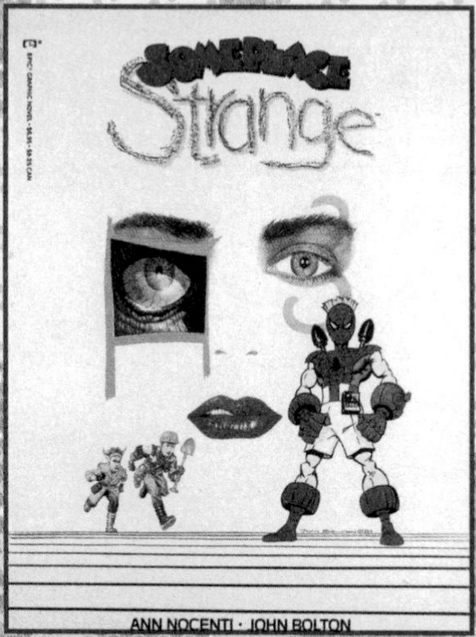
SOMEPLACE
Strange
ANN NOCENTI · JOHN BOLTON

SOMEPLACE STRANGE, published in August 1988, was an Epic Graphic Novel taking place in a surreal dreamscape.

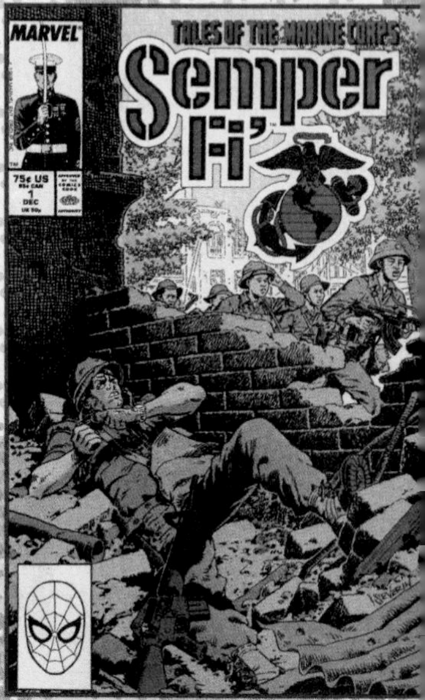
MARVEL
TALES OF THE MARINE CORPS
Semper Fi'
75¢ US
1
DEC

SEMPER FI' #1, published in August 1988, bega an ongoing series that told realistic tales of th U.S. Marine Corps.

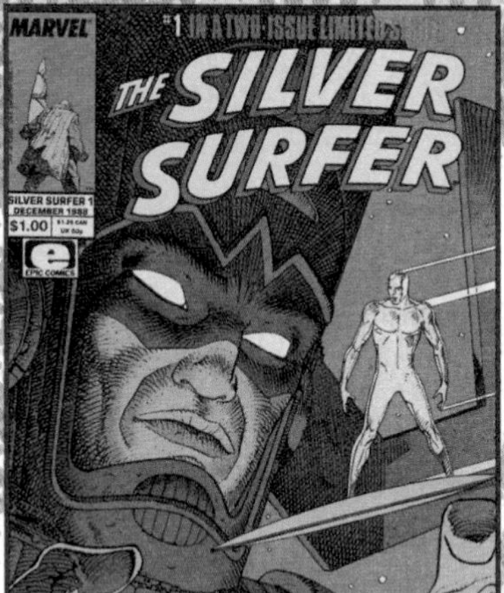
MARVEL
THE SILVER SURFER
SILVER SURFER 1
DECEMBER 1988
$1.00

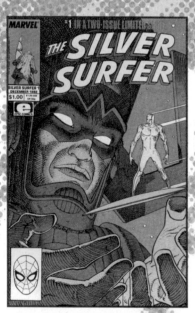

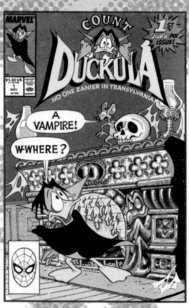

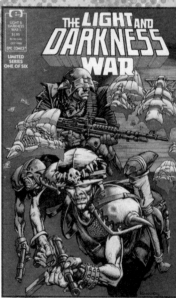

SILVER SURFER #1, published in August 1988, began an Epic miniseries starring the sentinel of the spaceways.

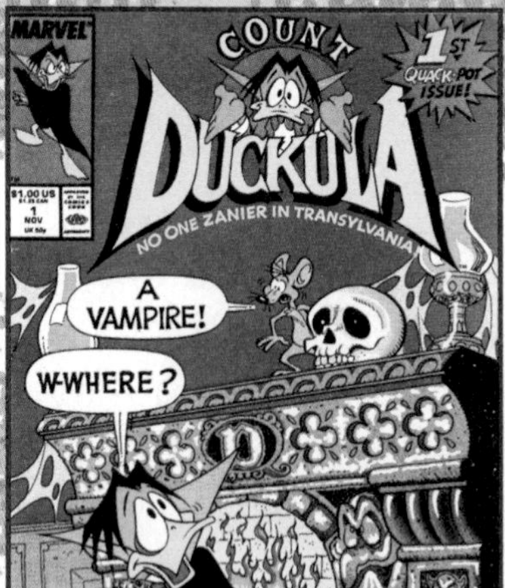
MARVEL
COUNT
DUCKULA
1ST QUACK-POT ISSUE!
$1.00 US
1
NOV
NO ONE ZANIER IN TRANSYLVANIA
A VAMPIRE!
W-WHERE?

COUNT DUCKULA #1, published in August 1988, began an ongoing Star series based on the Cosgrove Hall UK animated TV series.

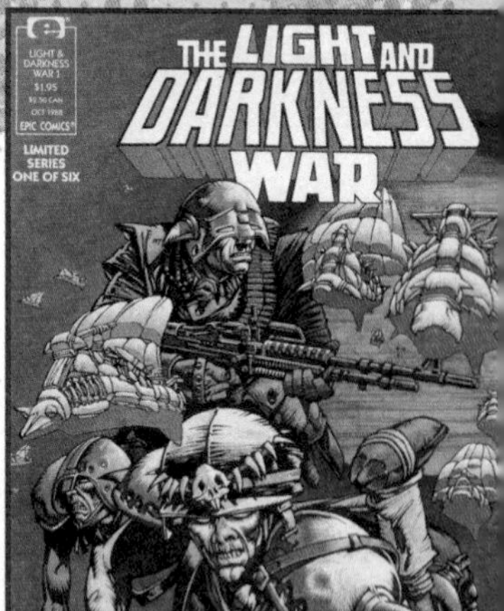
THE LIGHT AND DARKNESS WAR
EPIC COMICS
LIMITED SERIES ONE OF SIX

LIGHT AND DARKNESS WAR #1, published in August 1988, began an Epic miniseries starrin Tom Veitch and Cam Kennedy's creator-ownec characters.

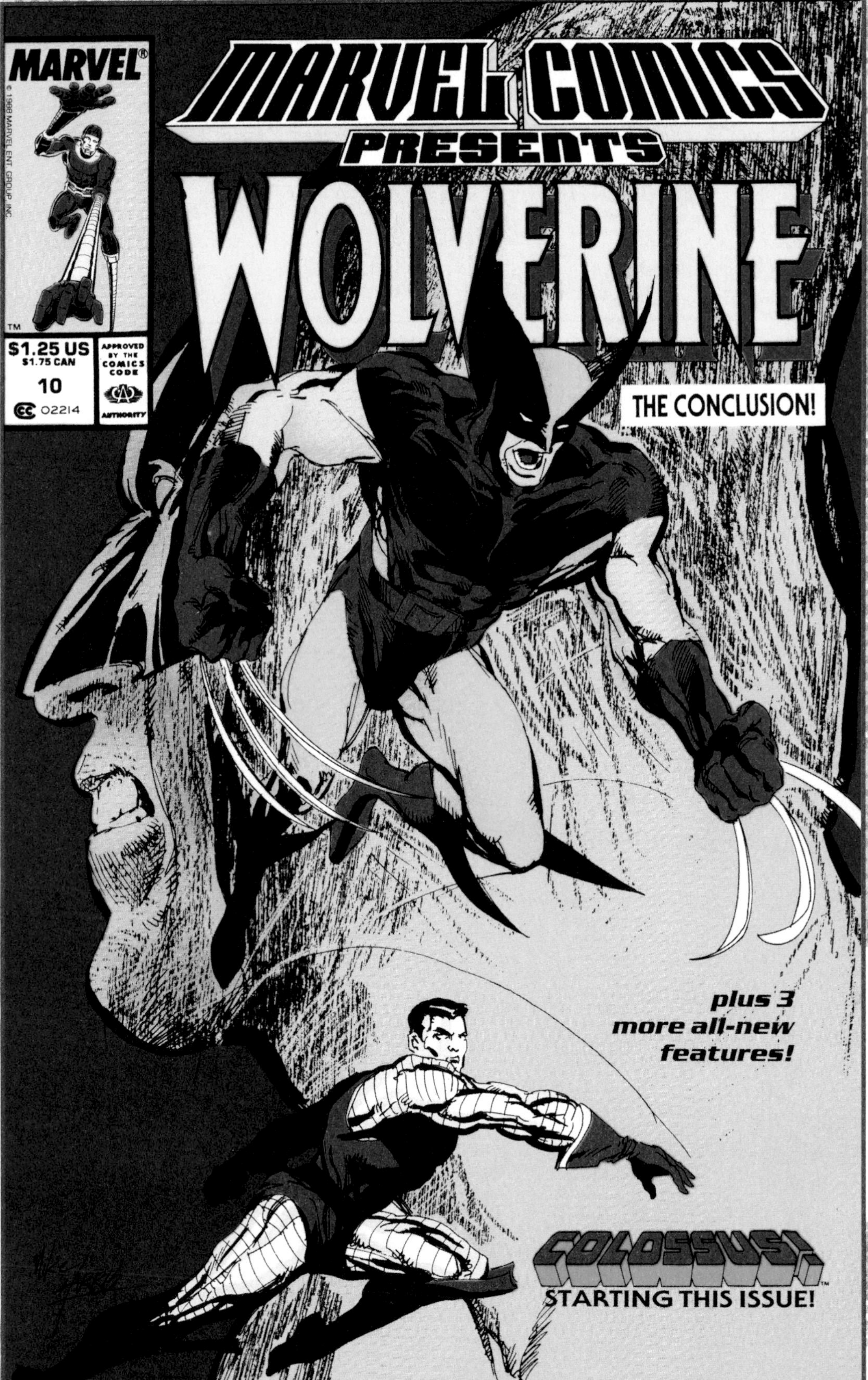
MARVEL®
© 1988 MARVEL ENT. GROUP, INC.
TM
$1.25 US
$1.75 CAN
10
02214
APPROVED BY THE COMICS CODE AUTHORITY
MARVEL COMICS
PRESENTS
WOLVERINE
THE CONCLUSION!
plus 3
more all-new
features!
COLOSSUS!
STARTING THIS ISSUE!

MARVEL COMICS PRESENTS #10, published in September 1988, began a limited serial starring the X-Men's Colossus.

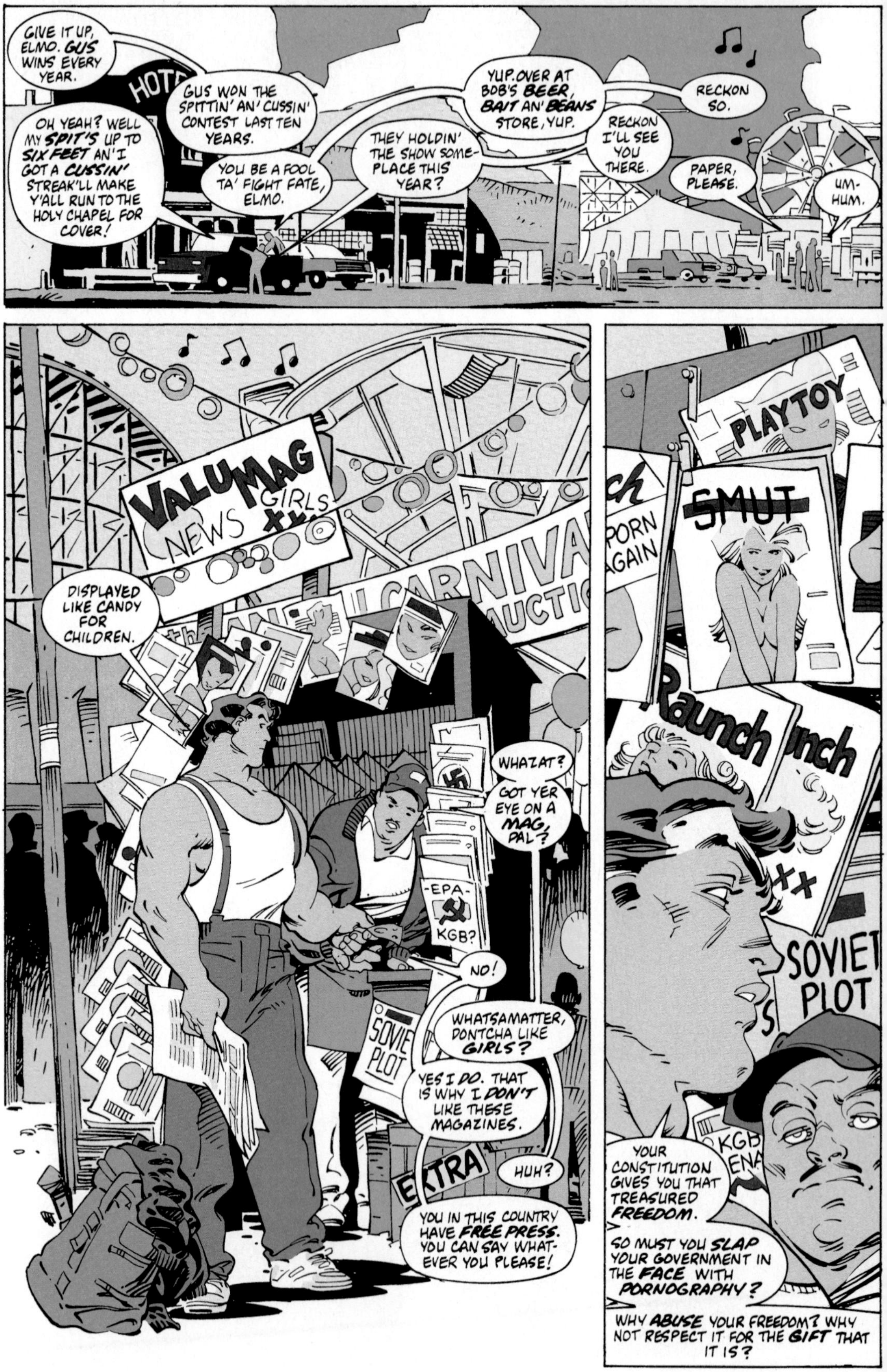

GIVE IT UP, ELMO. GUS WINS EVERY YEAR.
HOTE
OH YEAH? WELL MY SPIT'S UP TO SIX FEET AN' I GOT A CUSSIN' STREAK'LL MAKE Y'ALL RUN TO THE HOLY CHAPEL FOR COVER!
GUS WON THE SPITTIN' AN' CUSSIN' CONTEST LAST TEN YEARS.
YOU BE A FOOL TA' FIGHT FATE, ELMO.
THEY HOLDIN' THE SHOW SOME-PLACE THIS YEAR?
YUP. OVER AT BOB'S BEER, BAIT AN' BEANS STORE, YUP.
RECKON I'LL SEE YOU THERE.
RECKON SO.
PAPER, PLEASE.
UM-HUM.
VALU MAG
NEWS
GIRLS
CARNIVA
AUCTIO
DISPLAYED LIKE CANDY FOR CHILDREN.
WHAZAT?
GOT YER EYE ON A MAG, PAL?
EPA
KGB?
NO!
SOVIE PLOT
WHATSAMATTER, DONTCHA LIKE GIRLS?
YES I DO. THAT IS WHY I DON'T LIKE THESE MAGAZINES.
EXTRA
HUH?
YOU IN THIS COUNTRY HAVE FREE PRESS. YOU CAN SAY WHAT-EVER YOU PLEASE!
PLAYTOY
SMUT
PORN AGAIN
Raunch
SOVIET PLOT
YOUR CONSTITUTION GIVES YOU THAT TREASURED FREEDOM.
SO MUST YOU SLAP YOUR GOVERNMENT IN THE FACE WITH PORNOGRAPHY?
WHY ABUSE YOUR FREEDOM? WHY NOT RESPECT IT FOR THE GIFT THAT IT IS?

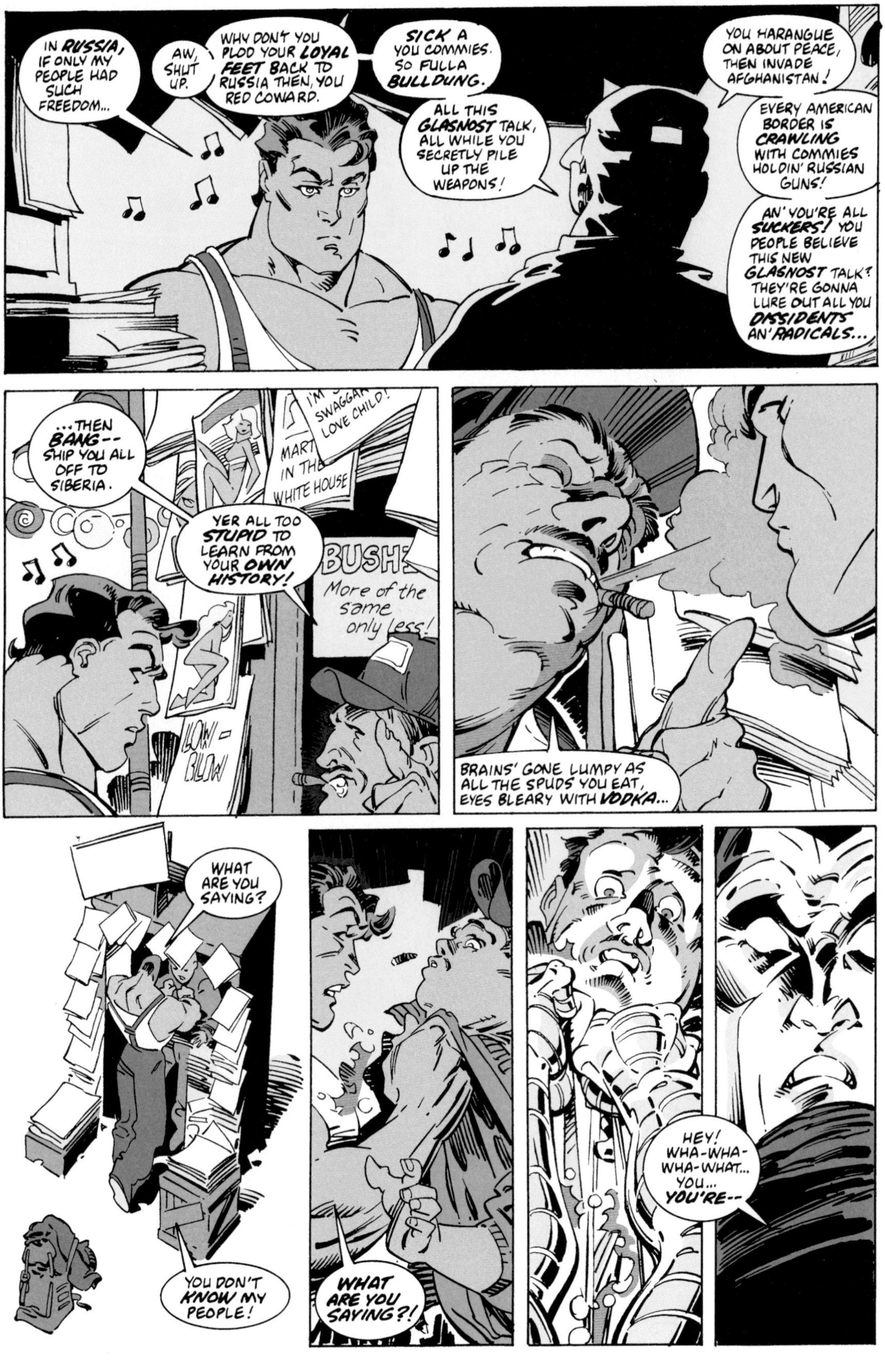
IN RUSSIA, IF ONLY MY PEOPLE HAD SUCH FREEDOM...
AW, SHUT UP.
WHY DON'T YOU PLOD YOUR LOYAL FEET BACK TO RUSSIA THEN, YOU RED COWARD.
SICK A YOU COMMIES. SO FULLA BULLDUNG.
ALL THIS GLASNOST TALK, ALL WHILE YOU SECRETLY PILE UP THE WEAPONS!
YOU HARANGUE ON ABOUT PEACE, THEN INVADE AFGHANISTAN!
EVERY AMERICAN BORDER IS CRAWLING WITH COMMIES HOLDIN' RUSSIAN GUNS!
AN' YOU'RE ALL SUCKERS! YOU PEOPLE BELIEVE THIS NEW GLASNOST TALK? THEY'RE GONNA LURE OUT ALL YOU DISSIDENTS AN' RADICALS...
...THEN BANG-- SHIP YOU ALL OFF TO SIBERIA.
MARTHA IN THE WHITE HOUSE
YER ALL TOO STUPID TO LEARN FROM YOUR OWN HISTORY!
BUSH More of the same only less!
BRAINS' GONE LUMPY AS ALL THE SPUDS YOU EAT, EYES BLEARY WITH VODKA...
WHAT ARE YOU SAYING?
YOU DON'T KNOW MY PEOPLE!
WHAT ARE YOU SAYING?!
HEY! WHA-WHA-WHA-WHAT... YOU... YOU'RE--

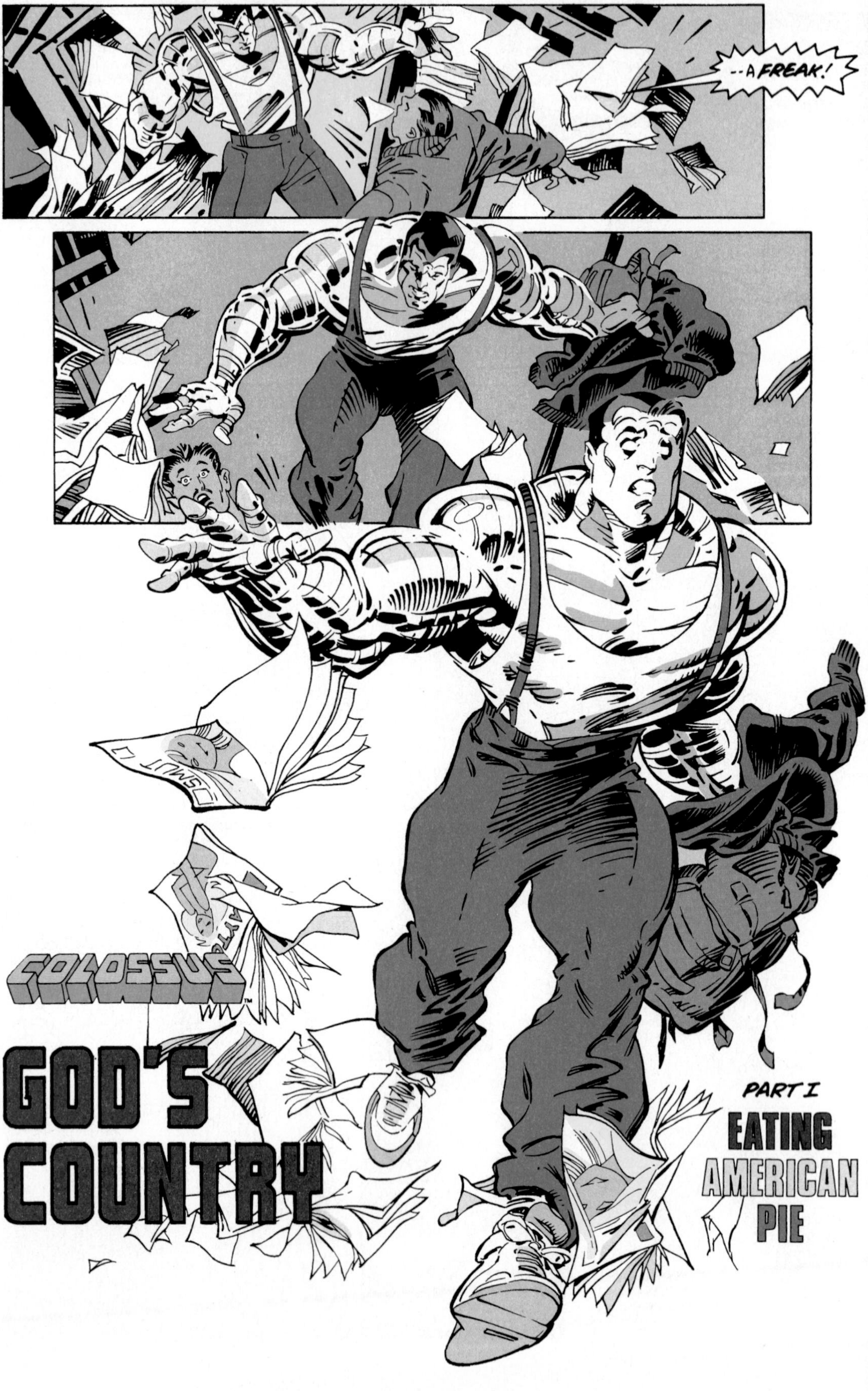
--A FREAK!
COLOSSUS
GOD'S COUNTRY
PART I
EATING AMERICAN PIE

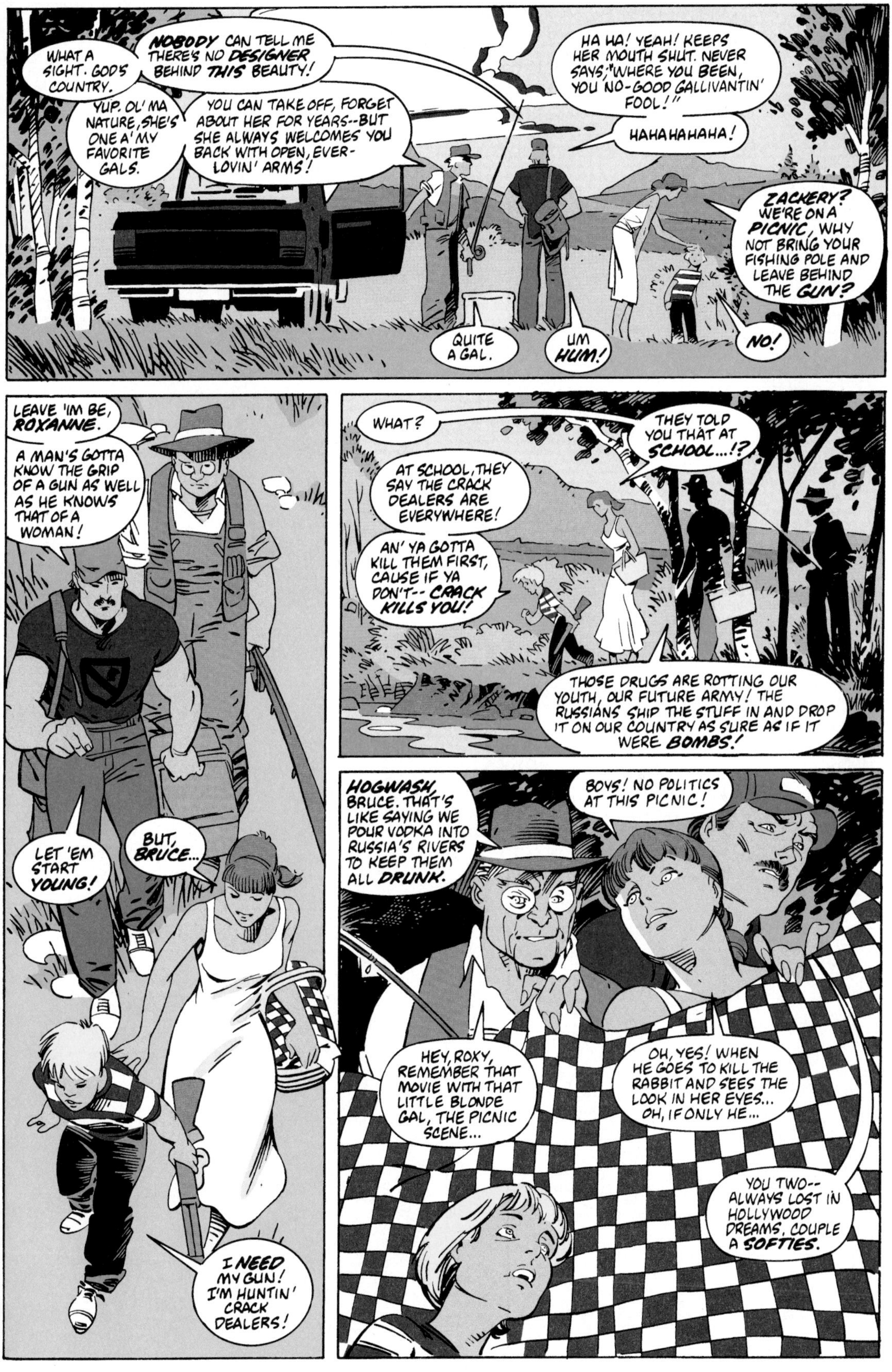
WHAT A SIGHT. GOD'S COUNTRY.
NOBODY CAN TELL ME THERE'S NO DESIGNER BEHIND THIS BEAUTY!
YUP. OL' MA NATURE, SHE'S ONE A' MY FAVORITE GALS.
YOU CAN TAKE OFF, FORGET ABOUT HER FOR YEARS--BUT SHE ALWAYS WELCOMES YOU BACK WITH OPEN, EVER-LOVIN' ARMS!
HA HA! YEAH! KEEPS HER MOUTH SHUT. NEVER SAYS, "WHERE YOU BEEN, YOU NO-GOOD GALLIVANTIN' FOOL!"
HAHAHAHAHA!
ZACKERY? WE'RE ON A PICNIC, WHY NOT BRING YOUR FISHING POLE AND LEAVE BEHIND THE GUN?
QUITE A GAL.
UM HUM!
NO!
LEAVE 'IM BE, ROXANNE.
A MAN'S GOTTA KNOW THE GRIP OF A GUN AS WELL AS HE KNOWS THAT OF A WOMAN!
LET 'EM START YOUNG!
BUT, BRUCE...
I NEED MY GUN! I'M HUNTIN' CRACK DEALERS!
WHAT?
THEY TOLD YOU THAT AT SCHOOL...!?
AT SCHOOL, THEY SAY THE CRACK DEALERS ARE EVERYWHERE!
AN' YA GOTTA KILL THEM FIRST, CAUSE IF YA DON'T-- CRACK KILLS YOU!
THOSE DRUGS ARE ROTTING OUR YOUTH, OUR FUTURE ARMY! THE RUSSIANS SHIP THE STUFF IN AND DROP IT ON OUR COUNTRY AS SURE AS IF IT WERE BOMBS!
HOGWASH, BRUCE. THAT'S LIKE SAYING WE POUR VODKA INTO RUSSIA'S RIVERS TO KEEP THEM ALL DRUNK.
BOYS! NO POLITICS AT THIS PICNIC!
HEY, ROXY, REMEMBER THAT MOVIE WITH THAT LITTLE BLONDE GAL, THE PICNIC SCENE...
OH, YES! WHEN HE GOES TO KILL THE RABBIT AND SEES THE LOOK IN HER EYES... OH, IF ONLY HE...
YOU TWO-- ALWAYS LOST IN HOLLYWOOD DREAMS, COUPLE A SOFTIES.

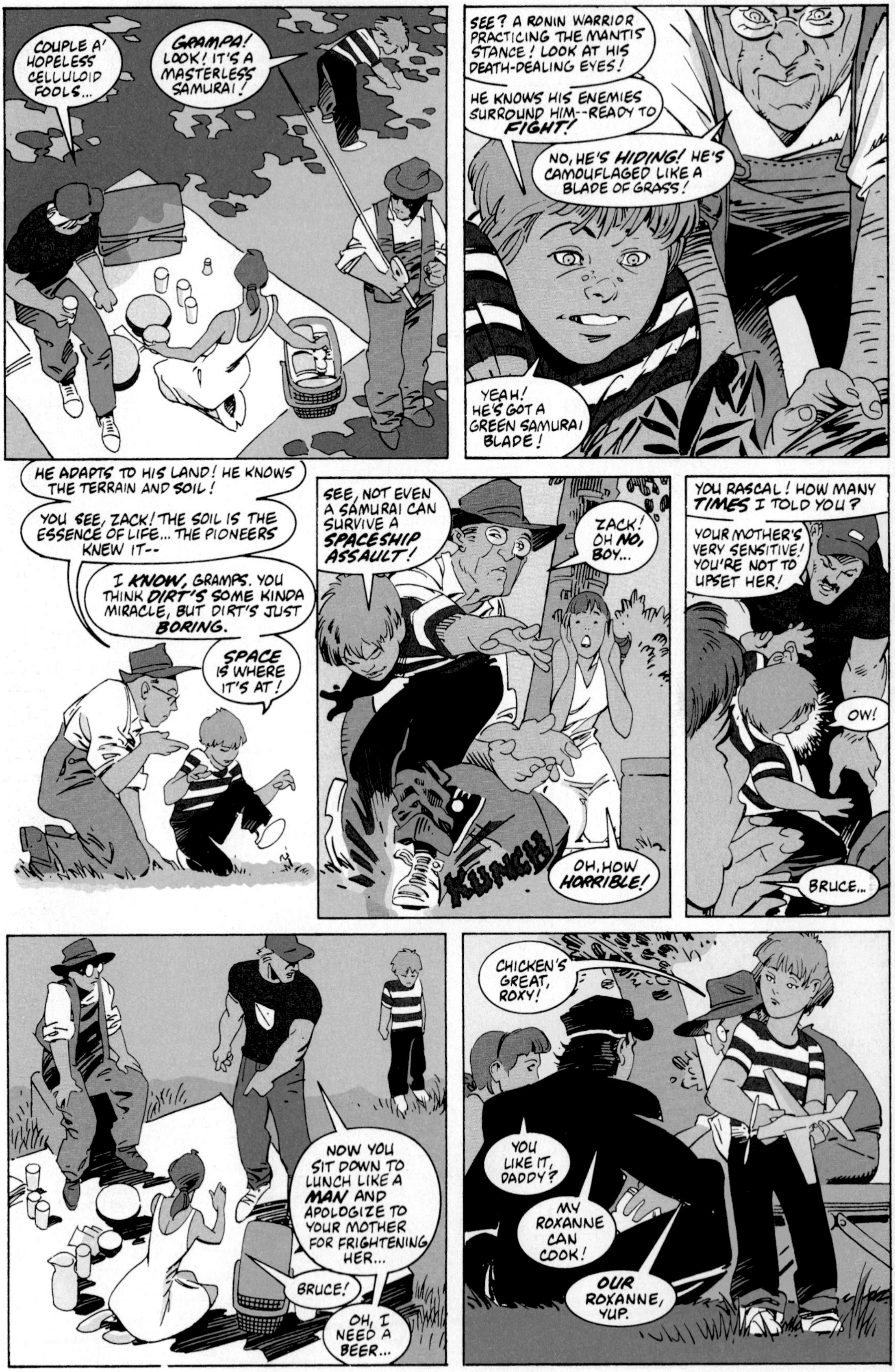
COUPLE A' HOPELESS CELLULOID FOOLS...
GRAMPA! LOOK! IT'S A MASTERLESS SAMURAI!
SEE? A RONIN WARRIOR PRACTICING THE MANTIS STANCE! LOOK AT HIS DEATH-DEALING EYES!
HE KNOWS HIS ENEMIES SURROUND HIM--READY TO FIGHT!
NO, HE'S HIDING! HE'S CAMOUFLAGED LIKE A BLADE OF GRASS!
YEAH! HE'S GOT A GREEN SAMURAI BLADE!
HE ADAPTS TO HIS LAND! HE KNOWS THE TERRAIN AND SOIL!
YOU SEE, ZACK! THE SOIL IS THE ESSENCE OF LIFE... THE PIONEERS KNEW IT--
I KNOW, GRAMPS. YOU THINK DIRT'S SOME KINDA MIRACLE, BUT DIRT'S JUST BORING.
SPACE IS WHERE IT'S AT!
SEE, NOT EVEN A SAMURAI CAN SURVIVE A SPACESHIP ASSAULT!
ZACK! OH NO, BOY...
KLUNCH
OH, HOW HORRIBLE!
YOU RASCAL! HOW MANY TIMES I TOLD YOU?
YOUR MOTHER'S VERY SENSITIVE! YOU'RE NOT TO UPSET HER!
OW!
BRUCE...
NOW YOU SIT DOWN TO LUNCH LIKE A MAN AND APOLOGIZE TO YOUR MOTHER FOR FRIGHTENING HER...
BRUCE!
OH, I NEED A BEER...
CHICKEN'S GREAT, ROXY!
YOU LIKE IT, DADDY?
MY ROXANNE CAN COOK!
OUR ROXANNE, YUP.

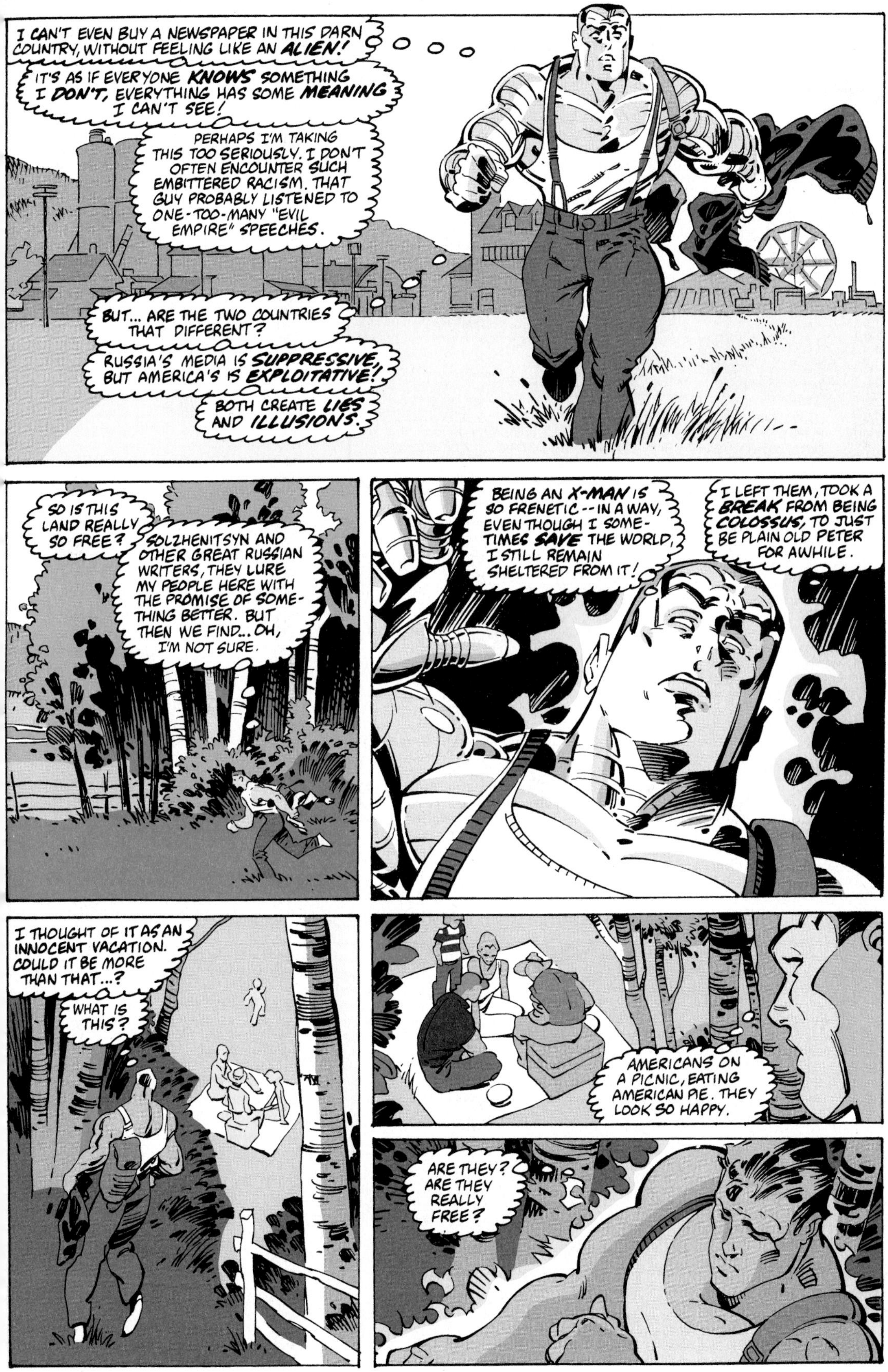

I CAN'T EVEN BUY A NEWSPAPER IN THIS DARN COUNTRY, WITHOUT FEELING LIKE AN ALIEN!
IT'S AS IF EVERYONE KNOWS SOMETHING I DON'T, EVERYTHING HAS SOME MEANING I CAN'T SEE!
PERHAPS I'M TAKING THIS TOO SERIOUSLY. I DON'T OFTEN ENCOUNTER SUCH EMBITTERED RACISM. THAT GUY PROBABLY LISTENED TO ONE-TOO-MANY "EVIL EMPIRE" SPEECHES.
BUT... ARE THE TWO COUNTRIES THAT DIFFERENT?
RUSSIA'S MEDIA IS SUPPRESSIVE, BUT AMERICA'S IS EXPLOITATIVE!
BOTH CREATE LIES AND ILLUSIONS.
SO IS THIS LAND REALLY SO FREE?
SOLZHENITSYN AND OTHER GREAT RUSSIAN WRITERS, THEY LURE MY PEOPLE HERE WITH THE PROMISE OF SOMETHING BETTER. BUT THEN WE FIND... OH, I'M NOT SURE.
BEING AN X-MAN IS SO FRENETIC -- IN A WAY, EVEN THOUGH I SOMETIMES SAVE THE WORLD, I STILL REMAIN SHELTERED FROM IT!
I LEFT THEM, TOOK A BREAK FROM BEING COLOSSUS, TO JUST BE PLAIN OLD PETER FOR AWHILE.
I THOUGHT OF IT AS AN INNOCENT VACATION. COULD IT BE MORE THAN THAT...?
WHAT IS THIS?
AMERICANS ON A PICNIC, EATING AMERICAN PIE. THEY LOOK SO HAPPY.
ARE THEY? ARE THEY REALLY FREE?

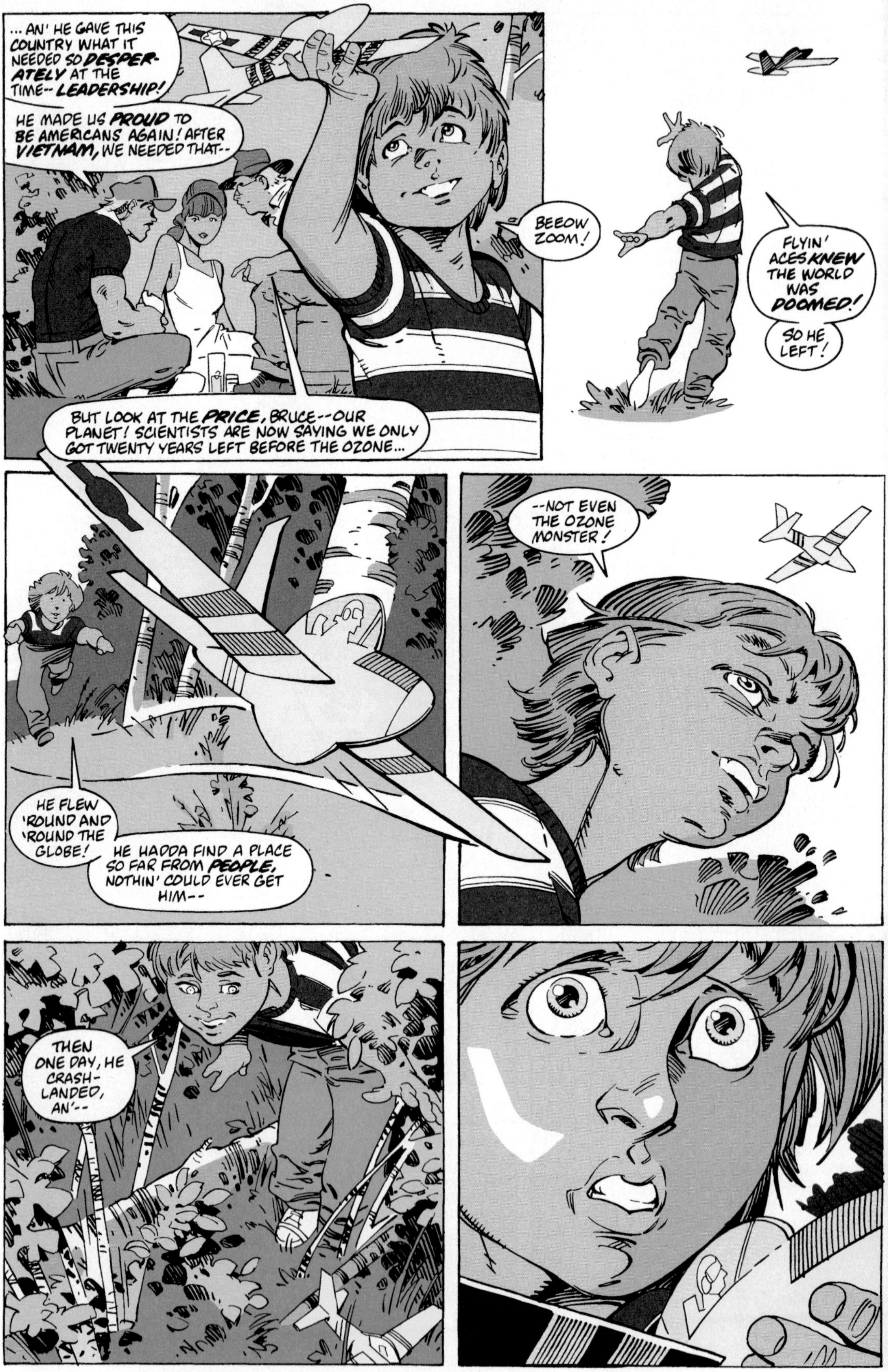

...AN' HE GAVE THIS COUNTRY WHAT IT NEEDED SO DESPERATELY AT THE TIME--LEADERSHIP!
HE MADE US PROUD TO BE AMERICANS AGAIN! AFTER VIETNAM, WE NEEDED THAT--
BEEOW ZOOM!
BUT LOOK AT THE PRICE, BRUCE--OUR PLANET! SCIENTISTS ARE NOW SAYING WE ONLY GOT TWENTY YEARS LEFT BEFORE THE OZONE...
FLYIN' ACES KNEW THE WORLD WAS DOOMED!
SO HE LEFT!
HE FLEW 'ROUND AND 'ROUND THE GLOBE!
HE HADDA FIND A PLACE SO FAR FROM PEOPLE, NOTHIN' COULD EVER GET HIM--
--NOT EVEN THE OZONE MONSTER!
THEN ONE DAY, HE CRASH-LANDED, AN'--

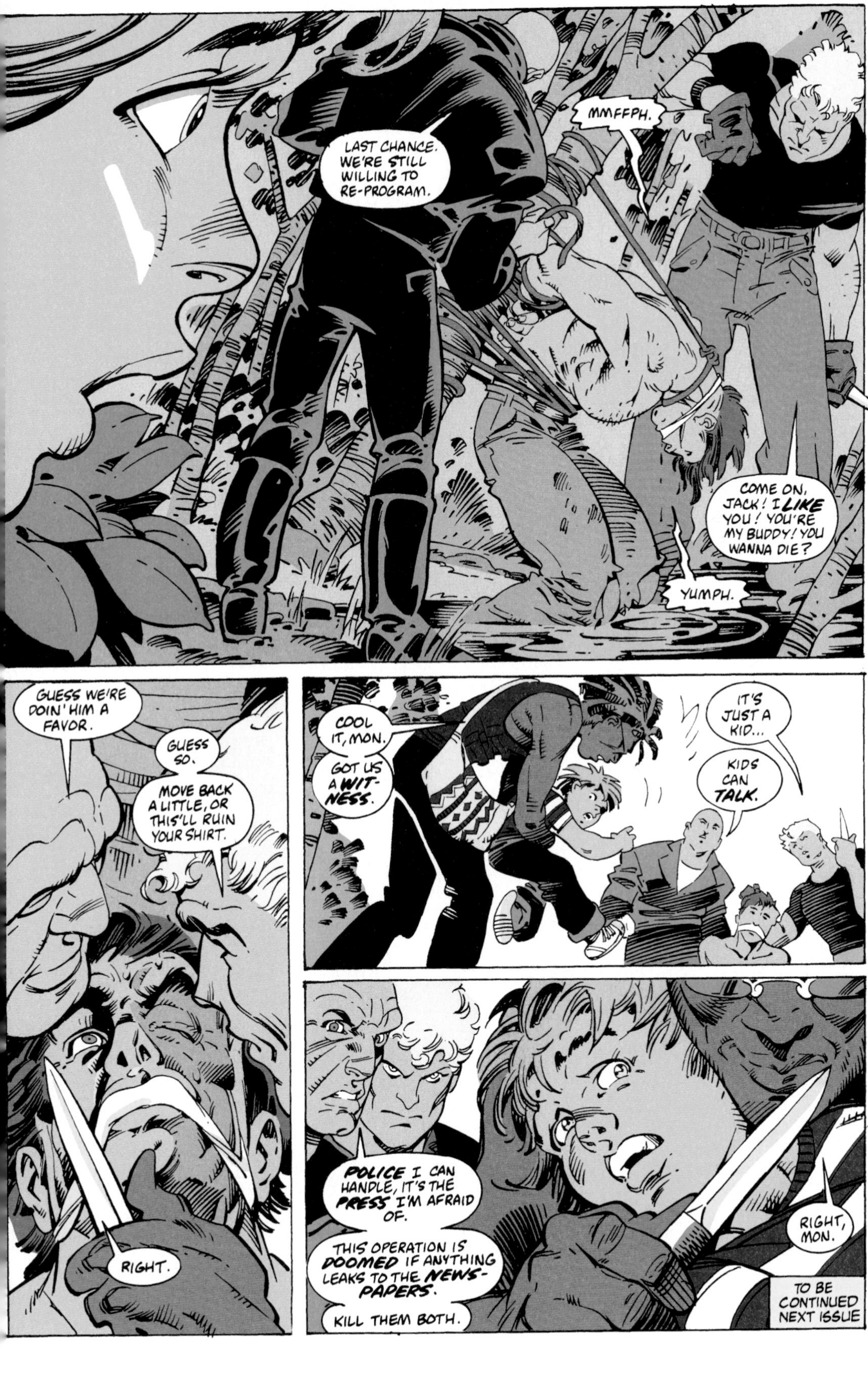
LAST CHANCE. WE'RE STILL WILLING TO RE-PROGRAM.
MMFFPH.
COME ON, JACK! I LIKE YOU! YOU'RE MY BUDDY! YOU WANNA DIE?
YUMPH.
GUESS WE'RE DOIN' HIM A FAVOR.
GUESS SO.
MOVE BACK A LITTLE, OR THIS'LL RUIN YOUR SHIRT.
RIGHT.
COOL IT, MON.
GOT US A WIT-NESS.
IT'S JUST A KID...
KIDS CAN TALK.
POLICE I CAN HANDLE, IT'S THE PRESS I'M AFRAID OF.
THIS OPERATION IS DOOMED IF ANYTHING LEAKS TO THE NEWS-PAPERS.
KILL THEM BOTH.
RIGHT, MON.
TO BE CONTINUED NEXT ISSUE

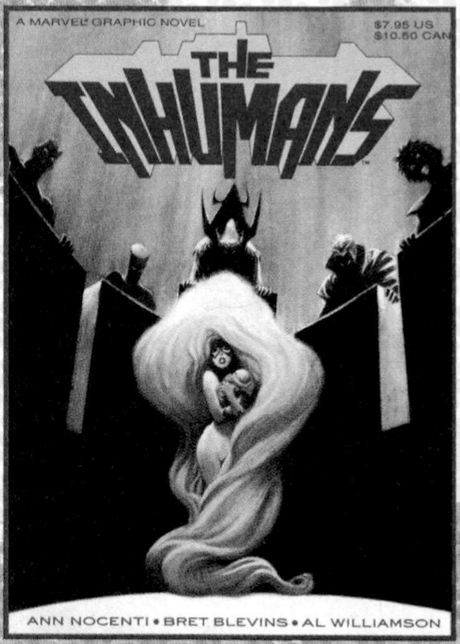
A MARVEL GRAPHIC NOVEL
$7.95 US
$10.50 CAN
THE INHUMANS
ANN NOCENTI • BRET BLEVINS • AL WILLIAMSON

Beginning with MARVEL GRAPHIC NOVEL: INHUMANS, published in August 1988, Marvel stopped attempting to apply a numbering system to the *Marvel Graphic Novel* line, and began publishing them as a series of one-shots.

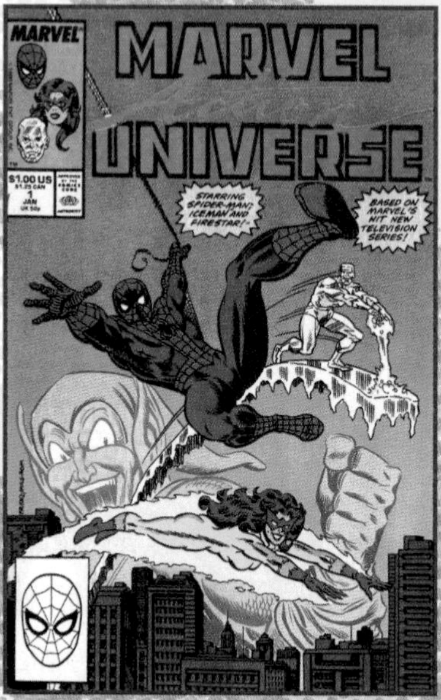
MARVEL
MARVEL UNIVERSE
$1.00 US
STARRING SPIDER-MAN! ICEMAN AND FIRESTAR!
BASED ON MARVEL'S HIT NEW TELEVISION SERIES!

MARVEL ACTION UNIVERSE, published in September 1988, was a reprint one-shot.

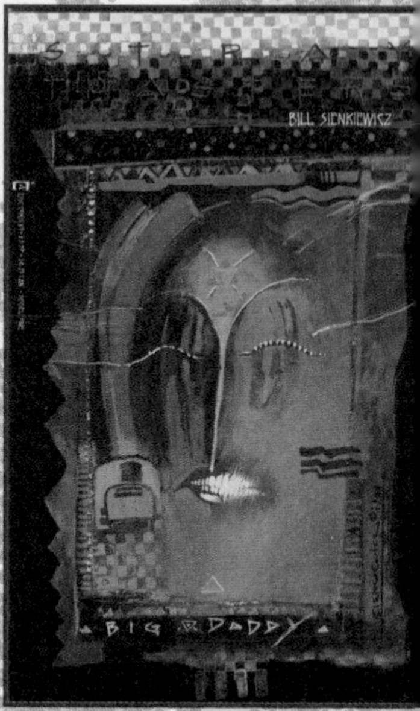
BILL SIENKIEWICZ
BIG DADDY

STRAY TOASTERS #1, published in Septembe 1988, began Bill Sienkiewicz's Epic miniserie

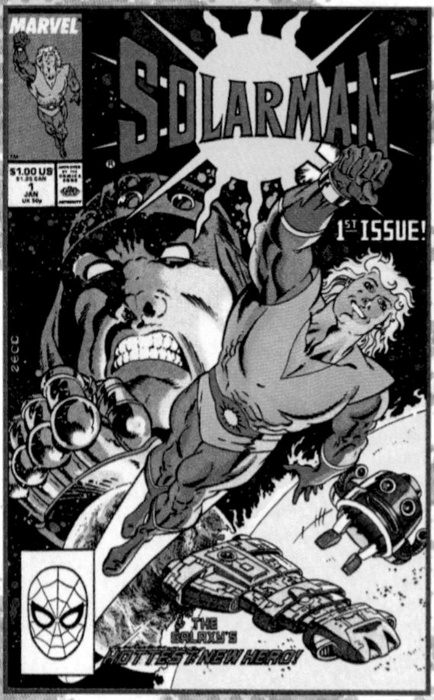
MARVEL
SOLARMAN
$1.00 US
1ST ISSUE!
THE GALAXY'S HOTTEST NEW HERO!

SOLARMAN #1, published in September 1988, began a short-lived series starring a solar-powered super hero.

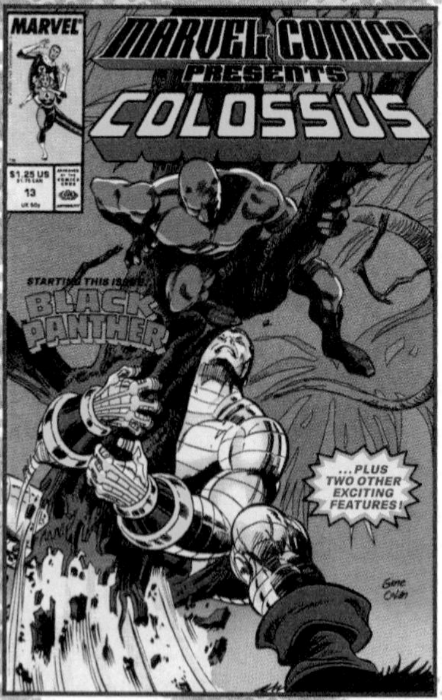
MARVEL
MARVEL COMICS PRESENTS
COLOSSUS
$1.25 US
13
STARTING THIS ISSUE: BLACK PANTHER
...PLUS TWO OTHER EXCITING FEATURES!
Gene Colan

MARVEL COMICS PRESENTS #13, published in October 1988, began a lengthy serial starring Black Panther.

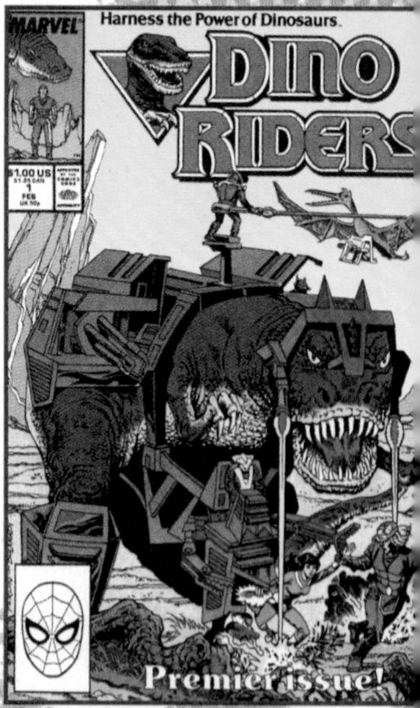
Harness the Power of Dinosaurs.
MARVEL
DINO RIDERS
$1.00 US
Premier issue!

DINO RIDERS #1, published in October 1988, beg a short series based on the Marvel Production animated TV series and the Tyco toy line.

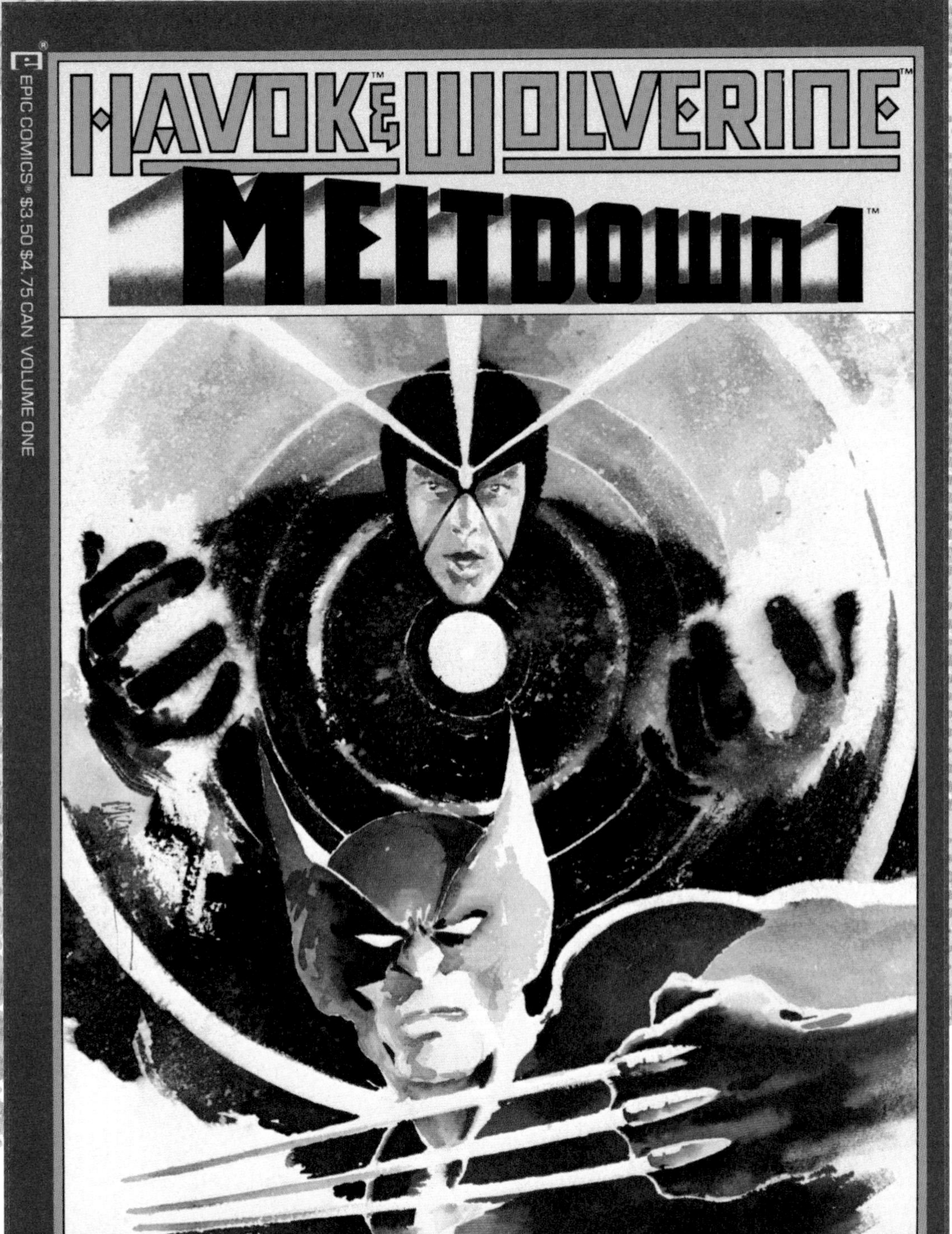
EPIC COMICS® $3.50 $4.75 CAN VOLUME ONE
HAVOK™ & WOLVERINE™
MELTDOWN 1™
WALTER SIMONSON • JON J MUTH
LOUISE SIMONSON • KENT WILLIAMS

HAVOK & WOLVERINE: MELTDOWN #1, published in November 1988, began an Epic limited series starring the two X-Men.

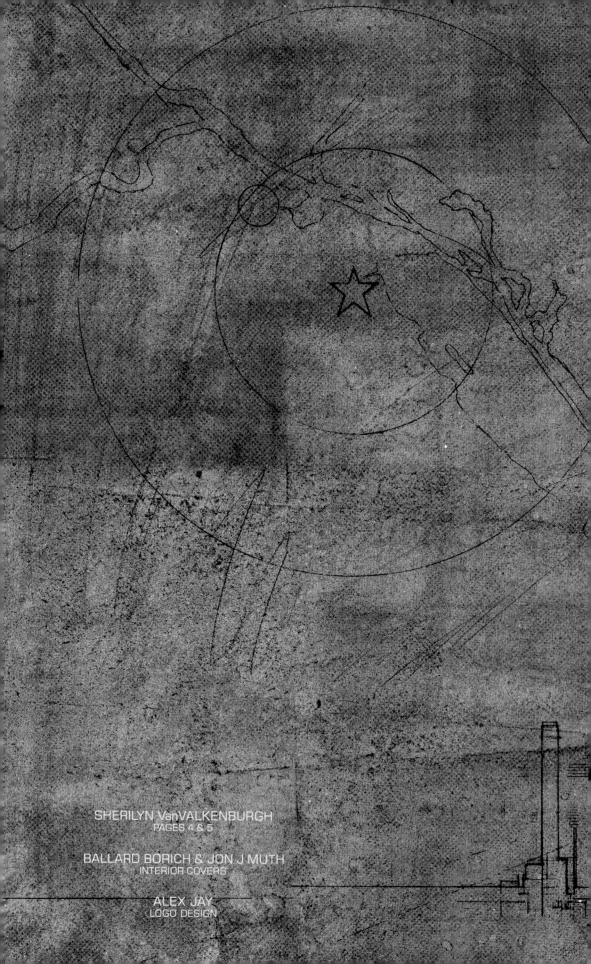

SHERILYN VanVALKENBURGH
PAGES 4 & 5

BALLARD BORICH & JON J MUTH
INTERIOR COVERS

ALEX JAY
LOGO DESIGN

WALTER SIMONSON
LOUISE SIMONSON
WRITERS

JON J MUTH
HAVOK ART

KENT WILLIAMS
WOLVERINE ART

BILL OAKLEY
LETTERER

R S BROSTERMAN
DESIGNER

MARGARET CLARK
STEVE BUCCELLATO
EDITORS

ARCHIE GOODWIN
EDITOR IN CHIEF

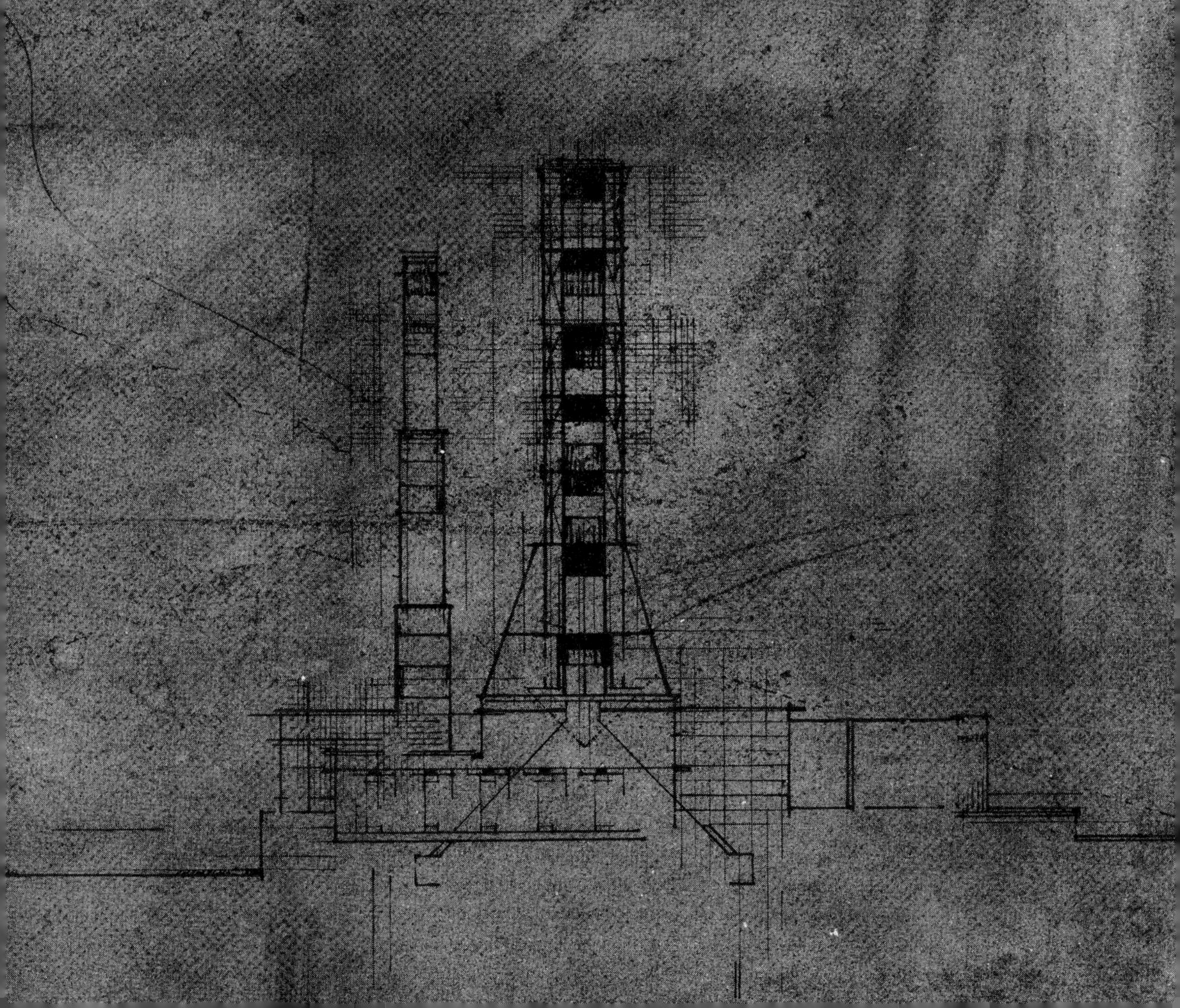

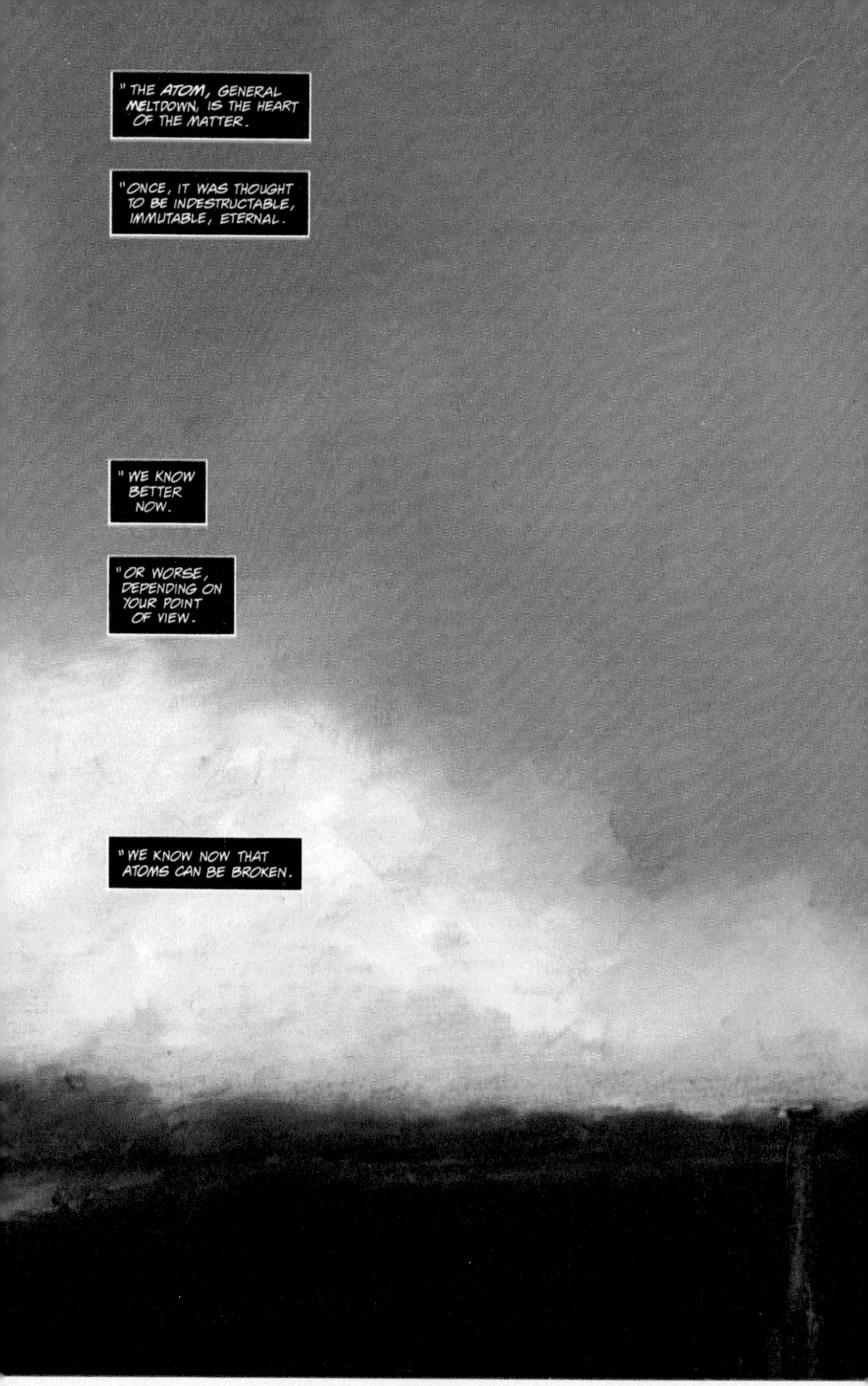
"THE ATOM, GENERAL MELTDOWN, IS THE HEART OF THE MATTER.
"ONCE, IT WAS THOUGHT TO BE INDESTRUCTABLE, IMMUTABLE, ETERNAL.
"WE KNOW BETTER NOW.
"OR WORSE, DEPENDING ON YOUR POINT OF VIEW.
"WE KNOW NOW THAT ATOMS CAN BE BROKEN.

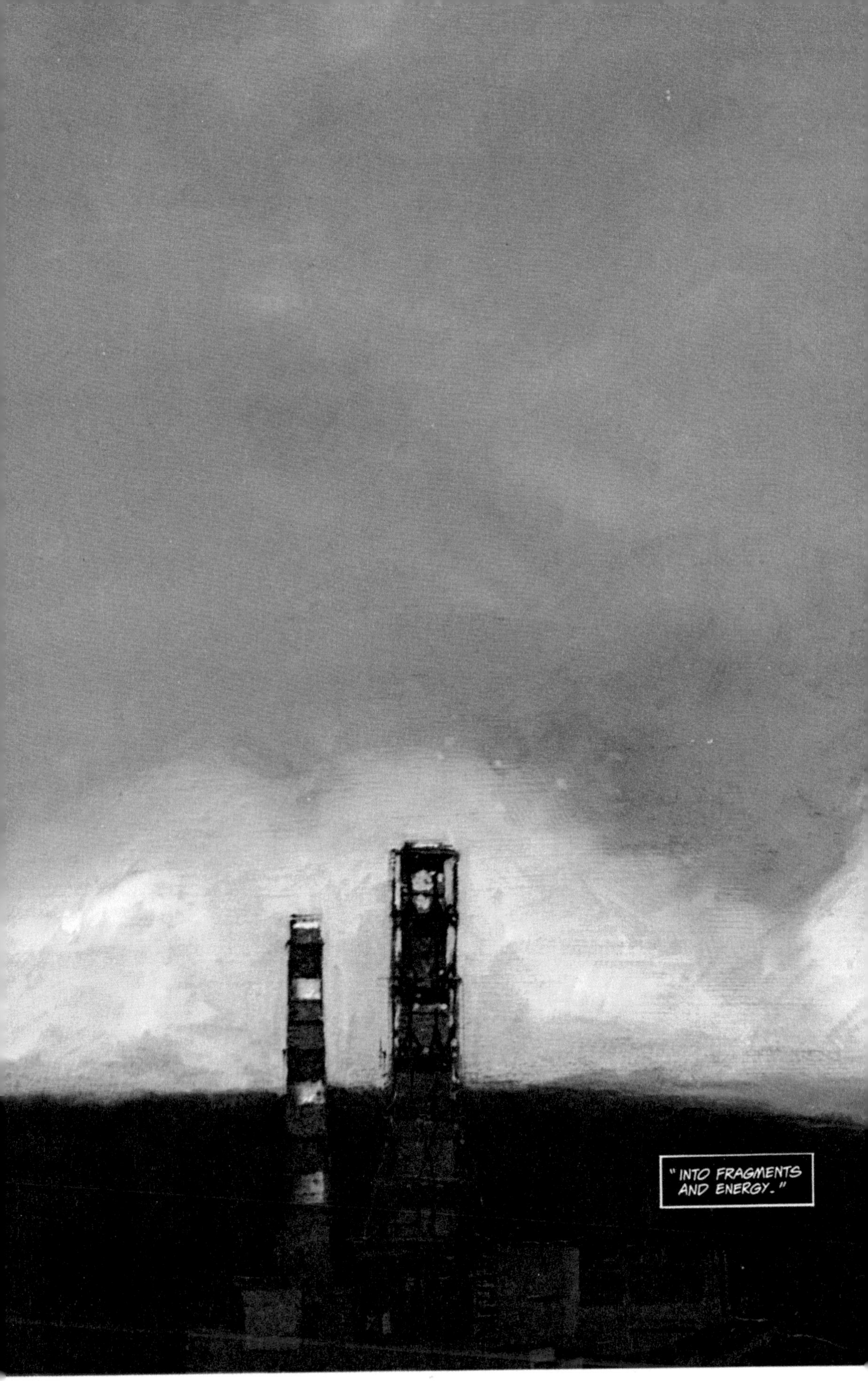
"INTO FRAGMENTS AND ENERGY."

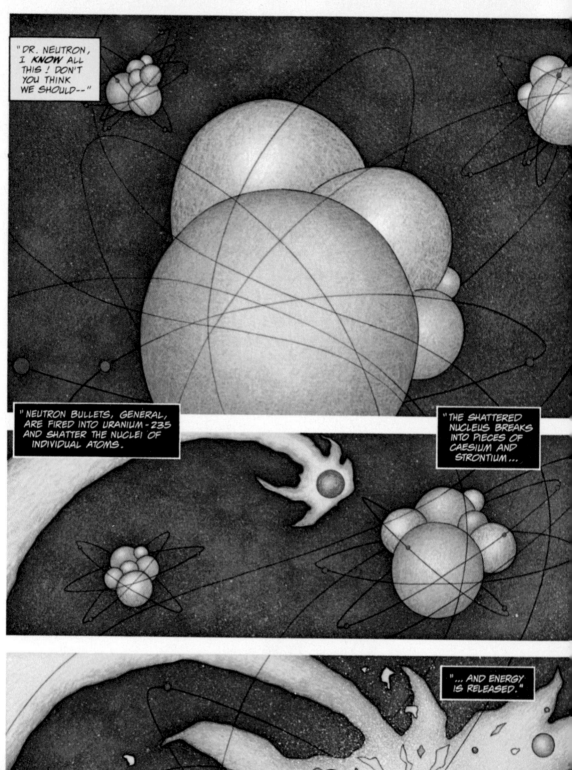

"DR. NEUTRON, I *KNOW* ALL THIS! DON'T YOU THINK WE SHOULD--"

"NEUTRON BULLETS, GENERAL, ARE FIRED INTO URANIUM-235 AND SHATTER THE NUCLEI OF INDIVIDUAL ATOMS.

"THE SHATTERED NUCLEUS BREAKS INTO PIECES OF CAESIUM AND STRONTIUM...

"...AND ENERGY IS RELEASED."

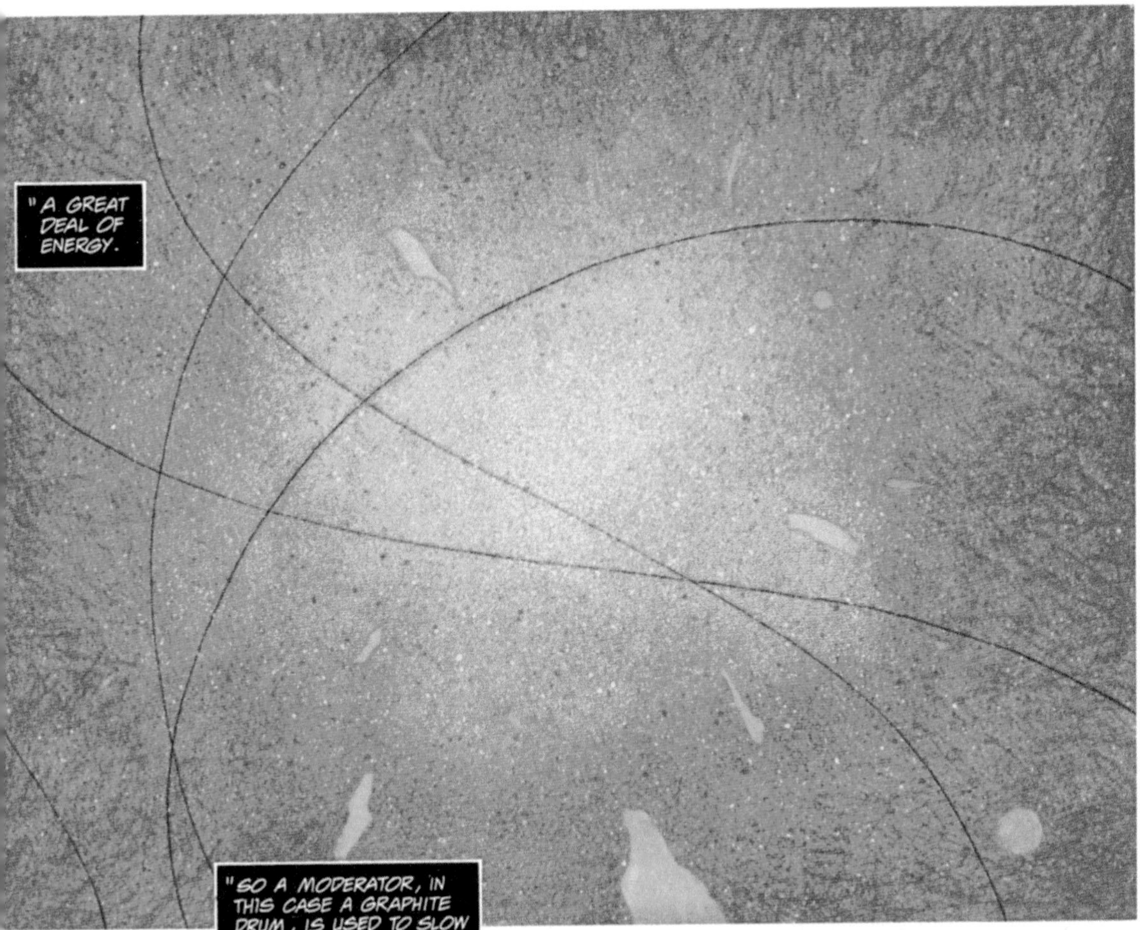
"A GREAT DEAL OF ENERGY.
"SO A MODERATOR, IN THIS CASE A GRAPHITE DRUM, IS USED TO SLOW THE NEUTRONS DOWN.

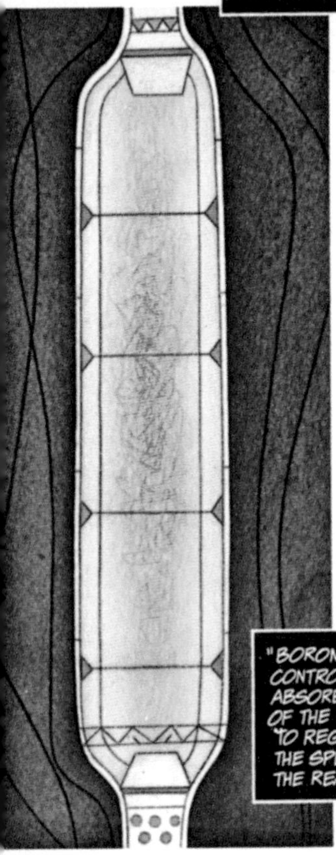
"BORON STEEL CONTROL RODS ABSORB SOME OF THE NEUTRONS TO REGULATE THE SPEED OF THE REACTION.

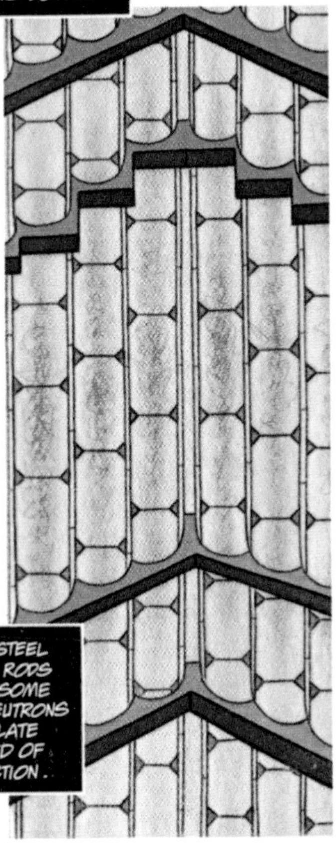

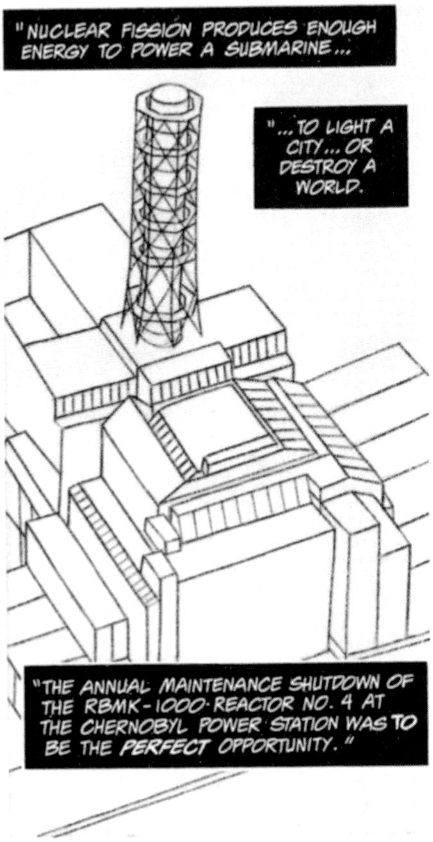
"NUCLEAR FISSION PRODUCES ENOUGH ENERGY TO POWER A SUBMARINE...
"...TO LIGHT A CITY... OR DESTROY A WORLD.
"THE ANNUAL MAINTENANCE SHUTDOWN OF THE RBMK-1000 REACTOR NO. 4 AT THE CHERNOBYL POWER STATION WAS TO BE THE *PERFECT* OPPORTUNITY."

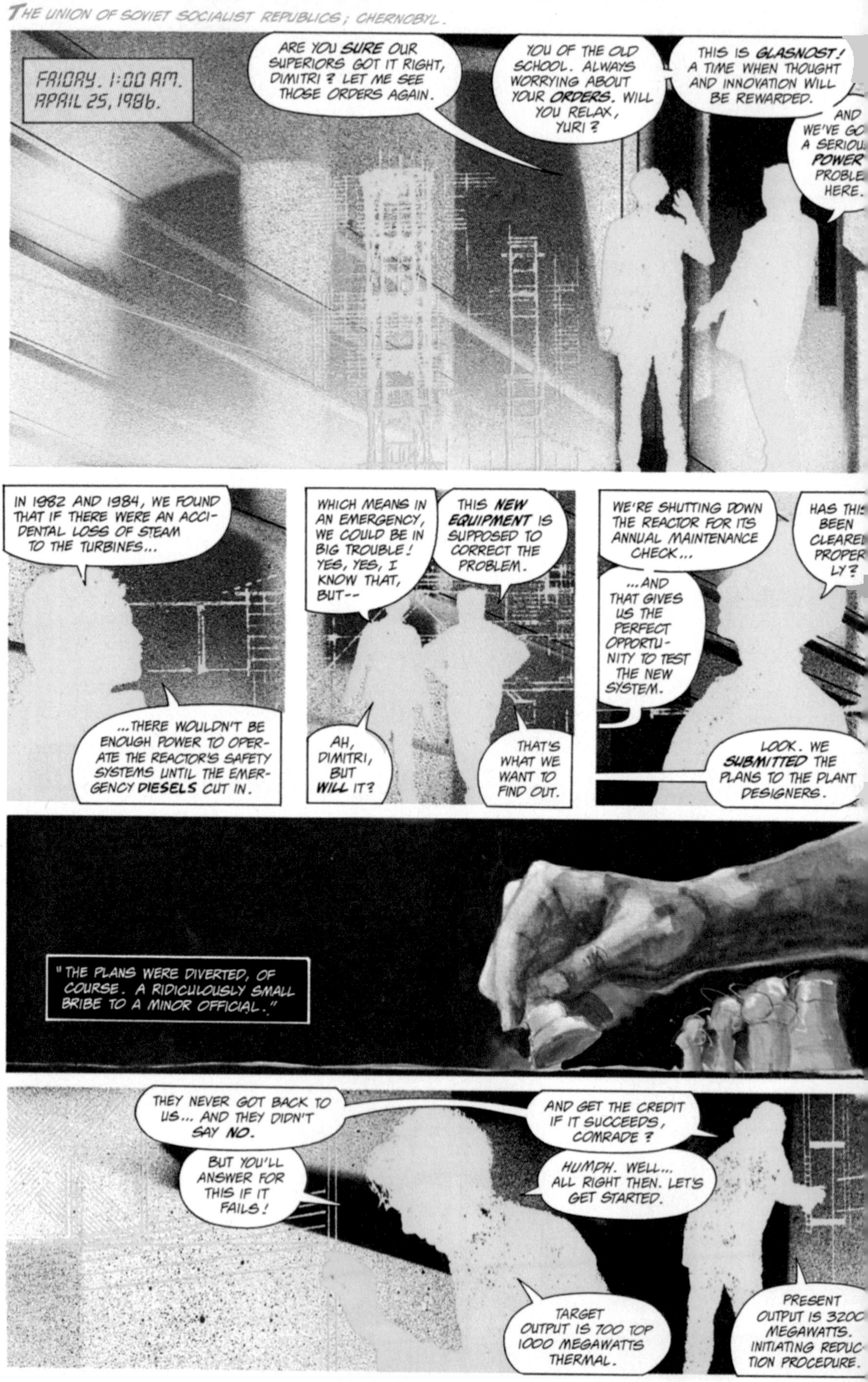
THE UNION OF SOVIET SOCIALIST REPUBLICS; CHERNOBYL.
FRIDAY. 1:00 AM. APRIL 25, 1986.
ARE YOU SURE OUR SUPERIORS GOT IT RIGHT, DIMITRI? LET ME SEE THOSE ORDERS AGAIN.
YOU OF THE OLD SCHOOL. ALWAYS WORRYING ABOUT YOUR ORDERS. WILL YOU RELAX, YURI?
THIS IS GLASNOST! A TIME WHEN THOUGHT AND INNOVATION WILL BE REWARDED.
AND WE'VE GO A SERIOU POWER PROBLE HERE.
IN 1982 AND 1984, WE FOUND THAT IF THERE WERE AN ACCIDENTAL LOSS OF STEAM TO THE TURBINES...
...THERE WOULDN'T BE ENOUGH POWER TO OPERATE THE REACTOR'S SAFETY SYSTEMS UNTIL THE EMERGENCY DIESELS CUT IN.
WHICH MEANS IN AN EMERGENCY, WE COULD BE IN BIG TROUBLE! YES, YES, I KNOW THAT, BUT--
THIS NEW EQUIPMENT IS SUPPOSED TO CORRECT THE PROBLEM.
AH, DIMITRI, BUT WILL IT?
THAT'S WHAT WE WANT TO FIND OUT.
WE'RE SHUTTING DOWN THE REACTOR FOR ITS ANNUAL MAINTENANCE CHECK...
HAS THI BEEN CLEARE PROPER LY?
...AND THAT GIVES US THE PERFECT OPPORTUNITY TO TEST THE NEW SYSTEM.
LOOK. WE SUBMITTED THE PLANS TO THE PLANT DESIGNERS.
"THE PLANS WERE DIVERTED, OF COURSE. A RIDICULOUSLY SMALL BRIBE TO A MINOR OFFICIAL."
THEY NEVER GOT BACK TO US... AND THEY DIDN'T SAY NO.
BUT YOU'LL ANSWER FOR THIS IF IT FAILS!
AND GET THE CREDIT IF IT SUCCEEDS, COMRADE?
HUMPH. WELL... ALL RIGHT THEN. LET'S GET STARTED.
TARGET OUTPUT IS 700 TOP 1000 MEGAWATTS THERMAL.
PRESENT OUTPUT IS 320C MEGAWATTS. INITIATING REDUC TION PROCEDURE.

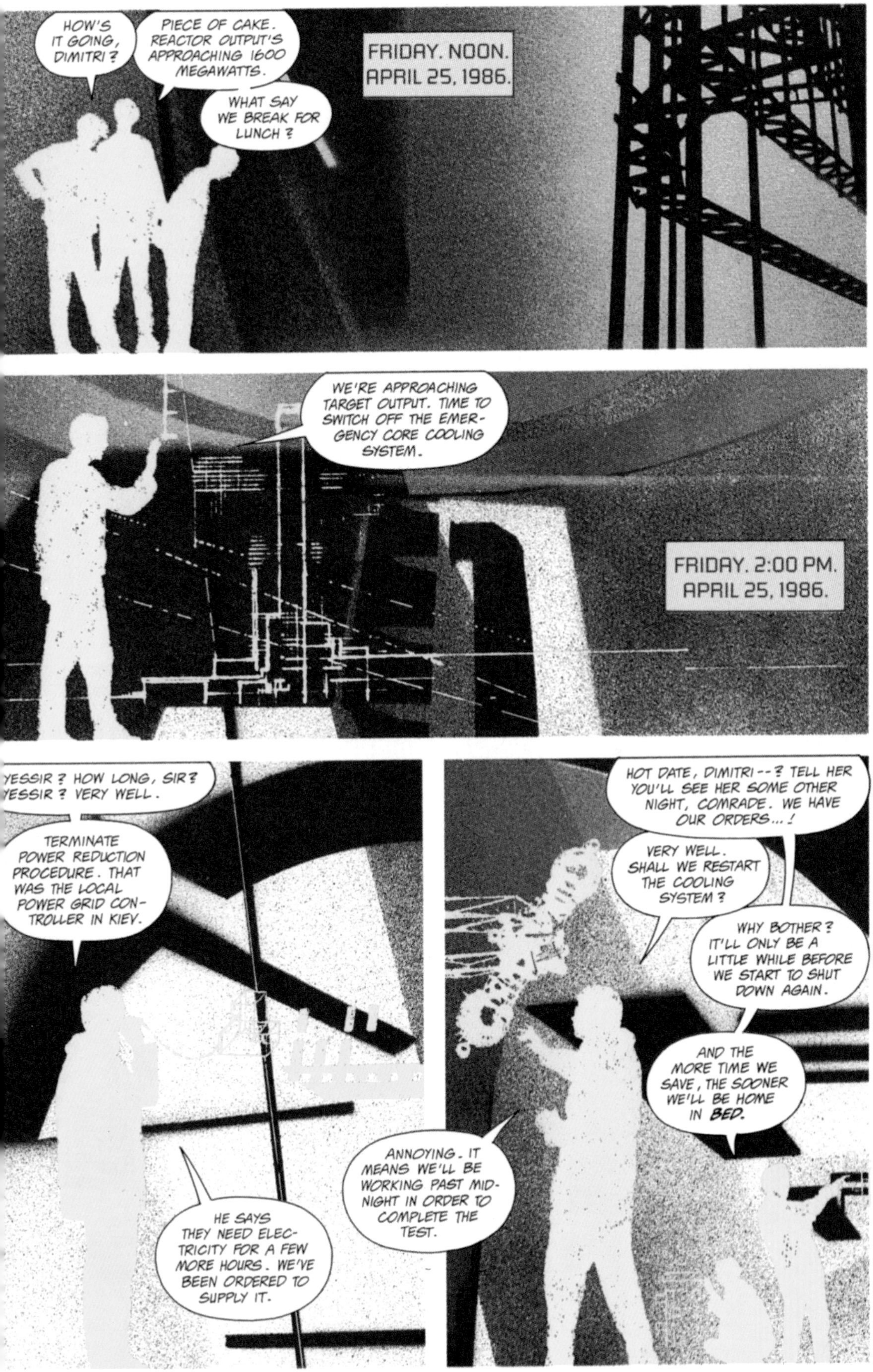
HOW'S IT GOING, DIMITRI?
PIECE OF CAKE. REACTOR OUTPUT'S APPROACHING 1600 MEGAWATTS.
WHAT SAY WE BREAK FOR LUNCH?
FRIDAY. NOON. APRIL 25, 1986.
WE'RE APPROACHING TARGET OUTPUT. TIME TO SWITCH OFF THE EMERGENCY CORE COOLING SYSTEM.
FRIDAY. 2:00 PM. APRIL 25, 1986.
YESSIR? HOW LONG, SIR? YESSIR? VERY WELL.
TERMINATE POWER REDUCTION PROCEDURE. THAT WAS THE LOCAL POWER GRID CONTROLLER IN KIEV.
HE SAYS THEY NEED ELECTRICITY FOR A FEW MORE HOURS. WE'VE BEEN ORDERED TO SUPPLY IT.
HOT DATE, DIMITRI--? TELL HER YOU'LL SEE HER SOME OTHER NIGHT, COMRADE. WE HAVE OUR ORDERS...!
VERY WELL. SHALL WE RESTART THE COOLING SYSTEM?
WHY BOTHER? IT'LL ONLY BE A LITTLE WHILE BEFORE WE START TO SHUT DOWN AGAIN.
AND THE MORE TIME WE SAVE, THE SOONER WE'LL BE HOME IN BED.
ANNOYING. IT MEANS WE'LL BE WORKING PAST MIDNIGHT IN ORDER TO COMPLETE THE TEST.

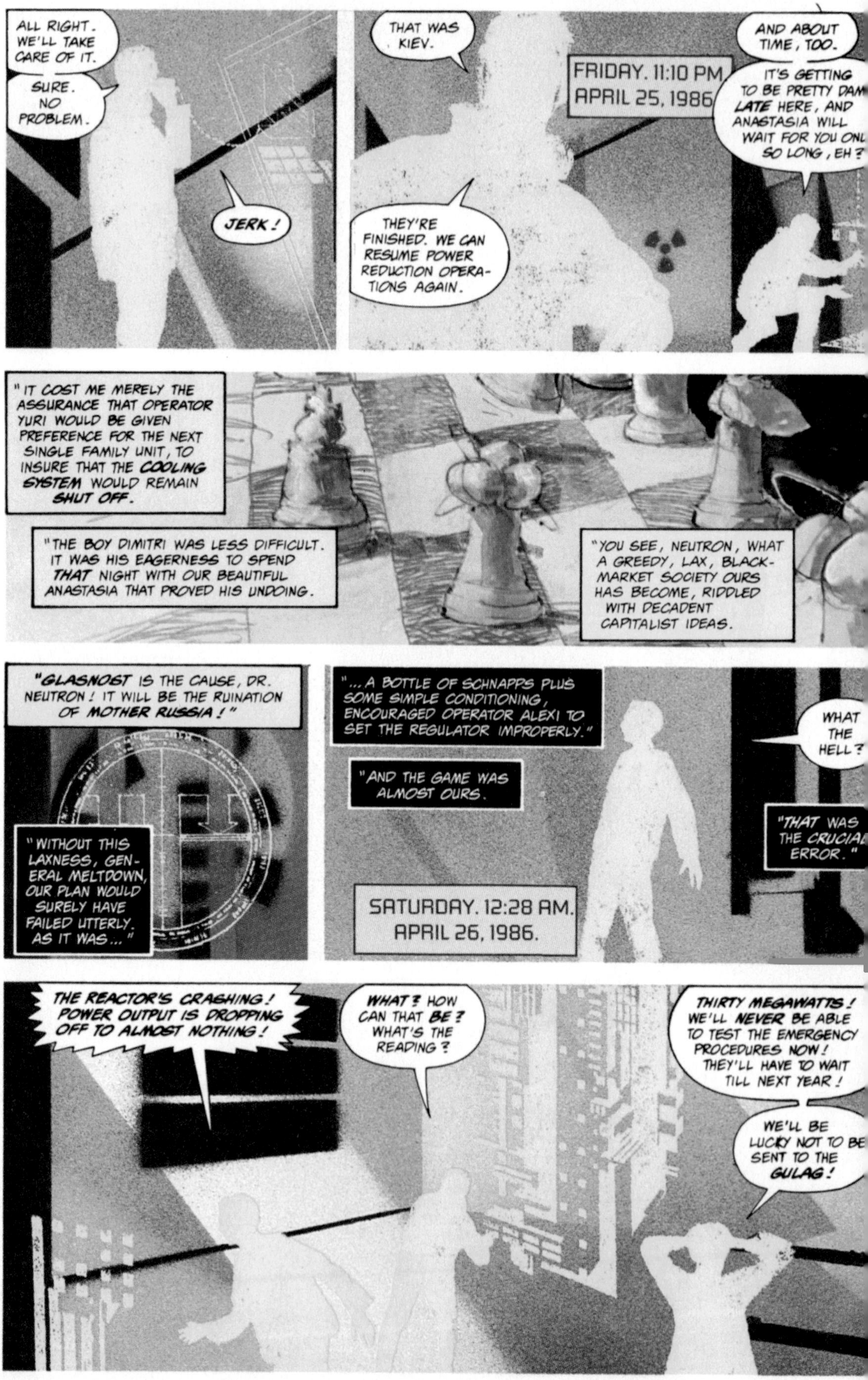
ALL RIGHT. WE'LL TAKE CARE OF IT.
SURE. NO PROBLEM.
JERK!
THAT WAS KIEV.
THEY'RE FINISHED. WE CAN RESUME POWER REDUCTION OPERATIONS AGAIN.
FRIDAY. 11:10 PM APRIL 25, 1986
AND ABOUT TIME, TOO.
IT'S GETTING TO BE PRETTY DAM LATE HERE, AND ANASTASIA WILL WAIT FOR YOU ONL SO LONG, EH?
"IT COST ME MERELY THE ASSURANCE THAT OPERATOR YURI WOULD BE GIVEN PREFERENCE FOR THE NEXT SINGLE FAMILY UNIT, TO INSURE THAT THE COOLING SYSTEM WOULD REMAIN SHUT OFF.
"THE BOY DIMITRI WAS LESS DIFFICULT. IT WAS HIS EAGERNESS TO SPEND THAT NIGHT WITH OUR BEAUTIFUL ANASTASIA THAT PROVED HIS UNDOING.
"YOU SEE, NEUTRON, WHAT A GREEDY, LAX, BLACK-MARKET SOCIETY OURS HAS BECOME, RIDDLED WITH DECADENT CAPITALIST IDEAS.
"GLASNOST IS THE CAUSE, DR. NEUTRON! IT WILL BE THE RUINATION OF MOTHER RUSSIA!"
"WITHOUT THIS LAXNESS, GENERAL MELTDOWN, OUR PLAN WOULD SURELY HAVE FAILED UTTERLY. AS IT WAS..."
"...A BOTTLE OF SCHNAPPS PLUS SOME SIMPLE CONDITIONING, ENCOURAGED OPERATOR ALEXI TO SET THE REGULATOR IMPROPERLY."
"AND THE GAME WAS ALMOST OURS.
SATURDAY. 12:28 AM. APRIL 26, 1986.
WHAT THE HELL?
"THAT WAS THE CRUCIAL ERROR."
THE REACTOR'S CRASHING! POWER OUTPUT IS DROPPING OFF TO ALMOST NOTHING!
WHAT? HOW CAN THAT BE? WHAT'S THE READING?
THIRTY MEGAWATTS! WE'LL NEVER BE ABLE TO TEST THE EMERGENCY PROCEDURES NOW! THEY'LL HAVE TO WAIT TILL NEXT YEAR!
WE'LL BE LUCKY NOT TO BE SENT TO THE GULAG!

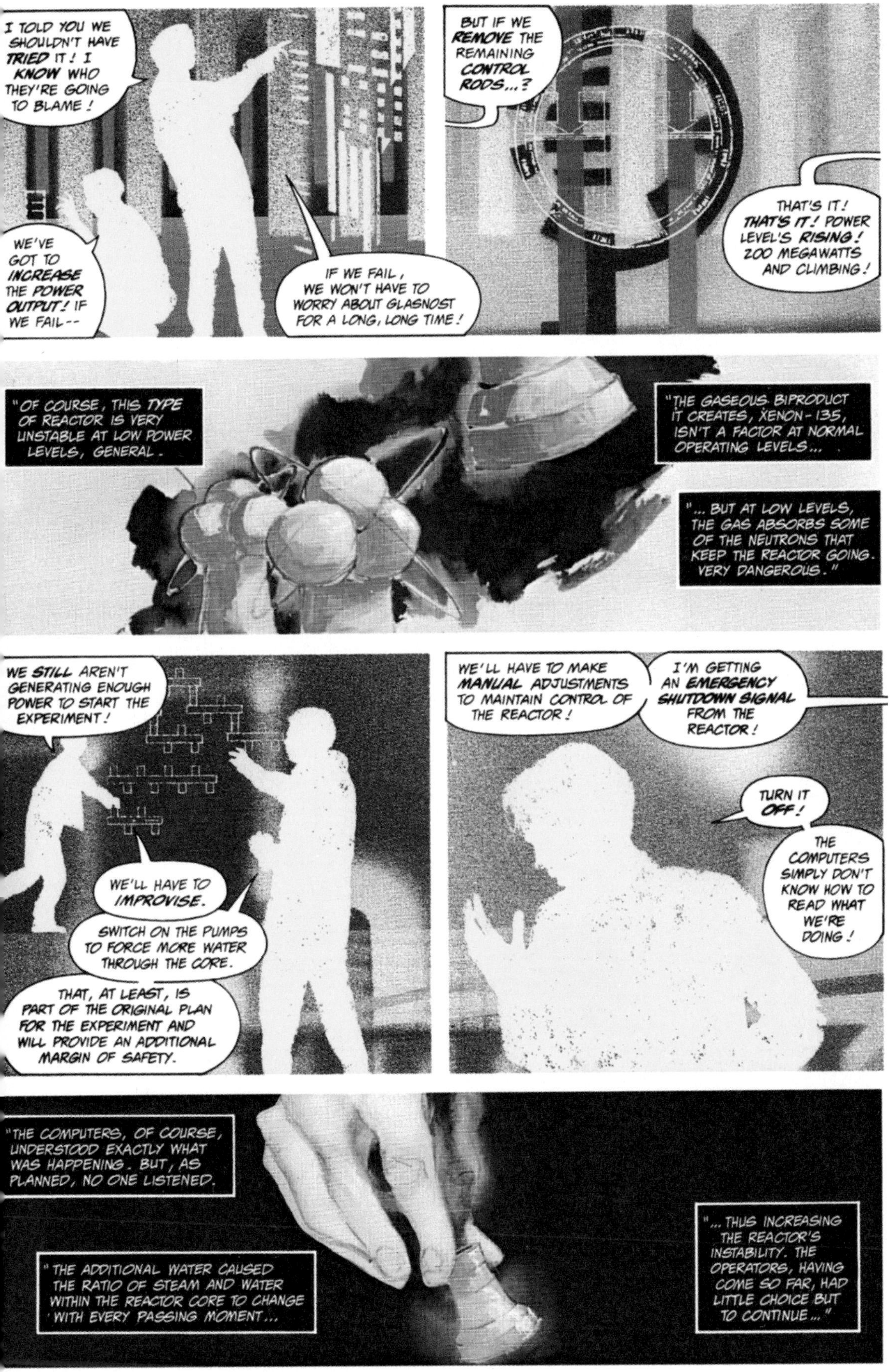
I TOLD YOU WE SHOULDN'T HAVE TRIED IT! I KNOW WHO THEY'RE GOING TO BLAME!
WE'VE GOT TO INCREASE THE POWER OUTPUT! IF WE FAIL--
IF WE FAIL, WE WON'T HAVE TO WORRY ABOUT GLASNOST FOR A LONG, LONG TIME!
BUT IF WE REMOVE THE REMAINING CONTROL RODS...?
THAT'S IT! THAT'S IT! POWER LEVEL'S RISING! 200 MEGAWATTS AND CLIMBING!
"OF COURSE, THIS TYPE OF REACTOR IS VERY UNSTABLE AT LOW POWER LEVELS, GENERAL.
"THE GASEOUS BIPRODUCT IT CREATES, XENON-135, ISN'T A FACTOR AT NORMAL OPERATING LEVELS...
"... BUT AT LOW LEVELS, THE GAS ABSORBS SOME OF THE NEUTRONS THAT KEEP THE REACTOR GOING. VERY DANGEROUS."
WE STILL AREN'T GENERATING ENOUGH POWER TO START THE EXPERIMENT!
WE'LL HAVE TO IMPROVISE.
SWITCH ON THE PUMPS TO FORCE MORE WATER THROUGH THE CORE.
THAT, AT LEAST, IS PART OF THE ORIGINAL PLAN FOR THE EXPERIMENT AND WILL PROVIDE AN ADDITIONAL MARGIN OF SAFETY.
WE'LL HAVE TO MAKE MANUAL ADJUSTMENTS TO MAINTAIN CONTROL OF THE REACTOR!
I'M GETTING AN EMERGENCY SHUTDOWN SIGNAL FROM THE REACTOR!
TURN IT OFF!
THE COMPUTERS SIMPLY DON'T KNOW HOW TO READ WHAT WE'RE DOING!
"THE COMPUTERS, OF COURSE, UNDERSTOOD EXACTLY WHAT WAS HAPPENING. BUT, AS PLANNED, NO ONE LISTENED.
"THE ADDITIONAL WATER CAUSED THE RATIO OF STEAM AND WATER WITHIN THE REACTOR CORE TO CHANGE WITH EVERY PASSING MOMENT...
"... THUS INCREASING THE REACTOR'S INSTABILITY. THE OPERATORS, HAVING COME SO FAR, HAD LITTLE CHOICE BUT TO CONTINUE..."

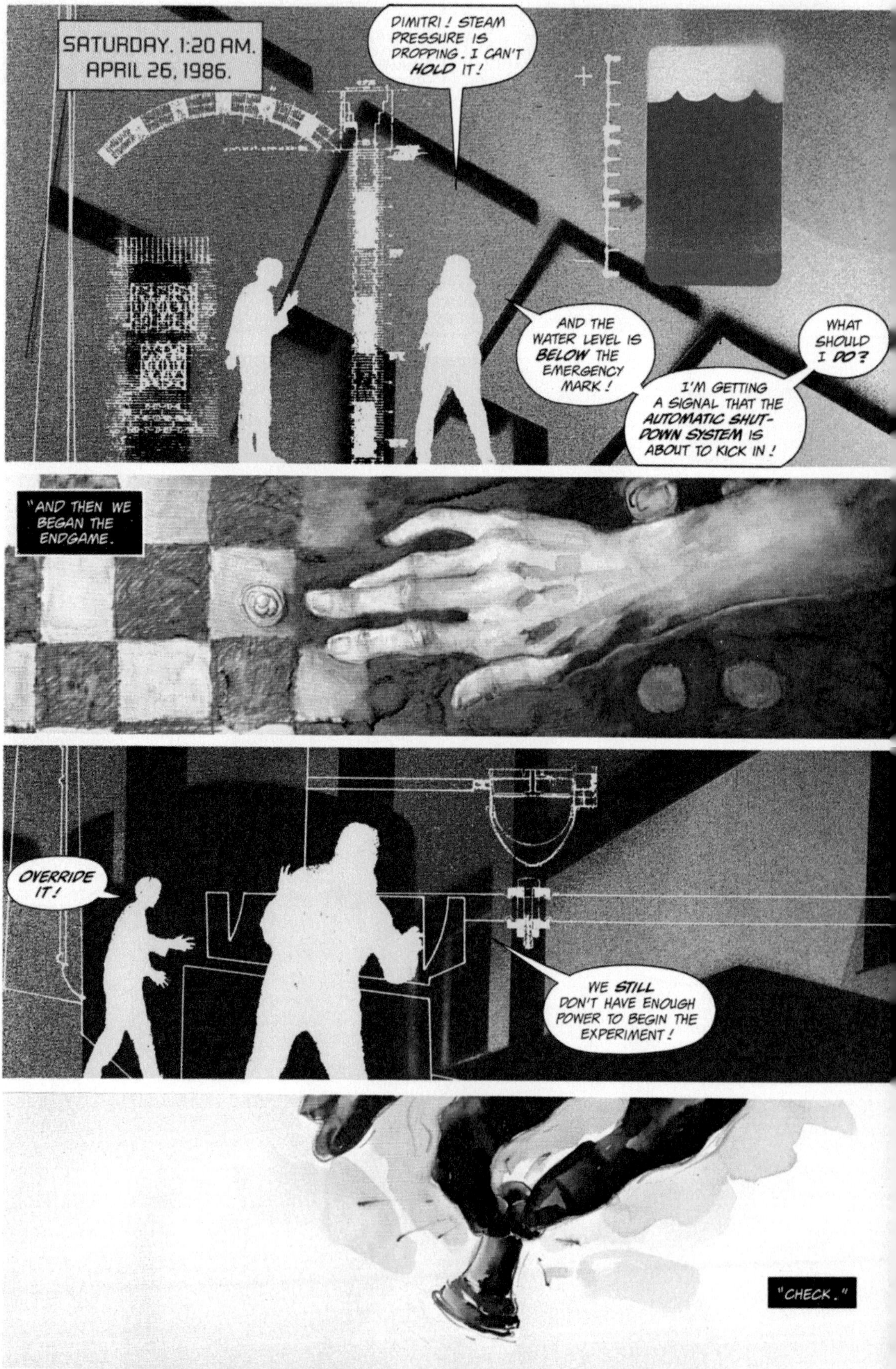
SATURDAY. 1:20 AM. APRIL 26, 1986.
DIMITRI! STEAM PRESSURE IS DROPPING. I CAN'T HOLD IT!
AND THE WATER LEVEL IS BELOW THE EMERGENCY MARK!
I'M GETTING A SIGNAL THAT THE AUTOMATIC SHUT-DOWN SYSTEM IS ABOUT TO KICK IN!
WHAT SHOULD I DO?
"AND THEN WE BEGAN THE ENDGAME.
OVERRIDE IT!
WE STILL DON'T HAVE ENOUGH POWER TO BEGIN THE EXPERIMENT!
"CHECK."

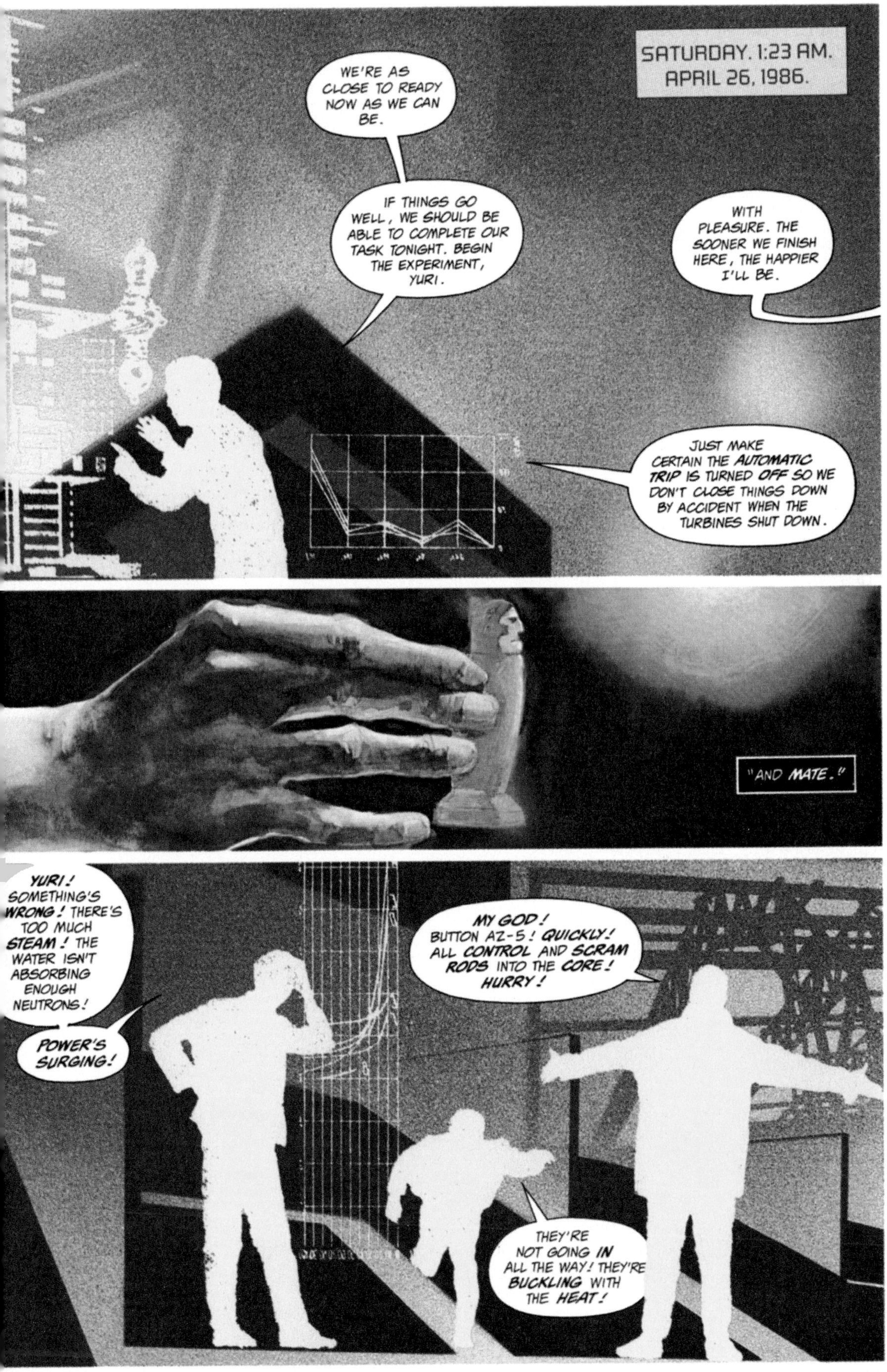
SATURDAY. 1:23 AM. APRIL 26, 1986.
WE'RE AS CLOSE TO READY NOW AS WE CAN BE.
IF THINGS GO WELL, WE SHOULD BE ABLE TO COMPLETE OUR TASK TONIGHT. BEGIN THE EXPERIMENT, YURI.
WITH PLEASURE. THE SOONER WE FINISH HERE, THE HAPPIER I'LL BE.
JUST MAKE CERTAIN THE AUTOMATIC TRIP IS TURNED OFF SO WE DON'T CLOSE THINGS DOWN BY ACCIDENT WHEN THE TURBINES SHUT DOWN.
"AND MATE."
YURI! SOMETHING'S WRONG! THERE'S TOO MUCH STEAM! THE WATER ISN'T ABSORBING ENOUGH NEUTRONS!
POWER'S SURGING!
MY GOD! BUTTON AZ-5! QUICKLY! ALL CONTROL AND SCRAM RODS INTO THE CORE! HURRY!
THEY'RE NOT GOING IN ALL THE WAY! THEY'RE BUCKLING WITH THE HEAT!

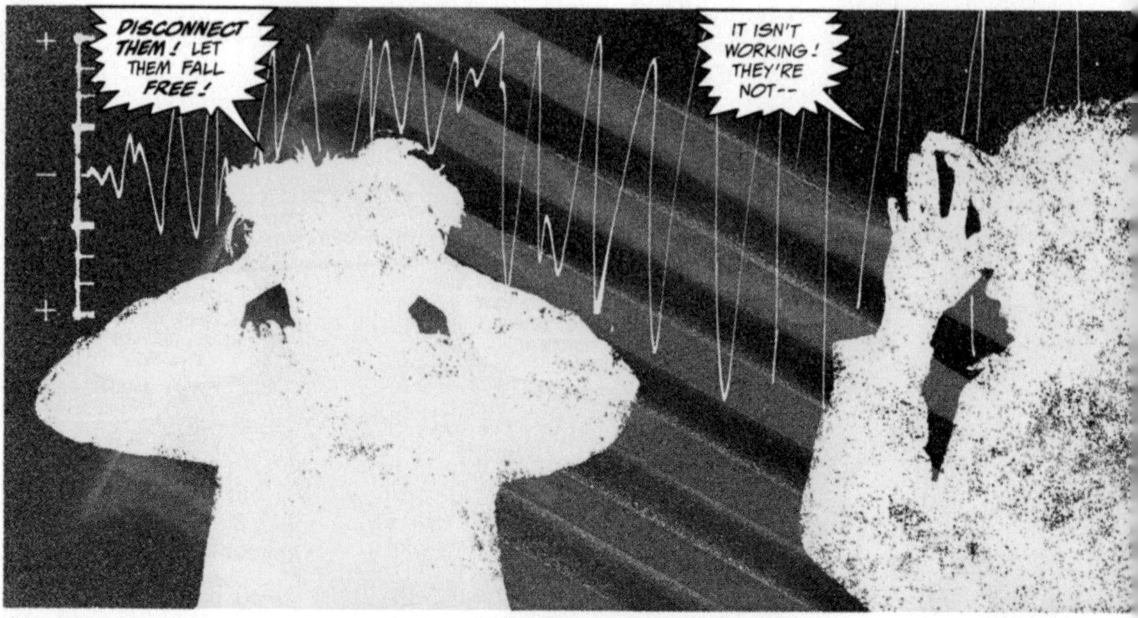
DISCONNECT THEM! LET THEM FALL FREE!
IT ISN'T WORKING! THEY'RE NOT--

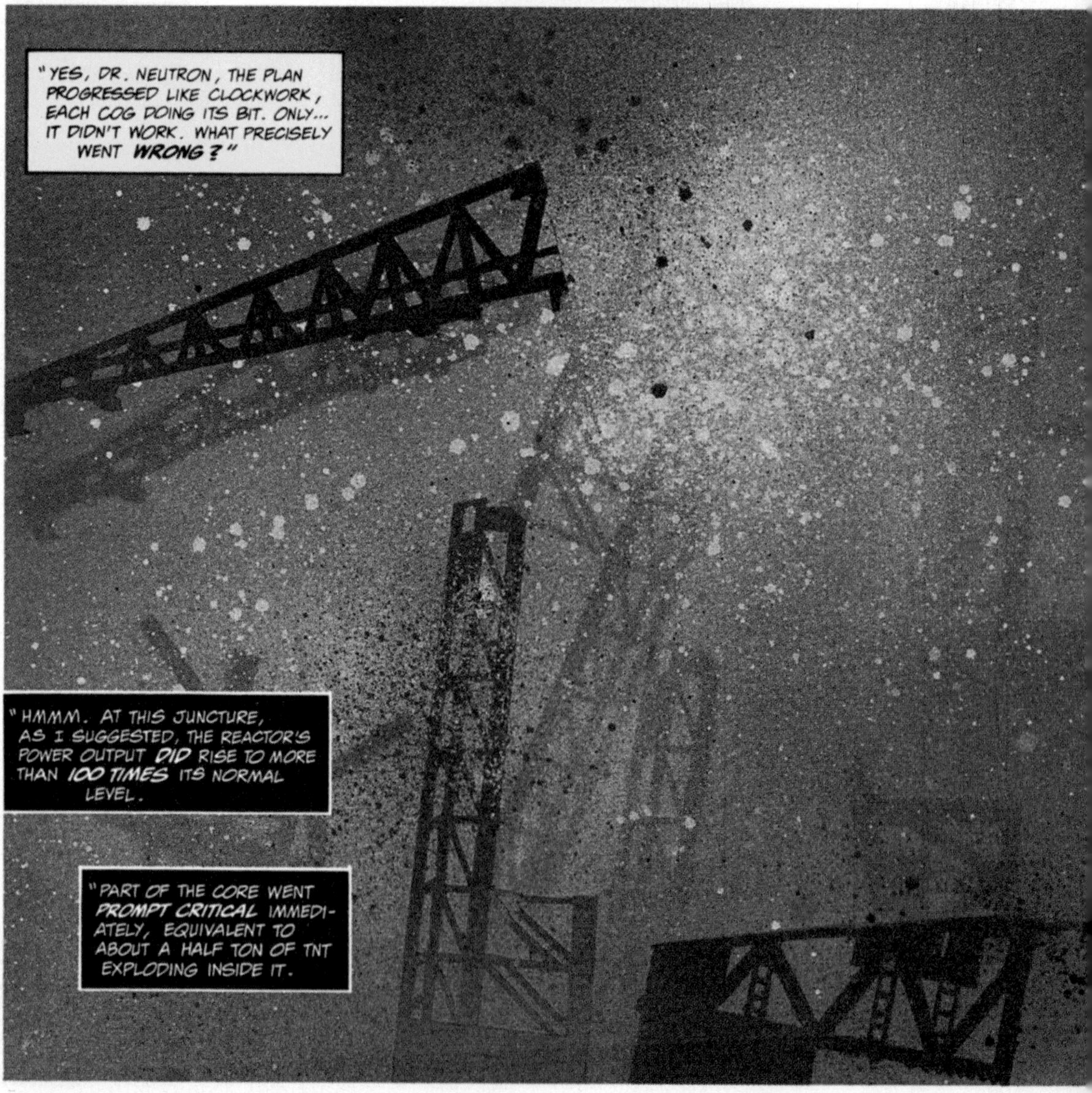
"YES, DR. NEUTRON, THE PLAN PROGRESSED LIKE CLOCKWORK, EACH COG DOING ITS BIT. ONLY... IT DIDN'T WORK. WHAT PRECISELY WENT WRONG?"
"HMMM. AT THIS JUNCTURE, AS I SUGGESTED, THE REACTOR'S POWER OUTPUT DID RISE TO MORE THAN 100 TIMES ITS NORMAL LEVEL.
"PART OF THE CORE WENT PROMPT CRITICAL IMMEDIATELY, EQUIVALENT TO ABOUT A HALF TON OF TNT EXPLODING INSIDE IT.

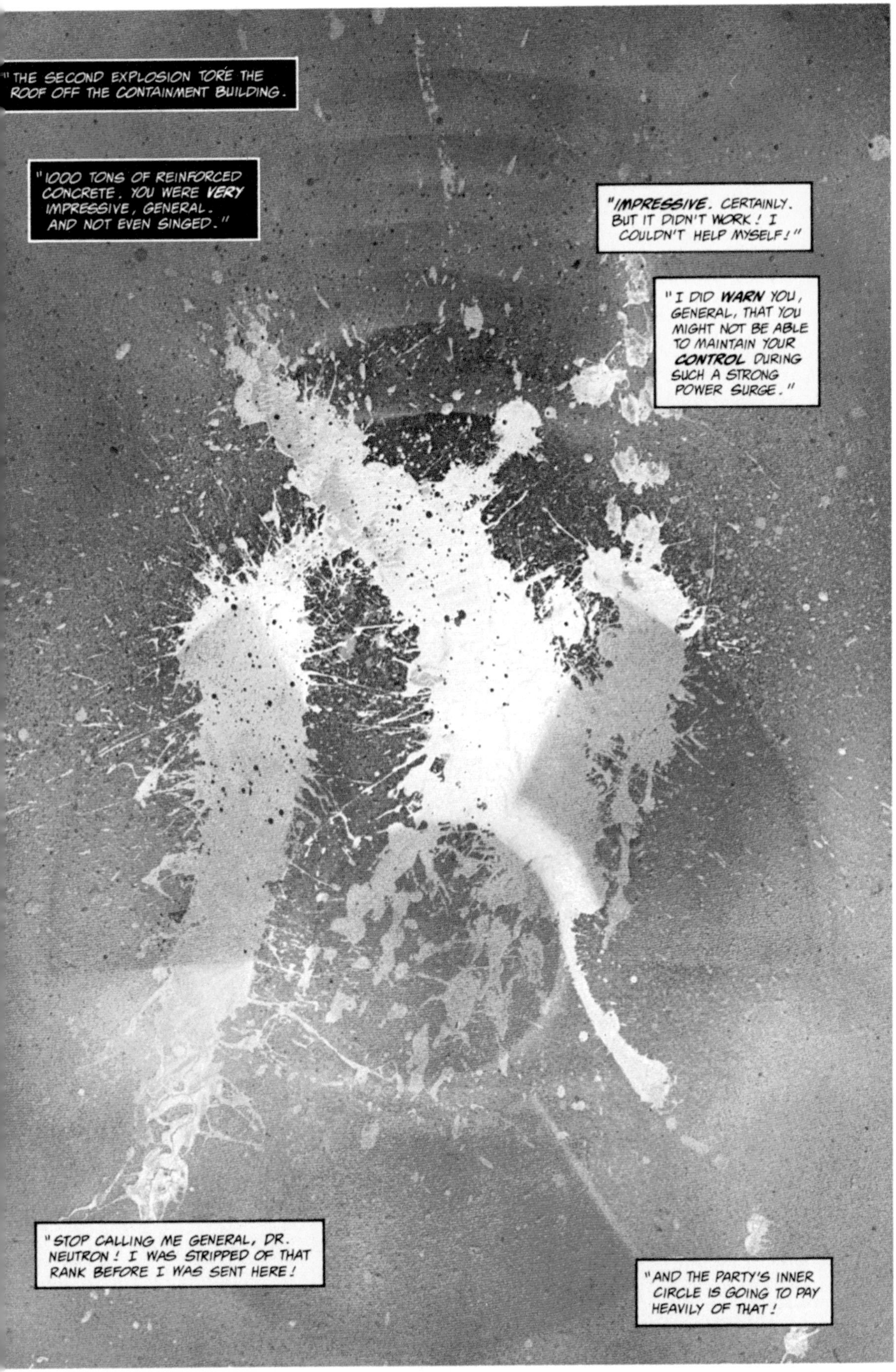
"THE SECOND EXPLOSION TORE THE ROOF OFF THE CONTAINMENT BUILDING.
"1000 TONS OF REINFORCED CONCRETE. YOU WERE VERY IMPRESSIVE, GENERAL. AND NOT EVEN SINGED."
"IMPRESSIVE. CERTAINLY. BUT IT DIDN'T WORK! I COULDN'T HELP MYSELF!"
"I DID WARN YOU, GENERAL, THAT YOU MIGHT NOT BE ABLE TO MAINTAIN YOUR CONTROL DURING SUCH A STRONG POWER SURGE."
"STOP CALLING ME GENERAL, DR. NEUTRON! I WAS STRIPPED OF THAT RANK BEFORE I WAS SENT HERE!
"AND THE PARTY'S INNER CIRCLE IS GOING TO PAY HEAVILY OF THAT!

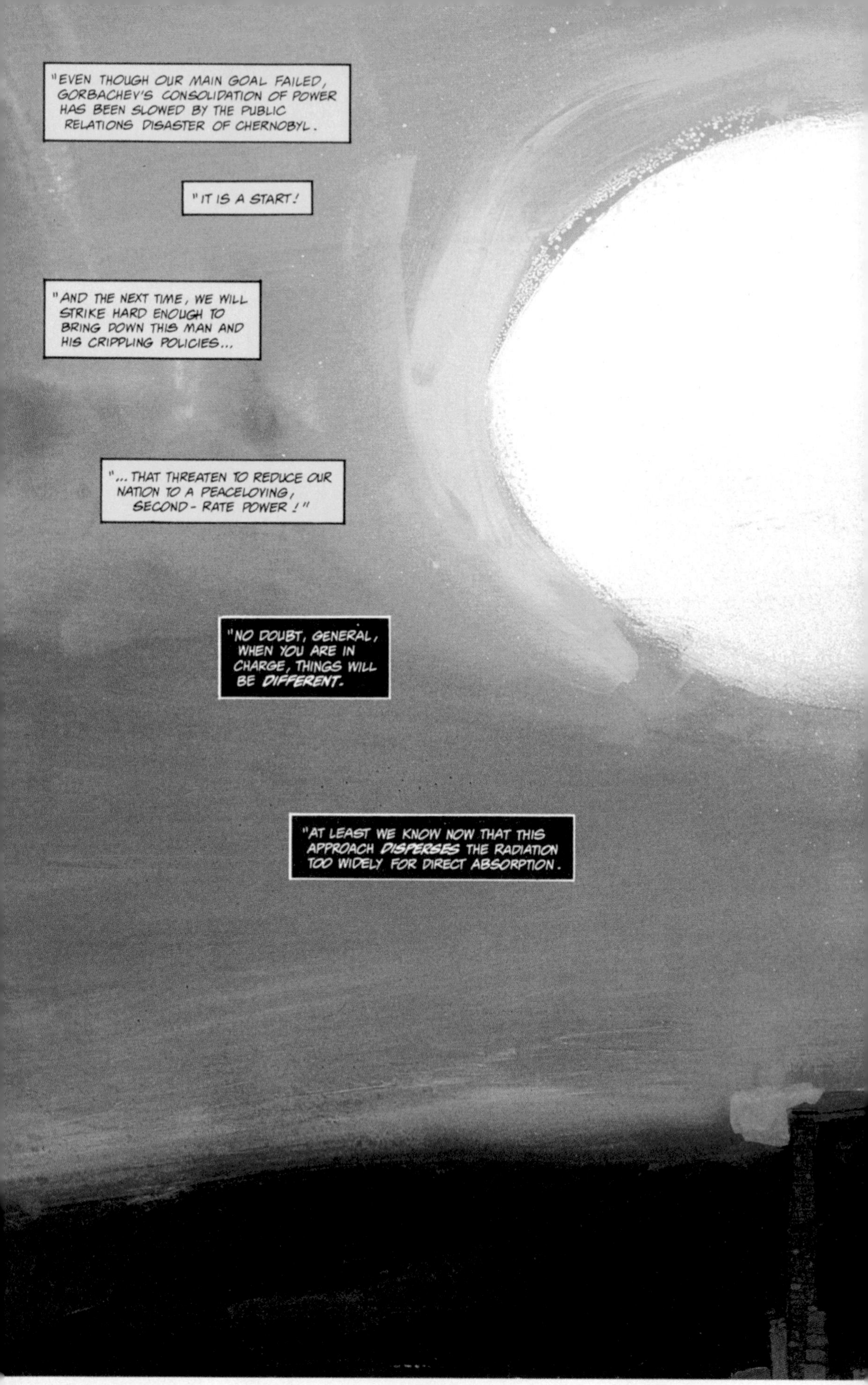
"EVEN THOUGH OUR MAIN GOAL FAILED, GORBACHEV'S CONSOLIDATION OF POWER HAS BEEN SLOWED BY THE PUBLIC RELATIONS DISASTER OF CHERNOBYL.
"IT IS A START!
"AND THE NEXT TIME, WE WILL STRIKE HARD ENOUGH TO BRING DOWN THIS MAN AND HIS CRIPPLING POLICIES...
"...THAT THREATEN TO REDUCE OUR NATION TO A PEACELOVING, SECOND-RATE POWER!"
"NO DOUBT, GENERAL, WHEN YOU ARE IN CHARGE, THINGS WILL BE DIFFERENT.
"AT LEAST WE KNOW NOW THAT THIS APPROACH DISPERSES THE RADIATION TOO WIDELY FOR DIRECT ABSORPTION.

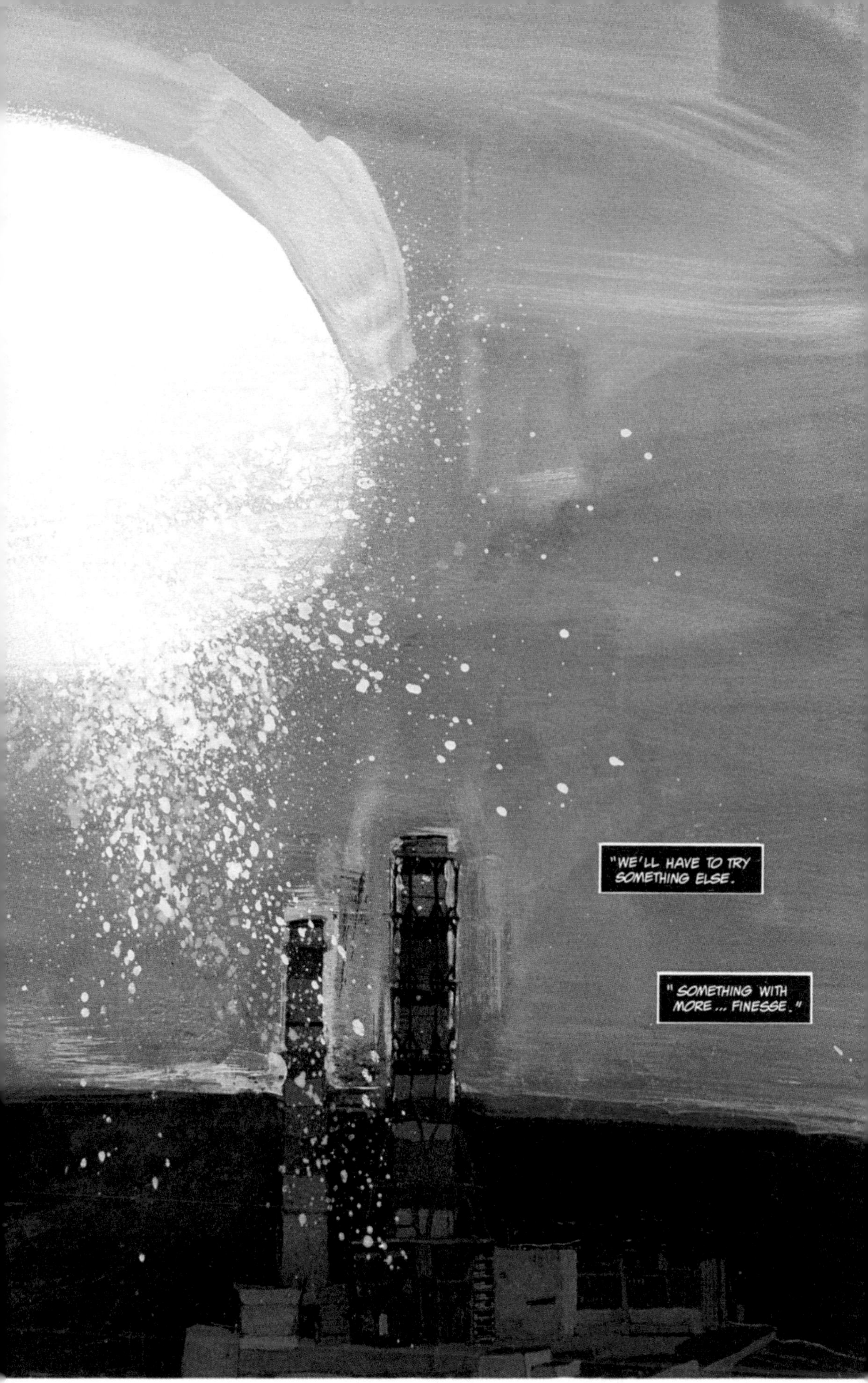
"WE'LL HAVE TO TRY SOMETHING ELSE.
"SOMETHING WITH MORE ... FINESSE."

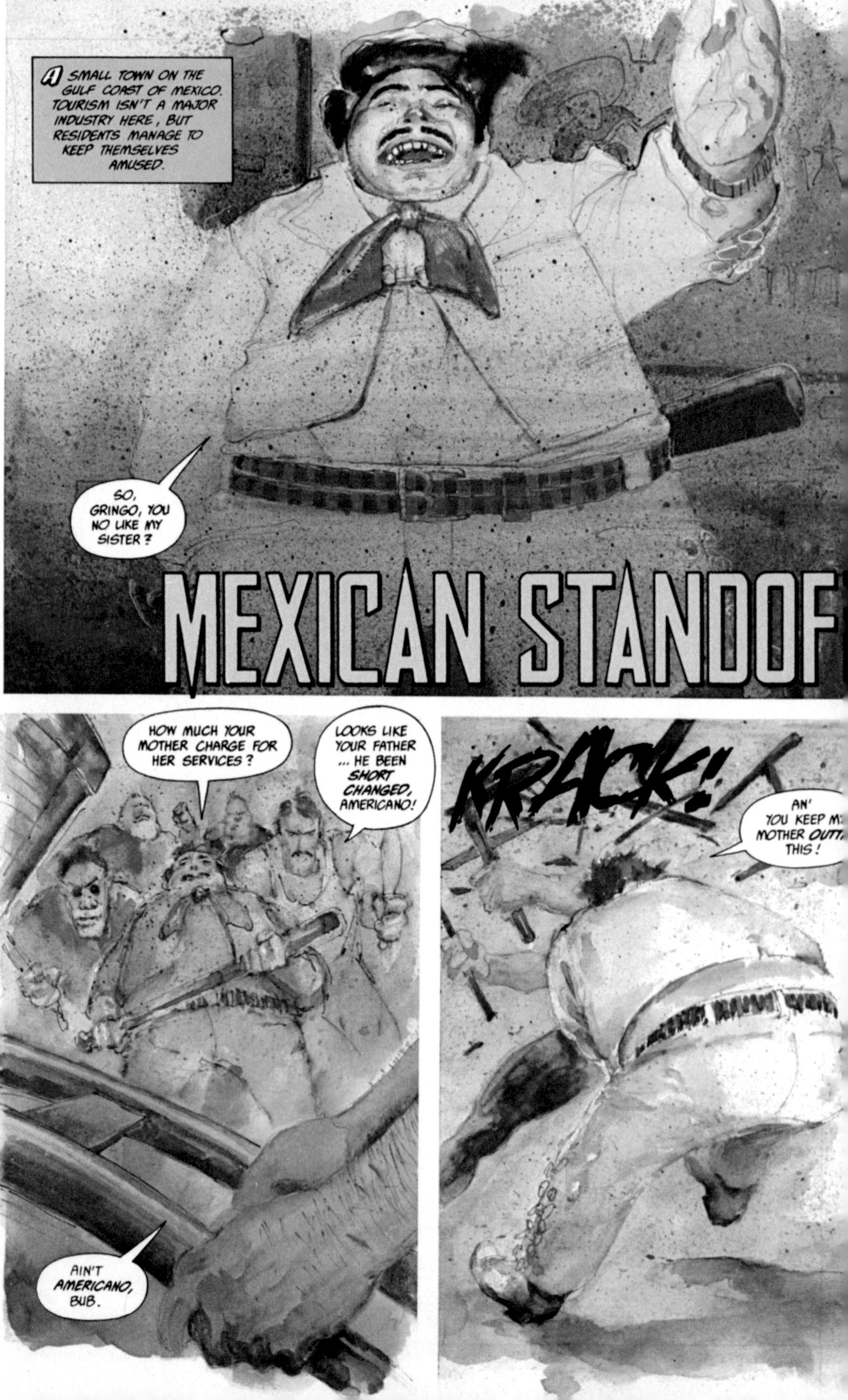
A SMALL TOWN ON THE GULF COAST OF MEXICO. TOURISM ISN'T A MAJOR INDUSTRY HERE, BUT RESIDENTS MANAGE TO KEEP THEMSELVES AMUSED.
SO, GRINGO, YOU NO LIKE MY SISTER?
MEXICAN STANDOF
HOW MUCH YOUR MOTHER CHARGE FOR HER SERVICES?
LOOKS LIKE YOUR FATHER ... HE BEEN SHORT CHANGED, AMERICANO!
AIN'T AMERICANO, BUB.
KRACK!!
AN' YOU KEEP M MOTHER OUTT THIS!

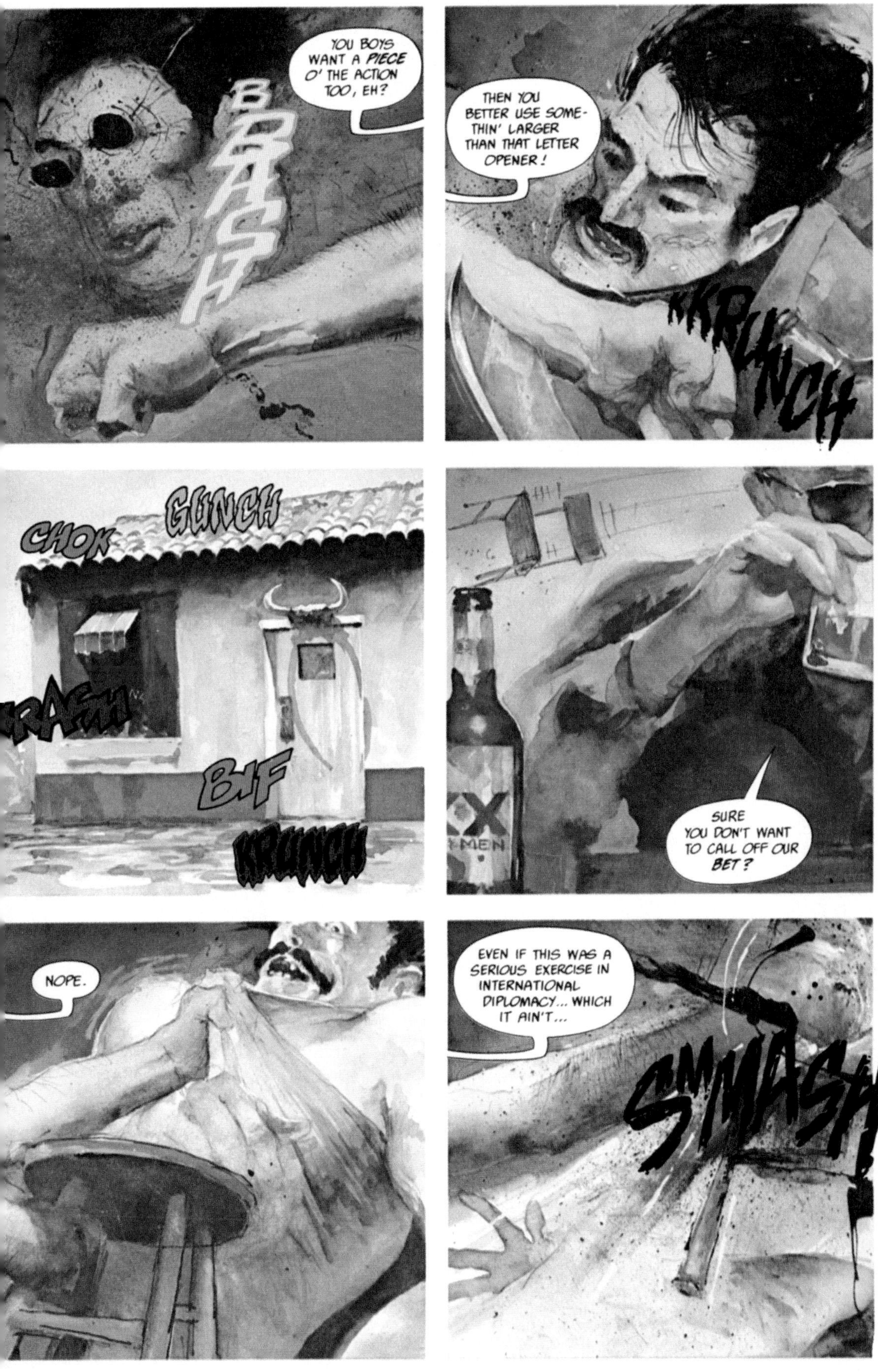
YOU BOYS WANT A PIECE O' THE ACTION TOO, EH?
BRASH
THEN YOU BETTER USE SOMETHIN' LARGER THAN THAT LETTER OPENER!
KKRUNCH
GUNCH
CHOK
RASH
BIF
KRUNCH
SURE YOU DON'T WANT TO CALL OFF OUR BET?
NOPE.
EVEN IF THIS WAS A SERIOUS EXERCISE IN INTERNATIONAL DIPLOMACY... WHICH IT AIN'T...
SMASH

...I WOULDN'T *NEED* CLAWS TA DEAL WITH THESE SUCKERS!

NO *WAY* I'M BUYIN' THE DRINKS THE REST OF OUR VACATION.

WHATEVER YOU SAY.

IT'S YOUR FIGHT. YOU STARTED IT.

ENJOY YOURSELF.

KRAKK!

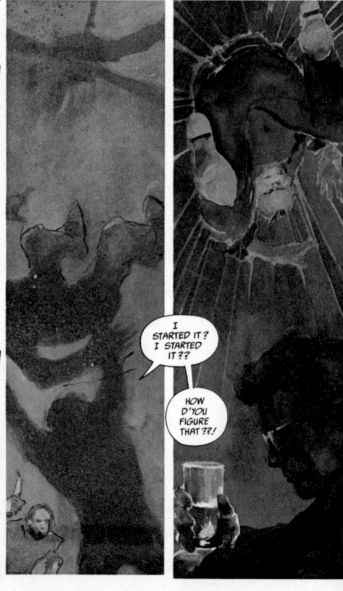

I STARTED IT? I STARTED IT??

HOW D'YOU FIGURE THAT??!

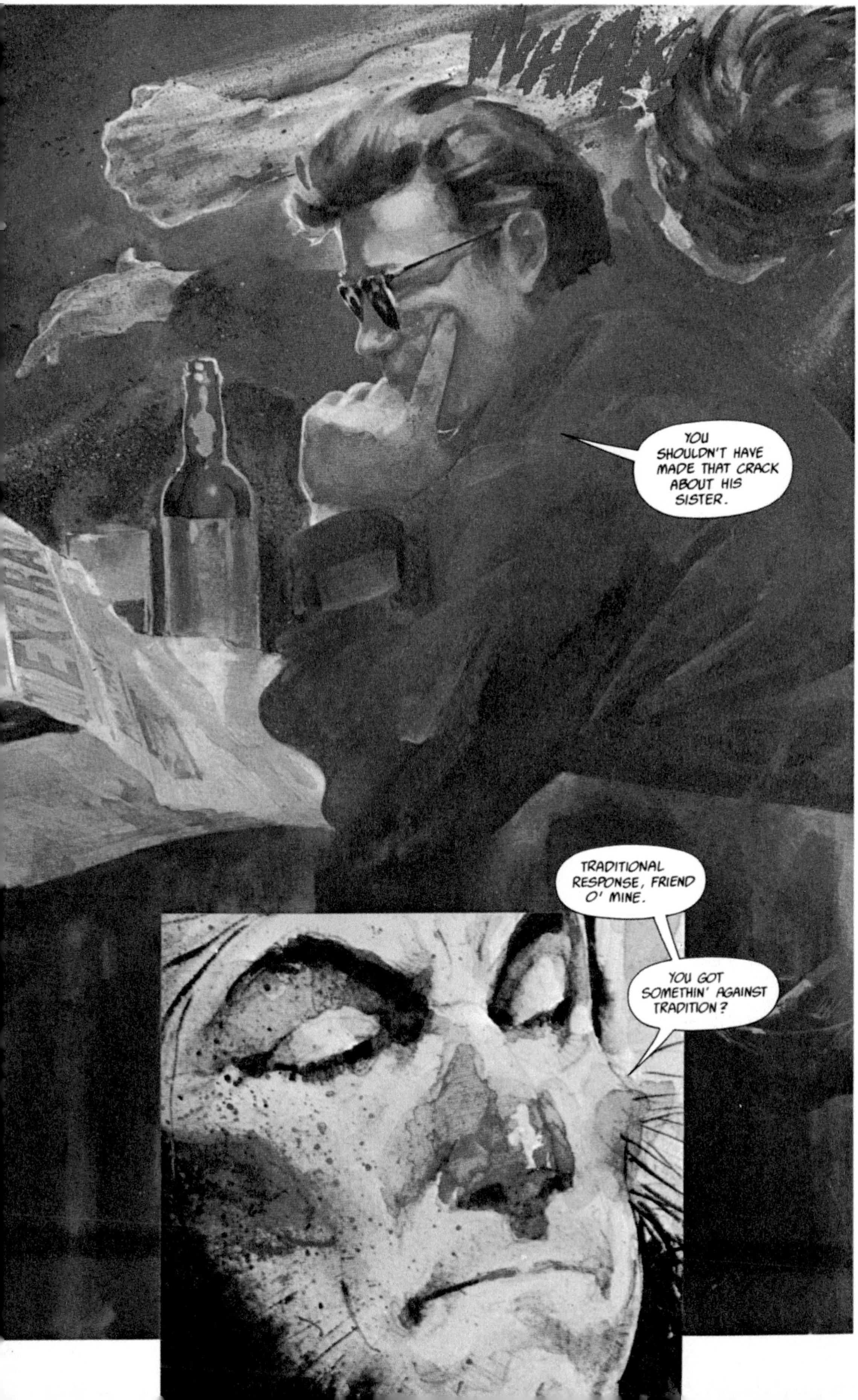
WHAK
YOU SHOULDN'T HAVE MADE THAT CRACK ABOUT HIS SISTER.
TRADITIONAL RESPONSE, FRIEND O' MINE.
YOU GOT SOMETHIN' AGAINST TRADITION?

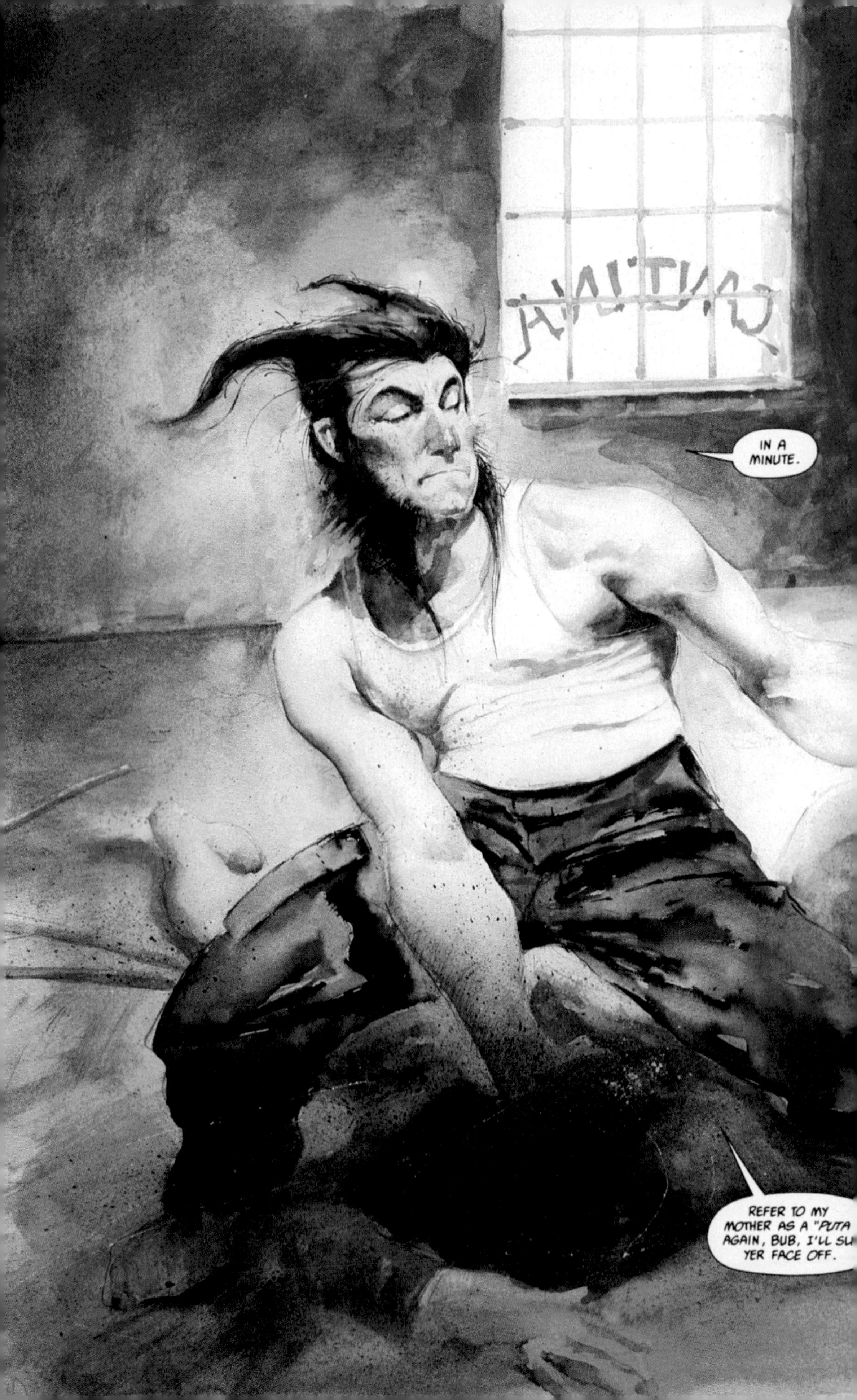
IN A MINUTE.
REFER TO MY MOTHER AS A "PUTA
AGAIN, BUB, I'LL SL
YER FACE OFF.

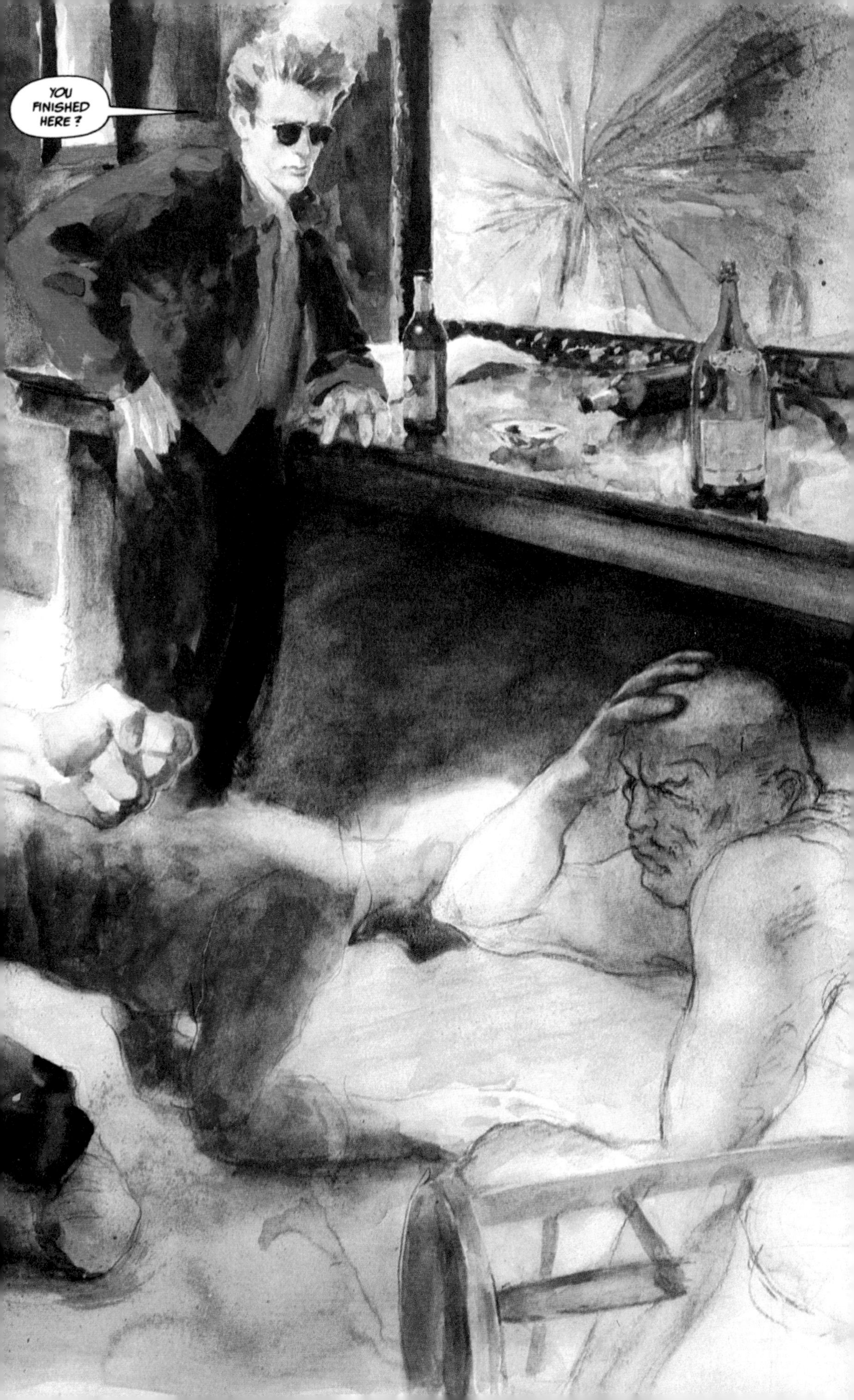
YOU FINISHED HERE?

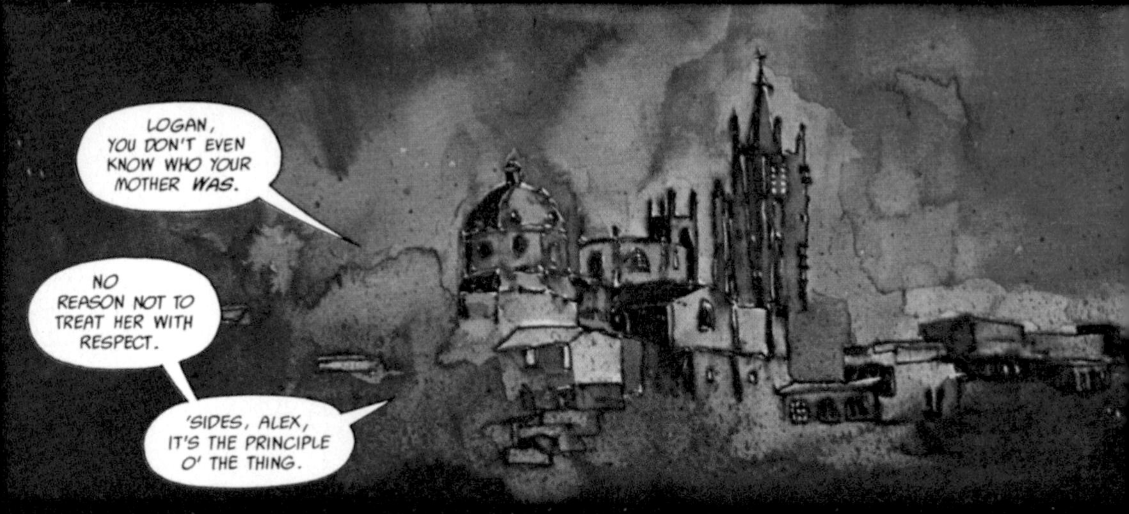
LOGAN, YOU DON'T EVEN KNOW WHO YOUR MOTHER *WAS*.
NO REASON NOT TO TREAT HER WITH RESPECT.
'SIDES, ALEX, IT'S THE PRINCIPLE O' THE THING.
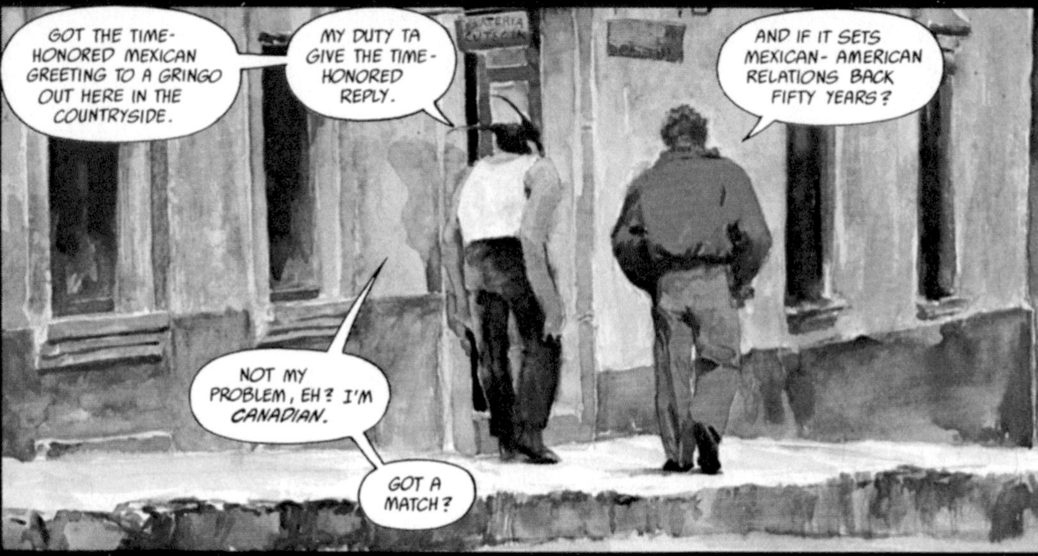
GOT THE TIME-HONORED MEXICAN GREETING TO A GRINGO OUT HERE IN THE COUNTRYSIDE.
MY DUTY TA GIVE THE TIME-HONORED REPLY.
AND IF IT SETS MEXICAN-AMERICAN RELATIONS BACK FIFTY YEARS?
NOT MY PROBLEM, EH? I'M *CANADIAN*.
GOT A MATCH?
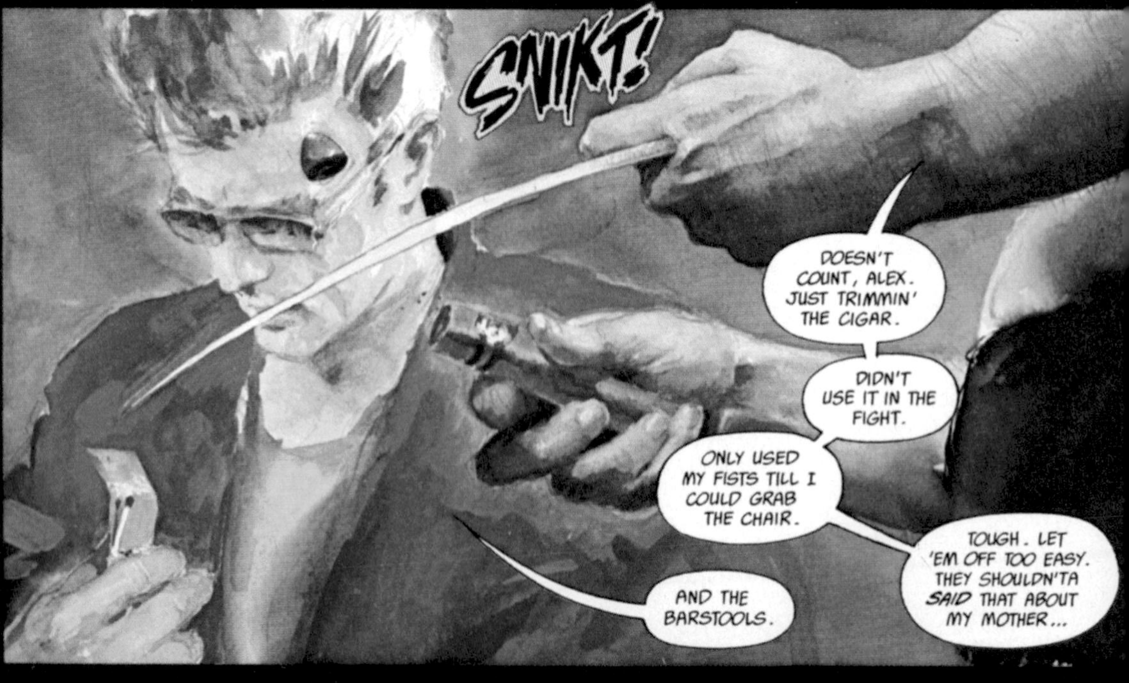
SNIKT!
DOESN'T COUNT, ALEX. JUST TRIMMIN' THE CIGAR.
DIDN'T USE IT IN THE FIGHT.
ONLY USED MY FISTS TILL I COULD GRAB THE CHAIR.
AND THE BARSTOOLS.
TOUGH. LET 'EM OFF TOO EASY. THEY SHOULDN'TA *SAID* THAT ABOUT MY MOTHER...

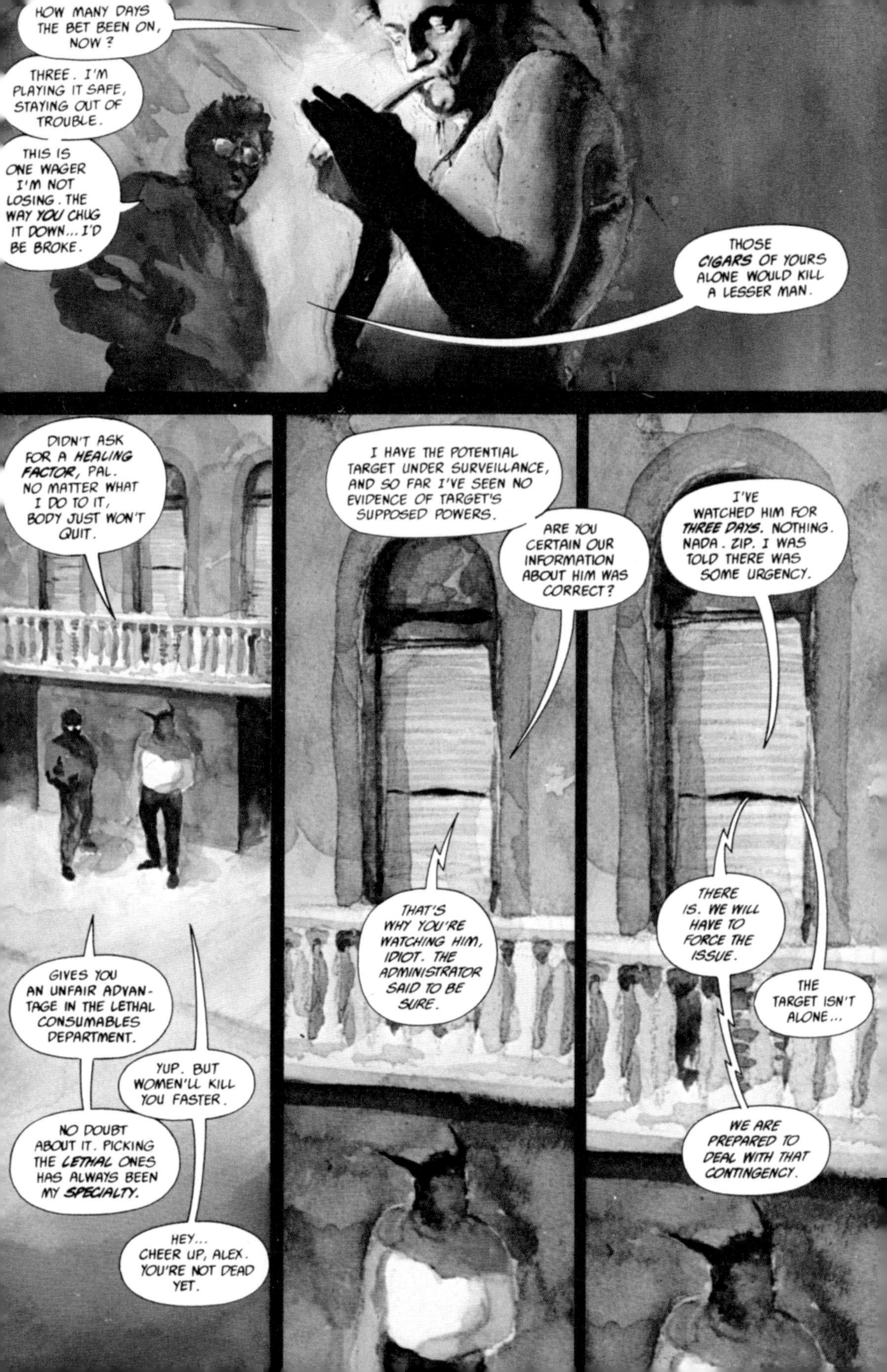
HOW MANY DAYS THE BET BEEN ON, NOW?
THREE. I'M PLAYING IT SAFE, STAYING OUT OF TROUBLE.
THIS IS ONE WAGER I'M NOT LOSING. THE WAY *YOU* CHUG IT DOWN... I'D BE BROKE.
THOSE ***CIGARS*** OF YOURS ALONE WOULD KILL A LESSER MAN.
DIDN'T ASK FOR A ***HEALING FACTOR***, PAL. NO MATTER WHAT I DO TO IT, BODY JUST WON'T QUIT.
GIVES YOU AN UNFAIR ADVANTAGE IN THE LETHAL CONSUMABLES DEPARTMENT.
YUP. BUT WOMEN'LL KILL YOU FASTER.
NO DOUBT ABOUT IT. PICKING THE ***LETHAL*** ONES HAS ALWAYS BEEN MY ***SPECIALTY***.
HEY... CHEER UP, ALEX. YOU'RE NOT DEAD YET.
I HAVE THE POTENTIAL TARGET UNDER SURVEILLANCE, AND SO FAR I'VE SEEN NO EVIDENCE OF TARGET'S SUPPOSED POWERS.
ARE YOU CERTAIN OUR INFORMATION ABOUT HIM WAS CORRECT?
THAT'S WHY YOU'RE WATCHING HIM, IDIOT. THE ADMINISTRATOR SAID TO BE SURE.
I'VE WATCHED HIM FOR ***THREE DAYS***. NOTHING. NADA. ZIP. I WAS TOLD THERE WAS SOME URGENCY.
THERE IS. WE WILL HAVE TO FORCE THE ISSUE.
THE TARGET ISN'T ALONE...
WE ARE PREPARED TO DEAL WITH THAT CONTINGENCY.

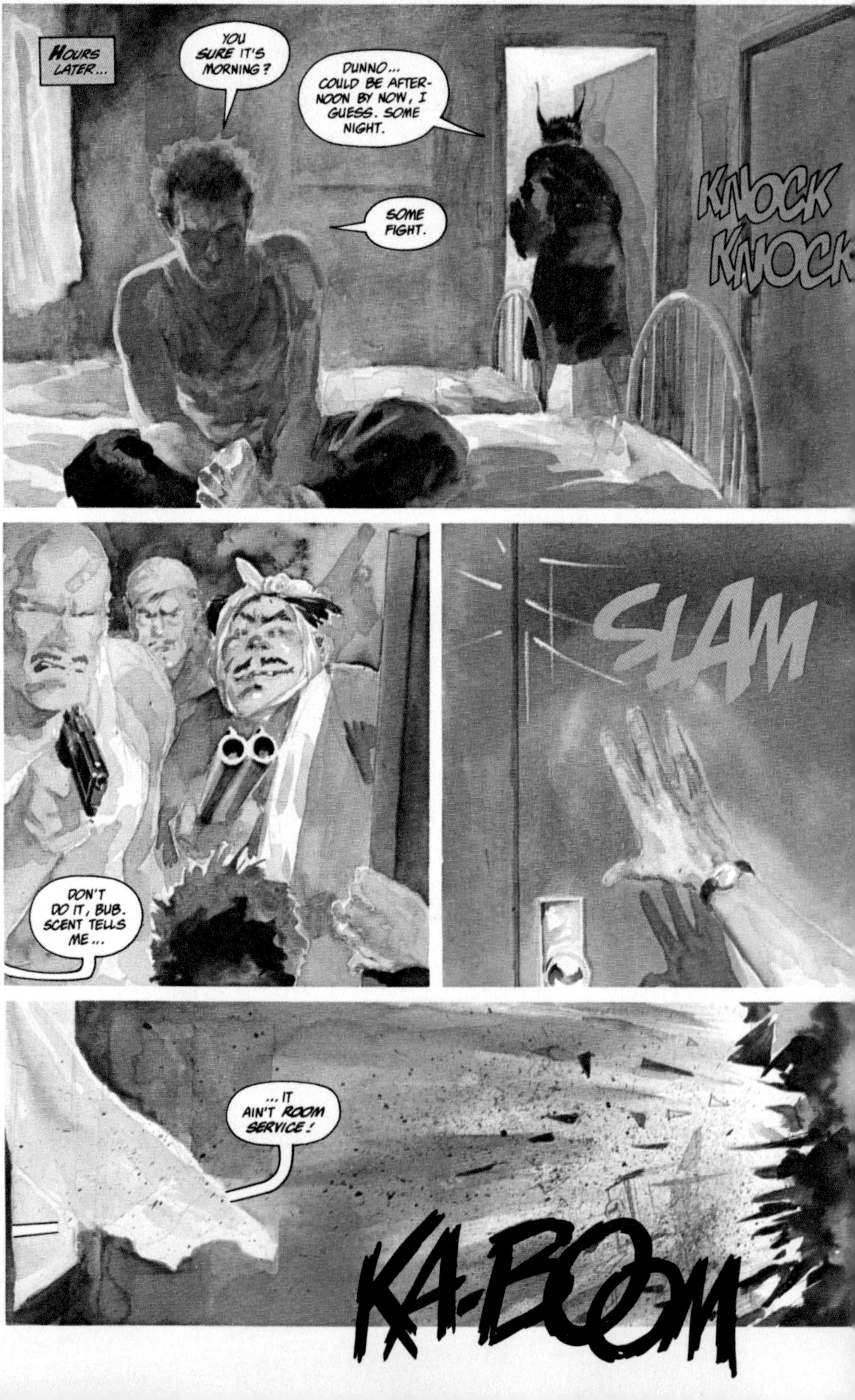
HOURS LATER...
YOU SURE IT'S MORNING?
DUNNO... COULD BE AFTER-NOON BY NOW, I GUESS. SOME NIGHT.
SOME FIGHT.
KNOCK KNOCK
DON'T DO IT, BUB. SCENT TELLS ME...
SLAM
...IT AIN'T ROOM SERVICE!
KA-BOOM

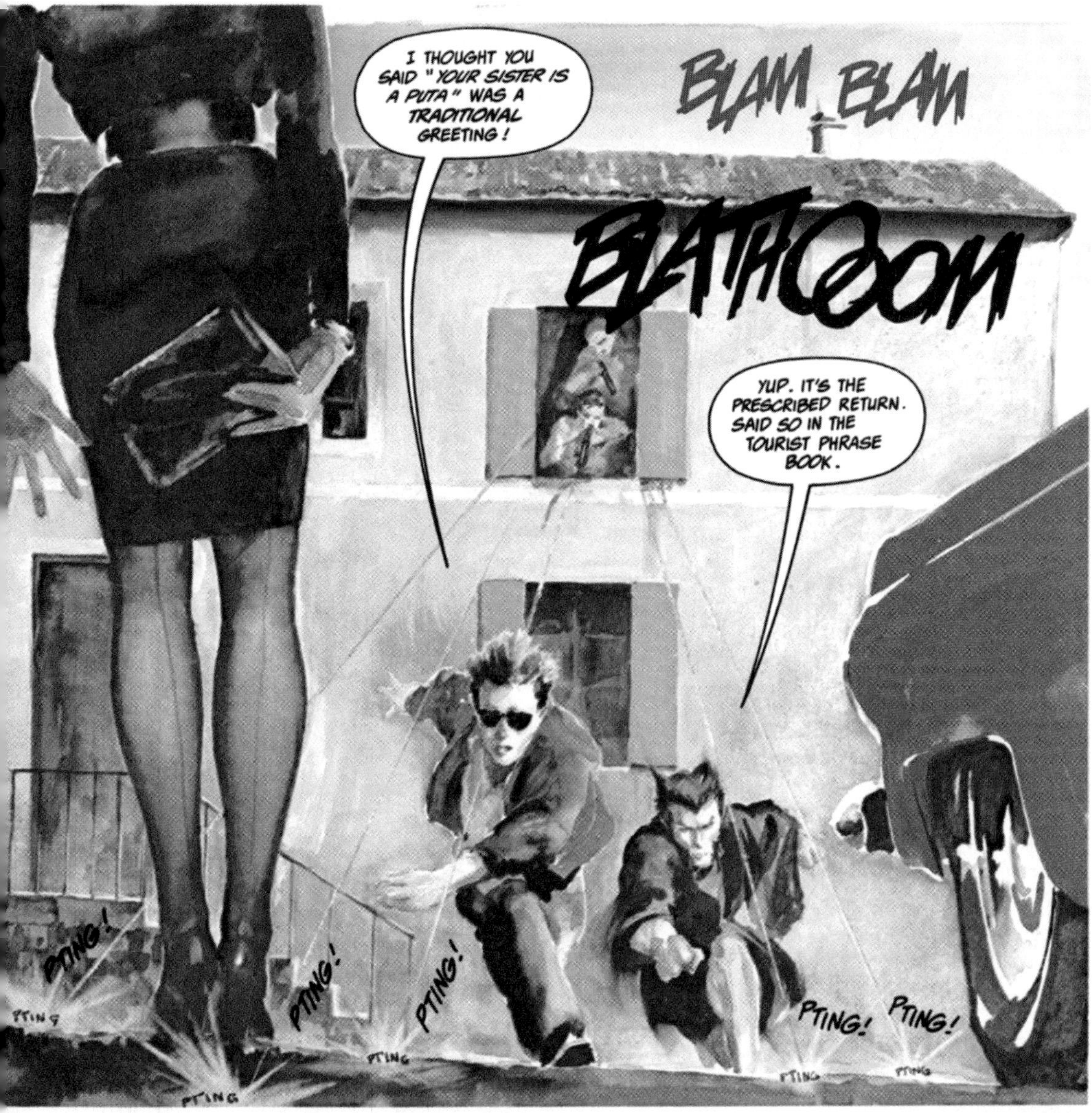
I THOUGHT YOU SAID "YOUR SISTER IS A PUTA" WAS A TRADITIONAL GREETING!
BLAM BLAM
BLATHOOOM
YUP. IT'S THE PRESCRIBED RETURN. SAID SO IN THE TOURIST PHRASE BOOK.
PTING!
PTING
PTING!
PTING!
PTING
PTING
PTING!
PTING!
PTING
PTING

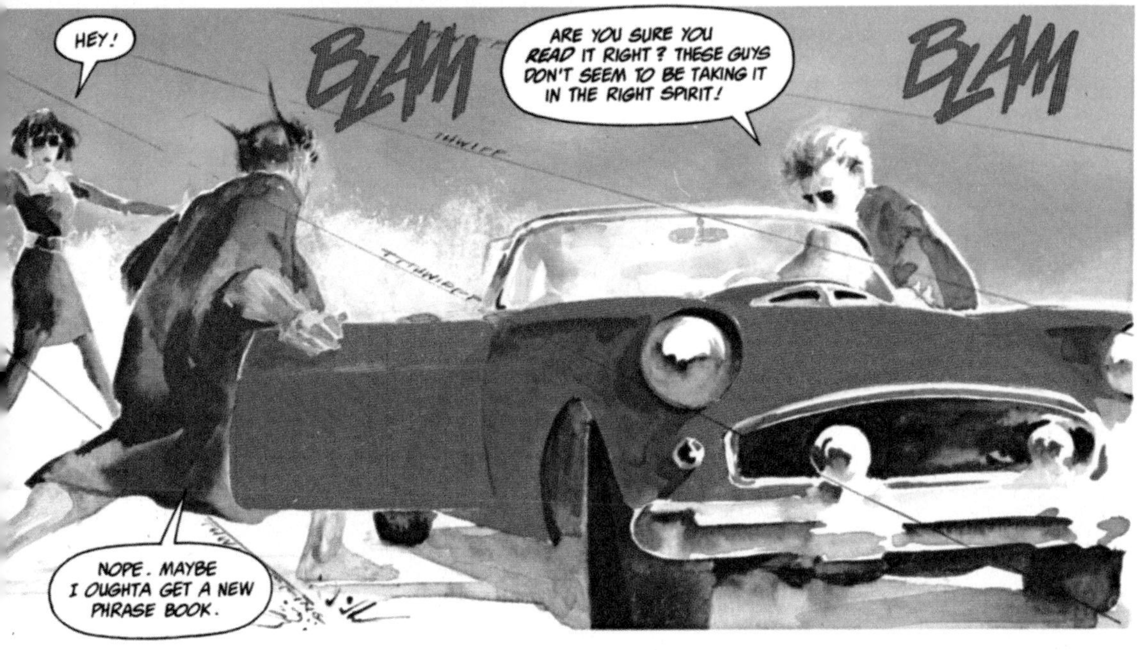
HEY!
BLAM
ARE YOU SURE YOU READ IT RIGHT? THESE GUYS DON'T SEEM TO BE TAKING IT IN THE RIGHT SPIRIT!
BLAM
NOPE. MAYBE I OUGHTA GET A NEW PHRASE BOOK.

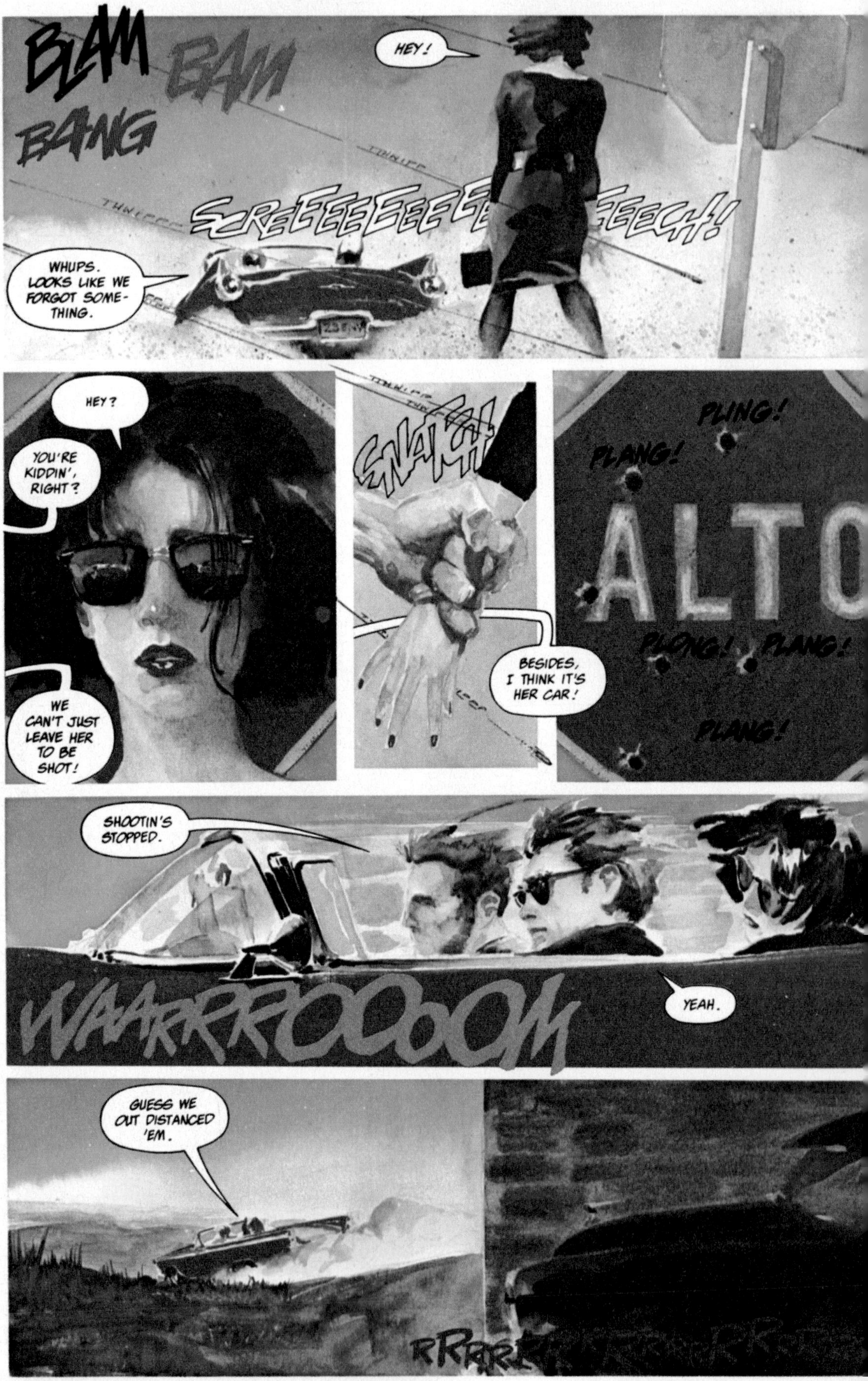
BLAM
BAM
BANG
HEY!
SCREEEEEEEEEEEEEEECH!
WHUPS. LOOKS LIKE WE FORGOT SOME-THING.
HEY?
YOU'RE KIDDIN', RIGHT?
WE CAN'T JUST LEAVE HER TO BE SHOT!
SNATCH
BESIDES, I THINK IT'S HER CAR!
PLING!
PLANG!
ALTO
PLONG!
PLANG!
PLANG!
SHOOTIN'S STOPPED.
WAARRROOOOM
YEAH.
GUESS WE OUT DISTANCED 'EM.

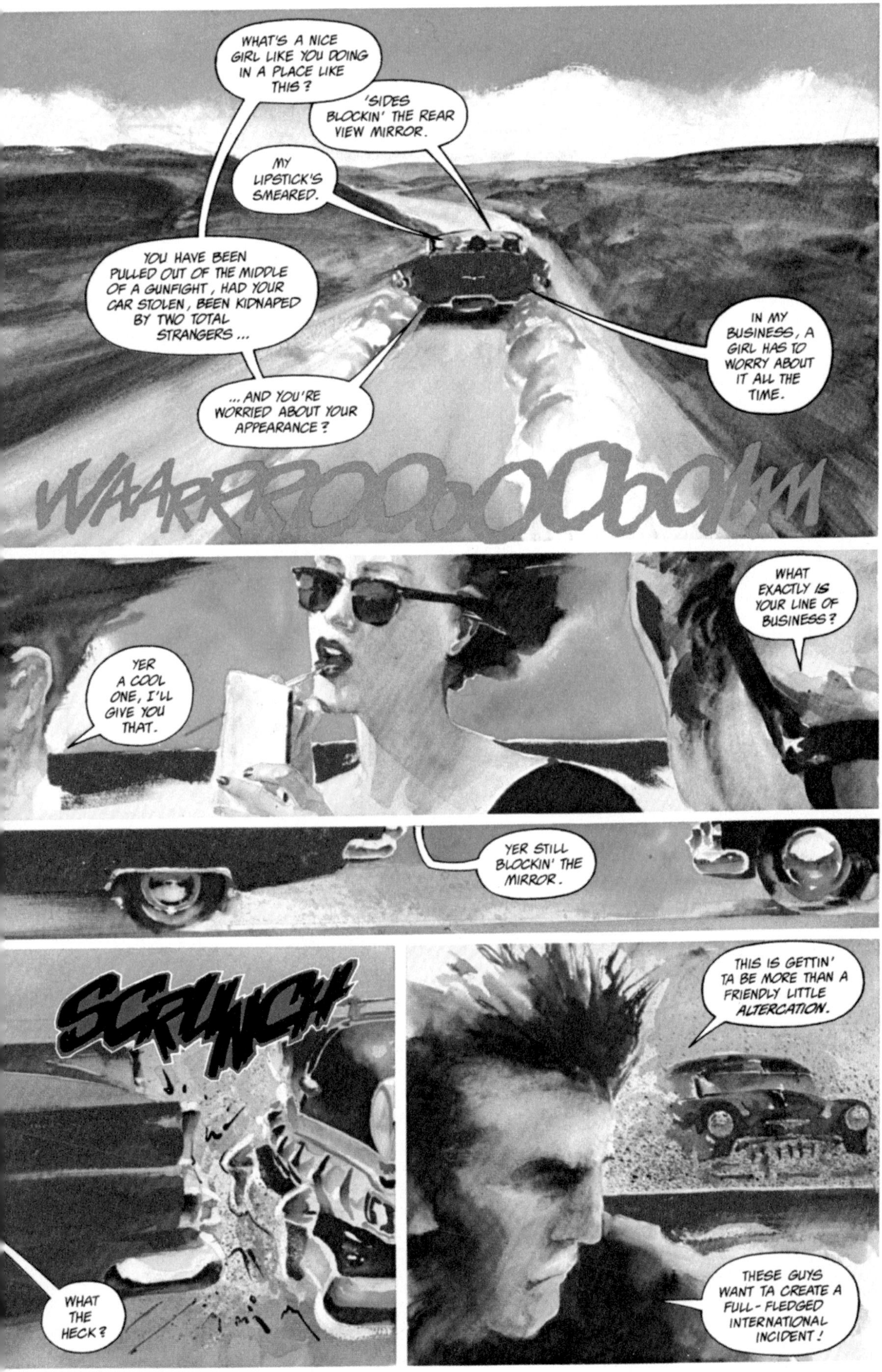
WHAT'S A NICE GIRL LIKE YOU DOING IN A PLACE LIKE THIS?
'SIDES BLOCKIN' THE REAR VIEW MIRROR.
MY LIPSTICK'S SMEARED.
YOU HAVE BEEN PULLED OUT OF THE MIDDLE OF A GUNFIGHT, HAD YOUR CAR STOLEN, BEEN KIDNAPED BY TWO TOTAL STRANGERS ...
... AND YOU'RE WORRIED ABOUT YOUR APPEARANCE?
IN MY BUSINESS, A GIRL HAS TO WORRY ABOUT IT ALL THE TIME.
WAARRROOOoOOOOoOM
YER A COOL ONE, I'LL GIVE YOU THAT.
WHAT EXACTLY IS YOUR LINE OF BUSINESS?
YER STILL BLOCKIN' THE MIRROR.
SCRUNCH
WHAT THE HECK?
THIS IS GETTIN' TA BE MORE THAN A FRIENDLY LITTLE ALTERCATION.
THESE GUYS WANT TA CREATE A FULL-FLEDGED INTERNATIONAL INCIDENT!

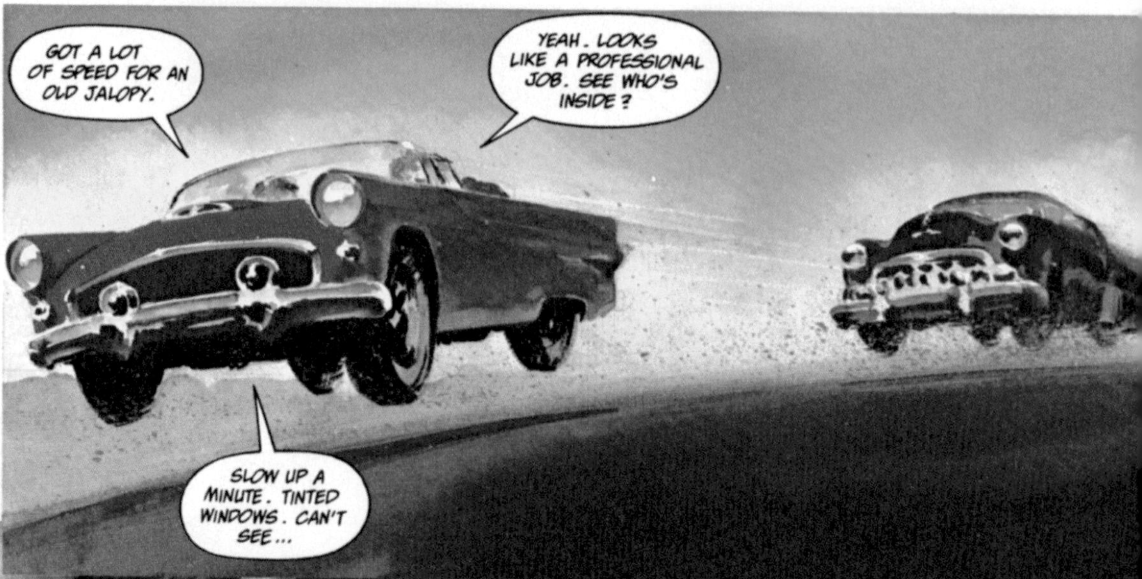
GOT A LOT OF SPEED FOR AN OLD JALOPY.
YEAH. LOOKS LIKE A PROFESSIONAL JOB. SEE WHO'S INSIDE?
SLOW UP A MINUTE. TINTED WINDOWS. CAN'T SEE...
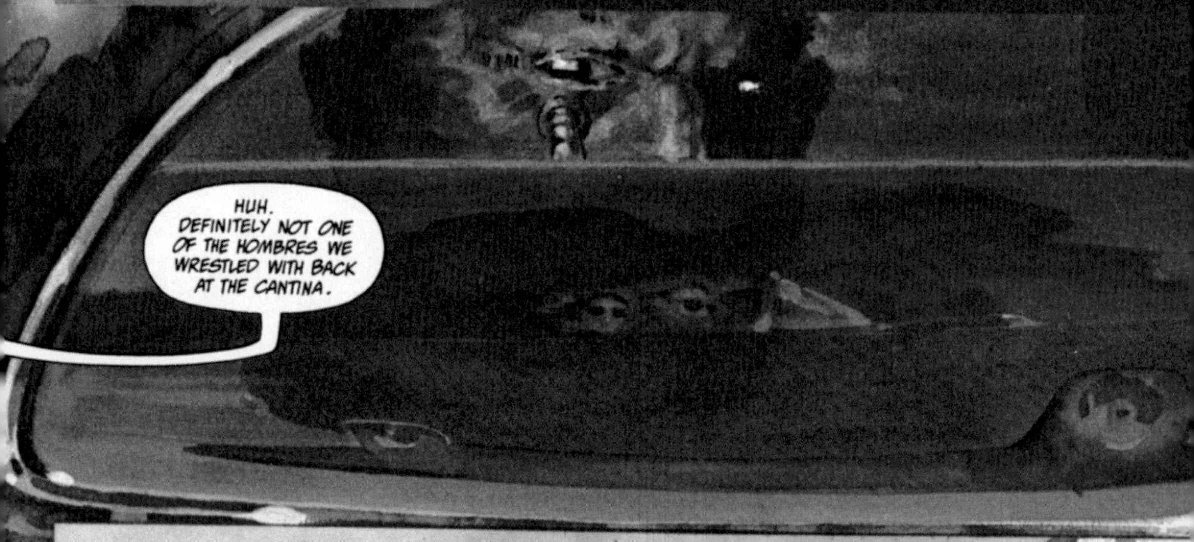
HUH. DEFINITELY NOT ONE OF THE HOMBRES WE WRESTLED WITH BACK AT THE CANTINA.
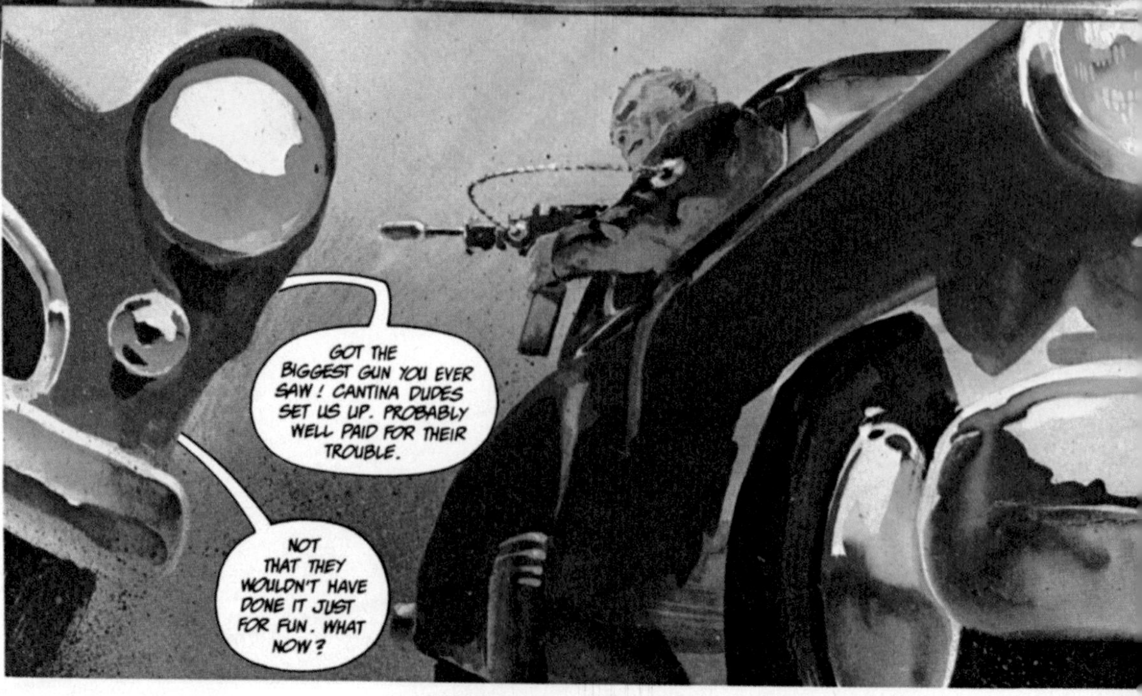
GOT THE BIGGEST GUN YOU EVER SAW! CANTINA DUDES SET US UP. PROBABLY WELL PAID FOR THEIR TROUBLE.
NOT THAT THEY WOULDN'T HAVE DONE IT JUST FOR FUN. WHAT NOW?

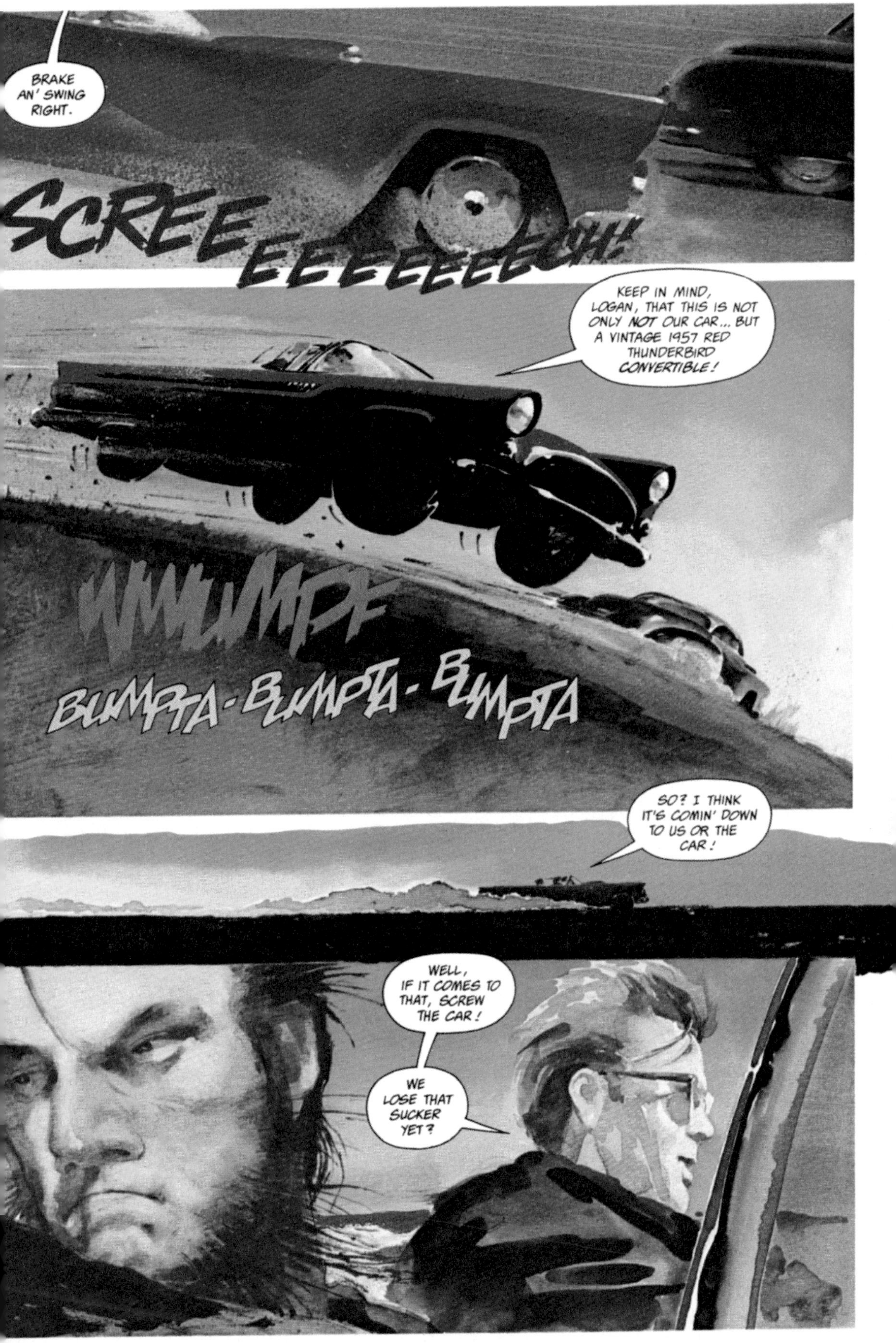
BRAKE AN' SWING RIGHT.
SCREEEEEEEEEECH!
KEEP IN MIND, LOGAN, THAT THIS IS NOT ONLY NOT OUR CAR... BUT A VINTAGE 1957 RED THUNDERBIRD CONVERTIBLE!
WWUMPF
BUMPTA-BUMPTA-BUMPTA
SO? I THINK IT'S COMIN' DOWN TO US OR THE CAR!
WELL, IF IT COMES TO THAT, SCREW THE CAR!
WE LOSE THAT SUCKER YET?

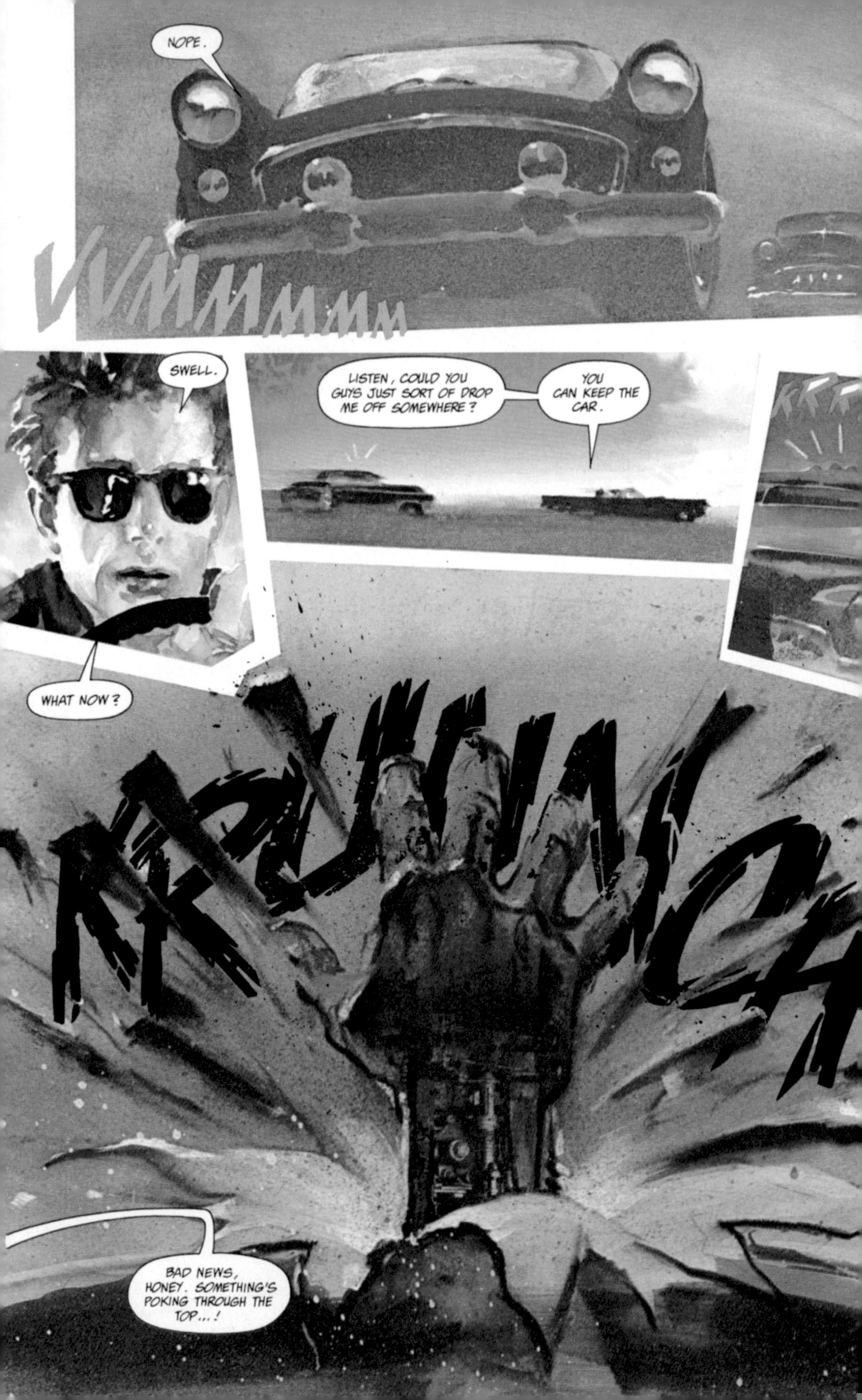
NOPE.
VVMMMMMM
SWELL.
WHAT NOW?
LISTEN, COULD YOU GUYS JUST SORT OF DROP ME OFF SOMEWHERE?
YOU CAN KEEP THE CAR.
BAD NEWS, HONEY. SOMETHING'S POKING THROUGH THE TOP...!

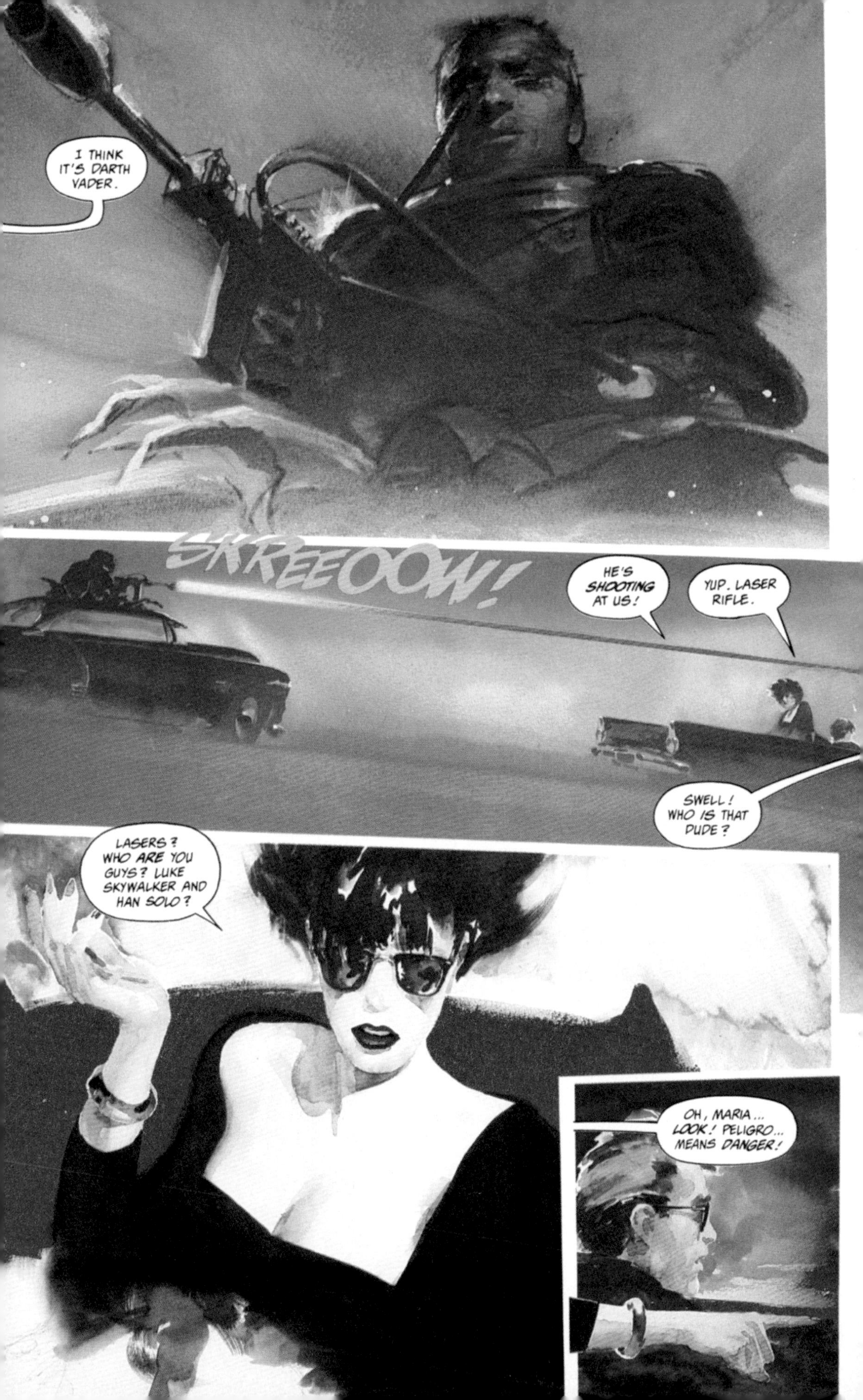
I THINK IT'S DARTH VADER.
SKREEOOW!
HE'S SHOOTING AT US!
YUP. LASER RIFLE.
SWELL! WHO IS THAT DUDE?
LASERS? WHO ARE YOU GUYS? LUKE SKYWALKER AND HAN SOLO?
OH, MARIA... LOOK! PELIGRO... MEANS DANGER!

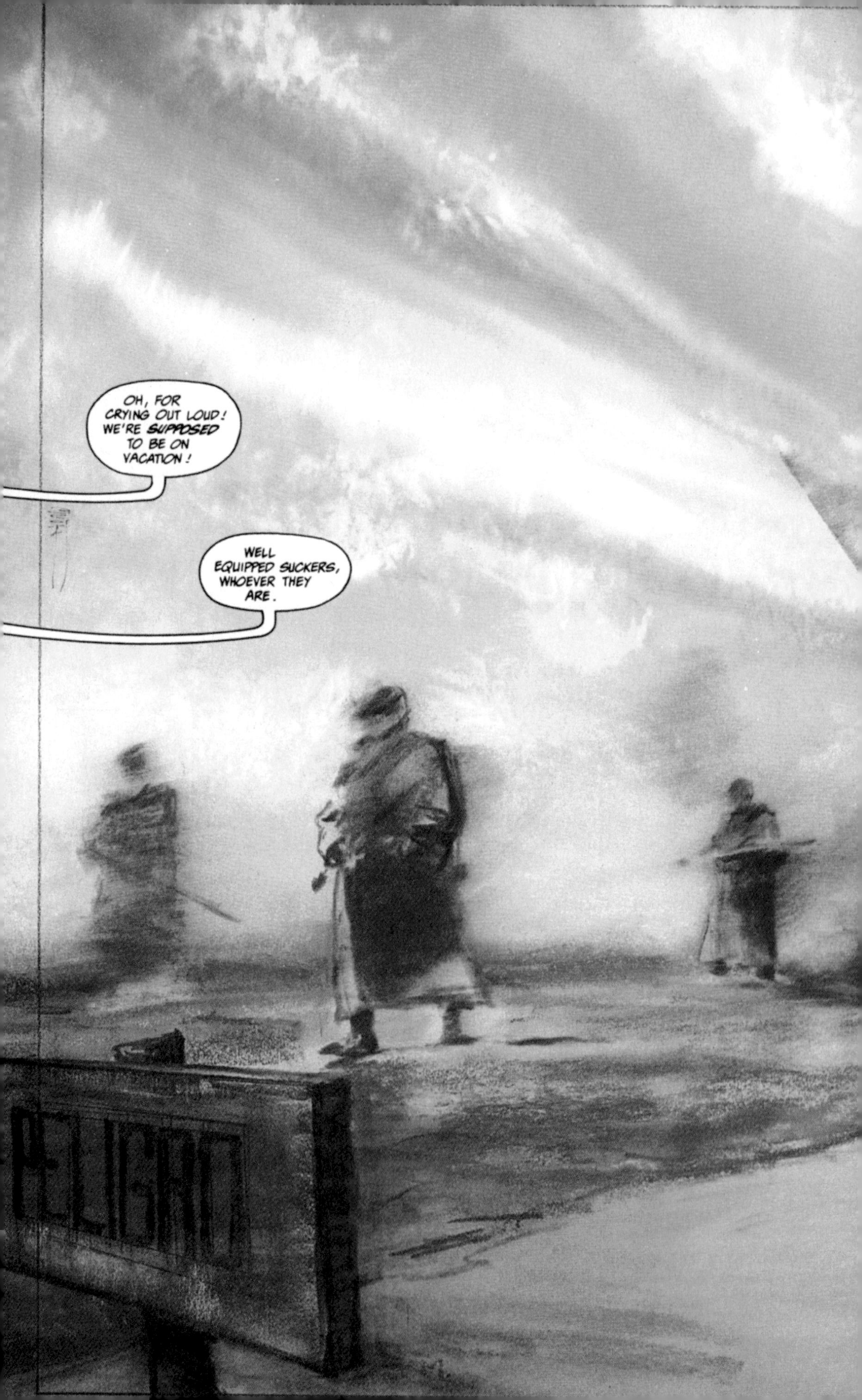
OH, FOR CRYING OUT LOUD! WE'RE SUPPOSED TO BE ON VACATION!
WELL EQUIPPED SUCKERS, WHOEVER THEY ARE.
PELIGRO

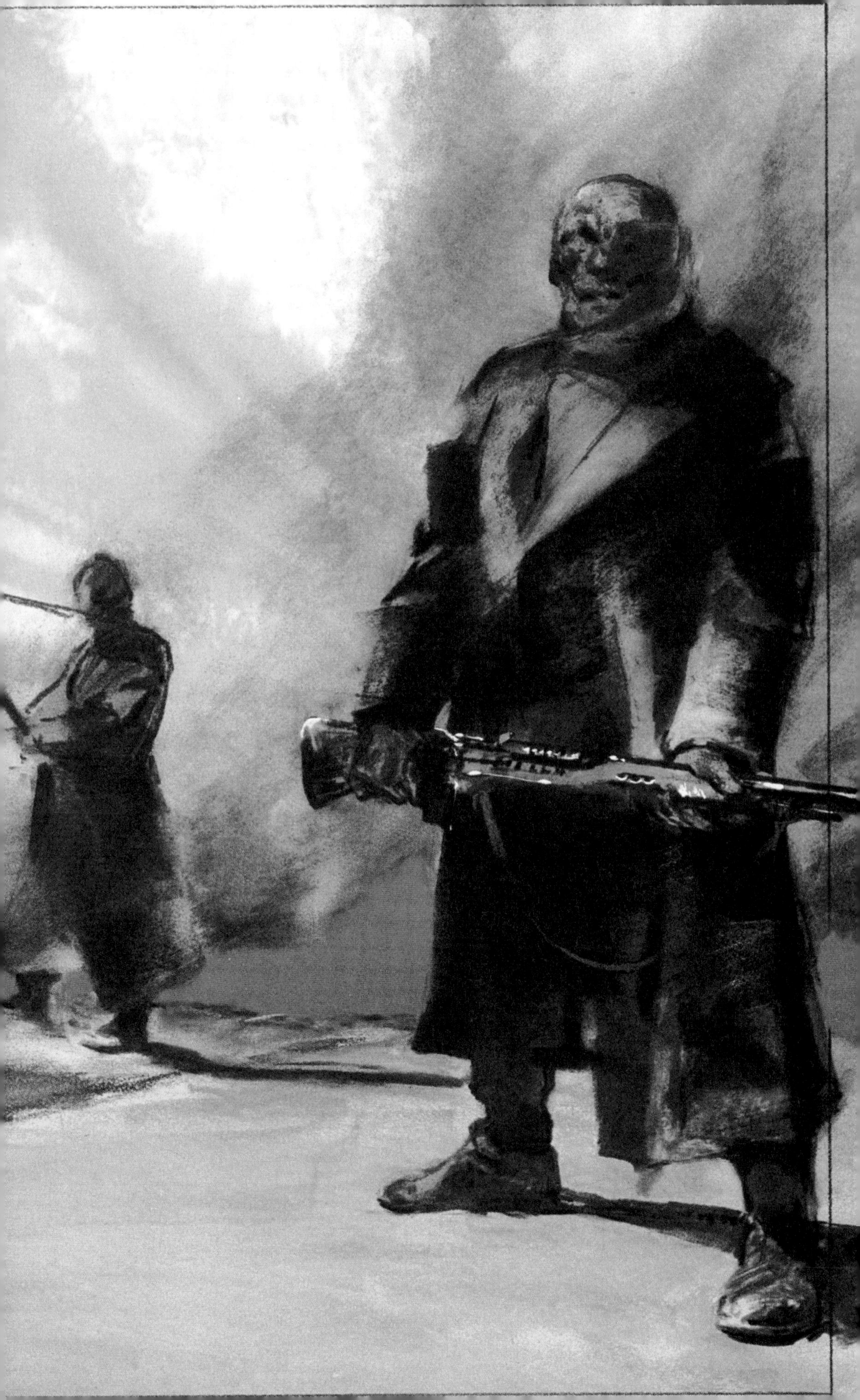

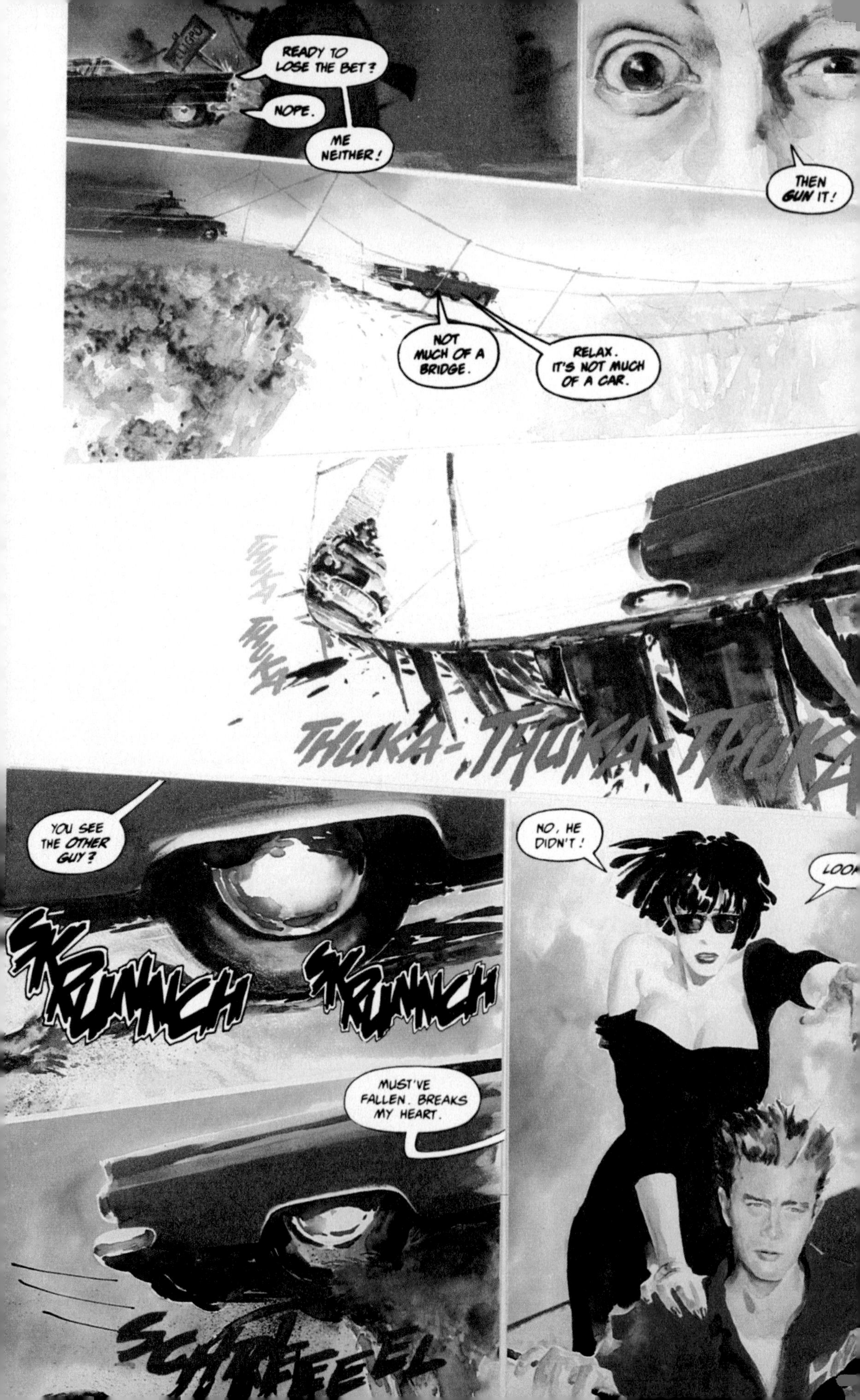
READY TO LOSE THE BET?
NOPE.
ME NEITHER!
THEN GUN IT!
NOT MUCH OF A BRIDGE.
RELAX. IT'S NOT MUCH OF A CAR.
THUKA THUKA
THUKA-THUKA-THUKA
YOU SEE THE OTHER GUY?
SKRUNNCH
SKRUNNCH
MUST'VE FALLEN. BREAKS MY HEART.
SCHREEEEL
NO, HE DIDN'T!
LOOK

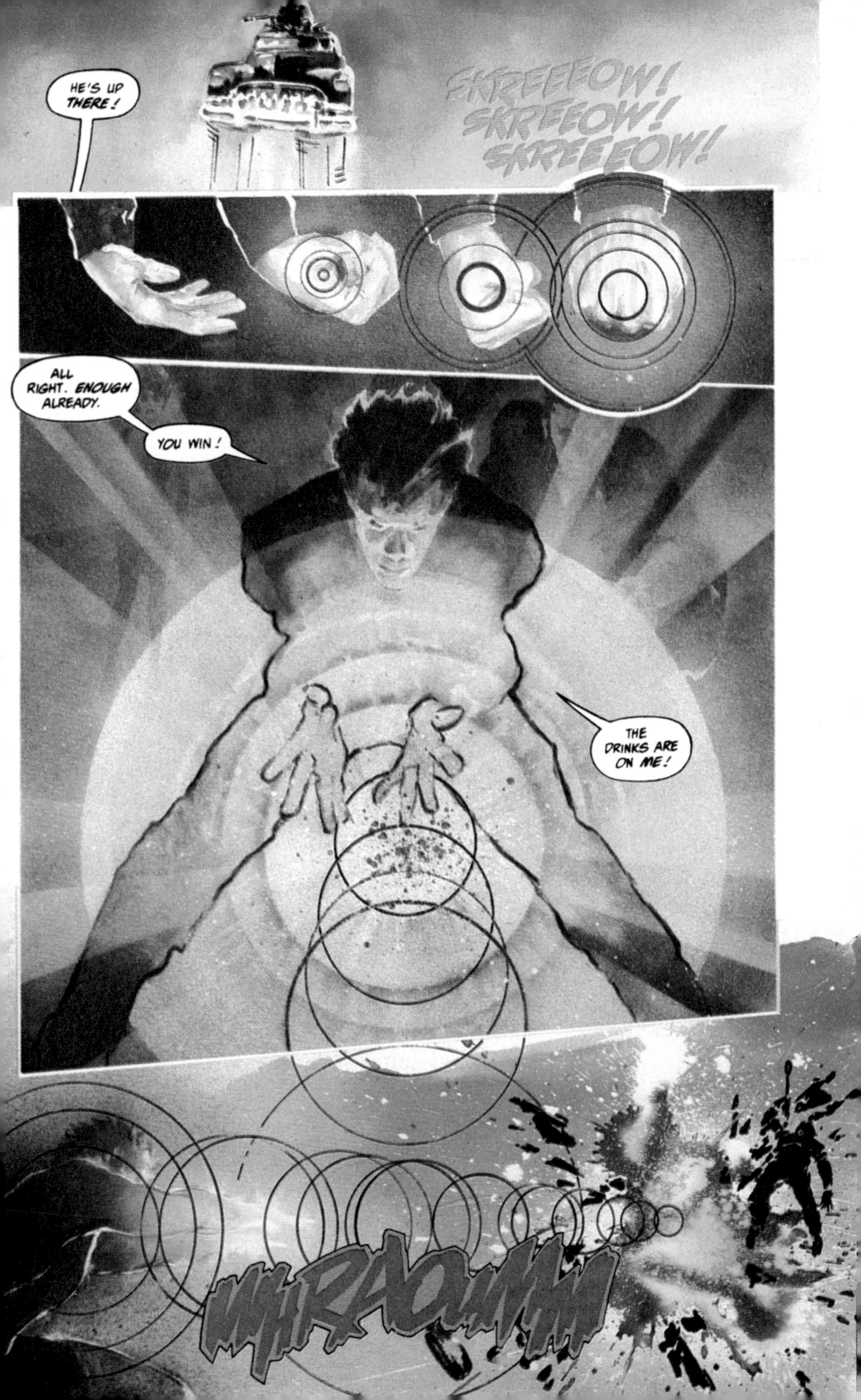
HE'S UP THERE!
SKREEEOW! SKREEOW! SKREEEOW!
ALL RIGHT. ENOUGH ALREADY.
YOU WIN!
THE DRINKS ARE ON ME!
WHRAOWM

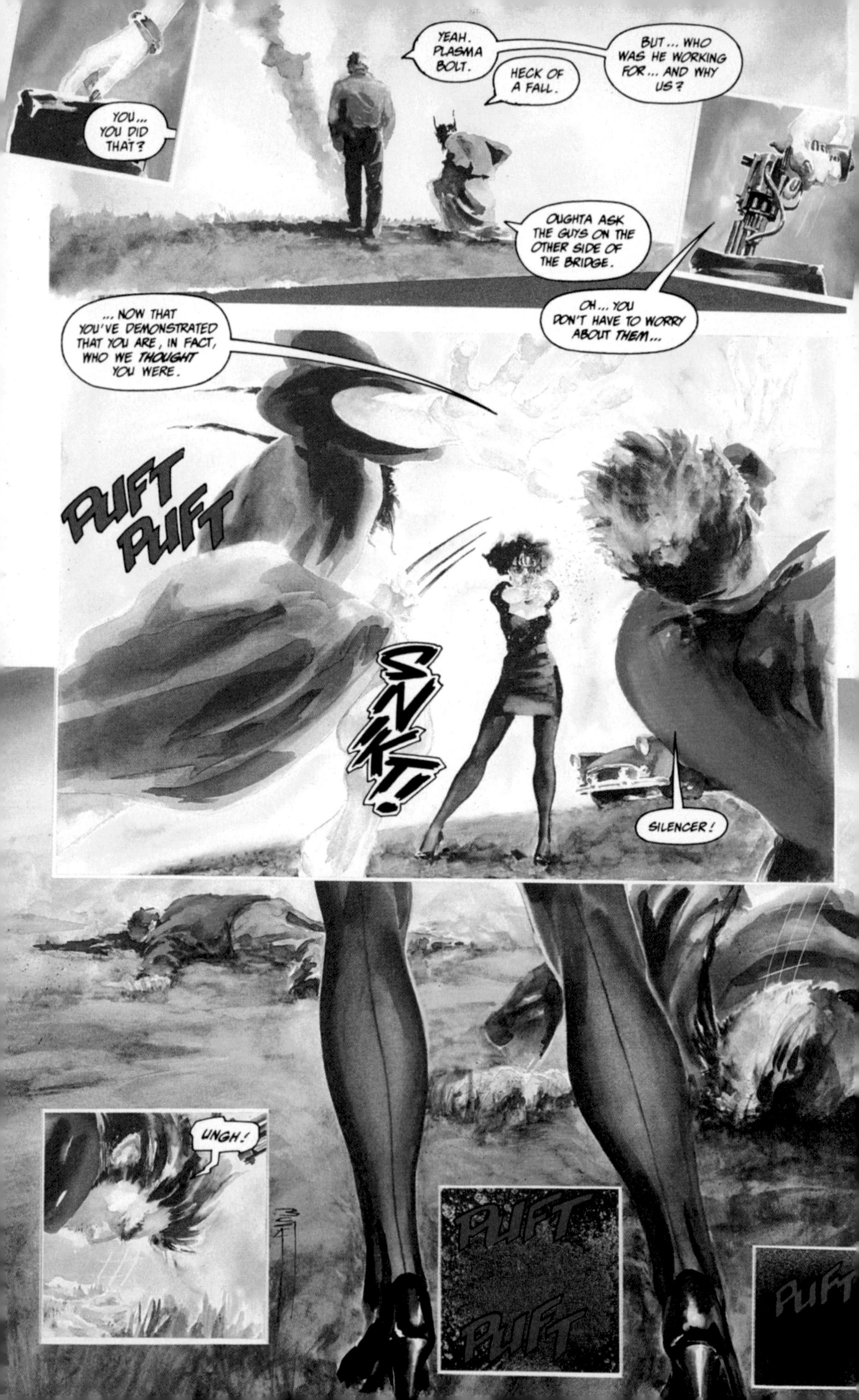
YOU... YOU DID THAT?
YEAH. PLASMA BOLT.
HECK OF A FALL.
BUT... WHO WAS HE WORKING FOR... AND WHY US?
OUGHTA ASK THE GUYS ON THE OTHER SIDE OF THE BRIDGE.
OH... YOU DON'T HAVE TO WORRY ABOUT THEM...
... NOW THAT YOU'VE DEMONSTRATED THAT YOU ARE, IN FACT, WHO WE THOUGHT YOU WERE.
PUFT PUFT
SNIKT!
SILENCER!
UNGH!
PUFT
PUFT
PUFT

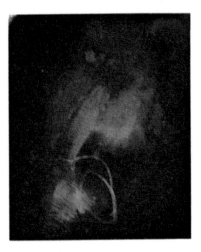

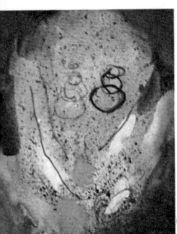

WHAT... HAPPENED?

BUBONIC PLAGUE.

EXCEPTIONALLY VIRULENT STRAIN.

MY... FRIEND? MI... AMIGO?

I... AM SORRY.

HE, TOO, HAD THE PLAGUE. HE WAS DEAD WHEN THEY FOUND YOU.

HE HAS ALREADY BEEN BURIED. YOU UNDER-STAND... BODIES OF PLAGUE VICTIMS MUST BE BURIED AS SOON AS POSSIBLE TO AVOID CONTAGION.

IT'S A MIRACLE THIS ONE IS STILL ALIVE!

HE WON'T BE FOR LONG. HE'LL BE DEAD BEFORE MORNING.

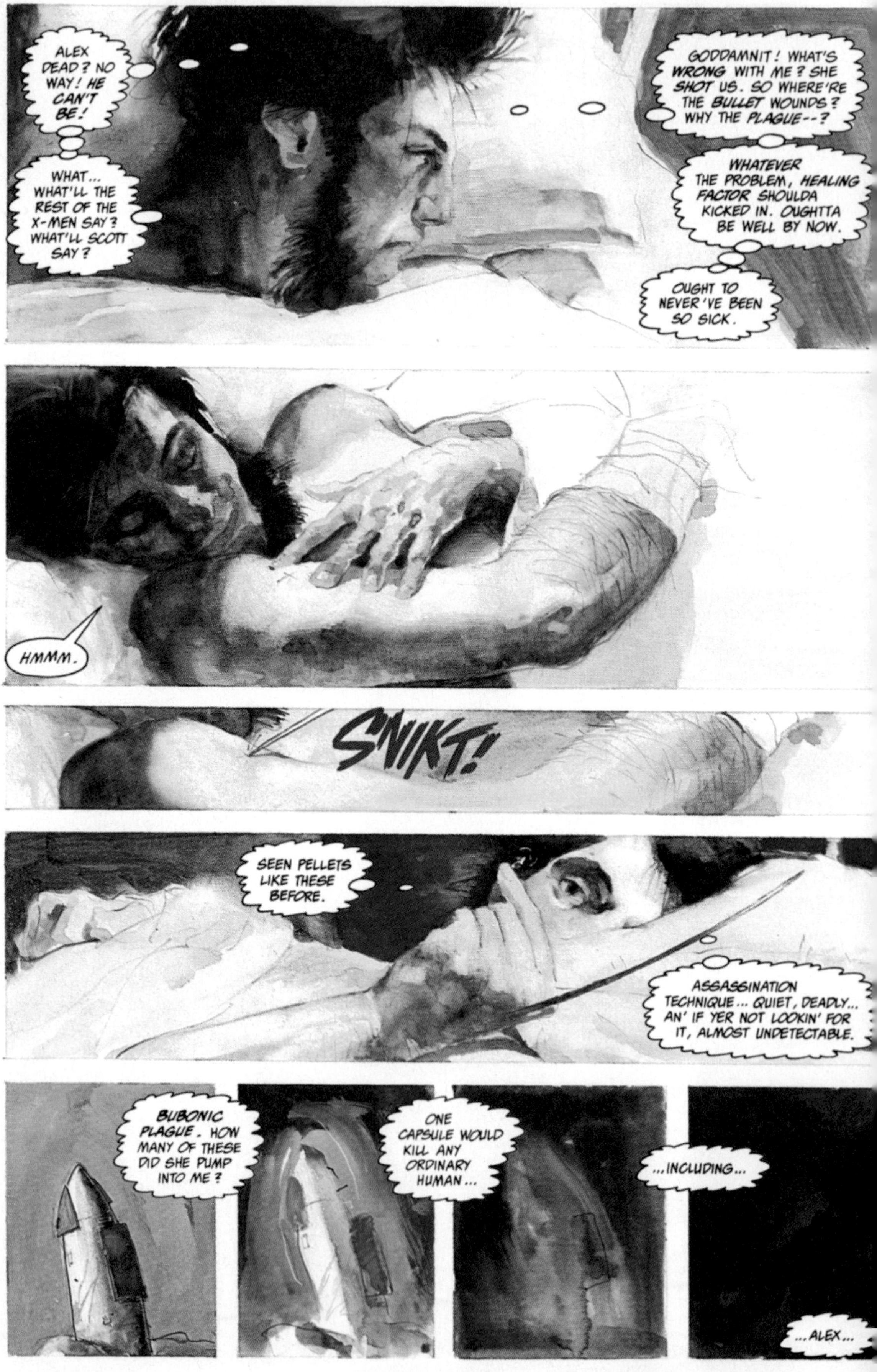
ALEX DEAD? NO WAY! HE CAN'T BE!
WHAT... WHAT'LL THE REST OF THE X-MEN SAY? WHAT'LL SCOTT SAY?
GODDAMNIT! WHAT'S WRONG WITH ME? SHE SHOT US. SO WHERE'RE THE BULLET WOUNDS? WHY THE PLAGUE--?
WHATEVER THE PROBLEM, HEALING FACTOR SHOULDA KICKED IN. OUGHTTA BE WELL BY NOW.
OUGHT TO NEVER'VE BEEN SO SICK.
HMMM.
SNIKT!
SEEN PELLETS LIKE THESE BEFORE.
ASSASSINATION TECHNIQUE... QUIET, DEADLY... AN' IF YER NOT LOOKIN' FOR IT, ALMOST UNDETECTABLE.
BUBONIC PLAGUE. HOW MANY OF THESE DID SHE PUMP INTO ME?
ONE CAPSULE WOULD KILL ANY ORDINARY HUMAN...
...INCLUDING...
...ALEX...

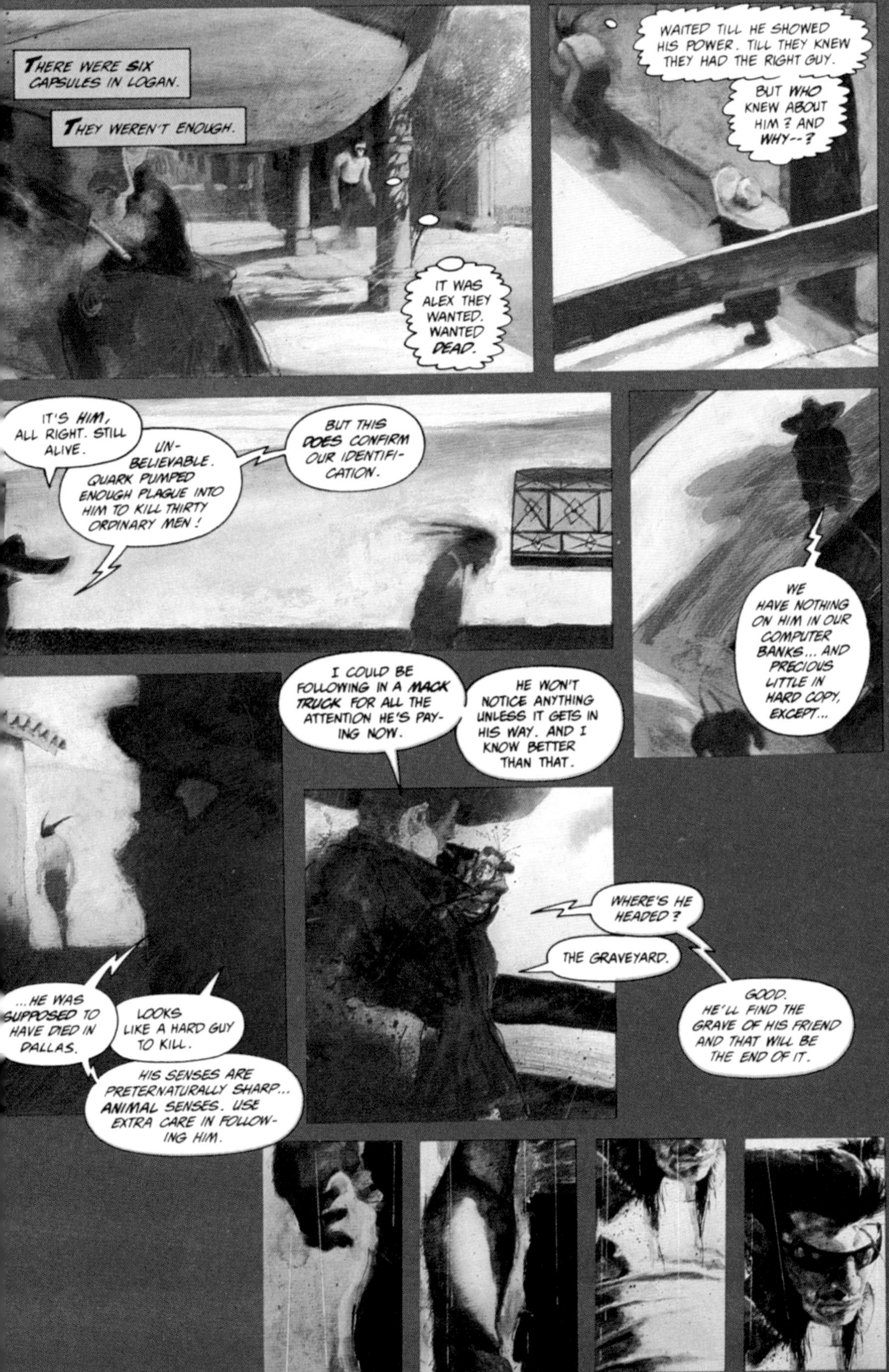
THERE WERE SIX CAPSULES IN LOGAN.
THEY WEREN'T ENOUGH.
IT WAS ALEX THEY WANTED. WANTED DEAD.
WAITED TILL HE SHOWED HIS POWER. TILL THEY KNEW THEY HAD THE RIGHT GUY.
BUT WHO KNEW ABOUT HIM ? AND WHY--?
IT'S HIM, ALL RIGHT. STILL ALIVE.
UN-BELIEVABLE. QUARK PUMPED ENOUGH PLAGUE INTO HIM TO KILL THIRTY ORDINARY MEN !
BUT THIS DOES CONFIRM OUR IDENTIFI-CATION.
WE HAVE NOTHING ON HIM IN OUR COMPUTER BANKS... AND PRECIOUS LITTLE IN HARD COPY, EXCEPT...
...HE WAS SUPPOSED TO HAVE DIED IN DALLAS.
LOOKS LIKE A HARD GUY TO KILL.
HIS SENSES ARE PRETERNATURALLY SHARP... ANIMAL SENSES. USE EXTRA CARE IN FOLLOW-ING HIM.
I COULD BE FOLLOWING IN A MACK TRUCK FOR ALL THE ATTENTION HE'S PAY-ING NOW.
HE WON'T NOTICE ANYTHING UNLESS IT GETS IN HIS WAY. AND I KNOW BETTER THAN THAT.
WHERE'S HE HEADED ?
THE GRAVEYARD.
GOOD. HE'LL FIND THE GRAVE OF HIS FRIEND AND THAT WILL BE THE END OF IT.

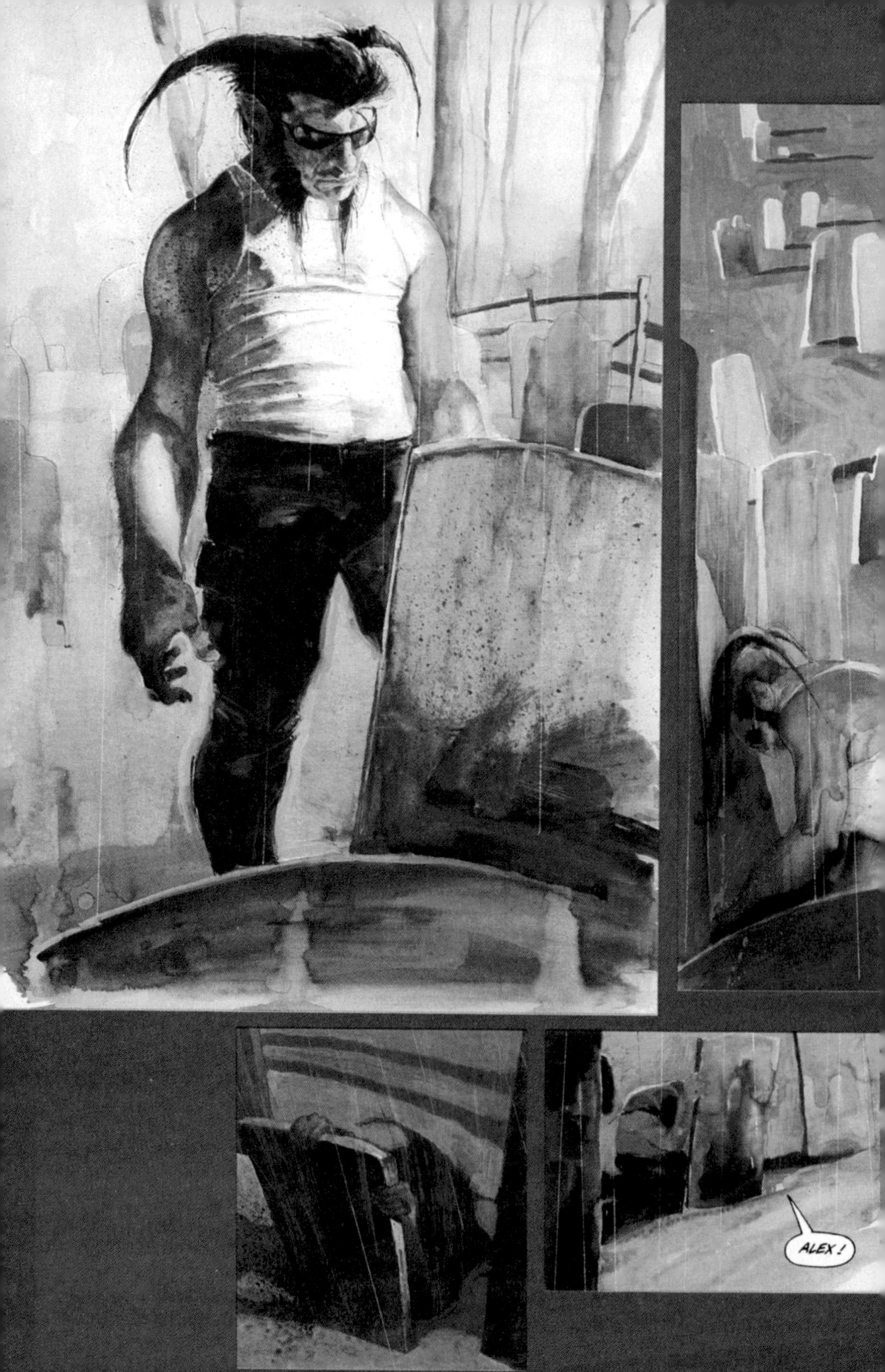
ALEX!

SNIFF?

SNIFF!
SNIFF!

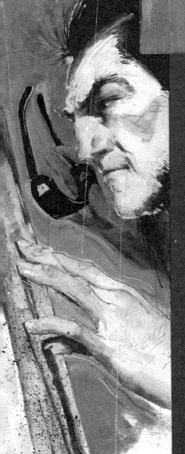

GGRRRRRRRRR

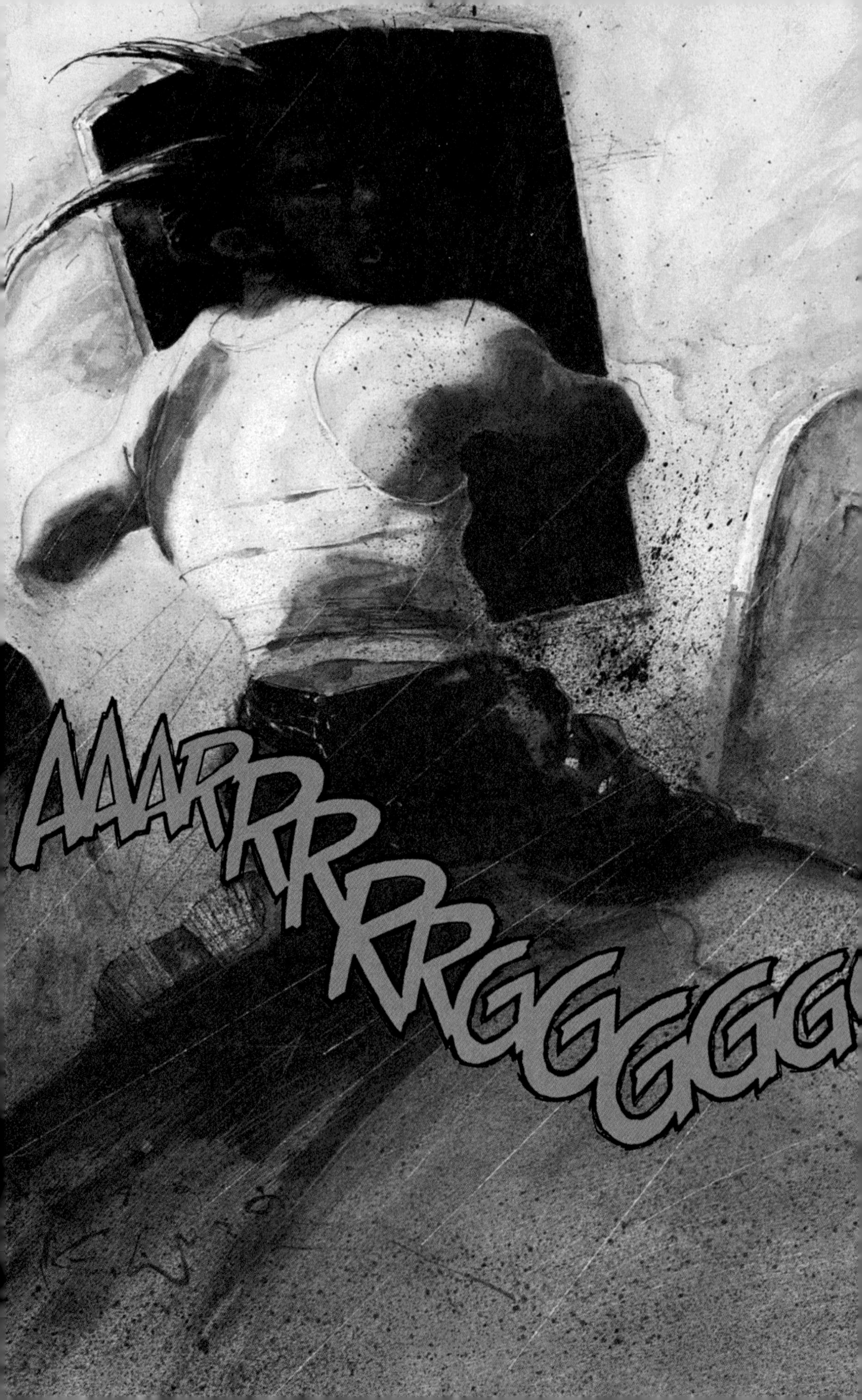
AAARRRRRGGGGG

AHHRRRGGHHH!

ALEX !

SNIKT!

SECHNNK

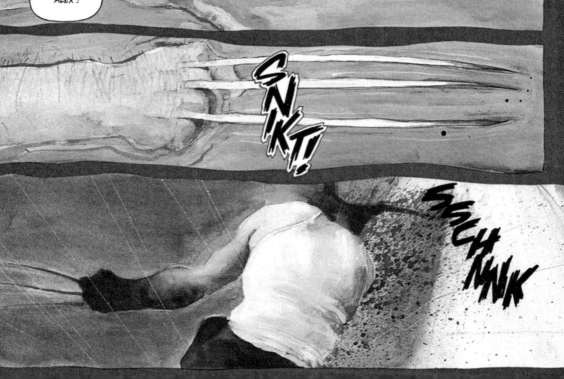

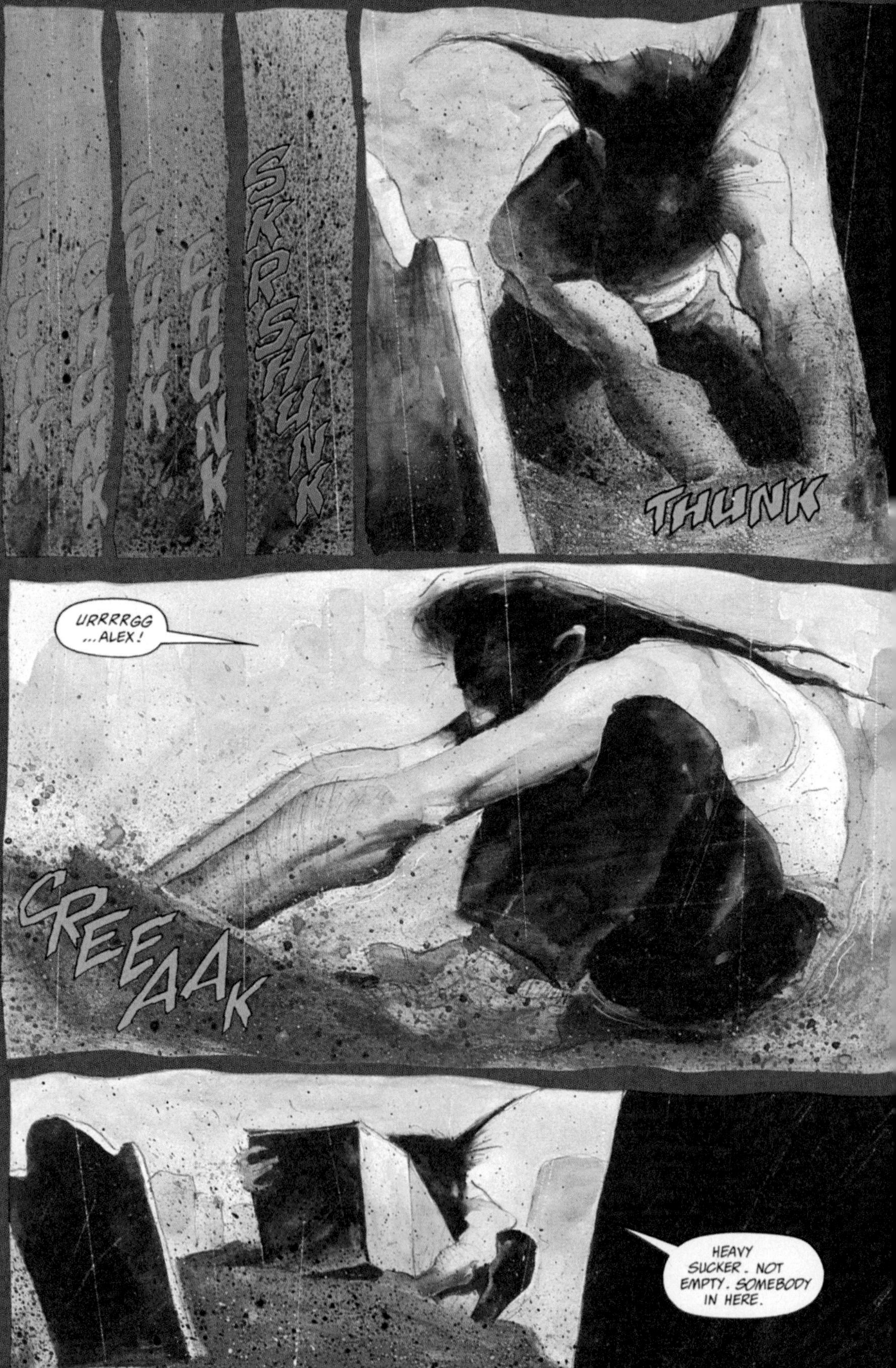
CHUNK
CHUNK
SKRSHUNK
THUNK
URRRRGG ...ALEX!
CREEAAK
HEAVY SUCKER. NOT EMPTY. SOMEBODY IN HERE.

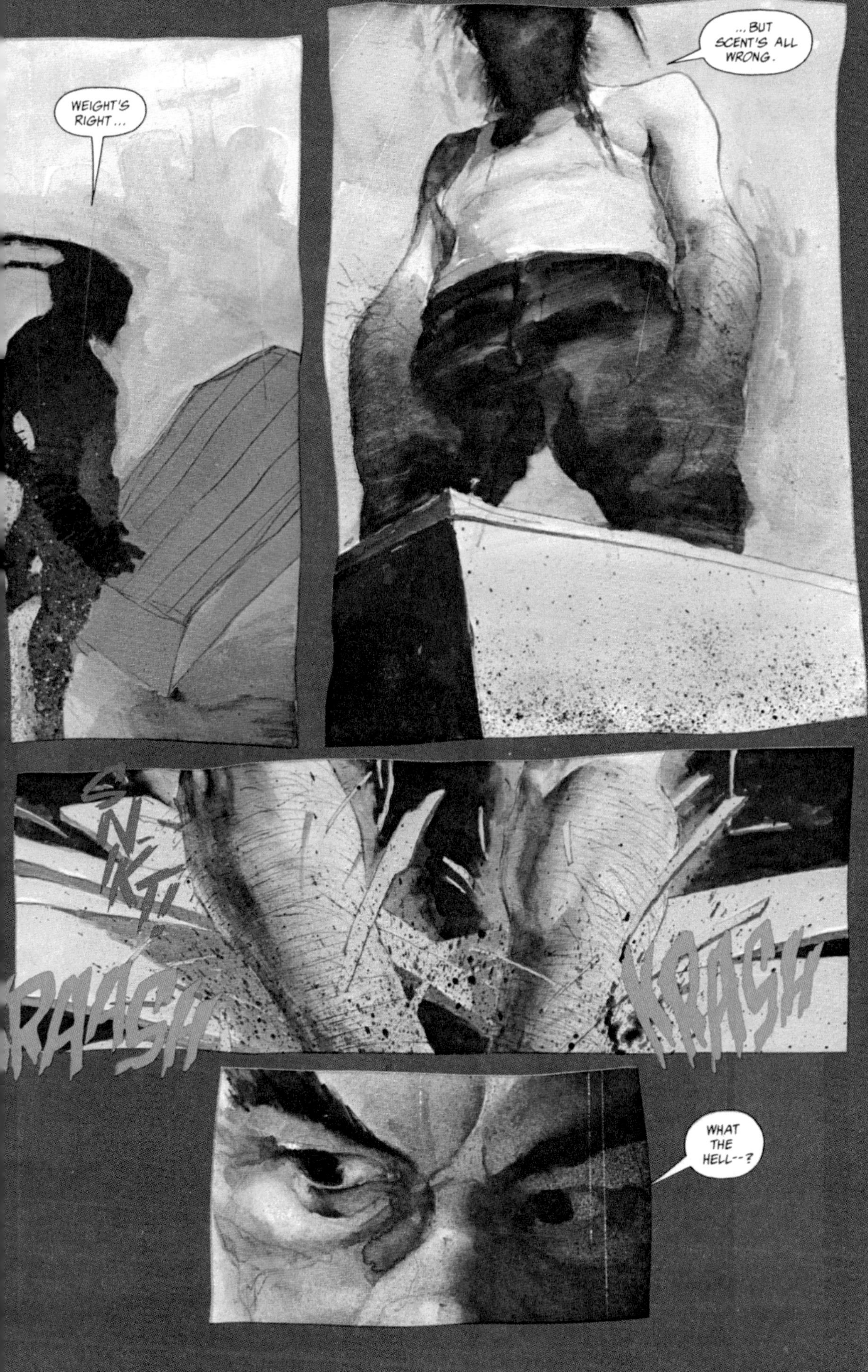
WEIGHT'S RIGHT...
...BUT SCENT'S ALL WRONG.
SNIKT!
RAASH
KRASH
WHAT THE HELL--?

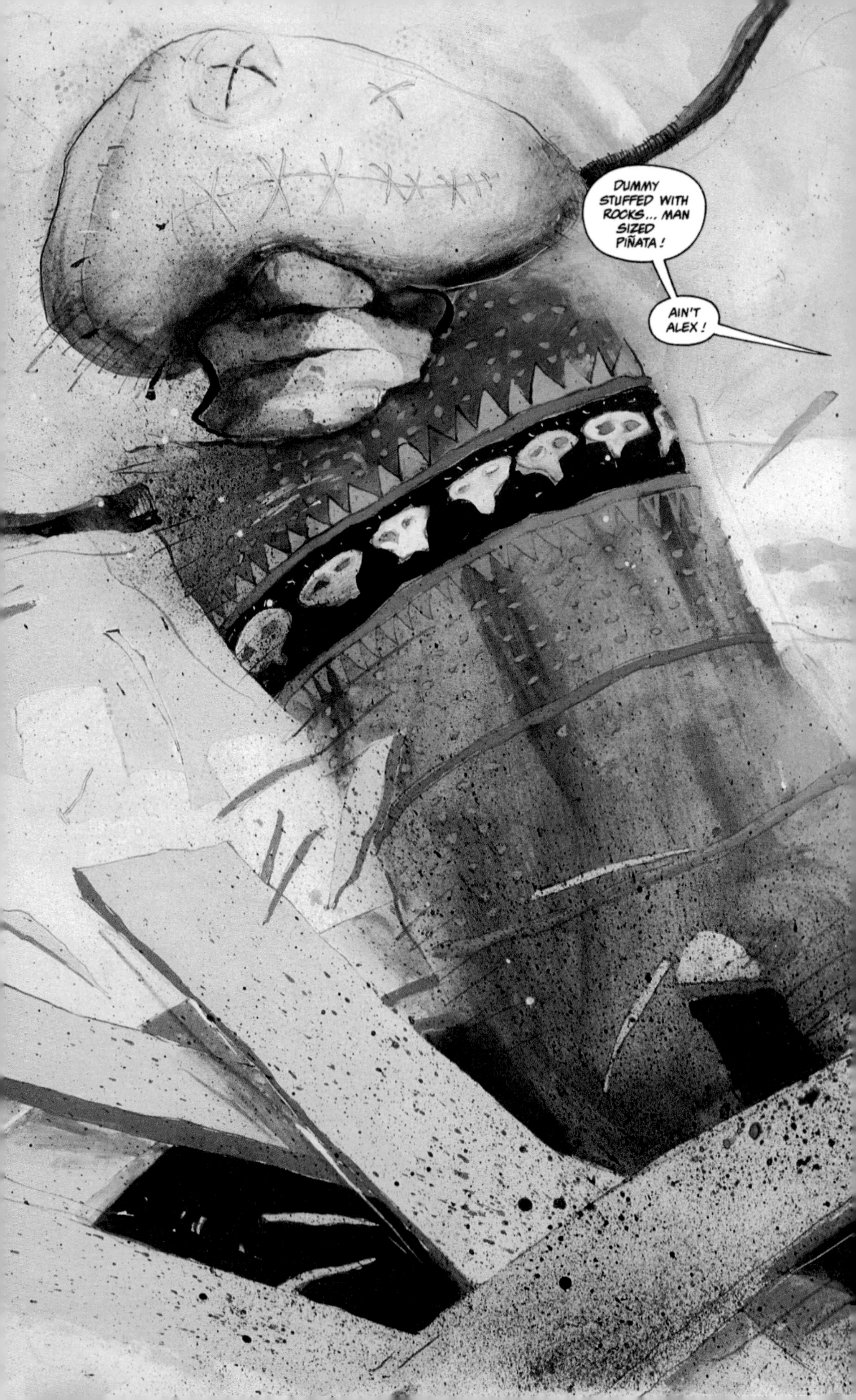
DUMMY STUFFED WITH ROCKS... MAN SIZED PIÑATA!
AIN'T ALEX!

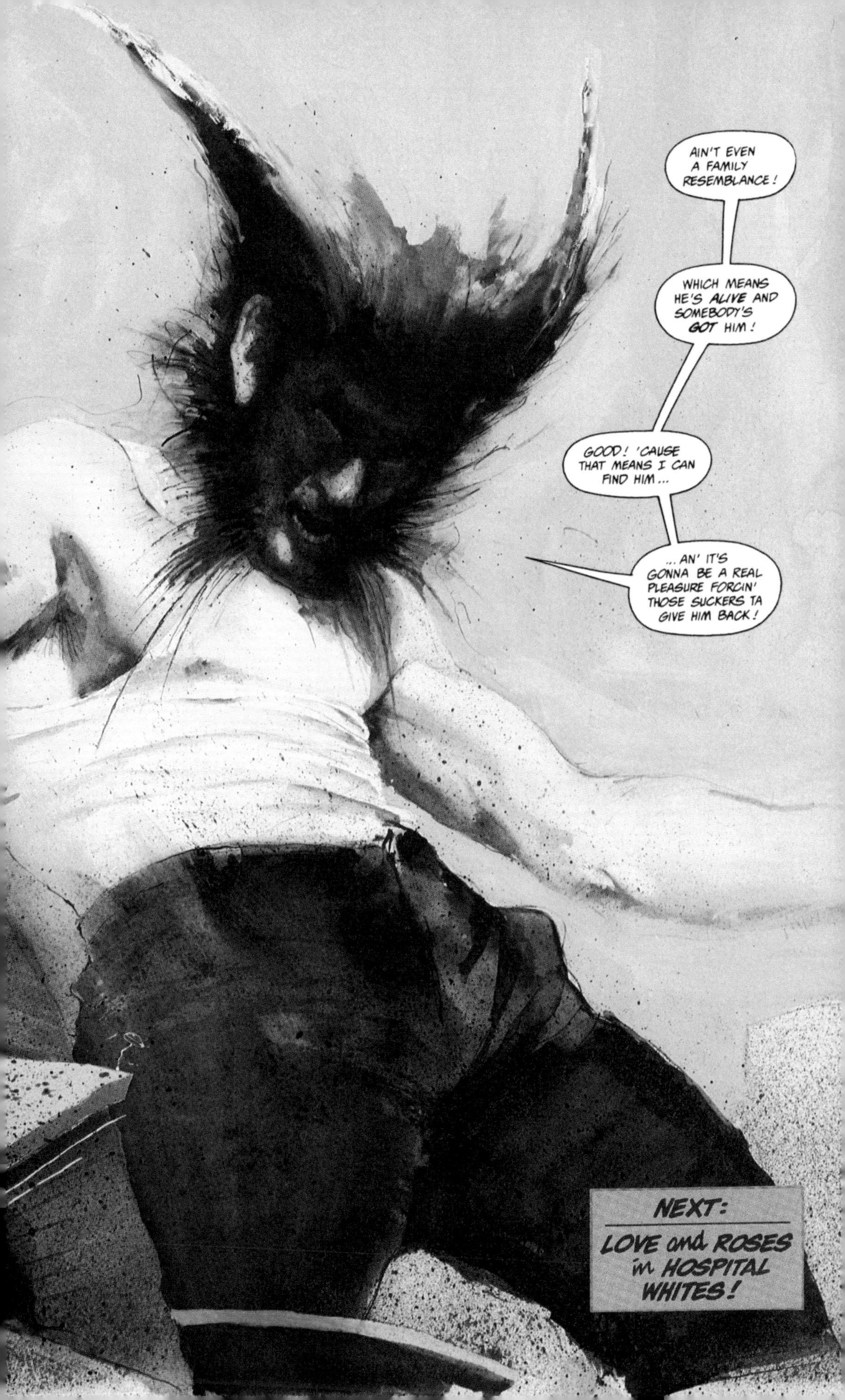
AIN'T EVEN A FAMILY RESEMBLANCE!
WHICH MEANS HE'S ALIVE AND SOMEBODY'S GOT HIM!
GOOD! 'CAUSE THAT MEANS I CAN FIND HIM...
...AN' IT'S GONNA BE A REAL PLEASURE FORCIN' THOSE SUCKERS TA GIVE HIM BACK!
NEXT:
LOVE and ROSES in HOSPITAL WHITES!

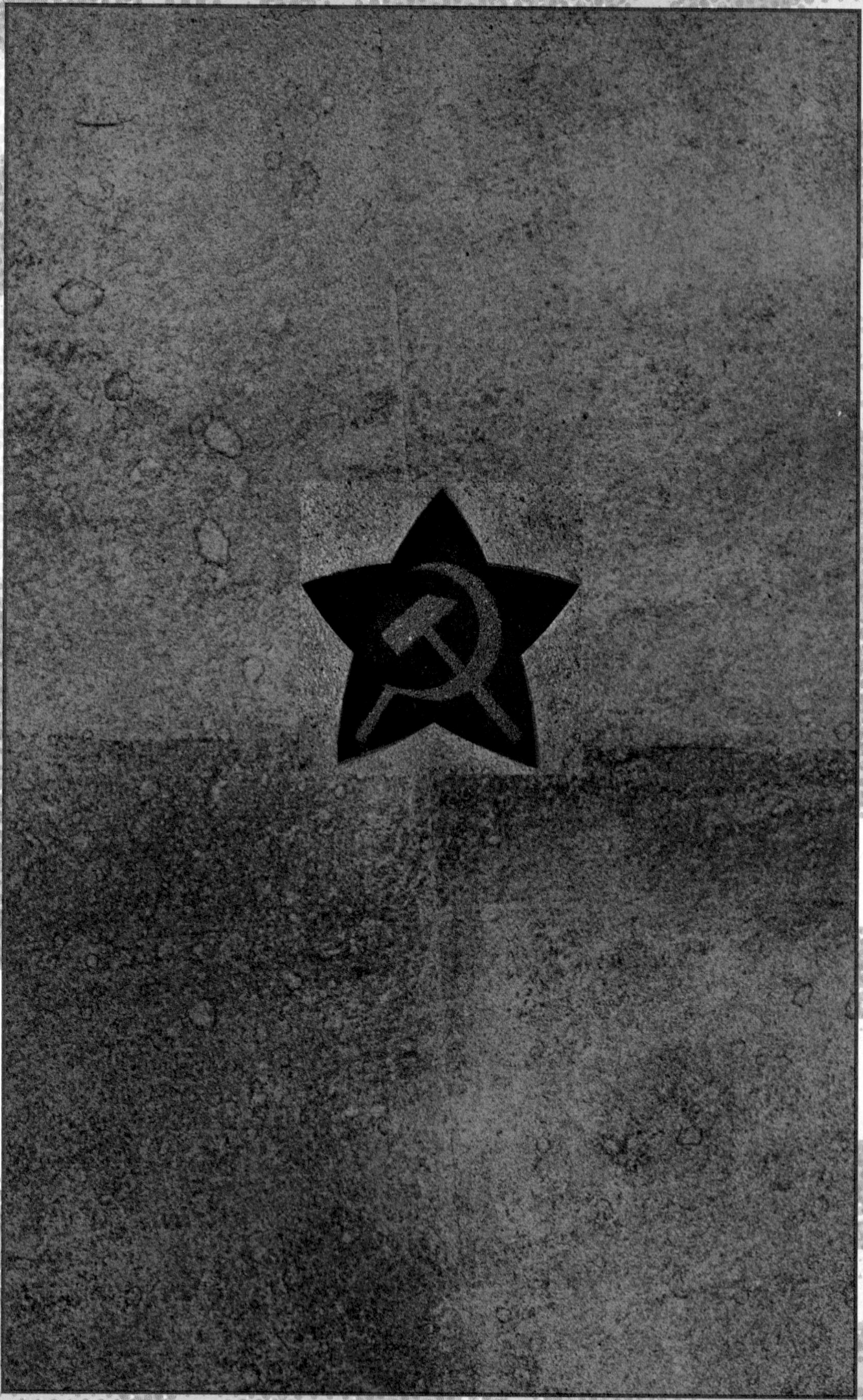

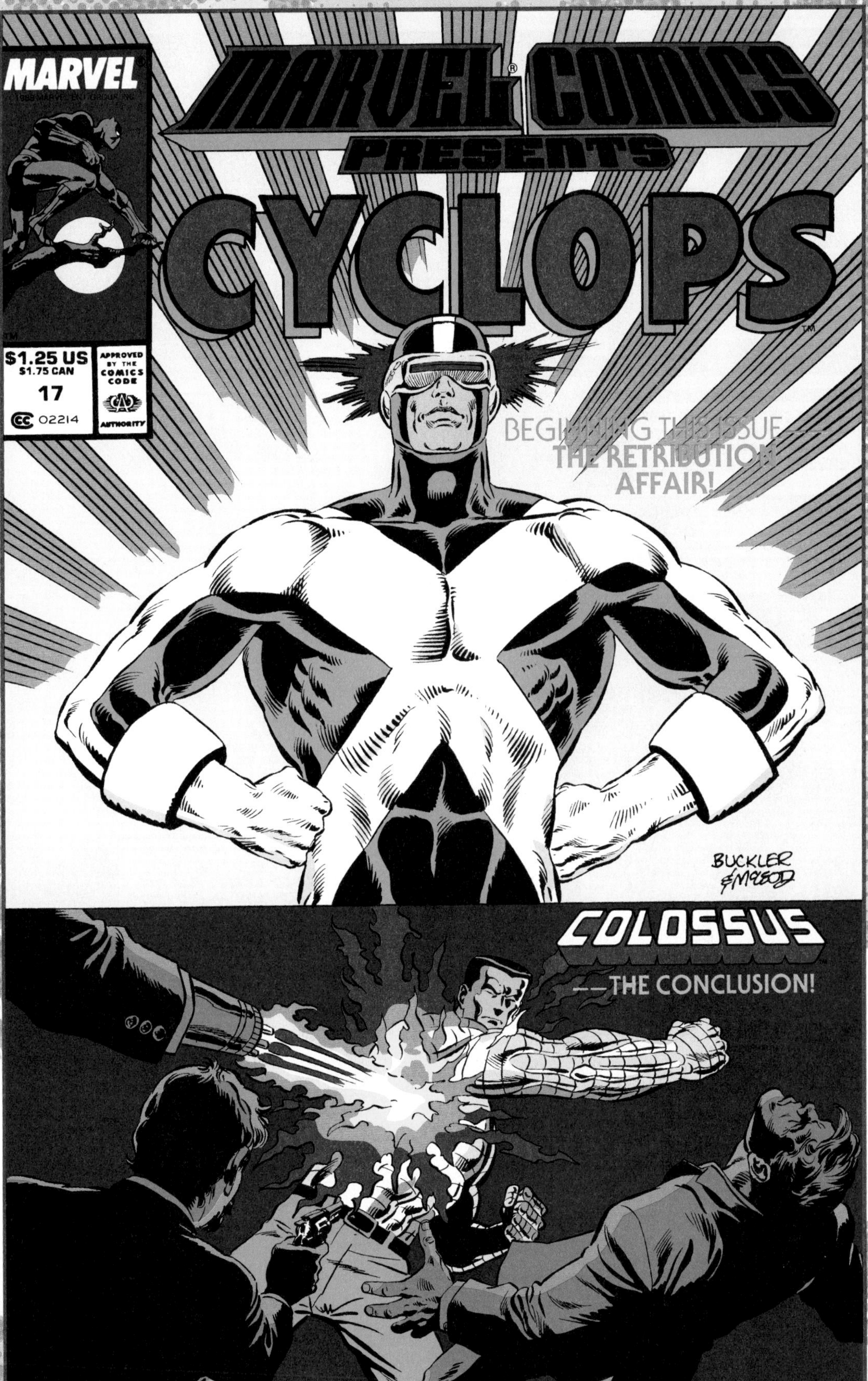
MARVEL
MARVEL COMICS PRESENTS
CYCLOPS
$1.25 US
$1.75 CAN
17
02214
APPROVED BY THE COMICS CODE AUTHORITY
BEGINNING THIS ISSUE—
THE RETRIBUTION AFFAIR!
BUCKLER & McLEOD
COLOSSUS
—THE CONCLUSION!

MARVEL COMICS PRESENTS #17, published in December 1988, began a limited serial starring Cyclops, then the leader of X-Factor.

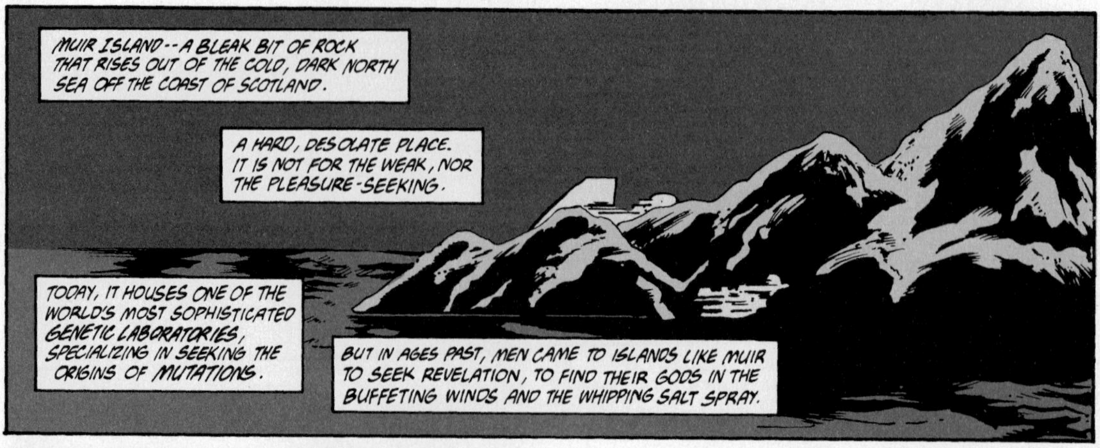
MUIR ISLAND--A BLEAK BIT OF ROCK THAT RISES OUT OF THE COLD, DARK NORTH SEA OFF THE COAST OF SCOTLAND.
A HARD, DESOLATE PLACE. IT IS NOT FOR THE WEAK, NOR THE PLEASURE-SEEKING.
TODAY, IT HOUSES ONE OF THE WORLD'S MOST SOPHISTICATED GENETIC LABORATORIES, SPECIALIZING IN SEEKING THE ORIGINS OF MUTATIONS.
BUT IN AGES PAST, MEN CAME TO ISLANDS LIKE MUIR TO SEEK REVELATION, TO FIND THEIR GODS IN THE BUFFETING WINDS AND THE WHIPPING SALT SPRAY.

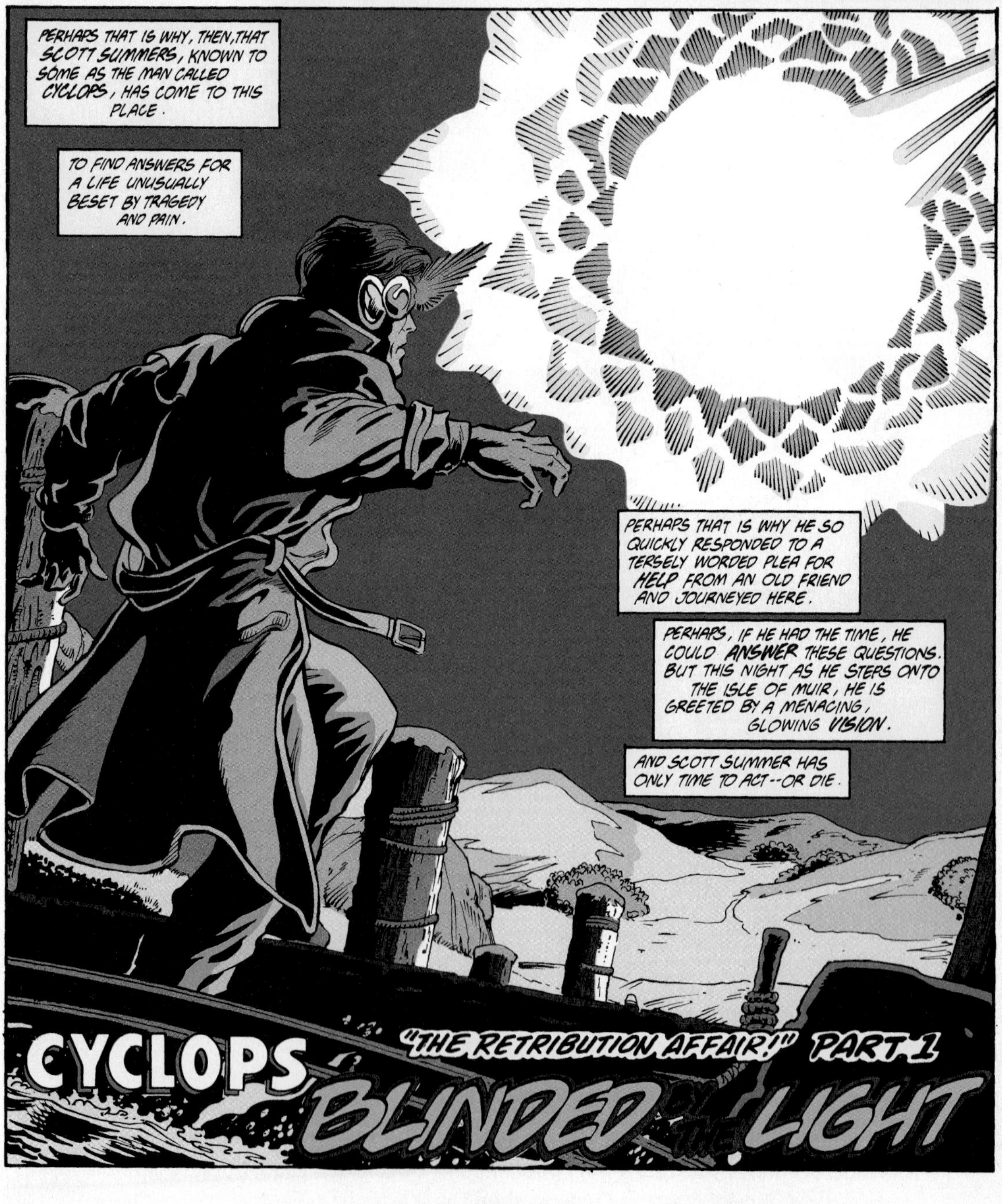
PERHAPS THAT IS WHY, THEN, THAT SCOTT SUMMERS, KNOWN TO SOME AS THE MAN CALLED CYCLOPS, HAS COME TO THIS PLACE.
TO FIND ANSWERS FOR A LIFE UNUSUALLY BESET BY TRAGEDY AND PAIN.
PERHAPS THAT IS WHY HE SO QUICKLY RESPONDED TO A TERSELY WORDED PLEA FOR HELP FROM AN OLD FRIEND AND JOURNEYED HERE.
PERHAPS, IF HE HAD THE TIME, HE COULD ANSWER THESE QUESTIONS. BUT THIS NIGHT AS HE STEPS ONTO THE ISLE OF MUIR, HE IS GREETED BY A MENACING, GLOWING VISION.
AND SCOTT SUMMER HAS ONLY TIME TO ACT--OR DIE.
CYCLOPS
"THE RETRIBUTION AFFAIR!" PART 1
BLINDED BY THE LIGHT

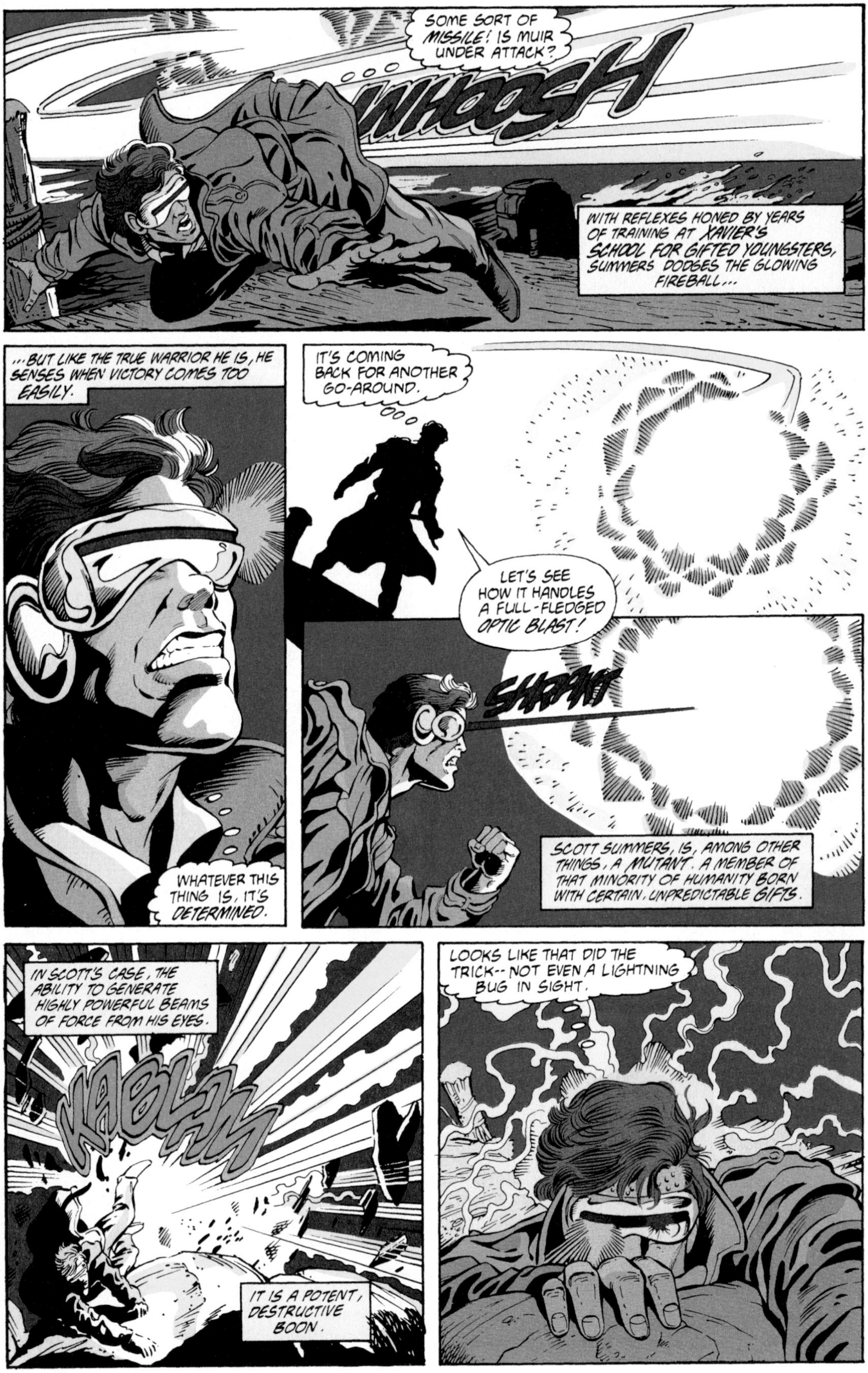

SOME SORT OF MISSILE! IS MUIR UNDER ATTACK?
WHOOSH
WITH REFLEXES HONED BY YEARS OF TRAINING AT XAVIER'S SCHOOL FOR GIFTED YOUNGSTERS, SUMMERS DODGES THE GLOWING FIREBALL...
...BUT LIKE THE TRUE WARRIOR HE IS, HE SENSES WHEN VICTORY COMES TOO EASILY.
WHATEVER THIS THING IS, IT'S DETERMINED.
IT'S COMING BACK FOR ANOTHER GO-AROUND.
LET'S SEE HOW IT HANDLES A FULL-FLEDGED OPTIC BLAST!
SHRAKT
SCOTT SUMMERS, IS, AMONG OTHER THINGS, A MUTANT. A MEMBER OF THAT MINORITY OF HUMANITY BORN WITH CERTAIN, UNPREDICTABLE GIFTS.
IN SCOTT'S CASE, THE ABILITY TO GENERATE HIGHLY POWERFUL BEAMS OF FORCE FROM HIS EYES.
JABLAM
IT IS A POTENT, DESTRUCTIVE BOON.
LOOKS LIKE THAT DID THE TRICK-- NOT EVEN A LIGHTNING BUG IN SIGHT.

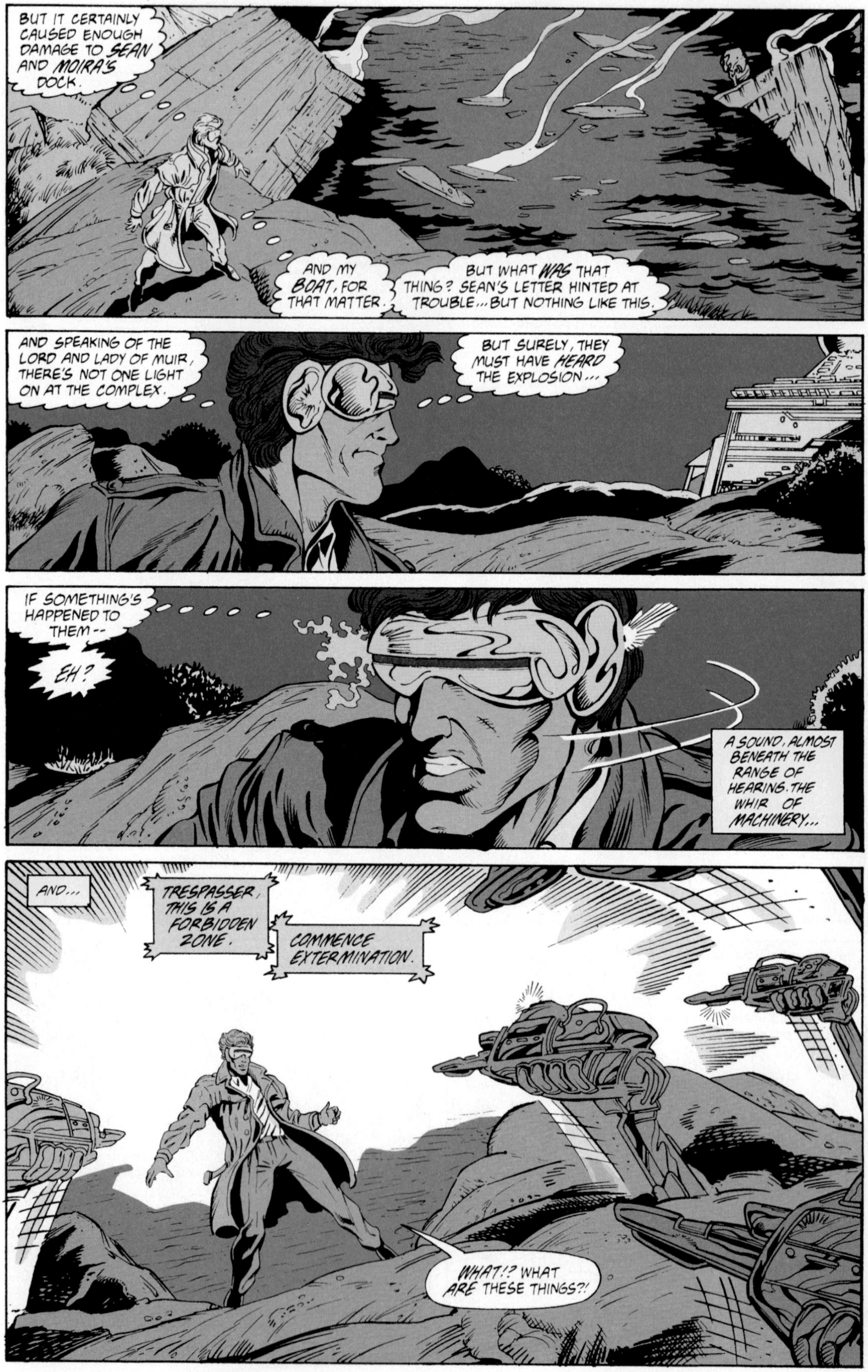
BUT IT CERTAINLY CAUSED ENOUGH DAMAGE TO SEAN AND MOIRA'S DOCK.
AND MY BOAT, FOR THAT MATTER.
BUT WHAT WAS THAT THING? SEAN'S LETTER HINTED AT TROUBLE... BUT NOTHING LIKE THIS.
AND SPEAKING OF THE LORD AND LADY OF MUIR, THERE'S NOT ONE LIGHT ON AT THE COMPLEX.
BUT SURELY, THEY MUST HAVE HEARD THE EXPLOSION...
IF SOMETHING'S HAPPENED TO THEM--
EH?
A SOUND, ALMOST BENEATH THE RANGE OF HEARING. THE WHIR OF MACHINERY...
AND...
TRESPASSER, THIS IS A FORBIDDEN ZONE.
COMMENCE EXTERMINATION.
WHAT!? WHAT ARE THESE THINGS?!

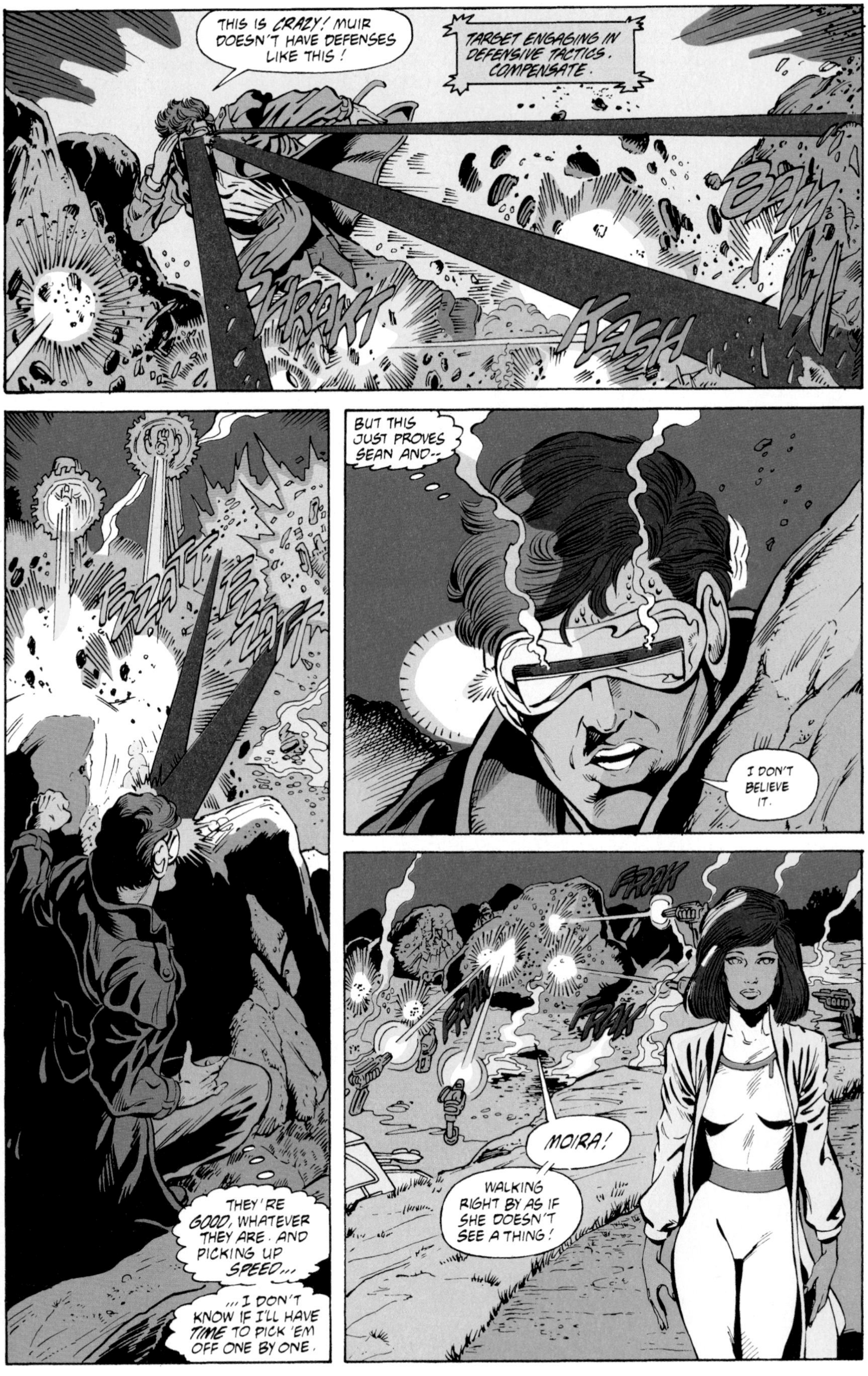
THIS IS CRAZY! MUIR DOESN'T HAVE DEFENSES LIKE THIS!
TARGET ENGAGING IN DEFENSIVE TACTICS. COMPENSATE.
SHRAKT
KASH
BAM
TZZZATT
TZZATT
THEY'RE GOOD, WHATEVER THEY ARE. AND PICKING UP SPEED...
...I DON'T KNOW IF I'LL HAVE TIME TO PICK 'EM OFF ONE BY ONE.
BUT THIS JUST PROVES SEAN AND--
I DON'T BELIEVE IT.
FRAK
FRAK
FRAK
MOIRA!
WALKING RIGHT BY AS IF SHE DOESN'T SEE A THING!

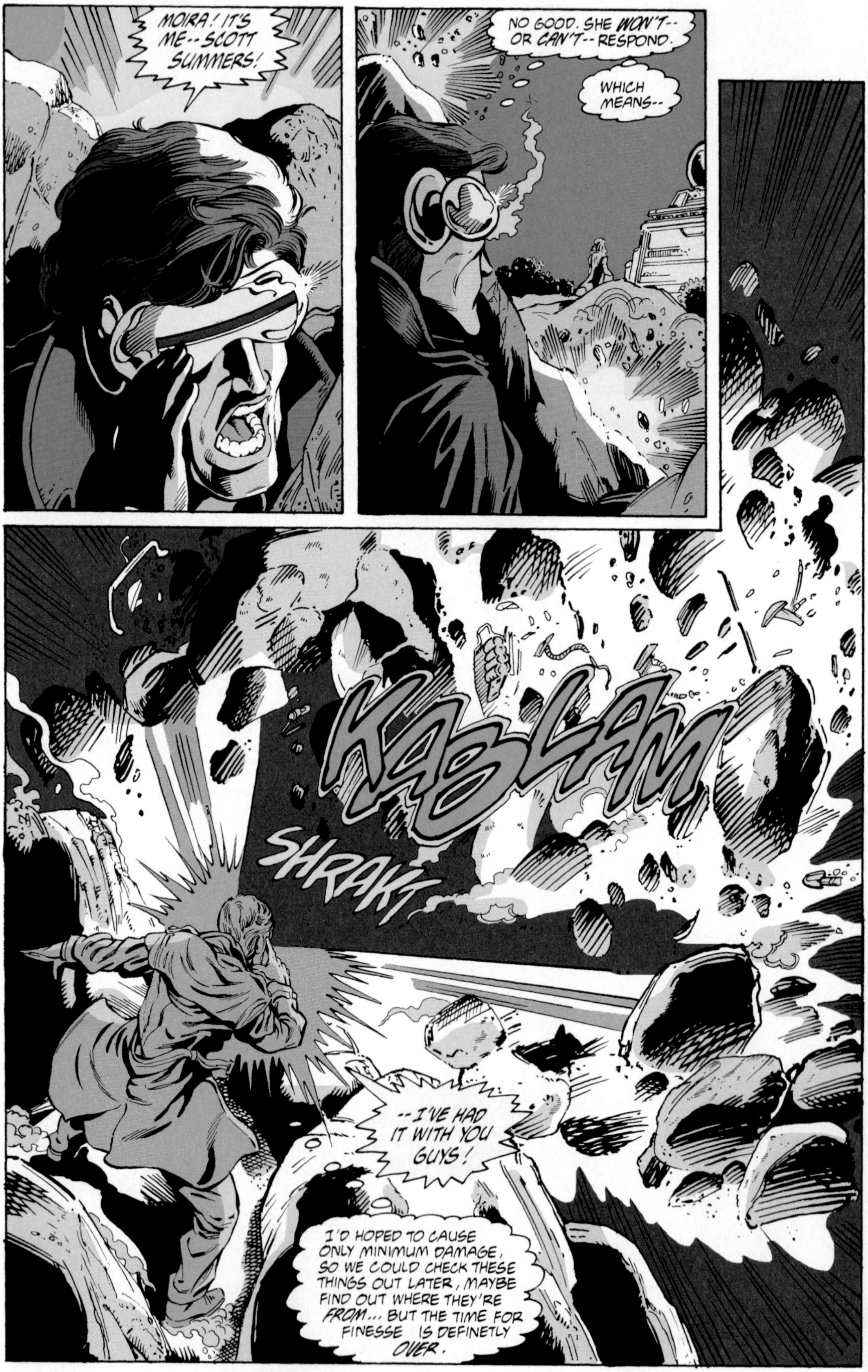
MOIRA! IT'S ME--SCOTT SUMMERS!
NO GOOD. SHE WON'T--OR CAN'T--RESPOND.
WHICH MEANS--
KABLAM
SHRAKT
--I'VE HAD IT WITH YOU GUYS!
I'D HOPED TO CAUSE ONLY MINIMUM DAMAGE, SO WE COULD CHECK THESE THINGS OUT LATER, MAYBE FIND OUT WHERE THEY'RE FROM... BUT THE TIME FOR FINESSE IS DEFINETLY OVER.

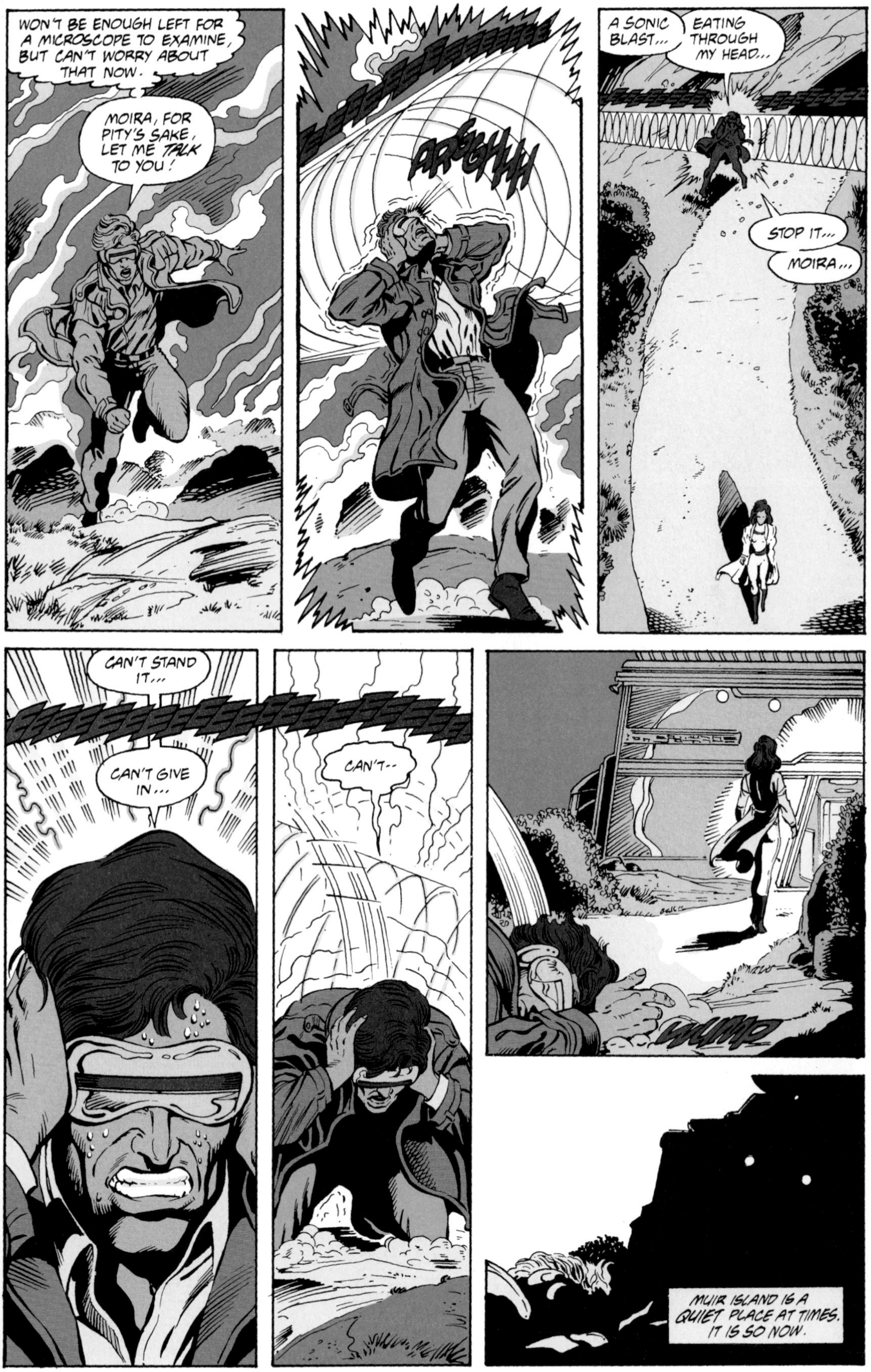
WON'T BE ENOUGH LEFT FOR A MICROSCOPE TO EXAMINE, BUT CAN'T WORRY ABOUT THAT NOW.
MOIRA, FOR PITY'S SAKE, LET ME TALK TO YOU!
ARRGHHH
A SONIC BLAST...
EATING THROUGH MY HEAD...
STOP IT...
MOIRA...
CAN'T STAND IT...
CAN'T GIVE IN...
CAN'T--
WUMP
MUIR ISLAND IS A QUIET PLACE AT TIMES. IT IS SO NOW.

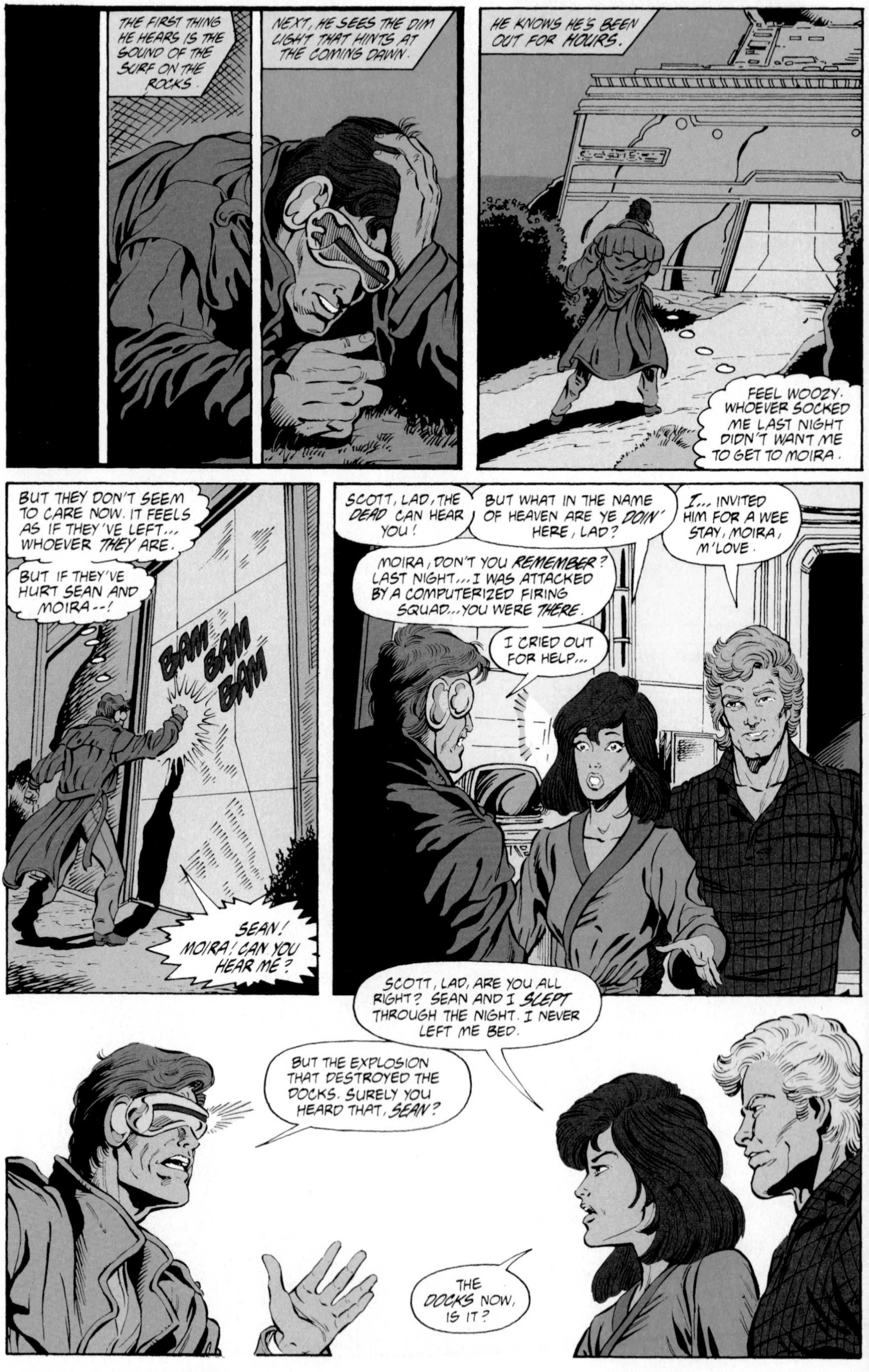
THE FIRST THING HE HEARS IS THE SOUND OF THE SURF ON THE ROCKS.
NEXT, HE SEES THE DIM LIGHT THAT HINTS AT THE COMING DAWN.
HE KNOWS HE'S BEEN OUT FOR HOURS.
FEEL WOOZY. WHOEVER SOCKED ME LAST NIGHT DIDN'T WANT ME TO GET TO MOIRA.
BUT THEY DON'T SEEM TO CARE NOW. IT FEELS AS IF THEY'VE LEFT... WHOEVER THEY ARE.
BUT IF THEY'VE HURT SEAN AND MOIRA--!
BAM BAM BAM
SEAN! MOIRA! CAN YOU HEAR ME?
SCOTT, LAD, THE DEAD CAN HEAR YOU!
BUT WHAT IN THE NAME OF HEAVEN ARE YE DOIN' HERE, LAD?
I... INVITED HIM FOR A WEE STAY, MOIRA, M'LOVE.
MOIRA, DON'T YOU REMEMBER? LAST NIGHT... I WAS ATTACKED BY A COMPUTERIZED FIRING SQUAD... YOU WERE THERE.
I CRIED OUT FOR HELP...
SCOTT, LAD, ARE YOU ALL RIGHT? SEAN AND I SLEPT THROUGH THE NIGHT. I NEVER LEFT ME BED.
BUT THE EXPLOSION THAT DESTROYED THE DOCKS. SURELY YOU HEARD THAT, SEAN?
THE DOCKS NOW, IS IT?

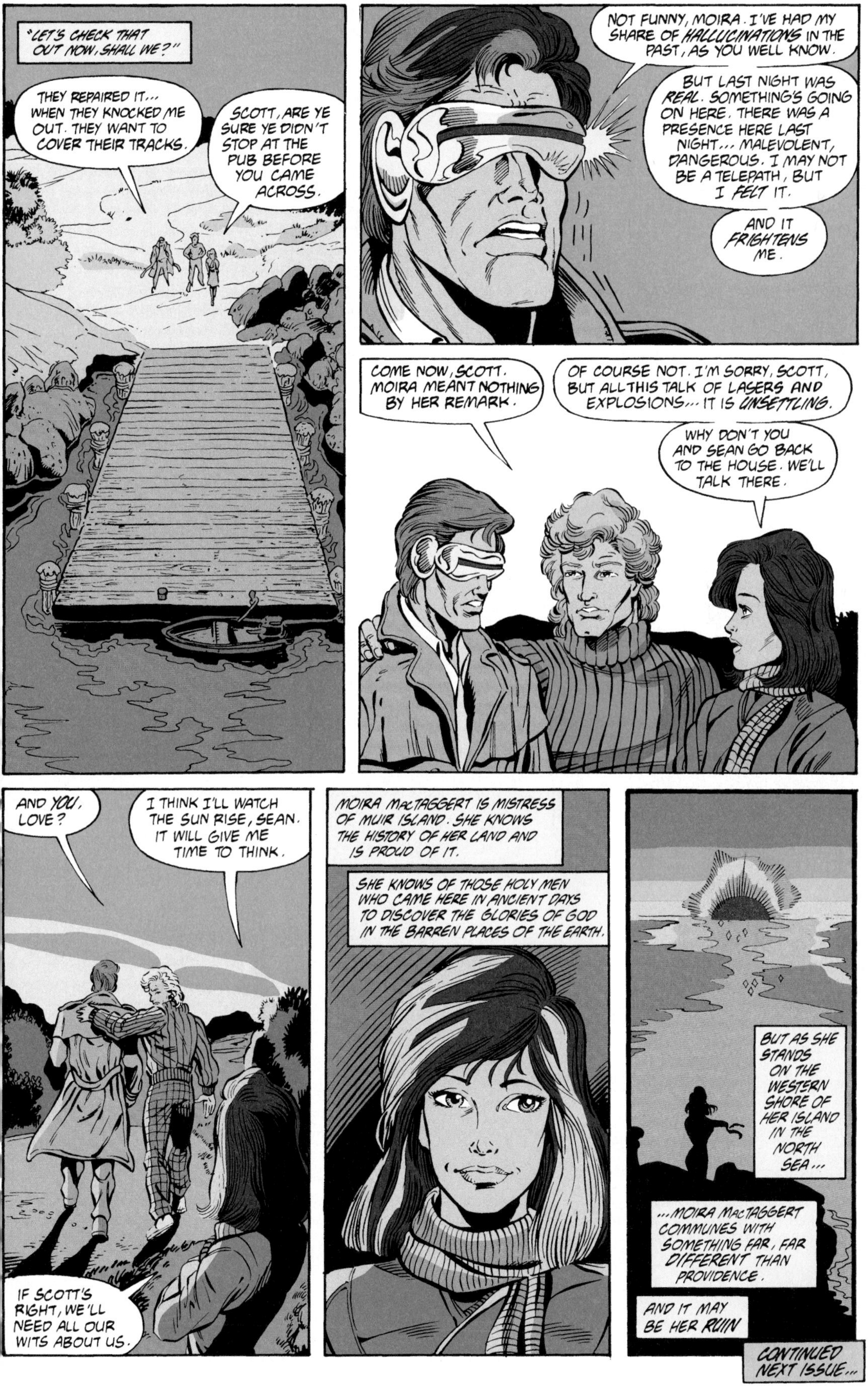
"LET'S CHECK THAT OUT NOW, SHALL WE?"
THEY REPAIRED IT... WHEN THEY KNOCKED ME OUT. THEY WANT TO COVER THEIR TRACKS.
SCOTT, ARE YE SURE YE DIDN'T STOP AT THE PUB BEFORE YOU CAME ACROSS.
NOT FUNNY, MOIRA. I'VE HAD MY SHARE OF HALLUCINATIONS IN THE PAST, AS YOU WELL KNOW.
BUT LAST NIGHT WAS REAL. SOMETHING'S GOING ON HERE. THERE WAS A PRESENCE HERE LAST NIGHT... MALEVOLENT, DANGEROUS. I MAY NOT BE A TELEPATH, BUT I FELT IT.
AND IT FRIGHTENS ME.
COME NOW, SCOTT. MOIRA MEANT NOTHING BY HER REMARK.
OF COURSE NOT. I'M SORRY, SCOTT, BUT ALL THIS TALK OF LASERS AND EXPLOSIONS... IT IS UNSETTLING.
WHY DON'T YOU AND SEAN GO BACK TO THE HOUSE. WE'LL TALK THERE.
AND YOU, LOVE?
I THINK I'LL WATCH THE SUN RISE, SEAN. IT WILL GIVE ME TIME TO THINK.
IF SCOTT'S RIGHT, WE'LL NEED ALL OUR WITS ABOUT US.
MOIRA MacTAGGERT IS MISTRESS OF MUIR ISLAND. SHE KNOWS THE HISTORY OF HER LAND AND IS PROUD OF IT.
SHE KNOWS OF THOSE HOLY MEN WHO CAME HERE IN ANCIENT DAYS TO DISCOVER THE GLORIES OF GOD IN THE BARREN PLACES OF THE EARTH.
BUT AS SHE STANDS ON THE WESTERN SHORE OF HER ISLAND IN THE NORTH SEA...
...MOIRA MacTAGGERT COMMUNES WITH SOMETHING FAR, FAR DIFFERENT THAN PROVIDENCE.
AND IT MAY BE HER RUIN
CONTINUED NEXT ISSUE...

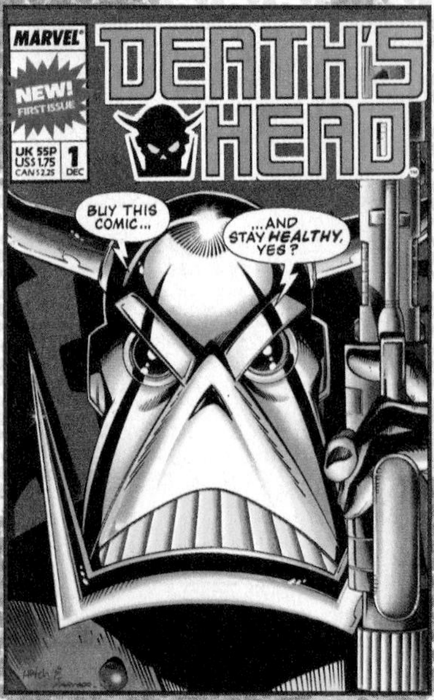
MARVEL
DEATH'S HEAD
NEW! FIRST ISSUE
UK 55P US$1.75 CAN $2.25
1 DEC
BUY THIS COMIC...
...AND STAY HEALTHY, YES?

DEATH'S HEAD #1, published in November 1988, began an ongoing UK series starring the freelance peacekeeping agent.

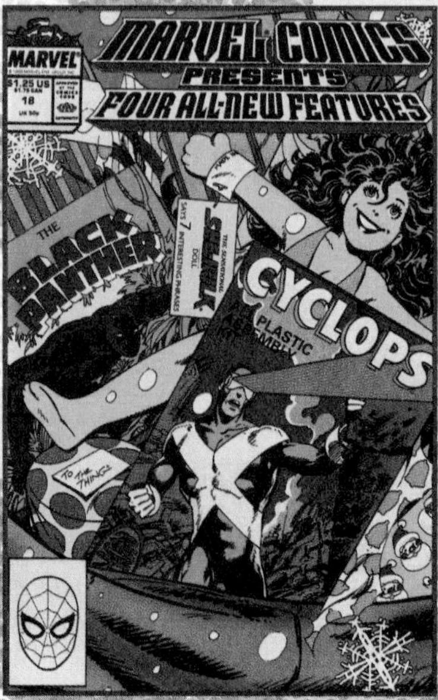
MARVEL COMICS PRESENTS
FOUR ALL-NEW FEATURES
MARVEL
$1.25 US
18
THE BLACK PANTHER
CYCLOPS
PLASTIC

MARVEL COMICS PRESENTS #18, published in December 1988, featured a She-Hulk story that led into her new ongoing series.

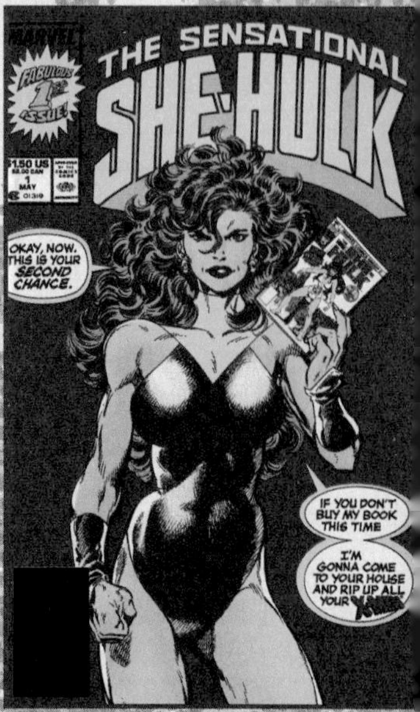
MARVEL
THE SENSATIONAL
SHE-HULK
FABULOUS 1st ISSUE!
$1.50 US
1 MAY
OKAY, NOW. THIS IS YOUR SECOND CHANCE.
IF YOU DON'T BUY MY BOOK THIS TIME
I'M GONNA COME TO YOUR HOUSE AND RIP UP ALL YOUR X-MEN

SENSATIONAL SHE-HULK #1, published i January 1989, began the jade giantess' second ongoing series.

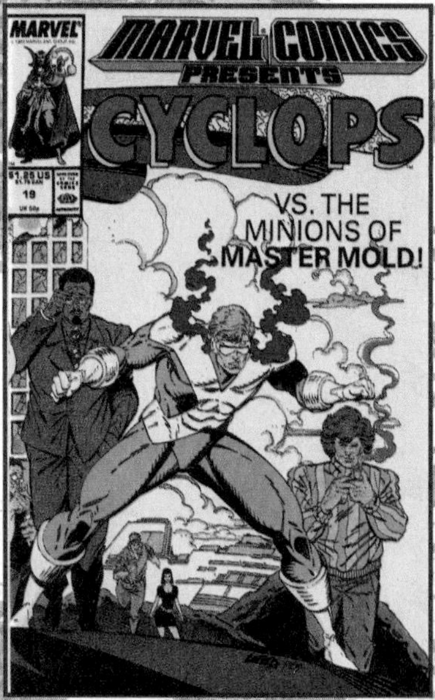
MARVEL COMICS PRESENTS
CYCLOPS
VS. THE MINIONS OF MASTER MOLD!
$1.25 US
19

MARVEL COMICS PRESENTS #19, published in January 1989, featured a Damage Control story that led into their miniseries.

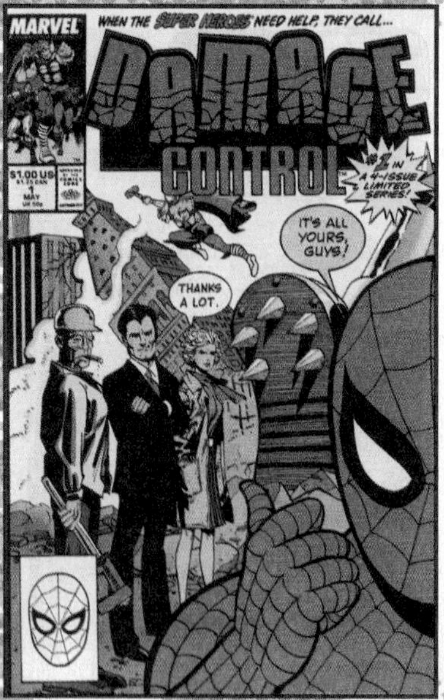
MARVEL
WHEN THE SUPER HEROES NEED HELP, THEY CALL...
DAMAGE CONTROL
#1 IN A 4-ISSUE LIMITED SERIES!
$1.00 US
1 MAY
IT'S ALL YOURS, GUYS!
THANKS A LOT.

DAMAGE CONTROL #1, published in January 1989, began the super hero cleanup company's first miniseries.

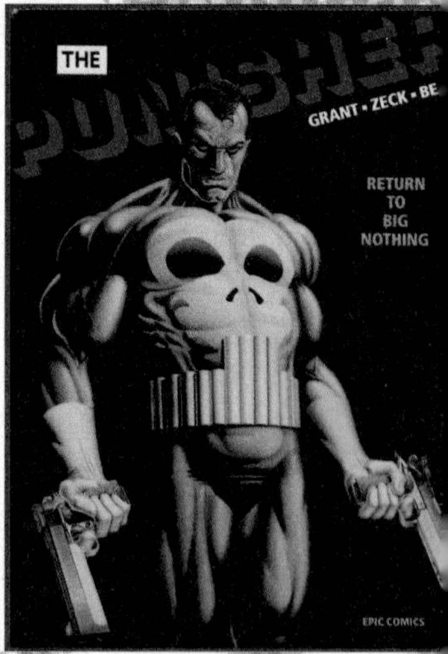
THE
PUNISHER
GRANT • ZECK • BE
RETURN TO BIG NOTHING
EPIC COMICS

PUNISHER: RETURN TO BIG NOTHING HC, published in January 1989, was a hardcover E Graphic Novel starring the lethal crimefighte

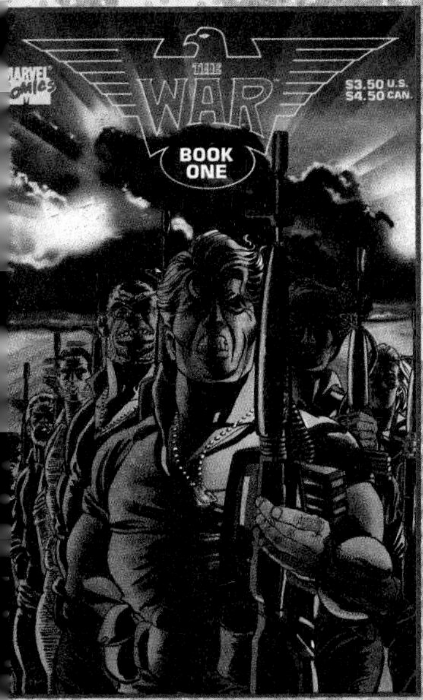
MARVEL COMICS
THE WAR
$3.50 U.S.
$4.50 CAN.
BOOK ONE

E WAR #1, published in February 1989, began a miniseries set in the New Universe.

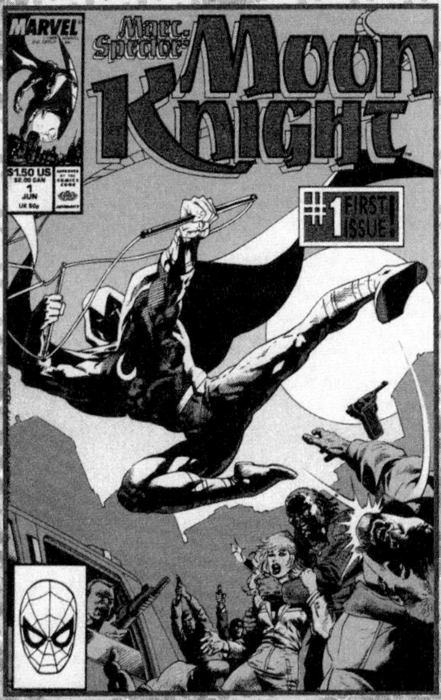
MARVEL
Marc Spector: Moon Knight
$1.50 US
1
JUN
#1 FIRST ISSUE!

MARC SPECTOR: MOON KNIGHT #1, published in February 1989, began Moon Knight's new ongoing series.

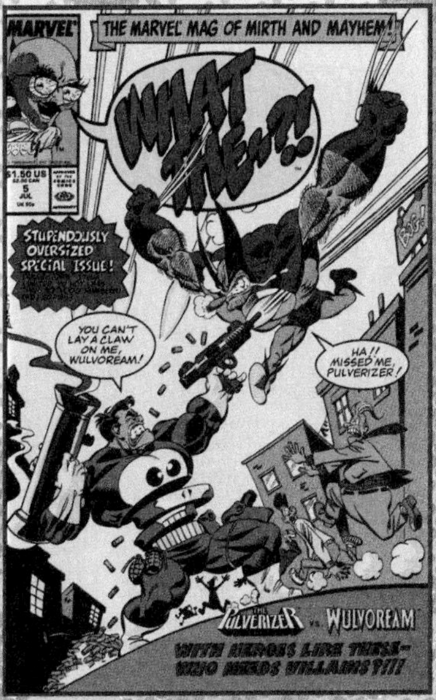
MARVEL
THE MARVEL MAG OF MIRTH AND MAYHEM!
WHAT THE--?!
$1.50 US
5
JUL
STUPENDOUSLY OVERSIZED SPECIAL ISSUE!
YOU CAN'T LAY A CLAW ON ME, WULVOREAM!
HA!! MISSED ME, PULVERIZER!
PULVERIZER vs. WULVOREAM
WITH HEROES LIKE THESE-- WHO NEEDS VILLAINS?!!

WHAT THE--?! #5, published in March 1989, revived the completed humor miniseries, extending it into an ongoing.

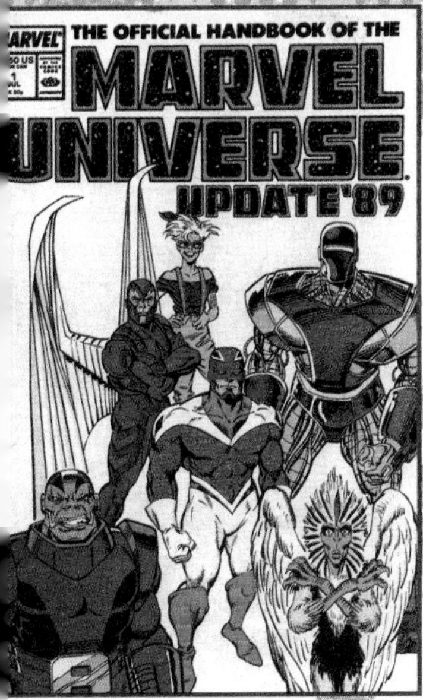
MARVEL
THE OFFICIAL HANDBOOK OF THE
MARVEL UNIVERSE
UPDATE '89

FFICIAL HANDBOOK OF THE MARVEL UNIVERSE: PDATE '89 #1, published in March 1989, began the Handbook's new miniseries.

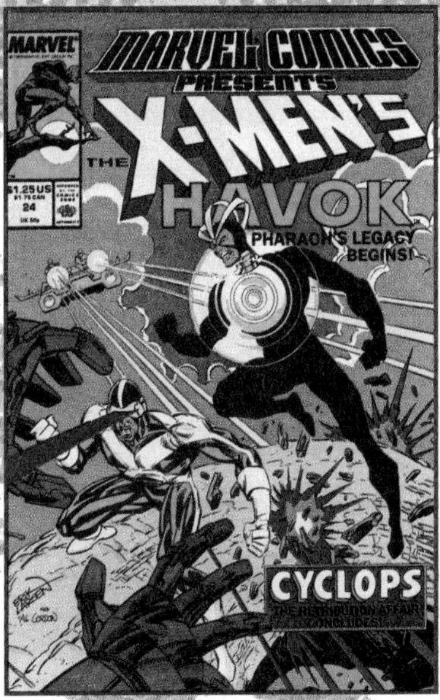
MARVEL
MARVEL COMICS PRESENTS
$1.25 US
24
THE X-MEN'S HAVOK
PHARAOH'S LEGACY BEGINS!
CYCLOPS

MARVEL COMICS PRESENTS #24, published in March 1989, began a limited serial starring Havok.

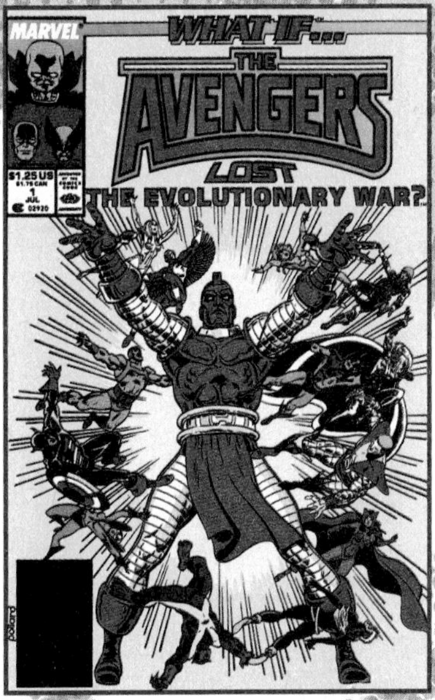
MARVEL
WHAT IF...
THE AVENGERS
LOST
THE EVOLUTIONARY WAR?
$1.25 US
1
JUL

WHAT IF? #1, published in March 1989, began the alternate-universe showcase's new ongoing series.

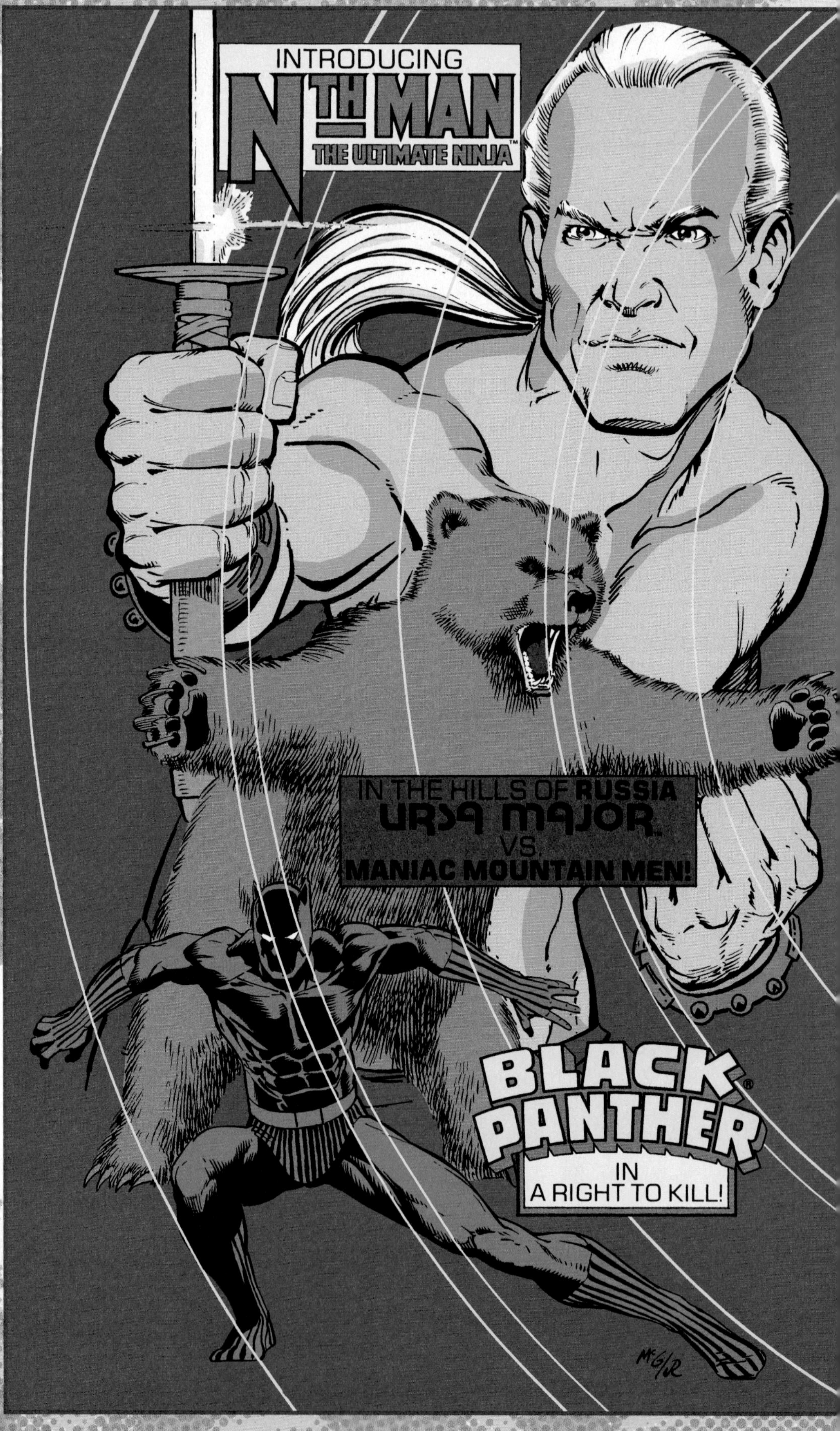
INTRODUCING
NTH MAN
THE ULTIMATE NINJA™
IN THE HILLS OF RUSSIA
URSA MAJOR™
VS.
MANIAC MOUNTAIN MEN!
BLACK PANTHER®
IN
A RIGHT TO KILL!
McG/R

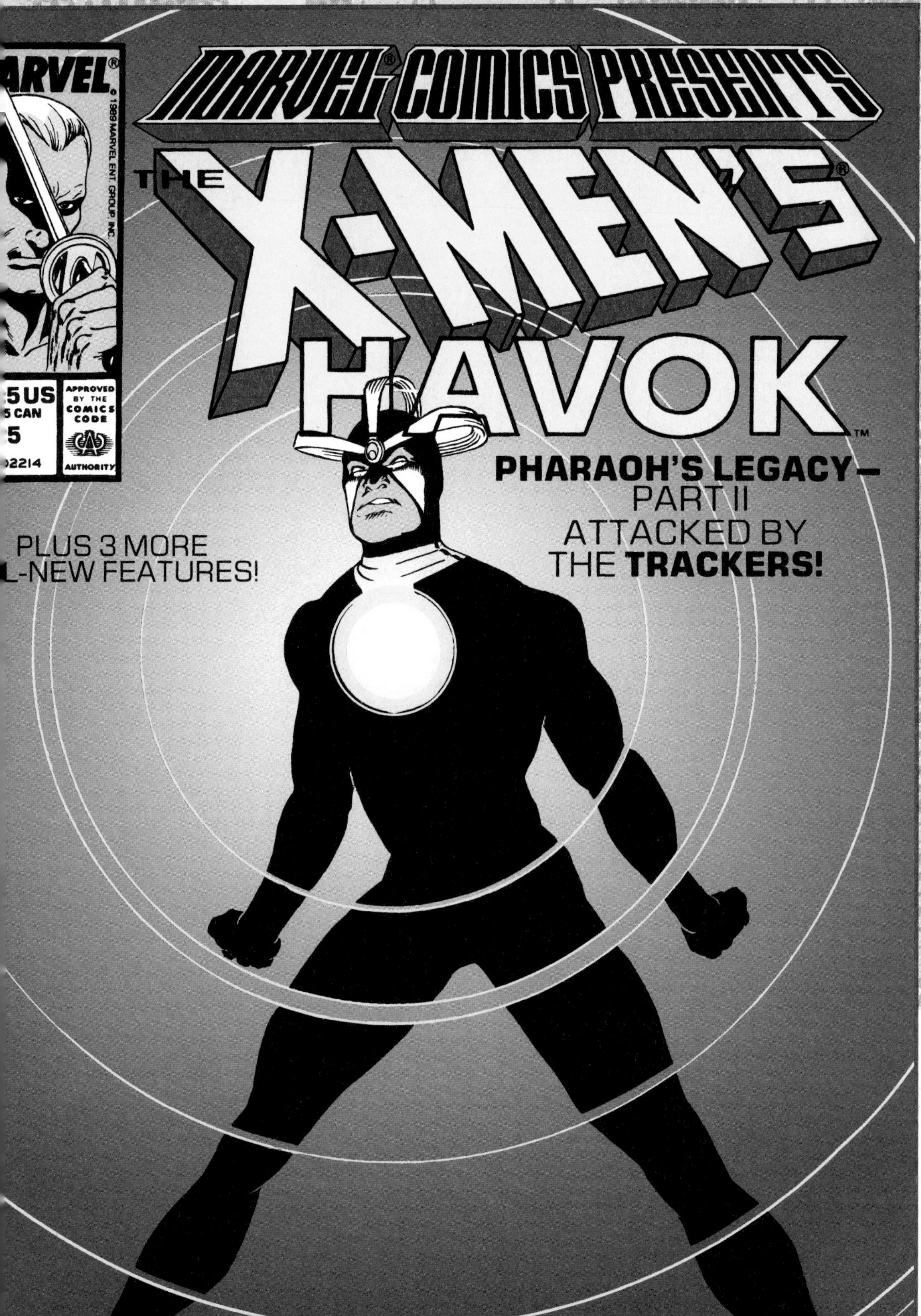
MARVEL
© 1989 MARVEL ENT. GROUP, INC.
APPROVED BY THE COMICS CODE AUTHORITY
MARVEL COMICS PRESENTS
THE X-MEN'S HAVOK
PHARAOH'S LEGACY— PART II ATTACKED BY THE TRACKERS!
PLUS 3 MORE

MARVEL COMICS PRESENTS #25, published in April 1989, introduced the ninja Nth Man; it was soon followed by an ongoing series.

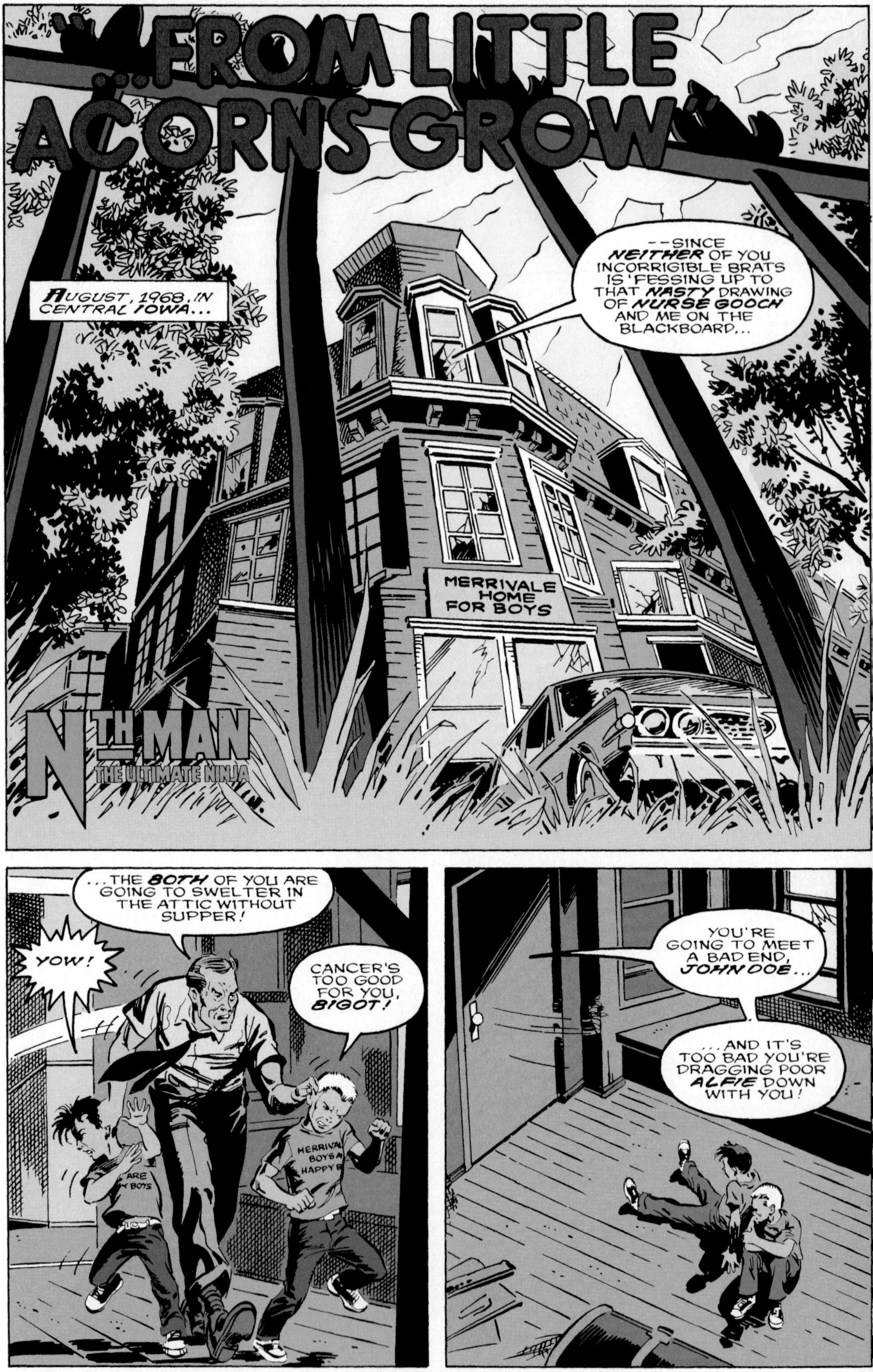
"...FROM LITTLE ACORNS GROW"
AUGUST, 1968, IN CENTRAL IOWA...
--SINCE NEITHER OF YOU INCORRIGIBLE BRATS IS 'FESSING UP TO THAT NASTY DRAWING OF NURSE GOOCH AND ME ON THE BLACKBOARD,...
MERRIVALE HOME FOR BOYS
Nth MAN
THE ULTIMATE NINJA
...THE BOTH OF YOU ARE GOING TO SWELTER IN THE ATTIC WITHOUT SUPPER!
YOW!
CANCER'S TOO GOOD FOR YOU, BIGOT!
YOU'RE GOING TO MEET A BAD END, JOHN DOE...
...AND IT'S TOO BAD YOU'RE DRAGGING POOR ALFIE DOWN WITH YOU!

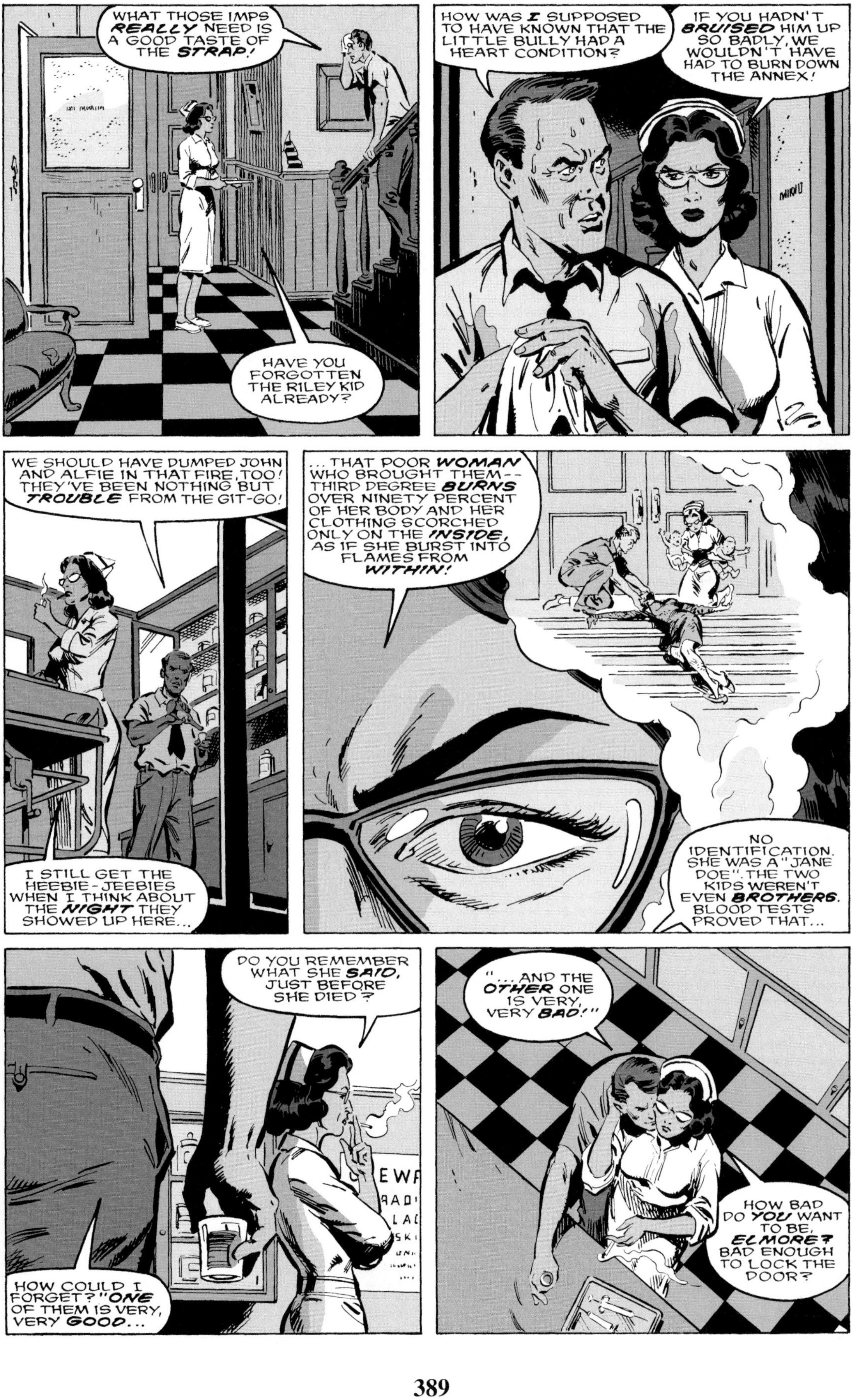

WHAT THOSE IMPS REALLY NEED IS A GOOD TASTE OF THE STRAP!
HAVE YOU FORGOTTEN THE RILEY KID ALREADY?
HOW WAS I SUPPOSED TO HAVE KNOWN THAT THE LITTLE BULLY HAD A HEART CONDITION?
IF YOU HADN'T BRUISED HIM UP SO BADLY, WE WOULDN'T HAVE HAD TO BURN DOWN THE ANNEX!
WE SHOULD HAVE DUMPED JOHN AND ALFIE IN THAT FIRE, TOO! THEY'VE BEEN NOTHING BUT TROUBLE FROM THE GIT-GO!
I STILL GET THE HEEBIE-JEEBIES WHEN I THINK ABOUT THE NIGHT THEY SHOWED UP HERE...
...THAT POOR WOMAN WHO BROUGHT THEM--THIRD DEGREE BURNS OVER NINETY PERCENT OF HER BODY AND HER CLOTHING SCORCHED ONLY ON THE INSIDE, AS IF SHE BURST INTO FLAMES FROM WITHIN!
NO IDENTIFICATION. SHE WAS A "JANE DOE". THE TWO KIDS WEREN'T EVEN BROTHERS. BLOOD TESTS PROVED THAT...
DO YOU REMEMBER WHAT SHE SAID, JUST BEFORE SHE DIED?
HOW COULD I FORGET? "ONE OF THEM IS VERY, VERY GOOD...
"...AND THE OTHER ONE IS VERY, VERY BAD!"
HOW BAD DO YOU WANT TO BE, ELMORE? BAD ENOUGH TO LOCK THE DOOR?

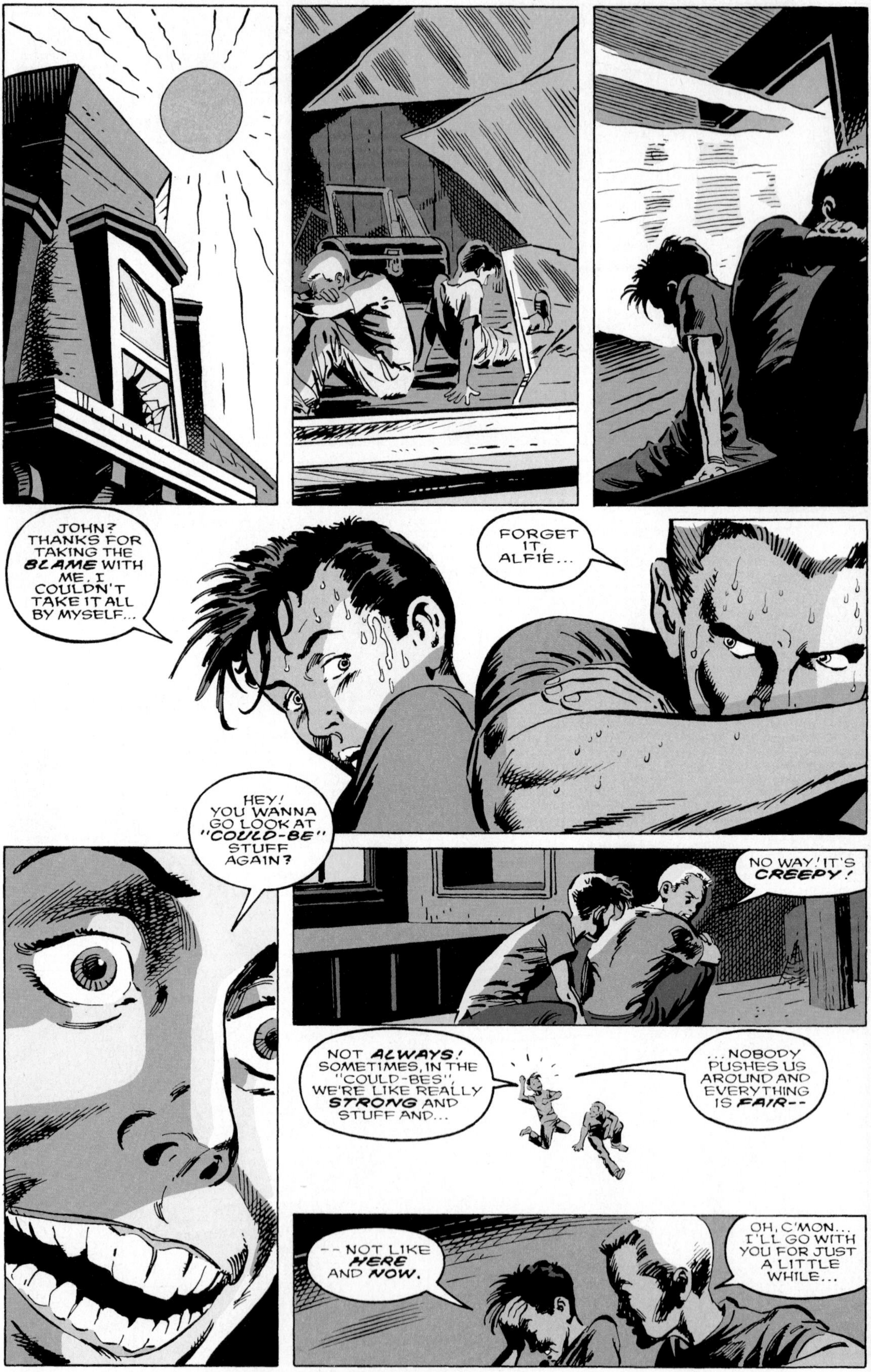

JOHN? THANKS FOR TAKING THE *BLAME* WITH ME. I COULDN'T TAKE IT ALL BY MYSELF...
FORGET IT, ALFIE...
HEY! YOU WANNA GO LOOK AT "*COULD-BE*" STUFF AGAIN?
NO WAY! IT'S *CREEPY!*
NOT *ALWAYS!* SOMETIMES, IN THE "COULD-BES", WE'RE LIKE REALLY *STRONG* AND STUFF AND...
...NOBODY PUSHES US AROUND AND EVERYTHING IS *FAIR*--
--NOT LIKE *HERE* AND *NOW*.
OH, C'MON... I'LL GO WITH YOU FOR JUST A LITTLE WHILE...

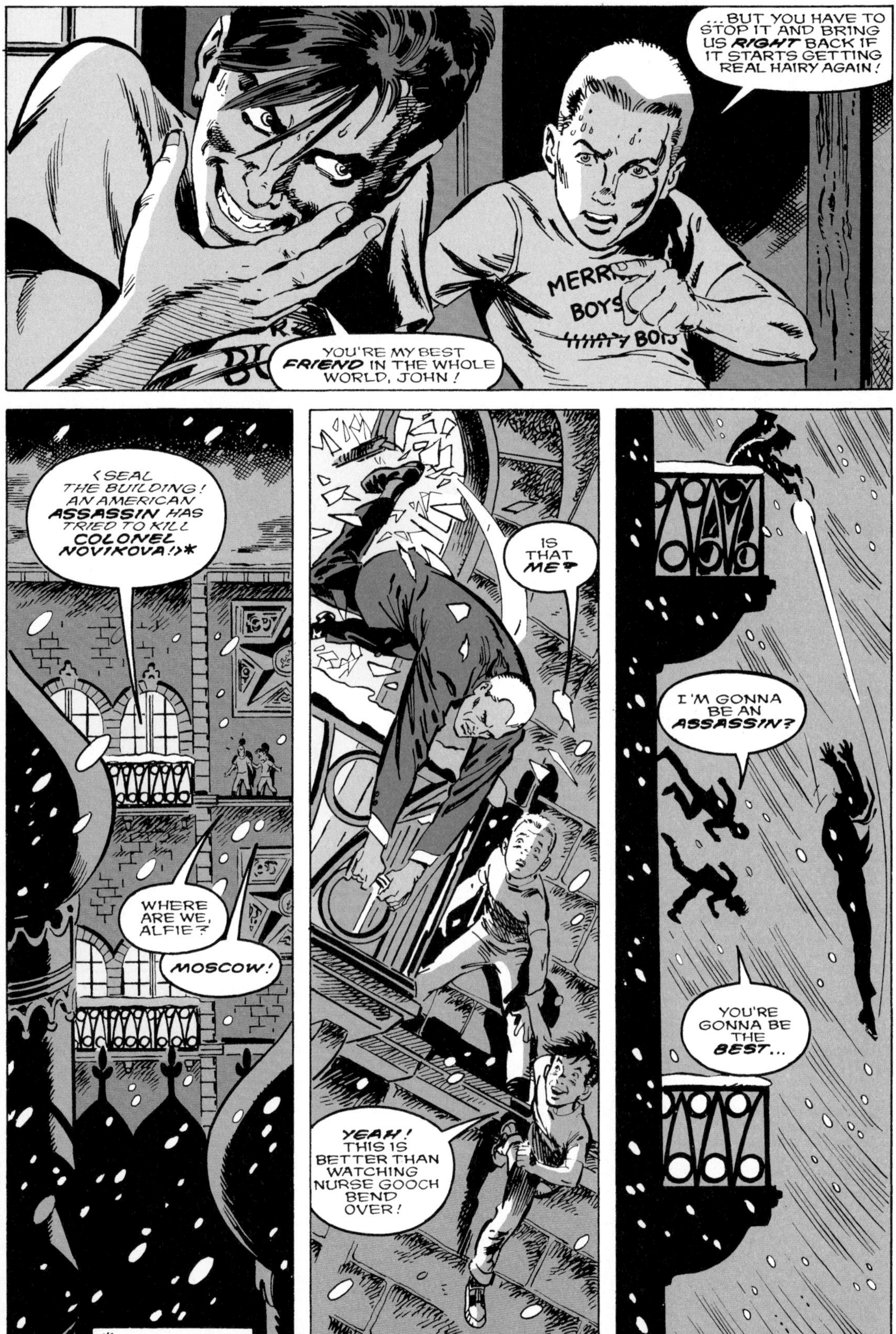
...BUT YOU HAVE TO STOP IT AND BRING US RIGHT BACK IF IT STARTS GETTING REAL HAIRY AGAIN!
YOU'RE MY BEST FRIEND IN THE WHOLE WORLD, JOHN!
MERRY BOYS
<SEAL THE BUILDING! AN AMERICAN ASSASSIN HAS TRIED TO KILL COLONEL NOVIKOVA!>*
WHERE ARE WE, ALFIE?
MOSCOW!
*TRANSLATED FROM THE RUSSIAN-- TERRY.
IS THAT ME?
YEAH! THIS IS BETTER THAN WATCHING NURSE GOOCH BEND OVER!
I'M GONNA BE AN ASSASSIN?
YOU'RE GONNA BE THE BEST...

"...THE *C.I.A.*'S HEAVY HITTER, NUMERO *UNO*--

"-- THE BLUE-EYED BOY OF COVERT OPERATIONS...

"...THE *BADDEST* BUTT-KICKER ON THE *BLOCK!*"

AIN'T THIS THE *COOLEST?!*

THEY'RE PASSING RIGHT *THROUGH* US!

THEY CAN'T *SEE* US EITHER...

"...HERE, WE'RE THE *PAST* OF A *COULD-BE!* THAT'S LESS THAN *NOTHING!*"

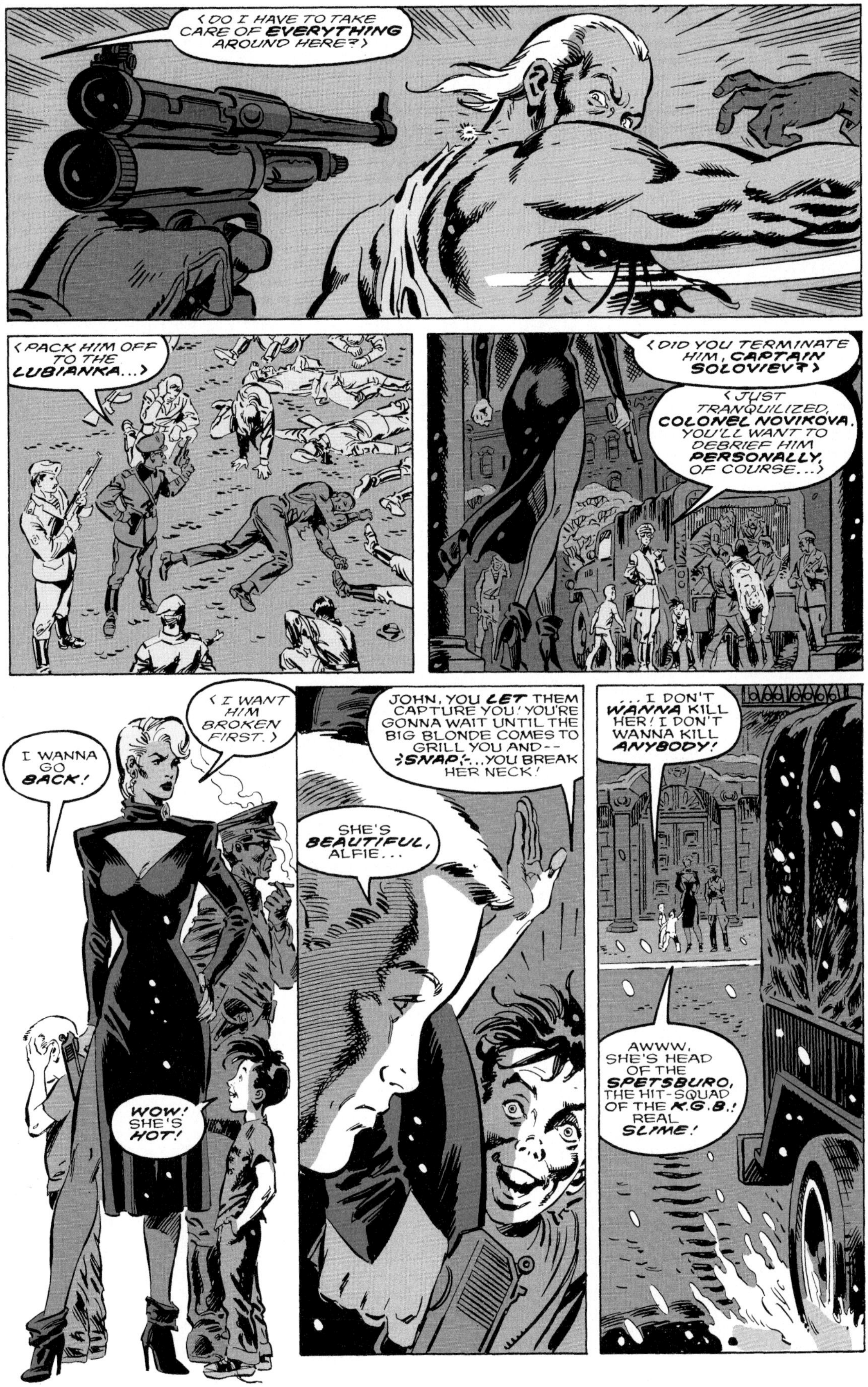
‹ DO I HAVE TO TAKE CARE OF **EVERYTHING** AROUND HERE? ›
‹ PACK HIM OFF TO THE **LUBIANKA**... ›
‹ DID YOU TERMINATE HIM, **CAPTAIN SOLOVIEV?** ›
‹ JUST TRANQUILIZED, **COLONEL NOVIKOVA**. YOU'LL WANT TO DEBRIEF HIM **PERSONALLY**, OF COURSE... ›
‹ I WANT HIM BROKEN FIRST. ›
I WANNA GO **BACK!**
WOW! SHE'S **HOT!**
JOHN, YOU **LET** THEM CAPTURE YOU! YOU'RE GONNA WAIT UNTIL THE BIG BLONDE COMES TO GRILL YOU AND-- **-:SNAP:-** ...YOU BREAK HER NECK!
SHE'S **BEAUTIFUL,** ALFIE...
...I DON'T **WANNA** KILL HER! I DON'T WANNA KILL **ANYBODY!**
AWWW, SHE'S HEAD OF THE **SPETSBURO,** THE HIT-SQUAD OF THE **K.G.B.!** REAL **SLIME!**

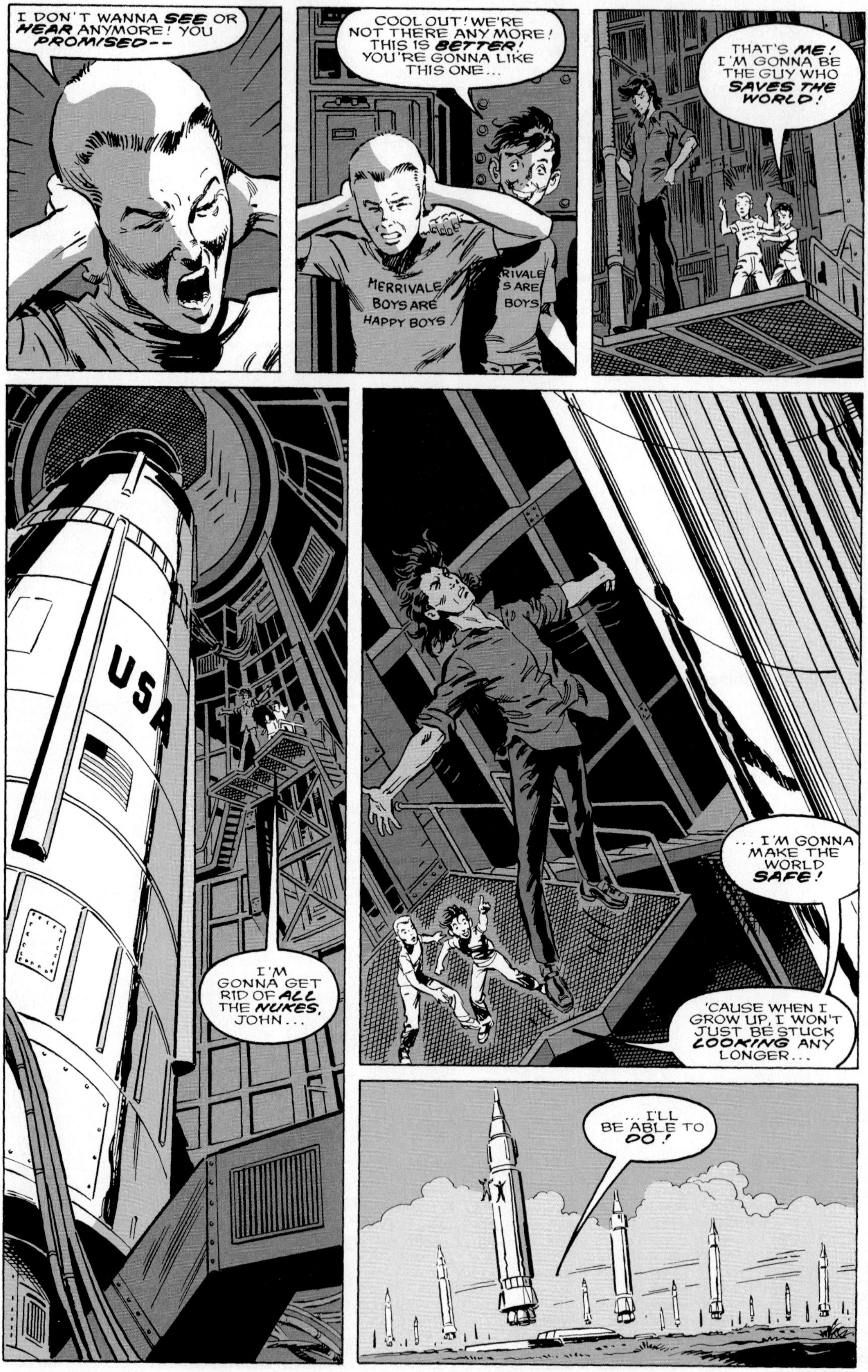

I DON'T WANNA SEE OR HEAR ANYMORE! YOU PROMISED--
COOL OUT! WE'RE NOT THERE ANY MORE! THIS IS BETTER! YOU'RE GONNA LIKE THIS ONE...
MERRIVALE BOYS ARE HAPPY BOYS
RRIVALE S ARE BOYS
THAT'S ME! I'M GONNA BE THE GUY WHO SAVES THE WORLD!
USA
I'M GONNA GET RID OF ALL THE NUKES, JOHN...
...I'M GONNA MAKE THE WORLD SAFE!
'CAUSE WHEN I GROW UP, I WON'T JUST BE STUCK LOOKING ANY LONGER...
...I'LL BE ABLE TO DO!

...I'LL HAVE THE *POWER*!

WAKE UP, ALFIE!

YOU REMEMBER THE *O'MEAGANS*?

THEIR PAPERWORK FINALLY CAME THROUGH...

...YOU'VE BEEN *ADOPTED*!

'REMEMBER THIS, JOHN...

MERRIVAL BOYS ARE HAPPY B

...NICE THINGS HAPPEN TO *GOOD* BOYS!

YOU MADE THE *RIGHT* CHOICE, FOLKS...

"...ALFIE'S A BOY WITH A LOT OF *POTENTIAL!*"

THE END...BUT THE *NTH MAN* STARS IN HIS OWN COMIC BOOK, ON SALE... NEXT WEEK.

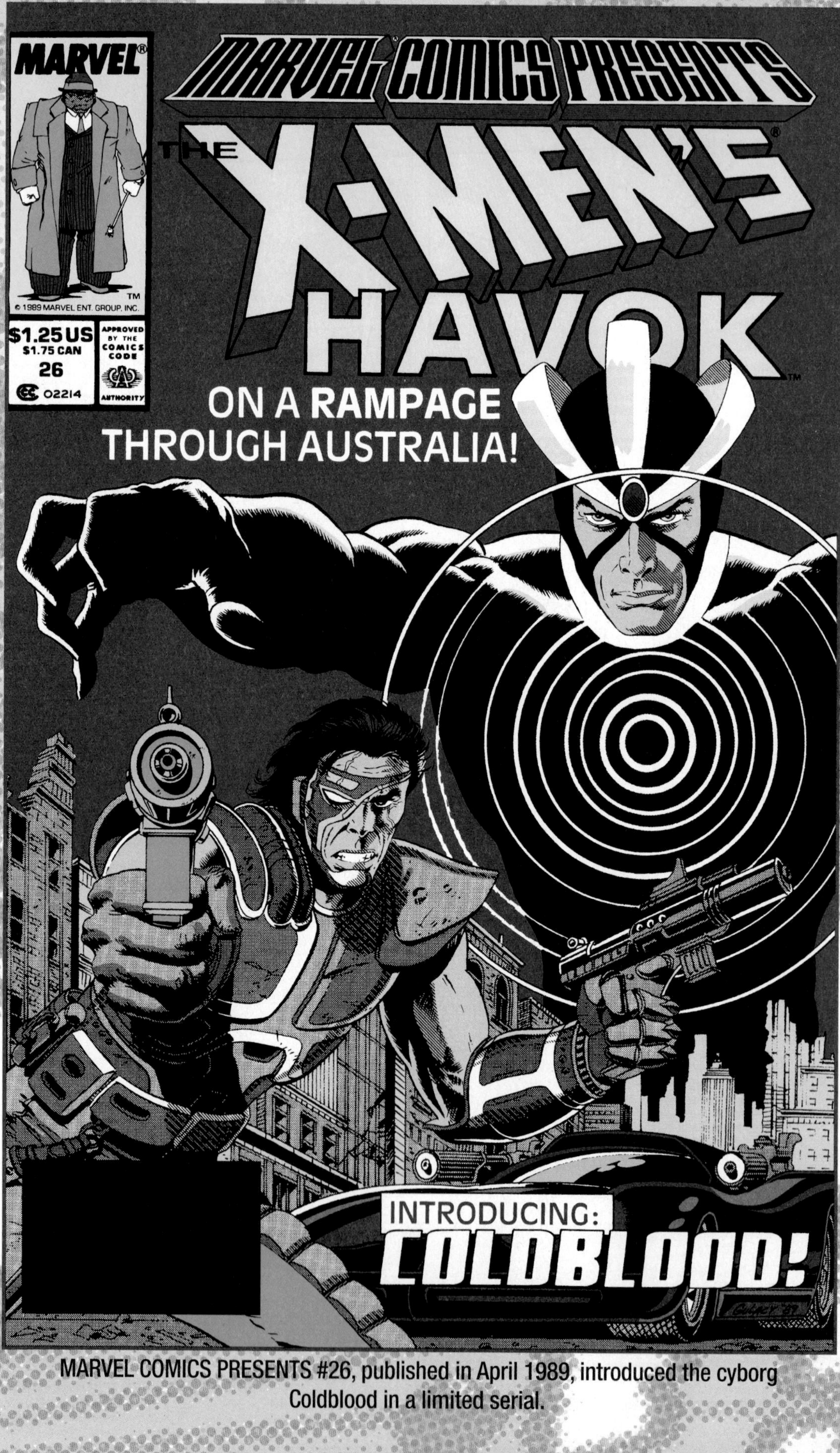
MARVEL
© 1989 MARVEL ENT. GROUP, INC.
$1.25 US
$1.75 CAN
26
02214
APPROVED BY THE COMICS CODE AUTHORITY
MARVEL COMICS PRESENTS
THE X-MEN'S
HAVOK
ON A RAMPAGE THROUGH AUSTRALIA!
INTRODUCING:
COLDBLOOD!

MARVEL COMICS PRESENTS #26, published in April 1989, introduced the cyborg Coldblood in a limited serial.

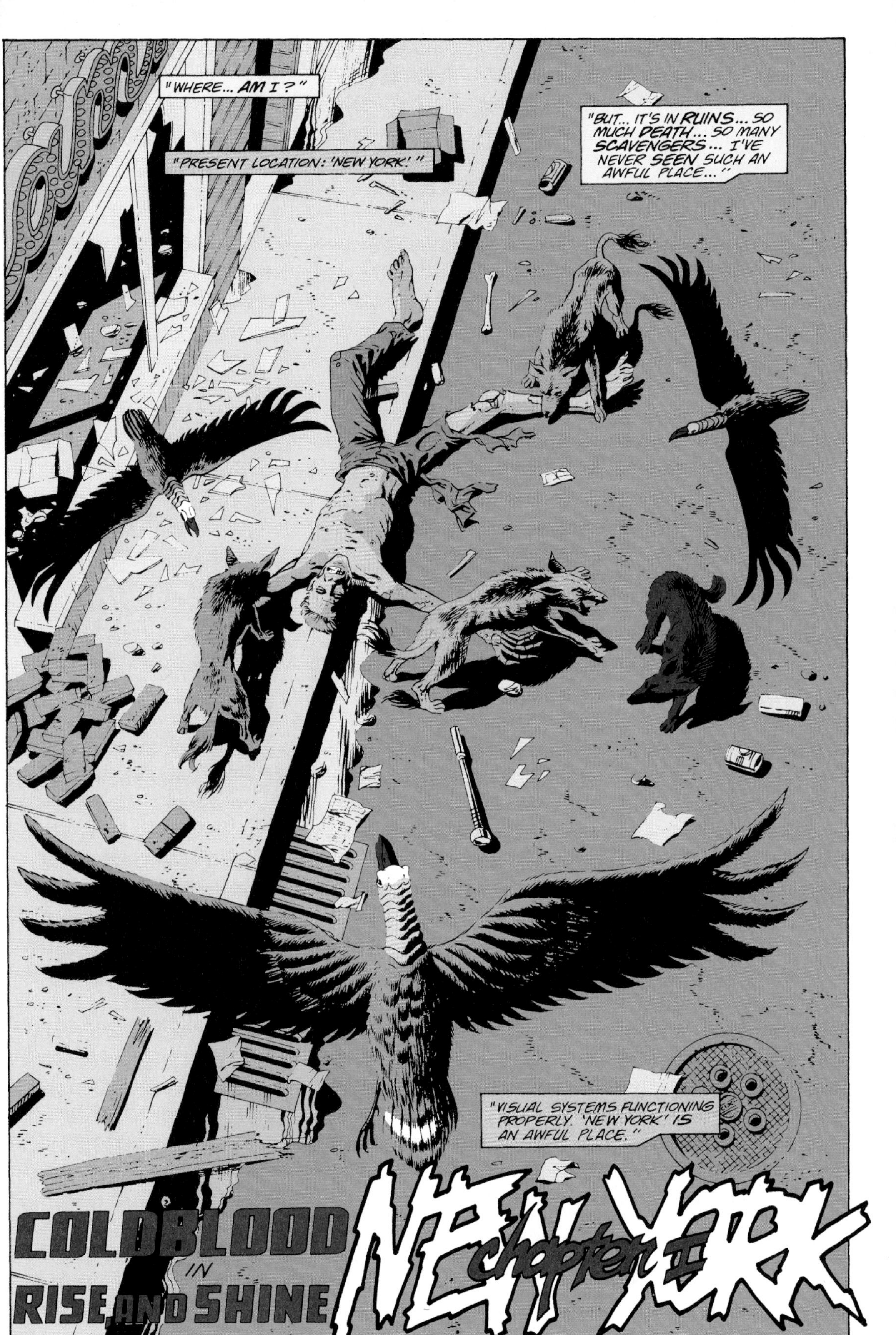
"WHERE... AM I?"
"PRESENT LOCATION: 'NEW YORK.'"
"BUT... IT'S IN RUINS... SO MUCH DEATH... SO MANY SCAVENGERS... I'VE NEVER SEEN SUCH AN AWFUL PLACE..."
"VISUAL SYSTEMS FUNCTIONING PROPERLY. 'NEW YORK' IS AN AWFUL PLACE."
COLDBLOOD IN RISE AND SHINE
NEW YORK chapter I

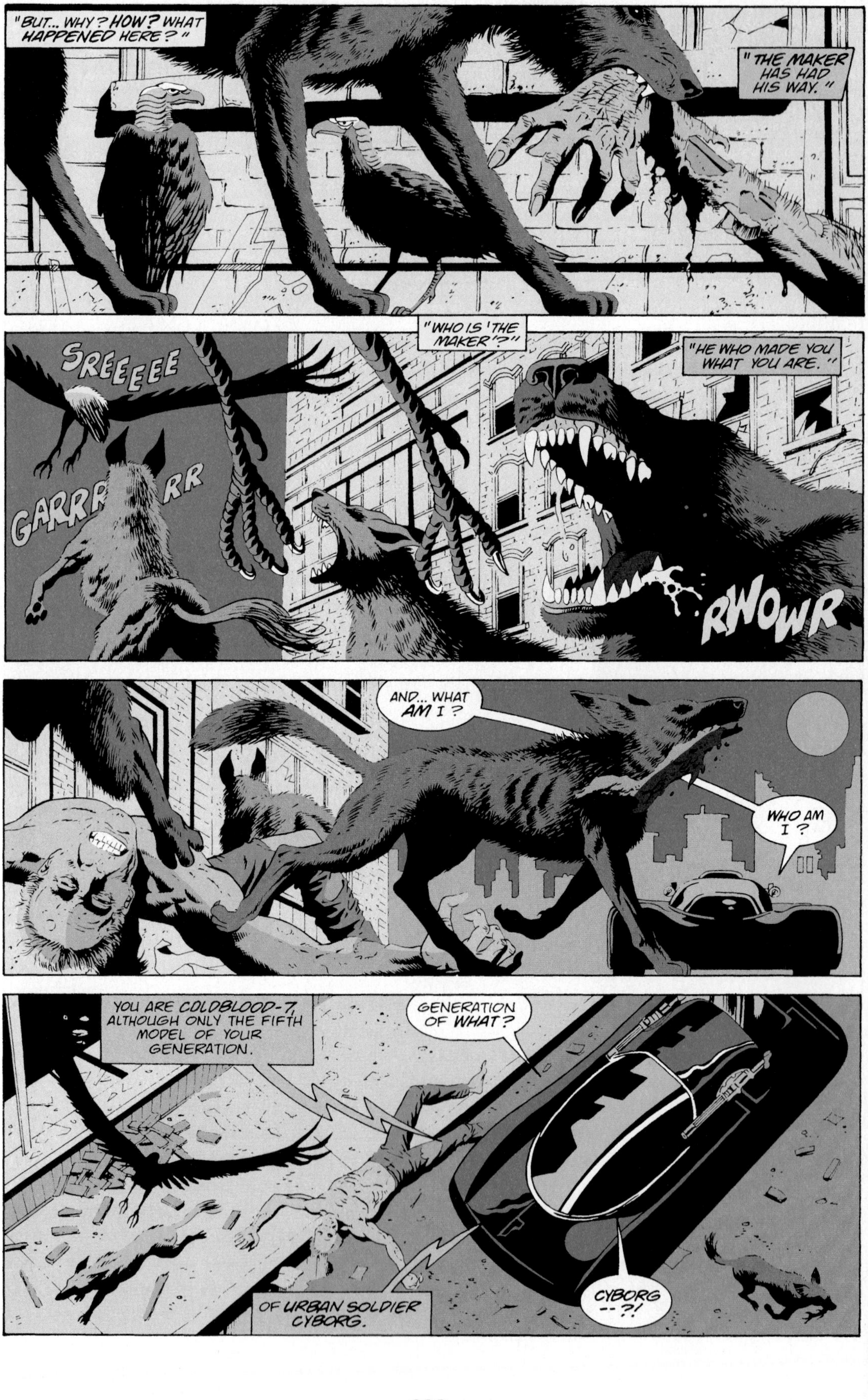
"BUT... WHY? HOW? WHAT HAPPENED HERE?"
"THE MAKER HAS HAD HIS WAY."
SREEEEEE
GARRRRRR
"WHO IS 'THE MAKER'?"
"HE WHO MADE YOU WHAT YOU ARE."
RWOWR
AND... WHAT AM I?
WHO AM I?
YOU ARE COLDBLOOD-7, ALTHOUGH ONLY THE FIFTH MODEL OF YOUR GENERATION.
GENERATION OF WHAT?
OF URBAN SOLDIER CYBORG.
CYBORG --?!

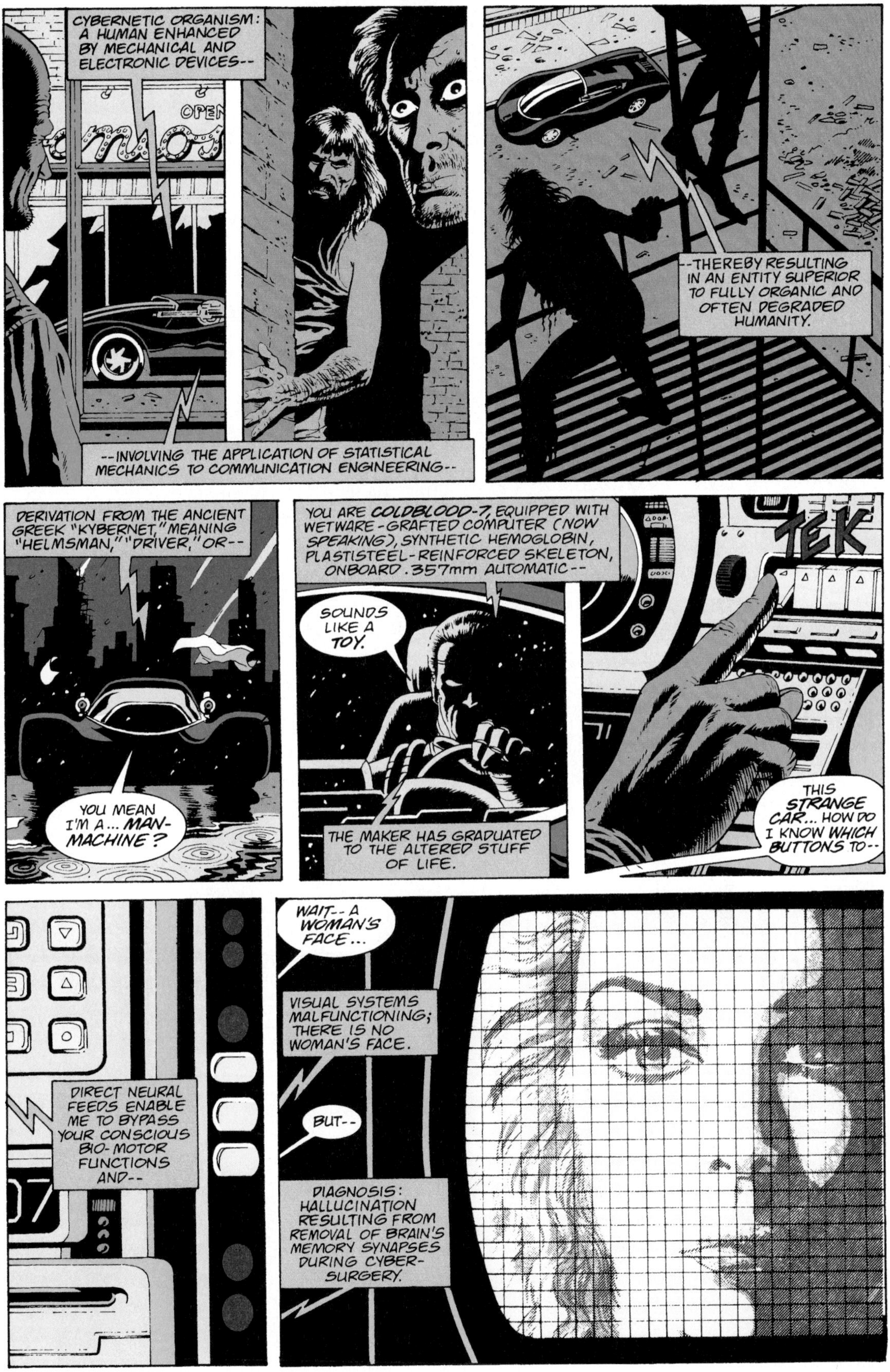
CYBERNETIC ORGANISM: A HUMAN ENHANCED BY MECHANICAL AND ELECTRONIC DEVICES--
OPEN
--INVOLVING THE APPLICATION OF STATISTICAL MECHANICS TO COMMUNICATION ENGINEERING--
--THEREBY RESULTING IN AN ENTITY SUPERIOR TO FULLY ORGANIC AND OFTEN DEGRADED HUMANITY.
DERIVATION FROM THE ANCIENT GREEK "KYBERNET," MEANING "HELMSMAN," "DRIVER," OR--
YOU MEAN I'M A... MAN-MACHINE?
YOU ARE COLDBLOOD-7, EQUIPPED WITH WETWARE-GRAFTED COMPUTER (NOW SPEAKING), SYNTHETIC HEMOGLOBIN, PLASTISTEEL-REINFORCED SKELETON, ONBOARD .357mm AUTOMATIC--
SOUNDS LIKE A TOY.
THE MAKER HAS GRADUATED TO THE ALTERED STUFF OF LIFE.
TEK
THIS STRANGE CAR... HOW DO I KNOW WHICH BUTTONS TO--
DIRECT NEURAL FEEDS ENABLE ME TO BYPASS YOUR CONSCIOUS BIO-MOTOR FUNCTIONS AND--
WAIT-- A WOMAN'S FACE...
VISUAL SYSTEMS MALFUNCTIONING; THERE IS NO WOMAN'S FACE.
BUT--
DIAGNOSIS: HALLUCINATION RESULTING FROM REMOVAL OF BRAIN'S MEMORY SYNAPSES DURING CYBER-SURGERY.

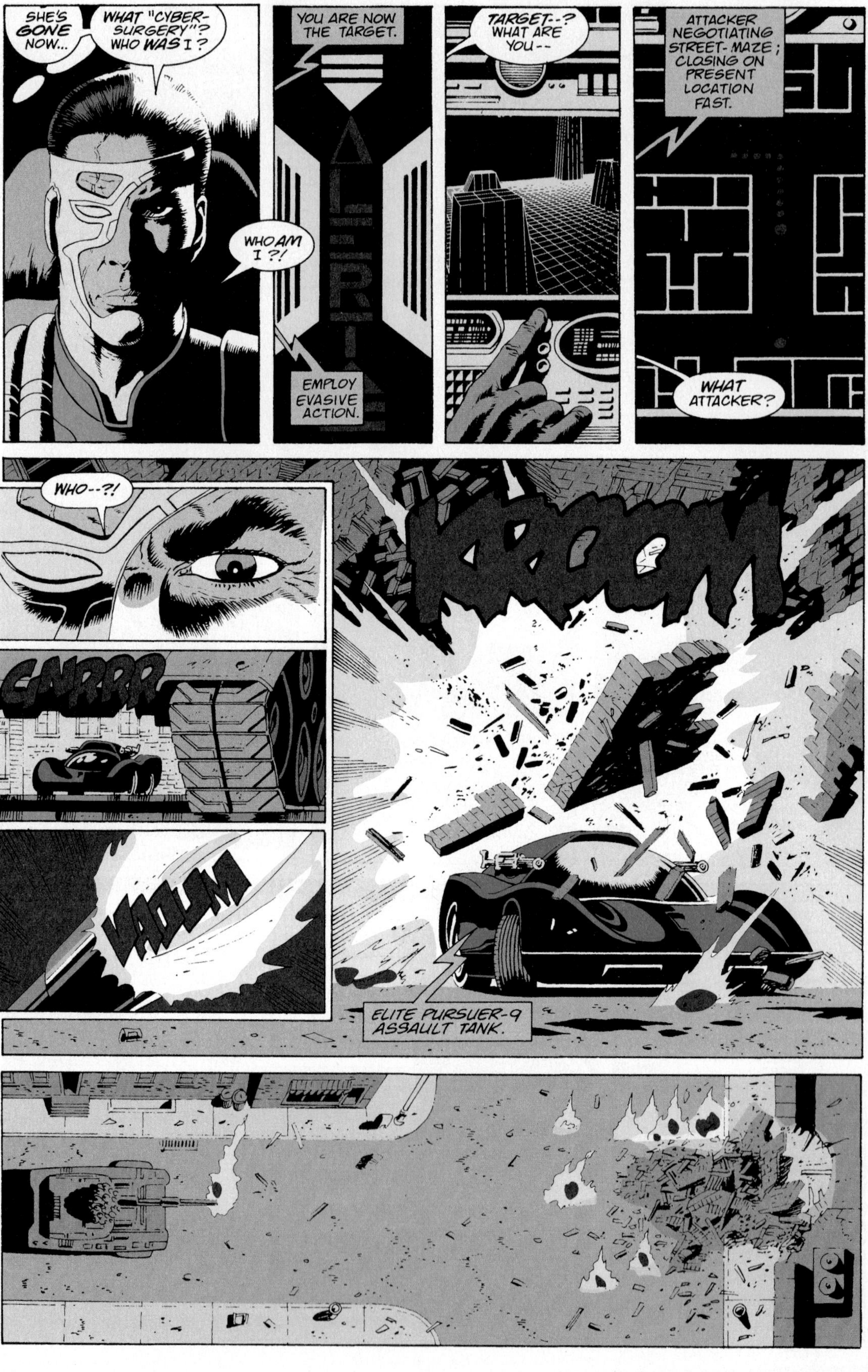
SHE'S GONE NOW...
WHAT "CYBER-SURGERY"? WHO WAS I?
WHO AM I?!
YOU ARE NOW THE TARGET.
ALERT
EMPLOY EVASIVE ACTION.
TARGET--? WHAT ARE YOU--
ATTACKER NEGOTIATING STREET-MAZE; CLOSING ON PRESENT LOCATION FAST.
WHAT ATTACKER?
WHO--?!
GNRRR
VROOM
KROOM
ELITE PURSUER-9 ASSAULT TANK.

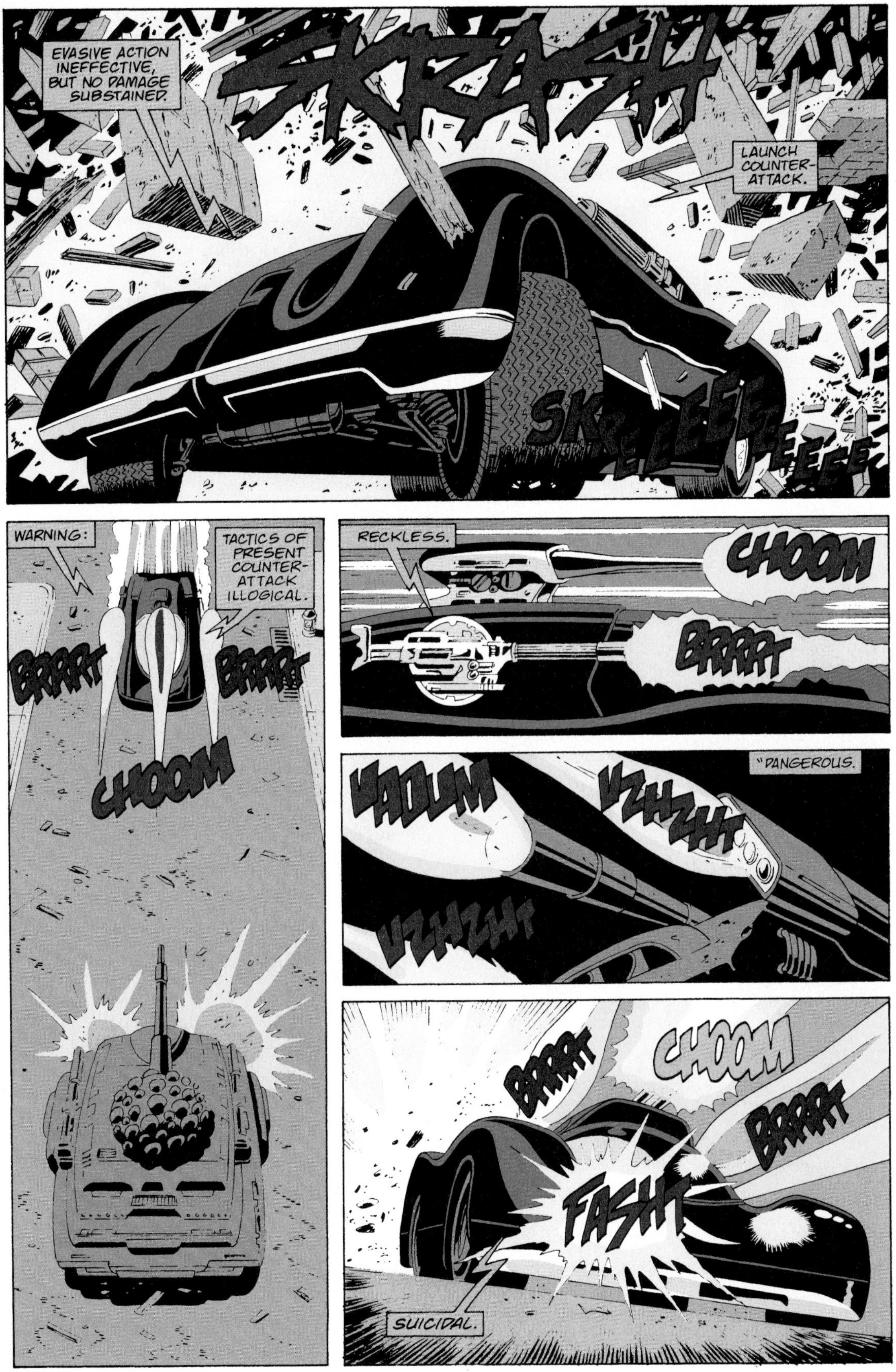
EVASIVE ACTION INEFFECTIVE, BUT NO DAMAGE SUBSTAINED.
SKRASH
LAUNCH COUNTER-ATTACK.
SKREEEEEEEEEEE
WARNING:
TACTICS OF PRESENT COUNTER-ATTACK ILLOGICAL.
BRRRRT
BRRRRT
CHOOM
RECKLESS.
CHOOM
BRRRRT
"DANGEROUS.
VADUM
VZHZHT
VZHZHT
BRRRRT
CHOOM
BRRRRT
FASHT
SUICIDAL.

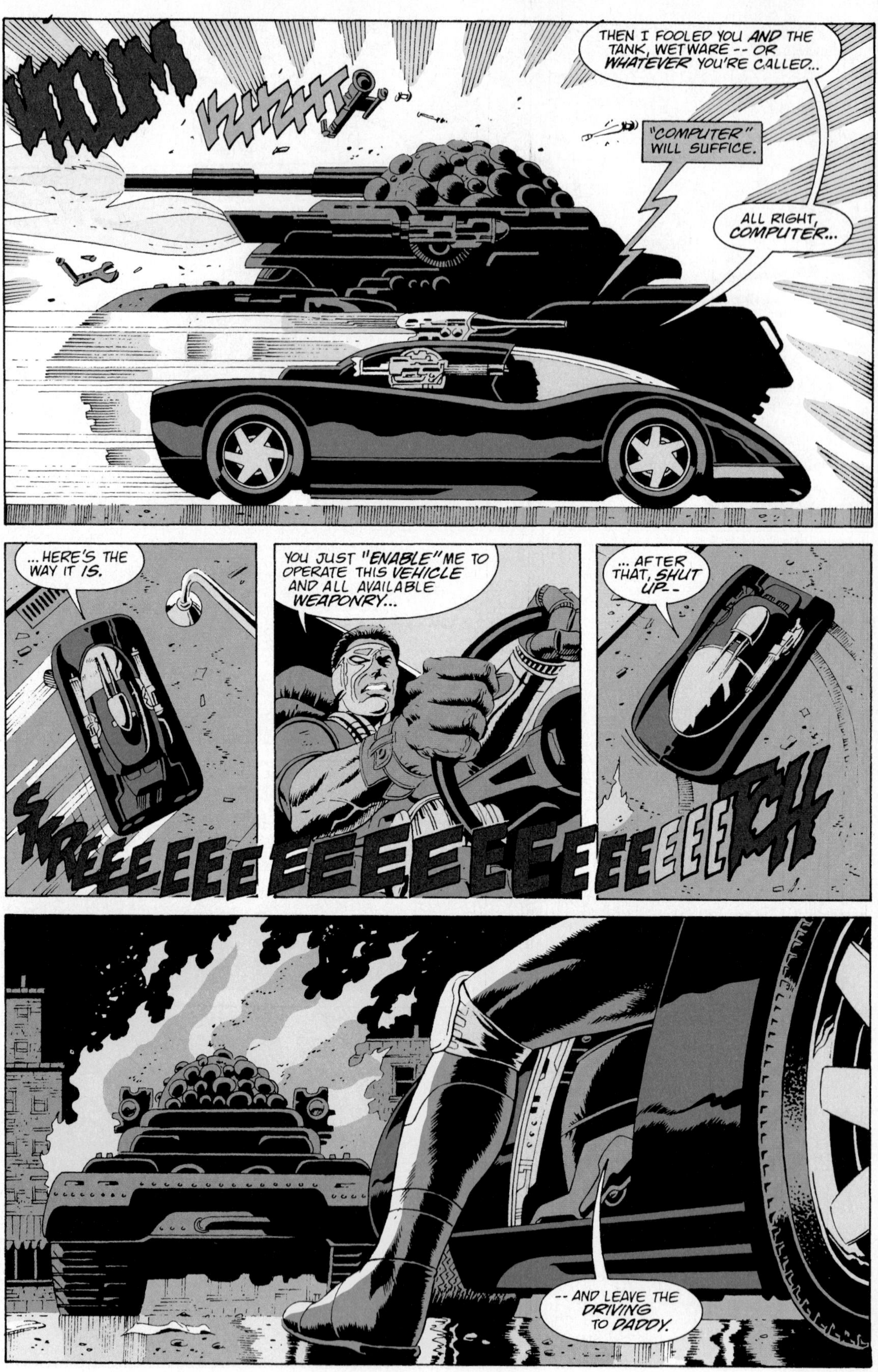
VOOM
VZZHT
THEN I FOOLED YOU AND THE TANK, WETWARE -- OR WHATEVER YOU'RE CALLED...
"COMPUTER" WILL SUFFICE.
ALL RIGHT, COMPUTER...
...HERE'S THE WAY IT IS.
YOU JUST "ENABLE" ME TO OPERATE THIS VEHICLE AND ALL AVAILABLE WEAPONRY...
...AFTER THAT, SHUT UP--
SKREEEEEEEEEEEEEEEEEEEEEEETCH
--AND LEAVE THE DRIVING TO DADDY.

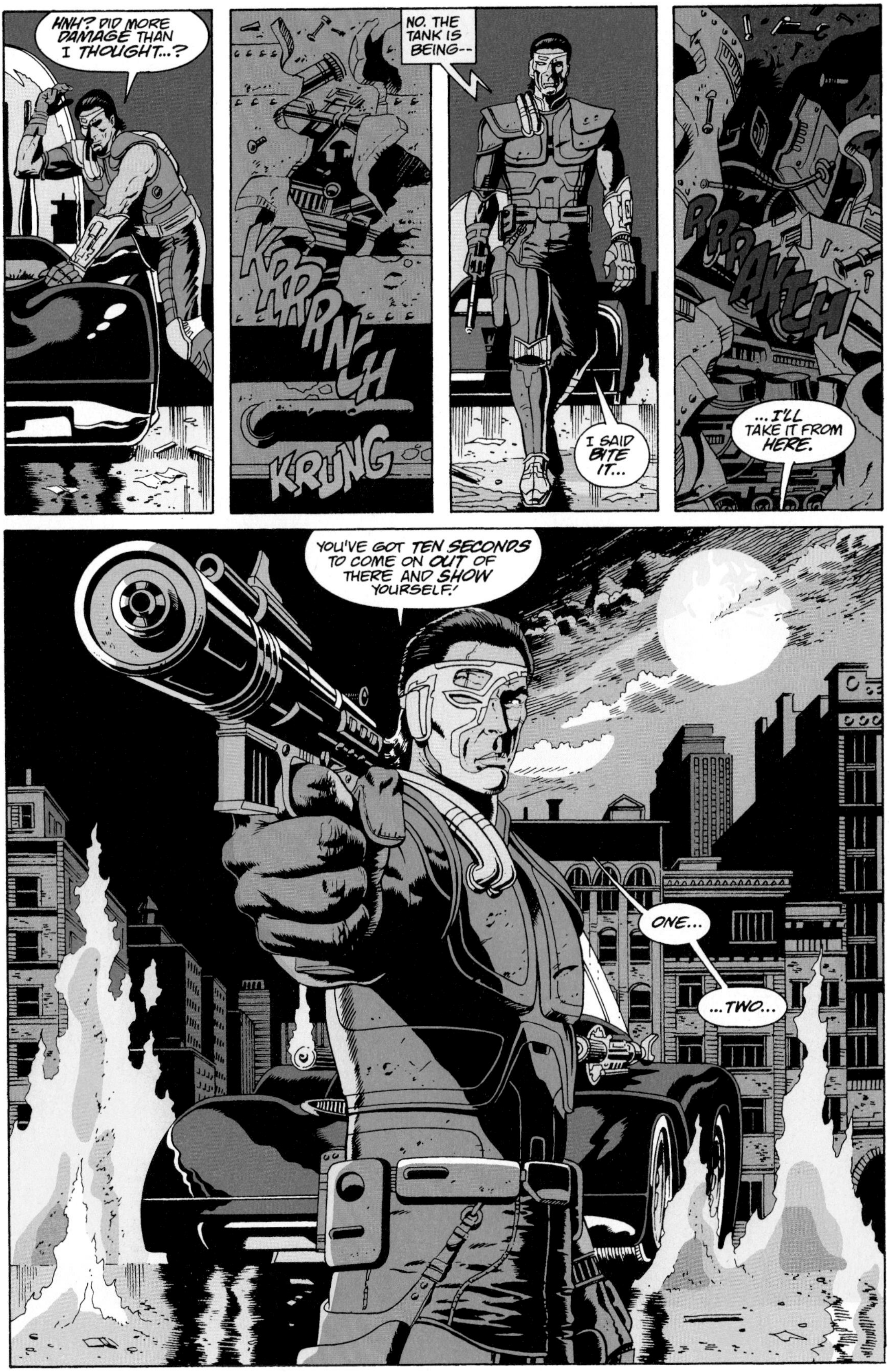
HNH? DID MORE DAMAGE THAN I THOUGHT...?
NO. THE TANK IS BEING--
KRRRNCH
KRUNG
I SAID BITE IT...
RRRAKKCH
...I'LL TAKE IT FROM HERE.
YOU'VE GOT TEN SECONDS TO COME ON OUT OF THERE AND SHOW YOURSELF!
ONE...
...TWO...

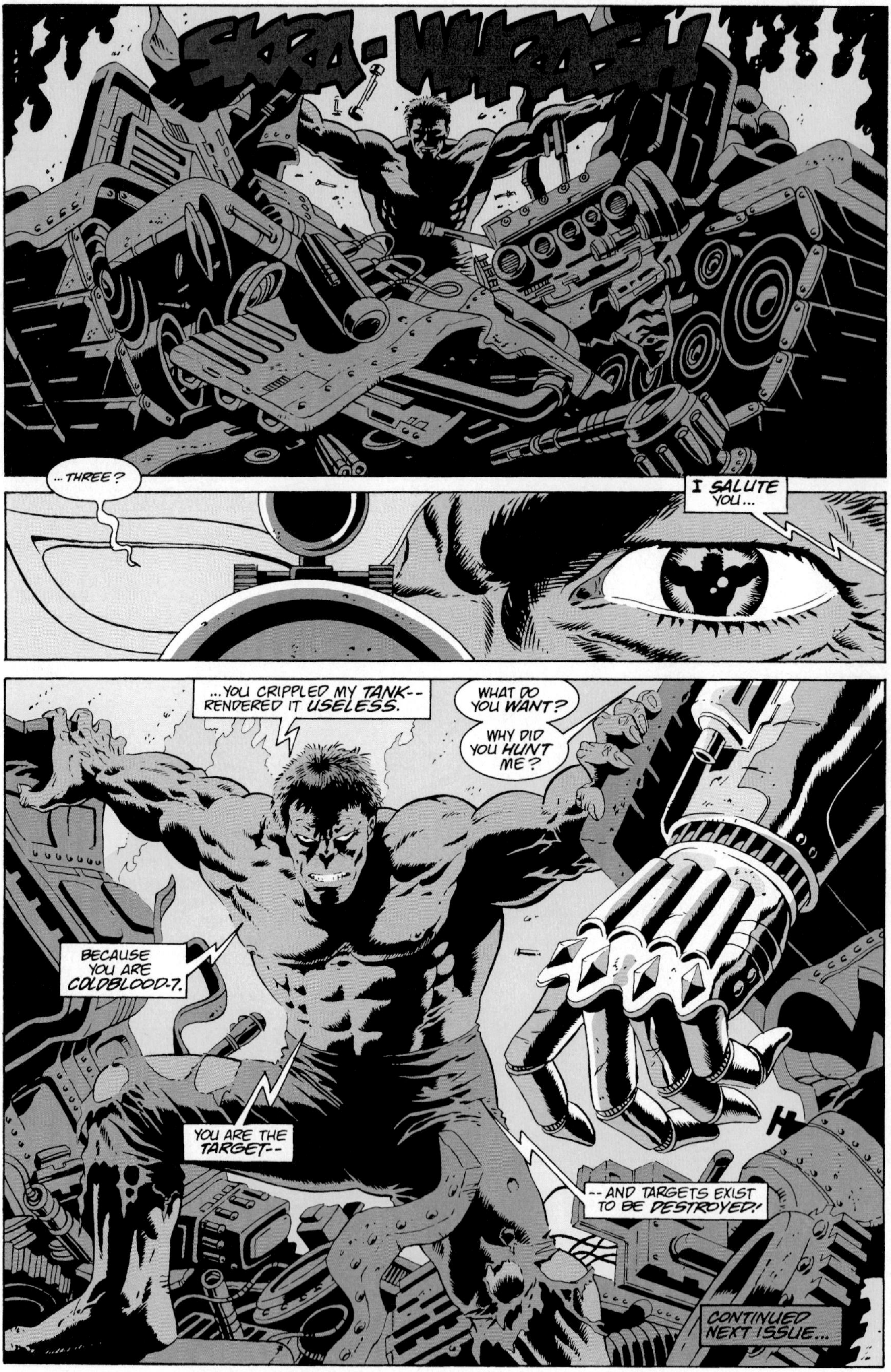
SKRA-WHRASH
...THREE?
I SALUTE YOU...
...YOU CRIPPLED MY TANK-- RENDERED IT USELESS.
WHAT DO YOU WANT?
WHY DID YOU HUNT ME?
BECAUSE YOU ARE COLDBLOOD-7.
YOU ARE THE TARGET--
--AND TARGETS EXIST TO BE DESTROYED!
CONTINUED NEXT ISSUE...

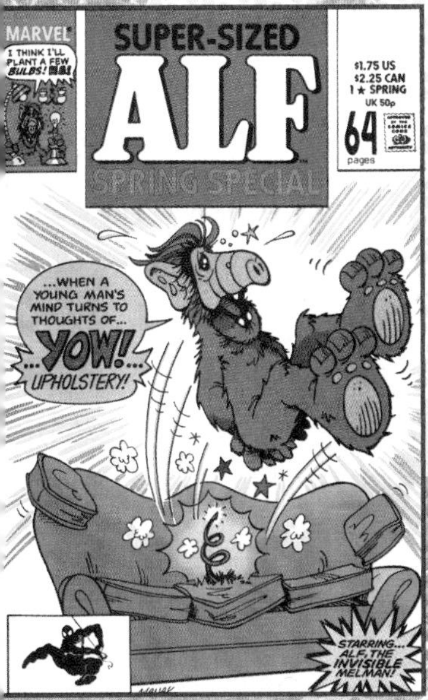
MARVEL
I THINK I'LL PLANT A FEW BULBS!
SUPER-SIZED
ALF
SPRING SPECIAL
$1.75 US
$2.25 CAN
1★ SPRING
UK 50p
64 pages
...WHEN A YOUNG MAN'S MIND TURNS TO THOUGHTS OF... ...YOW!... ...UPHOLSTERY!
STARRING... ALF, THE INVISIBLE MELMAN!

ALF SPRING SPECIAL, published in March 1989, was a humor one-shot.

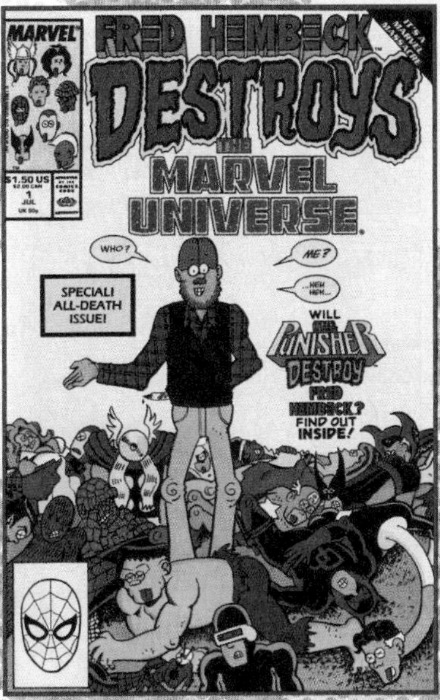
MARVEL
FRED HEMBECK
DESTROYS
THE
MARVEL UNIVERSE
$1.50 US
1
JUL
WHO?
ME?
...HEH HEH...
SPECIAL! ALL-DEATH ISSUE!
WILL THE PUNISHER DESTROY FRED HEMBECK? FIND OUT INSIDE!

FRED HEMBECK DESTROYS THE MARVEL UNIVERSE, published in March 1989, was a humor one-shot.

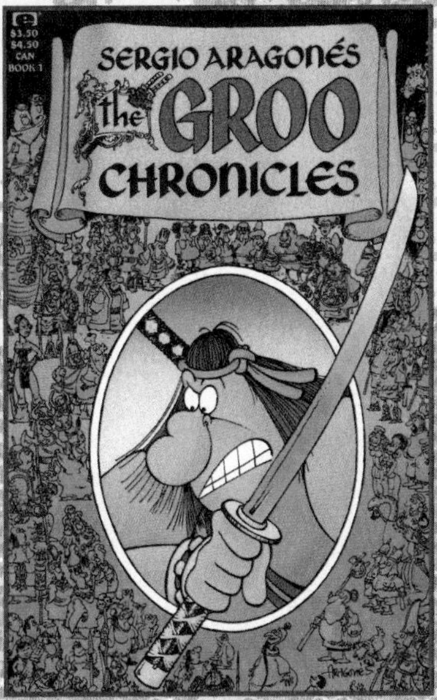
$3.50
$4.50
CAN
BOOK 1
SERGIO ARAGONÉS
the GROO
CHRONICLES

GROO CHRONICLES #1, published in March 1989, began a short Epic reprint series.

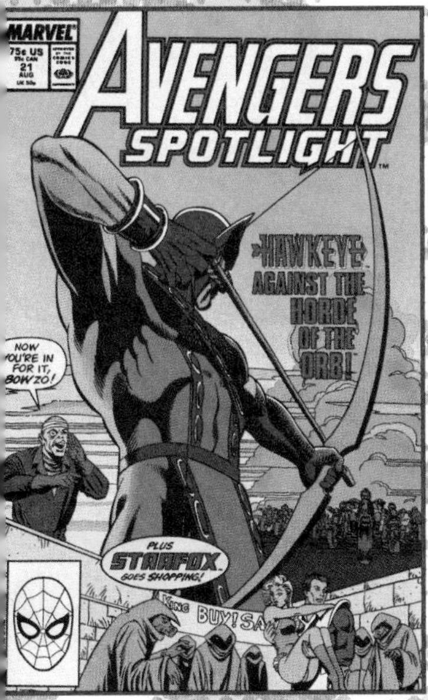
MARVEL
75¢ US
21
AUG
AVENGERS
SPOTLIGHT
HAWKEYE AGAINST THE HORDE OF THE ORB!
NOW YOU'RE IN FOR IT, BOWZO!
PLUS STARFOX GOES SHOPPING!

Solo Avengers changed its title to AVENGERS SPOTLIGHT with #21, published in April 1989.

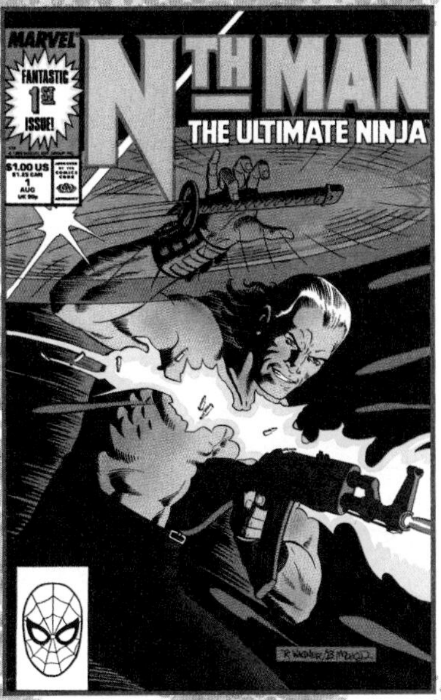
MARVEL
FANTASTIC 1ST ISSUE!
NTH MAN
THE ULTIMATE NINJA
$1.00 US
1
AUG

NTH MAN, THE ULTIMATE NINJA #1, published in April 1989, began the enigmatic ninja's ongoing series.

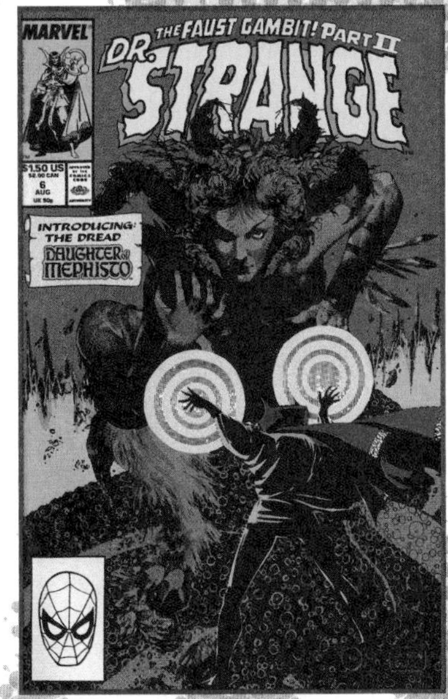
MARVEL
THE FAUST GAMBIT! PART II
DR. STRANGE
$1.50 US
6
AUG
INTRODUCING: THE DREAD DAUGHTER OF MEPHISTO

DR. STRANGE, SORCERER SUPREME #6, published in April 1989, began an ongoing Book of the Vishanti backup serial.

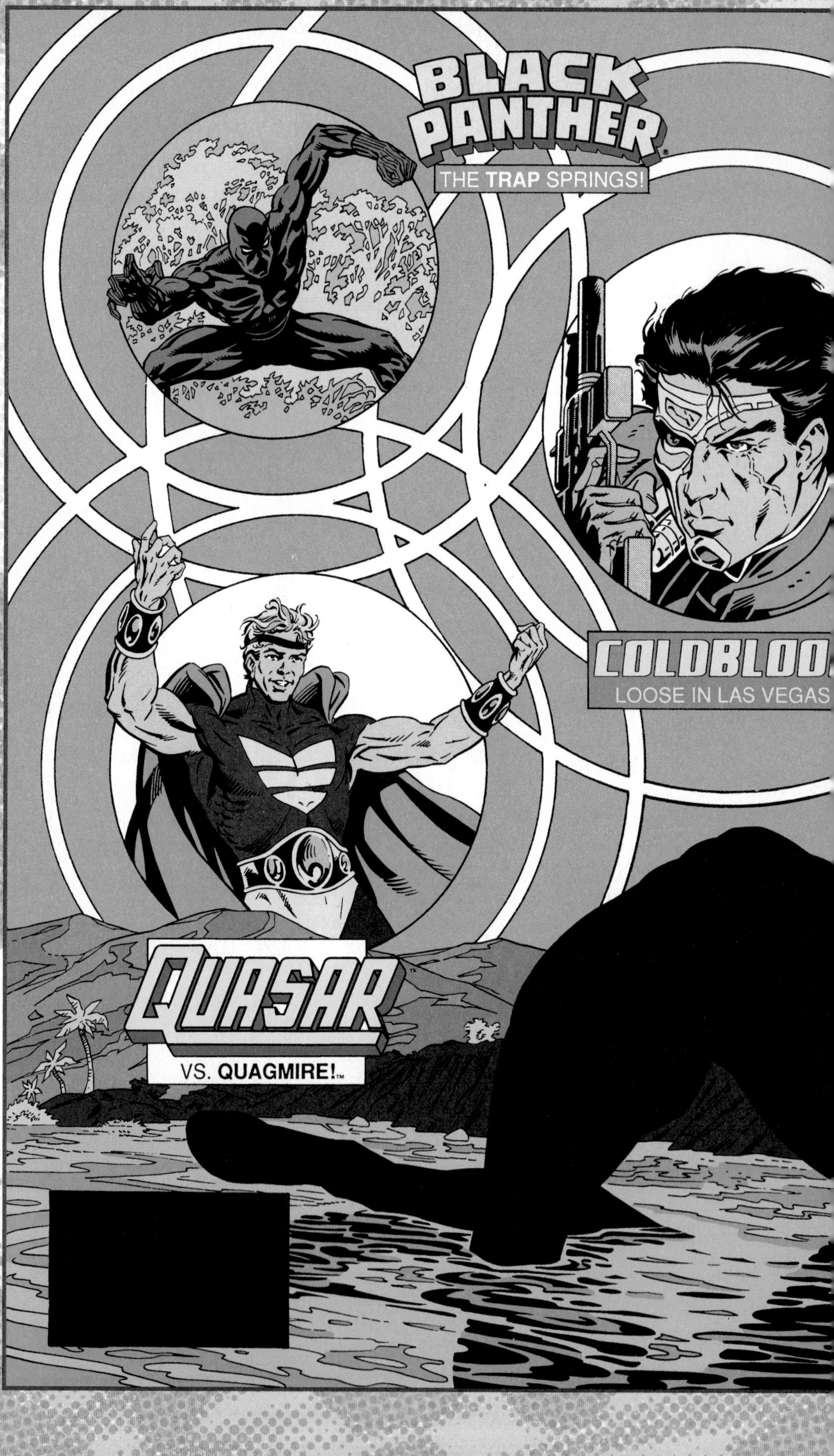
BLACK PANTHER
THE TRAP SPRINGS!
COLDBLOO
LOOSE IN LAS VEGAS
QUASAR
VS. QUAGMIRE!™

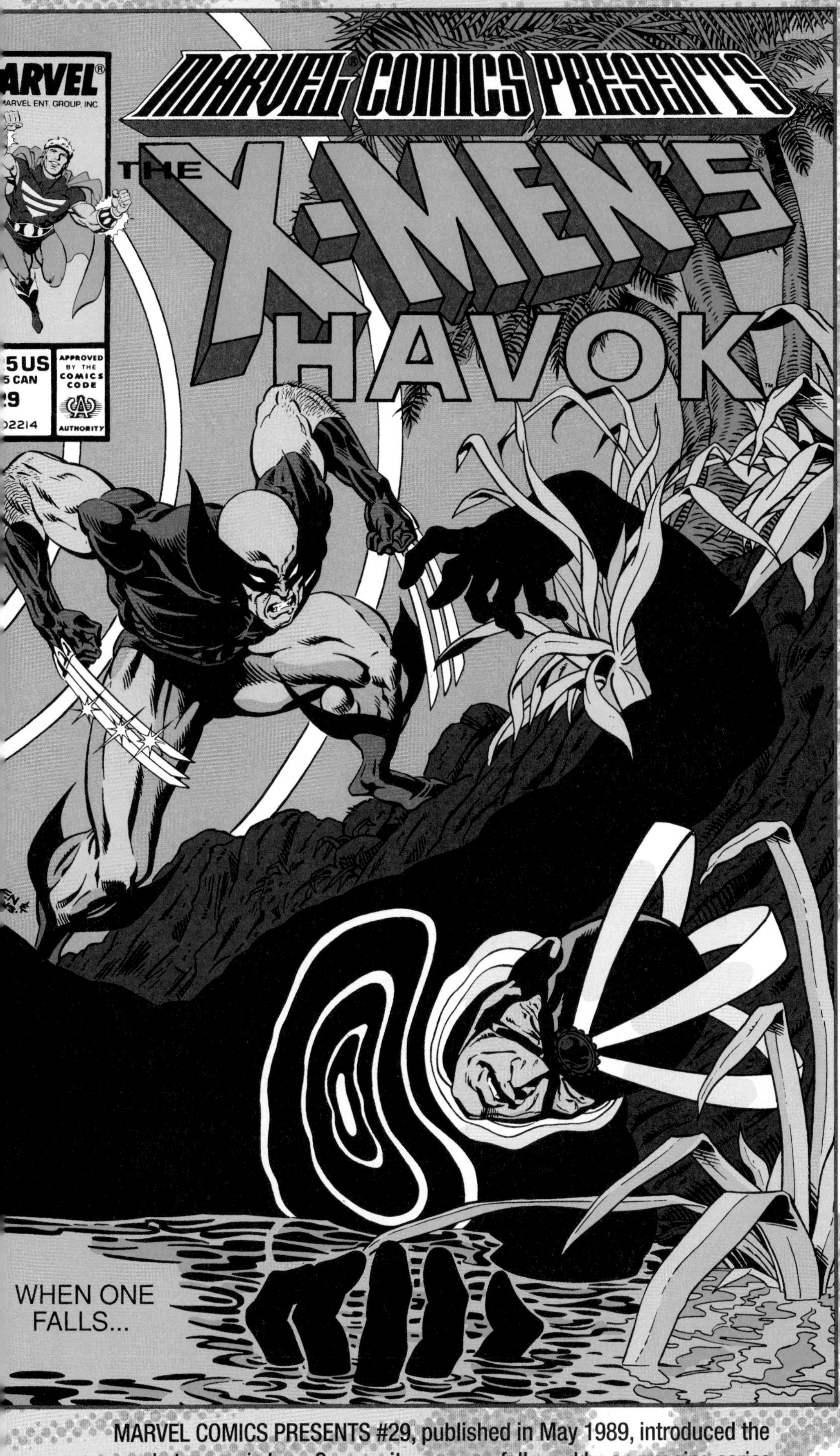
MARVEL COMICS PRESENTS
MARVEL ENT. GROUP, INC.
THE X-MEN'S
HAVOK
APPROVED BY THE COMICS CODE AUTHORITY
WHEN ONE FALLS...

MARVEL COMICS PRESENTS #29, published in May 1989, introduced the neophyte cosmic hero Quasar; it was soon followed by an ongoing series.

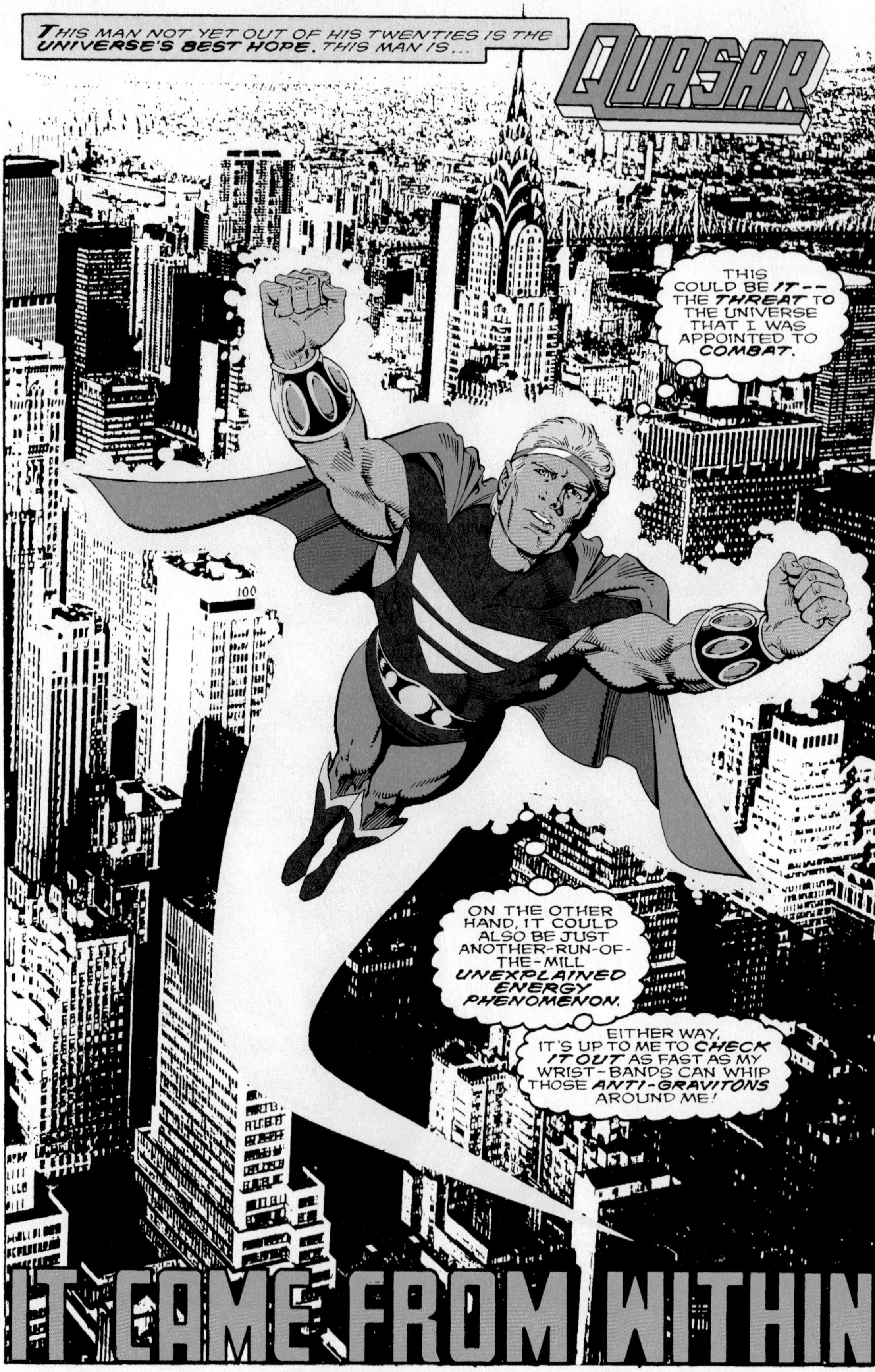
THIS MAN NOT YET OUT OF HIS TWENTIES IS THE UNIVERSE'S BEST HOPE. THIS MAN IS...
QUASAR
THIS COULD BE IT -- THE THREAT TO THE UNIVERSE THAT I WAS APPOINTED TO COMBAT.
ON THE OTHER HAND, IT COULD ALSO BE JUST ANOTHER-RUN-OF-THE-MILL UNEXPLAINED ENERGY PHENOMENON.
EITHER WAY, IT'S UP TO ME TO CHECK IT OUT AS FAST AS MY WRIST-BANDS CAN WHIP THOSE ANTI-GRAVITONS AROUND ME!
IT CAME FROM WITHIN

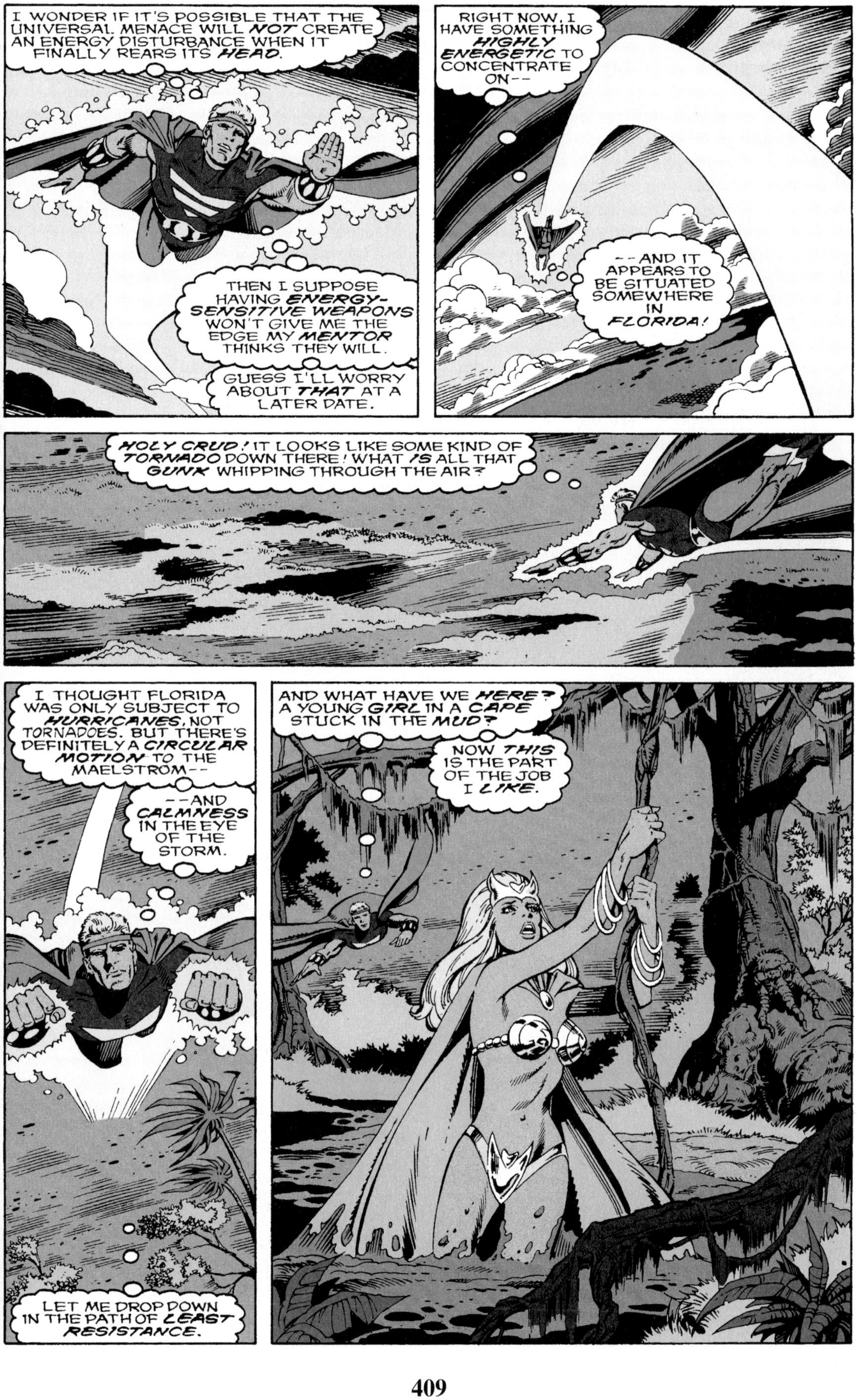
I WONDER IF IT'S POSSIBLE THAT THE UNIVERSAL MENACE WILL NOT CREATE AN ENERGY DISTURBANCE WHEN IT FINALLY REARS ITS HEAD.
THEN I SUPPOSE HAVING ENERGY-SENSITIVE WEAPONS WON'T GIVE ME THE EDGE MY MENTOR THINKS THEY WILL.
GUESS I'LL WORRY ABOUT THAT AT A LATER DATE.
RIGHT NOW, I HAVE SOMETHING HIGHLY ENERGETIC TO CONCENTRATE ON--
--AND IT APPEARS TO BE SITUATED SOMEWHERE IN FLORIDA!
HOLY CRUD! IT LOOKS LIKE SOME KIND OF TORNADO DOWN THERE! WHAT IS ALL THAT GUNK WHIPPING THROUGH THE AIR?
I THOUGHT FLORIDA WAS ONLY SUBJECT TO HURRICANES, NOT TORNADOES. BUT THERE'S DEFINITELY A CIRCULAR MOTION TO THE MAELSTROM--
--AND CALMNESS IN THE EYE OF THE STORM.
LET ME DROP DOWN IN THE PATH OF LEAST RESISTANCE.
AND WHAT HAVE WE HERE? A YOUNG GIRL IN A CAPE STUCK IN THE MUD?
NOW THIS IS THE PART OF THE JOB I LIKE.

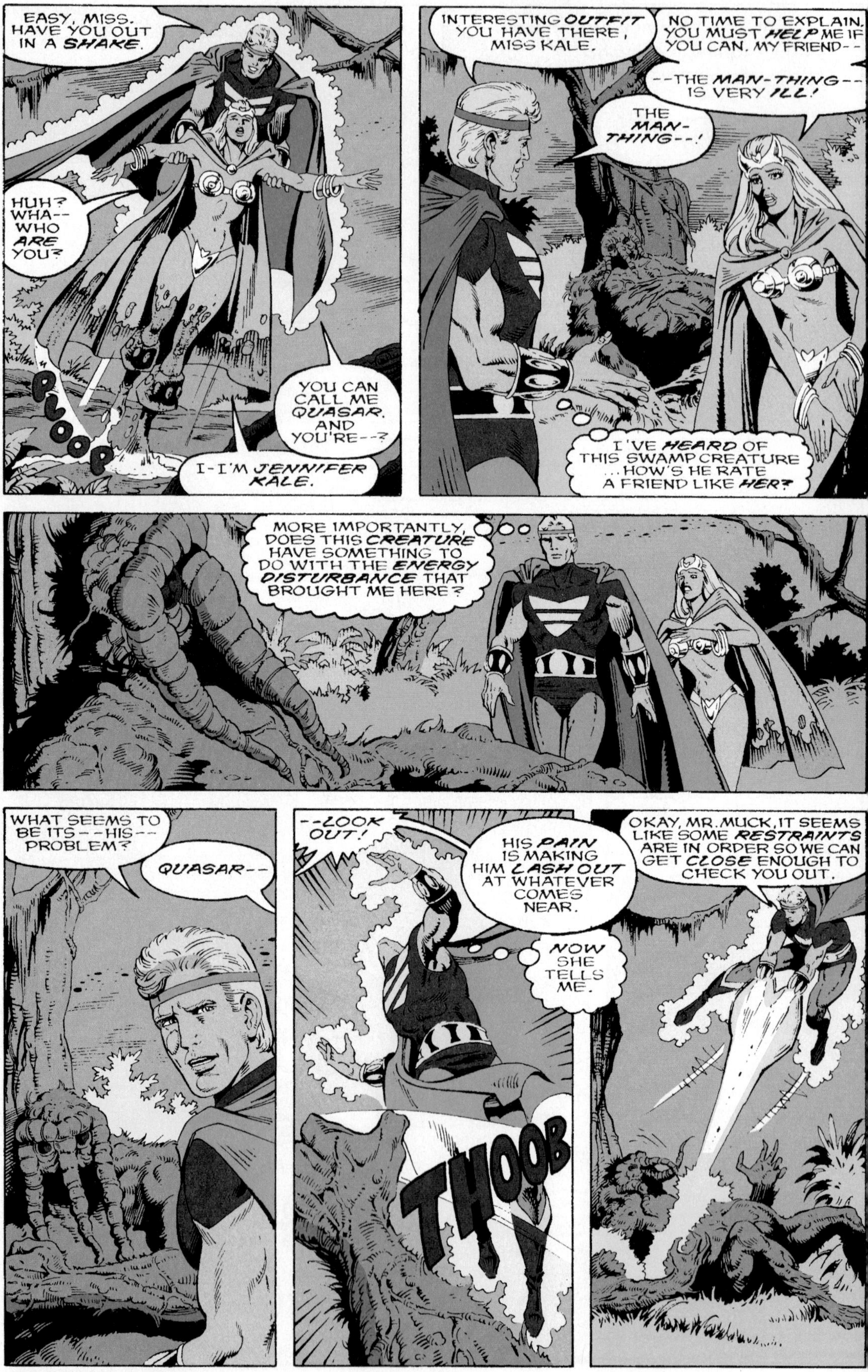
EASY, MISS. HAVE YOU OUT IN A SHAKE.
HUH? WHA-- WHO ARE YOU?
PLOOP
YOU CAN CALL ME QUASAR. AND YOU'RE--?
I-I'M JENNIFER KALE.
INTERESTING OUTFIT YOU HAVE THERE, MISS KALE.
NO TIME TO EXPLAIN. YOU MUST HELP ME IF YOU CAN. MY FRIEND--
--THE MAN-THING-- IS VERY ILL!
THE MAN-THING--!
I'VE HEARD OF THIS SWAMP CREATURE ...HOW'S HE RATE A FRIEND LIKE HER?
MORE IMPORTANTLY, DOES THIS CREATURE HAVE SOMETHING TO DO WITH THE ENERGY DISTURBANCE THAT BROUGHT ME HERE?
WHAT SEEMS TO BE ITS--HIS-- PROBLEM?
QUASAR--
--LOOK OUT!
HIS PAIN IS MAKING HIM LASH OUT AT WHATEVER COMES NEAR.
NOW SHE TELLS ME.
THOOB
OKAY, MR. MUCK, IT SEEMS LIKE SOME RESTRAINTS ARE IN ORDER SO WE CAN GET CLOSE ENOUGH TO CHECK YOU OUT.

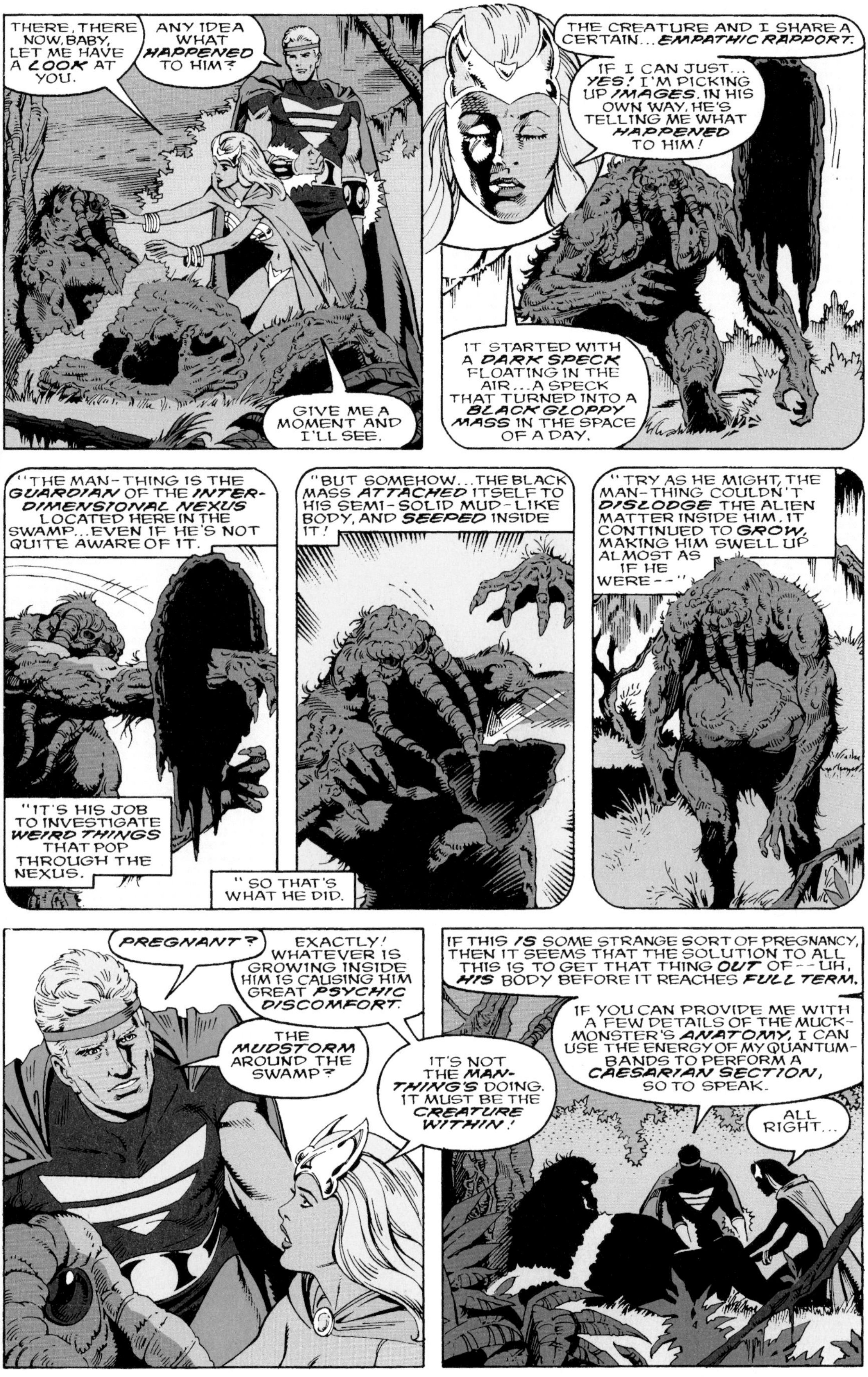
THERE, THERE NOW, BABY, LET ME HAVE A LOOK AT YOU.
ANY IDEA WHAT HAPPENED TO HIM?
GIVE ME A MOMENT AND I'LL SEE.
THE CREATURE AND I SHARE A CERTAIN... EMPATHIC RAPPORT.
IF I CAN JUST... YES! I'M PICKING UP IMAGES. IN HIS OWN WAY, HE'S TELLING ME WHAT HAPPENED TO HIM!
IT STARTED WITH A DARK SPECK FLOATING IN THE AIR... A SPECK THAT TURNED INTO A BLACK GLOPPY MASS IN THE SPACE OF A DAY.
"THE MAN-THING IS THE GUARDIAN OF THE INTER-DIMENSIONAL NEXUS LOCATED HERE IN THE SWAMP... EVEN IF HE'S NOT QUITE AWARE OF IT.
"IT'S HIS JOB TO INVESTIGATE WEIRD THINGS THAT POP THROUGH THE NEXUS.
" SO THAT'S WHAT HE DID.
"BUT SOMEHOW... THE BLACK MASS ATTACHED ITSELF TO HIS SEMI-SOLID MUD-LIKE BODY, AND SEEPED INSIDE IT!
"TRY AS HE MIGHT, THE MAN-THING COULDN'T DISLODGE THE ALIEN MATTER INSIDE HIM. IT CONTINUED TO GROW, MAKING HIM SWELL UP ALMOST AS IF HE WERE--"
PREGNANT?
EXACTLY! WHATEVER IS GROWING INSIDE HIM IS CAUSING HIM GREAT PSYCHIC DISCOMFORT.
THE MUDSTORM AROUND THE SWAMP?
IT'S NOT THE MAN-THING'S DOING. IT MUST BE THE CREATURE WITHIN!
IF THIS IS SOME STRANGE SORT OF PREGNANCY, THEN IT SEEMS THAT THE SOLUTION TO ALL THIS IS TO GET THAT THING OUT OF--UH, HIS BODY BEFORE IT REACHES FULL TERM.
IF YOU CAN PROVIDE ME WITH A FEW DETAILS OF THE MUCK-MONSTER'S ANATOMY, I CAN USE THE ENERGY OF MY QUANTUM-BANDS TO PERFORM A CAESARIAN SECTION, SO TO SPEAK.
ALL RIGHT...

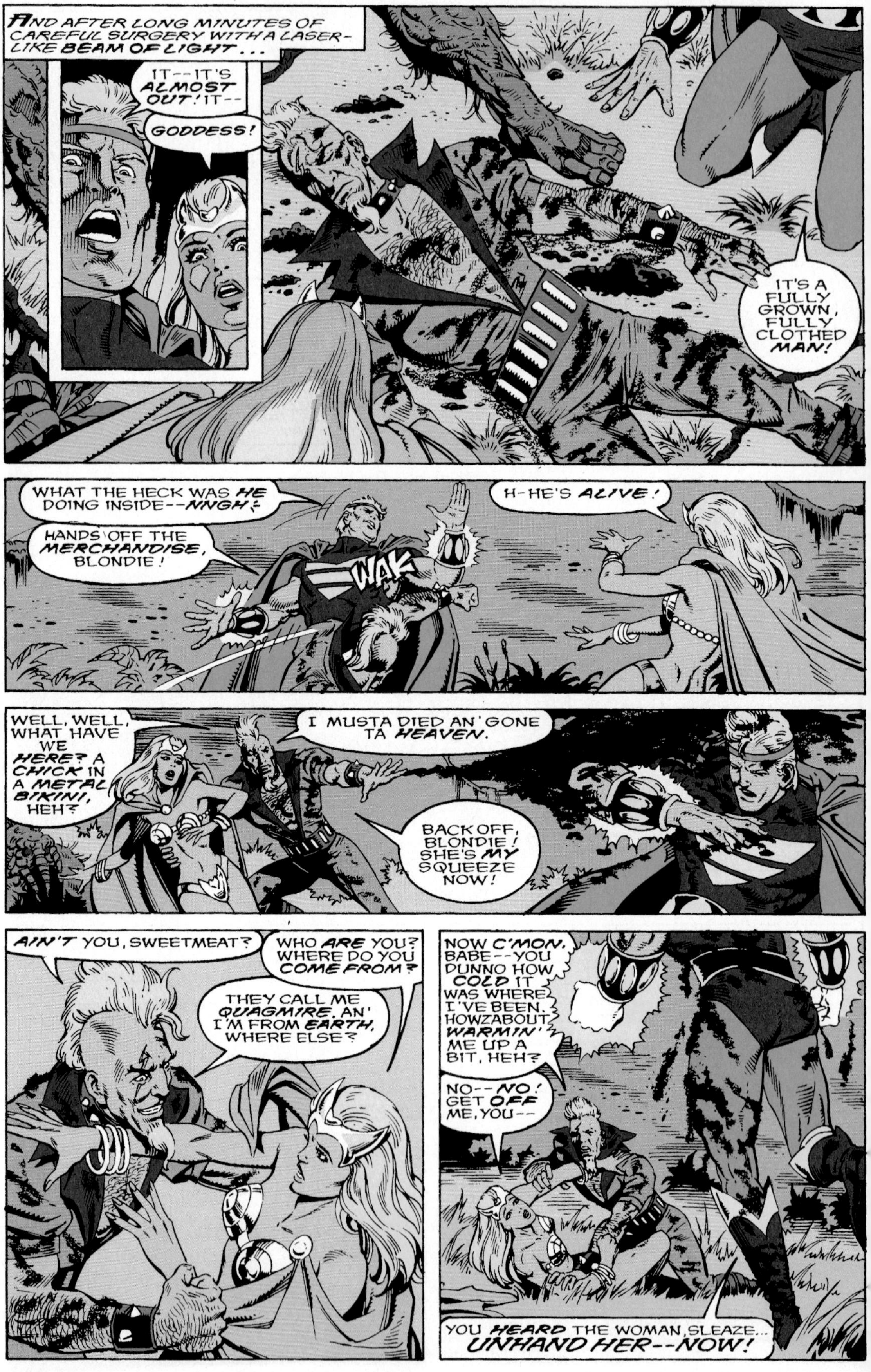
AND AFTER LONG MINUTES OF CAREFUL SURGERY WITH A LASER-LIKE BEAM OF LIGHT...
IT--IT'S ALMOST OUT! IT--
GODDESS!
IT'S A FULLY GROWN, FULLY CLOTHED MAN!
WHAT THE HECK WAS HE DOING INSIDE--NNGH!
HANDS OFF THE MERCHANDISE, BLONDIE!
WAK
H-HE'S ALIVE!
WELL, WELL, WHAT HAVE WE HERE? A CHICK IN A METAL BIKINI, HEH?
I MUSTA DIED AN' GONE TA HEAVEN.
BACK OFF, BLONDIE! SHE'S MY SQUEEZE NOW!
AIN'T YOU, SWEETMEAT?
WHO ARE YOU? WHERE DO YOU COME FROM?
THEY CALL ME QUAGMIRE. AN' I'M FROM EARTH, WHERE ELSE?
NOW C'MON, BABE--YOU DUNNO HOW COLD IT WAS WHERE I'VE BEEN. HOWZABOUT WARMIN' ME UP A BIT, HEH?
NO--NO! GET OFF ME, YOU--
YOU HEARD THE WOMAN, SLEAZE... UNHAND HER--NOW!

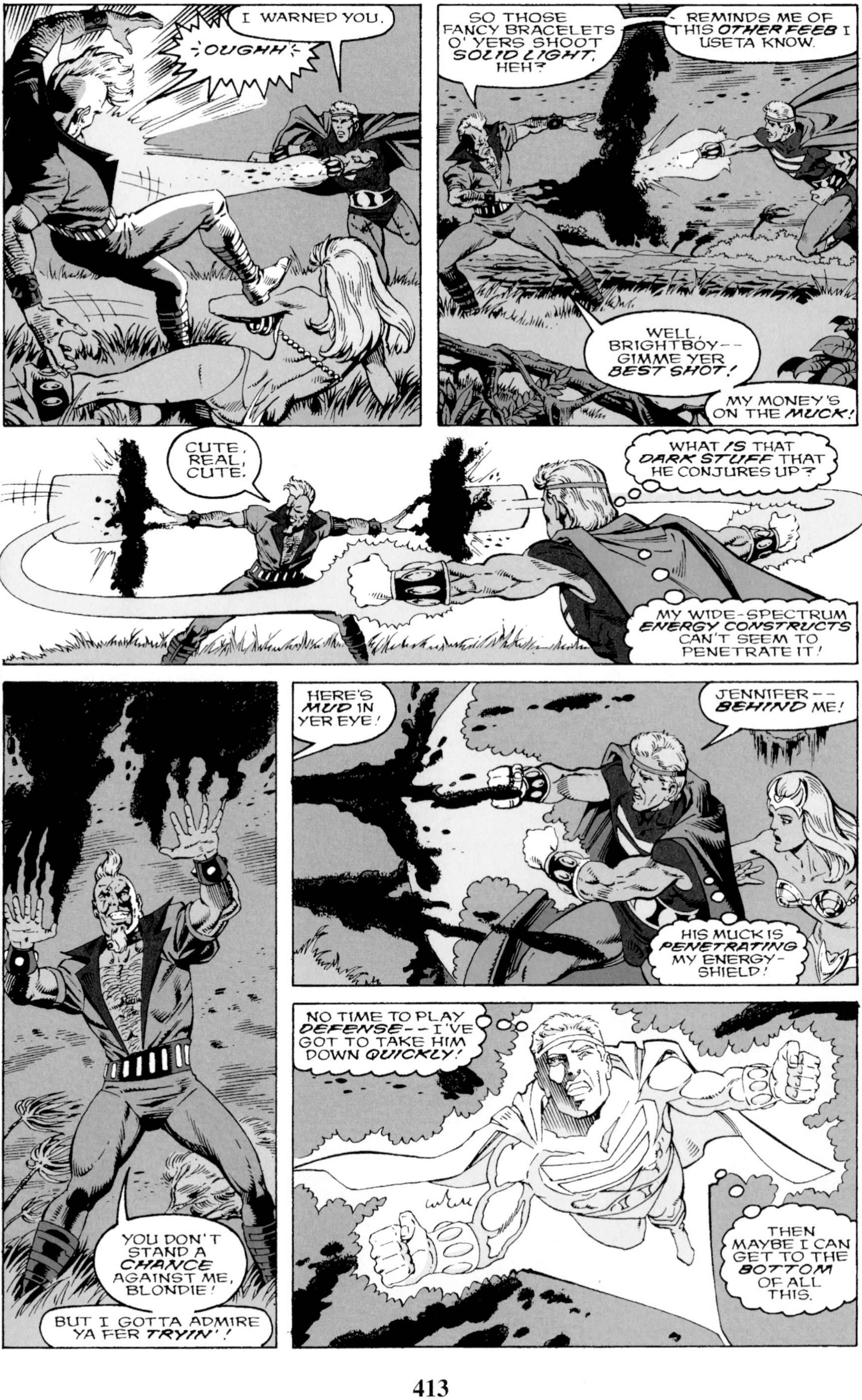

I WARNED YOU.
OUGHH
SO THOSE FANCY BRACELETS O' YERS SHOOT SOLID LIGHT, HEH?
REMINDS ME OF THIS OTHER FEEB I USETA KNOW.
WELL, BRIGHTBOY-- GIMME YER BEST SHOT!
MY MONEY'S ON THE MUCK!
CUTE, REAL, CUTE.
WHAT IS THAT DARK STUFF THAT HE CONJURES UP?
MY WIDE-SPECTRUM ENERGY CONSTRUCTS CAN'T SEEM TO PENETRATE IT!
YOU DON'T STAND A CHANCE AGAINST ME, BLONDIE!
BUT I GOTTA ADMIRE YA FER TRYIN'!
HERE'S MUD IN YER EYE!
JENNIFER-- BEHIND ME!
HIS MUCK IS PENETRATING MY ENERGY-SHIELD!
NO TIME TO PLAY DEFENSE-- I'VE GOT TO TAKE HIM DOWN QUICKLY!
THEN MAYBE I CAN GET TO THE BOTTOM OF ALL THIS.

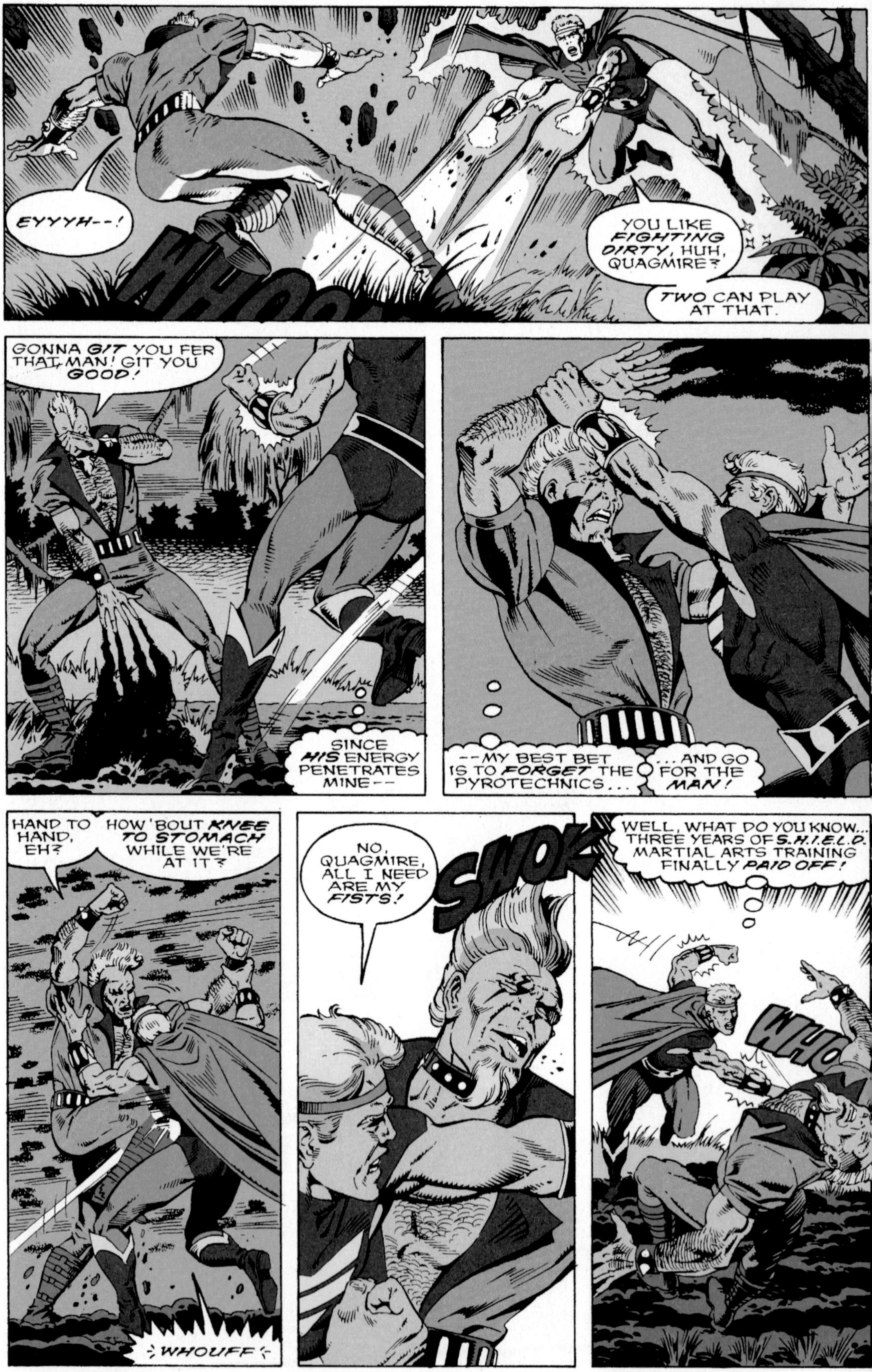
EYYYH--!
WHOO
YOU LIKE FIGHTING DIRTY, HUH, QUAGMIRE?
TWO CAN PLAY AT THAT.
GONNA GIT YOU FER THAT, MAN! GIT YOU GOOD!
SINCE HIS ENERGY PENETRATES MINE--
--MY BEST BET IS TO FORGET THE PYROTECHNICS...
...AND GO FOR THE MAN!
HAND TO HAND, EH?
HOW 'BOUT KNEE TO STOMACH WHILE WE'RE AT IT?
WHOUFF
NO, QUAGMIRE, ALL I NEED ARE MY FISTS!
SWOK
WELL, WHAT DO YOU KNOW... THREE YEARS OF S.H.I.E.L.D. MARTIAL ARTS TRAINING FINALLY PAID OFF!
WHO

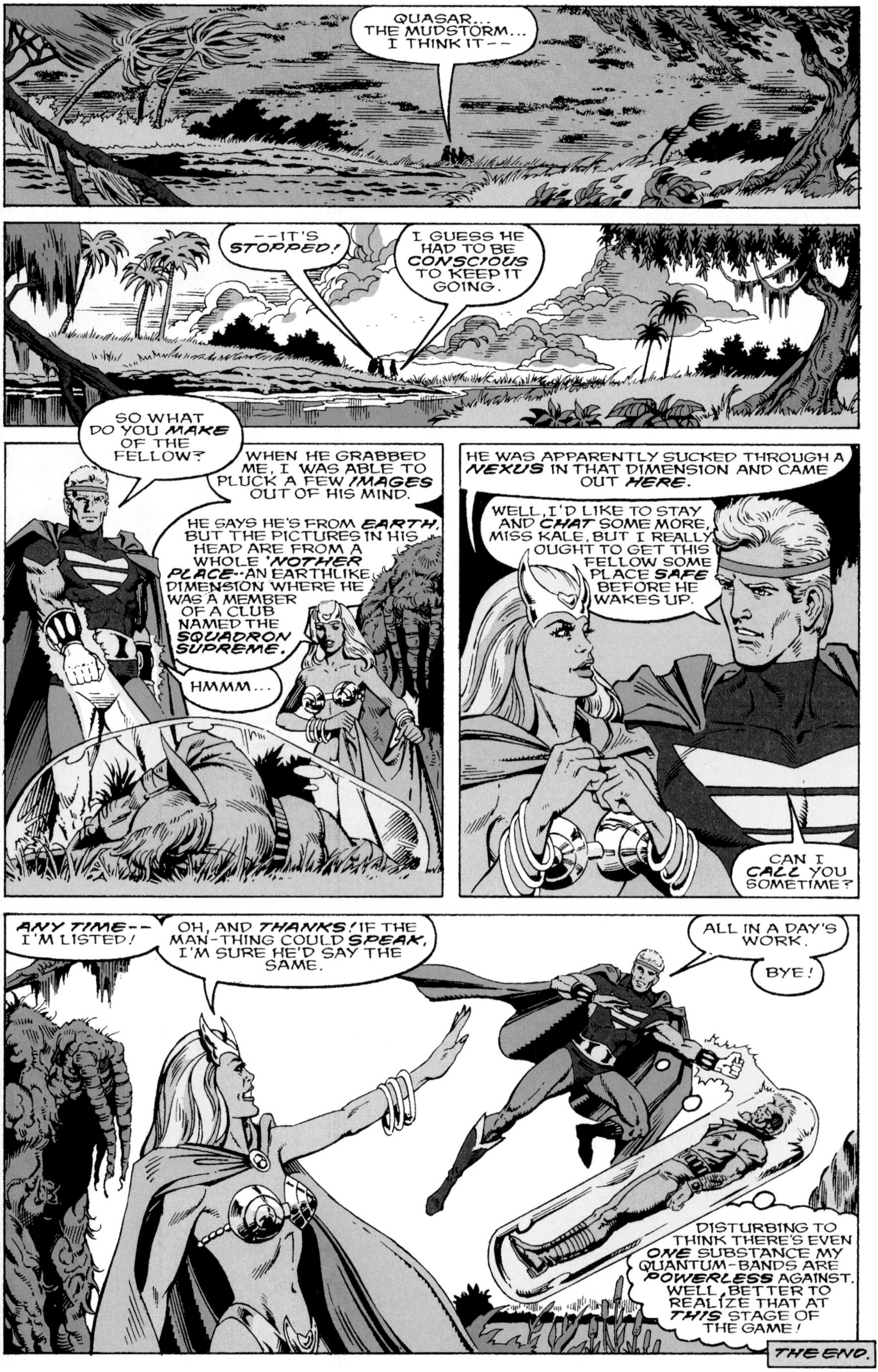

QUASAR... THE MUDSTORM... I THINK IT--
--IT'S STOPPED!
I GUESS HE HAD TO BE CONSCIOUS TO KEEP IT GOING.
SO WHAT DO YOU MAKE OF THE FELLOW?
WHEN HE GRABBED ME, I WAS ABLE TO PLUCK A FEW IMAGES OUT OF HIS MIND.
HE SAYS HE'S FROM EARTH, BUT THE PICTURES IN HIS HEAD ARE FROM A WHOLE 'NOTHER PLACE--AN EARTHLIKE DIMENSION WHERE HE WAS A MEMBER OF A CLUB NAMED THE SQUADRON SUPREME.
HMMM...
HE WAS APPARENTLY SUCKED THROUGH A NEXUS IN THAT DIMENSION AND CAME OUT HERE.
WELL, I'D LIKE TO STAY AND CHAT SOME MORE, MISS KALE, BUT I REALLY OUGHT TO GET THIS FELLOW SOME PLACE SAFE BEFORE HE WAKES UP.
CAN I CALL YOU SOMETIME?
ANY TIME-- I'M LISTED!
OH, AND THANKS! IF THE MAN-THING COULD SPEAK, I'M SURE HE'D SAY THE SAME.
ALL IN A DAY'S WORK.
BYE!
DISTURBING TO THINK THERE'S EVEN ONE SUBSTANCE MY QUANTUM-BANDS ARE POWERLESS AGAINST. WELL, BETTER TO REALIZE THAT AT THIS STAGE OF THE GAME!
THE END.

MARVEL
AVENGERS
WEST COAST
CAPTAIN AMERICA AND SHE-HULK HAVE FOUND THE SCARLET WITCH...
MAYBE NOT THE SMARTEST THING THEY EVER DID...

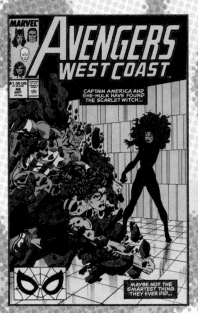

West Coast Avengers changed its title to AVENGERS WEST COAST with #48, published in May 1989.

MARVEL COMICS
THE
WOLVERINE
SAGA
BOOK ONE: BEGINNINGS

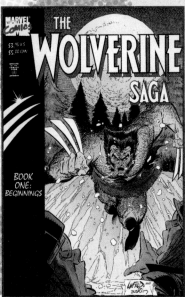

WOLVERINE SAGA #1, published in May 1989, began a miniseries providing an overview of Wolverine's history.

MARVEL COMICS
THE SENSATIONAL
SPIDER-MAN
NOTHING CAN STOP THE JUGGERNAUT

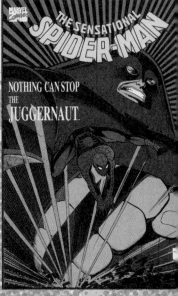

SENSATIONAL SPIDER-MAN: NOTHING CAN STO THE JUGGERNAUT, published in May 1989, was reprint one-shot.

MARVEL
THE BLOODSTONE HUNT
CAPTAIN AMERICA
PART 2 OF 6
TO RESCUE DIAMONDBACK, CAP ENTERS THE CAVERNS OF DEATH!

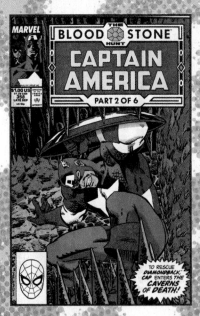

CAPTAIN AMERICA #358, published in May 1989, began a short backup serial starring U.S.Agent.

MARVEL
NICK FURY AGENT OF
SHIELD

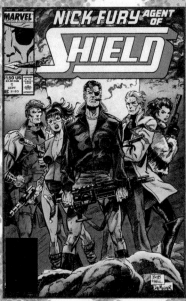

NICK FURY, AGENT OF S.H.I.E.L.D. #1, published in May 1989, began the spymaster's new ongoing series.

MARVEL
POWER
PACHYDERMS
$1.25 US
1
SEPT
WARNING! ANY SIMILARITY BETWEEN THIS BOOK AND THE X-MEN IS PROBABLY JUST A CHEAP COMMERCIAL PLOY!

POWER PACHYDERMS, published in May 1989, was a humor one-shot.

#1 IN A FOUR-ISSUE LIMITED SERIES
MARVEL
INDIANA JONES
and the LAST CRUSADE
$1.00 US
1
THE OFFICIAL COMICS ADAPTATION OF THE SPECTACULAR NEW MOVIE FROM LUCASFILM!
INDY'S FIRST ADVENTURE!

INDIANA JONES AND THE LAST CRUSADE #1, published in June 1989, began a miniseries reprinting Marvel's film adaptation.

A MARVEL MAGAZINE
THE PUNISHER
magazine
$2.25
1
SEPT
#1 FIRST ISSUE!

PUNISHER MAGAZINE #1, published in June 1989, began an ongoing magazine-sized reprint series.

MARVEL
PULSATING PREMIERE ISSUE!
QUASAR
$1.00 US
1
OCT
THE COSMIC AVENGER-- NOW IN HIS OWN BOOK!

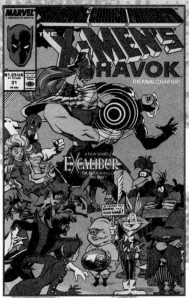

QUASAR #1, published in June 1989, began the neophyte hero's ongoing series.

MARVEL
MARVEL COMICS PRESENTS
THE X-MEN'S HAVOK
THE FINAL CHAPTER!
$1.25 US
31
A NEW SERIES
EXCALIBUR
THE BEGINNING OF THE END?!

MARVEL COMICS PRESENTS #31, published in June 1989, began a limited serial starring Excalibur.

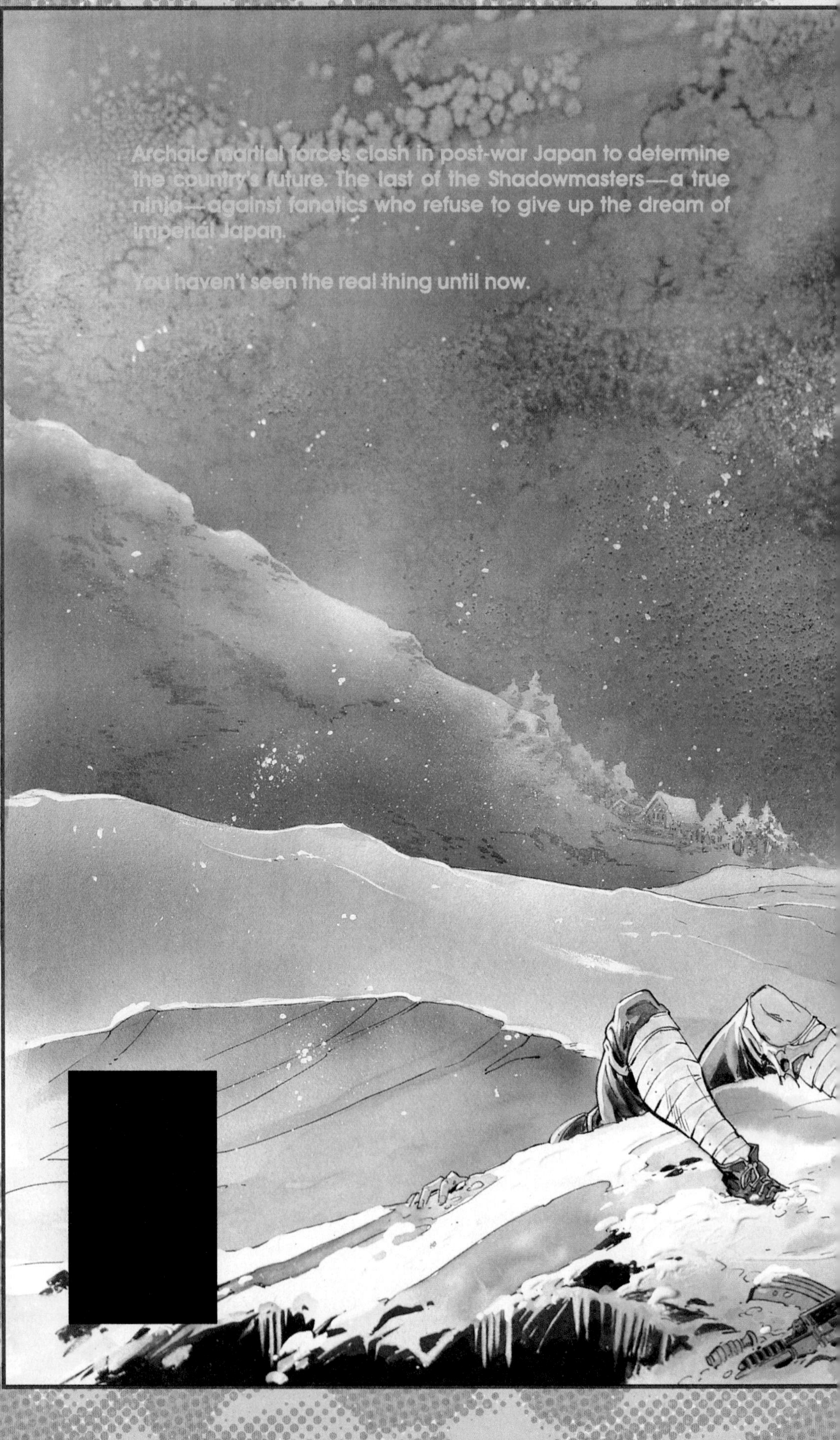
Archaic martial forces clash in post-war Japan to determine the country's future. The last of the Shadowmasters—a true ninja—against fanatics who refuse to give up the dream of imperial Japan.
You haven't seen the real thing until now.

[redacted]

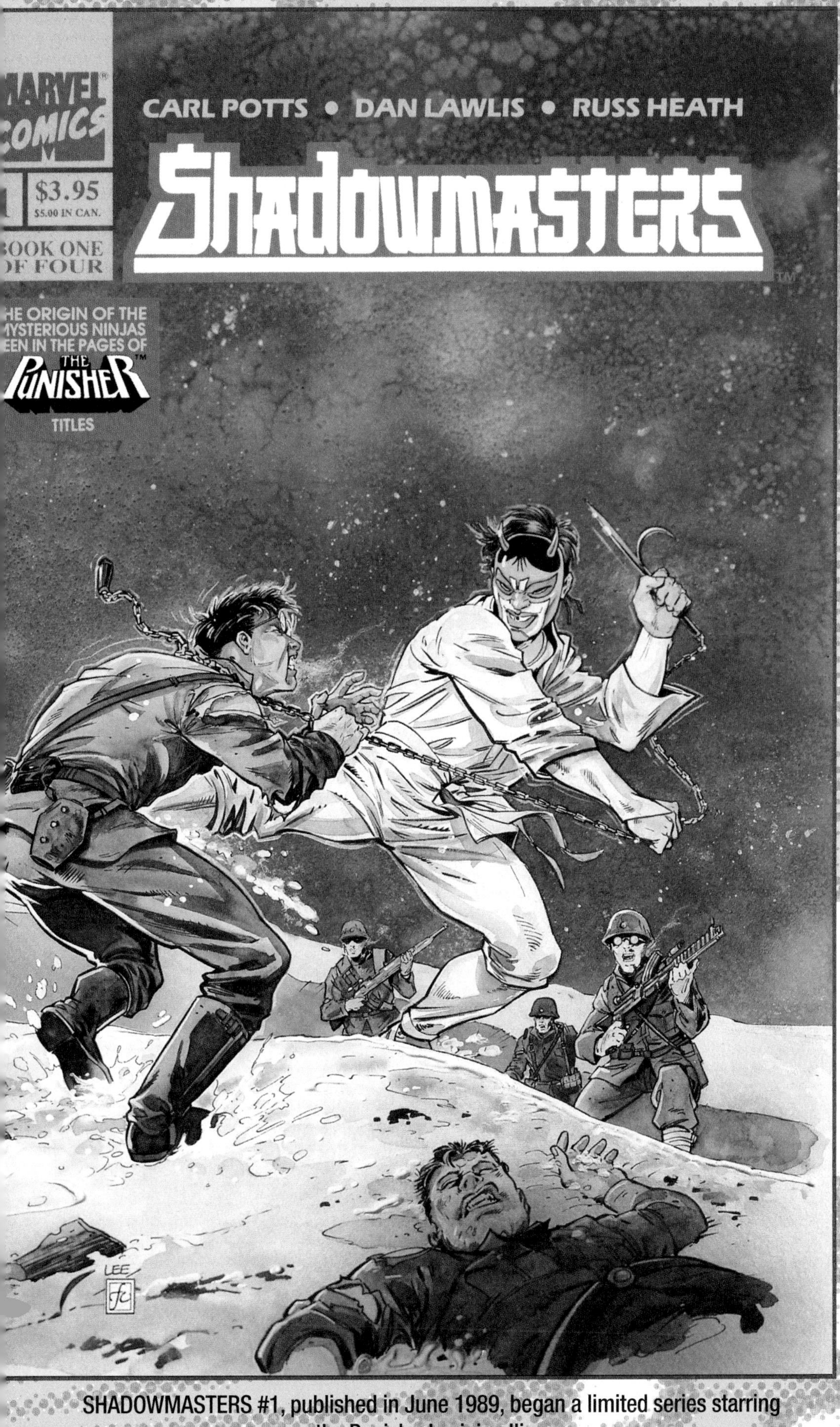
MARVEL COMICS
$3.95
$5.00 IN CAN.
BOOK ONE OF FOUR
CARL POTTS • DAN LAWLIS • RUSS HEATH
SHADOWMASTERS
THE ORIGIN OF THE MYSTERIOUS NINJAS SEEN IN THE PAGES OF
THE PUNISHER
TITLES
LEE

SHADOWMASTERS #1, published in June 1989, began a limited series starring the Punisher's ninja allies.

SHADOWMASTERS

CHAPTER ONE
OF FOUR

Shadows OF THE PAST

carl potts
WRITER/CREATOR

dan lawlis
PENCILER

russ heath
INKER

steve oliff
COLORIST

jim novak
LETTERER

allen milgrom
EDITOR

marc mc laurin
ASSISTANT EDITOR

tom de falco
EDITOR IN CHIEF

jim lee &
frank cirocco
COVER ART

SPECIAL THANKS TO:
jo duffy

TITLES DESIGN: C. POTTS

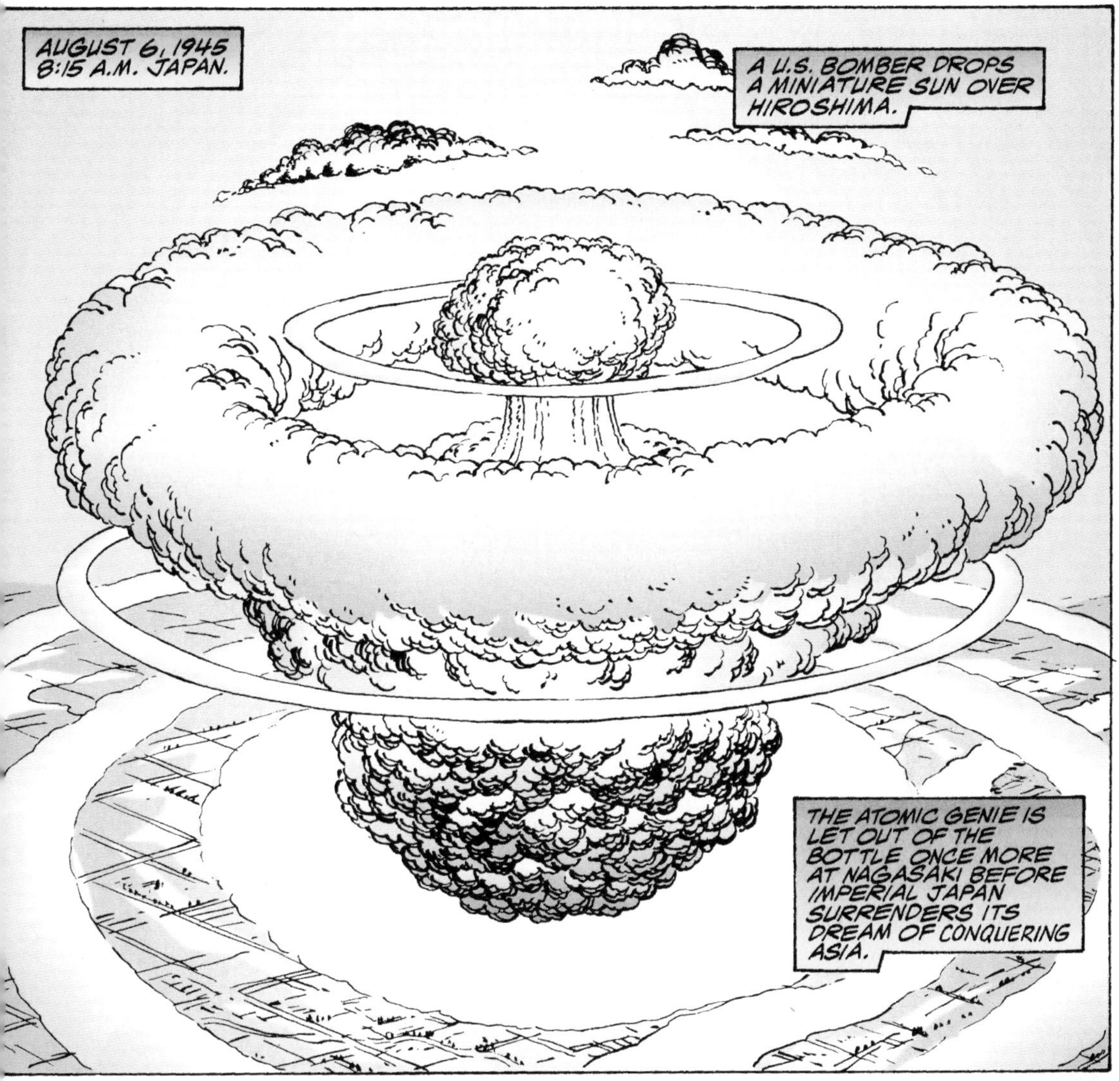
AUGUST 6, 1945
8:15 A.M. JAPAN.
A U.S. BOMBER DROPS A MINIATURE SUN OVER HIROSHIMA.
THE ATOMIC GENIE IS LET OUT OF THE BOTTLE ONCE MORE AT NAGASAKI BEFORE IMPERIAL JAPAN SURRENDERS ITS DREAM OF CONQUERING ASIA.

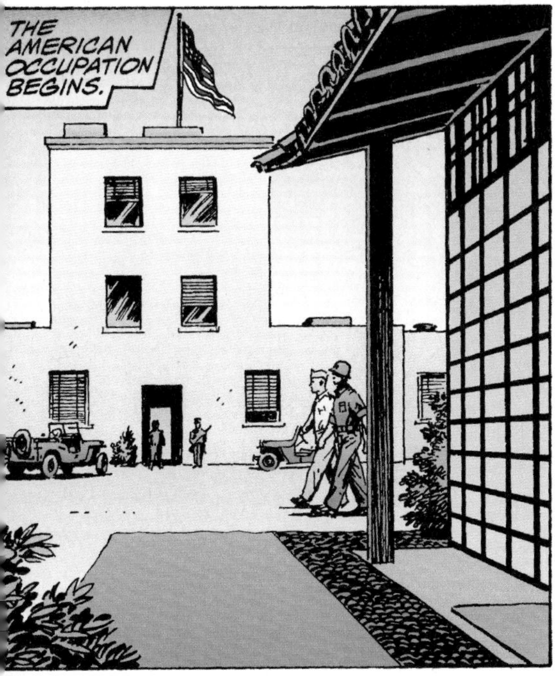
THE AMERICAN OCCUPATION BEGINS.

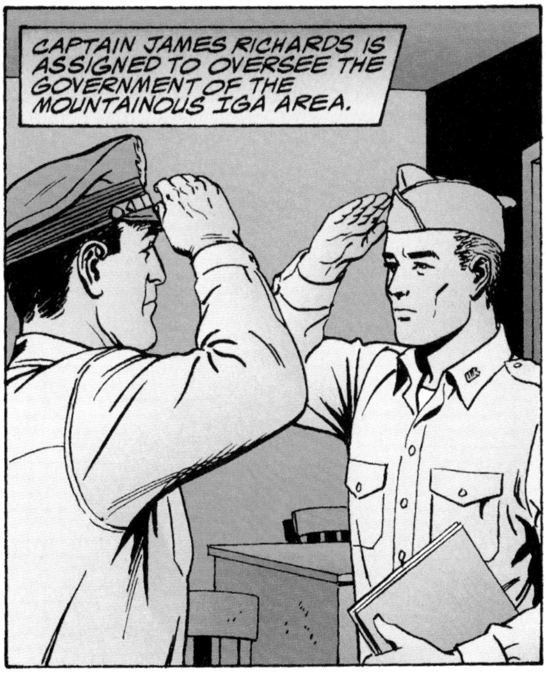
CAPTAIN JAMES RICHARDS IS ASSIGNED TO OVERSEE THE GOVERNMENT OF THE MOUNTAINOUS IGA AREA.

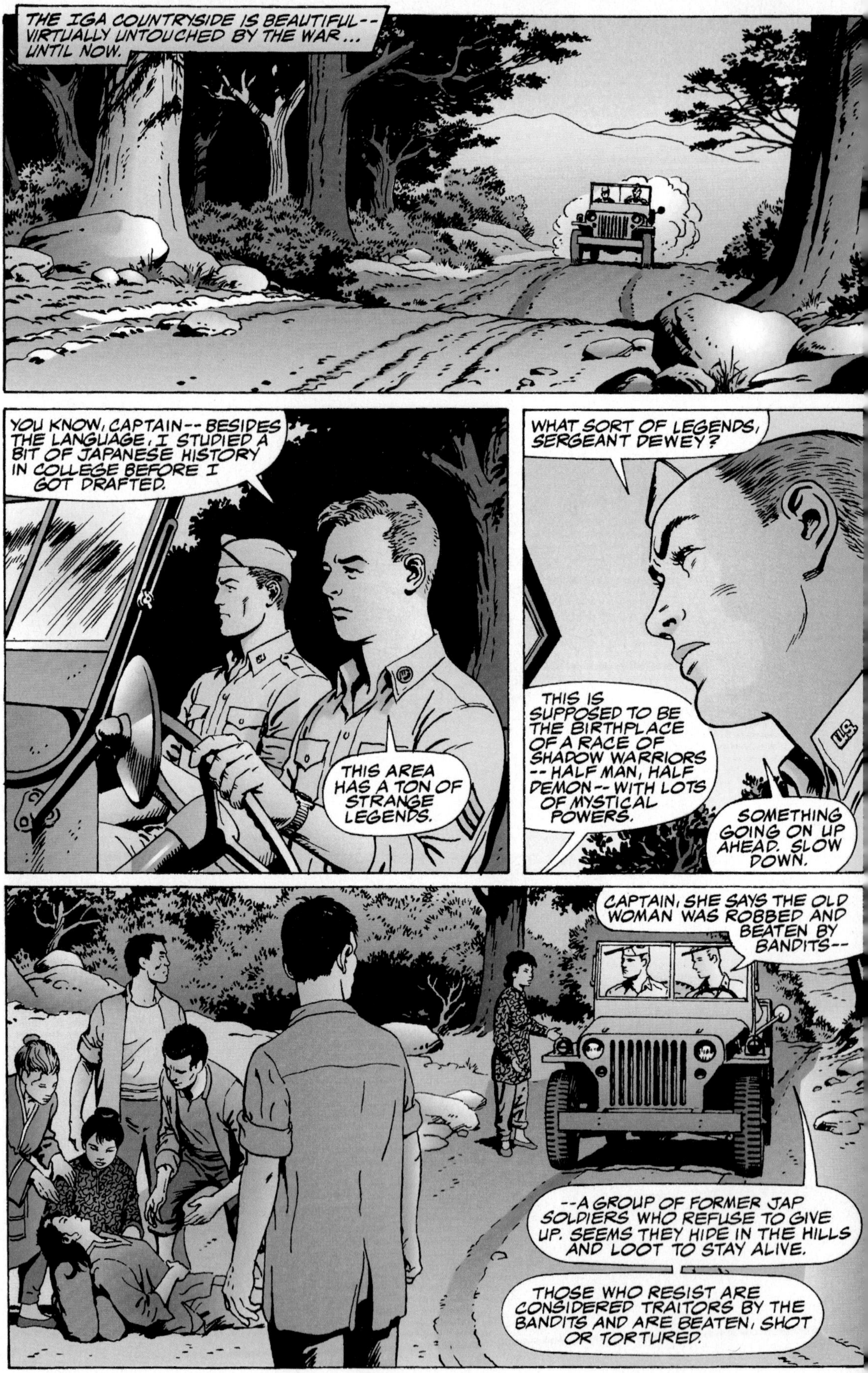
THE IGA COUNTRYSIDE IS BEAUTIFUL--VIRTUALLY UNTOUCHED BY THE WAR... UNTIL NOW.
YOU KNOW, CAPTAIN--BESIDES THE LANGUAGE, I STUDIED A BIT OF JAPANESE HISTORY IN COLLEGE BEFORE I GOT DRAFTED.
THIS AREA HAS A TON OF STRANGE LEGENDS.
WHAT SORT OF LEGENDS, SERGEANT DEWEY?
THIS IS SUPPOSED TO BE THE BIRTHPLACE OF A RACE OF SHADOW WARRIORS --HALF MAN, HALF DEMON--WITH LOTS OF MYSTICAL POWERS.
SOMETHING GOING ON UP AHEAD. SLOW DOWN.
CAPTAIN, SHE SAYS THE OLD WOMAN WAS ROBBED AND BEATEN BY BANDITS--
--A GROUP OF FORMER JAP SOLDIERS WHO REFUSE TO GIVE UP. SEEMS THEY HIDE IN THE HILLS AND LOOT TO STAY ALIVE.
THOSE WHO RESIST ARE CONSIDERED TRAITORS BY THE BANDITS AND ARE BEATEN, SHOT OR TORTURED.

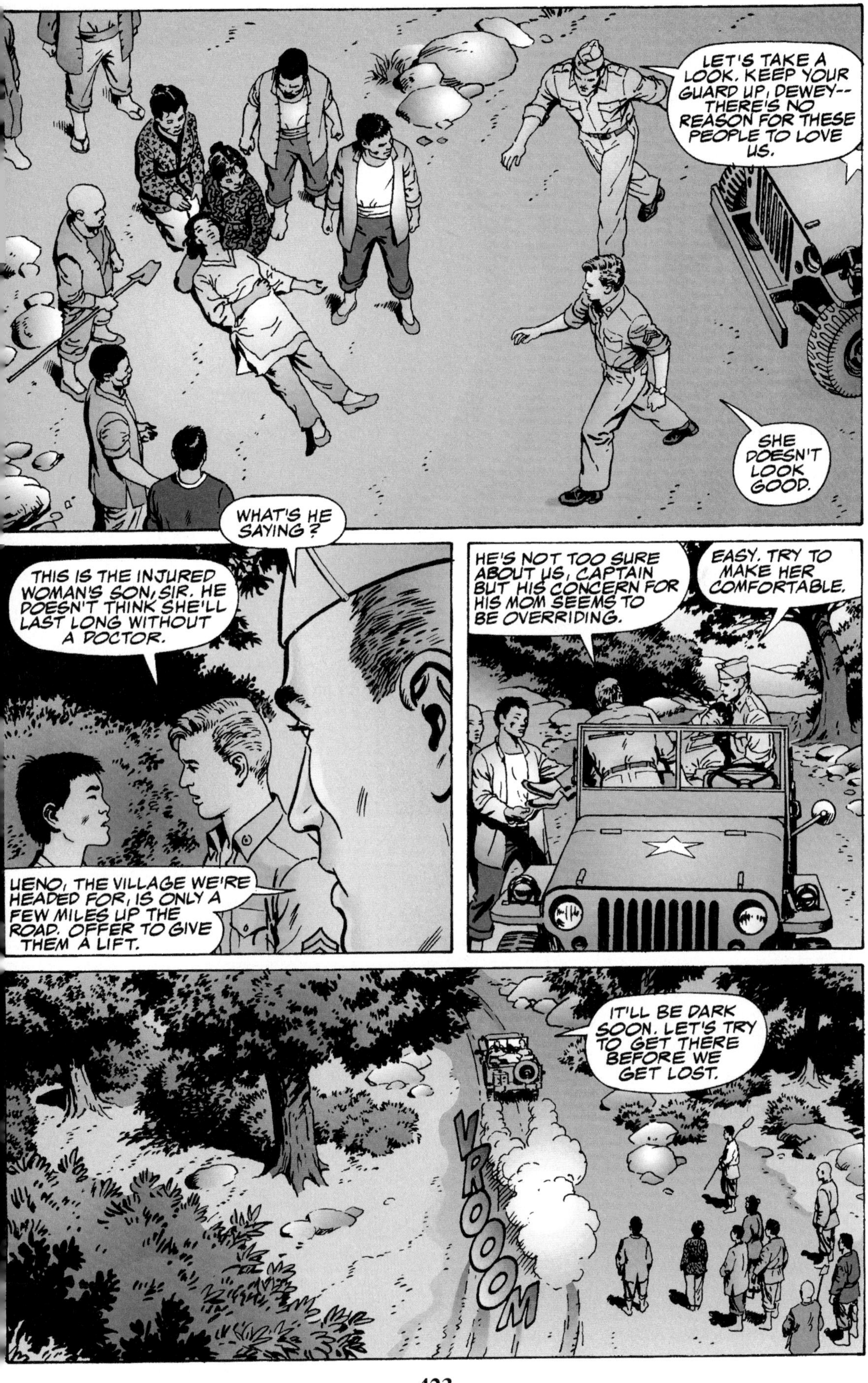
LET'S TAKE A LOOK. KEEP YOUR GUARD UP, DEWEY-- THERE'S NO REASON FOR THESE PEOPLE TO LOVE US.
SHE DOESN'T LOOK GOOD.
WHAT'S HE SAYING?
THIS IS THE INJURED WOMAN'S SON, SIR. HE DOESN'T THINK SHE'LL LAST LONG WITHOUT A DOCTOR.
UENO, THE VILLAGE WE'RE HEADED FOR, IS ONLY A FEW MILES UP THE ROAD. OFFER TO GIVE THEM A LIFT.
HE'S NOT TOO SURE ABOUT US, CAPTAIN BUT HIS CONCERN FOR HIS MOM SEEMS TO BE OVERRIDING.
EASY. TRY TO MAKE HER COMFORTABLE.
IT'LL BE DARK SOON. LET'S TRY TO GET THERE BEFORE WE GET LOST.
VROOOOM

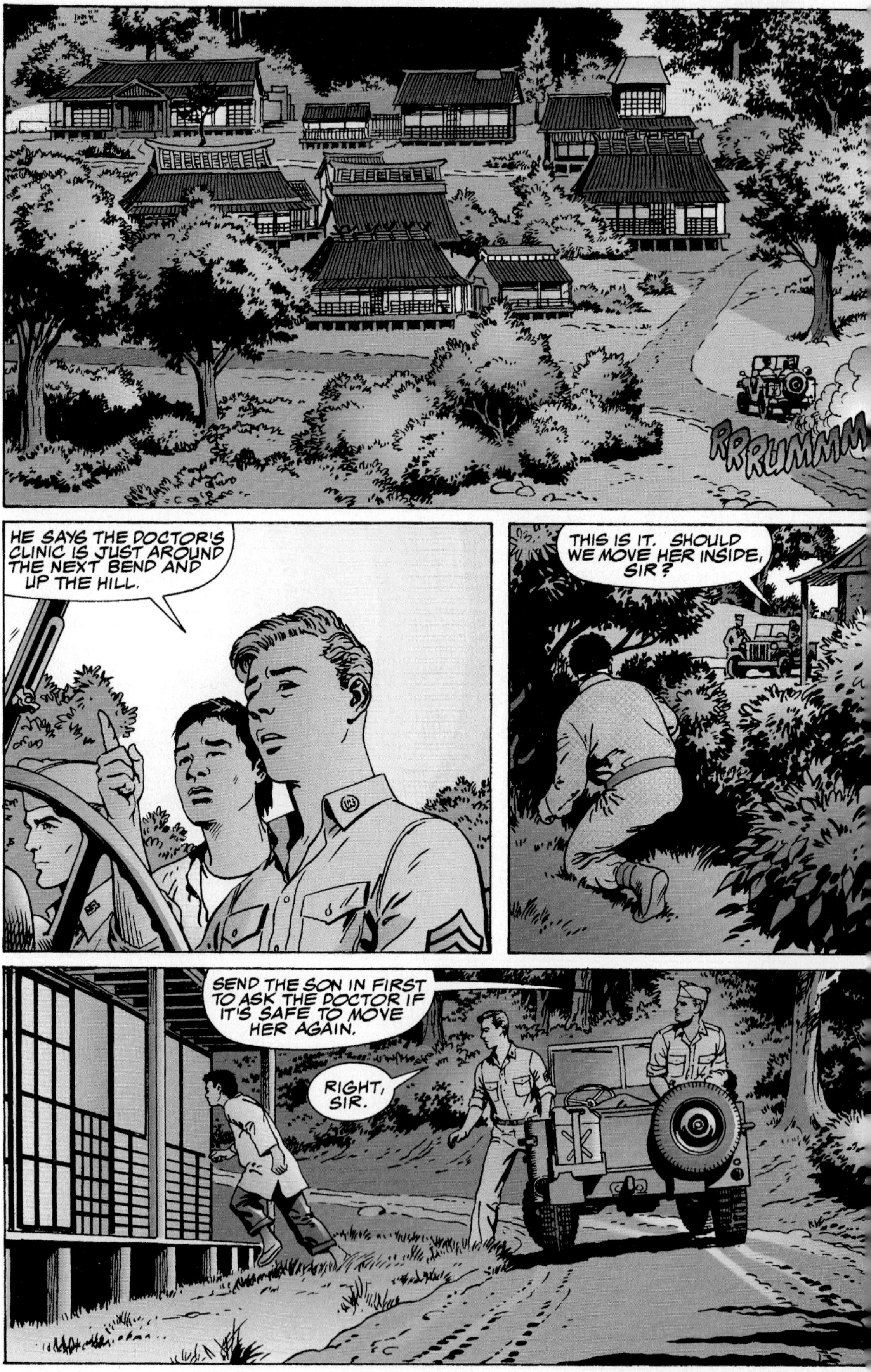
RRRUMMM
HE SAYS THE DOCTOR'S CLINIC IS JUST AROUND THE NEXT BEND AND UP THE HILL.
THIS IS IT. SHOULD WE MOVE HER INSIDE, SIR?
SEND THE SON IN FIRST TO ASK THE DOCTOR IF IT'S SAFE TO MOVE HER AGAIN.
RIGHT, SIR.

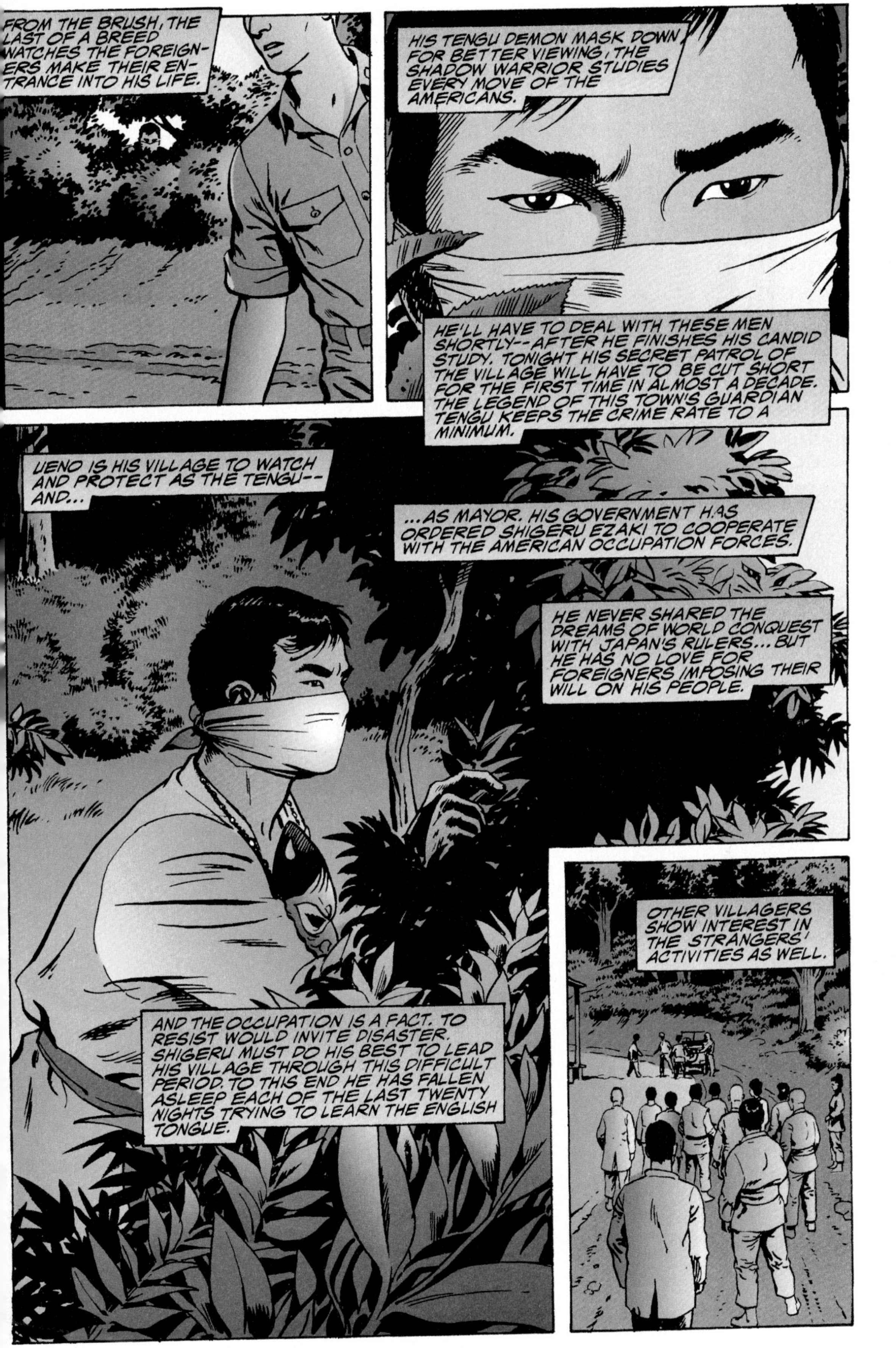
FROM THE BRUSH, THE LAST OF A BREED WATCHES THE FOREIGNERS MAKE THEIR ENTRANCE INTO HIS LIFE.
HIS TENGU DEMON MASK DOWN FOR BETTER VIEWING, THE SHADOW WARRIOR STUDIES EVERY MOVE OF THE AMERICANS.
HE'LL HAVE TO DEAL WITH THESE MEN SHORTLY--AFTER HE FINISHES HIS CANDID STUDY. TONIGHT HIS SECRET PATROL OF THE VILLAGE WILL HAVE TO BE CUT SHORT FOR THE FIRST TIME IN ALMOST A DECADE. THE LEGEND OF THIS TOWN'S GUARDIAN TENGU KEEPS THE CRIME RATE TO A MINIMUM.
UENO IS HIS VILLAGE TO WATCH AND PROTECT AS THE TENGU--AND...
...AS MAYOR. HIS GOVERNMENT HAS ORDERED SHIGERU EZAKI TO COOPERATE WITH THE AMERICAN OCCUPATION FORCES.
HE NEVER SHARED THE DREAMS OF WORLD CONQUEST WITH JAPAN'S RULERS... BUT HE HAS NO LOVE FOR FOREIGNERS IMPOSING THEIR WILL ON HIS PEOPLE.
AND THE OCCUPATION IS A FACT. TO RESIST WOULD INVITE DISASTER. SHIGERU MUST DO HIS BEST TO LEAD HIS VILLAGE THROUGH THIS DIFFICULT PERIOD. TO THIS END HE HAS FALLEN ASLEEP EACH OF THE LAST TWENTY NIGHTS TRYING TO LEARN THE ENGLISH TONGUE.
OTHER VILLAGERS SHOW INTEREST IN THE STRANGERS' ACTIVITIES AS WELL.

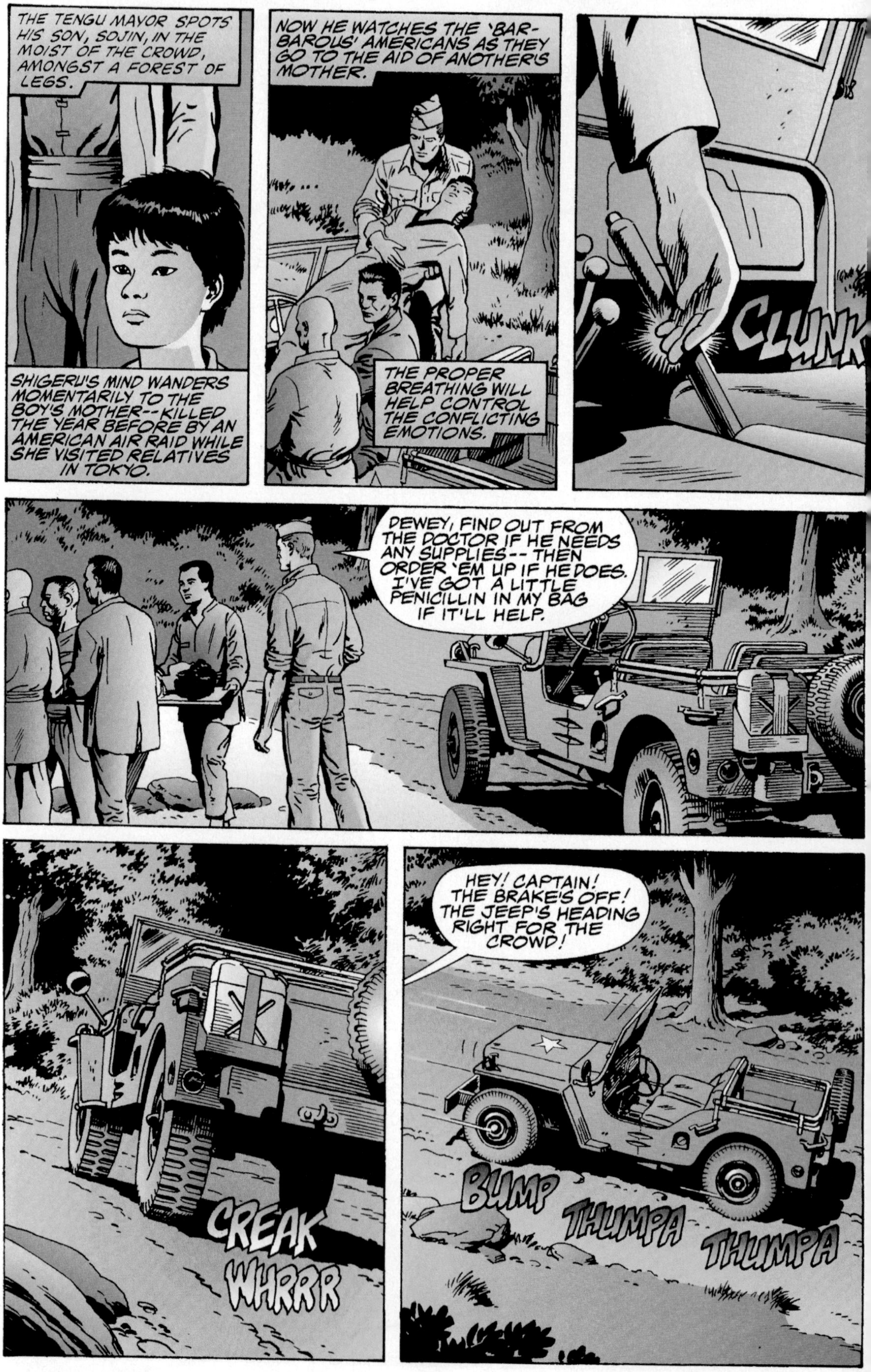
THE TENGU MAYOR SPOTS HIS SON, SOJIN, IN THE MOIST OF THE CROWD, AMONGST A FOREST OF LEGS.
SHIGERU'S MIND WANDERS MOMENTARILY TO THE BOY'S MOTHER-- KILLED THE YEAR BEFORE BY AN AMERICAN AIR RAID WHILE SHE VISITED RELATIVES IN TOKYO.
NOW HE WATCHES THE 'BARBAROUS' AMERICANS AS THEY GO TO THE AID OF ANOTHER'S MOTHER.
THE PROPER BREATHING WILL HELP CONTROL THE CONFLICTING EMOTIONS.
CLUNK
DEWEY, FIND OUT FROM THE DOCTOR IF HE NEEDS ANY SUPPLIES-- THEN ORDER 'EM UP IF HE DOES. I'VE GOT A LITTLE PENICILLIN IN MY BAG IF IT'LL HELP.
CREAK
WHRRR
HEY! CAPTAIN! THE BRAKE'S OFF! THE JEEP'S HEADING RIGHT FOR THE CROWD!
BUMP
THUMPA
THUMPA

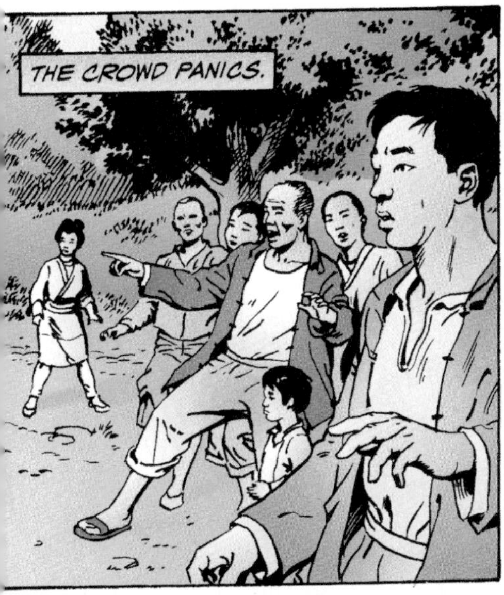
THE CROWD PANICS.

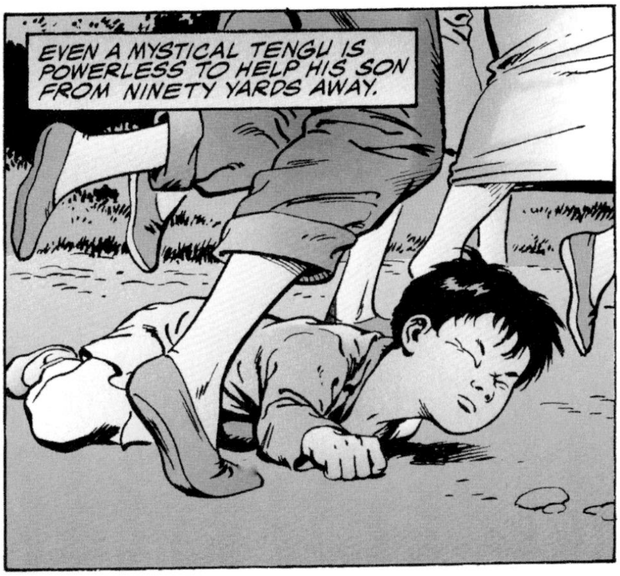
EVEN A MYSTICAL TENGU IS POWERLESS TO HELP HIS SON FROM NINETY YARDS AWAY.

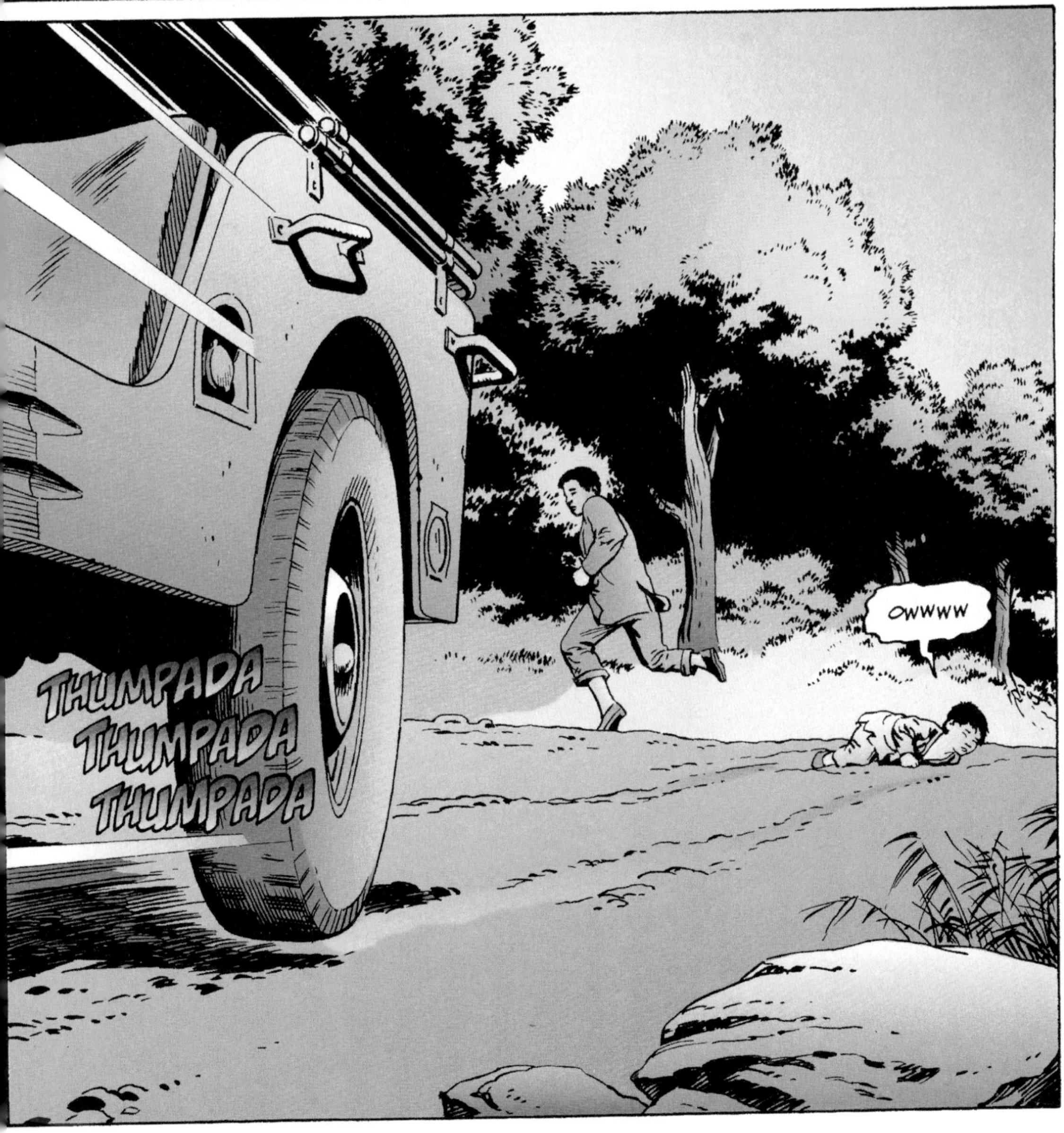
THUMPADA
THUMPADA
THUMPADA
OWWWW

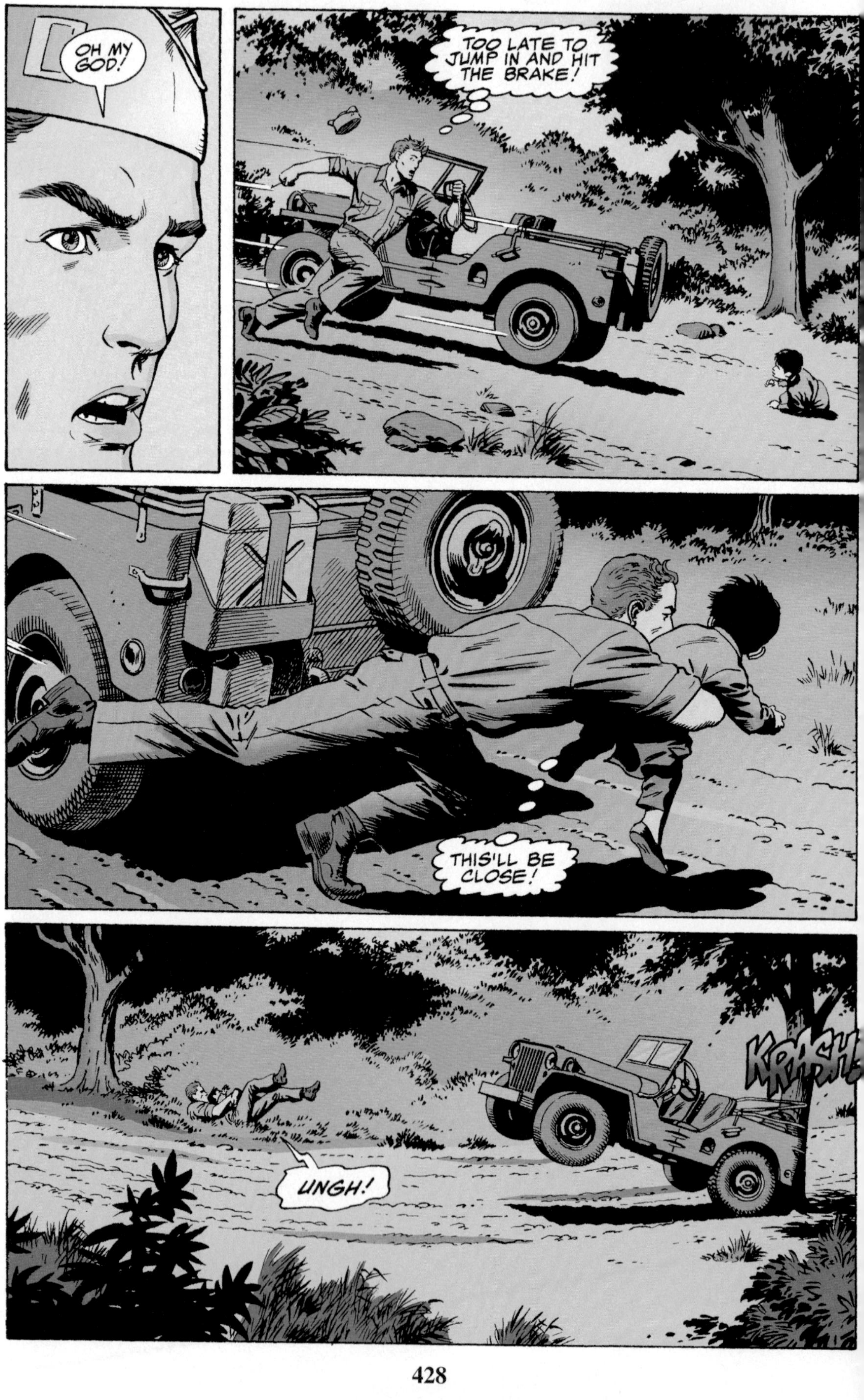
OH MY GOD!
TOO LATE TO JUMP IN AND HIT THE BRAKE!
THIS'LL BE CLOSE!
KRASH!
UNGH!

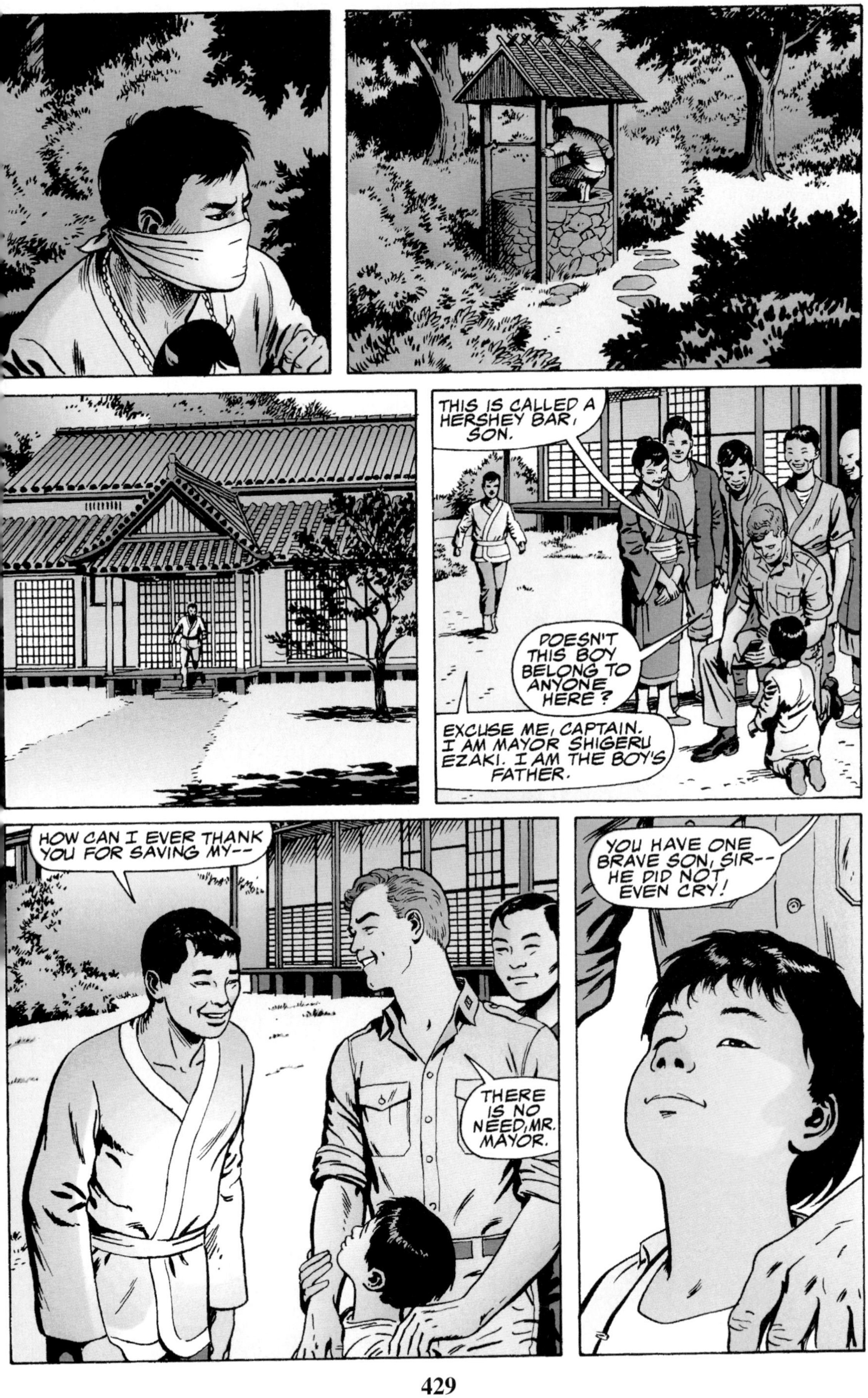
THIS IS CALLED A HERSHEY BAR, SON.
DOESN'T THIS BOY BELONG TO ANYONE HERE?
EXCUSE ME, CAPTAIN. I AM MAYOR SHIGERU EZAKI. I AM THE BOY'S FATHER.
HOW CAN I EVER THANK YOU FOR SAVING MY--
THERE IS NO NEED, MR. MAYOR.
YOU HAVE ONE BRAVE SON, SIR-- HE DID NOT EVEN CRY!

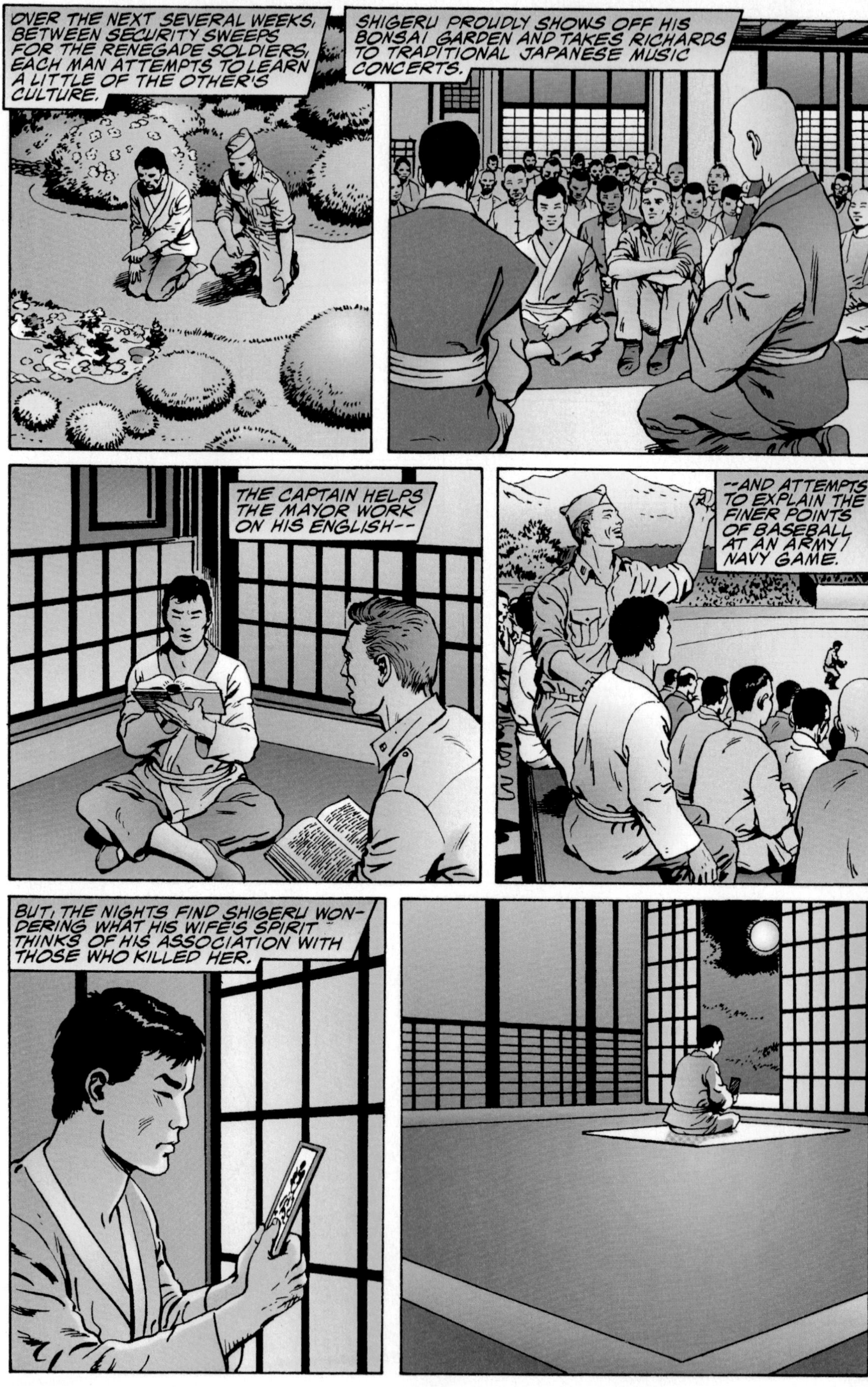
OVER THE NEXT SEVERAL WEEKS, BETWEEN SECURITY SWEEPS FOR THE RENEGADE SOLDIERS, EACH MAN ATTEMPTS TO LEARN A LITTLE OF THE OTHER'S CULTURE.
SHIGERU PROUDLY SHOWS OFF HIS BONSAI GARDEN AND TAKES RICHARDS TO TRADITIONAL JAPANESE MUSIC CONCERTS.
THE CAPTAIN HELPS THE MAYOR WORK ON HIS ENGLISH--
--AND ATTEMPTS TO EXPLAIN THE FINER POINTS OF BASEBALL AT AN ARMY / NAVY GAME.
BUT, THE NIGHTS FIND SHIGERU WONDERING WHAT HIS WIFE'S SPIRIT THINKS OF HIS ASSOCIATION WITH THOSE WHO KILLED HER.

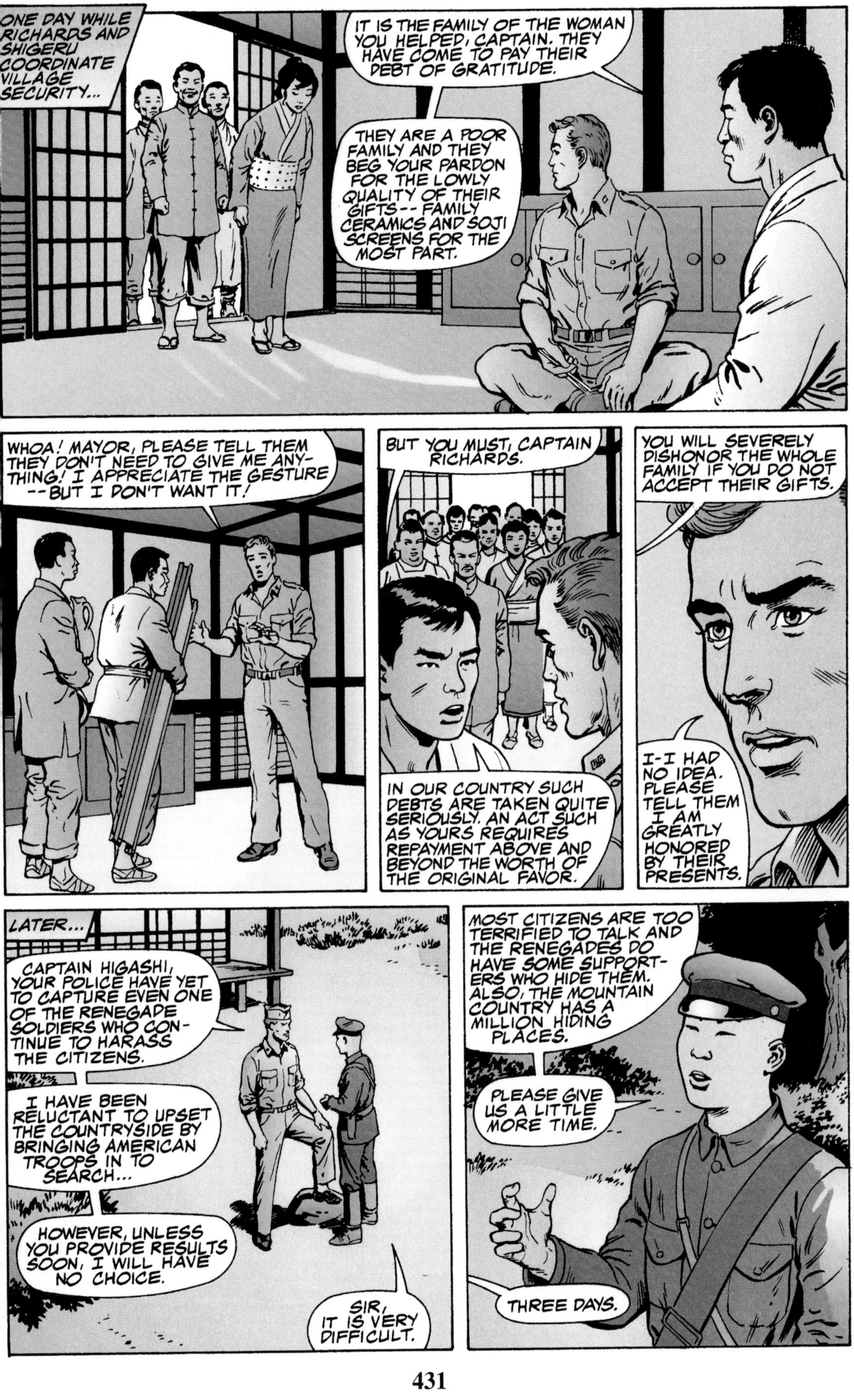
ONE DAY WHILE RICHARDS AND SHIGERU COORDINATE VILLAGE SECURITY...
IT IS THE FAMILY OF THE WOMAN YOU HELPED, CAPTAIN. THEY HAVE COME TO PAY THEIR DEBT OF GRATITUDE.
THEY ARE A POOR FAMILY AND THEY BEG YOUR PARDON FOR THE LOWLY QUALITY OF THEIR GIFTS-- FAMILY CERAMICS AND SOJI SCREENS FOR THE MOST PART.
WHOA! MAYOR, PLEASE TELL THEM THEY DON'T NEED TO GIVE ME ANYTHING! I APPRECIATE THE GESTURE --BUT I DON'T WANT IT!
BUT YOU MUST, CAPTAIN RICHARDS.
IN OUR COUNTRY SUCH DEBTS ARE TAKEN QUITE SERIOUSLY. AN ACT SUCH AS YOURS REQUIRES REPAYMENT ABOVE AND BEYOND THE WORTH OF THE ORIGINAL FAVOR.
YOU WILL SEVERELY DISHONOR THE WHOLE FAMILY IF YOU DO NOT ACCEPT THEIR GIFTS.
I-I HAD NO IDEA. PLEASE TELL THEM I AM GREATLY HONORED BY THEIR PRESENTS.
LATER...
CAPTAIN HIGASHI, YOUR POLICE HAVE YET TO CAPTURE EVEN ONE OF THE RENEGADE SOLDIERS WHO CONTINUE TO HARASS THE CITIZENS.
I HAVE BEEN RELUCTANT TO UPSET THE COUNTRYSIDE BY BRINGING AMERICAN TROOPS IN TO SEARCH...
HOWEVER, UNLESS YOU PROVIDE RESULTS SOON, I WILL HAVE NO CHOICE.
SIR, IT IS VERY DIFFICULT.
MOST CITIZENS ARE TOO TERRIFIED TO TALK AND THE RENEGADES DO HAVE SOME SUPPORTERS WHO HIDE THEM. ALSO, THE MOUNTAIN COUNTRY HAS A MILLION HIDING PLACES.
PLEASE GIVE US A LITTLE MORE TIME.
THREE DAYS.

THAT NIGHT, WHILE ON HIS NIGHTLY PATROL, SHIGERU COMES ACROSS A GROUP OF STRANGERS NOT FAR FROM THE HOUSE USED BY CAPT. RICHARDS.

〈TONIGHT WE BEGIN TO KILL THE AMERICAN *TRESPASSERS* WHO *INFECT* OUR GREAT LAND. WE START NOW WITH THIS YANKEE CAPTAIN WHO TRIES TO HAVE US HUNTED DOWN.〉

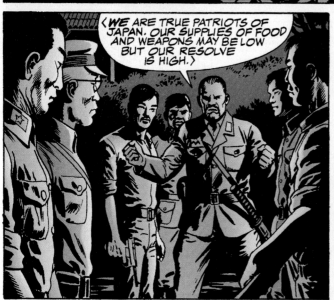

〈*WE* ARE TRUE PATRIOTS OF JAPAN. OUR SUPPLIES OF FOOD AND WEAPONS MAY BE LOW BUT OUR RESOLVE IS HIGH.〉

〈SOON, AS THE MASSES SEE OUR *SPIRIT* AND OUR *SUCCESSES*, THE *PEOPLE* WILL *RISE* TO DRIVE *OUT* THE *BARBARIAN* OCCUPIERS!〉

〈WE FEW SHALL LEAD THE REBIRTH OF IMPERIAL JAPAN.〉

〈THERE WILL BE A DAY WHEN IT WILL BE *AMERICANS* WHO HAVE TO ANSWER TO *JAPANESE* OVERSEERS!〉

THERE IS NO TIME FOR THE SHADOW WARRIOR TO CHANGE INTO A MAYOR AND WARN THE AMERICAN, INSTEAD HE BECOMES THE TENGU--

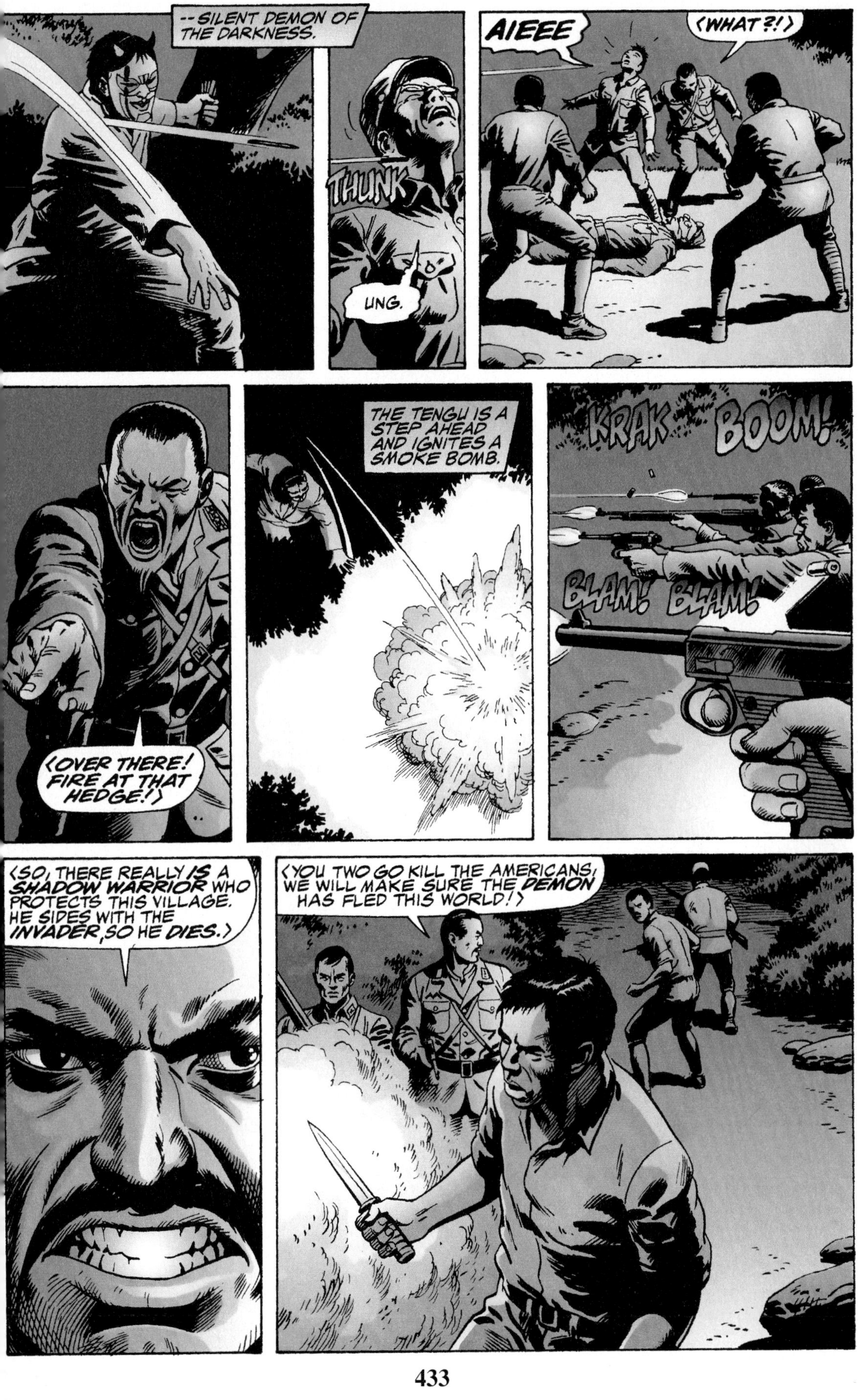
--SILENT DEMON OF THE DARKNESS.
THUNK
UNG.
AIEEE
⟨WHAT?!⟩
⟨OVER THERE! FIRE AT THAT HEDGE!⟩
THE TENGU IS A STEP AHEAD AND IGNITES A SMOKE BOMB.
KRAK
BOOM!
BLAM! BLAM!
⟨SO, THERE REALLY IS A SHADOW WARRIOR WHO PROTECTS THIS VILLAGE. HE SIDES WITH THE INVADER, SO HE DIES.⟩
⟨YOU TWO GO KILL THE AMERICANS, WE WILL MAKE SURE THE DEMON HAS FLED THIS WORLD!⟩

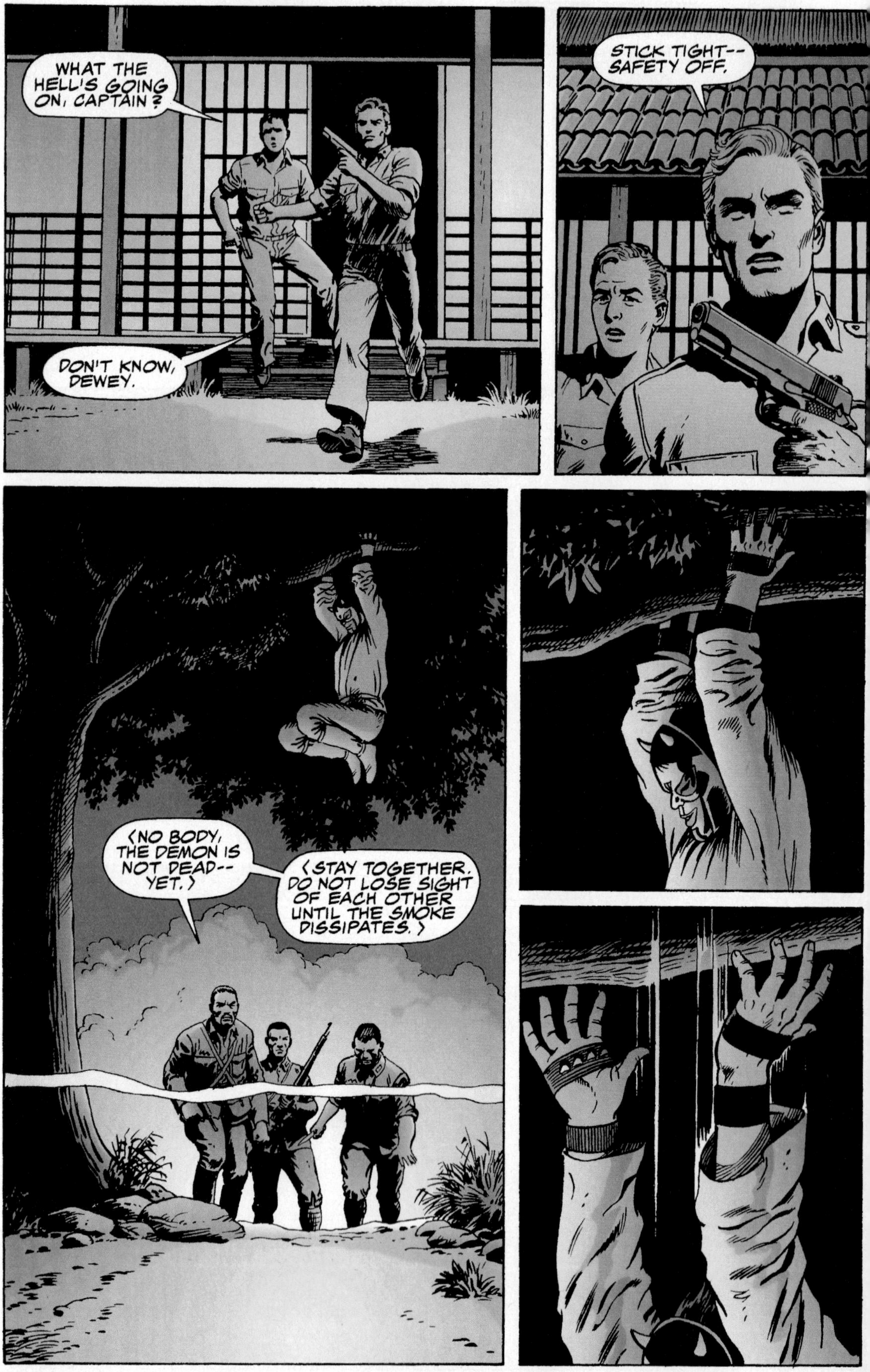
WHAT THE HELL'S GOING ON, CAPTAIN?
DON'T KNOW, DEWEY.
STICK TIGHT-- SAFETY OFF.
<NO BODY, THE DEMON IS NOT DEAD-- YET.>
<STAY TOGETHER. DO NOT LOSE SIGHT OF EACH OTHER UNTIL THE SMOKE DISSIPATES.>

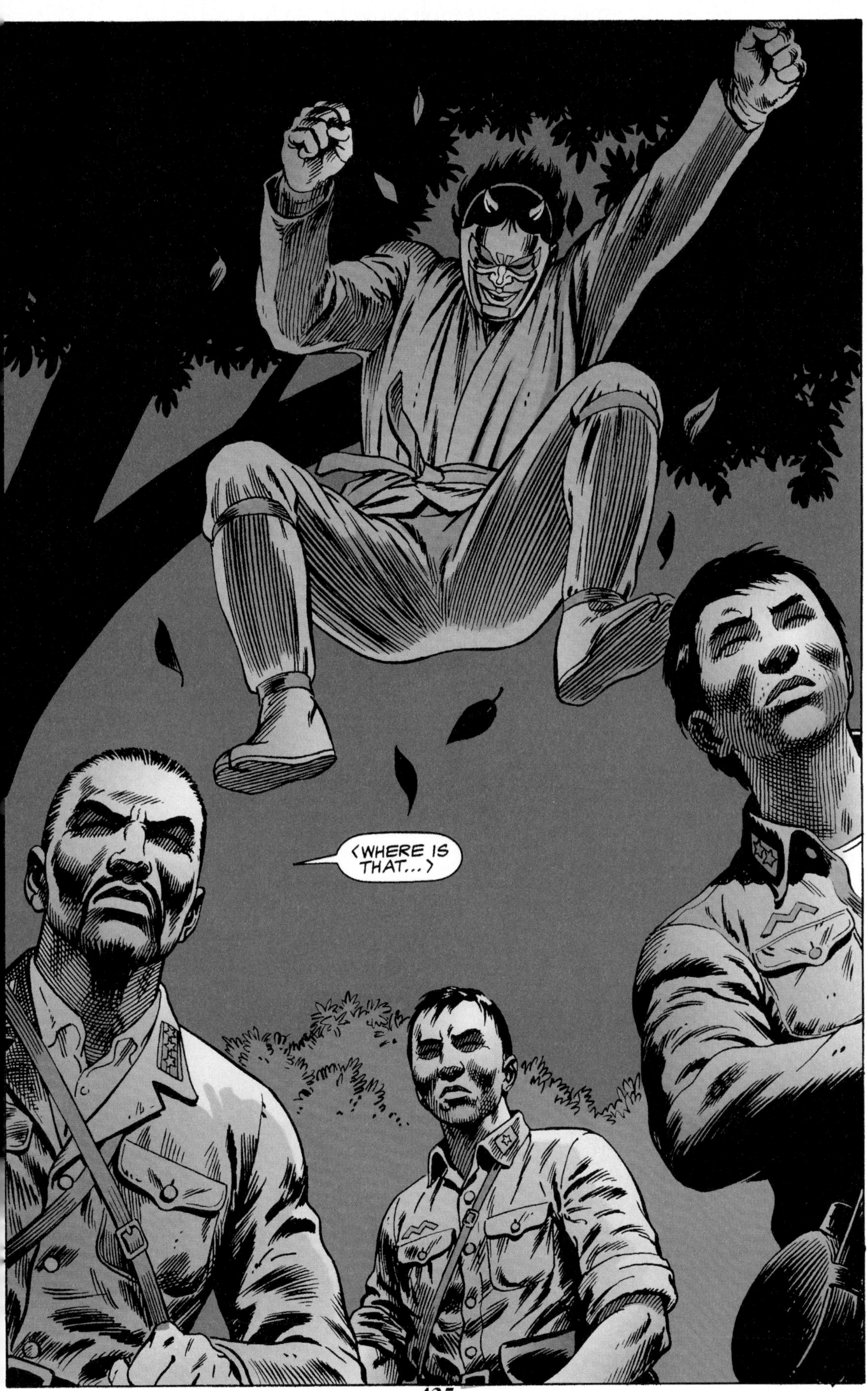

‹WHERE IS THAT...›

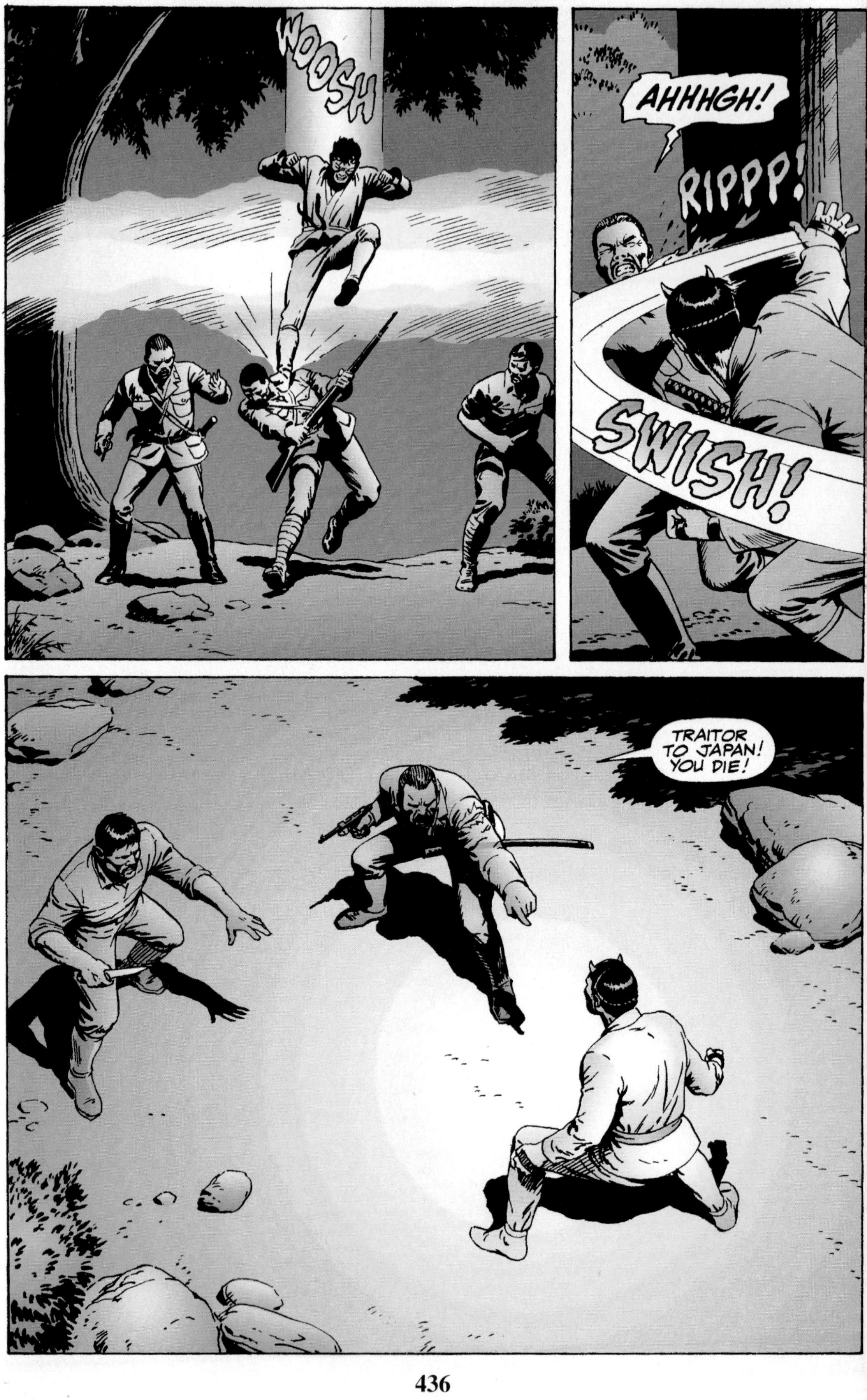
WOOSH
AHHHGH!
RIPPP!
SWISH!
TRAITOR TO JAPAN! YOU DIE!

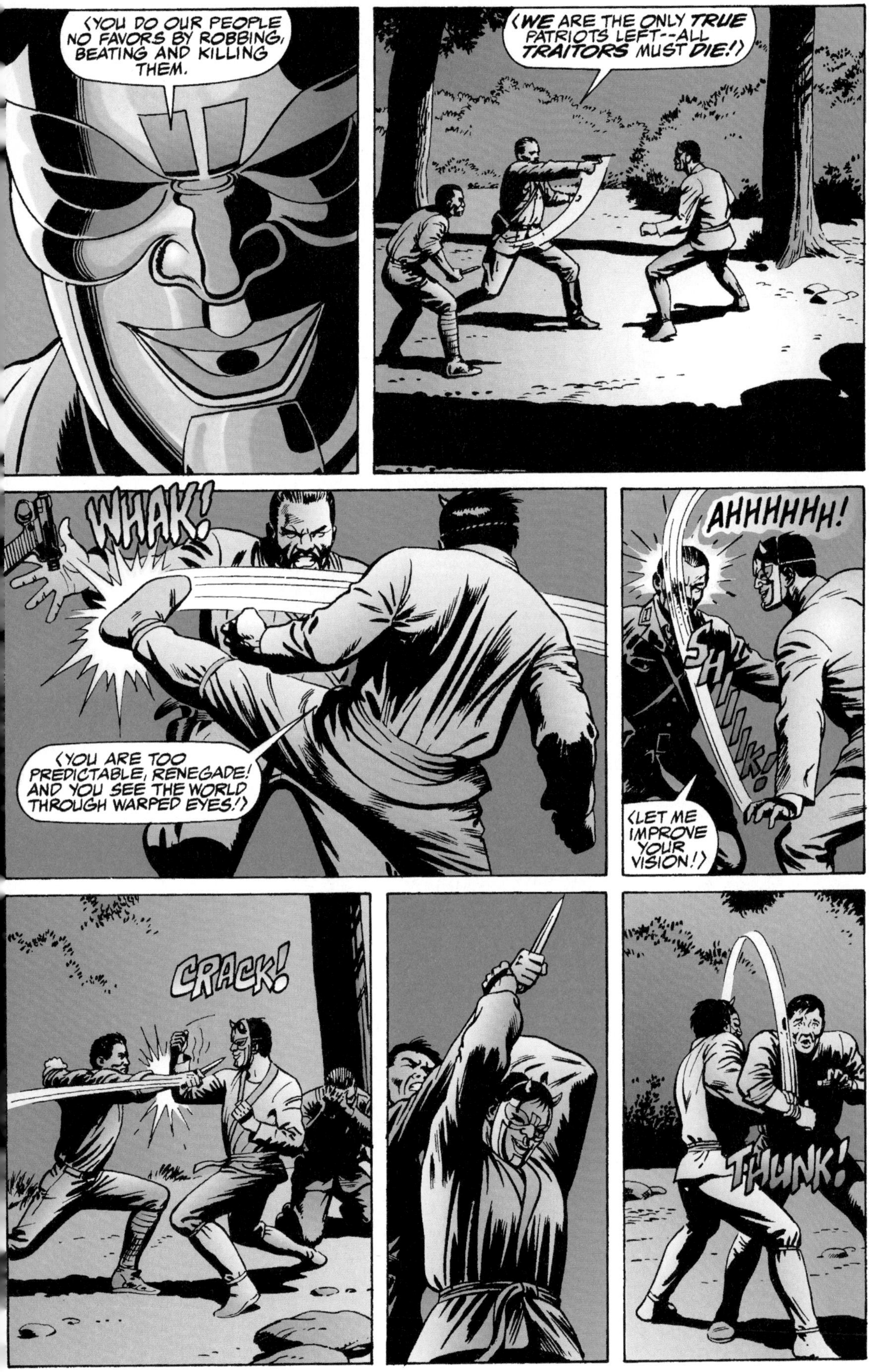
‹YOU DO OUR PEOPLE NO FAVORS BY ROBBING, BEATING AND KILLING THEM.
‹WE ARE THE ONLY TRUE PATRIOTS LEFT--ALL TRAITORS MUST DIE!›
WHAK!
‹YOU ARE TOO PREDICTABLE, RENEGADE! AND YOU SEE THE WORLD THROUGH WARPED EYES!›
AHHHHHH!
SHHHK!
‹LET ME IMPROVE YOUR VISION!›
CRACK!
THUNK!

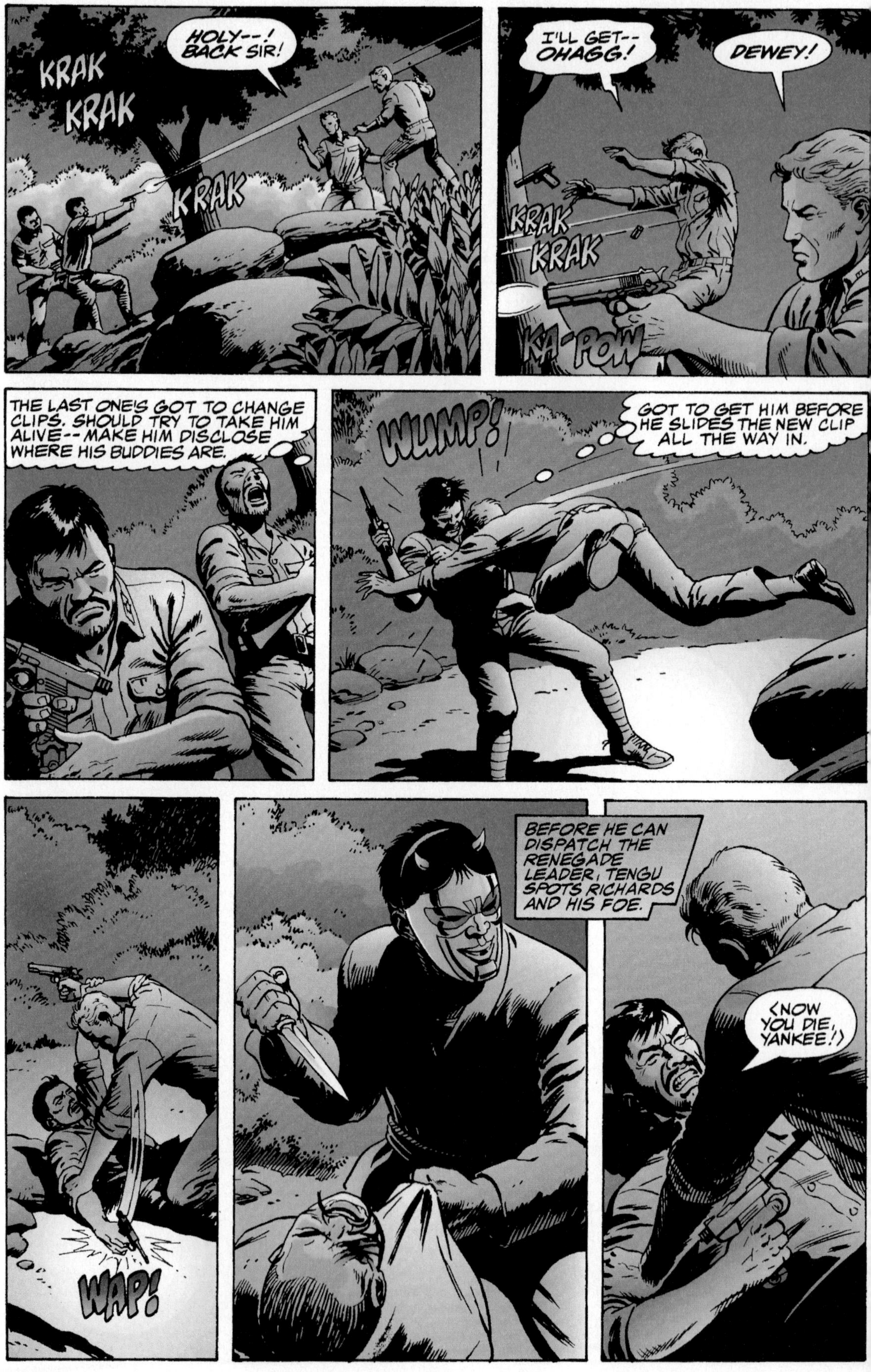
KRAK
KRAK
HOLY--! BACK SIR!
KRAK
I'LL GET-- OHAGG!
DEWEY!
KRAK
KRAK
KA-POW
THE LAST ONE'S GOT TO CHANGE CLIPS. SHOULD TRY TO TAKE HIM ALIVE--MAKE HIM DISCLOSE WHERE HIS BUDDIES ARE.
WUMP!
GOT TO GET HIM BEFORE HE SLIDES THE NEW CLIP ALL THE WAY IN.
WAP!
BEFORE HE CAN DISPATCH THE RENEGADE LEADER, TENGU SPOTS RICHARDS AND HIS FOE.
<NOW YOU DIE, YANKEE!>

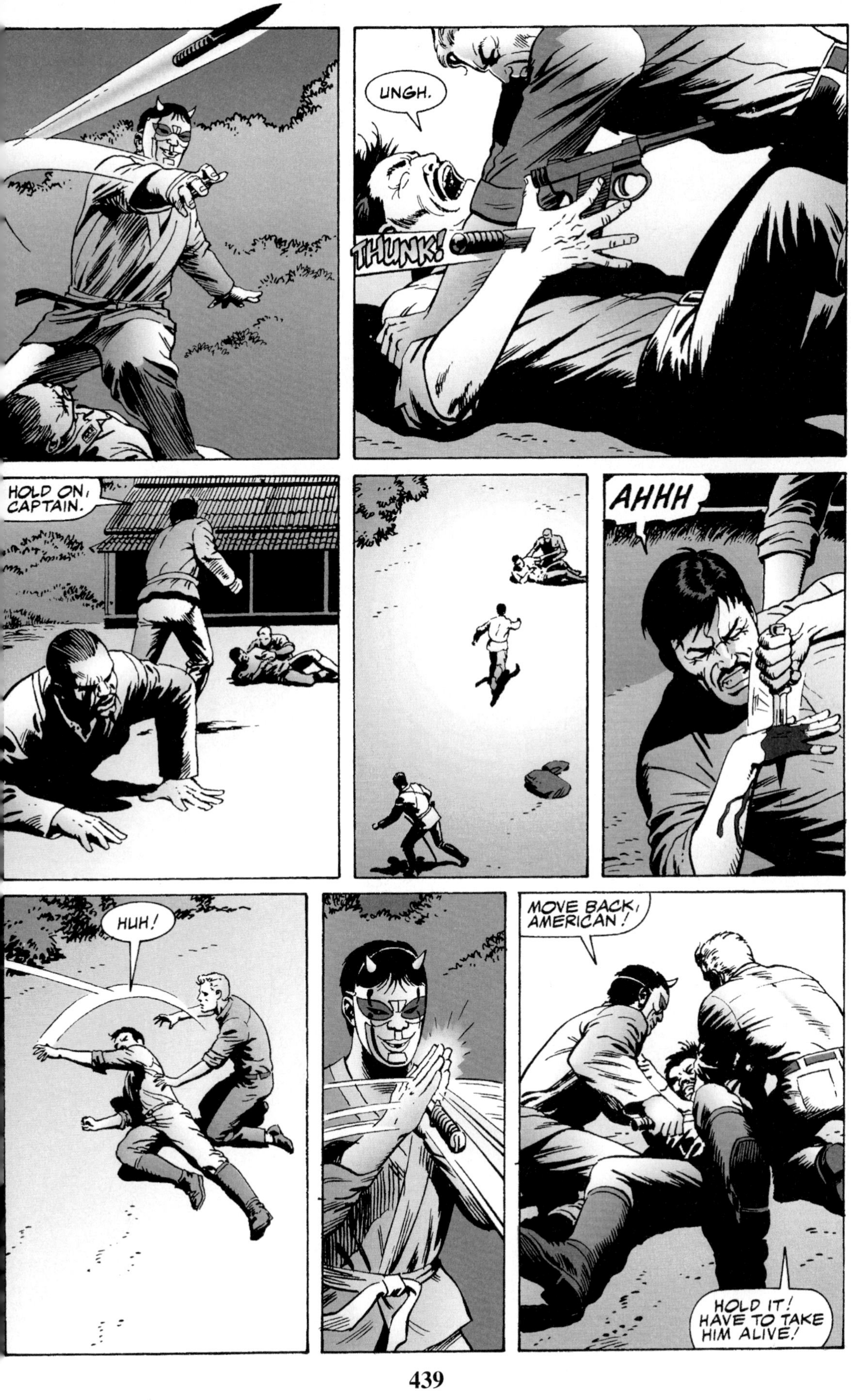
UNGH.
THUNK!
HOLD ON, CAPTAIN.
AHHH
HUH!
MOVE BACK, AMERICAN!
HOLD IT! HAVE TO TAKE HIM ALIVE!

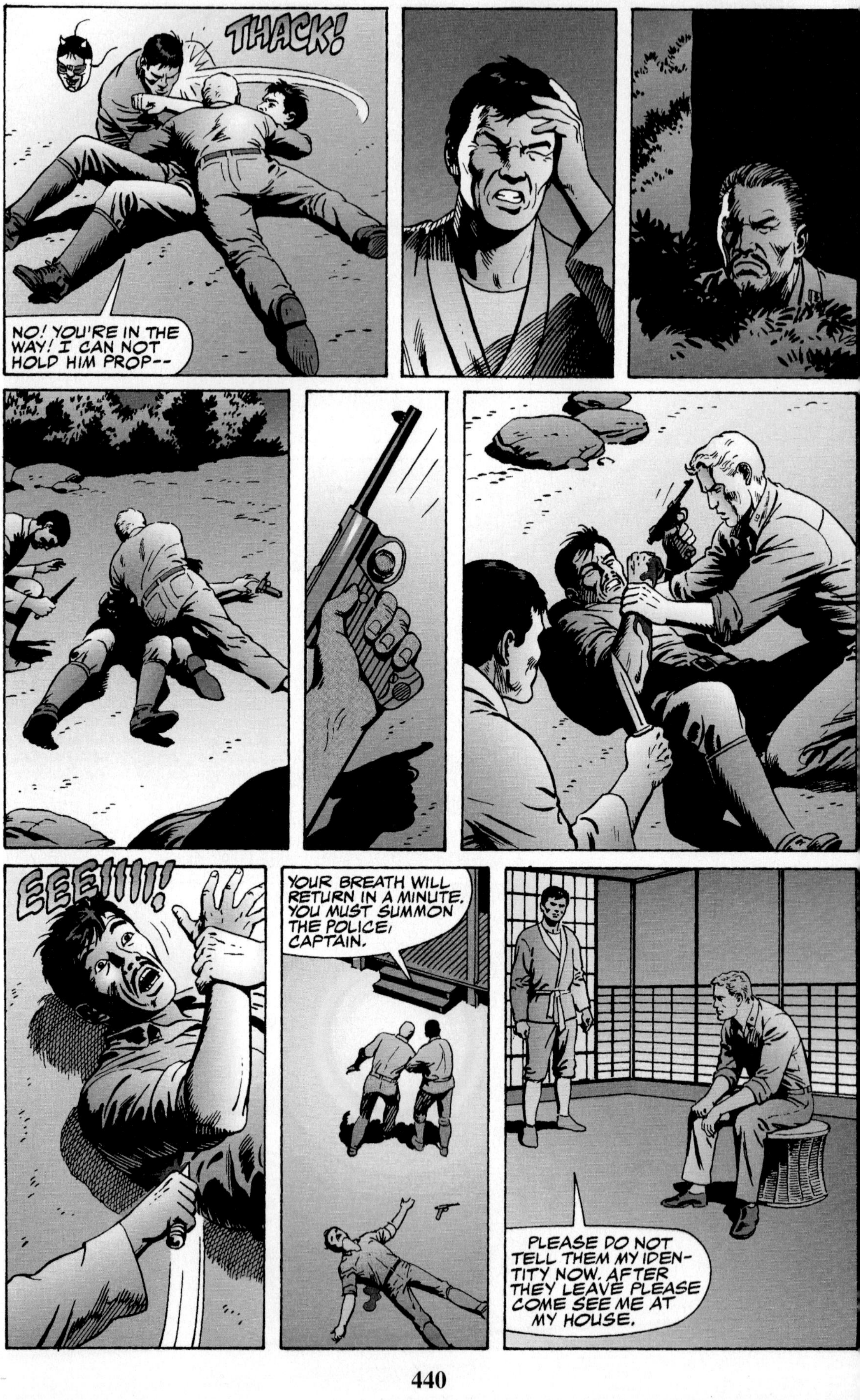
THACK!
NO! YOU'RE IN THE WAY! I CAN NOT HOLD HIM PROP--
EEEIIIII!
YOUR BREATH WILL RETURN IN A MINUTE. YOU MUST SUMMON THE POLICE, CAPTAIN.
PLEASE DO NOT TELL THEM MY IDENTITY NOW. AFTER THEY LEAVE PLEASE COME SEE ME AT MY HOUSE.

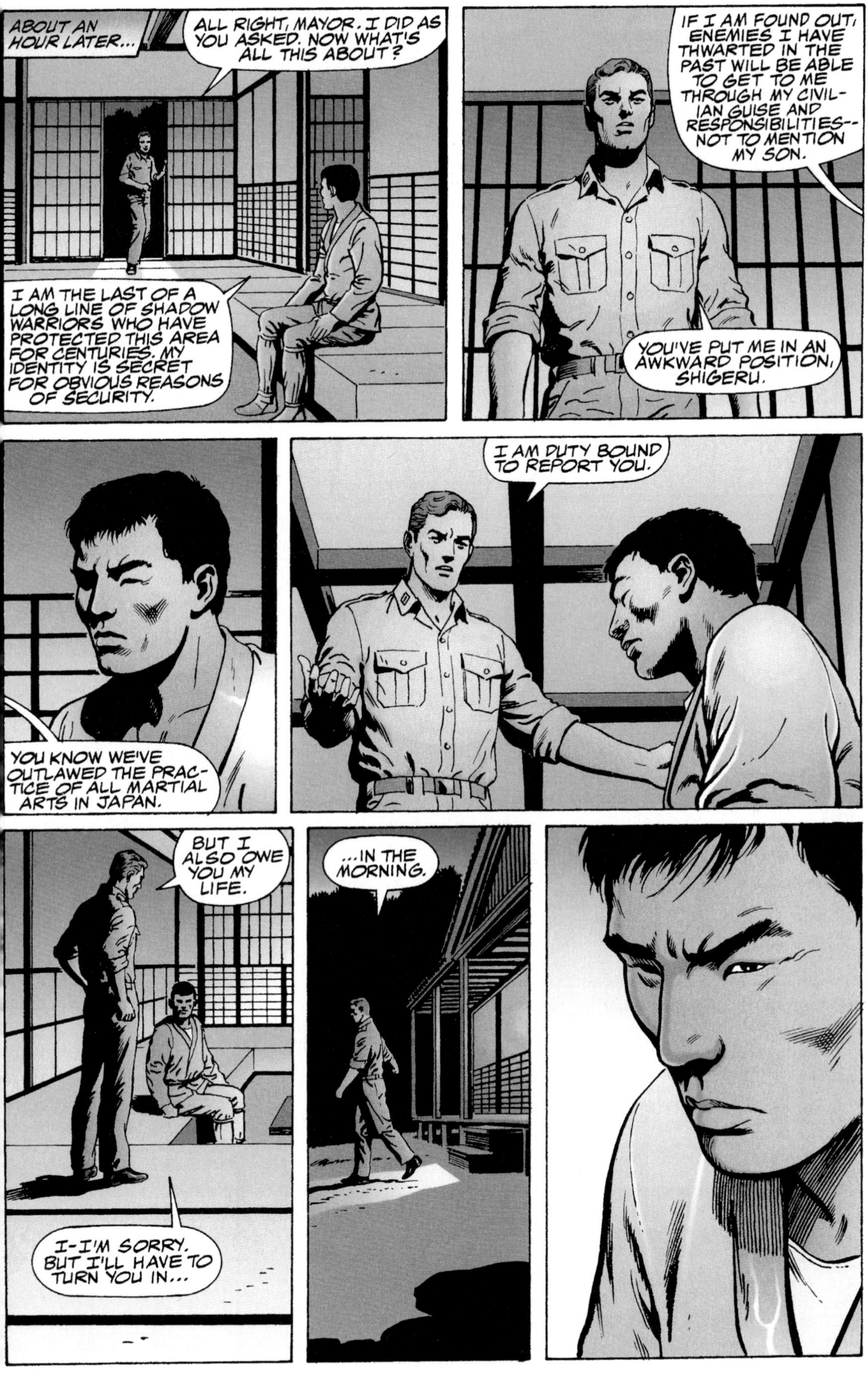
ABOUT AN HOUR LATER...
ALL RIGHT, MAYOR. I DID AS YOU ASKED. NOW WHAT'S ALL THIS ABOUT?
I AM THE LAST OF A LONG LINE OF SHADOW WARRIORS WHO HAVE PROTECTED THIS AREA FOR CENTURIES. MY IDENTITY IS SECRET FOR OBVIOUS REASONS OF SECURITY.
IF I AM FOUND OUT, ENEMIES I HAVE THWARTED IN THE PAST WILL BE ABLE TO GET TO ME THROUGH MY CIVILIAN GUISE AND RESPONSIBILITIES--NOT TO MENTION MY SON.
YOU'VE PUT ME IN AN AWKWARD POSITION, SHIGERU.
YOU KNOW WE'VE OUTLAWED THE PRACTICE OF ALL MARTIAL ARTS IN JAPAN.
I AM DUTY BOUND TO REPORT YOU.
BUT I ALSO OWE YOU MY LIFE.
I-I'M SORRY. BUT I'LL HAVE TO TURN YOU IN...
...IN THE MORNING.

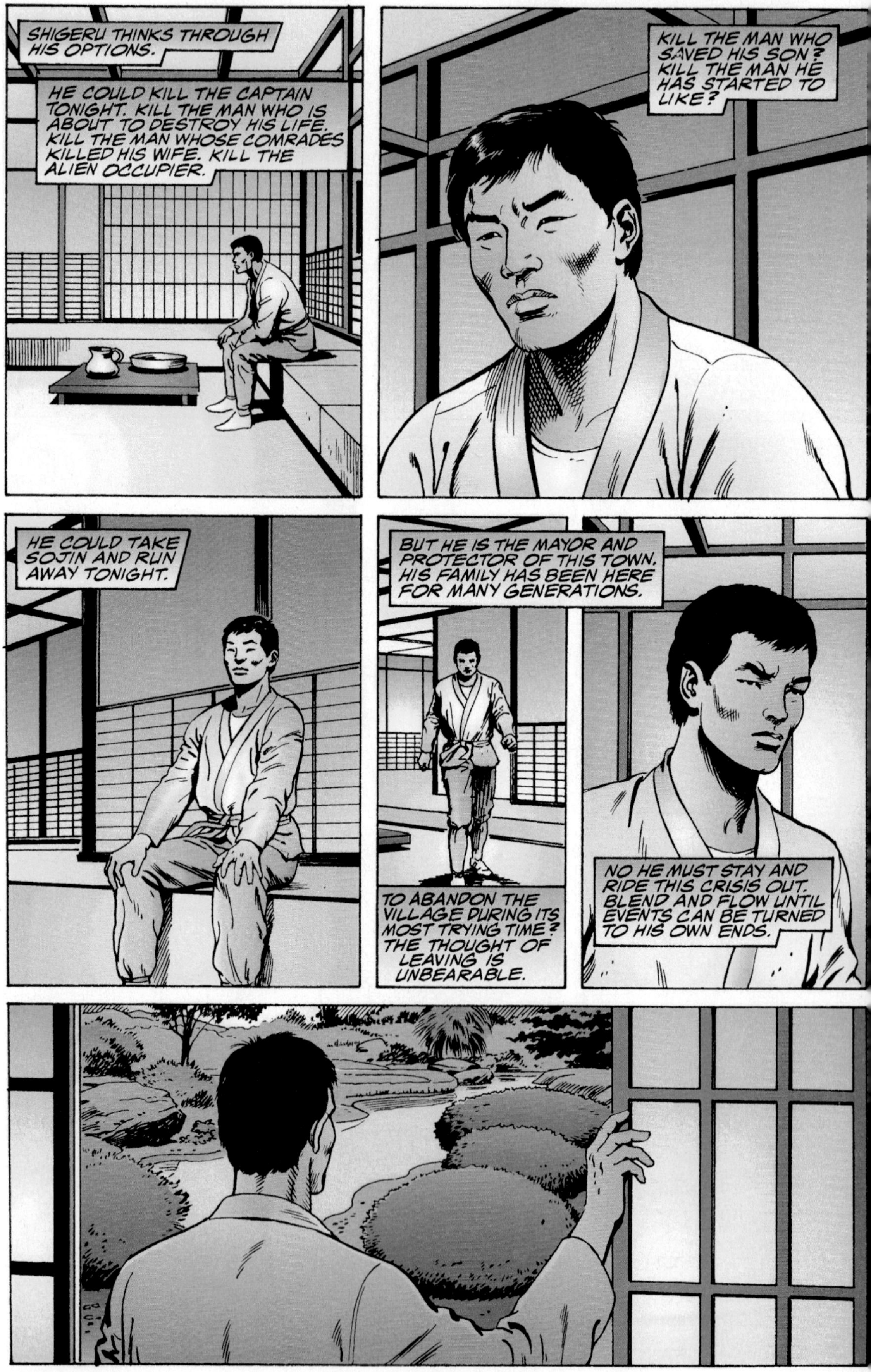
SHIGERU THINKS THROUGH HIS OPTIONS.
HE COULD KILL THE CAPTAIN TONIGHT. KILL THE MAN WHO IS ABOUT TO DESTROY HIS LIFE. KILL THE MAN WHOSE COMRADES KILLED HIS WIFE. KILL THE ALIEN OCCUPIER.
KILL THE MAN WHO SAVED HIS SON? KILL THE MAN HE HAS STARTED TO LIKE?
HE COULD TAKE SOJIN AND RUN AWAY TONIGHT.
BUT HE IS THE MAYOR AND PROTECTOR OF THIS TOWN. HIS FAMILY HAS BEEN HERE FOR MANY GENERATIONS.
TO ABANDON THE VILLAGE DURING ITS MOST TRYING TIME? THE THOUGHT OF LEAVING IS UNBEARABLE.
NO HE MUST STAY AND RIDE THIS CRISIS OUT. BLEND AND FLOW UNTIL EVENTS CAN BE TURNED TO HIS OWN ENDS.

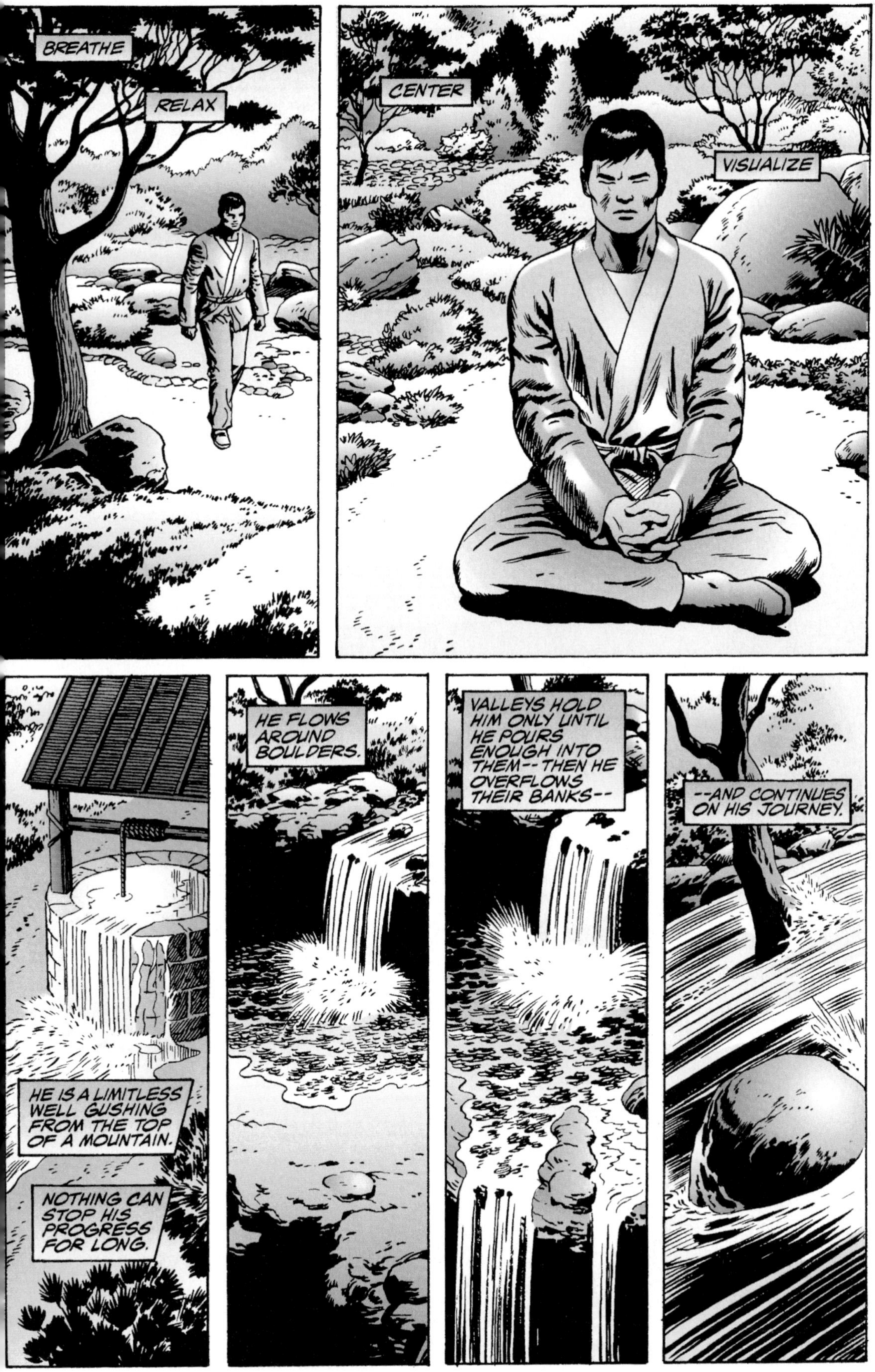
BREATHE
RELAX
CENTER
VISUALIZE
HE IS A LIMITLESS WELL GUSHING FROM THE TOP OF A MOUNTAIN.
NOTHING CAN STOP HIS PROGRESS FOR LONG.
HE FLOWS AROUND BOULDERS.
VALLEYS HOLD HIM ONLY UNTIL HE POURS ENOUGH INTO THEM--THEN HE OVERFLOWS THEIR BANKS--
--AND CONTINUES ON HIS JOURNEY.

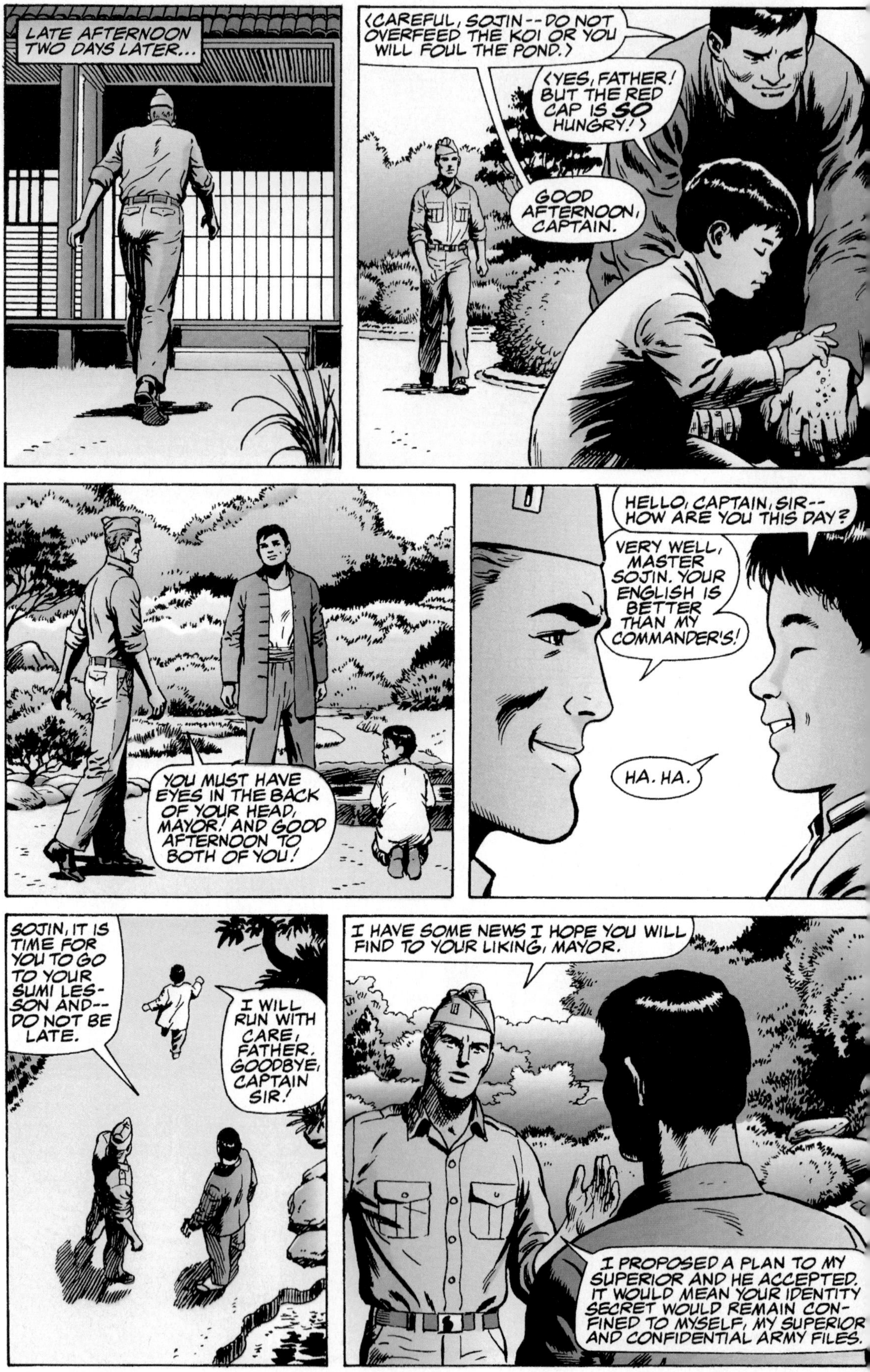
LATE AFTERNOON TWO DAYS LATER...
‹CAREFUL, SOJIN--DO NOT OVERFEED THE KOI OR YOU WILL FOUL THE POND.›
‹YES, FATHER! BUT THE RED CAP IS SO HUNGRY!›
GOOD AFTERNOON, CAPTAIN.
YOU MUST HAVE EYES IN THE BACK OF YOUR HEAD, MAYOR! AND GOOD AFTERNOON TO BOTH OF YOU!
HELLO, CAPTAIN, SIR-- HOW ARE YOU THIS DAY?
VERY WELL, MASTER SOJIN. YOUR ENGLISH IS BETTER THAN MY COMMANDER'S!
HA. HA.
SOJIN, IT IS TIME FOR YOU TO GO TO YOUR SUMI LES-SON AND-- DO NOT BE LATE.
I WILL RUN WITH CARE, FATHER. GOODBYE, CAPTAIN SIR!
I HAVE SOME NEWS I HOPE YOU WILL FIND TO YOUR LIKING, MAYOR.
I PROPOSED A PLAN TO MY SUPERIOR AND HE ACCEPTED. IT WOULD MEAN YOUR IDENTITY SECRET WOULD REMAIN CON-FINED TO MYSELF, MY SUPERIOR AND CONFIDENTIAL ARMY FILES.

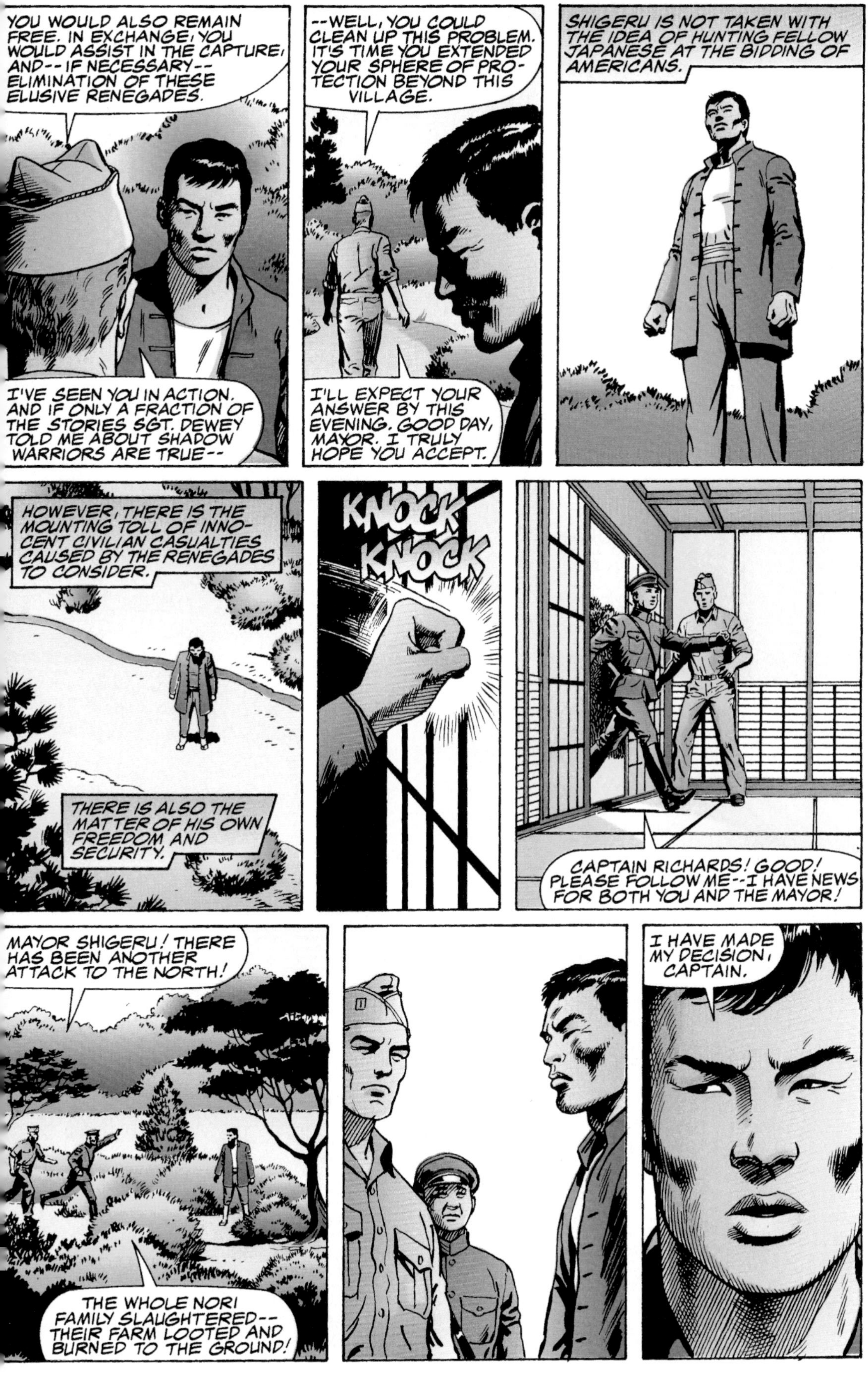

YOU WOULD ALSO REMAIN FREE. IN EXCHANGE, YOU WOULD ASSIST IN THE CAPTURE, AND-- IF NECESSARY-- ELIMINATION OF THESE ELUSIVE RENEGADES.
I'VE SEEN YOU IN ACTION. AND IF ONLY A FRACTION OF THE STORIES SGT. DEWEY TOLD ME ABOUT SHADOW WARRIORS ARE TRUE--
--WELL, YOU COULD CLEAN UP THIS PROBLEM. IT'S TIME YOU EXTENDED YOUR SPHERE OF PROTECTION BEYOND THIS VILLAGE.
I'LL EXPECT YOUR ANSWER BY THIS EVENING. GOOD DAY, MAYOR. I TRULY HOPE YOU ACCEPT.
SHIGERU IS NOT TAKEN WITH THE IDEA OF HUNTING FELLOW JAPANESE AT THE BIDDING OF AMERICANS.
HOWEVER, THERE IS THE MOUNTING TOLL OF INNOCENT CIVILIAN CASUALTIES CAUSED BY THE RENEGADES TO CONSIDER.
THERE IS ALSO THE MATTER OF HIS OWN FREEDOM AND SECURITY.
KNOCK
KNOCK
CAPTAIN RICHARDS! GOOD! PLEASE FOLLOW ME--I HAVE NEWS FOR BOTH YOU AND THE MAYOR!
MAYOR SHIGERU! THERE HAS BEEN ANOTHER ATTACK TO THE NORTH!
THE WHOLE NORI FAMILY SLAUGHTERED-- THEIR FARM LOOTED AND BURNED TO THE GROUND!
I HAVE MADE MY DECISION, CAPTAIN.

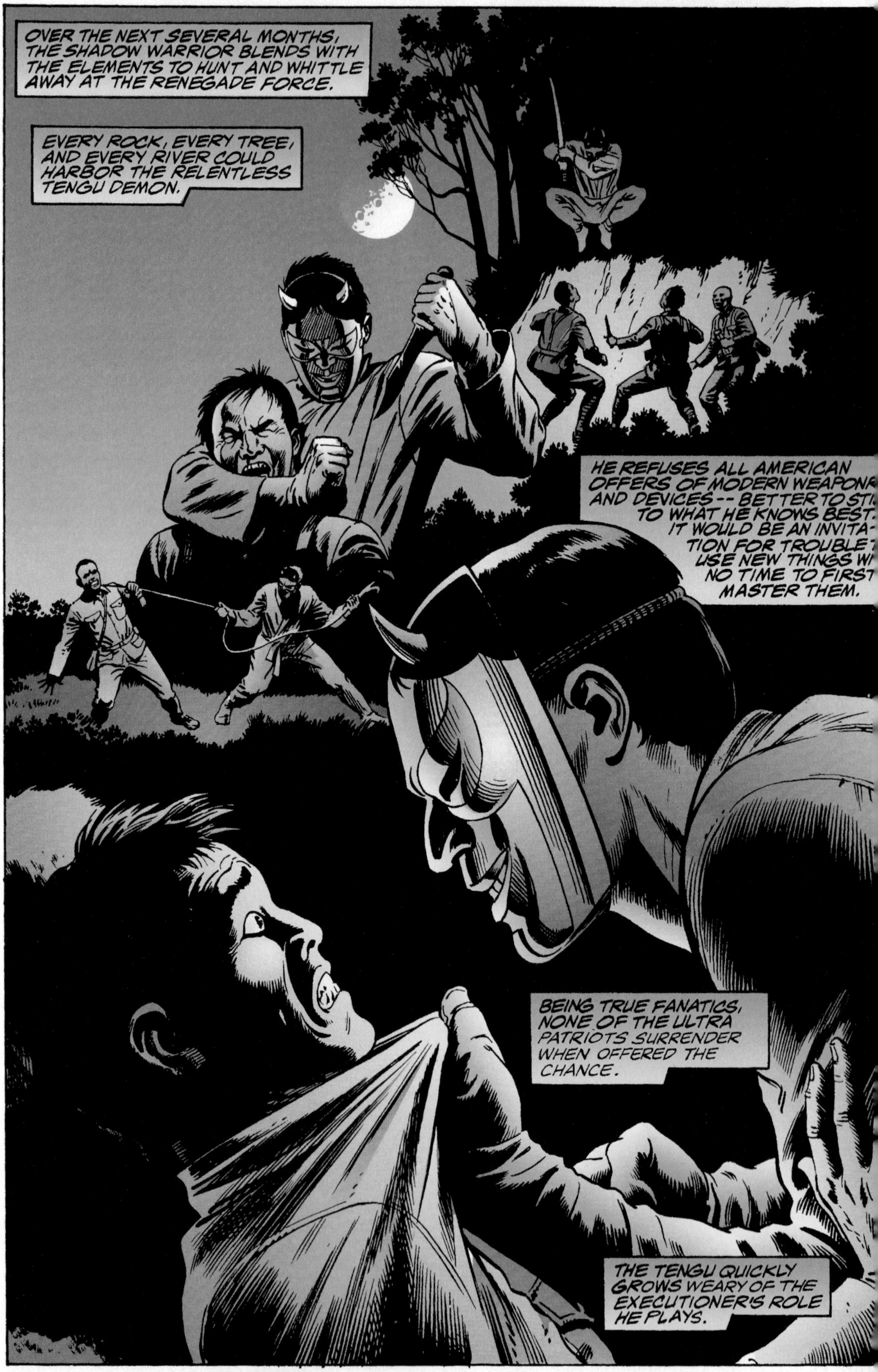
OVER THE NEXT SEVERAL MONTHS, THE SHADOW WARRIOR BLENDS WITH THE ELEMENTS TO HUNT AND WHITTLE AWAY AT THE RENEGADE FORCE.
EVERY ROCK, EVERY TREE, AND EVERY RIVER COULD HARBOR THE RELENTLESS TENGU DEMON.
HE REFUSES ALL AMERICAN OFFERS OF MODERN WEAPONR AND DEVICES -- BETTER TO STI TO WHAT HE KNOWS BEST. IT WOULD BE AN INVITA- TION FOR TROUBLE T USE NEW THINGS WI NO TIME TO FIRST MASTER THEM.
BEING TRUE FANATICS, NONE OF THE ULTRA PATRIOTS SURRENDER WHEN OFFERED THE CHANCE.
THE TENGU QUICKLY GROWS WEARY OF THE EXECUTIONER'S ROLE HE PLAYS.

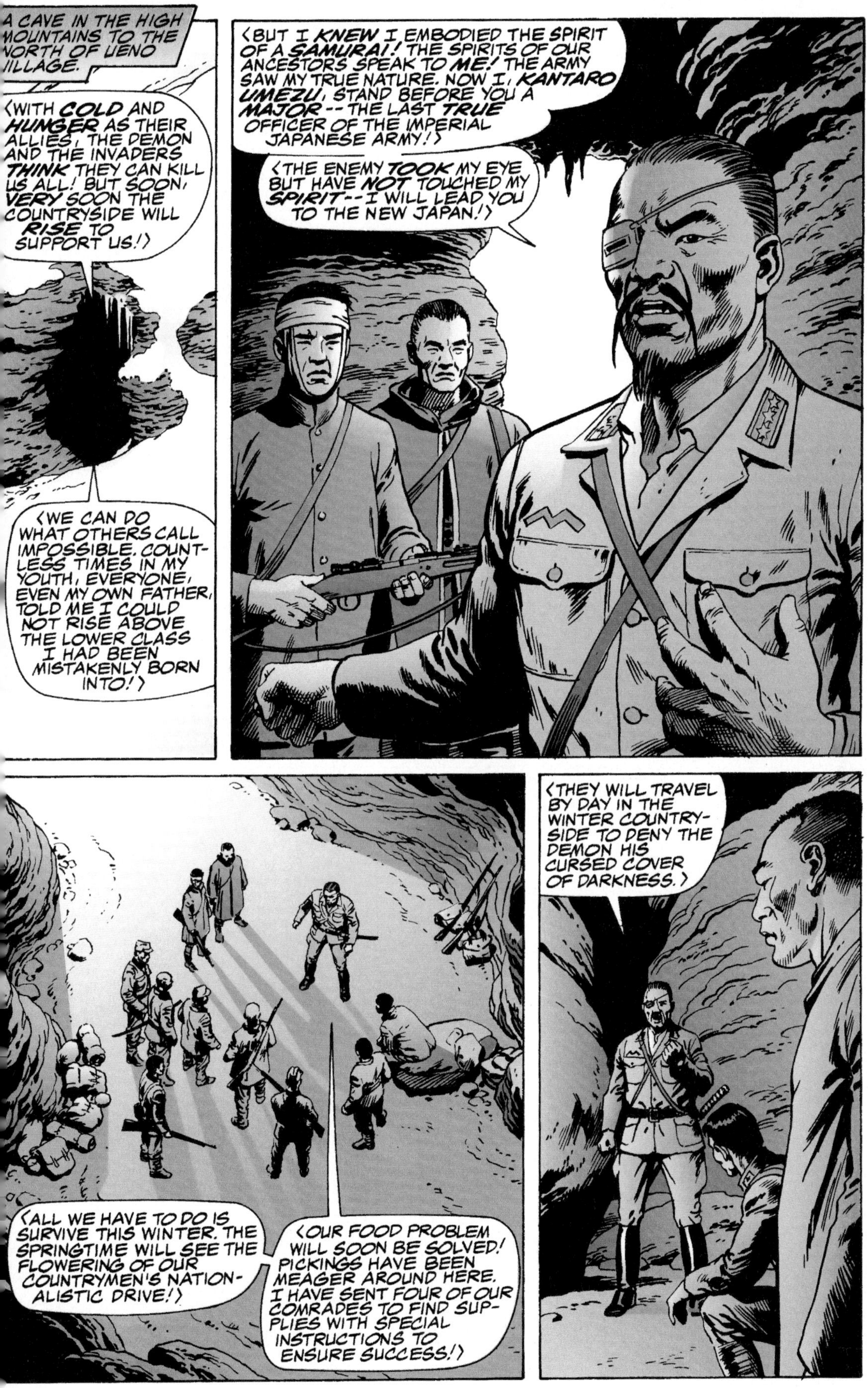
A CAVE IN THE HIGH MOUNTAINS TO THE NORTH OF UENO VILLAGE.
‹WITH COLD AND HUNGER AS THEIR ALLIES, THE DEMON AND THE INVADERS THINK THEY CAN KILL US ALL! BUT SOON, VERY SOON THE COUNTRYSIDE WILL RISE TO SUPPORT US!›
‹WE CAN DO WHAT OTHERS CALL IMPOSSIBLE. COUNTLESS TIMES IN MY YOUTH, EVERYONE, EVEN MY OWN FATHER, TOLD ME I COULD NOT RISE ABOVE THE LOWER CLASS I HAD BEEN MISTAKENLY BORN INTO!›
‹BUT I KNEW I EMBODIED THE SPIRIT OF A SAMURAI! THE SPIRITS OF OUR ANCESTORS SPEAK TO ME! THE ARMY SAW MY TRUE NATURE. NOW I, KANTARO UMEZU, STAND BEFORE YOU A MAJOR -- THE LAST TRUE OFFICER OF THE IMPERIAL JAPANESE ARMY!›
‹THE ENEMY TOOK MY EYE BUT HAVE NOT TOUCHED MY SPIRIT -- I WILL LEAD YOU TO THE NEW JAPAN!›
‹ALL WE HAVE TO DO IS SURVIVE THIS WINTER. THE SPRINGTIME WILL SEE THE FLOWERING OF OUR COUNTRYMEN'S NATIONALISTIC DRIVE!›
‹OUR FOOD PROBLEM WILL SOON BE SOLVED! PICKINGS HAVE BEEN MEAGER AROUND HERE. I HAVE SENT FOUR OF OUR COMRADES TO FIND SUPPLIES WITH SPECIAL INSTRUCTIONS TO ENSURE SUCCESS!›
‹THEY WILL TRAVEL BY DAY IN THE WINTER COUNTRYSIDE TO DENY THE DEMON HIS CURSED COVER OF DARKNESS.›

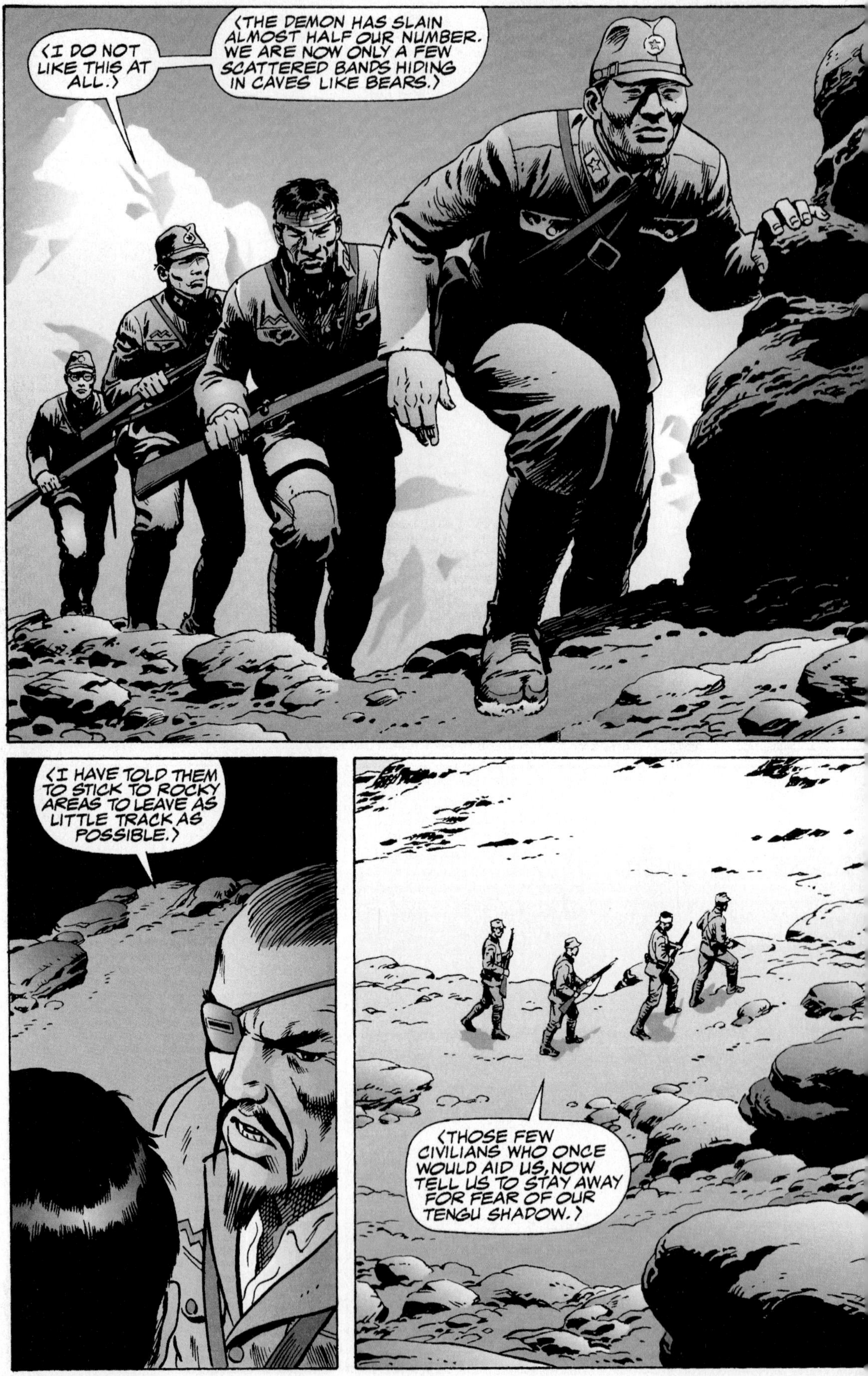
<I DO NOT LIKE THIS AT ALL.>
<THE DEMON HAS SLAIN ALMOST HALF OUR NUMBER. WE ARE NOW ONLY A FEW SCATTERED BANDS HIDING IN CAVES LIKE BEARS.>
<I HAVE TOLD THEM TO STICK TO ROCKY AREAS TO LEAVE AS LITTLE TRACK AS POSSIBLE.>
<THOSE FEW CIVILIANS WHO ONCE WOULD AID US, NOW TELL US TO STAY AWAY FOR FEAR OF OUR TENGU SHADOW.>

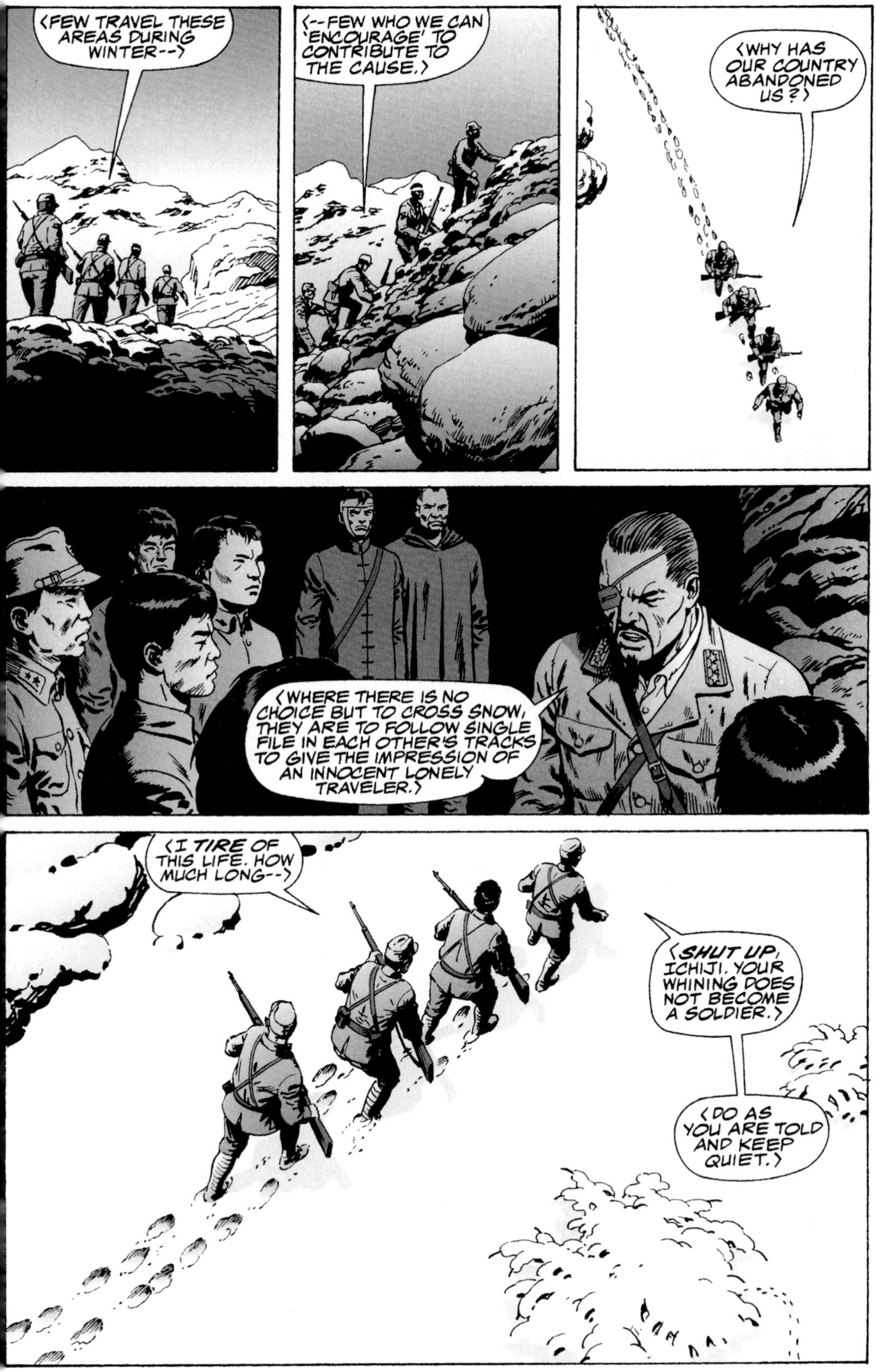

‹FEW TRAVEL THESE AREAS DURING WINTER--›
‹--FEW WHO WE CAN 'ENCOURAGE' TO CONTRIBUTE TO THE CAUSE.›
‹WHY HAS OUR COUNTRY ABANDONED US?›
‹WHERE THERE IS NO CHOICE BUT TO CROSS SNOW, THEY ARE TO FOLLOW SINGLE FILE IN EACH OTHER'S TRACKS TO GIVE THE IMPRESSION OF AN INNOCENT LONELY TRAVELER.›
‹I TIRE OF THIS LIFE. HOW MUCH LONG--›
‹SHUT UP, ICHIJI. YOUR WHINING DOES NOT BECOME A SOLDIER.›
‹DO AS YOU ARE TOLD AND KEEP QUIET.›

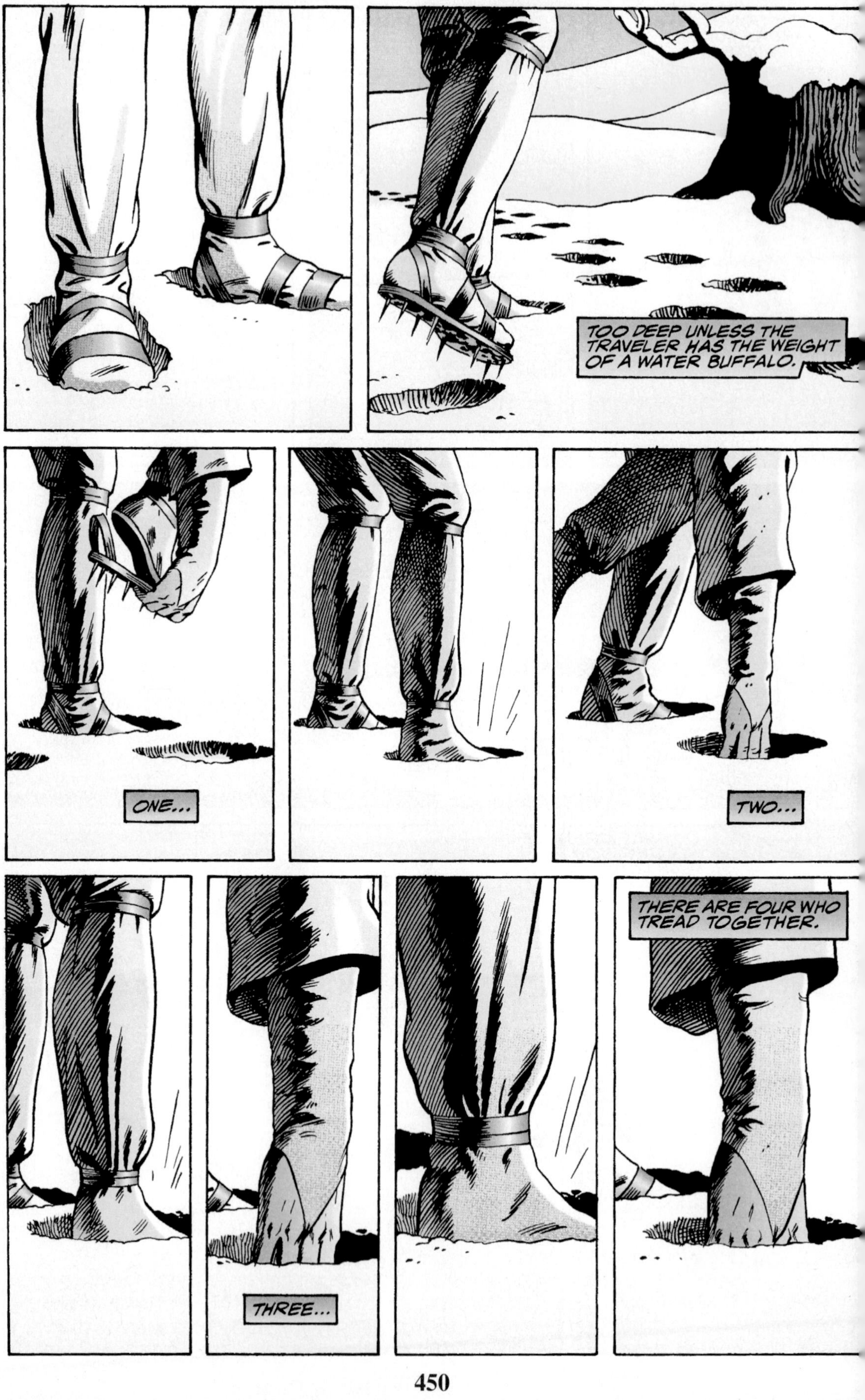
TOO DEEP UNLESS THE TRAVELER HAS THE WEIGHT OF A WATER BUFFALO.
ONE...
TWO...
THREE...
THERE ARE FOUR WHO TREAD TOGETHER.

‹OVER THAT RIDGE IT WILL BE FOUR KILO-METERS TO THE INN.›

‹ONLY THE INNKEEPER AND HIS FAMILY WILL BE THERE IN THIS MONTH.›

NOTHING. PERHAPS THE NEXT ROCK PILE WILL HOLD WHAT HE SEEKS.

‹AN EASY TARGET.›

‹EASY YOU CALL THIS?›

IT IS SLUGGISH WITH WINTER'S COLD.

451

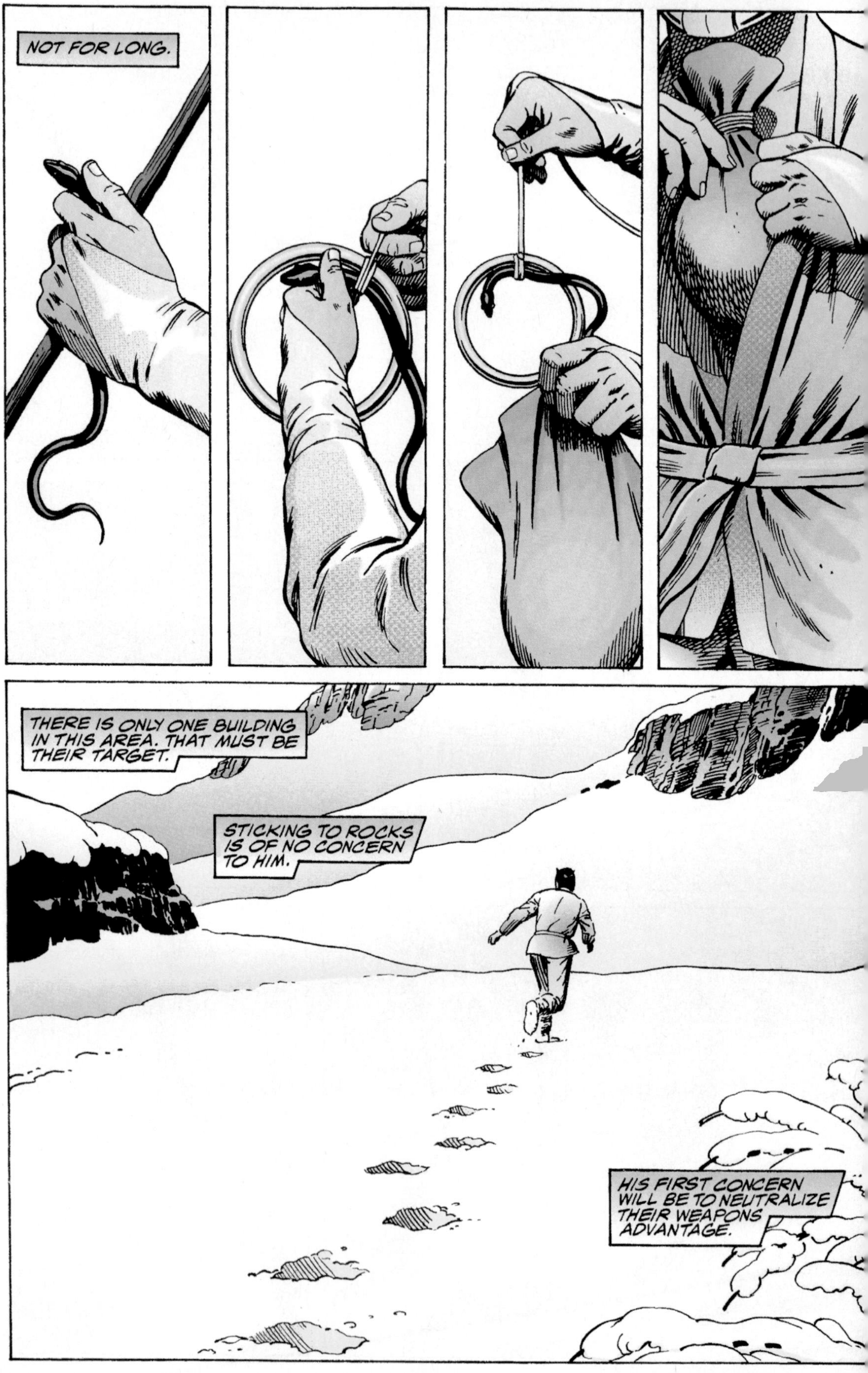
NOT FOR LONG.
THERE IS ONLY ONE BUILDING IN THIS AREA. THAT MUST BE THEIR TARGET.
STICKING TO ROCKS IS OF NO CONCERN TO HIM.
HIS FIRST CONCERN WILL BE TO NEUTRALIZE THEIR WEAPONS ADVANTAGE.

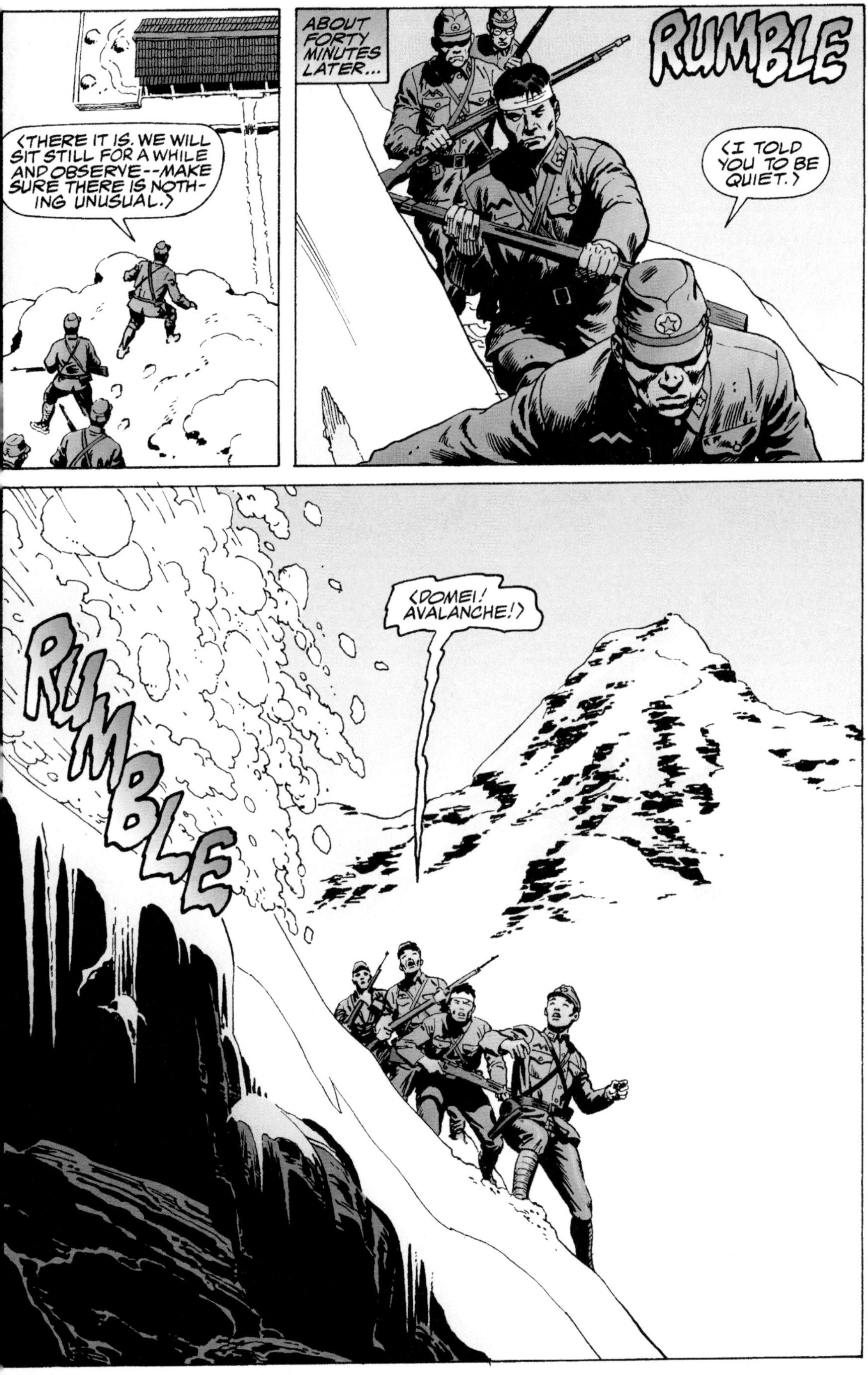
<THERE IT IS. WE WILL SIT STILL FOR A WHILE AND OBSERVE--MAKE SURE THERE IS NOTHING UNUSUAL.>
ABOUT FORTY MINUTES LATER...
RUMBLE
<I TOLD YOU TO BE QUIET.>
RUMBLE
<DOMEI! AVALANCHE!>

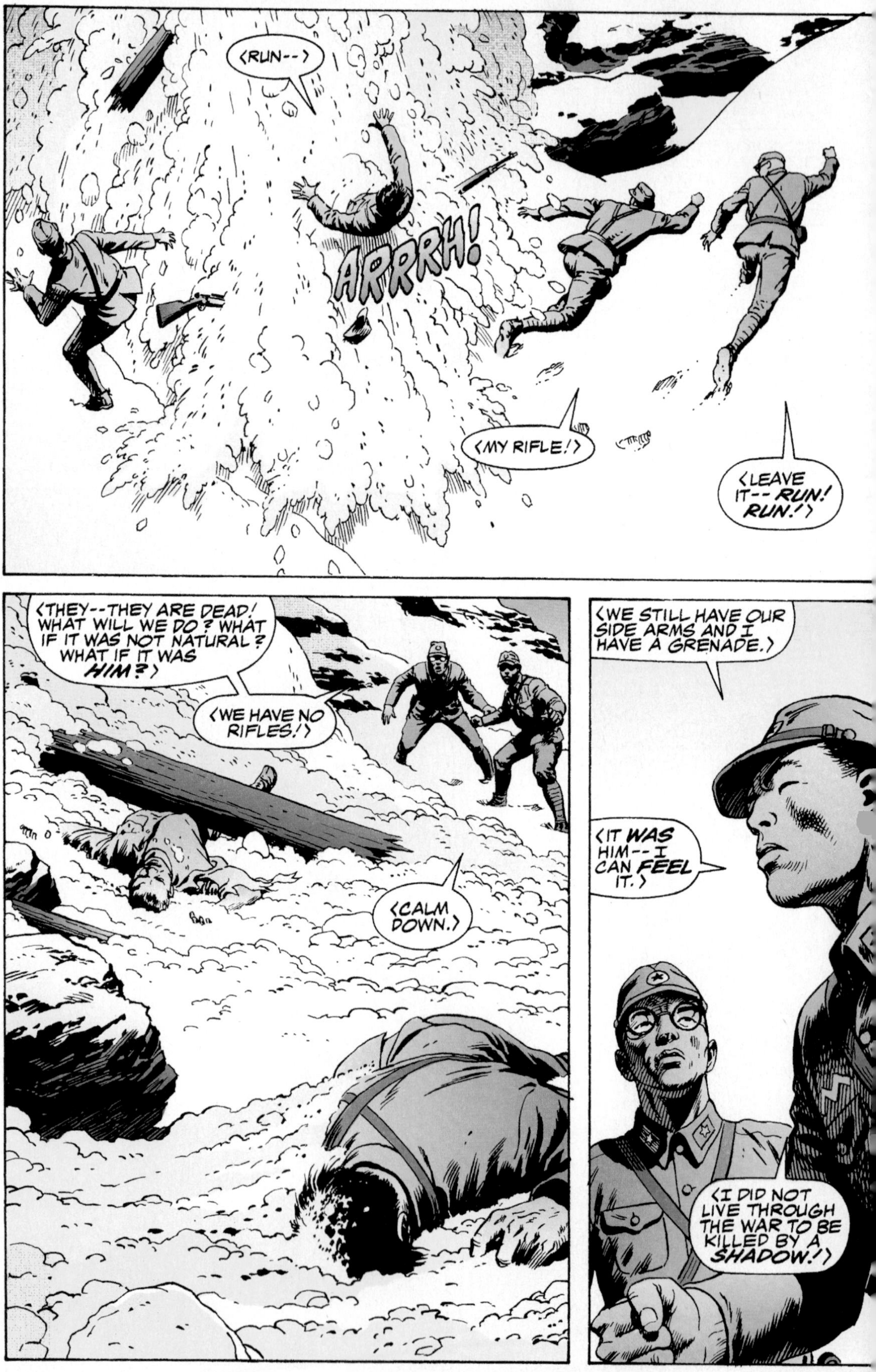
<RUN-->
ARRRH!
<MY RIFLE!>
<LEAVE IT-- RUN! RUN!>
<THEY--THEY ARE DEAD! WHAT WILL WE DO? WHAT IF IT WAS NOT NATURAL? WHAT IF IT WAS HIM?>
<WE HAVE NO RIFLES!>
<CALM DOWN.>
<WE STILL HAVE OUR SIDE ARMS AND I HAVE A GRENADE.>
<IT WAS HIM-- I CAN FEEL IT.>
<I DID NOT LIVE THROUGH THE WAR TO BE KILLED BY A SHADOW!>

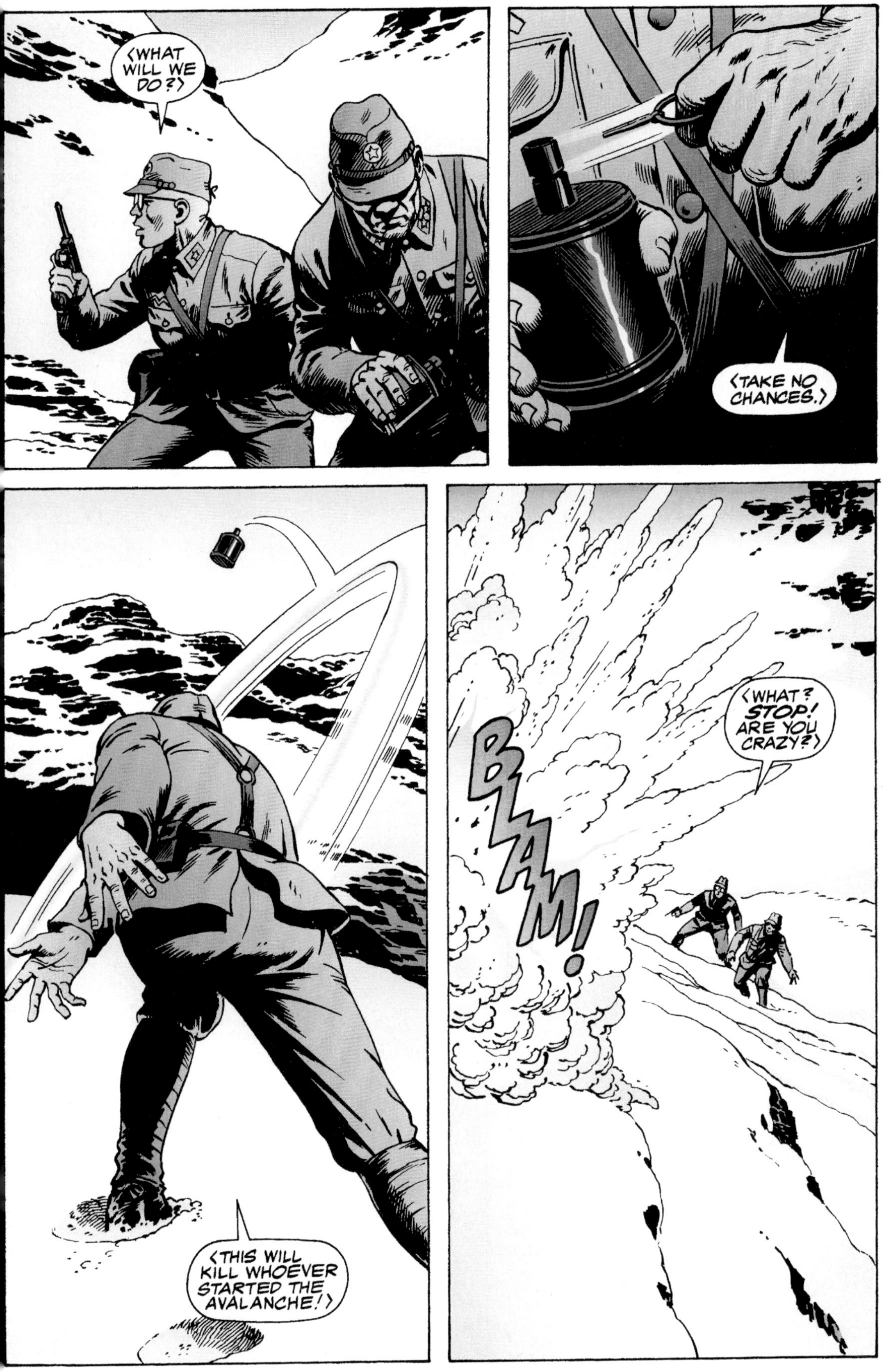
⟨WHAT WILL WE DO?⟩
⟨TAKE NO CHANCES.⟩
⟨THIS WILL KILL WHOEVER STARTED THE AVALANCHE!⟩
BLAM!
⟨WHAT? STOP! ARE YOU CRAZY?⟩

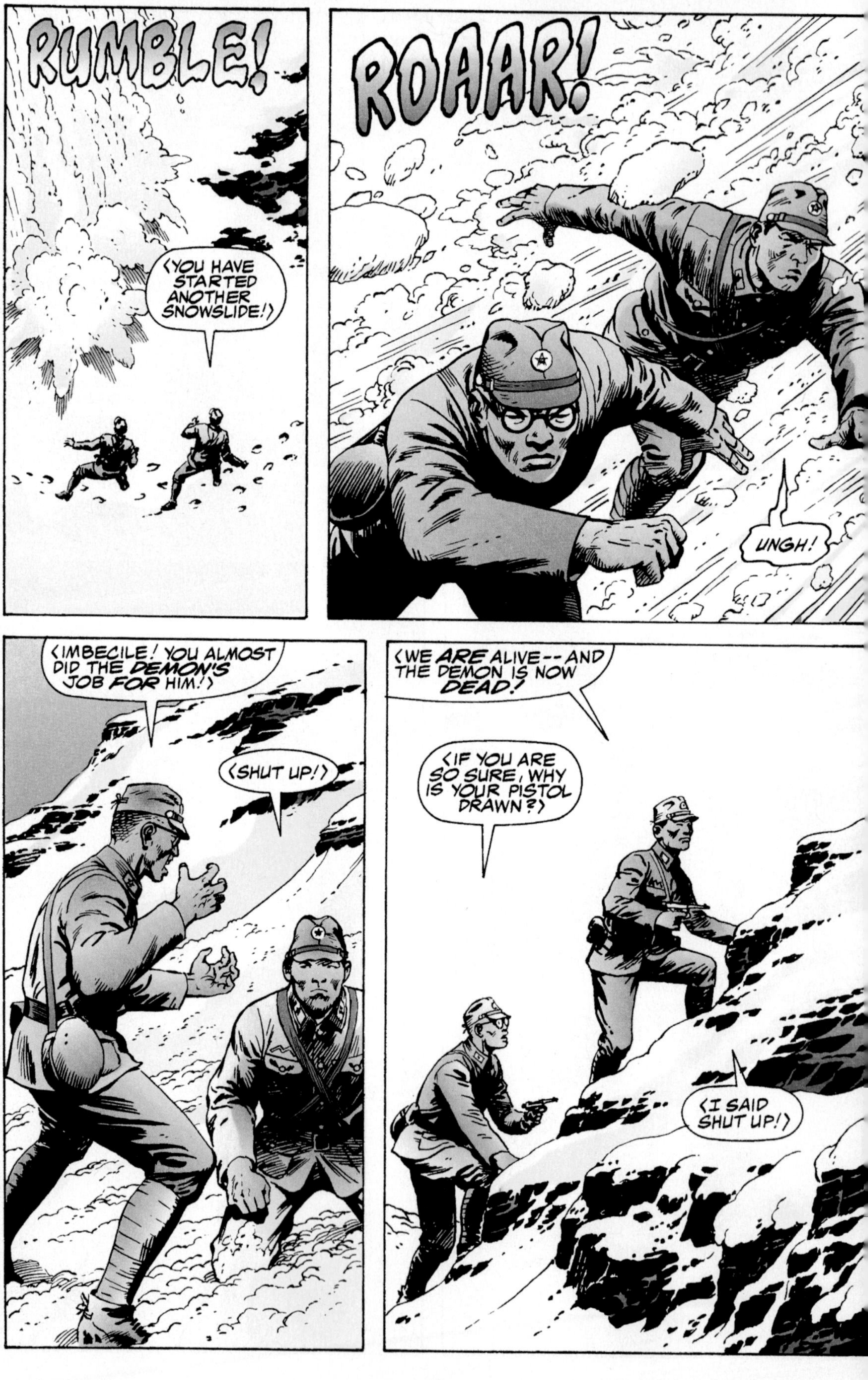
RUMBLE!
‹YOU HAVE STARTED ANOTHER SNOWSLIDE!›
ROAAR!
UNGH!
‹IMBECILE! YOU ALMOST DID THE *DEMON'S* JOB *FOR* HIM!›
‹SHUT UP!›
‹WE *ARE* ALIVE-- AND THE DEMON IS NOW *DEAD!*›
‹IF YOU ARE SO SURE, WHY IS YOUR PISTOL DRAWN?›
‹I SAID SHUT UP!›

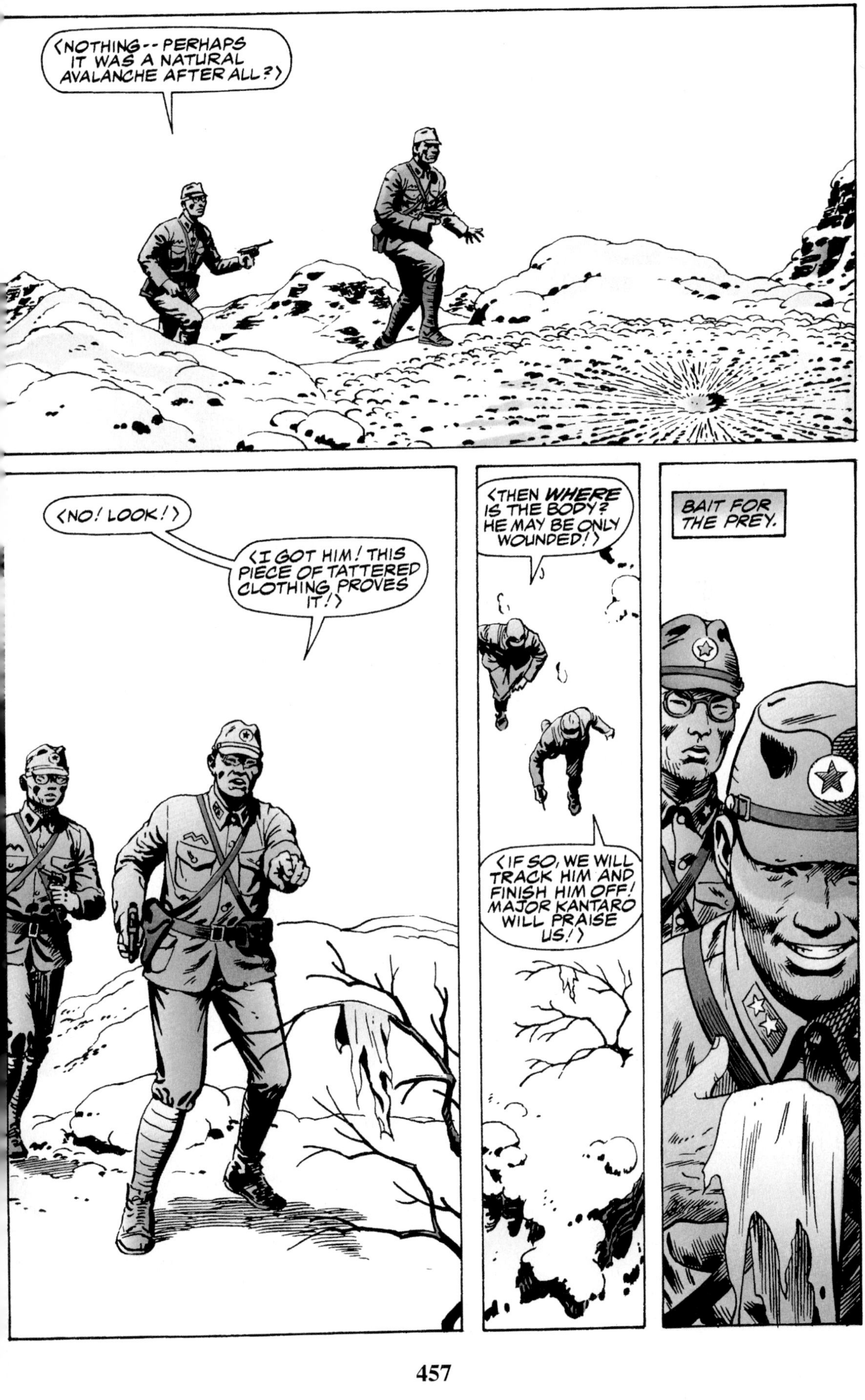

⟨NOTHING-- PERHAPS IT WAS A NATURAL AVALANCHE AFTER ALL?⟩
⟨NO! LOOK!⟩
⟨I GOT HIM! THIS PIECE OF TATTERED CLOTHING PROVES IT!⟩
⟨THEN WHERE IS THE BODY? HE MAY BE ONLY WOUNDED!⟩
⟨IF SO, WE WILL TRACK HIM AND FINISH HIM OFF! MAJOR KANTARO WILL PRAISE US!⟩
BAIT FOR THE PREY.

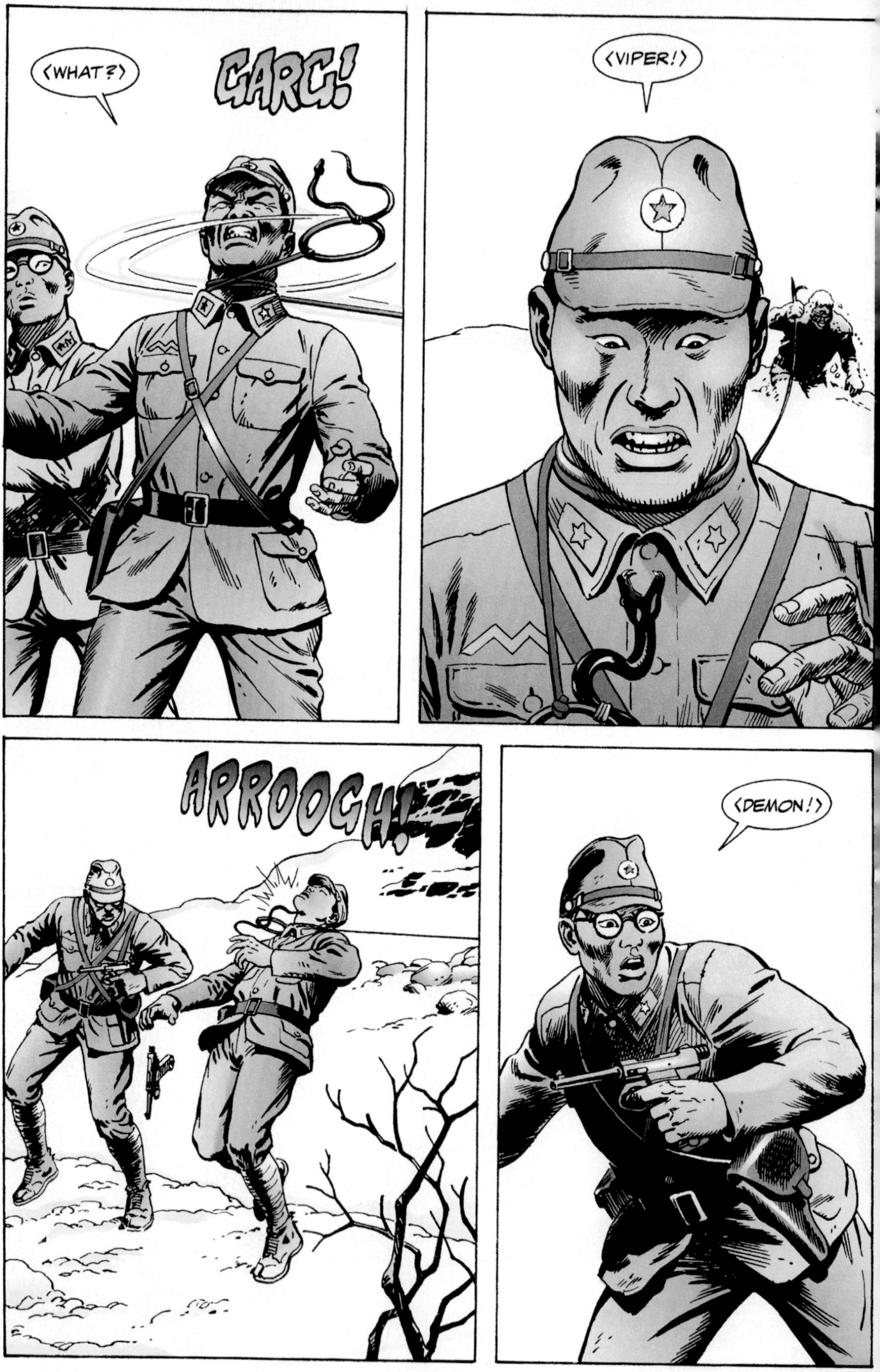
⟨WHAT?⟩
GARG!
⟨VIPER!⟩
ARROOGH!
⟨DEMON!⟩

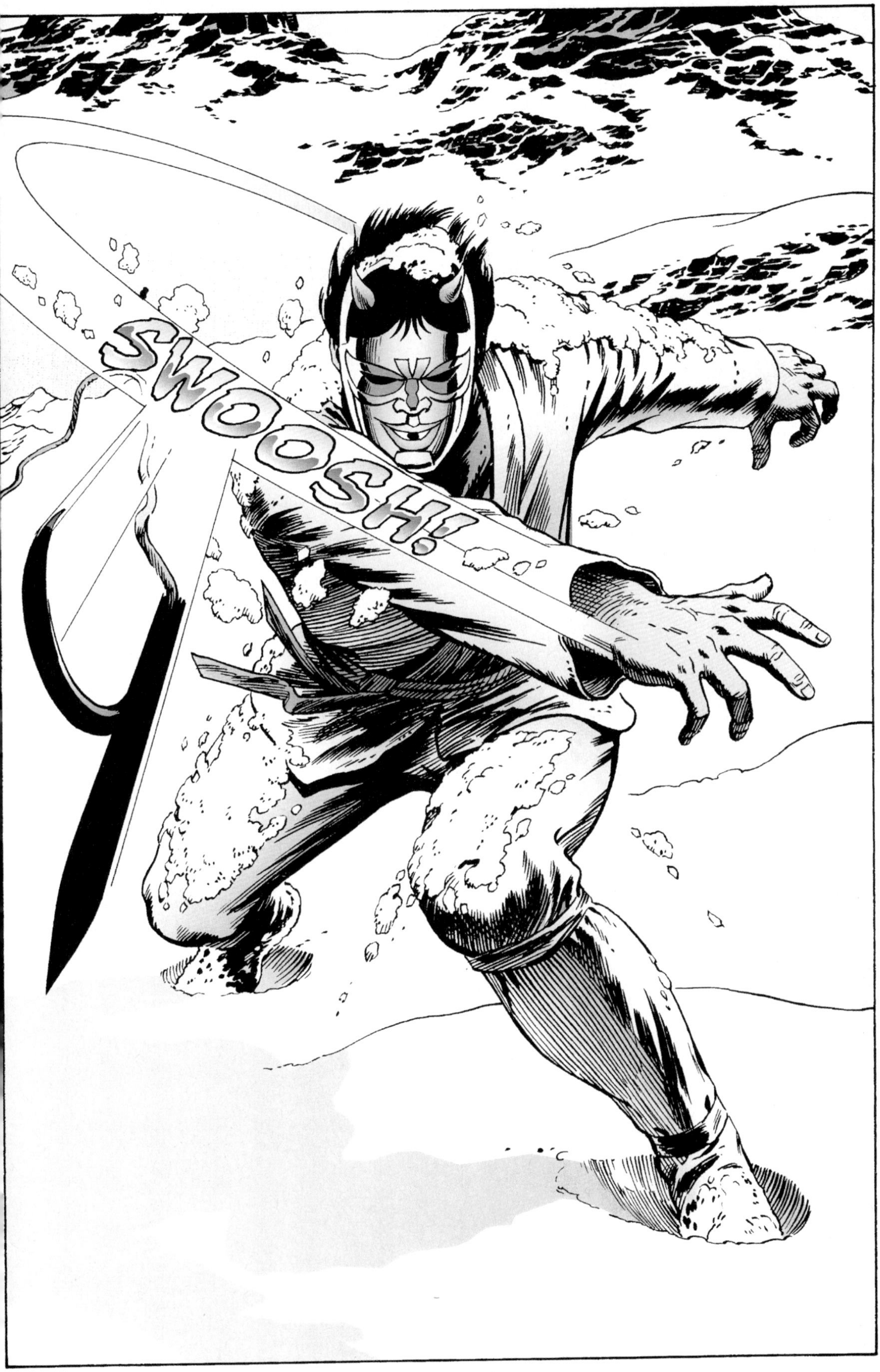
SWOOSH!

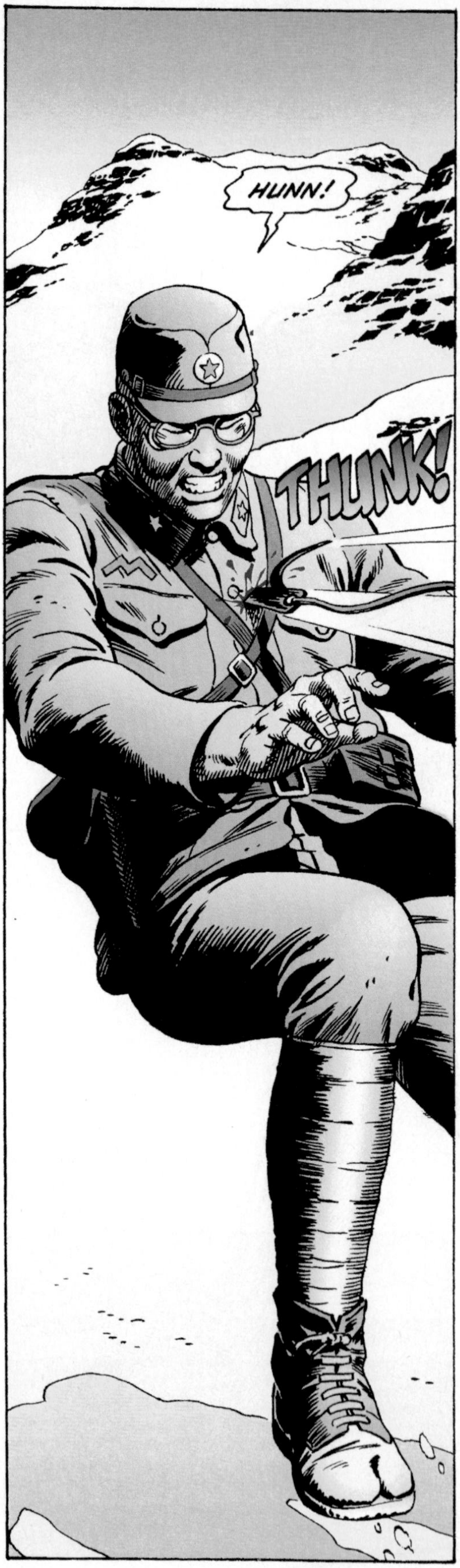
HUNN!
THUNK!

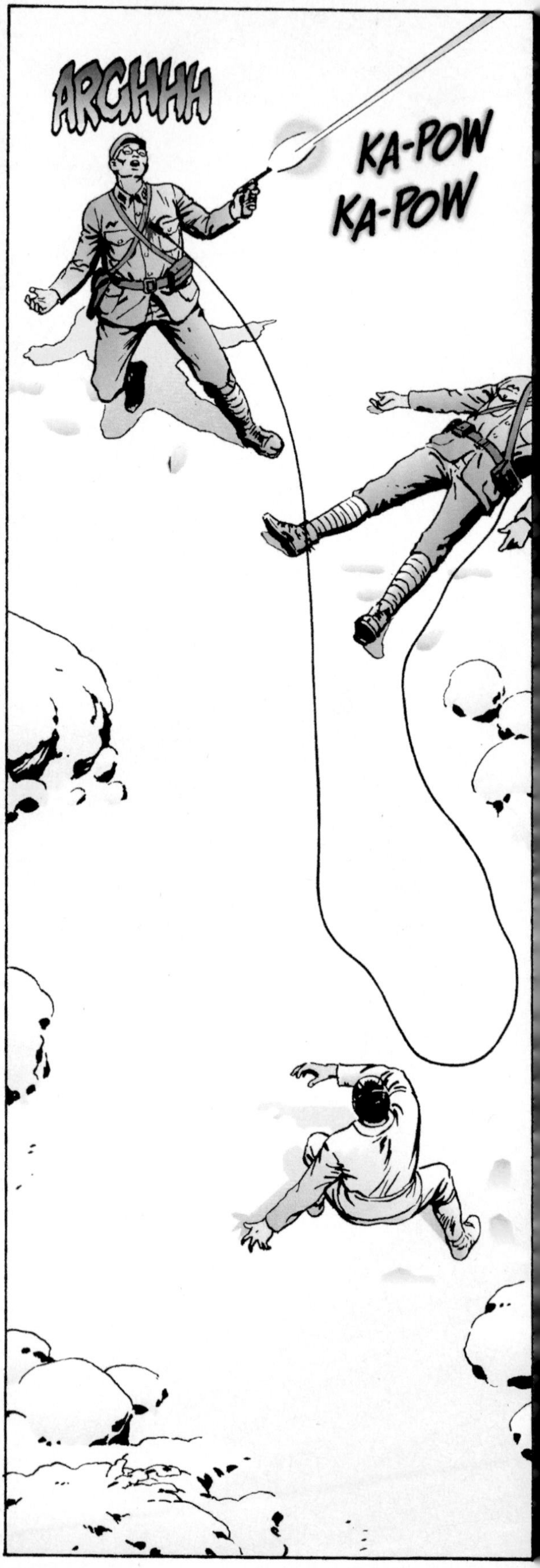
ARGHHH
KA-POW
KA-POW

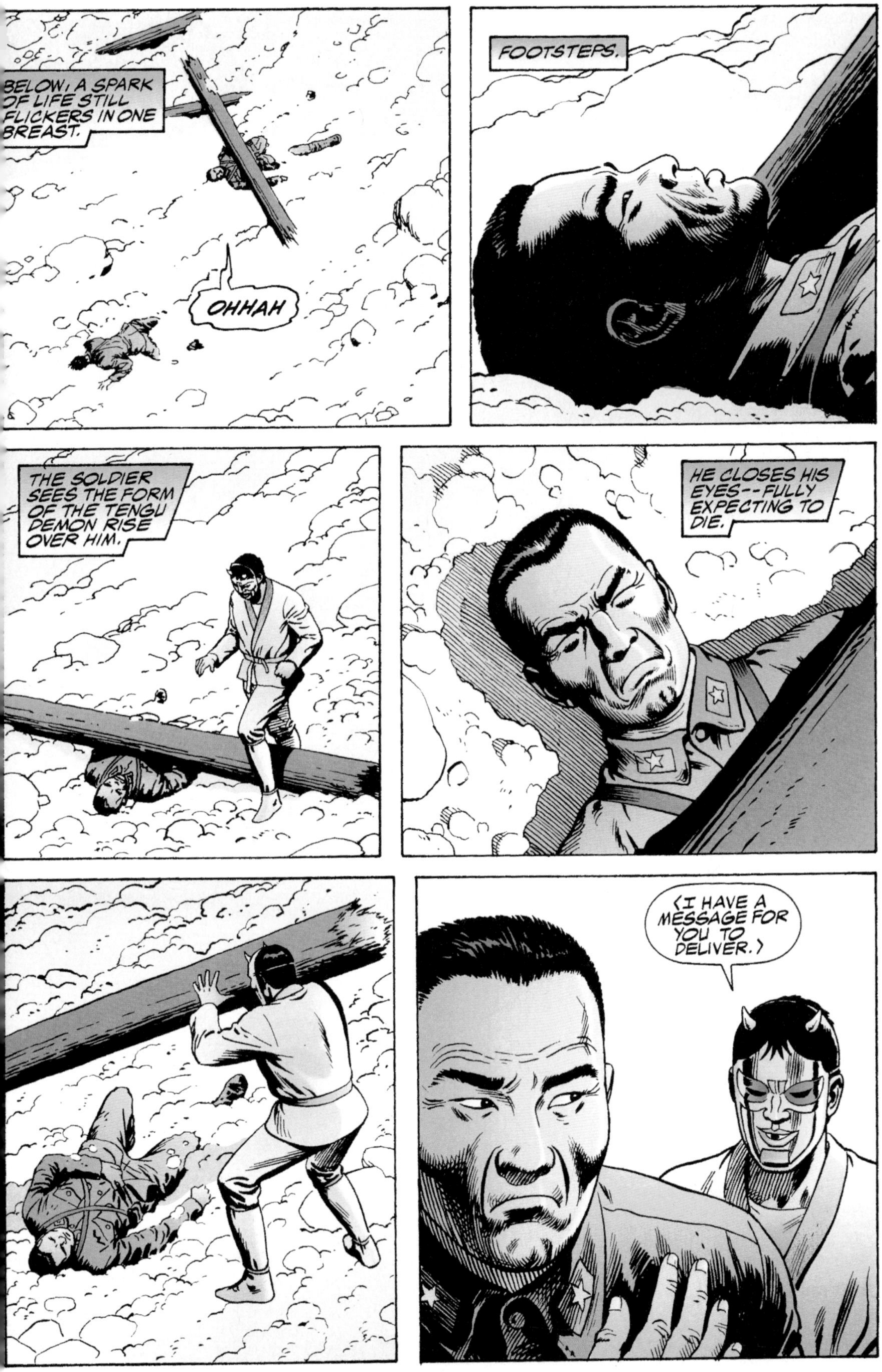
BELOW, A SPARK OF LIFE STILL FLICKERS IN ONE BREAST.
OHHAH
FOOTSTEPS.
THE SOLDIER SEES THE FORM OF THE TENGU DEMON RISE OVER HIM.
HE CLOSES HIS EYES--FULLY EXPECTING TO DIE.
⟨I HAVE A MESSAGE FOR YOU TO DELIVER.⟩

⟨FUJIMURA! WHAT HAS HAPPENED?⟩

⟨THE DEMON--KILLED THE REST--LET ME GO TO--TO GIVE YOU A MESSAGE.⟩

⟨YOU IDIOT! YOU COULD HAVE LED HIM RIGHT BACK HERE! HE COULD BE OUTSIDE RIGHT NOW SIGNALING HIS YANKEE ALLIES!⟩

⟨WE COULD BE SURROUNDED!⟩

⟨MAYOR, HE ALREADY KNEW OF THIS CAVE. HE SAYS HE IS TIRED OF KILLING US.⟩

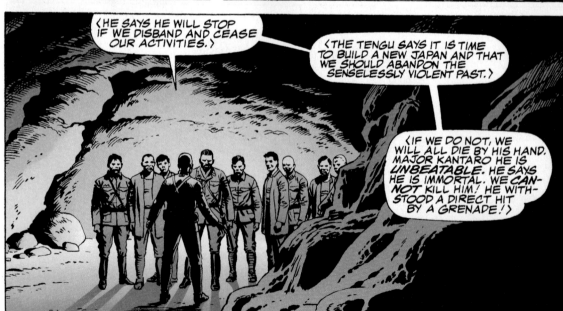

⟨HE SAYS HE WILL STOP IF WE DISBAND AND CEASE OUR ACTIVITIES.⟩

⟨THE TENGU SAYS IT IS TIME TO BUILD A NEW JAPAN AND THAT WE SHOULD ABANDON THE SENSELESSLY VIOLENT PAST.⟩

⟨IF WE DO NOT, WE WILL ALL DIE BY HIS HAND. MAJOR KANTARO HE IS UNBEATABLE. HE SAYS HE IS IMMORTAL. WE CANNOT KILL HIM! HE WITHSTOOD A DIRECT HIT BY A GRENADE!⟩

462

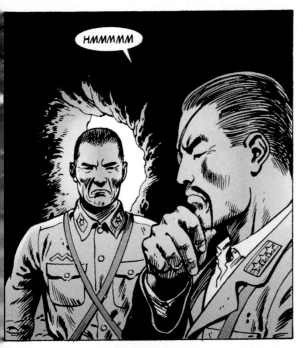

HMMMMM

⟨THERE IS A GRAIN OF WISDOM IN THE DEMON'S WORDS: "...ABANDON THE... VIOLENT PAST."⟩

⟨THE TENGU HAS SHOWN ME THE WAY TO OUR ULTIMATE VICTORY!⟩

⟨WE WILL BLEND INTO THIS 'NEW JAPAN'--BECOME A PART OF IT--⟩

⟨--BECOME LEADERS. SUBTLY STEER IT TOWARD OUR GOALS WHILE WE BECOME STRONG!⟩

⟨STRONG ENOUGH TO TAKE OVER COMPLETELY!⟩

⟨GO! INTEGRATE YOUR SELVES BACK INTO SOCIETY. USE FAMILY CONNECTIONS AND CUNNING TO WORK YOUR WAY INTO POSITIONS OF INFLUENCE!⟩

⟨IN SIX MONTHS WE MEET BACK HERE IN THE FIRST OF MANY PLANNING SESSIONS AND PROGRESS REPORTS!⟩

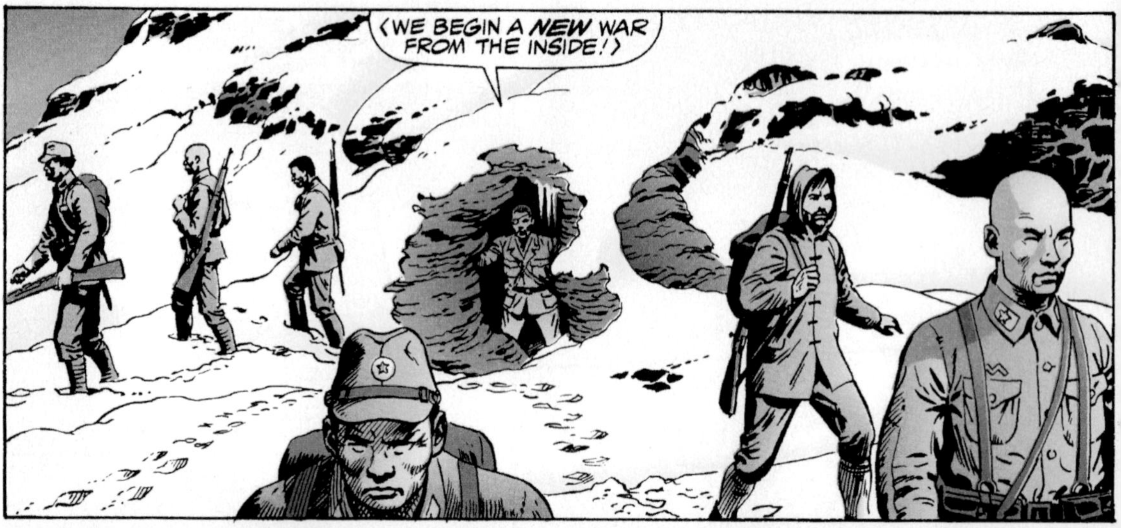
‹WE BEGIN A NEW WAR FROM THE INSIDE!›

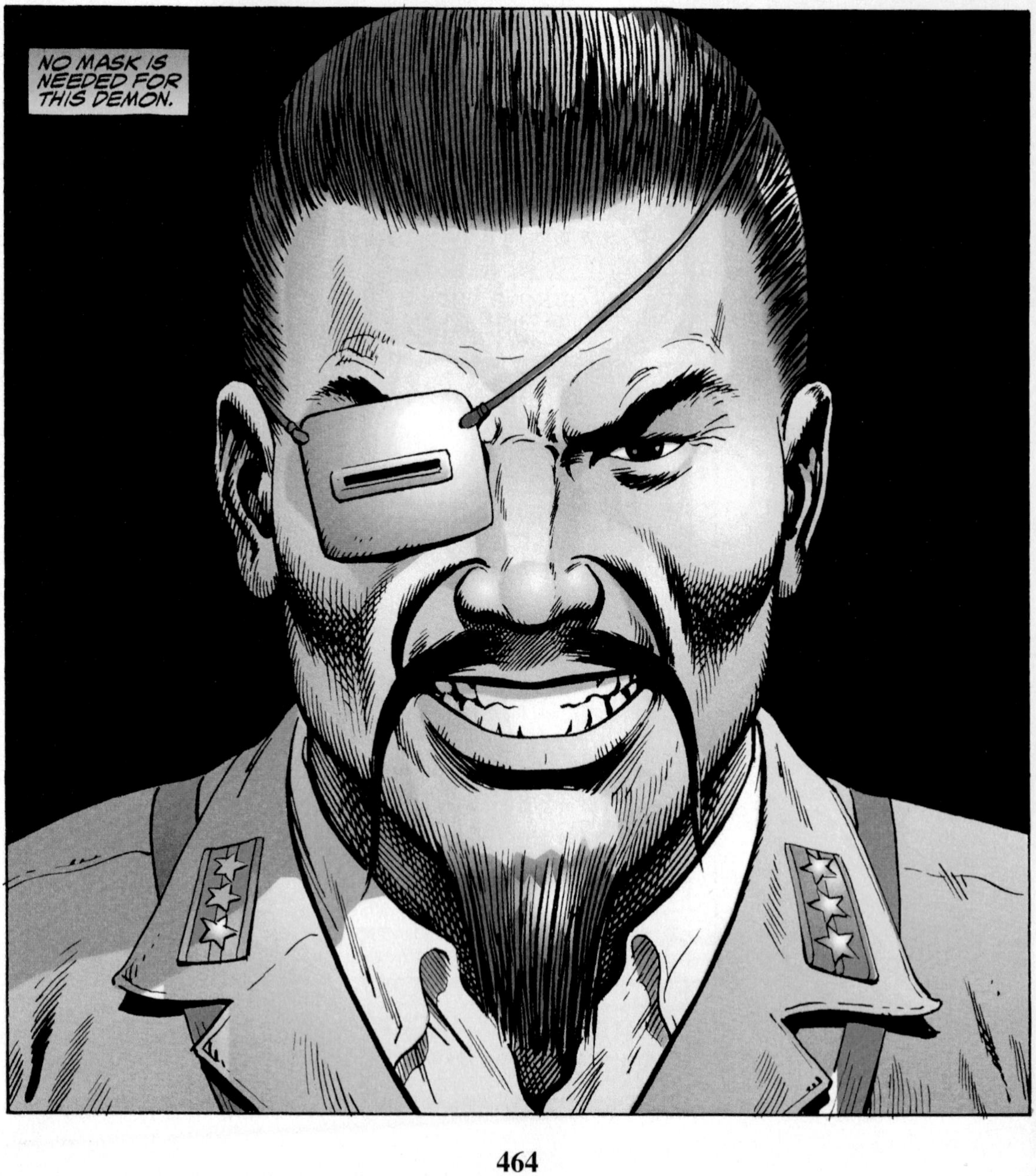
NO MASK IS NEEDED FOR THIS DEMON.

**END
CHAPTER
ONE**

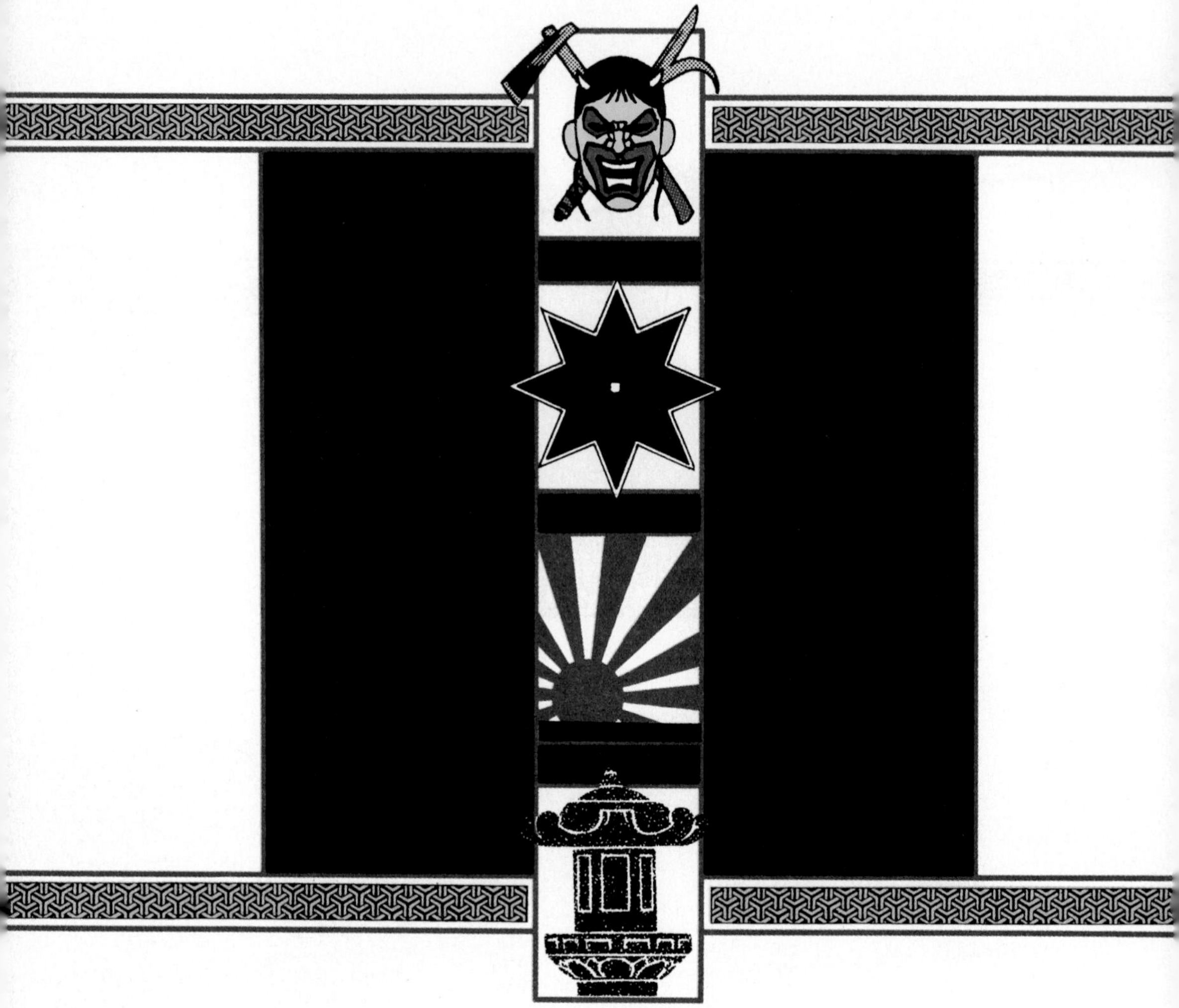

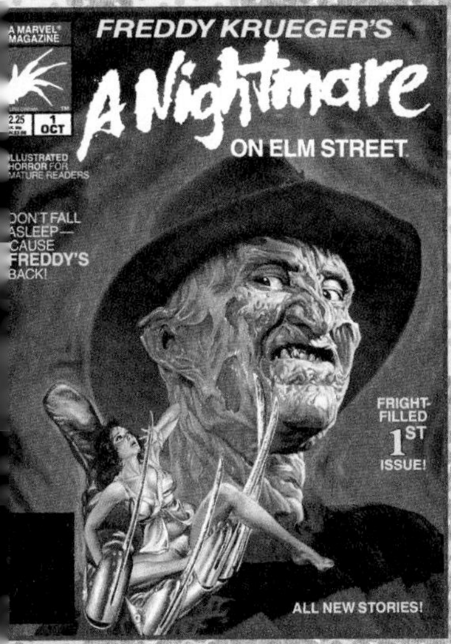
A MARVEL MAGAZINE
FREDDY KRUEGER'S
A Nightmare
ON ELM STREET
1 OCT
ILLUSTRATED HORROR FOR MATURE READERS
DON'T FALL ASLEEP— CAUSE FREDDY'S BACK!
FRIGHT-FILLED 1ST ISSUE!
ALL NEW STORIES!

FREDDY KRUEGER'S NIGHTMARE ON ELM STREET #1, published in July 1989, began a short magazine-sized series based on New Line Cinema's film franchise.

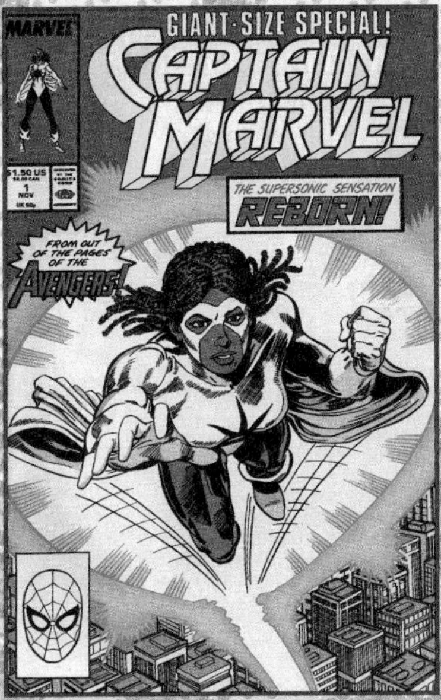
MARVEL
GIANT-SIZE SPECIAL!
CAPTAIN MARVEL
$1.50 US
1 NOV
THE SUPERSONIC SENSATION
REBORN!
FROM OUT OF THE PAGES OF THE AVENGERS!

CAPTAIN MARVEL #1, published in July 1989, was a one-shot starring the energy-wielding Monica Rambeau.

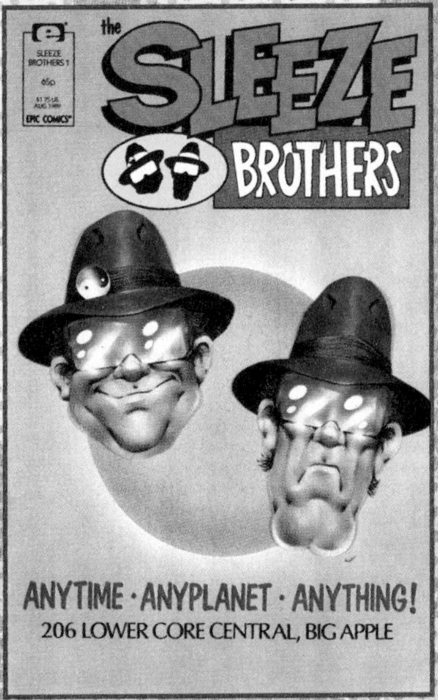
SLEEZE BROTHERS 1
EPIC COMICS
the
SLEEZE BROTHERS
ANYTIME · ANYPLANET · ANYTHING!
206 LOWER CORE CENTRAL, BIG APPLE

SLEEZE BROTHERS #1, published in July 1989, began John Carnell and Andy Lanning's short Epic series.

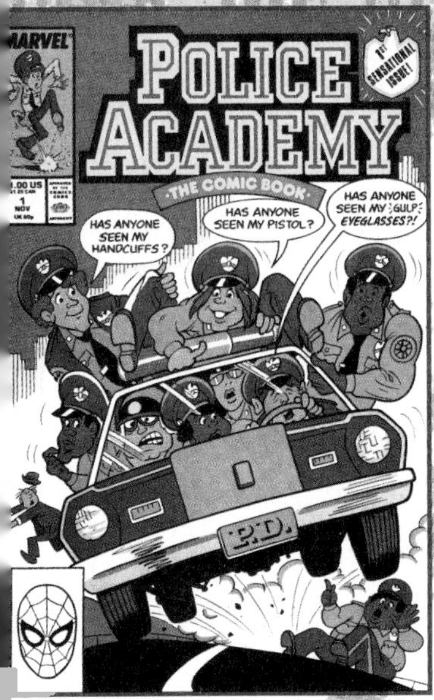
MARVEL
POLICE ACADEMY
1ST SENSATIONAL ISSUE!
1 NOV
THE COMIC BOOK
HAS ANYONE SEEN MY HANDCUFFS?
HAS ANYONE SEEN MY PISTOL?
HAS ANYONE SEEN MY GULP! EYEGLASSES?!
P.D.

POLICE ACADEMY #1, published in July 1989, began a short series based on the Warner Brothers film franchise and Ruby-Spears animated TV series.

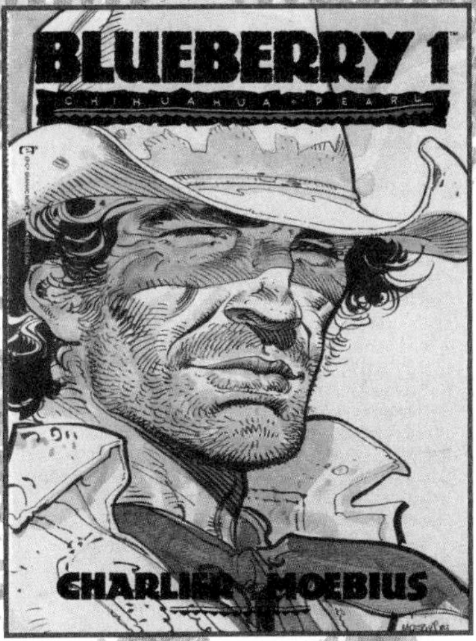
BLUEBERRY 1
CHIHUAHUA PEARL
CHARLIER MOEBIUS

BLUEBERRY #1, published in July 1989, began a series of Epic Graphic Novels reprinting and translating the French cowboy series.

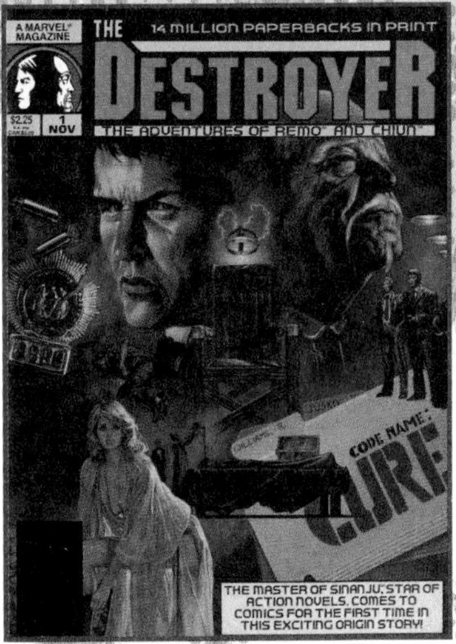
A MARVEL MAGAZINE
14 MILLION PAPERBACKS IN PRINT
THE DESTROYER
THE ADVENTURES OF REMO AND CHIUN
$2.25
1 NOV
CODE NAME: CURE
THE MASTER OF SINANJU, STAR OF ACTION NOVELS, COMES TO COMICS FOR THE FIRST TIME IN THIS EXCITING ORIGIN STORY!

DESTROYER #1, published in August 1989, began an ongoing magazine-sized series starring the characters from Warren Murphy and Richard Sapir's novels.

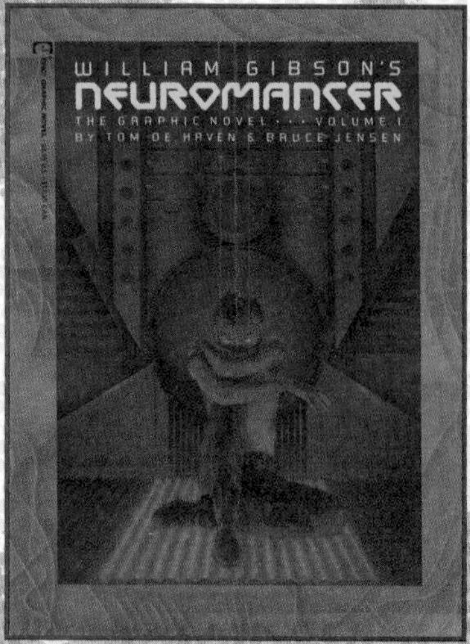
WILLIAM GIBSON'S
NEUROMANCER
THE GRAPHIC NOVEL · · · VOLUME I
BY TOM DE HAVEN & BRUCE JENSEN

NEUROMANCER, published in August 1989, was an Epic Graphic Novel adapting the first half of William Gibson's sci-fi novel.

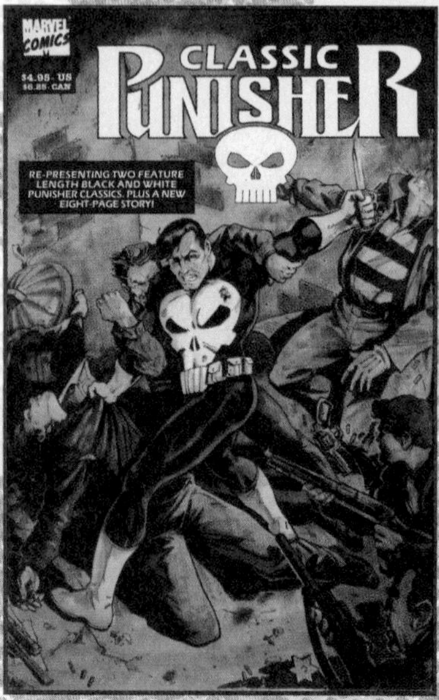
MARVEL COMICS
$4.95 US
$6.25 CAN
CLASSIC
PUNISHER
RE-PRESENTING TWO FEATURE LENGTH BLACK AND WHITE PUNISHER CLASSICS, PLUS A NEW EIGHT-PAGE STORY!

CLASSIC PUNISHER, published in August 1989, was a reprint one-shot.

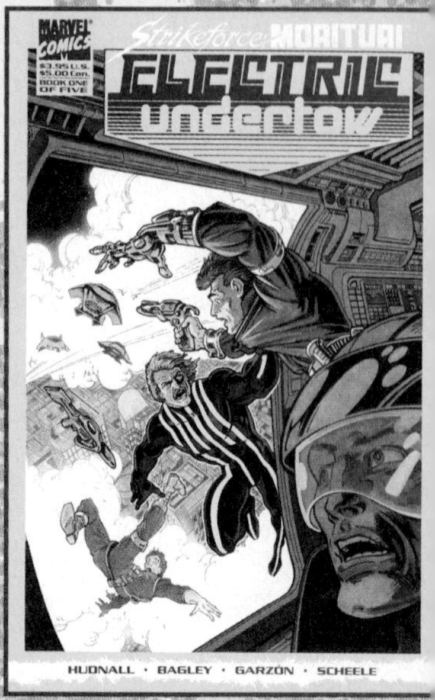
MARVEL COMICS
Strikeforce: MORITURI
ELECTRIC
undertow
$3.95 U.S.
$5.00 Can.
BOOK ONE OF FIVE
HUDNALL · BAGLEY · GARZÓN · SCHEELE

STRIKEFORCE MORITURI: ELECTRIC UNDERTOW #1, published in September 1989, began a miniseries starring the alien-fighting characters.

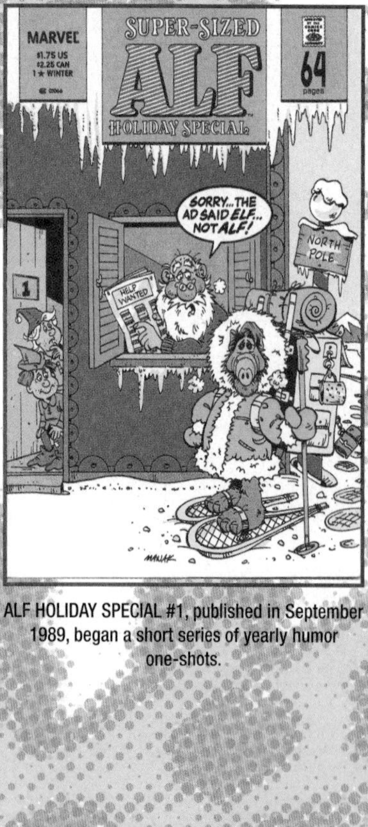
MARVEL
$1.75 US
$2.25 CAN
1 WINTER
SUPER-SIZED
ALF
HOLIDAY SPECIAL
64 pages
SORRY...THE AD SAID ELF... NOT ALF!
HELP WANTED
NORTH POLE
MANAK

ALF HOLIDAY SPECIAL #1, published in September 1989, began a short series of yearly humor one-shots.

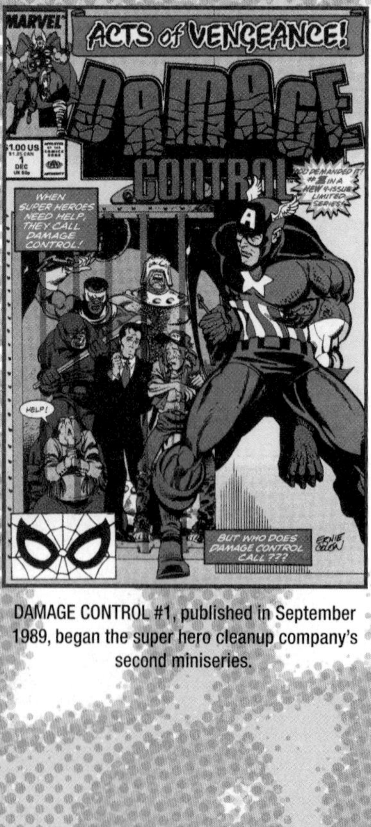
MARVEL
ACTS of VENGEANCE!
DAMAGE
CONTROL
$1.00 US
$1.25 CAN
1
DEC
UK 50p
YOU DEMANDED IT! #1 IN A NEW 4-ISSUE LIMITED SERIES!
WHEN SUPER HEROES NEED HELP, THEY CALL DAMAGE CONTROL!
HELP!
BUT WHO DOES DAMAGE CONTROL CALL???

DAMAGE CONTROL #1, published in September 1989, began the super hero cleanup company's second miniseries.

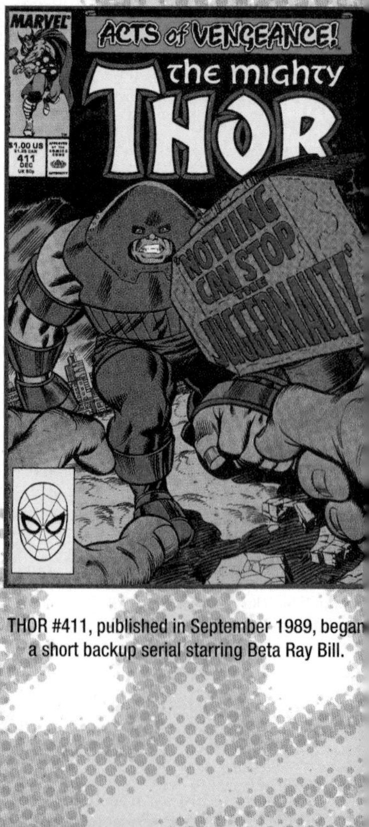
MARVEL
ACTS of VENGEANCE!
the mighty
THOR
$1.00 US
$1.25 CAN
411
DEC
UK 50p
NOTHING CAN STOP THE JUGGERNAUT!

THOR #411, published in September 1989, began a short backup serial starring Beta Ray Bill.

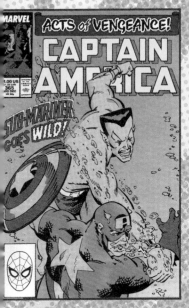

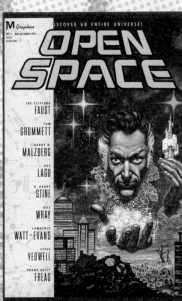

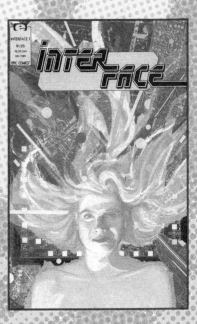

MARVEL
ACTS of VENGEANCE!
CAPTAIN AMERICA
SUB-MARINER GOES WILD!
CAPTAIN AMERICA #365, published in October 1989, began a short backup serial starring the villainous Cobra.

M Graphics
DISCOVER AN ENTIRE UNIVERSE!
OPEN SPACE
JOE CLIFFORD FAUST
TOM GRUMMETT
BARRY N. MALZBERG
RAY LAGO
G. HARRY STINE
BILL WRAY
LAWRENCE WATT-EVANS
STEVE YEOWELL
FRANK KELLY FREAS
OPEN SPACE #1, published in October 1989, began a short-lived sci-fi anthology series.

INTERFACE 1
$1.95
DEC 1989
EPIC COMICS
INTER FACE
INTERFACE #1, published in October 1989, began James D. Hudnall's ongoing Epic series.

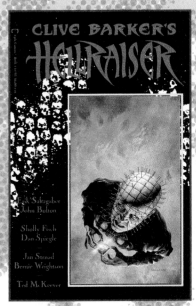

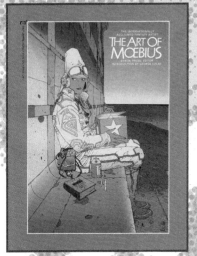

CLIVE BARKER'S
HELLRAISER
Erik Saltzgaber
John Bolton
Sholly Fisch
Dan Spiegle
Jan Strnad
Bernie Wrightson
Ted McKeever
HELLRAISER #1, published in October 1989, began an ongoing Epic series based on New World Pictures' film franchise.

THE ART OF MOEBIUS
ART OF MOEBIUS, published in October 1989, was a magazine-sized Epic one-shot spotlighting the work of Jean "Moebius" Giraud.

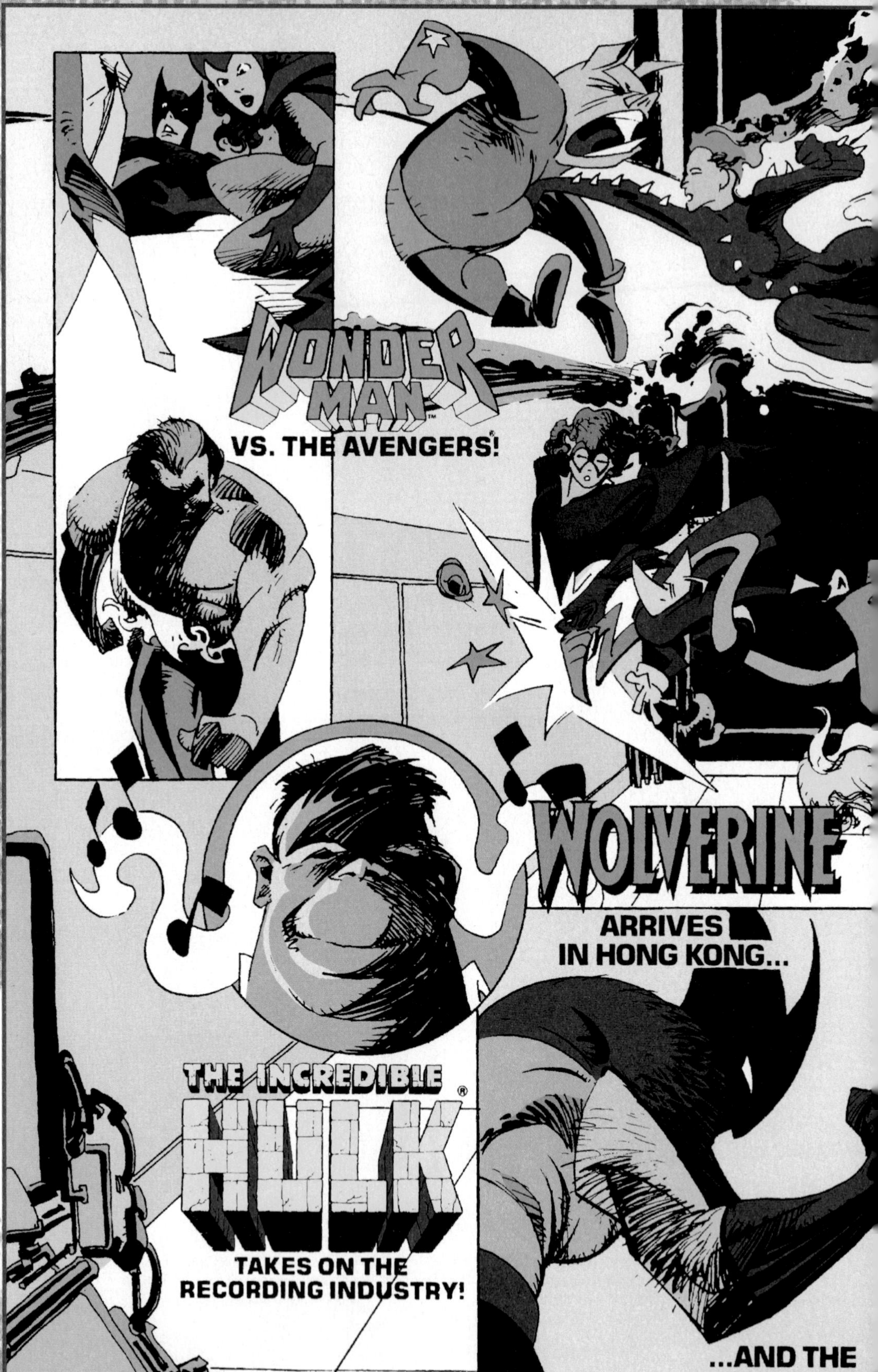

WONDER MAN™
VS. THE AVENGERS!®
WOLVERINE
ARRIVES IN HONG KONG...
THE INCREDIBLE HULK®
TAKES ON THE RECORDING INDUSTRY!
...AND THE ACTION BEGI

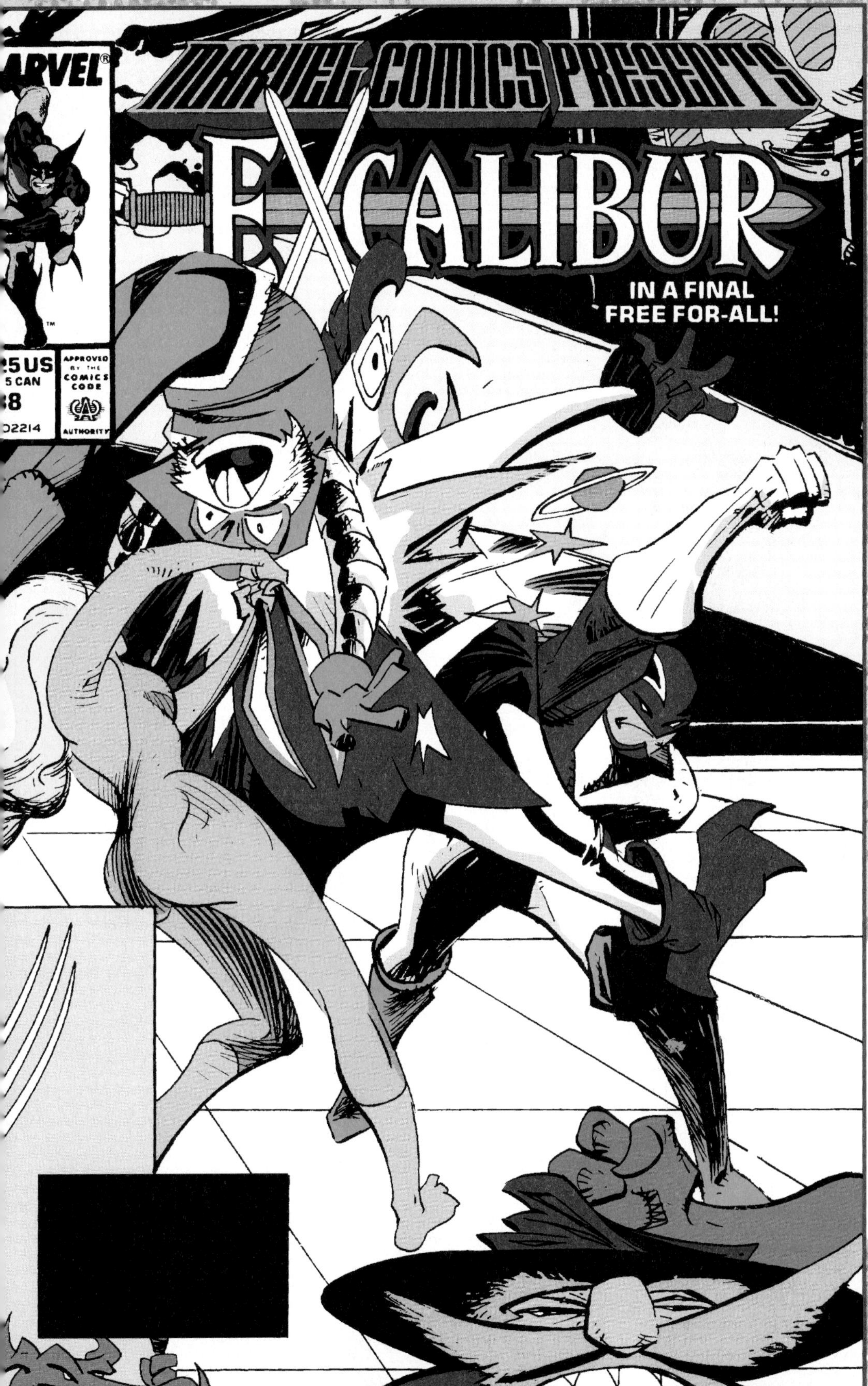
MARVEL
MARVEL COMICS PRESENTS
EXCALIBUR
IN A FINAL FREE FOR-ALL!
APPROVED BY THE COMICS CODE AUTHORITY

MARVEL COMICS PRESENTS #38, published in October 1989, began a limited serial starring the West Coast Avengers' Wonder Man.

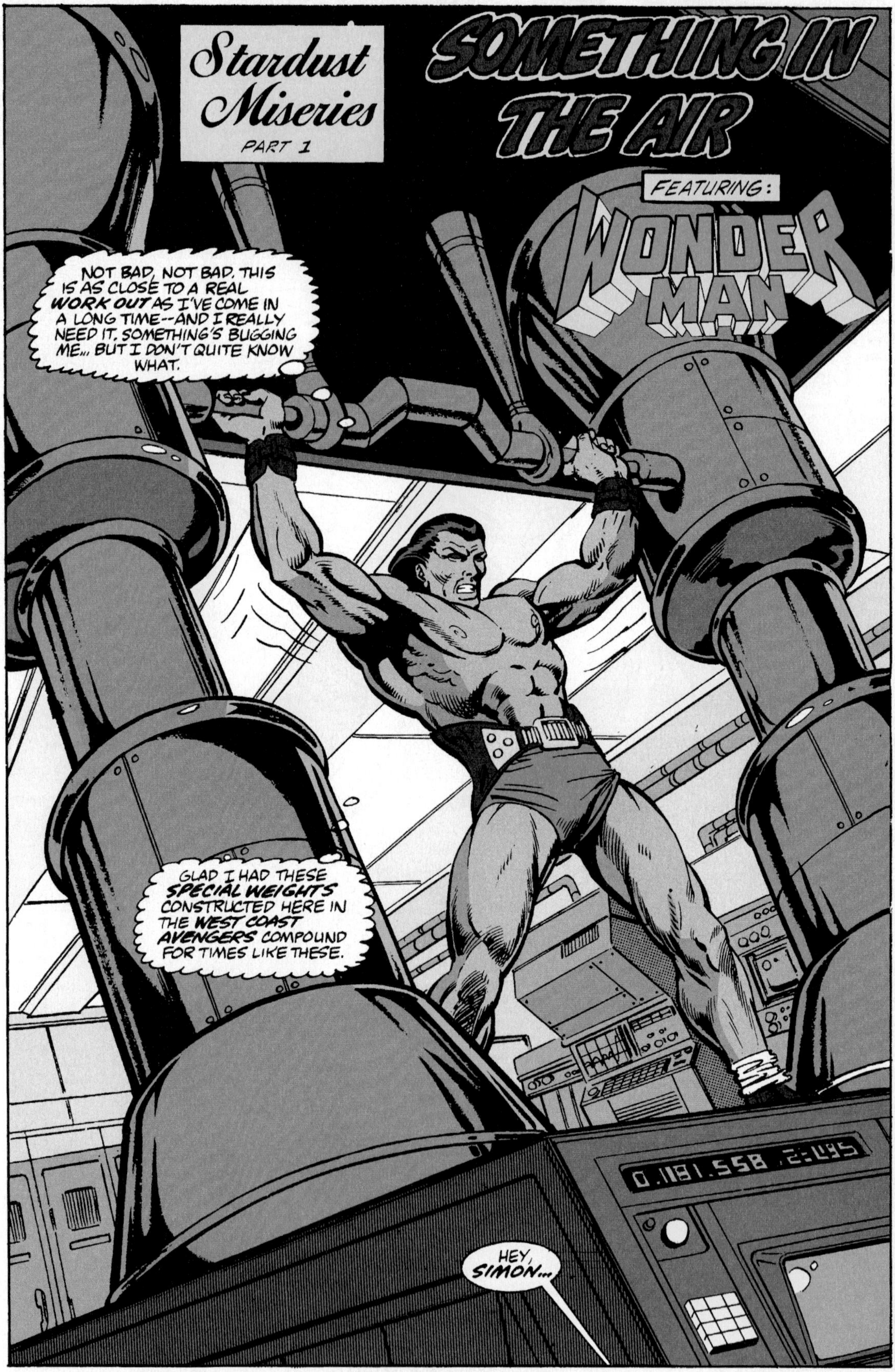
Stardust Miseries
PART 1
SOMETHING IN THE AIR
FEATURING:
WONDER MAN
NOT BAD, NOT BAD. THIS IS AS CLOSE TO A REAL WORK OUT AS I'VE COME IN A LONG TIME--AND I REALLY NEED IT. SOMETHING'S BUGGING ME... BUT I DON'T QUITE KNOW WHAT.
GLAD I HAD THESE SPECIAL WEIGHTS CONSTRUCTED HERE IN THE WEST COAST AVENGERS COMPOUND FOR TIMES LIKE THESE.
HEY, SIMON...

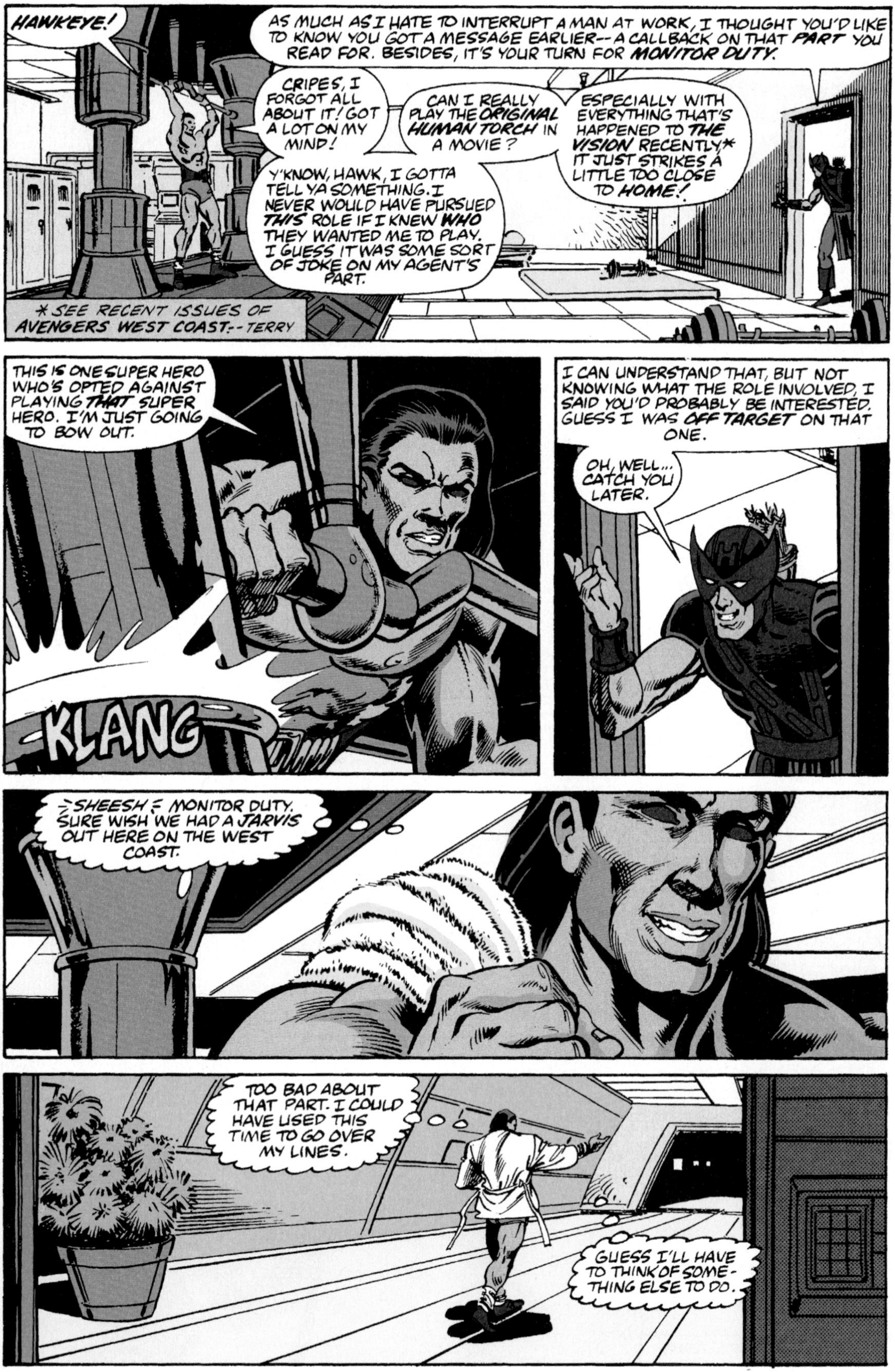
HAWKEYE!
AS MUCH AS I HATE TO INTERRUPT A MAN AT WORK, I THOUGHT YOU'D LIKE TO KNOW YOU GOT A MESSAGE EARLIER-- A CALLBACK ON THAT PART YOU READ FOR. BESIDES, IT'S YOUR TURN FOR MONITOR DUTY.
CRIPES, I FORGOT ALL ABOUT IT! GOT A LOT ON MY MIND!
Y'KNOW, HAWK, I GOTTA TELL YA SOMETHING. I NEVER WOULD HAVE PURSUED THIS ROLE IF I KNEW WHO THEY WANTED ME TO PLAY. I GUESS IT WAS SOME SORT OF JOKE ON MY AGENT'S PART.
CAN I REALLY PLAY THE ORIGINAL HUMAN TORCH IN A MOVIE?
ESPECIALLY WITH EVERYTHING THAT'S HAPPENED TO THE VISION RECENTLY,* IT JUST STRIKES A LITTLE TOO CLOSE TO HOME!
* SEE RECENT ISSUES OF AVENGERS WEST COAST.--TERRY
THIS IS ONE SUPER HERO WHO'S OPTED AGAINST PLAYING THAT SUPER HERO. I'M JUST GOING TO BOW OUT.
KLANG
I CAN UNDERSTAND THAT, BUT NOT KNOWING WHAT THE ROLE INVOLVED, I SAID YOU'D PROBABLY BE INTERESTED. GUESS I WAS OFF TARGET ON THAT ONE.
OH, WELL... CATCH YOU LATER.
SHEESH! MONITOR DUTY. SURE WISH WE HAD A JARVIS OUT HERE ON THE WEST COAST.
TOO BAD ABOUT THAT PART. I COULD HAVE USED THIS TIME TO GO OVER MY LINES.
GUESS I'LL HAVE TO THINK OF SOME-THING ELSE TO DO.

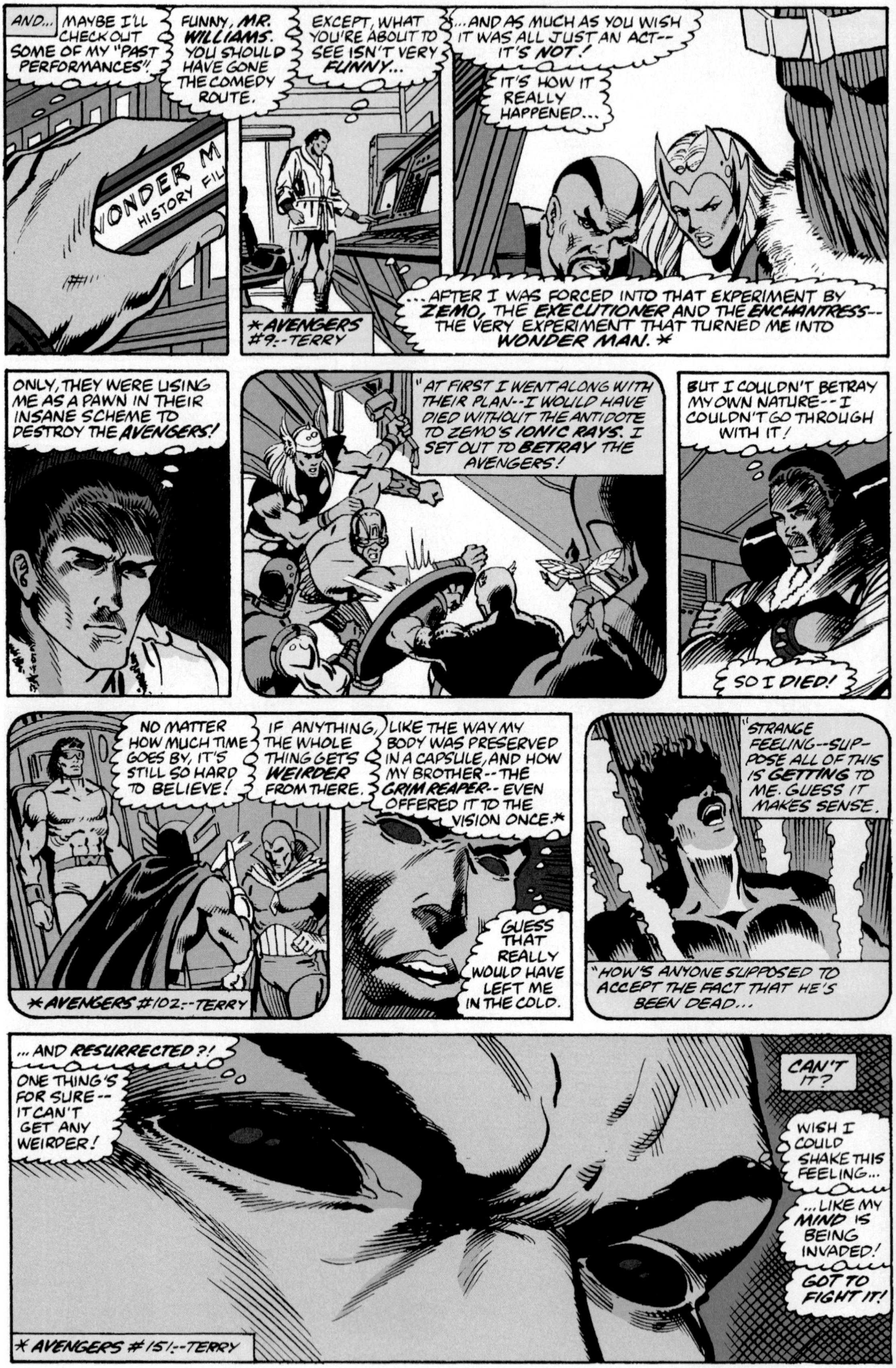
AND...
MAYBE I'LL CHECK OUT SOME OF MY "PAST PERFORMANCES".
WONDER M HISTORY FIL
FUNNY, MR. WILLIAMS. YOU SHOULD HAVE GONE THE COMEDY ROUTE.
EXCEPT, WHAT YOU'RE ABOUT TO SEE ISN'T VERY FUNNY...
*AVENGERS #9.--TERRY
...AND AS MUCH AS YOU WISH IT WAS ALL JUST AN ACT-- IT'S NOT!
IT'S HOW IT REALLY HAPPENED...
...AFTER I WAS FORCED INTO THAT EXPERIMENT BY ZEMO, THE EXECUTIONER AND THE ENCHANTRESS-- THE VERY EXPERIMENT THAT TURNED ME INTO WONDER MAN.*
ONLY, THEY WERE USING ME AS A PAWN IN THEIR INSANE SCHEME TO DESTROY THE AVENGERS!
"AT FIRST I WENT ALONG WITH THEIR PLAN--I WOULD HAVE DIED WITHOUT THE ANTIDOTE TO ZEMO'S IONIC RAYS. I SET OUT TO BETRAY THE AVENGERS!
BUT I COULDN'T BETRAY MY OWN NATURE-- I COULDN'T GO THROUGH WITH IT!
SO I DIED!
NO MATTER HOW MUCH TIME GOES BY, IT'S STILL SO HARD TO BELIEVE!
IF ANYTHING, THE WHOLE THING GETS WEIRDER FROM THERE.
*AVENGERS #102.--TERRY
LIKE THE WAY MY BODY WAS PRESERVED IN A CAPSULE, AND HOW MY BROTHER-- THE GRIM REAPER-- EVEN OFFERED IT TO THE VISION ONCE.*
GUESS THAT REALLY WOULD HAVE LEFT ME IN THE COLD.
"STRANGE FEELING--SUPPOSE ALL OF THIS IS GETTING TO ME. GUESS IT MAKES SENSE.
"HOW'S ANYONE SUPPOSED TO ACCEPT THE FACT THAT HE'S BEEN DEAD...
...AND RESURRECTED?!
ONE THING'S FOR SURE-- IT CAN'T GET ANY WEIRDER!
CAN'T IT?
WISH I COULD SHAKE THIS FEELING...
...LIKE MY MIND IS BEING INVADED!
GOT TO FIGHT IT!
*AVENGERS #151.--TERRY

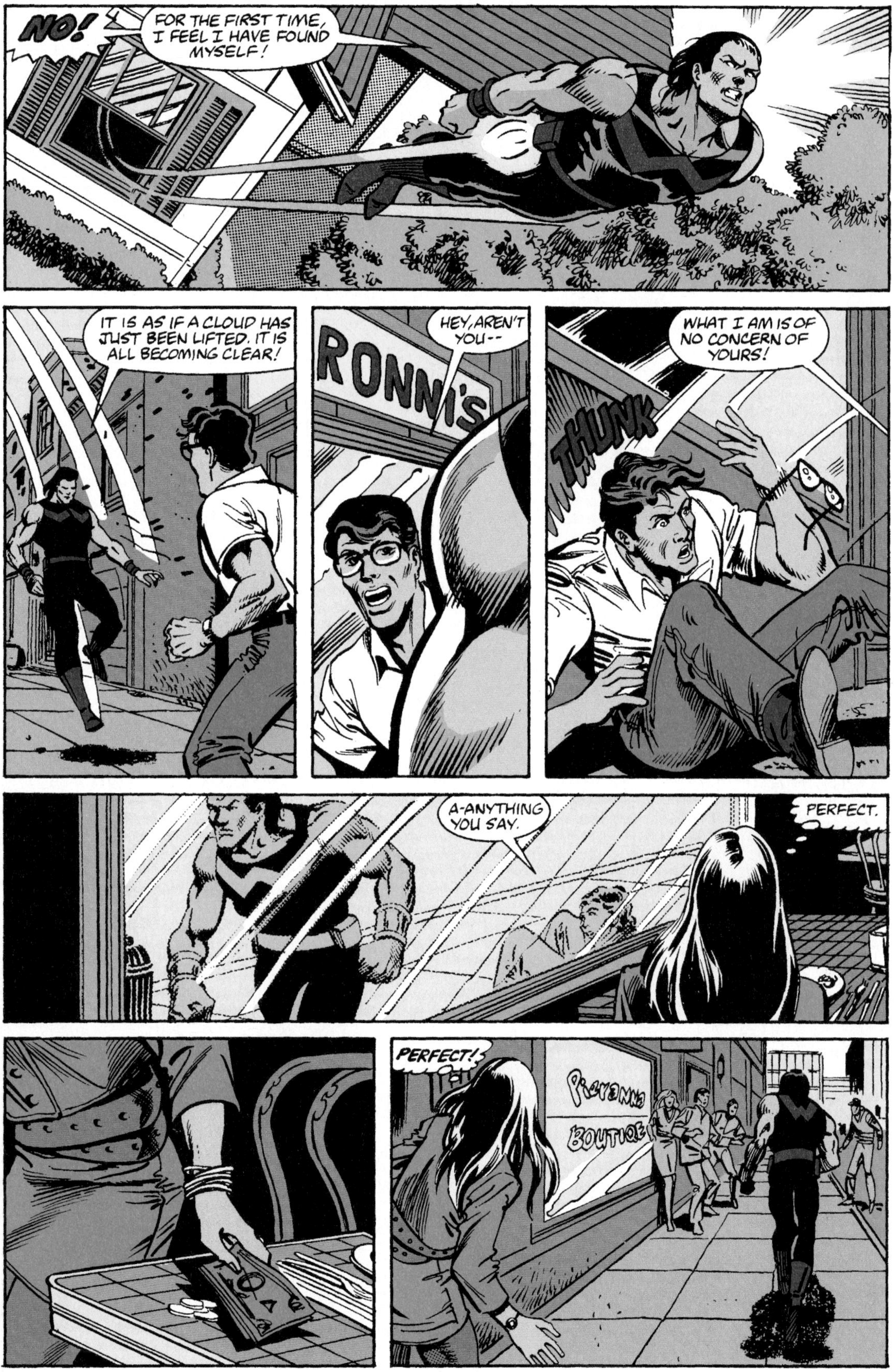
NO!
FOR THE FIRST TIME, I FEEL I HAVE FOUND MYSELF!
IT IS AS IF A CLOUD HAS JUST BEEN LIFTED. IT IS ALL BECOMING CLEAR!
RONNI'S
HEY, AREN'T YOU--
WHAT I AM IS OF NO CONCERN OF YOURS!
THUNK
A-ANYTHING YOU SAY.
PERFECT.
PERFECT!
BOUTIQUE

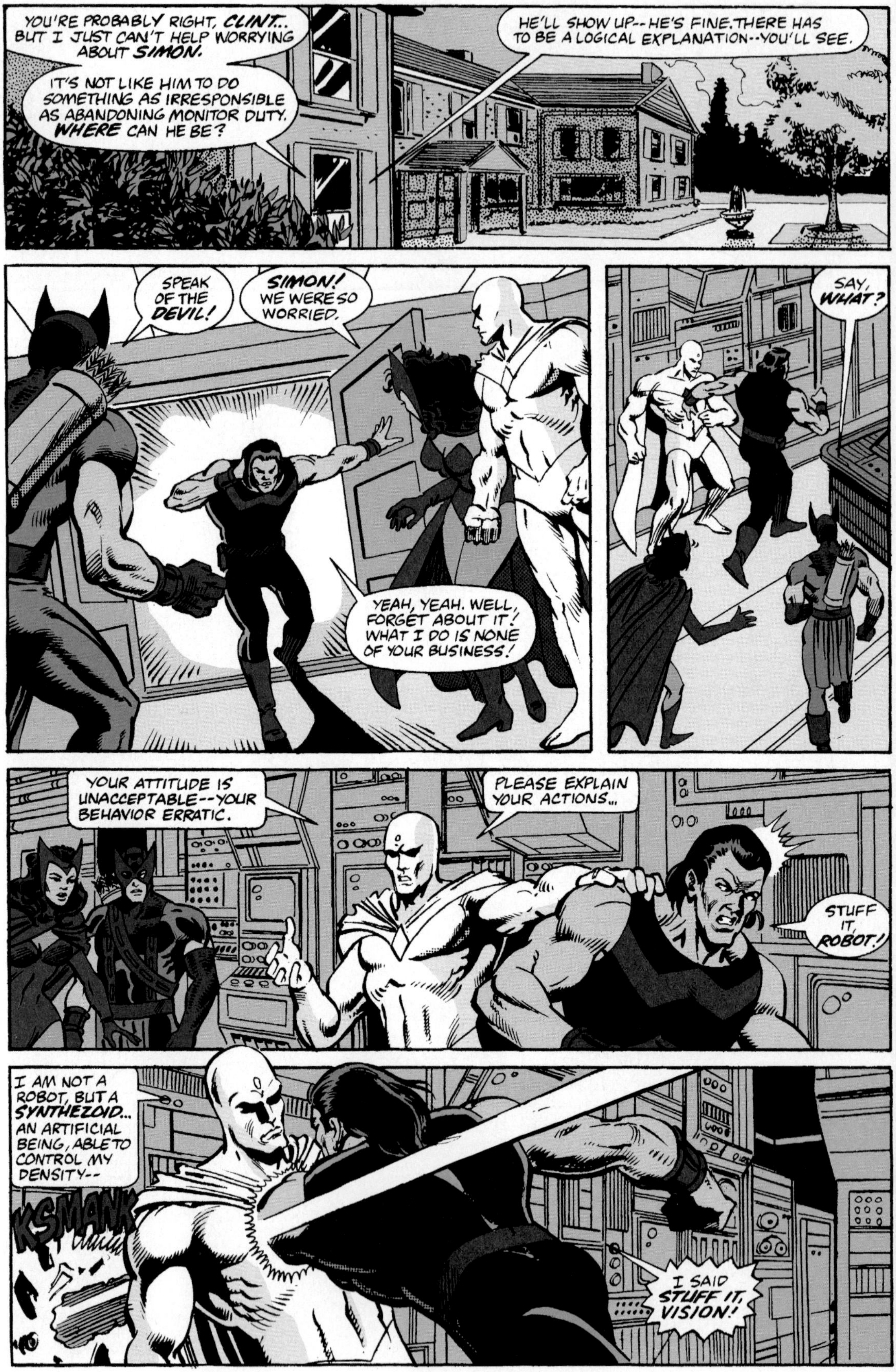

YOU'RE PROBABLY RIGHT, CLINT... BUT I JUST CAN'T HELP WORRYING ABOUT SIMON.
IT'S NOT LIKE HIM TO DO SOMETHING AS IRRESPONSIBLE AS ABANDONING MONITOR DUTY. WHERE CAN HE BE?
HE'LL SHOW UP--HE'S FINE. THERE HAS TO BE A LOGICAL EXPLANATION--YOU'LL SEE.
SPEAK OF THE DEVIL!
SIMON! WE WERE SO WORRIED.
YEAH, YEAH. WELL, FORGET ABOUT IT! WHAT I DO IS NONE OF YOUR BUSINESS!
SAY, WHAT?
YOUR ATTITUDE IS UNACCEPTABLE--YOUR BEHAVIOR ERRATIC.
PLEASE EXPLAIN YOUR ACTIONS...
STUFF IT, ROBOT!
I AM NOT A ROBOT, BUT A SYNTHEZOID... AN ARTIFICIAL BEING, ABLE TO CONTROL MY DENSITY--
KSMANK
I SAID STUFF IT, VISION!

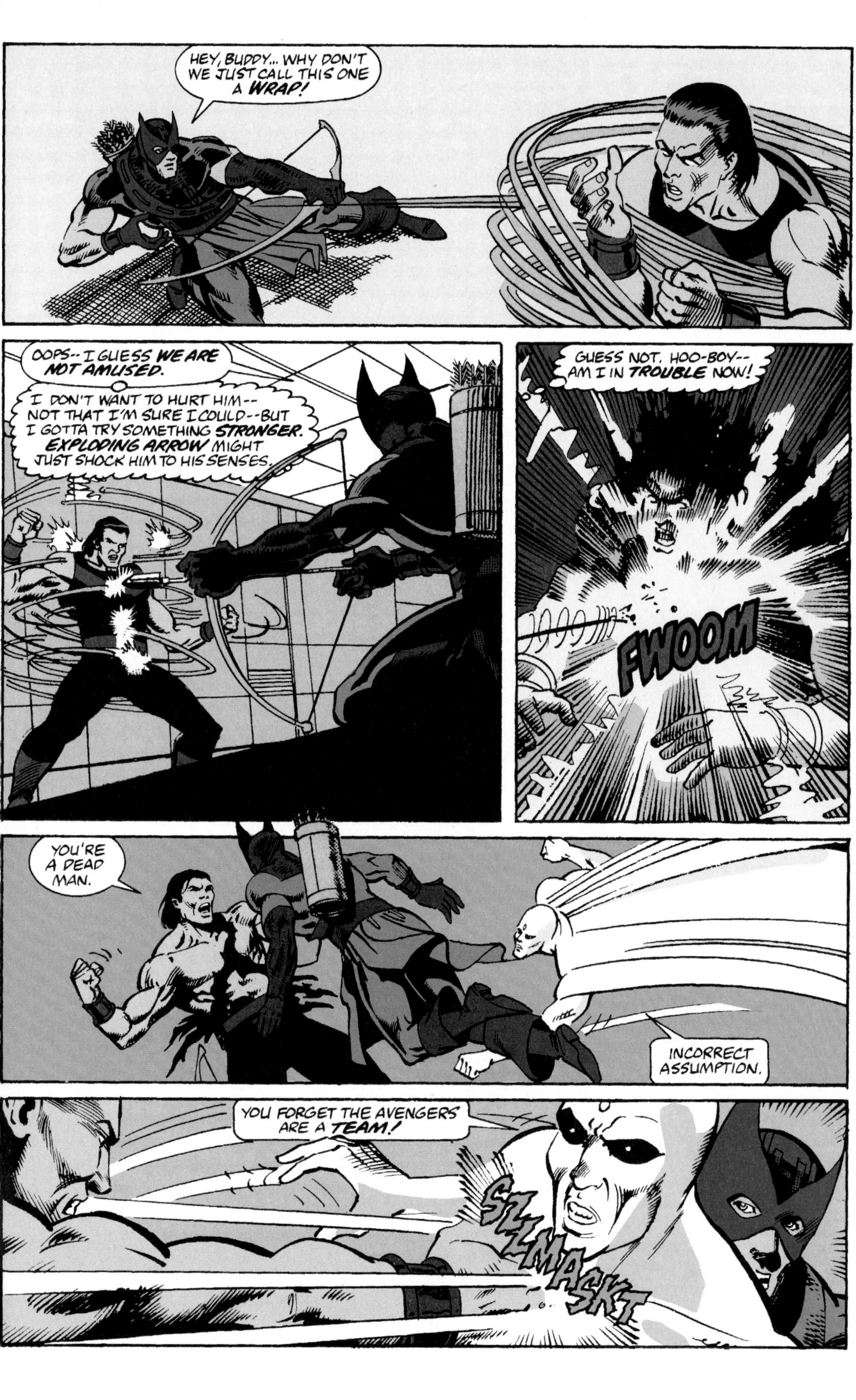
HEY, BUDDY... WHY DON'T WE JUST CALL THIS ONE A WRAP!
OOPS-- I GUESS WE ARE NOT AMUSED.
I DON'T WANT TO HURT HIM-- NOT THAT I'M SURE I COULD--BUT I GOTTA TRY SOMETHING STRONGER. EXPLODING ARROW MIGHT JUST SHOCK HIM TO HIS SENSES.
GUESS NOT. HOO-BOY-- AM I IN TROUBLE NOW!
FWOOM
YOU'RE A DEAD MAN.
INCORRECT ASSUMPTION.
YOU FORGET THE AVENGERS ARE A TEAM!
SZLMASKT

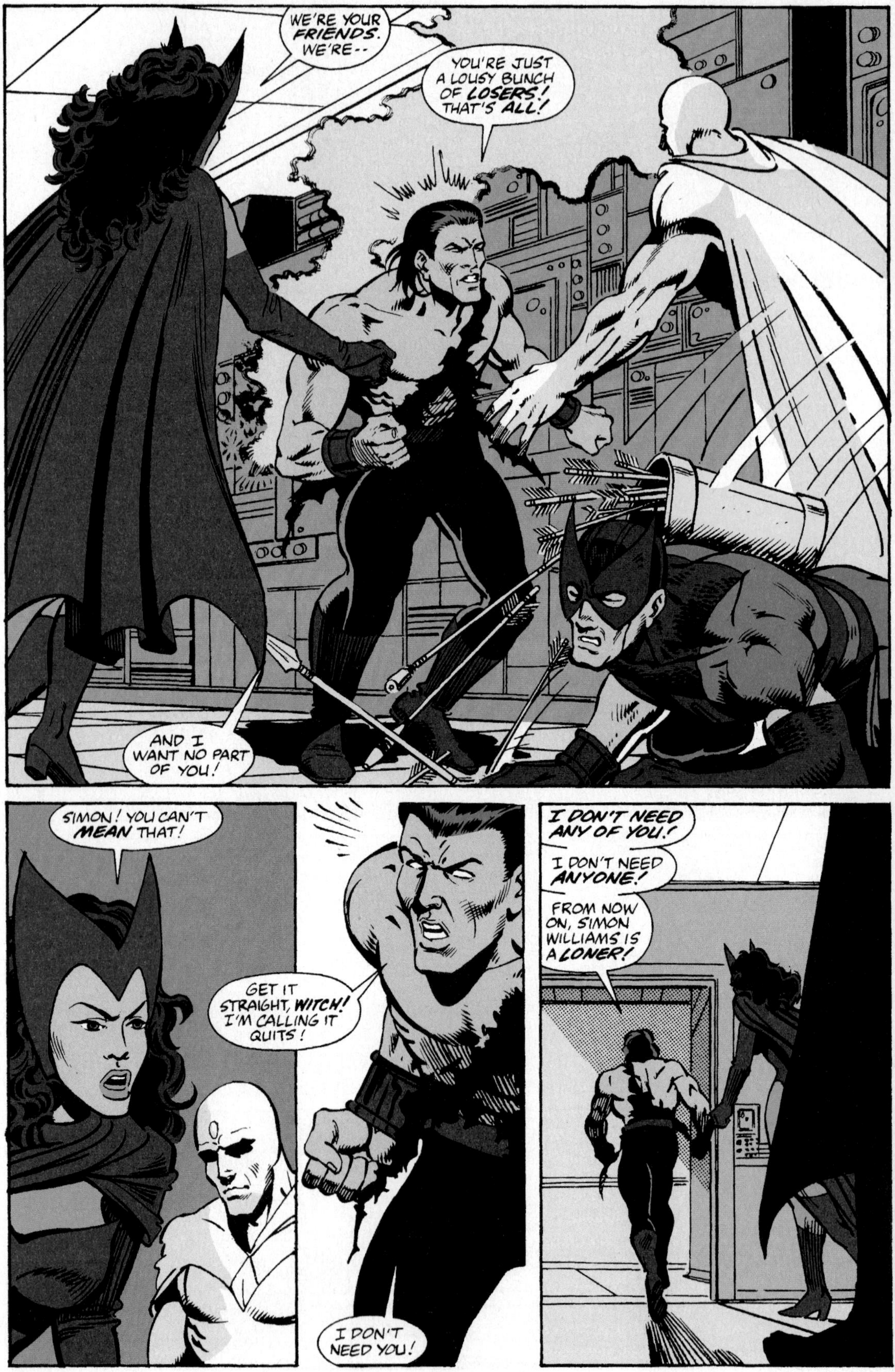
WE'RE YOUR FRIENDS. WE'RE--
YOU'RE JUST A LOUSY BUNCH OF LOSERS! THAT'S ALL!
AND I WANT NO PART OF YOU!
SIMON! YOU CAN'T MEAN THAT!
GET IT STRAIGHT, WITCH! I'M CALLING IT QUITS!
I DON'T NEED YOU!
I DON'T NEED ANY OF YOU!
I DON'T NEED ANYONE!
FROM NOW ON, SIMON WILLIAMS IS A LONER!

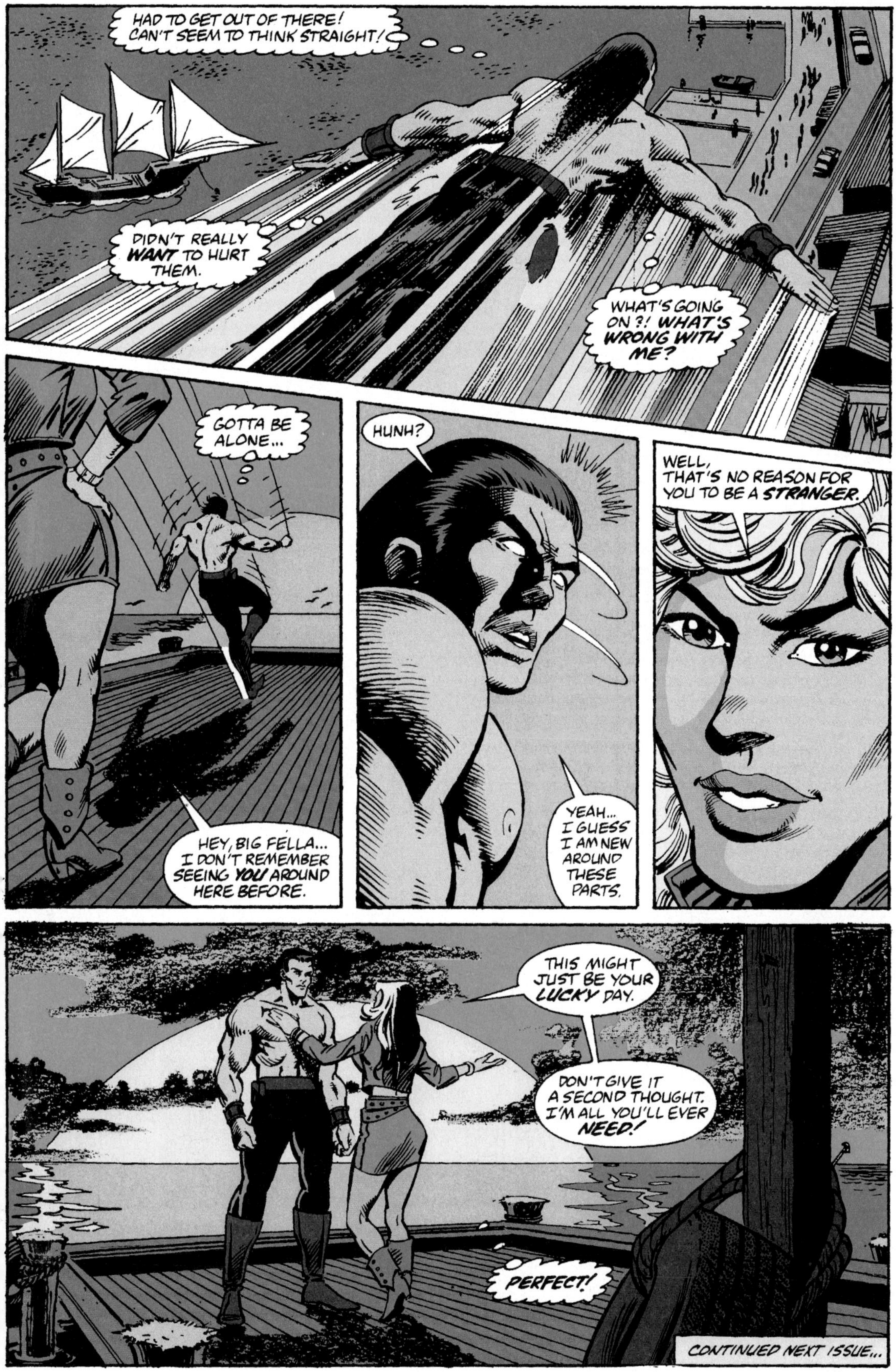
HAD TO GET OUT OF THERE! CAN'T SEEM TO THINK STRAIGHT!
DIDN'T REALLY WANT TO HURT THEM.
WHAT'S GOING ON?! WHAT'S WRONG WITH ME?
GOTTA BE ALONE...
HEY, BIG FELLA... I DON'T REMEMBER SEEING YOU AROUND HERE BEFORE.
HUNH?
YEAH... I GUESS I AM NEW AROUND THESE PARTS.
WELL, THAT'S NO REASON FOR YOU TO BE A STRANGER.
THIS MIGHT JUST BE YOUR LUCKY DAY.
DON'T GIVE IT A SECOND THOUGHT. I'M ALL YOU'LL EVER NEED!
PERFECT!
CONTINUED NEXT ISSUE...

MARVEL
MARVEL COMICS PRESENTS
WOLVERINE
$1.25US
39
SHADOW BOXING!
PLUS 3 MORE ALL-NEW FEATURES!

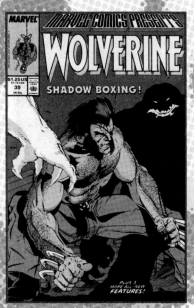

MARVEL COMICS PRESENTS #39, published in October 1989, began a short serial starring the Hercules of the future.

MARVEL COMICS
YUPPIES FROM Hell
DO YOU HAVE A HOUSE IN THE HAMPTONS, AN IRA, AND A TRUST FUND FROM EITHER OR BOTH OF YOUR PARENTS?
by Barbara Slate

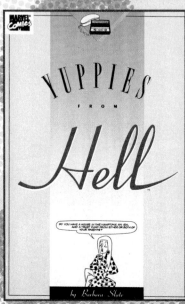

YUPPIES FROM HELL, published in October 1989, was a humor one-shot.

critica
mass

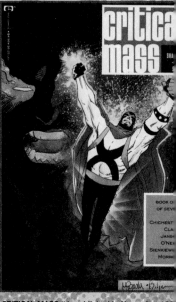

CRITICAL MASS #1, published in November 198
began an Epic miniseries featuring a crossove
between the Shadowline characters.

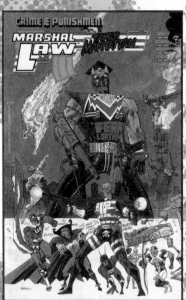

CRIME & PUNISHMENT
MARSHAL LAW
TAKES MANHATTAN

CRIME & PUNISHMENT: MARSHAL LAW TAKES MANHATTAN, published in November 1989, was a magazine-sized Epic one-shot starring the hero-hunting lawman.

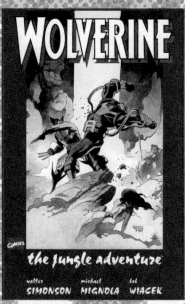

WOLVERINE
the jungle adventure
walter SIMONSON
michael MIGNOLA
bob WIACEK

WOLVERINE: THE JUNGLE ADVENTURE, published in December 1989, began a series of regular one-shots that supplemented the main *Wolverine* title.

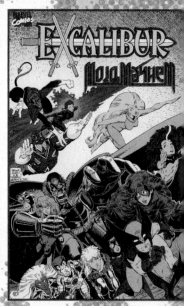

EXCALIBUR
MOJO MAYHEM

EXCALIBUR: MOJO MAYHEM, published in
December 1989, began a series of regular one
shots that supplemented the main *Excalibur* titl